Frommer's
1st Edition

FRUGAL TRAVELER'S GUIDES

California
FROM $60 A DAY

by Erika Lenkert, Matthew R. Poole, Stephanie Avnet & Elizabeth Hansen

Macmillan • USA

ABOUT THE AUTHORS

A native San Franciscan, **Erika Lenkert** worked for HarperCollins before becoming a freelance writer. She has contributed to dozens of travel guides and is currently seeking her fortune in both San Francisco and Hollywood. Her Siamese cats are along for the ride.

Combining the only three things he's good at—eating, sleeping, and criticizing—**Matthew R. Poole** has found a surprisingly prosperous career as a freelance travel writer. A native Northern Californian and author of nearly a dozen travel guides to California and Hawaii—including *Frommer's San Francisco,* with Erika Lenkert—Matt's looking forward to retiring at 30 but fears he won't be able to tell the difference. He currently lives in San Francisco and has no intention of writing a novel.

A native of Los Angeles and an avid traveler, antique hound, and pop history enthusiast, **Stephanie Avnet** believes that California is best seen from behind the wheel of a red convertible. She also authors *Frommer's Los Angeles* and is currently at work on *Wonderful Weekends from Los Angeles* (Macmillan Travel).

Longtime La Jolla resident **Elizabeth Hansen** is the author of *Frommer's San Diego* as well as multiple Frommer's guides to Australia and New Zealand.

MACMILLAN TRAVEL

A Simon & Schuster Macmillan Company
1633 Broadway
New York, NY 10019

Find us online at **http://www.mgr.com/travel** or
on America Online at Keyword: **Frommer's**

ISBN 0-02-861237-X
ISSN 1091-5761

Editors: Cheryl Farr, Alicia Scott
Thanks to Philippe Wamba
Contributors: Lisa Stone-Norman, Andrew Rice, Jim Moore, Mary Herczog, Steve Hochman, Heidi Siegmund Cuda, and John McKinney
Production Editor: Chris Van Camp
Design by Michele Laseau
Digital Cartography by Peter Bogaty, Roberta Stockwell, and Ortelius Design

SPECIAL SALES

Bulk purchases (10+ copies) of Frommer's and selected Macmillan travel guides are available to corporations, organizations, mail-order catalogs, institutions, and charities at special discounts, and can be customized to suit individual needs. For more information write to: Special Sales, Macmillan General Reference, 1633 Broadway, New York, NY 10019.

Manufactured in the United States of America

Contents

List of Maps

AN INVITATION TO THE READER

In researching this book, we discovered many wonderful places—hotels, restaurants, shops, and more. We're sure you'll find others. Please tell us about them, so we can share the information with your fellow travelers in upcoming editions. If you were disappointed with a recommendation, we'd love to know that, too. Please write to:

Frommer's California from $60 a Day
Macmillan Travel
1633 Broadway
New York, NY 10019

AN ADDITIONAL NOTE

Please be advised that travel information is subject to change at any time—and this is especially true of prices. We therefore suggest that you write or call ahead for confirmation when making your travel plans. The authors, editors, and publisher cannot be held responsible for the experiences of readers while traveling. Your safety is important to us, however, so we encourage you to stay alert and be aware of your surroundings. Keep a close eye on cameras, purses, and wallets, all favorite targets of thieves and pickpockets.

WHAT THE SYMBOLS MEAN

✪ Frommer's Favorites

Hotels, restaurants, attractions, and entertainment you should not miss.

⑤ Super-Special Values

Hotels and restaurants that offer great value for your money.

The following abbreviations are used for credit cards:

AE	American Express	ER	enRoute
ATM	Debit Cards	EU	Eurocard
CB	Carte Blanche	JCB	Japan Credit Bank
DC	Diners Club	MC	MasterCard
DISC	Discover	V	Visa

Area Code Changes Notice

Please note that a number of area codes in Southern California will be changing during the life of this edition:

- Effective January 25, 1997, portions of Los Angeles County, including Long Beach, are in the new **562** area code. You can dial 310 until July 26, 1997, after which you will have to use 562.
- Effective March 22, 1997, the area code for the desert regions, including the Palm Springs resorts, the desert parks, and San Diego's North County beach towns, is scheduled to change to **760**. You will be able to dial 619 until September 27, 1997, after which you will have to use 760.
- Effective June 14, 1997, the eastern portion of Los Angeles County's 818 area code—including Burbank, Glendale, and Pasadena—will change to **626**. You will be able to dial 818 until January 17, 1998, after which you will have to use 626.

These changes have also been noted throughout the text where appropriate.

The Best of California for the Frugal Traveler

by Erika Lenkert, Matthew R. Poole,
Stephanie Avnet, and Elizabeth Hansen

If ever a state embodied Americana, California does.

Sure, there's famous, fun stuff like Hollywood and the Golden Gate Bridge and miles of beach filled with nubile, tanned surf gods and volleyball goddesses à la *Baywatch.*

But look beyond the headlines. It's not all movie stars, earthquakes, and race riots.

The real California is also Yosemite and Big Sur, whale-watching and the Mojave Desert.

It's small-town pride and commitment, personified by the descendants of gold miners who use their painstakingly restored bed-and-breakfasts to eke the kind of living from the Sierra that eluded most of their ancestors.

And don't picture grizzled miners as whites only—legions of African, Asian, and Hispanic Americans also discovered riches there and elsewhere in the Golden State.

Move over, Ellis Island. Ever since Spain and England laid conflicting claims to the land originally populated by Native Americans and long home to Mexican ranchers, California's history has enjoyed a rainbow hue.

For visitors today, this rich cultural diversity offers literally hundreds of annual celebrations and beautiful monuments to enjoy, from Chinese New Year parades to a chain of 21 beautiful, Spanish-style missions.

Of course, the reigning California tradition is sun worship: Come prepared to enjoy the outdoors. Visitors who aren't content with some of the nation's best white-water rafting and downhill skiing can strap on a snowboard, in-line skates, or a bungee harness for the well-padded thrill of a lifetime.

Then again, other travelers may choose simply, and literally, to feast between gorgeous views of vineyards and sea cliffs.

From white-hatted gourmets of trendy California cuisine to traditional Mexican *cocineras,* amazing cooks serve up the fruits of sea and land with delicious variety and flair.

If you don't like bean sprouts, don't worry—the homegrown Burmese, Italian, Greek, Thai, and Lebanese cuisine is great, too, especially when washed down with the state's renowned wines and microbrewed suds.

And California's natural beauty and proud family traditions won't interfere if what you really want is to discover the state's reputation as the bad boy of popular culture.

Megamalls. Movie stars. Mud baths in Calistoga. Tattoo exhibitions and chain-saw jugglers on Venice Beach.

From Castroville's giant, plastic artichoke—roughly the size of a Volkswagen bug—to the astonishing opulence of San Simeon, California has kitsch, glitter, and breathtaking self-indulgence to share.

Come and see.

1 The Best of Natural California

- **Año Nuevo State Reserve:** Nature enthusiasts come from all over the world to this spot 22 miles north of Santa Cruz to view the elephant seal colony. Pups are born from December through March, and molting follows between April and August. You can also spot sea lions in spring and summer, whales in winter and spring, plus more than 250 bird species. See Chapter 6.
- **Point Reyes:** This extraordinarily scenic stretch of coast and wetlands is one of the best bird-watching spots in California for shore birds, songbirds, and waterfowl, as well as osprey and red-shouldered hawks. There's a rainbow-hued wildflower garden, too, and you might catch a glimpse of a whale from the Point Reyes Light-house. See Chapter 8.
- **Sonoma State Beaches:** Stretching about 10 miles from Bodega Bay to Jenner, these beaches attract more than 300 species of birds. From December to September, look for osprey. Seal pups can be spotted from March to June, and the gray whale from December to April. See Chapter 8.
- **Redwood National Park:** A wildlife enthusiast's dream. More than 300 bird species and 100 mammals can be seen, many of them year-round. Also watch (or watch out!) for black bears in summer. See Chapter 8.
- **Point Lobos State Reserve:** Take Calif. 1 about 4 miles south of Carmel to view harbor seals, sea lions, and sea otters at play. Gray whales pass by on their migration south from December to May. The area is filled with nature walks. See Chapter 12.
- **Cachuma Lake:** Situated on mountainous and scenic Calif. 154, halfway between Solvang and Santa Barbara, is this stunning winter home to dozens of American bald eagles. Loons, white pelicans, and Canada geese are some of the other migra-tory birds that call this glassy lake home part of the year. See Chapter 13.
- **Channel Islands National Park:** This is California in its most natural state. Paddle a kayak into sea caves; camp among indigenous island fox and seabirds; and swim, snorkel, or scuba dive tide pools and kelp forests teeming with wild-life. The channel waters are prime for whale watching, and May brings elephant seal mating season, when you'll see them and their sea lion cousins sunbathing on cove beaches. See Chapter 13.
- **Antelope Valley Poppy Reserve:** California's state flower, the poppy, blooms between March and May, carpeting the hillsides in brilliant hues of red, orange, and gold. This reserve, in the high desert near Los Angeles, is one of the poppy's most consistent natural growing sites. The fields extend for miles around—it's not uncommon to see motorists along Calif. 14 pull to the side of the road to marvel at the breathtaking spectacle. From Los Angeles, take I-5 north to Calif. 14; you'll know when you've arrived. See Chapter 16.
- **Joshua Tree National Park:** You'll find awesome rock formations, groves of flowering cacti and stately Joshua trees, ancient Native American petroglyphs, and shifting sand dunes in this desert wonderland—and a brilliant night sky, if you choose to camp here. See Chapter 16.

- **Death Valley National Park:** Its inhospitable climate makes it the state' likely tourist attraction. But the same conditions that thwarted settlers creat of the most dramatic landscapes you'll ever see. Mesmerizing rock formations, ever-changing dry lake beds, and often stifling heat provide the setting for relics of hardy 19th-century borax miners and (fool)hardy dwellers from the 1930s. See Chapter 16.
- **Torrey Pines State Reserve:** Poised on a majestic cliff overlooking the Pacific Ocean, this reserve is home to the rare torrey pine and numerous hiking trails. See Chapter 17.
- **Anza-Borrego Desert State Park:** The largest state park in the Lower 48 states attracts the most visitors during the spring wildflower season, when a kaleidoscopic carpet blankets the desert floor. Others come year-round to hike the more than 100 miles of designated trails. See Chapter 17.

2 The Best Beaches

- **San Francisco's Ocean Beach:** At the end of Golden Gate Park, on the western-most side of the city, Ocean Beach is gorgeous, but recommended for strolling and sunning only. Just offshore, the jagged Seal Rocks are inhabited by colonies of sea lions, among other creatures. See Chapter 5.
- **Stinson Beach:** Mount Tamalpais sweeps down to the sea at a point 6 treacher-ous miles north of Muir Beach on Highway 1. Chilly waters and the threat of sharks don't keep away thousands of sun worshippers and surfers. See Chapter 6.
- **Drake's Beach:** A massive stretch of white sand at Point Reyes National Seashore, west of Inverness. Winds and choppy seas make it rough for swimmers, but sun worshippers can have their Marin County tan for the day. If the rangers say it's all right, beach driftwood can make a romantic campfire in the early evening. See Chapter 8.
- **Manchester State Beach:** Take Calif. 1 eight miles north of Point Arena for a breezy introduction to the beaches of the far north. There are five miles of sand for beachcombing and surf fishing and huge driftwood logs along the beach. See Chapter 8.
- **Sand Dollar:** The best Big Sur beach lies beyond Pacific Valley—ideal for swim-ming and surfing, with a panoramic view of Cone Peak, one of the coast's high-est mountains. See Chapter 12.
- **Pfeiffer Beach:** This is one of Big Sur's best-kept secrets. It can be accessed via an unmarked paved road on the right-hand side of Calif. 1, one mile south of Pfeiffer State Park. There are no signs, so you'll have to do some sleuthing, but once you've parked behind the trail of cars on the side of the road and made it to the beach, you'll know why locals want to keep this spot all to themselves. See Chapter 12.
- **Santa Barbara's Cabrillo Beach:** This wide swath of clean, white sand hosts beach umbrellas, sand castle builders, and spirited volleyball games. A grassy, parklike median keeps the happy beachgoers insulated from busy Cabrillo Boulevard. On Sundays, local artists display their wares beneath the elegant palm trees. See Chapter 13.
- **Malibu's Legendary Beaches:** Zuma and Surfrider Beaches are the stretches of sand that were the inspiration for the 1960s surf music that embodies the South-ern California beach experience. Surfrider, just up from Malibu Pier, is home to Los Angeles's best waves. Zuma is loaded with amenities, including snack bars, rest rooms, and jungle gyms. In addition to some of the state's best sunbathing, you

can walk in front of the Malibu Colony, a star-studded enclave of multimillion-dollar homes set in this seductively curving stretch of coast. See Chapter 14.

- **Hermosa Beach:** This is one of Los Angeles's top beaches for family outings. It's also popular with the volleyball set. It offers wide sands, a paved boardwalk ("The Strand") that's great for strolling and biking, and loads of amenities, including plenty of parking. See Chapter 14.

- **La Jolla's Beaches:** *La Jolla* means "the jewel," and the beaches of La Jolla's cliff-lined coast truly are gems. Each has a distinct personality: Surfers love Windansea's waves; Torrey Pines and La Jolla Shores are popular for swimming and sunbathing; and Black's Beach is San Diego's unofficial (and illegal) nude beach. See Chapter 17.

- **Coronado Beach:** On the west side of Coronado extending to the Hotel del Coronado, this beautiful beach is uncrowded and great for watching the sunset. Marilyn Monroe romped in the surf here during the filming of *Some Like It Hot*. See Chapter 17.

3 The Best Walks

- **Golden Gate Park:** This walking tour lets you escape the bustle of San Francisco and takes you through an array of attractions, beginning with the 1878 Conservatory of Flowers, but also including museums and a Japanese Tea Garden, and even a 430-foot-high artificial island, Strawberry Hill. End your walk by renting a rowboat and taking it for a spin. See Chapter 5.

- **Point Reyes National Seashore:** In Marin County, west of Inverness and a quarter mile north of Drake's Beach, Point Reyes Lighthouse, 6 miles to the west, will be your final goal. The scenery is among the most beautiful and enticing in the Golden State, especially the hike to Chimney Rock (follow the signs on your way to the lighthouse). See Chapter 8.

- **Mendocino Headlands State Park:** Between Mendocino and the Pacific is one of the most scenic nature trails in the north. From December through March, the California gray whales pass by on their migration from the Arctic Ocean and Bering Sea to Baja California. Sunset vistas are worth the detour. See Chapter 8.

- **Yosemite National Park:** Relatively short and easy hikes will take you to Yosemite Falls, the highest waterfall in North America and the fifth highest in the world (upper falls at 1,430 feet), or to Bridalveil Falls, a ragged 620-foot cascade that can be wind-tossed as much as 20 feet from side to side. However, a more strenuous hike is a third option, the 3 1/2-mile Yosemite Falls Trail, which rises to a height of 2,700 feet for one of the most panoramic vistas in the West. See Chapter 10.

- **The Beachfront Trails at Big Sur:** Take towering cliffs, rock-strewn beaches, and a backdrop of redwood forests, and you have one of the most dramatic stretches for coastline hiking in the world. Begin your adventure about 8 miles south of Point Lobos. See Chapter 12.

- **Cabrillo Peak:** Morro Bay State Park offers a terrific day hike that culminates with a fantastic 360° view of surrounding hills and the distant ocean. There are hiking trails, but the best way to reach the top is by bushwhacking straight up the gentle slope. See Chapter 13.

- **Beverly Hills' "Golden Triangle":** Defined by Wilshire Boulevard, Crescent Drive, and Santa Monica Boulevard, this is a window-shopper's fantasyland of tiny shops with picture-perfect displays and sky-high price tags. It even boasts a cluster of shops built to resemble an Italian plaza, with its own faux cobblestone "streets." Despite what you've heard about Rodeo Drive tariffs (it's all true), don't worry: There are plenty of down-to-earth shops and eateries, plus an elegant Moorish-Mediterranean City Hall that's worth a look. See Chapter 14.

- **The L.A. Conservancy's Guided Walking Tours of Downtown Los Angeles:** The Conservancy conducts a dozen fascinating, information-packed tours of historic downtown Los Angeles, seed of today's sprawling metropolis. The most popular is "Broadway Theaters," a loving look at movie palaces; other intriguing ones include "Marble Masterpieces," "Art Deco," "Mecca for Merchants," and tours of the landmark Biltmore Hotel and City Hall. See Chapter 14.

- **Griffith Park:** This wooded enclave linking Hollywood with the San Fernando Valley has something for everyone. Be on the lookout for golf carts crossing near the picturesque Wilson and Harding golf courses, and for horseback riders from the nearby Equestrian Center. The L.A. Zoo and the Autry Museum lie at the northeast corner near I-5; the hills are loaded with hiking trails and picnic areas, and kids love the merry-go-round and pony rides. See Chapter 14.

- **From Crystal Pier (in Pacific Beach) South to the Jetty, and then North Along the Bay Side to the Catamaran Hotel:** During the first part of this walk, you'll share the sidewalk with joggers, cyclists, and in-line skaters, and surfers will be testing their skill on the waves to your right. After you cross over to the Mission Bay side of Mission Boulevard, you'll experience the more subdued side of things: quiet water lapping onto white sand beaches, and the local residents tending their gardens. A lovely way to spend the day in San Diego. See Chapter 17.

- **From the San Diego Convention Center to Harbor Island:** This delightful stroll takes you around the waterfront of San Diego Bay. Along the way you'll pass Seaport Village, Tuna Bay, the cruise ship terminal, the Embarcadero, and the Maritime Museum. The foot and cycle path offers a great view of Coronado and the ships plying the harbor. See Chapter 17.

4 The Best Budget Golf Courses

- **Coronado Municipal Golf Course** (San Diego): This 18-hole, par-72 municipal course overlooking Glorietta Bay is located to the left of the Coronado Bay Bridge. It's the first thing you see when you arrive in Coronado—a fabulous welcome for duffers. See Chapters 2 and 17.

- **Lincoln Park Golf Course** (San Francisco): The only problem with playing this course is that the views are so stunning, they may distract your game. For $23 to $28, you can tee off with the Golden Gate Bridge as a backdrop. If you want to play a few holes before sunset, nearby is the casual, but equally beautiful, nine-hole Golden Gate Park Course, where you can get nine in for a mere $10 to $13. See Chapter 5.

- **Lake Shastina Golf Resort** (near Mt. Shasta): For around $50, you can enjoy spectacular views of Mt. Shasta and 27 challenging holes designed by Robert Trent Jones Jr. See Chapter 9.

- **Lake Tahoe Golf Course** (Lake Tahoe): Set among California's pristine Sierra Nevada Mountains, this 18-hole tree-lined course on the South Shore will satisfy both hackers and scratch golfers. A round will cost about $40, and reduced rates are offered during the off-season. See Chapter 9.

- **Pacific Grove Municipal Golf Course:** In an area where most golfers cough up $200 to swing their clubs, this course offers golf at a price any duffer can afford. For a mere $24 to $28, you can play 18 holes overlooking the same beautiful ocean landscape that Pebble Beach does. See Chapter 12.

- **Santa Barbara Golf Club:** Unlike many municipal courses in California, this 6,009-yard, 18-hole course is well maintained and was designed to present a moderate challenge for the average golfer. Greens fees are $24 weekdays, and $28 on weekends ($17 for seniors). The driving range is an added bonus. See Chapter 13.
- **Rancho Park Golf Course** (Los Angeles): Although budget golf is almost an oxymoron in Los Angeles, Rancho Park, located smack-dab in the middle of the west side, offers a private-course atmosphere at public course prices. Greens fees are $17 Monday to Friday, and $21 on weekends. See Chapter 14.
- **Palm Springs Country Club:** The oldest public-access golf course within the city limits, this uniquely laid-out course is especially popular with budget-conscious golfers. With greens fees of only $40 to $50, this is about as cheap as it gets in the desert. See Chapter 16.
- **Torrey Pines Golf Course** (La Jolla): Two gorgeous 18-hole championship courses overlook the ocean and provide players with plenty of challenge. In February, the Buick Invitational Tournament is held here; the rest of the year these popular municipal courses are open to everybody. See Chapter 17.

5 The Best Offbeat Experiences That Won't Cost You a Fortune

- **Taking a Mud Bath in Calistoga:** In this town's famous volcanic-ash mud— mixed with mineral water—you can get buck naked and covered in gooey mud. At a dozen or so places you can immerse yourself in the mud bath, followed by a mineral-water shower and a whirlpool bath, then a steam bath. It's perhaps the most relaxing experience in California. See Chapter 7.
- **Discovering "The Lost Coast":** The terrain was so rugged the state of California couldn't extend Highway 1 along the Pacific between Rockport and Eureka. Today, this isolated region remains pristine, with redwood trees perched precariously on cliffs some 200 feet above the rock-strewn coastline. The 75-mile drive is entered from U.S. 101 at Garberville, or, better yet, from a paved road from Humboldt Redwoods State Park, 3 miles north of Weott. See Chapter 8.
- **Panning for Gold in the Gold Country:** In the southern Gold Country, you can dig into living history and pan for gold. Several companies, including **Gold Prospecting Expeditions** (☎ 800/596-0009 or 209/984-4653) in Jamestown, offer dredging lessons and gold-panning tours. You'll quickly learn that this is back-breaking labor, although an adventure. And who knows? You might get lucky and launch a new gold rush. See Chapter 11.
- **Taking a Gastronomic Road Trip Between Bakersfield and the Gold Country:** Calif. 99 passes through fertile agricultural land and a series of small towns, each with a distinct ethnic heritage. Basque sheep farmers and bakers, Dutch dairies, Swedish and Armenian enclaves near Fresno, Portuguese and Italians near Modesto, and a French sausage maker in Lodi. They all represent the delicious diversity of California's central region. See Chapter 11.
- **Riding the Amtrak Rails Along the Southern California Coast:** Relive the golden age of train travel and see the natural beauty of California, avoiding the crowded highways at the same time. Spanish-style Union Station, a marble-floored Streamline Moderne masterpiece, is the Los Angeles hub. Trains run between Los Angeles and the romantic mission towns of San Juan Capistrano, San Diego, Santa Barbara, and San Luis Obispo. The scenery includes lush valleys, windswept coastline, and the occasional urban stretch. Call **Amtrak** at **800/USA-RAIL** for information.

- **Discovering Downtown Los Angeles's Public Art:** The wealth of public art on display in downtown Los Angeles is one of the city's best-kept secrets. Some works make political or social commentary (the black experience as represented by the life of former slave Biddy Mason in a multimedia exhibit between Broadway and Spring Streets just south of 3rd Street, or Judd Fine's evolutionary chronicle *Spine* installed outside the Central Library). Others are abstract and open to a variety of interpretations. Pershing Square, a formerly untended eyesore bounded by 5th, 6th, Olive, and Hill streets, has been reincarnated as a modern sculpture garden. See Chapter 14.
- **Exploring Forest Lawn Memorial Park:** America's most famous cemetery is a wacky 300-acre park with more stars in the ground than Hollywood's Walk of Fame. In addition to Hollywood's most dearly departed, the cemetery contains 1,000 full-scale reproductions of Renaissance statuary, the enormous Great Mausoleum with its oversized stained-glass reproduction of *The Last Supper,* and the Church of the Recessional, where Ronald Reagan married his first wife, Jane Wyman. See Chapter 14.
- **Strolling Venice Beach:** All of humanity, for better and worse, is represented on a boardwalk framed by broad sands, swaying palms, and the sparkling blue Pacific. The day's carnival might include well-tanned body builders, outrageous street performers, scantily clad beach bunnies (bimbos *and* himbos), roving gangs of teens, psychedelic-era hippies, and much more. Experiment with style at the cheap sunglass stalls, grab an exotic dog at Jody Maroni's Sausage Kingdom, and make your way to the Santa Monica pier to check out the historic photo gallery and carousel. See Chapter 14.
- **Going to the Movies, San Diego Style:** Imagine sitting on the deck of the world's oldest merchant ship, watching a film projected on the "screen-sail"; floating on a raft in a huge indoor pool while a movie is shown on the wall; watching a silent movie accompanied by the San Diego Symphony; or sitting on the beach watching a movie that's projected on a floating barge. Only in San Diego! See Chapter 17.
- **Experiencing a San Diego Christmas:** Although visions of sugar plums don't dance in most people's heads when they think about San Diego, the area does offer a variety of unusual Christmas traditions. These include Christmas on the Prado in Balboa Park; the Coronado Christmas Celebration and Parade, where Santa arrives by ferry; and the Mission Bay Boat Parade of Lights and the San Diego Harbor Parade of Lights, where decorated boats of all sizes and types are the focus of attention. And it wouldn't be Christmas without the annual reading of Dr. Seuss's *How the Grinch Stole Christmas* at Loews Coronado Bay Resort. See chapters 2 and 17.

6 The Best Places to Get Away from It All

- **The Mt. Shasta Area:** The region around Mt. Shasta is a remote swath of Northern California. "Lonely as God and white as a winter moon," wrote Joaquin Miller in 1873, and it's still true at this 14,000-foot-plus dormant volcano, which Native Americans called "the resting place of the Great Spirit." Here, in the region at the top of California, you can wander away from everything and everybody. Go in late spring when the wildflowers first burst into bloom and the trout are jumping. See Chapter 9.
- **Sequoia and Kings Canyon National Parks:** They have only a fraction of Yosemite's crowds and they're stunningly beautiful. This is a land of grandiose

scenery separated by Kings Canyon, the deepest chasm in the continental United States. Virgin forests carpet the parks. Use them for hiking or wilderness camping almost unequaled in America. Autumn is our favorite time to visit. Almost everyone disappears, and you get to experience crisp days in fall colors and long, lingering Indian summers. See Chapter 10.

- **The Ventana Wilderness** (Big Sur): The U.S. Forest Service maintains 167,323 scenic acres straddling the Santa Lucia mountains. Cascading streams, waterfalls, deep pools, and thermal springs take you back to Eden. Bring your Adam or Eve so you won't get lonely in the midst of all this nature. See Chapter 12.
- **Channel Islands National Park:** Just off the coast of Ventura is a world removed from the bustle of Southern California. The islands are a wild and storm-blown region of sharp cliffs, curving grasslands, and rocky coves punctuated by the barking of elephant seals and sea lions. Camping among the archipelago's many endemic plant species and fascinating array of animals (including the endangered brown pelican and indigenous fox) is a splendid way to steep yourself in the beauty of this untamed preserve. See Chapter 13.
- **The Huntington Library, Art Collections, and Botanical Gardens** (near Pasadena): This daytime Pasadena area getaway is many treats in one. The former estate of railroad baron Henry Huntington is a spectacular botanical garden whose highlights include Japanese and Zen gardens, an oft-filmed statuary lawn, a camellia garden, and tranquil lily ponds. The Italianate main house is a gallery of European paintings, and scholars flock to study at the Huntington Library, one of the world's finest collections of rare manuscripts and first editions (including a Gutenberg bible). A superb bookstore and delightful tearoom round out this peaceful retreat. See Chapter 15.
- **The Pine Hills Area of Julian:** A half dozen bed-and-breakfast inns are located in this wonderfully quiet small town, where birdsong is the loudest sound you'll hear. See Chapter 17.

7 The Best Things to Do for Free

- **Beach It:** It wouldn't be a true California vacation if you didn't hit at least one of the state's beautiful beaches. See each coastal chapter for beach highlights.
- **Walking the Golden Gate Bridge:** Break out your windbreaker and walking shoes and venture across San Francisco's windy Golden Gate Bridge. On a sunny day, every view is spectacular. In dense fog, it can be bone-chilling, but still a mystical experience. See Chapter 5.
- **San Francisco's Midsummer Music Festival:** One of our all-time favorite ways to spend a sunny Sunday. Grab a picnic, a bottle of wine, a blanket, and head to Sigmund Stern Grove, where you'll get a real feel for San Franciscans and their love for culture and unity. Each summer there's an amazing lineup of talent, ranging from symphony orchestras to ballet, that's always accompanied by a feel-good atmosphere. The program runs from mid-June through August. Call **415/252-6252.** See Chapter 5.
- **Discovering Muir Woods, Stinson Beach, and Point Reyes:** If you're in or around the Bay Area and have wheels, indulge in this memorable side trip. Take Calif. 101 to the Stinson Beach exit and spend a few hours gawking at the monolithic redwoods at Muir Woods (this place is amazing); continue on to Stinson Beach, then head up the coast to the spectacular Point Reyes National Seashore. Rain or shine, you won't be disappointed. See Chapter 6.

- **Wine Appreciation Classes:** Goosecross Cellars (☎ 707/944-1986), a Napa Valley winery near Yountville, gives a free class each Saturday morning at 11am. In the course of a few hours, they can turn anyone into a budding sommelier. Ignorance being bliss, you even get to taste all kinds of yummy wines while you learn. See Chapter 7.
- **Whale Watching:** Gray whales travel along the California coast from late December to early February, and you don't need to get on a whale-watching boat to enjoy their fluid frolic. Point Reyes Lighthouse is a particularly good on-shore whale-watching spot. See Chapter 8.
- **Exploring Shasta Dam and Power Plant:** Located near Mt. Shasta, it's one of the best free tours in the state, and an entertaining way to beat the summer heat. Explore deep within the dam's many chilly corridors and below the enormous spillway. Call **916/275-4463** for details. See Chapter 9.
- **Yosemite:** Walk, hike, backpack, or just drive in and catch some rays. Whatever you do in Yosemite, bring your camera, because the landscape is nothing less than astounding. If you're the sporting type, you can get up close and personal with some of the largest waterfalls on earth; climb a gargantuan granite monolith; or swim in fresh snowmelt lakes. There's a nominal charge to enter the park, but once you're in, it's yours to explore. See Chapter 10.
- **Touring the State Capitol in Sacramento:** Looking very much like a scale model of the U.S. Capitol in Washington, D.C., this domed structure is the city's most distinctive landmark. Free guided tours, offered daily (every hour on the hour), shed light on the building's architecture and the workings of government. For information, call **916/275-4463**. See Chapter 11.
- **Cruising Pacific Grove's Ocean View Boulevard:** This coastal stretch, which starts near Monterey's Cannery Row and follows the Pacific Ocean south to Asilomar State Beach, offers coastal views as spectacular as those of 17-Mile Drive, but without the $6.50-per-car entrance fee. See Chapter 12.
- **SLO's Farmer's Market:** Spend a Thursday evening at the Farmer's Market in San Luis Obispo to get the true flavor of this somewhat earthy, intimate community. There's usually live music, barbecues, demonstrations, discussions, and plenty of places to plop down and watch this small town rejoice. See Chapter 13.
- **Santa Barbara Crafts Fairs:** Stroll along the promenade of East Beach by Stearns Wharf on a Sunday and you'll get a good dose of ocean air, sunshine, and fabulous art. Here dozens of arts and crafts vendors sell their wares. Don't bother paying $5 to park in the lot; if you continue south on Cabrillo Boulevard, you're likely to find free parking. See Chapter 13.
- **Watching the Sunset from a Southern California Pier:** Huntington, Hermosa, Malibu, Mission, or Pacific—nothing rivals the sensation of standing suspended over the swirling ocean, watching a glowing sun descend into the horizon. Wispy clouds reflect the reds, oranges, and pinks cast by the receding sun, and behind you waves crash upon meeting the sand. See chapters 14 and 17.
- **Spending an Afternoon at Los Angeles's Central Library:** The city is truly fond of the Central Library, for both its history and its architecture, and for the remarkable effort made by firefighters and philanthropists to save and restore it after a fire in 1986. Behind the familiar facade is a newly designed modern wing, housing most of the library's countless volumes, and a light-filled atrium with gigantic, whimsical chandeliers. Intriguing outdoor art adorns the front courtyard. Admission is free, of course, and weekend parking in the library's lot is just $2 with validation. See Chapter 14.

- **Attend an Organ Concert in Balboa Park** (San Diego): Free one-hour Sunday concerts are given at the Spreckels Organ Pavilion, home of the world's largest pipe organ; from June through August you can also attend free evening concerts here as part of the city's "Twilight in the Park" festival. See Chapter 17.
- **Discover California's Roots** (San Diego): The Golden State was born in what is now the Old Town State Historic Park in San Diego. A tour here (check out the original adobe dwellings) doesn't cost a dime—neither does the fabulous weekend entertainment at the Bazaar del Mundo featuring mariachis and folk dancers. See Chapter 17.

8 The Best Family Vacation Experiences

- **San Francisco:** Ride the cable cars that "climb halfway to the stars" and visit the Exploratorium, the California Academy of Sciences (which includes the Steinhart Aquarium), the zoo, the ships at the maritime museum, Golden Gate Park, and much more. The City by the Bay is filled with unexpected pleasures for all members of the family and all ages. See Chapter 5.
- **Marine World Africa USA:** One of Northern California's most popular attractions is located on Marine World Parkway at Vallejo, an hour's drive northeast of San Francisco. This 160-acre wildlife theme park features animals of the air, land, and sea. Killer whales, elephants, dolphins, and sea lions are all in the act and you get a close-up look. See Chapter 6.
- **San Jose:** There's the Children's Discovery Museum, the Tech Museum of Innovation, and especially the architecturally bizarre Winchester Mystery House and Paramount's Great America. See Chapter 6.
- **Lake Tahoe:** Lake Tahoe has piles of family fun things to do. Skiing, snowboarding, hiking, tobogganing, swimming, fishing, boating, waterskiing, mountain biking—the list is nearly endless. Even the casinos cater to kids while Mom and Pop play the slots. See Chapter 9.
- **Yosemite National Park:** Camping or staying in a cabin in Yosemite is a premier family attraction in California. Sites are scattered over 17 different campgrounds, and the rugged beauty of the Sierra Nevada surrounds you. During the day, the family calendar is packed with hiking, bicycling, white-water trips, and even mountaineering to rugged, snowy peaks. See Chapter 10.
- **Monterey:** It's been called "Disneyland-by-the-Sea" because of all its tourist activities, including those on Cannery Row and Fisherman's Wharf. Check out the state-of-the-art aquarium and have breakfast at the Bagel Bakery at 201 Lighthouse Blvd. (the best family bargain in town). See Chapter 12.
- **Big Bear Lake:** Families flock year-round to this lake in the San Bernardino Mountains, and not just for the skiing. Horseback riding, miniature golf, water sports, and the Alpine Slide (kind of a snowless bobsled) are fun alternatives, and you can see and learn about native wildlife at the Moonridge Animal Park. The newly expanded village has a movie theater, arcade, and dozens of cutesy bear-themed businesses. Most of the local lodging consists of clusters of woodsy cabins that are perfect for families. See Chapter 15.
- **Disneyland:** The "Happiest Place on Earth" is family entertainment at its best. Whether you're wowed by Disney animation come alive, thrilled by the roller-coaster rides, or interested in the history and hidden secrets of this pop-culture icon, you won't walk away disappointed. Stay at the nearby Disneyland Hotel (connected directly to the park by monorail), a wild attraction unto itself, which offers appealing packages including multiday access to the park that can really save

you some money. There's also a terrific extra bonus: On most days, gu___ hotel get to enter the park early and enjoy the major rides with no lines. But __ the hotel tariffs are still too rich for your blood, don't worry; we've recommended plenty of comfortable motels nearby. Call ahead for the day's schedule. See Chapter 15.

- **San Diego Zoo, Wild Animal Park, and Sea World:** San Diego boasts three of the world's best animal attractions. At the zoo, animals live in creatively designed habitats such as Tiger River and Hippo Beach. At the Wild Animal Park, 3,000 animals roam freely over 2,200 acres. And Sea World, with its ever-changing animal shows and exhibits, is an aquatic wonderland. See Chapter 17.

9 The Best of Small-Town California

- **St. Helena:** A small town in the heart of the Napa Valley, St. Helena is known for its Main Street, which is lined with Victorian storefronts featuring intriguing wares. In a horse and buggy, Robert Louis Stevenson and his new bride, the cantankerous Fanny, made their way down this street. Go here for the old-timey, tranquil mood and the wonderful food. See Chapter 7.
- **Mendocino:** An artist's colony with a New England flavor, Mendocino served as the backdrop for *Murder, She Wrote.* Perched on the clifftops above the Pacific Ocean, it's filled with small art galleries, general stores, weathered wooden houses, and elbow-to-elbow tourists. See Chapter 8.
- **Arcata:** If you're losing your faith in America, a few days spent at this Northern California coastal town will surely restore your patriotism. One of the best small towns in America, Arcata has it all: its own redwood forest and bird marsh, a charming town square, great family owned restaurants, and even its own minor-league baseball team, which draws the whole town together for an afternoon of pure camaraderie. See Chapter 8.
- **Nevada City:** The whole town is a national historic landmark and the best place to understand Gold Rush fever. Settled in 1849, it offers fine dining and shopping and a stock of multigabled Victorian frame houses of the Old West. Relics of the ill-fated Donner Party are on display at the 1861 Firehouse No. 1. See Chapter 11.
- **Pacific Grove:** Here you can escape from the crowds in Monterey, 2 miles to the west. Pacific Grove is known for its tranquil waterfront location and quiet, unspoiled air. Thousands of Monarch butterflies flock here between October and March to make their winter home in Washington Park. See Chapter 12.
- **Cambria:** Near Hearst Castle, Cambria benefits from a constant stream of visitors, who bring the right amount of sophistication to this picturesque coastal town. Moonstone Beach holds a string of seaside lodges, while the village itself is filled with charming B&Bs, artists' studios and galleries, and friendly shops. Don't miss Linn's Bakery and Restaurant, whose fresh olallieberry pies and other regional treats are well known throughout the Central Coast. See Chapter 13.
- **Ojai:** When Hollywood needed a Shangri-La for the movie *Lost Horizon,* they drove 1¹/₂ hours north to idyllic Ojai Valley, an unspoiled hideaway of eucalyptus groves and small ranches warmly nestled among soft, green hills. Ojai is the amiable village at the valley's heart. It's a mecca for artists, free spirits, and weary city folk in need of a restful weekend in the country. See Chapter 13.
- **Ventura:** This charming mission town is filled with colorful Victorians. It's also home to a pleasantly eclectic old Main Street lined with thrift and antique shops, used record stores, friendly diners, and even old-time saloons operating beneath

broken-down second-story hotels. Don't miss the historic mission on its landscaped plaza, and the deco-era Greek Revival San Buenaventura City Hall looming over the town, bedecked with smiling stone faces of the founding Franciscan friars. See Chapter 13.

- **Julian:** This old mining town in the Cuyamaca Mountains near San Diego is well known today for its wildflower fields, the fall apple harvest, and tasty flavored breads from Dudley's Bakery. There's plenty of pioneer history here, too, including a local history museum, a circa 1888 schoolhouse, and mining demonstrations. A smattering of antique shops, plenty of barbecue, and an old-fashioned soda fountain operating since 1886 round out the experience. See Chapter 17.

- **Temecula:** This charming town, located in Riverside County 60 miles north of San Diego, is best known for its wineries and the excellent vintages they produce, as well as the annual hot-air balloon festival at harvest time. Since the wineries here are smaller than their counterparts in Northern California, and are mostly family owned and operated, you're more likely to be able to meet and talk with the vintners here. See Chapter 17.

10 The Best California-Style Americana

- **Mel's Diner** (San Francisco): Kids from 6 to 60 love this quintessential '50s diner straight out of *American Graffiti*. Though the fare has advanced to meet today's demands (there's even a veggie burger on the menu), you can still stuff yourself with a big, juicy bacon cheeseburger, a side of "wet fries" (they're smothered in gravy), and a milkshake. There's plenty of chrome, miniature jukeboxes at each table with good ole American hits on them, and photo memorabilia from the movie that inspired the place. Kids will love the crayons and meal-in-a-car. See Chapter 5.

- **Phoenix Inn** (San Francisco; ☎ 800/248-9466): Get out your red heart-shaped sunglasses and you'll be ready for the funky Phoenix. An intentionally tacky-tropic oasis in the midst of one of the city's most colorful, and shady, neighborhoods, this '50s-style retro-chic motel hosts all walks of life, from famous rockers to politicians and movie stars who come for the anonymity, the kidney-shaped pool, and reggae at the adjoining festive restaurant. See Chapter 5.

- **Baseball in Arcata:** On Wednesday, Friday, and Saturday evenings between June and July, Arcata's semipro baseball team, the Humboldt Crabs, partakes in America's favorite pastime at Arcata Ballpark at 9th and F streets. For a $3.50 ticket, it's one of the best entertainment bargains on the North Coast. See Chapter 8.

- **Ponderosa Ranch** (Lake Tahoe; ☎ 702/831-0691): Remember Hoss and Little Joe Cartwright from the popular 1960s television show *Bonanza*? Well, their digs are still kickin', folks, so mosey on over to Tahoe to visit the original 1959 Cartwright Ranch House and western township, complete with blacksmith's shop and staged gun battles. There are also such activities as breakfast hay rides and pony rides. See Chapter 9.

- **Dennis the Menace Playground:** Just north of Monterey, at Camino El Estero and Del Monte Avenue, near Lake Estero, is an expansive, old-fashioned playground created by Pacific Grove resident and famous cartoonist Hank Ketcham. It has a pond, bridges to cross, tunnels to climb through, an authentic Southern Pacific engine car teeming with wanna-be conductors, and plenty of Dennis the Menace motifs. It's a must-see for families. See Chapter 12.

- **The Madonna Inn** (San Luis Obispo; ☎ **800/543-9666**): No, not *that* Madonna. This inn is named after Alex and Phyllis Madonna, who, though they have no ties to the pop star, share with her a wild, and tacky, sense of style. The entire hotel is one giant over-the-top fantasy, done up in Pepto Bismol pink, Flintstone-style rock, and whatever else catches their whim. You've got to see this place for yourself. See Chapter 13.
- **Solvang:** If the Dutch built a replica of a quaint Dutch village, Solvang would be it. This is not the kind of place where you'd want to hang out for a few days; it's more a quick stopover to grab a few supersweet pastries and gawk at the gingerbread houses, giant clogs, and cute little windmills. See Chapter 13.
- **Route 66** (east of Pasadena): Although much of America's historic "Mother Road" has been plowed under for superslab, multilane highways, there's a treasure trove of glorious relics to be seen between Pasadena and San Bernardino. Picture T-bird convertibles and "woody" station wagons pulling into low-profile motor courts with romantic names like Ken-Tuck-U-Inn, Rose Motel, Moana, Dragon, Sand and Sage, Sunset, 40 Winks, Redwing, and the truly unique Wigwam Motel (comprised of actual concrete wigwams). Old-style roadside diners, abandoned single-pump gas stations, and a bevy of drive-through dairies also abound. See Chapter 4.
- **The Wheel Inn Restaurant** (Cabazon; ☎ **909/849-7012**): What's different about this clean roadside diner and gas station on I-10 near Palm Springs? It's not the food (basic truck stop chow), but the looming presence of a four-story brontosaurus and his Tyrannosaurus rex pal. They were built in the 1960s by a sketch artist and sculptor from Knott's Berry Farm with a grandiose dream of an entire dinosaur amusement park. You can climb up into the belly of the larger one, where you'll find a remarkably spacious gift shop selling dinosaur toys, books, and souvenirs. See Chapter 16.
- **The Roy Rogers and Dale Evans Museum** (Victorville; ☎ **619/243-4547**): Housed in a replica old-West log fort, this tribute to the lives, films, family, and travels of the famous B-movie couple is best known for being the final resting place of Roy's faithful horse, Trigger, who is stuffed, mounted, and prominently displayed. Evoking both Las Vegas tackiness and the jam-packed attic of some wacky, well-traveled relative, the museum is one-of-a-kind, and well worth a one- or two-hour stop between Los Angeles and Las Vegas. See Chapter 16.

11 The Best Architectural Landmarks

- **The Civic Center** (San Francisco): The creation of designers John Bakewell Jr. and Arthur Brown Jr., it is perhaps the most beautiful beaux arts complex in America. See Chapter 5.
- **The Painted Ladies** (San Francisco): The so-called "Painted Ladies" are the city's famous, ornately decorated Victorian homes. Check out the brilliant beauties around Alamo Square. Most of the extant 14,000 structures date from the second half of the 19th century. See Chapter 5.
- **Winchester Mystery House** (San Jose): The heiress to the Winchester rifle fortune, Sarah Winchester, created one of the major "Believe It or Not?" curiosities of California, a 160-room Victorian mansion. It's been called the "world's strangest monument to a woman's fear." When a fortune teller told her she wouldn't die if she'd continue to build onto her house, her mansion underwent construction day and night from 1884 to 1922. She did die eventually and the hammers were silenced. See Chapter 6.

- **The Carson House** (Eureka): This splendidly ornate Victorian is one of the state's most photographed and flamboyant Queen Anne–style structures. It was built in 1885 by the Newsom brothers for William Carson, the local timber baron. Today it's the headquarters of a men's club. See Chapter 8.
- **Mission San Carlos Borromeo del Rio Carmelo** (Carmel): The second mission founded in California in 1770 by Father Junípero Serra (who is buried there) is perhaps the most beautiful. Its stone church and tower dome have been authentically restored, and a peaceful garden of California poppies adjoins the church. Sights include an early kitchen and the founding father's spartan sleeping quarters. See Chapter 12.
- **The Control Tower and Theme Building at Los Angeles International Airport:** The spacey Jetsons-style "Theme Building," which has always loomed over LAX, unmistakably signaling your arrival, has been joined by a brand-new silhouette. The main control tower, designed by local architect Kate Diamond to evoke a stylized palm tree, is tailored to present Southern California in its best light. Only authorized personnel are allowed to make the ascent, but you can still enjoy the view from the Theme Building's observation lounge. See Chapter 14.
- **Los Angeles's Central Library:** The city rallied to save the downtown library when an arson fire nearly destroyed it in 1986; the triumphant result has returned much of its original splendor. Working in the early 1920s, architect Bertram G. Goodhue employed the Egyptian motifs and materials popularized by the recent discovery of King Tut's tomb, combined with the more modern use of concrete block. See Chapter 14.
- **Tail o' the Pup** (Los Angeles): At first glance, you might not think twice about this hot dog–shaped bit of kitsch on West Hollywood's San Vicente Boulevard, just across from the Beverly Center. But locals adored this closet-sized wiener dispensary so much that when it was threatened by the developer's bulldozer, they spoke out en masse to save it. One of the last remaining examples of 1950s representational architecture, the "little dog that could" also serves up a great Baseball Special. See Chapter 14.
- **The Gamble House** (Pasadena): The Smithsonian Institution calls this Pasadena landmark, built in 1908, "one of the most important houses in the United States." Architects Charles and Henry Greene created a masterpiece of the Japanese-influenced Arts and Crafts movement. Tours are conducted of the spectacular interior, designed by the Greenes down to the last piece of teak furniture and coordinating Tiffany lamp, and executed with impeccable craftsmanship. After you're done, stroll the immediate neighborhood to view several more Greene and Greene creations. See Chapter 15.
- **Balboa Park** (San Diego): These Spanish/Mayan style buildings were originally built as temporary structures for the Panama-California Exposition between 1915 and 1916. Although many have been rebuilt over the years, a few of the original buildings still remain, and are worth seeking out. See Chapter 17.
- **Hotel Del Coronado** (Coronado): The "Hotel Del" stands in all its ornate Victorian red-tiled glory on some of the loveliest beach in Southern California. Built in 1888, it's one of the largest remaining wooden structures in the world. Even if you're not staying, stop by to take a detailed tour of the splendidly restored interiors, elegant grounds, and fascinating minimuseum of the hotel's spirited history. On your way to Coronado, you can't miss the Coronado Bay Bridge, an architectural landmark in its own right. Crossing the bridge by car or bus is an undeniable thrill because you can see Mexico, the San Diego skyline, Coronado, the naval station, and San Diego Bay. See Chapter 17.

12 The Best Museums

- **The Exploratorium** (San Francisco): The hands-on, interactive Exploratorium boasts 650 exhibits that help to show how things work. You use all your senses and stretch them to a new dimension. Every exhibit is designed to be useful. See Chapter 5.
- **The Oakland Museum:** This one might be dubbed the "Museum of California." The colorful people and history of the Golden State, and its sometimes overpowering art and culture, are here. Everything from the region's first inhabitants to today's urban violence is depicted. See Chapter 6.
- **California State Railroad Museum** (Sacramento): Old Sacramento's biggest attraction, the 100,000-square-foot museum was once the terminus of the transcontinental and Sacramento Valley railways. The largest museum of its type in the United States, it displays 21 locomotives and railroad cars, among other attractions. One sleeping car simulates travel, with all the swaying and flashing lights of lonely towns passed in the night. See Chapter 11.
- **Petersen Automotive Museum** (Los Angeles): This museum is a natural for Los Angeles, a city whose personality is so entwined with the popularity of the car. Impeccably restored vintage autos are displayed in life-size dioramas accurate to the last period detail (including an authentic 1930s-era service station). Upstairs galleries house movie-star and motion-picture vehicles, car-related artwork, and visiting exhibits. See Chapter 14.
- **J. Paul Getty Museum** (Malibu): This exact replica of a villa buried by Vesuvius in A.D. 79 is the perfect setting for a world-renowned collection of Greek and Roman antiquities. Fueled by a bottomless endowment from billionaire oil magnate J. Paul Getty, the foundation has built an awesome collection that also includes European paintings and furnishings. There's a surprisingly eclectic parade of visiting exhibits, as well as a splendid Pacific view from the Roman pool garden. See Chapter 14.
- **Autry Museum of Western Heritage** (Los Angeles): This is a treat for both young and old. Relive California's historic cowboy past, and see how the period has been depicted by Hollywood through the years, from Disney cartoon recreations to founder Gene Autry's "singing cowboy" films to popular 1960s TV series. Highlights include a life-size woolly mammoth and a glimmering vault of ornate frontier firearms. See Chapter 14.
- **Norton Simon Museum** (Pasadena): This Pasadena museum is seen by millions each January 1 as a picturesque backdrop for the Rose Parade. What TV viewers miss, however, are the treasures inside, carefully collected by wealthy art lover Norton Simon and his wife, actress Jennifer Jones. The collection, spanning 2,000 years, includes Asian art and works of the Renaissance Masters, but the museum's strength is its modern collection. Fine Impressionist (Cezanne, Renoir, van Gogh) and later (Kandinsky, Picasso) works are well complemented by the 19th- and 20th-century sculpture gardens, home to works by Rodin and others. See Chapter 15.
- **Museum of Contemporary Art** (San Diego): MCA is actually one museum with two locations: one in La Jolla, the other downtown. The museum is known internationally for its permanent collection, focusing primarily on work produced since 1950. See Chapter 17.
- **The Museums of Balboa Park** (San Diego): Located in a relaxed, verdant setting, the museums here offer unique cultural experiences. Highlights include the Aerospace Historical Center, Museum of Man, Museum of Photographic Arts, Model

...d Museum, Natural History Museum, and the Lily Pond and Botanical
...ng. Check in at the Hospitality Center for a map and "Passport to Balboa
...., a low-cost pass to a combination of the museums. See Chapter 17.

13 The Best Views

- **Coit Tower** (San Francisco): The round 1933 tower atop Telegraph Hill opens onto a panoramic 360° view of the City by the Bay. In the distance, the Marin Headlands unfold. In a city known for its views and vantage points, Coit Tower is the scenic show-stopper. See Chapter 5.
- **The Summit of Mount Tamalpais:** Twenty miles north of San Francisco, "Mount Tam" gives you a 100-mile panoramic sweep in all directions, from the foothills of the Sierras to the western horizon. The sunset there equals any Hemingway ever wrote about. See Chapter 6.
- **Mt. Shasta As Seen from Black Butte:** The view of venerable Mount Shasta is best from Black Butte, which sits next to the 14,000-foot-plus behemoth itself. The 6,325-foot dome of Black Butte is reached after a three-hour hike to the top. The majesty of the site turned fabled naturalist John Muir's "blood to wine." See Chapter 9.
- **Glacier Point in Yosemite National Park:** A sweeping 180° panorama of the High Sierra unfolds from 3,200 feet above the valley. Glacier Point looks out over Nevada and Vernal Falls, the Merced River, and the snow-covered Sierra peaks of Yosemite's backcountry. See Chapter 10.
- **San Joaquin Valley:** This fertile valley is part of California's geographic and economic center. Roadside stops along I-5 offer panoramic views of 11 million rich acres of grapes, figs, almonds, carrots, asparagus, corn, and more. See Chapter 11.
- **The Coastline at Garrapata State Park:** You'll see 4 miles of the California coastline from Garrapata State Park, a 2,879-acre preserve in the Big Sur area. Rock-strewn beaches, towering cliffs, and redwood forests combine to form what may be the world's most dramatic coastal panorama. See Chapter 12.
- **The Santa Barbara Mission:** Gazing seaward from the church's majestic steps, you can take in a panoramic view of Santa Barbara's delightful Spanish-style red-tile roofs, plus the California coast and azure Pacific in all their splendor. It is a postcard-worthy vista throughout the day, from the pastel shades of dawn to the midday shimmer of the sea to the fiery brilliance of sunset. See Chapter 13.
- **Griffith Observatory and Planetarium** (Los Angeles): For an outlook on urban Los Angeles without compare, head to this spot in the Hollywood Hills. Great ornate bronze doors lead into this 1935 Classic Moderne edifice (immortalized in *Rebel Without a Cause*). The view over the city from the hilltop balconies can, on a clear day, stretch to the Pacific. The lights of Hollywood below sparkle seductively at night, and the observatory's telescope can illuminate the myriad moons of Jupiter for you. See Chapter 14.
- **Rim of the World Highway** (Lake Arrowhead): This aptly named road winds toward Lake Arrowhead along a mountain ridge above San Bernardino. The view of the vast, flat valley floor beyond the evergreen fringe is breathtaking. At this altitude (about 5500 feet), where the air is crisp and clean, it's easy to imagine you're floating above the earth. See Chapter 15.
- **The Colorado Desert:** If you think the desert is barren and ugly, you'll quickly change your mind. From the sweeping panorama atop Mt. San Jacinto (accessible by the Palm Springs Aerial Tramway) to the vast, other-worldly wind-turbine

fields scattered throughout the valley, the visual splendor of this area mirrors the spirituality felt here by Native Americans and 20th-century spa-goers alike. From sunrise to sunset, natural light and shadow perform magic, transforming the shapes and colors of the arid hills. See Chapter 16.

- **Cabrillo National Monument** (near San Diego): From this vantage point, on the tip of Point Loma, you're treated to a spectacular vista of the ocean, San Diego Bay, Los Coronados Islands, and the mountains that ring the city to the east. Simply spectacular. See Chapter 17.
- **Mount Soledad** (San Diego): For a 360° view of La Jolla, Del Mar, downtown San Diego, inland San Diego, the Pacific Ocean, the mountains, and on a clear day, even Mexico, Mount can't be beat. And it can't be missed, either: This La Jolla landmark is topped by a large, white cross. See Chapter 17.

14 The Best Moderately Priced Hotels

- **Savoy Hotel** (San Francisco; ☎ 415/441-2700): This hotel is not only well appointed, affordable, and centrally located, but also has one of the city's better midrange restaurants adjoining the lobby. See Chapter 5.
- **St. Orres** (Gualala; ☎ 707/884-3303): Designed in a Russian style—complete with two Kremlinesque onion-domed towers—St. Orres offers secluded accommodations constructed from century-old timbers salvaged from a nearby mill. One of the most eye-catching inns on California's north coast. See Chapter 8.
- **Coloma Country Inn** (Coloma; ☎ 916/622-6919): Deep in the heart of California's northern Gold Country, this 1852 farmhouse stands on five acres of land. Rooms are decorated with stenciling and furnished with antiques, and old-fashioned country quilts cover the beds. Fresh flowers from the surrounding gardens brighten the house. See Chapter 11.
- **The Jabberwock** (Monterey; ☎ 408/372-4777): This place, only four blocks from Cannery Row, was once a convent. Set in its own gardens with waterfalls, it was named after an episode from Lewis Carroll's *Through the Looking Glass*. Each room is individually decorated; one even has a fireplace. See Chapter 12.
- **Bath Street Inn** (Santa Barbara; ☎ 800/341-BATH): This is one of the sweetest, most immaculate B&Bs in California. The inn makes special efforts to coddle guests and also has a wonderfully peaceful back deck shaded by an enormous wisteria. See Chapter 13.
- **Hollywood Roosevelt** (Los Angeles; ☎ 800/252-7466): This hotel, overlooking the Walk of Fame, is a legendary survivor from Hollywood's Golden Age. Centrally located for sightseeing, it offers terrific city views, one of the city's most elegant lobbies, and evening entertainment at the popular art deco Cinegrill. The first Academy Awards ceremony was held here in 1929, and legends claim the hotel is haunted by the ghosts of Marilyn Monroe and Montgomery Clift. See Chapter 14.
- **Casa Malibu** (Malibu; ☎ 800/831-0858): This beachfront motel will fool you from the front. Its cheesy 1970s entrance, right on noisy Pacific Coast Highway, belies the quiet, restful charm found within. Situated around the courtyard garden are 21 rooms, many with private decks above the Malibu sands. Rooftops and balconies are festooned with bougainvillea vines, creating an effect reminiscent of a Mexican seaside village. There's easy beach access, and one elegant suite that was Lana Turner's favorite. See Chapter 14.
- **Sommerset Suites Hotel** (San Diego; ☎ 800/962-9665): This terrific bargain is also a good choice for those who find traditional hotels too impersonal. The staff

is friendly and helpful, and in the late afternoon they serve complimentary snacks, soda, beer, and wine in the cozy guest lounge. See Chapter 17.

- **Ocean Park Inn** (San Diego; ☎ 800/231-7735): This three-story standout, located right on Pacific Beach's lively beach path, is visually appealing both inside and out. Behind the hotel's modern Spanish-Mediterranean facade is a sharply designed marble lobby that gives way to the less splendid, but completely comfortable, guest rooms. See Chapter 17.

15 The Best Places to Stay on a Shoestring

- **San Francisco International Hostel** (San Francisco; ☎ 415/771-7277): If you don't mind going communal, you'll be hard pressed to find cheaper accommodations in San Francisco. Throw in the view, location (near the Marina and Ghirardelli Square), and free parking, and you've got yourself a deal. See Chapter 5.
- **Golden Bear Motel** (Berkeley; ☎ 800/525-6770): If you're not dying to set up camp at one of the cheap motels on busy University Avenue or entrench yourself in the chaos of U.C. Berkeley, the Golden Bear is far enough away to make you feel like you're exploring a neighborhood, but close enough to the campus that you can drive there in less than 10 minutes. Added bonuses: It's across from Alice Waters's (of Chez Panisse fame) Cafe Fanny and close to Fourth Street shopping. See Chapter 6.
- **Napa Valley Railway Inn** (Yountville; ☎ 707/944-2000): This is one of our favorite, and most affordable, places to stay in the Wine Country. Guests get their own private caboose or railcar, each sumptuously appointed with comfy love seats, chairs, queen size brass beds, and full, tiled baths. The coup de grace is the bay windows and skylights, which let in plenty of California sunshine (surely the Pullman cars of yesteryear never had it this good). See Chapter 7.
- **Bodega Harbor Inn** (Bodega Bay; ☎ 707/875-3594): Thank Poseidon for this low-priced accommodation, set on a small bluff overlooking Bodega Bay. There's no better way to enjoy the day than plopping yourself in one the lawn chairs and watching the fishing boats bring in their daily catch. See Chapter 8.
- **Fools Rush Inn** (Little River; ☎ 707/937-5339): The name may be clever, but it's woefully inaccurate. In fact, you'd be a fool *not* to stay here, because these simple yet unarguably romantic cottages cost about half the going rate for a room on the North Coast. After a day of outdoor adventures, come home to a bottle of chilled champagne (each cottage has a kitchen), light the fire (each has a fireplace, too), settle into the sofa, and congratulate yourself for being no fool. See Chapter 8.
- **Bear Valley Inn** (Point Reyes; ☎ 415/663-1777): Ron and JoAnne Nowell's venerable two-story 1899 Victorian has survived everything from a major earthquake to a recent forest fire, which is lucky for you because you'll be hard pressed to find a better B&B for the price in Point Reyes. It's loaded with charm, from the profusion of flowers and vines outside to the comfy chairs fronting a toasty-warm wood stove inside. See Chapter 8.
- **Mt. Shasta Ranch Bed and Breakfast** (Mount Shasta; ☎ 916/926-3870): Built in 1923 as a private retreat and thoroughbred horse ranch for one of the country's most famous horse trainers and racing tycoons, this B&B offers one of the best deals anywhere: rates starting at $50 for a room (most with mountain views) *including* a big country breakfast. See Chapter 9.
- **Tamarack Lodge** (Lake Tahoe; ☎ 916/583-3350): This is one of the oldest lodges on the North Shore—so old it was a favorite haunt of Clark Gable and Gary Cooper. It's now one of the best bets for the cost-conscious traveler. Hidden

among a cadre of pines just east of Tahoe City, the Tamarack Lodge consists of a few old cabins, five "poker rooms," and a modern motel unit. The cabins can hold up to four guests, but the most popular rooms are definitely the hokey old poker rooms. See Chapter 9.

- **The Miner's Inn** (Nevada City; ☎ **916/265-2253**): Located about a mile from Nevada City's historic district, this cabinlike motel is cooled by the shade of a small tree-lined park. Considering all the standard amenities—TV, telephone, air-conditioning—and fantastic price, the cash-conscious traveler could hardly ask for more. See Chapter 11.

- **Gunn House Inn** (Sonora; ☎ **209/532-3421**): Built in 1850 by Dr. Lewis C. Gunn, this was the first two-story adobe structure in Sonora, and is now one of the best low-priced hotels in the Gold Country. It's easy to catch the '49er spirit here, as the entire hotel and grounds are brimming with quality antiques and turn-of-the-century artifacts. But what really makes the Gunn House one of our favorites is the hotel's beautiful pool and patio, surrounded by lush vegetation and admirable stonework. See Chapter 11.

- **Cypress Tree Inn** (Monterey; ☎ **408/372-7586**): The rates here are the best in town—and what you get for your money is a clean, spacious, like-new room with a firm bed. Added bonuses include in-room fridges and a shared outdoor hot tub. See Chapter 12.

- **Butterfly Grove Inn** (Pacific Grove; ☎ **408/373-4921**): Pacific Grove is far less stressful than Monterey on the mind and the wallet when it comes to accommodations. This basic motel offers rooms with kitchenettes, a pool, Jacuzzi, and peaceful verdant surroundings, where you'll stumble upon plenty of quiet, residential walks that ultimately wind to the nearby beach. See Chapter 12.

- **Adobe Inn** (San Luis Obispo; ☎ **800/676-1588**): The price of a motel combined with the hospitality of a B&B makes this inn a great option for the budget traveler. In addition to its cute and cozy rooms, El Adobe provides a substantial breakfast (with good coffee) and the owners are on hand to help you plan your activities while in town. See Chapter 13.

- **The Clamdigger** (Pismo Beach; ☎ **805/773-2342**): Take a walk back in time to when a luxury vacation was nothing more than a little shack on the ocean. Stock your fridge in the kitchen, bring a good book, and you'll have no reason to leave your cute little beachfront cabin—except maybe to pick up another bottle of sunscreen. See Chapter 13.

- **Franciscan Inn** (Santa Barbara; ☎ **805/963-8845**): You'd better really love the beach if you're on a budget and staying oceanfront in Santa Barbara, because after you pay for your room, building sand castles will be the only activity you can afford—except if you stay here. Clean, friendly, and full of extras, this hotel offers quite a deal. Rent one of the suites with a full kitchen and you'll save even more by making your own meals. See Chapter 13.

- **Banana Bungalow** (Hollywood; ☎ **800/4-HOSTEL**): Alongside the Hollywood Freeway nestled in the Cahuenga Pass, the Banana Bungalow is part hotel, part hostel, and draws a youthful, fun-loving international crowd—you'll often find them enjoying the arcade/game room, free movie theater, and of course, the bar. Doubles are only $45 and shared rooms just $12 to $18 per person. See Chapter 14.

- **Best Western Hollywood Motor Hotel** (Los Angeles; ☎ **800/287-1700**). If you're longing to stay near all the Hollywood attractions—the Wax Museum, Walk of Fame, Chinese Theater, movie studios, and Universal City—you'll be ideally located at this Best Western just off the U.S. 101 (Hollywood) Freeway and within walking distance of the renowned Hollywood and Vine intersection. Rates start around $70 (quite a bargain in Los Angeles). See Chapter 14.

- **Best Western Anaheim Stardust** (Anaheim; ☎ **800/222-3639**): Not willing to sacrifice *all* the comforts in your quest for an affordable Disneyland vacation? Then check out the Stardust, where the entire family can swim, sleep, enjoy a full breakfast, and shuttle to the Park (three blocks away) for as little as $58 a night—even the largest suite is less than $100. See Chapter 15.
- **Casa Cody** (Palm Springs; ☎ **619/320-9346**): You'll feel more like a private guest than a paying customer at this cozy compound just a couple of blocks from Palm Springs's main drag. Once owned by "Wild" Bill Cody's niece, it was built in the 1920s around two swimming pool courtyards with large lawns and shady fruit trees. Basic rooms, which come equipped with small kitchens, run $55 to $69, including breakfast and afternoon wine and cheese. See Chapter 16
- **The Cottage** (San Diego; ☎ **619/299-1564**): This two-room cottage is a private hideaway tucked away in a secret garden. It comes complete with its own tiny kitchen and a working wood-burning stove. See Chapter 17.
- **The Beach Cottages** (San Diego; ☎ **619/483-7440**): Located directly on the beach, these cozy lodgings offer great views and immediate access to the sand. Beware of bikes when crossing the boardwalk! See Chapter 17.

16 The Best Culinary Experiences

- **Dungeness Crab at Fisherman's Wharf** (San Francisco): Crabs, which are best consumed as soon as possible after being cooked, emerge right from boiling pots onto your plate. You crack the shells and pick the delectable meat out. Gastronomes treasure even the edible organs (crab butter) inside the carapace. See Chapter 5.
- **Steaks at Harris's** (San Francisco; ☎ **415/673-1888**): This is the great steak restaurant of San Francisco, a tradition since the founding of the Old West. Owner Ann Lee Harris, who grew up on a cattle ranch and married the owner of the largest feedlot in California, knows her steaks. They hang in a glass-windowed aging room, cut thick New York style or else as T-bones. Definitely worth a splurge. See Chapter 5.
- **Hong Kong Flower Lounge** (San Francisco; ☎ **415/668-8998**): For an unforgettable dim sum experience, skip the downtown tourist traps and head out to the avenues where real folks go to get their fill of these Chinese delicacies. See Chapter 5.
- **An Affordable Decadent Meal in the Wine Country:** Have yours at the fabled **Mustards Grill** (Yountville; ☎ **707/944-2424**); it's been called "the quintessential Napa Valley wine restaurant." It's noisy and fun as you sample the fare, many platters straight from a wood-burning oven. Try the grilled Sonoma rabbit, or calf's liver with caramelized onions. Make sure to finish with the Jack Daniel's chocolate cake. All this decadence doesn't have to cost a fortune: Main courses start at a very reasonable $8 (most are in the $14 to $16 range), and local wines start at $4 a glass. See Chapter 7.
- **Fresh Pacific Salmon:** Plump, firm, with a brightly colored flesh, salmon is best when consumed along the northern coast, especially in a restaurant at sunset overlooking the water. Memories are made of this. Although many species are available, the best known is the Chinook or king salmon. The leanest and most

delicately flavored salmon appears in the late spring. The fish is caught in the Pacific just prior to its migration upstream to spawn. This salmon is in prime condition, as it's been feeding for years on rich marine bounty. See Chapter 8.

- **Roadside Strawberries and Peaches in the Central Valley:** You can sail through the Golden State's rich agricultural heartland and fill your car or your mouth with some of the finest fruit (vegetables, too) grown in America. The peaches rival those of Georgia, and there are more than 150 varieties of nectarines grown in the valley. When you see baskets of strawberries, tipped so that their luscious scarlet fruit is spilling out, you'll slam on the brakes. See Chapter 11.

- **The Pastry Shops of Solvang:** It's easy to dismiss Solvang as a tacky tourist trap, but in truth, the town's bakeries are among California's very best. Many Santa Barbarans regularly make the 40-minute drive to this inland hamlet just to buy dessert. See Chapter 13.

- **A Sunset Horseback Ride Through Griffith Park to a Mexican Feast:** This culinary/equine excursion departs Friday evenings from Beachwood Stables in the Hollywood Hills just before dusk, winding up in Burbank at the modest but tasty—especially coming off the trail!—Viva Restaurant. Tie up your steed outside and saunter in for a steaming plate of enchiladas accompanied by an ice-cold *cerveza* (beer), just like the real *vaqueros* (cowboys). The cost is $35 per person, plus dinner. For information, call the **Sunset Ranch** at **213/464-9612.** See Chapter 14.

- **Grand Central Market** (Los Angeles; ☎ 213/624-2378): Fresh produce stands, exotic spice and condiment vendors, butchers and fishmongers, and prepared food counters create a noisy, fragrant, vaguely comforting atmosphere in this L.A. mainstay. The gem of this airy, cavernous complex is the fresh juice bar at the southwest corner. A market fixture for many years, it dispenses dozens of fresh varieties from an elaborate system of wall spigots (just like an old-fashioned soda fountain), deftly blending unlikely but heavenly combinations. See Chapter 14.

- **Sunday Champagne Brunch Aboard the *Queen Mary*** (Long Beach; ☎ **310/ 435-3511** or 310/499-1606): This elegant ocean liner was the largest, finest vessel when she was built in 1934, and the grandeur of those Atlantic crossing days remains. A sumptuous buffet-style feast, accompanied by harp soloist and ice sculpture, is presented in the richly wood-furnished first-class dining room. You'll be able to eat all you want for $22.95 ($7.95 for kids), and then walk off your overindulgence on the spectacular teak decks and through the art deco interiors. See Chapter 15.

- **A Date with the Coachella Valley:** Ninety-five percent of the world's dates are farmed here in the desert. While the groves of date palms make evocative scenery, it's their savory fruit that draws visitors to the National Date Festival in Indio each February. Amidst the Arabian Nights parade and dusty camel races, you can feast on an exotic array of plump Medjool, amber Deglet Noor, caramel-like Halawy, and buttery Empress. Throughout the rest of the year, date farms and markets throughout the valley sell dates from the season's harvest, as well as date milkshakes, sticky date coconut rolls, and more. See Chapter 16 and the "Calendar of Events" in Chapter 2.

- **San Diego County Farmers' Markets:** The bountiful harvest of San Diego County is sold on various days at moveable markets throughout the area. Finds are fresh local fruits, vegetables, and flowers, as well as specialty items such as raw apple cider (in the fall), macadamia nuts, and rhubarb pies. See Chapter 17.

17 The Best Dining Bargains

- **Mario's Bohemian Cigar Store** (San Francisco; ☎ 415/362-0536): It's not the Italian fare (although the eggplant sandwiches are quite tasty) but the atmosphere that makes this cafe a bargain hot spot. The place is almost always packed and offers both a vibe and a view that's ultimately San Franciscan. See Chapter 5.
- **Pasta Pomodoro** (San Francisco; ☎ 415/399-0300): Join the young, festive crowd for what is perhaps one of the best dinner bargains in town. Pasta Pomodoro's simple, airy dining room offers plenty of atmosphere and counter seating looking onto North Beach action, while the menu offers fresh pasta dishes at cheap prices. See Chapter 5.
- **Manora's Thai Cuisine** (San Francisco; ☎ 415/861-6224): No one can resist the savory sauces topping every mouth-watering dish that comes out of Manora's kitchen. The food here is so good, it almost makes up for the wait and the noise level. See Chapter 5.
- **Cha Cha Cha** (San Francisco; ☎ 415/386-5758): Go with a few friends, share sangria while you wait, and order from the tapas menu when you finally get seated at this eternally popular Haight Street haunt. Beware of overindulgence: The food is quite rich, and the pitchers of sangria may alter your judgment and break your budget. See Chapter 5.
- **Zona Rosa** (San Francisco; ☎ 415/668-7717): It's difficult not to develop an addiction to Zona Rosa's fresh, delicious burritos. But, since they're less than $5, you can afford to eat as many as you want (though you'll be lucky to polish off one of these big suckers). See Chapter 5.
- **Cafe Intermezzo** (Berkeley; ☎ 510/849-4592): Here, a salad really is a meal, and the fresh-baked bread comes in thick, spongy slabs. And you get to watch Berkeley's Telegraph Avenue going at full throttle. See Chapter 6.
- **Cafe Fanny** (Berkeley; ☎ 510/524-5447): Gourmet and budget rarely go hand in hand, but if you don't mind a sidewalk meal and aren't on a big breakfast binge, you'll be quite pleased with Berkeley's favorite breakfast stop. See Chapter 6.
- **Cantinetta** (St. Helena; ☎ 707/963-8888): Adjacent to the famed, and expensive, Tra Vigne Restaurant is this rustic little cafe, offering a small selection of inexpensive sandwiches, pizzas, and lighter meals (you've never had a better focaccia in your life). They can also pack your picnic basket for an impromptu lunch at your favorite winery. See Chapter 7.
- **Lucas Wharf Deli** (Bodega Bay; ☎ 707/875-3562): This place doles out steaming pints of fresh, tangy crab cioppino for only $5. It's a fabulously messy affair, best devoured at the picnic tables next door. When crab season is over, the cioppino special is replaced by an equally awesome pile of fresh fish-and-chips (easily big enough to feed two). See Chapter 8.
- **Samoa Cookhouse** (Samoa; ☎ 707/442-1659): When lumber was king, cookhouses were the hub of Eureka. Here the millmen and longshoremen came to chow down three hot meals before, during, and after their 12-hour work day. The Samoa is the last of the great cookhouses, and the food is still hearty, served up family style at long red-checkered tables; nobody leaves hungry. See Chapter 8.
- **The Fishwife at Asilomar Beach** (near Pacific Grove; ☎ 408/375-7107): This cozy little shack dating from the early 1800s serves wonderfully fresh fish complemented with hearty side dishes. Its out-of-the-way location and reasonable prices will make you feel like an insider. See Chapter 12.

- **Caffè Napoli** (Carmel; ☎ 408/625-4033): Tourists may be anxious to throw down big dollars for a dinner out in Carmel, but locals are definitely not. When they hit the town, the most popular spot is Caffè Napoli, a casual family restaurant with traditional Italian decor and reasonably priced, flavorful fare. See Chapter 12.
- **Cafe Kevah** (Big Sur; ☎ 408/667-2344): All the grandeur of the Big Sur coastline will cost you extra if you're seeing it from your table at a restaurant in Big Sur. But Cafe Kevah offers the same million-dollar view and a variety of tasty international dishes at a fraction of the price. See Chapter 12.
- **Farmer's Market** (San Luis Obispo): Who would guess that San Luis Obispo residents are so into barbecue? Head to the Thursday night Farmer's Market and taste for yourself—there are plenty of other cheap options, as well. See Chapter 13.
- **La Super-Rica Taqueria** (Santa Barbara; ☎ 805/963-4940): Even chefs and restaurateurs from San Francisco and beyond visit this hole-in-the-wall restaurant to get what many consider the best Mexican food this side of the border. See Chapter 13.
- **Montecito Cafe** (Santa Barbara; ☎ 805/969-3392): Their prices may not be rock bottom, but if you'd like a special night out, for the money you can't do better than this cafe a few miles south of downtown Santa Barbara. The feeling is California bistro and the fare, California nouveaux. See Chapter 13.
- **Grand Central Market** (Los Angeles; ☎ 213/658-5571): A splendid downtown fixture since 1917, this bustling market serves Latino families, enterprising restaurateurs, and home cooks in search of unusual ingredients and bargain fruits and vegetables. Prepared foods of every ethnicity are served up at counters throughout the market, from chile relleno burritos (around $2) to a complete Thai plate for under $5. Visit the fresh produce sellers for a natural dessert or to stock up for a picnic; we prefer the west end of the market with its fresh juice bar, where a tropical smoothie with the works is only $2.95. See Chapter 14.
- **The Original Pantry Cafe** (Los Angeles; ☎ 213/972-9279): Finicky eaters and snobbish gourmands, skip this listing. L.A. mayor Dick Riordan's round-the-clock downtown diner won't be winning any culinary awards, but still I've never driven past when there weren't a dozen or more folks lined up outside for a table. The reason? Hearty portions of simple American food at bygone-era prices, plus plenty of free munchies on each. See Chapter 14.
- **Bread and Porridge** (Santa Monica; ☎ 310/453-4941): A steady stream of locals will always be found milling outside this neighborhood cafe, reading their newspapers and waiting for a vacant seat. Once inside, you too can sample the delicious breakfasts, fresh salads and sandwiches, and super-affordable entrees—almost all are under $10. Menu items range from from Mexican omelettes to Cajun crab cakes to traditional pasta dishes. You really can't go wrong here. See Chapter 14.
- **Belisle's Restaurant** (Anaheim; ☎ 714/750-6560): After you've blown the family budget on Disneyland, haul your hungry brood a couple of miles to this unique diner, where they've been doling out "Texas-size" favorites like omelets and steaks since 1955. Portions are ridiculously enormous—desserts are so large they look like movie props (picture a chocolate eclair the size of a fireplace log). See Chapter 15.
- **Harry's Coffee Shop** (San Diego; ☎ 619/454-7381): You can't beat Harry's for an inexpensive, filling breakfast or lunch. This is a quintessential American coffee shop—the wait staff seems to have stepped out of a Norman Rockwell poster. See Chapter 17.

- **Point Loma Seafoods** (San Diego; ☎ 619/223-1109): Pick up a fresh seafood sandwich or salad here and enjoy a view that rivals the best restaurants in town. See Chapter 17.
- **Old Spaghetti Factory** (San Diego; ☎ 619/233-4323): Located in the Gaslamp District, this family friendly spot offers plentiful portions of the old standbys at bargain meals. See Chapter 17.

18 The Best Deals for Serious Shoppers

- **Aardvark's** (San Francisco; ☎ 415/621-3141): If you have a hot date but nothing to wear, stop by this new and used clothing store for everything from hair clips to leather jackets, suits, and ball gowns, all at absurdly low prices. See Chapter 5.
- **Catherine Clark Gallery** (San Francisco; ☎ 415/399-1439): Thanks to Catherine Clark, art is no longer a purchase reserved for those who own million-dollar homes in which to exhibit it. This gallery boasts an excellent selection of contemporary artists, many from California, whose works are sold at reasonable prices. There's even an interest-free layaway plan for up to one year. See Chapter 5.
- **Esprit Outlet** (San Francisco; ☎ 415/957-2550): Shoppers here pile their carts high with sweaters, shoes, bags, accessories, and children's clothes. The bargain bins are especially cheap, with many items priced from $5 to $10. See Chapter 5.
- **New West** (San Francisco; ☎ 415/882-4929): Between their own line of merchandise and the array of other designer clothing, shoes, and accessories, you can't help but leave here looking sharp. New shipments come in frequently and prices can be 75% less than those at department stores. See Chapter 5.
- **Wine Club San Francisco** (☎ 415/512-9086): Whether you've got $4 or $400 to spend, the Wine Club will direct you toward bargain bottles that are even cheaper than winery prices. See Chapter 5.
- **The American Tin Cannery Factory Outlet Center** (Pacific Grove; ☎ 408/372-1442): Although it's common knowledge now that most "designer" labels produce a cheaper line to sell specifically at outlets, this mall with 45 shops is still a favorite for those who have had enough of neighboring Monterey Bay Aquarium. See Chapter 12.
- **Downtown Los Angeles:** During the week, skyscrapers and big business rule downtown Los Angeles, but the weekends illuminate the bustling trade south of the concrete jungle (which actually goes on seven days a week). Angelenos in the know flock to the Jewelry Mart for wholesale prices on gold, diamonds, watches, and more; the California Mart and Cooper Building high-rises have floor upon floor of way-below-retail brand name clothes and accessories; and clothing designers shop alongside housewives on Maple Street for bargains on designer yardage. See Chapter 14.
- **Ocean Front Walk** (Venice): Whether it's designer-knockoff sunglasses, $5 ethnic-print fanny packs (and $10 backpack purses), Mexican woven huarache sandals, or supercheap sterling silver jewelry (including rings for a lot more than earlobes), the colorful vendors crammed together along the boardwalk are almost as interesting as the crazy quilt of humanity passing through. See Chapter 14.
- **Barneys New York Outlet** (Cabazon; ☎ 909/849-1600): Even if you detest outlet malls, you can't argue with the classy atmosphere and great deals at Barneys, the most appealing tenant at the Desert Hills Factory Stores. With a prime location just west of Palm Springs on the much-traveled artery I-10, Desert Hills has all the usual suspects, too: Coach, Eddie Bauer, Joan and David, Old Navy.

But Barneys is the true gem, filled with deals on off-the-rack fashions from New York, Paris, and Italy for men and women. See Chapter 16.

- **San Diego County Farmers' Markets:** The bountiful harvest of San Diego County is sold on various days at movable markets throughout the area. Finds include fresh local fruits, vegetables, and flowers, as well as specialty items such as raw apple cider (in the fall), macadamia nuts, and rhubarb pies. See Chapter 17.

- **Kobey's Swap Meet** (San Diego): Bargain hunters will enjoy cruising the aisles at this gigantic open-air market, where more than 3,000 vendors sell everything from blue jeans and T-shirts to fresh flowers and produce. See Chapter 17.

2 Planning an Affordable Trip to California

California has as many attractions as do some entire countries, and it can be bewildering to plan your trip with so many options vying for your attention. We've made this task easier for you by scouring the entire state from top to bottom. In the pages that follow, we've compiled everything you need to know to handle the practical details of planning your trip in advance—airlines, how to make camping reservations, a calendar of events, driving laws, and more.

But you may still be wondering: How can we see and do everything without going flat broke? You can, using our insider advice, money-saving tips, and recommendations on great places to stay and eat that can keep your basic living costs—a comfortable room and three meals a day—down to as little as $60 a day. (We assume that two adults are traveling together and that between the two of you, you have at least $120 a day to work with.) The costs of sightseeing, transportation, and entertainment are all extras, but don't worry; we'll provide tips on saving money in those areas as well.

1 Visitor Information & Money

VISITOR INFORMATION

For information on the state as a whole, contact the **California Office of Tourism,** 801 K St., Suite 1600, Sacramento, CA 95812 (☎ **800/862-2543**), and ask for their free information packet. In addition, almost every city and town in the state has a dedicated tourist bureau or chamber of commerce that will be happy to send you information on its particular parcel. These are listed under the appropriate headings in the chapters that follow.

Foreign travelers should also see Chapter 3, "For Foreign Visitors," for entry requirements and other pertinent information.

INFORMATION ON CALIFORNIA'S PARKS To find out more about California's national parks, contact the **Western Region Information Center,** National Park Service, Fort Mason, Building 201, San Francisco, CA 94123 (☎ **415/556-0560**).

For general state park information, contact the **Department of Parks and Recreation,** P.O. Box 942896, Sacramento, CA 94296-0001 (☎ **916/653-6995**). Ten thousand campsites are on the department's reservation system, and can be booked up to eight weeks in advance by calling **Mistix** at **800/444-7275.** In the past,

What Things Cost in Santa Barbara	U.S. $
Shuttle bus up State Street	.25
Double at the Hotel State Street (cheap)	50.00
Double at the Franciscan Inn (affordable)	80.00
Double at the Bath Street Inn (pricey)	145.00
Dinner for one at The Natural Cafe (cheap)	9.00
Dinner for one at Montecito Cafe (affordable)	16.00
Dinner for one at Pan e Vino (a splurge)	40.00
Coca-Cola	1.50
Beer (a pint)	3.00
Admission to the Santa Barbara Mission	3.00
Movie ticket	7.50

it's been practically impossible to get through to this line, and campers have complained long and loud. The Parks Department has finally heard their pleas, and in June 1995 some improvements were implemented, including additional operators. Hours for making reservations have been extended; you can now call Monday through Saturday from 8am to 8pm, and Sundays from 8am to 5pm (Pacific standard time). Plans are in the works for taking reservations by fax, and the Parks Department is also planning to post parks information, including a reservations form that can be mailed or faxed, on the Internet.

For information on fishing and hunting licenses, contact the **California Dept. of Fish and Game,** License and Revenue Branch, 3211 S St., Sacramento, CA 95816 (☎ **916/227-2244** for license information, or 916/227-2266 for 24-hour information).

MONEY

The ubiquitous Bank of America accepts Plus, Star, and Interlink cards, while First Interstate Bank is on-line with the Cirrus system. Both banks have dozens of branches all around California. For the location of the nearest ATM, dial **800/424-7787** for the Cirrus network or **800/843-7587** for the Plus system. You can also locate Plus ATMs on the World Wide Web at **http://www.visa.com** and Cirrus ATMs at **http://www.mastercard.com.** Most ATMs will make cash advances against MasterCard and Visa. American Express cardholders can write a personal check, guaranteed against the card, for up to $1,000 in cash at an American Express office (see "Fast Facts" in the city chapters for locations).

2 50 Money-Saving Tips

While planning your trip, don't get discouraged if you've almost blown your entire vacation budget on hotels before you've even packed your bags. The California coast is one of the most popular destinations in the world, and hotel prices prove that it's no secret. But there's good news, too. Once you get there, pay for your room, and head out to explore, you'll find that many activities and attractions won't cost you a dime. You can hike the Redwood Forest, bodysurf in Malibu, bike 17-Mile Drive, smell the flowers in Golden Gate Park, in-line skate along Venice Beach, or just kick back under a tree with a book.

The following are some tips to help keep your traveling costs to a minimum:

AIR TRAVEL

1. Visit a travel agent before your trip, and see what they can arrange in the way of airfares and packages that include hotels or car rentals; agents sometimes know about or arrange deals that you don't have access to independently. Since the services of a travel agent are free, it doesn't hurt to inquire.
2. Buy your ticket well in advance. Most flights have a few cheap seats, but they're always the first to sell out.
3. Check with airlines regularly, especially if you're booking close to your travel date. As the departure date draws near, more seats are sold at lower prices (no airline likes to fly with empty seats).
4. Always ask for the lowest fare, not just a discount fare. Ask about discounts for seniors, children, and students.
5. Read the advertisements in newspaper travel sections, which often feature special promotional fares and packages.
6. For the cheapest airfares, check your newspaper—the Sunday travel section is your best bet—for both consolidators ("bucket shops") and charter flights. Though tickets are usually heavily restricted (ask about all the details), you're likely to save a bundle—usually 20% to 35%. This can really be a great way to go if you're buying at the last minute. Consolidators you might try include **TFI Tours International** (☎ **800/745-8000,** or 212/736-1140 in New York State); **Cheap Tickets** (☎ **800/377-1000** or 212/570-1179); and **1-800-FLY-4-LESS.** Contact the Better Business Bureau before going with an unknown or questionable company.
7. Flying within California can be expensive, and in doing so you'll miss the sights along the way; in most cases, you're better off driving, especially since rental car rates are relatively low in California. If you do plan to fly from Southern California to Northern California or vice versa, check with **Shuttle By United** (☎ **800/ SHUTTLE**) or **Southwest Airlines** (☎ **800/435-9792**). Southwest usually has the lowest fares. However, do note that in the San Francisco area, Southwest only flies into Oakland International Airport; if this is a problem for you, you might want to go with another carrier.
8. Don't take a taxi from the airport. Almost every airport in California has a shuttle or bus that will take you to a central location near your destination for far less money; many hotels have shuttles to and from the airport as well. For further details, see the introductory sections in each chapter.

RENTING A CAR

9. If you're planning to rent a car, call all car-rental companies (use toll-free numbers; see "Getting Around" below and the appendix at the end of this book) to compare rates. Even after you've made your reservations, call again and check rates a few days or weeks later—you may stumble upon a cheaper rate.
10. Don't book a rental car through an airline without doing some research. Airlines do not offer the best rental car deals; they merely reserve a car for you.
11. Don't forget to check whether your credit card or personal auto insurance policy covers you when you rent a car. If you're covered by one or the other, you will be able to avoid the cost of collision-damage waivers (usually an additional $10 or $12 a day) that the car-rental agencies are eager to sell you.
12. Whether you're driving or not, it's a good idea to be a member of the **Automobile Association of America (AAA).** Members (only those that carry their cards with them) not only receive free roadside assistance, but also have access to a wealth of free travel information (detailed maps and guidebooks). Also, many hotels and

attractions throughout California offer discounts to AAA members—always inquire. Call **800/222-4357** or your local branch for membership information.

13. When renting a car, consider that weekly rates are usually cheaper; but if you return your car before the week is up, you'll be charged the daily (higher) rate. You're likely to stumble upon a much cheaper rate.

14. Don't let the car company talk you into a bigger (and more expensive) car than you need. If you can live with manual locks and windows, economy cars are usually just a little smaller than the next step up, and you're likely to save big bucks if you opt for one of them.

15. Beware: Some car-rental companies say they don't have any economy cars available, forcing you to rent a more expensive car. Insist on economy, reserve the cheapest option, and continue to shop around until you're satisfied with your choice.

16. Don't bother putting expensive gas in the tank. After all, it is a rental.

PUBLIC TRANSPORTATION

17. Inquire about money-saving **Amtrak** (☎ **800/USA-RAIL**) packages that include hotel accommodations, car rentals, and tours with your train fare.

18. Discounted train and bus fares, like airfares, are often based on advanced purchase, so make your reservation as far in advance as possible to obtain the lowest rates.

19. Ask Amtrak and **Greyhound** (☎ **800/231-2222**) about discounted fares for children and seniors.

20. If you're planning on using local public transportation to get around, inquire about day or week passes, which could seriously reduce your transportation costs. In San Francisco, a one-day Passport fare card allows unlimited rides on buses, Metro streetcars, and cable cars for only $6; three- and seven-day cards are just $10 and $15, respectively. San Diego's Day Tripper passes allow unlimited rides on all MTS bus and trolley routes, plus free passage on the San Diego–Coronado ferry, for just $5 per day (four days for $15).

ACCOMMODATIONS

21. The sooner you book a room, the better. The cheapest accommodations are always the first to go, so the further in advance you commit, the better your chances of scoring a bargain.

22. Whether you make a reservation or arrive on the spot, ask for the cheapest room. Also, inquire about what makes it worth less than other options (public versus private bathrooms) and be sure that's acceptable to you.

23. Always ask about promotions, weekly rates (if you're staying a while), and special discounts for students, government employees, military personnel, seniors, and corporate employees. If you belong to AAA or AARP, be sure to ask whether the hotel offers discounts to members; more often than not, they do.

24. Using toll-free numbers lets you compare hotel rates without spending a lot on long-distance phone calls; and some places, especially the chains, will give you a discount only when you use the 800 number.

25. Travel in the off-season (winter months in places other than ski areas, plus July and August in the cities) and you'll save a bundle on room rates, especially along the Monterey Peninsula and the Central Coast. The majority of city hotels, from budget to luxury, slash rates by as much as 50% in these months (be sure to call as far in advance as possible to get these discounts).

26. Bargain at the front desk. A hotel makes zero dollars per night on an empty room. Hence, most hotels are willing to bargain on rates. Haggling probably won't work too well during the high season, when hotels are almost 100% booked, but if

you're traveling off-season and the answer to that question is "no," try politely speaking with a manager, with whom you might be able to negotiate a better deal. An especially advantageous time to haggle for lower rates is late afternoon/early evening on the day of your arrival, when a hotel's likelihood of filling up with full-price bookings is remote.

27. Each town's visitors' bureau will either be able to provide you with hotel suggestions, or refer you to an accommodations service. But keep in mind that they will only recommend hotels who pay for bureau membership, and the small, cheaper hotels usually aren't members.

28. If you think "B&B" refers to "bargain and budget," think again. You're likely to pay higher prices to stay at one of these homey little spots than you are at many hotels and motels. Sharing a bathroom, however, will usually knock the price down a few bucks.

29. If your heart is set on a bed-and-breakfast, contact **Bed and Breakfast International,** P.O. Box 282910, San Francisco, CA 94128 (☎ **800/872-4500** or 415/696-1690), and let them find affordable accommodations for you. They book hundreds of B&Bs throughout California ranging from $60 to $150 per night. There's a two-night minimum. Also, check the "Accommodations" sections throughout this book for the destination(s) you want to visit. We recommend lots of great places to stay at low rates, and often list other companies that will help you find a hotel in your price range.

30. When booking your hotel, find out if there's an extra charge for parking. In cities like San Francisco and Los Angeles, stashing your car can cost up to $20 (sometimes more) per day. If there is a charge, be sure to ask about the availability of local street parking; hotel employees are usually more than happy to give you the lowdown on the local parking situation.

31. If you're traveling with children, try to secure a room at a hotel where they can stay in your room for free. Also, consider a suite accommodation; in some areas, such as Los Angeles, moderately priced suite accommodations abound. At first glance, the rate may seem high, but when you figure in the money you'll save by booking one room instead of two and by preparing some of your own meals (many come with kitchens), the savings start to add up.

32. Camping is one of the best, and cheapest, ways to experience California. California State Parks manages hundreds of campsites throughout the state and offers discounts to seniors, disabled persons, disabled veterans, and former prisoners of war. Call **DESTINET** (☎ **800/444-7275**) between 8am and 5pm to reserve a campsite or request a brochure. See each chapter's accommodations section for other camping options.

33. At budget hotels, if the first room you see is disappointing (all right, dismal), don't storm out. Ask to see other rooms; they often vary considerably.

34. Hotels often charge 75¢ for local calls, as well as inflated rates for long-distance calls. Even if you use your credit card for long-distance calls, you're often charged 50¢ to 75¢ for access. Save money by making your calls from a hotel lobby or nearby phone booth. If you're planning on making a lot of local calls for business or other reasons, find a hotel that offers free local calls.

DINING

35. Fixed-price menus and early bird dinners are big money savers. Look for restaurants that offer them. If you're traveling with children, find restaurants that offer reduced-price children's menus.

36. Consider hotels that include breakfast; you'll save money by not heading to a restaurant first thing in the morning. Or opt for a hotel that has rooms with kitchens, and do a little cooking (or a least heating up of leftovers) instead of eating out for every meal.
37. If you want to try out a restaurant that's beyond your budget for dinner, consider visiting at lunch. Often, the lunch menu is served until 4 or 5pm, and main courses, which are duplicated on the dinner menu, cost a few dollars less. You probably won't be hungry for the rest of the day, and will avoid spending a fortune for dinner.
38. Keep an eye out for happy hours. Aside from budget cocktails, many establishments provide a free snack spread that makes a good dinner replacement.
39. California is an outdoor, sporty kind of place. Instead of dining in restaurants, consider putting together a picnic breakfast, lunch, or dinner. There's an infinite number of celestial outdoor dining spots, and hundreds of phenomenal take-out joints that will help you create a cheap feast to go; even a gourmet spread can cost less than a meal in a restaurant.

SIGHTSEEING

40. The major convention and visitors bureaus usually offer free visitors guides, as well as information on freebies available in their area. Some visitors' centers, such as those in San Diego and San Francisco, offer booklets of money-saving coupons for restaurants, shops, and attractions in the area. Call or stop in to inquire.
41. Check out local alternative and tourist newspapers, many of which regularly run discounts and two-for-ones for restaurants and activities about town. In San Francisco, the *Bay Guardian* is a good bet.
42. Most museums are open to the public free one day per month (sometimes one day a week). Call the museum of your choice to find out which day is free day.
43. Many attractions offer discounts to seniors, students, or military personnel. Inquire before paying full admission, and be sure to bring your ID.

SHOPPING

44. If you live out of state and make a substantial purchase, it may be wise to have the store mail it to your home. You will have to pay a shipping charge, but you won't have to pay California sales tax or lug it along the rest of you trip.
45. Stock up on groceries and supplies before heading to vast wilderness areas such as Yosemite and Big Sur. Stores there tend to be smaller and more expensive than supermarkets in surrounding metropolitan areas.
46. Don't be afraid to bargain with antique dealers; they're almost always prepared to compromise with you.

NIGHTLIFE

47. In the major cities, avoid clubs with high cover charges. There are plenty of bars and dance clubs with cover charges of just a couple of dollars, some with no admission at all; many are recommended in the "After Dark" sections in this book.
48. If you want to see a musical or theatrical performance, contact the box office to inquire about discounted or matinee shows; some theaters and companies offer same-day reduced tickets, student discounts, and standing room rates.
49. Inquire about free concerts, films, and other evening programs at museums and attractions; many regularly offer these kinds of programs.
50. Just hang out. Stroll San Francisco's Chinatown, nurse a Coke or a cocktail in a glitzy L.A. bar, or kick up your feet at an outdoor cafe almost anywhere along the

coast and just watch the world go by—in California, there's no better way to spend an evening.

3 When to Go

California's climate is so varied that it's impossible to generalize about the state as a whole. However, the prime tourist areas, along the coast, tend to be mild year-round. This is good news for budget travelers, who can save a bundle by traveling in the off-season (the winter months, plus July and August in the cities).

San Francisco's temperate marine climate means relatively mild weather year-round. In summer, temperatures rarely top 70°F (pack sweaters, even in August), and the city's famous fog rolls in most mornings and evenings. In winter, the mercury seldom falls below freezing, and snow is almost unheard of. Because of San Francisco's fog, summer rarely sees more than a few hot days in a row. Head a few miles inland, though, and it's likely to be clear and hot.

The Central Coast shares San Francisco's climate, though it gets warmer as you get farther south. Seasonal changes are less pronounced south of San Luis Obispo, where temperatures remain relatively stable year-round. The northern coast is rainier and foggier; winters tend to be mild but wet.

Summers are refreshingly cool around Lake Tahoe and in the Shasta Cascades—a perfect climate for hiking, camping, and other outdoor activities and a popular escape for residents of California's sweltering deserts and valleys who are looking to beat the heat. Skiers flock to this area for terrific snowfall from late November through early April.

Southern California is usually much warmer than the Bay Area, and it gets significantly more sun. This is the place to hit the beach. Even in winter, daytime thermometer readings regularly reach into the 60s and warmer. Summers can be stifling inland, but Southern California's coastal communities are always comfortable. Don't pack an umbrella. When it rains, Southern Californians go outside to look at the novelty. It's possible to sunbathe throughout the year, but only die-hard enthusiasts and wet-suited surfers venture into the ocean in winter. The water is warmest in summer and fall, but even then, the Pacific is too chilly for many.

The Southern California desert is sizzling hot in summer; temperatures regularly top 100°F. Winter is the time to visit the desert resorts (and remember, it gets surprisingly cold at night in the desert).

San Francisco's Average Temperatures (°F)

	Jan	Feb	Mar	Apr	May	June	July	Aug	Sept	Oct	Nov	Dec
Avg. High	56	59	60	61	63	64	64	65	69	68	63	57
Avg. Low	46	48	49	49	51	53	53	54	56	55	52	47

Los Angeles's Average Temperatures (°F)

	Jan	Feb	Mar	Apr	May	June	July	Aug	Sept	Oct	Nov	Dec
Avg. High	65	66	67	69	72	75	81	81	81	77	73	69
Avg. Low	46	48	49	52	54	57	60	60	59	55	51	49

CALIFORNIA CALENDAR OF EVENTS

January

✪ **Tournament of Roses,** Pasadena. A spectacular parade down Colorado Boulevard, with lavish floats, music, and extraordinary equestrian entries, followed by the Rose

Bowl Game. Call **818/449-4100** for details or just stay home and watch it on TV (you'll have a better view). January 1.

- **Gold Discovery Celebration,** Coloma. A celebration of the fateful day that rocketed California to riches, with gold-panning demonstrations, musical entertainment, Gold Rush skits, and historic house tours. Call **916/622-6198.** January 24.
- **AT&T Pebble Beach National Pro-Am,** Pebble Beach. A PGA-sponsored tour where pros are teamed with celebrities to compete on three world-famous golf courses. Call **408/649-1533.** Lasts a week; dates vary.

February

❂ **Chinese New Year Festival and Parade.** The largest Chinese New Year Festival in the United States is San Francisco's, which includes a Golden Dragon parade with lion-dancing, marching bands, street fair, flower sale, and festive food. Call **415/982-3000.**

L.A.'s celebration is colorful as well, with dragon dancers parading through the streets of downtown's Chinatown. Chinese opera and other events are scheduled. For this year's schedule, contact the Chinese Chamber of Commerce at **213/617-0396.** Late January to early February.

- **National Date Festival and Riverside County Fair,** Indio. Coachella Valley dates and produce are featured at this annual desert festival, which also includes an Arabian Nights Pageant and camel and ostrich races. Call **619/863-8247** for details.
- ❂ **Fresno County Blossom Trail.** A 67-mile driving tour featuring the fruit and nut orchards in full bloom. Call **209/233-0836.** Occurs from late February to late March.

March

- **Snowfest,** Truckee. A 10-day winter carnival with parades, ski challenges, polarbear swim, children's carnival, and fireworks. Dates vary. Call **916/583-7625.**
- **Ocean Beach Kite Festival,** San Diego. Kite building, decorating, and flying are all demonstrated and contested. Phone **619/224-0189** for details. Early March.
- **Redwood Coast Dixieland Jazz Festival,** Eureka. Three days of jazz featuring 12 of the best Dixieland groups, including a variety of jam sessions. Call **707/445-3378.** Last weekend in March.
- **American Indian Festival and Market,** Los Angeles. A showcase and festival of Native American arts and culture at the L.A. Natural History Museum. The fun includes traditional dances, storytelling, and a display of arts and crafts as well as a chance to sample ethnic foods. Admission to museum includes festival tickets. For further details, call **213/744-3314.** Late March.

April

❂ **San Francisco International Film Festival.** One of America's oldest film festivals, featuring more than 100 films and videos from more than 30 countries. Tickets are relatively inexpensive, and screenings are very accessible to the general public during two weeks early in the month. Call **415/931-FILM.**

- **Toyota Grand Prix,** Long Beach. An exciting weekend of Indy-class auto racing and entertainment in and around downtown Long Beach, drawing world-class drivers from the United States and Europe. Contact the Grand Prix Association at **800/752-9524** or 310/436-9953. Mid-April.
- **Fisherman's Festival,** Bodega Bay. Fishing vessels, decorated with ribbons and banners, sail out for a Blessing of the Fleet, while landlubbers enjoy music, lamb, and an oyster barbecue, an arts and crafts fair, and a boat parade. End of month (dates vary).
- **Asparagus Festival,** Stockton. The spring harvest festival is celebrated with food and a variety of entertainment. Call **209/943-1987.** Late April.

✪ **Renaissance Pleasure Faire,** San Bernardino. One of America's largest Renaissance festivals, this annual happening, set in Glen Ellen Regional Park in L.A.'s relatively remote countryside, is a re-created Elizabethan marketplace with costumed performers and living history displays. For ticket information, phone **800/ 523-2473.** Weekends, April through June.

• **La Jolla Easter Hat Parade.** Prizes are awarded in several different categories. Call **619/454-2600** for more information. Easter Sunday.

✪ **Ramona Pageant,** Hemet. A unique outdoor pageant that portrays the lives of the Southern California Mission Indians. The play was adapted from Helen Hunt Jackson's 1884 novel *Ramona.* Call **909/658-3111** for details. Late April to early May.

• **Del Mar National Horse Show.** Horse and rider teams compete in national championships. Held at the Del Mar Fairgrounds. Call **619/792-4288** or 619/ 755-1161 for more information. Late April to early May.

May

✪ **Cinco de Mayo.** A week-long celebration of one of Mexico's most jubilant holidays takes place throughout the city of Los Angeles. The fiesta's Carnival-like atmosphere is created by large crowds, live music, dances, and food. The main festivities are held in El Pueblo de Los Angeles State Historic Park, downtown; other events around the city. Phone **213/628-1274** for information.

There's also a Cinco de Mayo celebration in San Diego, featuring folkloric music, dance, food, and historical reenactments. Held in Old Town. Call **619/ 296-3161** or 619/220-5422 for more information.

• **Redondo Beach Wine Festival.** The largest outdoor wine-tasting event in Southern California. For exact dates and this year's locations, contact the Redondo Beach Chamber of Commerce at **310/376-6912.** Early May.

• **Luther Burbank Rose Parade and Festival,** Santa Rosa. Marching bands, floats, food, and roses everywhere honor horticulturist Luther Burbank. Call **707/542- ROSE.** Mid-May.

• **Venice Art Walk,** Venice Beach. An annual weekend event that gives visitors a chance to take docent-guided tours, visit five artists' studios, or take a Sunday self-guided art walk through private studios and homes of more than 50 emerging and well-known artists. Phone **310/392-8630,** ext. 342. Mid-May.

• **Russian River Wine Festival,** Healdsburg. Five hours of superb tasting of wines, Sonoma County food specialties, and signature dishes from local chefs. Music and crafts, too, all on the Healdsburg Plaza. Call **707/433-6782.** Usually third Saturday in May.

• **Great Monterey Bay Squid Festival.** The squid in all its glory is the focus of the celebration here, which maintains that "a day without squid is a day in hell." Squid-cleaning and squid-cooking demonstrations are followed by a taste of the squid, which, as shown here, can be used in virtually everything but ice cream. Festival fare includes arts and crafts, educational exhibits, and the usual entertainment. Memorial Day weekend. Contact the festival at **408/649-6547.**

✪ **Calaveras County Fair and Jumping Frog Jubilee,** Angel's Camp. The event inspired by Mark Twain's story "The Celebrated Jumping Frog of Calaveras County." Entrants from all over the world arrive with their frog participants. Also children's parade, livestock competition, rodeo, carnival, and fireworks. Call **209/ 736-2561.** Third weekend in May.

• **Cross-County Kinetic Sculpture Race,** Arcata. Wild and crazy human-powered amphibious vehicles in a three-day race from Arcata to Ferndale across mud, sand, roadway, and water. Call **707/725-3851.** Memorial Day.

- **Bay to Breakers Foot Race,** Golden Gate Park, San Francisco. One of the city's most popular annual events, it's really more fun than run. Thousands of entrants show up dressed in their best Halloween-style costumes for the approximately 7¹/₂-mile run across the park. Call **415/777-7770.** Third Sunday of May.

- ✪ **Carnival,** San Francisco. The Mission District's largest annual event is a week-long series of festivities that culminates with a parade on Mission Street over Memorial Day weekend. More than a half-million spectators line the route, and the samba musicians and dancers continue to play on 14th Street, near Harrison, at the end of the march. Call the Mission Economic and Cultural Association at **415/826-1401.** Memorial Day weekend.

June

- **Music in the Mountains,** Nevada City. A three-week classical music festival. For information, call MIM at **916/265-6124.** Dates vary.

- **Playboy Jazz Festival,** Los Angeles. Bill Cosby is the traditional Master of Ceremonies, presiding over top artists at the Hollywood Bowl. Call **310/246-4000.** Mid-June.

- **Pony Express Celebration and Re-Ride,** Folsom. Horses and riders follow the same route that the Pony Express took, starting in Missouri and ending with a major celebration in Folsom, about 20 miles east of Sacramento. Much of the route parallels Calif. 50 in El Dorado County. Call **916/621-5885** or 916/985-2707. Dates vary.

- **Lesbian and Gay Freedom Day Parade.** It's celebrated all over the state, but San Francisco's party draws up to half a million participants. The parade's start and finish has been moved around in recent years to accommodate road construction but traditionally it begins and ends at Civic Center Plaza, where hundreds of food, art, and information booths are set up around several sound stages. Call **415/864-3733** for information. Usually the third or last weekend of June.

- **Mariachi USA Festival,** Los Angeles. A two-day family oriented celebration of Mexican culture and tradition at the Hollywood Bowl, where festival-goers pack their picnic baskets and enjoy music, ballet, folklorico, and related performances by special guests. Call **213/848-7717.** Late June.

July

- **Independence Day.** It's celebrated all over the state, of course, but it's terrific in Pasadena, which offers Southern California's most spectacular display of fireworks following an evening of live entertainment at the Rose Bowl. Phone **818/577-3100** for further information.

- ✪ **Festival of Arts and Pageant of the Masters,** Laguna Beach. A fantastic performance-art production in which live actors re-create famous Old Masters paintings. Ticket prices range from $15 to $40. Call **800/487-FEST** or 714/497-6582. Early July through late August.

- **Carmel Bach Festival.** A three-week festival honoring Johann Sebastian Bach and his contemporaries. It culminates in a candlelit concert in the chapel of the Carmel Mission. Call **408/624-1521.** Dates vary.

- **Gilroy Garlic Festival.** A gourmet food fair with more than 85 booths serving garlicky food from almost every ethnic background, plus close to 100 arts, crafts, and entertainment booths. Call **408/842-1625.** Last full weekend in July.

- **Mammoth Lakes Jazz Jubilee.** A three-day festival featuring 15 bands on 10 different stages, plus food, drink, and dancing—all under the pine trees and stars. Call **619/934-2478.** Dates vary.

- **Shakespeare at the Beach,** Lake Tahoe. A bewitching experience of the Bard at Sand Harbor on the shore beneath the stars. Call **702/832-1606.** Three weeks in late July and August.
- **International Surf Festival,** Los Angeles. Four beachside cities—Hermosa Beach, Manhattan Beach, Redondo Beach, and Torrance—collaborate in the oldest international surf festival in California. Competitions include surfing, boogie boarding, sand-castle building, and more. Contact the International Surf Festival Committee at **310/376-6911** for information. End of July.

August

- **Sonoma County Showcase and Wine Auction.** Four days of wine tastings and celebrations plus a wine auction. Held at the Sonoma County Wine and Visitors Center and at different wineries. Call **707/586-3795.** Usually first weekend in August.
- **Old Spanish Days Fiesta,** Santa Barbara. The city's biggest annual event, this five-day festival features a grand parade with horse-drawn carriages, two Spanish marketplaces, a carnival, a rodeo, and dancers. Call **805/962-8101.** Early August.
- **Nisei Week Japanese Festival,** Little Tokyo, Los Angeles. This week-long celebration of Japanese culture and heritage is held in the Japanese American Cultural and Community Center Plaza. Festivities include parades, food, music, arts, and crafts. Call **213/687-7193.** Mid-August.
- **California State Fair,** Sacramento. At the California Exposition grounds, a gala celebration, with livestock, carnival food, exhibits, entertainment on 10 different stages, plus thoroughbred racing and a 1-mile monorail for panoramic views over the scope of it all. Call **916/263-3000.** Late August to early September.

September

- **San Diego Street Scene.** The historic Gaslamp Quarter is transformed into an urban food and music festival. Call **619/557-8487** for more information. Early September.
- **Sausalito Art Festival.** A juried exhibit of more than 180 artists. It is accompanied by music provided by Bay Area jazz, rock, and blues performers and international cuisine enhanced by wines from some 50 different Napa and Sonoma producers. Parking is impossible; take the Red and White Fleet (☎ **415/ 546-2628**) ferry from Fisherman's Wharf to the festival site. Call **415/332-3555** for information. Labor Day weekend.
- ☻ **Monterey Jazz Festival.** Top names in traditional and modern jazz. One of the oldest annual jazz festivals in the world. Call **408/373-3366.** Mid-September.
- **San Francisco Blues Festival,** on the grounds of Fort Mason. The largest outdoor blues music event on the West Coast. Local and national musicians perform back-to-back during two marathon days. Call **415/826-6837.** Usually in mid-September.
- **Los Angeles County Fair.** Horse racing, arts, agricultural displays, celebrity entertainment, and carnival rides are among the attractions of the largest county fair in the world, held at the Los Angeles County Fair and Exposition Center, in Pomona. Call **909/623-3111** for information. Late September.
- **Cabrillo Festival,** San Diego. A week-long fair commemorating the exploration of the West Coast by Juan Rodriquez Cabrillo in 1542. A reenactment of the event takes place at the Cabrillo National Monument. Call **619/557-5450** for more information. Late September.
- **Catalina Island Jazz Trax Festival.** Great contemporary jazz artists travel to the island to play in the legendary Casino Ballroom. The festival is over two

---

Christmas in San Diego

Christmas in San Diego offers a number of unique activities:

- **Christmas on the Prado,** Balboa Park. Celebrated since 1977, this weekend of evening events is held the first Friday and Saturday in December. Includes Christmas carol sing-a-long and food booths. Free admission to all museums. First weekend. Call **619/239-0512** for information.
- **Coronado Christmas Celebration and Parade.** First Friday. Santa's arrival by ferry is followed by a parade along Orange Avenue. Call **619/437-8788** or 435-8895 for information.
- **Mission Bay Boat Parade of Lights,** from Quivira Basin in Mission Bay. Concludes with the lighting of a 320-foot tower of Christmas lights at Sea World. Saturday in mid-December. Call **619/276-8200** for information.
- **San Diego Harbor Parade of Lights,** from Shelter Island to Harbor Island to Seaport Village. Decorated boats of all sizes and types participate, and spectators line the shore and cheer for their favorites. Sunday in mid-December. Check local newspaper for exact day and time.

—Elizabeth Hansen

---

consecutive three-day weekends. Call **800/866-TRAX** or 619/458-9586 for more information. Late September or early October.
- **Watts Towers Day of the Drum Festival,** Los Angeles. Performances from Afro-Cuban folkloricos to East Indian tabla players. Phone **213/847-4646.** Late September.

October
- **Gold-Panning Championships and Historic Demonstration Day,** Coloma. Gold-panning contests, foods, crafts, music, and tours. Living history demonstrations of spinning, weaving, cooking, and doll-making. Call **916/622-6198.** Dates vary.
- **Sonoma County Harvest Fair.** A three-day celebration of the harvest with exhibitions, art shows, and annual judging of the local wines. At the Sonoma County Fairgrounds. Call **707/545-4203.** Dates vary.
- **Annual Bob Hope Celebrity Golf Tournament,** Riverside. Bob Hope is the honorary chairman of this annual event. For ticket and other information, contact the Riverside Convention and Visitors Bureau at **909/222-4700.**
- **Whale Festival,** Long Beach. Join in building a life-size whale from sand, and enjoy a family sand sculpture contest, food, crafts, children's activities, entertainment, booths on sea life and issues, and a watermelon feast. Call **310/548-7562.** Late October.
- **Halloween,** San Francisco. The City by the Bay celebrates with a fantastical parade organized at Market and Castro, and a mixed gay-straight crowd revels in costumes of extraordinary imagination.

November
- **Doo Dah Parade,** Pasadena. An outrageous spoof of the Rose Parade on the Sunday before Thanksgiving, featuring participants such as the Briefcase Brigade and a kazoo band. Call **818/449-3689.**
- **Hollywood Christmas Parade.** This spectacular star-studded parade marches through the heart of Hollywood the first or second Sunday after Thanksgiving. For information, phone **213/469-2337.**

- **San Diego Dixieland Jazz Festival.** More than 30 bands perform foot-stomping jazz at the Town and Country Hotel. Call **619/297-5277** for more information. Late November.

December
- **Truckers Christmas Light Convoy,** Eureka. Big rigs decorated and festooned with lights compete for cash prizes in this lumber town. Call **707/442-5744** for dates and times.

4 Getting There

BY PLANE

All major U.S. carriers serve the San Francisco, Sacramento, San Jose, Los Angeles, and San Diego airports. Domestic airlines flying in and out of these cities include **Alaska Airlines** (☎ 800/426-0333), **American Airlines** (☎ 800/433-7300), **Delta Air Lines** (☎ 800/221-1212), **Northwest Airlines** (☎ 800/225-2525), **Southwest Airlines** (☎ 800/435-9792), **TWA** (☎ 800/221-2000), **United Airlines** (☎ 800/241-6522), and **USAir** (☎ 800/428-4322). Foreign travelers should also see "Getting to the U.S." and "Getting Around the U.S." in Chapter 3 for a list of airlines offering overseas flights into California.

The lowest round-trip fares to the West Coast from New York fluctuate between about $400 and $500; from Chicago they range from $300 to $400. The lowest round-trip fare between Los Angeles and San Francisco is about $198. Sometimes it's even lower.

You might be able to get a great deal on airfare by calling a consolidator. One recommendable consolidator is **Unitravel,** 1177 N. Warson Rd. (P.O. Box 12485), St. Louis, MO 63132 (☎ **800/325-2222** or 314/569-0900).

BY CAR

Here are some handy driving times if you're on one of those see-the-U.S.A. car trips. From Phoenix, it's about six hours (okay, seven if you drive the speed limit) to Los Angeles on I-10. Las Vegas is 265 miles northeast of Los Angeles (about a four- or five-hour drive).

San Francisco is 227 miles southwest of Reno, Nevada, and 577 miles northwest of Las Vegas. It's a long day's drive 640 miles south from Portland, Oregon, on I-5.

Of course, if you have time on your hands, the ultimate nostalgic road trip into California is along Route 66, "America's Main Street," which runs from the shores of Lake Michigan and winds through eight states before ending at the L.A. coast.

Before you set out on a big car trip, you might want to join the **American Automobile Association (AAA)** (☎ **800/222-4357**), which has hundreds of offices nationwide. Members receive excellent maps (they'll even help you plan an exact itinerary) and emergency road service.

BY TRAIN

Amtrak (☎ **800/USA-RAIL**) connects California with about 500 American cities. Trains bound for both Northern and Southern California leave daily from New York and pass through Chicago and Denver. The journey takes about 3¹/₂ days, and seats fill up quickly. As of this writing, the lowest round-trip fare was $266 from New York and $240 from Chicago. These heavily restricted tickets are good for 45 days and allow up to three stops along the way.

The *Sunset Limited* is Amtrak's regularly scheduled transcontinental service, originating in Florida, and making 52 stops along the way as it passes through Alabama, Mississippi, Louisiana, Texas, New Mexico, and Arizona before arriving in Los Angeles. The train, which runs three times weekly, features reclining seats, a sightseeing car with large windows, and a full-service dining car. Round-trip coach fares begin at $286; sleeping accommodations are available for an extra charge.

Ask about special family plans, tours, and other money-saving promotions the rail carrier may be offering. Call for a brochure outlining routes and prices for the entire system.

BY BUS

Greyhound/Trailways (☎ **800/231-2222**) can get you here from anywhere cheaply, if not in great comfort. Round-trip fares vary depending on your point of origin, but few, if any, ever exceed $200.

5 Getting Around

BY CAR

California's freeway signs frequently indicate direction by naming a town rather than a point on the compass. If you've never heard of Canoga Park you might be in trouble, unless you have a map. The best state road guide is the comprehensive Thomas Bros. *California Road Atlas,* a 300-plus–page book of maps with schematics of towns and cities statewide. It costs $20 but is a good investment if you plan to do a lot of exploring. Smaller, accordion-style maps are handy for the state as a whole or for individual cities and regions. These foldout maps usually cost $2 to $3 and are available at gas stations, pharmacies, supermarkets, and tourist-oriented shops everywhere.

For road conditions, call **916/445-7623** in Northern California, **213/628-7623** in Southern California.

If you're heading into the Sierra or Shasta-Cascades for a winter ski trip, top up on antifreeze and carry snow chains for your tires (chains are mandatory in certain areas).

Here are a few sample distances between key California cities:

Los Angeles

96 miles SE of Santa Barbara
103 miles W of Palm Springs
120 miles NW of San Diego
332 miles SE of Monterey

379 miles SE of San Francisco
383 miles S of Sacramento
659 miles SE of Eureka

San Francisco

87 miles SW of Sacramento
115 miles NW of Monterey
278 miles SE of Eureka

321 miles NW of Santa Barbara
379 miles NW of Los Angeles
548 miles NW of San Diego

Sacramento

87 miles NE of San Francisco
185 miles NE of Monterey
304 miles SE of Eureka

383 miles N of Los Angeles
391 miles NE of Santa Barbara
484 miles NW of Palm Springs

RENTALS   California is one of the cheapest places in America to rent a car. The best-known firms, with locations throughout the state and at most major airports, include **Alamo** (☎ 800/327-9633), **Avis** (☎ 800/331-1212), **Budget** (☎ 800/527-0700), **Dollar** (☎ 800/421-6868), **Hertz** (☎ 800/654-3131), **National** (☎ 800/328-4567), and **Thrifty** (☎ 800/367-2277).

Most rental firms pad their profits by selling loss/damage waivers (LDW), which usually cost an extra $9 per day. Before agreeing to this, however, check with your insurance carrier and credit- and charge-card companies. Many people don't realize that they are already covered by either one or both. For renters, the minimum age is usually 19 to 25.

DRIVING RULES   California law requires both drivers and passengers to wear seat belts. Children under four years or 40 pounds must be secured in an approved child safety seat. Motorcyclists must wear a helmet. Auto insurance is mandatory; the car's registration and proof of insurance must be carried in the car.

You can turn right at a red light, unless otherwise indicated, but be sure to come to a stop first. Pedestrians *always* have the right-of-way.

BY PLANE

In addition to the major carriers listed above in "Getting There," several smaller airlines provide service within the state, including **America West** (☎ 800/235-9292), **American Eagle** (☎ 800/433-7300), **Skywest** (☎ 800/453-9417), **Southwest** (☎800/435-9792), **Shuttle by United** (☎ 800/241-6522), and **USAir Express** (☎ 800/428-4322).

BY TRAIN

Amtrak (☎ 800/USA-RAIL) runs trains up and down the California coast, connecting Los Angeles with San Francisco and all points in between. A one-way ticket can often be had for as little as $50. The coastal journey, aboard Amtrak's *Coast Starlight,* is a fantastically beautiful trip that runs from Seattle to Oakland; crosses Salinas, the artichoke capital of the world; climbs San Luis Obispo's bucolic hills; drops into Santa Barbara; then runs down the Malibu coast into Los Angeles. You can then continue on to San Diego. It's a popular journey—make reservations well in advance.

FAST FACTS: California

AAA   If you're a member of the American Automobile Association and your car breaks down, call **800/AAA-HELP** for 24-hour emergency roadside service.

American Express   To report lost or stolen traveler's checks, call **800/221-7282.** Local office locations are listed in the appropriate chapters throughout the book.

Driving Rules   See "Getting Around," earlier in this chapter.

Earthquakes   In the rare event of an earthquake, you should know about a few simple precautions that every California schoolchild is taught: If you're in a tall building, don't run outside; instead, move away from windows and toward the building's center. Crouch under a desk or table, or stand against a wall or under a doorway. If you're in bed, get under the bed or stand in a doorway, or crouch under a sturdy piece of furniture. When exiting the building, use stairwells, *not* elevators.

If you're in your car, pull over to the side of the road and stop, but wait until you're away from bridges or overpasses, and telephone or power poles and lines. Stay in your car.

If you're out walking, stay outside and away from trees, power lines, and the sides of buildings. If you're in an area with tall buildings, stand in a doorway.

Emergencies To reach the police, ambulance service, or fire department, dial **911** from any telephone. No coins are needed at pay phones.

Liquor Laws Liquor and grocery stores, as well as some drugstores, can legally sell packaged alcoholic beverages between 6am and 2am. Most restaurants, nightclubs, and bars are licensed to serve alcoholic beverages during the same hours. The legal age for the purchase and consumption of alcoholic beverages is 21; proof of age is strictly enforced.

Maps Local maps can usually be obtained free from area tourist offices. State and regional maps are sold at gas stations, in drugstores, and in tourist-oriented shops all around the state; the Thomas Bros. maps are the best.

Pets Many chain hotels and motels accept dogs (though some require a deposit or impose size restrictions). Some good bets, with their toll-free reservation numbers, include **Best Western** (☎ 800/528-1234), **Comfort Inns** (☎ 800/228-5150), **Holiday Inns** (☎ 800/HOLIDAY), **La Quinta Inns** (☎ 800/531-5900), **Red Lion Inns** (☎ 800/547-8010), and **Motel 6** (☎ 800/4-MOTEL6). But remember that managers of individual establishments are free to set or change their pet policy, so it's vital that you contact the hotel itself to confirm your dog's reservation instead of relying solely on these central reservation numbers.

It's not a good idea to bring your dog to any of California's national parks, for your pet's own protection. It's just not safe for dogs to wander in these areas, where they might have dangerous encounters with wildlife.

The *California Dog Lover's Companion* (Foghorn Press) is a huge and incredibly useful resource, with lodging recommendations plus ratings of hundreds of parks and beaches, plus details on where Fido is allowed to romp off-leash. You'll learn that San Francisco is an unusually dog-friendly destination, and that dogs are welcome at Pismo Beach and on the sands at Carmel. *On the Road Again with Man's Best Friend* (Macmillan) is another great reference tool, with detailed reviews of accommodations where dogs are welcome.

Taxes California's state sales tax is 7.75%. Some municipalities include an additional percentage, so tax varies throughout the state. Hotel taxes are almost always higher than tariffs levied on goods and services.

Time California and the entire West Coast are in the Pacific standard time zone, three hours earlier than the East Coast.

3 For Foreign Visitors

This chapter will provide some specifics about getting to the United States as economically and effortlessly as possible, plus some helpful information about how things are done in California—from sending mail to making a local or long-distance telephone call.

1 Preparing for Your Trip

ENTRY REQUIREMENTS

DOCUMENT REGULATIONS Canadian nationals need only proof of Canadian residence to visit the United States. Citizens of the United Kingdom and Japan need only a current passport. Citizens of other countries, including Australia and New Zealand, usually need two documents: a valid passport with an expiration date at least six months later than the scheduled end of their visit to the United States and a tourist visa available at no charge from a U.S. embassy or consulate.

To get a tourist or business visa to enter the United States, contact the nearest American embassy or consulate in your country; if there is none, you will have to apply in person in a country where there is a U.S. embassy or consulate. Present your passport, a passport-size photo of yourself, and a completed application, which is available through the embassy or consulate. You may be asked to provide information about how you plan to finance your trip or show a letter of invitation from a friend with whom you plan to stay. Those applying for a business visa may be asked to show evidence that they will not receive a salary in the United States. Be sure to check the length of stay on your visa; usually it is six months. If you want to stay longer, you may file for an extension with the Immigration and Naturalization Service once you are in the country. If permission to stay is granted, a new visa is not required unless you leave the United States and want to reenter.

MEDICAL REQUIREMENTS No inoculations are needed to enter the United States unless you are coming from, or have stopped over in, areas known to be suffering from epidemics, particularly cholera or yellow fever.

If you have a disease requiring treatment with medications containing narcotics or drugs requiring a syringe, carry a valid, signed generic prescription (as the brands you are accustomed to buying in your country may not be available here) from your physician to allay any suspicions that you are smuggling drugs.

CUSTOMS REQUIREMENTS   Every adult visitor may bring in, free of duty: 1 liter of wine or hard liquor, 200 cigarettes or 100 cigars (but no cigars from Cuba) or 3 pounds of smoking tobacco, and $100 worth of gifts. These exemptions are offered to travelers who spend at least 72 hours in the United States and who have not claimed them within the preceding six months. It is altogether forbidden to bring foodstuffs (particularly cheese, fruit, cooked meats, and canned goods) and plants (vegetables, seeds, tropical plants, and so on) into the country. Foreign tourists may bring in or take out up to $10,000 in U.S. or foreign currency with no formalities; larger sums must be declared to Customs on entering or leaving.

INSURANCE

Unlike most other countries, the United States does not have a national health system. Because the cost of medical care is extremely high, we strongly advise all travelers to secure health coverage before setting out on their trip.

You may want to take out a comprehensive travel policy that covers (for a relatively low premium) sickness or injury costs (medical, surgical, and hospital); loss or theft of your baggage; trip-cancellation costs; guarantee of bail in case you are arrested; and costs of accident, repatriation, or death. Such packages (for example, "Europe Assistance" in Europe) are sold by automobile clubs at attractive rates, as well as by insurance companies and travel agencies and at some airports.

MONEY

The U.S. monetary system has a decimal base: One American dollar ($1) = 100 cents (100¢). Dollar bills commonly come in $1 (a "buck"), $5, $10, $20, $50, and $100 denominations (the last two are not welcome when paying for small purchases and are usually not accepted in taxis or at subway ticket booths). There are six coin denominations: 1¢ (one cent or a "penny"), 5¢ (five cents or a "nickel"), 10¢ (ten cents or a "dime"), 25¢ (twenty-five cents or a "quarter"), 50¢ (fifty cents or a "half dollar"), and $1 pieces (which are relatively uncommon).

American Express, Thomas Cook, and Barclay's Bank traveler's checks in U.S. dollars are accepted at most hotels, motels, restaurants, and large stores. Sometimes picture identification is required.

Credit cards are the method of payment most widely used: Visa (BarclayCard in Britain), MasterCard (EuroCard in Europe, Access in Britain, Diamond in Japan), American Express, Discover, Diners Club, enRoute, JCB, and Carte Blanche, in descending order of acceptance. You can save yourself trouble by using "plastic" rather than cash or traveler's checks in 95% of all hotels, motels, restaurants, and retail stores. A credit card can also serve as a deposit for renting a car, as proof of identity, or as a "cash card," enabling you to draw money from automatic-teller machines (ATMs) that accept them.

You can telegraph money, or have it telegraphed to you very quickly using the **Western Union** system (☎ **800/325-6000**).

SAFETY

While tourist areas are generally safe, crime is on the increase everywhere, and U.S. urban areas tend to be less safe than those in Europe or Japan. Visitors should always stay alert. This is particularly true of large U.S. cities. It is wise to ask the city's or area's tourist office if you're in doubt about which neighborhoods are safe.

DRIVING   Recently more and more crime has involved cars and drivers. If you drive off a highway into a doubtful neighborhood, leave the area as quickly as possible. If you have an accident, even on the highway, stay in your car with the doors locked until you assess the situation or until the police arrive. If you are bumped from behind on the street or are involved in a minor accident with no injuries and the situation appears to be suspicious, motion to the other driver to follow you. Never get out of your car in such situations.

If you see someone on the road who indicates a need for help, do not stop. Take note of the location, drive on to a well-lighted area, and telephone the police by dialing **911.**

Park in well-lighted, well-traveled areas if possible. Always keep your car doors locked, whether attended or unattended. Never leave any packages or valuables in sight. If someone attempts to rob you or steal your car, do not try to resist the thief/carjacker—report the incident to the police department immediately.

2 Getting to the U.S.

A number of U.S. airlines offer service from Europe to the United States. If they do not have direct flights from Europe to California, they can book you straight through on a connecting flight. You can make reservations by calling the following numbers in London: **American** (☎ 0181/572-5555), **Continental** (☎ 4412/9377-6464), **Delta** (☎ 0800/414-767), and **United** (☎ 0181/990-9900).

And of course many international carriers serve Los Angeles International Airport and/or San Francisco International Airport. Helpful numbers to know include **Virgin Atlantic** (☎ 0293/747-747 in London), **British Airways** (☎ 0345/222-111 in London), and **Aer Lingus** (☎ 01/844-4747 in Dublin or 061/415-556 in Shannon). **Qantas** (☎ 008/177-767 in Australia) has flights from Sydney to Los Angeles and San Francisco; you can also take United from Australia to the West Coast. **Air New Zealand** (☎ 0800/737-000 in Auckland or 64-3/379-5200 in Christchurch) also offers service to Los Angeles. Canadian readers might book flights on **Air Canada** (☎ 800/268-7240 in Canada or 800/361-8620), which offers direct service from Toronto, Montréal, Calgary, and Vancouver to San Francisco, Sacramento, Los Angeles, and San Diego.

The visitor arriving by air, no matter what the port of entry, should cultivate patience and resignation before setting foot on U.S. soil. Getting through immigration control may take as long as two hours on some days, especially summer weekends, so have your guidebook or something else to read handy. Add the time it takes to clear customs and you will see you should make a very generous allowance for delay in planning connections between international and domestic flights—figure on two to three hours at least.

For the traveler arriving by car or by rail from Canada, the border-crossing formalities have been streamlined to the vanishing point. And if you're traveling by air from Canada, Bermuda, and some places in the Caribbean, you can sometimes go through customs and immigration at the point of departure, which is much quicker.

3 Getting Around the U.S.

On their transatlantic or transpacific flights, some large U.S. airlines offer special discount tickets for any of their U.S. destinations (American Airlines' Visit USA program and Delta's Discover America program, for example). The tickets or coupons are not on sale in the United States and must be purchased before you leave your point of departure. This system is the best, easiest, and fastest way to see the United States at low cost. You should obtain information well in advance from your travel agent or the office of the airline concerned, since the conditions attached to these discount tickets can be changed without advance notice.

International visitors can also buy a **USA Railpass,** good for 15 or 30 days of unlimited travel on Amtrak. The pass is available through many foreign travel agents. Prices in 1996 for a 15-day pass were $245 off-peak, $355 peak; a 30-day pass costs $350 off-peak, $440 peak (off-peak is August 21 to June 16). (With a foreign passport, you can also buy passes at some Amtrak offices in the United States including locations in San Francisco, Los Angeles, Chicago, New York, Miami, Boston, and Washington, D.C.) Reservations are generally required and should be made for each part of your trip as early as possible.

Visitors should also be aware of the limitations of long-distance rail travel in the United States. With a few notable exceptions, service is rarely up to European standards: Delays are common, routes are limited and often infrequently served, and fares are rarely significantly lower than discount airfares. Thus, cross-country train travel should be approached with caution.

The cheapest way to travel the United States is by bus. Greyhound/Trailways, the sole nationwide bus line, offers an **Ameripass** for unlimited travel for 7 days (for $179), 15 days (for $289), 30 days (for $399), and 60 days (for $599). Bus travel in the United States can be both slow and uncomfortable, so this option is not for everyone. In addition, bus stations are often located in undesirable neighborhoods.

FAST FACTS: For the Foreign Traveler

Automobile Organizations   Auto clubs will supply maps, suggested routes, guidebooks, accident and bail-bond insurance, and emergency road service. The major auto club in the United States, with 955 offices nationwide, is the **American Automobile Association (AAA).** Members of some foreign auto clubs have reciprocal arrangements with the AAA and enjoy its services at no charge. If you belong to an auto club, inquire about AAA reciprocity before you leave. The AAA can provide you with an International Driving Permit validating your foreign license, although drivers with valid licenses from most home countries don't really need this permit. You may be able to join the AAA even if you are not a member of a reciprocal club. To inquire, call **619/233-1000.** In addition, some automobile rental agencies now provide these services; inquire about their availability when you rent your car.

Business Hours   Offices are usually open weekdays from 9am to 5pm. Banks are open weekdays from 9am to 3pm or later and sometimes Saturday morning. Shops, especially those in shopping complexes, tend to stay open late: until about 9pm weekdays and until 6pm weekends.

Climate   See "When to Go," in Chapter 2.

Currency Exchange   The "foreign-exchange bureaus" so common in Europe are rare in the United States. They're at major international airports, and there are a few in most major cities, but they're nonexistent in medium-size cities and small towns. Try to avoid having to change foreign money, or traveler's checks denominated other than in U.S. dollars, at small-town banks, or even at branches in a big city. In fact, leave any currency other than U.S. dollars at home (except the cash you need for the taxi or bus ride home when you return to your own country). Your own currency may prove more nuisance to you than it's worth.

Drinking Laws   The legal age to drink alcohol is 21.

Electric Current   The United States uses 110–120 volts, 60 cycles, compared to 220–240 volts, 50 cycles, as in most of Europe. Besides a 100-volt converter, small appliances of non-American manufacture, such as hair dryers or shavers, will require a plug adapter, with two flat, parallel pins. The easiest solution to the power struggle is to purchase dual-voltage appliances, which operate on both 110 and 220 volts, and then all that is required is a U.S. adapter plug.

Embassies/Consulates   All embassies are located in Washington, D.C. Listed here are the West Coast consulates of the major English-speaking countries. The **Australian Consulate** is located at Century Plaza Towers, 19th floor, 2049 Century Park East, Los Angeles, CA 90067 (☎ 310/229-4800). The **Canadian Consulate** is at 550 South Hope St., 9th floor, Los Angeles, CA 90071 (☎ 213/346-2700). The **Irish Consulate** is located at 655 Montgomery St., Suite 930, San Francisco, CA 94111 (☎ 415/392-4214). The **New Zealand Consulate** is at 12400 Wilshire Blvd., Los Angeles, CA 90025 (☎ 310/207-1605). Contact the **U.K. Consulate** at 11766 Wilshire Blvd., Suite 400, Los Angeles, CA 90025 (☎ 310/477-3322).

Emergencies   Call **911** for fire, police, and ambulance. If you encounter such traveler's problems as sickness, accident, or lost or stolen baggage, call Traveler's Aid, an organization that specializes in helping distressed travelers. (Check local directories for the location nearest you.) U.S. hospitals have emergency rooms, with a special entrance where you will be admitted for quick attention.

Gasoline (Petrol)   One U.S. gallon equals 3.75 liters, while 1.2 U.S. gallons equals 1 Imperial gallon. A gallon of unleaded gas (short for gasoline), which most rental cars accept, costs about $1.30 if you fill your own tank (it's called "self-serve"); it's about 10¢ more if the station attendant does it (called "full-service").

Holidays   On the following national legal holidays, banks, government offices, post offices, and many stores, restaurants, and museums are closed: January 1 (New Year's Day), third Monday in January (Martin Luther King Jr. Day), third Monday in February (Presidents' Day), last Monday in May (Memorial Day), July 4 (Independence Day), first Monday in September (Labor Day), second Monday in October (Columbus Day), November 11 (Veterans Day/Armistice Day), last Thursday in November (Thanksgiving Day), and December 25 (Christmas Day). The Tuesday following the first Monday in November is Election Day.

Legal Aid   If you are stopped for a minor infraction of the highway code (such as speeding), never attempt to pay the fine directly to a police officer; you may be arrested on the much more serious charge of attempted bribery. Pay fines by mail or directly into the hands of the clerk of the court. If accused of a more serious offense, it is best to say and do nothing before consulting a lawyer. Under U.S. law, an arrested person is allowed one telephone call to a party of his or her choice. Call your embassy or consulate.

Mail   Mailboxes are blue with a red-white-and-blue logo and carry the inscription U.S. MAIL. Within the United States, it costs 20¢ to mail a standard-size postcard and 32¢ to send an oversize postcard (larger than $4^1/_4$ by 6 inches, or 10.8 by 15.4 centimeters). Letters that weigh up to 1 ounce (that's about five pages, 8 by 11 inches or 20.5 by 28.2 centimeters) cost 32¢, plus 23¢ for each additional ounce. A postcard to Mexico costs 30¢, a $^1/_2$-ounce letter 35¢; a postcard to Canada costs 30¢, a 1-ounce letter 40¢. A postcard to Europe, Australia, New Zealand, the

Far East, South America, and elsewhere costs 40¢, while a letter is 60¢ for each ¹/₂ ounce.

Taxes In the United States there is no value-added tax (VAT) or other indirect tax at a national level. There is a $10 Customs tax, payable on entry to the United States, and a $6 departure tax. Sales tax is levied on goods and services by state and local governments, however, and is not included in the price tags you'll see on merchandise. These taxes are not refundable.

Telephone and Fax Pay phones can be found on street corners, as well as in bars, restaurants, public buildings, stores, and at service stations. Some accept 20¢, most are 25¢. If the telephone accepts 20¢, you may also use a quarter (25¢), but you will not receive change.

In the past few years, many American companies have installed "voice-mail" systems, so be prepared to deal with a machine instead of a receptionist if calling a business number.

For long-distance or international calls, it's most economical to charge the call to a telephone charge card or a credit card; or you can use a lot of change. The pay phone will instruct you how much to deposit and when to deposit it into the slot at the top of the telephone box.

For long-distance calls in the United States, dial 1 followed by the area code and number you want. For direct overseas calls, first dial 011, followed by the country code (Australia, 61; Republic of Ireland, 353; New Zealand, 64; United Kingdom, 44; and so on), and then by the city code (for example, 71 or 81 for London, 21 for Birmingham, 1 for Dublin), and the number of the person you wish to call.

Before calling from a hotel room, always ask the hotel phone operator if there are any telephone surcharges. There almost always are, and they often are as much as 75¢ or $1, even for a local call. These charges are best avoided by using a public phone, calling collect, or using a telephone charge card.

For reversed-charge or collect calls and for person-to-person calls, dial 0 (zero, not the letter "O") followed by the area code and number you want; an operator will then come on the line, and you should specify that you are calling collect, or person-to-person, or both. If your operator-assisted call is international, immediately ask to speak with an overseas operator.

For local directory assistance ("Information"), dial **411;** for long-distance information dial 1, then the appropriate area code and **555-1212.**

Time California is on Pacific time, which is three hours earlier than on the U.S. East Coast. For instance, when it is noon in San Diego, it is 3pm in New York and Miami; 2pm in Chicago, in the central part of the country; and 1pm in Denver, in the midwestern part of the country. California, like most of the rest of the United States, observes daylight saving time during the summer; in late spring, clocks are moved ahead one hour and then are turned back again in the fall. This results in lovely, long summer evenings, when the sun sets as late as 8:30 or 9pm.

Tipping Some rules of thumb: bartenders, 10% to 15%; bellhops, at least 50¢ per bag, or $2 to $3 for a lot of luggage; cab drivers, 10% of the fare; cafeterias and fast-food restaurants, no tip; chambermaids, $1 per day; checkroom attendants, $1 per garment; theater ushers, no tip; gas-station attendants, no tip; hairdressers and barbers, 15% to 20%; waiters and waitresses, 15% to 20% of the check; valet parking attendants, $1.

4 On the Road: Seeing California by Car

The cult of the car was born in California. We've assumed that you'll be driving as you explore, and there's no better way to see this spectacular state. Perhaps the most famous scenic drive in the United States follows Calif. 1 as it twists and turns, hugging the Pacific Coast.

The great thing about driving, of course, is that you can go as you please, stopping to explore offbeat sights and little-known destinations. Here are three great drives that will get you started.

1 Ghost Towns of the Gold Country

by Lisa Stone-Norman

The scene of California's original get-rich-quick scheme is hundreds of miles from the fistfuls of money made today in Hollywood and Silicon Valley. The crannies of the Sierra foothills hide the real hardscrabble genesis of the Golden State, where a few gutsy pioneers accidentally shoveled pure gold in 1848.

In a brief decade, nearly 400,000 people stampeded to California to try to pan their piece of the Gold Rush. Long before the rush petered out, a small but lucky percentage of the famed forty-niners and others extracted millions of dollars in precious metal from the Mother Lode; most everybody else eventually went home, or stayed put, empty-handed.

Long before the gold was gone, however, the boomtowns of the Sierra became famous for the colorful characters who dug, drank, gambled, and lusted through their quest to eke precious gold out of its 200-million-year-old hiding place in the stony earth. Criminal Charles "Black Bart" Bolton shot up the towns and stole gold dust from a fledgling bank called Wells Fargo. Budding journalist Mark Twain wrote about it—but no one really knows if Twain ever wore a pair of the popular canvas pants cunningly riveted by young merchant Levi Strauss.

Today, the legacy of the famous and forgotten fortune seekers lives on in a chain of more than 100 ghost towns and abandoned mines that dot Calif. 49. Driving from Coloma to Columbia, you'll discover picturesque villages that are doing a better business now than in the old days, thanks to painstakingly restored boardwalks stocked

Ghost Towns of the Gold Country

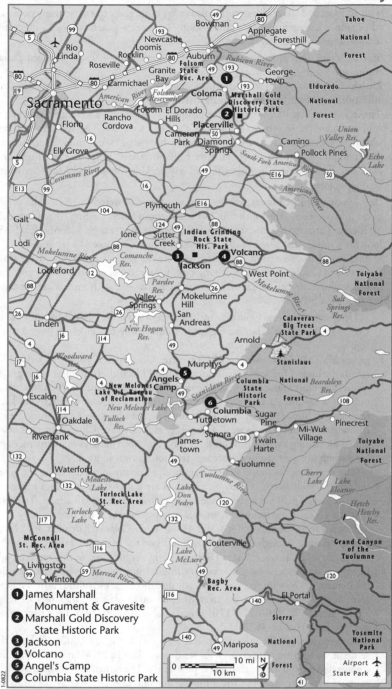

1. James Marshall
   Monument & Gravesite
2. Marshall Gold Discovery
   State Historic Park
3. Jackson
4. Volcano
5. Angel's Camp
6. Columbia State Historic Park

0 ____ 10 mi
  ____
0 ____ 10 km

Airport ✈
State Park 🌲

1-0822

with antiques and collectibles. You'll also enjoy quiet ghost towns, sparsely populated or empty testaments to how, not so long ago, a new generation of Californians scratched their way to a living.

Start: Coloma (32 miles east of downtown Sacramento—halfway between Sacramento and South Lake Tahoe).

Finish: Columbia (55 miles south of Sacramento, 39 miles east of Stockton, and 120 miles east of the San Francisco Bay Area).

Time: This one-day tour is perfect for visitors to Sacramento and South Lake Tahoe who are interested in seeing the heart of the Gold Country. The area also is accessible to visitors to the San Francisco Bay area who want a look at rural California and aren't afraid of a little driving. History buffs interested in staying overnight and exploring the twisting 120-mile stretch between Downieville and Mariposa won't be disappointed.

Begin your tour in **Coloma,** where gold was first discovered in 1848. The pretty ghost town overlooks the south fork of the American River. Getting there from U.S. 50 is easy: Turn north at the stoplight in Placerville, where signs advertise Calif. 49; look for a vintage, brick-red Southern Pacific Railroad caboose as a landmark.

The crowded, corrugated tin roofs that line the start of the 8-mile drive from Placerville to Coloma testify to a mining past. Closer to Coloma, the homes give way to windmills, cattle-grazing lands, and fruit orchards—the tools miners' descendants use to make a living nowadays.

Upon approaching Coloma, follow signs to the Marshall Monument, or Calif. 153 (California's shortest highway at three-tenths of a mile). At its end you'll find the:

1. **James Marshall Monument and Gravesite.** On a knoll beyond the parking lot stands the huge, bronze statue of James Wilson Marshall. It doubles as his gravestone and points to the spot where he discovered gold on January 24, 1848, while building a sawmill. As the story goes, the New Jersey carpenter managed to keep the news to himself for only a few minutes before he shouted to work crews. Although word of his find spread as far away as Mexico and China, Marshall never ended up making a dime from his discovery. He ended his days as a carpenter and blacksmith in nearby Kelsey, unrecognized for his contribution.

The view from the monument is beautiful, especially in spring, when the green hills sprout wildflowers. Nearby picnic tables are scattered beneath huge oak trees. The site and its public rest rooms are kept tidy by a resident park ranger. The state requests a $5 parking fee, which visitors may pay here or at the next stop.

Upon leaving the park, cross Calif. 49 and enter Coloma. Turn left onto Main Street and drive through the ghost town until on the left appears the:

2. **Marshall Gold Discovery State Historic Park.** A quick tour of this museum will bring you up to speed on gold country lingo, from "placer" gold, which erodes from quartz, to how miners "coyoted," or dug the metal out of the earth. You can learn how to pan for gold at the river and pick up an old-town walking tour map. The museum (☎ **916/622-1116**) is open from 10am to 5pm. (For park information, call **916/622-3470.**)

Coloma was quickly mined out, but its boom brought 10,000 people to the settlement and lasted long enough for residents to build a schoolhouse, a gunsmith, a general store, and a tiny, tin-roofed post office. The miners also planted oak and mimosa trees that shade the street during hot summers. A few stores open to sell light fare and jewelry from March to early fall; traditionally, a beer garden opens next to the restored Weller house, the last remaining evidence of the 13 guest houses the town boasted at its peak.

Farther up Main Street is a huge replica of the mill Marshall was building when he made his discovery. The largest building in town, the mill is powered by electricity during the summer months. Across the street are two restored stone buildings, all that remains of a large Chinese settlement that burned in an 1883 fire. Although the history of these early Californians is poorly recorded, proof remains that the Midas touch favored no race. Thousands of Chinese, Mexican, and African American miners worked their way to prosperity during the Gold Rush, boosting the state's multicultural flavor at the same time that Native American tribes, displaced and diseased by the influx of foreign people, died or moved on.

Leave Coloma by taking Main Street back to Calif. 49. Travel through Placerville and continue south along the twisting road.

☕ **TAKE A BREAK**   A few miles south of Placerville is the tiny boardwalk community of Diamond Springs, where Gold Country charm is served up alongside such urban comforts as cappuccino. Watch for the **Diamond Springs Hotel,** 545 Main St. (☎ **916/621-1730;** open 8am to 9pm daily). It's impossible to miss this huge red barn of a building with its white, wraparound porches. The hotel specializes in country breakfasts with huge homemade biscuits as authentic as the twangy music piped in to the dining room. Lunches are just as generous, and the children's menu offers everything from peanut butter and jelly to Jell-O.

About 12 miles after departing Diamond Springs on Calif. 49 South, you'll pass through bustling Amador City and Sutter Creek, former mining towns now devoted to modern commerce. Local merchants have made the most of a refurbished boardwalk and a few historic buildings; both villages are a shopper's paradise, with everything from antiques to art for sale. However, parking can be difficult, especially during the summer months, and travelers may opt to drive 5 miles farther to:

3. Jackson. Turn left off of Calif. 49 onto Jackson Gate Road, the back door of the town. After 3 or 4 miles, you'll pass the dramatic white St. Sava Serbian Orthodox Church and cemetery. Built in 1894, the church is the first of its kind in the United States.

A few hundred yards past St. Sava's, turn left onto Church Street. At no. 225 is the **Amador County Museum,** a huge brick building where Will Rogers filmed *Boys Will Be Boys* in 1920. Today the former home of Armstead Calvin Brown and his 11 children is filled with mining memorabilia and information on two local mines, the Kennedy and the Argonaut, that were among the deepest and richest in the nation. Behind the museum, tour a working large-scale model of the Kennedy for $1. The museum (☎ **209/223-6386**) is open Wednesday to Sunday from 10am to 4pm.

Turn right at the end of Church Street and head for downtown Jackson and Main Street.

Although the Kennedy and Argonaut mines ultimately produced more than $140 million in gold, Jackson initially earned its place in the gold rush as a supply center. That history is apparent in the town's wide Main Street, lined by tall buildings adorned with intricate iron railings. Make no mistake: This is no ghost town—Jackson is a modern minicity, but one that has worked to preserve its pre-Victorian influence. At the southern end of the street is the famous **National Hotel,** rumored to be California's oldest continuously operating hotel since it opened its doors in 1862. Today, the hotel's **Louisiana House Bar,** a cool, dark establishment where weary travelers can rest while a honky-tonk pianist beats out ragtime, does plenty of business.

Take a good look at the **Wells Fargo Club and Charcoal Broiler,** located diagonally across the street from the hotel. This two-story brick structure with its wooden balcony and awning is an original 1851 Wells Fargo Building.

Upon leaving Jackson, follow signs back to Calif. 49 South. Once back on the highway, begin looking immediately for Calif. 88 east. Turn left onto Calif. 88 and travel 12 miles to:

4. **Volcano.** Unrestored and beautiful, this is one of the most authentic ghost towns in the central Sierra. The town got its name in 1848, after miners mistook the origin of the enormous craggy boulders that lie in the center of the village. The dark rock and blind window frames of a few backless, ivy-covered buildings give the town's main thoroughfare a haunted look. Sprinkled between boarded up buildings, about a hundred residents do business in the same sagging wooden storefronts that a population of 8,000 frequented nearly 150 years ago.

The overwhelming thing you'll notice about Volcano is the silence of its streets. But the now-quiet tiny burg has a rich history: Not only was this boomtown once home to 17 hotels, courts of quick justice, and the state's first lending library, but Volcano gold supported the Union during the Civil War. Residents even smuggled a huge cannon to the front line in a hearse (it was never used). The story goes that had the enthusiastic blues fired it, **"Old Abe"** would have exploded, it was so overcharged. The cannon sits in the town center today, under a rusting weathervane.

Looming over the small buildings is the stately **St. George Hotel** (☎ 209/ **296-4458**), a three-story, balconied building that testifies to the $90 million in gold mined in and around the town. Its ivy-covered brick and shuttered windows will remind you of colonial New England. The 20-room hotel still operates from Wednesday through Sunday and serves meals and libations in its full bar and restaurant.

Take Calif. 88 back to Highway 49, and drive south 16 miles. Along the way, take note of the brick remains of **Butte Store.** The storefront is all that remains of Butte City, a camp that sprang up, and almost as quickly died, in the shadow of **Mokelumne Hill.** You'll want to stop at:

5. **Angel's Camp,** the site of "The Jumping Frog of Calaveras County," the Mark Twain story that made both him and the town famous overnight. It's a tale of frontier espionage—a champion frog croaks after being poisoned with buckshot by the competition. The town's Jumping Frog Jubilee is an annual celebration in the third week of May. Now you'll understand the recurring theme of amphibians painted on the boardwalk, which has flourished since 1860.

🍲 **TAKE A BREAK**   Stop for a late lunch at **Piaggi's Restaurant and the Frog Pond Creamery,** 1262 South Main St., where the settings and prices are modest, but no one has ever left the premises hungry. The homemade chili is great—order it with onions and cheese—as are the enormous hamburgers. (*Beware:* The regular patty weighs more than a pound and is easily twice the size of the large onion kaiser roll it comes on.)

Continue 7 miles down Calif. 49 to:

6. **Columbia State Historic Park,** an antique metropolis that has more standing relics of early mining days than almost any ghost town in the Gold Country. Allow at least two hours to explore it. Columbia is very popular, however, so expect crowds in the summer.

In Columbia's heyday, its 15,000 residents built 150 gambling houses, one of the first public schools in California, 17 dry-goods stores, and a full-fledged

Chinatown. Today, cars are banned from its dusty streets, giving the shady to an authentic and uncommercial feel. Merchants still do business behind some storefronts, as horse, stagecoach, and pedestrian traffic wanders by.

Start your tour at the beautiful, two-story **Fallon Hotel and Theater** (☎ 209/ **532-1470**). Like many buildings in Columbia, the hotel was built with bricks in 1857 to withstand the fires that regularly swept the town. The state has spent more than $1 million to restore the hotel and its antique furnishings, many of which are original to the Fallon. Its 14 rooms and full-service restaurant offer every convenience. Seasonal performances go on in the Fallon's quaint theater, courtesy of drama students from the University of the Pacific. The company rehearses down the street at Eagle Cotage (its traditional spelling), a former upscale boarding house for luckier miners.

Between the two buildings is the tiny office of the *Columbia Gazette,* the local paper that's still published once a year. The basement is home to a free museum on the history of California newspapers.

Up the road, on Main Street, is the **Wells Fargo Express** building. Constructed in 1858, the structure is notable for its lacework iron railing and, inside, a scale that gold-rush bankers used to weigh more than 1.4 million ounces of gold. The scale is fabled to be so precise that it can weigh a pencil signature on a piece of paper.

If you wait long enough in front of Wells Fargo, the **Columbia Stage** will pull up. The town's stables operate the stage and a livery year-round for visitors interested in a horse or pony tour of the town and cemetery. Call **209/532-0663** for information and reservations.

Nearby is an open-air example of how residents mined an estimated $90 million in gold in and around the town before 1870. An intricate system of miniature sawmills and tunnels delivers water to the area, where you can try your hand at panning for gold today. The large boulders and nearby grassy park make it perfect for children.

Kids will also get a kick out of the schoolhouse, built in 1861, which has been restored with desks and slates. Farther down Main Street is the **Columbia Museum** and another beautiful old guest house, the **City Hotel** (☎ 209/ **532-1479**), built in 1856. Behind the iron grillwork and French doors on the second floor are two of the hotel's 10 luxurious Victorian rooms.

WINDING DOWN Pull up a stool at the **Douglass Saloon** (open 10am to 5pm daily) on Columbia's Main Street. Inside the swinging doors of the classic Western bar you can sample homemade sarsaparilla and wild cherry, drinks the saloon has been serving since 1857. The storefront's large shuttered windows open onto a dusty Main Street, so put up your boots, relax awhile, and watch the stagecoach go by.

2 The Missions of the Central Coast

by Stephanie Avnet

For those of us who grew up along California's coast between the Bay Area and the Mexican border, grammar-school field trips to the beautifully restored old Spanish missions scattered throughout the region were a matter of course. For restless schoolkids, though, the day's greatest excitement was leaving the classroom temporarily behind. Many had more enthusiasm for scratching initials into the

k of a school bus seat than for learning about Franciscan friars who
h from Mexico more than 200 years ago.

..yone can remember similar school-age experiences. However, maybe
your boredom wasn't just a result of your pint-sized attention span. Maybe if those long-gone school trips were as interesting as this driving tour, we all would have lifted our heads from behind those school bus seats.

Today, take an extraordinary opportunity to step back in time—not just to relive what might be your own history, but California's as well—by seeking out the six historic missions along the central coast. What's more, the drive will give you a panoramic view of modern California. From surf-pounded coastlines to rich agricultural valleys, from upscale college towns to working-class farm communities and even sparsely populated ranchland, you'll see that the missions act as the chain linking everything together.

In fact, the 21 missions *were* originally laid out as links in a chain by the Spanish friars, led by Father Junípero Serra, who were the state's earliest European settlers. Serra, born on Majorca in 1713, was a Franciscan friar whose life work began when he was sent to the New World to administrate the church's missions in Baja (lower) California. Shortly after arriving, he was charged with founding missions at the ports of San Diego and Monterey in the little-explored Alta (upper) California, a Spanish territory populated with "heathen" natives and threatened by Russian imperialism. He was constantly thwarted by insufficient supplies, resistant natives, and Spanish bureaucratic red tape, yet Serra ultimately went on to found a total of nine thriving missions before his death in 1784. Recognized by many in both religious and secular circles for the role he played in spreading the Christian faith and establishing the strong Spanish legacy in California, Father Junípero Serra was a candidate for sainthood and was beatified by the Vatican in 1988.

Serra and his band of Spanish pilgrims spaced their colonial missions at roughly one-day intervals (on horseback, that is!) along *El Camino Real* (the royal road) that stretched up through California from Mexico. Present-day U.S. 101 runs true to this historic road along most of its blacktopped path. At several of the missions along this tour, you will be able to walk along portions of the original road used by the Spanish to supply and oversee these colony outposts.

Start: Santa Barbara (95 miles northwest of downtown Los Angeles).
Finish: San Juan Bautista (92 miles south of San Francisco and 35 miles east of Monterey Peninsula).
Time: Two days are recommended for seeing all six missions along this 270-mile drive. San Luis Obispo, Paso Robles, or Morro Bay are recommended for the overnight stop after seeing Mission San Luis Obispo.

Begin your tour in **Santa Barbara,** whose picturesque coastal location is complemented by the prevailing Spanish-Moorish architectural style, largely influenced by the city's imposing mission. From U.S. 101, exit at Mission Street and follow the beige-and-brown Historic Landmark signs, which are extremely well placed and helpful all along the drive, to the first stop on our tour. While cruising along Mission Street, notice the variety of architectural styles and eras. Just before the mission itself is **Plaza Junipero,** a small neighborhood of elegant Craftsman bungalows; two short stone replicas of a traditional mission *campanario* (bell tower) mark the gateway to the community. Just beyond Plaza Junipero is:

1. **Santa Barbara Mission Virgen y Martir.** Founded in 1786 and still inhabited by Franciscan friars, it is known as the "Queen of the Missions." The design of its imposing church, differing from the standard mission simplicity, incorporates

The Missions of the Central Coast

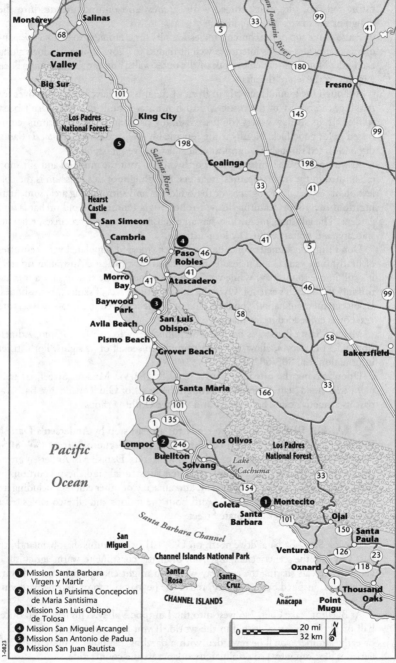

Monterey
Salinas
68
Carmel Valley
Big Sur
Los Padres National Forest
1
101
King City
198
Coalinga
33
41
Hearst Castle
San Simeon
Cambria
1
46
46
Paso Robles
41
41
Atascadero
58
Morro Bay
41
Baywood Park
1
San Luis Obispo
Avila Beach
Pismo Beach
Grover Beach
1
58
Bakersfield
Santa Maria
166
166
101
1
135
Lompoc
246
Los Olivos
Los Padres National Forest
Buellton
Solvang
Lake Cachuma
154
33
Goleta
Montecito
Santa Barbara
101
Ojai
150
Santa Paula
Ventura
126
23
San Miguel
Oxnard
118
Channel Islands National Park
Santa Rosa
Santa Cruz
Point Mugu
1
Thousand Oaks
CHANNEL ISLANDS
Anacapa

Salinas River
Salinas River
San Joaquin River
152
5
33
99
41
180
Fresno
145
99
41
5
99
Santa Barbara Channel

Pacific Ocean

1 Mission Santa Barbara Virgen y Martir
2 Mission La Purisima Concepcion de Maria Santisima
3 Mission San Luis Obispo de Tolosa
4 Mission San Miguel Arcangel
5 Mission San Antonio de Padua
6 Mission San Juan Bautista

0   20 mi
     32 km
N

1-0823

many Moorish and classical elements. Santa Barbara's residents embraced the church's distinctive look as the town grew during the 1920s and 1930s, incorporating red roof tiles, thick stucco walls, arches, and outdoor arcades into the design of the town's new buildings.

Pause at the top of the church's majestic stairs for a moment to behold the panorama of city and sea. Its interior is well lit thanks to a row of high windows along each side. Notice the extreme depth of the outer walls, and the single trompe l'oeil window to the left of the altar.

Although the grounds directly in front of the mission have been paved over for parking, the beauty of the rustic Moorish fountain, built in 1808, hasn't been spoiled. In its shallow waters you'll see fish, lily pads, and previous visitors' coins tossed in for good luck. Nearby is the remarkably well-preserved *lavanderia* (laundry basin), fed through a whimsical bear's head carved in stone.

As with most of the missions, it's worthwhile to tour the museum and gift shop established in the restored padres' quarters. A highlight of this museum is the collection of historical photographs of the buildings and surrounding area, some dating from the 1850s, featuring brown-robed friars tending the old orchards and gardens. The gift shop, meanwhile, has an extensive selection of crucifixes, religious statuary, and pottery crafted by local artisans.

Don't miss the cemetery outside the church, its yard populated with centuries of headstones, vaults, and mausoleums. Shaded by a majestic Australian fig tree, it's still in use to this day. While you're in the cemetery, be sure to take a minute to study the church's exterior. Over the door are three sets of skull and crossbones. Upon careful examination, you'll see that only one is carved in stone—two sets are *real* bones embedded in the plaster.

Mission Santa Barbara is open to the public daily from 9am to 5pm. Admission is $3 per person; allow 30 to 45 minutes to see all of its sights. For further information, call **805/682-4713.**

Upon leaving the mission, return to U.S. 101 via Mission Street, or take palm-tree–lined State Street west through the heart of Old Town Santa Barbara, past its attractive cafes, bookstores, and vintage clothing shops.

☕ **TAKE A BREAK**   If you're ready for a treat, stop by **Andersen's Danish Bakery and Restaurant,** at 1106 State St. near Figueroa Street (☎ **805/ 962-5085**). Reservations recommended on weekends. Danish Ms. Andersen greets you herself (when she's not baking) and offers substantial (and cheap!) portions of New York steak, chicken or crab salad, and an array of other edibles (including an honest-to-goodness smorgasbord). And both the indoor and alfresco tables offer great people-watching along State Street.

Leaving Santa Barbara, drive north on U.S. 101, which turns sharply inland just past Gaviota, the scenery changing from dramatic coastline to warm agricultural valleys. The cars sharing the roadway with you might change, too; many drivers in this area, inspired by the scenery, relive the heyday of motor touring with vintage autos.

At Buellton, take Calif. 246 west into the **Lompoc Valley.** This region produces half of all the flower seeds sold in the world. If you plan your trip for late spring or early summer, you'll be rewarded with a dazzling rainbow, as more than 200 varieties blossom into a colorful patchwork across the countryside.

After traveling 15 miles on Calif. 246, past ornate gateways to distant ranches and roadside produce stands, you'll reach:

2. **Mission La Purisima Concepcion de Maria Santisima,** founded 1787. Reconstructed in its still-rural setting, this is the most extensively, and authentically, rebuilt of the mission chain. During the Depression, the Civilian Conservation Corps (CCC) restored La Purisima, which is now a State Historic Park. Inside the museum, an interesting display documents the CCC and the restoration process.

La Purisima's open arrangement is unusual, varying from the standard "quadrangle" around a large inner yard. Allow at least one hour to tour the grounds. The reconstructed buildings and work stations clearly illustrate how the Spanish Empire used the clergy to colonize the "New World" with minimal military support (and expense) by establishing fully functional settlements for converting the native peoples. The mission's intricate water supply system, with its many elaborately decorated aqueducts and fountains, is still relatively intact. The pens of livestock and farm animals include some mighty impressive steers. Reportedly, the sheep are direct descendants of the original mission herds.

Between early spring and late autumn, costumed Park Service volunteers reenact daily life at the mission. You can enjoy the sights and smells of craft demonstrations (tortilla making, soap and candle making, leather working, blacksmithing, spinning, weaving, and pottery). On Sundays, the volunteers conduct nature walks of the park's diverse plant communities and wildlife habitats.

The grounds at Mission La Purisima are open to the public daily 7am to 6pm; the buildings close at 5pm. Admission is $5 per car; allow 60 to 90 minutes for your visit. For further information, including a schedule of living history events, call **805/733-3713.**

To leave the Lompoc Valley, follow Calif. 1 north. This route takes you through softly rolling hills past Vandenberg Air Force Base, which helps drive the local economy. Turn off at Calif. 135 and follow it toward Santa Maria for one mile. Exit at Clark Avenue and turn right. Follow Clark 2 miles to rejoin U.S. 101 north.

You'll certainly know when you've have entered the city limits of **San Luis Obispo**—who could miss the Pepto-Bismol–pink neon sign of the flamboyant **Madonna Inn?** Exit at Broad Street and follow the signs to the center of this attractive college town, where you'll find:

3. **Mission San Luis Obispo de Tolosa,** founded in 1772. Father Junípero Serra chose this valley for the site of his fifth mission based on tales told to him of friendly natives and bountiful food (including grizzly bears—yum!). Here, the traditional red-tile roof was first used atop a California mission, after the original thatched tule roofs repeatedly fell to hostile Native Americans' burning arrows.

Today, the site illustrates how a city growing up around historic structures can expertly incorporate new development without compromising historical value. Although the church has seen some disastrous restorations—the most offensive being the addition of wood siding and a New England–style steeple in 1880, since removed—in 1961 the city preserved the creek area fronting the mission, creating what is now the pedestrian **Mission Plaza.**

The former padres' quarters is an excellent museum chronicling both Native American and missionary life through all eras of the mission's use. Domestic and social artifacts are featured in the collection. The gift shop carries a fine selection of fired clay tiles with mission designs.

Mission San Luis Obispo is open to the public daily from 9am to 5pm from May through September and 9am to 4pm from October through April. Admission is $1 per person; allow 30 to 45 minutes to tour the mission and its grounds. For further information, call **805/543-6850.**

☕ **TAKE A BREAK**   Local art hangs on the walls and fresh, healthy cuisine is prepared using local ingredients at **Cafe Big Sky,** 1121 Broad St. (☎ **805/545-5401**). Most everything on the menu, like shrimp tacos, herb-infused roasted chicken, and lighter meals such as white bean and yellowtail tuna salad and a char-broiled eggplant sandwich, is inventive and tasty. The folk-artsy fervor of San Luis really shines here.

Twenty-five miles north of San Luis Obispo on U.S. 101 is the town of **Paso Robles,** so named for the region's plentiful oak trees. Almond orchards are also abundant, coloring the countryside pink and white during early spring. The valley's rich soils host many vineyards and award-winning wineries; most offer tours and tastings. Their wines and other local edibles are readily available and make great souvenirs and gifts. Eight miles north of Paso Robles is:

4. **Mission San Miguel Archangel,** founded in 1824. This mission, still run by the Franciscan order and inhabited by brown-robed friars, is less spoiled by restoration than many of its counterparts. Its modest exterior hides one of this tour's treats: The church interior is one of the most elaborate and well preserved of the entire chain. Painted and decorated by area Native Americans under the supervision of Spanish designer Estevan Munras, the walls and woodwork glow with luminous colors untouched since their original application. Behind the altar, and its statue of *San Miguel* (St. Michael), is splendid tile work featuring a radiant Eye of God.

Mission San Miguel is open to the public daily from 9:30am to 4:30pm; the church remains open until 5pm. Admission is $1 per family; allow 30 minutes to see the sights. For further information, call **805/467-3256.**

Fourteen miles north of San Miguel, turn off U.S. 101 onto County Hwy. G18 and follow it northwest for 30 minutes, past Jolon, to:

5. **Mission San Antonio de Padua,** founded 1771. The tranquil land upon which the mission sits was once part of the William Randolph Hearst ranch; it now belongs to Fort Hunter-Liggett, a U.S. military training base. **The Hacienda,** adjacent to the mission, is often mistaken for Mission San Antonio itself. Originally Hearst's secondary ranch house, designed by Julia Morgan to complement the opulent Hearst Castle, this mission-revival building now functions as an officers' club and VIP housing for Hunter-Liggett. If you visit on a weekday between 11am and 1pm, you can visit the Hacienda—the club welcomes civilians for lunch.

More than any other mission in the chain, San Antonio feels as though time has stood still. The countryside remains much as it was when the padres chose this setting among the oaks. The colonnade outside the original padres' quarters still shows brick exposed by cattle constantly rubbing themselves against the scratchy surface.

Restorative interest in the mission group began in the early 1900s, after painters and photographers were drawn to the picturesque decay of sites like San Antonio. Subsequent displays of their works stimulated tourist interest, followed by philanthropic campaigns to preserve the missions.

Be aware that much of the quadrangle is in use by today's Franciscans and is thus off-limits to visitors. You may not be aware when you see the friars at work; they usually cast aside their traditional robes for a more practical daily wardrobe of jeans and T-shirts. The rest of the mission, including its first-rate museum, is open to the public Monday to Saturday from 9:30am to 4:30pm and Sunday from 11am to 5pm. Admission is $1 per person; allow an hour to see the mission and its grounds. For further information, call **408/385-4478.**

To rejoin U.S. 101 after your visit, follow County Hwy. G14 north for 25 minutes to the intersection at King City. Sixty miles north on U.S. 101 is **San Juan Bautista,** your final destination on this tour.

San Juan Bautista is a charming mission town that works hard to retain the flavor of a 19th-century village. The mission complex is perched within a picturesque farming valley, surrounded by the restored buildings of the original city plaza. From U.S. 101, take Calif. 156 east (south) to the center of town and:

6. **Mission San Juan Bautista,** founded 1797. Here you'll see the largest church in the mission chain and the only one in unbroken service since its founding. Like San Luis Obispo, it once sported an incongruous wooden steeple but was mercifully decapitated by a storm in 1915. Inside, the church's three-aisle plan and large, theatrical altar inspired many Native Americans to convert, thus creating one of the largest congregations in all of California. The small museum contains many musical instruments and transcriptions, evidence of the mission's musical focus— it once boasted a formidable Native American boys' choir.

East of the church, perched at the edge of an abrupt drop created by the movement of the San Andreas Fault, is a marker pointing out the path of the old El Camino Real. Accompanying the marker are seismographic measuring equipment and an earthquake science exhibit.

There's much to see on the restored city plaza in addition to the mission. One Saturday morning, I witnessed wedding preparations at the church *and* a group of costumed historians reenacting a Spanish-American War battle on the center lawn. The **San Juan Bautista State Historic Park** comprises not only the old Plaza Hotel with its classic frontier barroom and furnished rooms, but also the Plaza Hall, its adjoining stables and blacksmith shop, and the Castro House, where the Breen family lived after traveling here with the ill-fated Donner Party in 1846. A local artist specializing in nostalgic portraiture still operates a studio on the Plaza Hotel's upper floor, accessible from the outside balcony.

Allow 90 minutes to two hours to see the entire plaza. Mission San Juan Bautista is open to the public daily from 9:30am to 5pm from May through October; it closes at 4:30pm the rest of the year. Admission is $2 per person. For further information, call **408/623-4528.** San Juan Bautista State Historic Park is open daily from 10am to 4:30pm. Admission to the park buildings is $2 per person (this charge is separate from your entrance fee to the mission). For further information (including events schedules), call **408/623-4881.**

🌀 **WINDING DOWN** At **Jardines De San Juan,** 115 Third St. (☎ **408/ 623-4466**), authentic Mexican food is served outdoors under graceful mulberry trees. Local entertainers (often a splendid guitar/mandolin duo) will entertain you as you enjoy enormous platters, all accompanied by coarse corn tortilla chips and two excellent homemade salsas. The restaurant is open for lunch and dinner daily. If you're not in the mood for Mexican food, more eateries and several fun antique shops line Third Street, the "Main Street" of San Juan Bautista.

3 Historic Route 66

by Stephanie Avnet

Route 66 has been immortalized in film, song, literature, and memory in the popular imagination. But is anything really left of this great snaking highway, a dependable, comforting spirit John Steinbeck called "the Mother Road"? What of the path to adventure traveled by Tod and Buz in their trademark red Corvette on the namesake 1960s TV series? Well, it's still there, if you're willing to look for it.

Until the final triumph of the multilane superslab in the early 1960s, Route 66 was the *only* route west, from the windy Chicago shores of Lake Michigan to Los Angeles's golden Pacific beaches, if you were traveling by car. "America's Main Street" rambled through eight states; today, in each one, there are enthusiastic organizations dedicated to preserving its remnants. California is fortunate to have a lengthy stretch of the original highway, many miles of which still proudly wear the designation "California State Highway 66."

Picturesque relics of a bygone era—single-story motels, friendly two-pump gas stations—exist beside their modern neighbors, inviting nostalgia for a slower, simpler time. So pop some Glenn Miller or Doris Day into the tape deck, eschew the fast pace of the present day, and prepare to transport yourself back to a time when the vacation began the moment you backed out of the driveway.

Start: Downtown San Bernardino (11 miles north of Riverside; 53 miles west of Palm Springs).
Finish: South Pasadena (6 miles northeast of downtown Los Angeles).
Time: Allow several hours to meander along this 59-mile stretch of the old route.

As Route 66 emerged from the Mojave Desert and wriggled through the Cajon Pass, hot and weary travelers strained for a glimpse of:

1. **San Bernardino,** the next friendly watering hole and a signpost that Los Angeles was now within range. Located in the northeast "elbow" where Interstate 10 meets Interstate 215, downtown San Bernardino is easily reached from Los Angeles, San Diego, the desert communities, and other points north and east. During the early 1900s, this land was fragrant with orange groves; the former Mormon settlement quickly prospered, earning the region a lasting sobriquet, "the Inland Empire."

   The year 1928 saw the grand opening of an elegant movie palace, **The California Theater** (562 West 4th St.), located one block from famous Route 66. From I-215, exit on Fifth Street east. Turn right at F Street, then make a left on Fourth Street, where you can pull over to view the theater. Lovingly restored and still popular for nostalgic live entertainment and the rich tones of its original Wurlitzer pipe organ, the California was a frequent site of Hollywood "sneak previews." Here humorist Will Rogers made his last public appearance in 1935. (Following his death, the highway was renamed the "Will Rogers Memorial Highway" in his honor, but it remains popularly known as Route 66.) Notice the intricate relief of the theater's stone facade, and peek into the lobby to see the red velvet draperies, rich carpeting, and gold bannistered double staircase leading up to the balcony.

   From the theater, turn left on E Street to Fifth Street, then turn left (west) and continue over the freeway. Although the first stretch is a little drab, have faith—after about a mile you'll enter the community of:

2. **Rialto.** Where Fifth Street becomes Foothill Boulevard, you'll need to be on the lookout for Meriden Avenue, site of the fanciful **Wigwam Motel.** Built in the

1950s (along with an identical twin motor court in Holbrook, Arizona), these stucco teepees lured many a road-weary traveler in for the night with their whimsy. Their catchy slogan, "Sleep in a wigwam, get more for your wampum," has been supplanted today by the more to-the-point "Do it in a teepee." But, as with many of the motor courts we'll pass on this drive, you need only picture a few large, shiny Buicks, T-bird convertibles, and "woody" station wagons pulling in for the night, and your imagination will begin to sense the welcoming charm of days gone by.

Continuing west on Foothill Boulevard, look for the **Golden Embers** restaurant. After that, you'll pass into the town of:

3. **Fontana,** whose name in Italian means "fountain city." There isn't too much worth stopping for along this stretch, but definitely slow down to have a look at the **motor court hotels** lining both sides of the road. They're of various vintages, all built to cater to the once vigorous stream of travelers passing through. Although today they're dingy, the melody of their names once again conjures up those glory days: **Ken-Tuck-U-Inn, Rose Motel, Moana, Dragon, Sand and Sage, Sunset, 40 Winks, Redwing.**

At 15395 Foothill is **Bono's Italian Deli,** here since 1936. Recently closed, it faces an uncertain future, for this stretch of highway is relatively desolate.

Soon you'll pass I-15 junction and be driving through:

4. **Rancho Cucamonga,** whose fertile soil still yields a reliable harvest. You might see impromptu **produce stands** springing up by the side of the road; stop and pick up a fresh snack. If you are blessed with clear weather, gaze north at the gentle slope of the **San Gabriel Mountains** and you'll understand how Foothill Boulevard got its name. The construction codes in this community are among the most stringent in California, designed to respect the region's heritage and restrict runaway development. All new buildings are Spanish-Mediterranean in style and amply landscaped.

Rancho Cucamonga has earnestly preserved two historic wineries. First you'll pass **The Virginia Dare Winery,** at the northwest corner of Haven Avenue, whose structures now house part of a large business park/shopping mall, but retain the flourish of the original (ca. 1830s) winery logo.

At Archibald Avenue, look near the northwest corner for the lonely remnants of a **1920s-era gas station.** Empty now, those service bays have seen many a Ford, Studebaker, or Packard in need of a helping hand. The **New Kansan** motel (on the northeast corner of Hellman) must have seemed welcoming to Dust Bowl refugees.

Next you'll see **Thomas Vineyards,** at the northeast corner of Vineyard Avenue, established in 1839. Legend holds that the first owner mysteriously disappeared, leaving hidden treasure still undiscovered on the property. The winery's preserved structures now hold two eateries (including the Roadhouse Cafe, below), a country crafts store, and a bookstore housed in the former brandy still.

☕ **TAKE A BREAK**   If all this driving has made you hungry, the **Roadhouse Cafe** (☎ 909/941-8793 open for lunch and dinner daily) offers hearty steaks, ribs, fish, and chicken in addition to salads and lighter lunches. Share one of their batter-dipped, deep fried whole onions, served with a zesty dipping sauce.

Farther up on the same side of Foothill Boulevard is the **Magic Lamp Inn,** 8189 Foothill Blvd. (☎ 909/981-8659), open for lunch and dinner Tuesday to Friday, dinner only Saturday and Sunday. Built in 1957, the Magic Lamp offers excellent continental cuisine (nothing nouvelle about Route 66!) in a setting that is part

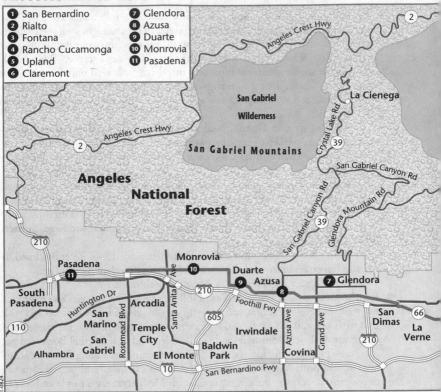

Historic Route 66

1 San Bernardino
2 Rialto
3 Fontana
4 Rancho Cucamonga
5 Upland
6 Claremont
7 Glendora
8 Azusa
9 Duarte
10 Monrovia
11 Pasadena

manor house and part *Aladdin* theme park. Dark, stately dining rooms lurk behind a funky banquette cocktail lounge punctuated by a psychedelic fountain/ fire pit and a panoramic view. The genie bottle theme is everywhere, from the restaurant's dinnerware to the plush carpeting, which would be right at home in a Las Vegas casino. Lovers of kitsch and hearty retro fare shouldn't pass this one up.

Even if you don't stop to eat, consider a stop at the shopping mall behind the Thomas Winery to tour **The Route 66 Territory Museum and Visitor's Bureau,** a minimuseum and gift shop. Stop in and look at the exhibits of old gas pumps, road signs, and other relics. You'll marvel at the array of books, maps, glassware, garments, jewelry, and other souvenirs. Many items bear the original black-on-white Route 66 shield, the ubiquitous highway marker purged from the old route by state transportation officials in 1984. The brown markers you see today were subsequently placed by the historical associations.

Leaving the Thomas Winery, pass underneath the railroad tracks and watch for the **Sycamore Inn,** nestled in a grove of trees and looking very much like an old-style stagecoach stop. This reddish-brown wooden house, dating from 1848, has formerly been a private home and gracious inn; today, it serves the community of Cucamonga as a restaurant and civic hall. Across the street, on the corner of San Bernardino Road, there's a wonderful old service station, now home to a flashy car stereo/cellular phone store.

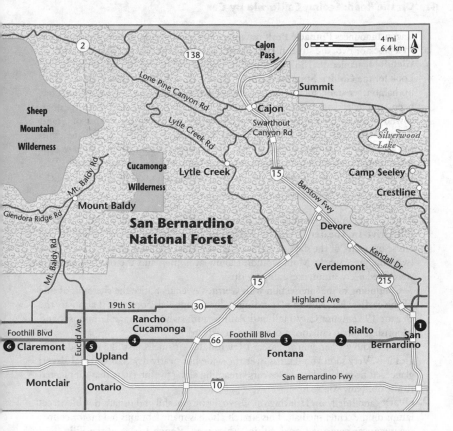

Continue driving, and soon you'll enter:

5. **Upland.** Look north at the intersection of Euclid Avenue for the regal **monument to pioneer women.** Just past San Antonio Avenue, keep your eyes open toward the right for a great old **Winchell's Donuts** sign set back from the street. The junk food theme continues nicely when you reach Benson Avenue, where a classic 1950s-style **McDonald's** stands on the southeast corner, its golden arches flanking a low, white walk-up counter with outdoor stools. The fast food chain has its roots in this region: Richard and Maurice McDonald opened their first burger joint in San Bernardino in 1939. The successful brothers expanded their business, opening locations throughout Southern California, until entrepreneur Ray Kroc purchased the chain in 1955 and franchised McDonald's nationwide.

Pretty soon you'll be in the community of:

6. **Claremont,** known these days for the highly respected group of **Claremont Colleges.** You'll pass several of them along this eucalyptus-lined boulevard. In days gone by, drivers would cruise along this route for mile upon mile, through orchards and open fields, the scenery punctuated only by ambling livestock or a rustic wood fence. You'll pass through **La Verne,** home of **La Paloma** Mexican cafe, a fixture on the Route for many years.

When you approach the start of I-210, keep to the left, passing under the on-ramp and into **San Dimas,** a ranchlike community where you must pay attention to the "horse crossing" street signs. At the corner of Cataract Avenue, a covered wagon announces **Pinnacle Peak** restaurant, guarded by a giant steer atop the roof. In a block or two, the street name changes to Alosta Avenue and you'll be in:

7. **Glendora,** named in 1887 by founder George Whitcomb for his wife Ledora. Look for the **Golden Spur** on the right-hand side. It began 70 years ago as a ride-up hamburger stand for the equestrian crowd; unfortunately, the restaurant has been remodeled in boring stucco, leaving only the original sign, with its neon cowboy boot, as a reminder of its colorful past. On the northeast corner of Grand Avenue stands the "world famous" **Derby East** restaurant. It's not affiliated with the legendary Hollywood watering hole, but was clearly built in the 1940s to capitalize both on its famous namesake and the nearby Santa Anita racetrack. Past the Derby is the **Palm Tropics,** one of the best-maintained old motels along the Route.

Soon you'll enter:

8. **Azusa,** where Alosta Avenue will curve to rejoin Foothill Boulevard at the **Foothill Drive-In Theater,** Southern California's last single-screen drive-in. As you cruise by, think of the days when our cars were an extension of our living rooms (with the great snacks Mom wouldn't allow at home), and the outdoor theaters were filled every summer evening by dusk.

Continuing to the intersection with Cerritos Avenue, notice the **skeleton of one of the earliest McDonald's,** standing sadly abandoned. Soon you'll also pass the elegant 1932 Azusa City Hall and Auditorium, whose vintage lampposts and Moorish fountain enhance a charming courtyard.

You'll know when you've entered **Irwindale**—it smells just like the industrial area it is. Very soon you'll cross over the wide but nearly dry **San Gabriel River;** glance left from the bridge to see cars streaming along the interstate that supplanted Route 66. Now you're in:

9. **Duarte,** and briefly on Huntington Drive, lit by graceful and ornate **double street lamps** on the center median. This stretch also has many fabulous old motor courts; see if you can spot the **Capri, Ohio, Evergreen, Ranch Inn,** and the **Filly.** Farther along, look for the **"Route 66" gas station** (at the corner of Mt. Olive), and yet another example of the "wagon wheel/Wild West" theme restaurants, **The Rails.** Its supertall dining sign will let you know when you're getting close.

Just inside the:

10. **Monrovia** city limits, turn right on Mountain Avenue to catch up with the 1930s alignment of Route 66. Make a left turn on Foothill Boulevard; you'll pass some splendid Craftsman bungalows and other historic homes.

Look for Magnolia Avenue and the outrageous **Aztec Hotel** on the northwest corner. Opened in 1925, the Aztec was a local showplace, awing guests with its overscale, dark Native American–themed lobby, garish Mayan murals, and exotic Brass Elephant bar. An arcade of shops once held the city's most prominent barber shop, beauty salon, and pharmacy. Little has changed about the interior, and a glance behind the front desk will reveal the original cord-and-plug telephone switchboard still in use. If you care to wet your whistle, stop into the bar before continuing on.

Nearby, at the southeast corner of Mayflower, a life-size plastic cow—a splendid example of this auto-age phenomenon—marks **Bob's Dairy.** If you've been observant, you'll have seen many drive-through dairies along our route (mostly Alta-Dena brand). Bob's has all the typical features, including the refrigerated island display case still bearing a vintage "Driftwood Dairy Products" price sign.

Continue west into the tree-lined residential streets of **Arcadia,** home to the **Santa Anita Racetrack** and the **Los Angeles Arboretum,** the picturesque former estate whose Queen Anne cottage has been the setting for many movies and TV shows.

Continue straight on Foothill Boulevard to Rosemead Boulevard; turn left and then right on Colorado Boulevard. This is your last chance to spot remaining motels like the **Hi-Way Host, Astro** (fabulous *Jetsons*-style architecture), **Siesta Inn, Swiss Lodge,** and **Saga Motor Hotel.** Colorado Boulevard leads into:

11. Pasadena, a charming city with many elegant historic buildings and a restored Old Town. If you're thinking about taking home some music reminiscent of your Route 66 experience, stop into **Canterbury Records** (☎ 818/792-7184; open seven days a week), at the corner of Hudson Avenue. They have Los Angeles's finest selection of big band and pop vocalists on CD and cassette; perhaps you'll choose one of the many renditions of Bobby Troup's homage, "(Get Your Kicks On) Route 66."

Continue along Colorado Boulevard, and turn left at Fair Oaks Avenue, keeping your eyes peeled as you pass the intersection with Green Street to see the rear view of the landmark **Castle Green Hotel.** Drive over the Pasadena Freeway (110) south on-ramp, which would take you onto L.A.'s historic first freeway, the **Arroyo Seco** (opened in 1940), to downtown Los Angeles. But continue instead along Fair Oaks Avenue to Mission Street and the **Fair Oaks Pharmacy** (☎ 818/799-1414; open seven days a week), a fixture on the northwest corner since 1915. If you share my belief that there is no finer end to a grand adventure than ice cream, stop for an authentic ice cream soda, sparkling phosphate, "Route 66" sundae, or old-fashioned malt (complete with the frosty mixing can), all served by today's fresh-faced "soda jerks" from behind the marble counter. They also serve soup, sandwiches, and other snacks. The Fair Oaks is still a dispensing pharmacy, and offers a variety of charming gifts, including an abundance of "Route 66"–themed items.

🌀 **WINDING DOWN**   From this point on, the path of Route 66 changed many times over the years as Los Angeles grew. It ran through downtown Los Angeles via either Mission Street/Figueroa or Huntington/Broadway, caught up with Sunset Boulevard for a stretch, and ended up cruising toward the beach on Santa Monica Boulevard. Most remnants have been obscured by the city's zealous development; of the few remaining in Santa Monica, most fell victim to the disastrous 1994 earthquake. But the *complete* Route 66 experience includes the final stretch into the city and that breathtaking first view of the ocean. So, if you decide to explore further, look for **Dolores Restaurant** (11407 Santa Monica Blvd.), the last of what was once a prominent chain of L.A.-area drive-ins. Near the ocean, notice the 1922 **Claude Short Dodge** dealership (1201 Santa Monica Blvd.), and the **Crocodile Cafe** at the corner of Ocean, which operated until recently as the Belle-Vue Restaurant, marking the unofficial "end of the line."

For more information, contact the **California Historic Route 66 Association** (☎ 714/289-8666) or the **U.S. Route 66 Association** (P.O. Drawer 5323, Oxnard, CA 93031). There's also a quarterly *Route 66 Magazine* (P.O. Box 66, Laughlin NV 89028-0066).

5 San Francisco

by Erika Lenkert and Matthew R. Poole

Consistently rated one of the top tourist destinations in the world, San Francisco is awash with multiple dimensions. Its famous, thrilling streets go up, and they go down; its multifarious citizens—and their adopted cultures, architectures, and cuisine—hail from San Antonio to Singapore; and its politics range from hyper-liberalism to an ever-encroaching wave of conservatism. Even something as mundane as fog takes on a new dimension as it creeps from the ocean and slowly envelopes San Francisco in a resplendent blanket of mist.

In a city so multifaceted, so enamored with itself, it's truly hard not to find what you're looking for. Feel the cool blast of salt air as you stroll across the Golden Gate. Stuff yourself on a Chinatown dim sum. Browse the Haight for incense and crystals. Walk along the beach, pierce your nose, see a play, rent a Harley—the list is endless. Like an eternal world's fair, it's all happening in San Francisco, and everyone's invited.

1 Orientation

ARRIVING
BY PLANE

Two major airports serve the Bay Area: San Francisco International and Oakland International. All the major national rental car companies have offices at these two locations (see "Getting Around" in Chapter 2).

SAN FRANCISCO INTERNATIONAL AIRPORT (SFO) San Francisco's major airport (☎ 415/761-0800) is 14 miles south of downtown directly on U.S. 101. For information on ground transportation to the city, call the airport's toll-free hot line (☎ 800/736-2008).

If you rent a car, it will take you about 40 minutes to get downtown during rush hour; otherwise it's 20 to 25 minutes. A cab will cost $25 to $30, plus tip.

The **SFO Airporter bus** (☎ 800/532-8405 or 415/495-8404) picks up passengers in front of the baggage claim area every 15 to 30 minutes daily from 6:20am to midnight and stops at several downtown hotels: the Grand Hyatt, San Francisco Hilton, San Francisco Marriott, Westin St. Francis, Parc Fifty-Five, Hyatt Regency, and Sheraton Palace. Reservations not needed. It costs

$9 one way, $15 round trip; and $5 each way for children 2 to 16 (accompanied by an adult).

Other private shuttle companies offer door-to-door airport service, in which you share a van with other passengers. **SuperShuttle** (☎ 415/558-8500) charges $11 to downtown; a second passenger pays only $8 each way; and you can rent the entire van for $38 with up to seven passengers. **Yellow Airport Shuttle** (☎ 415/282-7433) charges $10 per person. Each shuttle stops every 20 minutes or so to pick up passengers from the marked areas at the terminals' upper level. Reservations are required for the return trip to SFO only and should be made one day before departure. These shuttles usually reach downtown San Francisco in 45 to 60 minutes, but when leaving, make sure they pick you up 2 hours before your flight (3 during holidays).

The San Mateo County Transit system, **SamTrans** (☎ 800/660-4287 or 415/508-6200, within Northern California) runs two buses between the airport and the Transbay Terminal at First and Mission streets. The 7B bus costs $1 and takes about 55 minutes. The 7F bus costs $2 and takes only 35 minutes, but permits only one carry-on bag. Both buses run daily, every half hour from about 6am to 7pm, then hourly until about midnight.

OAKLAND INTERNATIONAL AIRPORT   Located about 5 miles south of downtown Oakland, at the Hegenberger Road exit on Calif. 17 (U.S. 880), Oakland International Airport (☎ 510/577-4000) is used primarily by passengers with East Bay destinations. Some San Franciscans, however, prefer this less-crowded airport when flying during busy periods.

Taxis into the center of San Francisco are expensive. The one-hour trip will cost about $45, plus tip.

If you make advance reservations, the **AM/PM Airporter**, P.O. Box 2902, Oakland, CA 94609 (☎ 510/547-2155), will take you from the Oakland Airport to your San Francisco hotel at any time of day. Allow about 50 to 60 minutes. The price depends on the number of passengers sharing the van, but it's usually $35 to $45 per person; get a quote when you call. There are also privately owned shuttle services waiting for passengers at the airport. Fares vary, but are usually less than $20 per person.

The cheapest way to get downtown is via **Bay Area Rapid Transit (BART).** The **AirBART shuttle bus** (☎ 510/562-8428) leaves about every 15 minutes from Terminals 1 and 2 en route to BART and costs $2. BART fares vary depending on your destination; the trip to downtown San Francisco costs $2.15 and takes 20 minutes. AirBART operates Monday through Saturday from 6am to midnight and on Sunday from 8am to midnight.

BY CAR

If you're driving in from the north, U.S. 101 crosses the Golden Gate Bridge at the northernmost tip of the peninsula and runs directly through the city. Approaching from the east, I-80 crosses the San Francisco-Oakland Bay Bridge and terminates in the city's South of Market (SoMa) district.

Both I-280 and U.S. 101 come up the peninsula from the south and drop into the city via several downtown off-ramps.

BY TRAIN

Passengers arriving by train will disembark at Amtrak's Emeryville depot just north of the East Bay side of the Bay Bridge. Free shuttles connect the depot with San Francisco's Ferry Building and CalTrain Station; they depart at 40-minute intervals and the trip takes about 45 minutes. For information call **Amtrak** (☎ 800/872-7245).

Since none of the major car-rental companies have an office at the train station, you'll have to pick up your car from downtown Oakland or San Francisco. **Hertz** (☎ **800/654-3131**) will reimburse your cab fare (up to $5) from the train station to its Oakland office at 1001 Broadway, 2 miles away.

BY BUS

Greyhound/Trailways (☎ **800/231-2222**) offers bus service in and out of San Francisco's Transbay Terminal at First and Mission streets.

VISITOR INFORMATION

The **San Francisco Visitor Information Center,** on the lower level of Hallidie Plaza, 900 Market St., at Powell Street (☎ **415/391-2000**), provides information in several languages (open Monday through Friday 9am to 5:30pm; Saturday 9am to 3pm; and Sunday 10am to 2pm). Call 415/391-2001 any time for a recorded message about special events.

The **Visitors Information Center of the Redwood Empire Association,** 2801 Leavenworth, San Francisco, CA 94103 (☎ **415/543-8334**), publishes an annual *Redwood Empire Visitors' Guide* ($3 by mail, free in person) that covers the city, Marin County, and some areas to the north. Open Monday through Friday from 9am to 5pm.

CITY LAYOUT

San Francisco occupies the tip of a 32-mile-long peninsula between San Francisco Bay and the Pacific Ocean. Its land area measures about 46 square miles. Twin Peaks, in the geographic center of the city, is more than 900 feet high.

San Francisco is easy to navigate. The downtown streets are arranged in a grid, except for Market Street and Columbus Avenue, which cut across the grid at right angles to each other. Hills sometimes appear to distort this pattern, which can be confusing. But as you learn your way around, these same hills will become your landmarks and reference points.

MAIN ARTERIES & STREETS

Market Street, with the tall office buildings of the Financial District at its northeast end, is the city's main thoroughfare. One block beyond lies the Embarcadero and the bay.

The **Embarcadero** curves north along San Francisco Bay, terminating at Fisherman's Wharf. Aquatic Park and the Fort Mason complex are located farther west around the bay, occupying the northernmost point of the peninsula. From the eastern perimeter of Fort Mason, **Van Ness Avenue** runs due south, back to Market Street.

The areas listed above form a rough triangle, with Market Street as its southeastern boundary, the waterfront as its northern, and Van Ness Avenue as its western. Within this triangle you'll find most of the city's major attractions.

STREET MAPS

The **San Francisco Visitor Information Center** (see above) gives away plenty of useful maps; if you intend to stick to the typical tourist areas, they will serve you well. The maps printed in the free tourist weeklies, *Bay City Guide* and *Key,* are also useful for visitors and can be found at most hotels, attractions, and at the visitor center. For a huge selection of street, topographical, and hiking maps of San Francisco and the state of California, stop by **Thomas Bros. Maps and Books,** 550 Jackson St. at Columbus Avenue (☎ **415/981-7520**).

THE NEIGHBORHOODS IN BRIEF

Union Square Union Square is the commercial hub of the city. Most major hotels and department stores are crammed into the area surrounding the actual square, which was named for a series of violent pro-Union demonstrations staged here on the eve of the Civil War. A plethora of upscale boutiques, restaurants, and galleries are tucked between the larger buildings.

Nob Hill Bounded by Bush, Larkin, Pacific, and Stockton streets, Nob Hill is one of the city's genteel, old-money districts, still home to the major power brokers and the social institutions they frequent. In the 1870s the Big Four built their mansions here, most of which were either destroyed by the 1906 earthquake or converted to hotels or private clubs like the Fairmont and the Flood mansions.

SoMa South of Market (dubbed "SoMa") is mostly warehouses and industrial spaces sprinkled with eclectic shops, galleries, restaurants, and clubs. It's officially demarcated by the Embarcadero, Calif. 101, and Market Street.

Financial District Northeast of Union Square, this area is bordered by the Embarcadero, Market, Third, Kearny, and Washington streets. It's the city's business district and stomping grounds for many major corporations. The TransAmerica Pyramid, at Montgomery and Clay streets, is one of the district's most conspicuous architectural features. To its east stands the sprawling Embarcadero Center, an $8^1/_2$-acre complex housing offices, shops, and restaurants. Even farther east is the World Trade Center, standing adjacent to the old Ferry Building. Ferries to Sausalito and Larkspur still leave from this point.

Chinatown The official entrance to Chinatown is marked by a large red and green gate on Grant Avenue at Bush Street. Beyond it lies a 24-block labyrinth, bordered by Broadway, Bush, Kearny, and Stockton streets, filled with restaurants, markets, temples, and shops—and of course, a substantial percentage of San Francisco's Chinese residents. Chinatown is a great place for urban exploration. Stroll along Stockton, Grant, and Portsmouth Square, and the alleys that lead off them like Ross and Waverly. This area is jam-packed so don't even think about driving around here.

Russian Hill Russian Hill extends from Pacific to Bay and from Polk to Mason. It is marked by steep streets, lush gardens, and high-rises housing the wealthy as well as the more bohemian. The San Francisco Art Institute is at the bottom of the hill at Chestnut and Jones.

North Beach The Italian quarter, which stretches from Montgomery and Jackson to Bay Street, is one of the best places in the city to sit down at a cafe, grab a coffee, and do some serious people-watching. The night life is equally happening; restaurants, bars, and clubs along Columbus and Grant avenues bring folks from all over the Bay Area here to fight for a parking place and romp through the festive streets. Down Columbus toward the Financial District are the remains of the city's beat generation landmarks, including Ferlinghetti's City Lights Bookstore and Vesuvio's Bar. Broadway, a short strip of sex joints, cuts through the heart of North Beach, while Telegraph Hill looms over the east side, topped by Coit Tower, one of San Francisco's best vantage points.

Fisherman's Wharf North Beach runs into Fisherman's Wharf, which was once the busy heart of the city's great harbor and waterfront industries. Today, it is a tacky tourist area with little if any authentic waterfront life, except for recreational boating and some friendly sea lions.

San Francisco at a Glance

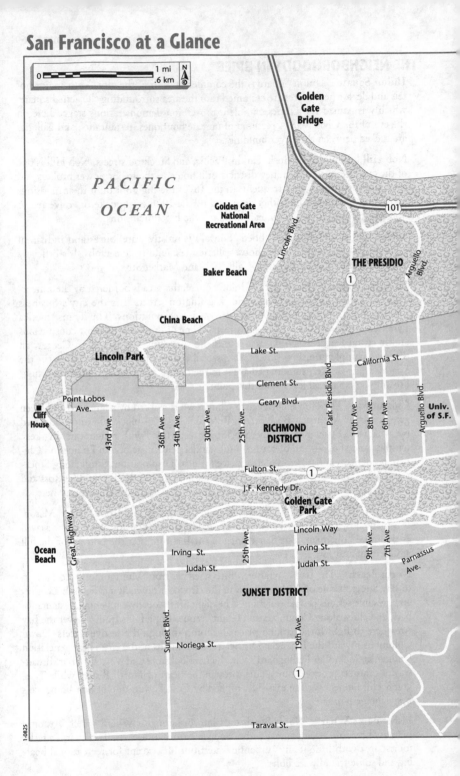

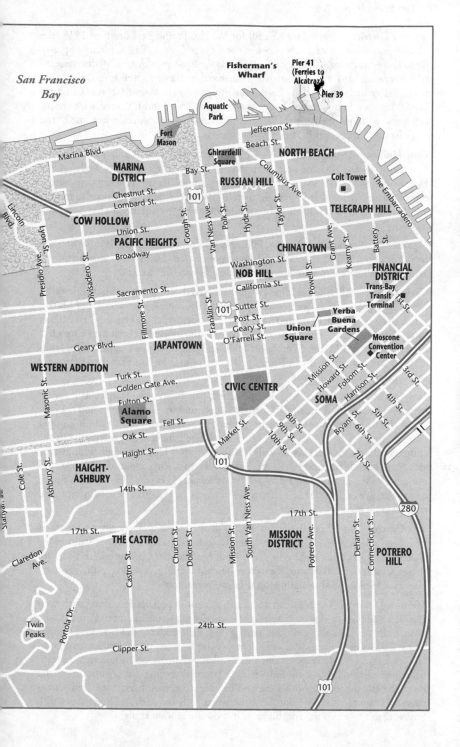

San Francisco Bay

Fisherman's Wharf

Pier 41 (Ferries to Alcatraz)

Pier 39

Aquatic Park

Fort Mason

Jefferson St.

Beach St.

Ghirardelli Square

NORTH BEACH

Marina Blvd.

MARINA DISTRICT

Bay St.

RUSSIAN HILL

Columbus Ave.

Colt Tower

Chestnut St.

Lombard St.

101

TELEGRAPH HILL

The Embarcadero

COW HOLLOW

Union St.

PACIFIC HEIGHTS

Broadway

Gough St.

Van Ness Ave.

Polk St.

Hyde St.

Taylor St.

CHINATOWN

Grant Ave.

Kearny St.

Battery St.

Lincoln Blvd.

Presidio Ave.

Divisadero St.

Fillmore St.

Washington St.

NOB HILL

California St.

Powell St.

FINANCIAL DISTRICT

Trans-Bay Transit Terminal

1st St.

Sacramento St.

Franklin St.

101

Sutter St.

Post St.

Geary St.

O'Farrell St.

Union Square

Yerba Buena Gardens

Geary Blvd.

JAPANTOWN

Moscone Convention Center

WESTERN ADDITION

Masonic St.

Turk St.

Golden Gate Ave.

CIVIC CENTER

Mission St.

Howard St.

Folsom St.

Harrison St.

3rd St.

Fulton St.

Alamo Square

Fell St.

SOMA

4th St.

Oak St.

8th St.

9th St.

10th St.

Bryant St.

5th St.

6th St.

Haight St.

Market St.

7th St.

Cole St.

Ashbury St.

HAIGHT-ASHBURY

101

14th St.

280

Stanyan St.

17th St.

17th St.

Claredon Ave.

THE CASTRO

Castro St.

Church St.

Dolores St.

Mission St.

South Van Ness Ave.

MISSION DISTRICT

Potrero Ave.

Deharo St.

Connecticut St.

POTRERO HILL

Portola Dr.

Twin Peaks

24th St.

Clipper St.

101

71

Marina District Created on landfill for the Pan Pacific Exposition of 1915, the Marina boasts some of the best views of the Golden Gate, as well as plenty of grassy fields alongside the San Francisco Bay. Streets are lined with elegant Mediterranean-style homes and apartments, which are inhabited by the city's well-to-do. Here too, is the Palace of Fine Arts, the Exploratorium, and Fort Mason Center. Chestnut Street, between Franklin and Lyon, is the main venue, and it's lined with shops, cafes, and boutiques. Because of its landfill foundation, the Marina was one of the city's hardest hit districts in the 1989 quake.

Cow Hollow Located west of Van Ness Avenue, between Russian Hill and the Presidio, this flat, grazable area supported 30 dairy farms in 1861. Today, Cow Hollow is largely residential and occupied by yuppies. Its two primary commercial thoroughfares are Lombard Street, known for its many relatively inexpensive motels; and Union Street, a flourishing shopping sector with restaurants, pubs, cafes, and shops.

Japantown Bounded by Octavia, Fillmore, California, and Geary, Japantown shelters only about 4% of the city's Japanese population, but it's still worthwhile to explore the shops and restaurants among these few square blocks.

Civic Center Although millions of dollars have been spent on brick sidewalks, ornate lampposts, and elaborate street plantings, the southwestern section of Market Street remains downright dilapidated. The Civic Center, at the "bottom" of Market Street, is an exception. This large complex of buildings includes the domed City Hall, the Opera House, Davies Symphony Hall, and the city's main library. The landscaped plaza connecting the buildings is the staging area for San Francisco's frequent demonstrations for or against just about everything.

Haight-Ashbury Part trendy, part nostalgic, part funky, The Haight, as it's most commonly known, was the soul of the psychedelic and free-loving 1960s and the center of the counterculture movement. Today, the neighborhood straddling upper Haight Street on the eastern border of Golden Gate Park is more gentrified, but the commercial area still harbors all walks of life. Leftover hippies mingle with grungy street kids outside Ben and Jerry's, probably still reminiscing about Jerry Garcia, and nondescript marijuana dealers whisper "buds" as shoppers pass. But you don't need to wear tie-dye or dye your hair chartreuse to enjoy the Haight: The food, shops, and bars cover all tastes.

The Castro One of the liveliest streets in town, Castro is practically synonymous with San Francisco's gay community, even though technically it is only a street in the Noe Valley district. Located at the very end of Market Street, between 17th and 18th streets, Castro supports dozens of shops, restaurants, and bars catering to the gay community. Open-minded straight people are welcome, too.

Mission District The Mexican and Latin American populations, along with their cuisines, traditions, and arts, make the Mission district a vibrant area to visit. Because some parts are poor and sprinkled with gangs, drug addicts, and homeless people, many tourists duck into Mission Dolores, cruise by a few of the 200 amazing murals, and head back downtown. But there's plenty more to see, including a substantial community of lesbians around Valencia Street; alternative arts organizations; and most recently the ultimate in young and hip nightlife. New bars, clubs, and restaurants are popping up on Mission Street between 18th and 24th and Valencia at 16th Street. Don't be afraid to visit this area, but do use caution at night.

2   Getting Around

BY PUBLIC TRANSPORTATION

The **San Francisco Municipal Railway,** better known as **Muni** (☎ 415/673-6864), operates the city's cable cars, buses, and Metro streetcars. The fare on buses and Metro streetcars is $1 for adults (payable in change or bills) and 35¢ for children ages 5 to 17 and seniors over 65. Cable cars cost $2 ($1 for seniors) from 9pm to midnight and from 6 to 7am. They're packed with tourists and exact change is required on all vehicles except cable cars.

For detailed route information, call Muni, check the map in the local Yellow Pages, or purchase a route map ($2) at the San Francisco Visitor Information Center; most bookstores and drugstores also sell these route maps.

Passports, fare cards allowing unlimited rides on buses, Metro streetcars, and cable cars, cost $6 for one day and $10 or $15 for three or seven consecutive days. They also entitle you to discounts at 24 of the city's major attractions, including the Museum of Modern Art, the Exploratorium, and the museums in Golden Gate Park. Get them at the Visitors Information Center or the TIX booth at Union Square.

BY CABLE CAR   There are three lines operating daily from 6:30am to 12:30am. The most scenic and exciting is the Powell-Hyde line, which follows a zigzag route from the corner of Powell and Market, over both Nob and Russian hills, to a turntable at Victorian Square in front of Aquatic Park. The Powell-Mason line starts at the same intersection and climbs over Nob Hill and down to Bay Street, just three blocks from Fisherman's Wharf. The California Street line begins at the foot of Market Street and runs straight through Chinatown and over Nob Hill to Van Ness Avenue. All riders must exit at the last stop and wait in line for the return trip.

BY BUS   Buses service the city, Marin County, and the East Bay. Some are powered by overhead electric cables; others use conventional gas engines. All are numbered and display their destinations on the front. Stops are designated by signs, curb markings, and yellow bands on adjacent utility poles. Many buses travel along Market Street or near Union Square and run daily from about 6am to midnight, after which there is infrequent all-night "Owl" service. For safety purposes, avoid taking buses late at night.

Popular tourist routes are covered by bus nos. 5, 7, and 71, all of which run to Golden Gate Park; nos. 41 and 45 travel along Union Street; and no. 30, operates between Union Square and Ghirardelli Square.

BY METRO STREETCAR   Five of Muni's six Metro streetcar lines, designated J, K, L, M, and N, run underground downtown, stopping at the BART stops along Market Street—Embarcadero, Montgomery, Powell, and the Civic Center—and in the outer neighborhoods. The J line goes to Mission Dolores; the K, L, and M to Castro Street; and the N parallels Golden Gate Park. Metros run about every 15 minutes (more frequently during rush hours), Monday to Friday from 5am to 12:30am, Saturday from 6am to 12:20am, and Sunday from 8am to 12:20am.

The most recent streetcar addition is not a newcomer at all, but San Francisco's beloved and rejuvenated 1930s cars. The beautiful green-and-cream colored F-Market line runs from downtown Market Street to the Castro and back.

BY BART   BART (☎ 415/992-2278) is a high-speed rail network connecting San Francisco with the East Bay—Oakland, Richmond, Concord, and Fremont—as well as southern Daly City. Market Street has four stations (see "By Metro Streetcar," above). Fares range from 90¢ to $3.55, depending on how far you go, and tickets are dispensed from machines in the stations. Children four and under ride free. Trains run every 15 to 20 minutes, Monday through Friday from 4am to midnight, on Saturday from 6am to midnight, and on Sunday from 8am to midnight. A line to the airport is scheduled to open in 1997.

BY CAR

You don't need a car to explore downtown San Francisco; in central areas it can be your worst nightmare. But if you plan to venture outside the city, driving is the way to go.

Cable cars always have the right-of-way, as do pedestrians at intersections and crosswalks. San Francisco's many one-way streets can create confusion, but most road maps of the city indicate which way traffic flows.

RENTAL CARS   Among the national car-rental companies operating in San Francisco are: **Alamo** (☎ 800/327-9633), **Avis** (☎ 800/331-1212), **Budget** (☎ 800/527-0700), **Dollar** (☎ 800/800-4000), **Hertz** (☎ 800/654-3131), **National** (☎ 800/227-7368), and **Thrifty** (☎ 800/367-2277).

In addition to the big chains, there are dozens of regional rental places in San Francisco, many of which offer lower rates. These include **A-One Rent-A-Car,** 434 O'Farrell St. (☎ 415/771-3977) and **Bay Area Rentals,** 229 Seventh St. (☎ 415/621-8989).

PARKING   Street parking is extremely limited and particularly tough in Chinatown, around Nob Hill, by Fisherman's Wharf, in North Beach, and on Telegraph Hill. If there are no meters, note the signs and curb colors indicating parking regulations. Red means no stopping or parking; blue is reserved for disabled drivers with a California-issued disabled plate; white means there's a five-minute limit; green indicates a 10-minute limit; and yellow and yellow-black curbs are for commercial vehicles only. Watch out, too, for street-cleaning signs. If you violate the law, you might be "booted" (immobilized) or towed away, and that can cost you as much as $100. Getting your car back is a huge hassle: You must obtain a release from the nearest district police department, then go to the towing company to pick up the vehicle.

When parking on a hill, apply the hand brake, put the car in gear, and turn your wheels—toward the curb when facing downhill, away from the curb when facing uphill. Curbing your wheels will not only prevent a possible "runaway" but will also keep you from getting a ticket, an expensive fine that is aggressively enforced.

Parking garages charge between $1 and $5 per hour (less by the day). In Chinatown, the cheapest place to park is the Portsmouth Square Garage at 733 Kearny St. (join the line to the entrance between Clay and Washington streets). At the Civic Center, try the Civic Center Plaza Garage between Polk and Larkin streets, and downtown, head for the Sutter-Stockton Garage at 330 Sutter St. At Fisherman's Wharf/Ghirardelli Square, try the garage on Beach Street between Hyde and Columbus, which charges $3.75 an hour to a $10 maximum; or the Ghirardelli Square Garage at 900 North Point, which offers 90 minutes of free parking with restaurant validation (60 minutes with retail validation).

BY TAXI

If you're downtown during rush hours or leaving from a major hotel, you can easily hail a cab. Otherwise, call one of the following companies to arrange a ride: **Veteran's Cab** (☎ 415/552-1300), **Desoto Cab Co.** (☎ 415/673-1414), **Luxor Cabs** (☎ 415/282-4141), **Yellow Cab** (☎ 415/626-2345), **City** (☎ 415/468-7200), and

Pacific (☎ 415/986-7220). Rates are approximately $2 for the first mile and $1.80 for each mile thereafter.

BY FERRY

The **Golden Gate Ferry Service** (☎ **415/923-2000**) operates between the San Francisco Ferry Building, at the foot of Market Street, downtown Sausalito (30 minutes), and Larkspur (45 minutes). Daily service to Sausalito is frequent (except New Year's Day, Thanksgiving Day, and Christmas Day). The ride takes a half hour and costs $4.25 for adults, $3.20 for kids ages 6 to 12, and $2.10 for seniors and the disabled.

The Larkspur ferry is primarily a weekday commuter service, with limited service on weekends. The 13-mile trip takes about 45 minutes and costs $2.50 for adults, $1.90 for kids ages 6 to 12, and $1.25 for seniors and people with disabilities; on weekends, prices rise to $4.25, $3.20, and $2.10 respectively.

The Blue and Gold Fleet, Pier 39, Fisherman's Wharf (☎ 415/705-5444 or 510/522-3300), operates daily from the Ferry Building and Pier 39 to Oakland, Alameda, and Vallejo. Fares are $3.75 for adults, $1.50 for children, and $2.50 for seniors to Oakland; $7.50, $4, and $6, respectively, to Vallejo. They'll also take you to Marine World Africa USA (see Chapter 6, "Side Trips from San Francisco") on a package trip that includes boat, bus shuttle, and admission.

The Red and White Fleet, Pier 41 and 43^1/$_2$ (☎ **800/229-2784** or 415/546-2700), operates from Pier 43^1/$_2$ to Sausalito and Tiburon. Ferries also operate to Angel Island and Vallejo daily in summer and weekends only in winter. On weekdays ferries operate from Tiburon to the Ferry Building. Round-trip fares are $9 for adults, $8 for children ages 12 to 18 and $4.50 for children ages 5 to 11. Sausalito/Tiburon fares are $11 for adults and seniors, $5.50 for kids. At press time, the Blue and Gold Fleet had just purchased the Red and White Fleet and schedule changes were yet to be determined. Call either number for updated schedules and fare changes.

FAST FACTS: San Francisco

American Express American Express has offices at 295 California St., at Battery Street (☎ 415/536-2686), and at 455 Market St., at 1st Street (☎ 415/536-2600) in the Financial District. Both are Monday to Friday from 9am to 5pm and Saturday from 9am to 2pm. To report lost or stolen traveler's checks, call **800/221-7282.**

Baby-Sitters Try **Temporary Tot Tending** (☎ **415/355-7377,** or 415/871-5790 after 6pm), which employs licensed teachers, and charges by the hour for children from 3 weeks to 12 years of age. It's open Monday to Friday from 6am to 7pm (weekend service is available only during convention times).

Dentist In an emergency, see your hotel concierge or contact the **San Francisco Dental Society** (☎ **415/421-1435**) for 24-hour referral to a specialist.

Doctor **Saint Francis Memorial Hospital,** 900 Hyde St., between Bush and Pine streets on Nob Hill (☎ **415/353-6566**), operates a physician-referral service.

Emergencies Dial **911** for police, ambulance, or the fire department. Emergency hot lines include the **Poison Control Center** (☎ **800/523-2222**) and **Rape Crisis** (☎ **415/647-7273**).

Hospitals **Saint Francis Memorial Hospital,** 900 Hyde St., between Bush and Pine streets on Nob Hill (☎ **415/353-6000**), provides 24-hour urgent-care service.

Liquor Laws   Liquor and grocery stores, as well as some drugstores, sell alcohol between 6am and 2am, as do bars and restaurants. The legal age for purchase and consumption is 21; proof of age is required.

Newspapers/Magazines   The city's two main dailies are the rather mediocre *San Francisco Chronicle* and the *San Francisco Examiner*. Get the combined Sunday edition for the Datebook of the week's events. The free weekly *San Francisco Bay Guardian* is indispensable for nightlife information; it's widely distributed on street corners and at city cafes and restaurants. *Key* and *San Francisco Guide* are also useful and are found in hotels and outlets in major tourist areas.

Police   Dial **911** in an emergency. For other matters, call 415/553-0123.

Post Office   The office closest to Union Square is inside Macy's department store, 121 Stockton St. (☎ **415/956-3570**).

Safety   We don't recommend walking alone late at night in the Tenderloin, between Union Square and the Civic Center; the Mission District, around 16th and Mission streets; the Fillmore area, around lower Haight Street; and the SoMa area south of Market Street.

Taxes   An 8.5% sales tax is added at the register for all goods and services purchased in San Francisco. The city hotel tax is 12%. There is no airport tax.

Transit Information   For 24-hour information, call **415/673-6864.**

Useful Telephone Numbers   These include: **American Express Global Assist** (for cardholders only; ☎ **800/554-2639**), highway conditions (☎ **415/557-3755**), **KFOG Entertainment Line** (☎ **415/777-1045**), **KMEL's Movie Phone Line** (☎ **415/777-FILM**), and the **Grateful Dead Hot Line** (☎ **415/457-6388**).

Weather   Call **415/936-1212** to find out when the next fog bank is rolling in.

3 Accommodations

San Francisco is an outstanding hotel town, especially considering its relatively small size. We can't cover them all in this guide, so if you'd like a larger selection, check out *Frommer's San Francisco,* which has dozens of other options.

Most of the city's 180 hotels are concentrated around Union Square, but there are also some smaller independent gems scattered around town. When reading over your options, keep in mind that prices listed are hotel rack rates (published rates) and you should always ask for special discounts or, even better, vacation packages. You're likely to get the room you want for $100 less than what's quoted here, except in summer when the hotels are packed and bargaining is close to impossible. San Francisco is sometimes referred to as "Convention City," so if you wish to secure rooms at a particular hotel during high season, which runs approximately from April through September, book well in advance.

Remember, to save the most, travel before or after summertime, book far in advance (but check later for newly added promotions), inquire about packages and special rates (AAA, AARP, military, etc.), and choose a place that doesn't charge for local calls and parking.

The hotels listed below are classified first by location and then by price, using the following categories: **Doubles for $60 or Less, Doubles for $80 or Less, Doubles for $100 or Less, Doubles for $130 or Less,** and **Worth a Splurge.** These categories reflect the price of an average double room during the high season. Read each of the entries carefully: Many hotels also offer rooms at rates above and below the price category that they have been assigned in this guidebook. Also note that prices listed below do not include state and city taxes, which total 12%, or hidden extras like parking and hefty telephone surcharges.

There are few hotels in San Francisco that charge less than $85 per night for a double. We have listed most of your best options below, but if all the hotels in your price range are booked and you don't mind going generic, you can always try **Motel 6** (☎ 800/4-MOTEL6); **Super 8** (☎ 800/800-8000); **Best Western** (☎ 800/528-1235); **Days Inn** (☎ 800/DAYS-INN); and **Travelodge** (☎ 800/ 367-2250).

If you're having reservations about your reservations, you might want to leave it up to one of the following pros:

Bed and Breakfast California, P.O. Box 282910, San Francisco, CA 94128 (☎ **800/872-4500** or 415/696-1690; fax 415/696-1699), offers a selection of B&Bs ranging from $60 to $150 per night (two-night minimum). Accommodations range from simple rooms in private homes to luxurious, full-service carriage houses, house-boats, and Victorian homes.

San Francisco Reservations, 22 Second St., San Francisco, CA 94105 (☎ **800/ 667-1550** or 415/227-1500), is a nifty World Wide Web site that allows Internet users to make their reservations on-line. Plug in at http://www.hotelres.com, and you can book rooms for more than 200 San Francisco hotels—often at discounted rates.

UNION SQUARE
DOUBLES FOR $60 OR LESS

AYH Hostel at Union Square. 312 Mason St. (between Geary and O'Farrell sts.), San Francisco, CA 94102. ☎ **415/788-5604.** 230 beds. $15 per person for Hostelling International members, $18 for nonmembers; $7 for persons under 18 when accompanied by a parent. Maximum stay 14 nights per year. MC, V. No parking on premises. A public parking lot on Mission between 4th and 5th sts. charges $12 per 24-hour period. Cable car: Powell-Mason line. Bus: 7B or 38.

If you don't give a darn for decor and want to save a fortune, you may want to consider a room here. Located a few blocks from Union Square, this hostel occupies five sparsely decorated floors of a quaint San Francisco–style building. Rooms are simple (we mean really simple!) and clean, each with two or three bunk beds, a sink, and a closet. Unlike most hostels, you can lock your room and take the key with you. Also, while most rooms share hallway baths, a few have private facilities (suite rooms are reserved for families). Freshly painted hallways are adorned with laminated posters, and there are several common rooms, including a reading room, a smoking room, and a large kitchen with lots of tables, chairs, and refrigerator space. There are laundry facilities nearby, and a helpful information desk offering tour reservations and sightseeing trips. The hostel is open 24 hours and reservations are essential during the summer. Persons under 18 may not stay without a parent unless they have a no-tarized letter, and then they must pay the adult rate.

Grant Plaza Hotel. 465 Grant Ave. (at the corner of Pine St.), San Francisco, CA 94108. ☎ **800/472-6899** or 415/434-3883. Fax 415/434-3886. 72 rms. TEL TV. $42–$65 double. MC, V. Parking $9.50. Cable car: Powell-Hyde and Powell-Mason lines (2 blocks west).

You won't find any free little bottles of shampoo here. What you will find are cheap and basic rooms right between Union Square and Chinatown. The lobby isn't easy on the eyes, but it's just a thoroughfare, so who cares? Many of the small rooms in this six-story building overlook Chinatown's main strip. Corner rooms on higher floors are both larger and brighter. Expect little more than a soap dispenser in the small bathroom. The Grant Plaza offers nothing more than decent value, but for 50 bucks, what do you expect? Visitors are not permitted in the rooms after 11pm, and no breakfast is served.

DOUBLES FOR $80 OR LESS

Amsterdam Hotel. 749 Taylor St. (between Sutter and Bush sts.), San Francisco, CA 94108
☎ 800/637-3444 or 415/673-3277. Fax 415/673-0453. 30 rms. TEL TV. $75–$79 double.
Rates include continental breakfast. AE, MC, V. Parking $13. Bus 2, 3, 4, or 76.

This hotel is one strange place. The lobby feels like that of a cheap motel, and the
rooms, though some are decorated with oak furnishings, are a mixture of old and
new, tasteful and tacky. The owners continue to remodel with Jacuzzi tubs, new
drapes and carpet, and marble or black lacquer bathrooms, but it's clear there's no
interior designer leading the way. The value is decent, though, and if you can race
past the peculiar disinfectant odor in the breakfast room, there's a small dining patio out back where you can enjoy your continental fare.

Brady Acres. 649 Jones St. (between Geary and Post sts.), San Francisco, CA 94102. ☎ **800/
627-2396** or 415/929-8033. Fax 415/441-8033. 25 rms. MINIBAR TEL TV. $60–$85 double.
MC, V. Weekly rentals Oct–Apr only; call for daily availability. Parking garage nearby. Bus: 2,
3, 4, 27, or 38.

Inside this small, four-story brick building is one of the best budget hotels in the city.
Enter through a black-and-gold door, with lamp sconces on either side. Inside, you'll
find small but well-kept rooms with microwave ovens, small refrigerators, toaster, and
coffeemaker; hair dryers and alarm clocks; direct-dial phones (with free local calls)
and an answering machine; color TVs and cassette players. Baths are newly remodeled, and a coin-operated washer and dryer are located in the basement, along with
free laundry soap and irons. Owner Deborah Liane Brady and her staff are usually
on hand to offer friendly, personal service. Keep in mind that weekly rentals are available between October and April.

Golden Gate Hotel. 775 Bush St. (between Powell and Mason sts.), San Francisco, CA 94108.
☎ **800/835-1118** or 415/392-3702. Fax 415/392-6202. 23 rms (14 with bath). TV. $65–$69
double without bath, $95–109 double with bath. Rates include continental breakfast. AE, CB,
DC, MC, V. Parking $12. Cable car: Powell-Hyde and Powell-Mason lines (1 block east). Bus:
2, 3, 4, 30, 38, or 45.

Among San Francisco's small, charming hotels occupying turn-of-the-century buildings are some real gems: the Golden Gate Hotel is one. It's two blocks north of Union
Square and two blocks down (literally) from the crest of Nob Hill, with cable car
stops at the corner for easy access to Fisherman's Wharf and Chinatown (the city's
theaters and best restaurants are also within walking distance). But the best thing
about the Golden Gate Hotel is that it's a family run establishment; John and Renate
Kenaston are hospitable innkeepers who take obvious pleasure in making their guests
comfortable. Each individually decorated room has handsome antique furnishings
(plenty of wicker) from the early 1900s, quilted bedspreads, and fresh flowers (request
a room with the claw-foot tub if you enjoy a good, hot soak). Most, but not all,
rooms have phones, and complimentary afternoon tea is served daily from 4 to 7pm.

The Sheehan. 620 Sutter St. (near Mason St.), San Francisco, CA 94102. ☎ **800/848-1529**
or 415/775-6500. Fax 415/775-3271. 68 rms (58 with bath). TEL TV. $62–$72 double without bath, $75–$105 double with bath. Rates include continental breakfast. AE, CB, DC, MC, V.
Parking $14. Cable car: Powell-Hyde and Powell-Mason lines (2 blocks east). Bus: 2, 3, 4, 30,
38, or 45.

Formerly a YWCA hotel, the Sheehan is just two blocks from Union Square, and you
can easily walk to most places in the downtown area. Rooms are pretty plain and
some walls could use a little paint, but the bathrooms are clean and new and rooms
have cable color TV. The hotel has a spiffy and pleasant lobby; a comfortable tea
room, open for light lunches and afternoon tea; and an indoor, heated lap-pool and
workout facility—a very good value.

DOUBLES FOR $100 OR LESS

Andrews Hotel. 624 Post St. (between Jones and Taylor), San Francisco, CA 94109. ☎ **800/926-3739** or 415/563-6877. Fax 415/928-6919. 43 rms, 5 suites. MINIBAR TEL TV. $86–$109 double; $119 petite suite. Rates include continental breakfast and evening wine. AE, DC, MC, V. Parking $15. Cable car: Powell-Hyde and Powell-Mason lines (3 blocks east). Bus: 2, 3, 4, 30, 38, or 45.

Two blocks west of Union Square, the Andrews was formerly a Turkish bath before its conversion in 1981. As is fitting with Euro-style hotels, the rooms are small but well maintained and comfortable; white lace curtains and fresh flowers in each room add a light touch. Some rooms have shower only, and bathrooms in general tend to be tiny, but for the location, a few blocks from Union Square, and price, the Andrews is a safe bet for an enjoyable stay in the city. An added bonus is the adjoining Fino Bar and Ristorante, which offers complimentary wine to its hotel guests in the evening.

Cornell Hotel. 715 Bush St. (near Mason St.), San Francisco, CA 94108. ☎ **800/232-9698** or 415/421-3154. Fax 415/399-1442. 60 rms. TEL TV. $85–$105 double. Rates include full breakfast (except Sun, when it's continental). Weekly room package including 7 breakfasts and 5 dinners, $600 double. AE, CB, DC, MC, V. Parking $12. Cable car: Powell-Hyde and Powell-Mason lines. Bus: 2, 3, 4, 30, or 45.

It's the quirks that make this hotel more charming than many in its price range. Rameau, the resident golden retriever, greets you at the door of this small French-style hotel; as you pass the office, a few faces will glance up in your direction with a smile; and then you embark on a ride in the old-fashioned elevator to get to your room. Each floor is dedicated to a French painter and is decorated with reproductions. Rooms are comfortable and individually decorated in a bland, modern style, with a desk and chairs. No smoking is allowed in any of them. A full breakfast is served in the cavernlike provincial basement dining room.

Hotel Beresford. 635 Sutter St. (near Mason St.), San Francisco, CA 94102. ☎ **800/533-6533** or 415/673-9900. Fax 415/474-0449. 114 rms. MINIBAR TEL TV. $99–$104 double. Rates include continental breakfast. Extra person $5. Children under 12 stay free in parents' room. Senior-citizen discounts available. AE, CB, DC, DISC, MC, V. Ask for special rates. Parking $15. Cable car: Powell-Hyde line (1 block east). Bus: 2, 3, 4, 30, 38, or 45.

Small and friendly, the seven-floor Hotel Beresford is a decent, moderately priced choice near Union Square. Rooms have a mishmash of furniture and a stocked minibar; some even have Jacuzzi tubs. Everything's well kept, but don't expect much more than a clean place to rest. The White Horse restaurant, an attractive replica of an old English pub, serves a complimentary continental breakfast, as well as lunch and dinner.

DOUBLES FOR $130 OR LESS

✪ **Commodore International.** 825 Sutter St. (at Jones St.), San Francisco, CA 94109. ☎ **800/338-6848** or 415/923-6800. Fax 415/923-6804. 113 rms. TEL TV. $69–$89 double or twin. AE, DC, MC, V. Parking $12. Bus: 2, 3, 4, 27, or 76.

If you're looking to pump a little fun and fantasy into your vacation, this is the place. Before its new owners revamped the aging Commodore from top to bottom, it hardly deserved mention. Then along came San Francisco hotelier Chip Conley, who, high on his success in transforming the Phoenix Hotel into a rocker's retreat, instantly recognized this eyesore's potential, added it to his collection, then let his hip-hop designers work their magic. The result? One groovy hotel. The Red Room, a Big Apple–style bar and lounge that reflects no other spectrum but ruby red (you gotta see this one), steals the show. The stylish lobby comes in a close second, followed by

👪 Affordable Family-Friendly Hotels

Hotel Beresford *(see p. 79)*   Ideally located in a quiet neighborhood between Union Square and the Theater District, this cheerful hotel offers spacious suites, some with fully equipped kitchens, at fair prices.

Brady Acres *(see p. 78)*   Not only is this one of the city's best budget hotels, it's also a great place for families; rooms come with microwaves, refrigerators, and other lifesaving amenities, and weekly rentals are available.

Stanyan Park Hotel *(see p. 88)*   A great moderately priced choice for families, the Stanyan Park is ideally located across from Golden Gate Park—for those times when your kids need to let off steam.

the adjoining Titanic Café, a cute little diner serving buckwheat griddlecakes and dragon fire salads. Catering to the masses, Chip left the first four floors as standard no-frills rooms, while dressing the top two floors in neo-deco overtones (well worth the extra $10 per night).

The Fitzgerald. 620 Post St., San Francisco, CA 94109. ☎ **800/334-6835** or 415/775-8100. Fax 415/775-1278. 42 rms, 5 suites. TEL TV. $79–$115 double. Rates include continental breakfast. Extra person $10. Lower rates in winter. AE, DISC, JCB, MC, V. Parking $15. Bus: 2, 3, 4, or 27.

The Fitzgerald was recently transformed from a dilapidated welfare hotel into a tasteful and clean establishment. A nook of a lobby gives way to the guest rooms outfitted with new, but generic, hotel furniture that's accented with bright bedspreads and patterned carpet. Small rooms and positively tiny closets are a drawback, and some dressers little over a foot from the bed. Suites, some of which are on no-smoking floors, include an additional sitting room furnished with a fold-out couch. Breakfasts include home-baked breads, scones, muffins, juice, tea, and coffee. A nearby off-premises swimming pool is available for guests at no charge. All in all, a good value.

⑤ Hotel Bedford. 761 Post St. (between Leavenworth and Jones sts.), San Francisco, CA 94109. ☎ **800/227-5642** or 415/673-6040. Fax 415/563-6739. 137 rms, 7 suites. MINIBAR TEL TV. $109–$129 double; from $175 suite. Continental breakfast $8.50 extra. AE, CB, DC, JCB, MC, V. Parking $18. Cable car: Powell-Hyde and Powell-Mason lines (4 blocks east). Bus: 2, 3, 4, or 27.

For the price and location (three blocks from Union Square) the Bedford offers one of the best deals in town. You won't be paying for lavish furniture, but you will find clean, large, sunny rooms, not to mention an incredibly attentive and professional staff. Each accommodation is well furnished with big beds, a VCR, writing desk, and armchair. Many rooms have priceless views of the city.

The hotel's Wedgewood Lounge is a small, beautiful mahogany bar opposite the registration desk. Canvas Café, under separate management, is an enormous eatery located behind the lobby, serving up basic American breakfasts for under $10. Hotel services include room service for breakfast only, valet parking, and complimentary wine in the lobby each evening from 5 to 6pm. There's a video library, and free morning limousine service to the Financial District.

✪ Hotel Diva. 440 Geary St. (between Mason and Taylor sts.), San Francisco, CA 94102. ☎ **800/553-1900** or 415/885-0200. Fax 415/346-6613. 98 rms, 12 suites. A/C TEL TV. $119 double; $139 junior suite, $300 villa suite. Rates include continental breakfast. AE, DC, DISC, JCB, MC, V. Parking $17. Bus: 38 or 38L.

Appropriately named, the Diva is the prima donna of San Francisco's modern hotels and one of our favorites. A showbiz darling when it opened in 1985, the Diva won "Best Hotel Design" by *Interiors Magazine* for its sleek, ultra-modern design. A stunning profusion of curvaceous glass, marble, and steel marks the Euro-tech lobby, while the rooms, each meticulously spotless, are significantly softened with fashionable Italian Modern furnishings. Nary a beat is missed with the amenities either: VCRs, Nintendo, pay-per-view, valet parking, room service, complimentary room-service breakfast, and on-site fitness and business centers complete the package.

Hot insider tip: Reserve one of the rooms ending in 09, which come with extra-large bathrooms with vanity mirrors and makeup tables.

Kensington Park Hotel. 450 Post St. (between Powell and Mason sts.), San Francisco, CA 94102. ☎ **800/553-1900** or 415/788-6400. Fax 415/399-9484. 82 rms, 2 suites. TEL TV. $115 double; $350 suite. Rates include continental breakfast. 50% discount for post-midnight check-in. Extra person $10. AE, CB, DC, MC, V. Parking $16. Cable car: Powell-Hyde and Powell-Mason lines (2 blocks east).

Old elegance comes at an affordable price at this hotel, which is just two blocks from Union Square. Rooms are a comfortable size and are adorned with mahogany furnishings and tapestry-style bedspreads. The small bathrooms are done in brass and marble, far more homey that most hotel bathrooms. The Royal Suite contains a canopy bed, fireplace, and Jacuzzi. Coffee and croissants are available on each floor every morning from 7 to 10am, and complimentary tea, sherry, and cookies are served every afternoon. On Thursday evenings the hotel treats its guests to a wine hour. Services include concierge, same-day laundry, room service, morning newspaper, complimentary morning limos to the Financial District, and fax and secretarial services. Access to an off-premises health club is also included in the price.

If you happen to arrive in the city late-night without a reservation, be sure to call here: The hotel offers 50% off rack rates to guests who arrive after midnight. (No advance reservations are accepted, and the offer is restricted to a one-night maximum.)

✪ Savoy Hotel. 580 Geary St. (between Taylor and Jones sts.), San Francisco, CA 94102. ☎ **800/227-4223** or 415/441-2700. Fax 415/441-2700. 70 rms, 13 suites. MINIBAR TEL TV. $115–$125 double; from $155 suite. Ask about package, government, senior, and corporate rates. Rates include continental breakfast. AE, CB, DC, DISC, MC, V. Parking $16. Bus: 2, 3, 4, 27, or 38.

Both travelers and *Travel and Leisure* agree that the Savoy is an excellent and affordable small hotel a few blocks off Union Square. The medium-size rooms are cozy French provincial, with 18th-century period furnishings, featherbeds, and goose down pillows—plus modern conveniences such as remote-control color TVs and hair dryers. Other perks include triple sheets, turndown service, full-length mirrors, and two-line telephones. Guests also enjoy concierge service and overnight shoe-shining free of charge. Rates include complimentary late-afternoon sherry and tea, plus a continental breakfast, served in the Brasserie Savoy, a seafood restaurant that lures even locals downtown for dinner (see "Dining" for more details).

WORTH A SPLURGE

Hotel Milano. 55 Fifth St. (between Market and Mission sts.), San Francisco, CA 94103. ☎ **800/398-7555** in the U.S., or 415/543-8555. Fax 415/543-5843. 108 rms. A/C MINIBAR TEL TV. $129–$189 double; extra person $19. Continental breakfast $6 extra. AE, DC, JCB, MC, V. Parking $19. All Market St. buses.

The Milano's contemporary Italian design, simple and elegantly streamlined rooms, and central location make it a popular choice for tourists and business people alike.

Guest rooms feature everything an executive could want, from fax/computer/modem hookups to Nintendo. Just off the lobby is the renowned Chef Michel Richard's Bistro M serving breakfast, lunch, and dinner in an equally modern setting.

Hotel Triton. 342 Grant Ave. (at Bush St.), San Francisco, CA 94108. ☎ **800/433-6611** or 415/394-0500. Fax 415/394-0555. 140 rms, 7 suites. A/C MINIBAR TEL TV. $119–$179 double; $199–$279 suite. Continental breakfast $7.75 extra. AE, DC, DISC, MC, V. Parking $20. Cable car: Powell-Hyde and Powell-Mason lines (2 blocks west).

Hotelier magnate Bill Kimpton commissioned a cadre of local artists and designers to "do their thing" to his latest acquisition, the Hotel Triton. As a result, it became San Francisco's first three-star hotel to finally break the boring barrier. Described as vogue, chic, retro-futuristic, and even neo-Baroque, the Triton begs attention from its Daliesque lobby to the sumptuous designer suites à la Jerry Garcia, Wyland (the ocean artist), Joe Boxer, and others.

A mild warning: Don't expect perfection; many of the rooms could use a little touching up here and there (stained curtains, chipped furniture), and service isn't as snappy as it could be.

Hotel Vintage Court. 650 Bush St. (between Powell and Stockton sts.), San Francisco, CA 94108. ☎ **800/654-1100** or 415/392-4666. Fax 415/433-4065. 106 rms, 1 suite. A/C MINIBAR TEL TV. $119–$159 double; $275 penthouse suite. AE, CB, DC, DISC, MC, V. Parking $16. Cable car: Powell-Hyde and Powell-Mason lines (direct stop). Bus: 2, 3, 4, 30, 45, or 76.

Consistent personal service and convenient location at this European-style hotel contribute to its growing and loyal clientele. The lobby, accented with dark wood, deep green, and rose, is welcoming enough to actually spend a little time in, especially when the nightly complimentary California wines are being poured. Each newly renovated and tidy room mimics a wine country establishment with floral bedspreads, matching drapes, and trellised carpeting. The hotel's dining room, Masa's, serves traditional French fare.

✪ **Petite Auberge.** 863 Bush St. (between Taylor and Mason sts.), San Francisco, CA 94108. ☎ **415/928-6000.** Fax 415/775-5717. 26 rms. TEL TV. $110–$160 double; $220 petite suite. Rates include continental breakfast. AE, DC, MC, V. Parking $17. Cable car: Powell-Hyde and Powell-Mason lines. Bus: 2, 3, 4, 30, 38, or 45.

The Petite Auberge is so pathetically cute we can't stand it. We want to say it's overdone, and that any hotel filled with teddy bears is absurd, but we can't. Bribed each year with a chocolate chip cookie from their never-empty platter, we make our rounds through the rooms and ruefully admit to ourselves that we're just going to have to use that word we loath to hear: *adorable.*

Nobody does French country like the Petite Auberge. Hand-crafted armoires, delicate lace curtains, cozy little fireplaces, adorable (there's that word again) little antiques and knickknacks—no hotel in Provence ever had it this good. Honeymooners should splurge on the Petite suite, which has its own private entrance, deck, spa tub, refrigerator, and coffeemaker. The breakfast room features a mural of a country market scene, terra-cotta tile floors, French country decor, and gold-yellow tablecloths. It opens onto a small garden where California wines and tea are served in the afternoon.

✪ **Sir Francis Drake.** 450 Powell St. (at Sutter St.), San Francisco, CA 94102. ☎ **800/227-5480** or 415/392-7755. Fax 415/677-9341. 412 rms, 5 suites. A/C MINIBAR TEL TV. $149–$199 double; $185–$600 suite. AE, CB, DC, DISC, MC, V. Parking $23. Cable car: Powell-Hyde and Powell-Mason lines (direct stop). Bus: 2, 3, 4, 45, or 76.

It took a change of ownership and a multimillion-dollar restoration to save the Sir Francis Drake from becoming a cafe, but now this stately old queen is once again housing guests in grand fashion. This venerable septuagenarian is still showing signs of age, but the price of imperfection is certainly reflected in the room rate: a good $100 less per night than its Nob Hill cousins. The new Sir Francis Drake is a hotel for people who are willing to trade a chipped bathroom tile or oddly matched furniture for the opportunity to vacation in almost-grand fashion. Allow the doorman to handle your bags as you make your entrance into the elegant, captivating lobby. Sip cocktails at the superchic Starlight Lounge overlooking the city. Dine at Scala's Bistro, one of the hottest new restaurants in the city. In short, live like the king or queen of Union Square without all the pomp, circumstance, and credit card bills.

NORTH BEACH/FISHERMAN'S WHARF
DOUBLES FOR $60 OR LESS

Green Tortoise Guesthouse. 494 Broadway (at Kearny St.), San Francisco, CA 94102. ☎ **800/867-8647** within U.S. and Canada, or 415/834-1000. Fax 415/956-4900. 100 beds, 5 private rms, 10 shared baths. Dorm beds $12–$17 per person; double $29–$35. Traveler's checks, cash only. Continental breakfast included. Bus: 9AX, 9X, BX, 15, 41, 30, 45, 83, or 30X.

You'll get an affordable dose of communal living at this bus-tour-company-cum-hostel hovering above Broadway's burlesque boulevard. Shack up dorm style in rooms that fit two to six persons (twin beds, linens, desk, and lamp included) or opt for a simple room with a queen-size bed. Either way, there's no chance you'll find a deal even remotely this good in the center of bustling North Beach. Aside from basic essentials in the rooms, guests enjoy the use of the TV lounge, an old ballroom with 20-foot ceilings, stained glass windows, VCR, and a pool table (it's also the only smoking area on the premises). Other bonuses include pay phones, a sauna, fully equipped kitchen, laundry facilities, safe deposit boxes, and coin-operated lockers. There's no curfew, so you can get a late-night dose of North Beach just steps outside your door.

A word of warning: Parking is downright treacherous in this area, so come without a car or expect to either hunt down a space or park in a garage (around $12 per day). As with most youth hostels, in summer most visitors are young Europeans; with winter comes a more diverse clientele.

⑤ San Remo. 2237 Mason St. (at Chestnut St.), San Francisco, CA 94133. ☎ **800-352-REMO** or 415/776-8688. Fax 415/776-2811. 59 rms (none with bath), 1 suite. $60–$70 double; $100 suite. AE, DC, MC, V. Parking $8. Cable car: Powell-Mason line. Bus: 15, 22, or 30.

Located in a quiet North Beach neighborhood and within walking distance of Fisherman's Wharf, the San Remo's rooms are small and its bathrooms shared, but all is forgiven when it comes time to pay the bill. Rooms are decorated in a cozy, country style with brass and iron beds, oak, maple, or pine armoires, and wicker furnishings. Most rooms also come equipped with ceiling fans. The shared bathrooms, each one immaculately clean, feature claw-foot tubs and brass pull-chain toilets.

DOUBLES FOR $100 OR LESS

Washington Square Inn. 1660 Stockton St. (between Filbert and Union sts.), San Francisco, CA 94133. ☎ **800/388-0220** or 415/981-4220. Fax 415/397-7242. 16 rms (5 with shared bath). TEL. $85–$95 with shared bath; $95–$165 with private bath; $180 with park view. Rates include continental breakfast. AE, DC, DISC, JCB, MC, V. Parking $17. Bus: 15, 30, 39, or 45.

Reminiscent of a traditional English inn, right down to the cucumber sandwiches served during afternoon tea, this small bed-and-breakfast is ideal for older couples who prefer a more quiet, subdued environment than the commotion of downtown San Francisco. It's located across from Washington Square in the North Beach District and within walking distance of Fisherman's Wharf and Chinatown. Each room is decorated in English floral fabrics with quality European furnishings and plenty of fresh flowers; a few rooms share baths. A continental breakfast is included, as are afternoon tea, wine, and hors d'oeuvres.

DOUBLES FOR $130 OR LESS

✪ Hotel Bohème. 444 Columbus St. (between Vallejo and Green sts.), San Francisco 94133 ☎ **415/433-9111.** Fax 415/362-6292. 15 rms. TEL TV. $115 double. AE, DISC, DC, MC, V. Parking $20 at nearby public garage. Cable car: Powell-Mason line. Bus: 12, 15, 30, 41, 45, or 83.

Although located on the busiest strip in North Beach, this recently renovated hotel's style and demeanor is more reminiscent of a prestigious home in upscale Nob Hill. The rooms are small but hopelessly romantic, with gauze-draped canopies and walls accented with lavender, sage green, black, and pumpkin. It's a few steps to some of the greatest cafes, restaurants, bars, and shops in the city, and Chinatown and Union Square are within walking distance.

COW HOLLOW/PACIFIC HEIGHTS
DOUBLES FOR $60 OR LESS

San Francisco International Hostel. Fort Mason Bldg., 240 Fort Mason, San Francisco, CA 94123. ☎ **415/771-7277.** Fax 415/771-1468. 155 beds. $13–$15. MC, V. Reservations up to 24 hours in advance.

Unbelievable but true, you can get front-row bay views for a mere $13 to $15 nightly. The hostel, sitting on national park property, provides dorm-style accommodations for 155 guests and easy access to the Marina's shops and restaurants. Rooms sleep three to four persons and include bedding and towels. The communal space includes a fireplace, pool table, kitchen, dining room, coffee bar, complimentary movies, laundry facilities, sundeck, and free parking. There's no curfew and smoking is not allowed. Slackers beware: Each guest is expected to do one quick, simple chore.

DOUBLES FOR $80 OR LESS

✪ Bed and Breakfast Inn. 4 Charlton Court (off Union St., between Buchanan and Laguna sts.), San Francisco, CA 94123. ☎ **415/921-9784.** 11 rms (4 with shared bath), 2 suites. $70–$90 double without bath, $115–$140 double with bath; $190–$275 suite. Rates include continental breakfast. No credit cards. Parking $10 a day at nearby garage. Bus: 41 or 45.

San Francisco's first bed-and-breakfast is composed of a trio of Victorian houses, all gussied up in English country style, hidden in a cul-de-sac just off Union Street. While it doesn't have quite the casual ambience of neighboring Union Street Inn, the Bed and Breakfast Inn is loaded with charm. Each room is uniquely decorated with family antiques, original art, and fresh flowers. The Garden Suite, highly recommended for families or groups of four, comes with a fully stocked kitchen, a living room with fireplace, two bedrooms, two bathrooms (one with a Jacuzzi tub), a study, and French doors leading out into the garden. Breakfast (freshly baked croissants; orange juice; and coffee, tea, or cocoa) is either brought to your room on a tray with flowers and a morning newspaper, or served in a sunny Victorian breakfast room with antique china.

Cow Hollow Motor Inn and Suites. 2190 Lombard St. (between Steiner and Fillmore sts.), at Steiner St., San Francisco, CA 94123. ☎ **415/921-5800.** Fax 415/922-8515. 117 rms, 12 suites. A/C TEL TV. $80 double, from $175 suite. Extra person $10. AE, DC, MC, V. Free parking. Bus: 28, 43, or 76.

If you're less interested in being downtown and romping in and around the beautiful bay-front Marina, check out this modest brick hotel smack in the middle of busy Lombard Street. There's no fancy theme here, but each room comes loaded with amenities like cable TV, free local phone calls, free covered parking, and in-room coffeemakers. All the rooms were renovated in 1996, so you'll be sure to sleep on a nice firm mattress surrounded by clean, new carpeting and drapes.

Francisco Bay Motel. 1501 Lombard (at Franklin), San Francisco, CA 94123. ☎ **415/ 474-3030.** Fax 415/567-7082. 38 rms. A/C TEL TV. Double $65–$95. AE, CB, DISC, MC, V. Bus: 82X, 30, 76, 30X, 47, 49, or 42.

Okay, so Lombard isn't exactly a quaint street lined with Victorians. In fact, aside from the famous winding section along Russian Hill, it's a major thoroughfare packed with motels, gas stations, and restaurants. But look on the bright side: It's five blocks from the Fisherman's Wharf area (better yet, the Marina); nearby Chestnut and Union Streets, which offer some of the best shopping, eating, and drinking action in town; and the price is half of what it'll cost you downtown. Rooms are nothing fancy, but they've been recently renovated (complete with coffeemakers) and a few come with radios and refrigerators. If you don't plan to spend all your time shopping downtown, this is the place to stay. You'll find this neighborhood to be one of San Francisco's most pleasant and scenic.

DOUBLES FOR $100 OR LESS

Chelsea Motor Inn. 2095 Lombard St. (between Fillmore and Webster sts.), San Francisco, CA 94123. ☎ **415/563-5600.** Fax 415/346-9127. 60 rms. A/C TEL TV. $83–$95 double. AE, CB, DC, MC, V. Free parking. Bus: 22, 28, 30, or 76.

An establishment on the "motel strip" that stretches from the Golden Gate Bridge to Van Ness Avenue, the Chelsea Motor Inn is perfectly located for a stroll along Union Street. Expect generic, clean motel accommodations, with coffeemakers in each room. No breakfast is offered, but there's complimentary coffee in lobby. Services offered include room service (from a local restaurant delivery service), concierge, laundry/valet, and massage.

WORTH A SPLURGE

Jackson Court. 2198 Jackson St. (at Buchanan St.), San Francisco, CA 94115. ☎ **415/ 929-7670.** 10 rms. TEL TV. $122–$170 double. Rates include continental breakfast. AE, MC, V. Parking on street only. Bus: 12, 24, 1, or 3.

If you crave a blissfully quiet vacation while swathed in elegant surroundings, this is the place. Each room is individually furnished with superior-quality antique furnishings; two have wood-burning fireplaces. The Blue Room, for example, features a brass and porcelain bed, a Renaissance-style sofa, and an inviting window seat, while the Garden Suite has hand-crafted wood paneling and a large picture window looking out at the private garden patio. After breakfast, spend the day browsing the shops along nearby Union and Fillmore Streets, then return in time for afternoon tea.

Union Street Inn. 2229 Union St. (between Fillmore and Steiner sts.), San Francisco, CA 94123. ☎ **415/346-0424.** Fax 415/922-8046. 5 rms, 1 cottage. TEL TV. $125–$175 standard double; $225 cottage. Rates include breakfast, hors d'oeuvres, and evening beverages. AE, MC, V. Parking $10. Bus: 22, 41, 45, or 47.

Who would have guessed that one of the most delightful B&Bs in California would be in San Francisco? This two-story Edwardian may front the perpetually busy (and trendy) Union Street, but it's quiet as a church on the inside. All individually decorated rooms are comfortably furnished with canopied or brass beds with down comforters, fresh flowers, bay windows (beg for one with a view of the garden), and private baths. A breakfast of fresh-baked croissants, fresh-squeezed orange juice, fruit, and coffee is served either in the parlor, in your room, or on an outdoor terrace overlooking a lovely English garden. The ultimate honeymoon retreat is the private carriage house behind the inn, but any room at this warm, friendly inn is guaranteed to please.

JAPANTOWN & ENVIRONS

✪ **Queen Anne Hotel.** 1590 Sutter St. (between Gough and Octavia sts.), San Francisco, CA 94109. ☎ **800/227-3970** or 415/441-2828. Fax 415/775-5212. 45 rms, 4 suites. TEL TV. $99–$150 double; $175 suite. Extra person $10. Rates include continental breakfast. AE, DC, MC, V. Parking $12. Bus: 2, 3, or 4.

Looking for old San Francisco charm combined with immaculate and lavish furnishings for half the price of downtown hotels? You've come to the right place. The Queen Anne is a majestic four-story 1890 Victorian that was restored in 1981 and renovated in 1995. Guests are welcome to walk under rich, red drapery to the immaculate "grand salon" lobby furnished in English oak paneling and period antiques. Rooms follow suit with antiques—armoires, marble-top dressers, and other Victorian pieces. Some have corner turret bay windows that look out on tree-lined streets, as well as separate parlor areas and wet bars; others have cozy reading nooks and fireplaces. All rooms have a telephone in the bathroom, a computer hook-up, and a refrigerator. There's a complimentary continental breakfast and services include concierge, morning newspaper, room service, and complimentary afternoon tea and sherry, as well as access to an off-premises health club with a lap-pool.

CIVIC CENTER
DOUBLES FOR $100 OR LESS

Abigail Hotel. 246 McAllister St. (between Hyde and Larkin sts.), San Francisco, CA 94102. ☎ **800/243-6510** or 415/861-9728. Fax 415/861-5848. 59 rms, 1 suite. TEL TV. $84 double; $129 suite. Extra person $10. Rates include continental breakfast. AE, CB, DC, MC, V. Parking $12. Muni Metro: all Market St. trams. All Market St. buses.

The Abigail is one of San Francisco's rare sleeper hotels. It doesn't get much press, but it's one of the better medium-priced hotels in the city. Built in 1925 to house celebrities performing at the world-renowned Fox Theater, what the Abigail lacks in luxury is more than made up in charm. The rooms, while on the small side, are clean, cute, and comfortably furnished with cozy antiques and down comforters. Morning coffee, pastries, and complimentary newspapers greet you in the beautiful faux-marble lobby, while lunch and dinner are served downstairs in the "organic" restaurant, the Millennium. Access to a nearby health club, as well as laundry and massage services, are available upon request.

✪ **Phoenix Inn.** 601 Eddy St. (at Larkin St.), San Francisco, CA 94109. ☎ **800/248-9466** or 415/776-1380. Fax 415/885-3109. 42 rms, 2 suites. TEL TV. $99–$109 double; $139–$150 suite. Rates include continental breakfast. AE, DC, MC, V. Free parking. Bus: 19, 31, or 38.

Situated on the fringes of San Francisco's less-than-pleasant Tenderloin District, this retro 1950s-style hotel has been described as the hippest hotel in town, a gathering place for visiting rock musicians, writers, and filmmakers who crave a dose of Southern California—hence the palm trees and pastel colors. The focal point is a small, heated outdoor pool adorned with a paisley mural by artist Francis Forlenza and ensconced by a modern-sculpture garden. The rooms, while far from plush, are comfortably equipped with bamboo furnishings, potted plants, and original local art. In addition to the usual amenities, the inn's own closed-circuit channel shows films exclusively made in or about San Francisco. Services include an on-site massage therapist, concierge, laundry, room service, and free parking. Adjoining the hotel is Miss Pearl's Jam House restaurant/club, featuring spicy island cuisine and the reggae sounds to go with it.

WORTH A SPLURGE

✪ **Inn at the Opera.** 333 Fulton St. (at Franklin St.), San Francisco, CA 94102. ☎ **800/ 325-2708** or 415/863-8400. Fax 415/861-0821. 30 rms, 18 suites. MINIBAR TEL TV. $140–$190 double; from $200 suite. Extra person $15. Rates include European buffet breakfast. AE, MC, V. Parking $19. Bus: 5, 21, 47, or 49.

Judging from its mild-mannered facade and offbeat location behind the Opera House, few would ever guess that the Inn at the Opera is one of San Francisco's, if not California's, finest small hotels. But don't take my word for it; Luciano Pavarotti, Placido Domingo, Mikhail Baryshnikov, and dozens of other stars of the stage throw their slumber parties here regularly, requisitioning the inn's luxurious restaurant and lounge, Act IV. Queen-size beds with huge stuffed pillows are standard in each pastel guest room, along with fresh flowers, elegant furnishings, and more amenities than you know what to do with. The larger rooms and suites are especially recommended for those who need elbow room; typical of small hotels, the least expensive "standard" rooms are short on space.

HAIGHT-ASHBURY
DOUBLES FOR $60 OR LESS

The Metro Hotel. 319 Divisadero St. (between Oak and Page). ☎ **415/861-5364.** Fax 415/863-1970. 24 rms. TEL TV. Double $50; queen $60; suite $74–$94. AE, DC, DISC, MC, V.

It's not exactly in the heart of the Haight, but from this remodeled Victorian you can walk to the Castro, Golden Gate Park, or upper or lower Haight in under 30 minutes. Buses stop a block away and blast downtown and to the Haight every few minutes (a 10-minute trip once on board). The neighborhood isn't the best in town, but it beats Civic Center by a long shot and has plenty of cheap restaurants nearby. The high-ceilinged hotel is reminiscent of a European pension—smallish rooms, nothing too fancy, but clean and friendly with everything you need to get by. There's a garden out back, too. *Take note:* Parking is free in the evenings, but you'll have to move your car off Divisadero (or keep feeding the meter) during the day.

DOUBLES FOR $80 OR LESS

Red Victorian Bed and Breakfast Inn. 1665 Haight St. (between Cole and Belvedere sts.), San Francisco, CA 94117. ☎ **415/864-1978.** 18 rms (4 with bath), 1 suite. TEL. $76–$110 double without bath, $120–$126 double with bath; $200 suite. Rates decrease based on length of stay. Extra person $15. Rates include continental breakfast and afternoon tea. MC, V. Guarded parking lot nearby. Muni Metro: N line. Bus: 7, 66, 71, or 73.

If you'd like to relive the sixties, the Red Vic, located in the heart of Haight, will give you a few memorable flashbacks. Owner Sami Sunchild, a confessed former flower child, runs this hotel and meditation center that honors the Summer of Love and Golden Gate Park. Rooms are inspired by San Francisco's history and are decorated accordingly—psychedelic posters and all. The Flower Child Room has a sun on the ceiling and a rainbow on the wall, while the Peacock Suite, though pricey, is one funky and colorful room, with red beads, a canopy bed, and a Persian temple light. The clincher is the bathtub which has a circular pass-through looking into the sitting area. Four guest rooms have private baths; the remaining accommodations share four bathrooms down the hall. In general, rooms and baths are clean, and the furnishings eccentric. This hotel is not for everybody, but if you're into it, it's pretty cool. Rates for longer stays are a great deal. Smoking is not permitted in the rooms.

DOUBLES FOR $100 OR LESS

Stanyan Park Hotel. 750 Stanyan St. (at Waller St.), San Francisco, CA 94117. ☎ **415/ 751-1000.** Fax 415/668-5454. 30 rms, 6 suites. TEL TV. $85–$105 double; from $135 suite. Rates include continental breakfast. Extra person $20. AE, CB, DC, DISC, MC, V. Parking $5. Muni Metro: N line. Bus: 7, 33, 71, or 73.

This charming, three-story establishment is decorated with antique furnishings, Victorian wallpaper, and pastel quilts, curtains, and carpets. The hotel has one- and two-bedroom suites that can sleep up to six comfortably—they're ideal for families. Each has a full kitchen, plus formal dining and living room, and tub/shower baths come complete with massaging shower head, shampoos, and fancy soaps. Complimentary tea and cookies are served each afternoon.

GAY & LESBIAN HOTELS

Most of the previously recommended hotels are undoubtedly "gay and lesbian friendly," but San Francisco also has a number of affordable hotels catering primarily to the gay traveler.

DOUBLES FOR $80 OR LESS

Castillo Inn. 48 Henry St., San Francisco, CA 94114. ☎ **800/865-5112** or 415/864-5111. Fax 415/641-1321. 4 rms (none with bath). $70 double; $160 suite. Suite rate negotiable depending on season and number of guests. Rates include American breakfast. MC, V. Muni Metro: F, K, L, or M. Bus: 8, 22, 24,or 37.

Just two minutes from the heart of the Castro District, this charming little house provides a safe, quiet, and clean environment for its clientele. Catering mostly to gay men (though anyone is welcome), the Castillo makes its guests feel at home. Bedrooms are small yet cozy, with hardwood floors and throw rugs. The Castillo also provides a large communal refrigerator and microwave in the kitchen. One enormous, two-bedroom suite that sleeps 4 comfortably has a full kitchen, two TVs, VCR, parking, and a deck. On Friday and Saturday nights, a two-night minimum stay is required.

Essex Hotel. 684 Ellis St. (between Larkin and Hyde sts.), San Francisco, CA 49109. ☎ **800/ 453-7739** in the U.S., 800/443-7739 in Canada, or 415/474-4664. Fax 415/441-1800. 100 rms. TEL TV. $69 double. AE, MC, V.

When guests enter the Essex Hotel, they are immediately greeted by a member of Jean Chaban's handpicked and trained staff, and a lobby with polished marble floors, fresh-cut flowers, ornate plaster ceilings, and French antiques. Bedrooms are traditional, clean, and safe, and are among the more reasonably priced in the area. The staff, or perhaps Jean Chaban himself, is always available to help guests and seems to truly care about the welfare of their clientele. Because some of the staff are fluent in French and German, European gays frequent this hotel. No breakfast is served.

DOUBLES FOR $100 OR LESS

Atherton Hotel. 685 Ellis St. (at Larkin St.), San Francisco, CA, 94109. ☎ **800/227-3608** in the U.S., or 415/474-5720. Fax 415/474-8256. 75 rms. TEL TV. $59–$99 double. Continental breakfast $6 extra. AE, MC, DC, V. Bus: 19, 38, or 72.

Across from the Essex (see above) and close to many gay clubs and restaurants in the more risqué and sometimes seedy section of Polk Street, this European-style hotel serves an equal mixture of gay and straight visitors. Totally refurbished in 1995 and 1996, it offers basic accommodation and each of the well-furnished bedrooms is complete with a private bath and shower. Complimentary weekday morning limo service is available and the staff will help secure theater tickets or book city or wine country tours.

The hotel's Abbey Room Bar is a relaxing place for a drink and perhaps a friendly conversation with a stranger. The hotel's Atherton Grill serves breakfast or lunch but only from Monday through Friday. Over the weekend a champagne brunch is featured here, attended by many gays who live in the nearby area.

✪ **Dolores Park Inn.** ℅ Bernie H. Vielwerth, 3641 17th St., San Francisco, CA 94114. ☎ **415/621-0482.** Fax is the same; please call before faxing. 4 rms (none with bath), 1 suite (with kitchenette). TV. $89 double; $165 suite. Rates include full breakfast. MC, V. Muni Metro: F, J, K, L, or M. Bus: 22 or 24.

For five years running, the Dolores Park Inn has been awarded for being one of the best B&Bs in the city. Conveniently located in the Castro, it's within walking distance of many gay shops and clubs as well as the downtown area. Each bedroom is individually decorated with beautiful antiques and a queen-size bed. Celebrities (Tom Cruise, members of the *Sister Act* cast, Robert Downey Jr., and others) have stayed here to avoid hype. The owner takes special care in providing a warm, hospitable, and romantic environment with excellent service. The suite has a 20-foot sundeck looking up at Twin Peaks and a four-posted bed. A two-night minimum stay is required, and there is no smoking.

Inn on Castro. 321 Castro (at Market St.), San Francisco, CA 94114. ☎ **415/861-0321.** 6 rms, 2 suites. TEL. $85–$120; suites $120. AE, MC, V. Rates include full breakfast and evening brandy. Muni Metro: Castro St.

One of the better choices in the Castro (just a half block away from all the action) is this Edwardian-style inn decorated with contemporary furnishings, original modern art, and fresh flowers. Almost all rooms have private baths and direct-dial phones; color TVs are available upon request. Most rooms share a small back patio, and the suite has its own private outdoor sitting area.

The Willows Inn. 710 14th St. (between Church and Market sts.), San Francisco, CA 94114. ☎ **415/431-4770.** Fax 415/431-5295. 10 rms (none with bath), 1 suite. $86–$96 double; $105–$125 suite. Rates include continental breakfast. AE, DISC, MC, V. Limited on-street parking. Muni Metro: Church St. (across the street). Bus: 8, 22, or 37.

Right in the heart of the gay Castro District, The Willows Inn employs a staff eager to greet and attend to visitors. The inn's willow furnishings, antiques, and Laura Ashley prints add a touch of romantic elegance. After a long day of sightseeing and shopping, followed by a night of dancing and cruising, you will be tucked in with a "sherry and chocolate turn-down." The staff will appear the next morning with your personalized breakfast delivered with a freshly cut flower and the morning newspaper. This place has a simple elegance and quality that attracts discriminating gay visitors. Extra amenities include direct-dial phones, alarm-clock radios, and kimono bathrobes.

4 Dining

San Francisco's dining is some of the finest in the world. We've included plenty of affordable options, as well as some renowned pricey establishments. If there is a way to eat elegantly, satisfy your appetite, and leave with some extra change in your pocket, we've made a point of noting it in the text.

The restaurants below are divided by area and by price (for a dinner), as follows: **Meals for $10 or Less, Meals for $20 or Less,** and **Worth a Splurge.** These categories reflect the cost per person for a main course and a drink or two—which means you *can* get away with spending that amount, but of course you can easily blow your budget if you go crazy on appetizers, cocktails, coffee, and dessert.

For other budget options, check out the cafes in the "Bar and Cafe Scene" section of this chapter. And don't forget: If you want a table at a top restaurant, make your reservation weeks ahead. Bon appétit!

UNION SQUARE/NOB HILL
MEALS FOR $10 OR LESS

Café Claude. 7 Claude Lane. ☎ **415/392-3505.** Reservations accepted. Main courses $5–$13. AE, MC, V. Mon–Fri 8am–10:30pm, Sat 10am–10:30pm. Cable car: Powell-Hyde and Powell-Mason lines. FRENCH.

Euro-transplants love Café Claude, a crowded and lively restaurant tucked in a narrow lane near Union Square. Seemingly everything—every table, every spoon, every saltshaker, and every waiter—is imported from France. There is usually live jazz on Tuesdays and Thursdays after 7pm, and Fridays and Saturdays after 11pm; outdoor seating is available when weather permits. With prices topping out at about $11 for main courses such as poussin rôti or the poisson du jour, Café Claude is a good value.

Dottie's True Blue Café. 522 Jones St. (at O'Farrell St.). ☎ **415/885-2767.** Reservations not accepted. Breakfast $4–$7; main courses $4.25–$7. DISC, MC, V. Wed–Mon 7:30am–2pm. Cable car: Powell-Mason line. Bus: 2, 3, 4, 27, or 38. AMERICAN.

This family-owned breakfast restaurant in the Pacific Bay Inn has only 10 tables and a handful of counter stools. A traditional coffee shop (with the exception of an espresso machine), Dottie's serves standard American fare (French toast, pancakes, bacon and eggs, omelets, and the like) on rugged, diner-quality plates and blue-and-white checkered tablecloths. Whatever you order comes with homemade bread, muffins, or scones. There are also daily specials and vegetarian dishes.

Emerald Garden. 1550 California St. (at Polk St.). ☎ **415/673-1155.** Main courses $7.95–$9. AE, DC, DISC, MC, V. Mon–Fri 11:30am–2:30pm, Daily 5–10pm. Bus: 1, 19, 47, 49, or 76. Cable car: California St. line. VIETNAMESE.

This is not one of our favorite parts of town (on the outskirts of Nob Hill bordering Polk Gulch), but one good reason to pass through is Emerald Garden. Most of this restaurant's seating area is actually a fashionably masqueraded alley wedged between two buildings. It may sound makeshift, but the fact is, this place is pretty darn cute with flowers and foliage in nooks and crannies and Asian sculpture and art adorning the walls. Start with the ever-popular green papaya salad or squash soup and if you happen to dine on a Friday, try the evening's special, a chicken breast stuffed with carrot and rice noodles served with a macadamia sauce—it's to die for. Free parking is available for 2¹/₂ hours at 1540 Pine St. (at Van Ness).

Emporio Armani Cafe. 1 Grant Ave. (at O'Farrell St., off Market St.). ☎ **415/677-9010.** $6–$13. AE, DC, DISC, MC, V. Lunch Mon–Sat 11:30am–4:30pm, Sun noon–4:30pm. All Union Square buses. ITALIAN.

All the hobnobbing of an elite dining club comes cheaply at the counter at Armani Cafe. It's nothing more than a circular counter located in the middle of Armani's ever-fashionable (and expensive) clothing store. But the fare and upscale/casual atmosphere is enough to lure folks who have lunch, not a new suit, on their minds. Local favorites include a homemade antipasto misto, artichoke heart salad with baby greens and shaved Parmesan, and penne with smoked salmon, tomato, vodka, mascarpone cheese, and chives. There's also a nice variety of sandwiches and as always, a large dose of attitude. Although there are a few dishes over $10, you can easily get by on a 10 spot. Outside seating is available when weather permits.

Family Inn Coffee Shop. 505 Jones St. (at O'Farrell St.). ☎ **415/771-5995.** Main courses $4–$6. No credit cards. Tues–Fri 7am–6pm; Sat 7am–4:30pm. Bus: 2, 3, 4, or 38. AMERICAN.

If you want a really inexpensive, hearty meal, it's hard to top the Family Inn. The menu varies daily, but homemade soups are the norm at lunch, along with a special entree served with mashed potatoes, a vegetable, bread, and dessert for less than $5. It's not the least bit fancy—just counter seats in front of a hard-working kitchen—but the food is wholesome and the price is right.

Salmagundi. 442 Geary St. (between Mason and Taylor sts.). ☎ **415/441-0894.** Soups and salads $3.50–$8.50. AE, MC, V. Tues–Sat 11am–11pm, Sun–Mon 11am–9pm. Cable car: Powell-Hyde and Powell-Mason lines. Bus: 2, 3, 4, or 38. AMERICAN.

If you're pinching pennies on this trip, there's no better deal on a meal in Union Square. Bright, pleasant, and sparkling clean, this cafeteria-style restaurant offers a variety of soups, salads, sandwiches, and occasional specials. Among the more unusual soup choices are English country cheddar, Hungarian goulash, North Beach minestrone, Barbary Coast bouillabaisse, and Ukrainian beef borscht. Seats in the rear look out onto a tiny garden.

Sears Fine Foods. 439 Powell St. (between Post and Sutter sts.). ☎ **415/986-1160.** Reservations not accepted. Breakfast $3–$8; salads and soups $1.80–$8; main courses $5–$10. No credit cards. Wed–Sun 6:30am–3:30pm. Cable car: Powell-Hyde and Powell-Mason lines. Bus 2, 3, 4, or 38. AMERICAN.

Sears would be the perfect place to breakfast on the way to work, but you can't always guarantee you'll get in the door before 9am. It's not just another pink-tabled diner run by motherly matrons; it's an institution that's famous for its crispy, dark-brown waffles, light sourdough French toast, and Swedish dollar-sized pancakes. As the story goes, Sears was founded in 1938 by Ben Sears, a retired clown. It was his Swedish wife Hilbur, however, who was responsible for the legendary pancakes, which are still whipped up according to her family's secret recipe.

✪ Tú Lan. 8 Sixth St. (at Market St.). ☎ **415/626-0927.** $3.50–$7. No credit cards. Mon–Sat 11am–9pm. Cable car: Powell-Hyde or Powell-Mason lines. Muni Metro: F, J, K, L, M, or N. Bus: 6, 7, 27, 31, 66, or 71. VIETNAMESE.

If you can handle walking down Sixth Street past the winos and weirdoes and you don't need a beautiful dining room to make you appreciate your meal, you won't find better (or cheaper) Vietnamese food than that of Tú Lan. The place is always packed. Even Julia Child (whose face graces the greasy old menus) has been known to pull up a chair at this shack of a restaurant to feast on imperial rolls on a bed of rice noodles, lettuce, peanuts, and mint (under $5). Take heart on the poor waiter who never seems to bring water no matter how many times you ask; he's been working here forever and is the only server. For the price, this has been one of our all-time favorite restaurants for more than a decade.

MEALS FOR $20 OR LESS

✪ Brasserie Savoy. In the Savoy Hotel, 580 Geary St. (at Jones St.). ☎ **415/474-8686.** Reservations recommended. Main courses $11–$17. AE, DC, DISC, JCB, MC, V. Daily 6:30–11am and 5:30–10pm. Bus 2, 3, 4, 27, or 38. CALIFORNIA/FRENCH.

A gourmet evening comes cheaply here, compared to neighboring establishments of the same caliber. Brasserie Savoy is a sophisticated French bistro, with a bright, busy dining room, black and white marble floors, and tables with leather chairs. But the convivial atmosphere is secondary to the food, which is consistent, affordable, and delicious. Choices may include beef tenderloin with port sauce and green peppercorn butter, or duck breast with mille feuille of potato and mushrooms served with a date puree and coffee sauce. On the lighter side, the crawfish risotto with red and green peppers, scallions, celery, and chive lemongrass butter is a perfect choice. Among the appetizers, the napoleon of braised rabbit with red onions, mushrooms, kalamata olives, and anise tuiles is highly recommended, if it's offered, or choose any one of several freshly made salads. For dessert, try the innovative crème brûlée.

Kuleto's. 221 Powell St. (between Geary and O'Farrell sts., in the Villa Florence Hotel). ☎ **415/ 397-7720.** Reservations recommended. Breakfast $3–$8; main courses $8–$18. AE, CB, DC, DISC, MC, V. Mon–Fri 7–10:30am, Sat and Sun 8–10:30am; daily 11:30am–11pm. Cable car: Powell-Hyde and Powell-Mason lines. Muni Metro: Powell. Bus: 2, 3, 4, or 38. NORTHERN ITALIAN.

Story has it the owners of this popular downtown bistro were so delighted with the design of their new restaurant that they named it after the architect, Pat Kuleto. Whatever the reason, Kuleto's is truly a beautiful place filled with beautiful people (don't come underdressed) who are here to see and be seen. The best plan is to skip the wait for a table, muscle a seat at the antipasto bar, and fill up on appetizers (which are often better than the entrees). For a main course, try the penne pasta drenched in a tangy lamb sausage marinara sauce, the clam linguini (overloaded with fresh clams), or any of the fresh fish specials grilled over hardwoods. If you don't arrive by 6pm, expect to wait—this place fills up fast.

Nob Hill Café. 1152 Taylor St. (Between Sacramento and Clay sts.). ☎ **415/776-6500.** Reservations not accepted. Main courses $7–$10.75. DC, MC, V. Daily 11:30am–10pm. Cable car: California St. line. Bus: 1. ITALIAN.

Considering the cost and formality of most meals on ultra-elite Nob Hill, it's no wonder that neighborhood residents don't mind waiting around for a table to open up at the Nob Hill Café. This is the kind of place where you can come wearing jeans, relax over a large bowl of pasta and a glass of merlot, and leave fulfilled without blowing a wad of dough. The dining room is split into two small, simple rooms, with windows looking on to Taylor Street and bright local art on the walls. Service is friendly and one of the owners is almost always on hand to satisfy your every need. When the kitchen is "on," expect fare worth at least twice its price; on an "off" day, it's still decent. Start with a salad or the decadent polenta with tomato sauce. Then fill up on the veal picatta, any of the pastas or pizzas, or petrole sole.

Puccini and Pinetti. 129 Ellis St. (at Cyril Magnin). ☎ **415/392-5500.** Reservations recommended. Main courses $5–$13. AE, CB, DC, DISC, MC, V. Daily 11:30am–3:30pm, Sun–Thurs 5–10pm, Fri–Sat 5–11pm. Cable car: Powell-Mason. Bus: 27 or 38. NORTHERN ITALIAN.

It takes some buco bravado to open an Italian restaurant in San Francisco, but partners Bob Puccini and Steve Pinetti obviously did their homework because this trendy little trattoria has been packed since the day it opened. The formula isn't exactly unique—good food at great prices. What really makes it work, though, is the upbeat, casual ambience, the colorful decor, and live music Monday through Friday nights— it's sort of like crashing a catered party. The menu features Italian standbys: pastas, salads, wood-fired pizzas, and grilled meats. The grilled salmon with sautéed spinach has been well received, along with the stuffed, oven-roasted portobello mushroom antipasti and fresh-baked focaccia sandwiches. The creamy tiramisu makes for a proper finish.

✪ **Rumpus.** One Tillman Place (off Grant Ave., between Sutter and Post sts.). ☎ **415/ 421-2300.** Reservations recommended. Main courses $11.95–$16.95. AE, DC, MC, V. Mon– Sat 11:30am–2:30pm; Sun–Thurs 5:30–10pm; Fri–Sat 5:30–11pm. Bus: 2, 9X, 30, 34, 45, or 76; all Union Square buses. CALIFORNIA.

Tucked into a small cul-de-sac off Grant Avenue, you'll find a fantastic restaurant serving well-prepared California fare at reasonable prices. The perfect place for a business lunch, shopping break, or dinner with friends, Rumpus is architecturally playful and always buzzing with conversation. Like most hip restaurants in town, ahi tuna tartare is on the starters list. It is, however, wonderfully fresh, savory, and spiced with wasabi caviar. The pan-roasted chicken's crispy crust is almost as delightful as the perfectly cooked chicken and mashed potatoes beneath it; and the quality cut of New York steak comes with a sweet-potato mash. If nothing else, make sure to stop in for one of the best desserts we've ever had: the puddinglike chocolate brioche cake.

⭘ **Scala's Bistro.** 432 Powell St. (at Sutter St.). ☎ **415/395-8555.** Reservations recommended. Breakfast $6–$9; lunch and dinner main courses $8–$17. AE, CB, DC, DISC, MC, V. Mon–Sun 6:30am–12am. Cable Car: Powell-Hyde. Bus: 2, 3, 4, 30, 45, or 76. FRENCH/ITALIAN.

Firmly entrenched at the base of the refurbished Sir Francis Drake Hotel, this latest venture by husband and wife team Giovanni (the host) and Donna (the chef) Scala is one of the best new restaurants in the city. The Parisian-bistro/old-world atmosphere blends just the right balance of elegance and informality, which means it's perfectly okay to have some fun here. Drawing from her success at Bistro Don Giovanni in Napa, Donna has put together a fantastic array of Italian and French dishes that are priced surprisingly low. Start with the Earth and Surf calamari appetizer (better than anything I've sampled along the Mediterranean) or the grilled portobello mushrooms. Generous portions of the moist, rich duck leg confit will satisfy hungry appetites, but if you can only order one thing, make it Scala's signature dish: the seared salmon. Finish with the creamy Bostini cream pie, a dreamy combo of vanilla custard and orange chiffon cake with a warm chocolate glaze.

Worth a Splurge

✪ **Charles Nob Hill.** 1250 Jones St. (at Clay St.). ☎ **415/771-5400.** Main courses $16–$26. AE, DC, MC, V. Daily 5:30–10pm. Cable car: California St. and Powell-Hyde lines. Bus: 1, 12, 27, or 83. FRENCH.

We never knew beef could actually melt in your mouth until Aqua owner Charles Condy bought the historic restaurant "Le Club" and introduced us to Aqua's executive chef Michael Mina's culinary magic. The "classically inspired light French fare" is served in two divided dining rooms with velvet banquettes, fresh floral arrangements, and the loud buzz of an older socialite crowd. Definitely start with the scallop and black truffle pot pie and for the main course you might choose the Poele of beef tenderloin with wild mushroom and potato torte, balsamic glazed onions, and foie gras, or a delicate seared red snapper with chive and preserved lemon, artichoke, and chanterelle ragout. No matter what, don't drive here unless you valet it; you may spend over an hour looking for parking.

✪ **Postrio.** 545 Post St. (between Mason and Taylor sts.). ☎ **415/776-7825.** Reservations required. Main courses $6–$15 breakfast, $14–$15 lunch, $20–$26 dinner. AE, CB, DC, DISC, MC, V. Mon–Fri 7–10am, 11:30am–2pm, and 5:30–10:30pm; Sat–Sun 9am–2pm; bar daily 11:30am–2am. Cable car: Powell-Hyde and Powell-Mason lines. Bus: 2, 3, 4, or 38. AMERICAN.

Rumor has it that ever since chefs Anne and David Gingrass left the kitchen to start their own enterprise, San Francisco's top restaurant isn't what it used to be. If its owners are crying, however, they're crying all the way to the bank, because it's a rare night when the kitchen doesn't perform to a full house. Eating, however, is only half the reason one comes to Postrio. After squeezing through the perpetually swinging bar, which dishes out excellent tapas and pizzas from a wood-burning oven, guests are forced to make a grand entrance down the antebellum staircase to the cavernous dining room below (it's everyone's 15 seconds of fame, so make sure your fly is zipped).

The menu, prepared by brothers Mitchell and Steven Rosenthal, combines Italian, Asian, French, and California styles with mixed results. When we last visited

Postrio, the sautéed salmon, for example, was a bit overcooked, but the accompanying plum glaze, wasabi mashed potatoes, and miso vinaigrette were outstanding. Despite the prime-time rush, service was friendly and infallible, as was the presentation.

FINANCIAL DISTRICT

Finding cheap eats, particularly for dinner, in the Financial District can be challenging since most diners in this neighborhood are footing the bill with corporate credit cards or expense accounts. Nevertheless, we've scouted out some affordable options.

MEALS FOR $10 OR LESS

Sophie's Cookhouse. 42 Columbus Ave. (at Jackson St.). ☎ 415/399-9254. No credit cards. Mon–Tues 11am–midnight Wed–Thurs 11am–2am. Fri– Sat 11am–3am; Sun 11am–5pm. Bus: 1, 15, 30X, 41, or 83. AMERICAN.

Locals may have grieved over the closure of Clown Alley, a historic late-night noshing spot once at this location; however, if it had to change hands, it couldn't have fallen into better ones. Much to the delight of San Francisco's thrifty gourmets, Paul Hodges (manager and wine steward extraordinaire formerly of Moose's and other SF faves), and Shawn Hall (interior designer of such hot spots as World Wrapps and Miss Pearl's Jam House) joined forces with Chef Mateo Granados (formerly at Masa's and 42 Degrees) to create an affordable and casual gourmet experience. What does that mean to your taste buds? Try succulent grilled fish sandwiches (bass, salmon, or halibut) for under six bucks. Or a burger, daily sausage, or roasted pork loin for under five. Salads, soups, and the "Sophie suggests" category guarantees something for everyone—vegetarians included. The cozy wine and beer bar, which stays open late, also makes this a great spot for a midnight snack.

MEALS FOR $20 OR LESS

Cafe Bastille. 22 Belden Place (between Pine and Bush sts.). ☎ 415/986-5673. Main courses $8–$16. AE, MC, V. Mon–Sat 11am to 11pm. Cable car: California St. line. Bus: 2, 3, 4, 9X, 15, 31AX, 31BX, 38AX, 38BX, or 81X. FRENCH.

Tucked in an adorable alley in the not-so-cute Financial District is a row of restaurants likely to conjure up memories of Europe. Cafe Bastille was clearly in sync with this ambience when they designed their bistro—French food and playfully Euro decor. The fare features soups, salads, crepes, sandwiches, and a small selection of entrees. The bustling upstairs and basement dining rooms and the live jazz (Thursday and Friday nights) make Europeans feel right at home and keep locals coming back.

✪ **Tadich Grill.** 240 California St. (between Battery and Front sts.). ☎ 415/391-1849. Reservations not accepted. Main courses $12–$19. MC, V. Mon–Fri 11am–9:30pm, Sat 11:30am–9:30pm. All Market St. buses. Muni Metro; All Market St. trams. SEAFOOD.

This venerated California institution arrived with the gold rush in 1849 and claims to be the very first to broil seafood over mesquite charcoal, back in the early 1920s. For a light meal you might try one of the delicious seafood salads, such as shrimp Louis. Hot dishes include baked avocado with shrimp diablo, baked casserole of stuffed turbot with crab and shrimp à la Newburg, and charcoal-broiled petrale sole with butter sauce, a local favorite. Almost everyone orders a side of the big, tasty French fries.

Yank Sing. 427 Battery St. (between Clay and Washington sts.). ☎ 415/781-1111. Dim sum $2–$4.75 for 3 to 4 pieces. AE, DC, MC, V. Mon–Fri 11am–3pm. Cable car: California St. line. Bus: 1 or 42. CHINESE.

Loosely translated as "a delight of the heart," Yank Sing does dim sum like no other restaurant in America, managing to be both first rate and affordable. Confident, experienced servers take the nervousness out of novices—they're good at guessing your gastric threshold. Most dim sum dishes are dumplings filled with savory concoctions of pork, beef, fish, or vegetables. Congees (porridges), spareribs, stuffed crab claws, scallion pancakes, shrimp balls, pork buns, and other palate-pleasers complete the menu. Like any good dim sum meal, you get to choose the small dishes from a cart that's continually wheeled around the dining room. *Tip:* Sit by the kitchen and you're guaranteed to get it while it's hot. There's a second location at 49 Stevenson St., off First Street (☎ 415/541-4949).

CHINATOWN
MEALS FOR $10 OR LESS

✪ **House of Nanking.** 919 Kearny St. (at Columbus Ave.). ☎ **415/421-1429.** Reservations not accepted. Main courses $4.95–$7.95. No credit cards. Mon–Fri. 11am–10pm, Sat noon–10pm, Sun 4–10pm. Bus: 9, 12, 15, or 30. CHINESE.

To the unknowing passerby, the shoe-box-sized House of Nanking has "greasy dive" written all over it. To its legion of fans, however, the wait, sometimes up to an hour, is worth what's on the plate. Located on the edge of Chinatown just off Columbus Avenue, this inconspicuous little diner is one of San Francisco's worst-kept secrets. When the line is reasonable, we drop by for a plate of pot stickers (still the best we've ever tasted) and chef/owner Peter Fang's signature shrimp-and-green-onion pancake, served with peanut sauce. Seating is tight, so prepare to be bumped around a bit, and don't expect good service; it's all part of the Nanking experience.

Sam Wo. 813 Washington St. (by Grant Ave.). ☎ **415/982-0596.** Reservations not accepted. Main courses $4–$5. No credit cards. Mon–Sat 11am–3am, Sun 12:30–9:30pm. Bus: 15, 30, 41, or 45. CHINESE.

A quick fix for late-night munchies, Sam's is a total dive that's well known and often packed. The restaurant's two pocket-size dining rooms are located on top of each other on the second and third floors—take the stairs past the first-floor kitchen. You'll have to share a table, but the mingling is almost as good as the food. The house specialty is jook, a thick rice gruel flavored with fish, shrimp, chicken, beef, or pork; the best is Sampan, made with rice and seafood. Try sweet-and-sour pork rice, wonton soup with duck, or a roast-pork/rice-noodle roll. More traditional fried noodles and rice plates are available too.

MEALS FOR $20 OR LESS

Brandy Ho's Hunan Food. 217 Columbus Ave. (at Pacific Ave.). ☎ **415/788-7527.** Reservations accepted. Main courses $8–$13. AE, DC, DISC, MC, V. Sun–Thurs 11:30am–11pm, Fri–Sat 11:30am–midnight. Bus: 15 or 41. CHINESE.

Fancy black-and-white granite tabletops and a large, open kitchen give you the first clue that the food here is a cut above the usual Hunan fare. Take our advice and start immediately with the fried dumplings (in sweet-and-sour sauce) or cold chicken salad. Next, move on to the fish-ball soup with spinach, bamboo shoots, noodles, and other goodies. The best main course is Three Delicacies, a combination of scallops, shrimp, and chicken with onion, bell pepper, and bamboo shoots, seasoned with ginger, garlic, and wine, and served with black-bean sauce. Most dishes here are quite hot and spicy, but the kitchen will adjust the level to meet your taste. There is a small selection of wines and beers, including plum wine and sake.

NORTH BEACH & FISHERMAN'S WHARF
MEALS FOR $10 OR LESS

Caffè Freddy's. 901 Columbus Ave. (corner of Lombard St.). ☎ **415/922-0151.** Reservations accepted. Main courses $2–$8 brunch; $4–$7 lunch; $5–$8 dinner. MC, V. Mon–Fri 10am–10pm, Sat 9am–10pm, Sun 9am–9pm. Bus: 15 or 41. ITALIAN.

Recognizable by the large, painted palms that flank the doorway, Caffe Freddy's attracts a young, hungry, and low-budgeted clientele that comes for the generous servings at generous prices. Pizzas, pastas, sandwiches, salads, and a large assortment of appetizers line the menu—try the antipasti plate of bruschetta, fresh melon, ham, sun-dried tomatoes, and pesto. Start with the warm cabbage salad with goat cheese, currants, walnuts, rosemary, and spinach, then move on to the house specialty: grilled polenta topped with a variety of meats, cheeses, and vegetables. It's not the best Italian food you'll ever eat, but it's good, cheap, and there's plenty of it.

Golden Boy Pizza. 542 Green St. (between Stockton and Grant aves.). ☎ **415/982-9738.** Slices $2–$2.75. No credit cards. Sun–Thurs 11:30am–11pm, Fri–Sat 11:30am–midnight. Bus: 15, 30, 45, 39, or 41. ITALIAN.

Pass by Golden Boy when the bars are hopping in North Beach and you'll find a crowd of inebriated sorts savoring steamy slices. But you don't have to be drunk to enjoy the big doughy Italian-style pizza that's served here. Locals have flocked here for years to fill up on one of the cheapest and cheesiest meals in town. Expect to take your feast to go—there are only a few bar seats inside.

Il Pollaio. 555 Columbus Ave. (between Green and Union sts.). ☎ **415/362-7727.** $5.50–$12.50. AE, MC, V. Mon–Sat 11:30am–9pm. Bus: 15, 30, 39, 41. Cable car: Powell-Mason line. ITALIAN/ARGENTINEAN.

Simple, affordable, and consistently delicious is a winning combination at Il Pollaio. The dining room is casual and the menu simple, but the tangy, rotisserie chicken is so moist it practically falls off the bone. Each meal is served with a choice of salads, and if you're not in the mood for chicken, opt for Italian sausage, rabbit, or lamb.

✪ L'Osteria del Forno. 519 Columbus Ave. (between Green and Union sts.). ☎ **415/982-1124.** Sandwiches $4.50–$8; pizzas $10–$13; main courses $2.50–$7.95. No credit cards. Mon–Wed 11am–10pm, Fri–Sat 11am–10:30pm, Sun noon–10pm. Bus: 15 or 41. ITALIAN.

L'Osteria del Forno may only be slightly larger than a walk-in closet, but it's one of the top three Italian restaurants in North Beach. Peer in the window facing Columbus Avenue, and you'll probably see two Italian women with their hair up, sweating from the heat of their brick-lined oven that cranks out the best focaccia and focaccia sandwiches in the city. There's no pomp or circumstance involved: Locals come here strictly to eat. The menu features a variety of superb pizzas and fresh pastas, plus a few daily specials (pray for the roast pork braised in milk). Small baskets of warm focaccia bread keep you going till the entrees arrive, which should always be accompanied by a glass of the house red.

⑤ Mario's Bohemian Cigar Store. 566 Columbus Ave. ☎ **415/362-0536.** Sandwiches $5–$6. No credit cards. Daily 10am–11pm. Closed Dec 24–Jan 1. Bus: 15, 30, 41, or 45. ITALIAN.

Across the street from Washington Square, Mario's is one of North Beach's most popular neighborhood hangouts. The century-old bar, which is small, well worn, and perpetually busy, is best known for its focaccia sandwiches, including meatball or eggplant. Wash it all down with an excellent cappuccino or a house Campari as you watch the tourists stroll by. And no, they don't sell cigars.

⑤ Pasta Pomodoro. 655 Union St. (at Columbus Ave.). ☎ **415/399-0300.** Main courses $3.95–$6.50. No checks or credit cards. Mon–Fri 11am–11pm, Sat noon–midnight, Sun noon–11pm. ITALIAN.

If you're looking for a good, cheap meal in North Beach, this place across from Washington Square can't be beat. There's usually a 20-minute wait for a table, but once seated you'll be promptly served. All dishes are fresh and sizable, and best of all, they cost a third of what you'll pay elsewhere. Winners include the spaghetti frutti di mare, with calamari, mussels, scallops, tomato, garlic and wine, or cavatappi pollo, with roast chicken, sun-dried tomatoes, cream, mushrooms, and Parmesan; both are under $7. Avoid the cappellini Pomodoro or ask for extra sauce—it tends to be dry. Their second location, at 2027 Chestnut St., at Fillmore (☎ 415/474-3400), is equally good, but cramped and noisy.

San Francisco Art Institute Cafe. 800 Chestnut St. (at Jones and Leavenworth sts.). ☎ **415/749-4567.** Main courses $4–$6. No credit cards. Fall–spring Mon–Fri 9am–9pm, Sat 9am–4pm, summer Mon–Sat 9am–2pm. Bus: 30. Cable car: Powell-Hyde and Powell-Mason lines. DELI.

One of the best kept secrets in San Francisco, this cafe offers fresh, affordable fare for Art Institute students and in-the-know residents and tourists. The food itself, though tasty, is not actually the draw; it's the view (you may have seen it in the movie *Copycat*—its exterior was the outside of Sigourney Weaver's ridiculously chic apartment). From here you'll get a sunny, birds-eye dose of the San Francisco Bay and a meal for around $5.

MEALS FOR $20 OR LESS

Gira Polli. 659 Union St. (at Columbus Ave.). ☎ **415/434-4472.** Reservations recommended. Main courses $7.50–$12.50. AE, MC, V. Mon–Sun 4:30–9:30pm. Bus: 15, 30, 39, 41, or 45. ITALIAN.

A favorite of ours is the Gira Polli Special: a foil-lined bag filled with half a wood-fired chicken (scrumptious), Palermo potatoes (the best in the city), a fresh garden salad, perfectly cooked vegetables, and a soft roll—all for under $10. *Tip:* On sunny days, there's no better place in North Beach for a picnic lunch than Washington Square right across the street.

WORTH A SPLURGE

Bix. 56 Gold St. (between Sansome and Montgomery sts.). ☎ **415/433-6300.** Reservations recommended. Main courses $5–$12 lunch, $11–$25 dinner. AE, CB, DC, DISC, MC, V. Mon–Thurs 11:30am–11pm, Fri–Sat 11:30am–midnight, Sun 5–10pm. Bus: 15, 30, 41, or 45. CALIFORNIA.

Bix is better known for its martinis than its menu. Curving Honduran mahogany, massive silver columns, and deco-style lighting set the stage for live music and dancing, though most locals settle for chatting with the friendly bartenders and noshing on appetizers. While the ultra-stylish setting tends to overshadow the food, Bix actually serves some pretty good grub. The lobster linguine with fresh prawns and mussels in a sun-dried tomato broth is the undisputed favorite, followed by the grilled filet mignon with mushrooms and chicken hash à la Bix.

Moose's. 1652 Stockton St. (between Filbert and Union sts.). ☎ **415/989-7800.** Reservations recommended. Main courses $8.50–$25. AE, CB, DC, MC, V. Mon–Thurs 11:30am–11pm; Fri–Sat 11:30am–midnight, Sun 10:30am–11pm. Bus: 15, 30, 41, or 45. CALIFORNIA.

This is where Nob Hill socialites and local politicians come to dine and be seen. But Moose's is not just an image. Everything that comes out of Moose's kitchen is way above par. The appetizers are innovative, fresh, and well-balanced (try Mediterranean fish soup with rouille and croutons that's cooked in the wood-fired oven), and the main courses (especially the meats) are perfectly prepared. The menu changes every few months and might include a grilled veal chop with potato galette and a variety of pasta, chicken, and fish dishes.

COW HOLLOW/PACIFIC HEIGHTS/THE MARINA DISTRICT

If you find yourself in this neck of the woods around lunchtime, you might opt for a picnic in the Marina Green, a popular recreational park with fantastic views of the

Bay. The **Marina Safeway,** 15 Marina Blvd. (☎ **415/563-4946**) is the perfect place to pick up fresh-baked breads, gourmet cheeses, and other foodstuffs.

MEALS FOR $10 OR LESS

✪ **Doidge's.** 2217 Union St. (between Fillmore and Steiner sts.). ☎ **415/921-2149.** Reservations accepted and essential on weekends. Breakfast $5–$10; lunch $5–$8. MC, V. Mon–Fri 8am–1:45pm, Sat–Sun 8am–2:45pm. Bus: 41 or 45. AMERICAN.

Doidge's is sweet, small, and always packed, serving up one of the better breakfasts in San Francisco since 1971. Doidge's fame derives from eggs Benedict; eggs Florentine runs a close second, prepared with thinly sliced Motherlode ham. Invariably the menu includes a gourmet omelet packed with luscious combinations, and to delight the kid in you, hot chocolate comes in your very own teapot. The six seats at the original mahogany counter are still the most coveted by locals.

✪ **La Canasta.** 2219 Filbert St. (at Fillmore St.). ☎ **415/921-3003.** Main courses $2.80–$6.15. No credit cards. Mon–Sat 11am–10pm. Bus: 22, 41, or 45. MEXICAN.

Unless you forge to the Mission District, burritos don't get much better (or bigger) than those served at this tiny take-out establishment where you can stuff yourself with a huge chicken burrito for a mere $4.80. There are no seats, though, so you'll just have to find another place to devour your grub; fortunately, the Marina Green is a short walk away and offers a million-dollar view of Golden Gate Bridge and the Bay. There's another location at 3006 Buchanan St. (☎ 415/474-2627).

✪ **Mel's Diner.** 2165 Lombard St. (at Fillmore St.). ☎ **415/921-3039.** Reservations not accepted. Main courses $4–$5.50 breakfast, $6–$8 lunch, $8–$12 dinner. No credit cards. Sun–Thurs 6am–3am; Fri–Sat 24 hr (Lombard location only). Bus: 22, 43, or 30. AMERICAN.

Sure, it's contrived, touristy, and not even that good, but when you get that urge for a chocolate shake and banana cream pie around midnight, no other place in the city comes through like Mel's. Modeled after a classic 1950s diner right down to the nickel jukebox at each table, Mel's harks back to the halcyon days when cholesterol and fried foods didn't stroke your guilty conscience with every greasy, wonderful bite. Too bad the prices don't reflect the '50s; a burger with fries and a coke runs about $8, and they don't take credit cards. There's another Mel's at 3355 Geary St., at Stanyan Street (☎ 415/387-2244).

Sweet Heat. 3324 Steiner St. (between Lombard and Chestnut sts.). ☎ **415/474-9191.** Reservations not accepted. All entrees under $6. MC, V. Daily 11am–midnight. Bus: 22, 28, 30, 30X, 43, or 76. MEXICAN.

If you're shopping on Chestnut Street and looking for a light lunch, check out this casual place offering healthful Mexican food. Far from traditional Mexican fare, Sweet Heat has capitalized on California's love affair with old-style food prepared in new ways, and the results are impressive. Prices are as low as $3.95 for a veggie burrito with grilled zucchini, eggplant, and roasted corn, or $4.25 for a tasty scallop burrito with green chile chutney. On a sunny day, the back patio is a great place to kick back and eat. The newest location, at 1725 Haight St. (☎ 415/387-8845), is equally popular and delicious.

World Wrapps. 2257 Chestnut St. (between Pierce and Scott sts.). ☎ **415/563-9727.** Burritos $3.95–$6.95. No credit cards. Daily 8am–11pm. Bus: 22, 28, 30, 43, 76. INTERNATIONAL.

You'll know you've found World Wrapps when you come upon a trendy, health-conscious crowd standing in line on yuppified Chestnut Street. It's yet another version of San Francisco's beloved burrito, only this time it's not Mexican-influenced, but rather a tortilla filled with your choice of foodstuffs from around the world (hence the name). Fresh ingredients and cheap prices make World Wrapps a perfect place for a quick bite.

✪ **Zinzino.** 2355 Chestnut St. (at Divisadero St.). ☎ **415/346-6623.** Reservations for 6 or more only. Main courses: $4–$9 brunch, $7.50–$9.50 lunch and dinner. MC, V. Tues–Fri. 5:30–10pm, Sat–Sun 10am–4pm, 5:30–10pm. Bus: 22 or 30. ITALIAN.

Zinzino may look like a tiny trattoria from the outside, but you could fit a small nuclear sub inside this former Laundromat. Italian movie posters, magazines, and furnishings evoke memories of past vacations, but we rarely recall the food in Italy being this good (and certainly not this cheap). Start off with the crispy calamari (second only to Scala's Earth and Turf) or the roasted jumbo prawns wrapped in crisp pancetta and bathed in a tangy balsamic reduction sauce. The perfect light lunch for two is a half eggplant, half house-spiced Italian sausage pizza (a mere $4.50 per person), complemented by the requisite glass of Chianti at the marble-topped wine bar. The huge focaccia sandwiches are also a big hit with the handful of locals who are privy to this San Francisco sleeper.

MEALS FOR $20 OR LESS

✪ **Greens Restaurant.** Building A, Fort Mason Center (enter Fort Mason opposite the Safeway at Buchanan and Marina sts.). ☎ **415/771-6222.** Reservations recommended 2 weeks in advance. Main courses $10–$13; fixed-priced dinner $38; brunch $7–$10. DISC, MC, V. Restaurant: Mon 5:30–9:15pm; Tues–Fri 11:30am–2pm, 5:30–9:15pm; Sat 11:30 am–2:30pm, 6–9pm; Sun 10am–2pm. Greens to Go: Mon–Fri 8:30am–9:30pm; Sat 8am–4pm; Sun 9am–3:30pm. Bus: 28 or 30. VEGETARIAN.

Executive chef Annie Somerville (author of *Fields of Greens*) cooks with the seasons using local organic produce, in an old warehouse with enormous windows overlooking the bridge and the bay. A weeknight dinner might feature such appetizers as tomato, white-bean, and sorrel soup, or grilled asparagus with lemon, Parmesan cheese, and watercress. Main courses might include spring vegetable risotto with asparagus, peas, shiitake and crimini mushrooms, and Parmesan cheese, or Sri Lankan curry made of new potatoes, cauliflower, carrots, peppers, and snap peas stewed with tomatoes, coconut milk, ginger, and Sri Lankan spices. A five-course dinner is served on Saturday, and an extensive wine list is available. The adjacent bakery sells homemade breads, sandwiches, soups, salads, and pastries to take home.

✪ **Pane e Vino.** 3011 Steiner St. (at Union St.). ☎ **415/346-2111.** Reservations recommended. Main courses $7.50–$18. AE, MC, V. Mon–Sat 11:30am–2:30pm; daily 5–10pm. Bus: 41 or 45. ITALIAN.

Pane e Vino is one of San Francisco's most authentic Italian restaurants. The food is consistently excellent (careful not to fill up on the outstanding breads), the prices reasonable, and the staff always smooth and efficient under pressure. The two small dining rooms, separated by an open kitchen that emanates heavenly aromas, offer only limited seating, so expect a wait even if you have reservations. Fare includes a hugely popular chilled artichoke stuffed with bread and tomatoes; an antipasti of mixed grilled vegetables, which always spurns a fork fight; and a broad selection of pastas. Other specialties are grilled fish and meat dishes. Top dessert picks are any of the Italian ice creams, the crème caramel, and, of course, the creamy tiramisu.

WORTH A SPLURGE

✪ **Harris'.** 2100 Van Ness Ave. (at Pacific Ave.). ☎ **415/673-1888.** Reservations recommended. Main courses $18–$30. AE, CB, DC, DISC, JCB, MC, V. Mon–Fri 6–11pm, Sat–Sun 5–11pm. Bus: 38 or 45. AMERICAN.

Proprietor Ann Lee Harris knows steaks; she grew up on a cattle ranch and married the owner of the largest feedlot in California. In 1976 the couple opened the Harris Ranch Restaurant on Interstate 5 in central California, where they built a rock-solid reputation up and down the coast. The steaks, which can be seen hanging in a glass aging room, are cut thick—either New York–style or T-bone—and are served with a baked potato and seasonal vegetables. Harris' also offers roast duckling, lamb chops, fresh fish, lobster, venison, buffalo, and other types of game. Those who like animal brains rave about the restaurant's sautéed beef brains in brown butter.

✪ La Folie. 2316 Polk St. (between Green and Union sts.). ☎ 415/776-5577. Reservations recommended. Main courses $22–$28. Five-course tasting menu $45. AE, DC, JCB, MC, V. Mon–Sat 5:30–10:30pm. Bus: 19, 41, 45, 47, 49, or 76. FRENCH.

The minute you walk through the door, you'll know why this is a local favorite. The country-French decor is tasteful but not too serious, with whimsical chandeliers and a cloudy sky painted overhead. The staff is friendly, knowledgeable, and very accommodating; the food is outstanding. Unlike many renowned chefs, La Folie's Roland Passot is in the kitchen nightly, and it shows. Each of his California-influenced French creations are architectural and culinary masterpieces. Best of all, they're served in a relaxed and comfortable environment. Start with an appetizer like roast quail and foie gras with salad. Main courses are not petite as in many French restaurants, and all are accompanied by flavorful and well-balanced sauces. Try the rôti of quail and squab stuffed with wild mushrooms and wrapped in crispy potato strings, or the roast venison with vegetables, quince, and huckleberry sauce.

✪ PlumpJack Café. 3127 Fillmore St. (between Filbert and Greenwich sts.). ☎ 415/563-4755. Reservations recommended. Main courses $14–$20. AE, MC, V. Mon–Fri 11:30am–2pm and 5:30–10:30pm, Sat 5:30–10:30pm. Bus: 41 or 45. CALIFORNIA/MEDITERRANEAN.

Wildly popular among San Francisco's trend-setters, this small Cow Hollow restaurant is the "in" place to dine, partly because it's run by one of the Getty clan (as in J. Paul), but mostly because chef Maria Helm's food is just plain good and the whimsical decor is a veritable work of art. Though the menu changes weekly, you might find roasted portobello mushroom with vegetable stuffing, reggiano, and cippolini onions; or roast local halibut with grilled asparagus and blood-orange chervil vinaigrette. Top it off with an apricot soufflé or the chocolate Kahlua torte. The extensive California wine list is sold at next to retail, with many wines available by the glass.

JAPANTOWN

Isobune. 1737 Post St. (in the Japan Center). ☎ 415/563-1030. Sushi $1.20–$2.95. MC, V. Daily 11:30am–10pm. Bus: 2, 3, 4, 22, or 38. SUSHI.

Unless you arrive early, there's almost always a short wait to pull up a chair around this enormous oval sushi bar. But once you're seated, the wait is over. Right before your eyes, plates and plates of sushi pass by on a circling sushi tug boat floating in a minuscule canal that encircles the bar. If you see something you like, just grab it (we mean food, of course), enjoy, and the wait person will tally up the damages at the end (they can tell how much you've eaten by the number of empty plates). It's not the best sushi in town, but it's relatively cheap and the atmosphere is fun.

Mifune. 1737 Post St. (in the Japan Center). ☎ 415/922-0337. Main courses $3.50–$14.50. AE, DC, DISC, MC, V. Daily 11am–9:30pm. Bus: 2, 3, 4, 22, or 38. JAPANESE.

Slide into one of the Japanese-style booths and order a homemade udon and soba noodles dinner—it's the house specialty. You might go for one of the donburi dishes or a full-blown tempura dinner. Mifune has been serving traditional Japanese food for 15 years and has a steady clientele of folks who are happy with the fare and ecstatic about the prices.

CIVIC CENTER & ENVIRONS
MEALS FOR $10 OR LESS

Hard Rock Café. 1699 Van Ness Ave. (at Sacramento St.). ☎ **415/885-1699.** Reservations sometimes accepted (depending on season). Main courses $5.50–$14. AE, MC, V. Sun–Thurs 11:30am–11pm, Fri–Sat 11:30am–midnight. Cable car: California St. line. Bus: 1. AMERICAN.

Like its affiliates around the world, this loud, nostalgia-laden establishment serves big portions of decent bar food (and plenty of blaring music) at moderate prices to an almost exclusively tourist clientele. Most courses come with salad and a side dish, so if you avoid the most expensive items, it's entirely possible to leave virtually stuffed for around $10.

Tommy's Joynt. 1109 Geary St. (at Van Ness Ave.). ☎ **415/775-4216.** Reservations not accepted. Main courses $4–$7. No credit cards. Daily 11am–2am. Bus: 2, 3, 4, or 38. AMERICAN.

With its colorful mural exterior, it's hard to miss Tommy's, a late-night favorite for those in search of a cheap and hearty meal. The interior is crammed with suspended hockey sticks, bamboo poles with attached stuffed birds, a mounted buffalo head, an ancient piano, rusty firearms, fading prints, a beer-guzzling lion, and Santa Claus masks. The cafeteria-style buffet offers a cornucopia of rib-clinging à la carte dishes, such as buffalo stew, corned beef, meatballs, and mashed potatoes. There's also tons of seating and almost 100 varieties of beer.

MEALS FOR $20 OR LESS

✪ **Hayes Street Grill.** 320 Hayes St. (near Franklin St.). ☎ **415/863-5545.** Reservations recommended. Main courses $13.50–$18.25 AE, DC, MC, V. Mon–Fri 11:30am–2pm and 5–8:30pm, Sat 6–10:30pm, Sun 5–8:30pm. Bus: 19, 31, or 38. SEAFOOD.

This small, no-nonsense seafood restaurant has built a solid reputation among San Francisco's picky epicureans for its impeccably fresh fish. Choices ranging from Hawaiian swordfish to Puget Sound salmon, cooked to perfection, naturally, are served with your choice of sauce (Szechuan peanut, tomato salsa, herb shallot butter) and a side of their signature french fries. Fancier seafood specials are available too, like bay scallops with chanterelle and shiitake mushrooms, and an impressive selection of dirt-fresh salads and local grilled meats. For dessert, indulge in the heavenly crème brûlée.

✪ **Zuni Café.** 1658 Market St. (at Franklin St.). ☎ **415/552-2522.** Reservations recommended. Main courses $16–$22.50. AE, MC, V. Tues–Sat 7:30am–midnight, Sun 7:30am–11pm. Muni Metro: All Market St. trams. Bus: 6, 7, 71, or 75. MEDITERRANEAN.

Zuni Café is one of our favorite places in the city to have lunch (when it's easier to refrain from a cocktail-and-oyster splurge at the bar). Its expansive windows and prime Market Street location guarantee good people-watching. For the full effect, sit at the bustling, copper-topped bar and peruse the foot-long oyster menu (half a dozen or so varieties on hand at all times); you can also sit in the stylish, exposed-brick dining room or on the outdoor patio. The changing menu always includes meat and fish, either grilled or braised in the kitchen's brick oven. *Warning:* The dinner bill can quickly become expensive, but if you're dying for the vibe, order the chicken for two, a whole bird served with Tuscan bread and salad. At $24 it's a bit of a rip-off, but the meal will definitely fill two and keep you within your budget. Also, the wait staff can sometimes be unpleasant.

SOUTH OF MARKET
MEALS FOR $10 OR LESS

Hamburger Mary's. 1582 Folsom St. (at Twelfth St.). ☎ **415/626-5767.** Reservations recommended. Breakfast $5–$9; main courses $6–$9. AE, DC, DISC, MC, V. Mon–Thurs 11am–1am, Fri 11:30am–2am, Sat 10am–2am, Sun 10am–1am. Bus: 9, 12, 42, or 47. AMERICAN.

San Francisco's most alternative burger joint serves everyone from the late-night SoMa dance club crowd to gays, lesbians, and bikers. The restaurant's kitsch decor includes thrift-shop floral wallpaper, family photos, garage-sale prints, stained glass, religious drawings, and Oriental screens. You'll get to know the bar well: It's where you'll stand with the tattooed masses while you wait for a table. Don't despair: They mix a good drink, and people-watching is what you're here for anyway. If you're not up for one their famous greasy burgers, there's a variety of sandwiches, salads, and vegetarian dishes.

Manora's Thai Cuisine. 1600 Folsom St. (at Twelfth St.). ☎ **415/861-6224.** Main courses $5.95–$10. MC, V. Mon–Fri 11:30am–2:30pm and 5–10:30pm; Sat 5–10:30pm; Sun 5–10pm. Bus: 9, 12, or 42. THAI.

Manora's cranks out some of the best Thai in town and is well worth a jaunt to its SoMa location. But this is no relaxed dining affair. It's perpetually packed (unless you come early) and you'll be seated sardinelike at one of the cramped and well-appointed tables. During the dinner rush, the noise level can make conversation almost impossible among larger parties, but the food is so good, you'll probably prefer to turn your head to your plate. Start with a Thai iced-tea or coffee and one of the tangy soups, or the chicken satay, which comes with a decadent peanut sauce. Follow up with any of the excellent dinner dishes, which should be shared, and a side of rice. The options are endless, including a vast array of vegetarian plates. Every dish arrives almost seconds after you order it, which is great if you're famished, a bummer if you were planning a long, leisurely dinner. Come before seven or after nine if you don't want a loud, rushed meal.

MEALS FOR $20 OR LESS

✪ **Bizou.** 598 Fourth St. (at Brannan St.). ☎ **415/543-2222.** Reservations recommended. Main courses $10.50–$17.50. AE, MC, V. Mon–Fri 11:30am–2:30pm; Mon–Thurs 5:30–10pm, Fri–Sat 5:30–10:30pm. Bus: 15, 30, 32, 42, or 45. FRENCH/ITALIAN.

Bizou's friendly and professional wait staff, fresh and creative fare, and sizable portions keep locals coming back again and again. The menu's starters include pizzas, grilled calamari with a citrus salsa and salsa verde, and batter-fried green beans with dipping sauce. As for main courses, you may find a sautéed sea bass with olive couscous, fennel, bay leaf, and dried orange peel; or grilled veal tenderloin with sautéed spinach, and garlic mashed potatoes in a buttery mustard sauce. Our only complaint is that almost every dish is so rich and flavorful (including the salads), you're likely to experience a bit of a sensory overload.

✪ **Fringale Restaurant.** 570 Fourth St. (between Brannan and Bryant sts.). ☎ **415/543-0573.** Reservations recommended. Main courses $9–$18; lunch $4–$12. AE, MC, V. Mon–Fri 11:30am–2:30pm; Mon–Sat 5:30–10:30pm. Bus: 30 or 45. FRENCH.

One of San Francisco's top restaurants, Fringale—French colloquial for "sudden urge to eat"—has enjoyed a week-long waiting list since the day chef/co-owner Gerald Hirigoyen first opened this small SoMa bistro. Sponged, eggshell-blue walls and other muted sand and earth tones provide a serene dining environment, which is all but shattered when the 15-table room inevitably fills with Hirigoyen's fans. For starters, try the potato and goat cheese galette with black olives. Among the dozen or so main courses you might discover a filet of tuna basquaise; pork tenderloin confit with onion and apple marmalade; or macaroni gratin with mushrooms. Desserts are worth savoring, too, particularly the hazelnut and roasted almond mousse cake or the signature crème brûlée with vanilla bean.

✪ **Lulu.** 816 Folsom St. (at Fourth St.). ☎ **415/495-5775.** Reservations recommended. Main courses $7–$13 lunch, $9–$17 dinner. AE, MC, V. Mon–Fri 7am–midnight, Sat 9am–midnight, Sun 9am–11pm. Bus: 15, 30, 32, 42, or 45. CONTINENTAL.

The energy created by the enormous, warehouse dining room, the pizzas sliding in and out of the wood-fired oven, and the chefs communicating via headsets that make a trip to Lulu's not a meal but a beloved event. The main room seats 170, but even while you sit amidst a sea of stylish diners, the room somehow feels warm and convivial. Don't pass up the roasted mussels piled high on an iron skillet; the chopped salad with lemon, anchovies, and tomatoes; or the pork loin with fennel, garlic, and olive oil. Everything is served "family style" and is meant to be shared. If you're carefully watching your cash, you'll survive unscathed by ordering a pizza and a few appetizers. Do save room for dessert and opt for the gooey chocolate cake.

WORTH A SPLURGE

✪ **Boulevard.** 1 Mission St. (at Embarcadero and Steuart St.). ☎ **415/543-6084.** Reservations recommended. Main courses $17.75–$22. AE, DC, MC, V. Mon–Fri 11:30am–2pm; daily 5:30–10:30pm. Bus: 15, 30, 32, 42, or 45. AMERICAN.

Art nouveau brick ceilings, floral banquettes, and fluid, tulip-shaped lamps set a dramatic scene for equally impressive dishes. Start with the delicate, soft egg ravioli with spinach, ricotta, and shaved white truffles; then embark on such wonderful concoctions as wood-oven roasted sea bass on a bed of sun-dried tomato and roasted garlic mashed potatoes. Vegetarian items, such as roasted portobello mushrooms layered with mashed sweet potatoes, are also offered.

HAIGHT-ASHBURY

✪ **Cha Cha Cha.** 1801 Haight St. (at Schrader St.). ☎ **415/386-5758.** Reservations not accepted. Tapas $4–$7; main courses $9–$13. No credit cards. Mon–Sun 11:30am–4pm; Sun–Thurs 5–11pm, Fri–Sat 5–11:30pm. Muni Metro: N line. Bus: 6, 7, 66, 71, or 73. CARIBBEAN.

Cha Cha Cha is not a meal, it's an experience. Put your name on the mile-long list, crowd into the minuscule bar, and drink sangria while you wait. When you do finally get seated (it usually takes at least an hour), you'll dine in a loud (and we mean loud) dining room with Santeria altars, banana trees, and plastic, tropical tablecloths. Order from the tapas menu and share the dishes family style (there are main courses, too). The fried calamari, fried new potatoes, Cajun shrimp, and mussels in saffron broth are all bursting with flavor and are accompanied by rich, luscious sauces. If your friends are in a partying mood, this is the kind of place you want to take them. If you want all the flavor without the festivities, come during lunch.

Ⓢ **Zona Rosa.** 1797 Haight St. (at Schrader St.). ☎ **415/668-7717.** Burritos $3.45–$4.83. No credit cards. Daily 11am–10:30pm. Muni Metro: N line. Bus: 6, 7, 66, 71, or 73. MEXICAN.

This is a great place to stop and get a cheap (and/or healthful) bite. The most popular items here are the burritos, which are made to order and include your choice of beans (refried, whole pinto, or black), meats, or vegetarian ingredients. You can sit on a stool at the window and watch the Haight Street freaks strolling by, relax at one of five colorful interior tables, or take it to go and head to Golden Gate Park (just two blocks away). Zona Rosa is one of the best burrito joints around.

THE RICHMOND DISTRICT
MEALS FOR $10 OR LESS

Fountain Court. 354 Clement St. (at Fifth Ave.). ☎ 415/668-1100. Reservations accepted. Most main courses $6.50–$10.50. AE, DC, MC, V. Daily 11am–3pm and 5–10pm. Bus: 2 or 44. SHANGHAI.

The decor is nothing special here, but the food is. We went with a crowd and ordered about a half-dozen dishes. Each was better than the next. Start with the pot stickers, which will arrive at your table in a bamboo steamer. A dining companion declared the garlic prawns better than sex—I don't know if I'd go that far, but they were pretty good. When we were here, the nightly specials were garlic crab (superb) and soft-shell turtle (less successful).

Ho and Ho Pastry. 309 Sixth Ave. (at Clement St.). ☎ 415/387-5700. 3 pieces for $1. No credit cards. Thurs–Tues 7am–6pm. Bus: 2, 4, 38, or 44. DIM SUM.

Step inside this tiny takeout shop where fresh-from-the-steamer dim sum is sold by the piece. Prices are ridiculously low, so buy plenty and head a few blocks north for a picnic in Golden Gate Park.

✪ **Hong Kong Flower Lounge.** 5322 Geary Blvd. (between 17th and 18th aves.). ☎ 415/668-8998. Most main dishes $5.95–$10.95; dim sum dishes $1.20–$3.20. AE, DISC, MC, V. Mon–Fri 11am–2:30pm, Sat–Sun 10am–2:30pm, daily 5–9:30pm. Bus: 1, 2, or 38. CHINESE/DIM SUM.

You know you're at a good Chinese restaurant when most people waiting for a table are Chinese. And if you come for dim sum (lunch only), be prepared to stand in line because you're not the only one who's heard this is the best in town. The Hong Kong Flower Lounge has been one of our very favorite restaurants for years. We never come for dinner, as it's pricey for Chinese, but come lunch time, it's a first-class budget banquet. Decor is upscale as Chinese restaurants go, and every little dish is nothing less than outstanding (and far less greasy than other dim sum spots). Don't pass up tarot cake, salt-fried shrimp, shark-fin soup, and the shrimp or beef crepes.

THE MISSION DISTRICT
MEALS FOR $10 OR LESS

La Cumbre. 515 Valencia St. (between 16th and 17th sts.). ☎ 415/863-8205. $3–$8. V, MC. Mon–Sat 11am–10pm, Sun noon–9pm. MEXICAN.

La Cumbre continually rates as one of the best spots for a San Francisco burrito. The ambience is nothing special; you order at the counter and eat at any of the available tables. But daytime or late night, you're sure to get a hearty, flavorful burrito here (there are plenty of other Mexican specialties, as well).

Roosevelt Tamale Parlor. 2817 24th St. (between Bryant and York sts.). ☎ 415/550-9213. $2–$8. No credit cards. Tues–Sun 10am–9:45pm. MEXICAN.

Roosevelt's may be the budget traveler's ultimate dream come true. As far as tamales go (and other Mexican dishes), the food here is nothing fancy, but it is certainly good. Best of all, you can fill yourself to the brim for under five bucks. The restaurant is dark, a little divelike, and filled with an eclectic mix: the young and the groovy, regular folks, and long-time customers. The place has been open since 1922.

MEALS FOR $20 OR LESS

✪ **Val 21.** 995 Valencia St. (at 21st St.). ☎ 415/821-6622. Reservations recommended. Main courses $11–$16. MC, V. Mon–Fri 5:30–10pm, Sat–Sun 10am–2pm and 5:30–10pm. Muni Metro: J line to 16th St. Station. CALIFORNIA.

Hip, eclectic decor, perpetually friendly service, and hefty portions of multiethnic fare have made Val 21 one of the Mission District's most popular restaurants. The menu changes frequently, although we've seen dishes like artichoke empanada, Southwestern blackened chicken, and grilled salmon in a red curry sauce; there's plenty of vegetarian plates, too. Sometimes the menu gets a little too creative, sending mixed messages to your taste buds, but the overall dining experience makes it worth the trip. Brunch is served on weekends.

WORTH A SPLURGE

Woodward's Garden. 1700 Mission St. (at Duboce Ave.). ☎ **415/621-7122.** Reservations required. Main courses $14–$17. MC, V. Four dinner seatings Wed–Sun 6, 6:30, 8, 8:30pm. Bus: 14, 26, or 49. AMERICAN.

If you find yourself parking along a dank industrial street where no decent restaurant would dare to set up shop, you're in the right place. Woodward's Garden, named after a turn-of-the-century amusement center in the same location, is the kind of gem many San Franciscans don't even know about. And it's a good thing: There are only nine tables in the entire place. Its simple decor and intimate (read tiny) environment make for romantic dining. And with so few tables, both the kitchen (formerly of Postrio and Greens) and the wait staff are attentive enough to make you feel they opened their doors just for you. Don't traipse down here without reservations or a car, for that matter.

AROUND TOWN
MEALS FOR $10 OR LESS

Pozole. 2337 Market St. (between Noe and Castro sts.). ☎ **415/626-2666.** Main courses $5.95–$7.95. No credit cards. Mon–Thurs 4–11pm, Fri–Sat noon–midnight, Sun noon–11pm. LATIN AMERICAN.

Beefcake waiters and waitresses in tank tops serve up fresh and healthy Latin American style food in this small, casual Upper Market restaurant. Both attitude and decor are vibrant here—Santeria altars and brightly colored walls are almost as flavorful as the fare. Local favorites include a quesadilla with black beans, roasted garlic, oven roasted tomatoes, and smoked chicken breast; chicken breast with a tangy mole sauce of dried fruit, dried chiles, and chocolate; or a snapper burrito with mango-jalapeño lime sauce.

The Ramp. 855 China Basin St. (at the end of Mariposa St.). ☎ **415/621-2378.** Main courses $4–$9.75. AE, MC. V. Food served daily 8am–4pm with live music and appetizers later in the day on Thurs–Sun; bar Sun–Thurs 8am–8pm, Fri–Sat 8am–1:30am. AMERICAN.

Lucky enough to be in San Francisco on one of those rare hot days? Well, don't waste those fleeting sunny moments lunching inside. Call for directions and head to The Ramp, one of in-the-know locals' favorite bay-side hangouts. Fare is of the basic-lunch variety: burgers, sandwiches, salads, and soups. But, the boatyard environment and patio seating make this an excellent place to dine in the sun (if you're especially ambitious you can head here for breakfast, too). In summer the place really rocks when live bands perform and tanned, cocktailing singles prowl the area.

5 The Top Attractions

✪ **Alcatraz Island.** Pier 41, near Fisherman's Wharf. ☎ **415/705-1045.** Admission (includes ferry trip and audio tour) $10 adults, $8.25 seniors 62 and older, $4.75 children 5–11. Winter daily 9:30am–2:45pm; summer daily 9:15am–4:15pm. Advance purchase advised. Ferries depart every half hour, at 15 and 45 minutes after the hour. Arrive at least 20 minutes before sailing time.

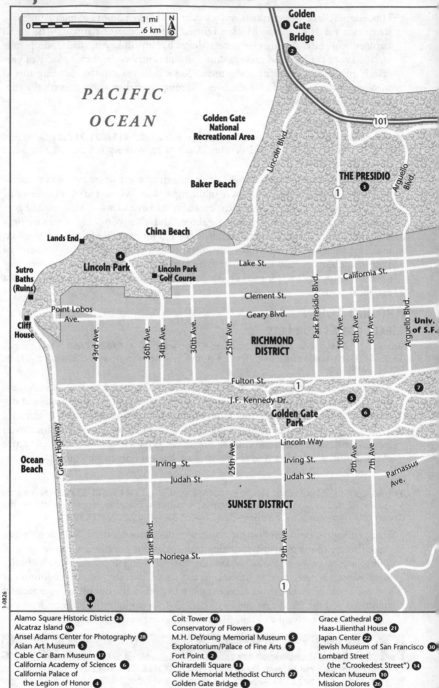

PACIFIC OCEAN

Golden Gate Bridge **1**

2

Golden Gate National Recreational Area

THE PRESIDIO **3**

Baker Beach

101

Lincoln Blvd.

Arguello Blvd.

China Beach

Lands End

Lincoln Park **4**

Lincoln Park Golf Course

Lake St.

California St.

Sutro Baths (Ruins)

Clement St.

Park Presidio Blvd.

Arguello Blvd.

Univ. of S.F.

Point Lobos Ave.

Geary Blvd.

Cliff House

43rd Ave.

36th Ave.

34th Ave.

30th Ave.

25th Ave.

10th Ave.

8th Ave.

6th Ave.

RICHMOND DISTRICT

Fulton St. **1**

7

J.F. Kennedy Dr. **5**

Golden Gate Park **6**

Lincoln Way

Great Highway

Ocean Beach

Irving St.

25th Ave.

Irving St.

9th Ave.

7th Ave.

Parnassus Ave.

Judah St.

Judah St.

SUNSET DISTRICT

Sunset Blvd.

19th Ave.

Noriega St.

1

8

1-0826

Alamo Square Historic District **24**
Alcatraz Island **9A**
Ansel Adams Center for Photography **28**
Asian Art Museum **5**
Cable Car Barn Museum **17**
California Academy of Sciences **6**
California Palace of
  the Legion of Honor **4**

Coit Tower **16**
Conservatory of Flowers **7**
M.H. DeYoung Memorial Museum **5**
Exploratorium/Palace of Fine Arts **9**
Fort Point **2**
Ghirardelli Square **13**
Glide Memorial Methodist Church **27**
Golden Gate Bridge **1**

Grace Cathedral **20**
Haas-Lilienthal House **21**
Japan Center **22**
Jewish Museum of San Francisco **30**
Lombard Street
  (the "Crookedest Street") **14**
Mexican Museum **10**
Mission Dolores **26**

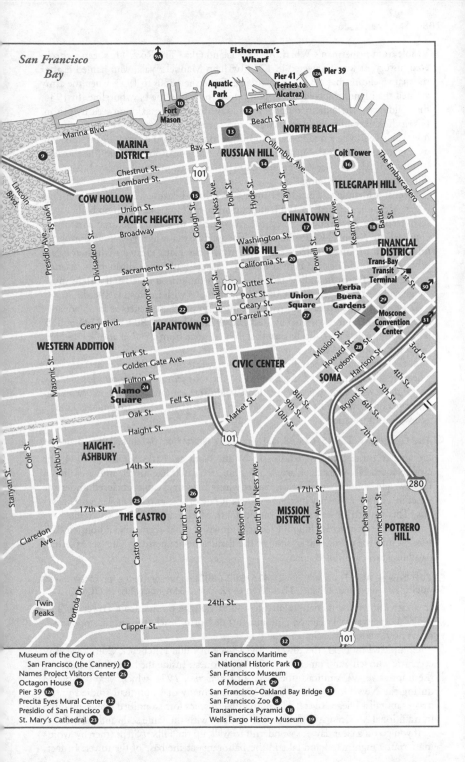

San Francisco Bay

Fisherman's Wharf

Aquatic Park

Fort Mason

Pier 41 (Ferries to Alcatraz)

Pier 39

Jefferson St.

Beach St.

NORTH BEACH

MARINA DISTRICT

Bay St.

RUSSIAN HILL

Coit Tower

Marina Blvd.

Chestnut St.

Lombard St.

Columbus Ave.

TELEGRAPH HILL

The Embarcadero

COW HOLLOW

Union St.

PACIFIC HEIGHTS

Broadway

Van Ness Ave.

Polk St.

Hyde St.

Taylor St.

CHINATOWN

Grant Ave.

Kearny St.

Battery St.

FINANCIAL DISTRICT

Lincoln Blvd.

Presidio Ave.

Divisadero St.

Sacramento St.

Washington St.

NOB HILL

California St.

Powell St.

Trans-Bay Transit Terminal

1st St.

Cough St.

Franklin St.

Sutter St.

Post St.

Geary St.

O'Farrell St.

Union Square

Yerba Buena Gardens

Moscone Convention Center

Fillmore St.

Geary Blvd.

JAPANTOWN

St. Mary's Cathedral

WESTERN ADDITION

Turk St.

Golden Gate Ave.

Fulton St.

CIVIC CENTER

Mission St.

Howard St.

Folsom St.

SOMA

Harrison St.

3rd St.

4th St.

5th St.

Masonic St.

Alamo Square

Fell St.

Oak St.

Haight St.

Market St.

8th St.

9th St.

10th St.

Bryant St.

6th St.

7th St.

Stanyan St.

Cole St.

Ashbury St.

HAIGHT-ASHBURY

14th St.

17th St.

South Van Ness Ave.

17th St.

280

Claredon Ave.

17th St.

THE CASTRO

Church St.

Dolores St.

Mission St.

MISSION DISTRICT

Potrero Ave.

Deharo St.

Connecticut St.

POTRERO HILL

Castro St.

Twin Peaks

Portola Dr.

24th St.

Clipper St.

101

Museum of the City of
 San Francisco (the Cannery) 12
Names Project Visitors Center 25
Octagon House 15
Pier 39 12A
Precita Eyes Mural Center 32
Presidio of San Francisco 3
St. Mary's Cathedral 23

San Francisco Maritime
 National Historic Park 11
San Francisco Museum
 of Modern Art 29
San Francisco–Oakland Bay Bridge 31
San Francisco Zoo 8
Transamerica Pyramid 18
Wells Fargo History Museum 19

Visible from Fisherman's Wharf, Alcatraz Island (aka "The Rock") has seen a checkered history. It was discovered in 1775 by Juan Manuel Ayala, who named it after the many pelicans that nested on the island. From the 1850s to 1933, when the army vacated the island, it served as a military post protecting the bay shoreline. In 1934, the buildings of the military outpost were converted into a maximum security prison. Given the sheer cliffs, treacherous tides, and currents, and frigid water temperatures, it was believed to be a totally escape-proof prison. Among the famous gangsters who were penned in cell blocks A through D were Al Capone, Robert Stroud (the so-called Birdman of Alcatraz because he was an expert in ornithological diseases), Machine Gun Kelly, and Alvin Karpis.

It cost a fortune to keep them imprisoned here because all supplies, including water, had to be shipped. In 1963, after an apparent escape in which no bodies were recovered, the government closed the prison, and in 1972 it became part of the Golden Gate National Recreation Area. The wildlife that was driven away during the military and prison years has begun to return—the black-crested night heron and other sea birds are nesting here again—and a new trail passes through the island's nature areas. Tours, including an audio tour of the prison block and a slide show, are given by park rangers, who entertain their guests with interesting anecdotes.

It's a popular excursion and space is limited, so purchase tickets as far in advance as possible. The tour is operated by **Red and White Fleet** (☎ 800/229-2784 or 415/ 546-2700); tickets may also be purchased in advance from the Red and White Fleet ticket office on Pier 41.

Wear comfortable shoes and take a heavy sweater or windbreaker because even when the sun's out, it's cold. Also, note that the tour requires climbing a lot of steps.

For those who want to get a closer look at Alcatraz without going ashore, two boat-tour operators offer short circumnavigation of the island. (See "Organized Tours," below, for information.)

✪ **The Cable Cars.** ☎ **415/673-6864.** Fares $2; $1 seniors from 6–7am and 9pm–midnight.

Designated official historic landmarks by the National Parks Service in 1964, the city's beloved cable cars clank across San Francisco's hills like mobile museum pieces. Each weighs about six tons and is hauled along by a steel cable, enclosed under the street in a center rail. They move at a constant rate of $9^1/_2$ m.p.h.—never more, never less. This may strike you as slow, but it doesn't feel that way when you're cresting an almost perpendicular hill and looking down at what seems like a bobsled dive straight into the ocean. But in spite of the thrills, they're perfectly safe (see "Getting Around," earlier in this chapter).

✪ **Coit Tower.** Atop Telegraph Hill. ☎ **415/362-0808.** Admission (to the top of the tower) $3 adults, $2 seniors and students, $1 children 6–12. Daily 10am–6pm. Bus: 39 ("Coit").

In a city known for its panoramic views and vantage points, Coit Tower is "The Peak." Located atop Telegraph Hill, just east of North Beach, the round, stone tower offers 360° views of the city and the Bay.

Completed in 1933, the tower is the legacy of Lillie Hitchcock Coit, a wealthy eccentric who left San Francisco a $125,000 bequest. Inside the base of the tower are the impressive WPA murals titled *Life in California, 1934,* which were completed during the New Deal by more than 25 artists, many of whom had studied under master muralist Diego Rivera. The individual frescoes form a unified whole, all done in traditional Mexican-style fresco, and all done with the same scale and palette.

If you go on a clear day, it's wonderful to walk up the Filbert Steps (thereby avoiding a traffic nightmare) and take in the panorama at the base of the tower. In fact, we'd recommend not paying the admission for going to the top; the view is just as good from the parking area and you can see the murals for free.

The Exploratorium. 3601 Lyon St., in the Palace of Fine Arts (at Marina Blvd.). ☎ **415/ 563-7337**, or 415/561-0360 for recorded information. Admission $9 adults, $7 senior citizens, $5 children 6–17, $2.50 children 3–5, free for children under 3; free for everyone first Wed of each month. Summer (Memorial Day to Labor Day) and holidays, Mon–Tues and Thurs–Sun 10am–6pm, Wed 10am–9:30pm; the rest of the year Tues and Thurs–Sun 10am–5pm, Wed 10am–9:30pm. Closed Mon after Labor Day to Memorial Day (except holidays), Thanksgiving Day, and Christmas Day. Bus: 30 from Stockton St. to the Marina stop.

This fun, hands-on science fair contains more than 650 permanent exhibits that explain everything from color theory to Einstein's Theory of Relativity. Optics are demonstrated in booths where you can see a three-dimensional bust of a statue, but when you try to touch it, you discover it isn't there! Every exhibit is designed to be used by visitors. You can whisper into a concave reflector and have a friend hear you 60 feet away, or design your own animated abstract art with sound.

✪ **Golden Gate Bridge.** ☎ **415/921-5858.** Bridge-bound Golden Gate Transit buses (☎ 415/332-6600) depart every half hour during the day from the Transbay Terminal at Mission and First sts., making stops at Market and Seventh sts., at the Civic Center, and along Van Ness Ave. and Lombard St. Consult the route map in the Yellow Pages of the telephone directory or phone for schedule information.

With its gracefully swung single span, spidery cables, and sky-high twin towers, the bridge looks more like a work of abstract art than the engineering feat that it is. Construction began in May 1937 and was completed less than five years later at the then-colossal cost of $35 million. Contrary to pessimistic predictions, the bridge neither collapsed in a gale or earthquake nor proved to be a white elephant. A symbol of hope when the country was afflicted with widespread joblessness, the Golden Gate single-handedly changed the Bay Area's economic life, encouraging the development of areas north of San Francisco.

The mile-long steel link, which reaches a height of 746 feet above the water, is an awesome bridge to cross. To view the bridge, park in the lot at the foot of the bridge on the city side and make the crossing by foot. Back in your car, continue to Marin's Vista Point, at the bridge's northern end. Look back and you'll be rewarded with one of the most famous cityscape views in the world. Millions of pedestrians walk across the bridge each year. You can walk out onto the span from either end. Note that it's usually windy and cold, and the bridge vibrates. Still, walking even a short way is one of the best ways to experience the immense scale of the structure.

Museum of Modern Art (MOMA). 151 Third St. (2 blocks south of Market St., across from Yerba Buena Gardens). ☎ **415/357-4000.** Admission $7 adults, $3.50 seniors and students 14–18, free for children 13 and under; free for everyone the first Tues of each month. Tues–Sun 11am–6pm (until 9pm Thurs). Tours offered daily. Closed Mon and holidays. Muni Metro: J, K, L, M to Montgomery Station. Bus: 15, 30, or 45.

Swiss architect Mario Botta, in association with Hellmuth, Obata, and Kassabaum, designed this $62 million museum, which opened South of Market in January 1995. The museum's collection consists of more than 15,000 works, including close to 5,000 paintings and sculptures by artists such as Henri Matisse, Jackson Pollock, and Willem de Kooning. Other artists represented include Diego Rivera, Georgia O'Keeffe, Paul Klee, the Fauvists, and exceptional holdings of Richard Diebenkorn. MOMA was also one of the first to recognize photography as a major art form; its extensive collection includes more than 9,000 photographs by such notables as Ansel Adams, Alfred Steiglitz, Edward Weston, and Henri Cartier-Bresson.

The Caffè Museo, located on the right of the museum entrance sets a new precedent for museum food with flavorful and fresh soups, sandwiches, and salads. Don't miss the Museum Store, which carries a wonderful array of architectural gifts, books, and trinkets. It's one of the best stores in town.

GOLDEN GATE PARK

This landmark urban green space is a narrow strip—3 miles long and 1 1/2 miles wide—that stretches from the Pacific coast inland. Enter the park at Kezar Drive, an extension of Fell Street, or take Bus 16AX, BX, 6, 7, 66, or 71. For information on the park, head first to the McClaren Lodge and Park Headquarters (open Monday through Friday). There are several special gardens in the park—notably the rhododendron dell, the rose garden, and at the western edge of the park a springtime array of thousands of tulips and daffodils around a Dutch windmill.

If you're planning to visit Golden Gate Park's museums (in San Francisco), pick up an **Explorer Pass.** For just $12.50 you'll have access to the California Academy of Sciences (and the Steinhart Aquarium), Japanese Tea Garden, Asian Art Museum, **De Young Museum,** and the Conservatory of Flowers. Call **415/750-7459** for further information.

Proceeding from east to west, you will come first to the **Conservatory of Flowers.** Built for the 1894 Midwinter Exposition, this striking glass structure was modeled on the famous glass house at Kew Gardens in London. It contains a rotating display of plants and shrubs at all times of the year. The orchids in particular are a highlight.

The **Japanese Tea Garden** is a quiet haven of cherry trees, shrubs, and bonsai, crisscrossed by winding paths and high-backed bridges crossing over pools of water. Focal points and places for contemplation include the massive bronze Buddha that was cast in Japan in 1790 and donated by the Gump family, the Shinto wooden pagoda, and the Wishing Bridge (its reflection in the water looks as if it completes a circle).

Six thousand plant species grow in the **Srybing Arboretum and Botanical Gardens,** among them some very ancient plants in a special "primitive garden" and a grove of California redwoods.

Strawberry Hill, a 430-foot-high artificial island, lies at the center of **Stow Lake.** A path encircles it leading from the rustic bridge around to the Chinese Pavilion. The boathouse on the lake rents pedal, row, and other boats.

In addition, the park contains numerous recreational facilities: tennis courts, baseball, soccer and polo fields, golf course, riding stables, fly-casting pools, and boat rentals at the Strawberry Hill boathouse. See Section 9, "Outdoor Activities," later in this chapter, for details on each facility.

The park is also home to the following:

M. H. De Young Memorial Museum. In Golden Gate Park (near 10th Ave. and Fulton St.). ☎ **415/750-3600,** or 415/863-3330 for recorded information. Admission (including the Asian Art Museum and California Palace of the Legion of Honor) $6 adults, $4 seniors over 65, $3 youths 12–17, free for children 11 and under (fees may be higher for special exhibitions); reduced admission for everyone the first Wed of each month. Wed–Sun 10am–4:45pm (first Wed of the month until 8:45pm). Bus: 44.

Best known for its American art, which spans from colonial times to the 20th century, this museum displays paintings, sculptures, furniture, and decorative arts by such

Golden Gate Park

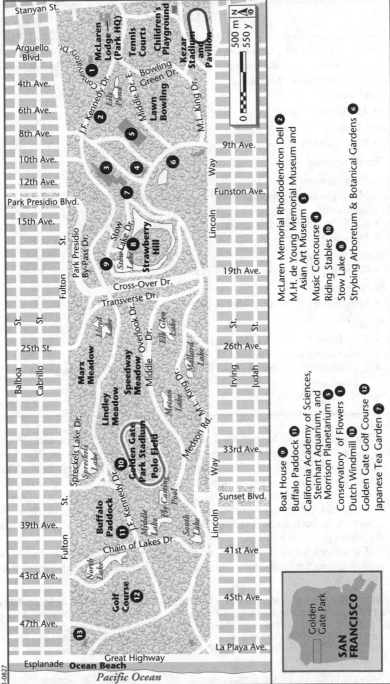

McLaren Memorial Rhododendron Dell ②
M.H. de Young Memorial Museum and
Asian Art Museum ③
Music Concourse ④
Riding Stables ⑩
Stow Lake ⑧
Strybing Arboretum & Botanical Gardens ⑥

Boat House ⑨
Buffalo Paddock ⑪
California Academy of Sciences,
Steinhart Aquarium, and
Morrison Planetarium ⑤
Conservatory of Flowers ①
Dutch Windmill ⑬
Golden Gate Golf Course ⑫
Japanese Tea Garden ⑦

1-0827

Free Culture

Almost all art galleries and museums are open free to the public one day of the month. The following list will help you learn how to plan your week around museums' free-day schedules (refer to the individual attractions listings for complete information on each museum).

First Monday
- The Jewish Museum

First Tuesday
- Museum of Modern Art

First Wednesday
- Exploratorium
- M. H. De Young Memorial Museum and Asian Art Museum (reduced admission)
- California Academy of Sciences
- Mexican Museum

Second Wednesday
- California Palace of the Legion of Honor

Every Thursday
- Yerba Center of the Arts Galleries (from 11am to 3pm)

Always Free
- The Names Project AIDS Memorial Quilt Visitors Center
- Cable Car Barn Museum
- San Francisco Maritime National Historical Park and Museum (there is a fee to board ships)
- Wells Fargo History Museum

diverse talents as Paul Revere, Winslow Homer, John Singer Sargent, and Georgia O'Keeffe. Note in particular the American landscapes, as well as the trompe l'oeil and still-life works from the turn of the century. There's also an important textile collection, with primary emphasis on rugs from Central Asia and the Near East. Other collections on view include ancient art from Egypt, Greece, and Rome; decorative art from Africa, Oceania, and the Americas; and British art by Gainsborough, Reynolds, Lawrence, Raeburn, and others. Special temporary exhibits are staged. Docent tours are offered daily; call for times.

The museum's Café De Young is exceptional. In summer, visitors can dine in the garden, among bronze statuary. The cafe is open Wednesday through Sunday from 10am to 4pm.

Asian Art Museum. In Golden Gate Park near 10th Ave. and Fulton St. ☎ **415/668-8921,** or 415/752-2635 for the hearing impaired. Admission (including the M. H. De Young Memorial Museum and California Palace of the Legion of Honor) $6 adults, $4 seniors 65 and up, $3 youth 12–17, free for children 11 and under (fees may be higher for special exhibitions); reduced admission for everyone the first Wed (all day) and first Sat (10am to noon) of each month. Wed–Sun 10am–4:45pm. Bus: 44.

Adjacent to the M. H. De Young Museum and the Japanese Tea Garden, this museum can only display about 1,800 pieces from the museum's vast collection of 12,000 at any given time. About half of the works exhibited are in the ground-floor

Chinese and Korean galleries, including sculptures, paintings, bronzes, ceramics, jades, and decorative objects. There is also a wide range of exhibits from Pakistan, India, Tibet, Japan, and Southeast Asia, including the world's oldest-known, dated Chinese Buddha. The museum's daily guided tours are recommended. Call for times.

California Academy of Sciences. On the Music Concourse of Golden Gate Park. ☎ **415/ 221-5100,** or 415/750-7145 for recorded information. Admission to aquarium and science exhibits, $7 adults, $4 students 12–17 and seniors 65 and up, $1.50 children 6–11, free for children under 6; free for everyone first Wed of every month. Planetarium shows $2.50 adults, $1.25 children under 18 and seniors 65 and up. Day before Labor Day to July 3 daily 10am–5pm. July 4 to Labor Day daily 10am–7pm. First Wed of every month 10am–9pm. Muni Metro: N line ("Judah") to Golden Gate Park. Bus: 5 ("Fulton"), 71 ("Haight-Noreiga"), or 44 ("O'Shaughnessy").

This group of three related museums—the Steinhart Aquarium, the Morrison Planetarium, and the Natural History Museum—is clustered around the Music Concourse. The Aquarium houses some 14,000 specimens, including amphibians, reptiles, marine mammals, and penguins. It contains a California tide pool and a hands-on area where children can touch starfish and sea urchins. The living coral reef is the largest display of its kind in the country and the only one in the West. In the Fish Roundabout, visitors are surrounded by fast-swimming schools of fish kept in a 100,000-gallon tank. Seals and dolphins are fed every two hours, beginning at 10:30am; the penguins are fed at 11:30am and 4pm.

The planetarium presents sky shows as well as laser-light shows. Approximately four major exhibits, with titles such as "Star Death: The Birth of Black Holes and The Universe Unveiled," are presented each year. Related exhibits are in the adjacent Earth and Space Hall. Call for show schedules and information.

At the Natural History Museum, the Wattis Hall of Human cultures traces the evolution of different human cultures and how they adapted to their natural environment. Visitors walk through an exhibit in McBean-Peterson Hall that traces the course of 3.5 billion years of evolution from the earliest life forms to the present day. Then you can experience a simulation of two of San Francisco's biggest earthquakes in the Hohfeld Earth and Space Hall, determine what your weight would be on other planets, see a real moon rock, and learn about the rotation of our planet at a replica of Foucault's Pendulum.

6 Exploring the City

Mission Dolores. 16th St. (at Dolores St.). ☎ **415/621-8203.** Admission $2 adults, $1 children 5–12. May–Oct daily 9am–4:30pm; Nov–Apr daily 9am–4pm; Good Fri 10am–noon. Closed Thanksgiving Day and Christmas Day. Muni Metro: J line to the corner of Church and 16th sts. Bus: 22.

This is the oldest structure in the city, built on order of Franciscan Father Junípero Serra by Fr. Francisco Palou. It was constructed of 36,000 sun-baked bricks and dedicated in June 1776, the northern terminus of El Camino Real, the Spanish road from Mexico to California. It's a moving place to visit to observe the cool, serene buildings with their thick adobe walls and most of all, the cemetery-gardens where the early settlers are buried.

The Names Project AIDS Memorial Quilt Visitors Center. 2362-A Market St. ☎ **415/ 863-1966.** Thurs–Tues noon–5pm, Wed noon–10pm. Muni Metro: J, K, L, or M line to Castro St. Station; F line to Church and Market sts.

The Names Project began in 1987 as a memorial to those who have died of AIDS. Sewing machines and fabric were acquired, and the public was invited to make coffin-sized panels for a giant memorial quilt. More than 28,000 individual panels now commemorate the lives of those who have died. Each has been uniquely designed and sewn by the victims' friends, lovers, and family members.

The quilt, which would cover 11 football fields if laid out end to end, was first displayed on the Capitol Mall in Washington, D.C., during a 1987 national march on Washington for Lesbian and Gay Rights. Although the quilt is often on tour throughout the world, portions of the heart-wrenching art project are on display here. A sewing machine and fabrics are also available here, free, for your use.

Lombard Street.
Known as the "crookedest street in the world," the whimsically winding block of Lombard Street, between Hyde Street and Leavenworth Street, puts smiles on the faces of thousands of visitors each year. The elevation is so steep that the road has to snake back and forth to make a descent possible.

The San Francisco Experience. At Fisherman's Wharf, on the waterfront at Embarcadero and Beach St. ☎ **415/388-6032.** Admission $7 adults, $6 seniors over 55, $4 children 5–16. Jan–Mar, shows daily every half hour 10am–8:30pm; rest of the year, shows daily every half hour 10am–9:30pm. Call for details; the show is relocating in the summer of 1997 to 828 Grant Ave., between Clay and Washington sts.

Two centuries of San Francisco history are condensed into about 30 minutes in this multimedia show that lets you see, hear, and experience events from the city's past. From the city's founding to the gold rush, the Great Earthquake, and the Summer of Love, the life and times of San Francisco are conveyed in a light and informative manner on a 70-by-35-foot screen. In addition, some unique city features and events are simulated in 3-D, including a San Francisco "fog" that really rolls in.

ARCHITECTURAL HIGHLIGHTS

The Alamo Square Historic District contains many of the city's 14,000 Victorian **"Painted Ladies,"** homes that have been restored and ornately painted by residents. The small area—bordered by Divisadero Street on the west, Golden Gate Avenue on the north, Webster Street on the east, and Fell Street on the south, about 10 blocks west of the Civic Center—has one of the city's largest concentrations of these. One of the most famous views of San Francisco, which you'll see on postcards and posters all around the city, depicts sharp-edged Financial District skyscrapers behind a row of Victorians. This view can be seen from Alamo Square at Fulton and Steiner streets.

Built in 1881 to a design by Brown and Bakewell, **City Hall** and the **Civic Center** are part of a City Beautiful complex done in the beaux arts style. The dome rises to a height of 308 feet on the exterior and is ornamented with occuli and topped by a lantern. The interior rotunda soars 112 feet and is finished in oak, marble, and limestone with a monumental marble staircase leading to the second floor.

The Flood Mansion, 1000 California St. at Mason, was built in 1885–86 for James Clair Flood who, thanks to the Comstock Lode, rose from a bartender to one of the city's wealthiest men. The house cost $1.5 million (the fence alone carried a price tag of $30,000!). It was designed by Augustus Laver and modified by Willis Polk after the earthquake to accommodate the Pacific Union Club.

The **Haas-Lilienthal House,** 2007 Franklin St. at Washington (☎ **415/441-3004**), is one of the city's most flamboyant Queen Anne–style Victorians. The 1886 structure features all the architectural frills of the period, including dormer windows, flying cupolas, ornate trim, and wistful turrets. The house is maintained by the Foundation for San Francisco's Architectural Heritage, which offers tours two days a week for $5 adults, $3 children 6–12, $3 seniors (open Wednesday from noon to 3:15pm, Sunday from 11am to 4:15pm).

The **Garden Court,** in the Sheraton Palace Hotel, 2 New Montgomery St. (☎ 415/392-8600), is an enclosed courtyard covered by a lofty iridescent glass roof that's supported by 16 Doric marble columns. Rebuilt in 1909 after the Great Earthquake and meticulously restored, it's worth seeing.

The **Octagon House,** 2645 Gough St. at Union Street (☎ 415/441-7512), is an eight-sided, cupola-topped house dating from 1861. Its architectural features are extraordinary, especially the circular staircase and ceiling medallion. Inside, you'll find furniture, silverware, and American pewter from the Colonial and Federal periods. There are also some historic documents, including signatures of 54 of the 56 signers of the Declaration of Independence. Even if you're not able to visit during open hours, this strange structure is worth a look. It's open on the second Sunday and second and fourth Thursday of each month from noon to 3pm; closed January and holidays.

The **Palace of Fine Arts,** on Baker between Jefferson and Bay Streets, is the only building to survive from the Pan Pacific Exhibition of 1915. Constructed by Bernard Maybeck, it was rebuilt in concrete using molds taken from the original in the 1950s.

The **TransAmerica Pyramid,** 600 Montgomery St., is the tallest structure in San Francisco's skyline—48 stories tall and capped by a 212-foot spire. It was completed in 1972.

Although the **San Francisco–Oakland Bay Bridge** (☎ 510/464-1148 for information) is visually less appealing than the Golden Gate Bridge (see "The Top Attractions," above), it is in many ways more spectacular. Opened in 1936, before the Golden Gate, it's 8¼ miles long, one of the world's longest steel bridges. It's not a single bridge at all, but actually a dovetailed series of spans joined in midbay, at Yerba Buena Island, by one of the world's largest (in diameter) tunnels. To the west of Yerba Buena, the bridge is really two separate suspension bridges, joined at a central anchorage. East of the island is a 1,400-foot cantilever span, followed by a succession of truss bridges.

Yerba Buena Center/Gardens, between Mission and Howard at Third, opened in 1993 adjacent to the Moscone Convention Center. It is the city's version of New York's Lincoln Center. The center consists of two buildings, a 755-seat theater designed by James Stewart Polshek, and the Arts Forum, which was conceived by Fumihiko Maki and which features three galleries and a space for dance. The complex also includes a five-acre garden featuring several art works, the most dramatic being a mixed-media memorial to Martin Luther King Jr. created by sculptor Houston Conwill, poet Estella Majoza, and architect Joseph de Pace. It features 12 glass panels, each inscribed with quotations from King, sheltered behind a 50-foot-high waterfall.

CHURCHES

Glide Memorial United Methodist Church. 330 Ellis St. ☎ 415/771-6300. Services held Sun 9 and 11am. Muni Metro: Powell. Bus: 37.

There would be nothing special about this plain Tenderloin-area church if it weren't for its exhilarating pastor, Cecil Williams. Williams's enthusiastic and uplifting preaching and singing with the homeless and poor people of the neighborhood has attracted nationwide fame. Go for an uplifting experience.

Cheap Thrills: What to See & Do for
Free (or Almost) in San Francisco

- **Riding the Outdoor Elevators at the Westin St. Francis Hotel.** Your heart may skip a beat as you race skyward at 1,000 feet per minute. The view, as you would expect, is dazzling, and no, you don't have to be a guest at the Westin (335 Powell St., at Union Square) to take a ride. Almost as thrilling is the glass elevator at the **Fairmont Hotel** (950 Mason St., at California Street). It's a lot slower, but the 360° view from the Crown Room restaurant and lounge is the best in the city.

- **Skating Golden Gate Park on a Weekend Day.** If you've never tried in-line skating before, there's no better place to learn than on the wide, flat street through Golden Gate Park, which is closed to vehicles on the weekends. **Skates on Haight,** 1818 Haight St. (☎ 415/752-8376), is the best place to rent in-line skates, and it's only one block away from the park. Protective wrist guards and knee pads are included in the cost: $7 per hour for in-line Rollerblades, $6 per hour for "conventionals."

- **Walking Across the Golden Gate Bridge.** It's simply one of those things you have to do at least once. Don't forget your jacket.

- **Riding on the Powell-Hyde or Powell-Mason Cable Cars.** It's the most fun you can have in San Francisco for only $3. Start on Market Street, then hang on to the brass rail for dear life as you whiz through the city toward Fisherman's Wharf.

- **Enjoying a Coke-on-the-Rocks at the Marriott Hotel's Atrium Lobby Lounge.** It takes a few stiff sodas to get the nerve to peer 40 stories straight down from the Marriott's Atrium Lounge (777 Market St., at Grant Avenue), where the only thing between you and the pavement is a piece of glass.

- **Strolling Haight Street between Stanyan and Masonic.** The San Francisco Zoo pales in comparison to some of the wildlife you'll see along lower Haight Street (don't worry, they won't bite). You'll also find plenty of colorful characters on Castro Street between Market and 19th.

- **Taking in a Sunday Sermon at Glide Memorial Church.** Reverend Cecil Williams's famous Sunday services attract a diverse audience (including the

MUSEUMS

Ansel Adams Center for Photography. 250 Fourth St. ☎ **415/495-7000.** Admission $4 adults, $3 students, $2 seniors and children 12–17. Tues–Sun 11am–5pm; until 8pm the first Thurs of each month. Muni Metro: Powell. Bus: 30, 45, or 9X.

This popular SOMA museum features five separate galleries for changing exhibitions of contemporary and historical photography. One area is dedicated solely to displaying the works and exploring the legacy of Ansel Adams.

Cable Car Barn Museum. Washington and Mason sts. ☎ **415/474-1887.** Free admission. Apr–Oct daily 10am–6pm; Nov–Mar daily 10am–5pm. Cable car: Both Powell St. lines stop by the museum.

If you've ever wondered how cable cars work, this nifty museum will explain (and demonstrate!) it all to you. Yes, this is a museum, but the Cable Car Barn is no stuffed shirt. It's the living powerhouse, repair shop, and storage place of the cable car system and is in full operation. The exposed machinery, which pulls the cables under San Francisco's streets, looks like a Rube Goldberg invention. Watch the massive

Clintons) that crosses all socioeconomic and religious boundaries. Held each Sunday between 9am and 11am at 330 Ellis St., it's one of the best free shows in town.

- **Taking the Ferry to Alcatraz.** San Francisco's all-time best tourist attraction has only gotten better. The new audio tour is excellent, and even the boat ride around the bay is fun; both are included in the $10 admission fee.
- **Walking the Coastal Trail from Fort Point to Cliff House.** If you think San Francisco is all cement and skyscrapers, take a walk along this 2¹/₂-mile route. From Fort Point, it takes you under the Golden Gate Bridge, around the Presidio cliffs, through Robin Williams's neighborhood (Sea Cliff), and to the Sutro Baths. Finish with a stroll along Ocean Beach.
- **Taking a Magical Mysteries–Explained Tour Through the Exploratorium.** Both kids and adults can spend the entire day at this huge, hands-on science museum and never get bored. Don't miss the incredible antique amusement machines at Musée Méchanique inside the Cliff House.
- **Pondering the Mission District Murals.** The Mission is one of the most ethnically colorful parts of the city. You could easily spend a day here seeking out the hundreds of vibrant murals. On Saturdays, you can take an hour-long tour, which highlights more than 70 murals. Contact the **Precita Eyes Mural Arts Center** at 348 Precita Ave., at Folsom Street (☎ **415/285-2287**).
- **Visiting the Marin Headlands.** Located just across the Golden Gate Bridge to the west, the Headlands are San Francisco's backyard; they shouldn't be left out of your itinerary. You'll discover the best views of the city from this glorious national park, in addition to a wealth of outdoor activities. Bird-watching, hiking, mountain biking—the list goes on—are all fair game (and free). Don't miss the Marine Mammal Center, a ward for injured or abandoned seals and sea lions. For more details, see Chapter 6.

groaning and vibrating winches as they thread the cable that hauls the cars through a huge figure eight and back into the system via slack-absorbing tension wheels. You can go through the room where you can see the cables operating underground. There's also a shop where you can buy a variety of cable-car gifts.

✪ **California Palace of the Legion of Honor.** In Lincoln Park (at 4th Ave. and Clement St.). ☎ 415/750-3600, or 415/863-3330 for recorded information. Admission (including the Asian Art Museum and M. H. De Young Memorial Museum) $6 adults, $4 seniors 65 and over, $3 youths 12–17, free for children 11 and under (fees may be higher for special exhibitions); free the second Wed of each month. Open Tues–Sun 10am–4:45pm; Open first Sat of the month until 8:45pm. Bus: 38 or 18.

Designed as a memorial to California's World War I casualties, the neoclassical structure is an exact replica of the Legion of Honor Palace in Paris, right down to the inscription *honneur et patrie* above the portal.

Reopened after a two-year, $29-million renovation and seismic upgrading project that was stalled by the discovery of almost 300 turn-of-the-century coffins, the museum's collection contains paintings, sculpture, and decorative arts from Europe, as well as international tapestries, prints, and drawings. The chronological display of more than 800 years of European art includes a fine collection of Rodin sculptures.

The Jewish Museum. 121 Steuart St. (between Mission and Howard sts.). ☎ **415/543-8880.** Admission $3 adult, $1.50 students and seniors; free the first Mon of each month. Mon–Wed noon–6pm, Thurs noon–8pm, Sun 11am–6pm. Closed Fri–Sat.

This museum hosts a variety of shows that concentrate on immigration, assimilation, and identity of the Jewish community in the United States and around the world. They are illustrated by paintings, sculptures, photographs, and installation art. The museum is moving in 1998 to the nearby Yerba Buena Gardens area.

Mexican Museum. Building D, Fort Mason, Marina Blvd. (at Laguna St.). ☎ **415/441-0404.** Admission $3 adults; $2 children over 10. Free to children under 10 and first Wed of the month. Wed–Sun noon–5pm. Bus: 76 to 28.

The gallery, which will be relocating to the Yerba Buena Center area in 1998, maintains a collection of art covering pre-Hispanic, Colonial, folk, Mexican fine art, and Chicano/Mexican American art. A recent show featured religious works by New Mexican women.

San Francisco Maritime National Historical Park and Museum. At the foot of Polk St. (near Fisherman's Wharf). ☎ **415/556-3002.** Admission museum free; ships $2 adults, $1 children 11–17, free for children under 11 and seniors over 62. Museum daily 10am–5pm; ships on Hyde St. Pier May 16–Sept 15 daily 10am–6pm, Sept 16–May 15 daily 9:30am–5pm. Closed Thanksgiving Day, Christmas Day, and New Year's Day. Cable car: Hyde St. line to the last stop. Bus: 19, 30, 32, 42, or 47.

Located near Fisherman's Wharf, the National Maritime Museum is filled with sailing, whaling, and fishing lore. Exhibits include intricate model craft, scrimshaw, painted wooden figureheads from old windjammers, and a collection of shipwreck photographs and historic marine scenes.

Two blocks east, at **Aquatic Park's Hyde Street Pier,** are several historic ships that are open to the public. The *Balclutha,* one of the last surviving square-riggers, was built in Glasgow, Scotland, in 1886. Visitors are invited to spin the wheel, squint at the compass, and imagine they're weathering a mighty storm. Kids can climb into the bunking quarters, visit the "slop chest" (galley to you, matey), and read the sea chanties (clean ones only) that decorate the walls. The 1890 *Eureka* was the last of 50 paddle-wheeled ferries that regularly plied the bay; it made its final trip in 1957. Restored to its original splendor, the side-wheeler is loaded with deck cargo, including antique cars and trucks. Other historic ships docked here include the tiny two-masted *Alma,* one of the last scow schooners to bring hay to the horses of San Francisco; the black-hulled, three-masted *C. A. Thayer,* built in 1895; the *Hercules,* a huge 1907 oceangoing steam tug; and several others.

At the pier's small-boat shop, visitors can follow the restoration progress of historic boats from the museum's collection. It's behind the maritime bookstore on your right as you approach the ships.

Wells Fargo History Museum. 420 Montgomery St. (at California St.). ☎ **415/396-2619.** Free admission. Mon–Fri 9am–5pm. Closed bank holidays. Muni Metro: Montgomery St. Bus: Any to Market St.

Wells Fargo, one of California's largest banks, was founded on the frontier, and this museum displays hundreds of frontier relics. In the center of the main room stands a Concord stagecoach, which opened the West as surely as the Winchester and the iron horse. On the mezzanine, you can take an imaginary ride in a replica stagecoach or send a telegraph message in code using a telegraph key and the codebooks, just the way the Wells Fargo agents did more than a century ago.

Yerba Center of the Arts Galleries. 701 Mission St. ☎ **415/978-2700.** Admission $4 adults, $2 seniors and students; free Thurs 11am–3pm. Tues–Sun 11am–6pm. Muni Metro: Powell or Montgomery. Bus: 30, 45, or 9X.

Cutting-edge computer art and multimedia shows are on view in the high-tech galleries. The initial exhibition, The Art of Star Wars, which featured the special effects created by George Lucas for the film, was a prime example.

EXPLORING SAN FRANCISCO'S NEIGHBORHOODS

THE CASTRO   Castro Street around Market and 18th streets is the center of the city's gay community, anchored by the bookstore A Different Light, and the many stores, restaurants, bars, and other institutions that cater to the community. Among the landmarks are Harvey Milk Plaza, the Names Project, and the Castro Theater, a 1920s movie palace. (See Section 7, "Organized Tours," later in this chapter, for details on a walking tour of the area.)

CHINATOWN   California Street to Broadway and Kearny to Stockton streets are the boundaries of today's Chinatown. San Francisco is home to the second-largest community of Chinese in the United States (about 33% of the city's population is Chinese), but the majority of them do not live and work in these 24 blocks, although they do return to shop and dine here on weekends.

The gateway at Grant and Bush marks the entry to Chinatown. Walk up Grant, which has become the tourist face of Chinatown, to California Street and Old St. Mary's. The square alongside it contains Bufano's monumental statue of Sun Yat-sen, founder of the Chinese Republic, who had an office in the Montgomery Block and worked toward the overthrow of the emperor from here.

The **Chinese Historical Society of America,** at 650 Commercial St. (☎ **415/ 391-1188**), has a small but interesting collection relating to the Chinese in San Francisco.

The heart of Chinatown is at **Portsmouth Square,** where the Chinese practice tai chi in the morning. This square was the center of early San Francisco and the spot where the American flag was first raised on July 9, 1846. From the square, Washington Street leads up to Waverly Place, where you can discover three temples.

A block north of Grant, Stockton Street is the main shopping drag of the community; it's lined with grocers, fishmongers, tea sellers, herbalists, noodle parlors, and restaurants. Here, too, is the Kon Chow Temple at No. 855 above the Chinatown Post Office.

Explore at your leisure, or see Section 7, "Organized Tours," later in this chapter, if you'd like to join a walking tour.

FISHERMAN'S WHARF & THE NORTHERN WATERFRONT   Few cities in America are as adept at wholesaling their historical sites as San Francisco, which has converted Fisherman's Wharf into one of the most popular tourist destinations in the world. Unless you come really early in the morning, you won't find any traces of the traditional waterfront life that once existed here; the only fishing going on around here is for tourist dollars.

Originally called Meigg's Wharf, this bustling strip of waterfront got its present moniker from generations of fishers who used to base their boats here. Today, the bay has become so polluted with toxins that bright yellow placards warn against eating fish from these waters. A small fleet of fewer than 30 boats still operates from here, but basically Fisherman's Wharf has been converted into one long shopping mall stretching from Ghirardelli Square at the west end to Pier 39 at the east. Some people love it, others can't get far enough away from it, but most agree that Fisherman's Wharf, for better or for worse, has to be seen at least once in your life.

What a Long, Strange Trip It's Been

San Francisco's rock bands were a key element of the counterculture scene that blossomed in the city in the mid-1960s; their free-form improvisation was one of the primary expressions of the hippies' "do-your-own-thing" principle. Until 1995, you could still experience something of that scene by attending a concert by the Grateful Dead, the quintessential psychedelic rock band. Amid all the tie-dye shirts and blissful smiles remained a set of musical values that dated from the days of Ken Kesey and his Merry Pranksters: a no-holds-barred reliance on spontaneous improvisation, even at the expense of clarity. San Francisco was deeply saddened in August 1995 by the death of the band's leader, Jerry Garcia, one of the city's cultural icons. Jerry played in a number of Bay Area bands before founding the Dead in 1965; they were soon headlining in counterculture strongholds like Bill Graham's Fillmore Theater in San Francisco. From June 1966 through the end of 1967, the Dead lived communally at 710 Ashbury St. in the Haight and played numerous free concerts there. As 1967's "Summer of Love" brought the flower children into full bloom, the Dead set the tone for one enormous citywide house party, liberally seasoned with ample doses of marijuana and acid.

The Grateful Dead played together for nearly 30 years. Over that span, they released numerous LPs; *American Beauty, Workingman's Dead,* and *Europe '72,* all on Warner Brothers, are some of their better records. If you ever caught one of their concerts, you got a small glimpse of Haight-Ashbury in 1967. For now, Haight Street windows are full of memorials to Jerry Garcia, and you'll find Dead memorabilia readily available in small shops throughout the neighborhood if you'd like to take home a reminder of the band that meant so much to San Francisco.

—Ian Wilker

Ghirardelli Square, at 900 North Point, between Polk and Larkin streets (☎ 415/775-5500), dates from 1864 when it served as a factory making Civil War uniforms, but it's best known as the former chocolate-and-spice factory of Domingo Ghirardelli. The factory has been converted into a 10-level mall containing 50-plus stores and 20 dining establishments. Scheduled street performers play regularly in the West Plaza. The stores generally stay open until 8 or 9pm in the summer and 6 or 7pm in the winter. Cable car: Powell-Hyde line to Aquatic Park.

The Cannery, at 2801 Leavenworth St. (☎ 415/771-3112) was built in 1894 as a fruit-canning plant and converted in the 1960s into a mall containing 50-plus shops and several restaurants and galleries, including **Jack's Cannery Bar** (☎ 415/931-6400), which features 83 beers on tap. Vendors' stalls and sidewalk cafes are set up in the courtyard amid a grove of century-old olive trees, and on summer weekends street performers are out in force entertaining tourists. The **Museum of the City of San Francisco** (☎ 415/928-0289), which traces the city's development with displays and artifacts, is on the third floor. The museum is free and is open Wednesday through Sunday from 10am to 4pm.

Pier 39, on the waterfront at Embarcadero and Beach Street (☎ 415/981-8030), is a 4¹/₂-acre waterfront complex, a few blocks east of Fisherman's Wharf. Ostensibly a re-creation of a turn-of-the-century street scene, it features walkways of aged and weathered wood salvaged from demolished piers. But don't expect a slice of old-time maritime life. This is the busiest mall of the group, with more than 100 stores. In addition, there are some 20 or so restaurants and snack outlets, some with good views of the bay. Two marinas accommodating 350 boats flank the pier and house the Blue and Gold bay sightseeing fleet.

In recent years some 600 California **sea lions** have taken up residence on the adjacent floating docks. They sun themselves and honk and bellow playfully. The latest major addition to Fisherman's Wharf is **Underwater World** (☎ 415/546-2700), a $38-million, 707,000-gallon marine attraction filled with sharks, stingrays, and more, all witnessed via a moving footpath that transports visitors through clear acrylic tunnels. The shops are open daily from 10:30am to 8:30pm. Cable car: Powell-Mason line to Bay Street.

THE MISSION DISTRICT   Once inhabited almost entirely by Irish immigrants, the Mission District is now the center of the city's Latino community, an oblong area stretching roughly from 14th to 30th streets between Potrero Avenue in the east and Dolores on the west. In the outer areas many of the city's finest Victorians still stand, though many seem strangely out of place in the mostly lower-income neighborhoods. The heart of the community lies along 24th Street between Van Ness and Potrero, where dozens of excellent ethnic restaurants, bakeries, bars, and specialty stores attract people from all over the city. Walking through the Mission District at night isn't a good idea, but it's usually quite safe during the day and highly recommended.

For an even better insight into the community, go to the **Precita Eyes Mural Arts Center** at 348 Precita Ave., at Folsom Street (☎ 415/285-2287) and take one of the hour-long tours conducted on Saturday, which cost $4 for adults, $3 for seniors, $1 for under-18s. You'll see 70 murals in an 8-block walk. Every year they also hold a Mural Awareness Week (usually the second week in May) when tours are given daily. Other signs of cultural life include a number of progressive theaters—Eureka, Theater Rhinoceros, and Theater Artaud, to name only a few.

At 16th and Dolores is the **Mission San Francisco de Assisi** (Mission Dolores), which is the city's oldest surviving building and the district's namesake.

NOB HILL   When the cable car was invented in 1873, this hill became the city's most exclusive residential area. The Big Four and the Comstock Bonanza kings built their mansions here, but the structures were all destroyed by the 1906 earthquake and fire. Only the Flood mansion, which serves today as the Pacific Union Club, and the **Fairmont** (which was under construction when the earthquake struck) were spared. Today the area is home to some of the city's most upscale hotels and also Grace Cathedral, which stands on the Crocker mansion site. Stroll around and enjoy the views, and perhaps pay a visit to **Huntington Park.**

NORTH BEACH   In the late 1800s, an enormous influx of Italian immigrants into North Beach firmly established this aromatic area as San Francisco's "Little Italy." Today, dozens of Italian restaurants and coffee houses continue to flourish in what is still the center of the city's Italian community. Walk down Columbus Avenue any given morning and you're bound to be bombarded with the wonderful smells of roasting espresso and savory pasta sauces. Though there are some interesting shops and bookstores in the area, it's the dozens of eclectic little cafes, delis, bakeries, and coffee shops that give North Beach its Italian-Bohemian character.

PARKS, GARDENS & ZOOS

In addition to Golden Gate Park (see Section 5, "The Top Attractions") and Golden Gate National Recreation Area and the Presidio (see Section 8, later in this chapter), San Francisco boasts more than 2,000 additional acres of parkland, most of which is perfect for picnicking.

Lincoln Park, Clement Street and 34th Avenue, a personal favorite, occupies 270 acres on the northwestern side of the city and contains the California Palace of the Legion of Honor (see "Museums," earlier in this section) and a scenic 18-hole municipal golf course. But the most dramatic features of the park are the 200-foot cliffs that overlook the Golden Gate Bridge and San Francisco Bay. Take bus no. 38 from Union Square to 33rd and Geary streets, then transfer to bus no. 18 into the park.

✪ **San Francisco Zoological Gardens and Children's Zoo.** Sloat Blvd. and 45th Ave. ☎ **415/753-7080.** Admission (main zoo) $7 adults, $3.50 seniors and youths 12–15, $1.50 for children 3–11, and free for children 2 and under if accompanied by an adult; (Children's Zoo) $1, free for children under 3. Main zoo daily 10am–5pm; Children's Zoo daily 11am–4pm. Muni Metro: L line from downtown Market St. to the end of the line.

Located between the Pacific Ocean and Lake Merced, in the southwest corner of the city, the San Francisco Zoo is among America's highest-rated animal parks. Most of the 1,000-plus inhabitants are contained in landscaped enclosures guarded by concealed moats. The innovative Primate Discovery Center is particularly noteworthy for its many rare and endangered species. Other highlights include Koala Crossing, which is linked to the new Australian WalkAbout exhibit that opened in 1995, housing kangaroos, emus, and walleroos; Gorilla World, one of the world's largest exhibits of these gentle giants; and Penguin Island, home to a large breeding colony of Magellanic penguins. The new Feline Conservation Center is a wooded sanctuary and breeding facility for the zoo's endangered snow leopards, Persian leopards, and other jungle cats. And the Lion House is home to rare Sumatran and Siberian tigers, Prince Charles, a rare white Bengal tiger, and the African lions (you can watch them being fed at 2pm Tuesday through Sunday).

The Children's Zoo, adjacent to the main park, allows both kids and adults to get close to animals. The barnyard is alive with strokable domestic animals such as sheep, goats, ponies, and a llama. Also of interest is the Insect Zoo, which showcases a multitude of insect species, including the hissing cockroach walking sticks.

7 Organized Tours

ORIENTATION TOURS

Gray Line, Transbay Terminal, First and Mission Streets (☎ **800/826-0202** or 415/558-9400), offers several daily itineraries with free transfers from centrally located hotels to departure points. Reservations are required for most tours.

THE 49-MILE SCENIC DRIVE

The self-guided, 49-mile drive is one easy way to orient yourself and to grasp the beauty of San Francisco and its extraordinary location. Beginning in the city, it follows a rough circle around the bay and passes virtually all the best-known sights from Chinatown to the Golden Gate Bridge, Ocean Beach, Seal Rocks, Golden Gate Park, and Twin Peaks. Originally designed for the benefit of visitors to San Francisco's 1939–40 Golden Gate International Exposition, the route is marked with blue-and-white seagull signs. Although it makes an excellent half-day tour, this miniexcursion can easily take longer if you decide, for example, to stop to walk across the Golden Gate Bridge or to have tea in Golden Gate Park's Japanese Tea Garden.

The San Francisco Visitor Information Center, at Powell and Market streets (see "Visitor Information," earlier in this chapter), distributes free route maps. Since a few of the Scenic Drive marker signs are missing, the map will come in handy. Try to avoid the downtown area during the weekday rush hours from 7 to 9am and 4 to 6pm.

BOAT TOURS

One of the best ways to look at San Francisco is from a boat bobbing on the bay.

Red and White Fleet, at Pier 41, Fisherman's Wharf (☎ **800/229-2784** or 415/546-2700), is the city's largest boat tour operator, offering more than half a dozen itineraries on the bay. You can't miss the observation tower ticket booths, at Pier 43½, located next to the Franciscan Restaurant. The Golden Gate Bay Cruise is a 45-minute cruise by the Golden Gate Bridge, Angel Island, and Alcatraz Island. Tours cost $16 for adults, $12 for juniors 12 to 18 and seniors 62 and older, and $8 for children 5 to 11. They depart from Pier 41 and Pier 43½ several times daily. The Blue and Gold Fleet acquired this company in 1996 so details may vary. Call for departure schedules.

Blue and Gold Fleet, at Pier 39, Fisherman's Wharf (☎ **415/705-5444**), tours the bay year-round. The fully narrated, 1¼-hour cruise passes beneath the Golden Gate and Bay bridges, and comes within yards of Alcatraz Island. Frequent daily departures from Pier 39's West Marina begin at 10am during summer and 11am in winter. Tickets cost $16 for adults, $8 for children 5 to 17, and seniors over 62; children under 5 sail free.

SPECIAL-INTEREST TOURS

FREE   City Guides (☎ 415/557-4266) offers more than two dozen **free** walking tours. Call for information or send a business-size self-addressed stamped envelope to City Guides, Friends of the Library, Main Library—Civic Center, San Francisco, CA 94102.

MOVING PARTY   Three Babes and a Bus (☎ 415/552-2582) is perhaps the world's hippest scheduled tour operator. This unique company runs regular night-club trips for out-of-towners and locals who want to experience the city's night scene. The Babes' ever-changing 3½-hour itinerary waltzes into four different clubs per night, cutting in front of every line with priority entry. The party continues en route, when the Babes entertain. Their bus departs on weekends only, at locations throughout the city. Phone for complete information and reservations. The tour costs $30, including club entrances, and departs Friday and Saturday nights only, from 9:30pm to 1:30am.

EXPLORING THE CASTRO   Cruisin' the Castro (☎ 415/550-8110) will give you a totally new insight into the gay community's contribution to the political maturity, growth, and beauty of San Francisco. Tours are personally conducted by Ms. Trevor Hailey, who was involved in the development of the Castro in the 1970s and knew Harvey Milk, the first openly gay politician elected to office in the United States.

Tours are conducted Tuesday through Saturday, from 10am to 1:30pm, and begin at Harvey Milk Plaza, atop the Castro Street Muni station. The cost includes lunch at the Lutie Pietia. Reservations are required. Prices are $30 adults, $25 seniors 62 and older and children 16 and under.

A HIPPIE TOUR   The Grateful Dead's crash pad, Janis Joplin's house, and other monuments to the Summer of Love—Rachel Heller will take you to the city's hippie haunts. Tours begin at 9:30am Tuesday and Saturday and cost $15 per person. For reservations call **Haight-Ashbury Walking Tours** at **415/221-8442.**

NORTH BEACH CAFE SOIREE   Javawalk is a two-hour walking tour by self-described "coffeehouse lizard" Elaine Sosa. Aside from visiting cafes, Javawalk also serves up a good share of historical and architectural trivia. Sosa keeps the tour interactive and fun, and it's obvious that she knows a dearth of tales and trivia about the history of coffee and its North Beach roots. Tours are Tuesday through Saturday at 10am. The price is $20 per person, kids 12 and under at half-price. For information and reservations call **415/673-WALK (9255).**

AN INSIDER'S TOUR OF CHINATOWN   Founded by author, TV personality, cooking instructor, and restaurant critic Shirley Fong-Torres, **Wok Wiz Chinatown Walking Tours** (☎ **415/355-9657**) takes you into nooks and crannies not usually seen by tourists. Each of her guides is intimately acquainted with all of Chinatown's backways, alleys, and small businesses. You'll learn about dim sum (a "delight of the heart") and the Chinese tea ceremony; meet a Chinese herbalist; stop at a pastry shop to observe rice noodles being made; watch artist Y. K. Lau do his delicate brush painting; learn about jook, a traditional Chinese breakfast; stop in at a fortune-cookie factory; and visit a Chinese produce market and learn to identify Chinese vegetables.

Tours are conducted daily from 10am to 1:30pm and include a Chinese lunch. The tour begins in the lobby of the Chinatown Holiday Inn at 750 Kearny St. (between Washington and Clay streets). Groups are generally limited to 12, and reservations are essential. Prices (including lunch) are $35 adults, $33 seniors 60 and older, $25 children under 12.

8 Golden Gate National Recreation Area & the Presidio

GOLDEN GATE NATIONAL RECREATION AREA

No urban shoreline is as stunning as San Francisco's. Golden Gate National Recreation Area, wrapping around the northern and western edge of the city and run by the National Parks Service, lets visitors fully enjoy it. Along this shoreline are several landmarks. From its edge visitors have views of the Bay and the Ocean. MUNI provides transportation to most sites, including Aquatic Park, the Cliff House, and Ocean Beach. For more information, contact the **National Park Service** at **415/556-0560.** For additional information, see Section 9, "Outdoor Activities," later in this chapter.

Here is a brief rundown of the major features of the recreation area, starting at the northern section and moving westward around the coastline:

Aquatic Park, adjacent to the Hyde Street Pier, is a small swimming beach, although it's not that appealing and the water's ridiculously cold.

Fort Mason Center occupies an area from Bay Street to the shoreline and consists of several buildings and piers, which were used during World War II. Today they are occupied by a variety of museums, theaters, and cultural, educational, and community organizations, as well as by Greens vegetarian restaurant, which affords views of the Golden Gate Bridge. For information about Fort Mason events, call **415/441-5705.** The San Francisco International Hostel is located here, too, overlooking the Bay. Park headquarters is also at Fort Mason.

Farther west along the Bay, **Marina Green,** at the northern end of Fillmore, is a favorite spot for kite-flying or watching the sailboats and the birds gliding above. Next stop along the Bay is the St. Francis Yacht Club. From here begins the 3 1/2-mile paved **Golden Gate Promenade,** a favorite biking and hiking path, which sweeps along Crissy Field, leading ultimately to Fort Point under the Golden Gate Bridge. This Promenade defines the outer limits of the **Presidio** (see below).

Fort Point (☎ **415/556-1373**), a National Historic Site that lies directly under the Golden Gate Bridge, was built in 1853 to protect the narrow entrance to the harbor. You might recognize it from Alfred Hitchcock's *Vertigo;* the master of suspense filmed some of the most important scenes here. During the Civil War, the brick Fort Point was manned by 140 men and 90 pieces of artillery to prevent a Confederate takeover of California. Rangers in Civil War regalia lead regular tours and sometimes fire the old cannons. Call **415/556-1693** for schedules and information.

Lincoln Boulevard sweeps around the western edge of the Bay to two of the most popular beaches in San Francisco. **Baker Beach,** a small and beautiful strand just outside the Golden Gate where the waves roll ashore, is a fine spot for sunbathing, walking, or fishing—packed on sunny days. Because of the cold water and the roaring currents that pour out of the bay twice a day, swimming is not advised here for any but the most confident. (You'll also see some nude sunbathers here.)

Here you can pick up the **Coastal Trail,** which leads through the Presidio (see below). A short distance from Baker, **China Beach** is a small cove where swimming is permitted. Changing rooms, showers, sundeck, and rest rooms are available.

A little farther round the coast appears **Lands End,** looking out to Pyramid Rock. Both a lower and an upper trail provide hiking opportunities amid windswept cypress and pine on the cliffs above the Pacific.

Still farther along the coast lies **Point Lobos,** the **Sutro Baths,** and the **Cliff House.** This last has been serving refreshments to visitors since 1863. Here you can view the **Seal Rocks,** home to a colony of sea lions and many marine birds. There's an information center here open daily 10am to 4:30pm (☎ **415/556-8642**), and the kids will enjoy the **Musée Mecanique,** an authentic old-fashioned arcade with 150 coin-operated amusements. Only traces of the Sutro Baths remain today northeast of the Cliff House. This swimming facility was a major summer attraction that could accommodate 24,000 people, but it burned down in 1966. A little farther inland at the western end of California Street is **Lincoln Park,** which contains a golf course and the Palace of the Legion of Honor. From the Cliff House, the Esplanade continues south along the 4-mile-long Ocean Beach, which is not suitable for swimming.

At the southern end of Ocean Beach is another area of the park around **Fort Funston** where there's an easy loop trail across the cliffs (call ranger station at **415/239-2366**). Here, too, you can watch the hang gliders taking advantage of the high cliffs and strong winds.

Farther south along Route 280, **Sweeney Ridge,** which can only be reached by car, affords sweeping views of the coastline from the many trails that crisscross this 1,000 acres of land. It was from here that the expedition led by Don Gaspar de Portolá first saw San Francisco Bay in 1769. It's in Pacifica and can be reached via Sneath Lane off Route 35 (Skyline Boulevard) in San Bruno.

THE PRESIDIO

In 1989 the Department of Defense announced what many had long thought impossible: The army, which had held the Presidio as a military base since before the Civil War, was pulling out and leaving the most prized piece of real estate in San Francisco to the National Parks Service as an example of post–Cold War retrofitting. Now an urban national park, it combines historical, architectural, and natural aspects.

The 1,480-acre area incorporates a variety of terrain—coastal scrub, dunes, and prairie grasslands that shelter many rare plants and more than 150 species of birds, some of which nest here. There are also more than 350 historic buildings to see, a scenic golf course to play, a national cemetery to visit, and a variety of landscapes and natural habitats to explore. The Park Service offers a number of walking and biking tours around the Presidio; reservations are required.

Golden Gate National Recreation Area

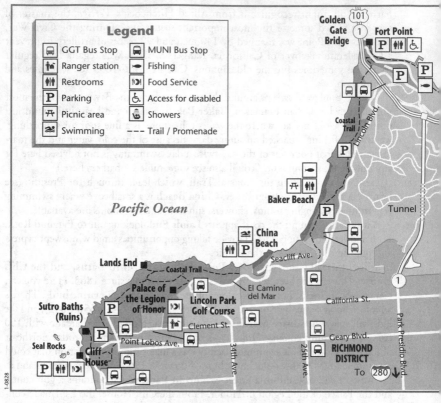

Legend

- GGT Bus Stop
- Ranger station
- Restrooms
- P Parking
- Picnic area
- Swimming
- MUNI Bus Stop
- Fishing
- Food Service
- Access for disabled
- Showers
- --- Trail / Promenade

Pacific Ocean

Golden Gate Bridge — 101 — 1 — Fort Point

Coastal Trail — Lincoln Blvd

Baker Beach

Tunnel

China Beach

Seacliff Ave.

Lands End

Coastal Trail

Palace of the Legion of Honor

El Camino del Mar

Lincoln Park Golf Course

California St.

Clement St.

Sutro Baths (Ruins)

Seal Rocks

Point Lobos Ave.

Cliff House

34th Ave.

25th Ave.

Geary Blvd.

RICHMOND DISTRICT

To 280

Park Presidio Blvd

Walkers and joggers will enjoy the forests of the Presidio. It was once a bleak field of wind-blasted rock, sand, and grass, but in a strangely humanitarian gesture, 60,000 trees were planted in the 1880s to make the place more livable for the troops. Today, on the 2-mile **Ecology Loop Trail,** walkers can see more than 30 different species of those trees, including redwood, spruce, cypress, and acacias. Hikers can follow the 2½-mile **Coastal Trail** from Fort Point along this part of the coastline all the way to Land's End. It follows the bluff top from Baker Beach to the southern base of the Golden Gate Bridge.

Anyone interested in the military history of the Presidio must stop at the **Presidio Army Museum,** loaded with military arcana from 200 years of base history. The museum, at the corner of Lincoln Boulevard and Funston Avenue (open Wednesday to Sunday from 10am to 4pm), tells its story in dioramas, exhibitions, and photographs.

Crissy Field is a former airfield that in recent years has become known as one of the see-and-be-seen proving grounds of California's windsurfing culture. Between March and October hundreds come to try their hand. The Crissy beach provides easy water access and plenty of room to rig up; it's not recommended for the inexperienced. This is also a popular place for joggers en route from the Marina District to Fort Point and back. At the west end of Crissy Field is a pier that can be used for fishing and crabbing.

For schedules, maps, and general information about ongoing developments at the Presidio, the best source is the **Golden Gate National Recreation Area**

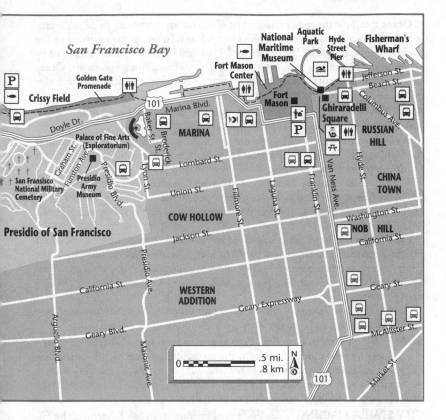

Headquarters at Fort Mason, Building 102, San Francisco, CA 94123 (☎ **415/ 556-2920**). It's on the west side of Montgomery Street, on the main parade ground. Open daily 10am to 5pm. Bus: 82X, 28, or 76.

9 Outdoor Activities

The prime places to enjoy all kinds of recreational activities in San Francisco have already been described earlier in this chapter. See Section 5, "The Top Attractions," for a complete description of Golden Gate Park; and Section 8, "Golden Gate National Recreation Area and the Presidio," for complete details on Golden Gate National Recreation Area and the Presidio, which comprise most of the city's shoreline.

BEACHES   There are only two beaches in San Francisco that are safe for swimming: **Aquatic Park,** which is adjacent to the Hyde Park Pier and not very memorable, and **China Beach,** a small cove on the western edge of the South Bay (changing rooms, showers, a sundeck, and rest rooms are available).

Baker Beach, a small, beautiful strand just outside the Golden Gate, isn't the best place for swimming due to strong currents, but it's popular for sunbathing (nude sunbathing in certain sections), walking, picnicking, or fishing. It's wonderful to sit here on a sunny day and take in the view of the bridge. You'll climb down a very long flight of stairs from the street to reach the beach.

Ocean Beach, at the end of Golden Gate Park, on the westernmost side of the city, is San Francisco's largest beach (4 miles long). Just offshore, at the northern end of the beach in front of Cliff House, are the jagged Seal Rocks, which are inhabited by various shore birds and a large colony of barking sea lions. Bring binoculars. Ocean Beach is for strolling or sunning, but don't swim here—tides are tricky, and each year bathers and surfers drown in the rough waters.

BICYCLING   Two city-designated bike routes are maintained by the recreation and parks department. One winds for $7^1/2$ miles through Golden Gate Park to Lake Merced; the other traverses the city, starting in the south, and follows a route over the Golden Gate Bridge. A bike map is available from the San Francisco Visitor Information Center and from bicycle shops all around town.

A massive new seawall, constructed to buffer Ocean Beach from storm-driven waves, doubles as a public walk and bikeway along five waterfront blocks of the Great Highway between Noriega and Santiago streets. It's an easy ride from Cliff House or Golden Gate Park.

Park Cyclery, 1749 Waller St. (☎ **415/752-8383**), is one of two shops in the Haight Street/Stanyan Street area that rent bikes. Next to Golden Gate Park, the cyclery rents mountain bikes exclusively, along with helmets, locks, and accessories. The charge is $5 per hour, $25 per day, and it's open Thursday through Tuesday from 10m to 6pm.

There's also great biking in the Presidio. From there you can venture across the Golden Gate Bridge and into the Marin hills.

BOATING   At **Golden Gate Park Boat House,** at Stow Lake (☎ **415/752-0347**), you can rent a rowboat or pedal boat by the hour and steer over to Strawberry Hill, a large, round island in the middle of the lake, for lunch. There's usually a line on weekends. It's open daily from June to September from 9am to 4pm; the rest of the year, it's Tuesday through Sunday from 9am to 4pm.

CITY STAIR-CLIMBING   You don't need Stairmaster in San Francisco. The **Filbert Street Steps,** 377 steps that run between Sansome Street and Telegraph Hill, scale the eastern face of Telegraph Hill, from Sansome and Filbert past charming 19th-century cottages and lush gardens. Napier Lane, a narrow wooden plank walkway, leads to Montgomery Street. Turn right, and follow the path to the end of the cul-de-sac where another stairway continues to Telegraph's panoramic summit.

The **Lyon Street Steps,** between Green Street and Broadway, comprise another historic stairway street, containing four steep sets of stairs totaling 288 steps. Begin at Green Street and climb all the way up, past manicured hedges and flower gardens, to an iron gate that opens into the Presidio. A block east, on Baker Street, another set of 369 steps descends to Green Street.

GOLF   Ⓢ **Golden Gate Park Course,** 47th Avenue and Fulton Street (☎ **415/751-8987**), is a nine-hole course over 1,357 yards and is par 27. All holes are par 3, tightly set, and well trapped with small greens. Greens fees are very reasonable: $10 per person Monday through Friday, $13 on Saturday and Sunday. The course is open daily from 9am to dusk.

Lincoln Park Golf Course, 34th Avenue and Clement Street (☎ **415/221-9911**), is San Francisco's prettiest municipal course and has terrific views and fairways lined with Monterey cypress trees. Its 18 holes encompass 5,081 yards, for a par 68. Greens fees are $23 per person Monday through Friday, $27 on Saturday and Sunday. The course is open daily from 9am to dusk.

RUNNING   The **Bay to Breakers Foot Race** is an annual 7.5-kilometer run from downtown to Ocean Beach. Around 80,000 entrants gather—many dressed in wacky, innovative, and sometimes X-rated costumes for what's considered one of San Francisco's favored trademark events. The event is sponsored by the *San Francisco Examiner* and is held the third Sunday of May. Call **415/777-7770** for details.

The **San Francisco Marathon,** held annually in the middle of July. For further information, contact **USA Track and Field** (☎ **415/391-2123**).

SKATING Although people skate in Golden Gate Park all week long, Sunday is best, when John F. Kennedy Drive, between Kezar Drive and Transverse Road, is closed to automobiles. A smooth "skate pad" is located on your right, just past the Conservatory. **Skates on Haight,** at 1818 Haight St. (☎ **415/752-8376**), is the best place to rent either in-line or conventional skates, and is located only one block from the park. Protective wrist guards and knee pads are included free. The cost is $7 per hour for in-line Rollerblades, $6 per hour for "conventionals." Major credit card and ID deposit are required. The shop is open Monday and Wednesday to Friday from 11:30am to 6:30pm, and Saturday and Sunday from 10am to 6pm.

10 Shopping

MAJOR SHOPPING AREAS

Union Square and Environs San Francisco's most congested and popular shopping mecca is centered around Union Square and enclosed by Bush, Taylor, Market, and Montgomery streets. Most of the big department stores and many high-end specialty shops are in this area. Be sure to venture to Grant Avenue, Post and Sutter streets, and Maiden Lane.

Chinatown Chinatown is the antithesis of Union Square, with shops along Grant Avenue selling an eclectic variety of cheap goods, T-shirts, knockoffs, and other tourist-oriented trinkets. Most stores in Chinatown are open daily from 10am to 10pm.

Union Street The Cow Hollow section of this trendy street, between Van Ness Avenue and Steiner Street, is the place for antiques, handcrafts, hip fashions, and deluxe glassware.

Haight Street The 6 blocks of upper Haight Street, between Central Avenue and Stanyan Street, are still the best place to shop for inexpensive, funky styles; antique and vintage clothing; Grateful Dead memorabilia; and kitsch. Along this street there's a healthy mix of boutiques, secondhand shops, and inexpensive restaurants.

Fillmore Street Some of the best shopping in town is packed into five blocks of Fillmore Street in Pacific Heights. From Jackson to Sutter streets, Fillmore is the perfect place to grab a bite and peruse the high-priced boutiques, craft shops, and incredible houseware stores.

Fisherman's Wharf and Environs The nonstop strip of waterfront malls that runs along Jefferson Street includes hundreds of shops, restaurants, and attractions. Ghirardelli Square, Pier 39, the Cannery, the Anchorage, and the San Francisco shopping center are the major complexes.

SHOPPING A TO Z
ART

Most of the city's major art galleries are clustered downtown, in the Union Square area, especially in the 400 and 500 blocks of Bush and Sutter. *The San Francisco Gallery Guide,* a comprehensive, bimonthly publication listing the city's current shows, is available free by mail. Send a self-addressed stamped envelope to **San Francisco**

Bay Area Gallery Guide, 1369 Fulton St., San Francisco, CA 94117 (☎ 415/ 921-1600), or pick one up at the San Francisco Visitor Information Center. Most of the city's major art galleries are clustered downtown in the Union Square area. Budget-minded art shoppers might want to swing by this unique gallery:

Catherine Clark Gallery. 49 Geary, 2nd Floor (between Grant and Kearny sts.). ☎ **415/ 399-1439.** Tues–Fri 10:30am–5:30pm, Sat 11am–5pm, first Thurs of the month 10:30am–7pm.

Catherine Clark's is a different kind of gallery experience: It's an affordable one. The gallery exhibits contemporary artists, mainly from California, and because Catherine and co-owner Jess Ghannam often show works from up-and-coming artists, the prices here make art a realistic purchase for everyone, not just the stinking rich. Catherine, who has an excellent eye for talent, is usually on hand and is dedicated not only catering to serious art buyers, but also to beginning art collectors. She even offers an unusual layaway plan where you may be able to pay off your piece interest-free over a full year. Don't come waving a deck of credit cards. She only accepts cash, checks, and American Express.

BOOKS

Charlotte's Web. 2278 Union St. (between Steiner and Fillmore). ☎ **415/441-4700.**

A children's bookstore, Charlotte's Web is known for its particularly knowledgeable owner, who sells everything from cloth books for babies to histories and poetry for young adults.

✪ City Lights Bookstore. 261 Columbus Ave. (at Broadway). ☎ **415/362-8193.**

Owned by Lawrence Ferlinghetti, the renowned beat poet, this excellent three-level bookshop prides itself on a comprehensive collection of fiction, art, poetry, and political paperbacks, as well as more mainstream books.

A Clean Well-Lighted Place. 601 Van Ness Ave. ☎ **415/441-6670.**

Voted best bookstore by the *San Francisco Bay Guardian,* this store has good new fiction and nonfiction sections as well as music, mystery, and cooking sections.

McDonald's Bookshop. 48 Turk St. ☎ **415/673-2235.**

San Francisco's biggest used-book shop claims to stock more than a million volumes, including out-of-print, esoteric, and hard-to-find books in all categories and languages.

Rand-McNally Map and Travel. 595 Market St. ☎ **415/777-3131.**

Hands down the best travel bookstore in the city, this corner shop features maps, atlases, and travel guides to all destinations, as well as educational games, toys, and globes.

Thomas Bros. Maps and Books. 550 Jackson St. (at Columbus Ave.). ☎ **800/969-3072** or 415/981-7520.

Thomas Bros. sells street, topographic, and hiking maps depicting San Francisco, California, and the world. A selection of travel-related books is also sold.

FACTORY OUTLETS

Esprit Outlet Store. 499 Illinois St. (at 16th St.). ☎ **415/957-2550.**

The Esprit collections and Susie Tompkins merchandise are available here starting at 30% off regular prices. In addition to clothes, the store sells accessories, shoes, and other assorted items. Open Monday through Friday from 10am to 8pm, Saturday from 10am to 7pm, and Sunday from 11am to 5pm.

New West. 426 Brannan St. (between Third and Fourth sts.). ☎ **415/882-4929.**

This SoMa boutique offers top designer fashions, from shoes to suits, at rock-bottom prices. There are no cheap knockoffs here, just good men's and women's clothes and accessories. New West also has their own stylish clothing line. Open Monday through Saturday from 10am to 5pm and Sunday from noon to 5pm.

The North Face. 1325 Howard St. (between Ninth and Tenth sts.). ☎ **415/626-6444.**

Reputed for its sporting, camping, and hiking equipment, this off-price outlet carries a good selection of high-quality skiwear, boots, sweaters, and other outdoor goods such as tents, packs, and sleeping bags.

FASHION
Children's Fashions
Minis by Profili. 2042 Union St. (between Webster and Buchanan). ☎ **415/567-9537.**

Christina Profili, a San Franciscan clothing maker who used to design for The Gap, owns this children's clothing store that features her line of pint-sized pants, shirts, and dresses.

Men's Fashions
Citizen Clothing. 536 Castro St. (between 18th and 19th sts.). ☎ **415/558-9429.**

Stylish (but not faddish) pants, tops, and accessories are sold here.

MAC. 5 Claude Lane (off Sutter St. between Grant Ave. and Kearny St.). ☎ **415/837-0615.**

There's no real bargain here, but if you've saved a few pennies for a special outfit, you might find it here where the more classic than corporate man shops for imported, tailored suits in new and intriguing fabrics. Their women's store is located at 1543 Grant Ave. (☎ 415/837-1604).

Women's Fashions
Métier. 50 Maiden Lane (at Grant Ave. and Kearny St.). ☎ **415/989-5395.**

Unless you recently won the lottery, hit this place when it's having a sale, and you'll find classic and sophisticated creations for women including European ready-to-wear lines and designer fashions at still high, but more reasonable, prices.

Solo Fashion. 1599 Haight St. (at Clayton St.). ☎ **415/621-0342.**

While strolling upper Haight, stop in here for a good selection of upbeat, contemporary, English-style street wear, along with a collection of dresses designed exclusively for this shop.

FOOD
Joseph Schmidt Confections. 3489 16th St. (at Sanchez St.). ☎ **415/861-8682.**

Chocolate takes the shape of exquisite sculptural masterpieces, for example, long-stemmed tulips and heart-shaped boxes, that are so beautiful, you'll be hesitant to take a bite. But once you do, you'll know why this is the most popular chocolatier in town. Prices are also remarkably reasonable, so you can take home an edible souvenir starting at $6.

Pure T. 2238 Polk St. (between Vallejo and Green sts.). ☎ **415/441-7878.**

If you're aching for a treat, it'd be a sin to miss out on what we consider the best ice cream shop in the city. The freshly made, all-natural ice creams redefine "gourmet." They're light, delicate and flavored with, you guessed it, pure tea. Gratify your taste buds with a scoop of black currant or Thai tea and you'll be hooked.

GIFTS

Exploratorium Store. In the Palace of Fine Arts, 3601 Lyon St. ☎ **415/561-0390.**

This fanciful store inside a hands-on science museum is the best museum gift shop in the city. Gifts include Space Age Super Balls, high-bouncing rubber balls that never seem to slow down; chime earrings and magnets; and other gizmos and gadgets.

Off Your Dot. 2241 Market St. (between Sanchez and Noe sts.). ☎ **415/252-5642.**

Wonderfully attractive and artistic handmade gifts cover almost every inch of this Castro-district store. There's everything from wall art to candles, picture frames, lamps, and glass works. Most of the merchandise is locally made, and it's tough to beat the prices.

Quantity Postcards. 1441 Grant St. (at Green St.). ☎ **415/986-8866.**

You'll find the perfect postcard for everyone you know here (there are hundreds of thousands), plus some depictions of old San Francisco, movie stars, and Day-Glo posters featuring concert-poster artist Frank Kozik.

HOUSEWARES

Fillamento. 2185 Fillmore St. (at Sacramento St.). ☎ **415/931-2224.**

Okay, it's far from cheap, but we can't exclude Fillamento's three floors of goodies. The store is always packed with shoppers searching for the most classic, artistic, and refined housewares. Whether you're looking to set a good table or revamp your bedroom, you'll find it all here. Although larger items might hurt your pocketbook, there are plenty of affordable trinkets.

The Wok Shop. 718 Grant Ave. (at Clay St.). ☎ **415/989-3797.**

This shop has every conceivable implement for Chinese cooking, including woks, circular chopping blocks, bamboo steamers—you name it—plus handmade linens from China.

Zinc Details. 1905 Fillmore St. (between Bush and Pine sts.). ☎ **415/776-2100.**

One of our favorite stores in the city, Zinc Details offers an amazing collection of locally hand-crafted glass vases, pendant lights, ceramics, and furniture. Each piece is a true work of art created specifically for the store (except vintage items). You're not likely to find anything under $25 here, but if you want to buy yourself one magnificent household gift, this is the place to find it.

JEWELRY

Pearl Empire. 127 Geary St. (between Stockton St. and Grant Ave.). ☎ **415/362-0606.**

The Pearl Empire has been importing jewelry directly from Asia since 1957. Specialists in unusual pearls and jade, they offer restringing on the premises.

MARKETS/PRODUCE

Farmers Market. Embarcadero, in front of the Ferry Building. ☎ **510/528-6987.**

Every Saturday from May to November fruit, vegetable, bread, and dairy vendors from North California join local restaurateurs in selling fresh delicious edibles. There's no better way to enjoy a bright San Francisco morning than strolling this gourmet street market and grazing your way through breakfast. You can also pick up locally made vinegars and oils; they make wonderful gifts.

VINTAGE CLOTHING

Ⓢ Aardvark's. 1501 Haight St. (at Ashbury St.). ☎ **415/621-3141.**

One of San Francisco's largest secondhand clothing dealers, Aardvark's has seemingly endless racks of shirts, pants, dresses, skirts, and hats from the last 30 years, all of which are dirt cheap.

Buffalo Exchange. 1555 Haight St. (between Clayton and Ashbury sts.). ☎ **415/431-7733.**

On upper Haight, this store is crammed with antique and new fashions from the 1960s, 1970s, and 1990s, including everything from suits and dresses to neckties, hats, handbags, and jewelry. A second shop is located at 1800 Polk St., at Washington Street (☎ 415/346-5741).

WINES

Ⓢ Wine Club San Francisco. 953 Harrison St. (between Fifth and Sixth sts.). ☎ **415/ 512-9086.**

What a bargain! The Wine Club is a discount warehouse that offers rock-bottom prices on over 1,200 domestic and foreign wines. Bottles—which are marked up only 6% to 12% over wholesale—start at $3.99 and go as high as $1,000.

11 San Francisco After Dark

To find out what's hot, check the *San Francisco Bay Guardian* and the *San Francisco Weekly,* available free at bars and restaurants, and from street-corner boxes. *Key,* a free tourist monthly available in hotels and at attractions, is also useful. Also check the Sunday edition of the *San Francisco Chronicle,* which contains a "Datebook" section.

THE PERFORMING ARTS

TIX Bay Area (☎ 415/433-7827) sells half-price tickets to theater, dance, and music performances on the day of the show only; tickets for Sunday and Monday events are sold on Saturday. They also sell advance, full-price tickets for most performances. Service charge is $1 to $3. Cash or traveler's checks only for half-price tickets. Tix is located on Stockton Street, between Post and Geary (open Tuesday through Thursday 11am to 6pm, Friday and Saturday from 11am to 7pm).

Tickets to most theater and dance events can also be obtained through **City Box Office,** 153 Kearny St., Suite 402 (☎ 415/392-4400) and **BASS Ticketmaster** (☎ 510/762-2277). You can also try Wherehouse stores throughout the city; the most convenient is at 30 Powell St.

From mid-June through August, one of the best free programs is the **Stern Grove Midsummer Music Festival,** 44 Page St., Suite 604D, San Francisco, CA 94102 (☎ 415/252-6252), held every Sunday during the summer at 2pm in Stern Grove Park. It opens traditionally with the San Francisco Symphony Orchestra; other performances include ballet, jazz, and theater. Stern Grove is located near 19th Avenue and Sloat Boulevard; arrive early for a good view, and bring a picnic.

CLASSICAL MUSIC

In addition to the San Francisco Symphony, there are a couple of other minor companies. Acclaimed by *The New York Times* as "the country's leading early music orchestra," the **Philharmonia Baroque Orchestra,** 57 Post St., Ste. 705 (☎ 415/ 391-5252), performs usually at Herbst Theatre from September to April. Tickets are $20 to $30. And the **San Francisco Contemporary Music Players,** 44 Page St.,

No. 604a (☎ **415/252-6235,** or 415/978-ARTS for box office), feature modern chamber works by international artists. Tickets are $14 for adults, $10 for seniors 65 and older, and $6 for students.

San Francisco Symphony. Performing in Louise M. Davies Hall, 201 Van Ness Ave. (at Grove St.). ☎ **415/864-6000.** Tickets $10–$68.

Founded in 1911, the internationally respected San Francisco Symphony is now under the baton of Michael Tilson Thomas. The season runs from September to May. Summer symphony activities include a Composer Festival and a Summer Pops series.

OPERA

In addition to the renowned San Francisco Opera, the **Pocket Opera,** 333 Kearny St., Suite 703 (☎ **415/989-1855**), performs from mid-February through mid-June on weekends. This comic company stages performances in English of well-known and not so well known operas accompanied by chamber orchestra. The staging is intimate and informal, lacking lavish costumes and sets. Tickets run $18 to $25.

○ **San Francisco Opera.** War Memorial Opera House, 301 Van Ness Ave. ☎ **415/864-3330.** Tickets $25–$135; $8 standing room tickets sold after 10:30am on day of performance.

The San Francisco Opera was the first municipal opera in the United States, and is one of the city's cultural icons. It features celebrated stars, along with promising newcomers in traditional and avant-garde productions, all with English supertitles. The season starts in September and runs 14 weeks, with nightly performances (except on Mondays) and matinees on Sundays. Performances in January and February 1997 will be performed elsewhere, due to retrofitting of the Opera House. The fall of 1997 will be the 75th anniversary season, which will be held in the newly restored Opera House.

THEATER

The theater district is concentrated on a few blocks west of Union Square. The city has a wide variety of offerings, many more than we have space to cover here—check the publications mentioned above to see what's currently in production. One good bet is **The Magic Theatre,** Building D, Fort Mason Center, Marina Boulevard at Buchanan Street (☎ **415/441-8822**), a highly acclaimed company that presents the works of new playwrights and has nurtured such luminaries as Sam Shepard and Jon Robin Baitz. The season usually runs from September to July with performances Wednesday through Sunday. Tickets cost $14 to $23; $12 for students, children, and seniors. There's also **Theatre Rhinoceros,** 2926 16th St. (☎ **415/861-5079**), which was America's first (and is still the foremost) theater ensemble devoted solely to works addressing gay and lesbian issues.

○ **American Conservatory Theater (A.C.T.).** Performing at the Geary Theater, 415 Geary St. (at Mason). ☎ **415/749-2228.** Tickets $14–$47.50.

The troupe is so venerated that A.C.T. has been compared to the British National Theatre, the Berliner Ensemble, and the Comédie Française. The season runs from October through May and features both classical and experimental works. The theater sustained severe damage in the 1989 earthquake and just reopened after undergoing renovation and seismic stabilization.

Lorraine Hansberry Theatre. 620 Sutter St. (at Mason). ☎ **415/474-8800.**

San Francisco's top African American theater group performs in a 300-seat theater in the Sheehan Hotel. Special adaptations from literature are performed along with contemporary dramas, classics, and world premieres.

DANCE

In addition to local companies, top traveling troupes such as the Joffrey Ballet and American Ballet Theatre make regular appearances. Primary modern dance spaces include the **Theatre Artaud,** 450 Florida St. at 17th Street (☎ **415/621-7797**); the **Cowell Theater,** at Fort Mason Center (☎ **415/441-3400**); **Dancer's Group/ Footwork,** 3221 22nd St., at Mission (☎ **415/824-5044**); and the **New Performance Gallery,** 3153 17th St. at Shotwell (☎ **415/863-9834**). Check the local papers for schedules or contact the theater box offices directly.

✪ **San Francisco Ballet.** 455 Franklin St. ☎ **415/861-5600** or 415/865-2000. Tickets $10–$75.

The San Francisco Ballet, which has won high international praise, is the oldest permanent ballet company in the United States. Under the artistic direction of Helgi Tomasson, the company performs an eclectic repertoire of full-length neoclassical and contemporary ballets. The season opens with performances of *The Nutcracker* in December and continues through May at the War Memorial Opera House, Van Ness Avenue and Grove Street. Tickets are $10 to $75.

As of January 1996 the Opera House is closed for 18 months for seismic renovations. The ballet will perform in alternate theaters.

CLUB & MUSIC SCENE

The hippest dance places are South of Market Street (SoMa), in former warehouses, whereas the most popular music and cafe culture is still centered in North Beach.

CABARET & COMEDY

Beach Blanket Babylon. At Club Fugazi, 678 Green St. ☎ **415/421-4222.** Tickets $18–$45.

A San Francisco tradition, Beach Blanket Babylon is a comedic musical send-up, best known for its outrageous costumes and oversize headdresses. It's been playing almost 22 years now and still almost every performance sells out. Persons under 21 are welcome at Sunday matinees at 3pm when no alcohol is served; photo ID is required for evening performances. It's wise to write for tickets at least three weeks in advance, or obtain them through TIX.

Cobb's Comedy Club. In the Cannery at Fisherman's Wharf, 2801 Leavenworth St. ☎ **415/ 928-4320.** Cover $5 Mon, $8–$15 Tues–Sun. 2-drink minimum required.

Cobb's features national headliners. There is comedy every night, including a 13-comedian All-Pro Monday showcase (a three-hour marathon). Open to those 18 and over, and to those 16 and 17 if they are accompanied by an adult.

Finocchio's. 506 Broadway (at Kearny St.). ☎ **415/982-9388.** Cover $12–15 (no drink minimum).

For more than 50 years this family run cabaret club has showcased the best female impersonators in a funny, kitschy show. Three different revues are presented nightly (usually Thursday through Saturday at 8:30, 10, and 11:30pm), and a single cover is good for the entire evening. Drinks begin at $2.75. Parking available next door at the Flying Dutchman.

Punch Line. 444 Battery St., plaza level (between Washington and Clay sts.). ☎ **415/ 397-4337,** or 415/397-7573 for recorded information. Cover $5 Sun, $6–$15 Mon–Sat (plus a 2-drink minimum nightly).

This is the largest comedy club in the city. Three-person shows with top national and local talent are featured Tuesday through Saturday. Showcase night is Sunday, when 15 to 20 rising stars take the mike. There's an all-star showcase or a special event on

Monday nights. Buy tickets in advance from **BASS Ticketmaster** outlets (☎ 510/762-2277) if you don't want to wait in line.

ROCK & BLUES CLUBS

The Fillmore. 1805 Geary Blvd. (at Fillmore). ☎ **415/346-6000.** Cover varies with performer.

Reopened after years of neglect, The Fillmore, made famous by promoter Bill Graham in the 1960s, is once again attracting big names. Check the local listings magazines, or call the theater for information on upcoming events.

The Saloon. 1232 Grant Ave. ☎ **415/989-7666.** Cover $3–$6 Fri–Sat.

An authentic Gold Rush survivor, this North Beach dive is the oldest extant bar in the city, popular with both bikers and daytime pinstripers. There's live blues several nights a week.

Slim's. 333 11th St. (at Folsom). ☎ **415/522-0333.** Cover $10–$20.

New Orleans–style Slim's is co-owned by Boz Scaggs, who sometimes takes the stage under the name "Presidio Slim." This glitzy restaurant/bar seats 300, serves California cuisine, and specializes in excellent American music—homegrown rock, jazz, blues, and alternative music—almost nightly.

JAZZ & LATIN CLUBS

Cesar's Latin Palace. 3140 Mission St. ☎ **415/648-6611.** Cover $5–$8.

Live Latin bands perform to a very mixed crowd—ethnically, economically, and generationally. Plenty of dancing and drinking.

✪ **Jazz at Pearl's.** 256 Columbus Ave. (at Broadway). ☎ **415/291-8255.** No cover, but 2-drink minimum.

One of the best venues for jazz in the city, where ribs and chicken go with the sounds. The live jams last until 2am nightly.

Mason Street Wine Bar. 342 Mason St. (at Geary). ☎ **415/391-3454.** No cover, except special performances.

This contemporary bar offers live jazz nightly. Small cabaret tables with black club chairs face a small stage. More than 100 different wines are served from the half-moon-shaped bar; glasses begin at $4.

330 Ritch. 330 Ritch (between Third and Fourth sts., off Townsend). ☎ **415/541-9574.**

If you can find this place, you must be cool. It's located on a two-block alley in SoMa and even locals have a hard time remembering how to get here. But once you do, expect happy-hour cocktails (specials on a few select mixed drinks and draft brews), pool tables, and a hip young crowd. Weekends, the place really livens up when live bands take center stage on Fridays and the Latin lovers salsa all night to the spicy beat.

Masons and the New Orleans Room. In the Fairmont Hotel, 950 Mason St. (at California St.). ☎ **415/772-5259.** Cover varies.

Cabaret reigns at Masons and the adjoining New Orleans Room features jazz. Call for information on featured entertainers.

DANCE CLUBS

The club scene is always changing. Most of the venues below are promoted as different clubs on various nights of the week, each with its own look, sound, and style. Discount passes and club announcements are often available at hip clothing stores and other shops along upper Haight Street.

Three Babes and a Bus (☎ 415/552-2582) runs regular nightclub trips on Friday and Saturday nights to the city's busiest clubs.

Club DV8. 540 Howard St. ☎ **415/777-1419,** or 415/957-1730 for recorded information. Cover $5 Thurs and Sun, $10 Fri–Sat; usually free before 10pm.

This SoMa club has been attracting the black-garb crowd longer than any other establishment. Two DJs spin music on separate dance floors. The decor mixes trompe l'oeil, pop art, candelabra, mirrors, and some extraordinary Daliesque props.

Club 1015. 1015 Folsom St. (at Sixth). ☎ **415/431-1200.** Cover $10–$15.

Three levels and three dance floors have made this a stylish stop along the nightclub circuit. Weekends are best, when the club is a carnival of hip people. Currently, **Dakota** (☎ 415/431-1200) is held on Fridays from 10pm to 6, featuring four different sounds—1970s, progressive house, funk, and rare groove. Saturday is gay night (☎ 415/431-BOYS). For other nights, call ahead.

Paradise Lounge. 1501 Folsom St. (at 11th St.). ☎ **415/861-6906.** Cover $3–$15.

Labyrinthine Paradise features three dance floors simultaneously vibrating to different beats. Smaller auxiliary spaces include a pool room with half a dozen tables. Poetry readings are also given.

Sound Factory. 525 Harrison (at 1st St.). ☎ **415/543-1300.** Cover $10; free before 10pm.

Herb Caen, who dubbed this the "mother of all discos," would never be found shaking it all night at this disco theme park. The maze of rooms and nonstop barrage of house, funk, lounge vibes, and club classics attracts swarms of young urbanites looking to rave it up until sometimes as late as 6am. Management tries to eliminate the riffraff by enforcing a dress code (no sneakers, hooded sweatshirts, or sports caps).

THE BAR & CAFE SCENE

Below is a good cross section of the best the city has to offer.

Edinburgh Castle. 950 Geary St. (between Polk and Larkin). ☎ **415/885-4074.**

Opened in 1958, this legendary Scottish pub is known for unusual British ales on tap and the best selection of single-malt scotches in the city. It's decorated with Royal Air Force mementos, steel helmets, and an authentic Ballantine caber, which was used in the annual Scottish games. Avoid Saturday nights unless you like bagpipes. Fish and chips are always available.

Gordon-Biersch Brewery. On the Embarcadero, 2 Harrison St. ☎ **415/243-8246.**

This is large brew-restaurant serving decent food and tasty brew to a lively yuppie crowd. There are several beers from which to choose, ranging from light to dark.

✪ **Harry Denton's.** 161 Steuart St. ☎ **415/882-1333.** Cover $3 Wed, $5 Thurs, $10 Fri–Sat; otherwise free.

Early evening it's filled with working "suits" and secretaries on the prowl. But when the stately restaurant with mahogany bar, red velvet furnishings, and chandeliers clears away dining utensils and turns up the music, a glitzy crowd shows up to valet with their boogie shoes on. The front lounge features R&B or jazz performers, and in the back room there's disco and pop dancing.

Johnny Love's. 1500 Broadway. ☎ **415/931-6053.**

This is the city's quintessential singles bar. There's a small dance floor and live music several nights a week; when it's jumping, this joint is a real scene. Love's serves decent food, too, but your money's best spent on drinks.

Julie's Supper Club. 1123 Folsom (at 7th St.). ☎ **415/861-0707.** Cover $5 Fri–Sat unless a full meal is ordered.

Crowded and lively, Julie's offers an array of appetizers and live music on Friday and Saturday nights.

The Redwood Room. In the Clift Hotel, 495 Geary St. ☎ **415/775-4700.**

This magnificent art deco–style room, completely done in redwood paneling, features a fabulous martini menu and a pianist who specializes in tunes from the 1930s and 1940s.

20 Tank Brewery. 316 11th St. (at Folsom). ☎ **415/255-9455.**

This huge, upscale bar is known for good ale, plus pizzas, sandwiches, chilis, and assorted appetizers. Live jazz is performed two nights a week. Other nights you can amuse yourself with darts, shuffleboard, and dice. Check them out on the Web: http://20tank.com.

NORTH BEACH BARS & CAFES

San Francisco in general, and North Beach in particular, is loaded with Italian-style cafes where patrons are encouraged to linger.

Caffe Trieste. 601 Vallejo St. ☎ **415/392-6739.**

Opera is always on the jukebox at this classic Italian coffeehouse, and on Saturday afternoons it's live when the family performs arias to the assembled crowd.

Caffè Greco. 423 Columbus Ave. ☎ **415/397-6261.**

Caffè Greco opened about eight years ago and has quickly become one of the best places to linger. Sophisticated and relaxed, it serves beer, wine, a good selection of coffees, focaccia sandwiches, and desserts.

Savoy Tivoli. 1434 Grant Ave. ☎ **415/362-7023.**

Eurotrash (and Eurotrash wanna-bes) crowds the few pool tables and indoor and outdoor seating to smoke cigarettes and look cool at this popular trendy bar.

Specs' Adler Museum Cafe. 12 Saroyan Place. ☎ **415/421-4112.**

Specs' is one of the liveliest and most likable pubs in North Beach. Maritime flags hang from the ceiling, while the exposed brick walls are lined with posters, photos, and various oddities.

Vesuvio. 255 Columbus Ave. ☎ **415/362-3370.**

This is one of North Beach's best beatnik-style hangouts. Popular with neighborhood writers, artists, songsters, and their wanna-bes, Vesuvio also gets its share of longshoremen, cab drivers, and business people. In addition to well-priced drinks, Vesuvio has good coffee/espresso.

COCKTAILS WITH A VIEW

The Carnelian Room. In the Bank of America Building, 555 California St. (between Kearny and Montgomery). ☎ **415/433-7500.**

This 52nd-floor room offers panoramic views of the city. In addition to cocktails, sunset dinners are served nightly, for about $45 per person. Jackets and ties are required for men. The restaurant has one of the most extensive wine lists in the city—1,275 selections to be exact.

Happy Hour, San Francisco Style

Good old happy hour. It's everyone's favorite time of day—and one of the best ways to save your pennies. Go ahead, put on your party hat and join them at this joyous time. Mingle. Joke. Rip on Southern California. Do whatever you'd like. It's happy hour, San Francisco style after all.

Whether you're on a bag lady's budget or a bacchanalian binge, the following establishments are some of the better places to fill your cup and your stomach when the sun starts heading over the Sunset District flatlands and beyond to the Pacific.

If greasy fingers, cold beer, and alternative rock is your kind of Sunday afternoon, wind your way to **Bottom of the Hill,** 2742 17th St., at Missouri (☎ **415/626-4455**), and fork over three bucks for the all-you-can-eat barbecue. The feast includes chicken, sausages, and a selection of salads. Drinks will cost you extra (though not much) and the music is free. This deal is on Sundays only from 4 to 7pm.

Wildly festive, **Cadillac Bar,** 325 Minna St. (☎ **415/543-8226**), is known for packing in tequila-shooting patrons who are looking to let their hair down. But come early before the suits are let loose and you'll have a somewhat mellow Mexican feast at the all-you-can-eat buffet. The fare is served Monday through Friday from 4pm to 6:30pm and usually includes such fire-starters as buffalo wings, chips and salsa, nachos, and ribs. Cool yourself off with a margarita or well drink for just $2.75.

Thank goodness there's an alternative to the disgusting—but addicting—pot of pink cheddar cheese and all-you-can-eat Ritz crackers that **Eddie Richenbacker's,** 133 Second St., between Howard and Mission, (☎ **415/543-3498**) otherwise always has on hand. Show up weekdays between 5 and 7pm (the earlier the better), elbow your way through the crowd of white collars, and indulge in the feast of freebies, which includes a selection of fresh seafood, pâté, sweet-and-sour pork, meatballs, and more. There is also a cool old train set overhead and a bunch of other knickknacks to peruse as you munch. Drinks range from $3 to $6.

The party on the patio is always in fashion at **El Rio,** 3158 Mission St., at Army St. (☎ **415/282-3325**), the Mission district's favorite dive. Every Friday from 5 to 7pm the place fills with the young and the thirsty who come for seriously cheap and *muy fuerte* (strong) margaritas and the all-you-can-eat oyster bar, which costs $10. Drinks run $2 to $3.50.

The yuppified **Holding Company,** Two Embarcadero Center (☎ **415/986-0797**), offers 21 on-tap beers, as well as barbecued beef, assorted veggies, and platters of fruit and cheese, Monday through Friday from 5 to 7pm. Folks also love the interactive televised trivia games.

Single professionals mingle with juicy baby back ribs (quickly clamor for them or miss out) along with an array of vegetables, chips and dip, and chicken wings at **MacArthur Park,** 607 Front St., at Jackson (☎ **415/398-5700**), every Monday through Friday from 5 to 7pm. *Hint:* The singles scene reaches its height on Fridays.

Last but not least, the **Tonga Room,** 950 Mason St., at California (☎ **415/772-5278**), is the Fairmont's version of an old-fashioned Disneyland attraction, complete with Polynesian theme and fruity cocktails. Happy hour is Monday through Friday from 5 to 7pm and features a $3 all-you-can-eat dim sum spread, as well as fruit and cheese and half-price cocktails.

✪ **Crown Room.** In the Fairmont Hotel, 950 Mason St., 24th floor. ☎ **415/772-5131.**

Of all the bars listed here, the Crown Room is definitely the plushest. Reached by an external glass elevator, the panoramic view from the top will encourage you to linger. In addition to drinks, dinner buffets are served for $31.

Harry Denton's Starlight Room. Sir Francis Drake Hotel, 450 Powell St., 21st Floor. ☎ **415/ 395-8595.** Cover $5–$10.

Tourists and locals sip cocktails at sunset and boogie down to live swing and big-band tunes after dark in this classic 1930s San Francisco room with red-velvet banquettes, chandeliers, and fabulous views. Jackets recommended.

✪ **Top of the Mark.** In the Mark Hopkins Hotel, California and Mason sts. ☎ **415/ 392-3434.**

One of the most famous cocktail lounges in the world opened here in 1939 and was renovated in 1996. During World War II countless Pacific-bound servicemen toasted their good-bye to the States here. The glass-walled room features an unparalleled view. Sunday brunch is served from 10am to 2pm for about $28.

GAY BARS & CLUBS

As with straight establishments, gay bars and clubs target varied clienteles. The major lesbian community is in Oakland, though there are a few hangouts in the city. In San Francisco, gay life is centered in the Castro, with some establishments South of Market (SoMa), along Polk Street, and in the Mission. Check the gay paper, *Bay Area Reporter,* or the *San Francisco Bay Guardian* for more information about what's currently hot.

Alta Plaza. 2301 Fillmore St. (at Clay St.). ☎ **415/922-1444.** Pacific Heights's wealthy gays flock to this classy Fillmore establishment with both bar and restaurant. It's especially festive on Fri and Sat during happy hour.

Castro Station. 456 Castro St. ☎ **415/626-7220.**

A well-known gay hangout, this bar is popular with the leather and Levi's crowd, and trendy boys from around the country show up here looking for action.

The Cinch Saloon. 1723 Polk St. (near Washington). ☎ **415/776-4162.**

Among the popular attributes of this cruising neighborhood bar are the outdoor patio, Sunday barbecue or buffet, and progressive music and videos. San Francisco 49ers fans also gather here for televised games. The bar attracts a mixed crowd of gays, lesbians (now that there are almost no exclusively lesbian bars left in San Francisco), and gay-friendly straight folk.

The End Up. 401 6th St. (at Harrison). ☎ **415/543-7700.** Cover varies.

It's a different night club every night of the week, but regardless of who's throwing the party, the place is always jumping with a DJ's blasting tunes. There are two pool tables, a fireplace, an outdoor patio, and a mob of gyrating souls on the dance floor. Some nights are straight so call for gay nights.

Metro. 3600 16th St. (at Market St.). ☎ **415/703-9750.**

With modern art on the walls, the Metro provides the gay community with high energy dance music and the best view of the Castro District from its large balcony. The bar seems to attract people of all ages who enjoy the friendly bartenders and the highly charged, cruising atmosphere. There's also a Chinese restaurant on the premises.

The Mint. 1942 Market St. (at Laguna). ☎ **415/626-4726.**

Come out of the closet and the shower and into The Mint where every night you can sing show tunes at this gay and lesbian-karaoke bar. Along with song, you'll encounter a mixed 20- to 40-something crowd who likes to combine cocktails with do-it-yourself cabaret.

Rawhide II. 280 Seventh St. (at Folsom). ☎ **415/621-1197.**

Gay or straight, this is one of the city's top country-western dance bars, patronized by both sexes. Free dance lessons are offered Monday through Thursday from 7:30 to 9:30pm.

The Stud. 399 Ninth St. (at Harrison). ☎ **415/863-6623.**

The Stud has been around for 30 years, and is one of the most successful gay establishments in town. It's mellow enough for straights as well as gays. Music here is a balanced mix of old and new; retro-disco for boys on Wednesdays and women's nights on Thursdays and Saturdays.

6

Side Trips from San Francisco

by Erika Lenkert and Matthew R. Poole

The Bay City is, without question, captivating, but don't let it ensnare you to the point of ignoring its environs, which contain a multitude of natural spectaculars like Mount Tamalpais and Muir Woods; scenic communities like Tiburon and Sausalito; and cities like gritty Oakland and its youth-oriented next-door neighbor, Berkeley. A little farther north stretch the valleys of Napa, Sonoma, and Alexander, the finest wine region in the nation. And to the south lies the digital wonderland of Silicon Valley and surf-city Santa Cruz.

1 Oakland

10 miles E of San Francisco

Although it's less than a dozen miles from San Francisco, the city of Oakland is worlds apart from its sister city across the bay. Originally little more than a cluster of ranches and farms, Oakland's size and stature exploded practically overnight as the last mile of transcontinental railroad track was laid down in 1869. Major shipping ports soon followed, and to this day Oakland has retained its hold as one of the busiest industrial ports on the West Coast.

The price for all this economic success, however, is Oakland's low-brow reputation as a predominantly working-class city, forever in the shadow of San Francisco's Eurochic spotlight. Even the city's NFL football team, the Oakland Raiders, has a proud and long-standing reputation for being mean, tough, and dirty (a cherished antithesis to their mortal enemy, the golden-boy 49ers). But with all its short-comings and bad press, Oakland still has a few pleasant surprises up its sleeve for the handful of tourists who venture this way. Rent a sailboat on Lake Merritt, stroll along the waterfront, explore the fantastic Oakland Museum—there are plenty of reasons to hop across the bay and spend a fog-free day exploring one of California's largest and most ethnically diversified cities.

ESSENTIALS

GETTING THERE   The **Bay Area Rapid Transit** (BART) makes the trip from San Francisco to Oakland through one of the longest underwater transit tunnels in the world. Fares range from 80¢ to $3, depending on your station of origin; children four and under ride free. BART trains operate Monday through Saturday, from 6am to midnight, and on Sunday from 9am to midnight. Exit at the 12th Street station for downtown Oakland.

If you're driving from San Francisco, take I-80 across the San Francisco–Oakland Bay Bridge and follow the signs to downtown Oakland. Exit at Grand Avenue South for the Lake Merritt area.

ORIENTATION   Downtown Oakland is bordered by Grand Avenue on the north, I-980 on the west, Inner Harbor on the south, and Lake Merritt on the east. Between these landmarks are three BART stations (12th Street, 19th Street, and Lake Merritt), in addition to City Hall, the Oakland Museum, Jack London Square, and several other sights.

INFORMATION   For a recorded update on Oakland's arts and entertainment happenings, phone **510/835-2787.**

WHAT TO SEE & DO

Lake Merritt is Oakland's primary tourist attraction along with Jack London Square (see below). Three and a half miles in circumference, the tidal lagoon was bridged and dammed in the 1860s and is now a wildlife refuge that is home to flocks of migrating ducks, herons, and geese. It's surrounded on three sides by the 122-acre **Lakeside Park,** a popular place to picnic, feed the ducks, and escape the fog. At the **Sailboat House** (☎ **510/444-3807**), in Lakeside Park along the north shore, you can rent sailboats, rowboats, pedal boats, and canoes for $6 to $12 per hour. They also run a tour boat that plies the lake on Saturdays and Sundays from 11am to 3pm; each trip is half an hour and only costs $1.75 for adults and 75¢ for kids and seniors.

Another site worth visiting is Oakland's **Paramount Theatre** (☎ **510/893-2300**), an outstanding example of art deco architecture and decor. Built in 1931 and authentically restored in 1973, it now functions as the city's main performing arts center. Guided tours of the 3,000-seat theater are given the first and third Saturdays of each month, excluding holidays. No reservations are necessary; just show up at 10am at the box office entrance on 21st Street at Broadway. Admission is $1.

Jack London Square. Broadway and Embarcadero. Take I-880 to Broadway, turn south, and go to the end. BART: 12th St. station; then walk south along Broadway (about half a mile) or take bus no. 51a to the foot of Broadway.

If you take pleasure from strolling sailboat-filled wharves or are a die-hard fan of Jack London, you might actually enjoy a visit to Jack London Square. Oakland's only patent tourist area, this low-key version of San Francisco's Fisherman's Wharf shamelessly exploits the fact that Jack London spent most of his youth along this waterfront. The square fronts the harbor, housing a tourist-tacky complex of boutiques and eateries that are about as far away from the "call of the wild" as you can get. Most are open Monday through Saturday from 10am to 9pm (some restaurants stay open later). In the center of the square is a small reconstructed Yukon cabin in which Jack London lived while prospecting in the Klondike during the gold rush of 1897.

In the middle of Jack London Square you'll find a more authentic memorial, **Heinold's First and Last Chance Saloon,** a funky, friendly little bar and historic landmark that's truly worth a visit. This is where London did some of his writing and most of his drinking; his corner table has remained exactly as it was nearly a century ago. Also in the square are the mast and nameplate from the USS *Oakland,* a ship that saw extensive action in the Pacific during World War II, and a wonderful museum filled with interesting London memorabilia.

Children's Fairyland. Lakeside Park, Grand Ave. and Bellevue Dr. ☎ **510/452-2259.** Admission $3 adults, $2.50 children 12 and under. Summer Sat–Sun 10am–5:30pm, Mon–Fri 10am–4:30pm; spring and fall, Wed–Sun 10am–4:30pm; winter Fri–Sun and holidays 10am–4:30pm. From I-580 south, exit at Grand Ave.; Children's Fairyland is at the far end of the park, on your left at Bellevue Ave. BART: Exit at 19th St. and walk north along Broadway; turn right on Grand Ave. to the park.

The Bay Area

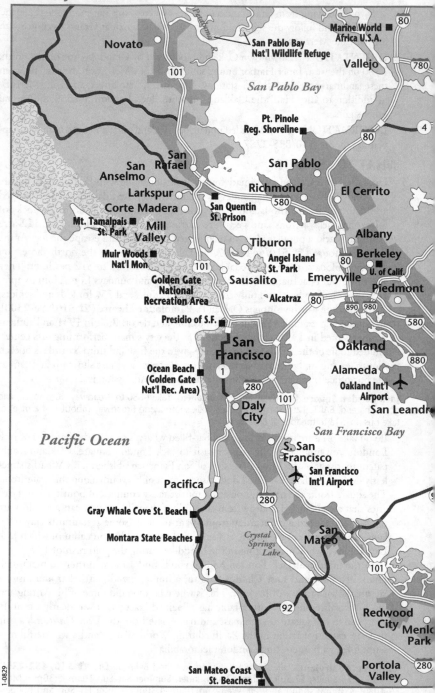

1-0829

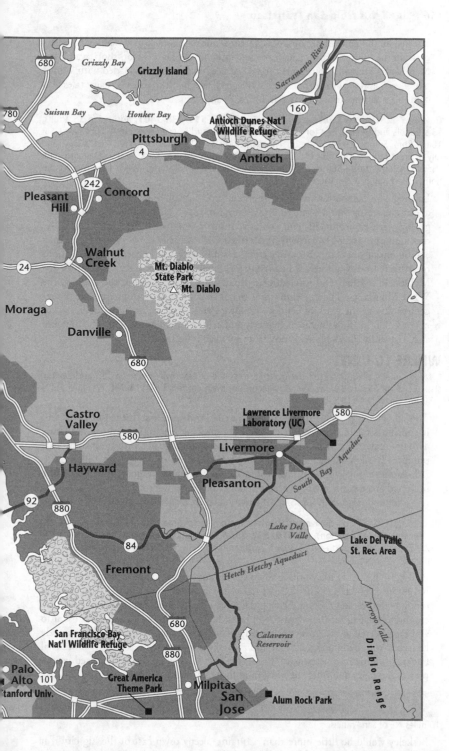

145

Located on the north shore of Lake Merritt is one of the most imaginative children's parks in the United States. Kids can peer into old Geppetto's workshop, watch the Mad Hatter eternally pouring tea for Alice, see Noah's Ark overloaded with animal passengers, and view Beatrix Potter's village of storybook characters. Fairy tales also come alive during puppet shows at 11am, 2, and 4pm.

Oakland Museum of California. 1000 Oak St. ☎ **510/238-3401.** Admission $5 adults, $3 students and seniors, free for children 6 and under and to everyone Sun 4–7pm. Wed–Sat 10am–5pm, Sun noon–7pm. Closed Thanksgiving Day, Christmas Day, New Year's Day, and July 4. From I-880 north, take the Oak St. exit; the museum is 5 blocks east at Oak and 10th sts. Alternatively, take I-580 to I-980 and exit at the Jackson St. ramp. BART: Lake Merritt station (1 block south of the museum).

Located 2 blocks south of the lake, the Oakland Museum of California includes just about everything you'd want to know about the state, its people, history, culture, geology, art, environment, and ecology. Inside a low-swept, modern building set down among sweeping gardens and terraces, it's actually three museums in one: exhibitions of works by California artists from Bierstadt to Diebenkorn; collections of artifacts from California's history, from Pomo Indian basketry to Country Joe McDonald's guitar; and re-creations of California habitats from the coast to the White Mountains. The museum holds major shows of California artists, like the recent exhibit of the work of ceramic sculptor Peter Voulkos, or shows dedicated to major California movements such as arts and crafts from 1890 to 1930. The museum also frequently shows photography from its huge collections.

WHERE TO DINE

Citron. 5484 College Ave. (off the northeastern end of Broadway between Taft and Lawton sts.). ☎ **510/653-5484.** Reservations accepted. Main courses $12–$18. MC, V. Daily 5:30–9:30pm. FRENCH/MEDITERRANEAN.

This adorable French bistro was an instant smash when it first opened in 1992, and it continues to draw raves for its small yet enticingly eclectic menu. Chef Craig Thomas draws the flavors of France, Italy, and Spain together with fresh California produce. Though the menu changes every few weeks, dishes range from grilled Colorado lamb sirloin with wild mushroom spoon bread and rosemary sauce, to white bean and green garlic ravioli with stewed artichokes, spring tomatoes, and sage butter. The fresh salads and Citron "40 clove" chicken are also superb.

Oliveto Café. 5655 College Ave. (off the northeastern end of Broadway at Keith St., across from the Rockbridge BART station). ☎ **510/547-5356.** Reservations accepted. Main courses $7–$12. AE, DISC, MC, V. Mon–Fri 11:30am–2pm, 5:30–9:30pm, Sat 5:30 –9:30pm, Sun 9:30am–2pm, 5:30–9:30pm. ITALIAN.

Paul Bertolli, chef at the world-renown Chez Panisse restaurant for the past 10 years, has jumped ship and opened one of the top Italian restaurants in the Bay Area and certainly the best in Oakland. During the week it's a madhouse at lunch, when BART commuters pile in for the wood-fired pizzas, house-made pastas, sausages, prosciutto and tapas served at the lower corner cafe. The main dining room upstairs—suavely bedecked with neoindustrial decor and partially open kitchen—is slightly more civil but significantly more expensive. Ergo, stay below: It's the reasonably priced pastas, pizzas, and tapas that offer the most tang for your buck.

2 Berkeley

10 miles NE of San Francisco

Berkeley would be little more than a quaint, sleepy town east of the big city if it weren't for the renowned University of California at Berkeley, which has produced

15 Nobel Prize winners (more than any other university) and spawned some of the largest and wildest student riots in U.S. history. Today, there's still hippie idealism in the air, but the radicals have aged, the '60s mostly lurk in tie-dye and paraphernalia shops, and the students have less angst. Still, it's a charming town teeming with a beautiful campus, vast parks, great shopping, and some incredible restaurants.

ESSENTIALS

The Berkeley BART station is two blocks from the university. The fare from San Francisco is under $3. If you're driving from San Francisco, take I-80 east to the University exit. Count on walking some distance because you won't find a parking spot near the university.

The **Berkeley Convention and Visitor's Bureau,** 1834 University Ave., 1st Floor, Berkeley, CA 94703 (☎ **510/549-7040**), can answer your questions and even find accommodations for you. Call their **Visitor Hot Line** (☎ **510/549-8710**) for general information on events and happenings in Berkeley.

EXPLORING THE UNIVERSITY & ENVIRONS

Hanging out is the preferred Berkeley pastime and the best place to do it is on **Telegraph Avenue,** the street that leads to the campus' southern entrance. Most of the action lies between Bancroft Way and Ashby Avenue where coffeehouses, restaurants, shops, great book and music stores, and craft booths swarm with life.

Pretend you're local: Plant yourself at a cafe, sip a latte, and ponder something intellectual while you survey the town's unique residents bustling by. Bibliophiles must stop at **Cody's Books,** 2454 Telegraph Ave., to peruse their gargantuan selection of titles, independent press books, and magazines. The avenue is also packed with street vendors selling everything from T-shirts and jewelry to I Ching and tarot-card readings.

UC Berkeley itself is worth a stroll as well. It's a beautiful old campus with plenty of woodsy paths, architecturally noteworthy buildings, and of course many of the 31,000 students scurrying to and from classes. Among the architectural highlights of the campus are a number of buildings by Bernard Maybeck, Bakewell and Brown, and John Galen Howard. The **Visitor Information Center** at 101 University Hall, 2200 University Ave. at Oxford Street (☎ **510/642-5215**), has free, regularly scheduled campus tours Monday, Wednesday, and Friday at 10am and 1pm (no tours are offered from mid-December to mid-January). The office also supplies self-guided walking tour brochures.

You'll find the university's southern entrance at the northern end of Telegraph, at Bancroft Way. Walk through the main entrance into **Sproul Plaza.** When school is in session, you'll encounter the gamut of Berkeley's inhabitants here: the colorful homeless, rambling political zealots, chanting Hare Krishnas, and ambitious students. You'll also find the Student Union, complete with a bookstore, cafes, and an information desk on the second floor where you can pick up a free map of Berkeley, as well as the local student newspaper (also found in dispensers throughout campus).

You might be lucky enough to stumble upon some impromptu musicians or a heated, and sometimes absurd, debate. There's always something going on, so stretch out on the grass for a few minutes and take in Berkeley's vibes.

For viewing more traditional art forms, there are some noteworthy museums here, too. The **Hearst Museum of Anthropology** is open from 10am to 5pm Wednesday, Friday, Saturday, and Sunday; 10am to 9pm Thursday. Admission is $2 for adults, $1 for seniors, and 50¢ children under 16. Thursdays are free. The **Lawrence Hall of Science** offers hands-on science exploration, is open from 10am to 5pm daily, and is a wonderful place to watch the sunset. Admission is $6 for adults, $4 for seniors and children 7 to 18, $2 for children 3 to 6. Finally, the **University Art Museum** is open from 11am to 5pm, Wednesday and Friday through Sunday. Thursday from 11am to 9pm. Admission is $6 for adults, $4 for seniors and children 12 to 17. This museum includes a substantial collection of Hans Hofmann paintings, a sculpture garden, and the Pacific Film Archive.

If you're interested in notable off-campus buildings, contact the **Berkeley Convention and Visitors Bureau** at **510/549-7040** for an architectural walking tour brochure.

OFF-CAMPUS ATTRACTIONS

Unbeknownst to many travelers, Berkeley has some of the most extensive and beautiful parks around. If you want to wear out the kids or enjoy hiking, swimming, or just getting a breath of California air and sniffing a few roses, jump in your car and make your way to **Tilden Park,** where you'll find plenty of flora and fauna, hiking trails, an old steam train and merry-go-round, farm and nature area for kids, and a chilly arbor-encircled lake. Call **510/843-2137** for further information. On the way, stop at the colorful terraced **Rose Garden,** located in north Berkeley on Euclid Avenue between Bay View and Eunice Street.

Another worthy nature excursion is the **University of California Botanical Garden,** in Strawberry Canyon on Centennial Drive, which features a vast collection of herbage ranging from cacti to redwoods. Call **510/642-3343** for details.

If you're itching to exercise your credit cards, head to one of two places: **College Avenue** from Dwight all the way down to the Oakland border is crammed with eclectic boutiques, antique shops, and restaurants. The other is **Fourth Street,** in west Berkeley just two blocks north of the University Avenue exit. This two-block expanse is the perfect place to go on a sunny morning to grab a cup of java and read the paper at a patio table.

You might also want to visit the factory of **Takara Sake USA,** at 708 Addison St. (☎ **510/540-8250**). The popular Sho Chiku Bai sake isn't Japanese: It's made here by America's largest sake maker. Unfortunately, there are no regularly scheduled tours of the plant, but you can learn about sake-making from a slide presentation and taste three different types of the rice wine. Open daily from noon to 6pm.

WHERE TO STAY

Bed and Breakfast International, P.O. Box 282910, San Francisco, CA 94128 (☎ **800/872-4500** or 415/696-1690; fax 415/696-1699), books visitors into more than 150 private homes and apartments in the San Francisco-Berkeley area. The cost ranges from $60 to $150 per night, and there's a two-night minimum.

DOUBLES FOR $60 OR LESS

Campus Motel. 1619 University Ave., (between McGee Ave. and California St.), Berkeley, CA 94703. ☎ **510/841-3844.** 23 rms. TEL TV. $56 double. AE, DISC, MC, V.

You won't be pampered with imported soaps or extrafluffy towels, but this basic motel only five blocks from the south end of campus offers clean, well-kept rooms with a full bath and coffeemaker at an almost unbeatable price. It's located on a busy strip that leads to the west end of campus and is surrounded by cheap ethnic restaurants. You probably won't want to hang around here during the day (there's not much to see), but with the campus and north Berkeley nearby, you won't miss out on anything if you stay here.

Golden Bear Motel. 1620 San Pablo Ave. (between University and Cedar sts.), Berkeley, CA 94702. ☎ **800/525-6770** or 510/525-6770. 42 rms. TEL TV. Doubles $49–$59; cottages $89–$125. Pets okay ($5 1-time fee). AE, DC, DISC, MC, V.

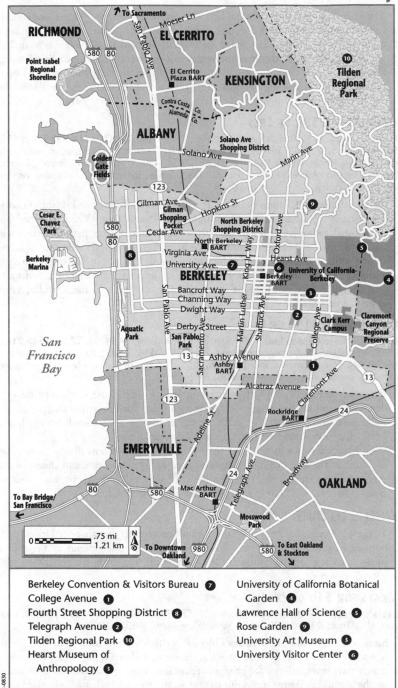

Berkeley

To Sacramento

Moeser Ln

RICHMOND

EL CERRITO

KENSINGTON

580 80

Point Isabel Regional Shoreline

San Pablo Ave.

El Cerrito Plaza BART

Tilden Regional Park ⑩

ALBANY

Contra Costa Co.
Alameda Co.

Solano Ave Shopping District

Solano Ave.

Marin Ave.

Golden Gate Fields

123

Gilman Ave.

Hopkins St.

Rose Garden ⑨

Cesar E. Chavez Park

580
80

Gilman Shopping Pocket

Cedar Ave.

North Berkeley Shopping District

Oxford Ave.

Berkeley Marina

⑧

Virginia Ave.

North Berkeley BART

Hearst Ave.

Lawrence Hall of Science ⑤

University Ave.

⑦

King Jr. Way

University of California-Berkeley

④

BERKELEY

Berkeley BART

University Visitor Center ⑥

Bancroft Way

Channing Way

Dwight Way

Martin Luther

Shattuck Ave.

③ University Art Museum

Claremont Canyon Regional Preserve

Aquatic Park

Derby Street

San Pablo Park

② Telegraph Avenue

Clark Kerr Campus

San Pablo Ave.

Sacramento Ave.

13

Ashby Avenue

Ashby BART

College Ave.

① College Avenue

San Francisco Bay

123

Alcatraz Avenue

Claremont Ave.

13

Rockridge BART

24

EMERYVILLE

Adeline St.

24

Telegraph Ave.

Broadway

OAKLAND

80 580

Mac Arthur BART

To Bay Bridge/ San Francisco

Mosswood Park

0   .75 mi
    1.21 km

N

To Downtown Oakland

980

To East Oakland & Stockton

580

1-0830

Berkeley Convention & Visitors Bureau ⑦	University of California Botanical Garden ④
College Avenue ①	
Fourth Street Shopping District ⑧	Lawrence Hall of Science ⑤
Telegraph Avenue ②	Rose Garden ⑨
Tilden Regional Park ⑩	University Art Museum ③
Hearst Museum of Anthropology ③	University Visitor Center ⑥

149

The price is right at this comfortable, 1950s Spanish-style motor lodge, located near Cafe Fanny and the new hip Fourth Street shops. Each room comes with either a queen or two twin beds, a dresser, a night stand, and a desk. For a few extra dollars you can opt for one of the three cottages, which have two bedrooms, a living room, and a full kitchen. Guests also enjoy free local calls. In the past, this area hasn't been the safest in town, but since Fourth Street's shops and restaurants have surfaced, the neighborhood is looking up.

DOUBLES FOR $80 OR LESS

French Hotel. 1538 Shattuck Ave., Berkeley, CA 94709. ☎ **510/548-9930.** Fax 510/ 548-9930. 18 rms. TEL TV. $68–$125 single or double. Government employee, university, and group rates available. Breakfast $4.50 extra. AE, CB, DC, MC, V. Free parking. From I-80 north, take the University Ave. exit and turn left onto Shattuck Ave.; the hotel is 6 blocks down on your left. BART: Berkeley.

This small hotel is in north Berkeley, the sleepier side of town, and is within crawling distance from the renowned restaurant Chez Panisse (see "Where to Dine," below). Guest rooms are light and airy, decorated in quiet rose carpeting, floral throw cushions, and all but three rooms have balconies. In lieu of a dresser, stacked sliding white baskets are provided for your personal things. No-smoking rooms are available. The downstairs cafe, a casual meeting place with exposed brick walls and outdoor tables, serves espresso, pastries, and other light items, or for lazy folks, many items can be delivered to your room.

DOUBLES FOR $130 OR LESS

Gramma's Rose Garden Inn. 2740 Telegraph Ave., Berkeley, CA 94705. ☎ **510/549-2145.** Fax 510/549-1085. 40 rms, all nonsmoking. TEL TV. $99–$165 double. Rates include breakfast. AE, DC, MC, V. Free parking. Take I-80 north to the Ashby exit and turn left onto Telegraph Ave.; the hotel is located 4 blocks up. BART: Ashby.

Gramma's restored Tudor-style mansion includes a main house, carriage house, garden house, and the Fay house, with guest rooms furnished in period antiques, floral wallpapers, and patchwork quilts. Accommodations in the restored carriage house overlook a garden and have fireplaces and king-size beds.

Guests are served a complimentary breakfast in the downstairs dining room or on the deck overlooking the garden, as well as complimentary wine and cheese in the evening. There's also fresh-brewed coffee and a bottomless cookie jar for any spontaneous sweet tooth. Dinner is served in the Greenhouse Cafe.

WHERE TO DINE

Telegraph Avenue has an array of small ethnic restaurants that are priced for student business (that means supercheap). Walk along, read the posted menus, and take your pick—keep in mind that a crowded restaurant hints that the fare is either especially good or dirt cheap.

MEALS FOR $10 OR LESS

Bette's Oceanview Diner. 1807A Fourth St. ☎ **510/644-3230.** Breakfast $5–7.50. Cash only. Mon–Thurs 6:30am–2:30pm; Fri–Sun 6:30am–4pm. AMERICAN.

Situated in the middle of Berkeley's blooming chic shopping area, Bette's may look like an old-style diner, but one glance at the menu and you'll know they've risen to match their surroundings. Sure there are pancakes, eggs, and all the breakfast basics on the menu, but Bette's leaves out the grease and substitutes it with advanced culinary style. Savor any of the fresh homemade morning buns or scones and move on to a delightful mound of an omelet filled with fresh ingredients like roasted red peppers with herbed cream cheese. Other specialties include soufflé pancakes (banana rum, apple brandy, fresh berry, and chocolate swirl), and grate-to-order potato pancakes.

Blondie's Pizza. 2340 Telegraph Ave. (at Durant Ave.). ☎ **510/548-1129**. Slices $1.50–$3. Mon–Thurs 10:30am–1am, Fri–Sat 10:30am–2am. No credit cards. PIZZA.

Blondie's is a Berkeley institution. It's where late-night fraternity/sorority folks stumble to grab a big, supercheesy slice and sop up their belly o' beer; it's also a quick, cheap place to grab lunch on the way to class; and it's where all the young street kids hang out and stop in for a bite on begged change. This is not a sit-down place, but it's a long-time favorite among all walks of life.

Blue Nile. 2525 Telegraph Ave. ☎ **510/540-6777.** Reservations required Fri–Sat. Main courses $6.50–$7.45. MC, V. Mon–Sat 11:30am–10pm, Sun 5pm–10pm. ETHIOPIAN.

Step through the beaded curtains and the African paintings and music will summon your appetite to other parts of the world. But the journey doesn't end there. Be prepared to savor the flavorful specialties such as doro wat (a spiced stew of beef, lamb, or chicken, served with a fluffy crepe injera) or gomen wat (mustard greens sautéed in cream) with no utensils other than your fingers. Sure, you could convince the wait staff to drum up a fork or two, but don't bother. No appetizers are served, but meals come with a small salad.

Brennan's. 4th St. (at University Ave. under the overpass). ☎ **510/ 841-0960.** Main courses $7. MC, V. Daily 11am– 9:30pm; bar Sun–Mon 11am–midnight, Tues–Thurs 11am–1am. Fri–Sat 11am–2am. Live music and dancing on weekends. AMERICAN.

This establishment has been kept in the family since its debut in 1959, and the prices seem to be somewhat unchanged as well. How about a hot roasted turkey sandwich with mashed potatoes, gravy, and bread for $5.25? Or a corned beef plate with hot veggies, mashed potatoes, bread, and butter for $6.35? Nothing on the menu is over $6.50, except a whole barbecued chicken for $8.25, and the fare focuses on fresh-carved meats, with a few stews, casseroles, and pasta dishes for variety. It's not a fancy place, just good old-fashioned food, cafeteria-style service, nine different draft beers, and infamous Irish coffees.

✪ **Cafe Fanny.** 1603 San Pablo (between Cedar and Virginia). ☎ **510/524-5447.** Breakfast items $1.52–$4.50, lunch $3–$6.25. MC, V. Mon–Fri 7am–3pm, Sat 8am–4pm, Sun 8am–3pm. Breakfast is served until 11am except for Sun when it's an all-day thing. FRENCH/ITALIAN.

Alice Waters's (of Chez Panisse fame) cafe is one of those local must-do breakfast traditions. Grab the morning paper, put on your Birkenstocks, and head here to wait in line for a simple, but masterfully prepared stand-up French breakfast. The menu offers such items as a soft-boiled farm egg with levain toast and house jam ($3.79), buckwheat crepes with jam ($3.79), and an assortment of sweet pastries. Lunch is more of an Italian experience featuring seasonal selections. Sandwiches, such as baked ham and watercress on focaccia; roasted eggplant with red peppers, mozzarella, aioli, and tapenade on a baguette; and grilled chicken breast wrapped in prosciutto, sage, and aioli on an Acme bread might convince you that you've never really had a sandwich before. There's also a selection of pizzettas, salads, and soup. Eat inside at the stand-up food bar (one bench), or outside at one of the cafe tables.

⑤ Cafe Intermezzo. 2422 Telegraph Ave. ☎ **510/849-4592.** Most items $3.25–$5.65. No credit cards. Daily 10:30am–10:30pm. SOUPS/SANDWICHES.

Pay no heed to the line out the door. Counter persons whip up orders with such fervor, you'll be happily munching in five to 10 minutes on what I consider the best and most enormous salads in the Bay Area. The dressings aren't any fancier than Italian or poppy seed, but each salad is literally a trough of fresh greens with kidney and garbanzo beans, sprouts, avocado, egg, and cucumber. One salad is a meal for two, and comes with thick slices of freshly baked bread and slabs of butter. Soups and sandwiches here are also delicious and one of the best deals around.

MEALS FOR $20 OR LESS

✪ **Cambodiana's.** 2156 University Ave. (between Shattuck and Oxford). ☎ **510/843-4630.** Reservations recommended, especially Fri–Sat. Main courses $7.50–$13; fixed-price dinner $10.95. AE, DC, JCB, MC, V. Mon–Fri 11:30am–3pm; nightly 5–10pm. CAMBODIAN.

For those who relish the spicy cuisine of Cambodia, this is quite a find. The decor is as colorful as the fare: brilliant blue, yellow, and green walls with Breur-style chairs set at tables. Especially tasty are the curry (chicken, beef, etc.) or Naga dishes with a sauce of tamarind, turmeric, lemongrass, shrimp paste, coconut milk galinga, shallot, lemon leaf, sugar, and green chile. This sauce may also be smothered on salmon, prawns, chicken, or steak. Another tempting dish is the chicken chaktomuk prepared with pineapple, red peppers, and zucchini in soy and oyster sauce. There's also an excellent value three-course, fixed-price dinner.

O Chamé. 1830 Fourth St. (near Hearst). ☎ **510/841-8783.** Reservations required Fri–Sat. Main courses $7–$16.50. AE, DC, MC, V. Mon–Fri 11:30am–3pm; Mon–Thurs 5:30–9pm, Fri–Sat 5:30–9:30pm. JAPANESE.

Spare and plain in its decor, with ochre-colored walls marked with etched patterns, this spot has a meditative air to complement the traditional and experimental Japanese-inspired cuisine. The menu, which changes daily, offers meal-in-a bowl dishes (from $7 to $11) that allow a choice of soba or udon noodles in a clear soup with a variety of toppings—from shrimp and wakame seaweed to beef with burdock root and carrot. Appetizers and salads include a flavorsome melding of grilled shiitake mushrooms and sweet peppers and portobello mushrooms, watercress and green onion pancakes, and the sashimi of the day. Specials range in price from $10 to $16.50 and always include a delicious roasted salmon.

Rivoli. 1539 Solano. ☎ **510/526-2542.** Reservations recommended. Main courses $10.25–$15. ATM, MC, V. Mon–Thurs 5:30–9:30pm, Fri 5:30–10pm, Sat 5–10pm, Sun 5–9pm. CALIFORNIA.

This small restaurant is one of the favored dinner destinations in the East Bay. It's not the well-appointed atmosphere, floral art, or small garden with magnolias that keeps the locals coming back (though the atmosphere is good); it's the food. If available, start with the portobello mushroom fritters with lemon aioli and shaved Parmesan, or the ahi tuna tartare with ginger vinaigrette. Next try the braised pork chile verde with tomatillos, cilantro, chipotle, sour cream, red onion salsa, and corn sticks; the grilled top sirloin with marsala sauce, gorgonzola gnocchi, and sautéed baby spinach; or the chicken breast with currants, red wine, and a saffron brioche stuffing. To finish, opt for the blood-orange granita or the bittersweet chocolate and walnut tart with butterscotch sauce and espresso cream.

WORTH A SPLURGE

✪ **Chez Panisse.** 1517 Shattuck Ave. (between Cedar and Vine). ☎ **510/548-5525.** Fax 510/548-0140. Reservations essential for restaurant—accepted a month in advance; cafe, accepted for lunch at 9am on the day, not accepted for dinner. Main courses in the cafe $13–$18; fixed-price dinner $35–$65. AE, CB, DC, MC, V. Restaurant, dinner seatings Mon–Sat at 6–6:30pm, 8:30–9:15pm. Cafe, Mon–Thurs 11:30am–3pm and 5–10:30pm, Fri–Sat 11:30am–4pm and 5–11:30pm. From I-80 north, take the University exit and turn left onto Shattuck Ave. BART: Berkeley. CALIFORNIA.

Okay, there's absolutely nothing budget about this restaurant. But if culinary adventure is an essential element of your vacation, you'd be a fool to pass up a meal from Alice Waters's kitchen. You can either put your conscience aside, or go for the more affordable choice: the cafe. In the dining room, the menu is fixed (it's cheaper and simpler earlier in the week, more expensive and extensive later in the week and on weekends). In the cafe, you order à la carte, enjoy equally fantastic fare, and will save a few bucks if you don't go overboard on appetizers, wine, and dessert.

The downstairs restaurant and the upstairs cafe both serve Mediterranean-inspired cuisine, most of which is made with organic produce and meat from local farms. The cafe has displays of pastries and fruit, and large bouquets of fresh flowers adorning an oak bar. At lunch or dinner you might find a delicately smoked gravlax or a roasted eggplant soup with pesto, followed by lamb ragout garnished with apricots, onions, and spices served with couscous. Dinner reservations are not taken for the cafe, so there will be a wait, but it's worth it.

The cozy downstairs restaurant, strewn with blossoming floral bouquets, is an appropriately warm environment to indulge in the fixed-price four-course gourmet dinner, which is served Tuesday through Thursday. Friday and Saturday, it's four courses plus an aperitif, and Monday is bargain night with a three-course dinner for $35. The menu, which changes daily, is posted outside the restaurant each Saturday for the following week. Meals are complemented by an excellent wine list ($20 to $200).

BERKELEY AFTER DARK

Blake's, 2367 Telegraph Ave. (☎ 510/848-0886), was recently voted the town's best bar by the student newspaper. Three floors provide a variety of entertainment ranging from a pool table and dancing, to an unspectacular but cheap full-service restaurant and bar. The draw here is the music, the affordable prices, and the down-home atmosphere, not the food.

There's also the **Triple Rock Brewery and Alehouse,** 1920 Shattuck Ave., at Hearst (☎ 510/843-2739), a top-notch Berkeley favorite that pipes its ale directly from the glass-enclosed brewery to the bar where sandwiches and chilies are also served. Play a game of shuffleboard or on a sunny afternoon head to the rooftop deck.

You can also wet your whistle (and wash down affordable pizza) amidst jazz and Berkeley hipsters at **Jupiter,** 2181 Shattuck Ave, at Center St. (☎ 510/843-8277), a beer and wine bar with more than a dozen beers on tap. Live music plays Thursday through Sunday, and if the weather's good, there may not be a better beer-drinking atmosphere than the courtyard patio.

The Sage of Aquarius

Are you curious about the direction your life is taking? Need a little assistance in making those important decisions? Consider spending an afternoon in Berkeley having an astrological consultation by the **Aquarius Astrological Services,** who are so renowned for their accuracy that even licensed psychologists have been known to drop in for a little astrological assistance. The AAS is run by a former world traveler who has solid academic credentials and an impressive 30-year background in astrology and Eastern religions. You can write for an appointment if you know that you're going to be in the area, or you can have them send you a 25-page report for your birth horoscope. Send your request to Aquarius Astrological Services, P.O. Box 894, Berkeley, CA 94701-0894, or call them at **510/549-3345.**

3 Sausalito

5 miles N of San Francisco

Just off the northern end of the Golden Gate Bridge is the eclectic little town of Sausalito, a slightly bohemian, nonchalant, and quaint adjunct to San Francisco. With approximately 7,500 residents, Sausalito feels rather like St. Tropez on the French Riviera—minus the starlets and the social rat race. It has its quota of paper millionaires, but they rub their permanently suntanned shoulders with a good number of hard-up artists, struggling authors, shipyard workers, and fishers. Next to the swank restaurants, plush bars, and antique shops and galleries, you'll see hamburger joints, beer parlors, and secondhand bookstores.

GETTING THERE

Ferries of the **Red and White Fleet** (☎ **800/229-2784** or 415/546-2700) leave from Pier 43½ (Fisherman's Wharf) and cost $11 round-trip, half price for kids 5 to 11. Boats run on a seasonal schedule; phone for departure information.

If you're driving from San Francisco, take U.S. 101 north, then take the first right after the Golden Gate Bridge (Alexander exit). Alexander becomes Bridgeway in Sausalito.

STROLLING & SHOPPING

Above all, Sausalito has scenery and sunshine. Once you cross the Golden Gate Bridge you're out of the San Francisco fog patch and under blue California sky. The town's steep hills are covered with houses that overlook a forest of masts on the waters below, but almost all the tourist action, which is primarily limited to window shopping and eating, takes place at sea level on Bridgeway.

The town is a mecca for shoppers seeking handmade, original, and offbeat clothes and footwear, as well as arts and crafts. The town's best shops are found in the alleys, malls, and second-floor boutiques reached by steep, narrow staircases on and off Bridgeway. Additional shops are found on Caledonia Street, which runs parallel to and one block inland from Bridgeway.

Village Fair, 777 Bridgeway, is Sausalito's closest approximation to a mall. It's a complex of 30 shops, souvenir stores, coffee bars, and gardens. Among them, **Quest Gallery** (☎ 415/332-6832) features fine ceramics, whimsical chess sets, contemporary glass, hand-painted silks, woven clothing, art jewelry, and graphics. The shop specializes in celebrated California artists, many of whom sell exclusively through this store. The complex is open daily from 10am to 6pm; restaurants stay open later.

Burlwood Gallery. 721 Bridgeway. ☎ **415/332-6550.**

Visit this gallery for one-of-a-kind redwood furniture plus fine jewelry, metal sculptures, hand-blown glass, Oriental rugs, and other interesting gifts. It's well worth browsing. Open daily from 10am to 6pm.

Magnet Madness. 795 Bridgeway. ☎ **415/331-9226.**

Finally, a store that sells something you can afford: refrigerator magnets. Thousands of colorful and creative little gems, from Airedales to zucchini, are backed with a magnet and stuck to the walls of this irresistibly inviting store. Open daily from 10am to 6pm.

Pegasus Leather Company. 28 Princess St. (off Bridgeway). ☎ **415/332-5624.**

Pegasus is a vendor of beautiful leather clothing and accessories. Along with jackets, coats, skirts, and blouses, there are handsome belts, gloves, and purses made from ultrasoft, richly colored leathers. Clothing can be custom made and altered for a perfect fit at no extra charge. Open daily from 10am to 5:30pm.

The Sausalito Country Store. 789 Bridgeway. ☎ **415/332-7890.**

This place sells oodles of handmade, country-style goods for the home and garden. Many of these items—ceramic, stuffed, and painted-wood animals, aprons, baskets, birdhouses, embossed quilt prints, and lithographs—are made by local artists and artisans. Open daily from 10am to 6pm.

WHERE TO DINE

Feng Nian Chinese Restaurant. 2650 Bridgeway. ☎ **415/331-5300.** Reservations accepted. Lunch specials $4–$5.50; main courses $6.55–$14. AE, DISC, MC, V. Mon and Wed–Thurs 11:30am–9:30pm, Fri–Sat 11:30am–10pm, Sun 12:30–9:30pm. From U.S. 101 north, take the first right after the Golden Gate Bridge (Alexander exit); Alexander becomes Bridgeway in Sausalito. The restaurant is located near the intersection of Bridgeway and Harbor Dr., before downtown Sausalito. CHINESE.

A pretty restaurant serving quality Chinese food, Feng Nian has such a wide selection of appetizers that a combination of them would make a delicious meal. The crispy roast duck is a personal favorite, but if you'd like an assortment, try the flaming combination (enough for two) that includes egg roll, fried prawn, paper-wrapped chicken, barbecued ribs, fried chicken, and teriyaki. There are nine soups, including a truly exceptional, rich crabmeat/shark's fin soup with shredded crab-leg meat.

Choosing one of the chef's suggestions isn't easy. The Peking duck requires about a half hour of preparation, but it's always delectable. If you enjoy seafood, try the Twice Sizzling Seafood, with prawns, scallops, squid, and fresh vegetables in oyster sauce; it's prepared at your table. Beef dishes are prepared in a variety of ways: Mongolian, Szechuan, Hunan, Mandarin; with ginger, curry, and broccoli, just to name a few. The restaurant offers more than 90 main dishes, including a number of vegetarian plates.

Guernica. 2009 Bridgeway. ☎ **415/332-1512.** Reservations recommended. Main courses $10–$17. AE, MC, V. Daily 5–10pm. From U.S. 101 north, take the first right after the Golden Gate Bridge (Alexander exit); Alexander becomes Bridgeway in Sausalito. FRENCH/BASQUE.

Established in 1976, Guernica is one of those old, funky restaurants that you'd probably pass up for something more chic and modern if you didn't know better. The legendary Paella Valencianais is definitely worth a visit; be sure to call ahead and order it in advance, and bring a friend or two because it's served for two but will feed three. Begin with an appetizer of artichoke hearts or escargots, and be sure to try the wonderful homemade bread. Other main courses are grilled rabbit with a spicy red diablo sauce, a hearty Rack of Lamb Guernica, and medallions of pork loin with baked apples and Calvados. Rich desserts include such in-season specialties as strawberry tart and peach Melba.

Horizons. 558 Bridgeway. ☎ **415/331-3232.** Reservations accepted weekdays only. Main courses $9–$15, salads and sandwiches $6–$8. AE, MC, V. Mon–Fri 11am–11pm, Sat–Sun 10am–11pm. SEAFOOD/AMERICAN.

Eventually every San Franciscan ends up at Horizons to meet a friend for Sunday Bloody Marys. It's not much to look at from the outside, but it gets better as you head past the funky dark-wood interior toward the waterside terrace. On warm days it's worth the wait for outside seating if only to watch dreamy sailboats glide past San Francisco's distant skyline. The food here can't touch the view, but it's well portioned and satisfying enough. Seafood dishes are the main items, including steamed clams and mussels, freshly shucked oysters, and a variety of seafood pastas. In fine Marin tradition, Horizons has an "herb tea and espresso" bar, and is a totally nonsmoking restaurant.

WHERE TO PUT TOGETHER A PERFECT PICNIC

Even Sausalito's naysayers have to admit that it's hard not to enjoy eating your way down Bridgeway on a warm, sunny day. If the crowds are too much or the prices too steep at the bay-side restaurants, grab a bite to go for an impromptu picnic in the park fronting the marina.

Small, clean, cute, and cheap, **Café Soleil,** 37 Caledonia St. (☎ 415/331-9355), whips up some savory soups, salads, and sandwiches along with killer smoothies. Order to-go at the counter, then take your goods a block over to the marina for a dock-side lunch. Open daily 7am to 6:30pm.

Caledonia Kitchen, 400 Caledonia St. (☎ 415/331-0220), is the sort of place you wish was just around the corner from your house—a beautiful little cafe serving a huge assortment of fresh salads, soups, chili, sandwiches, and inexpensive entrees like herbed roast chicken or vegetarian lasagna for only $4.95. Continental-style breakfast items and good coffee and espresso drinks are also on the menu. Open daily 8am to 8pm.

Like the name says, the specialty at tiny **Hamburgers,** 737 Bridgeway (☎ 415/ 332-9471), is juicy flame-broiled hamburgers, arguably Marin County's best. Look for the rotating grill in the window off Bridgeway, then stand in line and salivate (chicken burgers are a slightly healthier option). Order a side of fries, grab a bunch of napkins, then head over to the park across the street. Open daily 11am to 5 pm.

You can get anything from a snack to a meal at **The Stuffed Croissant,** 43 Caledonia St. (☎ 415/332-7103). There are all sorts of gourmet croissants, including those filled with almond-chicken salad as well as bagels, soups, and stews. Hot, cheap meals such as chicken curry with rice are also popular. For dessert there's carrot cake, pecan bars, fudge and peanut brownies, and more. Open Monday through Wednesday from 6:45am to 9pm, Thursday through Saturday 6:45am to 10pm, and Sunday 7:30am to 8pm.

Venice Gourmet Delicatessen, 625 Bridgeway (☎ 415/332-3544), is a classic old deli with all the makings for a superb picnic: wines, cheeses, fruit, stuffed vine leaves, mushroom and artichoke salad, quiche, delicious sandwiches (made to order on sourdough bread), olives, and fresh-baked pastries. Open daily 9am to 6pm.

4 Tiburon & Angel Island

8 miles N of San Francisco

A federal and state wildlife refuge, **Angel Island** is the largest of the San Francisco Bay's three islets (the others being Alcatraz and Yerba Buena). The island has been, at various times, a prison, a quarantine station for immigrants, a missile base, and even a favorite dueling site. Nowadays, though, most of the people who visit here are content with picnicking on the large green lawn that fronts the docking area. Loaded with the appropriate recreational supplies, they claim a barbecue, plop on the lush green grass, and wile away an afternoon free of phones, television, and traffic. Hiking, mountain biking, and guided tram tours are also popular options.

Tiburon, situated on a peninsula of the same name, looks like a cross between a fishing village and a Hollywood Western set—imagine San Francisco reduced to toy dimensions. This seacoast town rambles over a series of green hills and ends up at a spindly, multicolored pier on the waterfront, like a miniature Fisherman's Wharf. But in reality it's an extremely plush patch of yacht-club suburbia, as you'll see by both the boats and their owners' homes. Main Street is lined with ramshackle, color-splashed old frame houses that shelter chic boutiques, souvenir stores, antiques shops, and art galleries. Other roads are narrow, winding, and hilly, leading up to dramatically situated homes. The view of San Francisco's skyline and the islands in the bay is a good enough reason to pay the precious price to live here.

GETTING THERE

BY BOAT   Ferries of the **Red and White Fleet** (☎ **800/229-2784** or 415/546-2700) leave from Pier 43¹/₂ (Fisherman's Wharf) and travel to both Tiburon and Angel Island. Boats run on a seasonal schedule; phone for departure information. The round-trip fare is $11 to Tiburon, $9 to Angel Island; half price for kids 5 to 11. (*Note:* The Red and White Fleet may be converted into the Blue and Gold Fleet, but will probably keep the same schedule and fares.)

BY CAR   If you're driving from San Francisco, take U.S. 101 to the Tiburon/Calif. 131 exit, then follow Tiburon Boulevard all the way into downtown, a 40-minute drive from San Francisco. Catch the ferry (☎ **415/435-2131** or 415/388-6770) to Angel Island from the dock located at Tiburon Boulevard and Main Street. The 15-minute round-trip costs $5 adult, $3 children 5–11, and $1 for bikes.

WHAT TO SEE & DO ON ANGEL ISLAND

Passengers get off the ferry at **Ayala Cove,** a small marina abutting a huge lawn area equipped with tables, benches, barbecue pits, and rest rooms. Also at Ayala Cove is a small store, gift shop, cafe (with surprisingly good grub), and an overpriced mountain bike rental shop (helmets included).

Among the 12 miles of Angel Island's hiking and mountain bike trails is the **Perimeter Road,** a partly paved path that circles the island and winds its way past disused troop barracks, former gun emplacements, and other military buildings; several turnoffs lead up to the top of Mount Livermore, 776 feet above the bay. Sometimes referred to as the "Ellis Island of the West," Angel Island was used as a holding area for Chinese immigrants awaiting their citizenship papers from 1910 to 1940. You can still see some faded Chinese characters on the walls of the barracks where the immigrants were held. During the warmer months you can camp at a limited number of sites; reservations are required.

Also offered at Angel Island are guided sea kayak tours. The all-day trips, which include a catered lunch, combine the thrill of paddling stable one-, two-, or three-person kayaks with an informative, naturalist-led tour that encircles the island (conditions permitting). All equipment is provided, kids are welcome, and no experience is necessary. Rates run about $110 per person. Call **Sea Trek** (☎ **415/488-1000**) for more information.

For recorded information about **Angel Island State Park,** call **415/435-1915.** For camping information and reservations call **800/444-7275.**

WHAT TO SEE & DO IN TIBURON

The main thing to do in Tiburon is stroll along the waterfront, pop into the stores, and spend a fast $50 on drinks and appetizers before heading back to the city. For a taste of the wine country, stop in at **Windsor Vineyards,** 72 Main St. (☎ **800/214-9463** or 415/435-3113). Their Victorian tasting room dates from 1888, and 35 different wines are available for free tasting. Wine accessories and gifts—glasses, cork pullers, gourmet sauces, posters, carry-packs (they hold six bottles), and maps—are also available. Ask about personalized labels for your own selections. The shop is open daily from 10am to 6pm.

WHERE TO DINE IN TIBURON

Guaymas. 5 Main St. ☎ **415/435-6300.** Reservations accepted. Main courses $12–$18. AE, CB, DC, MC, V. Mon–Fri 11:30am–9:30pm, Sat 11:30am–10:30pm, Sun. 10:30am–9:30pm. From U.S. 101, exit at Tiburon/Calif. 131; follow Tiburon Blvd. 5 miles and turn right onto Main St. The restaurant is situated directly behind the bakery. Ferry: Walk about 10 paces from the landing. MEXICAN.

Guaymas offers authentic Mexican cuisine and a spectacular panoramic view of San Francisco and the Bay. If it's a nice day, the two outdoor patios will probably be packed with diners. Inside, the beige walls are covered with colorful Mexican artwork and to the rear is a beehive-shaped adobe fireplace.

Guaymas is named after a fishing village on Mexico's Sea of Cortez, and both the town and the restaurant are famous for their *camarones* (giant shrimp). In addition, the restaurant features ceviche, handmade tamales, and charcoal-grilled beef, seafood, and fowl. Save room for dessert, especially the outrageously scrumptious fritter with "drunken" bananas and ice cream. In addition to a good selection of California wines, the restaurant offers an exceptional variety of tequilas, Mexican beers, and mineral waters flavored with flowers, grains, and fruits.

Sam's Anchor Café. 27 Main St. ☎ **415/435-4527.** Reservations accepted. Main courses $8–$16. AE, MC, V. Mon–Thurs 11am–10pm, Fri 11am–10:30pm, Sat 10am–10:30pm, Sun 9:30am–10pm. From U.S. 101, exit at Tiburon/Calif. 131; follow Tiburon Blvd. 4 miles and turn right onto Main St. Ferry: Walk from the landing. SEAFOOD.

Summer Sundays are liveliest in Tiburon, when weekend boaters tie up to the docks at waterside restaurants like this one. Sam's is the kind of place where you and your cronies can take off your shoes and have a fun, relaxed time eating burgers and drinking margaritas outside on the pier. The fare is pretty typical—sandwiches, salads, and seafood—but the quality and selection of the food is inconsequential: Beers, burgers, and a designated driver are all you really need.

Sweden House Bakery-Café. 35 Main St. ☎ **415/435-9767.** Reservations not accepted. Omelets $6.50–$7; sandwiches $6–$8. MC, V. Mon–Fri 8am–6pm, Sat–Sun 8am–7pm. From U.S. 101, exit at Tiburon/Belvedere; follow Tiburon Blvd. 5 miles and turn right onto Main St. Ferry: Walk from the landing. SWEDISH/AMERICAN.

This small, cozy cafe with gingham-covered walls adorned with copperware is a local favorite. On sunny mornings there's no better seat in the Bay Area than on the bakery's terrace, where you can nurse an espresso and pastry while gazing out over the bay. Full breakfasts are served, too, all accompanied by toasted Swedish limpa bread; skip the eggs and bacon routine and go with the tasty Swedish pancakes made with lingonberry, blueberry, and apple. At lunch, there's typical American fare plus traditional open-face sandwiches, including avocado and bacon or asparagus tips rolled in Danish ham. Beer and wine are available.

5 Muir Woods & Mount Tamalpais

15 miles N of San Francisco

by Andrew Rice

Muir Woods is one of the best-preserved wilderness regions that lies in the shadow of a major U.S. metropolitan area. Leave San Francisco, cross the Golden Gate Bridge, and within 20 minutes you can experience the old-growth coastal redwoods of Northern California much as they were prior to the influx of European settlers in the 19th century.

While the rest of Marin County's redwood forests were being devoured to feed San Francisco's building boom around the turn of the century, the trees of Muir Woods, in a remote ravine on the flanks of Mount Tamalpais, escaped destruction. By 1905, however, lumber companies had designs on the 200-foot-tall, 800-year-old giants. They were thwarted when farsighted congressman, philanthropist, and conservationist William Kent purchased the grove for $45,000. But only two years later the trees faced a different threat: The local water agency sought to condemn the land and build a dam on Redwood Creek that would have inundated the forest. Kent appealed to President Theodore Roosevelt and in 1908 secured the woods as a national monument. It was on Kent's request that the park was named after John Muir.

Muir Woods is a small park, only 553 acres tucked in a V-shaped canyon, but the area is completely encircled by enormous **Mount Tamalpais State Park,** lending it a wildness beyond its size.

The monument is 17 miles north of San Francisco, with well-marked signs leading from U.S. 101. From 101 you can enter the park from either Calif. 1 or the Panoramic Highway. The national monument visitor center and the state park both sell good hiking maps for a small fee. Muir Woods is open every day from 8am to sunset. Admission is free. For more information, contact **Muir Woods National Monument,** Mill Valley, CA 94941 (☎ **415/338-2595**). There is no picnicking, camping, or accommodations in Muir Woods. The nearest campground is a first-come, first-served 13-site walk-in camp at Pan Toll Station, or the heavily wooded **Alice Eastwood Group Camp** (☎ **800/444-7275**) in Mount Tamalpais State Park. Reservations are required.

HIKING Most visitors take the easy, paved loop trail that leaves from the visitor center and circles along the banks of Redwood Creek into the heart of the monument's **Bohemian and Cathedral Groves.** Hikers seeking more solitude should consider the longer trails, such as **Fern Creek Loop,** 4 miles of spectacular canyon and redwood views; or the more strenuous **Dipsea Loop,** an 8-mile mix of shady creekside, high ridges, and ocean views. On busy weekends, when the 200-space visitor center parking area can be a real headache, consider choosing the **Hassle Free Loop,** which begins on the Panoramic Highway in Mount Tamalpais State Park and descends into the redwood grove and fern canyon via the Panoramic Trail, Ocean View Trail, and Fern Canyon Trail—a total of about 5 miles. The hike from this parking area to the top of **Mount Tamalpais** is short but steep, and the view is among the best in the Bay Area.

6 Marine World Africa USA

30 miles NE of San Francisco, 10 miles S of Napa

Marine World Africa USA, on Marine World Parkway, in Vallejo (☎ **707/643-6722**), is a kind of Disney-meets-Wild-Kingdom theme park, offering aquatic and other trained animal performances.

The **Blue and Gold Fleet** (☎ **415/705-5555**) operates high-speed ferries from Pier 41 at Fisherman's Wharf. The scenic cruise, past Alcatraz and the Golden Gate Bridge, takes 80 minutes, plus a brief bus ride. The round-trip, including park admission, is $39 for adults, $32 for seniors 62 and over and students 13 to 18, and $23.50 for kids 4 to 12. Service is limited; call for departure times.

If you're driving from San Francisco, take I-80 north to Calif. 37 and follow the signs to the park; the ride is less than an hour.

A variety of events are scheduled continuously throughout the day. There's a **Killer Whale and Dolphin Show,** where the front seven rows of seats are saved for guests who want a thorough drenching. **Shark Experience,** a moving walkway through a clear acrylic tunnel, brings visitors through a 300,000-gallon tropical shark-filled tank.

Cross a bridge over a waterfall, past the flamingos, and you enter **Africa USA.** Here you'll find the **Elephant Encounter,** where visitors can meet the park's 11 Asian and African elephants. In addition to shows, you can ride elephants for $3. At **Tiger Island,** you can see trainers and Bengal tigers playing and swimming together. An informative show about the park's exotic and endangered animals is performed in the **Wildlife Theater.**

The **Bird Show** is one of the park's best features and proves that birds' peanut-sized brains are capable of more than we think. There's also an enclosed Butterfly World, a Small Animal Petting Kraal (with llamas), and Gentle Jungle, a playground that combines education, fun, and adventure. Finally there's a 55-acre lake that is the stage for a **Waterski and Boat Show,** April through October.

Admission is $25.95 for adults, $17.95 for kids 4 to 12, and $21.95 for seniors over 60, free for children under 4. Credit cards are accepted. The park is open from Memorial Day through Labor Day, daily from 9:30am to 6pm; the rest of the year, Wednesday through Sunday from 9:30am to 5pm.

7 San Jose & Environs

45 miles SE o f San Francisco

THE HEART OF SILICON VALLEY: SAN JOSE

Some may mourn the San Jose of yesterday, a sleepy, small town of orchards, crops, and beef, but those days are long gone. Founded in 1717 and long dwelling in the shadows of San Francisco, San Jose is now Northern California's largest city. With surveys claiming San Jose to be one of the safest, sunniest cities in America, it's a force to be reckoned with. Today the prosperity of Silicon Valley has transformed an agricultural backwater into a thriving city of restaurants, shops, a state-of-the-art light rail system, a reputable art scene, and a sports arena (home to the popular San Jose Sharks, the city's NHL team).

ESSENTIALS

GETTING THERE   BART (☎ 510/793-2278) travels from San Francisco to Fremont in 1¹/₄ hours; you can take a bus from there). **Caltrain** (☎ 415/291-5651) operates frequently from San Francisco and takes about an hour and 25 minutes.

VISITOR INFORMATION   Contact the **San Jose Convention and Visitors Bureau,** 333 West San Carlos St., Suite 1000, CA 95110 (☎ 408/295-9600).

GETTING AROUND   Light Rail (☎ 408/321-2300) ⓘ best for getting around. A ticket is good for two hours and stops include Paramount's Great America, the Convention Center, and downtown museums. You can also use the historic trolleys, which operate in a loop around downtown (summer only). Tickets can be purchased at Light Rail stations.

MUSEUMS WORTH SEEKING OUT

Downtown San Jose has several museums worth mentioning. **The Tech Museum of Innovation,** 145 W. San Carlos St., between Market and Almaden Boulevard (☎ 408/279-7150), is a small-scale museum that allows visitors to grapple with modern technology. For example, visitors can use CAD (computer-aided design) to create a bicycle and then test it in a wind tunnel. Admission is $6 for adults, $4 children 6 to 18 and seniors; open Tuesday through Sunday from 10am to 5pm.

The **San Jose Museum of Art,** 110 S. Market St. (☎ 408/294-2787), is collaborating with New York's Whitney Museum of American Art for shows that trace the development of 20th-century American art. The series will include works by Franz Kline, Louis Nevelson, Andy Warhol, and many others. Look for renovations in the Historic Wing, opening in 1997. Admission is $6 adults, $3 children 6 to 17 and seniors. Open Tuesday through Sunday 10am to 5pm (until 8pm Thursday).

The **Children's Discovery Museum,** 180 Woz Way (☎ **408/298-5437**) offers more than 150 interactive exhibits, as well as shows and workshops for kids to explore science, humanities, arts, and technology. "ArtWorks Too!" is a studiolike art center with projects changing monthly, while an exhibit drawing rave review is "Bubbalogna," which highlights the whimsical and scientifically intriguing world of bubbles. Smaller kids enjoy dressing up in costumes and role-playing on the fire truck. Admission is $6 for adults, $5 for seniors, $4 for children 2 to 18. Open Tuesday through Saturday from 10am to 5pm, Sunday from noon to 5pm.

The **San Jose Historical Museum,** 1600 Senter Rd. (☎ **408/287-2290**), occu-pies 25 acres in Kelley Park and features 26 original and replica buildings that have been restored to represent San Jose life in the 1880s. The usual cast of characters is here—the doctor, the printer, the postmaster—with an occasional local surprise, such as the 1888 Chinese temple and the original Stevens fruit barn. Admission is $4 adults, $3 seniors, and $2 children 4 to 17. Open Monday through Friday from 10am to 4:15pm, Saturday and Sunday from noon to 4:15pm.

The **Rosicrucian Egyptian Museum and Planetarium,** 1342 Naglee Ave. (☎ **408/947-3636**), is associated with the Rosicrucian Order that traces its origins back to the Egyptians who believed strongly in the afterlife and reincarnation. On display are human and animal mummies, funerary boats, canopic jars as well as jew-elry, pottery, and bronze tools. There's also a replica of a noble Egyptian's tomb. Admission is $6.75 for adults, $4 for seniors, and $3.50 for children 7 to 15. Open daily from 9am to 5pm. Call for show times at the Planetarium, which is open week-days only. Admission is $4 for adults and $3 for children.

A Great Place to Take A Break

A great spot to rest your feet and wallow in the comfort of air-conditioning is the ven-erable **Fairmont Hotel,** 170 S. Market St., San Jose, CA 95113 (☎ **408/998-1900**). Ideally located near the Convention Center and the Center of Performing Arts, this landmark hotel, with its dwarfing crystal chandeliers, golden-marble columns, and plush furnishings, plays host to the likes of President Clinton, Luciano Pavarotti, Mike Wallace, and more. A popular spot to have afternoon tea or cocktails, the elegant lobby and gracious service attracts many who are just stopping in for a peek. For fun, slide up to the massive marble soda fountain, and have a frothing root beer float.

THEME PARK THRILLS

Paramount's Great America, Great America Parkway (off U.S. 101), Santa Clara (☎ **408/988-1776**), provides 100 acres of family entertainment. A pretty cool place to lose your lunch, the park includes such favorites as the Top Gun suspended jet coaster, the Days of Thunder auto-racing simulator, a three-acre Nickelodeon Cen-ter for children, and the new "Drop Zone," the world's tallest free-fall ride. Be sure to check for concerts and special events. Admission is $27.95 adults, $18.95 seniors, and $13.95 children 3 to 6. Open from March to October 22 on Saturdays and Sun-days from 10am to 9pm (hours are extended on Labor Day weekend). To get there from San Francisco, take U.S. 101 south for about 45 miles to the Great America Parkway exit.

WHERE TO STAY

A variety of chain motels are represented in San Jose. The best for budget travelers is the **Comfort Inn** (☎ 408/280-5300).

The Hensley House. 456 N 3rd St. San Jose, CA 95112 ☎ **408/298-3537.** 5 rms. TEL TV. $79–$175. AE, DC, MC, V.

"Location, location, location," is what innkeepers Sharon Layne and Bill Priest will tell you. The Hensley's proximity to museums, theaters, and restaurants certainly hasn't hurt business. This stately Queen Anne is a quiet getaway in a restored land-mark building, with beautiful antiques, crystal chandeliers, feather beds—all sur-rounded by dark wood. If you're up for more luxury and a little superstition, try the Judge's Chambers. Complete with wet bar, whirlpool, hand-painted ceiling and walls, fireplace, VCR, and its very own ghost (previous owner and superior court Judge Perley Gosbey), this room is quite an experience. Guests can also enjoy a complete breakfast, daily afternoon hors d'oeuvres, and high tea on Thursdays and Saturdays.

Hotel de Anza. 233 W. Santa Clara St., San Jose, CA 95113. ☎ **800/843-3700** or 408/286-1000. Fax 408/286-0500. 100 rms. A/C MINIBAR TEL TV. $155–$170 double, $295 suite. Special weekend rates available. AE, DC, MC, V.

Located downtown in a landmark art deco building, this hotel is small enough to provide personal service. The room decor may reflect a 1930s style in the furnish-ings, but the amenities are state of the art. There are three telephones in each room, including one with dedicated data line and fax port, plus voice-mail service. Com-puters and fax machines are supplied on request. Additional amenities include a VCR and complimentary tapes. Bathrobes, a hair dryer, a make-up mirror, a TV, and a telephone are available in each bathroom. There's room service, laundry/valet, com-plimentary shoeshine, nightly turndown, and a health club with Nautilus machines. There is a club lounge as well as La Pastaia restaurant, which serves fine Italian cuisine.

WHERE TO DINE

Meals for $20 or Less

Gordon Biersch. 33 E. San Fernando St. ☎ **408/294-6785.** Reservations recommended. Main courses from $7.50–$13.95. AE, DC, DISC, MC, V. Hours Sun–Wed 11am–11pm, Thurs 11am–midnight, Fri–Sat 11am–1am. ECLECTIC.

One of the original luxe brew-pub restaurants that are quickly spreading across Northern California, this place offers a little of everything. To complement the beer, the menu features some lighter fare, ranging from a Thai satay platter and goat cheese salads to molasses-glazed baby back ribs. Big burgers and filling pub grub is equally popular. A large outdoor patio and live music continues to attract a younger crowd. Four tasty home brews are always on tap, and locals are allowed to keep their own steins in wood lockers.

Il Fornaio. In the Hotel Sainte Claire, 302 S. Market St. ☎ **408/271-3366.** Reservations rec-ommended. Main courses $8–$11. AE, DC, MC, V. Mon–Fri 7–10:30am and 11:30am–10pm; Sat–Sun 8–10:30am and 11:30am–11pm. Live entertainment is offered Tues–Sat. NORTHERN ITALIAN.

Voted by readers of *San Francisco Focus* magazine as "Best Italian" and "Best Over-all Restaurant" three years running, this fine establishment is always a sure thing. This location isn't quite as inviting as the one in Palo Alto, but it's still a lovely place to dine. The specialties of the house include the mesquite-grilled fresh fish and the veal chop with sage and rosemary, as well as grilled pounded chicken breast with a purée of roasted garlic and rosemary. There are about ten pizzas to choose from; our favorite

The Winchester Mystery House

Begun in 1884, the **Winchester Mystery House,** at 525 S. Winchester Blvd., San Jose (☎ 408/247-2101), is a monument to one woman's paranoia. It's the legacy of Sarah L. Winchester, widow of the son of the famous rifle magnate. After the deaths of her husband and baby daughter, Mrs. Winchester consulted with a seer, who proclaimed that continuous building would appease the evil spirits of those killed with Winchester repeaters. Convinced that she'd live as long as construction went on, the widow used much of her $20 million inheritance to finance the construction, which went on 24 hours a day, 7 days a week, 365 days a year, for 38 years. If only she could be on *Ricki Lake* today.

It's immediately apparent that this is no ordinary home. With 160 rooms, it sprawls across a half dozen acres. And it's full of disturbing features: a staircase leading nowhere, a Tiffany window with a spider web design, and doors that open onto blank walls. There are 13 bathrooms, 13 windows and doors in the old sewing room, 13 palms lining the main driveway, 13 hooks in the seance room, and chandeliers with 13 lights. Such schemes were designed to confound the spirits that seemed to plague the heiress.

You can tour house and grounds for $12.95 adults, $9.95 seniors, and $6.95 for children 6 to 12. Tours leave about every 15 minutes. The house is open daily from 9am to 8pm.

comes topped with Maui onions, gruère and mozzarella cheese, smoked ham, and sage. For hearty appetites, there's an excellent and tender 22 oz. steak. Salads and appetizers, including a tasty grilled polenta with wild mushrooms provolone, round out the menu.

Paolo's. 333 W. San Carlos St. ☎ **408/294-2558.** Reservations recommended. Main courses $7–$20. AE, MC, V. Mon–Fri 11am–2:30pm; Mon–Sat 5:30–10pm. NORTHERN ITALIAN.

Paolo's occupies the ground floor of a high-rise office building. The restaurant attracts a business crowd at lunch and a rather cultured crowd in the evening. The cuisine is refined northern Italian, with innovative flourishes. Among the appetizers, for instance, the beef carpaccio is served with a piquant vegetable sauce. The main dishes might include sea scallops roasted with whole garlic, cherry tomatoes, and thyme, or a classic roasted quail with white raisins, grappa, and natural juices. Desserts also stretch beyond the typical Italian favorites to include a chocolate torte with orange caramel sauce, or a lemon curd tart with toasted coconut and pistachio nuts. An extensive wine list features 600-plus selections.

Worth a Splurge
Emile's. 545 S. 2nd St. ☎ **408/289-1960.** Reservations recommended. Main courses $16.50–$28. AE, MC, V. Tues–Sat 6–10pm. CONTEMPORARY EUROPEAN.

Chef/proprietor Emile Mooser uses local ingredients to produce a tasty, contemporary cuisine. To start, try the scallops and spinach wrapped in filo on citrus emulsion, or Mooser's interesting variation on French onion soup, made with gorgonzola and Gruyère cheese. Follow with a roasted, peppered pork tenderloin, served on roasted Granny Smith apples that bring out the flavor perfectly. Mirrors and recessed lighting and large, bold floral arrangements create an elegant atmosphere. For dessert, select the chocolate mousse flavored with dark rum and served with raspberry coulis.

OFF THE BEATEN TRACK: SARATOGA

To reach quaint Saratoga from San Jose, drive south on Calif. 17 for about 10 miles and take the Los Gatos Road exit (Calif. 9); head northwest on Los Gatos to the center of town.

Walk down Saratoga's Main Street and you're bound to get the feeling that the real world has yet to infiltrate this sprawl of expensive shops, restaurants, and homes—not unlike a miniature Carmel. Be sure to check out the many small wineries in the area such as **The Mountain Winery** (☎ 408/741-5183) and **Mariani Winery and Saratoga Vineyards** (☎ 408/741-2930).

WHERE TO STAY

Los Gatos Lodge. 50 Saratoga Ave., Los Gatos, CA 95032. ☎ **408/354-3300.** 127 rms. $48–$52. A/C TEL TV. AE, DC, DISC, MC, V.

If history is any indication of success, it should be known that the Los Gatos Lodge has held its own for the past four decades. Surrounded by dense woods, this rustic lodge, bar, and restaurant used to be a real pick-up joint in the 1970s. A great deal for the dollar, the place is loaded with amenities, including balconies, patios, a putting green, a pool, room service, kitchenettes, and shuffle board courts. For a small fee, you can even bring Fluffy along.

Madison Street Inn. 1390 Madison St. Santa Clara, CA 95050. ☎ **408/249-5541.** 6 rms. $60–$85. TEL. AE, DC, DISC, MC, V.

Conveniently located just minutes from downtown, this restored Victorian B&B is nestled among two gigantic pepper trees and ensconced by a white picket fence and rose garden. It has four rooms, each distinctively decorated with personal touches from the era. Special suites come with a claw-foot tub, brass beds, lace coverlets, and more; all come with private baths. Proprietors Ralph and Theresa Wigginton are willing to whip up custom dinners of California cuisine or serve you their hearty breakfast that might feature eggs Benedict, Belgian waffles, omelets, and home-baked muffins and breads.

WHERE TO DINE

Bella Mia. 14503 Big Basin Way, Saratoga. ☎ **408/741-5115.** Reservations recommended. Main courses $12–$20. AE, DC, DISC, MC, V. Mon–Fri 11:30am–9:30pm, Sat 10am–10pm, Sun 10am–3pm, 5–10pm. ITALIAN.

Customers come from far or near to enjoy the best pasta in town. Set in an attractive two-story Victorian in the center of town, this dining experience pleases all the senses. Dishes range from salmon ravioli in a creamy tomato-dill sauce; angel hair pasta with fresh tomatoes, basil, white wine, and garlic; and the meat-eaters fave, lasagna layered with ground beef, sausage, salami, and cheese. Tantalizing appetizers include a roasted prawn cocktail, bruschetta, and fried mozzarella. If you can't make Mia's for dinner, come by for their Sunday jazz brunch.

Pigalle. 27 N Santa Cruz Ave., Los Gatos. ☎ **408/395-7924.** Reservations strongly recommended. Main courses $7–$15. MC, V. 11am–10pm daily. FRENCH.

Local residents have affectionately dubbed this bistro "Pig Alley", but they mean it in only the nicest way. Due to its generous and reasonably priced portions, the nickname and popularity can not be questioned. A Parisian street scene painted on the wall sets the mood for the topnotch French country cuisine. Pigalle, named for Paris's red-light district, offers a small, yet wonderful, seasonal menu. For lunch try the seafood fettuccine with scallops and prawns or the chicken pie stuffed with artichoke hearts, mushrooms, and cream sauce wrapped in a puff pastry. For dinner enjoy the crisp roast duck in a caramelized raspberry sauce or a tender piece of rabbit with a mustard-sherry cream sauce. House specialties often include tempting French desserts, such as poached pears filled with mascarpone in a fruit reduction sauce. *C'est bon.*

DRIVING TO SANTA CRUZ VIA GILROY & MISSION SAN JUAN BAUTISTA

A short drive down U.S. 101 from San Jose, Gilroy is famous for its **garlic festival,** which is held in July. It's also becoming known for its outlet shopping, too. For information, contact the **Gilroy Visitor's Bureau** (☎ **408/842-6436**).

A little farther down, U.S. 101 brings you to the San Juan Bautista exit. This is an historic town with a definite Spanish-Mexican flavor. The B (open daily from 9:30am to 4:30pm) is filled with power and serenity. Its walls look out over meadowlands, and one can imagine how isolated it must have been when it was built in 1797. The interior walls are decorated with frescoes, while the reredos has six hand-carved painted wooden statues, including a life-size polychrome figure of San Juan Bautista. More than 4,000 Native Americans are buried in the cemetery beside the church.

A grassy plaza spreads in front of the mission and around it stand a nunnery (built in 1815), the Castro House, the Plaza Hotel (1858), and stables, which together constitute the **San Juan Bautista Historic Park** (☎ **408/623-4881**). Admission is $2 adults, $1 children; it's open Wednesday through Sunday from 10am to 4:30pm.

The Castro House was the home of the Mexican administrator, Jose Maria Castro. In 1848 it was purchased by the Breen family, members of the Donner party who had survived 111 days stranded in the snow-bound Sierra Nevada in 1846.

The Plaza Hotel was a major stop on the stagecoach route in the mid-1800s when 10 or so stages passed through here daily. Once the railroad bypassed the town in 1876, it became a quiet backwater, which is why it's survived intact. The town's main street is lined with antique stores that are worth browsing and several Mexican restaurants. The big event here is the Annual Flea market and Antique Show held in August. For additional information, contact the **San Juan Bautista Chamber of Commerce** at **408/623-2454.**

8 Santa Cruz

77 miles SE of San Francisco

To reach Santa Cruz directly from San Francisco, take Calif. 280 south toward San Jose, then take the well-marked turnoff to Calif. 17, which brings you right into the downtown area.

For a small bay-side city, Santa Cruz has a lot to offer. The main show, of course, is the Beach Boardwalk, the West Coast's only seaside amusement park that attracts millions of visitors each year. But past the arcades and cotton candy is a surprisingly diverse and energetic city that has a little something for everyone. The list of things to do here is almost endless—shopping, hiking, mountain biking, sailing, fishing, kayaking, surfing, wine tasting, golfing, whale watching—making Santa Cruz one of the premier family destinations on the California coast.

ESSENTIALS

For information, contact the **Santa Cruz County Conference and Visitors Council,** 701 Front St., Santa Cruz, CA 95060 (☎ **800/833-3494** or 408/425-1234). It's open Monday to Saturday from 9am to 5pm, Sundays from 10am to 4pm.

Special events include the **Santa Cruz Hot and Cool Jazz Festival** (☎ 408/ 662-1912; July); **Shakespeare Santa Cruz** (☎ 408/459-2121; July/August); and the **Cabrillo Music Festival** (☎ 408/426-6966; August).

WHAT TO SEE & DO: BEACHES, HIKING, FISHING & MORE

One of the top amusement parks in the nation, the privately owned **Santa Cruz Beach Boardwalk,** draws more than three million visitors a year to its 27 rides and multitudes of arcades, shops, and restaurants. Parents will remember the park's two national landmarks: a 1924 wooden Giant Dipper roller coaster and a 1911 carousel complete with hand-carved wooden horses and a 342-pipe band organ. It's open daily in the summer from Memorial Day weekend through Labor Day, and on weekends and holidays throughout the spring and fall, from 11am on. Admission to the boardwalk is free, but an all-day "unlimited rides" pass will set you back about $18. For more information, call 408/426-7433.

Here, too, at 400 Beach St. is **Neptune's Kingdom** (☎ **408/426-7433**), an enormous indoor family recreation center where the main feature is a two-story miniature golf course. Also on Beach Street is the **Municipal Wharf** (☎ **408/429-3628**) and pier, lined with shops and restaurants—visitors are serenaded by the sea lions below. (This is where you can pick up your UC-Santa Cruz Banana Slugs T-shirt, just like the one John Travolta sported in *Pulp Fiction*.) You can also crab and fish from here. Open daily from 7am to 9am. **Stagnaro's,** P. O. Box 7007 (☎ **408/ 427-2334**), also operates fishing and whale-watching trips from the pier from November through April.

Farther around West Cliff Drive, you'll come to a favorite surfing spot, **Steamers Lane,** where you can watch the surfers coasting into the beach. If you want to find out more about this local sport that's been practiced here for 100 years, then go to the memorial lighthouse, which contains the **Santa Cruz Surfing Museum** (☎ **408/429-3429**), open Thursday through Monday from noon to 4pm in winter and Wednesday through Monday from noon to 5pm in summer.

Continue along West Cliff and you'll eventually reach **Natural Bridges State Beach,** 2531 W. Cliff Dr. (☎ **408/423-4609**), a large sandy beach with nearby tide pools and hiking trails. It's also home to a large colony of Monarch butterflies that roost and mate in the nearby eucalyptus grove.

Other Santa Cruz beaches worth noting are: **Bonny Doon,** at Bonny Doon Road and Calif. 1, an uncrowded sandy beach and a major surfing spot accessible by a steep walkway; **Pleasure Point Beach,** East Cliff Drive at Pleasure Point Drive; and **Twin Lakes State Beach,** which is ideal for sunning and also provides access to Schwann Lagoon, a bird sanctuary.

In addition to many cultural and sporting events, the University of California at Santa Cruz also possesses the **Long Marine Laboratory and Aquarium,** 100 Shaffer Rd. (☎ **408/459-4308**), where you can observe the activities of marine scientists and the species kept in tide pool touch tanks and aquariums. Open Tuesday through Sunday from 1 to 4pm.

The **Santa Cruz Harbor,** 135 5th Ave. (☎ **408/475-6161**), is the place to head for boat rentals, open boat fishing (cod, shark, and salmon), and whale-watching trips. Operators include **Santa Cruz Sportfishing,** Santa Cruz Yacht Harbor, P.O. Box 3176, Santa Cruz, CA 95063 (☎ **408/426-4690**); and **Shamrock Charters,** 2210 E. Cliff Dr., Santa Cruz, CA 95062 (☎ **408/476-2648**).

There's a great bike ride along the 2-mile cliff walk. Bikes—mountain, kids, tandem, hybrid—are available by the hour, day, or week from the **Bicycle Rental and Tour Center,** 415 Pacific Ave. at Front St. (☎ **408/426-8687; open 10am** to 6pm in summer). Figure on paying $25 a day, which includes helmets, locks, and packs.

There are several public golf courses, the best being the **Pasatiempo Golf Club,** rated among the top 100 courses in the United States; 18 Clubhouse Rd. (☎ 408/459-9155).

Hikers, bikers, and birders in need of some direction can call **The Tour Center** (☎ 408/426-8687), whose experienced local guides specialize in hiking, biking, and birding, as well as water sport tours.

Sea kayaking is also fun. Outfitters include **Kayak Connection,** 413 Lake Ave. No. 4 (☎ 408/479-1121), and **Venture Quest** (☎ 408/425-8445), which has kayak, sail, and water-bike rentals available at Building no. 2 on the wharf.

Surfing equipment can be rented at the **Cowell's Beach 'n' Bikini Surf Shop,** 109 Beach St. (☎ 408/427-2355), and also from the **Club Ed Surf School,** Cowell Beach in front of the Dream Inn (☎ 408/459-9283). You could also soar above the bay on a parasailing trip courtesy of **Pacific Parasail,** 58 Municipal Wharf (☎ 408/423-3545). All of the outfitters above offer lessons.

South around the coast lies the small attractive community of **Capitola** at the mouth of the Soquel Creek, which is a spawning ground for steelhead and salmon. Here visitors can fish (no license required) from the **Capitola Wharf,** 1400 Wharf Rd. (☎ 408/462-2208). Fishing boats can be rented, too: call **Capitola Boat and Bait** at **408/462-2208.**

Capitola Beach fronts the Esplanade. Surf-fishing and clamming are popular pastimes at Capitola's **New Brighton State Beach,** 1500 State Park Dr. (☎ 408/475-4850), where camping is also allowed.

Other Capitola pastimes? Antiquing! Try the many stores along Soquel Drive between 41st and Capitola avenues.

Still farther south around the bay is Aptos, home to the 10,000-acre **Forest of Nisene Marks State Park** (☎ 408/724-1266), with hiking trails that wind through redwoods and past abandoned mining camps. It was also the epicenter of the 1989 earthquake.

About 25 miles north of Santa Cruz the **Año Nuevo State Reserve,** New Years Creek Road, off Calif. 1 in Pescadero (☎ 800/444-7275), offers guided walks into the Northern Elephant Seal rookery from December through March. The walks take $2^{1}/_{2}$ hours and cover 3 miles. Reservations are necessary. Self-guided walks are possible with a permit in summer.

In the redwood-forested mountains behind Santa Cruz, there are quite a few wineries, although visitors may not be familiar with the labels because the production is small and consumed locally. Most are clustered around Boulder Creek and Felton or around Capitola. All offer tours by appointment; some feature regular tasting, including the **Bargetto Winery,** 3535 North Main, Soquel (☎ 408/475-2258), which has a courtyard wine-tasting area overlooking the creek. For additional information, contact **Santa Cruz Mountains Winegrowers Association** at **408/479-WINE.**

WHERE TO STAY

Two **Travelodges** (☎ 800/578-7878), two **Best Westerns** (☎ 800/528-1234), two **Super 8s** (☎ 800/800-8000), and an **Econolodge** (☎ 800/553-2666) provide moderate and budget-priced accommodations in addition to the more inspiring choices below.

Casablanca Inn. 101 Main St. (at the corner of Beach), Santa Cruz, CA 95060. ☎ 408/423-1570. Fax 408/423-0235. 34 rms. TEL TV. $95–$300 double in high season; $58–$195 double in low season. AE, CB, DC, MC, V.

Saving in Santa Cruz

We think Santa Cruz is definitely worth a few days' stopover. So we've compiled a useful list of money-saving tips to make sure you won't break the bank while you're here.

- On Friday summer nights, head to the Santa Cruz Beach Boardwalk and check out the **free concerts.**
- Every summer after 5pm on Mondays and Tuesdays the Santa Cruz Beach Boardwalk holds **1907 Nights,** celebrating the year it opened by reducing prices to 50¢ a ride (that's $2.50 off). Hot dogs, sodas, and cotton candy are all marked down, too.
- Great **Mexican food** at cheap prices is served daily at the **El Palomar Restaurant's** taco bar, located inside the Pacific Garden Mall at 1336 Pacific Avenue (☎ **408/425-7575**). Last we heard, tacos and margaritas were only a buck apiece between 5 and 8pm on Tuesdays.
- To skip the $5 entrance fee to **Henry Cowell Redwoods State Park,** drive 1¹/₂ miles south of the main entrance on Calif. 9 to the Ox Road parking lot. Park for free, then follow the trail into the park, which takes you past a popular swimming hole called the Garden of Eden.
- A far better walk than the boardwalk is along the 2-mile oceanside paved path on **West Cliff Drive** (west of the wharf). The scenery is spectacular, particularly at sunset, and it won't cost you a penny.
- Parking at the **Santa Cruz Wharf** is free for the first 20 minutes, which is plenty of time to cruise the armada of schlocky shops and cafes.
- The **Carmelita Cottages,** 321 Main St. (☎ **408/423-8304**), is a hostel in Santa Cruz that reserves a few rooms just for couples and families. The gaggle of whitewashed Victorian cottages is a few blocks north of the boardwalk in a quiet residential neighborhood. It's not exactly Romance Central, but for only $30 a night at such a prime location, it's hard to complain.
- Don't you dare pay for parking in downtown Santa Cruz. Along Cedar, Pacific, and Front streets there are three parking garages and 16 surface lots that offer three hours of **free parking.**

Across from the wharf in a heavily trafficked area, this motel along the waterfront was once the Mediterranean-style Cerf Mansion, dating from 1918. Other motel-style accommodations have grown up around the main building. Originally the home of a federal judge, it offers individually decorated bedrooms, some with brass beds and velvet draperies. Some units contain fireplaces and terraces, and all are equipped with microwaves and coffeemakers. Most of the accommodations open onto views of the water. There's a restaurant on the premises (see "Where to Dine," below) that serves good seafood in a romantic ocean-view setting.

✪ **Darling House.** 314 W. Cliff Dr., Santa Cruz, CA 95060. ☎ **408/458-1958.** 8 rms (2 with private bath). $95 double without bath; $225 double with bath. AE, DISC, MC, V.

This lovely Spanish-style house, designed in 1910 by William Weeks, architect of Santa Cruz's Coconut Grove, has a panoramic location overlooking the Pacific Ocean in a quiet residential area within walking distance of the Boardwalk and Lighthouse. The house boasts fine architectural features throughout, such as beveled glass, antiques, and handsome fireplaces. Each of the eight rooms is individually decorated, and though all have sinks, only two come with private baths. The Pacific Ocean room, decorated like a sea captain's quarters, features a fireplace, telescope, and one of the finest ocean views in Santa Cruz. A backyard hot tub is available for guests. Breakfast includes oven-fresh breads and pastries, fruit, and homemade granola made with walnuts via Darling's own farm.

Edgewater Beach Motel. 525 Second St., Santa Cruz, CA 95060. ☎ 408/423-0440. 17 rms. TEL TV. $105–$185 double. AE, DC, DISC, MC, V.

If the other two inns listed here are booked, consider the Edgewater Beach Motel. It looks like a time capsule from the 1960s, which, oddly enough, makes it all the more appealing, as if your in a movie set for *Apollo 13* (how they kept the furnishings in such prime condition is a mystery). The motel offers a range of accommodations, from family suites with kitchens to nonsmoking rooms and rooms with fireplaces; most have microwaves and refrigerators. The Edgewater also sports a heated pool, sundeck, and barbecue area, but the real bonus is the location: The Santa Cruz Beach Boardwalk is only a block away. *Tip:* Inquire about the Edgewater's minivacation packages, which can save you a bundle on room rates.

WHERE TO DINE

✪ **Cafe Bittersweet.** 2332 Mission St. (near King St.) ☎ 408/423-9999. Reservations recommended. Main courses $10–$16. MC, V. Tues–Fri and Sun 5:30–9pm; Fri–Sat 5:30–10pm. MEDITERRANEAN.

In an unlikely small strip development, this light, airy restaurant occupies a single room with white walls and terra-cotta tile floors. It has developed a reputation for fine cuisine since it opened in 1992. The menu features only five main dishes, which ensures quality. Start with the grilled shrimp over greens with garlic, sage, and white beans, or one of the fresh salads. Follow with the richly flavored veal medallions with a brandied wild mushroom sauce. We also enjoyed the inventive mushroom moussaka, which layers eggplant and potatoes with a mixture of exotic mushrooms; the whole thing is topped with béchamel and kassari asiago and Parmesan cheeses.

Casablanca Restaurant. 101 Main St. (at Beach). ☎ 408/426-9063. Reservations recommended. Main courses $14–$20. AE, DC, MC, V. Sun–Thurs 5–9pm, Fri–Sat 5–10pm, Sun 9:30am–2pm. CONTINENTAL.

The candlelit dining room at Casablanca was obviously built for romance, right down to the stellar views of the shimmering bay. For a stimulating start, try the Sicilian red clam chowder or the fire-roasted Anaheim chile stuffed with herbed chèvre and served with tomatillo salsa. Among the 10 or so main courses, we'd recommend any of the fresh seafood dishes, perhaps the red snapper sautéed with capers, scallions, and lemon butter sauce. The award-winning book-length wine list is excellent.

✪ **O'Mei.** 2316 Mission St. ☎ 408/425-8458. Reservations suggested on Fri–Sat. Main courses $7–$11. AE, MC, V. Mon–Fri 11:30am–2pm; Mon–Thurs 5–9:30pm, Fri–Sat 5–10pm. SZECHUAN.

O'Mei's (pronounced oh-*may*) minimall location may not be very inviting, but the fantastic food served here more than makes up for it. The menu features some unusual specialties such as apricot-almond chicken and wine-braised chicken livers, along with more familiar dishes such as chicken with cashews or Szechuan shrimp. Dinner starts with a dim sum–style tray of exotic offerings such as sesame-cilantro-eggplant salad or pan-roasted peppers with feta cheese. Recommended choices are the sliced rock cod in black bean-sweet pepper sauce and the black date and sweet-potato chicken.

7

The Wine Country

by Erika Lenkert and Matthew R. Poole

California's adjacent Napa and Sonoma valleys are two of the most famous wine-growing regions in the world. The workaday valleys that are a way of life for thousands of vintners are also a worthy trip for any wine lover. Hundreds of wineries nestle among the vines of this beautiful countryside; most are open to visitors, and only a few of the larger wineries charge for tasting their premium wines (and even then it's only a few dollars).

Conveniently, most of the large wineries—as well as the majority of the hotels, shops, and restaurants—are located along a single road, Calif. 29, which starts at the mouth of the Napa River, near the north end of San Francisco Bay, and continues north to Calistoga and the top of the growing region. The Sonoma Valley towns and wineries are on the opposite side of the Mayacamas Mountain ridge, due west of Napa Valley along Calif. 12.

The best time to visit California's Wine Country is during the autumn harvest seasons when the grapes have ripened and all the wineries are in full production—it's quite a show. Spring has its own rewards: Both valleys are blanketed in wildflowers. Summer? Say hello to hot weather and heavy traffic.

For the budget traveler, the Wine Country has is advantages and disadvantages. If you pack a picnic lunch and avoid the wineries that charge a fee, you can literally cut your day's expenses down to a tank of gas. Lodging is a little more tricky, as most hotels and B&Bs start at $100 a night and go way up from there. There are, however, a handful of quality hotels in the region that offer exceptional values, as you'll soon find out.

1 Napa Valley

Many of the California wines you've been enjoying with your meals in San Francisco hail from this warm, narrow valley about 90 minutes north of the city. Napa Valley's fame as California's premier wine-growing region began with its cabernet sauvignon; except for the white chardonnay grape, more acreage is devoted to the growth of the cabernet grape than any other.

Napa Valley is home to more than 250 wineries. If you can, plan on spending more than a day here; it will take you a couple of days to tour even a small number of the valley's wineries. The valley is just 35 miles long, so any of the valley towns—Napa, Yountville,

The Wine Country

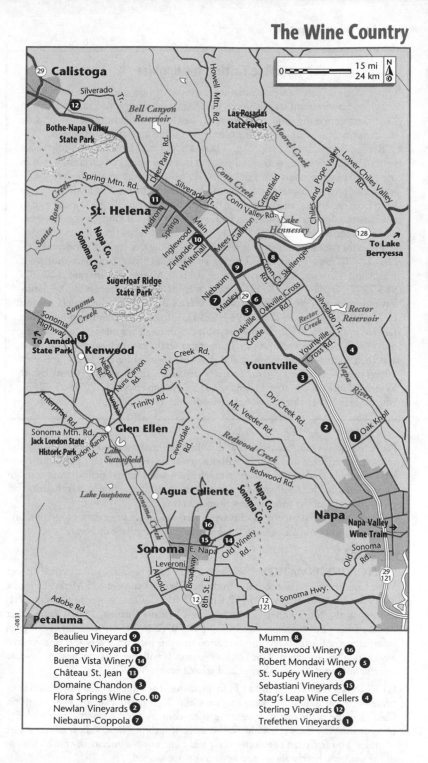

Calistoga 29
Silverado Tr.
12
Bell Canyon Reservoir
Las Posadas State Forest
Bothe-Napa Valley State Park
Moorel Creek
Lower Chiles Valley Rd.
Spring Mtn. Rd.
Deer Park Rd.
Conn Creek
Greenfield Rd.
Chiles and Pope Valley Rd.
Santa Rosa Creek
St. Helena 11
Madrona
Silverado Tr.
Conn Valley Rd.
Lake Hennessey
128
To Lake Berryessa
Napa Co.
Sonoma Co.
Spring
Inglewood
Zinfandel
Main
Whitehall
Mees
Calleron
Conn Cr. Rd.
8
Sugarloaf Ridge State Park
10
9
Niebaum
Manley
7
29
6
5
Oakville Cross Rd.
Skellenger
Silverado Tr.
Rector Creek
Rector Reservoir
Sonoma Creek
Oakville Grade
Yountville Cross Rd.
4
To Annadel State Park
13
Kenwood
12
Neligan Rd.
Nuns Canyon Rd.
Creek Rd.
Dry
Creek Rd.
Yountville
3
Napa River
Dunbar
Trinity Rd.
Dry Creek Rd.
2
1
Oak Knoll
Enterprise Rd.
Sonoma Mtn. Rd.
Glen Ellen
Mt. Veeder Rd.
Jack London State Historic Park
London Ranch Rd.
Lake Suttonfield
Cavendale Rd.
Redwood Creek
Redwood Rd.
Lake Josephone
Sonoma Creek
Agua Caliente
Napa Co.
Sonoma Co.
Napa
Napa Valley Wine Train
16
Old Winery Rd.
15
14
Sonoma
E. Napa
Sonoma Rd.
Leveroni
Broadway
8th St. E.
29 121
12
12 121
Sonoma Hwy.
Old Rd.
Adobe Rd.
Petaluma

1-0831

Beaulieu Vineyard 9	Mumm 8
Beringer Vineyard 11	Ravenswood Winery 16
Buena Vista Winery 14	Robert Mondavi Winery 5
Château St. Jean 13	St. Supéry Winery 6
Domaine Chandon 3	Sebastiani Vineyards 15
Flora Springs Wine Co. 10	Stag's Leap Wine Cellars 4
Newlan Vineyards 2	Sterling Vineyards 12
Niebaum-Coppola 7	Trefethen Vineyards 1

Wine Tasting for Rookies

Okay, admit it: You thought a cabernet was a dance show and merlot was a magician. You sip wines and say silly things like, "Ahhh, absurd yet flaccid." In fact, you barely know anything about wine, do you? Well fear not, fellow plebeians, because the majority of visitors to the wine country probably know less than you do.

Recognition is the first step. Say, "Okay, I admit it: I don't know diddly about wines." The second step is to enroll yourself in a wine appreciation class, which in the course of a few hours turns dummies like us into budding sommeliers. You'll learn, among many other things, what to look for in the color of a wine, what to learn from the aroma, and what *not* to do with the cork (smelling it is a sure sign of cluelessness). Ignorance being bliss, you even get to taste all kinds of yummy wines while you learn.

Prices for the classes range from free to $50. On the free end is **Goosecross Cellars** (☎ 707/944-1986), a small family winery at 1119 State Lane near Yountville, which hosts classes each Saturday morning at 11am. **Merryvale Vineyards** (☎ 707/ 963-7777), at 1000 Main St. in St. Helena, holds $5 wine seminars also on Saturday mornings at 10:30am. **Flora Springs Wine Co.,** 1978 W. Zinfandel Lane (off Calif. 29), St. Helena (☎ 707/963-5711), offers an excellent one-hour tour tailored to all levels of wine enthusiasts Monday through Saturday by appointment only. You'll trace the whole process, from grapes on the vine to beautiful, clear wine, and then learn to evaluate wines and pair them with different foods. Seasoned tasters may want to splurge on a variety of Napa's finest at **Edgewood Estate Winery,** 2 miles south of St. Helena at 401 St. Helena Hwy. (☎ 707/963-7293), which holds $45-per-person classes each Saturday from 10:30am to 12:30pm.

Rutherford, Oakville, St. Helena, and Calistoga—make a good base, allowing you to dine, wine, shop, and sightsee without traveling very far. Don't pass up the valley if you only have a day to spare, though; even a few hours spent driving through these manicured hills will introduce you to this beautiful region and its bounty and give you a taste of the wine-making process as well.

The Napa Valley wineries and towns listed below are organized geographically, from south to north, along Calif. 29, beginning in the village of Napa.

ESSENTIALS

VISITOR INFORMATION   While you're in San Francisco, you can pick up free Wine Country maps and brochures from the **Wine Institute** at 425 Market St., Suite 1000, San Francisco, CA 94105 (☎ 415/512-0151). Once you're in the Napa Valley, stop at the **Napa Valley Conference and Visitors Bureau,** 1310 Town Center Mall, off First Street, Napa, CA 94559 (☎ 707/226-7455), for a variety of local information. All over Napa and Sonoma, you can pick up a very informative free weekly publication called *Wine Country Review.* It will give you the most up-to-date information on the area's wineries and related events.

GETTING THERE   From San Francisco, cross the Golden Gate Bridge and continue north on Calif. 101. Turn east on Calif. 37 (toward Vallejo), then north on Calif. 29, the main road through the wine country (don't worry, there's plenty of signs showing the way). Calif. 29 runs the length of Napa Valley, which is just 35 miles. You really can't get lost—there's just one north-south road, on which most of the wineries, hotels, shops, and restaurants are located.

TOURING THE WINERIES

Touring the Wine Country takes a little planning. With more than 250 wineries, each offering a distinct wine, atmosphere, and experience, the best thing you can do is decide what you're most interested in and chart your path from there. Is it a specific wine you want to taste? A tour that interests you? Maybe it's the adjoining restaurant, picnic tables, or art collection that piques your interest. Whatever you do, take it slow. The Wine Country should never be rushed; like a great glass of wine, it should be savored.

Most wineries offer free tours daily from 10am to 5pm. Depending on the winery, the tour will chart the process of wine making from the grafting and harvesting of the vines to the pressing, blending, and aging of the wines in oak casks.

Our favorite wineries are listed below, organized geographically, from south to north along Calif. 29, beginning in the village of Napa.

Newlan Vineyards. 5225 Solano Ave., Napa. ☎ **707/257-2399.** Daily 9am–5pm.

This small, family-owned winery produces only about 10,000 cases a year. Cabernet sauvignon, Pinot Noir, Chardonnay, Zinfandel, and late harvest Johannesburg Riesling are produced. Tours are offered by appointment only, but you can stop for free wine tasting anytime during open hours.

Trefethen Vineyards. 1160 Oak Knoll Ave., Napa. ☎ **707/255-7700.** Daily 10am–4:30pm; tours by appointment year-round. From Calif. 29, take Oak Knoll Ave. east.

Listed on the National Register of Historical Places, the vineyard's main building was built in 1886, and remains Napa's only wooden, gravity-powered winery. Although Trefethen is one of the valley's oldest wineries, it didn't produce its first Chardonnay until 1973—but thank goodness it did. Their whites and reds are both award-winners and a pleasure to the palate. Tours are offered by appointment only; tastings are free.

Stag's Leap Wine Cellars. 5766 Silverado Trail, Napa. ☎ **707/944-2020.** Sales and tasting daily 10am–4pm; tours by appointment only. Silverado Trail parallels Calif. 29; go east on Trancas St. or Oak Knoll Ave., then north to the cellars.

Founded in 1972, Napa's Stag's Leap Wine Cellars shocked the oenological world in 1976 when its 1973 Cabernet won first place over French wines in a Parisian blind tasting. For $3 per person, you can be the judge of the winery's current releases.

Mumm. 8445 Silverado Trail, Rutherford. ☎ **707/942-3434.** Apr–Sept daily 10:30am–6pm; Oct–Mar daily 10:30am–5pm.

At first glance Mumm, housed in a big redwood barn, looks almost humble. But once you're in the front door, you'll know they mean big business. Just beyond the extensive gift shop (filled with all sorts of namesake mementos) is the tasting room, where you can purchase sparkling wine by the glass (ranging from $3.50 to $6) and take in the breathtaking vineyard and mountain views. The winery also has an art gallery exhibiting Ansel Adams photographs of the Wine Country. Unfortunately, there's no food or picnicking here, but during warm weather, with the open patio and a glass of champagne, you'll forget all about nibbling. Mumm also offers a 45-minute tour every hour from between 11am and 3pm daily.

Robert Mondavi Winery. 7801 St. Helena Hwy. (Calif. 29), Oakville. ☎ **800/MONDAVI** or 707/226-1395. May–Oct, daily 9:30am–5:30pm; Nov–Apr, daily 9:30am–4:30pm.

If you continue on Calif. 29 up to Oakville, you'll arrive at the ultimate high-tech Napa Valley winery, housed in a magnificent mission-style facility. Almost every processing variable in Mondavi's wine making is computer controlled—and absolutely fascinating to watch. Reservations are recommended for the guided tour. It's wise to make them one to two weeks in advance, especially if you plan to go on a weekend. After the guided tour, you can taste the results of all this attention to detail with selected current wines. The Vineyard Room usually features an art show, and you'll find some exceptional antiques in the reception hall. During the summer, the winery hosts some great outdoor jazz concerts.

St. Supéry Winery. 8440 St. Helena Hwy. (Calif. 29), Rutherford. ☎ **800/942-0809** or 707/963-4526. Daily 9:30am–4:30pm.

The outside may look like a modern corporate office building, but inside is a welcoming winery that encourages first-time wine tasters to learn more about oenology. On the self-guided tour, you can wander through the demonstration vineyard, where you'll learn about growing techniques. Inside, kids gravitate toward "SmellaVision," an interactive display about how to identify different wine ingredients. Adjoining is the Atkinson House, which houses more than 100 years of wine-making history. For $2.50, you'll get lifetime tasting privileges, and though they probably won't be pouring their ever-popular Moscato dessert wine, the Sauvignon Blanc and Chardonnay flow freely.

Beaulieu Vineyard. 1960 St. Helena Hwy. (Calif. 29), Rutherford, CA 94573. ☎ **707/963-2411.** Daily 10am–5pm; tours, daily 11am–4pm.

Bordeaux native Georges de Latour founded Napa's third-oldest continuously operating winery in 1900, and with the help of legendary oenologist André Tchelistcheff, produced world-class award-winning wines that have been served by every president of the United States since Roosevelt. The tasting room is not much to look at, but with Beaulieu's (say BOWL-YOU) stellar reputation, they have no need to visually impress. They do, however, offer you a complimentary glass of Chardonnay the minute you walk through the door. The Private Reserve Tasting Room offers tastes of reserve wines for a small fee. A free tour explains the wine-making process and the vineyard's history.

Niebaum-Coppola. 1991 St. Helena Hwy., Rutherford. ☎ **707/963-9099.** Daily 10am–5pm.

In March 1995, Hollywood met Napa Valley when Francis Ford Coppola bought historic Inglenook Vineyards. Although the filmmaker has been dabbling in wine production for years, this is his biggest endeavor yet. He's already plunked down millions to renovate the beautiful 1880s ivy-draped stone winery, and plans are to restore the entire property to its historic dimension—but it will, of course be accompanied by the glitz you'd expect from Tinsletown. On display are Academy awards and memorabilia from Coppola films *The Godfather* and *Bram Stoker's Dracula;* along more traditional lines is the Centennial Museum, which chronicles the history of the estate and its wine making. Throughout all the Hollywood hullabaloo, however, wine is not forgotten: The goal is to produce 75,000 cases a year of quality wine made from organically grown grapes. Wine tasting is $5; if you've had enough for the day, perk yourself up at the cappuccino bar. You're welcome to picnic at any of the designated (and beautiful) garden sites.

Beringer Vineyards. 2000 Main St., St. Helena. ☎ **707/963-7115.** Daily 9:30am–5pm.

Follow the line of cars just north of St. Helena's business district to Beringer Vineyards, where everyone stops at the remarkable Rhine House to taste wine and view the hand-dug tunnels carved out of the mountainside. This is the oldest continuously operating winery in the Napa Valley, open even during Prohibition, when the Beringer family kept afloat by making "sacramental" wines. Tasting of current vintages is conducted in the Rhine House; reserve wines are available in the Founders' Room (upstairs). A modest fee is charged per taste.

Sterling Vineyards. 1111 Dunaweal Lane (¹/₂ mile east of Calif. 29), Calistoga. ☎ **800/ 726-6136** or 707/942-3344. Daily 10:30am–4:30pm.

No, you don't need climbing shoes to reach this Mediterranean–style winery, perched 300 feet up on a rocky knoll: Just fork over $6 and you'll arrive via aerial tram, which offers exceptional views along the way. Once on land, follow the self-guided tour, which will take you through the fermenters and into the aging cellars. The winery produces more than 200,000 cases per year. Samples at the panoramic tasting room are included with the tram fare.

NAPA

Driving into Napa, you might wonder why you spent over an hour getting here only to find the Wine Country is really just a long strip of industrial spaces, motels, and cheesy discount stores. But have no fear: The town of Napa serves mainly as the commercial center of the Wine Country and the gateway to the Napa Valley, hence, the high-speed freeway that whips you right past it and on to the "tourist" towns of St. Helena and Calistoga. If you have plenty of time and a penchant for Victorian architecture, however, spend a few hours exploring the historic downtown area. At **Napa's Visitors Bureau,** 1310 Napa Town Center Mall (off First Street; ☎ **707/226-7459**), you will find free self-guided walking tours.

While Napa lacks the chi-chi resorts and four-star restaurants of its neighboring towns to the north, it does have a wealth of inexpensive hotels and restaurants. Ergo, a good plan of action for the budget traveler is to hole up in Napa and spend the day exploring the northern reaches of the Wine Country (which is why you're here, right?). Napa is also an excellent place to start your day by loading up on coffee and deli items for a picnic lunch at your favorite winery.

FARMER'S MARKETS

Grapes aren't the only thing grown in these verdant valleys. An enormous variety of fresh produce, much of it organically grown, is sold directly to the public at various farmer's markets within Napa and Sonoma valleys. One of the most popular is the **Napa Valley Farmer's Market** in St. Helena, held Friday mornings from 7:30 to 11:30am May through September in Crane Park. Other markets include the **Napa Downtown Farmer's Market,** held every Tuesday from 7:30 to noon at the parking lot on Pearl and West streets off Soscal, and the **Sonoma Farmer's Market** in Depot Park off First Street West, which takes places on Tuesdays from 5:30am to dusk May through November and Fridays from 9 to noon year-round.

A livelier option to the morning markets is Napa's **Chef's Market,** which takes place Friday evenings mid-May through October from 4pm to 9pm at the Napa Town Center (take First Street exit off Calif. 29 and head east to First and Coombs streets; ☎ **707/255-8073**). You get all the same farm-fresh produce as the regular farmer's markets along with live music, samplings from noted Napa Valley chefs, beer and wine gardens, arts and crafts displays, and a kids' hands-on area.

SEEING THE WINE COUNTRY BY RAIL

The Napa Valley Wine Train. McKinstry St. Depot, 1275 McKinstry St., near First St. and Soscol Ave. ☎ **800/427-4124** or 707/253-2111. Train fare without meals, $30 for daytime rides, $22 for evening rides. Supplement for brunch $22; supplement for lunch $25; supplement for dinner $39.50. Departures Sat–Sun and holidays at 8:30am; Mon–Fri at 11:30am, Sat–Sun and holidays at noon; Tues–Sun and holidays at 6pm. Reduced departure schedule during Jan and Feb.

You don't have to worry about drinking and driving if you do the Wine Country aboard the Wine Train, a rolling restaurant that makes a nonstop, three-hour, 36-mile journey through the vineyards of Napa, Yountville, Oakville, Rutherford, and St. Helena. (*Tip:* Sit on the west side of the train for the best views.) The vintage-style cars—finished with polished Honduran mahogany paneling and etched-glass partitions—hearken back to the opulent sophistication of the 1920s and '30s. Gourmet meals are served by an attentive staff, complete with all the appropriate details: damask linen, bone china, silver flatware, and etched crystal. Menus are fixed, consisting of three or four courses, which might include poached Norwegian salmon court bouillon or Black Angus filet mignon served with a cabernet and Roquefort sauce. If all this seems out of your price range, you can opt for just the ride alone for about half the price and satiate your hunger with a sampling of wines.

In addition to the dining rooms, the train pulls a wine-tasting car ($5 for four tastings), a deli car, and three 50-passenger lounges. *Warning:* Photos are taken before you board in case you want to capture the moment on film, so be prepared.

WHERE TO STAY

If you need help organizing your Wine Country vacation, contact **Wine Country Referrals** at P.O. Box 543 Calistoga, CA 94515 (☎ **707/942-2186;** fax 707/942-4681). It's a knowledgeable company that specializes in the area and offers extensive rental information on inns, hotels, motels, resorts, and vacation homes, as well as wineries, limousine tours, restaurants, spas, ballooning, gliders and train rides.

Cedar Gables Inn. 486 Coombs St., Napa, CA 94559. ☎ **800/309-7969** or 707/224-7969. Fax 707/224-4838. 6 rms. $109–$169 double ($10 less in winter). Rates include breakfast. AE, MC, V. From Calif. 29 north, exit onto First St. and follow signs to "Downtown." The house is at the corner of Oak St.

This is easily one of Napa's best buys, located on a quiet, tree-lined residential street. Cedar Gables is an imposing 1892 Victorian mansion made inviting by the personal attention of innkeepers Margaret and Craig Snasdell. The rooms, all with private baths, are decorated with tapestries and antiques, and gilded in rich, old-world colors. Some have fireplaces; four have whirlpool tubs; and all feature brass, wood, or iron queen-size beds. The inn's cozy sunken family room is home to a large-screen TV and roaring fireplace—the perfect place to cuddle up with your sweetie pie. Wine and cheese are served in the evening.

Napa Valley Budget Inn. 3380 Solano Ave., Napa, CA 94558. ☎ **707/257-6111.** 58 rms. A/C TEL TV. $56–$79 double. AE, DC, DISC, MC, V. Free parking. From Calif. 29 north, turn left onto the Redwood Rd. turnoff and go 1 block to Solano Ave.; then turn left and go half a block to the motel.

The best thing going for this no-frills motel is its excellent location—close to Calif. 29 for those forays into the Wine Country and just across the street from a shopping plaza for that extra bottle of aspirin. Rooms are simple, clean, and comfortable, but don't expect any frills other than free cable TV and access to a small heated pool. (*Tip:* Request a room away from Calif. 29, which gets a lot of noisy traffic during the day.) If the Budget Inn is booked, try the **Chablis Lodge** (☎ 707/257-1944) next door, which offers almost exactly the same rooms and amenities as its neighbor but at a slightly higher rate. Both motels allow small pets.

Tall Timbers Chalets. 1012 Darms Lane, Napa, CA 94558. ☎ **707/252-7810.** 8 cottages. A/C MINIBAR TV. Sun–Fri $105, Sat $150. Extra person $10. AE, MC, V. Free parking. From Calif. 29 north, turn left onto Darms Lane 8 miles north of Napa.

This group of eight whitewashed, roomy cottages surrounded by pines and eucalyptus is one of the best bargains in Napa Valley. The cottages, which are all nonsmoking, are decorated in a simple, homey fashion and well furnished; amenities include refrigerators, toaster ovens, and coffeemakers. It's pleasant to find, on your arrival, a basket of fresh fruit in the breakfast nook, breakfast treats in the refrigerator, and a complimentary bottle of champagne. There are no phones in the cottages, but you'll have access to one in the main office. Each unit can sleep four (there's a bedroom plus a queen sofa bed in the living room); several have decks. The Tall Timber Chalets won't appear in *Country Inns Magazine* anytime soon, but you'd be hard pressed to find a better deal for your dollar in the Wine Country.

Ⓢ **Wine Valley Lodge.** 200 S. Coombs St., between 1st and Imola sts., Napa, CA 94558. ☎ **707/224-7911.** 53 rms. A/C TV TEL. $50–$90 double, $75–$150 suites. AE, DISC, MC, V.

Dollar for dollar, the Wine Valley Lodge offers the most for the least in the entire Wine Country. Located at the south end of town in a quiet residential neighborhood, the Mission-style motel is extremely well kept and accessible, just a short drive from Calif. 29 and the wineries to the north. Soft pastels dominate the color scheme, featured prominently in the matching quilted bedspreads, furniture, and objets d'art. It's decor is reminiscent of Grandma's house, to be sure, but at these prices—$55 for a king-size bed Sunday through Thursday—who cares? The clincher on the whole deal is a fetching little oasis in the center courtyard, consisting of sundeck, barbecue, and swimming pool flanked by a cadre of odd tea cup-shaped hedges.

WHERE TO DINE

Bistro Don Giovanni. 4110 St. Helena Hwy. (just north of Salvador Ave.). ☎ **707/224-3300.** Reservations recommended on weekends. Main courses $11–$15. AE, DC, MC, V. Daily 11am–10pm. NORTHERN ITALIAN.

Donna and Giovanni Scala—who also run the fantastic Scala's Bistro in San Francisco—serve refined Italian fare prepared with top-quality ingredients and a California flair at this large, lively, Mediterranean-style restaurant. Terra-cotta tiles, an open kitchen, cafe-style chairs, and an enormous painting of the Italian flag set the scene. The menu features pastas, risottos, wood-burning oven-baked pizzas, and a half-dozen other main courses such as braised lamb shank and Niman Schell bistro burgers. Less traditional appetizers include a grilled pear with a frisé and arugula salad with blue cheese, caramelized walnuts, and bacon; and the matchstick zucchini sprinkled with Parmesan cheese has become a signature dish. Pasta lovers should go for the farfalle with asparagus, porcini, wild mushrooms, pecorino cheese, and truffle oil; the seared filet of salmon with tomato white wine and chive sauce is another winner. Alfresco dining among the vineyards is available (and highly recommended on a warm, sunny day).

Downtown Joe's. 902 Main St. at Second St. ☎ **707/258-2337.** Main courses $8–$14. AE, DISC, DC, MC, V. Lunch, dinner daily 11am–10pm, breakfast 8am–11am May–Oct, brunch Sat–Sun 9am–3pm. NAPA CUISINE.

Don't let the name fool you: Downtown Joe's is anything but a greasy diner. Working from a proven formula—good food and lots of it at a fair price—chef-owner Joe Ruffino has capitalized on a prime location in downtown Napa and created what is widely regarded as the best place in town to grub and groove. The menu is all over the place, offering everything from Porterhouse steaks to oysters, omelets, pasta, and seafood specials. The beers, such as their tart Lickety Split Lager, are made in-house, as are the breads and desserts. If the sun's out, request a table on the outside patio adjacent to the park. Thursday through Sunday nights, rock, jazz, and blues bands draw in the locals.

There's another great reason to visit Joe's: "Hoppy Hour" from 4 to 6pm, Monday through Thursday, features $2 pints, free appetizers, and they even have a drawing every 15 minutes so everyone has a chance to win free stuff.

First Squeeze Deli and Juice Bar. 1149 1st St. at Coombs St., ☎ **707/224-6762.** Deli items $3–$6. AE, MC, V. Mon–Fri 9am–5:30pm, Sat 9am–5pm, Sun 11am–5pm. DELI/JUICE.

After you fuel up on your requisite cup of Java at Napa Valley Coffee Roasting Co., located down the block from First Squeeze at 948 Main St. at 1st Street, head over here to load up on picnic supplies for the day's journey among the vineyards. Spartan furnishings (and decor to match) beg for a "to go" order, which is just as well because after one sip of their protein powder shake you can't hold still anyway. Wheat grass, spirulina, ginseng, bee pollen, brewer's yeast—it's a health nut's paradise. Our favorite is the Berry Bonds, a zingy combo of blackberry, strawberry, and apple juice and frozen yogurt. Sandwiches of every ilk are made big and bulky, best matched with a Stag's Leap '73 Cabernet Sauvignon (you wish).

The Red Hen Cantina. 5091 St. Helena Hwy. ☎ **707/255-8125.** Reservations recommended for large parties. Main courses $8–$14. AE, DC, MC, V. Sun–Thurs 11am–9pm, Fri–Sat 11am–10pm. MEXICAN.

This popular taqueria serving moderately priced food looks like a Swiss chalet that got lost somewhere south of the border. Seafood dishes supplement the traditional burritos, tacos, and pollo Mexicano (chicken strips sautéed in white wine, onion, mushrooms, and tomatoes). What you get isn't bad, but it loses something in the translation this far north. Your best bet is to rest your weary bones at a patio table adorned with chips, salsa, and a cool margarita.

YOUNTVILLE

Founded by George Calvert Yount, the first American to settle in the valley, Yountville lacks the small-town charm of neighboring St. Helena and Calistoga. For better or for worse, the town lacks a rambunctious Main Street, but it does serve as a good base for exploring the valley and has a handful of reasonably priced restaurants and inns.

WHAT TO SEE & DO BEYOND THE WINERIES

At the center of the village is **Vintage 1870** (☎ 707/944-2451), once a winery (from 1871 to 1955) and now a gallery with about 40 specialty shops selling antiques, wine accessories, country collectibles, and more; it's also home to three restaurants.

WHERE TO STAY

Napa Valley Railway Inn. 6503 Washington St., adjacent to the Vintage 1870 shopping complex, Yountville, CA 94599. ☎ **707/944-2000.** 9 rms. A/C TV. $65–$115 double. AE, MC, V.

This is one of our favorite places to stay in the Wine Country. Why? Because it's inexpensive and it's cute as all get out. Looking hokey as heck from the outside, The Railway Inn consists of two rows of sun-bleached cabooses and railcars sitting on a stretch of Yountville's original track and connected by a covered wooden walkway. Things get considerably better, though, as you enter your private caboose or railcar, each sumptuously appointed with comfy love seats, chairs, queen size brass beds, and tiled full baths. The coup de grace is the bay windows and skylights, which let in plenty of California sunshine (surely the Pullman cars of yesteryear never had it this good). The railcars are all suites, so if you're looking to save your pennies, opt for the cabooses. Adjacent to the inn is Yountville's main shopping complex, which includes wine tastings and some good low-priced restaurants.

WHERE TO DINE

The Diner. 6476 Washington St. (between Mission and Oak sts.) ☎ **707/944-2626.** Reservations not accepted. Breakfast $4–$8; lunch $6–$10; dinner $8–$13.25. No credit cards. Tues–Sun 8am–3pm and 5:30–9pm. AMERICAN/MEXICAN.

This down-home diner, decorated in pink and featuring a functioning Irish Waterford wood stove and rotating art exhibits, is presided over by hearty empress Cassandra Mitchell, a fourth-generation San Franciscan who believes in giving people good food and plenty of it. The menu is extensive, the portions huge, and the food satisfying. Breakfast offers such staples as oatmeal with walnuts and raisins, as well as French toast and standard egg dishes, but regulars tend to go for the local sausages, house potatoes, and cornmeal pancakes with house maple syrup. At lunch and dinner, there's an assortment of Mexican and American dishes such as roast free-range chicken with fresh vegetables (from the diner's own gardens, no less), giant burritos, big ole burgers, and thick sandwiches made with house-roasted meats and house-made organic bread. Vegetarians, calorie-counters, wine lovers, and beer snobs are all catered to here, as are children, who can select from their own special menu.

Mark Allen. 6795 Washington St. ☎ **707/944-0168.** Main courses $12.95–$18.95. AE, MC, V. Daily 11:30am–3pm; dinner 5–10pm. CALIFORNIA.

Pacific Rim–influenced California food has made its way up to the Wine Country at this quaint, airy restaurant in the heart of Yountville. Following a Wine Country trend, chef/owner Mark Allen (who formerly presided at San Francisco's Inn at the Opera) styled his restaurant and cafe in a casually sophisticated fashion, with ceramic and tile Mediterranean floors and modern formal table settings. The food is equally as interesting, with such choices as tempura-battered prawns with a spicy bean sprout salad in a soy-mustard vinaigrette starter, or main courses like grilled pork chop with butternut squash raviolis topped with maple/sun-dried-cherry sauce. A newcomer to the chi-chi restaurant scene (opened in late 1995), word around town is that Mark Allen is the new hot spot in Napa Valley.

☺ Mustards Grill. 7399 St. Helena Hwy. (1 mile north of Yountville on Calif. 29). ☎ **707/944-2424.** Reservations required. Main courses $8–$25. CB, DC, MC, V. Apr–Oct, daily 11:30am–10pm; Nov–Mar, daily 11:30am–9pm. CALIFORNIA.

Food critics writing about this place invariably call it "the quintessential Napa Valley wine restaurant." Opened in 1983 by a trio of innovators who also founded San Francisco's Fog City Diner, it just may be. Inside, you'll find a bilevel, black-and-white tiled dining room with cathedral ceilings, a small bar, and a glass-enclosed outer dining area. The atmosphere is often boisterous and noisy. The blue-jeaned, white-shirted servers are friendly and knowledgeable.

Starry, Starry Friday Nights

Somebody at **Stars Oakville Cafe** was thinking when they came up with this idea: Why not cook a pile of gourmet mesquite-barbecued grub, chill a few kegs of beer, and charge $15 a head for an all-you-can-eat-and-drink feast of the gods? Good idea. And while we're at it, why not have everybody bring a bottle of their favorite wine to share with everyone? Another good idea.

Last we heard, the party takes place in the restaurant's garden patio out back, starts at 6pm, and runs from June 14 through October. For reservations, call **707/944-8905.**

Among the appetizers are such gems as home-smoked salmon with pasilla corn cakes and crème fraîche, and garlicky goat cheese toasts with arugula and sun-dried tomatoes. Seasonal main courses range from wood-burning-oven specialties, like calf's liver with caramelized onions, bacon, and homemade chili sauce or smoked Long Island duck with 100-almond-onion sauce, to grilled items such as Sonoma rabbit with wild mushroom cacciatore and filet mignon with merlot sauce. The Jack Daniels chocolate cake with chocolate sauce or the crumble top banana cheesecake with caramel sauce are the top to-hell-with-the-calories desserts. Featured local wines range from $4 to $9 a glass. If you bring your own, there's a $10 corkage fee.

We've known this place since it opened, and, quite frankly, it has its good and bad days, but we keep coming back. A sign of their commitment to both quality and style: If you order a burger (they make superb ones here), it comes with homemade catsup. Not bad.

Red Rock Grill. 6525 Washington St., in front of the Vintage 1870 shopping complex. ☎ **707/944-2614.** Main courses $5–$10. AE, DISC, MC, V. Daily 9am–8pm. AMERICAN.

In a town silly with expensive restaurants, the Red Rock Grill is a refreshingly unpretentious oasis for the burger-'n'-beer crowd. Sporting a shiny new redwood deck, this homey little grill is packed with pooped tourists on the weekends. The menu is pretty basic—sandwiches, salads, burgers, and such—but at least you won't feel self conscious ordering a plain old beer.

OAKVILLE & RUTHERFORD

Driving farther north on the St. Helena Highway (Calif. 29) brings you to the Oakville Cross Road and the ✪ **Oakville Grocery Co.,** 7856 St. Helena Hwy., in Oakville (☎ **707/944-8802**), one of the finest, and most expensive, gourmet food stores this side of New York's Dean and Deluca. Here you can put together the provisions for a memorable picnic or for a very special custom gift basket. You'll find the best breads, the choicest selection of cheeses in the northern Bay Area, pates, fresh foie gras (domestic and French, seasonally), smoked Norwegian salmon, smoked sturgeon and smoked pheasant (by special order), fresh caviar (Beluga, Sevruga, Osetra), and an exceptional selection of California wines, of course. The grocery will prepare a picnic basket for you themselves with 24-hours' notice. Delivery service is available to some areas. It's open daily from 10am to 6pm.

If the Oakville Grocery Co. is a little too rich for your blood, across the proverbial (and literal) tracks is **Pometta's Delicatessen,** a raging antithesis to its high-brow neighbor. Smoked pheasant? Ha! More like barbecued chicken, Coke à la can, and a slice of Mama's Homemade Meat Loaf. But you sure can't beat the price, particularly for Susan Pometta's quartet of packaged picnic lunches such as The Oakville: Pometta's Famous Roasted Quarter Chicken, Choice of Two Salads, Baguette a nd Butter, and a Cookie, for $12.50. That's $6.25 each for a ready-to-go picnic basket; not a bad deal, folks. (Open Monday to Friday from 9am to 6pm, Saturday 10am to 5pm, Sunday 10am to 4pm. Visa and MasterCard are accepted; ☎ **707/ 944-2365.**)

WHERE TO DINE

✪ **Stars Oakville Cafe.** 7848 Calif. 29 at Oakville Cross Rd., Oakville. Reservations recommended. ☎ **707/944-8905.** Lunch $6–$10, dinner $12–$16. AE, MC, V. Mon, Thurs noon–9pm, Tues–Wed noon–6pm, Fri–Sat noon–10pm, Sun noon–9pm (winter hours vary; call ahead). CALIFORNIA.

This is the sort of cafe you wish someone would open in your neighborhood: stylish yet unpretentious, delicious yet affordable. Part of chef/restaurateur Jeremiah

Tower's trio of Stars establishments (the other two being in San Francisco), you probably won't find Robin Williams playing with his food at this lonely outpost, but you will find a reasonably priced array of gourmet dishes. The menu changes daily, but on our last visit we shared a heavenly slice of country spinach quiche with fresh garden greens, excellent bread, and a glass of good white wine for a mere $9. Other tempting choices included a sandwich of wood oven-roasted pork on focaccia bread with a side of spicy slaw and onion rings ($8.50), and a fresh cut pasta (and we do mean fresh) with English peas, Roma tomato, and farmer's cheese for $9.50. Dinner, as you would expect, runs a bit steeper, but it's still worth the splurge, particularly if you dine on the extraordinarily romantic garden patio on a typically sublime Wine Country evening.

ST. HELENA

Located 17 miles north of Napa on Calif. 29, this former Seventh Day Adventist village manages to maintain a pseudo–Old West feel while simultaneously catering to upscale shoppers with deep pockets—hence the Vanderbilt's, purveyor of fine housewares, at 1429 Main St. It's a quiet, attractive little town hosting a slew of beautiful old homes and first-rate restaurants and accommodations. Assuming you can find a parking space, a stroll along Main Street is highly recommended.

BIKING   The quieter northern end of the valley is an ideal place to rent a bicycle and ride the Silverado Trail. **St. Helena Cyclery,** at 1156 Main St. (☎ **707/963-7736**), rents bikes for $7 per hour or $25 a day, including rear rack and picnic bag.

WHERE TO STAY

Ⓢ **El Bonita Motel.** 195 Main St. (at El Bonita Ave.), St. Helena, CA 94574. ☎ **800/ 541-3284** or 707/963-3216. 26 rms. A/C MINIBAR TEL TV. $79–$120 double. AE, DC, MC, V.

This 1930s art deco motel was built a bit too close to Calif. 29 for comfort, but the 2¹/₂ acres of beautifully landscaped gardens behind the hotel (away from the road) help even the score. The rooms, while small, are spotlessly clean and decorated with new furnishings; all contain microwave ovens and coffeemakers, while some have kitchens or whirlpool baths. Families, attracted to the larger bungalows with kitchenettes, often consider El Bonita one of the best values in Napa Valley, especially considering the motel comes with a heated outdoor pool, Jacuzzi, sauna, and new massage facility.

Wine Country Inn. 1152 Lodi Lane, St. Helena, CA 94574. ☎ **707/963-7077.** Fax 707/ 963-9018. 24 rms. A/C TEL. $115–$248 double. Rates include breakfast. MC, V.

Just off the highway behind Freemark Abbey Vineyard, this attractive wood-and-stone inn—complete with a French-style mansard roof and turret—overlooks a pastoral landscape of Napa Valley vineyards. The rooms are furnished with iron or brass beds and pine country furnishings; most have fireplaces and private terraces overlooking the valley, while others have private hot tubs. One of the inn's best features, besides the absence of televisions, is the outdoor pool, which is attractively landscaped into the hillside. Sure, it's pretty expensive, but if you split the cost with your partner you're looking at a slice of paradise for as little as $60 night.

WHERE TO DINE

Brava Terrace. 3010 St. Helena Hwy. ☎ **707/963-9300.** Reservations recommended. Main courses $8–$15. AE, DC, DISC, MC, V. Thurs–Tues noon–9pm. CALIFORNIA/MEDITERRANEAN.

Fred Halpert earned acclaim as the head chef at the Portman Hotel in San Francisco; in 1991, he struck out on his own, setting up his shop in the Wine Country, where he became a hit almost at once. The main dining room has an open kitchen and handsome stone fireplace; there's also a glass-enclosed area and a large terrace with umbrella-covered tables. Halpert is always searching for new taste sensations; fortunately, that experimentation is backed up by a thorough training in the flavors and zest of Provence and other culinary locales.

The food is both good and reasonably priced. You can order a simple sandwich of grilled portobello mushrooms with mozzarella, red onions, and rosemary aioli, or go whole hog for such main courses as coq au vin or a grilled pork chop with barbecue sauce. There's always a fish, a pasta, and a risotto of the day. Be sure to try the spicy fries (a heartburn special) or the garlic-"smashed" potatoes. If your stomach can handle this wild and robust mixture of flavors and food, finish your meal with the chocolate chip crème brûlée. A dozen selections of wine by the glass are available. *Beware:* Service can be slow on weekends.

✪ **Terra.** 1345 Railroad Ave. (between Adams and Hunt sts.) ☎ **707/963-8931.** Reservations recommended. Main courses $14–$23. DC, MC, V. Sun–Thurs 6–9pm, Fri–Sat 6–10pm. CONTEMPORARY AMERICAN.

St. Helena's restaurant of choice and one that's worth the splurge, Terra is the creation of Lissa Doumani and her husband, Hiro Sone, a master chef who hails from Japan and once worked with Wolfgang Puck at Spago. Sone makes full use of the region's bounty; he seems to know how to coax every nuance of flavor from his fine local ingredients. The simple dining room is a perfect foil for Sone's extraordinary food. Among the appetizers, the terrine of foie gras with apple, walnut, and endive salad and the home-smoked salmon with cucumber dill salad, caviar, and sour cream are the stars of the show. The main dishes successfully fuse different cooking styles: Try the grilled salmon with Thai red-curry sauce or the sake-marinated sea bass with shrimp dumplings in shiso broth. A recommended finale? The apple crostata with vanilla bean ice cream and cinnamon apple cider sauce.

✪ **Tra Vigne Restaurant and Cantinetta.** 1050 Charter Oak Ave. (at Calif. 29). ☎ **707/ 963-4444,** or 707/963-8888 for the cantinetta. Reservations recommended. Main courses $12.50–$16; cantinetta $4–$8. CB, DC, DISC, MC, V. Daily 11:30am–9:30pm; cantinetta daily 11:30am–6pm. ITALIAN.

If you can only dine at one restaurant while visiting the Wine Country, make it Tra Vigne. Sure, there are a few fancier places in town, but there's no restaurant that measures up to the combined qualities of this restaurant's atmosphere, food, and pricing.

Even though it's tempting, don't fill up on the wonderful bread, served with housemade flavored olive oils, as soon as you're seated in the enormous dining room; instead, save plenty of room for the robust California dishes cooked Italian style that have made this place everyone's favorite. The menu features about seven or so pizzas, including a succulent version with caramelized onions, thyme, and gorgonzola. The dishes of the day might include a grilled and cedar-planked tuna with herb salad and roasted tomato vinaigrette or a grilled Sonoma rabbit with teleme cheese-layered potatoes, oven-dried tomatoes, and mustard pan sauce, and a dozen or so antipasti. Pastas are also tempting, including ceppo with sausage, spinach, potatoes, sun-dried tomatoes, and Pecorino. Desserts are equally delicious and might include a warm apple tart with candied walnut crust, sweet gorgonzola, and caramel sauce.

Adjacent to the Tra Vigne Restaurant is their rustic little cafe called the Cantinetta, which offers a small selection of inexpensive sandwiches, pizzas, and lighter meals (I've never had a better focaccia in my life). They can also pack your picnic basket and sell about 20 flavored olive oils infused with everything from roasted garlic to lavender, as well as other creative cooking ingredients (great for gifts). Guests are forced to dine alfresco, but we prefer the walled-in Mediterranean-style patio to the often cacophonous main dining room anyway.

CALISTOGA

Sam Brannan, entrepreneur extraordinaire and California's first millionaire, made his first bundle of wealth by providing miners with general supplies during the gold rush. Flushed with success, he went on to take advantage of the natural geothermal springs at the north end of the Napa Valley by building a hotel and spa here in 1859.

This small, simple resort town remains popular and uncomplicated today, particularly with city folk who come here to unwind. Calistoga's main street is only about six blocks long, and no building is higher than two stories. It's a great place to relax and indulge in mineral waters, mud baths, Jacuzzis, massages, and, of course, wine.

FIND THE NEW YOU: TAKE A CALISTOGA MUD BATH

The one thing you should do while you're in Calistoga is what people have been doing here for the last 150 years: Take a mud bath. The natural baths are composed of local volcanic ash, imported peat, and naturally boiling mineral water, all mulled together to produce a thick mud that simmers at a temperature of about 104°F.

Once you overcome the hurdle of deciding how best to place your naked body into the mushy stone tub, the rest is pure relaxation—you soak with surprising buoyancy for about 10 to 12 minutes. A warm mineral-water shower, a mineral-water whirlpool bath, and a mineral-water steam room visit follow. Afterward, a relaxing blanket-wrap will cool your delighted body down slowly. All of this takes about $1^1/2$ hours and costs about $45; with a massage, add another half hour and $20 (we recommend a full hour). The outcome is a rejuvenated, revitalized, squeaky-clean you. Mud baths aren't recommended for those who are pregnant or have high blood pressure.

The spas also offer other treatments, such as hand and foot massages, herbal wraps, acupressure face-lifts, skin rubs, and herbal facials. Prices range from $35 to $125, and appointments are necessary for all services; call at least a week in advance.

Indulge yourself at any of these Calistoga spas: **Dr. Wilkinson's Hot Springs,** 1507 Lincoln Ave. (☎ 707/942-4102); **Lincoln Avenue Spa,** 1339 Lincoln Ave. (☎ 707/942-5296); **Golden Haven Hot Springs Spa,** 1713 Lake St. (☎ 707/ 942-6793); and **Calistoga Spa Hot Springs,** 1006 Washington St. (☎ 707/ 942-6269).

BUDGET TIP   If you want to get down and dirty with your partner but can't afford the "dirt," don't sweat it. If you browse through the latest edition of *Inside Napa Valley,* a free listing of Napa's goings on that's distributed throughout the valley, you might just find a coupon for a mud bath for two for only $72, redeemable at either Golden Haven Hot Springs or Lincoln Avenue Spa (see above). Even without the coupon, they still offer some of the best body-soothing deals in the valley.

WHAT TO SEE & DO BEYOND THE MUD BATHS & WINERIES

There's plenty to do in Calistoga even beyond the world-famous mud baths and aforementioned wineries.

Calistoga Depot, at 1458 Lincoln Ave. (on the site of Calistoga's original 1868 railroad station), now houses a variety of shops, some of which are housed in six restored passenger cars dating from 1916 into the 1920s.

Old Faithful Geyser of California, at 1299 Tubbs Lane (☎ **707/942-6463**), is one of only three Old Faithful geysers in the world. It's been blowing off steam at regular intervals for as long as anyone can remember. The 350°F water spews out to a height of about 60 feet (20m) every 40 minutes or so, day and night (varying with natural influences such as barometric pressure, the moon, tides, and tectonic stresses). The performance lasts about three minutes. You'll learn a lot about the origins of geothermal steam on your visit. You can bring a picnic lunch with you and catch the show as many times as you wish. An exhibit hall, gift shop, and snack bar are open every day. Admission is $5 for adults, $4 for seniors, $2 for children ages 6 to 12, and free for children under 6. Open summer, daily from 9am to 6pm; winter, daily 9am to 5pm. To get there, follow the signs from downtown Calistoga; it's between Calif. 29 and Calif. 128.

You won't see thousands of trees turned into stone, but you'll still find many interesting petrified specimens at the **Petrified Forest,** 4100 Petrified Forest Rd. (☎ **707/942-6667**). Volcanic ash blanketed this area after the eruption of Mount St. Helena three million years ago. As a result, you'll find redwoods that have turned to rock through the slow infiltration of silicas and other minerals, as well as petrified seashells, clams, and marine life indicating that water covered this area even before the redwood forest. Admission is $3 for adults, $1 for children 4 to 11, free for children under 4. Open daily during the summer from 10am to 5:30pm; in winter, daily from 10am to 4:30pm. To get there from Calif. 128, turn right onto Petrified Forest Road, just past Lincoln Avenue.

BICYCLING   Cycling enthusiasts can rent bikes from **Getaway Bikes,** 1117 Lincoln Ave. (☎ **800/499-BIKE** or 707/942-0332). Full day tours ($89), which include lunch and a visit to three or four wineries, are available, as are downhill cruises ($39) for people who hate to pedal. On weekdays they'll even deliver bikes to you.

GLIDER RIDES   Calistoga offers a unique way of seeing its vineyard-filled valleys: from a glider. These quiet "birds" leave from the **Calistoga Gliderport,** 1546 Lincoln Avenue, Calistoga, CA 94515 (☎ **707/942-5000**). Twenty-minute rides are $79 for one, $110 for two (weight limits apply). Thirty-minute rides are also available.

WHERE TO STAY

Calistoga Inn. 1250 Lincoln Ave. at Cedar St., Calistoga, CA 94515. ☎ **707/942-4101.** 18 rms. $49–$60 double. AE, MC, V.

Would the fact that the Calistoga Inn has its own brewery influence our decision to recommend it? You betcha. Here's the deal: You're probably here for the spa treatments, right? Unfortunately, the guest rooms at almost every spa in town are lacking in the personality and warmth department. A better bet for the budget traveler is to book a room at this homey turn-of-the-century inn, then walk a few blocks up the street for your mud bath and massage. The only caveat is that the bathroom must be shared and the rooms above the inn's restaurant can be noisy, but otherwise you get a cozy little room with a double bed and continental breakfast for only $60 on the weekend (that's half the average room rate in these parts). What's more, they don't require a two-night minimum, and the best beer in town is served downstairs.

Dr. Wilkinson's Hot Springs. 1507 Lincoln Ave. (in downtown Calistoga), Calistoga, CA 94515. ☎ **707/942-4102.** 42 rms. A/C MINIBAR TEL TV. Winter, $59–$119 double. Summer, $79–$119 double. Weekly discounts and packages available. AE, MC, V.

This spa/resort was originally established by "Doc" Wilkinson, who arrived in Napa Valley just after World War II. Rooms range from Victorian-style units with sundecks and garden patios to rather basic and functional motel-like rooms, similar to Janet Leigh's room in *Psycho*. All rooms have drip coffeemakers and refrigerators; some have kitchens. Nonsmoking rooms are available. Facilities include three mineral water pools (two outdoor and one indoor), Jacuzzi, steam room, mud baths, and a health club. Facials and all kinds of body treatments are available in the salon.

Another good choice for a low-priced spa/resort is **Nance's Hot Springs,** 1614 Lincoln Ave. (☎ **707/942-6211**), located just down the road from Dr. Wilkinson's. Room rates are slightly less expensive, but the spa services are almost exactly the same. Be sure to request a room on the second floor overlooking the gliderport.

If both places are fully booked, try **Golden Haven Hot Springs Spa and Resort,** 1713 Lake St. (☎ **707/942-6793**). Located about three blocks off Main Street in a quiet residential neighborhood, it's slightly more downscale than its cousins across the way (okay, okay, it looks like a mobile home park), but for only $60 a night for spa-side lodging one shouldn't complain too loud.

Mount View Hotel. 1457 Lincoln Ave. (in downtown Calistoga), Calistoga, CA 94515. ☎ **707/942-6877.** Fax 707/942-6904. 22 rms, 8 suites, 3 cottages. A/C TEL TV. $110–$140 double; $155–$200 suite, $200 cottage. Packages available. AE, MC, V.

Listed on the National Register of Historic Places, the Mount View Hotel offers 1920s- and 1930s-style "European Eclectic" rooms, three self-contained cottages, and eight suites named for the movie idols of those eras—all of which are nonsmoking. The Carole Lombard Suite has peach-colored walls and light-green carpeting, while the Tom Mix Suite has a Western theme (of course). The cottages have queen-size beds, wet bars, private decks, and hot tubs; all rooms have a private bath, air-conditioning, and television. A heated swimming pool, European spa, and Jacuzzi are on the premises, as is one of our favorite Napa Valley restaurants, Catahoula (see "Where to Dine," below). Tennis courts, nature trails, and a nine-hole golf course are also nearby. *Be forewarned:* There's a two-night minimum during high-season weekends, and some of the mattresses are rumored to be a bit sagging.

WHERE TO DINE

✪ **All Seasons Café.** 1400 Lincoln Ave. (at Washington St.) ☎ **707/942-9111.** Reservations recommended on weekends. Main courses $13–$19 at dinner. MC, V. Thurs–Tues, 11am–3pm and 5:30–10pm, brunch Sat–Sun 9am–noon (wine shop, Thurs–Tues 11am–8pm). CALIFORNIA.

Wine Country devotees often wend their way to the All Seasons Café in downtown Calistoga because of its extensive wine list, knowledgeable staff, and a solid reputation among locals for serving outstanding food. The trick here is to buy a bottle of wine from the cafe's wine shop (say hi to Margaux for us), then bring it to your table: The cafe adds a corkage fee of $7.50 instead of tripling the price of the bottle (as they do at most restaurants). The menu is diverse, ranging from pizzas and pastas to such main courses as braised lamb shank "osso bucco" in an orange, Madeira, and tomato sauce. Anything with the house-smoked salmon or spiced sausages is also a safe bet. Chef John Coss saves his guests from any major faux pas by matching wines to his dishes on the menu, so you'll know what's just right for his grilled duck breast or duck confit pizza.

Catahoula. 1457 Lincoln Ave. ☎ **707/942-2275.** Reservations recommended. Main courses $11–$20. MC, V. Mon, Wed–Fri noon–2:30pm, Sat–Sun noon–3:30pm; Mon, Wed–Thurs, and Sun 5:30–10pm, Fri and Sat 5:30–10:30pm. AMERICAN/SOUTHERN.

Named after the official hound of the state of Louisiana, Catahoula features the beloved dog everywhere—on the metal sculptures over the bar and in the photos in the restaurant and the saloon. The domain of chef Jan Birnbaum, formerly of New York's Quilted Giraffe and San Francisco's Campton Place, this restaurant is the current favorite in town. And with good reason: It's the only place in Napa where you can get a decent rooster gumbo. You'd have to travel all over Louisiana to find another pan-fried jalapeño-pecan catfish like this one. Catahoula is funky and fun, and the food that comes out of the wood-burning oven—like the roast duck with chili cilantro potatoes or the whole roasted fish with lemon broth, orzo, and escarole—is exciting. Start with the spicy gumbo ya ya with andouille sausage, and finish with what may be a first for many non-Southerners: buttermilk ice cream.

Smokehouse Café. 1458 Calistoga Ave. (in downtown Calistoga). ☎ **707/942-6060.** Main courses $5–$15. No credit cards. Open daily 6am–10pm. REGIONAL AMERICAN.

Jack Hunter, Smokehouse Café's ebullient meat-master, guarantees you'll leave his restaurant neither hungry nor unsatisfied. And he's right. Who would've guessed that the best spareribs and house-smoked meats in Northern California would come from this little kitchen in Calistoga? Here's the winning game plan: Start with the Delta Crawfish cakes (better than any wimpy crab cakes you'll find in San Francisco) and husk-roasted Cheyenne corn, then move on to the slow pig sandwich, half-slab of ribs, or house-made sausages—all of which take up to a week for Jack to smoke. The clincher, though, is the fluffy all-you-can-eat cornbread dipped in pure maple syrup, which comes with every full-plate dinner. Kids are especially catered to—a rarity in these parts—and patio dining is available during the summer for breakfast, lunch, or dinner.

Wappo Bar and Bistro. 1226B Washington St. (off Lincoln Ave.) ☎ **707/942-4712.** Main courses $8.50–$14.50. AE, DC, MC, V. Wed–Mon 11:30am–2:30pm; Thurs–Mon 6–9:30pm. INTERNATIONAL.

One of the best alfresco dining experiences in the Wine Country is under Wappo's honeysuckle- and vine-covered arbor. You'll be comfortable inside this small bistro, too, at one of the well-spaced, well-polished tables. The menu offers a wide range of choices: roast vegetables with polenta, rabbit pie with wild mushrooms and puff pastry, and chicken with morels served with a side of chive mashed potatoes might give you an idea of what's going on here. The desserts of choice are the black-bottom coconut cream pie or the strawberry rhubarb pie.

2 The "Other" Wine Country: Sonoma Valley

Sonoma is often thought of as the "other" Wine Country, forever in the shadow of Napa Valley. Truth is, even though there are far fewer wineries here (and far, far fewer tourists), its wines have actually won more awards than Napa's. Sonoma County, which stretches west to the coast, is more rural and less traveled than its neighbor to the east. Small, family owned wineries are its mainstay, just like back in the old days of wine making when everyone started with the intention of going broke and loved every minute of it. Today, Sonoma is home to about 35 wineries and 13,000 acres of vineyards. Chardonnay is the variety for which Sonoma is most noted, representing almost one-quarter of the valley's acreage in vines. Tastings on the west side of the Mayacamas Mountains are usually free, low key, and come with plenty of friendly banter between the winemakers and their guests.

ESSENTIALS

VISITOR INFORMATION   Before you begin your explorations of the area, visit the **Sonoma Valley Visitors Bureau,** 453 First St. East, Sonoma, CA 95476 (☎ **707/996-1090;** fax 707/996-9212). The office, located right on the Plaza in the town of Sonoma, offers free maps and brochures about local happenings. It's open daily from 9am to 5pm in winter and 9am to 7pm in summer. An additional office has recently been added a few miles south of Sonoma at 25200 Arnold Dr. (Calif. 121; ☎ **707/996-1090**); it's open daily from 9am to 5pm.

The **Sonoma County Convention and Visitors Bureau,** 5000 Roberts Lake Rd., Suite A, Rohnert Park, CA 94928 (☎ **800/326-7666** or 707/586-8100; fax 707/ 586-8111), offers a free 48-page visitors guide with information about the whole county. They're also happy to provide lots of specialized information. Write as far in advance as possible. Open daily from 9am to 5pm.

GETTING THERE   From San Francisco, cross the Golden Gate Bridge and stay on Calif. 101 north. Exit at Calif. 37 (toward Vallejo); after 10 miles, turn north onto Calif. 121. After another 10 miles, turn north onto Calif. 12 (Broadway), which will take you into town. From the town of Napa, take Calif. 121 south to Calif. 12. Yeah, this all sounds confusing, but don't worry, the roads are well marked with signs.

TOURING THE WINERIES

The wineries here tend to be a little more spread out than they are in Napa, but they're still easy to find. The visitors bureaus listed above will provide you with maps to the valley's wineries. We've listed our favorite ones below; they, and the towns that follow, are listed roughly from south to north.

Ravenswood Winery. 18701 Gehricke Rd., Sonoma. ☎ **707/938-1960.** Fax 707/938-9459. Daily 10am–4:30pm. Reservations required for tours.

This small, traditional winery in the Sonoma Hills, built right into the hillside to keep it cool inside, crushed its first grapes in 1976 for its inaugural Zinfandel. The winery is best known for its reds, especially its big, bold Zinfandels, but it also produces a Merlot, a Cabernet Sauvignon, and some whites. You'll be able to taste these as well as some younger blends, which are less expensive than the older vintages. Tours follow the wine-making process from grape to glass and include the oak-barrel aging rooms. A "Barbecue in the Vineyards" is held each weekend from Memorial Day through the end of September (call for details).

Sebastiani Vineyards Winery. 389 Fourth St. E., Sonoma. ☎ **800/888-5532** or 707/ 938-5532. Daily 10am–5pm (last tour begins at 4pm).

Although Sebastiani doesn't occupy the most scenic setting or structures in Sonoma Valley, its place in the history and development of the region is unique, and it does offer an interesting and informative guided tour. The 25-minute tour, through aging stone cellars containing more than 300 carved casks, is well worth the time. You can see the winery's original turn-of-the-century crusher and press, as well as a large collection of oak-barrel carvings. If you don't want to take the tour, go straight to the tasting room, where you can sample an extensive selection of wines. A picnic area is adjacent to the cellars.

Buena Vista. 18000 Old Winery Rd. (P.O. Box 1842), Sonoma, CA 95476. ☎ **707/ 938-1266.** Daily 10:30am–4:30pm.

Buena Vista, the patriarch of California wineries, is located slightly northeast of the town of Sonoma. It was founded in 1857 by Count Agoston Haraszthy, the Hungarian émigré who is called the father of the California wine industry. A close friend of General Vallejo, the Mexican administrator who controlled the area when it was still part of Mexico, Haraszthy returned from Europe in 1861 with 100,000 of the finest vine cuttings, which he made available to all wine growers. Although Buena Vista's wine making now takes place in an ultramodern facility outside Sonoma, the winery still maintains a complimentary tasting room here, inside the restored 1862 Press House. There's also a self-guided tour that you can follow anytime during operating hours and a guided tour daily at 2pm.

Chateau St. Jean. 8555 Sonoma Hwy. (Calif. 12), Kenwood. ☎ **707/833-4134.** Self-guided tours, daily 10am–4pm; tasting room, daily 10am–4:30pm.

This winery, founded in 1973, is at the foot of Sugarloaf Ridge, just north of Kenwood and east of Calif. 12. A private drive takes you to what was once a 250-acre country retreat, built in 1920. Chateau St. Jean is notable for its exceptionally beautiful buildings, well-landscaped grounds, and elegant tasting room. A well-manicured lawn is now a picnic area, complete with a fountain and benches.

There's a self-guided tour with detailed and photographic descriptions of the wine-making process. When you've completed it, be sure to walk up to the top of the tower for a view of the valley. Back in the tasting room, Chateau St. Jean offers several Chardonnays, a Cabernet, a Fumé Blanc, a Merlot, a Riesling, and a Gewürztraminer.

The toll-free, interactive **Chateau St. Jean "wine line"** (☎ **800/332-WINE**) offers free recorded reports on the Sonoma Wine Country, including updated information on vineyard conditions, interviews with winemakers and growers, listings of special events at the winery, and descriptions of currently available wines.

SONOMA

Sonoma owes much of its appeal to Mexican Gen. Mariano Guadalupe Vallejo, who fashioned this pleasant, slow-paced town after a typical Mexican village, right down to the central plaza, Sonoma's geographical and commercial center. The Plaza sits at the top of a T formed by Broadway (Calif. 12) and Napa Street. Most of the surrounding streets form a grid pattern around this axis, making Sonoma easy to negotiate. The Plaza's Bear Flag Monument marks the spot where the crude Bear Flag was raised in 1846, signaling the end of Mexican rule; the symbol was later adopted by the state of California. The eight-acre park at the center of the Plaza, with two ponds frequented by ducks and geese, is perfect for an afternoon siesta in the cool shade.

WHAT TO SEE & DO BEYOND THE WINERIES

The best way to see the town of Sonoma is to follow the **Sonoma Walking Tour,** available from the Sonoma Valley Visitors Bureau (see "Visitor Information," above). Highlights include General Vallejo's 1852 Victorian-style home; Sonoma Barracks, erected in 1836 to house Mexican army troops; and the Blue Wing Inn, an 1840 hostelry built to accommodate tourists and new settlers while they erected homes in Sonoma—John Frémont, Kit Carson, and Ulysses S. Grant were all guests.

The **Mission San Francisco Solano de Sonoma,** on Sonoma Plaza at the corner of First Street East and Spain St. (☎ **707/938-1519**), was founded in 1823. It was the northernmost, as well as the last, mission built in California. It was also the only one established on the northern coast by the Mexican rulers, who wished to protect their territory against expansionist Russian fur traders. It's now part of Sonoma State Historic Park. Admission is $2 for adults, $1 for children 6 to 12, free for children under 6. Open daily 10am to 5pm except Thanksgiving, Christmas, and New Year's.

The **Arts Guild of Sonoma,** 140 E. Napa St. (☎ **707/996-3115**), showcases the works of local artists. Exhibits change frequently and include a wide variety of styles and media. Admission is free. Open Wednesday through Monday 11am to 5pm.

SHOPPING   Most of the town's shops, which offer everything from food and wines to clothing and books, are located around the Plaza, including **The Mercado,** a small shopping center at 452 First St. E. that houses several good stores selling unusual wares.

BICYCLING   You can rent a bike or in-line skates at the **Goodtime Bicycle Company,** 18503 Calif. 12 (☎ **707/938-0453**). They'll happily point you to easy bike trails. They also provide a picnic on request. Bikes cost $25 a day, $5 per hour. Bikes are also available from **Sonoma Valley Cyclery,** 20093 Broadway (☎ 707/ **935-3377**), for $20 a day, $6 per hour. For additional biking information in Sonoma County, call the friendly folks at **Dave's Bikes Sport,** 353 College Ave., Santa Rosa, CA 95402 (☎ **707/528-3283**).

WHERE TO STAY

El Dorado Hotel. 405 First St. W. (at W. Spain St.), Sonoma, CA 95476. ☎ **800/289-3031** or 707/996-3030 . Fax 707/996-3148. 27 rms. A/C TEL TV. Winter $85–$110 double, summer $105–$145 double. Rates include continental breakfast, split of wine. AE, MC, V.

If sleeping on a rickety antique bed and bathing in a cramped claw-foot tub isn't exactly your idea of a good time, consider the El Dorado Hotel—it may look like another old timer from the front, but inside it's all 20th-century deluxe. Each modern, handsomely appointed guest room—designed by the same folks who put together Auberge du Soleil—has French windows and small terraces; some offer lovely views of the Town Square, others overlook the hotel's private courtyard and heated pool. Each guest room has a canopy bed and a private bath with plush towels and hair dryers. The two rooms on the ground floor are off the private courtyard; each has its own partially enclosed patio. Services include concierge, laundry, in-room massage, bicycle rental, and access to a nearby health club. Breakfast, served either inside or out, includes coffee, fruits, and freshly baked breads and pastries. Within the hotel is Piatti, a popular restaurant serving regional Italian cuisine (see "Where to Dine," below).

El Pueblo Inn. 896 W. Napa St., Sonoma, CA 94576. ☎ **800/900-8844** or 707/996-3651. 38 rms. A/C TEL. May–Oct $70–$80 double; Mar–Apr and Nov $60–$70, Dec–Feb $59 except during holidays when rates are higher. AE, DISC, JCB, MC, V.

This isn't Sonoma's fanciest hotel, but it offers some of the best-priced accommodations around. Located on Sonoma's main east-west street eight blocks from the center of town, the rooms here are pleasant enough, with post-and-beam construction, exposed brick walls, light wood furniture, and geometric prints. A drip coffee machine with packets of coffee should be a comfort to early risers. An outdoor heated pool will cool you off in hot weather. If possible, reservations should be made at least a month in advance for the spring and summer months.

✪ **Sonoma Chalet.** 18935 Fifth St. W. (at the northwest end of town), Sonoma CA 95476. ☎ **707/938-3129.** 3 rms, 3 cottages, 1 suite. Apr–Oct $95–$140 double; Nov–Mar $80–$130 double. Rates include continental breakfast. AE, MC, V.

This is one of the few accommodations in Sonoma that is truly secluded; it's a bit out of town, in a peaceful country setting overlooking a 200-acre ranch. Accommodations are in a Swiss-style farmhouse and several cottages, but they're by no means rustic—all were delightfully decorated by someone with an eye for color and a concern for comfort. The rooms don't have TVs or phones, but are outfitted with claw-foot tubs, beds covered with country quilts, oriental carpets, comfortable furnishings, and private decks; some even have woodstoves. A breakfast of fruit, yogurt, pastries, and cereal is served either in the country kitchen or in your room (and the gaggles of ducks, chickens, and ornery geese will be glad to help you finish off the crumbs).

Sonoma Hotel. 110 W. Spain St. (at First St. W.), Sonoma, CA 94576. ☎ **800/468-6016** or 707/996-2996. Fax 707/996-7014. 17 rms (5 with bath). Winter, Sun–Thurs $65 double without bath, $95 double with bath; Fri–Sat $75 double without bath, $115–$125 double with bath.

Summer, $75–$85 double without bath, $115–$125 double with bath. Rates include continental breakfast. AE, MC, V. Free parking.

This cute little historic hotel on Sonoma's tree-lined Town Square first opened over a century ago and still retains the same ambience it did then. Each room is decorated in an early California style, with antique furnishings, fine woods, floral-print curtains, and an emphasis on European-style elegance and comfort. Some of the rooms feature brass beds, and all are blissfully void of phones and TVs. Five of the third-floor rooms share immaculate baths (and significantly reduced rates), while rooms with private baths have deep claw-foot tubs with overhead showers. Perks include nightly turndown, continental breakfast, and a bottle of wine on arrival. Also within the hotel is a small restaurant and bar.

WHERE TO DINE

Depot Hotel Restaurant and Garden. 241 First St. W. (3 blocks north of W. Spain St.). ☎ **707/938-2980.** Reservations recommended. Main courses $7–$16 at dinner. AE, DC, DISC, MC, V. Wed–Fri 11:30am–2pm; Wed–Sun 5–closing. NORTHERN ITALIAN.

Michael Ghilarducci has been the chef and owner here for the past 11 years, so you know he's either independently wealthy or a good cook. Fortunately, it's the latter. Located one block north of the Plaza in a handsome and historic 1870 stone building, the Depot Hotel offers pleasant outdoor dining in the Italian garden complete with a central reflection pool and cascading Roman fountain. The menu is unwaveringly Italian, filled with a plethora of classic dishes such as spaghetti Bolognese and veal alla parmigiana. Start with the bounteous antipasto misto and end the feast with a dish of Michael's handmade Italian ice cream and fresh fruit sorbets.

✪ **East Side Oyster Bar and Grill.** 133 East Napa St. ☎ **707/939-1266.** Reservations recommended. Main courses $9–$15. AE, DC, MC, V. Mon–Sat 11:30am–2:30pm, 5:30–9:30pm; Sun noon–9:30pm. Closed Tues–Wed in winter. INTERNATIONAL.

This is one of Sonoma's most popular restaurants, opened in 1992 by Charles Saunders, who gained fame and a following at the Sonoma Mission Inn and Spa. If possible, dine on the vine-entwined brick patio, which is warmed on cool nights by a fire. Saunders is blessed with an unerring sense of proportion and flavor; he knows how to keep both visiting and local foodies coming back for more. The emphasis is on seafood, although there will certainly be a local bird of the day—perhaps a pheasant or a local chicken—as well as sandwiches. Our favorite dishes are the drunken Manila clam linguini dunked in garlic, smoked chile peppers, Spanish chorizo sausage, oregano, and a splash of golden tequila. Top it all off with the New Orleans–style praline-meringue layered with chocolate ganache in a pool of bourbon spiked crème anglaise—wow!

Feed Store Café and Bakery. 529 First St. W. (at Napa St.). ☎ **707/938-2122.** Reservations recommended on Sun. Main courses $5–$9. MC, V. Daily 7am–4pm. CALIFORNIA.

This attractive, airy restaurant has a small fountain-cooled courtyard, a helpful staff, and first-rate, reasonably priced food served in bountiful portions. For breakfast, there are more varieties of eggs than you can imagine. For lunch, quesadillas, burgers, and the crowd-pleasing Jalisco club sandwich (a grilled chicken breast Mexican burrito) are all good choices.

Under the same roof is the **Bakery at the Feed Store,** offering a great selection of baked goods, from small coffee cakes and muffins to New York cheesecake. Their homemade breads are ideal for picnics.

La Casa. 121 E. Spain St. (at First St. E.) ☎ **707/996-3406.** Reservations recommended on weekends and summer evenings. Main courses $6–$11; AE, CB, DC, DISC, MC, V. Daily 11:30am–10pm. MEXICAN.

Where to Stock Up for a Gourmet Picnic, Sonoma Style

Sonoma has plenty of restaurants, but on a sunny day, the Wine Country is really the ideal place to picnic. Sonoma's Plaza Park is a perfect place to set up a gourmet spread; there are even picnic tables provided. Below are Sonoma's top spots for stocking up for such an alfresco fete.

If you want to pick up some specialty fare on your way into town, stop at **Angelo's Wine Country Deli,** 23400 Arnold Dr. (☎ **707/938-3688**). Angelo's sells all types of smoked meats, special salsas, and homemade mustards. The deli is known for its half-dozen types of homemade beef jerky. It's open daily from 9am to 6pm.

The Sonoma Cheese Factory, on the Plaza at 2 Spain St. (☎ **707/996-1000**), offers an extraordinary variety of imported meats and cheeses; a few are set out for tasting every day. The factory also sells caviar, gourmet salads, pâté, and homemade Sonoma Jack cheese. Sandwiches are available, too. While you're there, you can watch a narrated slide show about cheesemaking. The factory is open weekdays from 8:30am to 5:30pm and weekends from 8:30am to 6pm.

At 315 Second St. East, one block north of East Spain Street, is the **Vella Cheese Company** (☎ **800/848-0505** or 707/938-3232). Established in 1931, the folks at Vella pride themselves on making cheese into an award-winning science, their most recent victory being "U.S. Cheese Championship 1995–96" for their Monterey Dry Jack. Other cheeses range from flavorful High Moisture Jack to a mild Daisy and a razor-sharp Raw Milk Cheddar. Among other cheeses for which Vella has become famous is Oregon Blue, made at Vella's southern Oregon factory—rich, buttery, and even spreadable, one of the few premier blues produced in this country. Any of these fine handmade, all-natural cheeses can be shipped directly from the store. Vella Cheese Co. is open Monday to Saturday 9am to 6pm, and Sunday 10am to 5pm.

Of course, you're going to need something to wash down all of this gourmet fare. Head to the **Wine Exchange,** at the Mercado, 452 First St. East (☎ **707/ 938-1794**), which carries more than 600 domestic wines and has a full wine-tasting bar. The beer connoisseur who's feeling displaced in the Wine Country will be happy to find more than 280 beers from around the world here too, including a number of exceptional domestic beers. Open daily from 10am to 6pm, with wine and beer tastings daily.

This no-nonsense Mexican restaurant, on the Sonoma Town Square across from the mission, serves great enchiladas, fajitas, and chimichangas. To start, try the black bean soup or the ceviche made of fresh snapper, marinated in lime juice with cilantro and salsa, and served on crispy tortillas. Follow that with tamales prepared with corn husks spread with corn masa, stuffed with chicken filling, and topped with a mild red chile sauce. Or, you might opt for the delicious Suiza (deep-dish chicken enchiladas) or the fresh snapper Veracruz if it's on the menu. Wine and beer are available.

Piatti. 405 First St. W. (at W. Spain St.). ☎ **707/996-2351.** Reservations recommended. Main courses $7–$12. AE, MC, V. Mon–Thurs 11:30am–2:30pm and 5–10pm, Fri–Sat 11:30am–11pm, Sun 11:30am–10pm. ITALIAN.

This local favorite is known for serving reasonably priced food in a rustic Italian-style setting with delightful patio seating. The bright, sun-filled restaurant occupies the ground floor of the rejuvenated El Dorado Hotel, a 19th-century landmark. Good-tasting pizzas emerge from a wood-burning oven. There are also satisfying pastas, such as lasagna al pesto and spaghetti con agnello (with fresh mushrooms and lamb ragout). Other dishes include a wonderful roast vegetable appetizer, rotisserie chicken with creamy mashed potatoes, and a good scaloppini Pizzaiola. Granted, there are far fancier restaurants in the area, but not many that can fill you up at these prices.

Swiss Hotel. 18 W. Spain St. (at First St. W.) ☎ **707/938-2884.** Reservations recommended. Main courses $8–$16. MC, V. Daily 11:30am–2:30pm, 5–9pm. Bar daily 11am–2am. CONTINENTAL/NORTHERN ITALIAN.

The historic Swiss Hotel, located right in the town center, is a Sonoma landmark, complete with slanting floors and aged beamed ceilings. The turn-of-the-century long oak bar at the left of the entrance is adorned with black-and-white photos of pioneering Sonomans. The bright white dining room and rear dining patio are pleasant spots to enjoy pastas, sandwiches, and California-style pizzas (fired in a wood-burning oven) for lunch. Dinner might start with a warm winter salad of pears, walnuts, radicchio, and blue cheese. Main courses run the gamut; we like the prawn linguine with a spicy tomato sauce, the filet mignon wrapped in a cheese crust, and the duck in an orange honey sauce.

GLEN ELLEN

This small Wine Country town about 7 miles north of Sonoma hasn't changed much since the days when Jack London settled on his Beauty Ranch, about a mile west. Today, **Jack London State Park,** on London Ranch Road (☎ **707/938-5216**), is home to the House of Happy Walls, a museum built by Jack's wife, Charmian, to house a considerable collection of artifacts from the author's life. Jack London settled on his ranch here in 1913 and began building his 26-room Wolf Mansion, which was destroyed by fire shortly before completion. The cottage that the Londons occupied is still there, though, along with the ruins of the mansion and the Londons' graves. Admission is $5 per car, $4 per car for seniors over 62. The park is open daily in winter from 10am to 5pm, summer 10am to 7pm; museum, daily 10am to 5pm.

HORSEBACK RIDING   This is ideal riding country. The **Sonoma Cattle Company and Napa Valley Trail Rides** in Jack London State Park (☎ **707/996-8566**), offers guided tours on horseback. You'll ride on the same trails that London once followed, right past the writer's eucalyptus grove and wood-frame cottage on your way to the top of Mount Sonoma, where you'll have great views of the surrounding countryside. Rides are $40 for two hours and are available by appointment daily, weather permitting. For reservations, write P.O. Box 877, Glen Ellen, CA 95442.

WHERE TO STAY

Glenelly Inn. 5131 Warm Springs Rd., Glen Ellen, CA 95442. ☎ **707/996-6720.** 8 rms. $105–$140 double. Rates include breakfast and afternoon refreshments. MC, V. From Calif. 12, take Arnold Dr. to Warm Springs Rd.

Back in 1916, this was a wayside inn for train passengers. Today, the inn evokes that gentler time with its wicker-furnished, country-style, antique-filled rooms. The "Valley of the Moon" room on the upper level has a woodstove, brass bed, and pine armoire. Others have pine four-posters or sleigh beds; most have claw-foot tubs. Down comforters, bathrobes, ceiling fans, and good reading lamps add to the comfort of the immaculate peach and white rooms. Best of all, the guest rooms are all only steps away from the trellised gardens and hot tub.

Jack London Lodge. 13740 Arnold Dr. at the turnoff to Jack London State Park, Glen Ellen, CA 95442. ☎ **707/938-8510.** 22 rms. A/C TV. $55 double in winter, $75 in summer. MC, V.

In the summer you'll have to book a room far in advance if you want to stay at the Jack London Lodge in Glen Ellen. What's the attraction? The price, naturally: Moderately priced hotels in Sonoma Valley are a rarity, which makes this well-kept two-story motel a hot item. It's in a great location, just down the street from Jack London State Park, close to Sonoma, and surrounded by some of the best small wineries in the valley. Each room comes with a brass king-size bed (or two queens), private bath, and a pleasant country-antique decor. There's a swimming pool situated alongside Sonoma Creek, and a continental breakfast is included in the price on weekends, holidays, and daily during the summer.

WHERE TO DINE

Kenwood Restaurant and Bar. 9900 Sonoma Hwy. ☎ **707/833-6326.** Reservations recommended. Main courses $12.50–$23.50. MC, V. Tues–Sun 11:30am–9pm. CALIFORNIA/ CONTINENTAL.

This is what California Wine Country dining should be (and often, disappointingly, isn't). From the terrace, you can enjoy a view of the vineyards as you dine at umbrella-covered tables. On nippy days, you can retreat inside to the Sonoma-style roadhouse, with its shiny wood floors and pine ceiling. The decor—cushioned rattan chairs set at white cloth-covered tables—is discreetly simple, with a long oak bar on one side and painted vine on the wall behind.

The chef, Max Schacher, serves first-rate cuisine, supported by a reasonably priced wine list. The menu is perfectly balanced between tradition and innovation, and the finely crafted cooking is marked by the heightened, distinctive flavors of California's Wine Country. Great starters are the Dungeness crab cake with herb mayonnaise and the superfresh sashimi with ginger, soy, and wasabe, and the wonderful Caesar salad. Main dish choices might include poached salmon in a creamy sorrel sauce or braised Sonoma rabbit with grilled polenta. Fortunately, the Kenwood doesn't take itself too seriously: Sandwiches and burgers are also available (and considerably less expensive than the main menu items).

8 The Northern Coast

by Erika Lenkert and Matthew R. Poole

Heading north from San Francisco, you'll come upon a California that hardly resembles the southern half of the state. It's an entirely different landscape, in climate as well as flora and fauna. You can forget about the fabled surfing-and-bikini scene this far north; instead, you'll find miles and miles of rugged coastline with broad beaches and tiny bays harboring dramatic rock formations, from chimney stacks to bridges and blowholes, carved by the ocean waves.

The best time to visit the North Coast is in the spring or fall. In spring, the headlands are carpeted with wildflowers—golden poppy, iris, and sea foam—and in fall the sun shines clear, cool, and bright. Summers are typically damp and windy, with the ubiquitous fog burning off by the afternoon.

You'll think you've already arrived in Alaska by the time you hit the beaches of Northern California. Take a dip in the sea and you'll soon agree with the locals: When it comes to swimming, the Arctic waters along the north coast are best left to the seals. But that doesn't mean you can't enjoy the beaches, whether by strolling along the water or taking in the panoramic views of towering cliffs and seascapes. Unlike their southern cousins, the beaches along the north coast are not likely to be crowded, even in summer.

The most scenic way to reach Point Reyes, Mendocino, and points north is to drive from San Francisco along the coast via Calif. 1, one of the most beautiful (and treacherous in foggy weather) drives in the world. U.S. 101, which runs inland from San Francisco to the Oregon border, is much faster, but don't unpack the camera for this one. Unless you're determined to drive the entire stretch of Calif. 1—a grueling all-day event—start out on U.S. 101 to save time and gas, then choose the appropriate artery leading west toward Calif. 1 and your destination.

1 Point Reyes National Seashore

by Andrew Rice

Point Reyes is a 100-square-mile peninsula of dark forests, wind-sculpted dunes, endless beaches, and plunging sea cliffs. Aside from its beautiful scenery, it also boasts historical treasures that offer a window into California's coastal past, including lighthouses, turn-of-the-century dairies and ranches, the site of Sir Francis Drake's 1579 landing, plus a complete replica of a coastal Miwok Indian village.

The Northern Coast

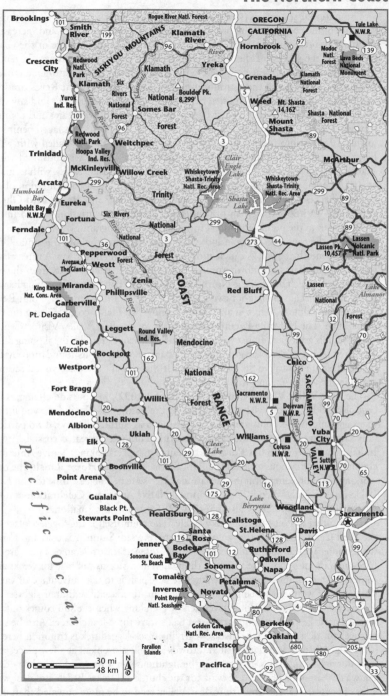

Brookings
101
Smith River
199
SISKIYOU MOUNTAINS
Rogue River Natl. Forest
Klamath River
OREGON
CALIFORNIA
Tule Lake N.W.R.
Crescent City
96
Klamath
Yreka
Hornbrook
97
Modoc Natl. Forest
139
Lava Beds National Monument
Redwood Natl. Park
Klamath
Six Rivers National Forest
Somes Bar
Boulder Pk. 8,299'
3
Grenada
5
Klamath National Forest
Shasta National Forest
Yurok Ind. Res.
101
96
National
Weed
Mt. Shasta 14,162'
Klamath River
Weitchpec
Forest
3
Mount Shasta
89
Trinidad
Redwood Natl. Park
Hoopa Valley Ind. Res.
Willow Creek
Whiskeytown-Shasta-Trinity Natl. Rec. Area
Clair Engle Lake
Whiskeytown-Shasta-Trinity Natl. Rec. Area
McArthur
McKinleyville
299
Trinity
89
Arcata
Humboldt Bay
Eureka
Six Rivers
National
Shasta Lake
299
89
Humboldt Bay N.W.R.
Fortuna
National
3
299
273
44
Lassen Pk. 10,457'
Lassen Volcanic Natl. Park
Ferndale
101
36
Pepperwood
Forest
Forest
5
36
Avenue of The Giants
Weott
Zenia
36
Lassen
Lake Almanor
Miranda
Phillipsville
Red Bluff
National
King Range Nat. Cons. Area
Garberville
Eel River
32
Forest
70
Pt. Delgada
Leggett
Round Valley Ind. Res.
Mendocino
99
Cape Vizcaino
Rockport
162
Chico
162
Westport
101
National
Sacramento N.W.R.
SACRAMENTO
99
Fort Bragg
Willits
Forest
Sacramento River
70
Mendocino
20
RANGE
5
Delevan N.W.R.
Little River
COAST
Yuba City
20
Albion
Ukiah
20
Williams
Colusa N.W.R.
VALLEY
Sutter N.W.R.
70
Elk
128
Clear Lake
29
20
65
Manchester
Boonville
16
113
Point Arena
29
Gualala
175
Lake Berryessa
Woodland
Black Pt.
Healdsburg
128
Calistoga
505
Sacramento
Stewarts Point
Santa Rosa
St. Helena
Davis
5
Jenner
116
Bodega Bay
101
12
Rutherford
128
80
99
Sonoma Coast St. Beach
Sonoma
Oakville
Napa
12
160
Tomales
Petaluma
12
Inverness
Novato
5
Point Reyes Natl. Seashore
1
80
Berkeley
Golden Gate Natl. Rec. Area
4
Oakland
4
San Francisco
680
580
205
Pacifica
101
92
33
Farallon Islands

Pacific Ocean

0   30 mi
      48 km
N

1-0832

195

The national seashore system was created to protect rural and undeveloped stretches of the coast from the pressures of soaring real estate values and increasing population, preserving both the natural features and unique culture of the coast. Nowhere is the success of the system more evident than at Point Reyes. Layers of human history coexist peacefully here with one of the world's most dramatic natural settings. Residents of the surrounding towns—**Inverness, Point Reyes Station, and Olema**—have steadfastly resisted runaway development. You won't find any strip malls or fast-food joints here—just laid-back coastal towns with cafes and country inns where gentle living prevails. The park, a 71,000-acre hammer-shaped peninsula jutting 10 miles into the Pacific and backed by Tomales Bay, is loaded with wildlife, ranging from tule elk, birds, and bobcats to gray whales, sea lions, and white sharks. During Audubon's annual Christmas bird count, Point Reyes, with as many as 350 different varieties, is regularly found to have the largest concentration of diverse bird species in the continental United States. The **Point Reyes Bird Observatory** (☎ **415/868-1221**), an ornithological research organization located in the park, is open to the public and offers tours and special programs.

Though the peninsula's people and wildlife live in harmony above the ground, the situation beneath the soil is much more volatile. The infamous San Andreas fault separates Point Reyes, the northernmost landmass on the Pacific Plate, from the rest of California, which rests on the North American Plate. Point Reyes is making its way toward Alaska at a rate of about two inches per year. In 1906, however, Point Reyes jumped north almost 20 feet in an instant, leveling San Francisco and jolting the rest of the state. The half-mile **Earthquake Trail,** near the Bear Valley Visitor Center, illustrates this geological drama with a loop through an area torn by the slipping fault. Shattered fences, rifts in the ground, and a barn knocked off its foundation by the quake illustrate how alive the earth is here. If that doesn't convince you, a seismograph in the visitor's center will.

The **Bear Valley Visitor Center** (☎ **415/663-1092**), just outside Olema, is the best place to begin your visit. In addition to the Earthquake Trail, here you'll find maps and information plus great natural history and cultural displays. Two particularly fascinating features of the center are **Kule Loklo,** a re-created coastal Miwok Indian village that often hosts displays of dancing, basket-making, Native American cooking, and indigenous art; and the Park Service's **Morgan Horse Ranch,** the only working horse-breeding farm in the national park system. The best time to visit Kule Loklo is during July when it hosts an annual **Native American Celebration** and the whole village comes to life. Call **415/479-3281** for more information.

The weather at Point Reyes is very fickle. The point itself is the foggiest place on the West Coast. Generally the seasons here are reversed: Summer is cold and foggy, while winter is clear and, if not exactly warm, often at least tolerable. There are no hard-and-fast rules about the weather, though. Winter storms can rage for weeks and sometimes the summer fog stays away. The best plan is to take advantage of variations in local weather by being flexible with your itinerary: Save indoor sightseeing for rainy or foggy days, and hit the beach or go hiking when the sun comes out. In wooded areas keep an eye out for poison oak's waxy three-leaf clusters. Also be sure to check for ticks as the Lyme disease–carrying black-legged tick is common here.

Though the park is heavily visited, crowds are only a problem at a few places and only during certain times. If you visit the lighthouse on a weekend or holiday during whale season, be prepared to wait for the shuttle at Drakes Beach and deal with a lot of people. Trails leaving from Bear Valley tend to be more crowded than others on weekends. Try the Five Brooks or Palomarin trailheads to avoid backcountry hordes.

Point Reyes National Seashore & Bodega Bay

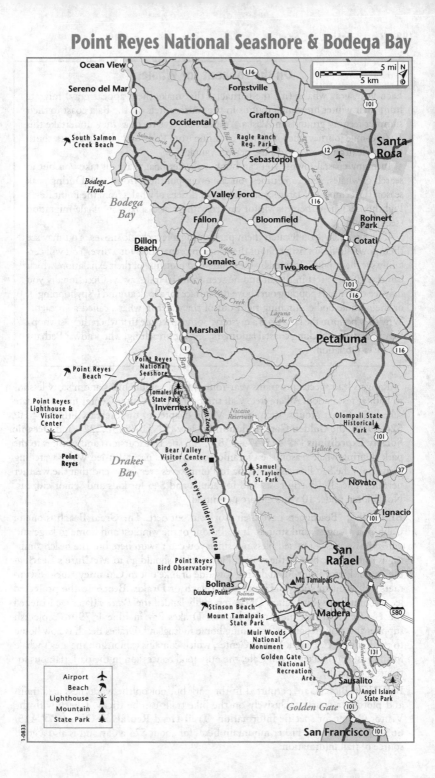

0   5 mi
0   5 km

N

Ocean View
Sereno del Mar
Forestville
116
Occidental
Grafton
101
South Salmon
Creek Beach
Ragle Ranch
Reg. Park
Santa
Rosa
Salmon Creek
Dutch Bill Creek
Sebastopol
12
Bodega
Head
Valley Ford
116
Bodega
Bay
Fallon
Bloomfield
Rohnert
Park
Dillon
Beach
Cotati
Walker Creek
Tomales
Two Rock
101
116
Tomales Bay
Chileno Creek
Laguna
Lake
Marshall
Petaluma
116
Point Reyes
Beach
Point Reyes
National
Seashore
Tomales Bay
State Park
Inverness
Rift Zone
Nicasio
Reservoir
Olompali State
Historical
Park
101
Point Reyes
Lighthouse &
Visitor
Center
Olema
Bear Valley
Visitor Center
Halleck Creek
Point
Reyes
Samuel
P. Taylor
St. Park
Novato
Drakes
Bay
Point Reyes Wilderness Area
1
Ignacio
101
San
Rafael
Point Reyes
Bird Observatory
Mt. Tamalpais
Bolinas
Duxbury Point
Bolinas
Lagoon
Corte
Madera
580
Stinson Beach
Mount Tamalpais
State Park
Muir Woods
National
Monument
131
Golden Gate
National
Recreation
Area
Sausalito
Angel Island
State Park
Golden Gate
San Francisco
101

Airport
Beach
Lighthouse
Mountain
State Park

1-0833

On the Lookout for Whales

Each year, gray whales (it's the barnacles that make them appear gray) migrate from their winter breeding grounds in the warm waters off the Baja coast to their summer feeding grounds in Alaska. You can observe them as they undertake this 10,000-mile journey; the California coastline from Redwood National Park south to the Mexican border offers the perfect vantage.

In many coastal towns, you can book a charter boat that will take you out in search of whales. And sometimes you can even spot them from land. During peak season (December to March), you might spot dozens of whales from the Point Reyes Lighthouse, where there's a visitor center with great displays on whale migration (see below).

If you're lucky, you'll catch them performing a few classic moves. You may see their powerful flukes rising out of the water in preparation for a dive. You will certainly see their spouts, formed by the condensed moisture of their exhalation, which can rise 10 to 15 feet in the air and be seen from 10 miles away. Occasionally you may see their heads popping out above the surface for a look around ("spyhopping"), or their whole bodies lurching right out of the water in what's called a "breach." Why they perform the last two is a mystery. Some speculate that when they "spyhop" they're actually checking coastal landmarks. As for breaching, who knows? Perhaps it's sheer jubilation.

Rangers lead special programs year-round, from wildlife hikes and history lessons to habitat restoration. All are free. Call the Bear Valley Visitor Center for up-to-date schedules. Other groups, such as the Marin chapter of the **Sierra Club** (☎ 510/526-8969), the **Golden Gate Audubon Society** (☎ 510/843-2222), and **Oceanic Society Expeditions** (☎ 415/474-3385), run special excursions and outings to the park. During whale season the Oceanic Society takes naturalist-led whale-watching boats from the San Francisco Marina to Point Reyes every weekend that the weather permits. The all-day trip costs $48 for adults and $46 for kids and senior citizens. No children under 10 years old are permitted.

BEACHES Beachgoers have their work cut out here. The **Great Beach** is one of California's longest sand strands. It is also one of the windiest and home to large and dangerous waves—a mixed blessing, since you can't swim here but the beachcombing is some of the best in the world. Tide poolers should go to **McClure's Beach** at the end of Pierce Point Road during low tide or hike out to **Chimney Rock.** Swimmers will want to stick to **Limantour Beach** or **Drakes Beach** in the protected lee of Point Reyes. Sir Francis Drake reputedly landed the *Pelican* (later rechristened the *Golden Hind*) on the sandy shore of Drakes Bay in June 1579, to replenish supplies and make repairs before sailing home to England. Drakes Beach is now home to the Kenneth C. Patrick Visitor Center, which contains exhibits on the area's whale fossil beds, and Drakes Beach Cafe, the only food concession in the park (famous for its great oysters).

BIKING Bicycles are permitted in the park but not on the wilderness area trails, and plotting a course exclusively on the bike trails can be tricky. Check with the Visitor Center for specific information. **Trail Head Rentals** in Olema (☎ 415/663-1958) rents nice Fisher mountain bikes for about $24 a day and is also a good source of trail information.

CAMPING & LODGING   The only lodging within Point Reyes is the rustic but affordable ($9 per night) **AYH Hostel** on Limantour Road (☎ 415/663-8811). A beautiful old ranch complex 2 miles from Limantour beach that was converted into bunkhouse sleeping quarters, the hostel fills up early. Reservations are recommended. Maximum stay three nights.

Camping within the park is limited to four hike-in camps. Two, **Wildcat Camp** (a 6½-mile hike) and **Coast Camp** (a 1.8-mile hike), sit just above the beach. They are often foggy and damp, so bring a good tent and sleeping bag. **Sky Camp** (1.7 miles) and **Glen Camp** (4.6 miles), set in the woods away from the sea, are more protected from the coastal elements. Individual sites hold up to eight people and have picnic tables and food lockers. Pit toilets and drinking water are available. Camping is free, but permits are required and stays are limited to four days. Sites can be reserved up to two months in advance by calling **415/663-1092** Monday through Friday from 9am to noon only. Dogs are not permitted on any trails or in the campgrounds.

HIKING   There's a little of everything for hikers here: 32,000 acres of the park contain 70 miles of trails and are set aside as wilderness where no motor vehicles or bicycles are allowed. The **Bear Valley Trail** leads through wooded hillsides until it reaches the sea at **Arch Rock,** about eight miles round-trip, where Coast Creek splashes into the sea through a "sea tunnel." More relaxing is the 4½-mile **Estero Trail,** a favorite with birders that meanders along the edge of Limantour Estero and Drakes Estero. *Estero* is the Spanish word for estuary and these brackish waters draw flocks of waterfowl and shorebirds as well as many raptors and smaller species. Near Wildcat Camp on the Coast Trail is **Alamere Falls,** also reached via the Palomarin Trail or Five Brooks Trail in the south of the park. **Tomales Point Trail,** 11 miles round-trip, gives hikers a tour of the park's rugged shoreline and also passes through wilderness that is home to the park's herd of tule elk.

WHALE WATCHING   During peak season (December to March) the park service runs a shuttle from Drakes Beach to the **Point Reyes Lighthouse,** where it is sometimes possible to see 100 whales in an afternoon. Even if the whales don't materialize, the lighthouse itself, a fabulous old structure teetering high above the sea at the tip of a knife-backed promontory, is worth a visit. The **Lighthouse Visitor Center** (☎ 415/669-1534) offers great displays on whale migration and maritime history. Two other spots, Chimney Rock and Tomales Point, offer just as many whales without the crowds.

WHERE TO STAY

Bear Valley Inn. 88 Bear Valley Rd., Olema, CA 94950. ☎ **415/663-1777.** 3 rms. $75–$135 double. Rates include breakfast. AE, MC, V.

Ron and JoAnne Nowell's venerable two-story 1899 Victorian has survived everything from a major earthquake to a recent forest fire, which is lucky for you because you'll be hard pressed to find a better B&B for the price in Point Reyes. Granted, the Bear Valley Inn isn't perfect: The rooms lack private baths and the main highway is a tad too close. But it's loaded with Victorian charm, right down to the profusion of flowers and vines outside and comfy chairs fronting a toasty-warm wood stove inside. It's in a great location, too, with three good restaurants only a block away, and the entire national seashore at your doorstep. Ron, who also runs a mountain bike rental shop next door, can set you up with wheels for about $25 a day and point you in the right direction.

Knob Hill. 40 Knob Hill Rd., Point Reyes Station. ☎ **415/663-1784.** 1 rm. $50–$60. No credit cards.

Sh. It's a secret. Atop a small bluff overlooking beautiful Point Reyes Mesa is Knob Hill, where horse trainer Janet Schlitt rents a small room and private cottage next to her stable. The separate cottage is a bit pricey, but attached to Janet's home is a small room with its own entrance, private bath, and garden area that she rents for only $60 a night. Granted, there's barely enough elbow room for a couple to change their minds, but it's simply adorable. Just down the street is a trail leading into Point Reyes. All in all, it's a great deal, particularly for horse lovers.

✪ **Manka's Inverness Lodge.** P.O. Box 1110, Inverness, CA 94937. ☎ **800/58-LODGE** or 415/669-1034. Fax 415/669-1598. 12 rms. $100–$165 double. AE, MC, V.

This immediately lovable old hunting lodge is one of our favorite places to stay and dine on the coast. Every room resembles the sort of rustic old mountain cabin you read about in Jack London novels, and the restaurant has that perfect balance of countrified charm and polished refinement. In addition to the standard rooms in the main lodge (which are anything but standard with their tree-limb bedsteads, billowy down comforters, and rustic furnishings), there are two luxuriously appointed cabins adjacent to the inn, a quartet of smaller, less-expensive rooms in the redwood annex (the budget traveler's first choice), and a drippingly romantic 19th-century hunting cabin located down the road.

The lodge's reputation is built on its restaurant, which dominates the bottom floor. The specialty of the house is game and fish, including oysters from Tomales Bay. Prices range from $18 to $22, but you can sneak by for under $10 if you stick to salads and appetizers. The limited menu might feature pheasant with a Madeira sauce, mashed potatoes, and a wild huckleberry jam, black buck antelope chops with sweet corn salsa, or everybody's favorite, pan-seared elk tenderloin. It's open for dinner Thursday through Monday with a brunch on Sunday.

Motel Inverness. 12718 Sir Francis Drake Blvd., Inverness, CA 94937. ☎ **415/669-1081.** 7 rms. TV. $59–$89 double. AE, DISC, MC, V.

Finding an inexpensive place to stay in Point Reyes is next to impossible, as hoity-toity B&Bs reign supreme. There is, however, one exception: Motel Inverness, a homey, well-maintained lodging fronting Tomales Bay. For the outdoor adventurer who plans on spending as little time indoors as possible, it's the perfect place to hole up, as the entire national seashore is at your doorstep. Those seeking a little romance on their vacation, however, should dig a little deeper in their wallets and opt for Manka's (see above). All of the guest rooms were completely renovated and refurnished in May 1996; each comes with a queen-size bed, linoleum floors, rosewood blinds, and a color television; smoking is strictly verboten. Attached to the hotel is a giant rec room, complete with pool table, pinball machine, and big-screen TV to distract the kids (who stay free), while parents can relax on the back lawn overlooking the bay, bird sanctuary, and rolling green hills beyond.

WHERE TO DINE

The Gray Whale. 12781 Sir Francis Drake Blvd., Inverness. ☎ **415/669-1244.** Main courses $5–$10. MC, V. Daily 11am–9pm. ITALIAN.

For more than a decade The Gray Whale cafe has been a popular pit stop for Bay Area residents heading to the lighthouse at Point Reyes. Why so popular? First off, it's cheap. Sandwiches such as the roasted eggplant with pesto and mozzarella are only $5, as are most of the salads and pastas. Second, it's pretty good. Personal favorites are the specialty pizzas, such as the Californian (artichoke hearts, fresh basil, and tomatoes) and the Vegetarian (baked eggplant, roasted onions and romas, broccoli, and piles of freshly grated Parmesan cheese). Veteran hikers and mountain bikers stop by for an espresso booster, sipped on the small patio overlooking the block-long town of Inverness.

Johnson's Oyster Farm. Off Sir Francis Drake Blvd., about 6 miles south of Inverness. ☎ **415/ 669-1149.** AE, DISC, MC, V. Tues–Sun, 8am to 4pm. OYSTERS.

Why pay $15 at a restaurant for a skimpy plate of oysters when you can buy them straight from the source for next to nothing? Johnson's may look (and smell) like a dump, but those tasty bivalves don't come any fresher. Our modus operandi is: Buy a couple of dozen, head for an empty campsite along the bay, fire up the barbecue pit (don't forget the charcoal), split and grill the little guys, slather them in Johnson's special sauce, and slurp them down.

✪ **Station House Cafe.** 11180 Main St., Point Reyes Station. ☎ **415/663-1515.** Reservations recommended. Breakfast $4–$6.50; main courses $9–$16. DISC, MC, V. Sun–Thurs 8am–9pm, Fri–Sat 8am–10pm. AMERICAN.

A local favorite, the Station House Cafe is known for its good food and lively atmosphere, particularly when the live music fires up on weekends. For breakfast, we recommend a fritatta with asparagus, goat cheese, and olives, which always seems to taste better while sitting outside on the shaded garden patio. Luncheon specials might include two-cheese polenta served with sautéed fresh spinach and grilled garlic-buttered tomatoes. Organically grown local beef is always on the menu, which changes every week, as is a good selection of fresh fish. Rounding out the menu are homemade chili, steamed clams, fresh soup made daily, and fish and chips. The cafe has an extensive list of fine California wines, plus local imported beers.

Taqueria La Quinta. 3rd and Main sts. in downtown Point Reyes Station. ☎ **415/663-8868.** Main courses $4–$6. No credit cards. Wed–Mon 11am–9pm. MEXICAN.

Fresh, good, fast, and cheap: What more could you ask for in a restaurant? The Taqueria has been one of our favorite lunch stops in downtown Point Reyes for years. A huge selection of Mexican American standards are posted above the counter, but those-in-the-know inquire about the seafood specials. Since it's all self-serve, you can skip the tip, but watch out for the salsa—this stuff is hot.

2 Along the Sonoma Coast

TOMALES BAY

From Point Reyes Station, Calif. 1 travels north along the eastern edge of Tomales Bay. Around the town of **Marshall,** stop in at one of the oyster farms and pick out some choice samples from the tanks. The **Tomales Bay Oyster Company,** for example, sells its wares by the dozen or in sacks of 100, should you be on your honeymoon. It's open daily from 9am to 5pm; 15479 Calif. 1, Tomales (☎ **415/ 663-1242**). The bay is also good for clamming, windsurfing, and kayaking and for hang gliding, especially at **Dillon Beach** at the mouth of the Bay. Kayak trips, including three-hour sunset outings, $3^{1}/_{2}$-hour full moon paddles, day trips, and longer excursions are organized by **Tomales Bay Kayaking** (☎ **415/663-1743**). Prices start at $45. Rentals begin at $16 for two hours for a single seater.

BODEGA BAY

Beyond the tip of the Point Reyes Peninsula, the road curves around toward the coastal village of Bodega Bay, which supports an active fishing fleet of about 300 boats. As you drive north, Bodega Bay is a good place to stop for lunch or to stroll around town. There are a handful of mildly entertaining shops and galleries, though the best show in town is at Tides Wharf, where the fishing boats come in to unload their daily catch, which is then promptly gutted and packed in ice.

Bodega Head State Park is a great vantage point for whale watching during the annual migration season from January through April. At **Doran Beach** there's a large bird sanctuary (willets, curlews, godwits, and more), and the University of California Marine Biology Lab next door conducts guided tours on Friday afternoon.

The **Bodega Harbour Golf Links,** 21301 Heron Dr. (☎ **707/875-3538**), enjoys a panoramic oceanside setting. It's an 18-hole Scottish-style course designed by Robert Trent Jones Jr. A new warm-up center and practice facility has been added, which is free of charge to registered golfers.

A few miles inland, the tiny town of **Bodega,** with a population of 100, is famous as the setting of Alfred Hitchcock's *The Birds;* fans will want to visit the Potter School House and St. Teresa's Church.

For more information, stop in at the **Bodega Bay Area Visitors Center,** 850 Calif. 1, Bodega Bay, CA 94923 (☎ **707/875-3422**). They have lots of brochures about the town and the surrounding area, including maps of the Sonoma Coast State Beaches and the best local fishing spots.

WHERE TO STAY

Ⓢ Bodega Harbor Inn. 1345 Bodega Ave., Bodega Bay, CA 94923. ☎ **707/875-3594.** 14 rms. TV. $48–$70 double. MC, V.

Thank Poseidon for the Bodega Harbor Inn, which, besides being the only low-priced accommodation in Bodega Bay, is also one of the best deals for your dollar on the North Coast. Set on a small bluff overlooking the bay, the inn consists of four single-story clapboard buildings surrounded by well-maintained lawns and gardens. The rooms, though small, are impeccably neat and tastefully decorated with unpretentious antique furnishings; double beds, private baths, and cable TV are all standard. (*Insider tip:* For only $10 more you can upgrade to room 12 or 14, which come with a small deck and ocean view.) The clincher, though, is the inn's private lawn area overlooking the bay: On sunny days, there's no better way to enjoy the day in Bodega Bay than situating your fanny in one the lawn chairs and watching the fishing boats bring in their daily catch.

WHERE TO DINE

Breakers Cafe. 1400 Calif. 1, Bodega Bay. ☎ **707/875-2513.** Main courses $6–$16. MC, V. Daily 9am–9pm. CALIFORNIA.

If you're a big breakfast eater, the Breakers Cafe is your best bet in Bodega Bay. Omelets, Belgian waffles, baked polenta, house-baked muffins, and even good ol' biscuits and gravy are served in a pleasant greenhouselike dining room filled with a profusion of healthy plants and diffused sunlight. The cafe also offers a modest lunch and dinner menu, ranging from above-average sandwiches and burgers to fresh pastas, locally caught seafood, and a small selection of vegetarian dishes. Prices run a bit steep for the seafood dishes (odd, considering the location), but the majority of menu items are under $10. If the weather's warm, ask for a table on the patio.

Ⓒ Lucas Wharf Deli. 595 Calif. 1, Bodega Bay. ☎ **707/875-3562.** Deli items $4–$10. DISC, MC, V. Daily 10am–7pm. DELI.

Whenever we find ourselves passing through Bodega Bay, this is one stop we always make. Most visitors don't even give it a glance as they head into the adjacent restaurant, but that's because they don't know about the big bowls of fresh, tangy crab cioppino they dole out for only $5 a pint—a third of what they charge at the restaurant. It's a fabulously messy affair, best devoured at the picnic tables next to the deli. When crab season is over, the cioppino special is replaced by an equally awesome pile of fresh fish-and-chips (easily big enough to feed two).

Tides Wharf Restaurant. 835 Calif. 1, Bodega Bay. ☎ **707/875-3652.** Main courses $10–$24 at dinner. AE, DISC, MC, V. Daily 7:30am–9:30pm (last order). SEAFOOD.

It isn't as secluded or intimate as you might have wanted (in summer, as many as 1,000 diners a day pass through here), but it evokes all the nostalgia of the 1950s, when it served as one of the settings for Hitchcock's *The Birds*. Don't expect the weather-beaten, board-and-batten luncheonette you saw in that movie: The place has been gentrified, enlarged, and redecorated many times since, although it retains the original bar used in that film. There are views over the water, and tables are cramped but convivial. The bill of fare is what you might expect at a chowderhouse in Boston, with fish and chips, barbecued oysters, oysters Rockefeller, and all the seafood that the owners (who send their own fishing boat out into the Pacific every day) can dredge up from the cold blue waters offshore. We enjoyed a terrific open-faced crab sandwich served with melted cheese on sourdough bread. Land-locked items such as prime rib and pasta are also available.

THE SONOMA COAST STATE BEACHES, JENNER & FORT ROSS STATE HISTORIC PARK

Along 13 winding miles of Calif. 1—from Bodega Bay to Goat Rock in Jenner—stretch the Sonoma Coast State Beaches. These beaches are ideal for walking, tide pooling, abalone picking, fishing, and bird watching for such species as blue heron, cormorant, osprey, brown and white pelicans, and more. Each is clearly marked from the road, and numerous pullouts are provided for parking. Even if you don't stop at any beach, the drive alone is spectacular.

At **Jenner,** the Russian River empties into the ocean. Penny Island, in the river's estuary, is home to otters and many species of birds, while out on the ocean rocks there's a colony of harbor seals. Goat Rock Beach is a popular breeding ground for the seals; pupping season begins in March and lasts until June.

From Jenner, a 12-mile climb along some very dramatic coastline will bring you to **Fort Ross State Historic Park** (☎ 707/847-3286), a reconstruction of the fort that was established here in 1812 by Russian seal and otter hunters (it was abandoned in 1842). At the visitor center you can view the silver samovars and elaborate table services that the Russians used. The fenced compound contains several buildings, including the first Russian Orthodox Church built on the North American continent outside Alaska. The park also offers beach trails and picnicking facilities on more than 1,000 acres. Admission is free, but parking is a hefty $5.

North from Fort Ross the road continues to **Salt Point State Park.** Its 3,500-acre expanse contains 30 campsites, 14 miles of hiking trails, dozens of tide pools, a pygmy forest, and old Pomo village sites. Your best bet is to pull off the highway wherever looks good and start exploring on foot. At the north end of the park, branch off inland on Kruse Ranch Road to the 317-acre **Kruse Rhododendron Reserve** (☎ 707/847-3221), positively a miracle in April and May. Some rhododendrons grow to a height of 18 feet under the redwood and fir canopy.

WHERE TO STAY

Murphy's Jenner Inn. 10400 Calif. 1, in downtown Jenner, CA 95450. ☎ **800/732-2377** or 707/865-2377. 13 rms. $75–$175 double. Rates include continental breakfast. AE, MC, V.

Coastal Cost-Cutters

Just about every restaurant and hotel on the North Coast seems to charge a small fortune, but after a little detective work we've unearthed a few great deals for your hard-earned dollars.

A room at the **Coast Guard House,** a wonderful B&B in Point Arena, normally goes for about $125 and up, but innkeeper Merita Whatley rents two of her smaller rooms for only $75 to $85. What's more, a gourmet continental breakfast is included, as is use of the ocean view hot tub. (695 Arena Cove, Point Arena; ☎ 800/524-9320 or 707/882-2442. MC, V.)

Bookends, a hybrid coffeehouse, bookstore, and community center, is Point Arena's most cerebral hangout. We consider it a mandatory stop for a sandwich (build your own from their "Sandwich Chekov List"), double mocha, and a new book. Breakfast is served until 1pm (try the tofu scramble), and the lunch counter runs daily until closing time. (265 Main St., Point Arena; ☎ 707/882-2287. Daily 7am to 9pm.)

A sit-down dinner at **Bridget Dolan's Dinner House** in the town of Elk will set you back at least $20, but if you sit at the bar you can dine on fresh mussels, sourdough bread, and a side of garlic and herb pasta for only $10. There's a good selection of beer, too. (5910 Calif. 1, Elk; ☎ 707/877-1820. Open daily 3 to 10pm).

Top-secret lunch tip: In the back of the **Little River Market,** located directly across from the Little River Inn, are a trio of small tables overlooking the Mendocino coastline. All you need for an invitation is to order a tamale, sandwich, or whatever else is on the menu at the tiny deli inside the market. On the way out, be sure to buy a loaf of the legendary Cafe Beaujolais bread sold at the front counter. (On Calif. 1 in Little River; ☎ 707/937-5133. Open daily 8am to 7pm.)

They call it Poor Man's Pebble Beach, but the majority of rooms at the **Little River Inn** golf and tennis resort are still priced beyond this book's range. There are, however, a few motel-like rooms with ocean views that go for about $85 a night (just follow the well-worn golf-shoe trail). Aside from the view, they lack even a semblance of luxury or romance—though the main lodge itself is exquisite—but if you want to knock the ball around without going broke it's here or nada. (7751 Calif. 1, Little River; ☎ 707/937-5942. MC, V.)

The worst-kept secret on the North Coast is Murphy's Jenner Inn, a hodgepodge of seven houses and cottages scattered along the coast and inland along Russian River. Couples from the Bay Area, who want to stay along the coast for a night but dread the long drive to Mendocino, usually wend their way here for an easy weekend getaway. Most of the houses are subdivided into suites, while second honeymooners vie for the ultraprivate oceanfront cottages. Wicker furniture, wood paneling, and private baths and entrances are standard, though each lodging has its own distinct personality: Some have kitchens, others have fireplaces, porches, or private decks. Naturally, the private cottages overlooking the Pacific are the priciest, but for about $80 most people are content with one of the small suites. A complimentary continental breakfast is served in the main lodge.

WHERE TO DINE

River's End. Calif. 1., Jenner. ☎ 707/865-2484. Reservations recommended. Main courses $13–$33 at dinner. MC, V. Mon–Fri 11am–9:30pm, Sat–Sun 10am–9:30pm. INTERNATIONAL.

Outwardly unpretentious yet deceptively urbane, this small seaside restaurant offers an artfully rustic setting where big windows overlook the California coast, the sea, and whatever seals and sea lions happen to be cavorting offshore. The menu is wonderfully eclectic, the product of a German-born chef who whips up versions of Indonesian bahmi goreng, a choice of Indian curries, beef sate, beef Wellington, seafood, and steaks. If the dinner menu is out of your price range ($53 for a rack of lamb for two), you'll be happy to know that lunch is far more affordable. A burger with fries, for example, is only $6, yet the million-dollar view remains the same.

Sizzling Tandoor. 9960 Calif. 1, at the south end of the Russian River Bridge, Jenner. ☎ **707/ 865-0625.** Main courses $6–$10. AE, MC, V. Lunch daily 11:30am–3pm, dinner Mon–Thurs 5–9:30pm, Fri–Sun 5–10pm. INDIAN.

Something of an anomaly along a rather desolate stretch of Calif. 1 between Bodega Bay and Jenner is this roadside restaurant serving huge, inexpensive plates of classic Indian cuisine. The lonely location, though peculiar, is superb. Perched high atop a windswept hill, it boasts an exquisite view of the Russian River far below. The large array of curries and kabobs is accompanied with a side of soup, vegetables, pulao rice, and the best nan (Indian bread) we've ever had. Even if you're not hungry, stop here anyway and order some nan to go: It makes the perfect road snack.

GUALALA & POINT ARENA

Back on Calif. 1 going north you'll pass through Sea Ranch, a series of condominium beach developments, until you reach Gualala (pronounced wah-*la*-la). Access to the beaches along this stretch of coast is across private property and may be restricted at any time. Still, there are about 10 or so public beaches that are ideal for walking.

The **Gualala River,** adjacent to the town of the same name, is suitable for canoeing, rafting, and kayaking since all power boats and jet skis are forbidden. Along its banks you're likely to see osprey, heron, egrets, and ducks as well as steelhead, salmon, and river otters in the waters. Canoes, kayaks, and bicycles can be rented for two hours, a half day, or full day in Gualala from **Adventure Rents,** P.O. Box 489 (☎ **707/884-4386**), behind the Gualala Hotel on Calif. 1. The cost ranges from $15 for a bike for two hours to $25 for a canoe (two to five persons) for a half day and $60 for a double kayak for the whole day. **Gualala Kayak,** 39175 South Calif. 1 next to the Chevron station (☎ **707/884-4705**), specializes in river and sea kayaking. A single kayak rents for $20 for two hours, $35 a day, a double for $65. Prices include everything from instruction to shuttle service.

Point Arena lies a few miles north of Gualala. Most folks stop here for the view at the **Point Arena Lighthouse,** which was built in 1870 after 10 ships ran aground here on a single night during a storm. A $2.50 fee covers parking, entrance to the lighthouse museum, and a tour of the six-story, 145-step lighthouse (which is surprisingly interesting). It's open daily from 11am to 3:30pm weekdays and winter, and 10am to 3:30pm weekends (☎ **707/882-2777**).

WHERE TO STAY & DINE

✪ Old Milano Hotel. 38300 Calif. 1, Gualala, CA 95445. ☎ **707/884-3256.** 6 rms (sharing 2 baths), 1 suite, 2 cottages. $85 double with garden view; $115 double with ocean view; $170 master suite; $140 cottages. Rates include breakfast. MC, V.

This romantic lodging lies just north of Gualala with a spellbinding view of Castle Rock from the front porch and sloping lawn. The inn was built in 1905 on three acres and is listed in the National Registry of Historic Places. It has enchanting flower and herb gardens and a superbly situated hot tub, from which you can look directly out to the ocean. The rooms are all decorated differently, often with rare antiques.

Upstairs, six rooms share two bathrooms, each with double showers. The most alluring units are the Vine Cottage, which has a sleeping alcove, reading loft, and wood stove; and an authentic caboose, a romantically private space with a wood stove and two upstairs brakeman's seats.

A full breakfast is served either in your room or in the parlor. Chef Madeleine Jordan also offers pricey California cuisine—rack of Sonoma lamb, poached salmon, roasted Peking duck—served in an intimate dining room lit by candlelight and, on cool nights, by roaring fires in the stone fireplaces.

✪ **St. Orres.** 36601 Calif. 1, Box 523, Gualala, CA 95445. ☎ **707/884-3303.** Fax 707/ 884-3903. 8 rms sharing 3 baths, 12 cottages. $65 double rooms on side, $80 with ocean view. $85–$270 double occupancy of cottages, depending on the size. MC, V.

An extraordinary building designed in Russian style—complete with two onion-domed towers—St. Orres lies 1 1/2 miles north of Gualala. The complex was built in 1972 with century-old timbers salvaged from a nearby mill. It offers secluded cottage-style accommodations on 42 acres, as well as eight rooms in the main building (these eight accommodations, the budget traveler's best choice, are handcrafted and share three bathrooms decorated in brilliant colors). Other accommodations are very private, though expensive. Some have a full bath, wet bar, sitting area with Franklin stove, and French doors leading to a deck with a distant ocean view. Seven creekside cottages lie beside St. Orres Creek and have exclusive use of a spa facility that includes a hot tub, sauna, and sun deck. The most luxurious is Pine Haven, which has two bedrooms, two redwood decks, two baths, a tiled breakfast area, a beach stone fireplace, and wet bar.

The hotel is especially well known for its intimate restaurant (The St. Orres), a 17-seat charmer set below the intricate inner works of one of the main building's onion domes. Light filters through stained-glass windows onto strands of ivy that cascade down from the upper balcony. The only offering is a $30 three-course fixed-price meal that features game from the surrounding fields and forests. Dishes are inspired by Pacific Northwest cuisine, and include wild boar, pheasant, venison, quail, and rack of lamb. Reservations are essential. It's open for dinner daily, and closed during the weekdays for the first two weeks of December. MasterCard and Visa are accepted for hotel guests only; otherwise, no credit cards.

The Food Company. 38411 Calif. 1 at Robinsons Reef Rd., Gualala. ☎ **707/884-1800.** Deli items $3–$9. MC, V. Sun–Thurs 8–10:30am, 11am–8pm, Fri–Sat 8–10:30am, 11am–9pm. DELI.

If the St. Orres restaurant is out of your price range, you'll be happy to know that you can have an equally romantic lunch or dinner just down the road for a fraction of the price. Place your order at the deli counter, grab a bottle of wine from the rack, then head to the adjacent garden and plop yourself down at one of the picnic tables. The menu offers a dizzying array of specials from around the globe—corn tamales, Greek moussaka, lamb curry, quiche lorraine, pasta puttanesca—as well as fresh baked breads, pastries, and sandwiches. Better yet, order it all to go and head for the beach.

NORTH FROM POINT ARENA

Driving north from Point Arena, you'll pass the small towns of **Elk, Manchester, Albion,** and **Little River** on your way to Mendocino. This stretch of Calif. 1 also has some of the most dramatic and beautiful coastline in California, so be sure to plan on frequent stops along the way.

Though most of these coastal communities have existed for more than a century in relative obscurity, the recent tourism boom in California (in addition to the fact that there's not enough realty left in Mendocino to build an outhouse) has resulted in an explosion of new restaurants and B&Bs. There are precious few direct inland routes from Calif. 101, but if you don't mind the extra drive, it's worth skipping the Mendocino masses for some true small-town R&R along the coast.

WHERE TO STAY

Ⓢ Fools Rush Inn. 7533 Calif. 1, just south of Van Damme State Park, Little River, CA 95456. ☎ **707/937-5339.** 9 rms. $60–$100 double. No credit cards.

The inn's name may be clever, but it's woefully inaccurate. In fact, you would be a fool *not* to stay here. The inn's savvy owner, fully aware that inexpensive lodgings are nigh impossible to find along the coast, has found his niche by providing simple yet inarguably romantic cottages for about half the going rate in these parts. Perched on a small knoll at the edge of the forest and overlooking the ocean, the inn is within walking distance of Van Damme State Park, a small golf course, and, of course, the beach. After a day of outdoor adventures, come home to a bottle of chilled champagne (each cottage has a kitchen), light the fire (yes, each cottage has a fireplace, too), settle into the sofa, and wonder why you didn't think of this before.

KOA Kamping Kabins. On Kinney Rd. off Calif. 1, 1.6 miles north of Point Arena. ☎ **707/882-2375.** 18 cabins. $38–$45. AE, DISC, MC, V.

What? You expect me to stay at a Kampgrounds of America? You bet. Once you see these adorable little log cabins, you can't help but admit that, rich or poor, this is one cool way to spend the weekend on the coast. The cabins come with one or two bedrooms, sleeping four to six people respectively on log-frame double beds and bunk beds for the kids. *Rustic* is the key word here: Mattresses, a heater, and a lightbulb are your standard amenities. After that, you're on your own, but basically all you need is some bedding (or a sleeping bag), cooking and eating utensils, and a bag of charcoal for the barbecue out on the front porch (next to the log porch swing). Hot showers, bathrooms, laundry facilities, a small store, and a swimming pool are a short walk away, as is Manchester Beach.

WHERE TO DINE

Ⓞ Pangaea. 250 Main St., Point Arena. ☎ **707/882-3001.** Reservations recommended. Main courses $8–$15. No credit cards. Wed–Sun 6–9pm. ECLECTIC CUISINE.

North Coast locals have been raving about this place since the day it opened. Chef/Owner Shannon Hughes, a veteran of St. Orres and Old Milano Hotel restaurants, decided it was time to do her own thing, and boy is she doing it well. Everything that comes out of her kitchen is wondrously fresh and inventive, such as the succulent pork confit, served on a potato tart with homemade apricot chutney. And how's this for a $3 salad: organic greens in a vinaigrette of toasted shallots, sherry vinegar, and Italian mountain gorgonzola. Even her burgers and fries are beyond reproach, made with Niman-Schell beef, organic cheese and greens, Thai chile sauce, garlic roasted red potatoes, and homemade ketchup (of all things). Desserts, which include strawberry rhubarb crisp à la mode and lemon curd tart with a blood orange sauce, are equally impressive, as is the hip decor. Highly recommended.

3 Mendocino

In terms of the sheer numbers of the visitors it attracts, Mendocino is *the* premier destination on California's North Coast. Despite (or perhaps because of) its relative isolation, it emerged as one of Northern California's major centers for the arts in the 1950s. It's easy to see why artists were, and still are, attracted to this idyllic community, a cluster of New England–style sea captain's homes and small stores set on headlands overlooking the ocean: Mendocino is so darn picturesque that it has been the backdrop for dozens of movies, as well as the TV series *Murder, She Wrote*.

At the height of the logging boom in the 1860s, Mendocino became an important and active port. Its population swelled to about 3,500, and eight hotels were built along with 17 saloons and more than a dozen bordellos. Today, Mendocino only has about 1,000 residents, most of whom reside on the north end of town. On summer weekends the population seems more like 10,000 as droves of tourists drive up from the Bay Area, but despite the crowds Mendocino still manages to retain its small-town charm.

ESSENTIALS

GETTING THERE   The fastest route from San Francisco is via U.S. 101 north to Cloverdale. From there, take Calif. 128 west to Calif. 1, then go north along the coast. It's about a four-hour drive. (You could also take U.S. 101 all the way to Ukiah or Willits, and cut over to the west from there.) The most scenic route from the Bay Area, if you have the time and you don't mind the twists and turns, is to take Calif. 1 north along the coast the entire way; it's at least a five- to six-hour drive.

INFORMATION   There's a small information office up the coast in Fort Bragg, stocked with lots of free brochures and maps available for purchase. Visit the **Fort Bragg/Mendocino Coast Chamber of Commerce,** 332 N. Main St., P.O. Box 1141, Fort Bragg, CA 95437 (☎ **800/726-2780** or 707/961-6300).

EXPLORING THE TOWN

Stroll through town, enjoying the architecture, and browse in the dozens of galleries and shops. Our favorites include the **Highlight Gallery** for its handmade furniture, pottery, and other crafts (45052 Main St., ☎ **707/937-3132**); **Old Gold,** which carries a great selection of antique and contemporary jewelry and watches (6 Albion St., ☎ **707/937-5005**); and the **Gallery Bookshop,** which has a wonderful collection of new and used books, including children's books (at Main and Kasten streets, ☎ **707/937-2665**). Another popular stop is **Robert's Jams and Preserves** at 440 Main St., which offers free tastings of their gourmet wares on little bread chips (☎ **707/937-1037**).

After exploring the town, walk out on the headlands that wrap around the town and constitute **Mendocino Headlands State Park.** (The visitor center for the park is in Ford House on Main Street.) Three miles of trails wind through the park, giving visitors panoramic views of sea arches and hidden grottoes. If you're here at the right time of year, the area will be blanketed with a carpet of wild flowers; when we last stopped by in August, you could pick fresh blackberries beside the trails. The headlands are home to many unique species of birds, including the black oyster-catchers. Behind the Mendocino Presbyterian Church on Main Street is a trail leading to stairs that take you down to the beach, a small but picturesque stretch of sand where driftwood formations have washed ashore.

On the south side of town, **Big River Beach** is accessible from Calif. 1; it's good for picnicking, walking, and sunbathing.

In town, stop by the **Mendocino Art Center,** 45200 Little Lake Rd. (☎ **707/ 937-5818**), the town's unofficial cultural headquarters. It's also known for its gardens, three galleries, and shops that display and sell local fine arts and crafts. Pick up a copy of *Arts and Entertainment,* which lists upcoming events throughout Mendocino. Admission is free; open daily from 10am to 5pm.

For a special treat, go to **Sweetwater Gardens,** 955 Ukiah St. (☎ **800/300-4140** or 707/937-4140), which offers group and private saunas and hot-tub soaks by the hour. Additional services include Swedish or deep-tissue massages. Reservations are recommended. Private tub prices are $8 per person per half-hour, $11 per person per hour. Group tub prices are $7.50 per person with no time limit. Special discounts are available on Wednesdays.

ENJOYING THE OUTDOORS

Explore the Big River by renting a canoe, sea cycle, kayak, or outrigger from **Catch a Canoe and Bicycles Too** (☎ 707/937-0273), located on the grounds of the Stanford Inn by the Sea (see "Where to Stay," below). If you're lucky you'll see some osprey, blue herons, harbor seals, deer, and wood ducks. The same store will also rent you a mountain bike (much better quality than your usual bike rental) so you can head up Calif. 1 and explore the nearby state parks on two wheels. Horseback riding (both English and Western) on the beach and into the redwoods is offered by **Ricochet Ridge Ranch,** 24201 N. Calif. 1, Fort Bragg (☎ 707/964-PONY).

Aside from Mendocino Headlands State Park, there are several other state parks near Mendocino; all are within an easy drive or bike ride and make for a good day's outing. Information on all the parks' features, including maps of each one, is found in a brochure called "Mendocino Coast State Parks," available from the visitor center in Fort Bragg. These areas include Manchester State Park, located where the San Andreas fault sweeps into the sea; Jug Handle State Reserve; and Van Damme State Park, which has a sheltered, easily accessible beach.

Our favorite of these parks, located directly on Calif. 1 just north of Mendocino, is **Russian Gulch State Park** (☎ 707/937-5804). It's one of the region's most spectacular parks, where roaring waves crash against the cliffs that protect the park's California coastal redwoods. The most popular attraction is the Punch Bowl, a collapsed sea cave that forms a tunnel through which waves crash, creating throaty echoes. Inland, there's a scenic paved biking path and visitors can also hike along miles of trails, including a gentle, well-marked 3-mile Waterfall Loop that winds past tall redwoods and damp green foliage to a 36-foot-high waterfall. Admission is $5. Thirty camping sites enjoy a beautiful setting and are available from April through mid-October ($14 per night). Call **800/444-7275** for reservations.

Fort Bragg is just a short distance up the coast; deep-sea fishing charters are available from its harbor.

WHERE TO STAY

The trick to doing this town cheaply is to spend your days in Mendocino and your nights in Fort Bragg, which is only about a 10-minute drive away. Why? Because Fort Bragg is full of cheap motels, most charging a *third* less than what you'll fork out for an average B&B. See Fort Bragg, below, for details.

Joshua Grindle Inn. 44800 Little Lake Rd., P.O. Box 647, Mendocino, CA 95460. ☎ **800/ GRINDLE** or 707/937-4143. 10 rms. Sun–Thurs in off-season $90–$155 double; July–Sept and weekends $95–$175. Rates include full breakfast. AE, MC, V.

When it was built in 1879, this stately Victorian was one of the most substantial and impressive houses in Mendocino, owned by the town's wealthiest banker. Today the Grindle is the oldest B&B in Mendocino, and is surrounded with redwood siding, a wraparound porch, and large emerald lawns. From its prettily planted gardens there's a view across the village to the distant bay. There are five rooms in the main house, two in an adjacent cottage, and three in a water tower. All have well-lighted, comfortably arranged sitting areas; some offer fireplaces. Each is individually decorated: the Library, for example, has a New England feel with its four-poster pine bed, floor-to-ceiling bookcase, and 19th-century tiles around the fireplace depicting many of Aesop's fables; the sunny and spacious master room has a wood-burning fireplace, granite whirlpool tub, and separate shower. Sherry is served in the parlor in front of the fireplace and breakfast is offered in the dining room.

Mendocino Hotel and Garden Suites. 45080 Main St., Mendocino, CA 95460. ☎ **800/ 548-0513** or 707/937-0511. Fax 707/937-0513. 51 rms (37 with bath), 6 suites. TEL. $65–$80 double without bath, $80–$160 double with bath; $190–$225 suite. Additional person $20. Rates slightly lower Dec–Mar and weekdays year-round. AE, MC, V.

Right in the heart of town, this 1878 hotel evokes California's Gold Rush days. Beveled-glass doors open into a Victorian-style lobby and parlor where you might expect to see Mae West. The hotel's decor combines antiques and reproductions, like the oak reception desk from a demolished Kansas bank. Remington paintings (what else would do?), stained-glass lamps, and Persian carpets contribute to the Wild West aura. Guest rooms feature hand-painted French porcelain sinks with floral designs, quaint wallpaper, old-fashioned beds and armoires, and photographs and memorabilia of historic Mendocino. About half the rooms are located in four handsome small buildings behind the main house. Many of the deluxe rooms have fireplaces or wood-burning stoves, as well as more modern bathrooms and good views. Suites have an additional parlor, as well as a fireplace or balcony.

Breakfast and lunch are served in the Garden Room, while dinner is offered in the Victorian-style dining room. Room service is available daily from 8am to 9pm.

Mendocino Village Inn. 44860 Main St. (P.O. Box 626), Mendocino, CA 95460. ☎ **800/ 882-7029** or 707/937-0246 . 13 rms (11 with bath), 1 suite. $75 double without bath; $90– $175 double with bath; $175 suite. Rates include full breakfast. No credit cards.

Although there is a street running between the Mendocino Village Inn and the ocean, the hotel is certainly close to the water. A garden of flowers, plants, and frog ponds fronts the large blue-and-white guest house, which was built in 1882 by a local doctor. It was later occupied by famed local artist Emmy Lou Packard.

Innkeepers Bill and Kathleen Erwin have decorated each room differently. The Queen Anne Room features a four-poster canopy bed, and the sentimental Maggie's Room is named for a child who etched her name in the window glass almost a century ago (you can still see it). Except for two attic rooms, all have private baths and four rooms have private outside entrances. Complimentary beverages are served in the evening.

WHERE TO DINE

955 Ukiah Street Restaurant. 955 Ukiah St., Mendocino. ☎ **707/937-1955.** Reservations recommended. Main courses $11–$18. MC, V. Wed–Sun 6–10pm. Closed after Thanksgiving weekend through Christmas, and 1 week in June. CALIFORNIA/FRENCH.

Shortly after the building that houses this restaurant was constructed in the 1960s, the region's most famous painter, Emmy Lou Packard, commandeered its premises as an art studio for the creation of a series of giant murals. Today, it's a large but surprisingly cozy restaurant, its decor accented with massive railway ties and vaulted ceilings. The tables on the mezzanine level can get a little cramped; if possible, request a window table overlooking the gardens. The cuisine is creative and reasonably priced, a worthy alternative to the perpetually booked Cafe Beaujolais next door. It's hard to recommend a particular main dish, although the phyllo-wrapped red snapper with pesto and lime has a zesty tang, and the crispy duck with ginger, apples, and a Calvados sauce so authentic it would find friends in Normandy.

Bay View Café. 45040 Main St., Mendocino. ☎ **707/937-4197.** Dinner $6–$15. No credit cards. Thurs–Mon 8am–9pm; Tues–Wed 8am–3pm. AMERICAN.

This reasonably priced cafe is one of the most popular in town, and the only place around besides the Mendocino Hotel that serves breakfast ("And we're *way* better," says the owner). From the second-floor dining area of the cafe there's a sweeping view of the Pacific and faraway headlands; to reach it, climb a flight of stairs running up the outside of the town's antique water tower, then detour sideways. Surrounded by dozens of ferns suspended from the ceiling, you'll find a menu with Southwestern selections (the marinated chicken breast is very popular), a good array of sandwiches (our favorite is the hot crabmeat with avocado slices), fish and chips, and the fresh catch of the day. Breakfast ranges from the basic bacon and eggs to eggs Florentine and honey-wheat pancakes.

✪ Cafe Beaujolais. 961 Ukiah St., Mendocino. ☎ **707/937-5614.** Reservations recommended. Main courses $16–$20 at dinner. No credit cards. Daily 5:45–9pm. AMERICAN/FRENCH.

Cafe Beaujolais has been owned and managed since 1977 by California chef and entrepreneur Margaret Fox. It's one of Mendocino's—if not Northern California's—top dining choices. The venerable French country–style tavern is the sort of place where everyone who's anyone has to dine at least once. On warm summer nights, request a table at the enclosed deck overlooking the "designer" gardens.

Though Cafe Beaujolais started out as a breakfast and lunch place, it's strictly a dinner house now (yes, their famed weekend brunch has been discontinued). The menu usually lists about five main courses, such as Yucatan-Thai crab cakes with spicy avocado salsa and achiote-roasted tomato sauce, or free-range chicken stuffed with eggplant, mushrooms, cheese, garlic, and fresh herbs from local organic farmers. Tuesday through Thursday the cafe offers a fixed-price country menu, which includes appetizer, entree (usually a meat dish), and dessert for $20 to $25—a pretty good deal for Beaujolais-quality cuisine.

Budget Lunch Tips

You'd be surprised what $5 will buy you for lunch in Mendocino if you know where to go. **Tote Fete Bakery** (☎ 707/937-3383), for example, has a wonderful little carry-out booth at the corner of Albion and Lansing streets. We prefer the foil-wrapped barbecue chicken sandwiches, but the pizza, foccacia bread, and twice-baked potatoes are also good choices. Dine at the stand-up counter, or opt for a picnic at the headlands down the street.

Burger lovers won't be let down at **Mendo Burgers** (☎ 707/937-1111), arguably the best burger joint on the North Coast. Beef, chicken, turkey, veggie, fish—whatever it's made with, it's still a great burger. A side of thick fresh-cut fries is mandatory, as are a pile of napkins. Hidden behind the Mendocino Bakery and Café at 10483 Lansing St., it's a little hard to find, but it's well worth searching out.

On the opposite spectrum of Mendo Burgers is **Lu's Kitchen** (☎ 707/937-4939), which uses only organically grown produce for their vegetarian burritos, salads, tacos, and quesadillas. The restaurant is little more than a small shack hidden at 45013 Ukiah St., between Lansing and Ford Street (look for the white plastic tables and chairs on the south side of the street), and can be hard to find.

The Mousse Café. 390 Kasten St., at Albion St., Mendocino. ☎ **707/937-4323.** Main courses $11–$16. No credit cards. Mon–Thurs 11:30am–9pm, Fri 11:30am–10:30pm, Sat 10am–10:30pm, Sun 10am–9pm. CONTINENTAL/CALIFORNIA.

The setting is a turn-of-the-century clapboard-sided house inspired by the architecture of New England, set within a pleasant garden. In 1995, the place was gutted and the interior was redone; the result is a brand-new, bright, streamlined appearance. The menu includes many local items, particularly organic herbs and vegetables (try the Caesar salad). We enjoyed roast chicken with garlic mashed potatoes, plus a swordfish special with fresh vegetables. The Blackout cake is a chocoholic's fantasy. The food is good and the service is friendly; our only complaint is that the tables are a bit too close together, especially if it's crowded.

4 Fort Bragg

Fort Bragg is Mendocino County's commercial center, hence the fast-food restaurants and supermarkets. Inexpensive motels and cheap eats used to be its only attraction, but over the past few years gentrification has quickly spread throughout the town as logging and fishing continue to decline. With no room left to open new shops in Mendocino, many gallery, boutique, and restaurant owners have moved up the road. The result is a huge increase in Fort Bragg's tourist trade, particularly during the annual Whale Festival in March and Paul Bunyan Days over Labor Day weekend.

To explore the town properly, make you first stop at the **Fort Bragg/Mendocino Coast Chamber of Commerce,** 332 N. Main St., P.O. Box 1141, Fort Bragg, CA 95437 (☎ **800/726-2780** or 707/961-6300), and pick up a free walking map. The friendly staff can also answer any other questions about Mendocino, Fort Bragg, and the surrounding region.

SHOPPING & EXPLORING

The town doesn't boast as many well-coifed stores and galleries as its dainty cousin to the south, but it does have some worthwhile shopping. Antique shops line the 300 block of North Franklin Street, one block east of Main Street, and the **old train depot,** at 401 N. Main St. (☎ 707/964-6261), has been turned into a shopping center and historical museum with logging equipment and restored steam trains.

For the Shell of It, 344 N. Main St. (☎ 707/961-0461), stocks handmade jewelry, baskets, and collectibles made of shells or designed around a nautical theme. **The Hot Pepper Jelly Company,** 330 N. Main St. (☎ 707/961-1422), is famous for the variety of Mendocino food products that it offers—dozens of varieties of pepper jelly, plus local mustards, syrups, and biscotti along with hand-painted porcelain bowls, unusual baskets, and more. The **Mendocino Chocolate Company,** 542 N. Main St. (☎ 707/964-8800), makes and sells homemade chocolates and truffles, and ships them worldwide. Painters, jewelers, sculptors, weavers, potters, and other local artists display their works at **Northcoast Artists,** 362 North Main St. (☎ 707/964-8266). At **Windsong,** 324 N. Main St. (☎ 707/964-2050), you'll find a clutter of colorful kites, cards, candles, and other gifts.

Fort Bragg is the county's sportfishing center. Just south of town, **Noyo's Fishing Center,** 3245 North Harbor, Noyo (☎ 707/964-7609), is a good place to buy or rent tackle, and the best source of information on local fishing boats. Lots of party boats leave from the town's harbor, as do whale-watching tours.

Lost Coast Adventures, North Coast Divers Supply, 19275 S. Harbor Dr. (☎ 800/961-1143 or 707/961-1143), offers scuba diving, fishing, and whale-watching expeditions, as well as kayak tours of the coastline and coastal rivers.

Fort Bragg is also the home of the **Mendocino Coast Botanical Gardens,** 18220 N. Calif. 1 (☎ **707/964-4352**), about 8 miles north of Mendocino. This clifftop public garden, set among the pines along the rugged coast, nurtures rhododendrons, fuchsias, azaleas, and a multitude of flowering shrubs. The area contains trails for easy walking, bridges, streams, canyons, dells, and picnic areas. Children under 12 must be accompanied by their parents. Admission is $5 adults, $4 seniors age 60 and over, $3 children ages 13 to 17, $1 children ages 6 to 12, free for children 5 and under (children under 18 must be accompanied by an adult). Open March to October daily from 9am to 5pm, November to February daily from 9am to 4pm.

From Fort Bragg, the **Skunk Train** (☎ **707/964-6371**) gives riders a fine view of the area's redwoods. Locals always said of the logging trains that, "You can smell 'em before you can see 'em," which explains the nickname (the old locomotives emit a noxious diesel-fume odor). The trains, which can be boarded at the Fort Bragg Depot at the foot of Laurel Avenue in Fort Bragg (two blocks from the Grey Whale Inn), travel 40 miles inland along the Redwood Highway (U.S. 101) to Willits. It's a scenic route through the redwood forest, crossing 31 bridges and trestles and cutting through two deep tunnels. The round trip takes six to seven hours, allowing plenty of time for lunch in Willits before you return on the afternoon train. Half-day trips are offered weekends throughout the year, and daily in summer from mid-June to early September. In summer call for reservations. The trains run year-round but schedules vary, so call for exact times. Tickets cost $26 round trip, $21 one way; children 5 to 11 board for half-price.

Three miles north of Fort Bragg off Calif. 1 lies **Mackerricher State Park** (☎ **707/937-5804**), a popular place for biking, hiking, and horseback riding. This enormous 1,700-acre park has 142 campsites and 8 miles of shoreline. For a true biking or hiking venture, travel the 8-mile-long "Haul Road," an old logging road that gives fine ocean vistas all the way to Ten Mile River. Harbor seals make their home at the park's Laguna Point Seal Watching Station, reached via a elevated wooden gangway (truly a pleasant walk).

CUTTING-EDGE THEATER COMES TO THE MENDOCINO COAST

Living proof that poor, maligned ole Fort Bragg is on the road to respect is the upstart new theatrical company, **Warehouse Repertory Theatre.** Determined to make Fort Bragg the Ashland of California, this cadre of highly talented professional actors from around the country have finally answered the age-old Mendocino County question of "So, what is there to do around here at night?" From Shakespeare to Shepard, no play is too shocking or sultry for artistic director Meg Patterson and her crew, who have been bathed in nothing but kudos for the fresh, significant works they have brought to the north coast.

The Warehouse's season runs from late February to December, Thursday through Saturday (and the occasional Monday) at 8pm, with Sunday matinees at 2pm. For information about current shows, future plays, or to reserve tickets, which range from $10 to $15, call the box office at **707/961-2940.**

WHERE TO STAY

If you're looking to save money, your best bet is to base yourself in Fort Bragg and explore the Mendocino from here. The town's best motels, most of which charge about $50 a night, are the **Coast Motel** (18661 Calif. 1; ☎ 707/964-2852); **Columbi Motel** (647 Oak St.; ☎ 707/964-5773); **Fort Bragg Motel** (763 N. Main St.; ☎ 800/253-9972 or 707/964-4787); and the **Ocean Breeze Lodge** (212 S. Main St.; ☎ 707/961-1177). Granted, you wouldn't want to spend your honeymoon here, but if all you're looking for is a clean, comfortable room, any of these motels will satisfy your basic needs without emptying your wallet.

Grey Whale Inn. 615 N. Main St., Fort Bragg, CA 95437. ☎ **800/382-7244** or 707/964-0640. Fax 707/964-4408. 11 rms, 5 suites. TEL. $100–$170 double; $180 suite. Winter rates available midweek Nov–Mar. Rates include buffet breakfast. AE, DISC, JCB, MC, V.

A comfortable B&B six blocks from the beach and two blocks from the Skunk Train depot (don't worry, you can't smell the trains from here), this 1915 landmark was originally built as a hospital. The spacious and airy redwood building has become a well-run, relaxed inn, furnished partly with antiques and plenty of local art. Each guest room is unique: Two have ocean views, three have a fireplace, and one has a whirlpool tub; two have private decks and one offers a shower with wheelchair access. The buffet breakfast includes homemade bread or coffee cake and fresh fruit. No smoking.

Pudding Creek Inn. 700 N. Main St., Fort Bragg, CA 95437. ☎ **800/227-9529** or 707/964-9529. Fax 707/961-0282. 10 rms. $70–$130 double. Rates include breakfast. AE, DISC, MC, V.

The Pudding Creek Inn is actually two separate houses, built in 1884 by a Russian count. They're connected by an enclosed pebbled garden court filled with flowering plants, a stone fountain, and patio furnishings. Although some of the rooms are rather small, each is uniquely decorated, comfortable and colorful, and comes with private bath. Despite its name, the Main House contains fewer rooms than the adjacent two-story annex. The Count's Room features a huge stone fireplace and a king-size brass bed. It's a beautiful room, but faces the noisy highway. Rooms in back are quieter; the best is called Interlude, and contains a king-size bed, oversize shower, and fireplace. The B&B's guest phone is located in the garden. There's a TV and recreation room, plus a parlor where afternoon tea, wine, and cheese are served. A full buffet breakfast is offered in an attractive room that contains tall bay windows, antique tables, and a fireplace.

WHERE TO DINE

North Coast Brewing Company. 444 N. Main St., Fort Bragg. ☎ **707/964-3400.** Reservations accepted for large parties only. Main courses $6–$17. DISC, MC, V. Tues–Fri 4–11pm; Sat 2–11pm; summer Tues–Sun 2–11pm. AMERICAN.

This homey brewpub is the most happening place in town, especially at happy hour when the bar and dark wood tables are occupied by boisterous locals. The building that contains it is a dignified, century-old redwood structure, which in previous lives has functioned as a mortuary, an annex to the local Presbyterian Church, an art studio, and administration offices for the College of the Redwoods. Beer is brewed on the premises, in large copper kettles that are displayed behind plate glass. A pale ale, a pilsner, a stout, and a fourth seasonal brew are always available. Standard brewpub fare such as burgers and barbecued chicken sandwiches are supplemented by more substantial dishes, ranging from linguini with smoked mushrooms to a hefty pile of country-style Carolina barbecued pork. After lunch, browse the retail shop or take a free tour of the brewery.

The Restaurant. 418 Main St., Fort Bragg. ☎ **707/964-9800.** Reservations recommended. Lunch, $6:50–$10, dinner $14–$20. MC, V. Thurs–Fri 11:30am–2pm, Sun 9am–1pm; Thurs–Tues 5–9pm. PACIFIC NORTHWESTERN/CALIFORNIA.

This authentic local restaurant is housed in a Victorian building. The art on the walls is by a local artist, who also plays jazz bass and who may well be performing here if you stop by on a weekend evening. The menu features four fish and four meat dishes, including chicken marsala and grilled halibut with sweet-pepper relish. There are also a few vegetarian specialties, including grilled polenta with melted mozzarella and sautéed mushrooms topped with tomato herb sauce and Parmesan cheese. Tangy appetizers are likely to include corn fritters with fresh pineapples and chili sauce, or shrimp relleno with green tomato sauce.

5 The Avenue of the Giants & Ferndale

From Fort Bragg, Calif. 1 continues north along the shoreline for about 30 miles before turning inland to Leggett and U.S. 101, aka the "Redwood Highway," that runs north to Garberville. Six miles beyond Garberville, the Avenue of the Giants begins around Phillipsville; it's an alternative route that roughly parallels U.S. 101, and there are about a half dozen interchanges between U.S. 101 and the Avenue of the Giants if you don't want to drive the whole thing. It's one of the most spectacular scenic routes in the west (Route 254), cutting along the Eel River through the 51,000-acre Humboldt Redwoods State Park. The Avenue ends just south of Scotia; from here, it's only about 10 miles to the turnoff to Ferndale, about 5 miles west of U.S. 101.

For more information or a detailed map of the area, go to the **Humboldt Redwood State Park Visitor Center** just north of Hidden Springs State Campground, 2 miles south of Weott (P.O. Box 276, Weott, CA 95571; ☎ 707/946-2263). **The Chimney Tree** (Avenue of the Giants, P.O. Box 395, Garberville, CA 95542; ☎ 707/923-2265) is another place to secure information about the area.

Thirty-three miles long, the **Avenue of the Giants** was left intact for sightseers when the freeway was built. The giants, of course, are the majestic coast redwoods (*Sequoia sempervirens*); more than 50,000 acres of them make up the most outstanding display in the redwood belt. Their rough-bark columns climb 100 feet or more without a branch and soar to a total height of more than 340 feet. They are immune to insects, and their bark is fire resistant, so they have survived for thousands of years. The oldest dated coast redwood is more than 2,200 years old.

The state park has three **campgrounds** with 248 campsites: Hidden Springs, half a mile south of Myers Flat; Burlington, 2 miles south of Weott, near park headquarters; and Albee Creek State Campground, five miles west of U.S. 101 on the Mattole Road north of Weott. You'll also come across picnic and swimming facilities, motels, resorts, restaurants, and numerous resting and parking areas.

Sadly, the route has several tacky attractions that attempt to turn the trees into some kind of freak show. Our suggestion is to skip these and appreciate the trees by taking advantage of the trails and the campgrounds off the beaten path. As you drive along, you'll see numerous parking areas with short loop trails leading into the forest. From south to north the first of these "attractions" is the **Chimney Tree** (☎ 707/923-2265), where J. R. R. Tolkien's Hobbit is rumored to reside. This living, hollow redwood is more than 1,500 years old. Nearby is a gift shop and a burger place. Then there's the **One-Log House,** a small apartment-like house built inside a log. At Myers Flat midway along the Avenue, you can also drive your car through a living redwood at the **Shrine Drive Thru Tree.**

A few miles north of Weott is **Founders Grove,** named in honor of those who established the Save the Redwoods League in 1918. Farther north, close to the end of the Avenue, stands the 950-year-old Immortal Tree, just north of Redcrest. Near Pepperwood at the end of the Avenue, the Drury trail and the Percy French trail are two good short hikes. The park itself is also good for mountain biking. Ask the rangers for details. For more information, contact **Humboldt Redwoods State Park,** P.O. Box 100, Weott, CA 95571 (☎ 707/946-2409).

Beyond the Avenue of the Giants and west of U.S. 101, the village of **Ferndale** has been declared a historic landmark because of its many Victorian homes and store-fronts, including a smithy and a saddlery. About 5 miles inland from the coast and close to the redwood belt, Ferndale is one of the best-preserved Victorian hamlets in Northern California. In spite of its unbearably cute shops, it is nonetheless a vital part of the northern coast tourist circuit (the budget traveler, however, will have to continue north to Eureka to find affordable lodging). The small town has a number of artists in residence, and is also home to one of the oddest California events, the **World Championship Great Arcata to Ferndale Cross-Country Kinetic Sculpture Race,** a bizarre three-day event run every Memorial Day weekend. The race, which draws more than 10,000 spectators, is run over land and water in whimsically designed human-powered vehicles. Stop in at the **Kinetic Sculpture Museum** at 780 Main St. if you want to see some recent examples.

WHERE TO DINE

Curley's Grill. 460 Main St., Ferndale. ☎ **707/786-9696.** Reservations recommended. Main courses $9–$18. DISC, MC, V. Daily 11:30am–9pm (last order). CALIFORNIA GRILL.

Set within what looks like a clapboard-sided Victorian farmhouse, across the street from Ferndale's Repertory Theater, this is a bright and lively restaurant that specializes exclusively in California-inspired grilled foods. Don't think for a moment that the menu is limited just to steaks: Owner Curley Tait offers items that you might never have considered grillable, including polenta with a sausage-tomato sauce, a medley of Pacific seafish, and some of the freshest vegetables on the California coast. The interior decor is a vaguely art deco setting showcasing local artists' works, but the best seating is behind the kitchen in the secluded back patio. Curley's also offers a small but interesting selection of California wines.

6 Eureka & Environs

EUREKA

On first glance, Eureka (pop. 27,000) doesn't look very appealing—fast-food restaurants, cheap motels, and shopping malls dominate the main thoroughfare. But if you turn west off U.S. 101 anywhere between A and M streets, you'll discover Old Town Eureka along the waterfront, which is worth exploring. It has a large number of Victorian buildings, a museum, and some good-quality stores and restaurants.

The **Clarke Memorial Museum,** 240 E St. (☎ 707/443-1947), has a fine collection of Native American baskets and other historic artifacts. The other popular attraction is the extraordinary architectural gem, the **Carson House,** built in 1884–86 for lumber baron William Carson. A three-story conglomeration of ornamentation, it's designed in a mélange of styles: Queen Anne, Italianate, Stick, and Eastlake. It took 100 men more than two years to build. Today it's a private club, so you can only marvel at the exterior of this 18-room mansion—said to be the most photographed Victorian home in America—from the sidewalk. Across the street stands the **"Pink Lady,"** a Victorian mansion designed for William Carson as a wedding present for his son. Both testify to the wealth that was once made in Eureka's lumber trade. As early as 1856 there were already seven sawmills producing two million board feet of lumber every month.

Humboldt Bay, where the town stands, was discovered by whites in 1850. In 1853 Fort Humboldt was established to protect the white settlements from local Native American tribes. Ulysses S. Grant was stationed here for five months until he resigned after serious disputes with his commanding officer about his drinking. Today the fort offers a self-guided trail past a series of logging exhibits, plus a reconstructed surgeon's quarters and a restored fort hospital, used today as a museum that houses Native American artifacts and military and pioneer paraphernalia. **Fort Humboldt State Historic Park** is at 3431 Fort Ave. (☎ **707/445-6567**). Admission is free; open daily from 9am to 5pm.

Humboldt Bay supplies a large portion of California's fish, and Eureka has a fishing fleet of about 200 boats. To get a better view (and perspective) of the bay and surrounding waters, you can board skipper Leroy Zerlang's *Madaket*—some claim it's the oldest passenger carrying vessel in operation in the U.S.—for a 75-minute **Humboldt Bay Harbor Cruise** (☎ **707/445-1910**), departing daily from the foot of C Street in downtown Eureka.

More active water recreation includes fishing for halibut, king salmon, steelhead, and even shark, depending on the season. A license is required and can be secured for one day. For information, contact **Larry's Guide Service,** 3380 Utah St. (☎ **707/444-0250**). Fishing information can also be obtained from the **Eureka Fly Shop,** 505 H St. (☎ **707/444-2000**), and you can rent kayaks and sailboats from **Hum Boats,** located at the foot of F Street (☎ **707/443-5157**).

Humboldt County is also suitable for biking, because it's comparatively uncongested. Bikes can be rented from **Pro Sport Center,** 508 Myrtle Ave. (☎ **707/443-6328**).

Humboldt Bay is an important stopover point along the Pacific Flyway and is the winter home for thousands of migratory birds. South of town, the **Humboldt Bay National Wildlife Refuge,** 1020 Ranch Rd., Loleta, CA 95551 (☎ **707/733-5406**), provides an opportunity to see many of the 200 or so species that live in the marshes and willow groves—Pacific black brant, western sandpiper, northern harrier, great blue heron, and green-winged teal. The egret rookery on the Bay is spectacular. (The last is best viewed from Woodley Island Marina across the bay en route to Samoa). Peak viewing for most species of waterbirds and raptors is between September and March. Entry to the refuge is off U.S. 101 north at the Hookton Road exit. Cross the overpass and turn right onto Ranch Road.

For information, contact the **Eureka/Humboldt County Convention and Visitors Bureau,** 1034 Second St., Eureka, CA 95501 (☎ **800/346-3482** or 707/443-5097; fax 707/443-5115), or the **Eureka Chamber of Commerce,** 2112 Broadway, Eureka, CA 95501 (☎ **800/356-6381** or 707/442-3738).

WHERE TO STAY

✪ **An Elegant Victorian Mansion.** 14th and C sts., Eureka, CA 95501. ☎ **707/444-3144.** Fax 707/442-5594. 5 rms. $85–$165 double. Rates include breakfast. MC, V.

For anyone interested in social history and design, this is a special experience. Those who just want comfort, service, a true gourmet breakfast, and a lovely garden to enjoy, will also find this lodging ideal. The 1888 house is the labor of love of owners Doug and Lily Vieyra, who have combed the country for the wallpapers, fabrics, and designs that now provide the most authentic Victorian atmosphere we have ever encountered in the United States. Doug has paid attention to every detail, from the butler who greets you in morning dress down to supplying the silent movies and period music on the phonograph. The rooms are individually furnished; the Lily Langtry room, for instance, named after the actress and king's mistress who stayed here when she performed locally, features a four-poster bed and Langtry memorabilia. Services include laundry and Swedish massage. Bikes and a sauna are available, and croquet is played on the manicured lawn, where ice cream sodas and lemonade are served in the afternoon. No smoking is allowed.

⑤ Bayview Motel. 2844 Fairfield St., Eureka, CA 95501. ☎ **707/442-1673.** 14 rms. TEL TV. $42–$46 double. AE, DISC, MC, V.

While nowhere near the caliber of the Victorian Mansion or Carter Hotel, the Bayview Motel has them soundly beat in the price category, charging less than half of either competitor's cheapest rooms. This is, without a doubt, one of the cleanest and most meticulously landscaped motels we have ever seen. Indeed, what it lacks in character it makes up for in cost and cleanliness. Poised on the top of a small knoll on the south side of Eureka, it *does* have a bay view, but you have to peer through a seedy industrial area to see it (a better view, actually, is of the gardens). Each room comes with the standard motel amenities, including a queen-size bed, remote-control TV, and private bath.

✪ Hotel Carter. Carter House and Bell Cottage, 301 L St., Eureka, CA 95501. ☎ **800/404-1390** or 707/445-1390. Fax 707/444-8062. 29 rms, 2 suites. TEL TV. $65–$145 double; $95–$225 suite. AE, DC, MC, V. From U.S. 101 north turn left onto L St. and go to 3rd.

At the north end of Eureka's Old Town is the original building that started the renowned Carter hostelry empire: the Carter House. Copied from a famous 1884 San Francisco Victorian, it was constructed by Mark Carter as a family home in 1982. Soon afterwards, Mark and his wife, Christi Carter, began taking guests, and before long they built another 20-room hotel across the street. Later, the pretty Victorian Bell Cottage was acquired. The 20 rooms in the large full-service hotel are furnished in modern style with pine four-poster beds. The suites have such luxury appointments as VCRs, fireplaces, and Jacuzzis and distant views of the waterfront from the Jacuzzi tubs. There are seven rooms in the original house, which is furnished with antiques, Oriental rugs, and modern artworks. The Bell Cottage's rooms are also individually decorated in fine style. Within the inn on ground level is one of Eureka's finest restaurants (see below).

WHERE TO DINE

Ramone's Bakery and Cafe. 209 E St., Eureka. ☎ **707/445-2923.** Main courses $4–$6. No credit cards. Mon–Sat 7am–6pm, Sun 8am–5pm. BAKERY.

Ramone's combines a bakery on one side with a small cafe on the other. The baked items are extraordinary—try any one of the croissants, Danish, or muffins and you won't be disappointed. Alas, the once-popular restaurant has closed down, but you can still find a few lunch specials to choose from among the breads and pastries. At any time of the day, it's a great place to stop in for a light, inexpensive meal and cup of coffee. There's a second location at 2223 Harrison St. in Eureka, as well as two more in Arcata: 600 F St., and 747 13th St. at Wildberries Marketplace.

✪ Restaurant 301. In the Hotel Carter, 301 L St., Eureka. ☎ **707/444-8062.** Reservations required in summer. Main courses $10–$18. AE, DC, DISC, MC, V. Daily 6–9pm. CALIFORNIA.

This large, bright, and airy dining room adjacent to the Hotel Carter's lobby has tall windows looking out over the waterfront. It's one of the best restaurants in the area, with most of the herbs and many of the vegetables picked fresh from the hotel's organic gardens across the street. Predominantly Californian, the cuisine displays Asian accents, as for example, in the tiger prawns with sesame, ginger, and soy, and the chicken with spicy peanut sauce. If you're an oyster lover, start with a few Humboldt Bay oysters roasted with barbecue sauce. The hotel's proprietor, Mark Carter, offers an excellent and extensive wine list, courtesy of his 301 Wine Shop within the hotel.

Samoa Cookhouse. Cookhouse Road, Samoa. ☎ **707/442-1659.** Main courses $10.95.
AE, MC, V. Mon–Sat 6am–3:30pm and 5–10pm, Sun 6am–10pm. From U.S. 101, take Samoa
Bridge to the end and turn left on Samoa Rd.; then take the first left. AMERICAN.

When lumber was king, cookhouses like this one dating from 1885 were common
and were the hub of the community. Here the mill workers and longshoremen at the
Hammond Lumber Company came to chow down three hot meals before, during,
and after their 12-hour work day. The food is still hearty, though not particularly
healthful, and served family style at long, red-check cloth-covered tables; nobody
leaves hungry. The price includes soup, salad, fresh-baked bread, the main course,
and dessert (usually pie). The lunch and dinner menu still features a different dish
each day: roast beef, fried chicken, or pork chops. Breakfast typically includes
eggs, sausages, bacon, pancakes, and all the orange juice and coffee you can drink.
Adjacent to the dining room is a small museum featuring memorabilia from the
lumbering era.

ARCATA

From Eureka it's only 7 miles to Arcata, one of our favorite towns on the Northern
Coast. Sort of a cross between Mayberry and Berkeley, is has an undeniable small-
town flavor, right down to the bucolic town square, yet possesses that intellectual and
environmentally conscious esprit de corps so characteristic of university towns (Arcata
is home base to Humboldt State University).

There's loads of things to do here. On Wednesday, Friday, and Saturday evenings
between June and July, Arcata's semipro baseball team, the **Humboldt Crabs,** partake in America's favorite pastime at **Arcata Ballpark** (☎ 707/822-3619) at 9th and
F streets. Also worth a stop is: the **Humboldt State University Natural History
Museum,** 1315 G St. (☎ 707/826-4479), which is open Tuesday to Saturday; **Tin
Can Mailman,** at 10th and H streets (☎ 707/822-1307), a wonderful used bookstore with more than 130,000 titles; **Redwood Park** (east end of 11th Street), which
has an outstanding playground for kids and miles of forested hiking trails; and the
Humboldt Brewing Company, at 10th and I streets (☎ 707/826-BREW), creators
of the heavenly Red Nectar Ale (call for tour information).

The **Arcata Marsh and Wildlife Sanctuary,** at the foot of South I Street (☎ 707/
826-2359) is another worthwhile excursion. The 154-acre sanctuary doubles as
Arcata's integrated wetland wastewater treatment plant. It's a popular stopover for
march wrens, egrets, and other waterfowl, including the rare Arctic loon. Each Saturday at 8:30am (rain or shine) the Audubon Society gives free one-hour guided tours
at the cul-de-sac at the foot of South I Street.

Heading east from Arcata, Route 299 affords access to the **Trinity River** in the
heart of **Six Rivers National Forest.** Willowcreek and Somes Bar are the prime
recreational centers for the area. Here visitors can sign up for canoeing, rafting,
and kayaking trips with such outfitters as **Aurora River Adventures,** P.O. Box 938,
Willow Creek, CA 95573 (☎ 800/562-8475 or 916/629-3843), which offers some
offbeat, educationally oriented adventures that are great for kids, as well as gnarly
Class V white-water trips for the insane. Other outfitters include **Laughing Heart
Adventures/Trinity Outdoor Center,** in Willow Creek (☎ 916/629-3516); **Big
Foot Rafting Company,** in Willow Creek (☎ 800/722-2223 or 916/629-2263);
and **Klamath River Outfitters,** 3 Sandy Bar Rd., Somes Bar (☎ 916/469-3349).

A few miles north of Willow Creek lies the Hoopa Indian Reservation. In the
Hoopa Shopping Center, the **Hoopa Tribal Museum** (open Monday to Friday from
8am to 5pm; ☎ 916/625-4110) preserves the culture and history of the native
peoples of Northern California with displays of their ceremonial regalia, basketry,
canoes, and tools.

Arcata on $30 a Day

You don't need much money to have a great day in Arcata. For example, you can start your morning off with a big three-course breakfast at **TJ's Classic Café,** 1057 H St. at 11th Street (☎ **707/822-4650**) for under $5. Next, catch a $3 matinee at the **Arcata Theatre,** 1039 G St. at 10th Street (☎ **707/822-5171**), which shows some classic college flicks as well as first-run movies. If you're the bookish type, pick up a used paperback at **Tin Can Mailman,** 1000 H St. at 10th Street (☎ **707/822-1307**), an incredible bookstore whose shelves hold more than 130,000 titles. Then head for the **Humboldt Brewing Company** (see above) for a free tour, followed by a fresh pitcher of their oh-so-sweet Red Nectar Ale and a burger.

If it's baseball season, $3.50 will buy you nine innings of America's favorite pastime at **Arcata Ballpark** (see above), home of the Humboldt Crabs. After a hike through Arcata's **Redwood Park** and **Marsh and Wildlife Sanctuary** (see above), end the day with a big plate of organic mushroom stroganoff and all the trimmings for under $10 at **Wildflower Café,** 1604 G St. at 16th Street (☎ **707/822-0360**).

That's a full-day's fun for under $30. Not bad, Arcata, not bad.

WHERE TO STAY

Fairwinds Motel. 1674 G St., at 17th St., Arcata, CA 95521. ☎ **707/822-4824.** 27 rms. TEL TV. $50–$60 double. AE, DISC, MC, V.

If you can afford it, stay at The Lady Anne (see below). If you can't, stay here. This is your classic American freeway-side AAA-rated motel, right down to the cheap framed prints and wall-to-wall carpeting, but the rates are low, HBO is free, and it's only a short walk from the town square and Humboldt campus (the only other lodgings in the area are miles down the road). The Fairwinds offers a choice of queen, king, and family units, as well as nonsmoking rooms.

Hotel Arcata. 708 9th St., Arcata, CA 95521. ☎ **800/344-1221** or 707/826-0217. Fax 707/826-1737. 32 rms. TEL TV. $110–$150 double. Rates include continental breakfast. AE, DC, DISC, MC, V.

This is the town's most prominent hotel, and many guests are parents visiting their ungrateful offspring at Humboldt State University. Located at the northeast corner of the town plaza, its handsome turn-of-the-century brick facade belies a rather bland, modern interior; few of its original furnishings remain. The bedrooms have a rather characterless decor, but they're safe and comfortable lodgings nonetheless. On the premises, under different management, is a Japanese restaurant, Tomo.

✪ **The Lady Anne.** 902 14th St., Arcata, CA 95521. ☎ **707/822-2797.** 5 rms. $90–$130 double. MC, V.

Easily Arcata's finest lodging, this Queen Anne–style bed and breakfast is kept in top-notch condition by innkeepers Sharon Ferrett and Sam Pennisi, who also served a term as Arcata's mayor. The large, cozy guest rooms are individually decorated with period antiques, lace curtains, Oriental rugs, and English stained glass. For honeymooners there's the Lady Sarah Angela room with its four-poster bed and pleasant bay view. The Cinnamon Bear room sleeps up to four on its king-size trundle beds, which makes it an obvious choice for parents with kids in tow. Breakfast is served in the grand dining room, warmed on winter mornings by a toasty fire. On summer afternoons, the recreation of choice is to lounge on the verandah with a book or play a game of croquet on the front lawn. Several good dining options are only a few blocks away at Arcata Plaza.

WHERE TO DINE

Abruzzi/Plaza Grill. 791 8th St. (at the corner of H St.), Arcata. ☎ **707/826-2345** (Abruzzi), or 707/826-0860 (Plaza Grill). Abruzzi, main courses $8–$18. Plaza Grill, platters and salads $5–$10. AE, DISC, MC, V. Plaza Grill: Sun, Mon 5–10pm, Tues–Fri 5–11pm. Abruzzi: lunch Thurs, Fri 11:30am–2pm, dinner daily 5–10pm.

The best way to review your dining options in Arcata is to ramble through the downtown area's most distinctive minimall, the Jacoby Storehouse (a deftly converted mid–19th-century warehouse) and peer into both of these restaurants. **Abruzzi,** on the street level, is the more formal and substantial of the two, and is generally acknowledged as the best restaurant in town. Menu items include chicken Frascati (with artichoke hearts, mushrooms, and marsala), pastas, veal dishes, and well-seasoned fillet steaks. On the building's third floor is the **Plaza Grill.** Despite efforts to make it more upscale, it can't seem to shake its image as a college-student burger joint. The menu, however, is more substantial than you'd think, with a choice of salads, sandwiches, fish platters, and burgers.

TRINIDAD & PATRICK'S POINT STATE PARK

Back on U.S. 101 north of Arcata, you'll come to **Trinidad,** a tiny coastal fishing village with a population of 400. On of the smallest incorporated cities in California, it occupies a peninsula 25 miles north of Eureka. If you're not into fishing, there's little to do in town expect poke around at the handful of shops, walk along the busy pier, and wish you owned a house here. Unfortunately, budget accommodations are nonexistent in these parts unless you arrive in the winter, when room rates drop dramatically.

Five miles north of Trinidad takes you to the 640-acre **Patrick's Point State Park,** 4150 Patrick's Point Dr. (☎ **707/677-3570**), which has one of the finest ocean access points in the north at sandy **Agate Beach.** It's suitable for driftwood picking, rockhounding, and camping on a sheltered bluff. The park contains a re-creation of a Sumeg Village, which is actively used by the Yurok people and neighboring tribes. A self-guided tour takes you to replicas of family homes and sweat houses.

WHERE TO STAY

✪ **The Lost Whale Inn.** 3452 Patrick's Point Dr., Trinidad, CA 95570. ☎ **800/677-7859** or 707/677-3425. Fax 707/677-0284. 8 rms. Summer $130–$160 double; winter $80–$130 double. Rates include country breakfast. AE, MC, V.

This modern version of a blue-and-gray Cape Cod–style house is set on four acres of seafront land studded with firs, alders, spruces, and redwoods. Its owners cater to children (there's a playground on the premises and minizoo up the street) and adults (there's also a Jacuzzi with a view of the sea), and claim (arguably) that their's is the only hotel in the state of California with its own private beach. Afternoon tea and an artfully designed breakfast are included in the rates. The decor is eclectic, with lots of statuary and paintings, and an outdoor deck facing the surf. Part of the grounds are devoted to a kitchen garden with fresh herbs and vegetables. Rooms are comfortable, and don't have phone or TVs, so you can escape from the rest of the world. Families should inquire about the furnished homes, including a wonderful farmhouse, that the innkeepers also rent out.

WHERE TO DINE

✪ **Larrupin Cafe.** 1658 Patrick's Point Dr., Trinidad. ☎ **707/677-0230.** Reservations required. Main courses $10–$20. No credit cards. Summer Wed–Mon 5–9pm; winter Thurs–Sun 5–9pm. AMERICAN.

On a quiet country road 2 miles north of Trinidad, this highly praised restaurant sports an eclectic blend of Indonesian and African artifacts mingled with paintings

by North California artists and massive bouquets of flowers. Cuisine is often barbecued over mesquite fires, and includes fish (halibut and ahi tuna, among others) that
are basted with lemon butter and served with a portion of mustard-flavored dill sauce.
Other items include barbecued Cornish game hen served with an orange-and-brandy
glaze. For appetizers, the barbecued oysters are perfectly delightful, especially in winter, when a fireplace casts a welcome warmth.

The Seascape Restaurant. Beside the pier at the foot of Bay St., Trinidad. Reservations
accepted. ☎ **707/677-3762.** Full dinners $9–$20. MC, V. Daily 7am–9pm. CALIFORNIA.

Established in the 1940s, this is an unpretentious cross between a cafe and a diner,
with three dining rooms, overworked but cheerful waitresses, and a nostalgic aura.
Folks pop in for coffee or snacks from early morning till after sundown, but by far
the biggest seller here is the Trinidad bay platter ($15.95). Heaped with halibut, scal-
lops, shrimp, and accompanied with salad and rice pilaf, it's even more popular than
the prawn brochette, which draws a close second.

ORICK

From Trinidad it's about another 15 miles to Orick. You can't miss it: Just look for
the dozens of burl stands alongside the road. Carved with chisels and chain saws, these
redwood logs take on the forms of just about every creature you can imagine—
perhaps a gift for your mother-in-law?

At the south end of Orick is its only saving grace, the sleek **Redwood National
Park Information Center,** P.O. Box 7, Orick, CA 95555 (☎ **707/488-3461**). If
you plan to spend any amount of time exploring the park, stop here first and pick
up a free map; the displays of fauna and wildlife aren't too bad, either. It's open daily
from 9am to 5pm.

The first of the parks that make up Redwood National Park, **Prairie Creek,** is
6 miles north of Orick. About 14 miles further on is the mouth of the **Klamath
River,** famous for its salmon, trout, and steelhead. Tours aboard a jet boat take visitors upriver from the estuary to view bear, deer, elk, osprey hawks, otters, and more
along the river banks. It's about $20 for a 30-mile trip. For information, contact **Kla-
math River Jet Boat Tours,** Klamath (☎ **800/887-JETS** or 707/482-7775). From
Klamath it's another 20 miles to Crescent City, gateway to the other parks that make
up Redwood National Park.

7 Crescent City: Gateway to Redwood National Park

Crescent City itself has little to offer, but it makes a good base for exploring Redwood National Park and the Smith River, one of the great recreational rivers of the
West. **The Battery Point Lighthouse,** which is accessible on foot only at low tide,
houses a museum about the coast's history. Tours of the lighthouse are offered
Wednesday through Sunday from 10am to 4pm, weather permitting, April to September (at the foot of A Street; ☎ **707/464-3089**).

Another local draw is the **Smith River Recreation Area,** east of Jedediah Smith
State Park and part of Six Rivers National Forest. The headquarters is at the **Gasquet
Ranger Station,** 10600 Hwy. 199, Gasquet, CA 95543 (☎ **707/457-3131**), which
is reached via Route 199 from Crescent City (19 miles, about a 30-minute drive).
Maps of the forest can be obtained here, at the Supervisor's Office in Eureka, or at
the Redwood National Park centers in Orick and Crescent City.

The 300,000-plus acres of wilderness offer camping at five modest-size campgrounds (all with less than 50 sites), along the Smith River. Sixteen trails attract hikers

from across the country. The easiest short trail is the **McClendon Ford,** which is 2 miles long and drops from 1,000 to 800 feet in elevation to the south fork of the river. Other activities include mountain biking, white-water rafting, kayaking, and fishing for salmon and trout.

For information, contact the **Crescent City-Del Norte County Chamber of Commerce,** 1001 Front St., Crescent City, CA 95531 (☎ **707/464-3174**).

WHERE TO STAY

Crescent Beach Motel. 1455 Redwood Hwy. S. (U.S. 101), Crescent City, CA 95531. ☎ **707/464-5436.** 28 rms. TV. Summer $63–$68 double; winter $49–$52 double. AE, DISC, MC, V.

Set beside the highway, about 2 miles south of town, this single-story structure is the only local motel set directly on the beach. It has simple, old-fashioned bedrooms, without phone or cooking facilities, but with an undeniably rustic, outdoorsy appeal. Four of the units face the highway; try to get one of the others, which all have decks and doors opening directly onto the sands. There's no restaurant or bar on the premises, but one of the city's most popular restaurants, the Beachcomber (☎ 707/464-2205), is located next door.

Curly Redwood Lodge. 701 Redwood Hwy. S., Crescent City, CA 95531. ☎ **707/464-2137.** 36 rms. TEL TV. Summer $59–$64 double; winter $37–$39 double. AE, DC, MC, V.

This hotel is a blast from the past, the kind of place where you might have stayed as a kid during one of those cross-country vacations in the family station wagon. It was built in 1959 on grasslands across from the town's harbor, and completely trimmed with lumber from a single ancient redwood. Although they're not full of the latest high-tech gadgets, the bedrooms are among the largest and best-soundproofed in town, and certainly the most evocative of a bygone, more innocent age. In winter, about a third of the bedrooms (the ones upstairs) are locked and sealed. Overall, the aura is more akin to Oregon than anything you might imagine in California.

WHERE TO DINE

Beachcomber. 1400 Calif. 101, Crescent City. ☎ **707/464-2205.** Reservations recommended. Main courses $6–$15. MC, V. Thurs–Tues 5–9pm. SEAFOOD.

The decor is as predictably nautical as its name implies: rough-cut planking, a scattering of artfully arranged driftwood, fishnets, and buoys dangling above a dimly lit space. The restaurant lies beside the beach, 2 miles south of Crescent City's center. Its fans cite it as one of the two best restaurants in town. The cuisine is a joy to fish lovers who prefer not to mask the flavor of their seafood with complicated sauces. Most of the dishes are grilled over madrone-wood barbecue pits, a technique perfected since this place was established in 1975. Pacific salmon, halibut, lingcod, Pacific snapper, oysters, and steamer clams are house specialties, dishes for which visitors line up, especially on Friday or Saturday night.

Harbor View Grotto Restaurant and Lounge. 150 Starfish Way, Crescent City. ☎ **707/464-3815.** Lunch $6–$9; dinner $8–$35. MC, V. Daily 11:30am–10pm. SEAFOOD/STEAKS.

This is the best-established nonchain restaurant in town, specializing in fresh seafood at market prices since 1961. Completely renovated in December 1995, it has pleasant views of the ocean and harbor from both the dining room and lounge. It's capped with a miniature lighthouse inspired by Crescent City's Battery Point Lighthouse, and staffed by the family of the original founders. The "light eaters" menu includes a cup of white chowder (made fresh daily), salad, a main course, and vegetables; heavy eaters can choose from three different cuts of prime rib. Menu items include fresh fish from local fishing fleets, such as Pacific snapper or salmon. Crab or shrimp Louis, as well as crabmeat or shrimp sandwiches, are perpetually popular.

8 Redwood National & State Parks

by Andrew Rice

When he was governor of California, Ronald Reagan once said that if you've seen one redwood, you've seen them all. He couldn't have been more wrong. Redwood National and State Parks are living proof. While he was right that a 367-foot-tall coast redwood (the world's tallest, located in the Tall Trees Grove) does in fact look pretty much like the next one, Reagan was guilty of not seeing the forest for the trees.

It's impossible to explain the feeling you get in the old-growth forests of Redwood National and State Parks without resorting to Alice-in-Wonderland comparisons. Like a tropical rain forest, the redwood forest is a multistoried affair, the tall trees being only the top layer. Everything is big, misty, and primeval; flowering bushes cover the ground, 10-foot-tall ferns line the creeks, and the smells are rich and musty. It's so *Jurassic Park* that you can't help but half expect to turn the corner and see a dinosaur.

The 110,000-acre park offers a lesson in bioregionalism. When the park was first created to protect the biggest coast redwoods, the federal government allowed loggers to clear much of the surrounding area. Redwoods in the park began to suffer as the quality of the Redwood Creek drainage declined from upstream logging. In 1978 the government purchased the entire watershed, having learned that you can't preserve individual trees without preserving the ecosystem they depend on. In April of 1994, the National Park Service and California Department of Parks and Recreation signed an agreement to manage the four Redwood parks cooperatively.

SEEING THE HIGHLIGHTS

A number of scenic drives cut through the park. Steep, windy **Bald Hills Road** will take you back into the Redwood Creek watershed and up to the shoulder of 3,097-foot Schoolhouse Peak. Don't even think of driving a motor home or pulling a trailer up here.

The partially paved 8-mile **Coastal Drive** wanders among redwood groves and along the banks of the Klamath River. The southern section is okay for RVs, but don't go past Alder Camp Road going north or Flint Ridge heading south. Watch for the old World War II radar tracking station disguised as a barn and farmhouse to fool the Japanese.

SPORTS & ACTIVITIES

No one has ever wanted for things to do at Redwood National and State Parks. Everything from river kayaking to bird-watching is available here. In addition to the redwoods, the park includes miles of coastline, several miles of rivers and streams, a herd of elk, three California state parks, and several small towns.

HIKING   The park map and guide, available at any of the information centers, provides a good map of hiking trails. Backpackers can tackle the **Coastal Trail,** which runs the entire length of the park, as near the ocean as possible. Manageable segments of the Coastal Trail can be hiked in a day. One of the nicest runs is from Crescent Beach south into the Del Norte Coast Redwoods State Park.

Redwood National & State Parks

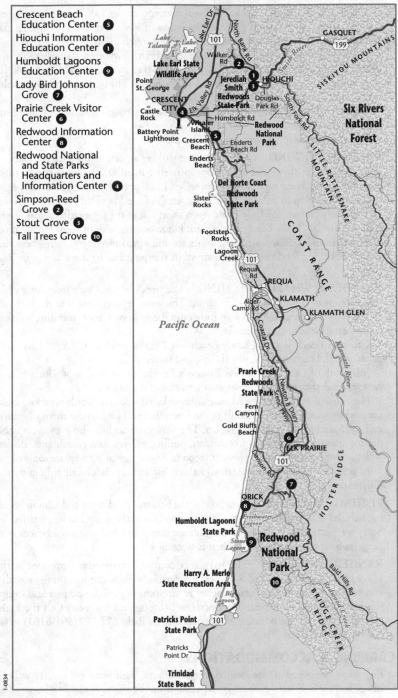

Crescent Beach
  Education Center ⑤
Hiouchi Information
  Education Center ①
Humboldt Lagoons
  Education Center ⑨
Lady Bird Johnson
  Grove ⑦
Prairie Creek Visitor
  Center ⑥
Redwood Information
  Center ⑧
Redwood National
  and State Parks
  Headquarters and
  Information Center ④
Simpson-Reed
  Grove ②
Stout Grove ③
Tall Trees Grove ⑩

1-0834

225

The 8-mile **Redwood Creek Trail** will take you to the Tall Trees Grove, where the tallest trees in the world grow on the banks of Redwood Creek. In winter two bridges are removed from the trail, making access much more difficult.

Smaller day hikes include the walk through **Fern Canyon,** an unbelievably lush grotto of sword, five-finger, and maidenhair ferns traversed by a babbling brook. It's only about a 1$^1/_2$-mile walk from Gold Bluffs beach, but be prepared to scramble across the creek several times on your way.

Ladybird Johnson Grove Loop is a short stroll through one of the park's lushest groves of redwoods.

Pets are prohibited on all of the park's trails.

WILDLIFE VIEWING One of the most striking aspects of the park is its herd of Roosevelt elk, usually found in the appropriately named Elk Prairie in the southern end of the park. These gigantic deer can weigh 1,000 pounds and the bulls carry huge antlers from spring to fall. Elk are also sometimes found at Gold Bluffs Beach—it's an incredible rush to suddenly come upon them out of the fog or after a turn in the trail. Nearly 100 black bears call the park home but are seldom seen. Unlike those at Yosemite and Yellowstone, these bears are still afraid of people. Keep them that way by observing food storage etiquette while camping and by disposing of garbage properly.

BEACHES & WHALE WATCHING The park's beaches vary from long white sand strands to cobblestone pocket coves. The water temperature is in the high 40s to low 50s year-round and it's often rough out there, so swimmers and surfers should be prepared for adverse conditions.

Crescent Beach is a long sandy beach just 2 miles south of Crescent City that's popular with beachcombers, surf fishers, and surfers.

Just south of Crescent Beach is **Endert's Beach,** a protected spot with a hike-in campground and tide pools at the southern end of the beach.

High coastal overlooks (like Klamath overlook and Crescent Beach overlook) make great whale-watching outposts during the December and January southern migration and the March/April return migration. The northern sea cliffs also provide valuable nesting sites for marine birds like auklets, puffins, murres, and cormorants. Birders will also thrill at the park's freshwater lagoons. These coastal lagoons are some of the most pristine shorebird and waterfowl habitat left and are chock-full of hundreds of different species.

FISHING The area streams are some of the best steelhead trout and salmon breeding habitats in California. Park beaches are good for surf casting but be prepared for heavy wave action. A California fishing license is required and you should check with rangers about any special closures before wetting a line.

RANGER PROGRAMS The park service runs interpretive programs at the Hiouchi, Crescent Beach, and Redwood information centers during summer months, and year-round at the park headquarters in Crescent City. State rangers lead campfire programs and numerous other activities throughout the year. Call the Parks Information service for both the National and State Parks (☎ 707/464-6101) to get current schedules and events.

CAMPING & ACCOMMODATIONS

Five small campgrounds are located in the national park proper. Four are walk-in camps and are free, but you must get a permit from the visitor center in advance. The fifth, a car-camping strip along the freeway at Freshwater Lagoon, requests an $8 donation. Most car campsites are in the **Prairie Creek and Jedediah Smith State**

Parks, which lie entirely inside the national park. Sites there are $14 per night and can be reserved by calling the state's infuriating **DESTINET reservation system** (☎ 800/444-7275), which requires an additional $6.75 reservation fee. Be prepared to deal with a truly annoying computer before you call and know exactly what campground and if possible which site you would like. (The state park service has promised improvements in this system, but we'll see.)

An interesting option is the **boat-in campground** at Stone Lagoon in Humboldt Lagoons state park. Reachable only by canoe, kayak, or rowboat, it is on the bank of the lagoon and a short walk from the ocean beach.

Farther from the park attractions but also farther from the crowds are four **National Forest Campgrounds** in the mountains above the park. Sites are $8 per night and can be reserved by calling **800/280-2267,** where an actual person can help you make decisions.

The **Redwood AYH Hostel** is the only lodging actually within the park. This turn-of-the-century inn has kitchen facilities, three showers, and 30 beds in shared rooms. The staff leads nature walks and is well versed in local history. It's very inexpensive, and located at 14480 U.S. 101, near Klamath (☎ 707/482-8265).

A number of B&Bs and funky roadside motels are available in the surrounding communities of Crescent City, Orick, and Klamath. **The Crescent City/Del Norte Chamber of Commerce** (☎ 800/343-8300) can steer you toward a proper match (also see the preceding two sections for our favorite recommendations).

JUST THE FACTS

Frankly, all those huge trees and ferns wouldn't have survived for 1,000 years if it didn't rain one heck of a lot. Just count on rain or at least a heavy drizzle, then go ecstatic when the sun comes out. It can happen anytime. Spring, of course, is the best season for wildflowers. Summer is foggy (it's called "the June gloom" but often includes July). Fall is the warmest, sunniest (relatively!) time of all, and winter isn't bad, though it is cold, wet (try 60 inches of rain), and some park facilities are closed. A storm can provide the most introspective time to see the park, since you'll probably be alone. And after a storm passes through, sunny days often follow.

The North Coast used to be one of those places where people left their keys in the ignition in case someone had to move their car. But no more. Lock your car and put valuables in the trunk or take them with you.

Admission to the national park is free, but to enter any of the three state parks (which contain the best redwood groves), you'll have to pay a $6 day-use fee. It's good at all three.

9

The Far North: The Shasta Cascades & Lake Tahoe

by Erika Lenkert and Matthew R. Poole

Dominated by the eternally snowcapped Mt. Shasta—visible for 100 miles around on a clear day—California's upper northern territory is among the least touristed sections of the state. Often referred to as "The Far North," this vast region stretches from the rice fields north of Sacramento all the way to the Oregon border. If fact, the area is so immense that the state of Ohio would fit comfortably within its borders.

The Far North is a virtual outdoor playground for the budget traveler, offering myriad inexpensive recreational activities such as hiking, climbing, skiing, white-water rafting, and mountain biking. Other attractions, both artificial and natural, range from the amazing Shasta Dam to Lava Beds National Monument, which has dozens of caves to explore, and Lassen Volcanic National Park, a towering laboratory of volcanic phenomena.

Directly south of the Cascade Range is one of the most popular recreational regions in the Golden State: Lake Tahoe. Lying 6,225 feet above sea level in the Sierra Nevada mountains, it straddles the border between Nevada and California. Although the lake has been marred by overdevelopment—particularly along the casino-riddled southern shore—the western and eastern coastlines still provides quiet havens for hiking and cycling. The surrounding mountains offer some of the best skiing in the United States at more than a dozen resorts.

1 Lava Beds National Monument

by Andrew Rice

Lava Beds takes a while to grow on you. It's a seemingly desolate, windy place with high plateaus, cinder cones, and rolling hills covered with lava cinders, sagebrush, and tortured-looking junipers. Miles of land just like it cover most of this corner of California. So why, asks the first-time visitor, is this a national monument? The answer lies underground.

The earth here is like Swiss cheese, so porous in places that it actually makes a hollow sound. When lava pours from a shield volcano it doesn't cool all at once; the outer edges cool first and the core keeps flowing, forming underground tunnels like a giant pipeline system.

More than 330 lava-tube caves lace the earth at Lava Beds, caves that are open to the public to explore on their own or with park rangers. Where most caves lend themselves to a fear of getting lost with their huge chambers, multiple entrances, and bizarre topography, these are simple, relatively easy-to-follow tunnels with little room to go wrong. The feeling once inside is that this would be a great place for a game of hide and seek.

SEEING THE HIGHLIGHTS

A hike to **Schonchin Butte** ($^3/_4$ mile, one way) will give you a good perspective on the wildly stark beauty of the Monument and nearby Tule Lake Valley. Wildlife lovers should keep their eyes peeled for terrestrial animals like mule deer, coyote, marmots, and squirrels, while watching overhead for bald eagles, 24 species of hawks, as well as enormous flocks of ducks and geese headed to the Klamath Basin, one of the largest waterfowl wintering grounds in the Lower 48. Sometimes the sky goes dark with ducks and geese during the peak migrations.

The caves at **Lava Beds** are open to the public with very little restriction or hassle. All you need to see most of them is a good flashlight or head lamp, sturdy walking shoes, and a sense of adventure. Many of the caves are entered by ladders or stairs, others still by holes in the side of a hill. Once inside, walk far enough to round a corner then shut off your light—a chilling experience, to say the least.

One-way **Cave Loop Road** just southwest of the visitor center is where you'll find many of the best cave hikes. About 15 lava tubes have been marked and made accessible. Two are ice caves, where the air temperature remains below freezing all year and ice crystals form on the walls. If exploring on your own gives you the creeps, check out **Mushpot Cave.** Almost adjacent to the visitor center, this cave has been outfitted with lights and a smooth walkway; you'll have plenty of company.

Hardened spelunkers will find enough remote and relatively unexplored caves in the monument, many requiring specialized climbing gear, to keep themselves busy.

Above ground, several trails crisscross the monument. The longest of these, the 8.2-mile (one way) **Lyons Trail** spans the wildest part of the monument, where you are likely to see plenty of animals. The **Whitney Butte Trail,** 3.4 miles (one way), leads from Merill Cave along the shoulder of 5,000-foot Whitney Butte to the edge of the Callahan Lava Flow and monument boundary.

PICNICKING, CAMPING & ACCOMMODATIONS

The 40-unit Indian Well Campground near the visitor center has spaces for tents and small RVs year-round, with water available only during the summer. The rest of the year you'll have to carry water from the nearby visitor center.

Two picnic grounds, Fleener Chimneys and Captain Jacks Stronghold, have tables but no water; open fires are prohibited.

There are no hotels or lodges in the monument but numerous services are available in nearby Tulelake and Klamath Falls. For more information call or write **Lava Beds National Monument,** P.O. Box 867, Tulelake, CA 96134 (☎ **916/ 667-2282).**

JUST THE FACTS

Park elevations range from 4,000 to 5,700 feet, and this part of California can get cold any time of year. Summer is the best time to visit, with average temperatures in the 70s; winter temperatures plunge down to about 40°F in the day and as low as 20°F by night. Summer is also the best time to participate in ranger-led hikes, cave trips, and campfire programs. Check at the visitor center for schedules.

2 Mt. Shasta & the Cascades

Chances are, your first glimpse of Mt. Shasta's majestic, snowcapped peak will result in a twang of awe. A dormant volcano with a 17-mile diameter base, it stands in virtual isolation 14,162 feet above the sea. When John Muir first saw Shasta from 50 miles away in 1874, he wrote: "[I] was alone and weary. Yet my blood turned to wine, and I have not been weary since." He went on to describe it as "the pole star of the landscape," which indeed it is.

For the budget traveler, Mt. Shasta and the Cascades offer a gold mine of opportunities. Dining and lodging here are the cheapest in the state, and most activities simply require an adventurous soul and a few outdoor toys (most of which can be rented for dollars a day). Don't forget to pack your binoculars—the endangered bald eagle is a common sight in these parts—and a pair of broken-in hiking boots.

ESSENTIALS

GETTING THERE   From San Francisco, take I-80 to I-505 to I-5 to Redding. From the coast, pick up Route 299 east a few miles north of Arcata to Redding.

Redding Municipal Airport, 6751 Airport Rd. (☎ 916/224-4331), is serviced by United Express. Amtrak stops in Dunsmuir and Redding.

VISITOR INFORMATION   Regional information can be secured from the following organizations: **Shasta Cascade Wonderland Association,** 14250 Holiday Rd., Redding, CA 96003 (☎ 800/326-6944 or 916/275-5555); **Mt. Shasta Chamber of Commerce,** 300 Pine St., Mt. Shasta, CA 96067 (☎ 800/926-4865 or 916/926-4865); **Redding Convention and Visitors Bureau,** 777 Auditorium Dr., Redding, CA 96001 (☎ 800/874-7562 or 916/225-4100); **Trinity County Chamber of Commerce,** 317 Main St., P.O. Box 517, Weaverville, CA 96093 (☎ 800/487-4648 or 916/623-6101).

WILLIAM B. IDE ADOBE STATE HISTORIC PARK

En route to Mt. Shasta from the south, you may want to stop near Red Bluff at **William B. Ide Adobe State Historic Park,** 21659 Adobe Rd. (☎ 916/529-8599), for a picnic along the Sacramento River. The three-acre park commemorates William B. Ide, California's first and only president, proclaimed on June 14, 1846, by those who led the Bear Flag Rebellion against the Mexicans who were excluding the Americans from California. The republic lasted only three weeks before the Mexican War and the American victory made California a state in the Union. The adobe home dates from 1852. Some historians say it was not the home of Mr. Ide, but it does give visitors an idea of frontier life. In the summer the park is open from 8am to sunset; the house is open noon to 4pm; call ahead in winter. Parking is $3 per vehicle.

REDDING & SHASTA

The major town and gateway to the region is Redding, the hub of the panoramic Shasta-Cascade region, lying at the top of the Sacramento Valley. From here you can either turn westward into the wilderness forest of Trinity and the Klamath Mountains, or north and east into the Cascades and Shasta Trinity National Forest.

In Redding, with its fast-food joints, gas stations, and cheap motels, summer heat generally hovers around 100°F. A city of some 60,000, Redding is the transportation hub of the upper reaches of Northern California. It has little of interest; it's mainly useful as a base for exploring the natural wonders nearby. Information is available from the **Redding Convention and Visitors Bureau** at 777 Auditorium Dr., west

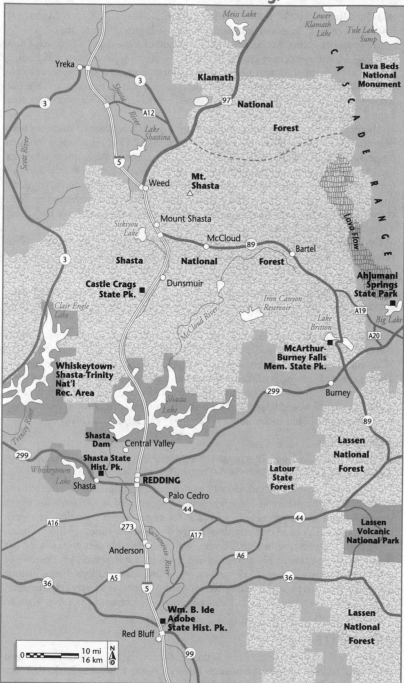

Meiss Lake

Lower Klamath Lake

Tule Lake Sump

Lava Beds National Monument

Yreka

3

Klamath

97

National

Shasta River

A12

Forest

5

Scott River

Lake Shastina

CASCADE RANGE

Weed

Mt. Shasta △

3

Siskiyou Lake

Mount Shasta

McCloud

89

Bartel

Lava Flow

Shasta

National

Forest

Ahjumani Springs State Park

Castle Crags State Pk.

Dunsmuir

Clair Engle Lake

McCloud River

Iron Canyon Reservoir

Lake Britton

A19

Big Lake

A20

Whiskeytown-Shasta-Trinity Nat'l Rec. Area

McArthur-Burney Falls Mem. State Pk.

Trinity River

Shasta Lake

299

Burney

89

Shasta Dam

Central Valley

Lassen National Forest

299

Whiskeytown Lake

Shasta State Hist. Pk.

REDDING

Latour State Forest

Shasta

Palo Cedro

44

A16

273

A17

44

Anderson

A6

Lassen Volcanic National Park

Sacramento River

A5

36

5

36

Lassen National Forest

Wm. B. Ide Adobe State Hist. Pk.

Red Bluff

99

0 ___ 10 mi
___ 16 km

N

1-0835

of I-5 on Route 299 (☎ **800/874-7562** or 916/225-4100). It's open Monday to Friday from 8am to 5pm and on Saturday and Sunday from 9am to 5pm.

Ahead and northeast, Mt. Shasta rises to a height of more than 14,000 feet. From Redding, I-5 cuts north over the Pit River Bridge, crossing Lake Shasta and leading eventually to the mount itself. Before striking north, however, you may want to explore Lake Shasta and see Shasta Dam. Another option is to take a detour west of Redding to Weaverville, Whiskeytown–Shasta Trinity National Recreation Area, and Lake Trinity (see below).

About 3 miles west, stop at the old gold mining town of **Shasta**, which has been converted into a **State Historic Park** (☎ **916/243-8194**). Shasta was founded on gold, and was the "Queen City" of the northern mines in the Klamath range. Its life, though, was short, and the town died in 1872 when the Central Pacific Railroad bypassed it in favor of Redding. Today the business district is a ghost town, complete with a restored general store and a Masonic hall. The 1861 courthouse has been converted into a museum where you can view the jail and a gallows out back, plus a remarkable collection of California art.

Continue along Calif. 299 west to Route 3 north, which will take you to Weaverville and then to the west side of the lake and Trinity Center.

WHERE TO STAY

Tiffany House Bed and Breakfast Inn. 1510 Barbara Rd., Redding, CA 96003. ☎ **916/244-3225.** 3 rms, 1 cottage. $75–$95 double, $125 cottage. Rates include breakfast. AE, DISC, MC, V.

Despite the fact that this two-story gray-and-white house wasn't built until 1939, everyone in town refers to it as a Victorian. You'll find a sweeping view of the Lassen Mountain Range from the oversize deck, which seems to float above a garden in back. There's also a swimming pool. Bedrooms have crocheted bedspreads, one has a claw-foot tub in the bathroom, and all contain some kind of reproduction Tiffany lamp, as the inn's name would imply. If the B&B were on the coast, a room would easily cost twice as much, but in Redding a little money can buy a lot of luxury.

WHERE TO DINE

Jack's Grill. 1743 California St. ☎ **916/241-9705.** Reservations not accepted. Main courses $7.25–$18.25. AE, DISC, MC, V. Mon–Sat 4–11pm. STEAK HOUSE.

This is a local favorite, established in 1938 in a building originally constructed as a secondhand clothing store in 1835. The second floor served as a whorehouse in the late 1930s, and an entrepreneur named Jack Young set up the main floor as a steak house (to service all of a body's needs over two floors of the same building). Today, it's an earthy, well-established steak house. Waiting for a table over drinks in the bar is part of the fun. Good old-fashioned red meat is supplemented by a couple of seafood dishes such as deep-fried jumbo prawns and ocean scallops. Prices include salad, hot garlic bread, and baked or french-fried potatoes. It's a very fetching spot, with good honest tavern food and a jovial crowd. Be prepared for a long wait on weekends.

WEAVERVILLE

Weaverville was a gold mining town in the 1850s, and part of its history is captured at the **Jake Jackson Memorial Museum-Trinity County Historical Park,** P.O. Box 333, Weaverville (☎ **916/623-5211**). It displays the usual collection of memorabilia, from firearms to household items. You'll learn some interesting facts about the residents of the town: Native Americans, miners, pioneers, and especially the Chinese.

Admission is free. It's open daily May 1 to October 31 from 10am to 5pm, November and April from noon to 4pm. Closed from December to March.

In the gold rush era, the town was half Chinese, with a Chinatown of about 2,500 residents. Across the parking lot, in fact, you can view the oldest continuously used Taoist temple in California at the **Joss House State Historic Park** (☎ **916/ 623-5284**). Although technically it's open 10am to 5pm Wednesday to Sunday, hours tend to be irregular, so call ahead. Admission is $2 adults, $1 children 6 to 13, free for children 5 and under.

WHERE TO DINE

Weaverville isn't exactly packed with exciting dining choices, so you take what you can get.

Mustard Seed. 252 S. Main St. ☎ **916/623-2922.** All items under $6.95. No credit cards. Mon–Sat 7am–3pm, Sun 8am–3pm. AMERICAN/MEXICAN.

This century-old, yellow-fronted Victorian house stands in the town's historic core. At breakfast the favorite items are the Belgian waffles with crushed almonds and the omelets—the best in town. Lunch brings an array of tacos, burritos, quiches, and veggie dishes for the dedicated cauliflower and broccoli lovers in the area.

The Pacific Brewery. 401 S. Main St. ☎ **916/623-3000.** Main courses $8–14. MC, V. Daily 6am–9pm. AMERICAN.

Good food at reasonable prices is served here—that is, if you can get a preoccupied staff member to pay you some attention. Start with the shrimp cocktail or the nachos, then follow with steak or pasta primavera, salmon steak, or breast of chicken in a mushroom garlic wine sauce. Mud pie is the traditional favorite conclusion. Several microbrews are available on tap. The decor consists of Americana; the same can be said for the diners.

THE TRINITY ALPS

West of Weaverville stretch the Trinity Alps, with Thompson Peak rising to more than 9,000 feet. This is the second-largest wilderness area in the state; it lies between the Trinity and Salmon rivers and contains more than 55 lakes and streams. Its alpine scenery makes it popular with hikers and backpackers. You can access the **Pacific Crest Trail** west of Mt. Shasta at Parks Creek, South Fork Road, Whalen Road, and also from Castle Crags State Park. For trail and other information, contact the **Forest Service** at Weaverville (☎ **916/623-2121**).

The Fifth Season, 300 N. Mt. Shasta Blvd., Mount Shasta (☎ **916/926-3606**), offers mountaineering and backpack rentals and will provide trail maps and other information concerning Shasta's outdoor activities.

Living Waters Recreation, Mt. Shasta (☎ **916/926-5446**), offers half-day to two-day rafting trips on the Upper Sacramento, Klamath, Trinity, and Salmon Rivers. **Trinity River Rafting Company** on Calif. 299W in Big Flat (☎ **916/ 623-3223**) also operates white-water trips along the Trinity, Salmon, and Klamath Rivers.

For additional outfitters and information, contact the **Trinity County Chamber of Commerce,** 317 Main St., Weaverville (☎ **800/487-4648** or 916/623-6101).

WHISKEYTOWN NATIONAL RECREATION AREA

In adjacent Shasta County, Whiskeytown National Recreation Area is on the eastern shore of Trinity Lake, a quiet and relatively uncrowded lake with 157 miles of shoreline. When this reservoir was created, it was officially named Clair Engle, after

the politician who created it. But locals insist on calling it Trinity after the name of
the river that used to rush through the region past the towns of Minersville,
Stringtown, and an earlier Whiskeytown. All of these were destroyed when the river
was dammed. They now lie under the lake's glassy surface.

Both Lake Trinity and the Whiskeytown National Recreation Area are in the
Shasta Trinity National Forest, 2.1 million acres of wilderness with 1,269 miles of
hiking trails. For information on trails, contact **Shasta Trinity National Forest,**
2400 Washington Ave., Redding (☎ **916/246-5222**).

LAKE SHASTA

Continuing north on I-5 from Redding, travel about 12 miles north and take the
Shasta Dam Boulevard exit to the ❾ **Shasta Dam and Power Plant** (☎ **916/
275-4463**), which has an overflow spillway that is three times higher than Niagara
Falls. The huge dam—3,460 feet long, 602 feet high, and 883 feet thick at its base—
holds back the waters of the Sacramento, Pit, and McCloud rivers. It's a dramatic
sight, as well as a vital component of the Central Valley water project. At the visitors center is a series of photographs and displays covering the dam's construction
period. You can either walk or drive over the dam, but far more interesting are the
free 45-minute tours given daily 9am to 5pm on the hour in the summer, and at
10am, noon, and 2pm from Labor Day to Memorial day. The guided tour takes you
deep within the dam's many chilly corridors (not a good place for claustrophobes)
and below the spillway. It's an entertaining way to beat the summer heat and one of
the best free tours in the state.

Lake Shasta has 370 miles of shoreline and attracts anglers (bass, trout, and king
salmon), water-skiers, and other boating enthusiasts—two million, in fact, in summer. The best way to enjoy the lake is aboard a houseboat, which can be rented from
several companies: **Antlers Resort and Marina,** P.O. Box 140, Antlers Rd.,
Lakehead, CA 96051 (☎ **800/238-3924**); **Packers Bay Marina,** 16814 Packers
Bay Rd., Lakehead, CA 96051 (☎ **800/331-3137**); and **Lakeshore Marina,**
20479 Lakeshore Drive, Lakehead, CA 96051 (☎ **916/238-2303**). Prices range
from $150 to $300 a day, but if you split it up among five friends, that's only $30
a pop for a full day of fun. For information and additional houseboat rentals,
contact the **Redding Convention and Visitors Bureau,** 777 Auditorium Dr.
(☎ **800/874-7562** or 916/225-4100).

While you're here, you can visit **Lake Shasta Caverns** (☎ **916/238-2341**). These
caves contain 20-foot-high stalactite and stalagmite formations—60-foot-wide curtains of them in the great Cathedral Room. To see the caves, drive about 15 miles
north of Redding on I-5 to the O'Brien/Shasta Caverns exit. A ferry will take you
across the lake and a short bus ride will follow to the cave entrance for an hour-long
tour. Admission is $12 adults, $6 children. The caverns are open daily year-round,
with tours every half hour in summer between 9am and 4pm, and every hour in winter from 9am to 3pm.

Farther north, off I-5 about 35 miles north of Redding, you'll reach **Castle Crags
State Park** (☎ **916/235-2684**), a 4,300-acre park with 64 campsites and 28 miles
of hiking trails. Here granite crags that were formed 225 million years ago tower
more than 6,500 feet above the Sacramento River. The park is filled with dogwood,
oak, cedar, and pine as well as tiger lilies, azaleas, and orchids in summer. You
can walk the 1-mile Indian Creek nature trail or take the easy 1½-mile Root Creek
trail.

Back on I-5 the road curves around past the old railroad town of Dunsmuir and
on into Mt. Shasta.

MT. SHASTA

A volcanic mountain with eight glaciers, $ Mt. Shasta is a towering peak of legend and lore. It stands alone, always snowcapped yet never shadowed by other mountains. Although dormant since 1786, the mighty volcano is far from extinct, as the hot sulfur springs bubbling at the summit will attest. It was these same springs, in fact, that saved John Muir on his third ascent of the mountain in 1875: caught in a severe snowstorm, he and his partner took turns submersing themselves in the hot mud to survive.

Many New Agers are convinced that Mt. Shasta is the center of an incredible energy vortex. These devotees, both young and old, arrive from all around the world to channel energy from what they firmly believe is one of the seven "power centers" of the world. In 1987 Mt. Shasta was the guest of honor for the worldwide Harmonic Convergence, calling for a planetary union and a new phase of universal harmony (yoga, massage, meditation, metaphysics, and crystals are all the rage here). These New Agers seem to live rather harmoniously with good old boys playing their country/western music, people who never get more metaphysical than hearing the lyrics in a George Strait song.

Those who don't want to climb Mt. Shasta can drive up to about 8,000 feet. From Mount Shasta City, head 14 miles up the Everitt Memorial Highway to the end of the road near Panther Meadow. Along the way you'll be able to stop and see the Sacramento River Canyon, the Eddy Mountains to the west, and glimpses of Mt. Lassen to the south. At the Everitt Vista Turnout, you can take the short hike through the forests to a lava outcrop overlooking the McCloud area.

Continue on to Bunny Flat, a major access point for climbers in the summer and also for cross-country skiing and sledding in winter. The highway ends at the Old Ski Bowl Vista, providing panoramic views of Mt. Lassen, Castle Crags, and the Trinity Mountains.

While in Mount Shasta, visit the **Fish Hatchery** at 3 N. Old State Rd. (☎ 916/ 926-2215), which was built in 1888. Here you can observe rainbow and brown trout being hatched to stock rivers and streams statewide—millions are produced here annually. You can feed them via coin-operated food dispensers, and on certain Tuesdays during the fall and winter observe the spawning process. Admission is free, and it's open daily 8am to sunset. Adjacent to the hatchery is the Sisson Museum, which displays a smattering of local history exhibits. It's open daily 10am to 5pm in summer, daily noon to 4pm in winter, and admission is also free.

OUTDOOR ACTIVITIES

SKIING   In winter, visitors can ski at **Mt. Shasta Ski Park,** 104 Siskiyou Ave., Mount Shasta, CA 96067 (☎ 916/926-8600); **Ski Lodge** (☎ 916/926-8610), which has 22 runs with 80% snowmaking and three chairlifts; a fourth lift is in the works. A day pass costs under $30. There's also a Nordic Ski center with 15 1/2 miles of groomed trails. In summer you can ride the chairlifts to scenic overlooks, mountain bike down the trails (all-day pass $9), or practice on the two-story climbing wall. Access to the chairlifts is 10 miles east on Mt. Shasta on its southern slopes via Calif. 89 from McCloud.

WATER SPORTS   Although the source of the headwaters of the Sacramento River is found here, water does not gush down from the mountain. Instead, it is accumulated at the base. At Shasta's base lies **Lake Siskiyou,** a popular lake for boating, swimming, fishing, and a great vantage point for photographs of Mt. Shasta and its reflection. Waterskiing is not allowed, but windsurfing is available, and boat rentals

are offered at **Lake Siskiyou Camp Resort,** 4239 W. A. Barr Rd., Mount Shasta
(☎ **916/926-2618**). For fishing information, go to **Hart's Guide Service,**
965 Lassen Lane (☎ **916/926-2431**), or contact **Mt. Shasta Fly Fishing** (☎ **916/
926-6648**).

GOLF & TENNIS Golfers should head for the 27-hole Robert Trent Jones Jr.
golf course at **Lake Shastina Golf Resort,** 5925 Country Club Dr., Weed (☎ **916/
938-3201**), or the 18-hole course at **Mt. Shasta Resort,** 1000 Siskiyou Lake Blvd.,
Mount Shasta (☎ **916/926-3030**). The resort also has tennis courts.

MOUNTAIN BIKING In and around Mount Shasta, you'll find a variety of sup-
pliers and sports outfitters, including the Fifth Season (see "The Trinity Alps," above).

The **Mt. Shasta Ski Park** (☎ **916/926-8610**) rents everything you'll need for a
complete day of mountain biking, including bike rentals and helmets. An all-day
chairlift pass in only $9.

WHERE TO STAY

Vacancies have been harder and harder to come by in these parts in both winter and
summer. If you find yourself in Mount Shasta, desperate for a room, try calling the
Mount Shasta Convention and Visitors Bureau at **800/926-4865.** Some other
good low-priced hotels are **Shasta Lodge Motel** (☎ **916/926-2815**); and **Evergreen
Lodge** (☎ **916/926-2143**).

Below is a list of what we consider the best deals:

Doubles for $60 or Less

⑤ Mt. Shasta Ranch Bed & Breakfast. 1008 W. A. Barr Rd., Mount Shasta, CA 96067.
☎ **916/926-3870.** 9 rms (4 with private bath), 1 cottage. TV. $50–$65 double with shared
bath; $85 double with private bath; $95 cottage for three. Rates include full country breakfast
(except cottage). AE, MC, V. Take Central Mt. Shasta exit off I-5 to W. A. Barr Rd.

Mt. Shasta Ranch offers one of the best deals anywhere: as low as $50 for a room
(most with mountain views) *including* a big country breakfast. The ranch was conceived and built by one of the country's most famous horse trainers and racing tycoons, H. D. ("Curley") Brown, in 1923 as the centerpiece of a private retreat and
thoroughbred horse ranch. Despite the encroachment of nearby buildings, the main
house and its annex are still available as a cozy B&B with touches of nostalgia and
the occasional antique. Four bedrooms (the ones with huge private baths) lie in the
main house; the remaining five share two bathrooms in the carriage house. It's a 30-
minute trek to the shores of nearby Lake Siskiyou, or you could stay here to enjoy
the hot tub, Ping-Pong and pool tables, or large veranda.

Mountain Air Lodge. 1121 S. Mt. Shasta Blvd., Mount Shasta, CA 96067. ☎ **916/
926-3411.** 38 rms. A/C TEL TV. $42–$125 double. AE, DC, DISC, MC, V.

As you drive into the town of Mount Shasta you see a row of cheap, mostly dingy
motels. The best of the lot is the Mountain Air Lodge, a sprawling green-on-green
motel mercifully shaded from the heat by a small cadre of pines. The rooms, tucked
well away from the main road, aren't worth writing home about, but they're big,
clean, and come with all the standard trappings such as cable TV, air-conditioning,
and a telephone. The clincher, though, is the enormous 8-by-14-foot Jacuzzi, just
the ticket after a long day of hiking or skiing. Skiers should inquire about special
lodging/lift ticket packages. Ping-Pong and pool tables within the main lobby provide nighttime entertainment.

Railroad Park Resort. 100 Railroad Park Rd., Dunsmuir, CA 96025. ☎ **916/235-4440.** Fax
916/235-4470. 28 rms, 4 cabins. A/C TEL TV. $60–$85 double. Additional person $5. AE, DISC,
MC, V. Take Railroad Park Exit off I-5, 1 mile south of Dunsmuir.

Lying ¹/₄ mile from the Sacramento River, this is an offbeat accommodation that kids enjoy. It's located at the foot of Castle Crags and contains several facilities—a restaurant and lounge, campground and RV park, and fishing ponds as well as the caboose motel. The railroad cabooses have been converted into rooms, leaving their pipes, ladders, and lofts in place. They're furnished with modern brass beds, table and chairs, dressers, and TV. They're located round the fenced-in kidney-shaped pool and whirlpool. The restaurant and lounge are also in vintage railroad cars.

Stewart Mineral Springs Resort. 4617 Stewart Springs Rd., Weed, CA 96094. ☎ **800/322-9223** or 916/938-2222. 3 teepees suitable for 1–4 persons; 4 dorm rooms suitable for 1–4; 6 motel rooms suitable for 1–2; 5 cabins with kitchens for 1–4; 1 large A-frame house suitable for 10–15 persons. $15 teepee for 1, $5 for additional persons up to 4; $30 dorm room for 1, $10 for additional persons up to 4; $37.50 motel room for 2; $45 cabin with kitchen for 2; $300 A-frame house for up to 15. MC, V. Closed Dec 1–Mar 1 or even later, if snows delay the reopening.

Stewart Mineral Springs is one of the most unusual health spas in California, loaded with lore and legends while making few concessions to modernity. It lies above coldwater springs that Native Americans valued for their healing powers. Don't expect anything approaching a European spa or big-city luxury here. Established in 1875, the site is deliberately rustic, with as few intrusions from the urban world as possible (no phones or TVs). Designed in a somewhat haphazard compound of about a dozen buildings, 4 miles west of the town of Weed, it occupies a 37-acre site of sloping, forested land accented with ponds, gazebos, and decorative bridges, and riddled with hiking and nature trails and freshwater streams. There are no restaurants on site.

Activities revolve around hiking, nature-watching, and taking the healing waters of the legendary springs. The bathhouse is the curative headquarters of the resort, and contains 13 private cubicles where water from the springs is heated and run into tubs for soaking. A staff member will describe the rituals involved in the immersion process: A 20-minute soak is followed with a visit to a nearby sauna, and an immersion in the chilly waters of Parks Creek, just outside the bathhouse. Other feel-good options include massages ($30 per half-hour session), herbal body wraps ($65 for a 90-minute experience), and facials ($15).

If you come here for the R&R, you won't be alone. Despite its rusticity, young Hollywood has discovered the place, including many soap-opera actors, members of the San Francisco 49ers, and local newscasters.

Ⓢ Stoney Brook Inn. 309 W. Colombero, P.O. Box 1860, McCloud, CA 96057. ☎ **800/369-6118** or 916/964-2300. 12 rooms, 6 suites. $20–$75 double. Additional person $8. MC, V. Take Calif. 89 east from I-5.

One of the few budget B&Bs in California and a highly recommended alternative to staying in Mount Shasta, the Stoney Brook Inn offers bunks for as low as $20 a night up to fully equipped kitchen suites for as little as $70. The former boarding house, located a few miles southeast of Mt. Shasta in the quiet little town of McCloud, pampers its guests with an outdoor hot tub and sauna, a wonderful pine-shaded wraparound porch, and a big ole fireplace for those chilly nights. Also part of the inn is Simply Vegetarian!, an organic vegetarian restaurant (the Stoney Brook is a meat-free environment), and a traditional Native American Sweat Lodge for those in need of purification and healing. Ski packages are also available.

Doubles for $80 or Less

Best Western Tree House. I-5 and Lake St. (P.O. Box 236), Mount Shasta, CA 96067. ☎ **800/545-7164** or 916/926-3101. Fax 916/926-3542. 95 rms. A/C TEL TV. $66–$149 double. AE, CB, DC, MC, V.

Just off the main highway, this motor inn offers rooms that are typically furnished with Scandinavian-style furnishings. Some accommodations have decks and refrigerators, which make them a family favorite. Facilities include a rustic dining room and lounge with a stone fireplace. There's also a huge indoor pool that's usually deserted, as well as an exercise room. Frankly, this is the best place to stay in the town of Mount Shasta far superior to its two main competitors, Finlandia and Swiss Holiday Lodge, and it keeps its prices low. Downhill and cross-country skiing is possible within a 10-mile drive.

😊 **McCloud Guest House.** 606 W. Colombero Dr. (P.O. Box 1510), McCloud, CA 96057. ☎ **916/964-3160.** 5 rms. $80–$95 double. Rates include continental breakfast. MC, V.

A veranda wraps around this bungalow-style house with dormer windows that is set among oak and pine trees on the lower slopes of Mt. Shasta, off Calif. 89, west of McCloud. The house was built in 1907 as a residence for the president of the McCloud River Lumber Company. In 1984 innkeepers Bill and Patti Leigh and Dennis and Pat Abreu restored it to fine condition. Upstairs there's a large comfortable parlor for guests with a pool table. Off the parlor are the five individually decorated rooms with white iron beds. Three of the rooms have claw-foot tubs and two have shower only.

On the ground floor there's a pleasant dining room with leaded- and stained-glass interior decoration. The menu offers a fine selection of Italian chicken, veal, pasta, and seafood dishes.

Wagon Creek Inn. 1239 Woodland Park Dr., Mount Shasta, CA 96067. ☎ **800/995-9260** or 916/926-0838. Fax 916/926-0855. 3 rms (1 with bath). $65 double without bath; $75 double with bath. Rates include continental breakfast. MC, V. From I-5 take the Central Mt. Shasta exit to Old Stage Rd. Turn right to Woodland Park Dr.

Loretta Lynn would feel at home in one of these country-style rooms within a log cabin home, located about 2¹/₂ miles from Mt. Shasta. The King Room has its own bath; the other two share. Guests can use the living room with fireplace, TV, and VCR. It's a homey, inexpensive place where pets, kids, and climbers are welcome.

WHERE TO DINE

Meals for $10 or Less

⑤ **The Bagel Cafe and Bakery.** 105 E. Alma St., Mount Shasta. ☎ **916/926-1414.** Main courses $4–$8. No credit cards. Daily 6:30am–9pm. AMERICAN.

This is the hands-down winner for a low-cost meal in Mount Shasta. Packed daily with locals, the lively little cafe serves the best coffee in the region, as well as wonderful vegetarian pizzas, soups, salads, sandwiches, and dinner plates, such as wok-fried veggies with tofu served over brown rice. Meat-eaters are welcome, too; try the fresh trout amandine with garlic butter and brown rice for only $7.95. Brunch is served daily until 3:30pm, and dinner starts at 4:30.

Wendie's Italian Restaurant. 610 S. Mt. Shasta Blvd., Mount Shasta. ☎ **916/926-4047.** Main courses $7–$15. AE, DISC, MC, V. Daily 6am–8:30pm. ITALIAN.

We don't know who Wendie is, but we know she thinks big. Her pancakes literally hang over the plate, and her house-made raviolis don't come in small portions either. Locals like to start their mornings here and head of to work with a slice of fresh pie in hand (her pies are supposedly legendary). Don't expect this place to be discovered by Julia Child anytime soon, but if your looking for hefty portions of good food at great prices, Wendie will take care of you.

Meals for $20 or Less

✪ **Lily's.** 1013 Mount. Shasta Blvd., Mount Shasta. ☎ **916/926-3372.** Reservations recommended. Main courses $9.50–$16. MC, V. Mon–Fri 7am–9pm, Sat–Sun 7am–9:30pm. ITALIAN.

Set within a white-clapboard, turn-of-the-century house in a residential neighborhood south of the town center, this friendly little restaurant—arguably the best in town—has porch and garden with fabulous view of Mt. Shasta. It's popular for breakfast, where chunky breads, omelets, potato pancakes, and enormous breakfast burritos start the morning off right. Lunch and dinner dishes lean toward seafood and pasta with a Venetian flair.

Michael's. 313 N. Mt. Shasta Blvd., Mount Shasta. ☎ **916/926-5288.** Main courses $13–$17. AE, MC, V. Tues–Fri 11am–2:30pm and 5–9pm, Sat noon–9pm. ITALIAN/AMERICAN.

Since 1980 Michael and Lynn Kobseff have enjoyed a devoted following of Shasta locals at their small but venerable restaurant. It stands across from a Hallmark store, in the midst of the town's main commercial street. The menu offers a variety of worthy Italian dishes along with steaks. Among the pasta dishes, opt for the manicotti or the cannelloni alla romana, with veal, chicken, spinach, and cheese in a marinara sauce. Dinners include soup, salad, garlic bread, and coffee. Thursdays, Fridays, and Saturdays feature Prime Rib Night.

MCARTHUR-BURNEY FALLS MEMORIAL STATE PARK

From Mt. Shasta, Calif. 89 east loops back south to ✪ **McArthur-Burney Falls Memorial State Park** (☎ **916/335-2777**), and eventually leads into Lassen Volcanic National Park. One of the spectacular features of this 768-acre park is a waterfall that cascades over a 129-foot cliff. Theodore Roosevelt once called the falls "the eighth wonder of the world." Giant springs lying a few hundred yards upstream feed the falls and keep them flowing, even during California's legendary dry spells.

The 1/2-mile **Headwater Trail** will take you to a good vantage point above the falls. If you're lucky you can observe the black swift that nest in the mossy crevices behind the cascade. Other birds to look for include barn and great horned owls, the belted kingfisher, the common flicker, and even the Oregon junco. The year-round park also has a mile-long nature trail, 128 campsites, picnicking grounds, and good fishing for bass, brown trout, rainbow trout, and brook trout. For camping reservations, call **800/444-7275.**

From here, Lassen Volcanic National park lies about 40 miles south.

3 Lassen Volcanic National Park

by Andrew Rice

Lassen Volcanic National Park is a remarkable reminder that North America is still forming, and that the ground below is alive with the forces of creation and, sometimes, destruction. Lassen Peak is the southernmost peak in a chain of volcanoes (including Mount St. Helens) that stretches all the way from British Columbia.

Though it's dormant, Lassen Peak is still very much alive. It last awakened in May 1914, beginning a cycle of eruptions that spit lava, steam, and ash until 1921. The eruption climaxed in 1915 when Lassen blew its top, sending a mushroom cloud of ash 7 miles high that was seen from hundreds of miles away. The peak itself has been dormant for nearly a century now, but the area still boils with a ferocious intensity: Hot springs, fumaroles, and mudpots are all indicators that Lassen hasn't had its last word. Monitoring of geothermal features in the park shows that they are getting hotter, not cooler, and some scientists take this as a sign that the next big eruption in the Cascades is likely to happen here.

Until then, the park gives visitors an interesting chance to watch a landscape recover from the massive destruction brought on by an eruption. To the northeast of Lassen Peak is the aptly named Devastated Area, a huge swath of volcanic destruction steadily repopulating with conifer forests. Botanists have revised their earlier theories that forests must be preceded by herbaceous growth after watching the Devastated Area immediately revegetate with a diverse mix of different conifer species.

The 106,000-acre park is a place of great beauty. The flora and fauna here is an interesting mix of species from the Cascade Range, which stretches north from Lassen, and species from the Sierra Nevada, which stretches south. The resulting blend accounts for an enormous diversity of plants; 715 distinct species have been identified in the park. Though it is snowbound in winter, Lassen is an important summer feeding ground for transient herds of mule deer and numerous black bears.

In addition to the volcano and all its geothermal features, Lassen Volcanic National Park includes miles of hiking trails, huge alpine lakes, large meadows, cinder cones, lush forests, a cross-country skiing, and great camping. Only one major road, Calif. 89 (the Park Road), crosses the park in a 39-mile half-circle with entrances and visitor centers at either end. Three-quarters of the park is designated wilderness.

SEEING THE HIGHLIGHTS

The highlight of Lassen is, of course, the volcano and all of its offshoots: hot springs, fumaroles, and mud pots. You can see many of the most interesting sites in a day, making it possible to visit Lassen as a short detour from I-5 or U.S. 395 on the way to or from Oregon. Available at park visitors centers (see "Just the Facts," below), the *Road Guide to Lassen Park* is a great traveling companion that will explain a lot of the features you'll see as you traverse the park.

Bumpass Hell, a 1¹/₂-mile walk off the Park Road in the southern part of the park, is the largest single geothermal site in the park—16 acres of bubbling mud pots cloaked in a stench of rotten-egg-smelling sulfur. The name comes from an early Lassen traveler, Bumpass, who lost a leg after he took a shortcut through the area while hunting and plunged into a boiling pool. Don't make the same error.

Sulfur Works is another stinky, steamy example of Lassen's residual heat. Two miles from the southwest park exit, the ground roars with seething gases.

Boiling Springs Lake and **Devil's Kitchen** are two of the more remote geothermal sites; they're located in the Warner Valley section of the park, which can be reached by hiking from the main road or entering the park through Warner Valley Road from the small town of Chester.

SPORTS & ACTIVITIES

HIKING   Most Lassen visitors drive through in a day or two, see the geothermal hot spots, and move on. That leaves 150 miles of trails and expanses of backcountry to the few who take the time to get off-road. The *Lassen Trails* booklet available at the visitor centers (see "Just the Facts," below) gives good descriptions of some of the most popular hikes and backpacking destinations. Anyone spending the night in the backcountry must have a wilderness permit issued at the ranger stations.

Probably the most popular hike is the 2¹/₂-mile climb from the Park Road to the top of **Lassen Peak.** The trail may sound short, but it's steep and generally covered with snow until late summer. At 10,457 feet in elevation, though, you'll get a view of the surrounding wilderness that's worth every step. On clear days you can see south all the way to the Sierra and north into the Cascades.

Lassen Volcanic National Park

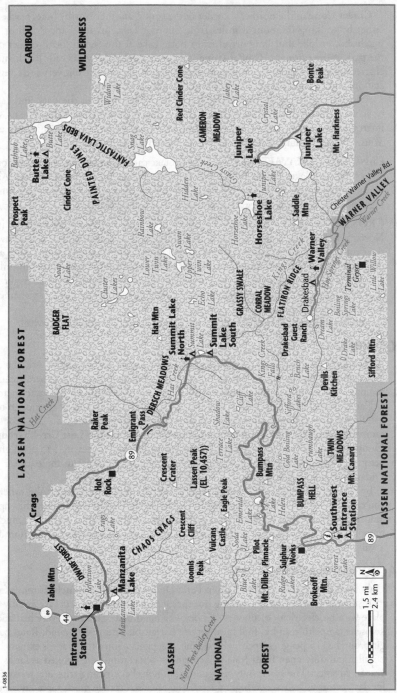

Cinder Cone in the northeast corner of the park is another worthy hike, reached either by walking in about 8 miles from Summit Lake on the Park Road, or a much shorter hike (but long drive) from Butte Lake at the far northeast corner of the park. Now dormant, Cinder Cone is approximately 250 years old. Black and charred-looking, Cinder Cone is bare of any sort of life (aside from very little vegetation) and surrounded by dunes of multihued volcanic ash.

A 17-mile segment of the **Pacific Crest Trail** cuts through the park and can be accessed via the Warner Valley Road or by a long hike from Hat Lake. The most interesting section of the trail for nonthrough hikers is the 5-mile segment south of Warner Valley leading to Boiling Springs Lake and Terminal Geyser.

CANOEING & KAYAKING   Paddlers can take canoes, rowboats, and kayaks on any of the park lakes except Reflection, Emerald, Helen, and Boiling Springs. All motors are strictly prohibited on all park waters. Park lakes are full of trout and fishing is popular. You must have a current California fishing license.

CROSS-COUNTRY SKIING   The park road usually closes due to snow in November, and most years it doesn't open until June, so cross-country skiers have their run of the park. Marked trails of all skill levels leave from Manzanita Lake at the north end of the park and Lassen Chalet at the south. You can ski the 30-mile course of the road in a long day or easy overnight. For safety reasons the park requires all skiers to register at the ranger stations before heading into the backcountry whether for an overnight or just the day.

Park staff also lead snowshoe hikes emphasizing ecology and winter survival.

CAMPING

Backcountry camping is allowed almost everywhere, and traffic is light. Ask about closed areas when you get your wilderness permit. If the park is packed, there are 43 campgrounds in surrounding Lassen National Forest, so you'll find a site somewhere.

Car campers have their choice of seven park campgrounds, more than enough to handle the half-million visitors who come to Lassen every summer. So few people camp in Lassen that there is no reservation system except for the **Lost Creek Group Campground,** and stays are granted a generous 14-day limit. Fees are $45 per night per group. Sites do fill up on weekends so your best bet is to get to the park early Friday to secure a place to stay.

By far the most "civilized" campground in the park is at **Manzanita Lake,** where you can find hot showers, flush toilets, and a camper store. When Manzanita fills up, rangers open the **Crags Campground** overflow camp about 5 miles away. It is much more basic. On the southern end of the park you'll find **Southwest Campground,** a walk-in camp directly adjacent to the Lassen Chalet parking lot.

ACCOMMODATIONS

Only one lodge operates within Lassen Park: **Drakesbad Guest Ranch.** Famous for its rustic cabins, lodge, and steaming hot spring pool, Drakesbad is deluxe as only a place with no electricity or phones can be, with handmade quilts on every bed and kerosene lamps to read by. Full meal service is available and is very good. Rates begin around $115 per guest, per night, double occupancy. Since the lodge is extremely popular and only open from June to September, reservations are booked as far as a year in advance. The spa is only for guests, but horseback riding trips are available for day visitors as well as overnight guests. You can also arrange meals for a day visit. Contact the **California Parks Co.,** 2150 N. Main St. No. 5, Red Bluff, CA 96080 (☎ **916/529-3376,** or 916/529-1512 in the off-season).

JUST OUTSIDE THE PARK

$ **The Bidwell House.** 1 Main St., P.O. Box 1790, Chester, CA 96020. ☎ **916/238-3338.**
14 rms (12 with private bath), 1 cottage with kitchenette. $60–$65 double without bath; $78–
$115 double with bath; cottage $153 for two. Rates include full breakfast. MC, V.

In 1901, Gen. John Bidwell, a California senator who made three unsuccessful bids
for the U.S. presidency, built a country retreat and summer home for his beloved
young wife, Annie. Although he died before ever living in the house, Annie eventually moved here and used it as a base for missionary work, converting scores of local
Native Americans to Christianity. After her death, when Chester had developed into
a prosperous logging hamlet, the building, with its farmhouse-style design and spacious veranda, was converted into the headquarters for a local ranch.

Today, the house sits at the extreme eastern end of Chester, adjacent to a rolling
meadow. The lake is visible across the road, and inside, Ian and Kim James maintain one of the most charming B&B inns in the region. Seven of the rooms have
Jacuzzi tubs, and two offer wood-burning stoves. Breakfast is presented with fanfare
and incorporates many gourmet touches, including home-baked breads and scrumptious omelets.

JUST THE FACTS

Most visitors enter the park at the Southwest Entrance Station, drive through the
park, and leave through the Northwest Entrance, or vice versa. Two other entrances
lead to remote portions of the park. Warner Valley is reached from the south on the
road from Chester. Butte Lake entrance is reached by a cut-off road from Calif. 44
between Calif. 89 and Susanville.

Ranger stations are clustered near each entrance and provide the full spectrum of
interpretive displays, ranger-led walks, informational leaflets, and emergency help.
The largest visitor center is located just outside the northwest entrance station before
Manzanita Lake. The park information number for all requests is **916/595-4444;** or
write **Lassen Volcanic National Park,** P.O. Box 100, Mineral, CA 96063-0100.

Because of the dangers posed by the park's thermal features, rangers ask that you
remain on trails at all times. Fires are allowed in campgrounds only; please make sure
they are dead before leaving them. Mountain bikes are prohibited on all trails.

Lassen is one of the least-visited parks in the Lower 48, so crowd control isn't as
big a consideration here as in other places. Unless you're here on the Fourth of July
or Labor Day Weekend, you won't encounter anything that could rightly be called
a crowd. Even then you can escape the hordes simply by skipping the popular sites
like Bumpass Hell or the Sulfur Works and heading a few miles down any of the
backcountry trails.

Modoc County (Lassen National Park does not lie in Lassen County) is one of the
coldest places in California. Winter begins in late October and doesn't release its grip
until June. Even in the summer you should plan for possible rain and snow. Temperatures at night can drop below freezing at any time. Winter, however, shows a
different and beautiful side of Lassen that more people are starting to appreciate. Since
most of the park is over a mile high and the highest point is 10,457 feet high, snow
accumulates in incredible quantities. Don't be surprised to find snowbanks lining the
Park Road into July.

4 Lake Tahoe

Lake Tahoe has long been California's most popular recreational playground. In summer you can enjoy boating and water sports, plus in-line skating, bungee jumping,

camping, ballooning, horseback riding, bicycling, parasailing, kayaking—the list is endless. In the winter, Lake Tahoe is transformed into a premier ski destination with its 13 downhill resorts and 15 cross-country skiing centers. There's also sleigh riding, ice-skating, snowmobiling, and increasingly, snowshoeing. Year-round activities include tennis, fishing, Vegas-style gambling, and big-name entertainment on the Nevada border. And that's not the half of it.

Then there's the lake. It's disputable whether Lake Tahoe is the most beautiful lake in the world, but it's certainly near the top of the list. It's famous for its 99.997% pure water (a white dinner plate at a depth of 75 feet would be clearly visible from the surface), and so immense that the water it contains—close to 40 trillion gallons—could cover the entire state of California with 14^1/$_2$ inches of water. Its average depth is 989 feet, although it reaches 1,645 feet in places, making it the second deepest lake in the United States (after Crater Lake in Oregon) and the eighth deepest in the world.

More important to the visitor, however, is the region's pristine beauty: The color of the lake oscillates throughout the day between a dazzling emerald and rich blues and purples; the snowy mountain tops reflecting off the water; the fresh, crisp air; and the deep green of the pine trees carpeting the expanse of the valley. It's a sight that no one should miss, and one that nobody forgets.

Though the private homes surrounding the lake are reserved for the wealthy—the price tag of most lakefront abodes starts in the millions—Lake Tahoe is by no means solely a rich person's retreat. Droves of college students on extended sabbatical account for a healthy portion of the population. As a result, cheap cafes and coffee houses catering to underpaid "lifties" (ski lift operators) and rafting guides line both ends of the lake, and a slew of inexpensive hotels continues to be built for the thousands of gamblers who make the pilgrimage here year-round.

So, what we're trying to say is that you don't need a bundle of cash to have a good time in Tahoe. What's more, some of the best things to see and do around the lake—hiking, mountain biking, cross-country skiing—are free. The trick is to know where to stay, eat, and play.

ESSENTIALS

GETTING THERE   From San Francisco (a 4-hour drive), take I-50 through Sacramento to the lake's south shore or I-80 to Calif. 89 to reach the lake's north shore. From Los Angeles, it's a grueling nine-hour drive; take I-5 through the San Joaquin Valley to I-80. If the weather is good and you can spare a few additional hours, it's really worth avoiding the interstate for the scenic drive on U.S. 395 and U.S. 50, which lie along the corridor between the towering peaks of the eastern Sierra and the Inyo Mountain Range.

Reno/Tahoe International Airport, 40 miles northeast of Lake Tahoe (about a 50-minute drive from the southern shore), offers regularly scheduled service from 13 national airlines, including **American** (☎ 800/433-7300), **Delta** (☎ 800/221-1212), and **United/United Express** (☎ 800/241-6522). **Trans World Express** (☎ 800/221-2000) has direct flights daily from many cities, including Los Angeles and San Francisco, to the tiny **South Lake Tahoe Airport** (☎ **916/542-6180**), just south of town, but these flights are usually very expensive.

Amtrak (☎ **800/USA-RAIL**) services Truckee, 10 miles north of the lake; shuttle service is available to North Lake Tahoe from the station. Trains connect with the rest of the state through Sacramento.

VISITOR INFORMATION   Call the **Tahoe North Visitors and Convention Bureau** in Tahoe City (☎ **800/824-6348** or 916/583-3495), or stop by the **North**

Lake Tahoe Chamber of Commerce, 245 North Lake Blvd., Tahoe City (☎ 916/581-6900). It's open Monday through Friday from 8:30am to 5pm, Saturday and Sunday from 9am to 4pm.

In South Lake Tahoe, contact the **South Lake Tahoe Visitors Authority,** 1156 Ski Run Blvd. (☎ 800/288-2463 or 916/544-5050), or the **South Lake Tahoe Chamber of Commerce,** 3066 Lake Tahoe Blvd. (☎ 916/541-5255), which is open Monday through Friday from 8:30am to 5pm and Saturday from 9am to 4pm (it's closed on major holidays).

NORTH SHORE VS. SOUTH SHORE

You wouldn't think the people and places on one end of the lake would be much different from the other, but ask any local: North Lake Tahoe and South Lake Tahoe, the two main destinations, have about as much in common as snow cones and sand castles. Don't let the "City" in North Shore's "Tahoe City" fool you: The entire town can be driven through in about 40 seconds. On the other hand, the South Shore is brimming with high-rise casinos, condominiums, and minimalls.

Which side you choose to stay on is important, because driving from one end of the lake to the other can be a two-hour affair on summer weekends and downright treacherous during snowstorms, so don't make the common mistake of thinking you can sleep for cheap on the South Shore and play all day on the North.

So which side is for you? If you're here to gamble, stay south: The selection of casinos is better and the lodging more abundant. If it's the great outdoors your after, or simply a little R&R under the shade of a Douglas fir, head north. Pound for pound, the North Shore offers a far better selection of quality lodgings, restaurants, and scenery, whereas the South Shore shoots for quantity, offering three times as many lodgings and restaurants at better rates.

SKIING & OTHER WINTER ACTIVITIES

Tahoe offers California's best skiing, with 13 downhill ski resorts and 15 cross-country centers. The ski season usually lasts from November to May, but frequently extends into summer—in 1993 and 1995 there was skiing until July 4th! Lift tickets usually cost about $42 per day, $30 per half day, and $6 for children under 13; midweek rates are often slightly lower. Five of the top areas—Alpine Meadows, Heavenly, Kirkwood, Northstar-at-Tahoe, and Squaw Valley—offer an interchangeable "Ski Lake Tahoe" lift pass for three to six days, which can be purchased at the Tahoe North Visitors and Convention Bureau (see above). Prices range from $132, for a three-day pass to $264 for six days. When used at one of the smaller resorts like Diamond Peak and Homewood, the pass buys two tickets for the price of one.

If you've come to ski, contact the visitors bureaus (see above) for information about ski packages offered by almost every hotel and resort on the lake—you're likely to save a bundle. The following are some of Tahoe's most popular resorts.

Alpine Meadows. P.O. Box 5279, Tahoe City, CA 96145. ☎ 800/441-4423 or 916/583-4232.

Six miles from Tahoe City, Alpine's high elevation (8,637 feet) gives it a long skiing season that lasts until Memorial Day. The midsized resort was ranked by readers of *Snow Country* as their favorite resort in California. It was the only major ski area left in Tahoe that didn't allow snowboarding. Alas, no longer: Snowboarding starts June 1, 1996. It's mainly a mountain for intermediate and advanced skiers, with 40% groomed for intermediate skiers, 35% for advanced, and 25% for beginners. There are no on-site lodgings or additional sports facilities.

Lake Tahoe & Environs

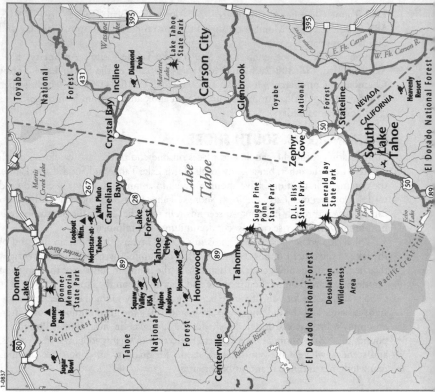

Diamond Peak. 1210 Ski Way, Incline Village, NV 89451. ☎ **702/832-1177** or 702/831-3249.

One of Tahoe's smaller, less-crowded and, most importantly, less expensive ski resorts, Diamond Peak plugs itself as the "premier family ski resort." Kids love the new snowboard park, and the Bee Ferrato Child Ski Center is one of the best on the lake. It's primarily a mountain for intermediates (49%), with 33% of the mountain groomed for advanced and 18% for beginners. The Peak recently installed the "Launch Pad," a carpeted conveyor belt that loads skiers on lifts more safely and efficiently—it was the first of its kind in North America. *Tip:* For a spectacular view of Lake Tahoe, head to the resort's mountain top Snowflake Lodge.

There's cross-country skiing, too, at a different location nearby, and lodging is available in Incline Village.

Heavenly Resort. P.O. Box 2180, Stateline, NV 89449. ☎ **702/586-7000.**

Celebrating its 40th anniversary, this South Lake Tahoe legend is one of the area's largest ski resorts, with 4,800 acres of ski terrain and snowmaking on 66% of the trails. The vertical drop is 3,500 feet, the steepest in the region. The terrain is 45% intermediate, 35% advanced, and 20% beginner. There are 25 lifts including a 50-passenger aerial tram and three high-speed detachable quads. It straddles the state borders. Heavenly West on the California side has easier trails than Heavenly North, which is predominantly intermediate territory. It's less crowded, however, on the Nevada side.

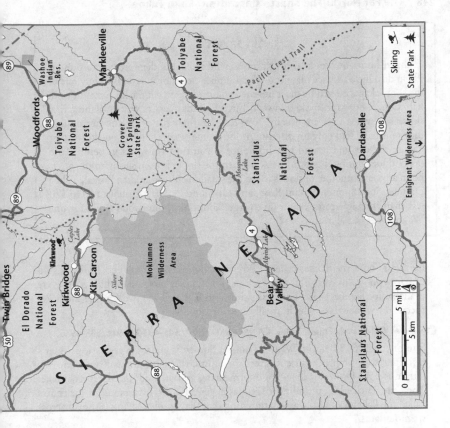

Kirkwood. P.O. Box 1, Kirkwood, CA 95646, off Calif. 88. ☎ **209/258-6000.**

Kirkwood's only drawback is that it's 30 miles (45 minutes) from South Lake Tahoe on Calif. 88; otherwise, this is one of the top ski areas in Tahoe, with the second-highest average snowfall after Squaw Valley (Alpine Meadows is third) and excellent spring skiing, which often runs into June. The 2,300 acres of skiable terrain is 50% intermediate, 35% advanced/expert, and 15% beginner. There are 11 lifts, including three triple chairs, accessing 65 trails.

Northstar-at-Tahoe. P.O. Box 129, Truckee, CA 96160. ☎ **800/466-6784** or 916/562-1010.

More than 50% snowmaking coverage and a full-time kids program make Northstar a top choice in Tahoe for families. It offers 2,000 acres of downhill skiing with 60 runs (half of which have snowmaking), 37 miles of cross-country trails, plus sleigh rides and snowmobiling. It has 12 lifts, including a six-passenger express gondola and four express quad chairs. Facilities include on-site lodging and five restaurants. It's only 45 minutes from the Reno-Tahoe airport.

Ⓢ Ski Homewood. P.O. Box 165, 5145 Westlake Blvd., Homewood, CA 95718. ☎ **916/525-2992.**

Homewood is one of my favorite small ski areas and one of the most affordable. It's a cozy, nostalgic little resort with lean lift lines and gorgeous views of the lake. Located 6 miles south of Tahoe City and 19 miles north of South Lake Tahoe on

---

Ski Savers

Yeah, we know, $42 for a ski lift ticket is awful steep, but there are ways around it if you do a little advance planning. The number-one money saver is to buy one of the ski packages offered by most hotels—you're likely to cut the lift ticket price in half. Other options are to ski midweek, buy a multiday pass, or wait until the spring ski season, when rates are usually 20% less. Half-day passes are another option; they're usually sold only for afternoons, but some resorts will let you ski the first half of the day and refund the difference if you turn your pass in before 1pm (a good idea during the spring season when the slopes get too slushy in the afternoon anyway). Another option is to ski the smaller, cheaper resorts: Boreal, Tahoe Donner, Soda Springs, Mount Rose, and Diamond Peak are all about $10 to $20 less than the big resorts. And don't forget about Ski Homewood's two-for-one Wednesdays (see above).

---

the West Shore, the ski area covers 1,260 acres and offers 57 trails and 10 lifts. Child care for two- to five-year-olds and a special ski and play program for kids 6 to 12 are available for families. Tip: The best ski deal in Tahoe is the two-for-one lift ticket special on Wednesdays, which usually start in January.

✪ **Squaw Valley USA.** Squaw Valley, CA 96146. ☎ **800/545-4350** or 916/583-6985.

Site of the 1960 Olympic Winter Games, Squaw is almost every serious skier's favorite resort, simply because it offers the most challenging array of runs. Squaw's terrain is 25% for beginners, 45% intermediate, and 30% advanced/expert/insane. There are 33 chairlifts, including a 120-passenger cable car. It's famous for the chutes called the Palisades and the acrobatic skiing that they inspire. Skiing is spread across six mountains.

The **Squaw Creek Cross-Country Ski Center** at the Resort at Squaw Creek (☎ **916/583-6300**) has 400 acres for touring and 28 miles of groomed trails.

Sugar Bowl. P.O. Box 5, Norden, CA 95724. ☎ **916/426-3651.**

Ranked by *Ski Magazine* in 1994 as one of the top 30 resorts in the nation, Sugar Bowl's *best* attribute is its location: If you're driving to Tahoe from the Bay Area via I-80, it's about an hour's drive closer than Squaw Valley. Known for its deep snowpack and powder skiing, the midsized resort has 58 runs serviced by eight lifts. Whether it's worth the drive from the lake is questionable, but anyone coming up from the valley should seriously consider this one. Should you choose to stay, lodging is available at the base of the resort.

CROSS-COUNTRY SKIING   Though it's a bit of a drive from South Lake, **Sorenson's Resort** in Hope Valley offers some of the best free cross-country skiing in the region. More than 60 miles of trials wind through the Toiyabe National Forest; lessons, rentals, tours, and trail maps are also available at the Hope Valley Cross-Country Ski Center, located within Sorenson's Resort. From U.S. 50 in Myers, take Calif. 89 South over the Luther Pass to the Calif. 88/89 intersection. Turn left then continue 1/2 mile to Sorenson's. For more information, call the **Ski Center** at **916/694-2266.**

Lakeview Cross Country (☎ **916/583-9353**) has 37 miles of groomed trails, a full-service day lodge, and three warming huts. It's only 2 miles from Tahoe City off Calif. 28 at Dollar Point Shell, making it very accessible.

The **Royal Gorge Cross-Country Ski Resort,** Soda Springs (☎ 800/500-3871 or 916/426-3871), is one of the largest cross-country facilities anywhere, with 88 trails (203 miles), including 28 novice trails and four ski lifts. Facilities include a day lodge and two wilderness lodges; ski school; 10 warming huts; and four trailside cafes. It's 1 mile off I-80 at the Soda Springs exit.

Sugar Pine Point State Park (☎ 916/525-7982) has cross-country skiing on well-maintained trails.

ICE-SKATING   One of the world's most unusual ice rinks is 8,200 feet above sea level at **Squaw Valley's High Camp** (☎ 916/583-6985). The open-air, tent-covered rink, which provides a wonderful view of the lake, is accessible only by cable car, a scenic ride that's included with rink admission. Skating costs about $20 for adults, $10 for children, including cable-car ride and skate rentals. After 4pm the prices drop to $9 for adults and $6 for children. The rink is open year-round, daily from 10am to 9pm. Call first, as the rink closes a few days in the spring and fall for repairs and hours may vary according to demand.

SUMMER ACTIVITIES

BICYCLING   There are miles of paved bike paths around the lake. The 3.4-mile Pope-Baldwin Bike Path on the south shore runs parallel to Calif. 89 and through Camp Richardson and the Tallac Historic Site. Another paved path in South Lake Tahoe runs from El Dorado Beach along the lake paralleling U.S. 50. Along the west shore there are 15 miles of paved pathways, extending from Tahoe City in three directions. On the northeast shore, Incline Village also has a 2¹/₂-mile trail from Gateway Park on Calif. 28.

You can rent bikes in Tahoe City at **Porter's Ski and Sport,** 501 N. Lake Blvd. (☎ 916/583-2314), and at the other **Porter's** in Incline Village, 885 Tahoe Blvd. (☎ 702/831-3500). In South Lake Tahoe go to **Anderson's Bike Rental** on the lake side of Calif. 89 at 13th Street (☎ 916/541-0500). Bike rentals usually cost $4 per hour, $11 for 4 hours, and $18 a day.

BOAT RENTALS   Several companies rent a variety of boats—canoes, power boats, and pedal boats. Among them are: **Zephyr Cove Resort Marina** (☎ 702/588-3833), which rents all three; **Paradise Watercraft** at Camp Richardson Resort (☎ 916/541-7272); **Tahoe Keys Boat Rentals** at Tahoe Keys Marina (☎ 916/544-8888 or 916/541-8405), which only rents power boats, and **North Tahoe Marina,** Calif. 28, 1 mile west of Calif. 267, Tahoe Vista (☎ 916/546-8248), which rents skis and tow lines along with 18- to 21-foot motor boats. Canoes and kayaks, far cheaper and more environmentally friendly, can be rented from **Tahoe Paddle and Oar** in Tahoe City (☎ 916/581-3029).

FISHING   Fishing in the crystalline clear waters of the lake presents a special challenge to anglers. Deep-water fishing for mackinaw trout is good year-round. Surface fishing for Kokanee salmon is best in May and June, whereas fishing for rainbow trout is ideal in the fall and winter months.

There are dozens of charter companies offering daily excursions on Lake Tahoe year-round. **Mickey's Big Mack Charters,** Tahoe City (☎ 800/877-1462 after 6pm, or 916/546-4444), is a well-respected outfit, led by experienced guide Mickey Daniels. All the fishing gear is provided, but you'll need a license, which can be purchased on the boat. Call for requirements and reservations. Mickey's boats depart from Sierra Boat Co., in Carnelian Bay, about 5 miles north of Tahoe City. Five-hour trips cost $65 per person and depart daily, in the early morning and late afternoon; exact times vary according to season. Other fishing specialists include: **Blue Ribbon Fishing**

Charters, South Lake Tahoe (☎ 916/541-8801), and **Tahoe Sportfishing,** Ski Run Marina, 900 Ski Run Blvd., South Lake Tahoe (☎ 916/541-5448). Don't bother with the Truckee River; even the best anglers have been skunked there for years.

GOLF   There are two Robert Trent Jones Jr. championship courses in the area: **Incline Village Championship Course,** 955 Fairway Blvd. (☎ 702/832-1144), and **Squaw Creek Golf Course,** at the Resort at Squaw Creek (☎ 916/583-6300), which is the most expensive course ($115 on weekends) around Tahoe. Other challenging courses include the **Northstar Golf Course,** Basque Drive (☎ 916/562-2490) and South Lake's **Edgewood Tahoe,** site of the Isuzu Celebrity Gold Championship, with 18 holes and a driving range (☎ 702/588-3566). Budget golfers, however, will fare better at the **Old Brockway Golf Course** in Kings Beach ($25 for nine holes; ☎ 916/546-9909); **Tahoe City Golf Course** ($20 for nine holes; ☎ 916/583-1516); the **Incline Village Executive Golf Course** ($45 for 18 holes; ☎ 702/832-1150), a challenging little mountain course (pars three and four only); or **Lake Tahoe Golf Course** ($40 for 18 holes, no cart; ☎ 916/577-0788) on the South Shore. Also, most resorts offer lower rates during the week and also for "twilight golf," which usually begins around 5pm.

HIKING   The mountains surrounding Lake Tahoe are crisscrossed with hiking trails graded for all levels of experience. If a guided hike interests you, **Tahoe Trips and Trails** (☎ 800/581-HIKE or 916/583-4506). For $25 to $60 an expert mountaineer will take anyone, from Grandpa to Rambo, on a hike specifically suited to your ability, from supereasy to hard core. Everything is provided, including a gourmet vegetarian-friendly lunch, drinks, transportation, and answers to any question you have about the history and geology of Lake Tahoe. It's truly a great outfit that guarantees a good time at a fair price.

If you want to set off on your own, you may wish to contact the local visitors bureau for a map and more in-depth information on particular trails. Serious hikers and backpackers should consult *Outside Magazine's Adventure Guide to Northern California* for more extensive treks in the area.

One of the best trails for novice hikers, the **Eagle Falls** walk offers a cascading reward. The trail begins at Eagle Picnic Area, directly on Calif. 89 across from Emerald Bay.

From the parking area, 1¹/₂ miles above Tahoe's prettiest inlet, you can hike down to **Vikingsholm,** a 38-room replica of a medieval Scandinavian castle. The trail begins at the parking area on the north side of Emerald Bay, on Calif. 89.

An easy but beautiful walk to three lakes, the **Loch Levon Trail** is perfect for hikers who wish to stay on the beaten path. To reach the trailhead, take I-80 to the Big Bend exit and look for the sign Private Road Public Trail across from the Big Bend ranger station.

In Squaw Valley, near the tram line, the excellent **Shirley Lake** hike has the advantage of a one-way adventure; you can take the tram up and hike down or vice versa. The trail begins at the end of Squaw Peak Road, next to the tram building.

IN-LINE SKATING   Although there are trails all around Lake Tahoe, the best ones for blading are the well-paved paths that hug the Truckee River and Calif. 89, between Tahoe City and Squaw Valley (you'll see signs that say Bicycles and Pedestrians Only). Rollerblades and other in-line skates can be rented from the nearby **Squaw Valley Sport Shop,** Tahoe City (☎ 916/583-6278). The shop charges $5 per hour (a $10 minimum) or $15 a day (the price covers wrist guards and other protective gear). Squaw Valley is open Sunday through Thursday from 9am to 6pm, Friday and Saturday from 9am to 7pm.

JET-SKIING The **Lighthouse Watersports Center,** 950 N. Lake Blvd., Tahoe City (☎ **916/583-6000**), rents jet skis, paddle boats, and canoes during summer months only. Reservations are recommended for jet-ski rentals. Jet skis cost $35 per half hour and $60 per hour; paddle boats and canoes go for $15 per half hour and $20 for two hours. The water sports center is open June through September, daily from 9am to 6pm.

In South Lake Tahoe, the place to rent is **Lakeview Sports,** 3131 U.S. 50, across from the El Dorado Campground (☎ **916/544-0183** or 916/541-8405). They also rent mountain bikes, in-line skates, and boats.

MOUNTAIN BIKING At both **Northstar** (☎ **916/562-1010**) and **Squaw Valley** (☎ **916/583-6985**), you can ride the cable car with your bike and take the trails all the way down. Call for complete information.

The most famous ride in the area, however, is actually in Nevada: the scenic and challenging **Flume Trail.** Parts of this trail are grueling, but the flume itself is awesome: 4$^{1}/_{2}$ miles of perfect single track looking out over Lake Tahoe. It begins at Spooner Lake Park, located on Tahoe's eastern shore off Calif. 28. Try to ride it on a weekday; it gets jammed on the weekends.

RIVER RAFTING For the first time this decade the Truckee River in North Lake Tahoe is open to commercial rafting operations. After six years of drought, Lake Tahoe's only outlet is now dumping plenty of water for a mostly gentle, leisurely ride down the river. Rafts seat anywhere between 2 to 14 people and cost about $25 for adults and $20 for kids (no kids under five); the season runs from Memorial Day weekend to Labor Day (May to October). Rafting outfits include **Truckee River Raft Rental** (☎ **916/583-0123**), **Fanny Bridge Rafts** (☎ **916/581-0123**), or **Truckee River Rafting/Mountain Air Sports** (☎ **916/583-7238**).

TENNIS All the major resorts have tennis courts open to the public on a fee basis. Call the **Resort at Squaw Creek** (☎ **916/583-6300**) and **Northstar** (☎ **916/ 562-0321**) for information and reservations.

Budget-minded players looking for good local courts should visit Tahoe Lake School, on Grove Street in Tahoe City, where two lighted courts are available free, on a first-come, first-served basis. South Tahoe Intermediate School, Lyons Avenue, off U.S. 50, has eight lighted courts. It charges a manageable $3 per hour.

WATERSKIING **North Tahoe Marina,** Calif. 28, 1 mile west of Calif. 267, Tahoe Vista (☎ **916/546-8248**), rents skis and tow lines along with 18- to 21-foot motor boats. Other powerboat toys, including tubes, kneeboards, and wetsuits, are also available. Rates are $65 to $95 per hour. Open May 1 through October 1, daily from 8am to 6pm.

LAKE CRUISES

The best way to experience the lake is to get out on it. **MS *Dixie II,*** Zephyr Cove Marina, NV (☎ **702/588-3508**), a 570-passenger vessel with bars, a dance floor, and a full dining room, offers daily cruises year-round, which may include breakfast, champagne brunch, and dinner. Zephyr Cove Marina is on U.S. 50, 4 miles north of Stateline in South Lake Tahoe. Bay cruises cost $14 adults, $5 children 11 and under; breakfast and brunch cruises, $18 adults, $9 children 11 and under; dinner cruises, $26 to $36 adults, $10 children 11 and under. Call for schedules.

The *Tahoe Queen* (☎ **800/238-2463** or 916/541-3364), a 500-passenger stern-wheeler, operates year-round, offering daily Emerald Bay cruises, sunset dinner dance cruises, and shuttle service between the lake's north and south shores during the ski season. There are large outdoor and indoor viewing decks and a glass bottom for peering deep into the lake. The Emerald Bay Cruise costs $14 adults, $5 children 11 and under; dinner cruise, $18 adults, $9.50 children 11 and under (dinner optional, menu selections from $14.95); round-trip North/South Shore Ski Shuttle $18 adults, $9 children 11 and under. The *Tahoe Queen* departs from Ski Run Marina, just west of Stateline. Call to confirm rates and schedules.

The North Shore version of *Tahoe Queen* is the **Tahoe Gal** (☎ **800/218-2464** or 916/583-0141), a Mississippi River paddlewheeler that departs from the Lighthouse Marina in Tahoe City (behind Safeway). Cruises include Emerald Bay ($18 adult, $8 child), Champagne Breakfast ($15 adult, $5 child), Sunset Cocktail ($15 adult, $5 child), Dinner ($35 adult, $17 child), and Scenic Shoreline ($15 adult, $5 child).

Woodwind Sailing Cruises, in the Zephyr Cove Resort, on U.S. 50, Zephyr Cove, NV (☎ **702/588-3000**), operates daily sailing trips aboard a 41-foot trihull craft that takes up to 30 passengers. The boat's glass bottom allows for good underwater viewing. Reservations are recommended. Trips cost $14 adults, $7 children under 12, under 2 free. It leaves daily at 11:30am and 1, 2:30, and 4pm from April through October. There's also a sunset champagne cruise for $20 adults only.

A DRIVE AROUND THE LAKE

The next best way to contemplate the lake is to drive the 72 miles around it, though at times it can be completely clogged with traffic. Although the lake has never frozen over, the roads that surround it do; many are closed in winter, making this trip possible during the summer season only. If your car sports a tape player, consider buying *Drive Around the Lake,* an drive-along audio cassette that contains facts, tales and legends, places of interest, and just about everything else you could possibly want to know about the lake. It's available at numerous gift shops or at the **South Lake Tahoe Chamber of Commerce,** 3066 Lake Tahoe Blvd. (☎ **916/541-5255**), which is open Monday through Friday from 8:30am to 5pm and Saturday from 9am to 4pm (it's closed on major holidays).

We'll start at the California/Nevada border in South Lake Tahoe and loop around the western shore on Calif. 89 to Tahoe City and beyond. U.S. 50, which runs along the south shore, is an ugly strip of motels and overdevelopment that obliterates any view of the lake unless you're staying at one of these developments. Keep heading west and you're soon free of this ugly zone.

Our first stop is the **Tallac Historic Site,** a cluster of rustic mansions that were built 100 years ago and are currently being restored by the Forest Service. A little farther on you'll find the Forest Services' **Lake Tahoe Visitors Center** located along Taylor Creek, which offers nature trails and also an opportunity to view Kokanee salmon making their way upstream to spawn.

From here the highway climbs northward. Soon you'll be peering down into beautiful **Emerald Bay,** a 3-mile-long inlet containing tiny Fanette Island, which has an old stone teahouse clearly situated at its peak. It was built by Ms. Lora Knight, who also built Vikingsholm (see below).

Across Calif. 89 from Emerald Bay, there's another parking area. From here it's a short steep quarter-mile hike to a footbridge above Eagle Falls. Then it's about 1 mile to Eagle Lake. Register at the trailhead. **Emerald Bay State Park** (☎ **916/988-0205**) offers 100 camping sites on the south side of the bay.

It's not surprising that someone chose to build a mansion right here overlooking the bay. **Vikingsholm,** Emerald Bay, Calif. 89 (☎ **916/525-7277** or 916/525-7232), was built in 1929, a replica of a medieval Viking castle. It is so striking that a paved parking area on the highway had to be built for all the gawkers. Tree branches shaped like spears jut out from the gutters to ward off evil spirits. Inside carved dragon heads decorate the ceiling beams. A layer of sod blankets the roof,

Cheap Thrills: What to See & Do for Free (or Almost) in Tahoe

Nothing beats a cheap thrill, and Tahoe is loaded with them. Your most affordable adventures will inevitably involve getting outside and taking in the area's natural wonders. Take a drive around the lake, hike to a scenic vista and have a picnic lunch, soak up some rays on the beach. Whatever you choose to do, if it's a sunny day (and it probably will be), we promise you won't be disappointed. Here's some other inexpensive and offbeat things to do in and around Tahoe:

At the **Headwall Cafe and Climbing** (☎ 916/583-ROPE), at the base of the Squaw Valley Tram off Calif. 89 in Squaw Valley, you can test your strength on an artificial 30-foot climbing wall for a mere $7. A sturdy harness prevents you from falling, which makes it perfectly safe for kids (who usually out-climb the adults). It's an exhilarating challenge, and the best part is that absolutely no experience is necessary. Open daily year-round.

If you visit in winter and skiing just isn't in the budget, revisit the childhood thrill of **sledding.** On the South Shore the best place to go is directly across from the tiny South Lake Tahoe Airport, which is about a 15-minute drive south of town on U.S. 50. Park in the lot, cross the street, and start lugging your sled up the hill. The slope is small but it's fast, fun and free of trees.

Now that the lake is full again, tourists can partake in Tahoe's cheapest and most popular thrill of all: feeding the trout that hang out below **Fanny Bridge** (located at the intersection of Calif. 28 and Calif. 89 in Tahoe City). Bring bread or crackers and join the others leaning over the rail. If you step back and take a look, you'll know where the bridge got its name.

At some point during your visit you should get out on the water. We recommend trolling along the shores on a sit-on-top sea kayak. They're almost uncapsizable and require no previous experience; you'll discover places you'd never see otherwise. **Tahoe Paddle and Oar,** 7860 N. Lake Blvd, King's Beach (☎ 916/581-3029), and **Kayak Tahoe,** 1900 Jameson Rd., Camp Richardson (☎ 916/544-2011), both rent boats for about $10 to $15 per hour.

If you feel the urge for golf but don't have the time or the money, consider miniature golf. The Putt-Putt season in Tahoe runs from mid-May through September (depending on the weather). On the North Shore head for **Magic Carpet Golf** at Carnelian Bay, 5167 North Lake Blvd. (☎ 916/546-4279); on the South Shore, there's **Fantasy Kingdom Miniature Golf,** 4046 Lake Tahoe Blvd. (☎ 916/544-3833).

At the end of the day, soak yourself at the **North Tahoe Beach Center,** 7860 North Lake Blvd., Kings Beach (☎ 916/546-2566). Besides offering a full line of exercise equipment, the center also boasts the largest spa on the lake, some 26 feet in diameter—all this for $7. It's open daily from 10am to 10pm.

Another spa that's popular with the locals is **Walley's Hot Springs Resort** (☎ 702/782-8155). You'll need wheels to get there (it's located 2 miles north of the east end of Kingsbury Grade at 2001 Foothill Blvd. in Nevada), but it's worth the drive to indulge in their six open-air pools (each a bit warmer than the next) and massage center. Last we checked, admission was only $12.

---

which sprouts wild flowers in the spring. You can visit Vikingsholm by hiking down a steep 1¹/₂-mile trail (but remember, you have to come back, too). The mansion is open for tours, every hour on the half hour, during summer only. Admission is $2 adults, $1 children 6 to 17, free for kids 5 and under. It's open July to Labor Day daily 10am to 4pm.

From here it's only about 2 miles to **D. H. Bliss State Park** (☎ **916/525-7277**), where you'll find one of the lake's best beaches. It gets very crowded in summer, so get there early before all the parking places are occupied. The park also contains 168 campsites and several trails, including one along the shoreline.

About 7 miles farther on, **Sugar Pine Point State Park** (☎ **916/525-7982**) is the largest (2,000 acres) of the lake's parks and also the only one that has year-round camping. In summer there are several beaches in the park plus a nature trail; in winter there's cross-country skiing on well-maintained trails.

For a thrill, sign up with **Cal'Vada Aircraft** (☎ **916/525-7143**), and fly in their small planes, which take off and land on the lake. Trips range from 20 minutes to an hour. There's usually a two-person minimum for each tour, and the cost is anywhere from $50 to $90 a person. Call for reservations. The seaplane base is in **Homewood,** on the west shore of the lake, 6 miles south of Tahoe City.

It's a clear drive through the small town of Homewood (site of the ski resort of the same name) to **Tahoe City,** which is smaller and much more appealing than South Lake Tahoe, although it, too, has its share of strip development.

At Tahoe City, Calif. 89 turns off to **Truckee,** and to Alpine Meadows and Squaw Valley ski resorts. **Squaw Valley** is only 5 miles out, and a ride on the Squaw Valley cable car (☎ **916/583-6985**) rewards visitors with incredible vistas, summer or winter, from 2,000 vertical feet above the valley floor. In addition to the views, visitors can enjoy ice-skating, swimming, tennis, and bungee jumping at the High Camp Bath and Tennis Club. The cable car operates year-round daily from 8am to 4pm. A ticket costs $12 adults, $5 children 4 to 12, $9 seniors 65 and older, under 3 free. From Squaw Valley, it's another 5 or so miles to the gritty, but nevertheless charming railroad town of Truckee and **Donner State Park,** with its museum and monument to the Donner Party Expedition of 1846.

If you continue around the lake on Calif. 28, you'll reach Carnelian Bay, Tahoe Vista, and Kings Beach before crossing the state line into Nevada to Crystal Bay, Incline Village, the Ponderosa Ranch, and Sand Harbor Beach. **Kings Beach State Recreation Area** (☎ **916/546-7248**) is 12 miles east of Tahoe City and is jammed with sunbathers and swimmers in summer. At the border in Crystal Bay, take note of the Cal-Neva Lodge, a landmark hotel/casino whose property is divided by the state line and was once owned by Frank Sinatra. From **Incline Village,** often referred to as "Income Village" by locals because of its huge lakefront homes, take the 4-mile side trip up the Mt. Rose Highway to an awesome overlook of the entire Tahoe Basin.

Remember Hoss and Little Joe Cartwright? The ✪ **Ponderosa Ranch,** Calif. 28, Incline Village (☎ **702/831-0691**), is a decidedly hokey but fun theme park inspired by the popular 1960s television show *Bonanza.* The original 1959 Cartwright Ranch House can be visited along with a Western township complete with blacksmith's shop and staged gun battles. There are also such activities as pony rides and a petting farm. The barbecue grill is almost always fired up, and breakfast hayrides on tractor-pulled wagons are offered for an extra $2. Admission is $9.50 adults, $5.50 children 5 to 11, under 5 free. It's open mid-April to October only, daily 9:30am to 5pm.

Not far from Incline is **Sand Harbor,** one of the best beaches on the lake (though it can get incredibly crowded in summer). If you're visiting in August, try to get tickets to Sand Harbor's renowned Shakespeare festival.

From here, if you wish, you can turn inland to Spooner Lake and Carson City, capital of Nevada, or continue south along the highway to an outcropping called Cave Rock, where the highway passes through 25 yards of solid stone. Farther along is **Zephyr Cove,** from which the tour boats depart. You'll then return to Stateline and South Lake Tahoe, your original starting point.

WHERE TO STAY
OFF-SEASON DEALS

Spring and fall are Tahoe's slowest seasons, when the snow hasn't quite melted (or fallen) and the summer's heat has yet to arrive (or leave). It's the lull every Tahoe business owner dreads, but a boon for visitors looking to save a bundle. To drum up some business, the **Tahoe North Visitors and Convention Bureau** (☎ 800/824-6348 or 916/583-3495) has put together two fantastic packages: **Spring Fling** and **Fall in Tahoe.** Spring Fling offers two-for-one skiing at Alpine Meadows (consecutive days), two-for-one lodging, two-for-one dining, and even two-for-one coupons for bicycle, ski, snowboard, and in-line skate rentals, sightseeing tours, massages, and lake cruises—all starting at $70 per person from April 15 through June 14.

Available from October 1 through December 14 and staring at $89, Fall in Tahoe includes two nights lodging at economy inns, B&Bs, or gaming resorts; one dinner (from selection of great restaurants); one breakfast or lunch; and one activity of choice per person, which ranges from horseback riding to lake cruises and guided hikes.

SOUTH SHORE/SOUTH LAKE TAHOE
Doubles for $60 or Less

Chamonix Inn. 913 Friday Ave. (at Manzanita Ave.), South Lake Tahoe, CA 96150. ☎ **800/447-5353** or 916/544-5274. 32 rms. TEL TV. $35–$68 double. AE, DISC, MC, V.

Although it invokes about as much French atmosphere as a filet-o-fish sandwich, the Chamonix Inn is a budget skier's paradise. Start the day fueling up at the on-premises coffee shop, then walk 20 yards to the free ski shuttle stop. After a hard day of skiing, relax in the toasty spa, then gear up for a night of gambling, courtesy of another free shuttle. Summer seductions include access to a private beach and a heated pool. The rooms aren't anything special, but the beds are firm, the cable TV works, and the phone works. Skiers should definitely inquire about the Chamonix's ski packages.

Emerald Motel. 515 Emerald Bay Rd./Calif. 89, South Lake Tahoe, CA 96150. ☎ **916/544-5515.** 9 rms. TEL TV. $45–$55 double. MC, V.

If you prefer to stay on the South Shore but want to distance yourself from the hustle and bustle of the casinos, this small green-and-white motel on the west side of town is the budget-minded traveler's best option. The rooms are rather ordinary, but they are all clean and come with the basics—queen beds, cable TV, microwaves, and coffeemakers. For a few dollars more you can get a room with a kitchenette or fireplace, a real deal for Lake Tahoe. Although the downtown area is out of walking range, there are a handful of good, inexpensive restaurants just down the street, including Cantina Los Tres Hombres, a local favorite. Also within hoofing distance are all the major ski shuttle stops, a supermarket, and movie theater.

Lamplighter Motel. 4143 Cedar Ave., South Lake Tahoe, CA 96159. ☎ **916/544-2936.** Fax 916/544-5249. 28 rms. TEL TV. $36–$55 double. AE, DISC, JCB, MC, V.

A diamond in the rough, this family run motel is everything the budget traveler could hope for: clean, cozy, and loaded with perks such as cable TV, in-room coffeemaker, bathtub, and a ceiling fan. It's in a great spot, only three blocks from the beach and 50 yards from the casinos, but why you would ever want to leave the open-air spa and sundeck is beyond us. Be sure to inquire about the terrific ski packages, and request a room with air conditioning in summer.

Doubles for $80 or Less

Lakeland Village Beach and Ski Resort. 3535 Lake Tahoe Blvd. (between Ski Run Blvd. and Fairway Ave.), P.O. Box 1356, South Lake Tahoe, CA 96150. ☎ **800/822-5969** or 916/544-1685. Fax 916/541-3539. 212 units. A/C TEL TV. $75–$345 double. AE, MC, V.

One mile northeast of the casino district, off U.S. 50 and a mile from Heavenly Valley, this condo complex is clustered on 19 lightly forested acres. The complex was built in the 1970s as one of the region's most ambitious developments, but only 60 of them were bought by full- or part-time residents. The developers' solution involved transforming the remaining condos into a hybrid (half residential apartment complex, half holiday resort). Though most are priced far beyond the budget traveler's allowance, the studios can be had for a little as $75 a night, which includes all the same perks as the big boys.

When you check in, be prepared for a baffling choice of layouts, as the resort's staff will present an array of floor plans. The units, ranging from studios to four-bedroom lakeside apartments, are streamlined California architecture, and many have upstairs sleeping lofts. There are no restaurants on the premises, although complimentary shuttle buses carry gamblers to the nearby casinos; a grocery store is within walking distance; and all suites have fully equipped kitchens. Perks include two outdoor pools, three saunas, tennis and volleyball courts, bicycle rentals, a health club, a large private beach opening directly onto the lake, and access to a boat dock.

Richardson's Resort. Calif. 89 at Jamison Beach, South Lake Tahoe, CA 96158. ☎ **800/544-1801** or 916/541-1801. Fax 916/541-2791. 29 rms, 39 cabins. $64–$74 double; cabins $495–$1,095 per week. AE, MC, V.

Rich or poor, this is one of the most enjoyable places to stay in Lake Tahoe. The resort is an collection of real log cabins, condominiums, hotel rooms, and tent/RV sites spread out over several acres of wooded grounds adjacent to the beach. If you're staying only a few nights, book a room in the classic old lodge, but for longer stays, particularly with families or groups, the homey little cabins are the only way to go. Activities on the premises include tennis, volleyball, hiking, biking, horseback riding, cross-country skiing, and swimming and sunbathing. Nearby facilities include a bike rental shop, general store, ice cream parlor, boat/jet-ski/kayak rental shop, full-service marina, casino shuttle service, and one of the best restaurants on the lake, The Beacon.

NORTH SHORE/TAHOE CITY

Doubles for $60 or Less

Family Tree Restaurant and Motel. 551 N. Lake Blvd., P.O. Box 551, Tahoe City, CA 96145. ☎ **916/583-0287.** 10 rms. TV. $43–$60 double. MC, V.

Smack dab in the middle of Tahoe City, the Family Tree is obviously a restaurant first and a hotel second (guests must register with the cashier), but nobody complains because they know they're getting a great deal. The rooms are located behind the restaurant, each clean, comfy, and ordinary with optional air-conditioning and a choice of a queen bed or two doubles. The best part, of course, is the location: Not only is the entire town at your doorstep, but the trip from your bed to the breakfast table (try the biscuits and gravy) can be measured in feet. Make reservations early as possible, folks, because this place fills up fast.

Lake of the Sky Motor Inn. 955 N. Lake Blvd., P.O. Box 227, Tahoe City, CA 96145. ☎ **916/583-3305.** 23 rms. Apr 30–June 13 $50–$65 double; June 14–Sept 21 $74–$89 double; winter $50–$89 double. AE, CB, DC, DISC, MC, V.

Not much more than a 1960s-style A-frame motel in the heart of Tahoe City, this inn offers decent accommodations in a central location, only steps away from shops and restaurants. The place is popular with budget travelers and skiers, some of whom can be seen grabbing a very early morning cup of coffee, itching to get outside. Rooms throughout have almost no style, but the housekeeping is good and the comfort level in tiptop motor inn tradition. There's a heated swimming pool as well as a barbecue area.

North Lake Lodge. 8716 N. Lake Blvd., P.O. Box 955, Kings Beach, CA 96143. ☎ **916/546-2731.** 21 rms, 8 bungalows, 4 cabins. TV. Rms $50–$65; bungalows $50–$60; cabins $65–$75. AE, MC, V.

Sure, the private lakeside cabins at North Lake Lodge are a little on the funky side, but for only $65 a night most people are willing to put up with a few blemishes here and there. This is truly a great deal: each unit, some dating from the 1920s, has its own bath, deck, and picnic facilities, and most have fully equipped kitchens and views of the lake (units without kitchens have refrigerators and microwaves). If the cabins are all booked, go for the bungalows next, and as a last resort the rooms in the lodge. There's a public beach nearby (as well as a boat ramp), and in the winter free shuttle buses from Alpine Meadows, Squaw, and Northstar swing by. Be sure to bring a bag of charcoal for the lodge's barbecue pits, and some chump change for the nearby casinos. Another good reason to stay here? Pets are welcome.

Tamarack Lodge. 2311 N. Lake Tahoe Blvd., P.O. Box 859, North Lake Tahoe, CA 96145. ☎ **916/583-3350.** 21 rms, 4 cabins. TV. Rms $35–$65; cabins $45–$110. DISC, MC, V.

One of the oldest lodges on the North Shore—so old it was a favorite haunt of Clark Gable and Gary Cooper—is now one of the best bets for the cost-conscious traveler. Hidden among a cadre of pines just east of Tahoe City, the Tamarack Lodge consists of a few old cabins, five "poker rooms," and a modern (and far less nostalgic) motel unit. Rooms are spartan but clean; knotty pine dominates the decor. The cabins can hold up to four guests, but the most popular rooms by far are the hokey old poker rooms. Complimentary coffee and tea are served in the lobby, and rollaway beds are available for only $5 extra. Though the beach is within walking distance, you'll need a car to make forays into town.

Doubles for $80 or Less

Meeks Bay Resort. P.O. Box 411, Tahoma, CA 96142 (summer); P.O. Box 70248, Reno, NV 89570 (winter). ☎ **916/525-7242** (summer), or 702/829-1997 (winter). 21 units. TEL. $75 double per day, $575–$3,000 per week. No credit cards. Closed Oct 1 to Memorial Day weekend.

Lying 10 miles south of Tahoe City on Calif. 89, Meeks Bay Resort is one of the oldest hostelries on the lake and something of a historical landmark. This wide, sweeping lakefront curve fronts the best fine-sand beach in Tahoe. Known centuries ago to the Washoe Indians, Meeks Bay was opened as a public campground in 1920. During the next 50 years the resort grew to include cabins and other improvements, and attracted many celebrities from Southern California. Acquired by the U.S. Forest Service in 1974, the property is now operated under a special-use permit and is closed during the winter. Most rentals are on a weekly basis and consist of cabins both on the lake and on the adjacent hillside. Units vary in size, sleeping 2 to 12, and are modest without being austere. Each has a full kitchen, and some have fireplaces. Facilities include a beachfront cafe and canoe and kayak rentals.

Rodeway Inn. 645 N. Lake Blvd. (P.O. Box 29), Tahoe City, CA 96145. ☎ **800/624-8590** or 916/583-3711. 51 rms. TEL TV. $66–$87 double. AE, DC, DISC, MC, V.

If you're a Holiday Inn kind of person (no frills, no surprises) traveling on a Motel 6 kind of budget, the Rodeway Inn is for you. Two people can share a perfectly comfortable room for about $35 each, which includes access to a hot tub, heated outdoor pool with sundeck, free shuttle service to the major ski resorts, and all the cable channels you could want. The location, right in the middle of Tahoe City, is great, but where the Rodeway Inn really shines is with its generous ski packages: For under $60 you can score a room and an all-day lift ticket to Alpine Meadows or Squaw Valley (Sunday through Thursday only).

WHERE TO DINE
SOUTH SHORE/SOUTH LAKE TAHOE
Meals for $10 or Less
Ernie's Coffee Shop. 1146 Emerald Bay Road/Calif. 89. ☎ **916/541-2161.** Main dishes $5–$8. No credit cards. Daily 6am–2pm. DINER.

The undisputed king of coffee shops in South Lake Tahoe is Ernie's, which has been serving huge plates of good old American grub to cholesterol-be-damned locals since the Nixon administration. Since the food is far from original (omelets, bacon and eggs, pancakes), it must be the perpetually friendly service, low prices, and huge portions that attracts the steady stream of customers. Another good reason to come here is that Ernie's is located next to the cheapest gas station in town, so you can top off your tummy and your tank in one stop.

Yellow Sub. U.S. 50 and 983 Tallac Ave. ☎ **916/541-8808.** Sandwiches $3–$6. No credit cards. Daily 10:30am–10pm. SANDWICHES.

When it comes to picnic supplies, there's stiff competition in South Lake Tahoe: There are three sandwich shops on this single block alone. Still, our favorite is Yellow Sub, with its 21 kinds of overstuffed subs, made in 6-inch and 12-inch varieties. The shop is hidden in a small shopping center across from the El Dorado Campground.

Meals for $20 or Less
Cantina Los Tres Hombres. 765 Emerald Bay Rd. ☎ **916/544-1233.** Main courses $7–$13. AE, MC, V. Daily 11:30am–10:30pm. MEXICAN.

While this restaurant's cavernous tiki-bar interior can easily be mistaken to represent the South Seas, the food is unmistakably south-of-the-border. The bar and adjacent dining area are two of the busiest rooms in South Lake Tahoe. The menu is well priced and extensive, although it sticks to the tried-and-true Californian-Mexican specialties such as tacos, burritos, and enchiladas. The chile rellenos (cheese-stuffed peppers, battered and fried) get a thumbs-up, as does the crabmeat- and mushroom-stuffed enchilada. The dishes are unimaginative but the portions are mountainous. Service is brisk but not unfriendly, and some patrons may have had more than their share of tequila.

Nepheles. 1169 Ski Run Blvd. ☎ **916/544-8130.** Main courses $12–$18. AE, MC, V. Daily 5–10pm. CALIFORNIA.

En route to the Heavenly Ski Resort, this old home, complete with stained-glass windows, stops traffic. The cuisine is basically Californian, using market-fresh ingredients deftly handled by the kitchen. To give you a taste of the north woods, nightly menu items feature whatever game's in season—venison, elk, or wild boar.

The menu wanders about, with the usual steaks for the old boys, but more exciting dishes include swordfish in a pineapple-garlic-cilantro salsa, or perhaps duck in the classic orange sauce (this one is enlivened with a healthy dash of bourbon).

Scusa! 1142 Ski Run Blvd. ☎ **916/542-0100.** Main courses $9–$15. MC, V. Daily 5–10pm. ITALIAN.

Also on the trail to the Heavenly Ski Resort, this cozy Italian eatery may have a decor that leans a little garishly on the neon side, but the food more than compensates. Dishes are interspersed with enough surprises to keep the locals happy. The place is civilized, basic, and clean, and the staff is usually cheerful and knowledgeable unless they're rushed or having a bad hair day. Among the specialties are a smoked chicken and ravioli made with cheese ravioli, sun-dried tomatoes, capers, black olives, and sage butter, and a savory baked penne with smoked mozzarella, prosciutto, roasted garlic, and foccacia crust.

The Swiss House. 787 Emerald Bay Rd. ☎ **916/542-1717.** Main courses $10–$17. AE, MC, V. Daily 5–9pm. SWISS/CONTINENTAL.

The ambience here is genuine enough and warmly appreciated by diners, especially skiers who arrive to find a fire blazing away. Despite its name, the place is not exactly into yodeling and cowbells, but the dishes are often alpine. The operation seems to run like Swiss clockwork, and, although we've had better Wiener schnitzels than this, the one served here is perfectly adequate. There's also cheese fondue and raclette to take you back to the old country; it's warmly flavored but so filling you might not be able to finish. Other dishes include steaks or something more refined like salmon en croûte.

NORTH SHORE/TAHOE CITY

Meals for $10 or Less

Bridgetender Tavern and Grill. 30 W. Lake Blvd. (at Fanny Bridge), Tahoe City. ☎ **916/583-3342.** $5–$7. No credit cards. Daily 11am–2am. PUB FOOD.

Though it's located in Fanny Bridge, one of the most popular tourist areas on the North Shore, the Bridgetender is a locals' hangout through and through. Still, they're surprisingly tolerant of out-of-towners, who come for the cheap grub and huge selection of draft beers. The tavern is built around a trio of Ponderosa pines that meld in with the decor so well you hardly notice. Big, burly burgers, salads, pork ribs, and such round out the menu, and the daily beer specials—posted on the wall in Day-Glo colors—are definitely worth a visit. During the summer months, dine outside among the pines.

☉ Fire Sign Cafe 1785 W. Lake Blvd., Tahoe City. ☎ **916/583-0871.** $4–$9. MC, V. Daily 7:30am–2pm. AMERICAN.

Choosing a place to have breakfast in North Tahoe is a no-brainer: Since the late 1970s the Fire Sign Cafe has been the locals' choice for starting the day, which explains the lines out the door on weekend mornings. Just about everything is made from scratch, such as the soft buttermilk biscuits and coffee cake that accompany the big plates of bacon and eggs or blackberry-buckwheat pancakes. Even the salmon for the chef/owner Bob Young's legendary salmon omelet is smoked in-house. Try the Firesign breakfast crepes filled with eggs and mushrooms and topped with hollandaise. Lunch—burgers, salads, sandwiches, burritos, and more—is also quite popular, particularly when the outdoor patio is open.

Izzy's Burger Spa. 100 W. Lake Blvd. (at Fanny Bridge), Tahoe City. ☎ **916/583-4111.** Burgers $3.50–$6. No credit cards. Mon–Fri 11am–7pm, Sat–Sun 11am–8pm. BURGERS.

It's just a simple, wooden A-frame building containing a small short-order grill, but Izzy's Burger Spa flips an unusually hefty and tasty burger and an equally enticing grilled chicken breast sandwich. On a sunny day the best seats are at the picnic tables set out front. The restaurant is directly across from the Tahoe Yogurt Factory (see below).

Tahoe Yogurt Factory. 125 W. Lake Blvd., Tahoe City. ☎ **916/581-5253.** Coffee $1; espresso $1.30–$2.60; yogurt $1.50–$3.25; sandwiches $2–$4. No credit cards. Daily 6am–6pm; summer daily until 10pm. YOGURT/SANDWICHES.

This small coffee shack, located at the "Y" in Tahoe City, is frequently mentioned as "the best little cafe in Tahoe"; perhaps an overstatement, but it does have its devotees. There's not much more to it than basic croissants, bagels, muffins, sandwiches, smoothies, and excellent java. Small tables are placed outdoors in the summer.

✪ **Za's.** 395 N. Lake Blvd. (across from the fire station), Tahoe City. ☎ **916/583-1812.** $6–$10. MC, V. Daily 4:30–9:30pm. ITALIAN.

The sign used to say "Pizza's" until half of it fell off, which is just as well because there's a whole lot more to Za's than just pizza. One of the most popular restaurants in North Tahoe, this little gem serves great Italian food at bargain prices. Example: A hefty plate of smoked chicken fettucini in a garlic cream sauce with roasted bell peppers, fresh artichoke hearts, and mushrooms sells for under $10. Start with Pudge's Plate, a pleasing platter of fresh roasted veggies doused in a balsamic vinaigrette, and a tumbler or two of Chianti, then take a pick from the wide range of pastas, calzones, and pizza. Za's is a bit hard to find (look behind Pete-n-Peter's Saloon), but it's worth the search.

Meals for $20 or Less

Sunnyside Restaurant. 1850 W. Lake Blvd., Tahoe City. ☎ **916/583-7200.** Main courses $13–$19. AE, MC, V. Oct–June daily 5:30–9:30pm; July–Sept daily 10am–10pm; Sun brunch 9:30am–2pm. SEAFOOD/AMERICAN.

Located about 2 miles south of Tahoe City, on Calif. 89, Sunnyside Restaurant, at the Sunnyside Lodge (see "Where to Stay," above) is worth a detour. In summer, when the sun is shining, the most desirable table in Tahoe is on Sunnyside's lakeside veranda. Guests can also dine in the lodge's more traditional dining room with its 1930s aura.

At lunch the menu has fresh pastas, burgers, chicken, and fish sandwiches, together with a variety of soups and salads. Nothing out of the ordinary here. Dinners are fancier, with such main courses as Australian lobster tail, oven-roasted shiitake pork tenderloin, and lamb chops (broiled and served with fresh mint). All dinners come with San Francisco–style sourdough bread, the chef's starch of the day, and a Caesar salad or cup of creamy chowder.

Tahoe House Restaurant. 625 W. Lake Blvd., Tahoe City. ☎ **916/583-1377.** Main courses $9–$18. AE, DISC, MC, V. Bakery daily 6am–10pm, deli lunch from 11am, dinner 5–10pm. SWISS/CALIFORNIA.

Serving Tahoe's skiers, boaters, and sun bathers for more than 18 years, Tahoe House is one of the oldest Swiss restaurants on the lake, located at the "Y" in Tahoe City. Though not a trendsetter, it is known locally as a reliable venue for good food at reasonable prices. Chef-owner Barbara Vogt's menu features some Swiss-German dishes such as Wiener schnitzel, Rahmschnitzel (veal with creamy mushroom sauce), grilled bratwurst, and pork cordon bleu. Steaks and seafood also satisfy, as do several pastas. The full-service European-style bakery items and desserts are wonderful, as exemplified by home-baked tortes, truffles, and chocolates. Dishes are based on the seasonal availability of ingredients, and usually only the freshest and best are used. In keeping with the new trend in healthy cooking, Vogt has added a selection of lighter choices, including vegetarian dishes straight from the Vogt's farm.

TAHOE AFTER DARK

Tahoe is not known particularly for its nightlife, although there's always something going on in the showrooms of the major casino hotels, located in Stateline, just east of South Lake Tahoe. Call **Harrah's** (☎ 702/588-6611), **Harvey's** (☎ 702/588-2411), **Caesars** (☎ 702/588-3515), and the **Lake Tahoe Horizon** (☎ 702/588-6211) for current show schedules and prices. Most cocktail shows cost $12 to $40, and headliners are likely to include the likes of Jay Leno or perhaps Johnny Mathis. Also, most of these hotels have several bars and even a disco or two, like Nero's at Caesars.

If you're going out on the North Shore, Tahoe City is where most of the action is; however, budget-minded gamblers (pardon the oxymoron) might want to try their luck at Crystal Bay's stateline casinos where the stakes are a little lower. The **Tahoe Biltmore,** Calif. 28 (☎ 702/831-0660), and the **Crystal Bay Club,** Calif. 28 (☎ 702/831-0512), have $2 (instead of the usual $5) black jack tables, where you'll be served complimentary cocktails. Even better, both offer a filling $1.35 to $1.40 breakfast (coffee, toast, bacon, home fries, and eggs) around the clock.

Back in Tahoe City, there's usually live music nightly in **Bullwhackers Pub,** at the Resort at Squaw Creek (☎ 916/583-6300), 5 miles west of Tahoe City. The **Pierce Street Annex,** 850 N. Lake Blvd. (☎ 916/583-5800), behind the Safeway in Tahoe City, has pool tables, shuffleboard, and DJ dancing every night. It's one of the livelier places around and popular with the 30-something scene. Right next door is the **Blue Water Brewery** (☎ 916/581-2583) where you can play pool, munch on Buffalo wings, and sample homemade ales in a nonsmoking environment.

The college crowd will feel at home at **Humpty's,** 877 N. Lake Blvd. (☎ 916/583-4867), which has the cheapest drinks in town—particularly during happy hour from 4 to 9pm—and live rock music most nights. Twenty-somethings also gather at the **Naughty Dog,** 255 N. Lake Blvd. (☎ 916/581-3294), where you and a friend (or two) can sip the bartender's potent concoctions from a plastic doggie dish; they also have frequent drink specials and tasty gourmet pizzas at equally pleasing prices.

If it's just a casual cocktail you're after, our favorite spot is the handsome fireside lounge at **River Ranch Lodge,** Calif. 89 at the entrance to Alpine Meadows, about 10 miles northwest of Tahoe City (☎ 916/583-4264), which cantilevers over a turbulent stretch of the Truckee River; complement your drink here with an affordable appetizer like the tasty blue cheese and garlic breadsticks.

10

The High Sierra: Yosemite, Mammoth Lakes & Sequoia & Kings Canyon

by Erika Lenkert and Matthew R. Poole

The national parks of California's Sierra are a mecca for travelers across the globe. The big attraction is Yosemite, of course, but the entire region is the stuff from which postcards are made.

It was in Yosemite that naturalist John Muir found "the most songful streams in the world . . . the noblest forests, the loftiest granite domes, the deepest ice sculptured canyons." Even today, few visitors would disagree with Muir's early impressions as they explore this land of waterfalls, towering cliffs, wilderness, snow fields, alpine lakes, river beaches, and waterfalls. The waterfalls, one of the most stunning sights, reach their peak in mid-May. Yosemite Valley is riddled with waterfalls, sheer walls, and domes and peaks reaching toward the sky. The valley is the most central and accessible part of the park, stretching for some 20 miles, all the way from Wawona Tunnel in the west to Curry Village in the east. If you visit during spring or early fall, you'll encounter fewer problems with crowds.

Across the heart of the Sierra Nevada in east central California sprawl Sequoia and Kings Canyon National Parks, administered as one entity. Their peaks stretch across some 1,300 square miles, taking in the giant sequoias for which they are fabled. It's a land of alpine lakes, granite peaks, and deep canyons. At 14,495 feet, Mount Whitney is the highest point in the Lower 48.

Another big attraction in the area is Mammoth Lakes, one of the major playgrounds of California, with dozens of recreational activities in a setting of lakes, streams, waterfalls, and rugged meadows evocative of Austria. As if they had giant knives, glaciers in unrecorded times carved out much of this panoramic region, as did volcanic activity.

Because of the vast popularity of the parks, facilities can be strained at peak visiting times. Always secure your reservations in advance if possible (and that definitely includes camping). You'll be glad you did.

1 Merced: Gateway to Yosemite

Merced is an ideal overnight stop en route to the park. It also has several sights worth visiting if you have the time.

For out-of-state visitors, what's compelling about Merced is its location at the center of the San Joaquin Valley (see Chapter 11), one of California's most important agricultural regions. For example, you can explore the **Buchanan Hollow Nut Company,** 6510 Minturn Rd., LeGrand (☎ 209/389-4594), a family owned nut-processing and packaging plant where you can purchase some of the produce or ship gift boxes home.

You can acquire an agricultural history on Calif. 140 en route to Yosemite. The **Merced Agricultural Museum,** 4498 E. Calif. 140 (☎ 209/383-1912), is a collection of assorted machinery that includes antique gas engines and horse-drawn buggies. Anyone who appreciates early technology will get a kick out of a visit. A donation is requested, and it's open Tuesday to Sunday from 10am to 4pm.

For a completely different experience, kids and flying enthusiasts will want to visit the **Castle Air Museum,** Santa Fe and Buhach roads, Atwater (☎ 209/723-2178). On display outside at this former air base are 42 historic aircraft, including the B-17, the workhorse of World War II, and the SR-71, which flies at three times the speed of sound. To reach the museum, take the Buhach exit off Calif. 99 to Santa Fe Drive and turn left. Admission is free, and it's open daily from 10am to 4pm.

ESSENTIALS

If you're driving from San Francisco, take U.S. 580 to I-5 south to Calif. 140. **Merced Municipal Airport,** 20 Macready Dr. (☎ 209/385-6873), is serviced by United Air Express. Amtrak, which operates along the Central Valley from Sacramento to Bakersfield, stops at Merced.

For information, contact the **Merced Conference and Visitors Bureau,** 690 West 16th St. (☎ 800/446-5353 or 209/384-3333).

WHERE TO STAY

Best Western Pine Cone Inn. 1213 V St. (at West 13th St.), Merced, CA 95340. ☎ **800/528-1234** or 209/723-3711. Fax 209/722-8551. 94 rms. A/C TEL TV. $62 double. Additional person $5, room with refrigerator/microwave $10 extra. AE, DC, MC, V.

Set about a mile north of Merced's center, relatively isolated from its neighbors, the two-story Pine Cone Inn was built in the 1960s and renovated in 1995. It's probably your best option in Merced. Bedrooms are cozy if bland and painted in shades of hunter green. Units contain two phones and a coffeemaker. There's a run-of-the-mill restaurant on the premises and a swimming pool. The inn's bar is open until 11pm.

Holiday Inn Express. 730 Motel Dr., Merced, CA 95340. ☎ **800/HOLIDAY** or 209/383-0333. Fax 209/383-0643. 65 rms. A/C TEL TV. $75 double. Rates include continental breakfast. 10% discounts for AAA or AARP members. AE, DC, MC, V.

Built in 1992, this is one of the newest hotels in Merced and was designed in the blandly anonymous Holiday Inn format. Its three stories rise about a mile south of the town center. It's a good choice for families. Bedrooms are hardly inspired, but they are clean and comfortable, with modern amenities. It may be so hot outside you'll literally worship the air-conditioning in your room and the hotel's outdoor pool. A continental breakfast is served, and several fast-food joints lie within walking distance. On-command movies go for $7.95 and computer jacks are in each room.

Ramada Inn. Calif. 99 and Childs Ave., Merced, CA 95340. ☎ **800-2RAMADA** or 209/723-3711. Fax 209/723-0127. 112 rms. A/C TEL TV. Sun–Thurs $69 double; Fri–Sat $79 double. AE, MC, V.

New owners are working hard to make this more than merely a safe and relatively inexpensive stopover en route to Yosemite. The rather unremarkable building lies 3 miles south from the center of Merced, and though some of the decor may be motel-bland, new textiles have been recently added and a few larger units now have marble bathrooms. On the premises is a swimming pool, which comes as a blessed relief during the real summer scorchers. There's also a fairly basic restaurant that will fill you up, nothing else.

WHERE TO DINE

The Branding Iron. 640 W. 16th St. ☎ **209/722-1822.** Reservations accepted. Main courses $13–$20. AE, MC, V. Mon–Fri 11:30am–2pm; daily 5:30–9pm. STEAK/SEAFOOD.

This is by far the most animated, most popular, and most frenetic steak and seafood house in Merced. Set in the heart of town, behind its trademark green awnings, it has plank-sided walls accented with burned-in marks from branding irons. The portions are massive. Prime rib is the most popular, although seafood, chicken, and lobster (the most expensive item) tie for close seconds. Soup, salad, potato, and vegetables all accompany the main course.

Lenny's. 1052 W. Main St. (at R St.). ☎ **209/722-0350.** Dinner platters $10–$16. AE, MC, V. Mon–Fri 7am–9:30pm, Sat 7am–10pm, Sun 9am–9pm.

This is one of the two most visible restaurants in Merced, feeding a stream of new-comers who tend to return after they've explored Yosemite. The menu proudly offers old-world recipes handed down from the owner's family for several generations, with lots of all-American twists. Loaded with pastas and at least 15 other dishes, the lunch time buffet is probably the region's best bargain ("awesome," pronounced one local). Dinners are more elaborate, usually featuring chicken, veal, pasta, and vegetarian dishes. All sauces, as well as all the sausages, are made on the premises in the style of long-ago Italy.

You won't lack for visual distraction here. Glass-fronted refrigerators, set end-to-end, display more than 150 kinds of beers, and one corner of the place is devoted to an espresso bar.

2 Yosemite National Park

by Andrew Rice

This area first became widely known to white men when a troop of U.S. soldiers in the Mariposa Battalion, sent to chase down a band of Native Americans, stumbled upon this natural wonder and were awestruck by its beauty. They regaled their friends with tales of its impossible geography when they got home, and Yosemite's popularity has been steadily increasing ever since.

It's a place of record-setting statistics: the highest waterfall in North America and three of the world's 10 tallest waterfalls (Upper Yosemite Falls, Ribbon Falls, and Sentinel Falls), the tallest and largest single granite monolith in the world (El Capitan), the most recognizable mountain (Half Dome), one of the world's largest trees (the Grizzly Giant in Mariposa Grove), and literally thousands of rare plant and animal species.

What most sets the valley apart is its incredible geology. The Sierra Nevada were formed between 10 and 80 million years ago when a tremendous geological uplift pushed layers of granite lying under the ocean up into an incredible mountain range. Cracks and rifts in the rock gave erosion a start at carving canyons and valleys. Then, during the last ice age, at least three glaciers flowed through the valley, sheering

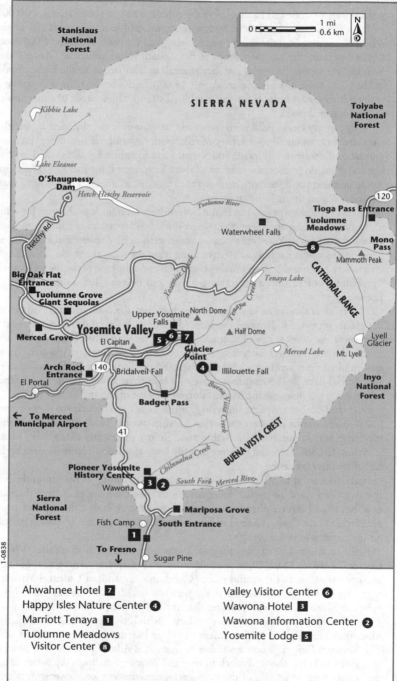

Yosemite National Park

0 ____ 1 mi
0 ____ 0.6 km

N

Stanislaus National Forest

Toiyabe National Forest

Kibbie Lake

SIERRA NEVADA

Lake Eleanor

O'Shaugnessy Dam

Hetch Hetchy Reservoir

Hetchy Rd.

Tuolumne River

120

Tioga Pass Entrance

Tuolumne Meadows

Waterwheel Falls

8

Mono Pass

Mammoth Peak

Big Oak Flat Entrance

Tuolumne Grove Giant Sequoias

Yosemite Creek

Tenaya Lake

Tenaya Creek

CATHEDRAL RANGE

Merced Grove

Upper Yosemite Falls

North Dome

Yosemite Valley

El Capitan

5 **6** **7**

Half Dome

Merced Lake

Mt. Lyell

Lyell Glacier

Glacier Point

4 Illilouette Fall

Arch Rock Entrance

140

El Portal

Bridalveil Fall

Buena Vista Creek

Inyo National Forest

Badger Pass

← **To Merced Municipal Airport**

BUENA VISTA CREST

41

Chilnualna Creek

South Fork Merced River

Pioneer Yosemite History Center

3 **2**

Wawona

Sierra National Forest

Fish Camp

Mariposa Grove

South Entrance

1

To Fresno
↓

Sugar Pine

1-0838

Ahwahnee Hotel **7**

Happy Isles Nature Center **4**

Marriott Tenaya **1**

Tuolumne Meadows
  Visitor Center **8**

Valley Visitor Center **6**

Wawona Hotel **3**

Wawona Information Center **2**

Yosemite Lodge **5**

vertical faces of stone and hauling away the rubble. The last glacier retreated 10,000 to 15,000 years ago, but left its legacy in the incredible number and size of the waterfalls pouring into the valley from hanging side canyons. From the 4,000-foot-high valley floor, the 8,000-foot tops of El Capitan, Half Dome, and Glacier Point look like the top of the world, but they're small in comparison to the highest peaks in the park, some of which reach almost 14,000 feet. The 7-square-mile valley is really a huge bathtub drain for the combined runoff of hundreds of square miles of snow-covered peaks.

High country creeks flush with snowmelt catapult over the abyss left by the glaciers and form an outrageous variety of falls, from tiny ribbons that never reach the ground to the torrents of Nevada and Vernal Falls. Combined with the shadows and lighting of the deep valley, the effect of all this falling water is mesmerizing. On a clear spring morning you'll see more rainbows than you can count and a base note of roaring water echoes through the entire valley.

All that vertical stone gets put to use by hundreds who flock to the park for some of the finest climbing anywhere. Sharp-eyed visitors will spot a lot of climbers hanging off the sheer faces of Yosemite's famous walls, such as El Capitan and Half Dome. Sometimes spending as long as 10 days slung from the rock, the world's best climbers are here to see and be seen proving their mettle. At the base of the big walls you'll find climbers of all abilities practicing moves and belaying techniques on smaller pitches.

The valley is also home to beautiful meadows and the Merced River. When the last glacier retreated it dammed the Merced River with glacial debris and formed a lake where the valley is now. Eventually sediment from the river filled the lake and created the rich and level valley floor we see today. Tiny Mirror Lake was created several hundred years ago by rockfall that dammed up Tenya Creek. The addition of an artificial dam in 1890 made it more of a lake than a pond. Rafters and inner tubers enjoy the slow-moving Merced during the heat of summer.

Deer and coyote frequent the valley, often causing vehicular mayhem as one heavy-footed tourist slams on the brakes to whip out the camcorder while another rubbernecker, mesmerized by Bambi too, almost drives right into him. Metal crunches, tempers flare, and the deer daintily hops away, doubtlessly amused at the stupidity it just witnessed.

Bears, too, are at home in the valley. The name "Yosemite" derives from the Native American word *Yohamite*, "killer among us." Grizzlies are gone from the park now, but black bears are plentiful and make their presence known through late-night plundering of ice chests and food in the campgrounds rather than by posing prettily for the cameras in broad daylight.

Right in the middle of the valley's thickest urban cluster is the **Valley Visitor Center** (☎ **209/372-0299**), with exhibits that will teach you about glacial geology, history, and the park's flora and fauna. Check out the **Indian Cultural Museum** next door for insight into what life in the park was once like. Excellent exhibits highlight the Miwok and Paiute cultures that thrived in the park; the museum has a great collection of baskets and other artifacts. Behind the center is a re-creation of Ahwahneechee village, a Native American village like those that once existed here. The Museum Gallery houses a number of fine Ansel Adams prints as well as other artists' work. You'll also find much history and memorabilia from the career of nature writer John Muir, one of the founders of the conservation movement. Muir's name is virtually synonymous with Yosemite. Muir came here from the Midwest in the late 1800s and ended up spending the rest of his life battling for the protection of Yosemite and the greater Sierra Nevada.

John Muir: Savior of Yosemite

John Muir was born in Dunbar, Scotland, in 1838 and came to the United States in 1848. After a couple of years studying at the University of Wisconsin in Madison, he dropped out. Carrying a plant press on his back, he began a 1,000-mile-long walk from Indiana to the Gulf of Mexico. Dissatisfied with Florida, he boarded a steamer and went via Panama to San Francisco in 1868.

On his arrival he asked a passerby for the nearest way out of town. The passerby asked him where he wanted to go. He replied, "To anyplace that is wild." And so John Muir was directed to the Oakland ferry and a journey that brought him eventually to the Sierra where he worked as a shepherd and lived simply in the wilderness.

From 1880 to 1890 he settled in Martinez and worked as a fruit rancher, becoming wealthy enough eventually to devote his life entirely to the wilderness that he loved. In 1892, he founded the Sierra Club and served as its first president. He wrote passionately about nature and conservation and enlisted the help of others to establish a system of national parks that would protect the wilderness for future generations. He saved Yosemite, but lost the battle to rescue Hetch Hetchy, which many say caused him to die of a broken heart in 1914. To secure its water supply, San Francisco dammed the Tulomne River, thereby denying future generations access to another valley as beautiful as Yosemite.

Two years after Muir's death the national parks legislation was passed, placing the parks under the protection of the federal government. Today, the battle to return Hetch Hetchy to its original state continues. The spirit of this great conservationist lives on, as the struggle to conserve what was dear to his heart continues.

Muir won the largest battle of his life when he formed the Sierra Club and convinced President Benjamin Harrison to declare Yosemite a national park in 1890. Later, though, he suffered a critical defeat when the city of San Francisco built a water diversion dam within the park, flooding Muir's beloved Hetch Hetchy Valley, the glacial splendor of which rivaled Yosemite Valley. Always the opportunist, Muir, lobbying the federal government to declare the entire Sierra Nevada a national park, once spent three days swapping tall tales, drinking, and sleeping on beds of pine boughs with the old rough rider himself, President Teddy Roosevelt.

While it's easy to let the tremendous beauty of the Valley monopolize your attention, remember that 95% of Yosemite is wilderness. Of the four million visitors who come to the park each year, very few ever get more than a mile from their car. That leaves most of Yosemite's 750,000 acres open for anyone adventurous enough to hike a few miles. Even though the valley is a hands-down winner for dramatic freak-of-nature displays, the high country offers a more subtle kind of beauty: glacial lakes, roaring rivers, and miles of granite spires and domes. In the park's southwest corner the Mariposa Grove is a striking forest of rare sequoias, the world's largest trees, as well as several meadows and the rushing south fork of the Merced River.

Tenaya Lake and Tuolumne Meadows are two of the most popular high country destinations, as well as starting points for many great trails to the backcountry. Whether you're here for a week or just a day, both are ideal places to spend the day fishing, climbing, or hiking among the spectacular granite of the high country. Since this area of the park is under snow from November through June, the short season we call summer is really more like spring. From snowmelt to the first snowfall, the high country explodes with wild flowers and long-dormant wildlife trying to make the most of the short season.

A NOTE ON CROWDS

Unfortunately, popularity isn't always the greatest thing for wild places. Over the last 20 years, tourist-magnet Yosemite Valley has set records for the worst crowding, noise, crime, and traffic in any California national park. More than 4.1 million visitors came in 1995.

The park covers more than 1,000 square miles, but most visitors flock to the floor of Yosemite Valley, a 1-mile-wide, 7-mile-long freak of glacial scouring that tore a deep and steep valley from the solid granite of the Sierra Nevada. It's still one of the most beautiful places on earth, but the Yosemite Valley becomes a total zoo anytime between Memorial Day and Labor Day. To make it worse, the Park Service, which once called for eliminating auto traffic in the valley and reducing infrastructure inside the park, has done the opposite, continuing to allow kitschy concession signs, rinky-dink curio shops, an auto repair garage, several hotels, a post office, small hospital, and last but certainly not least, a jail, to turn Yosemite Valley into an urban mess, albeit a pretty one. Cars line up bumper to bumper on almost any busy weekend. Until now, federal authorities did not show enough courage to implement one of several plans that would reduce traffic. But in 1995 Yosemite's new superintendent closed the entrances to the park 11 times between Memorial Day and mid-August when the number of visitors reached the park's quota; she turned away 10,000 vehicles. We'll see in future years whether or not she's successful in implementing measures to control crowds and preserve the quality of the visitor experience. In the meantime, to enjoy the reasons all those people flock to the valley without having to deal with the hordes themselves, my best advice is to try to come before Memorial Day or after Labor Day.

If you must go in summer, try to do your part to help out. It's not so much the numbers of people that are ruining the valley, but their insistence on driving from attraction to attraction within the valley. Once you're here, park your car and bike, hike, or ride the shuttle buses that go everywhere in the valley. **Curry Village** and **Yosemite Lodge** also both rent bikes in the summer (☎ **209/372-8367**). It may take longer to get from point A to point B, but you're in one of the most gorgeous places on earth, so why hurry?

SEEING THE HIGHLIGHTS
THE VALLEY

First-time visitors are often completely dumbstruck as they enter the valley from the west. The first two things you'll see are the delicate and beautiful **Bridal Veil Falls** and the immense face of **El Capitan,** a beautiful and anything-but-delicate 3,593-foot-tall solid granite rock. A short trail leads to the base of Bridal Veil, which at 620 feet tall is only a medium-sized fall by park standards, but one of the prettiest.

This is a perfect chance to get those knee-jerk tourist impulses under control early: Resist the temptation to rush around bagging sights like they're feathers for your cap. Instead, take your time and look around. One of the best things about the valley is that many of its most famous features are visible from all over. Instead of rushing to the base of every waterfall or famous rock face and a getting a crick in your neck from staring straight up, go to the visitor center and spend a half hour learning something about the features of the valley. Buy the excellent *Map and Guide to Yosemite Valley* for $2.50, which describes many excellent hikes and short nature walks. Then go take a look. Walking and biking are the best way to get around. To cover longer distances, the park shuttles run frequently and everywhere.

If you absolutely must see it all and want to have someone tell you what you're seeing, the **Valley Floor Tour** is a two-hour, narrated bus or open-air tram tour (depending on season) that provides an introduction to the valley's natural history, geology, and human culture for $15. Purchase tickets at valley hotels or call **209/ 372-1240** for advance reservations.

Three-quarters of a mile from the visitor center is the **Awahnee Hotel.** Unlike the rest of the hotel accommodations in the park, the Ahwahnee actually lives up to its surroundings. The native granite-and-timber lodge was built in 1927 and reflects an era when grand hotels were, well, grand. Fireplaces bigger than most Manhattan studio apartments warm the immense common rooms. Parlors and halls are filled with antique Native American rugs. Don't worry about what you're wearing unless you're going to dinner—this is Yosemite, after all.

The best single view in the valley is from **Sentinel Bridge** over the Merced River. At sunset, Half Dome's face functions as a projection screen for all the sinking sun's hues from yellow to pink to dark purple and the river reflects it all. Ansel Adams took one of his most famous photographs from this very spot.

VALLEY WALKS & HIKES Yosemite Falls is within a short stroll of the visitor center. You can actually see it better elsewhere in the valley, but it's really impressive to stand at the base of all that falling water. The wind, noise, and blowing spray generated when millions of gallons catapult 2,425 feet through space onto the rocks below is sometimes so strong you can barely stand on the bridge below.

If you want more, the **Yosemite Falls Trail** zigzags $3^1/2$ miles from Sunnyside Campground to the top of Upper Yosemite Fall. This trail gives you an inkling of the weird, vertically oriented world climbers enter when they head up Yosemite's sheer walls. As you climb this narrow switchbacked trail, the valley floor drops away until people below look like ants, but the top doesn't appear any closer. It's a little unnerving at first. Plan on spending all day on this 7-mile round-trip because of the incredibly steep climb.

A mile-long trail leads from the Valley Stables (shuttle bus stop 17; no car parking) to **Mirror Lake.** The already tiny lake is shrinking every year as it fills with silt, becoming a meadow, but the reflections of the valley walls and sky on its surface remain one of the park's most introspective sights.

Also accessible from the Valley Stables or nearby Happy Isles is the best valley hike of all: the **John Muir Trail** to Vernal and Nevada Falls. The John Muir Trail follows the Sierra crest 200 miles south to Mt. Whitney, but you only need go $1^1/2$ miles round-trip to get a great view of 317-foot Vernal Fall. Add another $1^1/2$ miles and 1,000 vertical feet for the climb to the top of Vernal Fall on the Mist Trail, where you'll get wet as you climb directly alongside the falls. On top of Vernal and before the base of Nevada Fall is a beautiful little valley and deep pool. For a truly outrageous view of the valley and one heck of a workout, continue on up the Mist Trail to the top of Nevada Fall. From 2,000 feet above Happy Isles where you began, it's a dizzying view straight down the face of the fall. To the east is an interesting profile perspective on Half Dome. Return either by the Mist Trail or the slightly easier John Muir Trail for a total 7-mile round-trip hike.

Half Dome may look insurmountable to anyone but an expert rock climber, but thousands every year take the popular cable route up the backside. It's almost 17 miles round-trip from Happy Isle on the John Muir Trail and a 4,900-foot elevation gain. Many do it in one day, starting at first light and rushing home to beat nightfall.

A more relaxed strategy is to camp in the backpacking campground in Little Yosemite Valley just past Nevada Fall. From there the summit is an easy striking distance to the base of Half Dome. Here you must climb up a very steep granite face using steel cables installed by the park service. During summer, boards are installed as crossbeams, but they're still far apart. Wear shoes with lots of traction and bring your own leather gloves for the cables. Your hands will thank you. The view from the top is an unbeatable vista of the high country, Tenaya Canyon, Glacier Point, and the awe-inspiring abyss of the valley below. When you shuffle up to the overhanging lip for a look down the face, be extremely careful not to kick rocks or anything else onto the climbers below who are earning this view the hard way.

THE SOUTHWEST CORNER

This corner of the park is densely forested and gently sculpted in comparison to the stark granite that makes up so much of the park. Coming from the valley, Calif. 41 passes through a long tunnel. Just before the tunnel entrance is **Tunnel View,** sight of another famous Ansel Adams photograph, and the best scenic outlook of the valley accessible by automobile. Virtually the whole valley is laid out below: Half Dome and Yosemite Falls straight ahead in the distance, Bridal Veil to the right, and El Capitan to the left.

A few miles past the tunnel, Glacier Point Road turns off to the east. Closed in winter, this winding road leads to a picnic area at **Glacier Point,** site of another fabulous view of the valley, this time 3,000 feet below. Schedule at least an hour to drive here from the valley and an hour or two to absorb the view. This is a good place to study the glacial scouring of the valley below; the Glacier Point perspective makes it easy to picture the valley below filled with sheets of ice.

Thirty miles south of the valley on Calif. 41 is the **Wawona Hotel** and the **Pioneer Yosemite History Center.** In 1879 the Wawona was the first lodge built in the state reserve that would later become the national park. Its Victorian architecture evokes a time when travelers spent several days in horse-drawn wagons to get to the park. What a welcome stop it must have been. The Pioneer center is a collection of early homesteading log buildings across the river from the Wawona.

One of the primary reasons Yosemite was first set aside as a park was the **Mariposa Grove** of sequoias. (Many good trails lead through the grove.) These huge trees have personalities that match their gargantuan size. Single limbs on the biggest tree in the grove, the Grizzly Giant, are 10 feet thick. The tree itself is 209 feet tall, 32 feet in diameter, and more than 2,700 years old. Totally out of proportion with the size of the trees are the tiny cones of the sequoia. Smaller than a baseball and tightly closed, the cones will not release their cargo of seeds until opened by fire.

THE HIGH COUNTRY

The high country of Yosemite has the most grandiose landscape in the entire Sierra Nevada. Dome after dome of beautifully crystalline granite reflects the sunlight above deep green meadows and icy-cold rivers.

Tioga Pass is the gateway to the high country. At times it clings to the side of steep rock faces; in other places it weaves through canyon bottoms. Several good campgrounds make it a pleasing overnight alternative to fighting summertime crowds in the valley, though use is increasing here, too. Unlike the valley, a car is vital to getting around as the only public transportation is the once-a-day bus to Tuolumne Meadows. Leaving the valley at 8am, the bus will let you off anywhere along the way. The driver waits two hours at Tuolumne Meadows, which isn't much time to see anything, then heads back down to the valley, returning around 4pm. One way fare is $12, or slightly less to intermediate destinations.

Tenaya Lake is a popular windsurfing, fishing, canoeing, sailing, and swimming spot. The water is very chilly. Many good hikes lead into the high country from here, and the granite domes surrounding the lake are popular with climbers. Fishing here varies greatly from year to year.

Near the top of Tioga Pass is stunning Tuolumne Meadows. This enormous meadow covering several square miles is bordered by the Tuolumne River on one side and spectacular granite peaks on the other. The meadow is cut by many stream channels full of trout, and herds of mule deer are almost always present. The Tuolumne Meadows Lodge and store is a welcome counterpoint to the overdeveloped valley. In winter the canvas roofs are removed and the buildings fill with snow. You can buy last-minute backpacking supplies here, and there is a basic burgers-and-fries cafe.

TUOLUMNE MEADOWS HIKES & WALKS   So many hikes lead from here into the backcountry that it's impossible to do them justice here. A good day hike is the 5-mile climb to Cathedral Lake. This steep but shady trail passes an icy-cold spring and traverses several meadows.

On the far bank of the Tuolumne from the meadow a trail leads downriver. Eventually this trail passes through the grand canyon of the Tuolumne and exits at Hetch Hetchy. Shorter hikes will take you downriver past rapids and cascades.

An interesting geological quirk is the Soda Spring on the far side of Tuolumne Meadow from the road. This bubbling spring gushes carbonated water from a hole in the ground. A small log cabin marks its site.

For a great selection of Yosemite high country hikes and backpacking trips, consult some of the specialized guidebooks to the area. Tuolumne Meadows, a hiking guide by Jeffrey B. Shaffer and Thomas Winnett, and Yosemite National Park by Thomas Winnett and Jason Winnett, both published by Wilderness Press, are two of the best.

YOSEMITE SPORTS & ACTIVITIES

BIKING   Biking is the perfect way to see the valley. Eight miles of bike paths in addition to the valley roads make this an even better option. You can rent one-speeds at the Yosemite Lodge or Curry Village for $5 per hour or $16.25 per day. If you want a fancier bike, you'll have to bring it from home. All trails in the park are closed to mountain bikes.

FISHING   The Merced River in the valley is catch and release only. Barbless hooks are required. High country lakes and streams are literally leaping with trout. A California license is required and available in the park at the Yosemite Village Sportshop.

HORSEBACK RIDING   Four stables offer scenic day rides and multiday pack excursions in the park. Yosemite Valley Stables (☎ 209/372-8348) is open spring through fall. The other three, Wawona (☎ 209/375-6502), White Wolf (☎ 209/372-1323), and Tuolumne Meadows (☎ 209/372-8427) only operate during summer. Day rides vary from $30 to $60 depending on length. Multiday backcountry trips cost roughly $100 per day and must be booked almost a year in advance. The park wranglers can also be hired to make resupply drops at any of the backcountry High Sierra camps if you want to arrange for a food drop while on an extended trip.

ICE-SKATING   In winter the Curry Village Ice Rink is a lot of fun. It's outdoors and melts quickly when the weather warms up. Rates are $5 for adults, $4.50 for children. Skate rentals are available.

SKIING   Yes, there is an alpine ski area in Yosemite, but it isn't much of one. The oldest operating ski area in California, Badger Pass (☎ 209/372-8430) opened in 1935. Four chairs and two T-bars cover a compact mountain of beginner and intermediate runs. At $28-per-day adults, $13 children on weekends, and about 20% cheaper midweek, it is a great place to learn how to ski or snowboard. If you are a good skier or boarder already, don't bother.

Yosemite is a better destination for cross-country skiers and snowshoers. The Badger Pass ski school and the mountaineering school run trips and lessons for all abilities, ranging from basic technique to transSierra crossings. If you're on your own, Crane Flat is a good place to go, as is the groomed track up to Glacier Point, a 20-mile round-trip.

CAMPING

Reservations for campgrounds in Yosemite can be reserved up to four months in advance through **DESTINET** (☎ **800/436-7275**). During the busy season all valley campsites sell out within hours of becoming available on the service.

VALLEY CAMPGROUNDS

The five car-campgrounds in the Valley are always full except in the dead of winter. All are located along the Merced River and cost $15 per night. All have drinking water, flush toilets, pay phones, fire pits, and a heavy ranger presence. Showers are available for a cost at Curry Village. Three—North Pines, Upper Pines, and Lower River—allow small RVs (less than 35 feet). Upper River is for tents only. If you are expecting a real nature experience, skip camping in the valley unless you like experiencing nature with 4,000 of your closest friends.

Sunnyside Campground is the only walk-in campground in the valley and fills up with climbers since it is only $3 per night. Hard-core climbers used to live here for months at a time, but the Park Service has cracked down on that. It's still a much more bohemian atmosphere than any of the other campgrounds.

ELSEWHERE IN THE PARK

Outside the valley, things start looking up for campers. Two campgrounds near the south entrance of the park, **Wawona** and **Bridal Veil Creek,** offer a total of 210 sites with all the amenities. Wawona is open year-round on a first-come first-serve basis. Because it sits well above snowline at more than 7,000 feet, Bridal Veil is open in the summer only. Both cost $10 per night.

Crane Flat, Hodgdon Meadow, and Tamarack Flat are all in the western corner of the park near the Big Oak Flat Entrance.

Crane Flat is the nearest to the valley, about a half-hour drive, with 166 sites, water, flush toilets, and fire pits. Its rates are $12 per night, and it's open from May to October. **Hodgdon Meadow** is directly adjacent to the Big Oak Flat entrance at 4,800 feet. It's open year-round and charges $12 per night. Facilities include flush toilets, running water, ranger station, and pay phone. It's one of the least crowded low-elevation car campgrounds, but there's not a lot to do here.

Tamarack Flat is a waterless, 52-site campground with pit toilets, open June through October. It's a bargain at $6 per night.

High-country car campers can choose between Tuolumne Meadows, White Wolf, Yosemite Creek, or Porcupine Flat. All are above 8,000 feet and open in the summer only.

Tuolumne Meadows is the largest campground in the park, with more than 300 spaces, but it absorbs the crowd well and has all the amenities, including campfire programs and slide shows in the outdoor amphitheater. Half the sites are reserved in advance. The rest are set aside on a first-come, first-served basis. Rates are $12 per night.

White Wolf, west of Tuolumne Meadows, is the other full-service campground in the high country, with 87 sites available for $10 per night. It offers a drier climate than the meadow and doesn't fill up as quickly.

Two primitive camps, **Porcupine Flat** and **Yosemite Creek,** are the last to fill up in the park. Both have pit toilets and no running water and charge $6 per night.

WHERE TO STAY
IN THE PARK

Curry Village (☎ 209/252-4848) is the valley's low-rent district. This compound of almost 200 cabins and 400 tent cabins varies widely in quality. Some have private baths. Others share campground-style bathrooms. Ironically, the oldest cabins are the nicest. Shoddy construction gives the others a slapped-together appearance, not to mention making them cold and drafty in winter. The tent cabins have wood floors and canvas walls. Without real walls to stop noise, the tent cabin areas lack any sort of privacy, but they're fun in that summer camp way. You'll have to sustain yourself with fast food from the Curry Village shopping center, as no cooking is allowed in the rooms. Rates are inexpensive to moderate.

An intriguing option bridging the gap between backpacking and staying in a hotel are Yosemite's five backcountry **High Sierra Camps.** These wilderness lodges are simple tent cabins and cafeteria tents located in some of the most beautiful, remote parts of the park. The five camps—Glen Aulin, May Lake, Sunrise, Merced Lake, and Vogelsang—make for good individual destinations. Or you can link several together, since they're arranged in a loose loop about a 10-mile hike from each other—a nice wilderness circuit. Overnight rates include a tent cabin, breakfast, dinner, bathrooms, and showers. High Sierra camp reservations are accepted beginning in December for the following summer and usually book solid by January. Contact **High Sierra Reservations,** Yosemite Park and Curry Co., 5410 E. Home Ave., Fresno, CA 93727 (☎ 209/454-2002).

Yosemite Lodge (☎ 209/252-4848) is another affordable choice in the Yosemite Valley. It's actually a huge complex, not a lodge, with an array of accommodations ranging from luxurious suites with outdoor balconies and striking views of Yosemite Falls, to one-room cabins with shared baths in a separate building. A pool is available to guests, and two restaurants and a cafeteria serve mediocre meals. Rates are moderate.

The **Wawona Hotel** (☎ 209/252-4848), near the south entrance, is a step up from the above lodgings, but it's still moderately priced. Now a National Historical Landmark, the Wawona is a romantic throwback to another century. That has its ups and downs. Private bathrooms were not a big hit yet in the 19th century, and rooms were small to hold in heat. Still, the Wawona is a great place to play make-believe. It offers a restaurant, pool, stables, and a lounge.

If you feel like splurging, the grand **Ahwahnee Hotel** (☎ 209/252-4848) is one of the most romantic and beautiful hotels in California. With its ballroom, pool, tennis, gourmet dining, outstanding views, and high-digit price tag, it's a special-occasion sort of affair. Rooms are booked a year in advance. Try to reserve one of the cottages, which cost the same as rooms in the main hotel but are more spacious.

OUTSIDE THE PARK

✪ **Tenaya Lodge.** 1122 Calif. 41, Fish Camp, CA 93623. ☎ **800/635-5807** or 209/683-6555. Fax 209/683-8684. 224 rms, 20 suites. A/C MINIBAR TEL TV. Winter Sun–Thurs $89 double; Fri–Sat $129 double. Summer Sun–Thurs $199 double; Fri–Sat $219 double. Suite supplement $20–$80. Buffet breakfast $10 per couple. Children stay free in parents' room. AE, DC, MC, V.

This three- and four-story resort opened in 1990 on a 35-acre tract of forested land loaded with hiking trails. It's the centerpiece of a village (Fish Camp) whose only other attraction is a gas station and a general store. Inside, the decorative theme is a cross between an Adirondack hunting lodge and a Southwestern pueblo. The lobby is dominated by a massive river-rock fireplace rising three stories. This is probably the best resort outside the southern entrance to Yosemite, with a likable and helpful staff. Rooms are ultramodern, with three phones and other amenities including in-room safes.

Dining/Entertainment: All three restaurants are well recommended, and since there aren't lots of other options in town, they draw huge crowds.

Services: Room service.

Facilities: Indoor and outdoor swimming pools, on-site massage specialists, a health club, games room, and, depending on the season, sleigh and hay rides.

JUST THE FACTS

ENTRY POINTS   There are four main entrances to the park. Most valley visitors enter through the Arch Rock Entrance Station on Calif. 140. The best entrance for Mariposa Grove and Wawona is the South Entrance on Calif. 41 from Mariposa. If you're going to the high country you'll save a lot of time by coming in through the Big Oak Flat Entrance, which puts you straight onto Tioga Road without forcing you to deal with the congested valley. The Tioga Pass Entrance is only open in summer and is only really relevant if you're coming from the east side of the sierra (in which case it's your only choice). A fifth, little-used entrance is the Hetch Hetchy Entrance in the euphonious Poopenaut Valley, on a dead-end road.

FEES   It's $5 per car per week to enter the park or $3 per person per week. Annual Yosemite Passes are a steal at only $15. Wilderness permits are free, but reserving them requires a $3 fee.

VISITOR CENTERS & INFORMATION   There is a central, 24-hour recorded information line for the park (☎ 209/372-0200). All visitor-related service lines including hotels, and information can be accessed by Touch-Tone phone at **209/ 372-1000.**

By far the biggest visitor center is the **Valley Visitor Center** (☎ 209/372 0299). The **Wawona Ranger Station** (☎ 209/372-0564) and **Big Oak Flat Information Center** (☎ 209/372-0615) give general park information. For interesting biological and geological displays about the high sierra, as well as trail advice, the **Tuolumne Meadows Visitor Center** (☎ 209/372-0263) is great. All three can provide you with maps plus more newspapers, books, and photocopied leaflets than you'll ever read.

REGULATIONS   Rangers in the Yosemite Valley spend more time being cops than being rangers and they have their own jail: Don't do anything here you wouldn't do in your home town—this isn't the Wild West. Despite the pressure, park regulations are pretty simple. Wilderness permits are required for all overnight backpacking trips. Fishing licenses are required. Use proper food storage methods in bear country. Don't collect firewood around campgrounds. No off-road bicycle riding. Dogs are allowed in the park but must be leashed and are forbidden from trails. Don't feed the animals.

SEASONS   Winter is one of the nicest times to visit the valley. It isn't crowded, as it is during summer, and a dusting of snow accentuates the stark contrasts of all that granite. To see the waterfalls at their best, come in spring when snowmelt is at its peak. Fall can be cool, but it's beautiful and much less crowded than summer.

The high country is under about 20 feet of snow from November through May, so unless you are snow camping, summer is pretty much the only season. Even in summer, thundershowers are an almost-daily occurrence and snow is not uncommon. Mosquitoes can be a plague during the peak of summer but get better after the first freeze.

AVOIDING THE CROWDS Crowds and summer in the valley go together like salt and french fries, and both will cause your blood pressure to soar. Help alleviate crowding and help yourself by doing whatever you can to visit the valley anytime but between Memorial Day and Labor Day—and avoid those holidays like the plague! Otherwise, the best way to avoid the crowd is to head for the backcountry.

RANGER PROGRAMS Even though they are overworked just trying to keep the peace, Yosemite's wonderful rangers also take time to lead a number of educational and interpretive programs ranging from backcountry hikes to fireside talks to snow country survival clinics. Call the main park information number with specific requests for the season and park area you'll be visiting. Also a great service are the free painting, drawing, and photography classes offered spring through fall and holiday weekends in winter at the Art Activity Center next to the Museum Gallery.

3 Mammoth Lakes

High in the Sierra, just southeast of Yosemite, Mammoth Lakes is surrounded by glacier-carved peaks that soar up from flower-filled meadows and are covered with dense pine forest. It's an alpine region of sweeping beauty and one of Californians' favorite playgrounds for hiking, biking, horseback riding, skiing, and more. It's also home to one of the top-rated ski resorts in the world.

ESSENTIALS

It's a six-hour drive from San Francisco via the Tioga Pass in Yosemite (closed in winter), five hours outside Los Angeles, and three hours south of Reno, Nevada. In winter, Mammoth is accessible via U.S. 395 from the north or the south.

Sierra Mountain Airways (800/22-GO-FLY) and **Mountain Air Express (800/788-4247)** service **Mammoth Lakes Airport** on U.S. 395.

For visitor information, contact the **Mammoth Lakes Visitors Bureau,** Calif. 203 (P.O. Box 48), Mammoth Lakes, CA 93546 (☎ **800/367-6572** or 619/934-2712).

ENJOYING THE OUTDOORS

Mammoth Lakes is at the heart of several wilderness areas and is cut through by the San Joaquin and Owens rivers. Mammoth Mountain overlooks the Ansel Adams Wilderness Area to the west and the John Muir Wilderness Area to the southeast and beyond to the Inyo National Forest and the Sierra National Forest.

Mammoth Mountain Ski Area, P.O. Box 24, Mammoth Lakes, CA 93546 (☎ **800/832-7320** or 619/934-2571), is the central focus for both summer and winter activities. Visitors can ride the lifts to see panoramic vistas; those who want an active vacation have a world of options. If you do hit the slopes in winter, you may want to contact **Mammoth Area Shuttle (MAS)** (☎ **619/934-0687**) for transportation to and from town and the ski area. The shuttle is free, makes many stops throughout town, and eliminates the long wait in traffic you might encounter if you take your own car.

SKIING In winter, Mammoth Mountain has more than 3,500 skiable acres, a 3,100-foot vertical drop, 150 trails (22 with snowmaking), and 31 lifts, including two high-speed quads. The terrain is 30% beginner, 40% intermediate, and

30% advanced. It's known for power sun, ideal spring skiing conditions, and a snow base anywhere from 8 to 12 feet. **Cross-country ski centers** are at **Tamarack Lodge** (☎ 619/934-2442) and **Sierra Meadows Ski Touring Center** (☎ 619/934-6161). There's also snow-mobiling, dog sledding, snowshoeing, and sleigh rides.

June Mountain Ski Area (☎ 619/648-7733), 20 minutes north of Mammoth, is smaller and offers many summer activities. It has 500 skiable acres, a 2,590-foot vertical drop, 35 trails, and 8 lifts, including two high-speed quads. The terrain is 35% beginner, 45% intermediate, and 20% advanced. It's at the center of a chain of lakes—Grant, Silver, Gull, and June—that can be viewed on a scenic driving loop around Calif. 158. It's especially beautiful in the fall when the aspens are ablaze with gold.

WARM-WEATHER ACTIVITIES   In summer, the mountain becomes one huge bike park and climbing playground. The **Bike Center** at the base of the mountain has rentals and accessories. The bike park is famous for its Kamikaze Downhill trail, the obstacle arena where riders can test their balance and skill, and the slalom course. There's also an area designed for kids. A pass granting unlimited access to the gondola and the trail system is $23 adult, $12 children 12 and under; to trails only, it's $12 adult, $6 children. The park operates daily 9am to 6pm, from about July 1 to September 29 and then weekends only to October 13. In town, mountain bikes can also be rented from **Footloose Sports Center** at the corner of Canyon and Minaret (☎ 619/934-2400). The **NORBA National Mountain Bike Championships** are held here in the summer.

Mammoth Lakes Basin sits in a canyon a couple of miles west of town. Here are the lakes—Mary, Mamie, Horseshoe, George, and Twin—that have made the region known for **trout fishing.** Southeast of town, Crowley Lake is also famous for trout fishing and so too are the San Joaquin and Owens Rivers. In addition, there are plenty of other lakes in which to try your reel. For fishing information and guides, contact **Rick's Sport Center,** at the corner of Calif. 203 and Center Street (☎ 619/934-3416); **The Trout Fitter,** Shell Mart Center, corner of Main Street and Old Mammoth Road (☎ 619/924-3676); and **Kittredge Sports,** Main Street and Forest Trail (☎ 619/934-7566), which rents equipment, supplies guides, teaches fly-fishing, and offers backcountry trips and packages.

At Crowley Lake, visitors can rent **kayaks** from **Caldera Kayaks** (☎ 619/935-4942) for $30 a day. This outfit also offers half- and full-day trips on Crowley and on Mono Lake and provides instruction, as well.

The region is also an equestrian's paradise, and numerous outfitters offer **pack trips.** Among them are: **Red's Meadows Pack Station,** Red's Meadows, past Minaret Vista (☎ 800/292-7758 or 619/934-2345); **Mammoth Lakes Pack Outfit,** Lake Mary Road, past Twin Lakes (☎ 619/934-2434), which offers one- to six-day riding trips and semiannual horse drives, plus other wilderness workshops; and **McGee Creek Pack Station,** McGee Creek Rd., Crowley Lake (☎ 619/935-4324).

Hiking and backpacking are also stellar activities. Trails abound in the Mammoth Lakes Basin area. They include the half-mile-long **Panorama Dome Trail,** which is just past the turnoff to Twin Lakes on Lake Mary Road, leading to the top of a plateau that provides a view of the Owens Valley and Lakes Basin. Another trail of interest is the 5-mile-long **Duck Lake Trail,** starting at the end of Coldwater Creek parking lot with switchbacks across Duck Pass past several lakes to Duck Lake. The **Inyo Craters** trailhead is reached via gravel road, off the Mammoth Scenic Loop Road. This trail takes you to the edge of these craters and a sign that explains how they were created.

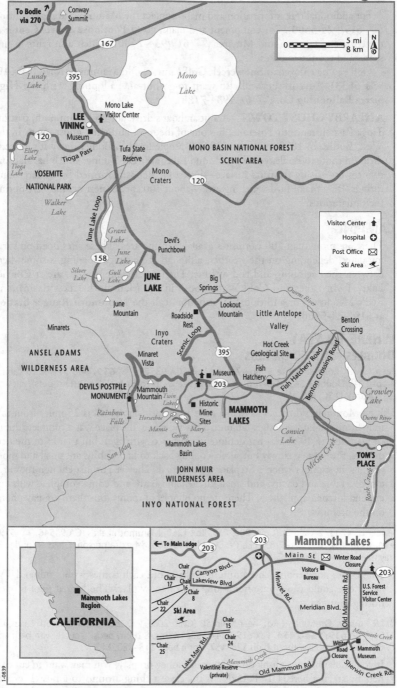

Mammoth Lakes Region

To Bodie via 270

Conway Summit

167

395

Lundy Lake

Mono Lake

Mono Lake Visitor Center

LEE VINING

Museum

120

Ellery Lake

Tioga Lake

Tioga Pass

YOSEMITE NATIONAL PARK

Walker Lake

Tufa State Reserve

MONO BASIN NATIONAL FOREST SCENIC AREA

Mono Craters

120

Grant Lake

June Lake Loop

158

Silver Lake

Gull Lake

June Lake

JUNE LAKE

Devil's Punchbowl

Big Springs

Lookout Mountain

Little Antelope Valley

Owens River

Benton Crossing

June Mountain

Roadside Rest

Minarets

Scenic Loop

Inyo Craters

Minaret Vista

ANSEL ADAMS WILDERNESS AREA

DEVILS POSTPILE MONUMENT

Mammouth Mountain

Twin Lakes

Rainbow Falls

Horseshoe

Mamie

George

Mary

Mammoth Lakes Basin

San Joaq

395

Hot Creek Geological Site

Fish Hatchery

Museum

203

MAMMOTH LAKES

Historic Mine Sites

Convict Lake

Fish Hatchery Road

Benton Crossing Road

Crowley Lake

Owens River

TOM'S PLACE

McGee Creek

Rock Creek

JOHN MUIR WILDERNESS AREA

INYO NATIONAL FOREST

Visitor Center	
Hospital	
Post Office	
Ski Area	

0   5 mi   8 km

N

Mammoth Lakes

To Main Lodge

203

Main St   Winter Road Closure

203

Visitor's Bureau

U.S. Forest Service Visitor Center

Chair 7

Chair 17

Chair 16

Chair 8

Canyon Blvd.

Lakeview Blvd.

Minaret Rd.

Old Mammoth Rd.

Meridian Blvd.

Chair 22

Ski Area

Chair 15

Chair 24

Chair 25

Lake Mary Rd.

Valentine Reserve (private)

Mammoth Creek

Old Mammoth Rd.

Winter Road Closure

Mammoth Museum

Sherwin Creek Rd.

CALIFORNIA

Mammoth Lakes Region

1-0839

For additional trail information and maps, contact the **Mammoth Ranger Station** (☎ **619/924-5500**). For equipment and maps, go to **Footloose Sports Center** at the corner of Canyon and Minaret (☎ **619/934-2400**), which also rents in-line skates and mountain bikes.

Golf can be enjoyed at **Snowcreek Golf Course,** Old Mammoth Road (☎ **619/ 934-6633**). Adventurers will also want to go hot-air ballooning with the **High Sierra Ballooning Co.** (☎ **619/934-7188**).

A NEARBY GHOST TOWN   About an hour's drive north of Mammoth, past the Tioga Pass entrance to Yosemite, lies one of the most authentic ghost towns in the West, **Bodie.** In 1870 more than 10,000 people lived in Bodie; today it's an eerie shell. En route to Bodie, you'll pass Mono Lake, near Lee Vining, which has startling tufa towers arising from its surface—limestone deposits formed by underground springs. It's a major bird-watching area—about 300 species nest or stop here during their migrations.

CAMPING

There are more than 700 campsites available in the area. These sites open on varying dates, depending on the weather, although the average opening is somewhere between the beginning and end of June. The largest campgrounds are at Convict Lake, Twin Lakes and Cold Water (both in the Mammoth Lakes Basin), and Red's Meadow. For additional information, call the **Mammoth Ranger Station** at **619/924-5500.**

WHERE TO STAY
DOUBLES FOR $60 OR LESS

Fern Creek Lodge. Route 3, Box 7, June Lake, CA 93529. ☎ **619/648-7744.** 10 cabins, 4 apts. TV. Doubles $45, 4-bedroom cabins (sleeps up to 8) $192. "Certain pets" allowed ($10 extra). DISC, MC, V.

June Mountain skiing is less than a mile away and Mammoth is 25 miles from this fully furnished budget lodge. Up until a few years ago, the place was a complete dump (it was built in 1927 and has definitely weathered with age), but thanks to the new owners, the lodge is slowly but surely coming back to life. Cabins are small and more popular in summer when a fireplace isn't needed. They've got just enough room for a bed, a table and chairs, and small kitchen and bath, and come complete with linens and kitchen appliances. There are no phones in rooms, but there is a pay phone on the premises.

Motel 6. 473372 Main St./Calif. 203, P.O. Box 1260, Mammoth Lakes, CA 93546. ☎ **619/ 934-6660.** Fax 619/934-6989. TEL TV. Double $46–$60. $4 extra person. Children under 17 stay free. AE, DC, DISC, MC, V.

Bare bones hotel rooms cost a minimum here, but each comes with a tub and TV. What else could you want after a long day of snow play? The heated pool is open during summer.

ULLR Lodge. On Minaret Rd., near Main St. (Calif. 203), P.O. Box 53, Mammoth Lakes, CA 93546. ☎ **619/934-2454.** Fax 619/934-3353. 17 rms, 8 dorm beds. Double with bath and TV $29–$57, double without bath $26–$57, dorm beds $13–$20. MC, V.

If you're planning to plunk down all your money on play, you may want to cut corners by staying here. ULLR Lodge is the closest thing around to a hostel (expect plenty of young folks), but does offer private rooms and bonuses like use of the fireplace lounge (with TV), community kitchen, and sauna. For $20 don't expect the

Ritz, but rather older, rustic accommodations run by a kindhearted staff. A few nice bonuses: Everyone gets keys to their rooms (even dorm rooms, which also have a private locker for each person). Pay phones are on the property and the desk takes messages. Reserve well in advance in winter.

DOUBLES FOR $80 OR LESS

Tamarack Lodge. P.O. Box 69 (Twin Lakes Rd., off Lake Mary Rd.), Mammoth Lakes, CA 93546. ☎ **800/237-6879** or 619/934-2442. 10 rms (5 with bath), 25 cabins. TEL. Double without bath $80 in winter, $70 in summer; double with bath $95–$140 in winter, $85–$105 in summer; cabin $110–$300 in winter, $85–$260 in summer. Special packages available. DISC, MC, V.

This rustic lakeside retreat is the kind of place your parents would've taken you when you were little (if you were the traveling kind). The lodge and cabin accommodations are nothing fancy, but that's exactly what's kept guests coming here since the 1920s. Folks relax in front of a fire burning in the stone hearth in the sitting room or hang out in their rooms, which are intentionally rustic with knotty-pine walls and modern furnishings. The cabins, which can accommodate two to nine persons, are dotted around the property and offer a variety of configurations, from studios with wood-burning stove and shower, to two-bedroom, two-bath accommodations with fireplace. Each cabin has a fully equipped kitchen, but there is no daily maid service (fresh towels are provided at the front desk). In the main lodge there are rooms with private baths and with shared bath.

The lodge has a very popular cross-country ski center with more than 25 miles of trails and skating lanes, ski rentals, and ski school. Boat and canoe rentals also available. The dining room, overlooking Twin Lakes, offers Californian/continental fare.

DOUBLES FOR $100 OR LESS

Snow Goose Inn. 57 Forest Trail (P.O. Box 946), Mammoth Lakes, CA 93546. ☎ **800/874-7368** or 619/934-2660. Fax 619/934-5655. 15 rms, 2 suites. TEL TV. Winter Sun–Thurs $78 double, $148 suite; Fri–Sat $98 double, $168 suite. Summer $68 double; $98 suite. Doubles with kitchens $5–$10 extra. Special packages available. Rates include breakfast, evening wine, and appetizers. AE, MC, V.

This place is managed by owners who run it as if it were a bed-and-breakfast rather than a traditional hotel. Set a half block off the main street, near a number of restaurants, the Snow Goose was built in two separate two-story buildings in 1967. Bedrooms are comfortably and attractively furnished, and two offer kitchens. The two-bedroom suites can accommodate four in a two-story space with dinette, kitchen, and living room complete with a fireplace. Antiques add a graceful note to some of the public rooms, and the staff is helpful and will direct you to cross-country and downhill skiing possibilities three miles away.

White Horse Inn. 2180 Old Mammoth Rd. (P.O. Box 2326), Mammoth Lakes, CA 93456. ☎ **800/982-5657** or 619/924-3656. 5 rms. Winter $75–$135; summer $90–$105. Rates include breakfast. DISC, MC, V.

Set about a mile southwest of the resort's center, this establishment occupies a gray-and-white gabled house built in the 1950s. Unlike its competitors, there's no flowery Laura Ashley theme here. Each accommodation is furnished eclectically and with wit, each with a distinct theme (such as all-Chinese antiques or a furniture ensemble from Austria and Mexico). A country breakfast is included as part of the price, and in nice weather, you'll enjoy it on an outdoor deck. Wine and cheese are served near a billiard table during the early evening. There's a hot tub on the premises, and a communal kitchen reserved for the use of guests.

WORTH A SPLURGE

Mammoth Mountain Inn. Minaret Rd., P.O. Box 353, Mammoth Lakes, CA 93546. ☎ **800/ 228-4947** or 619/934-2581. Fax 619/934-0701. 173 rms, 40 condos. A/C TEL TV. Winter $110–$210 double; summer $99–$130 double. 1-bedroom condos winter from $225; summer from $145 (suitable for up to four persons). Special ski and mountain biking packages available. AE, MC, V.

Conveniently located opposite the ski lodge, this modern accommodation started out in 1954 as only one building, but was enlarged a decade later into a newer, glossier complex. It was last remodeled in the early 1990s. With a certain rustic charm, it looks very much like a mountain resort with wood siding. Bedrooms are well equipped and pleasantly furnished, but not inspired. It's a definite bet for families and actively pursues that market, offering supervised children's activities, free cribs, a playground, box lunches for picnics, a game room, and even picnic tables.

You'll have your pick of sports facilities, including bicycles, fishing or hiking guides, downhill or cross-country skiing, sleighing, horseback riding, and even haywagon rides. The hotel has a snack bar and offers barbecues, and room service is also available. The rather standard restaurant serves from 7am to 2pm and reopens for dinner nightly from 5:30 to 9:30pm. (No one stays up late here.) Extras include free airport transportation and occasional entertainment. A whirlpool spa is also on-site.

✪ **Sierra Lodge.** 3540 Main St. (Calif. 203), Mammoth Lakes, CA 93546. ☎ **800/356-5711** or 619/934-8881. Fax 619/934-7231. TEL TV. Winter Sun–Thurs $100–$130 double, Fri–Sat $120–$150 double; summer Sun–Thurs $75 double, Fri–Sat $85 double. MC, V.

Opened in 1991 in the heart of the resort near the ski shuttle, this two-story inn deliberately abandoned the tried-and-true rustic-woodsy theme used in the area's other hotels in favor of a glossy, big-city decor of pop-modern prints, track lighting, streamlined detailing, and, as a concession to the mountains, rock-built fireplaces in the public areas. Breakfast is the only meal served, but many restaurants are nearby. Bedrooms, in sync with the public areas, are glossy and modern, proud of their divergence from the town's rustic tone. Rooms are spacious and furnished in typical contemporary styling, each equipped with a kitchenette. Facilities include an outdoor Jacuzzi and a fireside room for relaxing. Smoking is not allowed.

WHERE TO DINE
MEALS FOR $10 OR LESS

Grumpy's Saloon and Eatery. 37 Mammoth Rd. ☎ **619/934-8587.** Main courses $5.95–$14.95. AE, MC, V. AMERICAN.

Don't let the name fool you, Grumpy's is actually a fun-loving saloon with an Old West feel (minus the big-screen TVs, pool tables, and video games). The bar serves a great selection of beers on tap, and the hearty and affordable grub features burgers (go for the Grumpy Burger), tasty barbecued ribs, homemade chili, a handful of Mexican items, and the famous quarter-pound Dogger, an unbelievably enormous hot dog. Everything on the menu comes with a choice of fries, coleslaw, or barbecued baked beans, so trust us when we say you won't leave hungry. Stop by for happy hour when there's usually a free buffet of hors d'oeuvres that may include Buffalo wings, cheese and crackers, or mini-quesadillas.

Roberto's Cafe. 271 Old Mammoth Rd. ☎ **619/934-3667.** Main courses $6.75–$9.75. DC, DISC, MC, V. Sun–Thurs 11am–9pm, Fri–Sat 11am–10pm. MEXICAN.

Plunk down on a wooden bench and table at this small restaurant for the best Mexican food in town. The decor features hand-painted tiles and original Mexican art, and the menu is pretty simple. Just choose one of the combination plates of chicken or beef tacos, burritos, chimichangas, or enchiladas; all, of course, come with rice and beans. You can also order à la carte ($3.75 to $4.95). Wednesday night is "Locos Night," when draft beers go for a measly 75¢, and you can order a whole pitcher for $3.75.

MEALS FOR $20 OR LESS

✪ **Anything Goes Café.** 645 Old Mammoth Rd. ☎ **619/934-2424.** Main courses $13–$18. MC, V. Thurs–Tues 7am–3pm; Thurs–Mon 5:30–9:30pm. CALIFORNIA.

It lies about a half mile outside of town, near the golf course, within an old "but not antique" building. Customers order lunch directly at the counter, which helps retain the low noontime prices. Overstuffed deli sandwiches, salads, and platters of California-inspired chicken and pastas are all the rage. Despite the informality of the lunch hour, it's obvious that the hardworking owners are directing the seasonings from their perch in the kitchens.

Dinners, however, are more formal, with table service, tablecloths, candlelight, and more attention to the nuances of the cuisine. The menu changes weekly, but the dinner menu will feature about six or so main courses. For example, you might find breast of chicken marinated in orange juice, ginger, shallots, garlic, and soy, then oven roasted until crispy; or lamb shanks braised with figs, pinot noir, and garlic, then finished with Dijon mustard. Special attention is paid to desserts here, with emphasis on pies (peach or strawberry-apricot are especially good) and other homemade sweets.

Berger's Restaurant. Minaret Rd. ☎ **619/934-6622.** Reservations recommended on weekends. Main courses $8.25–$14.95. MC, V. Daily 11am–9:30pm. AMERICAN.

If after all that slope swishing you're looking to fill your tummy with a big slab of meat, head to Berger's, the best in American cuisine. Its cabinlike interior fits its surroundings and has local photographs on the wooden walls. Portions are huge and include an array of burgers, steak, ribs, chicken, and sandwiches, and there are even a few hefty salads to satisfy a more health-conscious hunger. Entrees include salad, garlic bread, and either fries or a baked potato. Sandwiches, which cost up to $7 and come with salad and fries, will also easily fill you up without emptying your wallet. The children's menu is the ultimate bargain, offering an array of kid-friendly feasts for under $6. The daily lunch specials are most coveted by locals, but if you want to try one, come early—they almost always sell out.

Old Mammoth Pasta House. 549 Old Mammoth Rd. (Meridian). ☎ **619/934-8088.** Reservations for 5 or more. Main courses $6.25–$12.25. DC, DISC, MC, V. Sun–Thurs 4:30–9pm, Fri–Sat 4:30–10pm. ITALIAN.

Talk about carbo loading! With 22 different pasta dishes on the menu—and the massive helpings of each—there's no way you can leave here hungry. Portions are so large that unless you have a trench of a stomach, you'll do just fine with a half order, which will cost you a mere $5.25 to $11.25 and still comes with all the extras (soup or salad, and bread with garlic herb butter). Other options include salads, pizza, and sandwiches.

Whiskey Creek. 18 Main St. (at corner of Minaret Rd.), Mammoth Lakes. ☎ **619/934-2555.** Main courses $9–$16. AE, DC, MC, V. Daily 5:30–10pm. AMERICAN.

If you favor The Chart House wherever you go, you've found your dining spot. It's not exactly a culinary adventure, but the fare is hearty and the view is splendid. The building is designed with wraparound windows to encompass a sweeping vista over the snow-clad mountains. Isolated on a corner lot about ³/₄ mile from the town center, it combines a rustic, but elegant restaurant with a rock-and-roll club. Live music begins every night at 9pm and continues till at least 1am, and entrance is free unless there's a well-known band (then the cover is no more than $5 per person).

Although this restaurant is known for its beef, there are some other fine dishes on the menu, including rack of lamb with a jalapeño mint jelly and even meat loaf with a mild horseradish sauce. People lust after the smashed potatoes. For an appetizer, try the duck quesadilla with roasted peppers, jack cheese, and tomatillo salsa. A micro brewery, the Mammoth Brewing Company (tours available) is a welcome addition to an already bubbly atmosphere.

Worth a Splurge

✪ **Nevados.** Main St. (at Minaret Rd.). ☎ **619/934-4466.** Reservation recommended. Main courses $14–$23. AE, MC, V, DC, DISC. Open daily 6pm– 9:30pm. EUROPEAN/CALIFORNIA.

What is it that makes this restaurant a favorite with the locals? Well, the owner/host Tim Dawson is on hand nightly to ensure their every need is met, the innovative cuisine is fresh and homemade, and the moist and tasty bread is house-baked. The clincher though is the fixed-price meal for $25.95. It consists of a first course, perhaps soft-shell crab, salad, or an ahi-tuna-and-California spring roll; the main course, which might be linguini with wild mushrooms, snow peas, red bell peppers and herbs, or roasted medallions of elk, lamb, or pork with warm cranberry-onion marmalade and a red currant cabernet sauce; and dessert (we loved the warm pear and almond tart). Throw in the casual-but-sweet ambience, which is accented with white table-cloths, candles, and French country murals, and the extensive selection of wines, single-malt scotches, and single-batch bourbons, and it's no wonder this is *the* hangout for ski instructors and race coaches.

✪ **Skadi.** 587 Old Mammoth Rd. (in the Sherwin Plaza III Shopping Mall). ☎ **619/934-3902.** Reservations recommended. Main courses $9.50–$20. AE, MC, V. Daily 5:30–10pm. ECLECTIC.

The minimall where this restaurant is located (a half-mile south of the town center) may not be the ideal home of the Viking goddess of skiing and hunting that the restaurant is named after, but she wouldn't care once she saw the view, which encompasses mountains for what seems like miles around. Everybody likes this place—it's the perfect spot for an aprés-ski cocktail or an appetizer, or a full-blown gourmet dinner. The decor evokes a big-city, postmodern aura that's a welcome change after all that local alpine rusticity. Main courses are self-proclaimed "alpine cuisine" and include such dishes as smoked trout Napoleon or grilled venison with lingonberries and a game sauce. Finish the evening with crème brûlée or the frozen macadamia nut parfait.

4 Devils Postpile National Monument

by Andrew Rice

Just a few miles outside the town of Mammoth Lakes, Devils Postpile National Monument is home to one of nature's most curious geological freak shows. Formed when molten lava cracked as it cooled, the 60-foot-high blue-gray basalt columns that form the postpile look more like some sort of enormous eerie pipe organ or a jumble of giant pencil leads than anything you'd expect to see made from stone. The three-to seven-sided columns formed underground and were exposed when glaciers scoured this valley in the last ice age some 10,000 years ago. Similar examples of columnar basalt are found in Ireland and Scotland.

Because of its high elevation (7,900 feet) and heavy snowfall, the monument is open only from summer until early fall. Weather in the summer is usually clear and warm, but afternoon thundershowers can soak the unprepared. Nights are still cold, so bring good tents and sleeping bags if you'll be camping. The Mammoth Lakes region is famous for its beautiful lakes—but unfortunately all that water also means lots of mosquitoes. Plan for them.

From late June until early September cars are prohibited in the monument between 7:30am and 5:30pm due the small roads' inability to handle the traffic. Visitors must take a shuttle bus from the Mammoth Mountain Inn to and from locations in the monument. While it takes some planning, the resulting peace and quiet is well worth the trouble and makes you wonder why the Park Service hasn't implemented similar programs at the Yosemite Valley and other traffic hot spots.

HIKING

There's more to Devils Postpile than a bunch of rocks, no matter how impressive they might be. Located on the banks of the San Joaquin River in the heart of a landscape of granite peaks and crystalline mountain lakes, the 800-acre park is a gateway to a hiker's paradise. Short paths lead from here to the top of the postpile, and to Soda Springs, a spring of cold carbonated water.

A longer hike (about 1 1/4 miles) from the separate Rainbow Falls trailhead will take you to spectacular **Rainbow Falls,** where the entire middle fork of the San Joaquin plunges 101 feet off a lava cliff. From the trail a stairway and short trail lead to the base of the falls and swimming holes below.

The **John Muir Trail,** which connects Yosemite National Park with Kings Canyon and Sequoia National Park, and the **Pacific Crest Trail** are located here. Named after famous conservationist and author John Muir, who is largely credited with saving Yosemite and popularizing the Sierra Nevada as a place worth preserving, the 211-mile Muir Trail traverses some of the most rugged and remote parts of the Sierra. There are two accesses to it in Devils Postpile, one via the ranger station, the other from Rainbow Falls Trailhead. From here you can hike as far as your feet will take you north or south.

Note that mountain bikes are not permitted on trails.

CAMPING

While most visitors stay in or around Mammoth Lakes, the monument does maintain a 21-site campground with piped water, flush toilets, fire pits, and picnic tables on a first-come, first-served basis. Rates are $8 per night. Bears are common in the park, so proper food storage measures must be taken. Leashed pets are permitted on trails and in camp. Call the **Park Service** (☎ 619/934-2289) for details. There are several other Forest Service campgrounds nearby including **Red's Meadow** and **Upper Soda Springs** (☎ 619/924-5500).

5 Visalia: Gateway to Sequoia & Kings Canyon

Visalia is the gateway to Sequoia and Kings Canyon National Parks. It's halfway between the coast and the Sierras and halfway between Los Angeles and Sacramento. The town is pleasant enough, and it has some very fine Victorian and Colonial revival homes. Pick up a walking tour pamphlet at the Visitors Bureau if you're interested in strolling.

In stride with its surroundings, Visalia has consciously preserved its natural wilderness in the form of 18 public parks, which cover almost 400 acres. Especially popular is the **Mooney Grove Park,** at 2700 South Mooney Blvd., which is filled with the remainder of a great oak forest that once reigned here. There's also a lagoon with islands, boathouse, and fish ponds. Another of the park's monuments to the past is the famous and moving statue *The End of the Trail* by James Earle Fraser. It depicts a battle-weary brave, head dropped to his chest, spear tip down, astride an exhausted pony. In 1968 the original was removed to the National Cowboy Hall of Fame in Oklahoma City and replaced by this copy cast in bronze.

The **Tulare County Museum,** also in the park, at 2700 S. Mooney Blvd. (☎ 209/733-6616), displays some fine collections and several restored historic buildings, including the Visalia Jail and Witt's Blacksmith Shop where C. V. Witt designed his world-famous cattle brands. Admission is $2 adults, $1 children under 13. It's open Wednesday to Monday from 10am to 4pm.

At the **Central California Chinese Cultural Center,** 500 S. Akers (☎ 209/625-4545), a temple complex and museum, the Chinese in the valley gather to preserve their traditions and cultural heritage. Visitors can view Chinese artifacts, archaeological objects, and paintings inside the center, and contemplate the eight-foot bronze statue of Confucius in the courtyard. Admission is free and it's open year-round. Call in advance for open hours.

ESSENTIALS

From San Francisco, take U.S. 580 to I-5 south to Calif. 298. For information, contact the **Visalia Convention and Visitors Bureau,** 815 W. Center St., Visalia, CA 93291 (☎ **800/524-0303** or 209/738-3435).

WHERE TO STAY

✪ **Ben Maddox House.** 601 N. Encina St., Visalia, CA 93291. ☎ **800/401-9800** or 209/739-0721. 4 rms. TEL TV. $60 double without bath; $75–$90 double. Rates include breakfast. AE, MC, V.

Set in a residential street of Victorian homes, 4 blocks from the town's main street, the Ben Maddox House is an impressive sight with its triangular gable, punctuated with a round window and two extremely tall palm trees looming over the front yard. The house, built in 1876, is constructed of redwood and its rooms retain their original dark-oak trim and white-oak floors. Guest rooms are decorated with late 18th-and 19th-century furnishings, and the two front rooms have French doors leading to two small porch sitting areas. A swimming pool and hot tub are open to guests in the back, and a full breakfast is served.

Radisson Hotel. 300 S. Court St., Visalia, CA 93291. ☎ **800/333-3333** or 209/636-1111. Fax 209/636-8224. 201 rms, 7 suites. A/C MINIBAR TEL TV. $100–$130 double; $225–$450 suite. Additional person $15. AE, CB, DC, MC, V.

Lying 7 blocks from the town center, this eight-story chain hotel is the finest in Visalia. It's a family favorite, and is often visited by those en route to Sequoia and Kings Canyon. Cribs are provided free, thankfully, as some of the attractively furnished rooms open onto balconies. This is certainly not the most glamorous Radisson in California, but it is serviceable in every way, and contains a whirlpool and wet bar in suites, and even offers room service until 2am. Free airport transfers are arranged as well. There is exercise equipment, and the hotel also maintains a fleet of bikes. The restaurant serves long hours, beginning with breakfast at 6am, with the last dinner orders going in at 10pm. You can also patronize the local bar, and entertainment is provided on Friday and Saturday nights. The hotel has a pool with poolside service.

🄢 **The Spalding House.** 631 N. Encina St., Visalia, CA 93291. ☎ **209/739-7877.** Fax 209/625-0902. 3 suites. $85 double. Rates include breakfast. MC, V.

This Colonial-revival house built in 1901 has been carefully restored by owners Wayne and Peggy Davidson. Hand-crafted beveled glass doors lead into the entry hall and the music room, which has a 1923 Steinway player grand piano. Readers will particularly enjoy the library, which is lined with more than 1,500 books. There's a

TV in the living room and Oriental rugs and antiques are combined with classic reproductions throughout the house. All of the rooms are suites with sitting room, bedroom, and private bath, but no phone. It's totally nonsmoking.

WHERE TO DINE

Michael's on Main. 123 W. Main St. ☎ **209/635-2686.** Main courses $15–$22. AE, DC, MC, V. Mon–Fri 11am–3pm; Mon–Thurs 5–10pm, Fri–Sat 5–11pm. CALIFORNIA.

Join the debate in Visalia—some claim that Michael's on Main is better than The Vintage Press (see below). The main dishes at Michael's range from fresh seafood such as blackened ahi tuna to grilled items including pork tenderloin with port wild mushroom sauce or grilled filet of rabbit. In season, game is available. There are also several luscious pastas, a favorite being the rigatoni bellini tossed with wild mushrooms, sun-dried tomatoes, smoked duck, and *quattro formaggi* (four cheese) sauce.

✪ **The Vintage Press.** 216 N. Willis St. ☎ **209/733-3033.** Main courses $12–$25. AE, CB, DC, MC, V. Mon–Sat 11:30am–2pm; Mon–Thurs 6–10:30pm, Fri–Sat 6–11pm. AMERICAN/CONTINENTAL.

This is the best restaurant within a surrounding 100-mile radius, a culinary stopover of widely acknowledged merit in the gastronomic wasteland between Los Angeles and San Francisco. Everything about it was designed to imitate a fin de siècle gin mill in gold-rush San Francisco, with a bar imported from that city manufactured by the Brunswick Company (of bowling-alley fame), lots of antiques bought at local auctions, and glittering panels of leaded glass and mirrors. The place is big enough (250 seats) to feed a boatload of gold-rush hopefuls and has a bustling bar/lounge where live music from a piano player is presented Thursday through Saturday from 5:30 to 9pm.

The menu is supplemented by daily specials—a zesty rack of lamb roasted in a cabernet sauce with rosemary and pistachios, for example. The regular menu offers about a dozen meat and fish dishes, with steaks supplemented by such dishes as red snapper with lemon, almonds, and capers or pork tenderloin with Dijon mustard, red chili, and honey. To start, we recommend a selection of farm-raised fresh oysters on the half shell or the wild mushrooms with cognac in puff pastry.

6 Sequoia & Kings Canyon National Parks

by Andrew Rice

It's only about 200 road miles between Yosemite and Sequoia and Kings Canyon National Parks, but the two Sierra Nevada parks are worlds apart. Where the Park Service has taken every opportunity to modernize, accessorize, and urbanize Yosemite, leading to a frenetic tourist scene much like the cities so many of us strive to escape, at Sequoia and Kings Canyon they've treated the wilderness beauty of the park with respect and care. Only one road loops through the park, the Generals Highway, and no road traverses the Sierra here. The park service doesn't recommend vehicles over 22 feet long use the steep and windy stretch between Potwisha Campground and the Giant Forest in Sequoia National Park. As a result, the park is much less accessible by car than most, but spectacular for those willing to head out on foot.

Technically two separate parks, Sequoia and Kings Canyon are contiguous and managed jointly from the park headquarters near Ash Mountain off Calif. 198 east of Visalia.

The Sierra Nevada tilts upward as it runs south. **Mt. Whitney,** the highest peak in the Lower 48 (at 14,495 feet), is just one of many high peaks in Sequoia and Kings Canyon. The Pacific Crest Trail reaches its highest point here too, crossing north to south through both parks. Besides the rocky, snow-covered peaks, Sequoia and Kings Canyon are also home to the largest groves of giant sequoias in the Sierra Nevada, as well as the headwaters of the Kern, Kaweah, and Kings rivers. A few small, high-country lakes are home to some of the only remaining pure-strain golden trout. Bear, deer, and numerous smaller animals and birds depend on the park's miles of wild habitat for summer breeding and feeding grounds.

SEEING THE HIGHLIGHTS

There are some 75 groves of giant sequoias in the park, but the easiest places to see the park's big trees are **Grant Grove,** in Kings Canyon near the park entrance on Highway 180 from Fresno, or **Giant Forest,** a huge grove of trees containing 40 miles of footpaths 16 miles from the entrance to Sequoia National Park on Calif. 198. Saving the sequoias was the reason Sequoia National Park was created in 1890 at the request of San Joaquin Valley residents, making it America's second-oldest national park.

The 2-mile **Congress Trail** loop in the Giant Forest starts at the base of the **General Sherman tree,** the largest living thing in the world. Single branches on the General Sherman are more than seven feet thick. Each year the General Sherman grows enough wood to make a 60-foot-tall tree of normal dimensions. Other trees in the grove are nearly as large and many of the peaceful-looking trees have also been saddled with strangely militaristic and political monikers like General Lee and Lincoln. Longer trails lead to remote reaches of the grove and nearby meadows.

Unlike the coast redwoods, which reproduce by sprouting or by seeds, giant sequoias only reproduce by seed. The tiny cones require fire to open, so decades can pass between generations. Adult sequoias don't die of old age and are protected from fire by thick bark. Most die when they topple in high winds or heavy snows. The huge trees have surprisingly shallow roots. These groves, like the ones in Yosemite, were first explored by conservationist and nature writer John Muir.

Besides the sequoia groves, Sequoia and Kings Canyon are home to the most pristine wilderness in the Sierra Nevada. At Roads End on the Kings Canyon Highway (open from May to November) you can stand by the banks of the Kings River and stare up at 5,000-foot-tall granite walls rising above the river, the deepest canyon in the United States.

Near Giant Forest Village, **Moro Rock** is a 6,725-foot-tall granite dome formed by exfoliation of layers of the rock. A quarter-mile trail scales the dome for a spectacular view of the adjacent Kaweah Canyon. The trail gains 300 feet in 400 yards, so be ready for a climb.

Boyden Cavern on Calif. 180, in neighboring Sequoia National Forest, is a large cave where you can take a 45-minute tour to see stalactites and stalagmites. A fee is charged; call **209/736-2708** for details.

Crystal Cave, is located 15 miles from the Calif. 198 park entrance and an additional 7 miles to cave parking. Here you can take a 50-minute tour of Crystal's beautiful marble interior. The tour costs $4 for adults and children 12 and older, $2 for children 6 to 11 and senior citizens, and free under six. Tickets are not sold at the cave and must be purchased at Lodgepole or Foothills visitors centers at least an hour and a half in advance. Be sure to wear sturdy shoes and bring a jacket.

HIKING THE PARK

Hiking and backpacking are what this park is really all about. Seven hundred miles of trails connect canyons, lakes, and high alpine meadows and snow fields.

Sequoia & Kings Canyon National Parks

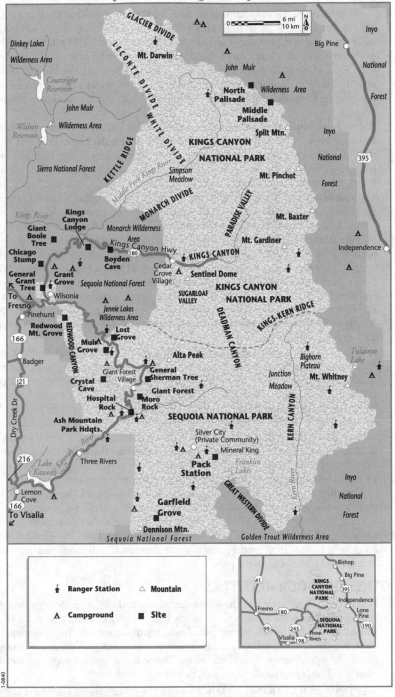

GLACIER DIVIDE

Dinkey Lakes
Wilderness Area

Courtright
Reservoir

John Muir

Wishon
Reservoir

Wilderness Area

Sierra National Forest

Kings River

Giant
Boole
Tree

Chicago
Stump

General
Grant
Tree

To
Fresno

Pinehurst

Badger

Dry Creek Dr

Lemon
Cove

To Visalia

Mt. Darwin

North
Palisade

Middle
Palisade

Split Mtn.

KINGS CANYON

NATIONAL PARK

Simpson
Meadow

MONARCH DIVIDE

Kings
Canyon
Lodge

Monarch Wilderness
Area
Kings Canyon Hwy

Boyden
Cave

Grant
Grove

Wilsonia

Redwood
Mt. Grove

Muir
Grove

Crystal
Cave

Hospital
Rock

Ash Mountain
Park Hdqts.

Three Rivers

Garfield
Grove

Dennison Mtn.

John Muir

Wilderness Area

Mt. Pinchot

KINGS CANYON

Cedar
Grove
Village

Sentinel Dome

SUGARLOAF
VALLEY

Sequoia National Forest

Jennie Lakes
Wilderness Area

Lost
Grove

Giant Forest
Village

General
Sherman Tree

Giant Forest

Moro
Rock

SEQUOIA NATIONAL PARK

Silver City
(Private Community)

Mineral King

Pack
Station

Lake
Kaweah

Kaweah River

Big Pine

Inyo

National

Forest

Inyo

National

Forest

Mt. Baxter

Mt. Gardiner

KINGS CANYON

NATIONAL PARK

DEADMAN CANYON

Alta Peak

KINGS-KERN RIDGE

Bighorn
Plateau

Junction
Meadow

Mt. Whitney

Franklin
Lakes

KERN CANYON

Kern River

Independence

395

Tulainyo
Lake

Inyo

National

Forest

GREAT WESTERN DIVIDE

Sequoia National Forest

Golden Trout Wilderness Area

Legend

- 🛉 **Ranger Station**
- ⚠ **Campground**
- △ **Mountain**
- ■ **Site**

Bishop

41

KINGS
CANYON
NATIONAL
PARK

Big Pine

395

Independence

Lone
Pine

Fresno

180

245

SEQUOIA
NATIONAL
PARK

190

99

Visalia

198

Three
Rivers

1-0840

287

Some of the park's most impressive hikes start in the **Mineral King** section in the southern end of Sequoia. Beginning at 7,800 feet, trails lead onward and upward to destinations like Sawtooth Pass, Crystal Lake, and the old White Chief Trail to the now-defunct White Chief Mine. Once an unsuccessful silver mining town in the 1870s, Mineral King was the center of a pitched battle in the late 1970s and early 1980s when developers sought to build a huge ski resort here. They were defeated when Congress added Mineral King to the park, and the wilderness remains unspoiled.

The **John Muir Trail,** which begins in Yosemite Valley, ends here just below Mount Whitney. For many miles it coincides with the **Pacific Crest Trail** as it skirts the highest peaks in the park. This is the most difficult part of the **Pacific Crest,** remaining above 10,000 feet most of the time and crossing 12,000-foot-tall passes.

Other hikers like to explore the end of the park from Cedar Grove and Roads End. The **Paradise Valley Trail** is a fairly easy day trip by park standards leading to beautiful Mist Falls. **Copper Creek Trail** immediately rises into the high wilderness around Granite Pass at 10,673 feet, one of the most strenuous day hikes in the park.

If the altitude and steepness are too much for you at these trailheads, try some of the longer hikes in the **Giant Forest** or **Grant Grove.** These forests are woven with interlocking loops that allow you to take as short or as long a hike as you want. The 6-mile **Trail of the Sequoias** in Giant Forest will take you to the grove's far eastern end where some of the finest trees are. In Grant Grove, a fascinating side trip, is the 100-foot walk through the hollow trunk of the Fallen Monarch. The fallen tree has been used for shelter for more than 100 years and is tall enough inside that you can walk through without bending over.

Perhaps the most traversed trail to the park is the **Whitney Portal Trail.** It runs from east of the park near Lone Pine, through Inyo National Forest, to the summit of Mt. Whitney. Overnight and day-use permits are required. They're limited and available by writing to **Wilderness Office,** Sequoia and Kings Canyon National Parks, Three Rivers, CA 93271 (permits are required for all overnight trips to the backcountry). Call **209/565-3708** for information. Though it is a straightforward walk to the summit and possible to bag it in a very long day hike, you'd better be in really good shape before attempting it. Almost half the people who attempt Whitney, including those who camp part way up, don't reach the summit. Weather, altitude, and fatigue can all conspire to stop even the most prepared party.

The official park map and guide gives good road maps for the parks, but for serious hiking you'll want to check out *Sierra South: 100 Back-Country Trips* by Thomas Winnett and Jason Winnett (Wilderness Press). Another good guide is *Kings Canyon Country,* a hiking handbook by Ginny and Lew Clark. The Grant Grove, Lodgepole, Cedar Grove, and Foothills visitors centers all sell a complete selection of maps and guidebooks to the park.

OTHER OUTDOOR ACTIVITIES

FISHING   Trout fishing in the lower altitudes is fairly limited, mostly along the banks of the Kings and Kaweah rivers. A few high-country lakes are refuges for trout and are not stocked with hatchery fish. Before venturing into the high country, inquire at a ranger station about the area you'll be visiting to find out about closures or specific regulations. A California fishing license is required for everyone over 16 years old. Tackle and licenses are available at several park stores.

RAFTING & KAYAKING   Only recently have professional outfitters begun taking experienced rafters and kayakers down the class IV and V Kaweah and Upper Kings rivers outside the parks. Contact **Sequoia National Forest** at

Winter Driving in the Sierras

Winter driving in the Sierra Nevada range can be dangerous. While the most hazardous roads are often closed, others are negotiable by four-wheel drive or with chained tires. Be prepared for sudden blizzards, and protect yourself by taking these important pretrip precautions:

- Check road conditions before setting out by calling **800/427-7623.**
- If you're driving a rental car, let the rental company know you're planning to drive in snow, and ask whether the antifreeze is prepared for cooler climates.
- Make sure your heater and defroster work.
- Always carry chains. If there is a blizzard, the police will not allow vehicles without chains on certain highways. You will have to pay about $40 to "chain up" at the side of the road.
- Recommended items include an ice scraper, a small shovel, sand or burlap for traction if you get stuck, warm blankets, and an extra car key (it's surprisingly common for motorists to lock their keys in the car while putting on tire chains).

209/784-1550 for a current listing of companies running trips. This is only for the very adventurous.

SKIING & SNOWSHOEING **Sequoia Ski Touring** (☎ **209/565-3381**), near Giant Forest Village, offers complete rentals and trail maps for 35 miles of Sequoia backcountry trails. In Kings Canyon, **Sequoia Ski Touring in Grant Grove** (☎ **209/335-2314**) provides the same services and an even wider selection of trails. People with their own equipment are welcome on all trails in the park at no cost. Trail maps are available at the visitor centers. On winter weekends park rangers lead introductory snowshoe hikes (snowshoes provided for $1) at both areas. The roads to Cedar Grove and Mineral King are closed in the winter.

CAMPING & ACCOMMODATIONS

There are 13 campgrounds in the park, offering the most convenient and economical accommodations here, although none have hookups. Only one accepts reservations: **Lodgepole Campground** on the Kaweah River in Sequoia. Others are first-come, first-served and often fill up on weekends. Three campgrounds, Azalea, Lodgepole, and Potwisha are year-round. The rest are open from snowmelt through September. Even in summer campers should prepare for rain and cold temperatures. Bring a good tent and warm sleeping bags.

Two large campgrounds in Sequoia are **Dorst** and Lodgepole. Both are close to the Giant Forest. Lodgepole is within a short stroll of a restaurant, gas station, and a visitor center. With more than 200 sites each, they tend to be the noisiest campgrounds in Sequoia. Lodgepole is the most expensive in the park at $14 per site. Dorst is $12.

Smaller and more peaceful are **South Fork, Potwisha, Buckeye Flats, Atwell Mill,** and **Cold Springs.** South Fork, Atwell Mill, and Cold Springs have pit toilets and are $6 per night. The others, with flush toilets, running water, and public phones, charge $12.

Campers in the remote Cedar Grove area of Kings Canyon National Park near the Kings River gorge can choose from **Moraine, Sentinel, Sheep Creek,** and **Canyon View,** a group camp. All four have flush toilets and are convenient to some of the park's best hiking. The small Cedar Grove Village offers a restaurant, store, showers, and gas. Sites are $12.

Three campgrounds in the Grant Grove area will put you near the sequoias without the noise and crowds of Giant Forest Village. All three, **Sunset, Azalea,** and **Crystal Springs,** have flush toilets and phones. Azalea has an RV disposal site and ranger station. Showers are nearby. Rates are $12 per site.

Lodging in the parks ranges from rustic one-room cabins with no bath or heat to a luxury motel. None of the complexes are very big. All lodging in the park is operated by the park concessionaire, **Sequoia Guest Services,** P.O. Box 789, Three Rivers, CA 93271 (☎ **209/561-3314** for information and reservations).

The heaviest concentration of accommodations is in Giant Forest, where you'll find something in every price and taste range. Grant Grove offers a variety of cabins with private or shared baths. Cedar Grove is the site of an 18-room motel. Each room has its own bath and two queen-size beds.

JUST THE FACTS

Most visitors make a loop through the parks by entering at Grant Grove and leaving through Ash Mountain, or vice versa.

ENTRANCE FEES   A $5 per car fee is good for one week's worth of entry at any park entrance. An annual pass is $15.

VISITOR CENTERS   Lodgepole and Grant Grove visitor centers are the largest, with a full selection of park information and displays about the history, biology, and geology of this incredible place. Some time spent here will pay off by letting you decide which parts of the widely dispersed park you most want to concentrate on.

AVOIDING THE CROWDS   To escape the crowds and see less used areas of the park, enter on one of the dead-end roads to Mineral King, South Fork, or Cedar Grove. The lack of through traffic makes these parts of the park incredibly peaceful even at full capacity, and they are gateways to the parks' best hiking.

RANGER PROGRAMS   Park rangers lead hikes, campfire talks, and slide shows at several campgrounds and visitor centers during the summer.

REGULATIONS   Wilderness permits are required for all backpacking trips. You can reserve permits in advance by writing the park headquarters. Mountain bikes and dogs are forbidden on all park trails (dogs are only permitted in developed areas , but must be leashed). The park service allows firewood gathering at campgrounds, but removing wood from living or standing trees is forbidden.

RESERVATIONS   You can reserve permits for Mt. Whitney and Inyo National Forest by phone, fax, or mail from **Wilderness Reservations,** P.O. Box 430, Big Pine, CA 93513 (☎ **888-374-3773** or 619/938-1136; fax 619/938-1137).

THE SEASONS   In the middle to high altitudes, where most Sequoia and Kings Canyon visitors are headed, summer is short and the winters are cold. Spring can come as early as April and as late as June. Snow is not unheard of in July and August. Afternoon showers are common. Only the main road through the parks is usually open during winter months when the climate can range from bitter cold to pleasant and changes minute by minute. Be ready for anything if you head into the backcountry on skis. Mosquitoes, poison oak, and rattlesnakes are common in lower elevations during summer.

The Gold Country & the Central Valley

11

by Erika Lenkert and Matthew R. Poole

On the morning of January 24, 1848, a carpenter named James Marshall came across a shiny yellow nugget on the south fork of the American River while working on John Sutter's mill in Coloma. Despite Sutter's wishes to keep the discovery a secret, word leaked out, a word that would change the fate of California, and John Sutter, almost overnight: Gold! The news spread like wildfire, and a frenzy seized the nation; the gold rush was on. Within three years, the population of the state grew from a meager 15,000 to more than 265,000. Most of these newcomers were single men under the age of 40, and not far behind were the thousands of merchants, bankers, and women who made their fortunes catering to these miners.

Sacramento grew quickly as a supply town at the base of the surrounding gold mines. Although boom time for the Gold Country ended less than a decade later and many towns diminished or disappeared, Sacramento continued to grow and the Central Valley to the south found another form of riches by becoming the vegetable and fruit garden of the nation.

A trip along Calif. 49 from the northern mines to the southern mines will give visitors a sense of what it must have been like on the rough and ready mining frontier. Nobody knows how many movies have been shot in the towns along the route—it's certainly into the hundreds, perhaps even the thousands. The main streets are familiar to everyone, with their raised wooden sidewalks, double-porched buildings, ornate saloons, and Victorian storefronts. Each town tells a similar story of sudden wealth and explosive growth, yet each has left behind a different imprint.

For the budget traveler, the Gold Country offers a wealth of inexpensive hotels and restaurants. Most towns along Calif. 49 depend on tourism as their main source of income (the gold mining business has pretty much run dry) and hotel rates are fairly competitive. As long as you avoid the higher-end B&Bs, which charge up to $150 a night, you can easily keep expenses down to about $70 a day and still live like a Comstock king.

In stark contrast to the Gold Country's rolling hills and winding roads is the broad, flat Central Valley. This is California's market garden, the source of much of its bounty that is shipped across the nation and overseas. Much of the history of California has revolved around the struggle for control of the water used to irrigate the valley (it receives less than 10 inches of rainfall per year) and to make this inland desert bloom: Orange and pistachio groves, grape vines, and strawberry fields stretch in an impressive panorama uninterrupted for miles. Tourists are a rarity in these parts, as there are few artificial attractions to visit and the scalding summer heat saps the wandering spirit out of most folks. But campers, backpackers, and anyone with a love for the outdoors will find a hidden slice of heaven among the national parks and wilderness areas to the southeast—rugged lands so remote that most Californians haven't even heard of, much less visited, them.

1 Sacramento

Sacramento, with a population of 370,000, is one of the state's fastest-growing cities. In addition to being the state capital, it is a thriving shipping and processing center for the fruit, vegetables, rice, wheat, and dairy goods that are produced in the fertile Central Valley. It's a prosperous and politically charged city, with broad, tree-shaded streets lined with some impressive Victorians and craftsman-style bungalows. At its heart sits the Capitol building, Sacramento's main attraction, in a well-maintained park replete with flower gardens and curious squirrels. Aside from Old Sacramento, site of the world-renowned Dixieland Jazz Jubilee, the city doesn't have a whole lot to offer tourists, but even the locals enjoy spending the day poking through the shops of Old Sacramento or floating down the American River.

ESSENTIALS

GETTING THERE   If you're driving from San Francisco, Sacramento is located about 90 miles east, a straight shot on I-80. From Los Angeles, take I-5 through the Central Valley directly into Sacramento. From North Lake Tahoe, get on I-80 west, and from South Lake Tahoe take U.S. 50.

Sacramento Metropolitan Airport (☎ 916/929-5411), 12 miles northwest of downtown Sacramento, is served by about a dozen airlines, including **American** (☎ 800/433-7300), **Continental** (☎ 800/525-0280 or 916/369-2700), **Delta** (☎ 800/221-1212 or 916/446-3464), **Northwest** (☎ 800/225-2525), and **United** (☎ 800/241-6522). AAA Taxi and Shuttle Service (☎ 916/334-5555) will get you from the airport to downtown; they charge a flat rate of $15 to the capital. A taxi will cost about $30 from the airport to downtown.

Amtrak (☎ 800/USA-RAIL) services Sacramento daily.

ORIENTATION   Suburbia sprawls around Sacramento, but its downtown area is relatively compact. Getting around the city is made easy by a gridlike pattern of streets that are designated by numbers or letters. The state capitol, on 10th Street between N and L streets, is the key landmark. From the front of the capitol, M Street, which is at this point called Capitol Mall, runs 10 straight blocks to Old Sacramento, one of the city's oldest sections.

VISITOR INFORMATION   The **Sacramento Convention and Visitors Bureau,** 1421 K St., Sacramento, CA 95814 (☎ **916/264-7777,** fax 916/264-7788), provides plenty of information. Once in the city, visitors can stop by the **Sacramento Visitor Center,** 1104 Front St. (☎ **916/264-7777,** or 916/442-7644 on weekends and holidays), in Old Sacramento. It's usually open daily from 9am to 5pm.

EXPLORING THE CAPITOL & ENVIRONS

The American and Sacramento rivers lie nearby, and rafting is immensely popular, especially on warm weekends. Several Sacramento area outfitters rent rafts for 4 to 15 persons, along with life jackets and paddles. Their shuttles drop you and your

Downtown Sacramento

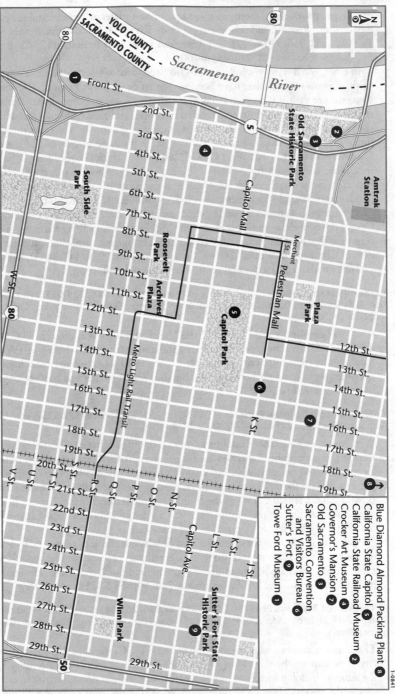

Yolo County
Sacramento County

Sacramento River

South Side Park

Roosevelt Park

Archives Plaza

Capitol Park

Capitol Mall

Plaza Park

Merchant St.

Pedestrian Mall

Amtrak Station

Old Sacramento State Historic Park

Metro Light Rail Transit

Winn Park

Sutter's Fort State Historic Park

Front St.
2nd St.
3rd St.
4th St.
5th St.
6th St.
7th St.
8th St.
9th St.
10th St.
11th St.
12th St.
13th St.
14th St.
15th St.
16th St.
17th St.
18th St.
19th St.
20th St.
21st St.
22nd St.
23rd St.
24th St.
25th St.
26th St.
27th St.
28th St.
29th St.

12th St.
13th St.
14th St.
15th St.
16th St.
17th St.
18th St.
19th St.

V St.
U St.
T St.
R St.
Q St.
P St.
O St.
N St.
L St.
K St.
J St.

Capitol Ave.
K St.
29th St.

Blue Diamond Almond Packing Plant 8
California State Capitol 5
California State Railroad Museum 2
Crocker Art Museum 4
Governor's Mansion 7
Old Sacramento 3
Sacramento Convention and Visitors Bureau 6
Sutter's Fort 9
Towe Ford Museum 1

293

entourage upstream and meet you three to four hours later at a predetermined point downstream. Recommended outfitters include **River Rat,** 4053 Pennsylvania Ave., Fair Oaks (☎ **916/966-6777**), and **American River Raft Rentals,** 11257 S. Bridge St., Rancho Cordova (☎ **916/635-6400**).

In town, you'll want to stroll around **Old Sacramento,** 4 square blocks at the foot of the downtown area that have become the city's major attraction. The blocks contain more than 100 restored buildings, including restaurants and shops. Although the area has cobblestoned streets, wooden sidewalks, and gold rush–era architecture, the high concentration of T-shirt shops and other gimmicky stores has turned it into a sort of historical Disneyland. While you're there, be sure to stop at the new **Discovery Museum** at 101 I St. (☎ **916/264-7057**), which houses dozens of hands-on exhibits and demonstrations on California's history, as well as plenty of fascinating scientific and technological gizmos and doodads. It's open Tuesday through Sunday from 10am to 5pm; admission is $3.50 for adults, $2 for kids 6 to 17.

Sacramento is as flat as a tortilla, which makes it perfect for exploring by bicycle. One of the best places to ride is along the 22-mile American River Parkway, which runs right through Old Sacramento. If you didn't bring your own wheels, the friendly guys at **City Bicycle Works,** 2419 K St. at 24th St. (☎ **916/447-2453**), will rent you one for about $15 a day and point you in the right direction.

California State Capitol. 10th St. (between N and L sts.). ☎ **916/324-0333.** Free admission. Daily 9am–4pm. Tours offered every hour on the hour. Closed Thanksgiving, Christmas, and New Year's Day.

Closely resembling a scale model of the U.S. Capitol in Washington, D.C., the domed California state capitol, built in 1869 and massively renovated in 1976, is Sacramento's most distinctive landmark. Daily guided tours, offered every hour on the hour, provide insight both into the building's architecture and the workings of the government it houses.

California State Railroad Museum. 125 I St. (at 2nd St.). ☎ **916/552-5252**, ext. 7245. Admission $5 adults, $2 children 6–12. Daily 10am–5pm.

Well worth visiting, this museum is one of the highlights of Old Sacramento. Bypass the memorabilia displays and head straight for the museum's 21 shiny locomotives and rail cars, beautiful antiques that are true works of art. Afterward, there's a film on the history of western railroading that's actually quite good; related exhibits tell the amazing story of the building of the transcontinental railroad. This museum is not just for train buffs; even the hordes of schoolchildren that overrun it almost every day shouldn't dissuade you from visiting.

April through September weekends and holidays, steam locomotive rides depart on the hour from 10am to 5pm from the Central Pacific Passenger Station at K and Front streets. Fares are $5 for adults, $2 for children 6–12. For more information, including off-season and holiday excursions, call **916/552-5252**, ext. 7245.

✪ **Crocker Art Museum.** 216 O St. (at 3rd St.). ☎ **916/264-5423.** Admission $4.50 adults, $2 ages 7–17, children under 6 free. Wed and Fri–Sun 10am–5pm, Thurs 10am–9pm. Closed major holidays.

This museum houses a truly outstanding collection of California art. Donated to the city of Sacramento by the widow of Judge E. B. Crocker more than a century ago, the museum building itself is an imposing Italianate, with an ornate interior of carved and inlaid woods. The Crocker Mansion Wing, the museum's recent addition, is modeled after the Crocker family home and contains works by Northern California artists from the 1960s to the present day.

Sutter's Fort State Historic Park. 2701 L St. ☎ **916/445-4422.** Admission $2 adults, $1 children 6–12; free for children 5 and under. Daily 10am–5pm.

John Augustus Sutter established this outpost in 1839. It has been restored to its 1846 appearance. The usual exhibits are on hand—blacksmith, cooper, bakery, jail—on a self-guided audio tour. Historic demonstrations are staged daily.

FOR KIDS: WHERE THE WILD THINGS ARE

In my experience, the best place to take your kid on a sunny afternoon in Sacramento is **Humpty Dumpty's Fairytale Town** (☎ 916/264-5885), in **William Land Park,** which is at the corner of Land Park Drive and Sutterville Road. How do I know? Because I grew up here, and I can still remember dragging my poor parents through the stone archway, guarded by a perilously perched Humpty Dumpty (now just a shell of a man). After riding *all* the rides and climbing and kicking everything in sight, we would cross the street to the **Sacramento Zoo,** buy a big spool of cotton candy, and see *all* the animals.

WHERE TO STAY

Within walking distance of the state capitol is another reliable, affordable choice, the **Sacramento Vagabond Inn,** 909 Third St. (☎ **800/522-1555** or 916/446-1481).

Abigail's Bed and Breakfast. 2120 G St., Sacramento, CA 95816. ☎ **800/858-1568** or 916/441-5007. Fax 916/441-0621. 5 rms. A/C TEL TV. $100–$160 double. Rates include breakfast. AE, DISC, MC, V.

A boarding house for women during World War II, this 1912 Colonial Revival mansion has since been converted into a quaint and comfortable B&B. There are several pretty sitting areas, an outdoor spa in the rear garden, and two house cats, Sabrina and Abigail. The home's five rooms, all with private baths, are furnished with queen-size wood or brass beds and an assortment of antiques, including a chair or small settee. Anne's Room, the B&B's best, contains an enormous mahogany four-poster bed. Every room comes with terry robes and reproductions of antique radios. A telephone and TV are available upon request.

✪ **Amber House Bed and Breakfast.** 1315 22nd St., Sacramento, CA 95816. ☎ **800/755-6526** or 916/444-8085. Fax 916/552-6529. 9 rms. A/C TEL TV. $99–$219 double. Rates include breakfast. AE, CB, DC, DISC, MC, V.

Just 8 blocks from the capitol, Michael and Jane Richards' bucolic 1905 Amber House has individually decorated rooms named for famous artists and writers. Accommodations are located in two adjacent historic houses: the Poet's Refuge, a 1905 craftsman-style home (five rooms) and the Artist's Retreat, a 1913 Mediterranean-style home. The Renoir Room is the B&B's best, containing a canopied, king-size bed and a Jacuzzi big enough for three. All rooms have marble bathrooms—eight with whirlpool bathtubs for two—hair dryers, VCRs, and phones with computer jacks and voice mail.

A beautiful living room and intimate library are available for guests' use. A full breakfast is served at the time and location you request, either in your room, at the large dining room, or outside on the veranda. Coffee is brought to your door early every morning along with a newspaper. Additional perks include room, concierge, and laundry service, as well as free use of bicycles.

Americana Lodge. 818 15th St. (at I St.). Sacramento, CA 95814. ☎ **916/444-3980.** 41 rms. A/C TEL TV. $39–$49. AE, DC, DISC, MC, V.

All of the Americana's rooms have been freshly remodeled and have air-conditioning (a must during Sacramento's summers). The lodge also has a swimming pool and is within walking distance of just about everything worth seeing in town. Granted, the Americana's no architectural masterpiece, but for rates starting at $40 a night at a prime location, nobody's complaining.

⑤ **Best Western Ponderosa Inn.** 1100 H St., Sacramento, CA 95814. ☎ **800/528-1234** or 916/441-1314. Fax 916/441-5961. 98 rms. A/C TEL TV. $75–$135 double. Rates include continental breakfast. AE, CB, DC, DISC, MC, V.

You'd never know from the plain motel-like exterior that this is one of the best values in Sacramento. Rooms here are as up-to-date as any offered by upscale players like Hilton and Sheraton, and include well-coordinated furnishings, in-room movies, voice-mail telephones, and valet and laundry service. There's a courtyard-enclosed swimming pool on the second floor, and complimentary coffee and Danish are served each morning in the lobby.

Delta King **Riverboat.** 1000 Front St., Old Sacramento, CA 95814. ☎ **800/825-5464** or 916/444-5464. 44 rms, 1 suite. A/C TEL TV. Sun–Thurs $99 double, $400 captain's quarters; Fri–Sat $139 double, $400 captain's quarters. Rates include continental breakfast. AE, DC, DISC, MC, V.

The *Delta King* carried passengers between San Francisco and Sacramento in the 1930s. Permanently moored in Sacramento since 1984, it underwent a $9 million restoration that enlarged all the staterooms and refurbished its popular restaurant. Staying here can be fun, but the hotel's novelty wears thin in the boat's cramped quarters, especially if you're planning to spend a lot of time in your room. All rooms are nearly identical and have private baths and low ceilings. The captain's quarters, a particularly pricey suite, is a unique, mahogany-paneled stateroom, complete with an observation platform and private deck.

The *Delta King's* Pilothouse Restaurant is popular for local office parties. When the weather is nice, there is dining on outside decks with views of Old Sacramento. The Paddlewheel Saloon, which overlooks the boat's 17-ton paddle wheel, regularly features live entertainment.

⑤ **Sacramento International Hostel.** 900 H St. (at 9th St.), Sacramento, CA 95814; ☎ **916/443-1691.** $12.75 for HI-AYH members, $15.75 for nonmembers. Family and couple rooms available. Check-in 7–9:30am, 5–10pm. Curfew 11pm.

Recuperating nicely from a $2 million facelift, this hostel, housed in a 12,000-square-foot Victorian mansion, is a real beauty (in fact, it's regarded as one of the finest hostels in the country). Yeah, yeah, we know: You don't want to share a room with snoring strangers. But if you happen to be towing a family along, you'd be hard pressed to find a better place for your money than the private rooms reserved for cash-conscious clans. There are three "couples" rooms, one with a double bed and two with three beds, that go for $33.50 a night. There's also three "family" rooms with five beds each, most of which are bunk beds. As for amenities, there are none: just a light and the beds—that's it. Everything else—bathroom, kitchen, rec room—is down the hall. Naturally, the rooms are a hot item, so make reservations as far in advance as possible.

WHERE TO DINE

Capitol Grill. 2730 N St. ☎ **916/736-0744.** Reservations recommended. Main courses $6.50–$19. AE, DC, DISC, MC, V. Mon 11am–10pm, Tues–Fri 11am–11pm, Sat 5–11pm, Sun 5–10pm. AMERICAN/SEAFOOD.

One of the liveliest restaurants in the city, Capitol Grill is popular with Sacramento's see-and-be-seen crowd—a good-looking throng of 20- and 30-somethings but without the Los Angeles–style snotty attitude. An excellent selection of well-prepared

---

Sacramento's Best Budget Dining

- **Best Artery Clogger: Tommy Burgers,** 2415 16th St. between Broadway and X Street (☎ 916/444-2006), a takeoff on L.A.'s Tommy Burgers, slathers everything in so much chili and cheese that heavy-duty paper towel dispensers are mandatory equipment. Open late most nights.

- **Best Vegetarian: Greta's Cafe,** 1831 Capital Ave. at 19th St. (☎ 916/442-7382), is silly with salads, offering a dozen choices along with fresh baked pastries and mondo sandwiches for under $4.

- **Best Coffee Joint:** A tough one, since there are so many great new coffee joints springing up, but one that's been popular forever and will probably remain that way is **Java City** (☎ 916/444-4422), at the corner of Capitol Avenue and 18th Street. Sure, there's plenty of bums around, but at least they keep the yuppies at bay.

- **Best Mexican: Taco Loco Taqueria,** 2326 J St. at 24th Street (☎ 916/444-0711). Try the charbroiled black-tip shark taco, big ole shrimp burrito, or snapper ceviche tostado, all so fresh they don't even own a freezer. Wash it all down with a Los Cabos Margarita while soaking up the sun on the front patio. There's another location at 1122 11th St. at L Street (☎ 916/447-TACO).

- **Best Breakfast:** Whenever we tell our friends about **Cornerstone Restaurant,** 2330 J. St. at 24th Street (☎ 916/441-0948), they always come back for more. The choices are all standard American, but the servings are huge, the service is friendly, and the price is right. A four-egg omelet with home fries, toast, and fruit costs less than $5.

- **Best Brewery:** Breweries seem to be popping up like weeds these days, but the **Rubicon Brewing Company,** 2004 Capitol Ave. at 19th Street (☎ 916/441-0948), still remains our favorite hangout. A pitcher of India Pale and a side of fries is guaranteed to do the trick.

---

dishes includes sea scallops with grilled scallions and ginger-soy butter, grilled lamb loin with French lentils, fried artichokes, and garlic sauce. Recommended starters are the shrimp pot stickers or chicken quesadilla.

✪ **Harlow's.** 2714 J St. ☎ **916/441-4693.** Main courses $10–$17. AE, DC, MC, V. Mon–Fri 11:30am–2pm; Mon–Thurs 6–9:30pm, Fri–Sat 6–10pm. ITALIAN/CALIFORNIA.

This comfortable, casual, and very popular spot has an ultrasleek 1930s air that might have pleased Jean Harlow herself. If you've got a hot date for the night, suggest meeting at the bar: It's the place to see and be seen in Sacramento. The pastas are superb here, ranging from the simple cannelloni in a rich meat sauce to the gnocchi in gorgonzola cream sauce. The main dishes are equally well prepared, such as the scampi diavola, which has a piquant horseradish mustard cream sauce. Top it all off with the chocolate pâté, then whip out your Macanudo and join the party upstairs at the Cigar Room, where you can often find some of Sacramento's best jazz bands.

Paragary's Bar and Oven. 1401 28th St. ☎ **916/452-3335.** Reservations recommended for 6 or more. Main courses $10–$17. AE, DC, DISC, MC, V. Mon–Thurs 11:30am–11pm, Fri 11:30am–midnight, Sat 5pm–midnight, Sun 5–10pm. ITALIAN.

Occupying two distinct dining rooms just across the street from Capitol Grill, Paragary's vies with its neighbor for best restaurant status in Sacramento's downtown.

The fireplace room is more formal than the brighter cafe, which is outfitted with bentwood chairs and white Formica tables. The same menu is served no matter where you sit, with the best dishes coming from the kitchen's wood-burning oven. Some of the more unusual gourmet pizza toppings are prosciutto, new potatoes, goat cheese, roasted garlic, artichokes, and smoked salmon. On warm summer nights we like to sit outside on the sidewalk and inhale bucketfuls of mussels.

Tower Cafe. 1518 Broadway. ☎ **916/441-0222.** Reservations recommended for parties of 8 or more. Main courses $7–$12. AE, MC, V. Mon–Fri 7–11am and 11:30am–4pm; Sun–Thurs 4:30–10pm, Fri–Sat 4:30–11pm; Sun 8am–2pm. Open later for dessert and drinks only.

The Tower Cafe gets its name from the building in which it's located: a grand old 1939 movie house with a tall art deco spire. The restaurant occupies the same space in which a small mom-and-pop music store once stood. This former resident, Tower Records, has since grown into America's second-largest record retailer. While it's unlikely that Tower Cafe will share the phenomenal success of its predecessor, it's not because of the food or surroundings. Both are good, and even with perpetually sluggish service this restaurant remains our favorite place for lunch in Sacramento. On warm days it seems as if everyone in the city is lunching here, and crowd-watching can be a real treat. Indeed, President Clinton and his staff were recently served here. Dishes reflect international flavors, from the Jamaican jerk chicken and African piri piri to the Thai pad Thai and Brazilian chicken salad.

2 The Gold Country

Cutting a swath for 350 miles along Calif. 49, the Gold Country stretches from Sierra City almost to the foothills of Yosemite. It still looks like a Western movie set, with its mine sites, caverns, and Wild West saloons, along with ghost towns and architecture that would make Gene Autry or Roy Rogers feel right at home.

Drive along Calif. 49 and stop wherever your mood dictates. We've gone there before you to highlight some of the best places to explore. We found the drive best in April, when most of the wildflowers burst into bloom. Motels, fast-food joints, and various convenience stores await you all along the route.

Placerville, on Calif. 50 to the east of Sacramento, sits in the approximate middle of the Gold Country. The northern Gold Country incorporates Placerville itself and other towns in the north. The southern Gold Country along Calif. 49 will take you to such towns as Amador City, Sutter Creek, and Jackson.

If you'd like to follow a very structured driving tour, see Chapter 4, "On the Road: Seeing California by Car."

THE NORTHERN GOLD COUNTRY: NEVADA CITY & GRASS VALLEY

Lying about 60 miles northeast of Sacramento, Nevada City and Grass Valley might be your best centers here. If you're driving from San Francisco, take I-80 to Calif. 49 and follow the signs. For information about the area, go to the **Grass Valley/Nevada County Chamber of Commerce,** 248 Mill St., Grass Valley, CA 95945 (☎ **916/273-4667**), or the **Nevada City Chamber of Commerce,** 132 Main St., Nevada City, CA 95959 (☎ **916/265-2692**).

These two towns were at the center of the hard-rock mining fields of Northern California. Grass Valley, in fact, was California's richest mining town, producing more than $400 million worth of gold in a century. Both are attractive to visit, although we would rank Nevada City number one. Its wealth of Victorian homes and

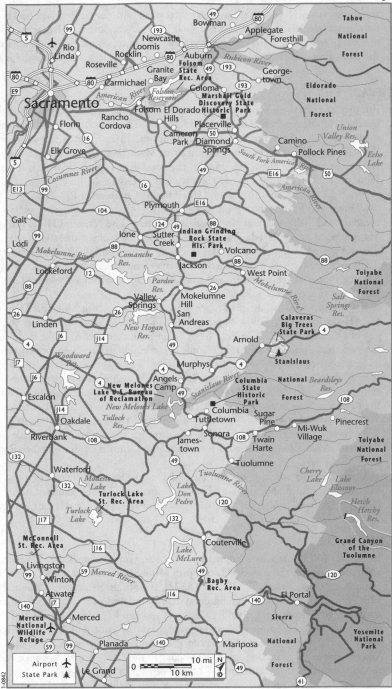

Tahoe National Forest

Bowman

Applegate
Foresthill

Newcastle
Loomis
Rocklin
Roseville
Rio Linda
Granite Bay
Auburn
Folsom State Rec. Area
Rubicon River
Georgetown
Eldorado National Forest

Carmichael
Sacramento
American River
Folsom Reservoir
Coloma
Marshall Gold Discovery State Historic Park
Union Valley Res.
Echo Lake

Florin
Rancho Cordova
Folsom
El Dorado Hills
Placerville
Camino
Pollock Pines

Elk Grove
Cameron Park
Diamond Springs
South Fork American
E16
American River

Cosumnes River

Galt
E13
Plymouth
E16

Lodi
Ione
Sutter Creek
Indian Grinding Rock State His. Park
Volcano

Lockeford
Mokelumne River
Comanche Res.
Jackson
West Point
Toiyabe National Forest

Valley Springs
Pardee Res.
Mokelumne Hill
Mokelumne River
Salt Springs Res.

Linden
New Hogan Res.
San Andreas
Calaveras Big Trees State Park

Arnold
Stanislaus

Woodward Res.
Murphys

Escalon
New Melones Lake U.S. Bureau of Reclamation
Angels Camp
Stanislaus River
Columbia State Historic Park
National Forest
Beardsleys Res.

Oakdale
New Melones Lake
Tullock Res.
Columbia
Tuttletown
Sugar Pine
Mi-Wuk Village
Pinecrest

Riverbank
James-town
Sonora
Twain Harte
Toiyabe National Forest

Waterford
Modesto Lake
Turlock Lake St. Rec. Area
Tuolumne
Cherry Lake
Lake Eleanor

Turlock Lake
Lake Don Pedro
Tuolumne River
Hetch Hetchy Res.

McConnell St. Rec. Area
Couterville
Lake McLure
Grand Canyon of the Tuolumne

Livingston
Winton
Merced River
Bagby Rec. Area
El Portal

Atwater
Sierra

Merced National Wildlife Refuge
Merced
National
Yosemite National Park

Planada
Mariposa
Forest

Airport
State Park
Le Grand
0   10 mi
10 km
N

storefronts makes it one of the most appealing small towns in California. The whole downtown has been designated a National Historic Landmark. It has attracted a number of artists and writers in recent years and there are several fine bookstores on the main street, a good selection of restaurants, and some high-quality shops to browse through.

NEVADA CITY

Rumors of miners pulling a pound of gold a day out of Deer Creek brought hundreds of fortune-seekers to the area in 1849. Within a year, it was a boisterous town of 10,000. In its heyday, everyone who was anyone visited this rollicking Western outpost with its busy red-light district: Mark Twain lectured here in 1866, telling the audience about his trips to the Sandwich Islands (Hawaii), former President Herbert Hoover also lived and worked here as a gold miner.

Pick up a walking tour map at the **Chamber of Commerce,** 132 Main St., and stroll the streets lined with impressive Victorian buildings, including the Firehouse, complete with bell tower and gingerbread decoration. The **National Hotel** (1854–56) is here, as is the **Nevada Theatre** (1865), one of the oldest theaters in the nation and still operating as such. Today it is home to the Foothill Theatre Company. **The Firehouse** contains a museum that displays mementos from the Donner Party, a Maidu Indian basket collection, and an altar from a temple originally located in the Chinese section of Grass Valley.

If you want to see the source of much of the city's wealth, visit **Malakoff Diggins State Historic Park,** 23579 N. Bloomfield Rd. (☎ 916/265-2740), 26 miles northeast of Nevada City. In the 1870s, North Bloomfield, then located in the middle of this park, had a population of 1,500. Some of the buildings have been reconstructed and refurnished to show what life was like then. The 3,000-acre park also offers several hiking trails, swimming at Blair Lake, and 30 campsites that can be reserved through **Mistix** by calling **800/444-7275.** The museum is open daily in summer from 10am to 5pm, but in winter is open only on weekends from 10am to 4pm. To reach the park, take Calif. 49 for 11 miles toward Downieville. Turn right onto Tyler-Foote Crossing Road for 17 miles. The name will change to Curzon Grade and then to Backbone. When the road turns into gravel, turn right onto Derbec Road and into the park.

Another 6 miles up Calif. 49 from the Malakoff Diggins turnoff will bring you to Pleasant Valley Road, the exit that will take you (in about 7 miles) to one of the most impressive **covered bridges** in the country. Built in 1862, it's 225 feet long and was crossed by many a stagecoach.

GRASS VALLEY

In contrast to Nevada City's "tourist town" image, Grass Valley is the commercial and retail center of the region. The **Empire Mine State Historic Park,** 10791 E. Empire St., Grass Valley (☎ 916/273-8522), is just outside of town. This mine, which once had 367 miles of underground shafts, produced an estimated 5.8 million ounces of gold between 1850 and 1956. Here you can look down the shaft of the mine, walk around the mine yard, and stroll through the gardens of the mine owner. From March through November, tours are given daily and a mining movie is shown. You can also enjoy picnicking, cycling, or hiking in the 784-acre park. It's open year-round. Admission to the museum is $2 for adults, $1 for children.

In town, visitors can pick up a walking tour map at the Chamber of Commerce and explore the historic downtown historic area along Mill and Main streets. There are also a couple of museums that history buffs will want to visit: the **Grass Valley**

Museum, in Mount Saint Mary's Convent and Chapel on S. Church Street (☎ 916/272-4725), and the **North Star Mining Museum** (☎ 916/273-4255).

Grass Valley was, for a time, the home of Lola Montez, singer, dancer, and paramour of the rich and famous. A replica of the **home** that she bought and occupied in 1853 can be viewed at 248 Mill St. (☎ 916/273-4667). It now houses the chamber of commerce, but it does contain some memorabilia of her two-year stay. Down the street, Lotta Crabtree, Montez's famous protégée, lived at 238 Mill St., now an apartment house. Also pop into the **Holbrooke Hotel,** at 212 Main St., to see the signature of Mark Twain, who stayed here. The saloon has been in continuous use since 1852, and it's the place to meet the locals and have a tall, cold one.

The surrounding region offers many recreational opportunities on its rivers and lakes and in the Tahoe National Forest. You can enjoy fishing, swimming, and boating at **Scotts Flat Lake** near Nevada City (east on Calif. 20), and at **Rollins Lake** on Calif. 174, between Grass Valley and Colfax. White-water rafting is available on several rivers. **Tributary Whitewater Tours,** 20480 Woodbury Dr., Grass Valley, CA 95949 (☎ 800/672-3846 or 916/346-6812), offers half- to three-day trips from March to October. In winter you can ski at Sugar Bowl Ski resort and Royal Gorge (only 45 minutes away), or at Squaw Valley, Alpine Meadows, and Northstar, a little more than an hour away over the Donner Pass (see Chapter 10). The region is also ideal for mountain biking. The chambers of commerce publish a trail guide, but there's nowhere to rent a bike in either Nevada City or Grass Valley—bring your own wheels. For regional hiking information, contact **Tahoe National Forest headquarters** at Coyote Street and Calif. 49 in Nevada City (☎ 916/265-4531).

From Nevada City, you have two choices about where to drive. You can take the 160-mile Yuba Donner Scenic Loop north along Calif. 49 through Downieville and Sierra City to Truckee before heading back to Nevada City via I-80 and Calif. 20. Alternatively, you can drive from Nevada City to Grass Valley in 15 minutes, and from there pick up Calif. 49, the Gold Country route, south to Auburn.

WHERE TO STAY
Nevada City
✪ **Deer Creek Inn Bed and Breakfast.** 116 Nevada St., Nevada City, CA 95959. ☎ 800/655-0363 or 916/265-0363. Fax 916/265-0980. 5 rms. A/C. $95–$140 double. Rates include breakfast. MC, V.

An 1887 three-floor Victorian overlooking Deer Creek and within walking distance of downtown Nevada City, this inn feels like a warm home away from home. The individually decorated rooms, all with private verandas facing the creek or town, are furnished with assorted antiques and four-poster or canopy beds with down comforters. The ceiling fans are adequate coolers in summer; most bathrooms have claw-foot tubs. A full breakfast is served either out on the deck or in the formal dining room. Guests are invited to try a little panning of their own, fish, play croquet, or simply relax and enjoy the lawn and landscaped gardens along the creek.

⑤ **Miner's Inn.** 760 Zion St., Nevada City, CA 95959. ☎ 916/265-2253. 20 rms. A/C TEL TV. $50–$55 double. Cabins also available. AE, MC, V.

Surely no '49er miner had it this good: his own cabinlike motel room cooled by the shade of a small tree-lined park. Granted, the rooms are a bit small and simple, but considering all the standard amenities—TV, telephone, air-conditioning—and the price, the cash-conscious traveler could hardly ask for more. The inn also rents three fully furnished cabins, popular with families and groups, that cost $95 to $120 a night, which is an outstanding deal for such a prime location—about a mile from

Nevada City's historic district. After a hard day's touring, rest your dry, weary bones at the restaurant and cocktail lounge next door.

National Hotel. 211 Broad St., Nevada City, CA 95959. ☎ **916/265-4551.** 43 rms (30 with private bath). A/C TEL TV. $68 double without bath, $113 double with bath. AE, MC, V.

You can't miss this classic three-story Victorian, the oldest hotel in continuous operation west of the Rocky Mountains. Once the town's red-light district centered across from where the parking lot is today. The lobby is full of mementos from that era, hence the grandfather clock and early square piano. The suites are replete with gold rush–era antiques and large, cozy beds. Most rooms have private baths, and some of them come with canopy beds and romantic love seats. A definite bonus on typically sweltering summers is the secluded swimming pool filled with cool mountain water.

The dining room also has a gold rush atmosphere; tables are lit with coal oil lamps. You'll find traditional items such as prime rib, steaks, and lobster tail. The hotel makes its own desserts, and provides live entertainment on Friday and Saturday nights. There's also a popular Sunday brunch, one of the best in the county.

✪ **Red Castle Inn.** 109 Prospect St., Nevada City, CA 95959. ☎ **916/265-5135.** 7 rms. $100–$150 double. Rates include breakfast. MC, V.

This hillside inn occupies a four-story Gothic Revival brick house built in 1860; it's situated in a secluded spot with a panoramic view of the town. It has an elegant but comfortable air, and the owners have a love of literature and music. The highlight of the week is the Sunday afternoon "Conversations with Mark Twain" in which guests can engage the great author (or at least a reasonable facsimile thereof—a costumed actor) in conversation while enjoying such specialties as lemon tarts and a choice cup of tea. The house has retained its original woodwork, plaster moldings, ceiling medallions, and much of the handmade glass. It lacks any modern intrusions such as televisions and telephones. Guests enjoy bountiful five-course buffet breakfasts, and can relax on the verandas that encircle the first two floors of the house. Our favorite rooms are the Garden Room, which features a canopy bed and has French doors leading into the gardens, and the air-conditioned three-room garret unit tucked under the eaves, furnished with sleigh beds and featuring Gothic arched windows.

Grass Valley

Another inexpensive option is the modern, fully equipped **Holiday Lodge,** 1221 E. Main St. (☎ **800/742-7125** or 916/273-4406).

Holbrooke Hotel. 212 West Main St., Grass Valley, CA 95945. ☎ **800/933-7077** or 916/273-1353. Fax 916/273-0434. 26 rms, 2 suites. A/C TEL TV. $55–$106 double; $95–$145 suite. AE, DC, DISC, MC, V.

This Victorian-era white-clapboard building was a rollicking saloon during the gold rush days, and then evolved into a place for exhausted miners to "rack out." It's the oldest and most historic hotel in town. It has hosted a number of legendary figures since it opened its doors: Ulysses Grant, Benjamin Harrison, Grover Cleveland, and Gentleman Jim Corbett, among others. Nineteen of the rooms lie within the main building. The remainder are within an historic annex, actually a house occupied long ago by the hotel's owner. The rooms have high ceilings; the front rooms are large and have access to the balconies. Each is decorated with eclectic old pieces of furniture appropriate to the era.

✪ **Murphy's Inn.** 318 Neal St., Grass Valley, CA. 95945. ☎ **916/273-6873.** 8 rms. A/C TV. $95–$140 double. Rates include breakfast. AE, MC, V.

This 1866 Colonial Revival house that was built for Edward Coleman, owner of the North Star mine, has been turned into a crackerjack B&B. Today it stands at the center of well-tended gardens complete with fountains, a fish pond, and a tall sequoia. Guests can relax in the gardens, on the porch, where trimmed ivy baskets hang decoratively, or in two very well furnished and comfortable living rooms with fireplaces. The rooms are equally alluring, all decorated in a chintzy Victorian style, but each with its own unique charm. Some have fireplaces, others offer private balconies, and two, the Maid's Quarters and the East Room, have skylights. Two of the most spacious units, both with fireplaces and one with a full kitchen, are in the Donation Day House.

WHERE TO DINE
Nevada City
Friar Tuck's. 111 N. Pine St. ☎ **916/265-9093.** Reservations accepted. Main courses $14–$20. AE, MC, V. Daily 5–9:30pm, weekends until 10pm. INTERNATIONAL.

A local favorite, this restaurant offers a series of rustic, dimly lit rooms furnished with high-backed oak booths. The menu is eclectic, offering everything from cheese fondues and Swiss meatballs to teriyaki steak, Tuck's bouillabaisse, or duck with raspberry sauce; the accompanying wine list is surprisingly impressive. With the flavor and ambience of a British pub, the bar is a popular local hangout, complete with a guitar player who entertains nightly from 7pm.

⑤ Gourmet to Go. 110 York St. ☎ **916/265-5697.** Lunch items $4–$8. No credit cards. Mon–Fri 11am–3pm. DELI.

Little more than a small room with a counter and barely enough room for a cooler of soft drinks, the Gourmet to Go is just that: a seatless deli serving homemade gourmet offerings to go at low prices. Excellent sandwiches, salads, pastas, soups, espresso, desserts, and a handful of specials are wrapped for the road. Don't know where to go with your goods? Ask the deli staff, who will probably send you to nearby Pioneer Park for an impromptu picnic among the pines.

✪ Potager. 320 Broad St. ☎ **916/265-5697.** Reservations accepted. Main courses $13–$24. AE, MC, V. Tues–Thurs 6–9pm, Fri 6–9:30pm, Sat 5:30–9:30pm, Sun 5–9pm. INTERNATIONAL.

Formerly Peter Selaya's California Restaurant, Potager (pronounced poh-ta-zhay) offers the most creative and cosmopolitan cuisine in town, served in a woodside setting enhanced with private dining niches. Natural meats and organic produce are the mainstay here, such as the Bradley Ranch Beef Wellington, wrapped in a puff pastry and topped with mushroom duxelle and cabernet foie gras sauce. Another recommended choice is the house-made wild boar sausage, served with Potager's prize-winning chipotle cherry sauce, grilled polenta, and fresh vegetables from the chef's own kitchen garden. Other hand-made items include a superb ravioli and top-notch desserts.

Grass Valley
The Dining Room at the Holbrooke Hotel. 212 W. Main St. ☎ **916/273-1353.** Reservations recommended on Fri–Sat nights. Main courses $12–$19. AE, DC, DISC, MC, V. Daily 11:30am–2pm and 5:30–9pm; Sun brunch 10am–2pm. AMERICAN.

This hotel dining room is the most formal place in town—an ironic twist, given its past life as a gold rush saloon and a flophouse for drunken miners. In its way, it's the most authentic and nostalgic restaurant in a town filled with hardworking competitors. Menu items include free-range chicken topped with proscuitto and Gruyère cheese, roasted duck breast in a cranberry honey sauce, and a changing

Cheap Eats, Right Here, Right Now

If you're the type whose wallet can't sit still through a four-course dinner, here are some reliable eateries in the northern Gold Country that specialize in good food that's served fast and priced fair:

Mrs. Dubblebee's Pasties Miners who emigrated from England didn't think much of the local grub, so between digging for dust they baked their own. Hence, the Cornish pasty, a gut-filling mix of beef and veggies topped with a buttery crust (251 C South Auburn St., Grass Valley; ☎ 916/272-7700).

Tofanelli's The closest you'll get to a hippie hangout in these parts, flesh-free burgers and tofu burritos are their angle (you get the idea), along with a darn good cuppa java (302 W. Main St., Grass Valley; ☎ 916/272-1468).

Cowboy Pizza Garlic lovers will find a slice of heaven here, usually in the form of artichoke heart pizza with fresh tomatoes, feta cheese, black olives, and, of course, garlic. There's a good selection of microbrewed beer, too (315 Spring St., Nevada City; ☎ 916/265-2334).

Gourmet to Go We mentioned it already in "Where to Dine," but it's so good it deserves a second billing. See the full entry above for more details. (110 York St., Nevada City; ☎ 916/265-5697).

assortment of dishes inspired by the whim of the chef, Andres Chavez. And should your arteries need further hardening, Saturday and Sunday are "prime rib" nights.

ⓈThe Old California. 341 East Main St. ☎ 916/273-7341. Main courses $5–$14. MC, V. Mon–Fri 11:30am–2pm; Sun–Thurs 5–9:30pm, Fri–Sat 5–10pm. PRIME RIB/AMERICAN.

Set about a half mile east of the commercial center of town, this restaurant has a very loyal clientele that swears by the prime rib. It occupies a sprawling, turn-of-the-century building that once housed a bordello that thrived for a while beginning around 1901. Inside, you'll find lots of old-time memorabilia and photos of earlier and lustier eras. A platter of prime rib, with salad and vegetables, is a bargain at $8.95, although other choices include boneless breast of chicken, vegetarian pastas, prawns, calamari steak, and such fish platters of the day as herbed and grilled filets of red snapper. The most expensive item on the menu, priced at $13.95, is a heaping platter with 16 ounces of prime rib cooked any way you like it.

ⓈPasta Luigi. 760 South Auburn St. ☎ 916/477-0455. Reservations recommended. Main courses $8–$13.50. AE, MC, V. Tues–Sun 5–9pm. ITALIAN.

This is the closest thing to a neighborhood Italian restaurant in town. It's a thoroughly charming, unpretentious spot, packed most nights with happy locals who couldn't care less about the less-than-trendy location. Menu items include a zesty cioppino; linguine *zingarella*, a "gypsy sautée" of Italian sausages, peppers, garlic, and onions; a classic veal scaloppini; and *cappellini alla contadina*, with diced chicken, fresh basil, olive oil, and tomatoes.

AUBURN, COLOMA & PLACERVILLE

From Grass Valley it's a short drive along Calif. 49 south to Auburn. If you're driving straight from San Francisco, take I-80 to U.S. 50 and follow the signs from there.

For information, contact the **Auburn Area Chamber of Commerce,** 601 Lincoln Way, Auburn (☎ 916/885-5616); **Placer County Tourism,** 13460 A Lincoln Way,

Auburn (☎ 916/887-2111); or **El Dorado County Chamber of Commerce,** 542 Main St., Placerville (☎ 916/621-5885).

In Auburn you might want to linger in the Old Town and browse the stores. Auburn also has the **Placer County Museum** (101 Maple St.; ☎ **916/889-6500**), a state-of-the-art exhibit on the history of Placer County, including a remarkable Native American collection, a restored sheriff's office, and mining displays. The museum is open Tuesday through Sunday, 10am to 4pm. Admission is free.

Auburn is en route to the site of the original discovery that started it all: **Coloma,** where gold was discovered in 1848. About 70% of the quiet, appealing town lies in **The Marshall Gold Discovery State Historic Park** (☎ **916/622-3470**), which preserves the spot where James Wilson Marshall discovered gold along the banks of the south fork of the American River. Although Marshall and his partner, John Sutter, tried to keep the discovery secret, the word soon leaked out. Sam Brannan, who ran a general store at Fort Sutter, secured some gold samples himself, and then lit out for San Francisco, where he ran through the streets shouting, "Gold! Gold! Gold! From the American River!" San Francisco was soon half-emptied as men rushed off to seek their fortunes. A self-guided trail leads to the site of this momentous event.

Other attractions in the park include the Gold Discovery Museum, which relates the story of the gold rush, and a number of Chinese stores, all that remain of the once sizable local Chinese community. The park also offers three picnic areas, four trails, recreational gold panning, and a number of buildings and exhibits relating the way of life that prevailed here in the 19th century. Admission is $5 per vehicle, and it's open daily 10am to 5pm, except on major holidays.

Folks also come here for white-water thrills on the American River. **White Water Connection,** Coloma (☎ **916/622-6446**), offers half- to three-day trips on the American, Klamath, Salmon, and Stanislaus rivers. Sure, the prices are a little steep for the budget traveler, but the half-day trips start at only about $50.

Eight miles south of Coloma is **Placerville.** Although its main street has a string of historic Victorian buildings, don't come here expecting a cute mining town—it's a modern commercial center. There is, however, the **El Dorado County Historical Museum,** 100 Placerville Dr. (☎ **916/621-5865**), which features a large collection of Native American baskets, plus some remarkable examples of the transportation that won the west. Admission is free and it's open Wednesday to Saturday from 10am to 4pm, Sunday from noon to 4pm. The other attraction is **Hangtown's Gold Bug Park,** 2501 Bedford Ave. (☎ **916/642-5238**), a 61-acre park where visitors can follow a self-guided tour through the gold mine. Admission is $2, and it's open daily in summer from 10am to 4pm (weekends only in spring, fall, and winter).

East of Placerville, Highway 50 leads out to the small towns of Camino and Pollock Pines. This hilly and forested area is worth visiting to explore **Apple Hill,** which has close to 30 apple and other fruit orchards, plus a number of small, family-operated wineries, including **Boeger Winery,** 1709 Carson Rd., Placerville (☎ **916/622-8094**), which has an atmospheric tasting room and produces Merlot and Zinfandel; **Lava Cap,** 2221 Fruitridge Rd., Placerville (☎ 916/621-0175), which produces a wide range of varietals; **Madrona Vineyards,** High Hill Rd., Camino (☎ **916/644-5948**), which produces Chardonnay, Riesling, and Zinfandel; and **El Dorado,** 3551 Carson Rd., Camino (☎ **916/644-2854**), which specializes in Chardonnay, Cabernet, and Merlot.

For a free map listing all of El Dorado County's wineries, call the **El Dorado Winery Association** at **916/446-6562** or 800/306-3956.

WHERE TO STAY

Auburn

Auburn Inn. 1875 Auburn Ravine Rd., Auburn, CA 95603. ☎ **800/272-1444** or 916/885-1800. Fax 916/888-6424. 78 rms, 3 suites. A/C TEL TV. $60–$66 double; $100–$120 suite. Rates include buffet continental breakfast. AE, DC, DISC, MC, V. From I-80, take Auburn Ravine Rd./Forest Hill exit.

Set on the town's eastern outskirts, near the highway leading to Reno, Nevada, this hotel is better maintained and equipped than some of its newer competitors. It has a two-story motel-style design and a vaguely Colonial Revival decor, and was completely remodeled in 1995 with all new furniture. There's also a swimming pool on the premises, and a Jacuzzi-style spa. Close attention is paid to security and locks, and there are rooms and facilities for the disabled. There are lots of nearby choices for dining.

Coloma

✪ **Coloma Country Inn.** 345 High St., Coloma, CA 95613. ☎ **916/622-6919.** 5 rms (3 with private bath), 2 suites. $88–$99 double; $120–$170 suite. No credit cards.

In the middle of the state park, this restored 1852 country farmhouse situated on five landscaped acres is a very romantic place to stay and is made even more so by the warmth of innkeepers Alan and Cindi Ehrgott. The rooms are very prettily decorated with stenciling and plenty of fresh flowers from the surrounding gardens, and furnished with antiques and quilts. The two suites in a separate cottage, one of which has a full kitchen, are exceptionally appealing. Afternoon tea and lemonade are served in the garden gazebo, and guests have free use of bicycles, and also of the comfortable parlor and front porch. There's an old pond on the property where kids can feed the ducks. A breakfast of fresh fruit, fresh baked goods, and juice and coffee is served in the formal dining room. If you're bringing children, advance notice is needed. Smoking is not permitted on the premises.

✪ **Vineyard House.** Cold Springs Rd., Coloma, CA 95613. ☎ **916/622-2217.** 7 rms (2 with private bath). $95 double without bath, $130 double with bath. AE, MC, V.

Adjacent to Marshall Gold Discovery Park off Calif. 49, this inn occupies a large Italianate house that was built between 1876 and 1878; it was once the social center of the area, the home of a state senator, and it's on the site of an award-winning winery. Downstairs it features a large granite-walled wine cellar, which now makes a very atmospheric saloon.

The rooms are all furnished differently, based on characters from the gold rush era. The Lola Montez room, for example, is decorated in rich reds and Spanish lace and has a private bath with a claw-foot tub. The restaurant, which consists of five period-furnished rooms, serves traditional fare such as chicken and dumplings and prime rib. There's bluegrass/jazz entertainment on Fridays and Saturdays in the saloon.

Placerville

⑤ **Cary House Hotel.** 300 Main St., Placerville, CA 95667. ☎ **916/622-4271.** 34 rms. A/C TV. $45–$65 double. DISC, MC, V.

People who stay at all the boring chain motels in Placerville obviously don't know about the Cary House Hotel, which has been housing its guests in style and comfort since 1857. Granted, it's a little hokey with its armada of gold rush–era knickknacks lining the walls, but Holy Eureka! what a great price for such spankingly clean and comfy rooms, each draped in odd but effective period decor. (We have to admit our room smelled a bit like Grandma's house, but, hey, maybe that's what it smelled like back then.) The clincher is the location: right in the middle of Old Town Placerville with its cadre of antique stores, boutiques, and cafes.

Chichester-McKee House. 800 Spring St., Placerville, CA 95667. ☎ **916/626-1882.** 3 rms. A/C. $80–$90 double. AE, DC, MC, V. Turn off Calif. 49 at Coloma St.; turn right on High St., then right again on Wood St. to the parking area behind the house.

A handsome Victorian featuring fretwork and stained glass, this home—the first in Placerville to have indoor plumbing—was built in 1892 for a lumber baron. Today it is furnished with the doll collection and other personal effects of innkeepers Bill and Doreen Thornhill, who are happy to give sightseeing advice. Each room contains a brass or iron bed, Oriental rugs, crocheted bedspread or quilt, country-oak furnishings, as well as bathrobes for the shared bath down the hallway (though each room has its own sink and toilet). Guests can relax in the parlor or the library. An elaborate breakfast of crepes, quiches, eggs Benedict, and "Bill's Special Blend" coffee is served in the dining room.

WHERE TO DINE
Auburn
✪ **The Headquarter House.** 14500 Musso Rd. ☎ **916/878-1906.** Reservations recommended. Main courses $9–$20. AE, DC, MC, V. Daily 11am–9:30 or 10pm. Drive northeast from Auburn's center along I-80, exit at Bell. AMERICAN/INTERNATIONAL.

Three miles east of Auburn's center is one of the area's most popular and consistently reliable restaurants. Many of its windows overlook the eighth hole of a nine-hole golf course; it's the unofficial watering hole and celebration site of anyone playing on the nearby course. A pianist performs every Thursday to Sunday from 6 to around 10pm. If you prefer to dine outside, there's a deck with a half dozen individual gazebos, each suitable for up to six diners. Menu items include steaks, prime rib, and such seafood dishes as salmon from the nearby Middlefork River, served in a lobster/pink peppercorn sauce. Smoking is not allowed inside.

Placerville
⑤ **Li'l Mama D. Carlo's.** 482 Main St. ☎ **916/626-1612.** Reservations accepted. Main courses $8–$15. MC, V. Sun–Thurs 3pm–9pm, Fri–Sat 3pm–10pm. ITALIAN.

If you're in the mood for Italian tonight, there's a little *ristorante* on Placerville's Main Street that has been placating hungry locals for the past 17 years. Just about everything coming out of the kitchen at Li'l Mama D. Carlo's is made from scratch, such as their giant ravioli hand-stuffed with ricotta, Parmesan, and spinach, or their tangy lasagna with seasoned pork sausage and thick layers of fresh Parmesan and mozzarella cheese. All entrees come with a choice of salad or minestrone soup, made fresh daily, and garlic bread. The best part, however, is the price: most pastas are under $10, and the entire selection of El Dorado County wines is under $15.

Smith Flat House. 2021 Smith Flat Rd. ☎ **916/621-0667.** Main courses $11–$16. AE, DC, MC, V. Mon 11:30am–2pm, Tues–Sat 11:30am–2pm and 5–9pm, Sun 5–9pm. Saloon Mon–Sat 10:30am–midnight, Sun 3pm–midnight (till 1:30am on Fri–Sat). AMERICAN.

Set at the western end of Placerville's historic center, behind a balcony where desperado shoot-outs might have taken place, this is probably the first building you'll see as you drive east into town from Sacramento. If there's a local favorite in Placerville, it must be Smith Flat House. Fabled as the final milepost on the Lake Tahoe Wagon Trail, this place has lived through many incarnations. It's been everything from a Pony Express depot drop-off to a dance hall with "wicked" show girls. Beginning in 1853, it fed whiskey and (probably unpalatable) food to miners and cattle farmers streaming in from the surrounding fields. Today it revels in nostalgia for the Old West. There's a cellar-level saloon, with a circular mine shaft that's said to lead to the heart of the Mother Lode. Reasonably well-prepared meals are served in the street-level restaurant. The food is hearty and very American, and no one leaves here hungry. Mainly steaks, chicken, and grilled or deep-fried seafood or fish fill the limited dinner menu.

Zachary Jacques. 1821 Pleasant Valley Rd. ☎ **916/626-8045.** Reservations recommended. Main courses $14–$20. AE, MC, V. Wed–Sat 5:30–9:30pm, Sun 5–8:30pm. FRENCH.

Zachary Jacques is easily the best restaurant in town. The French cuisine, which changes with the seasons, is well prepared and carefully presented, with an emphasis on fresh vegetables and fish. Start with the *champignons farcis en croûte,* mushroom caps stuffed with spinach, Brie, sun-dried tomatoes, and basil, then baked in puff pastry. Specialties include Rack of Lamb *Valréas,* with Dijon mustard, rosemary, and garlic, and *Lapin Ardèchoise,* fresh rabbit sautéed with leeks and served with whole-grain mustard sauce. Wednesday diners have a bonus option: *Cassoulet Maison,* a classic country dish with white beans, duck, sausages, and lamb.

THE SOUTHERN GOLD COUNTRY

From Placerville, continue south along Calif. 49 via Plymouth and Drytown to reach three appealing mining towns: Amador City, Sutter Creek, and Jackson. If you're coming straight here from San Francisco, take I-80 to Route 4. You can either follow Calif. 4 all the way to Angels Camp to pick up Calif. 49 north, or you can turn off Calif. 4 to Calif. 99 and pick up Calif. 88 to Jackson.

For information, contact the **Amador County Chamber of Commerce,** 125 Peek St., Jackson (☎ **209/223-0350**).

Before you reach these towns you may want to turn off Calif. 49 to explore the Shenandoah Valley around Plymouth. Take Shenandoah Road east to discover the **Amador County Wine Country,** which is known for its zinfandel and more recently for sauvignon blanc and chenin blanc. The wineries are small and family owned; any tour or tasting will most likely be given by the owner. There are several wineries on Shenandoah Road (Sonny Grace, Sobon Estate, and Vino Noceto), Bell Road (Karly and Story), and Steiner Road (with at least six). Bell and Steiner both branch off from Shenandoah.

Although **Amador City** sounds large and impressive, it is in fact tiny. Basically, it's a widening in the road with a few very browsable shops and the Imperial Hotel, which has one of the finest dining rooms in the area.

Sutter Creek is a small, attractive town with lots of 19th-century homes and worthwhile antique stores.

Jackson, the Amador County seat, is livelier. Take time to stroll through the town, browsing in the stores and noting the Victorian buildings.

South of Jackson on Calif. 49 is one of the most evocative mining towns of the region: **Mokelumne Hill.** There's just one street overlooking a valley with a few old buildings, but somehow its sad, abandoned air has the mark of authenticity. It's not gussied up; it's just the unvarnished way it was. At one time the hill was dotted with tents and wood and tar-paper shacks, and the town boasted a population of 15,000, including an Old French quarter and a Chinatown. But now many of its former residents are merely memorialized in the town's Protestant, Jewish, and Catholic cemeteries.

WHERE TO STAY

Amador City

Imperial Hotel. Main St. (P.O. Box 195), Amador City, CA 95601. ☎ **800/242-5594** or 209/ 267-9172. 6 rms. A/C. $80–$95 double. AE, MC, V.

Right on Calif. 49, this hotel occupies a brick Victorian that was built in 1879. The individually decorated rooms, all with private baths, are upstairs above the dining room and are furnished with brass, iron, or pine beds; two come with private balconies. Our favorite room is one containing hand-painted furnishings by local artist John Johannsen. Amenities include hair dryers and heated towel bars in all rooms, as well as newspaper delivery and in-room massage upon request. The restaurant, serving American/continental cuisine, has a sterling reputation, and hotel guests can take advantage of room service when it's open.

Drytown

Old Well Motel. 15947 Calif. 49, P.O. Box 187, Drytown, CA 95699. ☎ **209/245-6467.** 11 rms. A/C TV. $39–$65 double. MC, V.

Just up the road from Amador City is the don't-blink-or-you'll-miss-it community of Drytown, which, oddly enough, was built next to a swiftly moving creek. There's only a handful of buildings here, one of which is this small, 11-room motel that surprisingly few people know about. If it's Old West ambience you're after, you'll be happier at the Imperial Hotel down the street. But if all you need is a cheap, clean place to hang your hat for the night, the Old Well Motel will do. Next to the motel is a small diner and swimming pool, and you can even test your panning skills along the creek that ambles past your room.

Sutter Creek

Gold Quartz Inn. 15 Bryson Dr., Sutter Creek, CA 95685. ☎ **800/752-8738** or 209/ 267-9155. Fax 209/267-9170. 24 rms. A/C TEL TV. $80–$150 double. AE, DISC, MC, V.

Just off Calif. 49 outside Sutter Creek is one of the town's premier B&Bs, a modern establishment designed in Queen Anne style. Its amenities and first-class bedrooms make it comparable to a deluxe small hotel. The rooms are decorated with antique reproductions and iron or brass beds, and all have private baths. Some units have their own porches, the only place where smoking is allowed. Afternoon tea and a full breakfast are served daily in the dining rooms; the adjacent parlor offers an array of sofas and a VCR with a movie library. Services include a courtesy laundry.

Jackson

Jackson Holiday Lodge. 850 Calif. 49, P.O. Box 1147, Jackson, CA 95642. ☎ **209/ 223-0486.** A/C TEL TV. $45–$70 double. AE, DISC, MC, V.

If you're willing to forgo even the slightest hint of Old West ambience, the Jackson Holiday Lodge offers all the familiar trappings of a modern motel at a third of the cost of most B&Bs. We recommend it for the swimming pool alone, which comes in real handy on those sweltering Gold Country summer days. The price includes a continental breakfast (served in the lobby), in-room coffeemakers, and free local calls. Dollar for dollar, it's one of the best deals around.

WHERE TO DINE

Amador City

Imperial Hotel. Main St. (Calif. 49). ☎ **209/267-9172.** Main courses $14–$21. AE, MC, V. Daily 5–9pm. AMERICAN/CONTINENTAL.

This restored 1879 hotel has been recommended already, but even if you aren't staying here, its restaurant is worth a detour. There are only about seven main dishes offered on the seasonal menu, but whatever you choose will be tasty and well prepared. To start, try the sun-dried tomato polenta, topped with prosciutto and Parmesan, and served with a roasted tomato sauce. To follow, you might select the local version of cioppino, a tomato-based fresh seafood stew accented with zinfandel. If you put your name on the waiting list for their New Year's celebration, you might get a seat by the year 2000—it's that popular.

Sutter Creek

Ron and Nancy's Palace. 76 Main St. ☎ **209/267-1355.** Reservations recommended on weekends. Main courses $9–$16. AE, DC, MC, V. Daily 11:30am–3pm and 5–9pm (last order). AMERICAN/CONTINENTAL.

Set within a rustic building originally built in 1884 as a stable, this is the palace of Ron and Nancy Gottheiner, San Francisco restaurateurs of long experience. Many visitors come just for the two-fisted drinks served in the bar/lounge, where a battle for your attention will rage between the Elvis memorabilia favored by Nancy and the Oakland Raiders memorabilia prized by Ron. (The bar, incidentally, remains open through the afternoon, even when the restaurant area is closed.) In the three dining rooms, light from the windows is filtered through panels of stained glass.

Most dishes are enhanced with a dash of vermouth, marsala, or California wines. One of the most popular lunchtime platters is a steak croissant, whose ingredients are sautéed in marsala and flavored with onions and herbs. Dinner items include linguine, prime rib, and a wildly popular pan-fried scampi with veal strips.

Jackson

Mel and Faye's Diner. 205 Calif. 49 at Main St., Jackson. ☎ **209/223-0853.** Menu items $3–$6. No credit cards. Daily 4:45am–10pm. AMERICAN.

How can anybody not love a classic old diner? In business since 1956, Mel and Faye have been cranking out the best diner food in the Gold Country for so long that it's okay to not feel guilty for salivating over the thought of a sloppy double cheeseburger smothered with onions and special sauce and washed down with a large chocolate shake and could you please add a large side of fries with that and how much is a slice of pie? It's a time-honored Jackson tradition.

Michael's. In the National Hotel, 2 Water St. ☎ **209/223-3448.** Reservations recommended. Main courses $11–$19. AE, MC, V. Fri–Sat 5:30–10pm, Sun 10:30am–2pm and 5:30–8:30pm.

The best and brightest aspect of the faded National Hotel is this restaurant down in the basement. Chef Michael Golsie offers well-prepared food that is traditional enough to appeal to assorted tastes. For example, there's veal with an Amador County zinfandel raspberry sauce and shiitake mushrooms, and orange roughy with a light lemon wine sauce. In addition, there's always a vegetarian plate and a pasta of the evening.

CONTINUING SOUTH TOWARD JAMESTOWN

From Mokelumne Hill, Calif. 49 continues south via San Andreas for about 20 miles to **Angel's Camp.** This is where Mark Twain heard the story that inspired his "Celebrated Jumping Frog of Calaveras County." The frog jump contest started in 1928 to mark the paving of the town's streets, and to this day the "ribiting" competition continues every third weekend in May. The record jump of 21 feet, 5³/₄ inches was achieved in 1986 by "Rosie the Ribiter," who beat the old world record by 4¹/₂ inches. Livestock exhibitions, pageants, cook-offs, arm-wrestling tournaments, carnival rides, and plenty of beer and wine keep the spectators entertained between jump-offs. For more information and entry forms ($3 per frog), call the **Jumping Frog Jubilee** headquarters at **209/736-2561.**

Angel's Camp is built on hills that are honeycombed with mine tunnels. In the 1880s and '90s, five mines were located along Main Street: Sultana, Angels, Lightner, Utica, and Stickle. The town was bursting with the noise of the mills, as more than 200 stamps crushed the ore. Between 1886 and 1910 the five mines generated close to $20 million.

From Angel's Camp, take a detour east along Calif. 4 to **Murphys,** a smaller and less commercial town than those along Calif. 49. Just off Calif. 4, 1 mile north of Murphys, are **Mercer Caverns** (☎ 209/728-2101), off Sheep Ranch Road. The caverns were discovered in 1885 by Walter Mercer and contain a variety of formations—stalactites, stalagmites, columns, curtains, flowstone, and more. Tours take 45 minutes; the caverns are open daily from Memorial Day through September from 9am to 5pm, weekends only October through May from 11am to 4pm. Admission is $5 adults, $4.50 children under 11.

Fifteen miles beyond Murphys on Calif. 4 is **Calaveras Big Trees State Park,** where you can see California's fabled giant sequoias. Open daily, admission is $5 per car for day use.

From Murphys, get back on Calif. 49, crossing the Stanislaus River bridge over the Melones Reservoir to the most remarkable attraction in the area, **Columbia State Historic Park** (☎ 209/532-4301), one of the best preserved gold rush towns in the Mother Lode (even if it is somewhat commercialized). The whole town has been preserved and functions as it did in the 1850s, with stagecoach rides, Western–style Victorian hotels and saloons, a newspaper office, a working blacksmith, and a Wells Fargo express office. The whole town comes to life in summer.

The county seat, **Sonora,** only a few miles south, is set on ravines and hillsides. It's the Gold Country's largest and most congested town, which becomes painfully obvious as traffic comes to a halt on summer weekends. One of Sonora's most popular attractions is the **Tuolumne County Museum and History Center,** 158 W. Bradford Ave. (☎ 209/532-1317), which is located in the 1857 county jail. Admission is free, and it's open daily year-round from 10am to 4pm.

About 4 miles southwest of Sonora is **Jamestown,** one of our favorite stops along Calif. 49. Looking much like it did back in the halcyon days of the gold rush, it's a popular backdrop for westerns, including *Butch Cassidy and the Sundance Kid.* Jamestown is also the home of the Sierra Railroad Company, famous for its **Railtown 1897 State Historic Park** (☎ 209/984-3953), which features three original Sierra steam locomotives. These great machines were used in many a movie and TV show, including *High Noon, Bonanza,* and *Little House on the Prairie.* Rides are given on weekends from March to November. Open daily year-round.

From Jamestown, Calif. 49 continues south across the huge Don Pedro Reservoir and through Coulterville and Bear Valley to **Mariposa,** on the fringes of Yosemite. It's another attractive hilly mining town with plenty of atmosphere.

WHERE TO STAY
Angel's Camp
Cooper House Bed and Breakfast Inn. 1184 Church St. (P.O. Box 1388), Angel's Camp, CA 95222. ☎ **800/225-3764,** ext. 326, or 209/736-2145. 3 rms. A/C. $90 double. Rates include breakfast. AE, DISC, MC, V.

Once the home and office of a prominent community physician, Dr. George P. Cooper, the Cooper House is Angel's Camp's only B&B, a small Arts and Crafts home mercifully positioned well away from the hustle and bustle of the town's Main

How to Pan for Gold

Find a gold pan, ideally a 12- to 15-inch steel pan. Place the pan over an oven burner, or better yet, in a camp fire. This will darken the pan, making it easier to see any flakes of placer gold. Find some gravel, sand, or dirt in a stream that looks promising or feels lucky. Fill the pan nearly full and then place it under water and keep it there while you break up the clumps of mud and clay and toss out any stones. Then grasp the pan with both hands. Holding it level, rotate it in swirling motions. This will cause the heavier gold to loosen and settle to the bottom of the pan. Drain off the dirty water and loose stuff. Keep doing this until gold and heavier minerals called "black sand" are left in the pan. Carefully inspect the black sand for nuggets or speck traces of gold. You just might be lucky.

You can dredge for gold from June 1 to October 15. A dredging permit is required. Apply for one at **Regional 2 Headquarters,** Calif. Dept. of Fish and Game, 1701 Nimbus Rd., Rancho Cordova, CA 95670 (☎ **916/355-0978**). Or you can sign up for one of the many dredging lessons and gold-panning tours offered in the Gold Country towns. Try calling **Gold Prospecting Expeditions** (☎ **800/596-0009** or 209/984-4653) for dredging lessons and gold-panning tours.

Street. Owners/innkeepers Tom and Kathy Reese maintain three guest rooms, all with private baths. The Zinfandel Suite has its own private entrance and deck (alas, the bed is only a double), whereas the Chardonnay Suite has a king-size bed and antique claw-foot bathtub. Mamma Bear would be the Cabernet Suite, with its queen bed, adjoining sunroom, and splendid garden view.

Murphys

✪ **Dunbar House, 1880.** 271 Jones St. (P.O. Box 1375), Murphys, CA 95247. ☎ **800/692-6006** or 209/728-2897. 3 rms, 1 suite. A/C TEL TV. $115 double; $155 suite. Rates include breakfast. AE, MC, V.

This pretty Italianate home, built in 1880 for the bride of a local businessman, is one of the finest in the Gold Country. The inviting front porch, which overlooks the exquisite gardens, is decorated with hanging baskets of ivy and wicker furnishings. Inside, the emphasis is on comfort and elegance. The rooms are furnished with quality antiques and equipped with every possible amenity you could wish for. Beds have lace-trimmed linens and down comforters, and each room has a wood-burning stove and a personal refrigerator stocked with mineral water and a complimentary bottle of wine. Other unexpected extras include a TV/VCR (well hidden), make-up mirror, and hair dryer, plus his-and-her reading lamps. The most expensive room, the Cedar, is a two-room suite with a private sun porch and whirlpool bath where a bottle of complimentary champagne awaits you. Lemonade and cookies are offered in the afternoon, appetizers and wine in the early evening. Breakfast is served either in your room, the dining room, or the garden.

Columbia

City Hotel. Main St., Columbia State Park (P.O. Box 1870), CA 95310. ☎ **209/532-1479.** Fax 209/532-7027. 10 rms (all with shared bath). A/C. $75–$100 double. Rates include breakfast. AE, MC, V.

This atmospheric hostelry has been operating since 1856. Guests have access to a large parlor furnished with Victorian sofas, antiques, and Oriental rugs. The largest units are the two balcony rooms overlooking Main Street; the rooms off the parlor are also spacious. The hallway rooms are smaller but still nicely furnished with Renaissance Revival beds and antique pieces. Each room has a sink and toilet.

A large buffet breakfast is served in the dining room. The hotel has a full restaurant and also the What Cheer saloon, which boasts its original cherrywood bar.

Fallon Hotel. Washington St. (P.O. Box 1870), Columbia State Park, CA 95310. ☎ **209/532-1470.** 14 rms. A/C. $55–$95 double. Rates include breakfast. AE, MC, V.

This hotel, which opened in 1857, has been restored and decorated to evoke the 1890s, when Columbia experienced a second boom. A classic two-story building with an upper balcony, the hotel has retained many of its original antiques and furnishings. The largest rooms are the front balcony rooms. Each unit has a private half bath with showers nearby down the hall. The rooms are decorated with high-back Victorian beds, marble-top dressers, rockers, and similar oak pieces. A continental breakfast is served in the downstairs parlor.

Sonora

Ⓢ **Gunn House Hotel.** 286 South Washington St., Sonora, CA 95370. ☎ **209/532-3421.** 20 rms. A/C TV. $45–$75 double. AE, DISC, MC, V.

Built in 1850 by Dr. Lewis C. Gunn, the Gunn House was the first two-story adobe structure in Sonora, built to house his family, who sailed around Cape Horn from the East Coast to join him in the gold rush. Painstakingly restored by its present owners, Margaret Dienelt and her daughter Peggy, it's now one of the best low-priced hotels in the Gold Country. It's easy to catch the '49er spirit here, as the entire hotel and grounds are brimming with quality antiques and turn-of-the-century artifacts. Rare for a building this old, each guest room has a private bath and air-conditioning. What really makes the Gunn House one of our favorites, though, is the hotel's beautiful pool and patio, surrounded by lush vegetation and admirable stonework. Also within the hotel is the Josephine Room, a small, elegant Italian restaurant and bar where guests are served their complimentary continental breakfast.

Jamestown

Jamestown Hotel. Main St. (P.O. Box 539), Jamestown, CA 95327. ☎ **209/984-3902.** Fax 209/984-4149. 7 rms, 1 suite. A/C. $70–$95 double; $125 suite. Rates include breakfast. AE, DISC, MC, V.

Originally built in 1858, the Jamestown Hotel, the most worked-over building in town, burned down and was reconstructed twice before 1915. Even the brick-fronted Victorian look it sports today required ripping out a lot of stucco and Spanish-revival paraphernalia before its current owners were satisfied with its old-timey look.

Much of the interior is devoted to the restaurant, which is recommended separately below. The second floor, however, contains cozy bedrooms outfitted with antiques acquired along both coasts of North America. Each accommodation is larger than you might have expected, and contains a claw-foot tub and lots of nostalgic charm.

National Hotel. 77 Main St. (P.O. Box 502), Jamestown, CA 95327. ☎ **800/894-3446** or 209/984-3446. Fax 209/984-5620. 11 rms (5 with private bath). A/C. $65 double without bath, $80 double with bath. Rates include continental breakfast. AE, MC, V.

Located in the center of town, this two-story classic Western hotel has been operating as a hotel since 1859, it's one of the 10 oldest continuously operated hotels in the state. The saloon has its original 19th-century redwood bar, and you can imagine what it must have been like when miners traded gold dust for drinks. The rooms above are now furnished with oak pieces and brass beds made up with quilts. Some

rooms have private baths. Others have a bath down the hall and are provided with
bathrobes for guests' convenience. The restaurant serves traditional American and
continental food.

WHERE TO DINE

Jamestown

Jenny Lind Room at the Jamestown Hotel. Main St. ☎ **800/205-4901** or 209/984-3902.
Reservations recommended. Main courses $10–$17. Mon–Sat 11am–3pm; Sun brunch 10am–
3pm; daily 5–9pm. AMERICAN/INTERNATIONAL.

The Jenny Lind Room may not be the best restaurant in the Gold Country, but it's
certainly the most authentic looking, a dark-wood affair with stuffed wingback chairs,
a fireplace, and dozens of old photos. There are about 15 tables, plus another 13 on
an outdoor deck, which is open only during clement weather. Menu items include
escargot in mushroom caps cooked in garlic butter, and breast of chicken "Jerusalem,"
with artichokes, mushrooms, and lemon-scented cream sauce. There's also a Sunday
champagne brunch served until 3pm, and live music on weekend nights.

⭐ **Michelangelo.** 18228 Main St. ☎ **209/984-4830.** Reservations recommended. Main
courses $11–$13. DISC, MC, V. Mon and Wed–Sat 5–10pm, Sun 4–9pm. ITALIAN.

Marble-top tables, bentwood chairs, and drop halogen lights over the tables set the
modern Milan–style scene for the Italian cuisine, which ranges from pasta and
pizza to more complex dishes such as veal with lemon and caper sauce or chicken
saltimbocca. Among the pizzas, our favorite is topped with fresh apple, chicken
sausage, and roasted red peppers. Service is polite and professional. Also part of the
Michelangelo operation is the **Smoke Cafe** across the street, a stylish Tex-Mex
restaurant best known for its lively bar and wicked "After Burner" cocktail.

Sonora

Diamondback Grill. 110 S. Washington St. ☎ **209/532-6661.** Main courses: $5–$10. Open
daily 6am–9pm. AMERICAN.

This modest little family owned diner whips up one doozy of a burger: the Diamondback. The mesquite-grilled half-pounder comes with all the works, *including* fries,
for only five bucks. There's about a dozen other burgers to choose from, as well as
gourmet sandwiches (go for the grilled eggplant with fresh tomato and mozzarella);
house-made soups and pecan pies; a zesty black bean-and-steak chili; and great
specials listed daily on the board, most of which are well under $10.

But wait, it gets better: They also do breakfast. Their three-egg artichoke heart and
mushroom omelet is only $4.95, and a full stack of whole wheat honey hotcakes costs
just $3.25. There's also a good selection of beers and wines by the glass, but we prefer
to finish our feast with a thick chocolate shake from Jim Town Frosty, located at the
north end of Main Street in Jamestown.

⭐ **Good Heavens.** 49 N. Washington St. ☎ **209/532-3663.** Main courses $5–$9. No credit
cards. Tues–Sun 11am–2:30pm. AMERICAN.

This lunch-only cafe, with bentwood chairs and blue floral-patterned tablecloths, is
known for offering only homemade items. The menu features a variety of unique
sandwiches—cucumber and pesto cream, turkey and cranberry orange, plus an
array of delicious soups, salads, and desserts. There are also several daily specials listed
on the board outside, from chile rellenos to crepes and pastas. Each meal starts with
fresh herb-and-cheese biscuits and a choice of freshly made jams, such as the
decadent raspberry-chocolate or tart orange marmalade. For heaven's sake, don't leave
without purchasing a jar or two of the jams, which are sold at the counter.

Hemingway's. 362 Stewart St. ☎ **209/532-4900.** Reservations accepted. Main courses $13–$15. AE, MC, V. Tues–Fri 11:30am–2pm, 5pm–close; Sat–Sun 5pm–close.

What's going to be on the menu at Hemingway's this season is anyone's guess. Last year it was a California/French theme, with dishes ranging from mahogany duckling with Grand Marnier glacé to lobster Newburg. This time around it's the "classic foods of Spain," such as paella à la Velenciana, cordero al chilindron (chicken with orange sauce), and an array of tapas, sopas, and ensaladas. The trick is to call ahead and see what's on the menu: if it sounds good, it probably *is* good, for this place does a brisk business at night. On weekend nights the wait staff—semiprofessional musicians moonlighting to make ends meet—takes the occasional break to get behind the piano and bring a little extra atmosphere to your dinner.

3 The Central Valley & Sierra National Forest

The Central Valley (also known as the San Joaquin Valley) is about as far as you can get from California's movie-stars-in-stretch-limos image. This hot, flat strip stretches for some 225 miles of tract homes, fast-food joints, cheap motels, and minimalls, separating Los Angeles and San Francisco from the Sierra Nevada. Between the coastal foothills and the western slopes of the Sierra Nevada mountain range, this 18,000-square-mile valley is central to the economy of the Golden State, in part because of its cultivated and irrigated fields, orchards, pastures, and vineyards.

The major traffic arteries are Calif. 99 and I-5. Calif. 99 links the agricultural communities, while I-5 provides access routes to the roadside attractions in the valley. Rivers cutting through the valley offer recreation from houseboating on the delta to white-water rafting, and from fishing to boating on one of the lakes. Many visitors drive through in spring just to view the orchards in bloom.

Frankly, although each town in the Central Valley has some attractions, nearly all of them are minor. Consider the towns along the way merely places to grab a quick bite or find a bed for the night while you're pursuing your real interest in the area, which is adventure and communion with nature in one of the national forests.

The Central Valley towns and cities stand at the doorstep to some of America's greatest attractions, including Yosemite. See Chapter 10 for information on two Central Valley towns, Merced and Visalia, which are good gateways to Yosemite and Sequoia and Kings Canyon, respectively.

Fresno, although not much in itself, is a gateway to the Sierra National Forest (the big one), and to such nearby attractions as the Millerton Lake State Recreation Area.

FRESNO

The joke in California is that Fresno is the "gateway to Bakersfield." Although for most visitors Fresno is just a place to pass through en route to the state parks, it can be a good place to stop for food and lodging.

Founded in 1874, in the geographic center of the state, Fresno lies in the heart of the Central Valley and has experienced incredible growth in recent years, followed by an increase in crime, drugs, and urban sprawl.

As the seat of Fresno County, however, it handles more than $3 billion annually in agricultural production. It also contains Sun Maid, the world's largest dried-fruit packing plant, and Guild, one of the country's largest wineries.

Fresno has some good hotels and some surprisingly good restaurants (see below). However, be careful if you're looking for a bargain and plan to check into one of the cheap motels along the highway. Security may be questionable.

If you have any reason at all to be in Fresno, try to come between late February and late March to drive the **Fresno County Blossom Trail.** This 67-mile tour is self-guided and takes in the beauty of California's agrarian bounty at its peak. It lays out a trail through the fruit orchards in full bloom, and the citrus groves with their lovely orange blossoms. The **Visitor's Bureau,** 808 M St. in Fresno (☎ **800/788-0836** or 209/233-0836), will supply full details, including a map.

WHERE TO STAY

San Joaquin. 1309 W. Shaw Ave., Fresno, CA 93711. ☎ **800/775-1309** or 209/225-1309. Fax 209/225-6021. 68 suites. A/C TEL TV. $82–$89 junior suite; $129 1-bedroom suite with kitchen; $165 2-bedroom suite with kitchen; $195 3-bedroom suite with kitchen. Rates include breakfast. AE, DC, MC, V.

Set on the northern edge of Fresno, this hotel was conceived as an apartment complex in the 1970s. Around 1985, a lobby was added, the floor plans adjusted, and the place was reconfigured as an all-suite hotel. Each is outfitted in a slightly different style, with light, contemporary colors and furniture. Room service is available from an independently managed restaurant down the street.

WHERE TO DINE

Nicola's. 3075 N. Maroa Ave. ☎ **209/224-1660.** Reservations recommended. Main courses $9.75–$33.95. AE, DC, MC, V. Mon–Fri 11:30am–4pm; Mon–Thurs 5–10pm, Fri–Sat 5–11pm, Sun 4–10pm. ITALIAN/AMERICAN.

Restaurants come and go in Fresno, but Nicola's remains the enduring favorite of many a discriminating diner. It's also evidence that not everything in Fresno is fast food. Inside you're likely to meet the town's district attorney and a judge or two in a well-upholstered, masculine setting where you can indulge in a stiff cocktail before dinner. The place prides itself on its stuffed steak: a hearty slab of beef layered with ham and cheese, and drizzled with a white wine and mushroom au jus sauce. (Health food it isn't.) Other choices include veal scaloppini, cioppino, *capellini pescatore* (angel-hair pasta with shellfish); and beefsteak with gorgonzola.

✪ **Veni, Vidi, Vici.** 1116 N. Fulton. ☎ **209/266-5510.** Reservations recommended. Main courses $16–$19. MC, V. Wed–Sun 5:30–10pm. Closed two weeks in early Jan. NORTHERN CALIFORNIA.

The most innovative and creative restaurant in Fresno occupies a prominent position about 6 miles south of the commercial center, in a funky neighborhood known as the Tower District. The place's rustic exterior strikes an interesting contrast to the polished and artful interior on the other side of the 15-foot doors, where the decor is accented with exposed antique brick walls, hanging mirrors, and chandeliers-cum-sculpture fashioned from twisted wire and metal leaves.

The menu changes with the inspiration of the chef, but might include roasted loin of pork with Chinese black bean and citrus-flavored glaze, served with grilled portobello mushrooms, sun-dried tomatoes, risotto, and red-pepper coulis; or a vegetarian moussaka with a ragout of crimson lentils and fresh cucumber-yogurt sauce. This is the only restaurant in Fresno that makes its own ice cream (the flavor of the day when we arrived was Technicolor lime sorbet). A perennial favorite is the bittersweet chocolate cake.

SIERRA NATIONAL FOREST

Leaving Fresno's taco joints, used-car lots, and tract houses behind, an hour's drive east delivers you to the gateway to the Sierra National Forest, a land of lakes and coniferous forests lying between Yosemite and Sequoia/Kings Canyon national parks.

Development—some of it, unfortunately, beside the bigger lakes and reservoirs—is confined to the park's western side. The entire eastern portion is still wilderness protected by the government.

The 1.3 million-acre forest contains 528,000 acres of wilderness. The Sierra's five wilderness areas include Ansel Adams, Dinkey Lakes, John Muir, Kaiser, and Monarch (see below).

The forest, under certain guidelines, offers plenty of opportunities for fishing, swimming, sailing, boating, camping, water-skiing, white-water rafting, kayaking, and horseback riding. Downhill and cross-country skiing, as well as hunting, are also possible, depending on the season. Backpackers seeking to retreat to the wilderness will find solace here, as there are hiking trails galore, some 1,100 miles of them in all.

In the lower elevations, summer temperatures can frequently reach 100°F, but in the higher elevations, more comfortable 70s and 80s are the norm.

After visiting the ranger station at Oakhurst (see below), you'll be at Calif. 41, which links up with Calif. 49, providing the major road into the northern part of the national forest. This is more convenient for visitors approaching the park from Northern California. Calif. 168 via Clovis is the primary route from Fresno if you're headed for Shaver Lake. There is no approach road from the eastern Sierras, only from the west.

To learn about hiking, camping, or other activities, or to obtain fire and wilderness permits needed for backcountry jaunts, visit one of the ranger stations in the park's western section. These include: **Mariposa Ranger District,** 43060 Calif. 41, Oakhurst (☎ 209/683-4665); **Minarets Ranger Station,** 57003 North Fork (☎ 209/877-2218); **Kings River District,** 34849 Maxon Rd., Sanger, near the Pine Flat Reservoir (☎ 209/855-8321); or the **Pineridge Ranger Station,** 29688 Auberry Rd., Prather (☎ 209/855-5355).

Shaver Lake is one place to stock up on goods and supplies if you're going into the wilderness, although stores in Fresno carry much of the same stuff at lower prices. Even the town of Clovis outside Fresno (which you must pass through en route to the forest) has cheaper supplies, especially at its Peacock Market, Tollhouse Road (3rd Street) and Sunnyside Avenue (☎ **209/299-6627**).

OUTDOOR ACTIVITIES

CAMPING   The Sierra National Forest seems like one vast campsite. Possibilities include everything from primitive wilderness camps to developed and often crowded campgrounds with hookups for RVs, snack bars, flush toilets, and bath houses. For information and reservations, call the National Forest Reservation Center at **800/280-CAMP.**

Campgrounds are virtually everywhere, the major ones being the Shaver Lake area (first-come, first-served); the Huntington Lake area (six family campgrounds; reserved camping from the end of June through Labor Day); the Florence and Edison Lake area (first-come, first-served); the Dinkey Creek area (family and group camping by special permit); the Wishon and Courtright area (four campgrounds, first-come, first-served); the Pine Flat Reservoir (in the Sierra foothills, with two campgrounds available; first-come, first served); and Upper Kings River, east of Pine Flat Reservoir (family campgrounds on a first-come, first-served basis).

FISHING   The best freshwater angling is in the Pineridge and Kings River Rangers District. Lower elevation reservoirs such as Shaver Lake, Bass Lake, and Pine Flat Reservoirs are known for their black bass fishing. The many streams of the Sierra are home to rainbow, golden, brown, and brook trout. Questions about fishing in the national forest can be directed to the **California Department of Fish and Game,** 1235 E. Shaw Ave., Fresno, CA 93710 (☎ **209/222-3761**).

SKIING   Lying 65 miles northeast of Fresno on Calif. 168, in the Sierra National Forest, the **Sierra Summit Ski Area** is known for its alpine skiing. It also offers marked trails for cross-country skiing and snowmobiling. Information about the district is available from the Pineridge Ranger Station, 29688 Auberry Road, Prather (☎ **209/855-5355**).

The resort area has two triple and three double chairlifts, plus four surface lifts and 25 runs, the longest of which extends for 2¼ miles. There's a vertical drop-off at 1,600 feet. Other facilities include a snack bar, cafeteria, restaurant, and bar, plus a lodge. These facilities are open daily from mid-November until mid-April. For a ski report, call **209/893-3311.**

The ranger district has developed several marked cross-country trails along Calif. 168. They range from a 1-mile tour for beginners to a 6-mile trail for more advanced skiers.

WHITE-WATER RAFTING   The Upper Kings River, east of Pine Flat Reservoir, offers a 10-mile rafting run through Garnet Dike to Kirch Flat Campground. Rafting season is from late April to mid-July, with the highest waters in late May and early June. The location is about 63 miles east of Fresno; access is via Belmont Avenue in Fresno, heading east toward Pine Flat Reservoir.

Commercial rafting companies offering guided rafting trips on the Kings River include **Kings River Expeditions** (☎ **209/233-4881**), and **Zephyr River Expeditions** (☎ **209/532-6249**).

THE MAJOR WILDERNESS & RECREATION AREAS

First, we'll preview the five major wildernesses, then we'll run down the other major scenic highlights of the forest system.

THE ANSEL ADAMS WILDERNESS   Divided between the Sierra and Inyo National Forests, this wilderness area covers 228,500 acres. Elevations range from 3,500 to 13,157 feet. The frost-free period extends from mid-July through August, the best time for a visit to the park's upper altitudes.

Ansel Adams is splashed with scenic alpine vistas, including steep-walled gorges and barren granite peaks. There are several small glaciers in the north, and some fairly large lakes on the eastern slope of the precipitous Ritter Range. This vast wilderness has excellent stream and lake fishing, especially for rainbow, golden, and brook trout, and the Minarets Range poses a worthwhile challenge for recreational mountain climbers. Approach roads to the wilderness include Tioga Pass Road in the north, and U.S. 395 and Reds Meadow Road in the east; the Minarets Highway in the west, and Calif. 168 to High Sierra in the south.

DINKEY LAKES WILDERNESS   On the western slope of the Sierra Nevada southeast of Huntington Lake, and just northwest of Courtright Reservoir, the 30,000-acre Dinkey Lakes area was created in 1984. Most of the wilderness is 8,000 feet above sea level, reaching its highest point of 10,619 feet at Three Sisters Peak. Sixteen lakes are clustered in the west central region. Most of the wilderness consists of timbered, rolling terrain. Access is via Kaiser Pass Road (north), Red/Coyote Jeep Road (west), Rock Creek Road (southwest), or Courtright Reservoir (south east). The wilderness is generally accessible from mid-June to late October.

JOHN MUIR WILDERNESS   Cutting across some 584,000 acres in the Sierra and Inyo National Forests, John Muir Wilderness, named after the turn-of-the-century naturalist, extends along the crest of the Sierra Nevada from Mammoth Lakes southeasterly for 30 miles before forking around the boundary of Kings Canyon National Park to Crown Valley and Mt. Whitney. Elevations range from 4,000 to 14,496 feet at Mt. Whitney. Many peaks surpass 12,000 feet.

Split by deep canyons, the wilderness is also a land of meadows (especially beautiful when wildflowers bloom), and many lakes and streams. The South and Middle Forks of the San Joaquin River, the North Fork of Kings River, and many creeks draining into Owens Valley begin in the John Muir. Mountain hemlock, red and white fir, whitebark, and western pine dot the park's landscape. Temperatures vary widely throughout any 24-hour period: Summer temperatures range from 25° to 85°F, and the only really frost-free period is between mid-July and August. The higher elevations are marked by barren expanses of granite dotted with many glacially carved lakes.

KAISER WILDERNESS   Immediately north of Huntington Lake and some 70 miles northeast of Fresno, Kaiser is a 22,700-acre forest tract commanding a view of the central Sierra Nevada. It was named after Kaiser Ridge, which divides the area into two different regions. The northern half is much more open than the forested southern half. Four trailheads provide easy access in the northern half, and the primary point of entry is from the Sample Meadow Campground. All other lakes are approached cross-country. Winter storms begin to blow in late October, and the grounds are generally covered with snow until early June.

MONARCH WILDERNESS   This area extends across 45,000 acres in the Sierra and Sequoia National Forests. The Sierra National portion of the region, about 21,000 acres, is very rugged and hard to traverse. Steep slopes extend up from the Middle and Main Forks of Kings River, with elevations going from 2,400 to more than 10,000 feet. Rock outcroppings are found throughout Monarch, and most of the lower elevations are mainly chaparral covered with pine stands near the tops of the higher peaks.

HUNTINGTON LAKE RECREATION AREA   At an elevation of 7,000 feet, this area is a two-hour drive east of Fresno via Calif. 168. The lake is one of the reservoirs in the Big Creek Hydroelectric System, and has 14 miles of shoreline. It's a popular recreational area, offering such activities as camping, hiking, picnicking, sailing, swimming, windsurfing, fishing, and horseback riding. Or you can visit just to appreciate the beauty. The main summer season stretches from Memorial Day to Labor Day. There are seven campgrounds and four picnic areas in the Huntington Lake Basin, plus numerous hiking and riding trails. For information, stop in at the **Easterwood Visitor Center** (☎ 209/893-6611), open only from May through September.

✪ NELDER GROVE OF GIANT SEQUOIAS   This 1,540-acre tract in the Sierra National Forest contains 101 mature giant sequoias in the center of the Sequoia range, south of Yosemite National Park. A visitors center stands near the Nelder Grove Campground, with historical relics and displays, including two restored log cabins. The Bull Buck Tree, at one time thought to be the largest tree in the world, has a height of 246 feet and a circumference at ground level of 99 feet. There's a 1-mile-long, self-guided walk along the "Shadow of the Giants" National Recreational Trail in the southwest corner of the grove.

The Monterey Peninsula & Big Sur Coast

by Erika Lenkert and Matthew R. Poole

Located about 120 miles south of San Francisco, the Monterey Peninsula and Big Sur coast comprise one of the world's most coveted shorelines. Skirted with cypress, rugged shores, and crescent-shaped bays, the indescribably beautiful marine backdrop has made this entire stretch of coastline a favorite seaside playground for travelers worldwide. Monterey also reels in visitors with its Monterey Bay Aquarium and unparalleled outdoor activities; Pacific Grove is so peaceful and quaint that butterflies choose it as their yearly mating ground; tiny Carmel-By-The-Sea, though packed with tourists who come for the beaches, shops, and restaurants, somehow remains romantic and sweet; and Big Sur's dramatic and majestic coast, backed by pristine redwood forests and rolling hills, is one of the most breathtaking sites on earth.

Monterey and Pacific Grove occupy the northern half of the peninsula overlooking Monterey Bay. Pebble Beach and Carmel-By-The-Sea look out over Carmel Bay and hug the peninsula's south coast. Between the north and south coasts, which are only about 5 miles apart, are at least eight golf courses, some of the state's most stunning homes and hotels, and 17-Mile Drive, one of the most scenic coastal roads in the world. Inland lies Carmel Valley, with its elegant inns and resorts, golf courses, and guaranteed sunshine, even when the coast is blanketed in fog.

Farther down the coast is Big Sur, a stunning 90-mile stretch of coast south of the Monterey Peninsula and west of the Santa Lucia Mountains.

1 Monterey

While its neighbors are romantic coastal hideaways, Monterey is the antithesis. A harbor-town-cum-tourist-trap, it's big enough that you have to drive from downtown to Cannery Row and affected enough that chain hotels and restaurants have put the squeeze on boutiques. Plenty of history remains, but you'll have to weed through minimalls to find it. Its saving grace is the fantastic aquarium and beautiful Monterey Bay, where sea lions and otters still frolic.

If you're interested in saving money, you can stay in an inexpensive motel in Monterey and easily drive into pricier Carmel-By-The-Sea to shop and go to the beach, but if you want the full charm of the area, set up camp in Pacific Grove and make Monterey a day trip.

Originally settled in 1770, Monterey was one of the West Coast's first European settlements. The town was the capital of California under the Spanish, Mexican, and American flags and California's Constitution was drafted here in 1849, paving the way for the state's admission to the Union a year later. Many architectural buildings from the early colonial era still stand. A major whaling center in the 1800s, it also became a sardine center when the first packing plant was built in 1900. By 1913 the boats were bringing in 25 tons of sardines a night. Whenever they landed, the residents thronged down to the canneries to work.

Back then Cannery Row was home to 18 canning factories, and its life was captured in John Steinbeck's famous novel of the same name. After the sardines disappeared, the town and the peninsula went after tourist dollars instead.

ESSENTIALS

GETTING THERE & GETTING AROUND   The region's most convenient runway, at **Monterey Peninsula Airport** (☎ 408/373-1704), is 3 miles east of Monterey on Calif. 68. **American Eagle** (☎ 800/433-7300), **Northwest Airlines** (☎ 800/225-2525), **Skywest** (☎ 800/453-9417), **United** (☎ 800/241-6522), and **USAir** (☎ 800/428-4322) schedule daily flights in and out of Monterey.

Many area hotels offer free airport shuttle service. If you take a taxi, it will cost about $20 to $25 to get to a peninsula hotel. Several national car rental companies have airport locations, including **Dollar** (☎ 800/800-4000) and **Hertz** (☎ 800/654-3131).

Once in town, the **Waterfront Area Visitor Express** (WAVE), operates each year from Memorial Day weekend through Labor Day and takes passengers to and from the aquarium and other waterfront attractions. Stops are located at many hotels and motels in Monterey and Pacific Grove. For $1 (50¢ for kids and seniors), you can have unlimited rides all day between 9am and 6:30pm and eliminate the stress of parking downtown. Call **Monterey Salinas Transit** for further information at **408/899-2555.**

VISITOR INFORMATION   The **Monterey Peninsula Visitors and Convention Bureau,** 380 Alvarado St. (☎ **408/649-1770**), has good maps and free pamphlets and publications, including an excellent visitors' guide and the magazine *Coast Weekly*. The office is near the intersection of Pacific Street and Del Monte Avenue.

SEEING THE SIGHTS

The **Steinbeck Center Foundation,** 371 Main St., Salinas (☎ **408/753-6411**), offers a self-guided tour or information on docent-led tours of "Steinbeck Country," which show visitors sites once frequented by the renowned American author and local legend John Steinbeck.

Cannery Row. Monterey Bay (between David and Drake aves.). ☎ **408/649-6690.**

Once an industrious sardine-packing Mecca immortalized by John Steinbeck in his 1945 novel *Cannery Row,* the area he described as "a poem, a stink, a grating noise, a quality of light, a tone, a habit, a nostalgia, a dream" is today better portrayed as "a strip congested with wandering tourists, tacky gift shops, overpriced seafood restaurants, and an overall parking nightmare."

What changed it so dramatically? The silver sardines suddenly disappeared from Monterey's waters in 1948 as a result of overfishing, changing currents, and pollution. Fishers left, canneries closed, and the Row fell into disrepair. But curious tourists continued to visit Steinbeck's fabled area and where there are tourists, there are capitalists.

The Monterey Peninsula

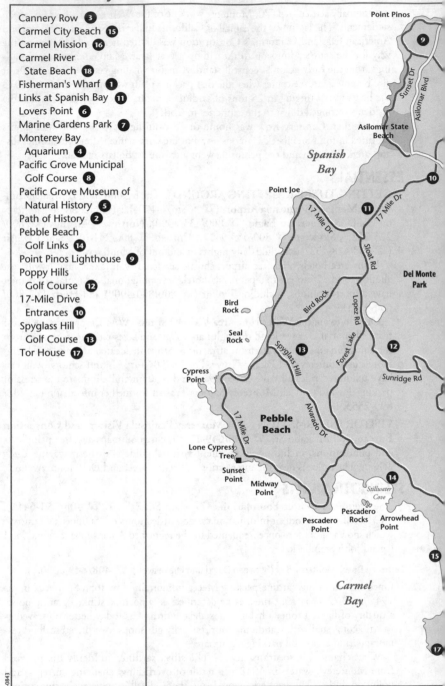

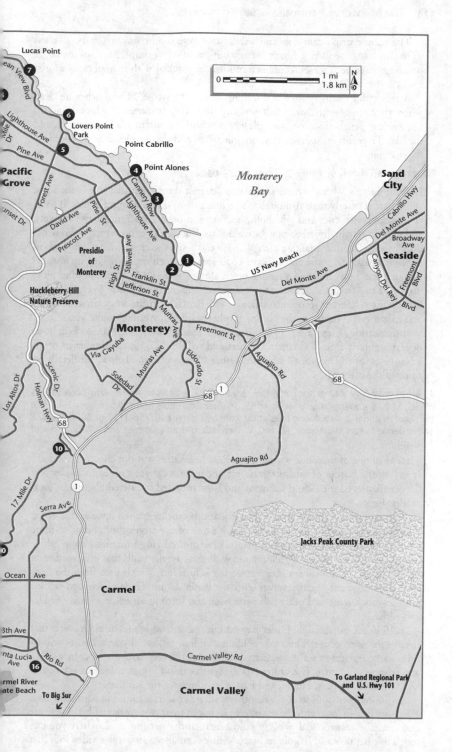

Lucas Point

Ocean View Blvd

7

6

Lovers Point Park

Point Cabrillo

Lighthouse Ave

5

Pine Ave

4 Point Alones

3

Cannery Row

Pacific Grove

Forest Ave

David Ave

Sunset Dr

Prescott Ave

Pine St

Stillwell Ave

Lighthouse Ave

Presidio of Monterey

High St

Franklin St

2

1

Jefferson St

Huckleberry Hill Nature Preserve

Monterey

Munras Ave

Via Gayuba

Munras Ave

Soledad Dr

Eldorado St

Freemont St

68

1

68

Los Altos Dr

Scenic Dr

Holman Hwy

68

10

17 Mile Dr

1

Serra Ave

Aguajito Rd

Ocean Ave

Carmel

8th Ave

Santa Lucia Ave

Rio Rd

16

Carmel River State Beach

To Big Sur

1

Carmel Valley Rd

Carmel Valley

Monterey Bay

Sand City

Cabrillo Hwy

Del Monte Ave

Broadway Ave

Seaside

Canyon Del Rey

Freemont Blvd

US Navy Beach

Del Monte Ave

1

Blvd

Aguajito Rd

Jacks Peak County Park

To Garland Regional Park and U.S. Hwy 101

0   1 mi
         1.8 km

N

The seaside strip's canneries and warehouses were soon renovated and converted to restaurants, art galleries, hotels, factory outlets, and gift shops. Many of the larger buildings have become self-contained minimalls, stocked with myriad tacky tourist shops and eateries.

After visiting Cannery Row in the 1960s, Steinbeck wrote, "The beaches are clean where they once festered with fish guts and flies. The canneries which once put up a sickening stench are gone, their places filled with restaurants, antique shops, and the like. They fish for tourists now, not pilchards, and that species they are not likely to wipe out."

Fisherman's Wharf. 99 Pacific St. ☎ **408/373-0600.**

Is "Fisherman's Wharf" synonymous with "tourist trap?" Just like San Francisco's, this wharf is exactly that. Although it's an honest-to-goodness wooden pier, it's still jam-packed with craft and gift shops, boating and fishing operations, fish markets, and seafood restaurants all baiting tourist dollars. But don't get me wrong—this wharf does have redeeming qualities; after all, who can resist the charm of a sunny harbor, bobbing boats, and surfacing sea lions? Grab some clam chowder sogging up its sourdough bread bowl and find a seaside perch along the pier. Or when the wind picks up, find a bay-front seat at one of the seafood restaurants (see "Where to Dine," below for specific restaurant recommendations). The natural surroundings are so beautiful you might not even notice the hordes of other tourists hovering around you.

If the seaside sights have got you itching to set sail, don't remain landlocked; boats depart regularly from Fisherman's Wharf and will lead you on a number of ocean adventures. See "Deep-Sea Fishing & Other Offshore Fun," below, for details on some of the offerings.

✪ **Monterey Bay Aquarium.** 886 Cannery Row. ☎ **408/648-4888.** Admission $13.75 adults, $11.75 students and seniors over 65, $6 disabled visitors and children ages 3–12, free for children under 3. Avoid long lines at the gate by calling 800/756-3737 or 800/225-2277 and ordering tickets in advance. AE, MC, V. Daily 10am–6pm (summer and holidays open at 9:30am).

The site of one of the world's most spectacular aquariums was not chosen at random. It sits on the border of one of the largest underwater canyons on earth (wider and deeper than even the Grand Canyon) and is surrounded by incredibly diverse local marine life.

Opened in 1984, the Monterey Bay Aquarium quickly gained fame as one of the best exhibit aquariums in the world, and it's one of the largest, too, home to more than 350,000 marine animals and plants. One of the living museum's main exhibits is a three-story, 335,000-gallon tank, with clear acrylic walls that give visitors an unmatched look at local sea life. A towering kelp forest, which rises from the floor of this oceanic zoo, gently waves with the water as hundreds of leopard sharks, sardines, anchovies, and other fish swim back and forth in an endless game of hide-and-seek.

In 1996 the outstanding Outer Bay exhibit opened, which features creatures that inhabit the open ocean. This tank, holding a million gallons of water, houses yellowfin tuna, a large green sea turtle, barracuda, sharks, the very-cool giant ocean sunfish, and schools of bonito. The Outer Bay's jellyfish exhibit is guaranteed to amaze and kids will love Flippers, Flukes, and Fun, a learning area for families.

Additional wet exhibits re-create other undersea habitats found in Monterey Bay. Everyone falls in love with the sea otters playing in their two-story exhibit. There are also coastal streams, tidal pools, a sand beach, and a petting pool, where you can touch live bat rays and handle sea stars. Visitors can also watch a live video link that regularly transmits from a deep-sea research submarine maneuvering thousands of feet below the surface of Monterey Bay.

THE PATH OF HISTORY

About a dozen antique buildings are clustered around Fisherman's Wharf and the adjacent town. Collectively, they comprise the Path of History, and many are a part of the **Monterey State Historic Park,** 20 Custom House Plaza (☎ **408/649-7118**). A self-guided walking tour booklet is available that describes the route. You can pick up a copy at clearly marked points along the path, including Cooper-Molera Adobe and Colton Hall (see below).

The path's best buildings are featured below; many do not have formal addresses, so they're listed according to the streets or street corners they fill. Path of History building hours vary and change frequently, although in most cases they're open daily from 10am to 4pm in winter, and 10am to 5pm in summer. Call the Monterey State Historic Park for the latest information or go to the State Park Visitor Center at Stanton Center, 5 Custom House Plaza. A film on the history of Monterey is shown here free every 20 minutes, and guided walking tours of the Path leave from here daily at 10:15am, 12:30 and 2:30pm. The price is $2 for adults, $1.50 for youths 13 to 18, and $1 for children 6 to 12. A $5 ticket guarantees admission over any two-day period into each of the four buildings that charge admission fees (the Cooper-Molera Adobe, Casa Soberanes, Larkin House, and Stevenson House). Otherwise, entrance to those four buildings costs $2 each.

The Monterey Maritime Museum and History Center This museum, at 5 Custom House Plaza (☎ **408/373-2469**), lets you view ship's models and other collections that relate the area's seafaring history. Admission is $5 adults, $3 youths 13 to 18, $2 children 6 to 12, free for kids 5 and under. Open Tuesday to Sunday from 10am to 5pm (daily in July and August).

The Custom House Dating from about 1827, this is the oldest government building in California, used by Mexican officials to inspect and tax ships trading on the California coast. It was here that Commodore John Sloat raised the stars and stripes to claim California for the United States.

California's First Theatre/Jack Swan's Tavern In 1847, Jack Swan built a lodging house and tavern at Scott and Pacific streets. Three years later several U.S. soldiers decided to produce plays as a business venture. They used blankets as curtains, barrels and boards as benches, and turned a healthy profit on their very first night. Today the troupers of the Gold Coast Theater Company stage authentic 19th-century melodramas here. Call for reservations after 1pm Wednesday through Saturday at **408/375-4916.** Tickets cost $8 for adults, $7 for children 13 to 19 and seniors over 60, and $5 for kids 12 and under. Show times are Wednesday through Saturday at 8pm in July and August, and Friday and Saturday at 8pm the rest of the year.

Cooper-Molera Adobe This house at the corner of Polk and Munras streets was the home of Capt. John Rogers Cooper, a successful merchant. It was built in the 1820s and 1830s, but was expanded and improved upon as he became wealthier. Today it's furnished with antiques that reveal much about his lifestyle.

Casa Soberanes This colonial-era adobe at 336 Pacific St., at Scott Street, was built during the 1840s. The home's cantilevered balcony and tile roof are of particular interest, as is the well-maintained interior, decorated with early New England furnishings and modern Mexican folk art.

Larkin House   Built in 1835, this balconied two-story adobe house at 510 Calle Principal, at Jefferson Street, was the home of Thomas Oliver Larkin, the U.S. consul to Mexico from 1843 to 1846. The house doubled as the consular office and is furnished with many fine antiques including some original pieces. Next door is the house that was used by William Tecumseh Sherman; it now contains a museum depicting the roles of the two men in California history.

Stevenson House   Robert Louis Stevenson rented a second-floor room here during the autumn of 1879. He wrote *The Old Pacific Capital,* an account of Monterey in the 1870s, during his stay. Today this building on Houston Street has been restored and several rooms are devoted to Stevenson memorabilia.

Pacific House   Built in 1847, Pacific House, at 10 Custom House Plaza, was first used for military offices and supplies. Horses were corralled behind the building, which was also a popular spot for Sunday bull and bear fights. Pacific House later sheltered several small stores, and served successively as a public tavern, a courtroom, county clerk's office, newspaper office, law offices, a church, and a ballroom. The first floor now houses a museum of California history; the second floor has an extensive collection of Native American artifacts.

Colton Hall   This structure, at 522 Pacific St., was originally built as Monterey's town hall and public school. California's constitutional congress convened here in 1849. Old Monterey Jail adjoins the property, its grim cell walls still marked with prisoners' scribblings.

Casa del Oro   Built by Thomas Oliver Larkin and used as a store by Joseph Bosta, this two-story adobe stands at the corner of Scott and Oliver streets. Today, Casa del Oro is again a general store, which is operated by the volunteers of Historic Gardens of Monterey.

DEEP-SEA FISHING & OTHER OFFSHORE FUN

Cast away your hook and your cares on a deep-sea fishing expedition. Among the operators are **Chris' Fishing Trips,** 48 Fisherman's Wharf (☎ **408/375-5951**), which offers large party boats. Cod and salmon are the main catches, with separate boats leaving daily. Call for a complete price list and sailing schedule. Full-day excursions cost $27 to $40 per person.

  Sam's Fishing Fleet, 84 Fisherman's Wharf (☎ **408/372-0577**), offers fishing excursions for cod, salmon, and whatever else is running, as well as whale-watching tours (seasonal). Make reservations and bring lunch. Departures are at 7:30am Monday through Friday (salmon-fishing boats leave earlier) and at 6:30am on Saturday and Sunday. Check-in is 45 minutes before departure, and weekday prices are $27 adults, $15 children under 12; $30 adults, $19 children under 12 on weekends and holidays. Equipment is an extra $16.

  Kayaks can be rented from several outfitters for a spin around the bay. Contact **Monterey Bay Kayaks,** 693 Del Monte Ave. (☎ **800/649-5357** or 408/373-5357), on Del Monte Beach north of Fisherman's Wharf, which offers instruction, plus natural history tours that introduce visitors to the Monterey Bay National Marine Sanctuary. Prices start at $45 for the tours, $25 for rentals. Want to know more? Check them out on-line at http://montereykayaks.com/tour.

  Adventures by the Sea, at 299 Cannery Row, Monterey (☎ **408/372-1807**), also rents kayaks and provides similar tours. Bikes (including free pickup and delivery) and in-line skates are also available for rent. Bikes cost $6 per hour or $24 a day; kayaks are $25 per person; and skates are $12 for 2 hours, $24 a day. Adventures also has other locations at 201 Alvarado Mall (☎ **408/648-7235**) at the Doubletree Hotel and on the beach at Lovers Point in Pacific Grove.

Experienced scuba divers with their own equipment and one tank can contact **Twin Otters** (☎ 408/394-4235), which specializes in scuba-diving trips along the reefs of Monterey and Carmel Bays.

KID STUFF

Feeling playful? The **Dennis the Menace Playground** at Camino El Estero and Del Monte Avenue (☎ 408/646-3866), near Lake Estero, is an old-fashioned playground created by Pacific Grove resident and famous cartoonist Hank Ketcham. It has bridges to cross, tunnels to climb through, and an authentic Southern Pacific engine car teeming with wanna-be conductors. There's also a hot dog and burger stand, and a big lake where you can rent paddleboats or feed the ducks. The park is open daily from 10am to sunset.

WHERE TO STAY

It seems there are only three types of choices for accommodations in Monterey: lace-and-flowers B&Bs; large corporate-cum-beachy hotels; or run-of-the-mill motel digs. And if you're on a strict budget, your choices are even more limited. The two things you should consider when making your reservations are how much you want to spend and which area you'd like to be in (beach, Cannery Row, wharf, secluded, central). For the most part, budget accommodations are scarce and are located on the periphery of town (and even these are hardly a bargain during high season). But don't let that discourage you: The entire area from north Monterey to Carmel is within a 15-minute drive. For more scenic budget options, check out what's available in adjoining Pacific Grove before booking in north Monterey.

DOUBLES FOR $60 OR LESS

Del Monte Beach Inn. 1110 Del Monte Ave., (at Park), Monterey, CA 93940. ☎ **408/649-4410.** 19 rooms. Sept 30–Jan 1 double with shared bath $45–$55 Mon–Thurs, double with private bath $65–$70; Fri–Sun double with shared bath $50–$55, double with private bath $70–$75. Jan–June double with shared bath $35–$45, double with private bath $55. June–Sept Mon–Thurs double with shared bath $55–$60, double with private bath $75–$80, Fri–Sun double without bath $60–$65, double with private bath $85–$90. Discounts for divers and AAA members (except during special events). AE, MC, DISC, V.

Less than a mile away from all the action of downtown Monterey, 6 blocks from the wharf, and a block away from the beach, you'll find one of the cheapest places to stay in the entire area (if you're willing to share a bath). This hotel was built in the late 1800s as a private residence, and though it's on a busy street, many tourists will still appreciate it as a respite from the hordes of tourists crowding up and down the even busier Cannery Row. The inn models itself after European B&Bs, with period reproductions and other homey furnishings, as well as an extended continental breakfast included in the price. Bathrooms are shared (except for two rooms that have a private bath) and parking is free. There are no phones or TVs in your room, but there is a pay phone inside the inn and a TV in the library. Another plus is the sunny balcony out back that overlooks the garden. Three rooms have wharf and ocean views.

DOUBLES FOR $80 OR LESS

Munras Avenue and northern Fremont Avenue are lined with inexpensive family-style motels, some independently owned and some chains. They are not as central as downtown options, but if transportation is not an issue, you can save a bundle staying in one of these areas. If the selection below is full, try calling **Best Western** (☎ 800/528-1234), **Motel 6** (☎ 800/4-MOTEL6), or **Super 8** (☎ 800/800-8000), for several other options. There's also the **Cypress Gardens Inn,** 1150 Munras Ave.

(☎ 408/373-2761), which offers a pool, hot tub, free movie channel, and continental breakfast, and welcomes dogs.

The Arbor Inn. 1058 Munras Ave., Monterey, CA 93940. ☎ **408/372-3381.** Fax 408/372-4687. 54 rms. A/C TEL TV. Mon–Thurs $39–$69 double, Fri–Sat $49–$129 double. AE, DC, DISC, MC, V.

If life were a musical you'd hear a *Brady Bunch* riff when you opened the door and peered into your guest room at this motel. Rooms are large, clean, and many have fireplaces, but the funky brown carpet, plaid couches, and '70s color scheme aren't exactly in vogue. There's a hot tub on the property that looks a little worn, but is tucked into a quiet spot away from the parking lot. A continental breakfast is served in a country-style dining room, complete with fireplace. Rates are darn good here considering the motel is close to downtown and the waterfront; since it just changed hands, expect some changes in the coming year.

DOUBLES FOR $100 OR LESS

Best Western DeAnza Inn. 2141 North Fremont St., Monterey, CA 93940. ☎ **800/858-8775** or 408/646-8300. Fax 408/646-8130. 41 rms, 2 suites. TEL TV. Double $65–$129; suites $100–$165. Extra person $8. Senior discounts. AE, DC, DISC, MC, V.

The common areas of this north Monterey motel are more modern and elaborate than most Best Westerns I've seen, but the rooms, though newly decorated don't venture far beyond your generic motel style. They are clean and new, however, which always makes for better accommodations. Amenities include in-room coffee, and microwaves and refrigerators are available upon request ($10 extra for each). There's also a heated pool and Jacuzzi on the premises. The only drawback is the motel's location a few miles north of all of Monterey's action; downtown's a quick and easy drive, but if you prefer great strolling grounds outside your door, opt for one of Best Western's other more centrally located properties. (There are 10 Best Westerns in the area, including the oceanfront Monterey Beach Hotel, which offers rooms on the beach for $59 to $179. Call the 800 number provided above for details.)

☉ Cypress Tree Inn. 2227 North Fremont St., Monterey, CA 93940. ☎ **408/372-7586.** Fax 408/372-2940. 55 rms (9 with hot tubs). TEL TV. $58–$92 double. Senior and AAA discounts. MC, V.

Although it's not exactly centrally located (2 miles from downtown), if you're on a budget and have transportation, you won't be sorry you saved your pennies by staying here. Rooms are spotless, large and have tub-showers (except one). There's no shampoo, hair dryer, or in-room treats (other than the taffy left by the maid), but the property does have a hot tub, sauna, and a coin-op laundry.

El Adobe Inn. 936 Munras (at El Dorado), Monterey, CA 93940. ☎ **800/433-4732** or 408/372-5409. Fax 408/375-7236. 26 rms. TEL TV. $85–$105 double. Continental breakfast included. AARP, AAA, senior, and corporate discounts. AE, DISC, MC, V.

A far cry from an authentic adobe, this basic motor lodge is close to downtown, is simple and clean, not too tacky, and offers perks that make it an overall good deal. Many rooms have ocean views (distant though they may be), and all have alarm clocks and a free movie channel. "Deluxe" rooms have coffeemakers and refrigerators. There's a small Jacuzzi on the premises and pets are welcome.

Fireside Lodge. 1131 10th St., Monterey, CA 93940. ☎ **408/373-4172.** Fax 408/655-5640. 24 rms. TEL TV. $69–$149 double. Rates include continental breakfast. AE, DC, DISC, MC, V.

Location is the primary draw of this hotel near Fisherman's Wharf and downtown. Room furnishings are relatively standard but attempt at coziness with wicker chairs set around the gas-heated brick fireplace. Amenities include an in-room tea- and coffeemaker, a hot tub on the premises, and a continental breakfast served daily in the hotel's lobby.

Travelodge, Downtown Monterey. 675 Munras Ave., Monterey, CA 93940. ☎ **408/ 373-1876.** Fax 408/373-8693. 49 rms. TEL TV. $49–$99 double. AARP, AAA, and corporate discounts available. AE, DC, DISC, MC, V.

You already know what to expect from Travelodge, so if you're hankering for lace window curtains and fresh flowers by the bed, you'd better bring 'em yourself. What you will find here are recently redecorated rooms (very clean!) with tidy seashell bedspreads, a table and chairs, a vanity, and shower baths (six have tubs). Extra perks such as hair dryers, free HBO, in-room coffeemakers, free local calls, free parking, and free newspapers in the lobby make this Travelodge a good deal (comparatively). There's even a small swimming pool (which unfortunately overlooks the street). This hotel is closer to downtown than the North Fremont options.

WORTH A SPLURGE

The Jabberwock Bed and Breakfast. 598 Laine St., Monterey, CA 93940. ☎ **408/ 372-4777.** Fax 408/655-2946. 7 rms (3 with private bath). $105 double without bath, $190 double with bath. Rates include full breakfast, afternoon appetizers, and bedtime cookies. MC, V.

One of the favored B&Bs in the area, the Jabberwock (named after an episode in Lewis Carroll's *Through the Looking Glass*) is four short blocks back from Cannery Row. Although centrally located, the property is tranquil and its half-acre garden with waterfalls is a welcome respite from the downtown crowds. The seven rooms are all furnished differently, some more elegantly than others, but all with goose-down comforters and pillows. The Toves room has a huge walnut Victorian bed; the Borogrove has a fireplace and a view of Monterey Bay; The Mimsey has a fine ocean view from its window seat, while the Wabe has an Austrian carved bed. Almost all rooms come with a shower, but no tub. A full breakfast is served in the dining room or in your own room. Evening hors d'oeuvres are also offered on the veranda, and each guest gets tucked in with cookies and milk.

Monterey Bay Inn. 242 Cannery Row, Monterey, CA 93940. ☎ **800/424-6242** or 408/ 373-6242. Fax 408/373-7603. 47 rms. MINIBAR TEL TV. $119–$329 double. Rates include continental breakfast delivered to your room. AE, CB, DC, DISC, MC, V. Free parking. From Calif. 1 take the Pacific Grove Del Monte Ave. exit and follow signs to Cannery Row. The hotel is near the aquarium.

I'd been under the impression that aside from Cannery Row's central locale (a short walk from the aquarium), there's no reason to stay there—it's noisy, teeming with tourists, and expensive. But when I stepped out onto my private patio at the Monterey Bay Inn and saw otters splashing around below me, my criticism melted into tranquil admiration. If you don't spend all your time on the balcony, you'll be pleased to discover that rooms escape appearing corporate and have a light beachy decor and old Monterey photos on the walls. Accommodations are spacious and most have king-size beds and sofa beds as well as dressing areas and combination baths (terry cloth robes included). Amenities include a refrigerator, VCR, and binoculars. Unfortunately, but not surprisingly, ocean-view rooms cost substantially more than those that look onto a park, harbor, or Cannery Row. Parents with small children should take precautions with the sliding glass doors, which open to a minimal balustrade.

Services: Room service from 5 to 10pm.

Facilities: Sauna, fitness room, scuba facilities, beach and dive access, two hot tubs (one's open 24 hours and the other, though its hours are limited, boasts romantic bay views).

❂ **Old Monterey Inn.** 500 Martin St., Monterey, CA 93940. ☎ **800/350-2344** or 408/375-8284. Fax 408/375-6730. 9 rms, 1 cottage. $170–$240 double; $240 cottage. Rates include American breakfast. MC, V. Free parking. From Calif. 1, take the Soledad Dr. exit and turn right onto Pacific Ave., then left onto Martin St.

Ann and Gene Swett have done a masterful job of converting their comfortable family home into a three-story, half-timbered, vine-clad country inn. Away from the surf, on a one-acre site off Pacific Avenue, it's a good choice for romantics, with rose gardens, a bubbling brook, and brick and flagstone walkways shaded by a panoply of oaks. Each guest room enjoys peaceful garden views and is equipped with cozy beds with goose-down comforters and pillows. Most rooms have feather beds and wood-burning fireplaces; two open onto private patios. Accommodations are charmingly furnished and unique in character, but all in the debt of Laura Ashley or Ralph Lauren. Special touches are evident throughout, including fresh fruit, flowers, and candies; sachets by the pillow; and books and magazines to read. Three rooms are wired for cable TV, where it is available on request, and though there are no phones in the rooms, cordless phones are provided in public areas. Bathrooms come with a complete toiletry package and hair dryers.

Breakfast is also stellar, consisting of perhaps a soufflé or Belgian waffles. It is served in your room, the dining room, or the rose garden. If you want to lunch on the beach, the Swetts provide guests with picnic baskets and towels. At 5pm guests are invited to have wine and hors d'oeuvres in front of a blazing fireplace.

WHERE TO DINE
MEALS FOR $10 OR LESS
❸ **Papá Chano's Taqueria.** 462 Alvarado St. (at Bonifaceo Pl. near Franklin). ☎ **408/646-9587.** Mexican plates $2.80–$5.95. No credit cards. Daily 10am–midnight. MEXICAN.

Considering the cavernous ceilings, unadorned walls, and plain wooden tables and brick floors, this is the last place you should go if you're looking for atmosphere. It's all about volume in this taqueria, so don't expect cloth napkins, a formal waiter (or any waiter for that matter), or quiet music surrounding your ears. You can, however, count on fresh ingredients, fast service, and dirt-cheap Mexican food: burritos, quesadillas, tacos, nachos, and *platillos especiales* (steak, pork, chicken, or chile relleno plates served with rice, beans, cheese, lettuce, tomato, salsa, sour cream, guacamole, and tortillas) all for under six bucks.

Rosine's. 434 Alvarado St. (at Franklin). ☎ **408/375-1400.** Reservations not accepted. Main courses breakfast $3.50–$8.25, lunch $5.50–$7.95, dinner most dishes $5.75–$8.50. AE, DC, DISC, MC, V. Mon–Thurs 7:30am–9pm, Fri 7:30–10pm, Sat 8am–10pm, Sun 8am–9pm. AMERICAN.

Everything about this place is simple, from its upscale cafeteria feel, to its menu filled with your basic entrees. Lunch features an extensive list of salads and sandwiches and dinner offers an array of pastas, burgers, and more expensive items such as rack of lamb ($16.95) and prime rib ($14.95). Other than steak and seafood, most entrees hover around $8 and include side salads and/or potatoes. Sugar fiends will appreciate the huge cakes behind glass as you walk in the front door (yes, you can buy them by the slice).

MEALS FOR $20 OR LESS
Cafe Fina. 47 Fisherman's Wharf. ☎ **408/372-5200.** Reservations recommended. Main courses $12.95–$18.95. AE, DC, MC, V. Mon–Fri 11:30am–2:30pm, Sat–Sun 11:30am–3pm; daily 5–10pm. Free parking at Heritage Harbor (at Scott and Pacific). ITALIAN/SEAFOOD.

While other pierside restaurants lure in tourists with little more than an outstanding view, Cafe Fina's mesquite-grilled meats, well-prepared fresh fish, brick-oven–baked pizzas, and an array of delicious salads and pastas give even locals a reason to head to the wharf. Combine the food with a million-dollar vista and a casual atmosphere and Cafe Fina is hands down the best choice on the pier.

Wharfside Restaurant and Lounge. 60 Fisherman's Wharf. ☎ **408/375-3956.** Reservations recommended. Main courses $9–$18. AE, CB, DC, DISC, MC, V. Daily 11am–9:30pm. Closed first two weeks of Dec. SEAFOOD.

A banner out front promises a "taste of Monterey," which translates into a decent helping of fresh seafood served a la tourist trap. While the fare is okay, the real flavor is the Wharfside's casual nautically themed dining room upstairs, where you'll get a great view from the end of Fisherman's Wharf. There's also downstairs and upper-deck outdoor seating where you can choose from seven different varieties of ravioli (made on the premises), such specialties as a Monterey bouillabaisse, or any of the house-made desserts. Daily specials usually include fresh seasonal fish, beef, and pasta; clam chowder, sandwiches (including hot crab), and pizzas are on the regular menu.

WORTH A SPLURGE

✪ **Fresh Cream.** Heritage Harbor, 99 Pacific St. ☎ **408/375-9798.** Reservations recommended. Main courses $21–$30. AE, DC, MC, V. Fri only 11:30am–2pm; daily 6–10pm. FRENCH/CALIFORNIA.

Consistently rated one of the best places in California for fresh and innovative cuisine, Fresh Cream is a sure thing if you're looking for a memorable meal. Decor in the five dining rooms is elegantly understated to emphasize on the food, though fresh flowers, oil lamps, and some tables with wharf views can't help but create ambiance. But once the food comes out of the kitchen, you're liable to forget your surroundings entirely and become entranced by every well-presented and perfectly prepared plate. Start with the lobster ravioli with lobster butter and black and gold caviar or the grilled prawns on whipped white beans with Castroville artichokes, pancetta bacon, and bouillabaisse. Venture on to a main dish such as the blackened ahi tuna sweetened with a pineapple rum sauce; duck richly flavored with black currant sauce; or veal loin with wild mushrooms and white wine butter. Save room for a fluffy Grand Marnier soufflé or the sinful *sac au chocolat.*

✪ **Montrio.** 414 Calle Principal (at Franklin). ☎ **408/648-8880.** Reservations recommended. Main courses lunch $6.45–$9.50, dinner $13.95–$19. AE, DISC, MC, V. Mon–Thurs 11:30am–3pm and 5:30–10pm; Fri–Sat 11:30am–11pm; Sun 10am–10pm. AMERICAN BISTRO.

Big city sophistication met old Monterey when Montrio hit the ground running here in March of 1995. The enormous dining room is definitely the sharpest in town, mixing chic style with a playful canopy vineyard of modern light fixtures, clouds hanging from the ceiling, and the buzz of well-dressed diners. You can watch chefs scurry around in the open kitchen, but you're more likely to keep your eyes on the tasty dishes, such as the crispy Dungeness crab cakes with spicy rémoulade, hot goat cheese salad with marinated veggies and toasted pumpkin seeds, a succulent grilled pork T-bone with apple, pear, and currant compote, or an oven-roasted portobello mushroom with polenta and ragout of vegetables. Finish the evening with chocolate bread pudding with warm banana compote and vanilla ice cream.

Whaling Station Inn. 763 Wave St. (between Prescott and Irving aves.). ☎ **408/373-3778.** Reservations recommended on weekends. Main courses $15–$30. AE, DC, DISC, MC, V. Daily 5–10pm. From Calif. 1, take the Soledad Dr. exit and follow signs to Cannery Row, turn left on Wave St. one block before Cannery Row. CONTINENTAL.

If you insist on eating on Cannery Row, come to this touristy old-fashioned dining house known for its New York, porterhouse, and other steaks grilled over oak and mesquite. A 25-year tradition guarantees you an artichoke vinaigrette appetizer before your main course, which ranges from salad to pasta and the inevitable seafood dish. Famished folk will appreciate the $27 fixed-price menu, which includes a salad or gnocchi, fresh fish or filet mignon with garlic mashed potatoes and garlic sauce and dessert.

2 Pacific Grove

Some compare 2.6-square-mile Pacific Grove, or "P.G." as the locals call it, to Carmel 20 years ago. Although tourists wind their way through here on oceanfront trails and dining excursions, the town remains quaint and peaceful—amazing considering Monterey is a stone's throw away (a quarter of the Monterey Bay Aquarium is actually in Pacific Grove). While neighboring Monterey is comparatively congested and cosmopolitan, Pacific Grove is a community sprinkled with historic homes, blooming flowers, and the kind of tranquility that inspires butterflies to flutter and frolic and deer to fearlessly meander across the road in search of another garden to graze.

ESSENTIALS

ORIENTATION   Lighthouse Avenue is Pacific Grove's principal thoroughfare, running from Monterey to the lighthouse at the very point of the peninsula. Lighthouse Avenue is bisected by Forest Avenue, which runs from Calif. 1 (where it is called Holman Highway, or Calif. 68), to Lover's Point, a finger that sticks out into the bay in the middle of Pacific Grove.

VISITOR INFORMATION   Although the town is small, Pacific Grove has its own chamber of commerce, at the corner of Forest and Central avenues (☎ 408/373-3304).

EXPLORING THE TOWN

Pacific Grove is a town to be strolled, so put on your walking shoes, park the car, and make an afternoon of it. Meander around **George Washington Park** and along the waterfront around the point. **Point Pinos Lighthouse** (☎ 408/648-3116), at the tip of the peninsula on Ocean View Boulevard, is the oldest working lighthouse on the West Coast; it dates from 1855 when Pacific Grove was little more than a pine forest. The museum and grounds are open free to visitors on Thursday, Saturday, and Sunday from 1pm to 4pm.

Marine Gardens Park, a stretch of shoreline along **Ocean View Boulevard** on Monterey Bay and the Pacific, is renowned not only for its ocean views and colorful flowers, but also for its fascinating tide pool seaweed beds. Walk out to Lover's Point (named after lovers of Jesus, not groping teenagers), and watch the sea otters playing in the kelp beds and cracking an occasional abalone shell for lunch.

An excellent alternative, or complement, to the 17-Mile Drive (see Section 3 later in this chapter) is the scenic drive (or bike ride) along Pacific Grove's **Ocean View Boulevard.** This coastal stretch starts near Monterey's Cannery Row and follows the Pacific around to the lighthouse point. There it turns into Sunset Drive, which runs along secluded Asilomar State Beach. Park on Sunset and explore the trails, dunes, and tide pools of this sandy stretch of shore. Look for purple shore crabs, green anemone, sea bats, starfish, and limpets, as well as all kinds of kelp and algae. The 11 buildings of the conference center established here by the YWCA in 1913 are historic landmarks that were designed by noted architect Julia Morgan. If you follow this route during winter months, a furious sea rages and crashes against the rocks.

Seeing the Monarch Butterflies

Pacific Grove is widely known as "Butterfly Town, U.S.A.," a reference to the thousands of monarch butterflies that migrate here each winter from November to February, traveling from as far away as Alaska to settle in the eucalyptus groves. The butterflies settle in the Monarch Grove sanctuary on Grove Acre Avenue off Lighthouse Avenue. George Washington Park, at Pine Avenue and Alder Street, is also famous for its "butterfly trees." To reach these sites the butterflies may travel as far as 2,000 miles, covering 100 miles a day at an altitude of 10,000 feet.

Collectors beware: The town imposes strict fines for molesting the butterflies.

To learn more about the marine and other natural life of the region, stop in at the **Pacific Grove Museum of Natural History,** 165 Forest Ave. (☎ **408/648-3116**). It has displays about the monarch butterflies and their migration and also stuffed examples of the local birds and mammals. Admission is free and it's open Tuesday to Sunday from 10am to 5pm.

GOLF

Just as Ocean View Boulevard serves as an alternative to the 17-Mile Drive, the ✪ **Pacific Grove Municipal Golf Course,** 77 Asilomar Ave., Pacific Grove (☎ **408/ 648-3177**), serves as a reasonably priced alternative to the high-priced courses at Pebble Beach. The back nine holes of this 5,500-yard, par-70 course overlook the sea and offer the added challenge of coping with the winds. Views are panoramic, and the fairways and greens are better maintained than most semiprivate courses. There's a restaurant, pro shop, and driving range. Greens fees are $24 Monday through Thursday, and $28 Friday through Sunday; optional carts cost $23. Visa and MasterCard are accepted for greens fees, but not rental equipment.

FACTORY-OUTLET SHOPPING

The **American Tin Cannery Factory Outlet Center,** 125 Ocean View Blvd., Pacific Grove (☎ **408/372-1442**), is a warehouse of 45 factory outlet shops. Labels represented here include Anne Klein, Joan and David, Bass Shoes, Carter's children's wear, Royal Doulton, Maidenform, London Fog, and Carole Little.

WHERE TO STAY

Hate making decisions? Call **Vacation Centers Reservations** at **408/466-6283** or **Resort II Me** at **800/449-1499;** both will help you choose a hotel and make a reservation.

DOUBLES FOR $80 OR LESS

Bide-A-Wee. 221 Asilomar Blvd., Pacific Grove, CA 93950. ☎ **408/372-2330.** Fax 408/ 372-3947. 8 rms, 9 family units. TV. $49–$89. Weekly rates. AE, MC, V.

Bide-A-Wee's accommodations may be a little worn, but the price and its location (a block from the beach along a quiet wooded street) makes this a charming out-of-the-way hotel option. Rooms are comfortable and individually decorated in country-rustic style, come with coffeemakers and coffee, and allow pets. Some have ocean views and/or a refrigerator. For a few extra bucks you can rent a family unit, which comes with a kitchenette (one has a fireplace).

Butterfly Grove Inn. 1073 Lighthouse Ave., Pacific Grove, CA 93950. ☎ **408/373-4921.** Fax 408/373-7596. 22 rms. TEL TV. $65–$95 double. AE, DC, DISC, MC, V.

More like a motor lodge than an inn, accommodations here are run-of-the-mill, but the amenities are not; some rooms come with refrigerators, kitchenettes, and/or fireplaces and guests have access to the property's pool, spa, Jacuzzi, and shuffleboard, croquet, and volleyball courts. (Don't get too excited: This is no California spa, but it is in one of the sweeter, and quieter, parts of Pacific Grove, and a pool is a pool after all.) Folks traveling with the family opt for one of the six family units tucked into a Victorian house. If you tire of the sporting life, just meander out your door and you're likely to see a soiree of butterflies (during winter), who migrate here each year, as well as deer who wander the streets from time to time.

ⓢ The Wilkies Inn. 1038 Lighthouse Ave., Pacific Grove, CA, 93950. ☎ **408/372-5960.** Fax 408/655-1681. 24 rms. TEL TV. $55–$95 double. Extra person $8. AE, DC, MC, V. Discounts available for seniors. 2-night minimum on weekends. Rates include continental breakfast during summer only.

Decor at this inn is basic motel style, but the owners did splurge on stylish bedspreads and special amenities for divers. All of the squeaky-clean rooms come with coffeemakers and free movies and local calls; some have microwaves or partial ocean views, two have a full kitchen, and you can have a refrigerator for a few extra dollars. Considering that this place consistently charges less than the other hotels in town, gets an A-plus for service, and is located on a quiet tree-lined street in Pacific Grove (I watched a deer cross the street midday), it's a great choice for the budget traveler.

DOUBLES FOR $100 OR LESS

Centrella Inn. 612 Central Ave., Pacific Grove, CA 93950. ☎ **800/233-3372** or 408/372-3372. Fax 408/372-2036. 19 rms, 4 suites, 5 cottages. $95–$159 double; from $178 suite; from $195 cottage. Rates include buffet breakfast. MC, V.

A couple of blocks from the waterfront, and 2 blocks from Lover's Point Beach, the two-story Centrella is an old turreted Victorian that has been standing here since 1889, when it was built as a boarding house. Today the rooms are decorated in a Victorian style, but they're somewhat plain—iron beds, plus side table, floor lamp, and armoire—although the bathrooms do have claw-foot tubs. In the back, connected to the house by brick walkways, are several private cottages and suites with living rooms with fireplaces, wet bars, TV, and a separate bedroom and bath. Two have private decks; the others offer decks facing the rose garden and patio, which is set with umbrella tables and chairs. Cheese and hors d'oeuvres are served in the evening. If you decide to spend big bucks on a room ($159), you'd be better off at Green Gables, Maritine, or Seven Gables, which are all oceanfront properties.

Gosby House. 643 Lighthouse Ave., Pacific Grove, CA 93950. ☎ **800/527-8828** or 408/375-1287. Fax 408/655-9621. 22 rms (20 with bath). TEL. $85–$100 double without bath, $150 double with bath. Rates include full breakfast. AE, MC, V. From Calif. 1, take Calif. 68 to Pacific Grove, where it turns into Forest Ave. Continue on Forest to Lighthouse Ave.; turn left and go three blocks.

Only a few rooms qualify as less than $100, but if you can get one of them and don't mind sharing a bath, the Gosby House is a pleasant place to stay.

Originally a boarding house for Methodist ministers, this Victorian was built in 1887, three blocks from the bay. It's one of the oldest homes in the neighborhood, and it's still one of the most charming Victorians on the Monterey Peninsula. Each room is uniquely decorated, with floral-print wallpapers, lacy pillows, and antique furnishings. Twelve guest rooms have fireplaces, some have TVs, and all come with the inn's trademark teddy bears.

The house has a separate dining room and parlor, where guests gather for breakfast and complimentary wine and snacks in the afternoon. Other amenities include complimentary newspaper, twice daily maid service, and bicycles. Smoking is not allowed.

☢ Green Gables Inn. 104 5th St., Pacific Grove, CA 93950. ☎ **800/722-1774** or 408/ 375-2095. Fax 408/375-5437. 11 rms (7 with bath), 1 suite. TEL TV. $100 double without bath, $160 double with bath. Rates include buffet breakfast. AE, MC, V. From Calif. 1, take the Pacific Grove exit (Calif. 68) and continue to the Pacific Ocean; turn right on Ocean View Blvd., and drive ¹/₂ mile to 5th St.

A Queen Anne–style mansion resembling an English country inn, this hotel dates from 1888, when a judge from Pasadena built it to shelter his mistress from the prying eyes of his hometown. Managed by hospitable innkeepers, this little gem may not be fancy, but it is comfortable. Rooms are divided between the main building and the less atmospheric carriage houses behind it. (The carriage-house rooms are better for families.) Most have an ocean view and are individually decorated with dainty furnishings, including some antiques and the occasional four-poster bed. Carriage rooms enjoy private baths; most of those in the front house share two immaculate bathrooms. There's an antique carousel horse in the comfortable parlor, where complimentary wine, tea, and hors d'oeuvres are served each afternoon. Teddy bears populate every nook and cranny and cookies and coffee are always at hand. No smoking.

WORTH A SPLURGE

Martine Inn. 255 Ocean View Blvd., Pacific Grove, CA 93950. ☎ **800/852-5588** or 408/ 373-3388. 20 rms. TEL. $135–$240 double. Rates include full breakfast. AE, DISC, MC, V.

One glance at the lavish Victorian interior and the incredible bay views and you'll know why this Mediterranean-style hotel is one of the best B&Bs in the area. Enjoy the vista with the binoculars the management leaves out for guests or stroll the bay-front promenade. Expect rooms, which have always been above par, that have been recently redecorated yet still maintain Victorian style. You'll blow your budget if you want a fireplace and ocean view. A full breakfast is served in the large front room at lace-covered tables; hors d'oeuvres are served in the evening. Guests also have access to two additional sitting rooms—a small room downstairs overlooking the ocean, and a larger room with shelves of books—and to a conference room equipped with a TV. Amenities include newspaper delivery, free coffee and refreshments, Jacuzzi, and a billiards table.

☢ Seven Gables Inn. 555 Ocean View Blvd., Pacific Grove, CA. 93950. ☎ **408/372-4341.** 14 rms. $105–$225 double. Rates include breakfast and afternoon tea. MC, V. Two-night minimum on weekends.

On the coast road overlooking the sea, this sprawling compound of Victorian buildings was constructed in 1886 by the Chase family (as in Chase Manhattan Bank) and has been a B&B since 1982. It's named after the seven gables that cap the hotel and its interior is graced with a valuable collection of mostly European antiques. Everything here is opulent and gilded, including the rooms, which are scattered amid the main house, cottages, and the guest house and all have ocean views. Accommodations are linked with verdant gardens filled with roses and marble sculpture. Pay phones are available and guests can watch TV in the parlor. Rates include breakfast and afternoon tea accompanied by an array of pastries and homemade chocolates. If this hotel is fully booked, ask about the Grand View Inn, a comparable B&B next door that's run by the same owners.

WHERE TO DINE

MEALS FOR $10 OR LESS

The First Awakening. In the American Tin Cannery, 125 Ocean View Blvd. ☎ **408/372-1125.** Reservations not accepted. Breakfast $4–$7; lunch $5–$8. AE, DC, MC, V. Daily 7am–2:30pm. From Calif. 1, take the Pacific Grove exit (Calif. 68) and turn right onto Lighthouse Ave. After 1 mile turn left onto Eardley Ave. and take it to the corner of Ocean View Blvd. AMERICAN.

What was once a dank canning factory is now a bright, huge, open restaurant, flooded with light from an entire wall of windows. Ceilings don't get much taller than these, and they're topped with an enormous skylight and hung with plants and industrial overhead fans.

Breakfast, the most important meal of the day here, includes 11 varieties of omelets; granola with nuts, fruit, and yogurt; walnut and wheat pancakes; and raisin French toast. At lunch there's a fine choice of salads and a foot-long list of sandwiches that encompasses everything from albacore to zucchini.

Toastie's Cafe. 702 Lighthouse Dr. ☎ **408/373-7543.** Breakfast dishes $5.95–$7.25. MC, V. Mon–Sat 6am–3pm, Sun 7am–2pm. AMERICAN.

At a time when most restaurants' success depends not only on food, but also on clever decor and elaborate presentation, Toastie's shrugs its traditional-style shoulders and continues to pack 'em in. What's the attraction? A good old-fashioned breakfast served in a no-frills casual dining room. Some rave about the eggs Benedict (with roasted potatoes) or the hefty, sinful waffles. Others indulge in one of the many other expected options. Regardless of what you order, one thing's for sure, this place serves up what everyone wants from breakfast: lots of selections, good service, plenty of coffee refills, and a heaping plate of food.

MEALS FOR $20 OR LESS

Ⓢ **The Fishwife at Asilomar Beach.** 1996¹⁄₂ Sunset Dr. (at Asilomar Beach). ☎ **408/375-7107.** Reservations accepted. Main courses lunch $4.95–$8.50, dinner $8.25–$12.50. AE, DISC, MC, V. Mon and Wed–Sat 11am–10pm; Sun 10am–10pm. From Calif. 1, take the Pacific Grove exit (Calif. 68) and veer left until it becomes Sunset Dr. The restaurant will be on your left about 1 mile ahead, as you approach Asilomar Beach. SEAFOOD.

This restaurant dates from the 1830s, when an enterprising sailor's wife started a small food market that became famous for its Boston clam chowder. Today locals still return for the savory soup as well as some of the finest seafood in Pacific Grove. Two bestsellers at dinner are calamari steak sautéed with shallots, garlic, tomatoes, and white wine; and prawns Belize, presented sizzling with red onions, tomatoes, fresh serrano chiles, jicama, lime juice, and cashews. There are also steak and pasta dishes on the menu and all main courses come with fresh vegetables, bread, black beans, and rice or potatoes. Kids get their own color-in menu, which has smaller portions for under $6.

Peppers Mexicali Cafe. 170 Forest Ave. ☎ **408/373-6892.** Reservations recommended. Main courses $5.50–$11. AE, DC, MC, V. Mon 11:30am–10pm Wed–Thurs 11:30am–10pm, Fri–Sat 11:30am–11pm, Sun 4–10pm. MEXICAN/LATIN AMERICAN.

Peppers is the kind of place where you can't help but feel at home. The dining room is casual and inviting, with wooden floors and tables, pepper art visible from every viewpoint, and a perpetual crowd of diners who come to suck up beers and savor spicy specialties such as well-balanced seafood tacos and fajitas or housemade tamales and chile rellenos. Other fire-starters include the snapper Yucatán, which is cooked with chiles, citrus cilantro, and tomatoes, and grilled prawns with lime-cilantro dressing. Add a substantial selection of suds, an addicting compilation of chips and salsa, and a friendly wait staff, and your taste buds are bound to bellow "Olé!"

WORTH A SPLURGE

✪ **Fandango.** 223 17th St. ☎ **408/372-3456.** Reservations recommended. Main courses $11–$19; fixed-price dinner $20. AE, CB, DC, DISC, MC, V. Mon–Sat 11am–3:30pm; brunch Sun 10am–2:30pm; daily 5–9:30pm. From Calif. 1, take the Pacific Grove exit (Calif. 68), turn left on Lighthouse Ave., and continue a block to 17th St. MEDITERRANEAN.

The term *fandango*, a Spanish dance, takes on new meaning here where it's not your feet that are rejoicing, but rather your tongue. Provincial Mediterranean specialties, that range in origin from Spain to Greece to North Africa, spice up the menu with such specialties as seafood paella with North African Couscous (the recipe has been in the owner's family for almost 200 years), cassoulet maison, cannelloni Niçoise, and a Greek-style lamb shank. Along with the fare, the atmosphere takes you straight to Europe in a fiesta of five upstairs and downstairs dining rooms cozied by fireplaces, wood tables, and antiqued walls. There is a very good international wine list, and a dessert menu that includes a Grand Marnier soufflé with fresh raspberry puree sauce and profiteroles.

In winter, ask to be seated in the fireplace dining room. In summer, request the terrace room, but whenever you come expect everything here to be lively and colorful, from the regional decor to the owner himself.

✪ **Melac's.** 663 Lighthouse Ave. ☎ **408/375-1743.** Reservations required. Main courses $19–$25. AE, DC, MC, V. Tues–Fri 11:30am–2pm; Tues–Sat 5:30–9:30pm. FRENCH.

Take an intimate dining room with brick walls and hand-painted French-country murals, formally set tables, and combine it with a husband and wife team (she's a graduate from Paris's Cordon Bleu, he's the friendly French host) and you've got Pacific Grove's favorite French restaurant. Elegant yet unpretentious, this is the place to romance alongside a fireplace, ordering from a limited menu of finely prepared classic dishes, without the stuffiness often associated with French establishments. For starters, expect such preparations as a delicious lobster ravioli appetizer with a tarragon lobster sauce or gratin of baby leeks and chanterelles with Reggiano Parmesan and Dijon mustard. Main courses range from Atlantic salmon poached on a bed of dilled vegetables julienne and lemon caper basmati rice pilaf, to veal sweetbreads roasted between layers of puff pastry with minced wild mushrooms and cognac cream (each entree is served with a dinner salad). If you want to go all out, opt for the fixed-price menu, and choose between the four-course "Petite" or six-course "Grande Aventure," $28 and $45 respectively.

3 The 17-Mile Drive

Fork over $6 to enter the drive and prepare to see some of the most exclusive coastal real estate in California. The drive can be entered from any of three gates: Pacific Grove to the north, Carmel to the south, or Monterey to the east. The most convenient entrance from Calif. 1 is just off the main road at the Holman Highway exit. Admission to the drive includes an informative map that points out 26 points of interest along the way. (You may beat traffic by entering at the Carmel Gate and doing the tour backwards.) Aside from the homes of the ultrarich and the pristine greens of that elite golfer's paradise, Pebble Beach, highlights include Seal and Bird Rocks, where you can see countless gulls, cormorants, and other offshore birds as well as seals and sea lions; and Cypress Point Lookout, which on a clear day affords a 20-mile view all the way to the Big Sur lighthouse. Also visible is the famous Lone

Cypress tree, an inspiration to so many artists and photographers, which you can stop and admire from afar, but can no longer approach. The drive also traverses Del Monte Forest, thick with tame black-tailed deer, and often compared to some "billionaire's private game preserve." One of the best ways to see the 17-Mile Drive is by bike, but the ride toward Carmel is all downhill so unless you're in great shape, arrange for a ride back or simply do it by car. If you're planning to make a day of it, bring a picnic lunch or you're doomed to blow your budget at one of the resort restaurants.

If you prefer to avoid the $6 fee, either ride a bike (you must enter from Pacific Grove) or walk into 17-Mile Drive.

4 Carmel-By-The-Sea

If you visited here dozens of years ago, you're likely to be of the school that criticizes its overcommercialization. Carmel-By-The-Sea, once an artist colony that attracted such luminaries as Robinson Jeffers, Sinclair Lewis, Robert Louis Stevenson, Ansel Adams, William Rose Benet, and Mary Austin, began its life as a nonconformist town where residents resisted assigning street numbers and lighting (they carried lanterns, which they considered more romantic).

Today Carmel-By-The-Sea may not be the bohemian artists' village seasoned travelers remember, but it is still an adorable (albeit touristy) town that knows how to celebrate its surroundings; vibrant wildflower gardens flourish along each residential street, gnarled cypress trees reach up from white sandy beaches, and at the beginning and end of each day, tourists magically disappear and the town for a split second seems undiscovered.

It's still intimate enough that there's no need for street numbers and commercial establishments are a small collection of inns, restaurants, boutiques, and a surprisingly high number of art galleries, all of which are only identified by cross streets. It's not the town itself, but such hints as Saks Fifth Avenue, convertible roadsters cruising through town, intolerable traffic, and the sky-high price tags on B&Bs that remind us we're not in Kansas anymore. Instead, Carmel-By-The-Sea is a rather well-preserved and thoroughly upscale tourist haven.

ESSENTIALS

The **Carmel Business Association** is above the Hog's Breath Inn on San Carlos between 5th and 6th Streets (P.O. Box 4444), Carmel, CA 93921 (☎ **408/624-2522**). It distributes local maps, brochures, and publications. It's open in June, July, and August, Monday to Friday from 9am to 6pm, Saturday from 11am to 6pm, and Sunday noon to 4pm. In winter it closes on Sunday and is only open until 5pm on the other days. Pass by to pick up a copy of the *Carmel Gallery Guide* and a schedule of local events.

EXPLORING THE TOWN

Carmel Beach City Park, a wonderful stretch of white sand backed by cypress trees, is a small bit of heaven on earth, though parking can be closer to that other hotter postmortem destination. There's plenty of room for families, surfers, and dogs with their owners (yes, pooches are allowed to run off-leash here). If the parking lot is full, there are some spaces on Ocean Avenue.

Farther south around the promontory, Carmel River State Beach is a less-crowded option with white sand and dunes, plus a bird sanctuary where brown pelicans, black oystercatchers, cormorants, gulls, curlews, godwits, and sanderlings make their home.

Carmel Mission, on Basilica Rio Road at Lasuen Drive (off Calif. 1; ☎ 408/
624-3600), is the burial ground of Father Junípero Serra and the second-oldest of
the 21 Spanish missions he founded. Founded in 1771 on a scenic site overlooking
the Carmel River, it remains one of the largest and most interesting of California's
missions. The present stone church, with its gracefully curving walls and Moorish bell
tower, was begun in 1793. Its walls are covered with a lime plaster made of burnt
seashells. The old mission kitchen, the first library in California, the high altar, and
the flower gardens are all worth visiting. More than 3,000 Native Americans are buried in the adjacent cemetery; their graves are decorated with seashells. A $2 donation
is requested. The mission is open daily from June 1 to August 31 from 9:30am to
7:30pm; at other times Monday to Saturday from 9:30am to 4:30pm, Sunday from
10:30am to 4:30pm.

One of Carmel's prettiest homes and gardens is **Tor House,** 26304 Oceanview
Ave. (☎ **408/624-1813,** or 408/624-1840 Friday and Saturday only), built by California poet Robinson Jeffers. On Carmel Point, the house dates from 1918 and includes a 40-foot tower containing stones from around the world, which are embedded
in the walls (there's even one from the Great Wall of China). Inside, an old porthole
is reputed to have come from the ship on which Napoléon escaped from Elba in
1815. Admission is by guided tour only, and reservations are required. It's $5 for
adults, $3.50 for college students, and $1.50 for high school students (no children
under 12). Open Friday to Saturday from 10am to 3pm.

If shopping is more your bag, leave the car at the hotel or park and check
out the town on foot. You'll be surprised at the amount of shops packed into
this small town; more than 500 boutiques offering unique fashions, baskets,
housewares, and imported goods and a veritable cornucopia of art galleries (don't
expect many bargains, however). All the commercial action is packed into the small
stretch of Ocean Avenue between Junipero and San Antonio avenues. If you want
to tour the galleries, pick up a copy of the *Carmel Gallery Guide* from the Carmel
Business Association. Shoppers will enjoy Carmel Plaza, a multilevel complex of
boutiques, craft stores, restaurants, and gourmet food outlets on Ocean Avenue at
Junipero Street, or The Barnyard, on Calif. 1, at Carmel Valley Road (you'll have
to take the car to this authentic early California barn housing 60-plus shops and
restaurants).

WHERE TO STAY

You're not going to find a room for much less than $100 in Carmel-By-The-Sea
unless it's off-season. It doesn't hurt to give the hotels here a try, but you'll be just
as happy staying in cozy Pacific Grove and cruising down to Carmel (a 10-minute
drive, traffic permitting) for daytime visits.

If you'd like some guidance in choosing your room, contact the **Tourist Information Cente**r at Mission Street (between 5th and 6th, ☎ **800/847-8066** or 408/
624-1711).

DOUBLES FOR $80 OR LESS

The Homestead. Lincoln St. (at 8th Ave.), Carmel, CA 93921. ☎ **408/624-4119.** 8 rms,
4 cottages. TV. Doubles $65–$90, cottages $85 to $95. Two-night minimum during high
season. MC, V.

This remodeled home with private entrances and private baths is most likely the
cheapest place to stay in Carmel. Rooms are individually decorated in "Old Carmel"
(classic country) style and come with either a tub/shower or just a shower bath.
The six nearby cottages have kitchens and fireplaces. All guests have access to the

peaceful gardens, a pay phone, and the beach, which is just 6 blocks away. Smoking is allowed on the patio only.

DOUBLES FOR $100 OR LESS

Traveling with Fido? **The Cypress Inn,** at Lincoln Street and 7th Avenue (☎ 408/ 624-3871), owned by actress Doris Day, is a lovely Mediterranean–style inn that goes to great lengths to make your pooch feel at home.

✪ **Vagabond House.** 4th and Dolores, (P.O. Box 2747), Carmel-By-The-Sea, CA 93921. ☎ **800/262-1262,** 408/624-7738, or 800/221-1262 in Canada. Fax 408/626-1243. 11 rms, 1 suite. TEL TV. Doubles $85–$95, with kitchen and/or fireplace $115–$165. Two-night minimum. Pets welcome. 20% discount weeknights between Thanksgiving and Christmas. AE, MC, V.

This place is so ridiculously cute and cozy that even the ultrafriendly woman at the front desk will remind you of your long lost grandmother. Attention is paid to every element of this place, from the lobby adorned with knickknack antiques and a welcoming decanter of sherry to the wonderfully lush garden courtyard that's draped with greenery and dotted with bloom. Each room is warm and homey, decorated in country decor, and has a private entrance and a refrigerator; all have fireplaces except two, which means the $85 rooms book quickly, so call ahead if you want one. Guests are welcomed with a basket of fruit and the extended continental breakfast is delivered to your room, but you'll most likely prefer to enjoy it on the garden patio.

⑤ **Village Inn.** Ocean Ave. (at Junipero St.; P.O. Box 5275), Carmel, CA 93921. ☎ **800/ 346-3864** in California, or 408/624-3864. Fax 408/626-6763. 34 rms, 2 suites. TEL TV. $69–$145 double; $89–$189 triple or quad; from $89 suite. Rates include continental breakfast. AE, MC, V. From Calif. 1 exit onto Ocean Ave. and continue straight to Junipero St.

Well run and centrally located, the Village Inn is nothing more than a motor lodge. Rooms, arranged around a courtyard/parking lot lined with potted geraniums, are outfitted with bland but functional decor. In addition to French country–style furniture, guest rooms come equipped with refrigerators. Breakfast, accompanied by the morning newspaper, is served in the downstairs lounge. This place is hardly splurge worthy, but it is one of the more affordable motels in town.

WORTH A SPLURGE

✪ **La Playa.** Camino Real and 8th Ave. (P.O. Box 900), Carmel, CA 93921. ☎ **800/582-8900** or 408/624-6476. Fax 408/624-7966. 72 rms, 3 suites, 5 cottages. TEL TV MINIBAR. $120–$220 double; $215–$395 suite; $215–$495 cottage. AE, DC, MC, V.

Only two blocks from the beach and yet within walking distance of town, the four-story La Playa is a romantic Mediterranean-style villa built in 1904 with a Bermudan-pink facade. Norwegian artist Christopher Jorgensen ordered its construction for his bride, an heiress of the Ghirardelli chocolate dynasty. Rooms are arranged around a lawn and garden with a pool at the center. The stylish lobby, with a white marble fireplace, sets the elegant tone with its terra-cotta floors enhanced with Oriental rugs. The room furnishings are Spanish in style. Beds have carved headboards; windows are shielded with white shutters. The cottages—some of which sleep as many as eight adults, making them a good deal if you're traveling as a family or in a group—have full kitchens, wet bar, garden patios, and wood-burning fireplaces.

Dining/Entertainment: The Terrace Grill, a riot of color, serves California cuisine and summer dining out on the alfresco terrace overlooking the gardens is very relaxing.

Services: Room service and nightly turndown (excluding cottages).

○ **Mission Ranch.** 26270 Dolores St., Carmel, CA 93923. ☎ **800/538-8221** or 408/624-6436. Fax 408/626-4163. 29 rms, 2 cottages. TEL TV. $85–$225 double; $125 cottage. Rates include continental breakfast. AE, MC, V.

This venerable inn, constructed in the 1850s as a dairy farm, was purchased and restored by Clint Eastwood, Carmel's former celebrity mayor, who wanted to preserve the vista of the nearby wetlands stretching out to the bay. The view today is inspiring, saved from condo development.

Millions went into the restoration of the historic property, and there are several rooms scattered amid different structures, both old and new. As befits a ranch, even this one, accommodations are decorated in a provincial style, with high-carved wooden beds dressed with handmade quilts. Homespun is the rule here. Some fixtures from the highly acclaimed Eastwood film *Unforgiven*, including a potbellied stove, are on display.

Rooms range from so-called regular in the main barn (less desirable) to meadow-view units, each with a vista across the fields to the bay. All are equipped with whirlpool baths, fireplaces, and decks or patios. The Martin Family farmhouse contains six of the units, all arranged around a central parlor, while the "Bunkhouse," the oldest structure on the property, contains separate living and dining areas, bedrooms, and a full kitchen.

Dining/Entertainment: The Restaurant at Mission Ranch serves American cuisine.

Facilities: Tennis courts, exercise room, pro shop.

Normandy Inn. Ocean Ave. (between Monte Verde and Casanova St.). P.O. Box 1706, Carmel, CA 93921. ☎ **800/343-3825** in California, or 408/624-3825. Fax 408/624-4614. 41 rms, 4 suites, 3 cottages. TEL TV. $100–$150 double; $180–$200 suite; $250–$350 cottage (sleeps up to eight). Additional person $10. Rates include continental breakfast. AE, MC, V. From Calif. 1, exit onto Ocean Ave. and continue straight for 5 blocks past Junipero St.

This hotel's French Normandy architecture is like something out of a storybook, especially with the array of colorful flowers that brighten up this white Tudor with a brown shingled roof. Rooms match the exterior with French country decor and down comforters. Some rooms have fireplaces and/or kitchenettes, and tub/showers; all come with coffeemakers. There's a small heated pool banked by a sweet flower garden, self-service laundry, and newspapers are delivered to your room daily.

Basic rooms aren't exactly "Worth a Splurge," but the larger family style units and three cottages are an especially good deal if you're traveling in a large group (they can accommodate up to eight). Each cottage has three bedrooms, two bathrooms, a fully equipped kitchen, dining room, living room with a fireplace, and a back porch. Be sure to reserve far in advance, especially in summer.

WHERE TO DINE
MEALS FOR $10 OR LESS

Carmel Bakery. Ocean (between Dolores and Lincoln). ☎ **408/626-8885.** Sandwiches $3.25–$4.95. No credit cards. Daily 6:30am–7pm. BAKERY/DELI.

The fanciest of the few bakeries along this main street leading down to the beach serves espresso, soup, sandwiches, and pastries. It's also the most festive and well decorated, with a few tables and chairs, and music playing from speakers overhead. Most grab their grub and go. For a more formal (and a mite more expensive) encounter with espresso and the like, head down the block to Il Fornaio.

The Hog's Breath Inn. San Carlos St. (between 5th and 6th aves.). ☎ **408/625-1044.** Reservations not accepted. Main courses: most lunch items $4.75–$6.75, dinner $9.50–$23.

AE, DC, MC, V. Mon–Fri 11:30am–3pm, Sat–Sun 11am–3pm and daily 5–10pm. From Calif. 1, take the Ocean Ave. exit and turn right onto San Carlos St. AMERICAN.

What's in a name? Well, if Clint Eastwood didn't own this place, I don't know what would inspire tourists to eat at a place named after something that sounds anything but aromatic (how very Clint!). But clamor they do for one of the tree-trunk tables with plastic chairs along a brick patio. Tables in the wood-paneled dark and rustic dining room decorated with farm implements fill up, too, though they're not as lively as the outdoor seats. Fare here isn't remotely as legendary as the eatery's owner (who you're not likely to see), but it's the perfect place to nosh on afternoon snacks and throw back a few brewskies. The small dark bar with sports on the tube is the best place to pull up a stool and get loaded on a rainy day (or a sunny one for that matter). Don't bother coming for dinner. Your buck will go a lot farther on the luncheon menu, where you can choose from a variety of burgers, sandwiches, and other basic favorites.

Katy's Place. Mission St. (between 5th and 6th). ☎ **408/624-0199.** Breakfast $4–$10. No credit cards. 7am–1:30 or 2pm. AMERICAN.

Breakfast can be far from cheap (depending on what you order), but it's available all day, the helpings are big, and the tree-shaded patio overlooking the street is a great place to stretch out and enjoy the down-home atmosphere. You can fill up on a waffle, French toast, or pancakes for around $6, but even looking at eggs will cost you close to $10.

Little Swiss Cafe. 6th (between Lincoln and Mission). ☎ **408/624-5007.** Reservations not accepted. $4.75–$7.50. No credit cards. Mon–Sat 7:30am–3pm, Sun 8am–2pm. CONTINENTAL.

Locals led me to this quirky little eatery designed to look like a Swiss cottage. Kids may love the decor (old-fashion Grandma cute) but the grown-ups come for what they consider the best homemade blintzes and pancakes in town. Late risers rejoice: Breakfast is served all day. Lunch is pleasantly affordable and features sandwiches, which are served with potato salad, mixed green salad, or soup ($5 to $7); salads; and an array of unusual entrees such as Swiss sausage with smothered onions, crepes filled with creamed chicken, calves liver sauté, and filet of red snapper with a rémoulade sauce.

Neilsen's Brothers. San Carlos (at 7th). ☎ **408/624-6263** (deli), or 408/624-6441 (market). Picnic items $3–$5. MC, V. Mon–Sat 8am–8pm, Sun 10am–7pm. DELI.

Why bother burning away precious midday vacation minutes indoors when you can dine alfresco at Carmel Beach? Duck a few blocks off the main drag to Neilsen Brothers market and you'll find everything you could want to fill your picnic basket, including sandwiches, barbecued chicken and ribs, pasta salads, and a vast selection of cheeses. You can even get french fries, veggie and meat burgers, and corn dogs (from noon to 6pm), but expect a 10-minute wait—they cook to order. Call and order over the phone or drop in.

MEALS FOR $20 OR LESS

⑤ **Caffè Napoli.** Ocean Ave. (between Dolores and Lincoln). ☎ **408/625-4033.** Reservations recommended. Most main courses $8–$12. MC, V. Daily 11:30am–4pm, 5–10pm. ITALIAN.

The decor here is so quintessentially Italiana, with flags, gingham table cloths, garlic and baskets overhead, I expected a flour-coated potbellied Padrino Napoli to emerge from the kitchen, embrace me wholeheartedly, and exclaim " *Mangia!*

Mangia!" as he slapped down a bowl overflowing with sauce-drenched pasta. Of course there is no Padrino here and I received no welcoming hug, but I did indulge in the fine Italian fare that keeps locals coming back for more. If the wait is too long, the host will direct you to a sister restaurant, Little Napoli, around the corner, which serves the same food, but in a slightly more upscale setting. The menu is straight Italian and includes seven salad choices, antipasti, pizza, and pasta.

✪ **Flying Fish Grill.** In Carmel Plaza, Mission St. (between Ocean and 7th aves.). ☎ **408/ 625-1962.** Reservations recommended. Main courses $14.50–$19.50. AE, DISC, MC, V. Daily 5–10pm. PACIFIC RIM SEAFOOD.

I always feel more confident when a restaurant's kitchen is actually run by its owner, and a dinner experience here will confirm that chef/proprietor Kenny Fukumoto is in the house. Dark, romantic, and Asian-influenced, the dining room's atmosphere is intimate and unique with redwood booths (built by Kenny) and fish hanging (flying?) from the ceiling. Cuisine features fresh seafood with exquisite Japanese accents. Start with some sushi, tempura, or any of the other exotic and tantalizing taste teasers. Then prepare yourself for seriously sensational main courses. House favorites include a savory rare peppered ahi, which is blackened and served with mustard sesame-soy vinaigrette and angel hair pasta, and a pan-fried almond sea bass with whipped potatoes, Chinese cabbage, and rock shrimp stir fry.

Il Fornaio. Ocean Ave. (at Monte Verde). ☎ **408/622-5100;** bakery 408/622-5115. Reservations accepted. Main courses $7.95–$14.95. AE, DC, MC, V. Mon–Fri 7am–10:30pm, Sat–Sun 8am–11pm. ITALIAN.

I don't care if it is a chain, Il Fornaio is still one of my favorite restaurants. Why? Because I know I'm guaranteed a well-prepared mocha and thick chocolate-dipped biscotti at every outpost. There's also a great selection of salads (go with the simple house salad with shaved Parmesan, croutons, and a tangy light dressing—I always do); pastas; pizzas; and rotisserie chicken, duck, and rabbit fresh from the brick oven. The housemade breads and seeded breadsticks alone are enough of a reason to come through the door. I must admit I was disappointed with tasty but measly $11 lasagna, so skip it and start with the seared swordfish antipasti with roast pepper and Dijon mustard, or decadent grilled polenta with sautéed wild mushrooms, provolone cheese, and Italian truffle oil. Move on to a gourmet pizza or a pasta, such as the lobster-filled ravioli with ricotta cheese, leeks, and a lemon cream sauce, or spaghetti with fresh shrimp, mussels, imported tuna, black olives, and garlic and tomato sauce. The large airy dining room and sunny terrace offer charming and diverse atmospheres. The Panetteria, a retail bakery, is the perfect place to pick up a gourmet picnic.

⑤ **La Bohéme.** Dolores St. (at 7th Ave.). ☎ **408/624-7500.** Reservations not accepted. Fixed-price 3-course dinner $19.75. MC, V. Daily 5:30–10pm. Closed 2 weeks before Christmas. From Calif. 1, exit onto Ocean Ave. and turn left on Dolores St. FRENCH COUNTRY.

La Bohéme mimics a French street with cartoonlike asymmetrical shingled house facades and a painted blue sky overhead. Dining here is utterly romantic French, served at cramped tables set with floral-print cloths in bright colors, hand-painted dinnerware, and vibrant floral bouquets. Dinner is a three-course, fixed-price feast, consisting of a large salad, a tureen of soup, and a main dish (perhaps breast of chicken with ginger-shallot sauce or filet mignon with cognac-cream sauce). Vegetarian specials are available nightly. Homemade desserts and fresh coffee are sold separately, and are usually worth the extra expense. Dress is casual. Curious on-line folks can learn more at http://www.carmelnet.com/laboheme.

WORTH A SPLURGE

✪ Crème Carmel. San Carlos St. and 7th Ave. ☎ **408/624-0444.** Reservations recommended. Main courses $16.75–$21.75. AE, DC, MC, V. Daily 5:30–9pm in July–Aug; closed Sun rest of the year. CALIFORNIA/FRENCH.

The discreet location of Crème Carmel (tucked into a courtyard) has not hurt its business any—it's still one of the most popular upscale dining spots for both tourists and locals. Art, fresh flowers, and a soaring tongue-and-groove ceiling provide a sweet setting for an evening robust with California-French flavor. The menu lists an array of decadent wonderful starters, such as prawn and goat cheese tart with a jalapeño and shallot sauce, lobster with Maui onion pancakes and lobster sauce, or melt-in-your-mouth Sonoma foie gras. Main courses are equally special and might include Pacific salmon with roasted leeks and fresh basil sauce or beef tenderloin with a cabernet sauce, fresh horseradish, and potato cake.

5　Carmel Valley

Inland from Carmel stretches Carmel Valley, where wealthy folks retreat beyond the reach of the coastal fog and mist. It's a scenic and perpetually sunny valley of rolling hills dotted with manicured golf courses and many a horse ranch.

Hike the trails in **Garland Regional Park,** 8 miles east of Carmel on Carmel Valley Road (dogs are welcome off-leash). The sun really bakes you out here, so bring lots of water. You can also sign up for a trail ride at **The Holman Ranch,** 60 Holman Rd. (☎ **408/659-2640**), 12 miles east of Calif. 1. Golf is offered at several resorts/facilities in the valley, notably at **Quail Lodge,** 8000 Valley Green Dr. (☎ **408/624-2770**), and **Rancho Canada Golf Club,** Carmel Valley Rd. (☎ **408/624-0111**). While you're in the valley, taste the wines at the **Château Julien Winery,** 8940 Carmel Valley Rd. (☎ **408/624-2600**), which is open daily.

WHERE TO STAY

Robles del Rio. 200 Punta del Monte, Carmel Valley, CA 93924. ☎ **800/833-0843** or 408/659-3705. 26 rms, 2 suites, 5 cottages. TV. $89–$145 double; from $200 suite; from $170 cottage. Rates include buffet breakfast. AE, MC, V.

On a mountaintop set among oak trees, this rustic resort has beckoned many a luminary since its 1928 opening (Arthur Murray, Red Skelton, and Alistair Cook, for example). Whether the rooms are in the main lodge or in the cottages, the furnishings have a simple, rustic style with iron or wicker beds and either feature knotty-pine walls or a Southern Colonial look. The cottages have fireplaces, plus a kitchen or kitchenette. The restaurant opens onto panoramic views of the Carmel Valley. There's also a well-landscaped pool, outdoor hot tub, tennis, horseback riding, hiking, and jogging trail.

CAMPING

Saddle Mountain. 27625 Schulte Rd., Carmel, CA 93923. ☎ **408/624-1617.** 50 sites. Basic sites $22, full hook-up, tent cabins, and teepees $32. MC, V.

The cheapest way to stay in exorbitant Carmel is to camp at Saddle Mountain. It may not be oceanside (it's 4¹/₂ miles east of Calif. 1 in Carmel Valley), but its sites are surrounded by natural beauty, offer a cornucopia of free activities, and are especially good for families. Twenty-five sites come complete with full hookups (water, sewer, electric, and even cable, if you brought the TV). Bring your own tent and you'll save 10 bucks a night, or pay extra for a teepee or tent-cabin (canvas tent cabin on wooden platform). Amenities include bath and shower facilities; a 24-yard heated pool; plenty of ocean view hiking trails; a clubhouse with TV, couches, and video games; a natural redwood children's playground; and volleyball and basketball courts. Call a month in advance to reserve in summer.

WHERE TO DINE

✪ **Fish Ranch Restaurant.** The Crossroads shopping center, 245 Crossroads Blvd. ☎ **408/ 625-1363.** Reservations recommended. Most main courses lunch $4.50–$9.50, dinner $11.95–$17.95. AE, MC, V. Daily 11:30am–4pm, 5–10pm. SEAFOOD.

Steven Spielberg, Clint Eastwood, Jason Priestly, and Brad Pitt are just a few of the celebrities who've been sighted recently at the hottest new restaurant in the Monterey Bay area. But star grazing is not the only attraction here—it's the stellar seafood served in one of the best dining rooms around that attracts most patrons. The atmosphere offers the kind of clever sophistication you'd expect from one of San Francisco's finer haunts (look up at the ceiling—you'll notice an underwater fish-eye view, complete with a boat's bottom in a running stream and a passing rainbow trout overhead). Tables are dispersed throughout the warm, handsome dining room with whimsical light fixtures and a large fireplace, and on the sunny patio overlooking the mountains. The menu starts off with "Lures," or appetizers, such as Monterey Bay calamari served with wasabi tartare, or sautéed clams and mussels with leeks, tomatoes, and saffron crème fraîche sauce. Main courses are arranged on a "Field and Stream" list and include ranch-made crab and ricotta ravioli in a tomato and basil nagé or cabernet-marinated lamb shank, minted rosemary sauce, and northern white beans. Don't worry if you're not fish-inclined; there's plenty of other options on the menu. Come on a weekend night for live music.

Rio Grill. 101 Crossroads Blvd. ☎ **408/625-5436.** Reservations required. Main courses $10–$17. AE, DISC, MC, V. Daily 11:30am–11pm. From Calif. 1, take the Rio Rd. exit west. After 1 block, turn right onto Crossroads Blvd. AMERICAN.

You won't mind waiting to be seated here: The lively lounge is one of the best in Carmel, attracting an interesting crowd. It's decorated with a cartoon mural of famous locals such as Clint Eastwood and the late Bing Crosby, as well as playful sculpture, cactus, and other vibrant art. The whimsical nature of the modern, Santa Fe–style dining room belies the kitchen's serious preparations, which include home-made soups; a rich quesadilla with almonds, cheeses, and smoked tomato salsa; bar-becued baby back ribs from a wood-burning oven; and fresh fish from an open oak grill. Don't let the costlier main courses scare you away: You can get all the flavor for less money if you come at lunch or stick with appetizers, salads, and sandwiches, all which run between $3.70 and $9. The restaurant's good selection of wines includes some rare Californian vintages and covers a broad price range. As usual in this town, dress is casual.

6 The Big Sur Coast

Big Sur is more than a drive along one of the most dramatic coastlines on earth or a peaceful evening amidst a forest of towering California redwoods. It's a stretch of vast wilderness so ominously beautiful (especially when the fog glows in the moonlight), it inspires all who walk its majestic paths.

Although there is an actual Big Sur Village approximately 25 miles south of Carmel, "Big Sur" refers to the famous 90-mile stretch of coast between Carmel and San Simeon, blessed on one side by the majestic Santa Lucia Range and on the other by the rocky Pacific coastline. It's one of the most romantic and relaxing places on earth, where there's little more to do than explore the mountains and beaches and perch yourself atop the cliffs at one of the few world-renowned resorts that take in the California sea air.

Vacationing in Big Sur can be both exorbitantly expensive and remarkably cheap at the same time. Unless you're camping, you aren't going to find ultracheap lodgings here, and since there are only a handful of restaurants, there's little alternative to paying hand-over-fist for a romantic night out. However, the good news is that the only thing to do here is enjoy the land and sea, so once you've forked over a few bucks for a good book and some sunblock (if the fog's not looming), the majority of your time here won't cost you a dime.

ESSENTIALS

ORIENTATION   Most of this stretch is state park, and Calif. 1 runs its entire length, hugging the ocean the whole way. Restaurants, hotels, and sights are easy to spot—most are situated directly on the highway—but without major towns as reference points, their addresses can be a little obscure. For the purposes of orientation, we will use the River Inn as our mileage guide. Located 29 miles south of Monterey on Calif. 1, the inn is generally considered the northern end of Big Sur.

VISITOR INFORMATION   The **Monterey Peninsula Visitors and Convention Bureau,** 380 Alvarado St., Monterey (☎ **408/649-1770**), also has specialized information on places and events in Big Sur.

WHAT TO SEE & DO

Big Sur offers visitors unspoiled tranquillity and unparalleled wild natural beauty, ideal for hiking, picnicking, camping, fishing, and beach combing. The first white settlers arrived here only a hundred years ago, and the present access highway was only built in 1937. Electricity only arrived in the 1950s, and is still not available in the remote inland mountains. Big Sur's mysterious, misty beauty has inspired several modern spiritual movements, the most famous being the "human potential" movement founded in Esalen. Even the tourist board bills the area as a place in which "to slow down, to meditate, to catch up with your soul." Take the board's advice and take your time—nothing better lies ahead.

The region affords a bounty of wilderness adventure opportunities. The inland ✪ **Ventana Wilderness,** which is maintained by the U.S. Forest Service, is comprised of 167,323 acres straddling the Santa Lucia mountains and is characterized by V-shaped valleys between steep-sided ridges. The streams that cascade through the area are marked by waterfalls, deep pools, and thermal springs. The wilderness offers 237 miles of hiking trails that lead to 55 designated trail camps—a backpacker's paradise. One of the easiest trails into the park is the **Pine Ridge Trail** at Big Sur station (☎ **408/667-2315**).

From Carmel the first stop along Calif. 1, 3 miles south of Carmel, is **Point Lobos State Reserve** (☎ **408/624-4909**), famous for the sea lions, harbor seals, sea otters, and thousands of seabirds that make the 550-acre reserve home. You can see whales in season, too. Trails follow the shoreline and lead to hidden coves. (Note that parking is limited. On weekends especially, you need to arrive early to secure a place.)

From here, cross the Soberanes Creek, passing **Garrapata State Park,** a 2,879-acre park with 4 miles of coastline. It's unmarked and undeveloped. To explore the trails you'll need to park at one of the turnouts on Calif. 1 near Sobranes Point and hike in.

Ten miles south of Carmel, you'll arrive at North Abalone Cove. From here, Palo Colorado Road leads back into the wilderness to the first of the Forest Service camping areas at Bottchers Gap ($12 to camp, $5 to park overnight).

Continuing south, you'll cross two dramatic bridges at Rocky Creek and Bixby Creek, which will bring you to the Point Sur Lighthouse, at the 18¹/₂-mile marker.

The Big Sur Coast

The **Bixby Bridge,** 13 miles south of Carmel, towers nearly 260 feet above Bixby Creek Canyon. It offers canyon and ocean views and several observation alcoves at regular intervals along the bridge. The lighthouse, which sits 361 feet above the surf on a volcanic rock promontory, was built in 1887–89, when only a horse trail provided access to this part of the world. Tours, which take two to three hours and involve a steep half-mile hike each way, are scheduled on most weekends. For information call **408/625-4419.** Admission is $5 adults, $3 ages 13 to 17, and $2 ages 5 to 12; free 4 and under.

About 3 miles south of the lighthouse is **Andrew Molera State Park** (☎ **408/ 667-2315**), the largest state park on the Big Sur Coast (4,800 acres), but much less crowded than Pfeiffer Big Sur. Miles of trails meander through meadows, and along beaches and bluffs. Hikers and cyclists use the primitive trail camp about $1/3$ mile from the parking area. **Molera Big Sur Trail Rides** (☎ **408/625-5486**) offers coastal trail rides on horseback for riders of all levels of experience. The $2^1/2$-mile-long beach, which is sheltered from the wind by a bluff, is accessible via a mile-long path strewn with wildflowers in spring. You can walk the entire length of the beach at low tide; otherwise take the Bluff trail above the beach. The park also has campgrounds.

Back on Calif. 1 heading south from Andrew Molera State Park, you'll soon reach Big Sur, where commercial services are available. Twenty-six miles south of Carmel will bring you to the U.S. Forest Service Ranger Station, where you can pick up maps and other information about the region. It's located in **Pfeiffer Big Sur State Park**

(☎ 408/667-2315), an 810-acre park that offers 218 camping sites along the Big Sur River, and picnicking, fishing, and hiking. It's a scenic park of redwoods, conifers, oaks, and open meadows. For this reason, it gets very crowded. The Lodge in the park has cabins with fireplaces and other facilities (see below). Sycamore Canyon Road (unmarked, it's the only paved road west of Calif. 1 between the Big Sur post office and the state park entrance) will take you 2 miles down the road to sandy Pfeiffer Beach, which has an arch-shaped rock formation just offshore. It's open for day use only and is the only beach in the park accessible by car. Admission to the park is $6, and it's open daily dawn to dusk.

Calif. 1 continues south for 11 miles, past Sea Lion Cove, to Julia Pfeiffer Burns State Park. High above the ocean is the famous **Nepenthe** restaurant, the retreat bought by Orson Welles for Rita Hayworth in 1944, and a few miles farther south is the **Coast Gallery,** the premier local art gallery, which also shows lithographs of works by Henry Miller. Miller fans will also want to stop at the **Henry Miller Memorial Library,** Calif. 1, 30 miles south of Carmel, ¼ mile south of Nepenthe Restaurant (☎ **408/667-2574**). The library displays and sells books and artwork by Henry Miller and houses a permanent collection library of first editions. It also serves as a community art center, hosting concerts, poetry readings, and art exhibitions. The rear gallery room is a video-viewing space where films about Henry Miller can be seen. There is a sculpture garden, plus tables on the adjacent lawn where visitors can rest and enjoy the surroundings. Admission is free and it's open Tuesday to Sunday from 11am to 5pm.

Julia Pfeiffer Burns State Park (☎ 408/667-2315) encompasses some of Big Sur's most spectacular coastline. To get a closer look, take the trail from the parking area at McWay Canyon, which leads under the highway to a bluff overlooking an 80-foot-high waterfall that drops directly into the ocean. It's less crowded here than at Pfeiffer Big Sur, and there are miles of trails to explore in the 3,580-acre park. Scuba divers can apply for permits to explore the 1,680-acre underwater reserve.

From here, the road skirts the Ventana Wilderness, passing Anderson and Marble Peaks and the Esalen Institute, before crossing the Big Creek Bridge to Lucia and several campgrounds farther south. Kirk Creek Campground, about three miles north of Pacific Valley, offers camping with ocean views and beach access. Beyond Pacific Valley, Sand Dollar Beach picnic area is a good place to stop and enjoy the coastal view and take a stroll. A half-mile trail leads down to the sheltered beach, from which there's a fine view of Cone Peak, one of the coast's highest mountains. Two miles south of Sand Dollar is Jade Cove, a popular spot for rock hounds. From here, it's about another 27 miles past the Piedras Blancas Light Station to San Simeon.

WHERE TO STAY

Want to stay within your budget? Well, break out the tent and sleeping bag, because the only affordable walls surrounding you here will be the towering redwood trees around your campsite. But hey, if you're not into the wilderness, there's no real reason to be here anyway. So either drum up a few of your favorite campfire songs or dig deep into your pockets and pay premium prices for rustic accommodations. Whichever you choose, Big Sur is especially busy in summer, so make reservations well in advance.

CAMPING

If you plan to camp, be sure to stock up on food before you enter Big Sur. There are no supermarkets here (the closest is around 30 miles out) and small stores have limited supplies and high prices.

Big Sur Campground and Cabins. Calif. 1, 26 miles south of Carmel (¹/₂ mile south of the River Inn). ☎ **408/667-2322.** 81 tent sites (40 with electricity and water hookup), 17 cabins (all with shower). $24 tent site double; $24 RV hookup, plus $3 extra for electricity and water; $72–$144 double cabin. Rates include entrance for car. MC, V.

Each campsite here has its own wood-burning fire pit, picnic table, and fresh-water faucet within 25 feet of the pitching area. Facilities include bathhouses with hot showers, laundry facilities, a river for swimming, a playground area, a volleyball/basketball court, and a grocery store. Open year-round.

Fernwood. Calif. 1, 31 miles south of Carmel (2 miles south of the River Inn). ☎ **408/667-2422.** 86 sites (39 with electricity). $24 double without electricity; $27 double with electricity. Additional person $3. RV hookup $27 for 2. Car entrance $5 extra. MC, V.

This campground on 23 woodland acres has 86 sites, each of which has running water and a fire pit. About half the sites overlook the river. The restaurant on the premises is open daily from 11:30am to 10pm and serves burgers, ribs, and other summer camp fare. An adjacent bar/cocktail lounge features live music on the weekends, and a grocery store sells wood, ice, beer, and other essentials.

Ventana Campground. Calif. 1, 28 miles south of Carmel (4¹/₄ miles south of the River Inn). ☎ **408/667-2688.** 75 sites. $24 double. Additional person $5. $5 charge for a dog. Rates include entrance fee for car. No credit cards.

The 70 campsites on 40 acres of a redwood canyon are spaced well apart for privacy. Each has a picnic table and fire ring, although there's no electricity and no RV hookups. Three bathhouses with hot showers (25¢) are conveniently located. The closest coastal access is at Pfeiffer Beach, 3 miles away. The entrance to Ventana Campground is adjacent to the entrance to the resort of the same name (see below). To reserve a space, send one night deposit ($24), dates you'd like to stay, and a stamped, self-addressed envelope at least two weeks in advance.

DOUBLES FOR $100 OR LESS

Deetjen's Big Sur Inn. Calif. 1, Big Sur, CA 93920. ☎ **408/667-2377.** 20 rms (15 with bath). Sun–Thurs from $70 double without bath, from $100 double with bath; Fri–Sat from $85 double without bath, from $115 double with bath. MC, V.

In the 1930s before Calif. 1 was built, this homestead was an overnight stopping place on the coastal wagon trail. It was begun by Norwegian homesteader Helmuth Deetjen, who over the years built several accommodations constructed out of hand-hewn logs and lumber. The rooms are simple, rustic, and short on creature comforts, but they're set in a redwood canyon and make for a peaceful retreat. Single-wall construction means that the rooms are far from soundproof so children under 12 are only allowed if families reserve both rooms of a two-room building. The cabins are not insulated, so prepare to crank up the fire- or wood-burning stove.

The restaurant consists of four intimate rooms lit by candlelight; they're made even more inviting by the classical music playing in the background. The cuisine runs to classic American/continental favorites—steaks, lamb chops, grilled fish, and some vegetarian dishes.

WORTH A SPLURGE

Big Sur Lodge. Pfeiffer-Big Sur State Park, Calif. 1, Big Sur, CA 93920. ☎ **800/424-4787** or 408/667-3100. Fax 408/667-3110. 61 cabins. $79–$139 double; $99–$159 double with kitchen or fireplace; $109–$179 double with kitchen and fireplace. Rates include park entrance fees. MC, V. From Carmel take Calif. 1 south 26 miles.

A family friendly place to stay, Big Sur Lodge, sheltered by towering redwoods, sycamores, and broad-leafed maples, is situated in the state park. The rustic accommodations are motel-style cabins, which are all quite large, with high peaked cedar- and redwood-beamed ceilings. They are clean and heated, and have private baths and reserved parking spaces; some have fireplaces and/or kitchenettes (bring your own cooking utensils, though). All offer porches or decks with views of the redwoods or the Santa Lucia Range. Cabins 34 to 50 will put you in Siberia.

An advantage to staying here is that you are entitled to free use of all the facilities of the park, including hiking, barbecue pits, and picnic areas. In addition, the lodge has its own large, outdoor heated swimming pool, gift shop, grocery stores, and laundry facilities. The lodge dining room is open for breakfast and dinner (and lunch in the summer). Evening menus, only slightly better than summer-camp food, feature fresh seafood, steaks, and pasta dishes. Reservations are recommended and should be made far in advance during summer months.

WHERE TO DINE
MEALS FOR $10 OR LESS

Cafe Kevah. Calif. 1 (3 miles south of Pfeiffer-Big Sur State Park). ☎ **408/667-2344.** Main courses $6–$10. AE, MC, V. Mon–Fri 9am–3pm food, 3–4pm coffee and pastries; Sat–Sun 9am–3:30pm food, 3:30–4pm coffee and pastries. INTERNATIONAL.

Cafe Kevah is the affordable way to enjoy the same view offered from the Nepenthe restaurant, as well as dine on a more varied selection of fresh, wholesome dishes. Surprisingly reasonable, Cafe Kevah serves up salads, interesting internationally influenced main courses (such as chile relleno custard) and pastries and espresso drinks in a relaxed, peaceful sundeck setting—the perfect place to fill your stomach and your soul without emptying your wallet.

⑤ Coast Gallery Cafe. Above the Coast Art Gallery, Calif. 1, 33 miles south of Carmel, 3 miles south of Nepenthe. ☎ **408/667-2301.** Main courses $4–$8. AE, MC, V. Daily 9am–5pm, closed Christmas and Thanksgiving. CALIFORNIA.

Coast Gallery Cafe is situated in an interesting structure built out of three converted water tanks. The casual indoor/outdoor cafe has a view of the ocean from 600 feet above the water, and if you come in season, you might catch a glimpse of migrating whales as you munch on a roast beef or turkey sandwich, teriyaki chicken, pizza, or any of the leafy salads. Dessert is a sweet affair: Pastries and coffee drinks perfectly polish off a leisurely day in Big Sur. After your meal, you might want to peruse the art gallery, which features art, sculpture, and high-end crafts, or browse in the boutique and candle shop (candles are made on the premises).

WORTH A SPLURGE

Nepenthe. Calif. 1, 30 miles south of Carmel (5 miles south of the River Inn). ☎ **408/667-2345.** Reservations accepted for parties of 5 or more. Lunch $9–$11.50, dinner $10–$25. AE, MC, V. Daily 11:30am–10pm. AMERICAN.

I scoff at a $10 burger and a $4 draft beer even when I am in the finest of San Francisco restaurants (and that's not including french fries, which at Nepenthe are a whopping $5.50 for a big basket full). But I'd cough up the cash all over again for an encore lunch on the terrace at Nepenthe. Think of it as a nominal admission fee for dining at heights only angels usually enjoy; 808 feet above sea level along the cliffs overlooking the ocean, Nepenthe's atmosphere is naturally celestial, especially when fog lingers above the water below.

Thankfully, the restaurant was intentionally constructed of redwood and adobe to unite it with the landscape and earth it stands on. The result? An unobtrusive wooden dining room (big wood-burning fireplace, redwood ceilings, and all) and large windows that frame the unearthly view.

The fare, though good, will not send you to gastronomic heaven, but if the sun is shining and you're sipping a chardonnay on the patio, who cares? Lunch is basic: burgers, sandwiches, and salads. Dinner main courses include steak, broiled chicken, and fresh fish prepared any number of ways.

WHERE TO STOCK UP FOR A PICNIC

Can't stand another night of high-priced dining? Don't worry, there are plenty of little stores throughout Big Sur where you can pick up some goodies for a picnic. You'll pay a little more for your Pepperidge Farm cookies, baguette, salami, and cheese than you would at a supermarket, but you'll still save a fortune if you avoid dining out. Your best budget bet, however, is to stock up on edibles before you head to this neck of the woods.

Big Sur Deli. Calif. 1, 26¹/₂ miles south of Carmel. ☎ **408/667-2225.** Sandwiches $4. AE, ATM, DISC, DC, MC, V. Daily 8am–8pm.

Sandwiches, a selection of pasta and chicken salad, rice, and other picnic necessities join basic grocery store and gift shop items here, at one of the cheaper stores around.

Big Sur Lodge Grocery. Pfeiffer-Big Sur State Park, Calif. 1. ☎ **408/667-3106.** Sandwiches $4–$4.50. AE, MC, V. Daily 8am–9pm summer; hours vary in winter.

Ready-made ham and cheese and vegetarian sandwiches, along with some camping supplies, beer, ice, wood, and other sundries can be found at this small convenience store.

Big Sur River Inn General Store. Pheneger Creek (Calif. 1, 25 miles south of Carmel). ☎ **408/667-2700.** Sandwiches $4.50. MC, V. Summer daily 7:30am–9pm, winter hours vary.

This is one of the only natural/organic food stores in the area. You can pick up ready-made sandwiches, and a selection of regular and natural organic foods, including bulk bins full of granola, trail mixes, and other snackables. There's also a decent supply of camping goods.

The Center Deli. Calif. 1, next to the Big Sur Post office. ☎ **408/667-2225.** Sandwiches $2.50–$3.95. AE, ATM, DC, DISC, MC, V. During summer open daily 8am–8pm, winter 8am–7pm.

Talk about one-stop shopping. This full-service deli not only sells fresh baked goods, a variety of salads, wine, beer, and a slew of more substantial options (such as fettuccine, calzones, enchiladas, and barbecue chicken), it also rents videos and has a grocery store. Sandwiches are made to order, or you can grab a ready-made hoagie or vegetarian portobello mushroom on a roll. Treats and coffee drinks are available, as well. Everything from the deli is made on the premises.

Fernwood. Calif. 1, 26 miles south of Carmel. ☎ **408/667-2422.** Sandwiches $3–$4. MC, V. Daily 8am–midnight.

A small grocery store, Fernwood also offers a variety of ready-made sandwiches.

7 Pinnacles National Monument

by Andrew Rice

Once a little-known outpost of the national monument system, Pinnacles National Monument has become one of the most popular weekend climbing destinations in central California over the last 10 years. The mild winter climate and plentiful routes make this a perfect off-season training ground for climbers. It's also a popular haven for campers, hikers, and nature lovers. One of the most unique chaparral ecosystems in the world supports a large community of plant and animal life here, including one of California's largest breeding populations of raptors.

The Pinnacles themselves, hundreds of towering crags, spires, and hoodoos, are seemingly out of place in the voluptuously rolling hills of the coastal range. And they are, in fact, out of place, part of the eroded remains of a volcano formed 23 million years ago 195 miles south in the middle of the desert. It was carried here by the movement of the San Andreas Fault, which runs just east of the park. The other half of the volcano remains in the Mojave. Because of this distinctive geology, Pinnacles was set aside as a national monument on January 16, 1908, though it wasn't developed for visitor use until the 1930s and 1940s.

You could spend days here without getting bored, but it's possible to cover the most interesting features in a weekend. With a single hike you can go from the lush oak woodland around the Bear Gulch Visitor Center to the dry and desolate crags of the high peaks, then back down through a half-mile-long cave complete with underground waterfalls.

Two entrances lead to the park. The West Entrance from Soledad and U.S. 101 is a dry, dusty, winding single-lane road (not suitable for trailers) with the best drive-up view of the park. It does not connect with the east side. The alternate route is via the East Entrance. Unless you're coming from nearby, take the longer drive on Calif. 25 to enter through the east. Because most of the peaks of the Pinnacles face east, and the watershed drains east, most of the interesting hikes and geologic features are on this side. No roads cross the park.

The first place you should go after entering the park from the east is the **Bear Gulch Visitor Center** (☎ 408/389-4485). This small center is rich with exhibits on the park's history, wildlife, and geology, and also has a great selection of nature handbooks and climbing guides for the Pinnacles. Climbers should check with rangers about closures and other information before heading out: Many routes are closed during hawk and falcon nesting season, and rangers like to know how many climbers are in the park.

Adjacent to the visitor center, the Bear Gulch picnic ground is a great place to fuel up before setting out on a hike or, if you're not planning on leaving your car, one of the best places to gaze up at dramatic spires of the high peaks (the ultimate spot is on the west side).

HIKING/SEEING THE HIGHLIGHTS

To see most of the park in a single, moderately strenuous morning, take Condor Gulch Trail from the visitor center. As you climb quickly out of the parking area, the Pinnacles' wind-sculpted spires seem to grow taller. In less than 2 miles you are among them and Condor Gulch intersects with the High Peaks Trail. The view from the top spans miles: the Salinas Valley to your west, the Pinnacles below, and miles of coast to the east. After traversing the high peaks (including stretches where footholds are carved in steep rock faces) for about a mile, the trail drops back toward the visitor center via a valley filled with eerie-looking hoodoos.

In another 1^1/$_2$ miles, you'll reach the reservoir marking the top of Bear Gulch Cave. You'll need your flashlight and might get wet, but this 0.6-mile-long talus cave is a thrill. At the end of the cave you're just a short walk, through the most popular climbing area of the park, from the visitor center. It's also possible to just hike Bear Gulch and the cave, then return via Moses Spring Trail. It's about 2 miles round-trip, but you'll miss the view from the top.

If you're coming from the west entrance, the Juniper Canyon Trail is a short (1.2 miles), but very steep, blast to the top of the high peaks. You'll definitely earn the view. Otherwise, try the short Balconies Trail to the monument's other talus cave, Balconies Cave. Flashlights are required here too.

CAMPING

The national monument campground on the west side is just an open field with a few pit toilets and picnic tables. What's more, it's not open on spring weekends, prime visiting season. Rates are $10 per night (☎ 408/389-4485).

The campground on the east side, privately run **Pinnacles Campground** (☎ 408/389-4462; $6 per person) is just outside the park (off Calif. 25, 32 miles south of Hollister) and offers lots of privacy and space between sites, and is equipped with showers, a store, and a pool. It is close enough that you can hike into the park from the campground, but it will add a few miles to your outing. Though private campgrounds are often overdeveloped, the management here saw the benefits of leaving the surroundings natural. Park rangers hold campfire programs here on weekends. Dogs are not recommended.

JUST THE FACTS

Beware of poison oak, particularly in Bear Gulch. Rattlesnakes are common throughout the park but rarely seen. Bikes and dogs are prohibited on all trails, and there is no backcountry camping allowed anywhere in the park.

Hiking through this variety of landscapes demands versatility. Come prepared with a good pair of hiking shoes, snacks, lots of water, and a flashlight.

Daytime temperatures often exceed 100°F in summer, so the best times of year to visit are spring, when the wild flowers are blooming, followed by fall. Crowds are common during spring weekends.

13 The Central Coast

by Erika Lenkert and Matthew R. Poole

California's Central Coast—a spectacular amalgam of beaches, lakes, and mountains—is the state's most diverse region. The narrow strip of coast that runs for more than 100 miles from San Simeon to Ventura spans several climate zones and is home to an eclectic mixture of students, middle-class families, retirees, farmers, computer techies, and fishermen. The ride along Calif. 1, which follows the ocean cliffs, is almost always packed with rental cars, recreational vehicles, and bicyclists. Traffic may give your brakes a workout, but it also allows you take longer looks at one of the most spectacular vistas in the world.

Whether you're driving from Los Angeles or San Francisco, Calif. 1 is the most scenic and leisurely route (U.S. 101 gets you there faster, but is less picturesque). Most bicyclists peddle from north to south, the direction of the prevailing winds. Those in automobiles may prefer to drive south to north, so they can get a better look at the coastline as it unfolds toward the west. No matter which direction you drive, break out the old camera: You're about to experience unparalleled beauty, California style.

1 San Simeon: Hearst Castle

Few places on earth compare to Hearst Castle. This 165-room estate of publishing magnate William Randolph Hearst, situated high above the coastal village of San Simeon atop a hill he called La Cuesta Encantada ("the Enchanted Hill"), is an ego trip par excellence. One of the last great estates of America's Gilded Age, it's an astounding, completely over-the-top monument to wealth and to the power that money brings with it.

Hearst Castle is a sprawling compound of structures, constructed over 28 years in a Mediterranean Revival architectural style, set in undeniably magical surroundings. The focal point of the estate is the you-have-to-see-it-to-believe-it **Casa Grande,** a 100-plus-room mansion brimming with priceless art and antiques. Hearst bought the majority of his vast European Collection via New York auction houses, where he bought entire rooms (including walls, ceilings, and floors) and shipped them here. The result is an old-world castle done in a priceless mix-and-match style. You'll see fantastic 400-year-old Spanish and Italian ceilings, enormous 500-year-old fireplace mantels, 16th-century Florentine bedsteads, Renaissance paintings, Flemish tapestries, and innumerable other treasures. And

The Central Coast

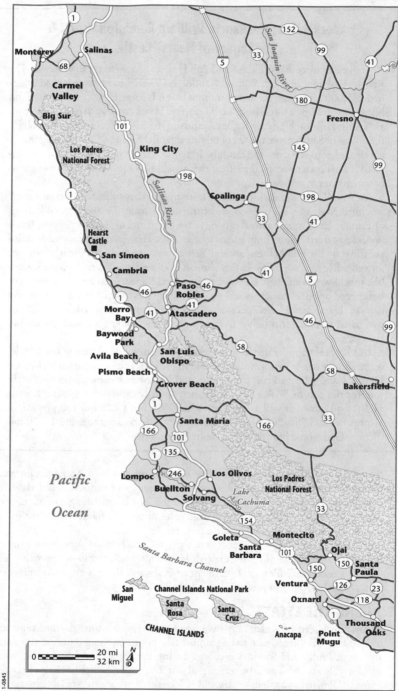

Monterey
Salinas
68
Carmel Valley
Big Sur
Los Padres National Forest
101
King City
Hearst Castle
San Simeon
Cambria
1
46
46
Paso Robles
41
Morro Bay
41
Atascadero
Baywood Park
Avila Beach
San Luis Obispo
Pismo Beach
Grover Beach
58
1
166
Santa Maria
101
166
1
135
Lompoc
246
Los Olivos
Buellton
Solvang
Lake Cachuma
Los Padres National Forest
33
154
Goleta
Montecito
Santa Barbara
Ojai
101
150
150
Santa Paula
Ventura
126
23
Oxnard
118
1
Thousand Oaks
Point Mugu
Anacapa

San Miguel
Channel Islands National Park
Santa Rosa
Santa Cruz
CHANNEL ISLANDS

Santa Barbara Channel

Pacific Ocean

San Joaquin River
152
33
99
41
5
180
Fresno
145
99
198
Coalinga
33
41
41
5
46
99
58
58
Bakersfield
33

Salinas River

0   20 mi
        32 km

N

1-0845

Weekends at the Ranch: William Randolph Hearst & the Legacy of Hearst Castle

The lavish palace that William Randolph Hearst always referred to simply as "The Ranch" took root in 1919. William Randolph ("W.R." to his friends) had inherited 275,000 acres from his father, mining baron George Hearst, and was well on his way to building a formidable media empire. He often escaped to a spot known as "Camp Hill" on his newly acquired lands in the Santa Lucia Mountains above the village of San Simeon, the site of boyhood family outings. Complaining that "I get tired of going up there and camping in tents," Hearst hired Paris-trained architect Julia Morgan to design the retreat that would become one of the most famous private homes in the world.

An art collector with indiscriminate taste and inexhaustible funds, Hearst overwhelmed Morgan with interiors and furnishings from the ancestral collections of Europe. Each week, railroad cars carrying fragments of Roman temples, lavish doors and carved ceilings from Italian monasteries, Flemish tapestries, hastily rolled paintings by the Old Masters, ancient Persian rugs, and antique French furniture arrived—five tons at a time—in San Simeon. *Citizen Kane*, which depicts a Hearst-like mogul with a similarly excessive estate called Xanadu, has a memorable scene of hoarded priceless treasures warehoused in dusty piles, stretching as far as the eye can see. Like Kane, Hearst, once described as a man with an "edifice complex," purchased so much that only a fraction of what he bought was ever installed in the estate.

In 1925, Hearst separated from his wife and began to spend time in Los Angeles overseeing his movie company, Cosmopolitan Pictures. His principal starlet, Marion Davies, became his constant companion and hostess at Hearst Castle—her main role for the rest of W.R.'s life. The ranch soon became a playground for the Hollywood crowd as well as dignitaries like Winston Churchill and playwright George Bernard Shaw, who is said to have wryly remarked of the estate that "this is the way God would have done it if He had the money."

then there are the swimming pools: The Roman-inspired indoor pool has intricate mosaic work, Carrara marble replicas of Greek gods and goddesses, and alabaster globe lamps that create the illusion of moonlight. The breathtaking outdoor Greco-Roman Neptune pool, flanked by marble colonnades that frame the distant sea, is one of the mansion's most memorable features.

In 1957, in exchange for a massive tax write-off, the Hearst Corporation donated the estate to the state of California (while retaining ownership of approximately 80,000 acres); the California Department of Parks and Recreation now administers it as a State Historic Monument.

TOURING THE ESTATE

Hearst Castle can be visited only by guided tour. Four distinct daytime tours are offered on a daily basis, each lasting almost two hours. Evening tours are also available most Friday and Saturday evenings during the spring and fall months. Wear comfortable shoes—you'll be walking about 1$^1/_2$ miles, which includes between 150 and 350 steps to climb or descend. (Wheelchair tours are available by calling **805/927-2020** at least 10 days in advance.)

Tour 1, recommended for the first-time visitor, includes part of the gardens, a guest house, and the ground floor of the main house, including the movie theater,

Despite its opulence, Hearst promoted "The Ranch" as a casual weekend home. He regularly laid the massive refectory table in the dining room with paper napkins and bottled ketchup and pickles to invoke a rustic, camplike atmosphere. Folklore has it that the only formal dinner held here was in honor of Calvin Coolidge. In Hearst's beautiful library, his priceless collection of ancient Greek pottery—one of the greatest collections of its kind in the world—is arranged casually among the rare volumes, like knickknacks.

The Hollywood crowd would take Hearst's private railway car from Los Angeles to San Luis Obispo, where a fleet of limousines waited to transport them to San Simeon. Those who didn't come by train were treated to a flight on Hearst's private plane from the Burbank Airport (MGM head Irving Thalberg and wife Norma Shearer preferred this mode of transportation). Hearst, an avid aviator, had a sizable landing strip built; Charles Lindbergh used it when he flew up for a visit in the summer of 1928.

Oh, if the walls could talk. Atop one of the castle's looming towers are the hexagonal Celestial Suites. One was a favorite of Clark Gable and Carole Lombard, who would be startled out of their romantic slumber by the clamor of 18 carillon bells directly overhead. David Niven, a frequent guest, was one of the unknown number who defied teetotaler Hearst's edict against liquor in private rooms. Niven was called upon more than once to explain the several "empties" under the bed (which Cardinal Richelieu once owned and slept in) in his customary suite.

W.R. and Marion Davies hosted frequent costume parties at the ranch, which were as intricately planned as a movie production. The most legendary, the Circus Party, was held to celebrate W.R.'s 75th birthday on April 29, 1938. Much of Hollywood attended to honor the tycoon, including grand dame Bette Davis—dressed as a bearded lady.

—Stephanie Avnet

where you'll see Hearst's home movies. **Tour 2** takes in the upper part of the main house, including Hearst's private suite and study, the library, guest rooms, the kitchen, and the pools. **Tour 3** visits the north wing of Casa Grande, with its 10 guest suites and sitting rooms, pools, and gardens; it deals with construction changes over a 20-year period. **Tour 4,** offered April through October only, does not go inside La Casa Grande itself; it focuses on the grounds and gardens and includes the wine cellar and two floors of the largest guest house. **Tour 5,** the Evening Tour, is available during the spring and fall and is led by docents in period dress. This tour highlights Casa Grande, the pools and gardens, the largest guest cottage, and a 1930s newsreel shown in the theater.

Tours are conducted daily, beginning at 8:20am, except Thanksgiving Day, Christmas Day, and New Year's Day. Two to six tours leave every hour, depending on the season. Allow two hours between starting times if you plan on taking more than one tour. Reservations are recommended and can be made up to eight weeks in advance. Tickets can be purchased by telephone through **DESTINET** (☎ **800/444-4445**). Daytime tours cost $14 for adults, $8 for children ages 6 to 12. The evening tour costs $25 for adults, $13 for children ages 6 to 12.

Hearst Castle is located directly on Calif. 1, about 42 miles north of San Luis Obispo and 94 miles south of Monterey. From San Francisco or Monterey, take

U.S. 101 south to Paso Robles, then Calif. 46 west to Calif. 1, and Calif. 1 north to the Castle. From Los Angeles, take U.S. 101 north to San Luis Obispo, then Calif. 1 north to the Castle. Park in the visitor center parking lot; a tour bus will take you 5 miles up the hill to the estate.

WHERE TO STAY

After driving for close to an hour without passing anything but lush green hills and nature at its most glorious, it's a remarkably quaint surprise to roll into the adorable coastal minitowns of Cambria or nearby San Simeon. Cambria, in particular, is so charming that the town itself is reason enough to make the drive. With little more than two streets worth of shops, restaurants, and a handful of B&Bs, Cambria is the perfect place to escape the everyday, enjoy the endless expanses of pristine coastal terrain, and meander through little shops selling local artwork.

Gray whales pass though the area from late December to early February, and for the past few years, much to the delight of locals and nature enthusiasts, hundreds of elephant seals have made the shore along Moonstone Beach Drive their year-round playground (do not approach them, but rather watch them from the bluffs; they are wild animals and will bite if molested). The beaches and coves are a wonderful place for humans to frolic as well—stone collectors will be especially enamored of the natural bounty of jade and moonstones mingled with the sand.

DOUBLES FOR $60 OR LESS

Cambria Palms Motel. 2662 Main St., Cambria, CA 93428. ☎ **805/927-4485.** 18 rms. TV. $30–$62 double. AE, DISC, MC, V.

When heading into Cambria, you'll know you've arrived at this motel when you see the British flag and a sign reading "Best Deal in Town"—and indeed it is, depending on what your idea of a deal is. You'll be paying substantially less to stay here than anywhere else in the vicinity, but you do get what you pay for. Saving $20 means you're a few blocks outside of the nook of shops and B&Bs which constitutes the center of town. You'll be subjected to downright tacky decor (vinyl-covered lamps, old lackluster desks), and there are no phones in the rooms. You'll pay a bit more for a queen or king-size bed, as well as any of the four rooms with kitchenettes ($5 to $8 extra). Some rooms have TV and/or coolers, and all have coffeemakers. Ask for a room with a creek-side and pasture view—it will help divert your attention from your boring room.

San Simeon Creek Campgrounds/Washburn Campgrounds. Calif. 1, 2 miles north of Cambria. ☎ **805/927-2035** for information, or DESTINET 800/444-7275 for reservations. San Simeon Creek has 132 sites, Washburn 70 sites. San Simeon sites up to $18 (high season), Washburn sites up to $11 (high season). MC, V.

Not far from the beach are almost 200 California State Parks' camping sites in two open areas (read: not wooded). The San Simeon Creek grounds are "developed" with coin-op showers (25¢ for three minutes); they're also closer to the beach and a little more sheltered than the Washburn Campgrounds. Washburn has chemical flush toilets and no showers, but does offer a good view of the ocean and hills. There's about a mile between the two campgrounds. Sites can be reserved from one day up to seven months in advance through DESTINET.

DOUBLES FOR $80 OR LESS

Creekside Inn. 2618 Main St., Cambria, CA 93428. ☎ **800/269-5212** or 805/927-4021. 21 rms. Double $45–$85. Extra person $5. DISC, MC, V.

Of the bare-bones accommodation choices in the area, Creekside's newer rooms are one of the safest bets. Its motel style and decor aren't nearly as charming as many of the authentic inns in the neighborhood, but ask for a room that faces the hills and has a small deck, and you're liable to forget all about the concrete promenade out front.

DOUBLES FOR $100 OR LESS

Best Western Cavalier Inn. 9415 Hearst Dr. (Calif. 1), San Simeon, CA 93452. ☎ **800/ 826-8168** or 805/927-4688. 90 rms. TEL TV. $64–$149 double. AE, DISC, MC, V.

The terms *oceanfront* and *budget* are generally a contradiction, but this family-friendly hotel offers the best of both. Aside from the basics, rooms are all outfitted with VCRs, refrigerators, computer jacks, hair dryers, and cable with HBO. Other bonuses include two outdoor heated pools, an exercise room, two restaurants, a launderette, a shopping center, and a video arcade.

California Seacoast Lodge. 9215 Hearst Dr., San Simeon, CA 93452. ☎ **805/927-3878.** Fax 805/927-1781. 57 rms. TEL TV. Sept 16–May, $50–$60 double; from $185 suite. June– Sept 15, $85–$95 double; from $185 suite. Additional person $5 extra. Rates include continental breakfast. AE, MC, V.

You'll find clean, newly renovated accommodations at this hotel located 3 miles from the entrance to Hearst Castle. There is an array of options here; you can go budget with a basic room, kick in a few extra bucks for one of the most expensive doubles (which comes with a king-size bed and fireplace), or splurge on a minisuite that's stocked with a fireplace, Jacuzzi, canopied bed, and French furnishings. There's also a glass-enclosed pool on the premises.

WORTH A SPLURGE

Blue Dolphin Inn. 6470 Moonstone Beach Dr., Cambria, CA 93428. ☎ **805/927-3300.** 18 rms. TV. $75–$225 double. Rates include continental breakfast. AE, MC, V.

Voted one of the best moderately priced California accommodations by *Los Angeles Times* readers in 1996, the Blue Dolphin offers high-quality rooms along the Cambria coastline. Designed in English country style, guest rooms brim with frilly opulence and include gas fireplaces, refrigerators, hair dryers, and VCRs. Rooms 111, 112, and 113 have good ocean views (a road, however, sits between you and the surf) from their patios.

○ **Olallieberry Inn.** 2476 Main St., Cambria, CA 93428. ☎ **805/927-3222.** Fax 805/ 927-0202. 6 rms, 1 cottage suite. $85–$140 double; $165 suite in separate cottage. Rates include evening wine and hors d'oeuvres and full breakfast. MC, V.

The minute I walked into this 1873 Greek Revival house located on Cambria's main street, I knew this was my kind of place. The grounds were perfectly manicured but whimsically blooming with flora, and the air smelled of baked brie and homemade bread (I'd come during the afternoon wine hour). You'll soon discover that the owners have a passion for cooking and gardening (the herb garden was recently featured in *Sunset Magazine*). In the meantime, decor doesn't fall by the wayside: Victorian floral-and-lace reigns, guest rooms are lovingly and individually appointed, and each has a private bath although not all are ensuite (some are across or down the hall). Follow the deck off the dining area to the backyard, and you'll find suites in a newer building overlooking a creek—they're remarkably charming and have fireplaces and private decks. The full breakfast—accompanied by olallieberry jam, of course— is guaranteed to impress.

WHERE TO DINE
MEALS FOR $10 OR LESS
Soto's Market and Deli. 2244 Main St. ☎ **805/927-4411.** Mon–Thurs 7am–8pm, Fri–Sat 7am–9pm, Sun 8am–6pm. DISC, MC, V. DELI.

When the sun is shining down on the mountainous coast of Cambria, there's no better way to "do lunch" than to grab a picnic and head for the hills (or the ocean). This small-town supermarket's deli will help you fill your basket with made-to-order sandwiches for $3.95, meat loaf, and a good selection of cheeses and salads. They'll also tell you how to get to a scenic luncheon spot.

MEALS FOR $20 OR LESS
Robin's. 4095 Burton Dr., Cambria. ☎ **805/927-5007.** Reservations recommended. Main courses $9–$14. MC, V. Mon–Sat 11am–9pm, Sun 5–9:30pm. ECLECTIC.

It's surprising to find such a culinarily adventuresome restaurant in a small town, but after hearing everyone rave about the salmon bisque appetizer, porcini raviolis with roasted pepper cream sauce, fresh spinach, basil, and Parmesan, and other flavorful combinations, it became clear that both residents and visitors here have discerning palates. Robin's is a restaurant with something for everyone, from exotic dishes from Mexico, India, Thailand (try the Thai prawns in green curry with basmati brown rice, fruit chutney and chapati), and beyond, to more straightforward preparations like a tasty salad or juicy steak and an array of vegetarian dishes. Don't miss dessert—try the espresso-soaked cake with mascarpone mousse and shaved chocolate or vanilla custard bread pudding. Tempt your taste buds on line at www.Cambria-online.com.

The Sow's Ear Cafe. 2248 Main St., Cambria. ☎ **805/927-4865.** Reservations recommended. Main courses $13–$18. AE, DISC, MC, V. Nightly 5pm–8 or 9:30pm depending on business. AMERICAN COUNTRY.

The name may not be romantic, but the dining room definitely is. It's a casually elegant spot, lit just enough to catch the warmth of its rustic wooden surroundings—the perfect place to lean over a bottle of California red, fresh baked bread, and a hearty plate of beer-spiced shrimp, chicken and dumplings, or baby pork ribs, and whisper travel fantasies to a companion. Early dinner specials range from $10.25 to $12.25 and might consist of honey lime barbecued chicken, a fresh catch, and a vegetarian dish.

WORTH A SPLURGE
✪ **Ian's.** 2150 Center St., Cambria. ☎ **805/927-8649.** Reservations highly recommended. Main courses $7.95–$21.95. AE, MC, V. Daily 5–9pm. CALIFORNIA.

Ask a local where they'd prefer to dine and they're likely to mention Ian's. The menu, which changes daily, reflects chef Mark Sahaydak's take on the local bounty. His individual artistry is apparent in dishes like porcini mushroom ravioli with spicy Italian sausage, and sautéed scallops in a crème fraîche and chardonnay sauce flavored with sun-dried tomatoes. Ian's wine list reflects the very best of local and regional vineyards.

2 Morro Bay

Don't get the wrong impression when you first enter Morro Bay via U.S. 101. It may look like an industrial town accented with one remarkable rock protruding from the shoreline; but aside from one absurdly placed oceanfront electrical plant and a motel strip, it's a wonderfully sleepy seaside town.

Morro Bay is separated from the ocean by a long peninsula of sand dunes, which can reach up to 85 feet tall. It's best known for dramatic Morro Rock, an enormous egg-shaped monolith that juts out of the water just offshore. Part of a chain of long-extinct volcanoes, the huge domed rock is a winter and fall sanctuary for thousands of migrating birds, including cormorants, pelicans, sandpipers, and the rare peregrine falcon. It's wonderful to watch them from the beach or from a window table of a restaurant with a bay view.

Stop here for lunch, a little shopping (it's far more upscale here than in nearby Pismo Beach), and a walk around amazing Morro Rock. Some visitors make Morro Bay their base while visiting the area, but families seem to gravitate toward Pismo Beach, where there's another great stretch of sandy shoreline.

ESSENTIALS

The **Morro Bay Chamber of Commerce,** 895 Napa St., Suite A-1, Morro Bay, CA 93442 (☎ **800/231-0592** or 805/772-4467), offers armfuls of area information. It's open Monday through Friday from 8am to 5pm and Saturday 10am to 3pm.

EXPLORING THE AREA

Most visitors come to Morro Bay to ogle **Morro Rock,** the much-photographed Central Coast icon known as the "Gibraltar of the Pacific." It's definitely worth a gander (actually you couldn't miss it if you wanted to) and a few snapshots, but there's more to do in the area beyond this *morro,* or miniature volcanic peak.

BEACHES

Popular **Atascadero State Beach,** just north of Morro Rock, has gentle waves and lovely views. Rest rooms, showers, and dressing rooms are available. Just north of Atascadero is **Morro Strand State Beach,** a long, sandy stretch with normally gentle surf. Rest rooms and picnic tables are available here. Morro Strand has its own campgrounds; for information, call **805/772-2560,** or reserve a spot through **DESTINET** (☎ **800/444-7275**).

NEARBY STATE PARKS

Cabrillo Peak, a morro located in the lovely **Morro Bay State Park** (☎ 805/772-7434), makes for a terrific day hike and offers fantastic 360° views from its summit. There is a faint zigzagging trail, but the best way to reach the top is by bushwhacking straight up the gentle slope—a hike that takes about two hours round-trip. To reach the trailhead, take Calif. 1 south and turn left at the Morro Bay State Park/Montana de Oro State Park exit. Follow South Bay Boulevard for ³/₄ mile, then take the left fork another ¹/₂ mile to the dirt parking lot, located on your left.

Montana de Oro State Park ("mountain of gold") is fondly known as "petite Big Sur" because of its stony cliffs and rugged terrain. There's great swimming at Spooner's Cove and lots of easy hiking trails here, including a number that lead to spectacular coastal vistas or hidden forest streams. The Hazard Reef trail will take you up on the Morro Bay Sandspit dunes. The park's campground is in the trees, across from the beach. For information, call the park rangers at **805/528-0513** or 805/772-7434, or reserve a spot through **DESTINET** (☎ **800/444-7275**).

IN TOWN

In addition to soaking up the local color at the Embarcadero, visit the **Morro Bay Aquarium** (☎ 805/772-7647), which takes in injured and abandoned sea otters and seals and nurses them back to health, eventually releasing the recovered animals back to the sea. Open in summer, daily 9am to 6pm; in winter, 9am to 5pm.

WHERE TO STAY
DOUBLES FOR $80 OR LESS

Sea Air Inn. 845 Morro Ave. (at Morro Bay Blvd.), Morro Bay, CA 93442. ☎ 805/772-4437. 40 rms (34 suites to be added). TEL (MINIBAR TEL TV in suites). Doubles from $58–$68. AE, MC, V. From Calif. 1, take Morro Bay Blvd. exit and head straight for the water.

There's no beach out front, but this hotel has a close-up view of looming Morro Rock and a key location (you can walk down the steps to the waterfront Embarcadero). The view inside is not so extraordinary—clean, but lackluster furnishings, which includes two-tone '70s-style carpeting and generic headboards fastened to the wall. Perks include direct-dial phones and coffee and tea in each room. Over the next year, the hotel is adding 34 suites, which will all have minibars, fireplaces, Jacuzzis, VCRs, refrigerators, and microwaves. These new additions will debut in late 1997 and will undoubtedly cost more than existing standard rooms.

DOUBLES FOR $100 OR LESS

Baywood Bed-and-Breakfast Inn. 1370 2nd St., Baywood Park, CA 93042. ☎ 805/528-8888. 5 rms, 10 suites. TEL TV. $80–$110 double, $110–$150 suite. Extra person $15. Rates include breakfast. MC, V.

Rarely will you find such affordable accommodations with so many extras. Each room at this two-story bay front inn, located in Baywood Park just south of Morro Bay, is decorated in a distinct theme, so you can cuddle in a floral and light wood country cottage, stretch out in a stately 19th-century English chamber, or saddle down in a Southwestern suite. Each room has a private entrance, gas fireplace, microwave, coffeemaker, and refrigerator stocked with complimentary sodas and snacks; all but a few have ocean views. Breakfast is brought to your room, which tops off an already romantic and pleasurable experience, or you can dine at the hotel's new Waterside Cafe, which also serves lunch, dinner, and Sunday brunch.

WORTH A SPLURGE

The Inn at Morro Bay. 60 State Park Rd., Morro Bay, CA 93442. ☎ 800/321-9566 or 805/772-5651. Fax 805/772-4779. 96 rms. TEL TV. $95–$265 double (highest rates charged only on weekends). AE, MC, V.

One of the most upscale hotels on the San Luis coast is strategically sandwiched along the shoreline between monumental Morro Bay and an 18-hole golf course. Two-story Cape Cod–style buildings house guests and have contemporary interiors tempered by blond wood cabinetry, polished brass fittings and beds, and reproductions of 19th-century European furnishings. The best rooms enjoy unobstructed views of Morro Rock; those in back face the swimming pool and gardens.

WHERE TO DINE

Hoppe's at 901. 901 Embarcadero. ☎805/772-9012. Reservations recommended. Main courses $12–$22. AE, DISC, MC, V. Fri–Sun 11am–2pm; Wed–Mon 5–9pm. CALIFORNIA.

Ask a local where to go for a special meal in Morro Bay, and they're likely to send you to Hoppe's. Not only do diners get a stellar view of Morro Rock, but also an opportunity to savor chef/owner Wilhelm Hoppe's seasonally inspired cuisine. Favorites include the lobster ravioli appetizer with red curry in a peanut sauce, or such entrees as smoked sea scallop lasagna with proscuitto and sun-dried tomatoes, and roasted duck breast with tamarind, ginger, and mango.

3 San Luis Obispo

Because the actual town of San Luis Obispo is not visible from U.S. 101, even many Californians don't know that it's more than a McDonald's-and-gasoline stopover on the way to Southern California. But its secret location is exactly what keeps San Luis the quaint little Central Coast jewel that it is.

San Luis Obispo is neatly tucked into the mountains about halfway between San Francisco and Los Angeles. It's surrounded by green pristine mountain ranges and filled with college kids and friendly locals. The atmosphere is small-town casual, making it the perfect place to meander and ponder a simpler, more carefree existence.

The town grew up around an 18th-century mission, and its dozens of historical landmarks, quaint Victorian homes, shops, and restaurants, are its primary tourist attractions. Today, it's still quaint and best explored on foot. It also makes a good base for an extensive survey of the region as a whole. To the west of town, a short drive away, are some of the state's prettiest swimming beaches; turning east, you enter the Central Coast's wine country, home to dozens of respectable wineries (see "Vintage: Central Coast," below).

ESSENTIALS

GETTING THERE   U.S. 101 runs right through San Luis Obispo; it's the fastest land route here from anywhere. If you're driving down along the coast, Calif. 1 is the way to go for its natural beauty and oceanfront cliffs. If you're entering the city from the east, take Calif. 46 or Calif. 41.

ORIENTATION   San Luis Obispo is about 10 miles inland, at the junction of Calif. 1 and U.S. 101. The downtown is laid out in a grid, roughly centered around the historic mission and its Mission Plaza (see below). Most of the main tourist sights are around the mission, within the small triangle created by U.S. 101 and Santa Rosa and Marsh streets.

VISITOR INFORMATION   The **San Luis Obispo County Visitors and Conference Bureau,** 1041 Chorro St., Suite E, San Luis Obispo, CA 93401 (☎ **800/ 634-1414** or 805/541-8000; fax 805/543-9498), is located downtown, between Monterey and Higuera streets. This helpful office is one of the best-run visitors bureaus I have ever come across. Ask for a "Path of History" map, which details many of the sights listed below. The visitors center can also make reservations and issue tickets for Hearst Castle. It's open Tuesday to Friday 8am to 5pm, and Monday, Saturday and Sunday 10am to 5pm.

EXPLORING THE TOWN

The Ah Louis Store. 800 Palm St. (at Chorro St.). ☎ **805/543-4332.** Usually open Mon–Sat 2–5:30pm; hours vary.

This establishment, practically unchanged since its opening in 1874, is still in the hands of the original Cantonese family owners. Entrepreneurial Mr. Ah Louis was lured to California by gold fever in 1856, but emerged from the mines empty-handed. Instead, he began a lucrative career as a labor contractor, hiring and organizing Chinese crews to work on the railroad, and later, he opened the store. Ah Louis also founded one of the country's first brickyards, built county roads, ran a vegetable and flower-seed business, bred racehorses, and oversaw eight farms.

Today, you can chat with Ah Louis's heir, Howard, while you browse through the clutter of Asian merchandise. Ask for a free brochure detailing the family's history. Hours are somewhat irregular, though, since Howard often just closes up and goes fishing.

✪ **Farmer's Market.** Higuera St. (between Osos and Nipomo sts.). Thurs 6:30–9pm.

If you're lucky enough to be in town on a Thursday, there's no better activity than taking an evening stroll down Higuera Street, when the state's largest weekly street fair fills four downtown city blocks. You'll find much more here than fresh-picked produce. There's an ever-changing array of street entertainment, open-pit barbecues, food stands, and market stalls selling fresh flowers, cider, and other seasonal goodies. Nibble from all the cheap food vendor's booths and barbecues, and you'll get an inexpensive and delicious meal while getting to know SLO residents. Surrounding stores stay open until 9pm.

Mission San Luis Obispo de Tolosa. 782 Monterey St. ☎ **805/543-6850.** $1 donation requested. Winter 9am–4pm; summer 9am–5pm (sometimes later).

Founded by Father Junípero Serra in 1772, California's fifth mission was built with adobe bricks by Native American Chumash people. The mission remains one of the prettiest and most interesting structures in the Franciscan chain. For further details on the mission, see "The Missions of the Central Coast" driving tour in Chapter 4.

Mission Plaza, a pretty garden with brick paths and park benches fronting a meandering creek, still functions as San Luis Obispo's town square. It's the focal point for local festivities and activities, from live concerts to poetry readings and theater productions. Check at the visitors center to see what's on when you're in town. At Mission Plaza you'll also find the **San Luis Obispo Art Center** (☎ **805/ 543-8562**), where three galleries display and sell an array of California-made art. Admission is free.

San Luis Obispo Children's Museum. 1010 Nipomo St. ☎ **805/544-KIDS.** Admission $3 for adults and children 2 and older; kids under 2 free. Sept–June Thurs–Fri 1–5pm, Sat 10am–5pm, Sun noon–5pm; Mon 10am–5pm; July–Aug Thurs–Tues 10am–5pm.

This terrific children's museum features a playhouse of interesting manipulatives for toddlers, an authentic reproduction of a Chumash cave dwelling, a music room, computer corner, a pint-sized bank and post office, and more. Special events like mask making, sing-alongs, and stage makeup classes are scheduled regularly; call for a current schedule.

SHOPPING

Don't expect New York's Fifth Avenue here, but rather a few charming boutiques (and many uninteresting ones) scattered throughout town. The best place to exercise your credit cards is on the downtown streets surrounding the mission, specifically the five blocks of Higuera Street from Nipomo to Osos streets as well as a short stretch of Monterey Street between Chorro and Osos streets. On Higuera Street, check out **Hands Gallery** (at 777 Higuera St., ☎ **805/543-1921**), which has a bright and playful collection of local and international art. Trinkets range from glass candies to vases, jewelry, and ceramics.

You might also want to check out **The Creamery,** 570 Higuera St., at Nipomo Street (☎ **805/541-0106**), which functioned as one of the state's most important milk-producing centers for more than 40 years. Restored, remodeled, and opened as a shopping and restaurant mall, the complex is centered around the creamery's old cooling tower. Antique freezer doors, overhead workhouse lights, and milk-can lamps pointedly remind visitors of the structure's original function.

Central Coast wineries are producing some excellent wines, some of which are available for tasting at the **Central Coast Wine Room,** 10 Old Creamery Rd., Harmony (☎ **805/927-7337**). If you don't mind wading through the mediocre ones, you'll find some excellent selections from Paso Robles and the Edna Valley that compete favorably with those of the Napa Valley. The tasting room is open daily from 11am to 5pm; tastings are $1.

WHERE TO STAY

In addition to what's listed below, San Luis is also home to the following reliable chains: There's a pristine branch of **Holiday Inn Express** (☎ 800/465-4329 or 805/544-8600); the **Best Western Olive Tree** (☎ 800/528-1234 or 805/544-2800) offers apartment–style accommodations that are a good value; and the reliable **Motel 6** (☎ 800/466-8356 or 805/541-6992) is a great budget choice.

DOUBLES FOR $60 OR LESS

Budget Motel. 345 Marsh St., San Luis Obispo, CA 93401. ☎ **805/543-6443.** Fax 805/545-0951. 51 rms, 2 two-bedroom suites. TEL TV (A/C in some rooms). Doubles $34–$50, suites $48–$78. Senior discount. Rates include continental breakfast. AE, CB, DC, DISC, MC, V.

True to its name, the Budget Motel offers decent accommodations 2 miles from the downtown area and includes free cable TV. Don't worry when you get your first glimpse of the place (the exterior is done in '60s brown and orange); its interior has been updated a bit since those days. The cheapest rooms have no tubs, but are clean and have a vanity and credenza. A small bump up in price promises newer rooms with plush carpeting, better-fashioned motel furnishings, and a tub.

DOUBLES FOR $80 OR LESS

Ⓢ **Adobe Inn.** 1473 Monterey St., San Luis Obispo, CA 93401. ☎ **800/676-1588** or 805/549-0321. Fax 805/549-0383. 15 rms (8 with kitchenette, but no stove). TEL TV. $45–$95 double. Extra person $6. Rates include breakfast. Seasonal discounts available. AE, DISC, MC, V.

Okay, it's not *actually* adobe, or even remotely close for that matter, but Michael and Ann Dinshaw have taken this old motor inn, given it a creatively homey atmosphere, and made it available to guests at unbeatable prices. Each spotless accommodation is named after a cactus, has a corresponding hand-painted sign on its door, and is individually decorated in Southwestern style with quirky additions such as playfully painted cupboards or a window-side reading nook. Breakfast is served in a clean dining area that unfortunately faces the street, but coffee snobs will delight in a cup of locally roasted coffee. Plants adorn the inn's exterior, and there's a mini cactus garden and fountain beyond the parking lot. Michael or Ann are usually on-site and go out of their way to make guests happy, offering a slew of packages that explore the surrounding areas and attractions. A great bargain all in all.

Ⓢ **Lamp Lighter Inn.** 1604 Monterey St. (at Grove St.), San Luis Obispo, CA 93401. ☎ **800/547-7787** or 805/547-7777. Fax 805/547-7787. 29 rms, 11 suites. A/C TEL TV. $45–$80 double; suites from $69. Rates include continental breakfast. AE, DISC, MC, V.

Even if you're not looking for a bargain, you'll be pleasantly surprised with the value of your dollar at this motel. Rooms boast traditional motel style and colors, but look brand new, are squeaky clean, and have firm mattresses. Other bonuses are coffee-makers, refrigerators (except in three rooms), and a heated pool and whirlpool. Breakfast is served in the lobby by an amazingly enthusiastic staff.

WORTH A SPLURGE

Apple Farm Inn. 2015 Monterey St., San Luis Obispo, CA 93401. ☎ **800/255-2040** or 805/544-2040. Fax 805/546-9495. 69 rms. A/C TEL TV. $95–$200 double. AE, DISC, MC, V.

The ultrapopular Apple Farm Inn is a peaceful getaway in a Disney plantation kind of way. Every square inch of the immaculate Victorian-style farmhouse is cheek-pinchingly cute with floral wallpaper, fresh flowers, and sugar-sweet touches. No two rooms are alike, though all have a gas fireplace, large well-equipped bath-room, pine antiques, lavish country decor, and a canopy, four-poster, or brass bed.

Some bedrooms open onto cozy turreted sitting areas with romantic window seats; others have bay windows and a view of San Luis Creek, where a working mill spins its huge wheel to power an apple press. An outdoor heated swimming pool and Jacuzzi are open year-round. Service here is outstanding and includes nightly turn-down and a morning wake-up knock, delivered with complimentary coffee or tea, and a newspaper. Complimentary cribs and train and airport shuttle service are also provided. Cider is always on hand in the lobby.

✪ **Madonna Inn.** 100 Madonna Rd. (off U.S. 101), San Luis Obispo, CA 93405. ☎ **800/543-9666** or 805/543-3000. Fax 805/543-1800. 109 rms, 25 suites. TEL TV. $87–$180 double; from $145 suites. Corporate discounts available. MC, V.

This one you've got to see for yourself. The creative imaginations of Madonna Inn's owners Alex and Phyllis Madonna gave birth to the wildest and most superfluously garish fantasy world this side of Graceland. The only decor consistency through-out the hotel is its color scheme, which is perpetual pink. Beyond that, it's a free-for-all. Every nook and cranny has been built to delight—even the men's room has a rock waterfall urinal and clamshell sinks. Each room offers a different thematic fantasy far beyond a creative paint job. One room features a trapezoid bed—it's five feet long on one side and six feet long on the other. "Rock" rooms with zebra- or tiger-patterned bedspreads and stone-like showers and fireplaces conjure up thoughts of a Flintstones' Playboy palace. There are also blue rooms, red rooms, over-the-top Spanish, Italian, Irish, Alps, Currier and Ives, Native American, Swiss, and hunting rooms. Even the coffee shop, dining room, and two cocktail lounges are outlandishly ornate. Even if you don't stay here, stop by and check it out.

WHERE TO DINE

Like the town itself, San Luis' restaurants are modest and affordable, which means you can afford to eat anywhere you like while you're here. Don't hesitate to stop and ask locals their favorite places to eat, and keep an eye out for public barbecues, especially at the Thursday night farmers' market. SLO folks love their barbecues, and they're liable to make you a fan, too.

MEALS FOR $10 OR LESS

Big Sky Cafe. 1121 Broad St. ☎ 805/545-5401. Reservations accepted for large parties. Main courses dinner $6–$11; lunch $6–$8; salads and sandwiches $5–$6; breakfast $4–$6. MC, V. Mon–Sat 7am–10pm, Sun 8am–4pm. AMERICAN.

The folk-artsy fervor of San Luis really shines at this Southwestern mirage where local art and an eclectic decor surround diners who come for fresh, healthy food. Almost everything on the menu, such as shrimp tacos and herb-infused roasted chicken, is created with local ingredients. Lighter meals, such as black bean vegetarian chili, char-broiled eggplant sandwich, and white bean and yellowtail tuna salad are equally in-ventive and tasty. Excellent breakfasts include buttermilk pancakes, a jambalaya omelet, turkey hash, and huevos rancheros.

Linnaea's Cafe. 1110 Garden St. (near Marsh St.). ☎ 805/541-5888. Reservations not accepted. Lunch main courses $3–$5.75. No credit cards. Daily 7am–midnight. VEGETARIAN.

New carpets, tables, and a chef from the Culinary Institute guarantees that Linnaea's will remain the reigning champ among budget breakfast and lunching folk. Morn-ing meals include waffles and French toast, plus breakfast burritos, delicious pastries, and more. In the afternoon, the most coveted dishes are soup, main course salads, and SLO roll sandwiches. Lunch is served until it's gone; the rest of the evening is devoted to coffee drinks and delectable desserts. Food for the soul is always available in the form of local art, and acoustic music and poetry join in on the weekends.

SLO Brewing Company. 1119 Garden St. ☎ **805/543-1843.** Reservations accepted. Main courses $5.95–$8.95. AE, MC, V. Mon–Wed 11:30am–10:30pm, Thurs–Sat 11:30am–12:30am, Sun noon–5pm.

This brewpub's homemade beer has created such a buzz that it's now distributed nationally in addition to being downed locally. Three distinct variations, Pale Ale, Amber Ale, and Porter are brewed from all-natural ingredients and wash down the menu's burgers and fried fare perfectly. Join the festive collegiate crowd at night, stop by for lunch, or check the place out on the web at http://www.slobrew.com.

⑤ Thai Classic. 1101 Higuera St. (at Osos), San Luis Obispo. ☎ **805/541-2025.** Reservations recommended on weekends. Most dishes $6–$11. DISC, MC, V. Sun–Thurs 11am–10pm, Fri–Sat 11am–11pm. THAI.

This place is not much to look at, that's for sure—but stare past the cheesy white booths and plain walls and focus on what's coming out of the kitchen and you won't be sorry you came. There's an extensive vegetarian selection and trademark Thai appetizers such as satay with peanut and cucumber sauces, pad Thai, and spring rolls. Locals favor the pineapple fried rice with shrimp chicken and cashews as well as the curry plates, all of which should be eaten family-style. Lunch specials on weekdays are a real bargain at $3 to $4 for soup, salad, spring roll, fried wonton, steamed rice, and one of 21 main courses.

MEALS FOR $20 OR LESS

Buona Tavola. 1037 Monterey St., San Luis Obispo. ☎ **805/545-8000.** Reservations recommended. Main courses $8.25–$16.95. DC, DISC, MC, V. Mon–Fri 11:30am–2:30pm, Sun–Thurs 5:30–9:30pm, Fri–Sat 5:30–10pm. NORTHERN ITALIAN.

While most eateries in town are burger-and-sandwich casual, Buona Tavola offers well-prepared Italian food in a more upscale environment. It's still the kind of place where you can stroll in wearing jeans, but the sweet dining room with checkerboard floors and original artwork is more intimate and warm than other spots in town. There's also backyard-terrace seating where you can enjoy your meal surrounded by magnolia, ficus, and grapevines. The menu lists a number of salads and antipasti. Favorite pastas include Agnolotti de scampi allo zafferano, which is homemade, filled with scampi, and served in a cream-saffron sauce, and the spaghettini scoglio d'oro, which comes with lobster, sea scallops, clams, mussels, shrimp, and diced tomatoes in a saffron sauce. Others opt for the pollo scamiciato alla Vinaggia—a grilled boneless chicken marinated with garlic and herbs and served with a rosemary mustard sauce. Don't worry, once you get through trying to pronounce your desired dish, the rest of the evening should be both relaxing and satisfying.

4 Pismo Beach

Just outside of San Luis Obispo, Pismo Beach is home to a 23-mile stretch of prime California beach where flip-flops are the shoes of choice and most clothing shops feature the latest in surf fashion. It's all about beach life here so bring your board, a good book, or if nothing else, your bathing suit.

If building sand castles or tanning isn't your idea of a tantalizing time, explore isolated dunes, cliff-sheltered tide pools, and old pirate coves. Bring your dog (Fido's welcome here) and play an endless game of fetch or go fishing—it's permitted from Pismo Beach Pier, which also offers arcade entertainment, bowling, and billiards. Pismo is also the only beach in the area that allows all-terrain vehicles (ATVs) to drive the dunes.

The town itself is not particularly interesting and consists of little more than tourist shops and surf-and-turf restaurants. If you want to stay in the area, San Luis Obispo is far more charming, but if you want a few days on a beautiful beach at half the price of an oceanfront stay in Santa Barbara, Pismo is a perfect choice.

ESSENTIALS

The **Pismo Beach Chamber of Commerce and Visitors Bureau,** 581 Dolliver St., Pismo Beach, CA 93449 (☎ **800/443-7778** in California, or 805/773-4382), is open Monday through Friday from 9:30am to 5pm, Saturday 10am to 4pm, and Sunday noon to 4pm, or you can peruse their information on the Internet at **http://webmill.com/pismo.**

WHAT TO SEE & DO
SEEING THE BUTTERFLIES

From late November through February, tens of thousands of migrating monarch butterflies take up residence in the area's Eucalyptus and Monterey Pine tree groves. The colorful butterflies form dense clusters on the trees, each hanging with its wings over the one below it, providing warmth and shelter for the entire group. During the monarchs' stay, Pismo State Beach naturalists conduct 45-minute narrative walks every Saturday and Sunday at 11am and 2pm. The majority of the "butterfly trees" are located on Calif. 1, between Pismo Beach and Grover Beach, to the south. Call **805/772-2694** for tour information.

BEACHES

Beaches in Pismo are exceptionally wide, making them some of the best in the state for sunning and playing. The beach north of Grand Avenue is popular with families and well suited to jogging and strolling. North of Wadsworth Street, the coast becomes dramatically rugged as it rambles northward to Shell Beach and Pirates Cove. Some areas of the beach are open to ATVs and automobiles.

OUTDOOR ACTIVITIES

CLAMMING　Pismo Beach was one of the most famous places in America for clamming, before the clam population was depleted almost to extinction. Government intervention has saved the clams, and you're now permitted to pick them up in limited numbers directly from the sand. Clams must measure at least $4^1/2$ inches in diameter, and catches are limited to 10; you'll need to dig down about a foot to find them. Clam forks can be rented at **Pismo Bob's True Value Hardware,** 930 Price St. (☎ **805/773-6245**) for $5 per day.

FISHING　No license is required to drop a line from Pismo Pier. Catches here are largely bottom fish like red snapper and ling cod. There's a bait and tackle shop on the pier.

HIKING　You can trek along the Guadalupe-Nipomo Dunes year-round. This 18-mile strip of coastline 20 minutes south of Pismo has the highest beach dunes in the West. It's a great place for hiking and observing native plants and birds, including the California brown pelican, one of 200 species that migrate here each year.

HORSEBACK RIDING　**Livery Stables,** 1207 Silver Spur Place (☎ **805/489-8100**), in Oceano (about 5 minutes south of Pismo Beach), is one of the very few places in the state that rents horses for riding on the beach. These are not guided rides; you rent the horses for $15 per hour and go at your own pace.

WHERE TO STAY
DOUBLES FOR $80 OR LESS

The Clamdigger. 150 Hinds Ave., Pismo Beach, CA 93449. ☎ **805/773-2342.** 10 studio cabins, one 1-bedroom cottage, 4 motel suites. TV. $50–$75 cabin; cottage from $110; suites $60–$90. 7th night free. AE, DISC, DC, MC, V.

This adorable cluster of cabins just south of the pier offers a true old-style California beach vacation. Who cares about hair dryers, VCRs, and plush new furnishings? What more do you need than a one-room shack on the beach (okay, there's a bathroom, too). Each cabin welcomes you with a stained-glass ship on the door, a queen-size bed, cable TV, a kitchenette with gas stove, coffeemaker (no coffee), and basic furniture. The cottage has a queen and a hide-a-bed, a private deck, and sleeps up to four. Motel suites sleep up to six. The place has some history, too—even Valentino stayed here when he filmed on-location in the 1920s.

DOUBLES FOR $100 OR LESS

Surf Motel. 250 Main St., Pismo Beach, CA 39449. ☎ **800/472-7873** or 805/773-2070. 33 rms. TEL TV. $65–$85 double (lower on off-season weekends). Rates include continental breakfast. MC, V.

Strategically located just a half block from the beach, the Surf Motel is a good bet if you want basic, clean accommodations. All rooms have refrigerators; some have fully stocked kitchenettes, and the indoor swimming pool is open year-round. However, unless you prefer modern and new motel amenities, you'll get more of Pismo's true flavor at the rustic oceanfront cottages of the Clamdigger.

WORTH A SPLURGE

SeaVenture Resort. 100 Ocean View Avenue, Pismo Beach, CA 93449. ☎ **800/662-5545** or 805/773-4994. Fax 805/773-0924. 50 rms. MINIBAR TV TEL. $99–$249 double. Rates include continental breakfast. AE, DC, DISC, MC, V. Calif. 101 to Price St. exit. Drive west on Ocean View (at the beach).

If luxury accommodations overlooking the beach and an outdoor spa on your private deck sound like heaven to you, you can have them, and you don't have to die to get there. SeaVenture, a brand-new resort, provides the most luxurious accommodations in Pismo, most of which look directly onto the beach. Once in your room you need only to drag your tired traveling feet through the thick forest of green carpeting, past the white country furnishings, and turn on your gas fireplace to begin what promises to be a relaxing stay. Then either opt for renting a movie from the video library, schedule a massage, or simply bathe your weary bones in your own outdoor hydrotherapy spa tub. With the beach right outside your door, there's not much more you could ask for. There *is*, in fact, more provided: a wet bar, refrigerator, coffeemaker, continental breakfast delivered to your room, and a pool and restaurant on the premises. Most rooms have ocean views; many have a private balcony overlooking the beach. Other bonuses include room service from 4pm to 10pm, massage, and laundry.

WHERE TO DINE
MEALS FOR $10 OR LESS

Rosa's Italian Restaurant. 491 Price St. ☎ **805/773-0551.** Reservations recommended on weekends. Main courses $8–$12.25. AE, DISC, MC, V. Mon–Fri 11:30am–2pm and 4–9:30pm, Sat–Sun 4–10pm. ITALIAN.

Look beyond the boring decor and you'll find that Rosa's is the finest Italian American restaurant in town. It ain't Italy, but fresh bread is made on the premises, as are the ravioli, cannelloni, and other pastas. Veal Parmesan, chicken cacciatore, and the fresh seafood dishes are dependably tasty dishes, but will cost a few bucks more than the pizzas and pastas, which are mostly under $10. Children's plates will barely set you back at all; they're all under $5. There are a few tables on a small heated patio, and though there's no ocean view, the food will be a welcome change from the overly abundant local surf and turf fare.

Splash Cafe. 197 Pomeroy St. (near Pismo Pier). ☎ **805/773-4653.** Main courses $2.50–$5.75. No credit cards. Daily 10am–8pm. AMERICAN.

This beachy burger stand, with a short menu and just a few tables, gets high marks for its excellent clam chowder, served in a sourdough bread bowl. Fish and chips, burgers, hot dogs, and sandwiches are also available; almost everything is under $5.

MEALS FOR $20 OR LESS

PierSide Seafood. In the Boardwalk Plaza Mall, 175 Pomeroy St. ☎ **805/773-4411.** Reservations recommended on weekends. Main courses $9–$20. AE, D, MC, V. Daily 10am–11pm summer; 11am–9pm winter. AMERICAN.

If food here is simply decent and the menu offers the same fare as everyone else in town (surf and turf), why bother writing it up? Well, first of all, this two-story restaurant is practically on top of Pismo Pier, which provides it with an unparalleled dining view. Secondly, the decor is fun: Mermaids and surfboards hang overhead and an array of trinkets and an ocean mural keep the eye wandering and interested throughout the meal. Finally, on a sunny day, there's no better place to kick back than at one of the outdoor umbrella-topped tables. The place is *tourist maximus*, but then again, what place in this area isn't?

5 En Route to Santa Barbara: The Santa Ynez Valley

The compact and beautiful Santa Ynez Valley (surrounded by mountains of the same name) is located between San Luis Obispo and Santa Barbara. The valley is home to five small towns: Buellton, Santa Ynez, Los Olivos, Ballard, and Solvang, the region's top tourist draw.

SOLVANG

Founded by Danish Americans in 1911, the town of Solvang ("sunny valley") has cashed in on its Scandinavian heritage by making it the lure for a popular and tacky tourist trap. The original intention of Solvang's founders was to preserve the townspeople's heritage. As the town's popularity grew, however, cultural celebration became its primary economic engine. The "quaint" village now looks as if Disney did Denmark, with white-and-blue fringed buildings housing hokey import shops and numerous pastry and pancake restaurants. Solvang's immense popularity has cost the town its charm. A trip here wouldn't ordinarily be worth going out of your way, but since it's well located, right on an inland shortcut, it wouldn't hurt much to arrive in time for lunch; despite Solvang's tackiness, its bakeries are still among California's very best.

To get there from U.S. 101 south, turn east (left) onto Calif. 246 at Buellton; the trip to Solvang is a well-marked 20-minute drive along an extremely scenic two lane road. From Santa Barbara, take U.S. 101 to Calif. 154, a truly breathtaking 45-minute drive over San Marcos Pass.

OTHER VALLEY ATTRACTIONS

✪ **Cachuma Lake Recreation Area.** Santa Barbara County Parks Department, Star Route, Santa Barbara, CA 93105. ☎ **805/688-4658.** On Calif. 154, between Solvang and Santa Barbara.

Cachuma Lake is both the primary town reservoir for Santa Barbara and a particularly beautiful habitat for the American bald eagle. In the winter months, dozens of bald eagles migrate here from as far north as Alaska, where food is plentiful for them and human development is minimal. Over the last few years, some have chosen to remain at Cachuma to raise their young. Perching on treetops and branches overlooking the water, the eagles hunt for trout and waterfowl. Other migratory birds also come in large numbers, including loons, white pelicans, and Canada geese.

You can simply drive into the Recreation Area and go birding on your own, or you can board the *Osprey* (☎ 805/568-2460), a 48-foot boat with viewing platforms at both the bow and stern. Two-hour Eagle Cruises are offered from November through February, Wednesday to Sunday at 10am; additional tours are offered on Fridays and Saturdays at 2pm. Wildlife Cruises, from which you can view deer, bobcats, and mountain lions, are offered from March through October on Fridays at 3pm, Saturdays at 10am and 3pm, and Sundays at 10am. All cruises cost $10 for adults, $5 for children under 12; reservations are recommended.

Old Mission Santa Ines. 1760 Mission Dr., Solvang. ☎ **805/688-4815.** $3 donation requested. Summer, Mon–Sat 9am–7pm, Sun 1:30–7pm; winter, Mon–Sat 9am–4:30pm, Sun 1:30–4:30pm. From downtown Solvang, take Calif. 246 one mile east to Mission Dr.

Founded in 1804, this perfectly restored mission is by far the oldest structure in town. The main building contains early Native American artifacts, and relics once belonging to the missionaries. Like many other missions, Santa Ines still maintains an active congregation; the church, chapel, museum, and grounds are open to the public.

WHERE TO STAY

There's no real reason to stay here since there are so many great places to stay just to the north and south, but if you've just got to wake up here to eat more pastries, try Solvang's comfortable **Royal Scandinavian Inn** (☎ **800/624-5572** or 805/688-8000) or the good-value **Motel 6** (☎ **800/466-8356** or 805/688-7797), just west of Solvang in Buellton.

6 Santa Barbara

Between the Santa Ynez Mountains and the Pacific, charming, spoiled Santa Barbara is coddled by wooded mountains, caressed by baby breakers, and sheltered from tempestuous seas by rocky offshore islands. And it's just far enough from Los Angeles to make the Big City seem at once remote and accessible. There are few employment opportunities and real estate is expensive, so demographics have favored college students and rich retirees, thought of by the locals as the "almost wed and almost dead."

Downtown Santa Barbara is distinctive for its Spanish-Mediterranean architecture; all the structures sport matching red-tile roofs. But it wasn't always this way. Santa Barbara had a thriving Native American Chumash population for hundreds, if not thousands, of years. The European era began in the late 18th century, around a Presidio (fort) that's been reconstructed in its original spot. The earliest architectural hodgepodge was destroyed in 1925 by a powerful earthquake that leveled the business district. Out of the rubble rose the Spanish-Mediterranean town of today, a stylish planned community that continues to rigidly enforce its strict building codes.

ESSENTIALS

GETTING THERE   U.S. 101 runs right through Santa Barbara; it's the fastest, and most direct, route from north or south (two hours outside Los Angeles and six hours from San Francisco).

The **Santa Barbara Municipal Airport** (☎ 805/967-7111) is located in Goleta, about 10 minutes north of downtown Santa Barbara. Airlines serving Santa Barbara include **American Eagle** (☎ 800/433-7300), **Skywest/Delta** (☎ 800/453-9417), **United** (☎ 800/241-6522), and **USAir Express** (☎ 800/428-4322). **Yellow Cab** (☎ 805/965-5111) and other metered taxis line up outside the terminal; the fare is about $20 to downtown.

Amtrak (☎ 800/USA-RAIL) offers daily service to Santa Barbara. Trains arrive and depart from the **Santa Barbara Rail Station,** 209 State St. (☎ 805/963-1015); fares can be as low as $20 from Los Angeles.

ORIENTATION   State Street, the city's primary commercial thoroughfare, is the geographic center of town. It ends at Stearns Wharf and Cabrillo Street; the latter runs along the ocean and separates the city's beaches from touristy hotels and restaurants.

VISITOR INFORMATION   The **Santa Barbara Visitor Information Center,** 1 Santa Barbara St., Santa Barbara, CA 93101 (☎ 800/927-4688 to order a free destination guide, or 805/965-3021) is on the ocean, at the corner of Cabrillo Street. They distribute maps, literature, an events calendar, and excellent advice. Be sure to ask for their handy guide to places of interest and public parking. The office is open Monday through Saturday from 9am to 4pm and Sunday from 10am to 4pm; it closes one hour earlier in winter and one hour later in July and August. A second **Visitor Information Center,** open Monday through Friday from 9am to 5pm, is located at 504 State St., in the heart of downtown. Be sure to pick up a free copy of *Things to See and Do* at one of the offices.

Also make sure you pick up a copy of *The Independent,* an excellent free weekly paper with a comprehensive listing of events. It's available in shops and from sidewalk racks around town.

SEEING THE SIGHTS

County Courthouse. 1100 Anacapa St. ☎ **805/962-6464.** Free admission. Mon–Fri 8am–5pm, Sat, Sun, and holidays 10am–5pm. Free tours Mon–Sat 2pm and Wed–Fri 10:30am.

The courthouse is the most flamboyant example of Spanish-Mediterranean architecture in the entire city. Built in 1929 to mimic a much older style, the ornate courthouse is Santa Barbara's literal and figurative centerpiece. There are great views of the ocean, mountains, and the city's terra-cotta tile roofs from the observation deck atop the clock tower. A free guided tour is offered on Wednesday and Friday at 10:30am and Monday through Saturday at 2pm.

Moreton Bay Fig Tree. Chapala and Montecito sts.

Santa Barbara's best-known tree has a branch-span that would cover half a football field, and its roots run under more than an acre of ground. It has been estimated that well over 10,000 people could stand in the tree's shade. Planted in 1877, it's a native of Moreton Bay in eastern Australia. The tree is related to both the fig tree and the rubber tree, but produces neither figs nor rubber. It is, hands down, the largest of its kind in the world. Once in danger of being leveled (for a proposed gas station) and later threatened by excavation for nearby U.S. 101, the revered tree is now protected as a historical landmark and is the unofficial home of Santa Barbara's homeless community.

Downtown Santa Barbara

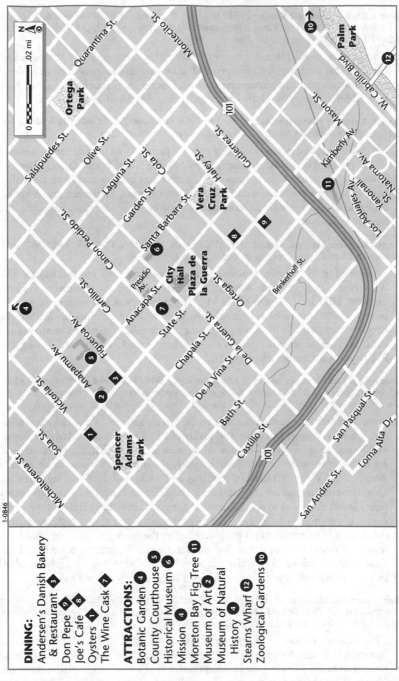

DINING:
Andersen's Danish Bakery & Restaurant 3
Don Pepe 9
Joe's Cafe 8
Oysters 1
The Wine Cask 7

ATTRACTIONS:
Botanic Garden 4
County Courthouse 5
Historical Museum 6
Mission 4
Moreton Bay Fig Tree 11
Museum of Art 2
Museum of Natural History 4
Stearns Wharf 12
Zoological Gardens 10

1-0846

Santa Barbara Botanic Garden. 1212 Mission Canyon Rd. ☎ **805/682-4726.** Admission $3 adults, $2 children 13–19 and seniors (over 64), $1 children 5–12, children under 5 free. Mon–Fri 9am–5pm, Sat–Sun 9am–6pm.

The gardens, about 1½ miles north of the mission, encompass 65 acres of native trees, shrubs, cacti, and wild flowers, and more than five miles of trails. They're at their aromatic peak just after spring showers. Docent tours are offered daily at 2pm, with additional tours on Thursday, Saturday, and Sunday at 10:30am.

Santa Barbara Historical Museum. 136 E. De La Guerra St. ☎ **805/966-1601.** Free admission; donation requested. Tues–Sat 10am–5pm, Sun noon–5pm.

Local-lore exhibits include late 19th-century paintings of the California missions by Edwin Deakin; a 16th-century carved Spanish coffer from Majorca, home of Junípero Serra; and objects from the Chinese community that once flourished here, including a magnificent carved shrine from the turn of the century. A knowledgeable docent leads an interesting free tour every Wednesday, Saturday, and Sunday at 1:30pm.

Santa Barbara Mission. Laguna and Los Olivos sts. ☎ **805/682-4713** or 805/682-4151. Admission $3 adults, free for children under 16. Daily 9am–5pm.

Established in 1786 by Fr. Junípero Serra and built by the Chumash Indians, this is a very rare example of the blending of Indian and Hispanic spirituality in physical form. Called the "Queen of the Missions" for its twin bell towers and graceful beauty, this hilltop mission overlooks the town and the Channel Islands beyond. Brochures are available in six languages and docent-guided tours can be arranged in advance ($1 extra per person). See "The Missions of the Central Coast" driving tour in Chapter 4 for further details.

Santa Barbara Museum of Art. 1130 State St. ☎ **805/963-4364.** Admission $4 adults, $3 seniors (over 65), $1.50 children 6–16, children under 6 free. Free for everyone Thurs and the first Sun of each month. Tues–Sat 11am–5pm, Thurs 11am–9pm, Sun noon–5pm.

A trip here feels like an exclusive visit to the private galleries of a wealthy art collector. Works by Monet and other midquality oils by Dalí, Picasso, Matisse, Chagall, and Rousseau are displayed on a rotating basis in rooms that, for the most part, are ample, airy, and well lit. Quantitatively, the museum's strengths lie in early 20th-century Western American paintings and 19th- and 20th-century Asian art. Qualitatively, the best are the antiquities and Chinese ceramics collections. Many pieces are often on loan to other museums, but good temporary exhibits show a high degree of reciprocity. Some awkward arrangements don't always make sense, and lighting could be improved on the placards. For the most part, though, SBMA is a jewel of a museum. Free docent-led tours are given Tuesday to Sunday at 1pm. Focus tours are held on Wednesday and Saturday at noon. A new wing is being added in 1997, which will include more galleries, a larger gift shop, and a cafe.

Santa Barbara Museum of Natural History. 2559 Puesta del Sol Rd. (2 blocks uphill from the mission). ☎ **805/682-4711.** Admission $5 adults, $4 seniors and teens, $3 children. Mon–Sat 9am–5pm, Sun and holidays 10am–5pm.

This museum focuses on the study and interpretation of Pacific Coast natural history, which includes mammals, birds, marine life, plants, and insects and displays ranging from fossil ferns to the complete skeleton of a blue whale. Native American history is emphasized in exhibits that include basketry, textiles, and a full-size replica of a Chumash canoe. An adjacent planetarium projects sky shows every Saturday and Sunday.

Santa Barbara Zoological Gardens. 500 Ninos Dr. ☎ **805/962-5339,** or 805/962-6310 for a recording. Admission $5 adults, $3 seniors and children 2–12, children under 2 free. Daily 10am–5pm; last admission is 1 hour before closing. Closed Thanksgiving, Christmas.

When you're driving around the bend on Cabrillo Beach Boulevard, look up—you might spot the head of a giraffe poking up through the palms. This is a thoroughly charming, pint-sized place, where all 700 animals can be seen in about 30 minutes. Most of the animals live in natural, open settings. The zoo has a children's Discovery Area, a miniature train ride, and a small carousel. The picnic areas (complete with barbecue pits) are underused and especially recommendable.

Stearns Wharf. At the end of State St.

In addition to a small collection of second-rate shops, attractions, and restaurants, the city's 1872 vintage pier offers terrific inland views and good drop-line fishing. The Dolphin Fountain at the foot of the wharf was created by local artist Bud Bottoms for the city's 1982 bicentennial.

BEACHES

Santa Barbara has an array of beaches perfect for stretching out on a towel, hitting around a volleyball (a very popular sport around here), or frolicking seaside. Two good choices are **Hendry's Beach,** which is located at the end of Cliff Drive and is popular with families, boogie-boarders who come to ride the excellent beach breaks, and sunset strollers; and **Cabrillo Beach,** a wide swath of clean, white sand that hosts beach umbrellas, sand-castle builders, and spirited volleyball games. A grassy, parklike median keeps the noise of busy Cabrillo Boulevard away. On Sundays, local artists set up shop beneath the palms. **East Beach,** by Stearns Wharf, is not incredibly interesting, and you'll have to pay $5 to park your car unless you find parking on the street. It is, however, a great place to stroll on Sundays when dozens of arts and crafts vendors exhibit their wares.

OUTDOOR PURSUITS

BICYCLING   A relatively flat, palm-lined 2-mile coastal pathway runs along the beach and is perfect for biking. More adventurous riders can peddle through town, up to the mission, or to Montecito, the next town over. The best mountain bike trail begins at the end of Tunnel Road and climbs up along a paved fire road before turning into a dirt trail to the mountain top.

Beach Rentals, 22 State St. (☎ **805/966-6733**), rents well-maintained one-speeds. They also have tandem bikes and surrey cycles that can hold as many as four adults and two children. Rates vary depending on equipment. Bring an ID (driver's license or passport) to expedite your rental. They're open daily from 8am to dusk.

GOLF   At the **Santa Barbara Golf Club,** 3500 McCaw Ave., at Las Positas Road (☎ **805/687-7087**), there's a great 6,009-yard, 18-hole course and driving range. Unlike many municipal courses, the Santa Barbara Golf Course is well maintained and was designed to present a moderate challenge for the average golfer. Greens fees are $24 Monday to Friday and $28 on weekends ($17 for seniors). Optional carts rent for $20 for 18 holes, $10 for nine.

HIKING   The hills and mountains surrounding Santa Barbara have excellent hiking trails. One of my favorites begins at the end of Tunnel Road. Take Mission Canyon Road past the mission, turn right onto Foothill Road, and take the first left onto Mission Canyon Drive. Bear left onto Tunnel Road and park at the end (where all the other cars are). You can buy a trail map at the Santa Barbara Visitor Information Center.

HORSEBACK RIDING   Several area stables rent horses, including **Circle Bar B Ranch,** 1800 Refugio Rd. (☎ **805/968-3901**), and Rancho Oso, Paradise Road, off Calif. 154 (☎ **805/964-8985**).

SKATING   The paved beach path that runs along Santa Barbara's waterfront is perfect for skating. **Beach Rentals,** 22 State St. (☎ **805/966-6733**), located nearby, rents both in-line and conventional roller skates. The $5 per hour fee includes wrist and knee pads.

SPORT FISHING, DIVE CRUISES & WHALE WATCHING   **Sea Landing,** at the foot of Bath Street and Cabrillo Boulevard (☎ **805/963-3564**), makes regular sport fishing runs with specialized boats. They also offer a wide variety of other fishing and diving cruises. Food and drink are served on board, and rods and tackle are available for rent. Rates vary according to the excursion; call for reservations.

Whale-watching cruises are offered from February through April, when the California gray whale makes its migratory journey from Baja California to Alaska. Tours are $24 for adults and $14 for children; sightings of large marine mammals are guaranteed.

SHOPPING

State Street from the beach to Victoria Street is the city's main thoroughfare and has the largest concentration of shops. Many specialize in T-shirts and postcards, but there are a number of boutiques as well. If you get tired of strolling, hop on one of the electric shuttle buses (25¢) that run up and down State Street at regular intervals.

Also check out **Brinkerhoff Avenue** (off Cota Street, between Chapala and De La Vina streets), Santa Barbara's "antique alley"; most shops are open Tuesday to Sunday 11am to 5pm. **El Paseo** (814 State St.) is a picturesque shopping arcade reminiscent of an old Spanish street. Built around an 1827 adobe home, the mall is lined with charming shops and art galleries. Don't count on any great steals here, however.

WHERE TO STAY

Before you even begin calling around for reservations, keep in mind that Santa Barbara's accommodations are expensive, especially during summer. Then decide whether you'd like to stay beachside (even more expensive) or downtown; the town is small, but not small enough to happily stroll between the two areas. There is, however a shuttle that will cart you back and forth.

Hot Spots Accommodations, 36 State St., Santa Barbara, CA 93101 (☎ **805/564-1637**), is a one-stop shop for hotel and B&B rooms that can help you find a room in your price range. There's no charge for their services. Significantly discounted rates are often available at the last minute, when hotels need to fill their rooms.

Another option is **Accommodations Reservations Service** (☎ **800/292-2222**), a company that books rooms along California's coast from Oxnard to Monterey. The service is free and has information on all price ranges.

In addition to those listed below, other highly recommendable, moderately priced accommodations are offered at the **Best Western Encina Lodge and Suites** (☎ **800/526-2282** or 805/682-7277) and **Tropicana Inn and Suites** (☎ **800/468-1988** or 805/966-2219).

DOUBLES FOR $60 OR LESS

Hotel State Street. 121 State St. (one block from the beach), Santa Barbara, CA 93101 ☎ **805/966-6586.** Fax 805/962-8459. 51 rms without bath, 2 rms with toilet, 1 rm with full bath. TV. Double in winter $30–$50, summer $40–$75. Rates include continental breakfast. AE, MC, V. Free parking.

Goleta

Young travelers and Europeans fill this hotel in the summer, but it's clean and well kept enough to make any budget traveler rest easy. The hotel makes an effort to be homey and stylish while maintaining its cheap rates by providing rooms with firm mattresses, a sink and hand towels, and prints on the walls. The feel here is a little reminiscent of a boarding house, but that's half the fun—imagine the worldly people you'll meet on your way to the shower. Extra bonuses include a continental breakfast of sweet rolls, coffee, tea, and fruit, as well as free parking, and a one-block stroll to East Beach. Phones have yet to be installed in rooms, but they're working on it. The only other drawback is that trains pass nearby and blow their whistles (it can be quite loud); they usually quiet down after 10pm, but have been known to wake folks from time to time, and can start up again as early as 7am.

DOUBLES FOR $100 OR LESS

All the best buys fill up fast in the summer months, so be sure to reserve your room well in advance. This is true even if you're just planning to stay at the nice, reliable **Motel 6** (☎ **800/466-8356** or 805/564-1392) near the beach or the good-value **Sandpiper Lodge** (☎ **805/687-5326**) just a little farther away.

Casa del Mar. 18 Bath St., Santa Barbara, CA 93101. ☎ **800/433-3097** or 805/963-4418. Fax 805/966-4240. 14 rms, 7 suites. TEL TV. $79–$154 double; suite from $114. Extra persons $10. Rates include continental breakfast and wine & cheese social. Midweek and corporate discounts available. $10 extra per pet. AE, DC, DISC, MC, V. Free parking. From U.S. 101 north, take the Cabrillo exit, turn left onto Cabrillo, and head toward the beach. Bath is the second street on right after the wharf. From U.S. 101 south take the Castillo exit, turn right on Castillo, left on Cabrillo, and left at Bath.

Very similar to the Franciscan Inn and just a half block away (even closer to the beach), Casa del Mar is another good-value motel with one and two room suites. Decor is old Spanish Mediterranean with a mishmash of furnishings. Many rooms have kitchenettes, refrigerators, and stoves. The Jacuzzi here stays open half an hour later than the Franciscan's.

ⓢ Franciscan Inn. 109 Bath St. (at Mason St.), Santa Barbara, CA 93101. ☎ **805/963-8845.** Fax 805/564-3295. 53 rms, 25 suites. TEL TV. $65–$99 double; suites from $85. Additional person $8 extra. Rates include continental breakfast. AE, CB, DC, MC, V. Free parking.

One of the best beachside bargains can be found one block from the shore at the Franciscan. The exterior looks like a motel, and inside the rooms are a quirky combination of country pine furnishings and floral and plaid prints. In some cases, the decor just doesn't work, but the immaculate, recently renovated rooms and the price more than make up for it. Several rooms have fully equipped kitchenettes and/or balconies, and most bathrooms come with a tub. All have coffeemakers, computer jacks, and VCRs, and hair dryers are available upon request. Suites come complete with a living room, a separate kitchen, and sleeping quarters for up to four adults; one has a fireplace. Breakfast, afternoon appetizers, and a complimentary newspaper are included in the price, as is the use of the heated outdoor pool, Jacuzzi, and coin-operated laundry. Reservations should be made well in advance, especially for May through September.

Mount View Inn. 3055 De La Vina St. (at State St.), Santa Barbara, CA 93105. ☎ **805/687-6636.** 34 rms. A/C TEL TV. Late Sept–May, $60–$75 double. June–early Sept, $75–$87 double. 2-night minimum on weekends. Rates include continental breakfast. AE, CB, DC, MC, V. Free parking.   *1-805-964-3596*

It may be a ways from downtown action and on a busy street corner, but Mount View's price and amenities make it worth considering. The very clean rooms are arranged motel-style, decorated in an attempt at brightness (fresh flowers, lace

motel 6 State Street   1-805-682-5400

curtains), and have firm mattresses, a refrigerator, and a table and chairs. Bathrooms are small, and some of the furniture looks a little weathered; but there is a pool, and rates include a continental breakfast, which is served in the lobby.

Orange Tree Inn. 1920 State St., Santa Barbara, CA 93101. ☎ **800/LEM-ORNG** or 805/ 569-1521. 44 rms, 2 suites. A/C TEL TV. $65–$150 double; suites from $90. AAA, AARP, and corporate discounts available. AE, DISC, MC, V. Free parking.

I'd prefer to stay by the beach, but if you want cheap downtown accommodations, you're safe with the Orange Tree. Don't get too excited, though. It is a motel, after all. Still, rooms are newly renovated and have new carpets, bedspreads, and TVs. Most have a balcony or patio, but only some have bathtubs. Guests also get free local calls and use of the pool.

WORTH A SPLURGE

✪ **Bath Street Inn.** 1720 Bath St. (north of Valerio St.), Santa Barbara, CA 93101. ☎ **800/ 341-BATH,** 800/549-BATH in California, or 805/682-9680. 12 rms. TEL TV. $95–$175 double. Up to 25% off midweek. Rates include breakfast. AE, MC, V.

This is one of the cutest, most meticulously cared for B&Bs I've ever seen. The minute I walked in, a gracious innkeeper guided me to the redwood patio for a glimpse of an amazing wisteria canopy in bloom (lucky guests can have breakfast beneath the flowers). I was then treated to fresh-baked cookies, which are served with tea and wine each afternoon. After my snack, I wandered from room to room, astonished by the exquisite details of each nook and cranny throughout the three-story Victorian (two unique features include a semicircular "eyelid" balcony and a hipped roof). Each adorable (and immaculate) room is intimately and individually decorated with antiques, colorful wall paper, fresh flowers, and a private bath. Some include a Jacuzzi and/or a VCR. Common areas are equally sweet and include a third-floor reading nook with a VCR (there's a video library downstairs). No smoking is allowed in the house.

WHERE TO DINE
MEALS FOR $10 OR LESS

Andersen's Danish Bakery and Restaurant. 1106 State St. (near Figueroa St.). ☎ **805/ 962-5085.** Reservations recommended on weekends. Breakfast $4–$8; lunch $5–$8. No credit cards. Wed–Mon 8am–8pm. DANISH.

Remember how ice cream parlors used to look? Well, pink and frilly does not describe this bakery's sweets, but rather the old-style decor of this family restaurant. Grandma will feel at home here, and kids won't have a problem finding something they like on the menu (especially when it comes to dessert). Authentically Danish Ms. Andersen greets you herself (when she's not baking) and offers substantial (and cheap!) portions of New York steak, chicken or crab salad, and an array of other edibles (including an honest-to-goodness smorgasbord). Seating provides great State Street people-watching from both indoor and outdoor tables.

Follow Your Heart Natural Foods Market and Cafe. 19 South Milpas St. ☎ **805/966-2251.** Sandwiches and salads $4.50–$5.50. MC, V. Daily 9am–8pm store, 9am–9pm cafe. DELI.

This supermarket is a health freak's dream come true. Everything wholesome you can possibly eat can be found here (including sea kelp snacks and sugarless candy). The deli features dozens of vegetarian options, as well as soups, pasta salads, pizzas, calzones, sandwiches, stuffed potatoes, Mexican dishes, veggie burgers, cookies and breads, smoothies, and a vast selection of breakfast options—all of which you can take to go. The cafe, a casual room connected to the store, offers the same fare, and nothing on the menu is over $6.95. Beware of pasta salads with oil-based dressing: They tend to be too greasy.

Joe's Cafe. 536 State St. (at Cota St.). ☎ **805/966-4638.** Reservations recommended. Pasta $4.50–$6.50, most main courses $9–$11, steaks $12.50–$18.25. AE, DISC, MC, V. Mon–Thurs 11am–11:30pm, Fri–Sat 11am–12:30am, Sun noon–9pm. AMERICAN.

Joe's may not be the hottest gourmet eatery in town, but it's been around so long (since 1928), it seems that coming here is a generationally inherited habit with locals and college students alike. Maybe it's because Joe's is dependable and reasonably priced, or perhaps it's the strong drinks served at the full bar. Whatever the reason, folks seem to love the hunting lodge-cum-picnic ambience and the fare you'd expect from such an old-school establishment. There are plenty of red meat dishes on the menu (five different steak options), Southern-fried chicken, and a shrimp dish and garden burger thrown in for good measure. Meals come with a barrage of side dishes. Steaks will cost you upward of $20, but all the other main courses are closer to $10—and talk about a real bargain, how about a big plate of pasta for $6? Weekends here are especially popular with partying students.

La Super-Rica Taqueria. 622 N. Milpas St. (between Cota and Ortega sts.). ☎ **805/963-4940.** Reservations not accepted. Main courses $3–$6. No credit cards. Sun–Thurs 11am–9:30pm, Fri–Sat 11am–10pm. MEXICAN.

Following celebrity chef Julia Child's lead, aficionados have deemed this place the state's best Mexican eatery. Excellent soft tacos are the restaurant's real forte. Unfortunately, portions can be quite small—you have to order two or three items in order to satisfy the average appetite. There's nothing grand about La Super-Rica except the food; you might want to get your order to go and take it to the beach.

Main Squeeze Cafe and Juice Bar. 138 East Canon Perdido St. ☎ **805/966-5365.** $4.35–$7.25. No credit cards. Mon–Fri 11am–10pm, Sat–Sun 10am–10pm. DELI.

Health food has come a long way since wheatgrass juice and alfalfa sprouts, and you can experience its evolution here at this quintessential no-nonsense, health-conscious California cafe. The fare goes far beyond rabbit food and includes a variety of substantial sandwiches and soups, soft tacos, and special plates, as well as a good selection of smoothies. Hard-core carnivores who crave something heavier than chicken beware: The only burgers you'll find on the menu are of the soy or garden variety. This place is less hippielike than many other cafes in town. Diners order at the counter and then grab a table inside or out.

The Natural Cafe and Juice Bar. 508 State St., Santa Barbara, CA 93101. ☎ **805/962-9494.** Main courses $4.50–$6.25. No credit cards. Sun–Thurs 10am–10pm, Fri–Sat 10am–11pm.

Groovy granola types mix with tourists, students, and other locals at this casual, very healthy cafe (there's plenty of 'em in this town). Voted best lunch and health food in a readers' poll, fare runs the good-for-you gamut, including nine types of salad ($5.25 and under), sandwiches (tofu hot dog anyone?), and heftier servings such as vegetarian lasagna, chicken enchiladas, and fish tacos. Most menu items hover around $5, and a smoothie will run you $2.50. You can pull up a worn blue chair inside amid dried flowers and hardwood floors, but the best seating is outside on State Street where you can people-watch. Save room for a huge, moist chunk of carrot cake and a cappuccino. Afterward, you can take your satiated self next door and stimulate your soul at the way-groovy Super Natural vitamin, herb, and gift store.

State & A Bar and Grill. Corner of State St. and Anapamu. ☎ **805/966-1010.** Reservations not accepted. Main courses $4.95–$10.95. AE, DISC, MC, V. Food daily 11am–midnight, bar open until 2am. AMERICAN.

Perfect for families or young folks in search of a cheap brew, State & A is a casual joint that's infamous for its huge portions and festive glass-encased street-front patio (there's indoor seating, as well). The menu includes an array of appetizers (nachos, chicken strips, hot wings), hefty salads (including a grilled mahi, Indonesian, and classic Caesar), Southwestern fare such as fajitas and enchiladas, burgers, steak, and pasta. Cocktailers especially appreciate happy hour, Monday through Friday from 3:30 to 6:30pm, where pints pour for $1.25 and well drinks, $2.25.

MEALS FOR $20 OR LESS

Brophy Bros. Clam Bar and Restaurant. Yacht Basin and marina (at Harbor Way). ☎ **805/966-4418.** Reservations not accepted. Main courses $9–$16. AE, MC, V. Sun–Thurs 11am–10pm, Fri–Sat 11am–11pm. SEAFOOD.

First-class seafood combined with an unbeatable view of the marina makes dining here a favorite for both tourists and locals. Dress is casual, service is excellent, portions are huge, and everything on the menu is good. Favorites include New England clam chowder, cioppino (California fish stew), and any one of an assortment of seafood salads. The scampi is consistently good, as is all the fresh fish. A nice assortment of beers and wines is available. *But be forewarned:* The wait at this small place can be up to two hours on a weekend night.

✪ **Montecito Cafe.** 1295 Coast Village Rd. (off Olive Mill Rd.). ☎ **805/969-3392.** Reservations recommended. Main courses $6.95–$12.95. AE, MC, V. Daily 11:30am–2:30pm, 5:30–10pm. CALIFORNIA NOUVEAUX.

Overlooking Montecito's shopping street, the light and airy Montecito Cafe provides diners with a high-quality California culinary experience at an affordable price (some say it's the best value in town). Menu items include broiled oysters with lemon cream and goat cheese, a walnut-filled pork chop with lemon herb sauce, and penne pasta with scallops, shrimp, and mussels in a saffron broth. The petite dining room itself is pleasantly simple, with well-set tables, a wall of windows, plants, a small fountain, and original art. It's the perfect place to impress a date.

✪ **Pan e Vino.** 1482 E. Valley Rd., Montecito. ☎ **805/969-9274.** Reservations required. Pastas $8–$10; meat and fish dishes $11–$18. AE, MC, V. Mon–Sat 11:30am–9:30pm, Sun 5:30–9:30pm. ITALIAN.

The perfect Italian trattoria, Pan e Vino offers food as authentic as you'd find in Rome. The simplest dish, spaghetti topped with basil-tomato sauce, is so delicious it's hard to understand why diners would want to occupy their taste buds with more complicated concoctions. But this kitchen is capable of almost anything. A whole artichoke appetizer, steamed, chilled, and filled with breading and marinated tomatoes, is absolutely fantastic. Pasta puttenesca, with tomatoes, anchovies, black olives and capers, is always tops. Pan e Vino gets high marks for its terrific food, attentive service, and casual atmosphere. Although many diners prefer to eat outside on the intimate patio, some of the best tables are in the charming, cluttered dining room.

Your Place. 22A N. Milpas St. (at Mason St.). ☎ **805/966-5151.** Reservations recommended. Main courses $7–$13. AE, DC, MC, V. Tues–Thurs and Sun 11am–10pm, Fri–Sat 11am–11pm. THAI.

There is an unusually large number of Thai restaurants in Santa Barbara, but when locals argue about which one is best, Your Place invariably ranks high on the list.

Traditional dishes are prepared with the freshest ingredients and represent a wide cross section of Thai cuisine. It's best to begin with tom kah kai, a hot-and-sour chicken soup with coconut milk and mushrooms, ladled out of a tableside hotpot, enough for two or more. Siamese duckling, a top main dish, is prepared with sautéed vegetables, mushrooms, and ginger sauce. Like other dishes, it can be made mild, medium, hot, or very hot.

WORTH A SPLURGE

✪ **Wine Cask.** 813 Anacapa, in El Paseo center. ☎ **805/966-9463.** Reservations recommended. Main courses lunch $7.95–$11.95; dinner $16.95–$27. AE, DC, MC, V. Mon–Thurs 10am–9pm, Fri–Sat 10am–10pm, Sun 10am–9pm. ITALIAN.

Take a 15-year-old wine shop, a large dining room with a big stone fireplace, a few large abstract paintings, a historic hand-stenciled ceiling decorated with gold leaf, and outstanding Italian fare. Mix them with an attractive staff and clientele and you've got the Wine Cask, the most popular upscale dining spot in Santa Barbara. Whether you go for the dining room (request a fireside table for romance) or patio dining (yes, there are heat lamps), you'll be treated to such heavenly creations as lamb sirloin with twice-baked au gratin potatoes, green beans, baby carrots, port wine and a roasted garlic demiglaze; potato and proscuitto-wrapped local halibut with sautéed spinach and shiitake mushrooms, cioppino sauce and rouille; or grilled marinated chicken breast in a red-wine reduction with prosciutto, wild mushrooms, fresh rosemary and sage. The wine list reads like a novel, lists more than 1,000 wines (ranging from $14 to $1400), and has deservedly received the *Wine Spectator* award for excellence. To avoid breaking the bank, come for lunch. There's also a happy hour at the beautiful maple bar from 4 to 6pm daily, which offers half-price wine and $2 to $4 well drinks. This place is so in-the-know they sells cigars, too.

SANTA BARBARA AFTER DARK

To find out what's going on in the theater scene while you're in town, check the free weekly *Independent,* available around town.

Backstage. 18 E. Ortega. ☎ **805/730-7383.** Cover free–$7.

Santa Barbara's most cutting-edge alternative nightclub enjoys a Los Angeles–style warehouse setting and a mixed gay/straight crowd. Under high ceilings are two bars, a pool table, an indoor fountain, and one of the largest dance floors in town. Regular theme nights are interspersed with occasional live performances by local bands.

Madhouse. 434 State St. ☎ **805/962-5516.** No cover.

Young singles pack into this warehouse-cum-cocktail lounge that's eclectically decorated with Eastern rugs and interesting trinkets hanging overhead. Order a drink from one of the beautiful young bartenders or forge your way to the back room, a heated covered patio that's jazzed up with colorful hanging lamps, where there's another bar and a little extra elbow room.

Mel's. 6 W. De La Guerra St. (in the Paseo Nuevo Mall). ☎ **805/963-2211.** No cover.

This is an old drinking room dive in the heart of downtown. The compact bar attracts a good cross section of regulars.

The Wildcat Lounge. 15 W. Ortega. ☎ **805/962-7970.** No cover.

On a side street off State downtown, this small bar with retro funky decor, a CD jukebox, and a pool table keeps young local singles coming back for more.

Vintage: Central Coast

Have a penchant for Pinot Noir? Craving a Sauvignon Blanc? You don't have to go all the way to Napa for a day of picnicking among the grapes, rambling the offbeat roads, and wandering the California wineries—the Central Coast is a varietal gold mine.

Central California's dewy green hillsides and sun-kissed valleys are the perfect climate for grape growing. Though this budding wine country can't boast hundreds of wineries or as many awards as its Northern California neighbors, it's definitely coming into its own. And even if you don't know the difference between a jug of Ernest and Julio Gallo and a magnum of Dom Perignon, this region is a wonderful place to spend a relaxing day in rural California, and it's not nearly as costly as a visit to Napa or Sonoma.

There are two distinct wine regions in Central California. Close to Cambria and San Luis Obispo is the Paso Robles Wine Country area. There are more than 25 known and not-so-well-known wineries here, with more than 100 vineyards that vary in elevation from 700 to 1,900 feet. **Arciero Winery,** located at Calif. 46 East, 6 miles east of U.S. 101 (P.O. Box 1287, Paso Robles, CA 93447; ☎ 805/239-2562), is open 10am to 5pm daily and 10am to 6pm during weekends in summertime; **Bonny Doon,** located at Sycamore Farms on Calif. 46 West, 3 miles west of U.S. 101 (☎ 805/239-5614), is open from 10:30am to 5:30pm; and **Wild Horse,** located at 1437 Wild Horse Winery Court, Templeton, CA 93465 (☎ 805/434-2541), is open daily 11am to 5pm and closed most major holidays.

For information on wine events, wineries, accommodations, and a winery map, write or call the **Paso Robles Vintners and Growers Association** at P.O. Box 324, Paso Robles, CA 93447 (☎ 805/239-VINE). Also contact the **San Luis Obispo**

7 The Ojai Valley

by Stephanie Avnet

In a crescent-shaped valley between Santa Barbara and Ventura, surrounded by mountain peaks, lies Ojai (pronounced "O-high"). It's a magical place, selected by Frank Capra as Shangri-La, the legendary utopia of his classic 1936 film *Lost Horizon.* The spectacularly tranquil setting has made Ojai a mecca for artists and a particularly large population of New Age spiritualists, both drawn by the area's mystical beauty.

Life is low-key in the peaceful Ojai Valley. Perhaps the most excitement in town is during the first week of June, when the **Ojai Music Festival** draws world-renowned contemporary jazz artists to perform in Libbey Bowl amphitheater.

You'll also hear folks wax poetic about something called the "pink moment." It's a phenomenon first noticed by the earliest Indian valley dwellers, when the brilliant sunset over the nearby Pacific is reflected onto the mountainside creating an eerie and beautiful pink glow.

ESSENTIALS

GETTING THERE   The 45-minute drive south from Santa Barbara to Ojai is along two-lane Calif. 150, a beautiful road that's as curvaceous as it is stunning. From Los Angeles, take U.S. 101 north to Calif. 33, which winds through eucalyptus groves to meet Calif. 150; the trip takes about 90 minutes.

County Visitors and Conference Bureau at 1041 Chorro St., Suite E, San Luis Obispo, CA 93401 (☎ **800/634-1414** or 805/541-8000) for a free "Bounty of the County" food and wine tour map.

The Santa Ynez Mountains combined with coastal fog and ocean breezes make Santa Barbara county another prime grape-growing spot. There are more than 10,000 acres of vineyards here and dozens of wineries. The drive over the hills hovering above Santa Barbara alone makes it worth the trip. But once you hit the wine country, you'll find some well-respected wineries amid the gorgeous Central California mountain range.

You'll be best off picking up a wine country touring map, which offers information on locations, hours of operation, and picnic and touring facilities. It's free at many hotels and shops around town, including **The Wine Cask** (see Santa Barbara, "Where to Dine," above). You can also order it by mail from the Santa Barbara County Vintners Association (P.O. Box 1558, Santa Ynez, CA 93460 ☎ **800/218-0881** or 805/688-0881).

A few recommended stops include: **Fess Parker Winery,** located at 6200 Foxen Canyon Rd., Los Olivos (P.O. Box 910, Santa Ynez, CA 93460; ☎ **805/688-1545**), which is open daily 10am to 4pm; **The Gainey Vineyard,** located at 3950 East Highway 246, Santa Ynez (P.O. Box 910, Santa Ynez, CA 93460; ☎ **805/688-0558**); **Firestone Vineyard,** at 5017 Zaca Station Rd., Los Olivos (P.O. Box 244, Los Olivos, CA 93441; ☎ **805/688-3940**), which is open daily from 10am to 4pm; and **Sunstone Vineyards and Winery,** located at 125 North Refugio Rd., Santa Ynez, CA 93460 (☎ **800/313-WINE** or 805/688-WINE), which is open daily from 10am to 4pm.

VISITOR INFORMATION The **Ojai Valley Chamber of Commerce,** 338 E. Ojai Ave., Ojai, CA 93023 (☎ **805/646-8126**), distributes free area maps, brochures, and a *Visitor's Guide to the Ojai Valley,* which lists galleries and current events. Open Monday to Friday from 9:30am to 4:30pm, Saturday and Sunday 10am to 4pm.

ORIENTATION Calif. 150 is called Ojai Avenue in the town center and is the village's primary thoroughfare.

EXPLORING TOWN & VALLEY

The main appeal of the Ojai Valley is its naturally beautiful setting, which provides the perfect opportunity for the budget traveler to enjoy a day-long excursion for the price of a tank of gas. Another bargain is to camp at Lake Casitas in the foothills overlooking the valley (see below), and split your time between enjoying the town and lakeshore recreation.

When Ronald Coleman saw Shangri-La in *Lost Horizon,* he was really admiring the Ojai Valley. To visit the breathtakingly beautiful spot where Coleman stood for his view of **Shangri-La,** drive east on Ojai Avenue, up the hill, and stop at the stone bench near the top; the view is spectacular.

Residents of the Ojai Valley *love* their equine companions—miles of bridle paths are painstakingly maintained, and "horse crossing" signs are everywhere. If you'd like to explore the equestrian way, call the **Ojai Valley Inn's Ranch & Stables** (☎ 805/646-5511 ext. 456).

Ojai is home to more than 35 artists working in a variety of media; most have home studios and are represented in one of several galleries in town. The best for jewelry and smaller pieces is **HumanArts**, 310 E. Ojai Ave. (☎ 805/646-1525); they also have a home accessories annex **HumanArts Home**, 246 E. Ojai Ave. (☎ 805/646-8245). One weekend each October (the weekend of October 11th and 12th in 1997), artisans band together for an organized **Artists' Studio Tour** (☎ 805/646-8126 for information). It's fun to drive from studio to studio at your own pace, meeting various artists and perhaps purchasing some of their work. Ojai's most famous resident is world-renowned **Beatrice Wood,** who celebrated her 103rd birthday in 1996 while overseeing a traveling exhibition of her whimsical sculpture and luminous pottery.

Strolling the Spanish arcade shops downtown and the surrounding area will yield a treasure trove, including open-air used book emporium **Bart's Books,** Matilija Street (at Canada Street; ☎ 805/646-3755), an Ojai fixture for many years; **Local Hero Books/Cafe,** 254 E. Ojai Ave. (☎ 805/646-3165), carries a large selection of New Age and philosophical titles and hosts readings and musical performances.

Ojai has long been a haven for several esoteric sects of metaphysical and philosophical beliefs. The **Krotona Institute and School of Theosophy,** Calif. 33/150 (at Hermosa Road; ☎ 805/646-2653), has been in the Valley since moving from Hollywood in 1926, and visitors are welcome at their library and bookstore.

LAKE CASITAS RECREATION AREA

Incredibly beautiful Lake Casitas (☎ **805/649-2233** for information) boasts nearly 32 miles of shoreline and was the site of the 1984 Olympic canoeing and rowing events. You can rent rowboats and small powerboats year-round from the boathouse (☎ **805/649-2043**) or enjoy picnicking and camping by the lakeside. Because the lake serves as a domestic water supply, swimming is not allowed. To get there from Calif. 150, turn left onto Santa Ana Road, and follow the signs to the recreation area.

✪ WHEELER HOT SPRINGS SPA & RESTAURANT

Nestled in a canyon and shaded by rustling palms, Wheeler Hot Springs, 16825 Maricopa Hwy. (Calif. 33, 7 miles north of downtown; ☎ **800/9-WHEELER** or 805/646-8131; fax 805/646-9787), is the place to purge all your inner demons. You'll be so relaxed after their pampering treatments that the walk across the gravel driveway to their world-class restaurant will be all you can manage. We recommend you enjoy their famed mineral baths *à deux* in private redwood lined and skylighted chambers, each containing hot bubbling and cold plunge wooden tubs; a half-hour session of dunking back and forth is just $10, but long enough for you to experience the water's legendary restorative effects. The full spa package for two (including hot tub, massage, and dinner) runs $139 to $165. Full-day, weekend brunch, and other combinations are also available, as are spa services à la carte.

WHERE TO STAY

Best Western Casa Ojai. 1302 E. Ojai Ave., Ojai, CA 93023. ☎ **800/255-8175** or 805/646-8175. Fax 805/640-8247. 45 rms. A/C TEL TV. $66–$115 double. AE, MC, V.

This pleasant-enough two-story motel is on the main road through town; although it's a mile or so from the hubbub, street traffic can get a little noisy at times. The rooms are light and airy, however, and come with coffeemakers; some have refrigerators as well. There's a heated pool and whirlpool, plus a wooded public golf course across the street. Midweek rates and free stays for kids 12 and under make the Casa Ojai a good family option.

Ojai Manor Hotel Bed & Breakfast. 210 E. Matilija, Ojai, CA 93023. ☎ **805/646-0961.** 6 rms (all with shared baths). $90–$100 double. MC, V. Rates include breakfast and evening wine and spirits.

Conveniently located a block off Ojai Avenue, this comfortable wood clapboard B&B was built as a schoolhouse in 1874; it's Ojai's oldest building. A cozy parlor and inviting wraparound porch help make up for no private baths (the six rooms share three baths), and a cottage on the grounds houses a friendly beauty and massage salon. A typical guest room is simply furnished with wrought-iron beds and throw rugs on the wooden floors. Children over 12 are welcomed.

Ojai Rancho Motel. 615 W. Ojai Ave. (at Country Club Dr.), Ojai, CA 93023. ☎ **800/ 362-1434** or 805/646-1434. 12 rms (2 with fireplace). A/C TEL TV. Rooms $80-$135. AE, DISC, MC, V.

This classic ranch-style motel has been well kept and presents an attractively rustic alternative to the pricey country club around the corner, but don't expect gracious service from the cranky front office. Rooms all come with microwave, refrigerator, and coffeemaker, and there's a heated outdoor pool, sauna, and Jacuzzi. The rooms in back look out over ranch land and tend to be quieter than front rooms near the street.

WHERE TO DINE
MEALS FOR $10 OR LESS

Boccali's. 3277 Ojai-Santa Paula Rd. ☎ **805/646-6116.** Reservations not taken. Pizza $9–$16, pasta $6–$9. No credit cards. Mon–Tue 4pm–9pm, Wed–Sun noon–9pm. ITALIAN.

This small, wood-frame restaurant set among citrus groves is a pastoral pleasure spot where patrons eat outside at picnic tables under umbrellas and twisted oak trees or inside on tables covered with red-and-white checked oilcloths. Pizza is the main dish served here, topped in California style with the likes of crab, garlic, shrimp, and chicken. Fresh lemonade, squeezed from fruit plucked from local trees, is the usual drink of choice, though both Miller and Michelob are available on tap.

Tottenham Court. In the downtown shopping arcade, 242 E. Ojai Ave. ☎ **805/646-2339.** Reservations recommended for weekend tea. Main courses $5–$10. AE, MC V. Daily 9:30am– 5:30pm. ENGLISH TEAROOM.

Beside being purveyors of a variety of British imports, Tottenham Court is a delightful change of pace for breakfast or lunch, offering a menu of quiches, salads, sandwiches, and pastries in addition to a traditional afternoon English tea service. They have a selection of English beers, and the store itself sells food items, gifts, and housewares imported from the U.K.

MEALS FOR $20 OR LESS

Roger Keller's Restaurant. 331 E. Ojai Ave. ☎ **805/646-7266.** Reservations recommended on weekends. Main courses $8–$22. AE, MC, V. Daily 11:30am–10pm. AMERICAN/ CONTINENTAL.

Installed in a former storefront in the center of downtown, Roger Keller's has a casual ambience with exposed brick walls, bare wooden tables, and works by local artists. The food is rich in both American and European bistro tradition; the linguini tossed with pesto and sun-dried tomatoes, topped with rock shrimp and bay scallops, is fantastic. We also like the filet mignon encrusted in cracked peppercorns and flamed with brandy. The small but well-selected wine list includes several good buys, and live piano music enhances the mood each Friday and Saturday evening.

Lanna Thai. 849 E. Ojai Ave. ☎ **805/646-6771.** Reservations recommended on weekends. Main courses $8–$17. MC, V. Mon–Sat 11:30am–2:30pm and 4:30–9:30pm. THAI.

Chiedo Latawan Lopez, a Northern Thailand transplant, runs this cheerful, casual restaurant with a garden-style decor. His dishes contain little sugar and no MSG, but otherwise they're Thai traditionals. Fresh salmon poached in a spicy and sour broth, the house specialty, is terrific. Also worth trying is pla goong salad—grilled shrimp on spikes with julienned vegetables, lemon grass, mint, cilantro, and hot chilies. A children's menu is available.

WORTH A SPLURGE

The Ranch House. South Lomita Ave. ☎ **805/646-2360.** Reservations recommended. Main courses $19–$24. AE, CB, DC, DISC, MC, V. Wed–Sat 6pm–8:30pm, Sun 11am–7:30pm. Lunch served Wed–Sat Apr–Sept; call for hours. CALIFORNIA.

This restaurant has been placing emphasis on using the freshest vegetables, fruits, and herbs in their cuisine since it opened its doors in 1965, long before the practice became a national craze. Freshly snipped sprigs from the restaurant's lush herb garden will aromatically transform your simple meat, fish, or game dish into a work of art. From an appetizer of cognac-laced liver pâté served with the restaurant's own chewy rye bread to leave-room-for-desserts like fresh raspberries with sweet Chambord cream, the ingredients always shine through. And you'll dine in a magical setting— The Ranch House offers alfresco dining year-round on the wooden porch facing the scenic valley, as well as in the romantic garden amidst twinkling lights and stone fountains. Definitely worth the splurge.

8 En Route to Los Angeles: Ventura

by Stephanie Avnet

Nestled between gently rolling foothills and the sparkling blue Pacific, Ventura boasts a picturesque setting and clean sea breezes typical of California coastal towns. Southland antique hounds know about the town's quirky collectible shops, and time-pressed vacationers zip up to charming B&Bs just an hour from Los Angeles. Ventura is also the headquarters and main point of embarkation for Channel Islands National Park (see below).

Most travelers don't bother exiting U.S. 101 for a closer look. But think about stopping to while away a couple of hours around lunchtime; sleepy Ventura's charm might even convince you to spend a night.

ESSENTIALS

If you're traveling southbound on U.S. 101, take the Main Street exit; northbound, exit at California Street. Don't let the directionals throw you off; because of the curve of the coastline, the ocean is not always to the west, but often southward.

Stop in at the **Ventura Visitors & Convention Bureau,** 89-C S. California St., Ventura, CA 93001 (☎ **805/648-2075**).

EXPLORING THE TOWN

Charming seaside **Main Street,** the town's historic center, grew outward from the Spanish Mission of San Buenaventura (see below). The best section for strolling is between the mission (to the north) and Fir Street (to the south).

Founded in 1782 (the current buildings date from 1815) and still in use for daily services, **Mission San Buenaventura,** 225 East Main St. (☎ **805/643-4318**), lent its style to the contemporary civic buildings across the street. Step back in time by touring the inside garden, where you can examine the antique water pump and olive press once essential to daily life here. Good for a quick history fix. Open Monday to Saturday from 10am to 5pm and Sunday from 10am to 4pm. Pick up a self-guided tour brochure in the adjacent gift shop for the modest donation of $1 for adults, 50¢ for children.

The majestic neoclassical **San Buenaventura City Hall,** 501 Poli St. (☎ 805/658-4726), sits on the hillside, regally overlooking old downtown and the ocean. To either side on Poli Street are some of Ventura's best preserved and most ornate late 19th- and early 20th-century houses. Full of architectural detail (like the carved heads of Franciscan friars adorning the facade) inside and out, City Hall can be fully explored by an escorted tour, offered every Saturday from May to September from 11am to 1pm ($4 for adults, $3 for seniors; free for children 6 and under).

Ventura County Museum of History & Art, 100 East Main St. (☎ 805/653-0323), is worth visiting for its rich Native American Room, filled with Chumash treasures, and its Pioneer Room, which contains a collection of artifacts from the Mexican-American War (1846–48). Open Tuesday to Sunday from 10am to 5pm. Admission is $3 for adults, free for children 16 and under.

Although Ventura stretches south to one of California's most picturesque little harbors (the jumping-off point for the Channel Islands), the town has its own simple pier at the end of California Street. Favored by area fishermen, the wooden pier is charming and old-fashioned. It's fun to walk out over the water and gaze back at Ventura nestled against the hills.

WHERE TO STAY

Bella Maggiore Inn. 67 S. California St. ($^1/_2$ block south of Main St.), Ventura, CA 93001. ☎ **800/523-8479** or 805/652-0277. 24 rms and suites. TEL TV. $75–$150 double; suites $100–$130. Extra adult $10, extra child (under 12) $5. Rates include full breakfast and afternoon refreshments and appetizers. AE, DISC, MC, V.

This intimate Italian–style inn offers simply furnished rooms (some with fireplaces, balconies, or bay window seats) that overlook a romantic courtyard or roof garden. Breakfast is served around the patio fountain. A kind of European elegance pervades all but the reasonable rates here; ask about midweek specials.

La Mer European Bed & Breakfast. 411 Poli St. (west of City Hall), Ventura, CA 93001. ☎ **805/643-3600.** 5 rms, 4 with private entrance. $105–$155 double. Rates include full breakfast and wine in room. MC, V.

This cozy little cottage is perfect for a romantic getaway. The 1890 Cape Cod–style home has spectacular ocean views from the parlor and two of the guest rooms, each of which is furnished in a different international style. The generous midweek packages for couples can include gourmet candlelit dinners, cruises to Anacapa Island, country carriage rides, and therapeutic massages . . . or all of the above. No children accepted.

WHERE TO DINE

Rosarito Beach Cafe. 692 E. Main St. (at Fir St.). ☎ **805/653-7343.** Main courses $10–$19. AE, DISC, MC, V. Tue–Sat 11:30am–2pm; Tues–Thu, Sun 5:30–9pm; Fri–Sat 5–10pm. MEXICAN.

Diners in the know bring their palates to this 1938 Aztec Revival Moderne building and its welcoming outdoor patio for superb Baja–style cuisine whose tangy elements are borrowed from the Caribbean. The handmade tortillas are delicious. A culinary sophistication rare in modest Ventura.

The Sportsman. 53 California St. ($^1/_2$ block south of Main St.). ☎ **805/643-2851.** Main courses $4–$14. AE, MC, V. Mon–Fri 11am–10pm; Sat 9am–2pm, 5–10pm; Sun 4–10pm. AMERICAN.

You might walk right by the inconspicuous facade of Ventura's oldest (since 1950) restaurant. Like the "retro" lettering on their awning, the interior hasn't changed a lick since then. The Sportsman looks fancy but is quite affordable, especially at breakfast and lunch; they serve up fine hearty breakfasts, burgers, steaks, and other grilled specialties. You can wet your whistle with $2.50 well drinks from the bar.

Yolie's Fresh Mex Grill. 26 S. Garden St. (at Main St., west of the mission). ☎ **805/ 652-0338.** Main courses $5–$13. AE, DISC, MC, V. Mon–Thu, Sun 11am–9pm; Fri–Sat 11am– 10pm. MEXICAN.

This colorful cantina is better than its nondescript exterior leads you to believe. Yolie offers an impressive fresh salsa bar (authentic and delicious) as well as an admirable beer, margarita, and tequila menu. The kitchen quickly sends out traditional combination plates (as well as lighter and/or vegetarian adaptations). Yolie's all-day hours make it a good road-trip rest stop.

9　Channel Islands National Park

by Andrew Rice

There's nothing like a visit to the Channel Islands for discovering the sense of awe the first European explorers to set foot on them must have felt nearly 400 years ago. This is a wild and empty land. It's miraculous what 25 miles of ocean can do. Whether you approach the islands by sea or air, you'll be bowled over by how untrammeled they remain, despite being next-door neighbors with Southern California's teeming masses.

Channel Islands National Park encompasses the five northernmost islands of the eight-island chain: Santa Barbara, Anacapa, Santa Cruz, Santa Rosa, and San Miguel. Tiny Santa Barbara Island sits very much by itself, about 46 miles off the Southern California coast. The other four are clustered in a 40-mile-long chain that begins in the east with tiny Anacapa; it continues with Santa Cruz, then Santa Rosa, and ends with wild and windy San Miguel at the western end of the chain. The park boundaries extend 1 mile offshore from each island. The National Marine Sanctuary extends 6 miles around each island.

The islands are the meeting point of two distinct marine ecosystems: The cold waters of Northern California and the warmer currents of Southern California swirl together here, creating an awesome array of marine life. On land, the relative isolation from mainland influences has allowed distinct species, like the island fox and the night lizard, to develop and survive here. The islands are also the most important seabird nesting area in California, and home to the biggest seal and sea lion breeding colony in the United States.

ANACAPA

Most people who visit the park come to Anacapa. It's only 11 sea miles from Ventura, an easy half-day trip. At only 1.1 square miles, Anacapa—actually three small islets divided by narrow stretches of ocean—is only marginally larger than Santa Barbara and, consequently, not a place for those who need a lot of space to roam around. Only East Anacapa is open to visitors (though Middle Anacapa is accessible via ranger-escorted walks), as the other two islets are important brown pelican breeding areas. Several trails on the island will take you to beautiful overlooks of clear-watered coves, wild ocean, and tide pools. Arch Rock, a natural land bridge, is visible from the landing cove, where you'll clamber up 154 stairs to the island's flat top.

JUST THE FACTS

GETTING THERE   Each of the five islands is relatively distinct. Odds are you're going to visit only one island on a given trip, so it's a good idea to study your options before going.

Visit the **Channel Islands National Park Headquarters and Visitor Center,** 1901 Spinnaker Dr., Ventura, CA 93001 (☎ **805/658-5700**), to get acquainted with the various programs and individual personalities of the islands through a film, maps, and displays. Rangers run interpretive programs both on the islands and at the center year-round. **Island Packers,** next door to the Visitor Center at 1867 Spinnaker Dr. (☎ **805/642-7688** or 805/642-1393), is the park's concessionaire for boat transportation to and from the islands; they're another great source of information.

There are no park fees, but getting to the islands is expensive since you must boat or fly out: anywhere from $20 to $120 per person. Island Packers will take you on a range of regularly scheduled boat excursions, from $3^1/_2$-hour non-landing tours of the islands ($21 per person) to full-day tours of individual islands led by naturalists ($37 to $49 per person).

Island Packers also arranges small group tours by sea kayak to all five Channel Islands. Half- and whole-day excursions allow you to enjoy the rugged coastline, sea lions, and teeming tide pools of Anacapa, Santa Barbara, and Santa Rosa islands. Bring a picnic lunch. Fares range from $21 to $65 for adults, $14 to $45 for children 12 and under. Two-day adventures to secluded and unspoiled San Miguel Island can also be arranged, with meals and berth accommodations included, for $215 to $235.

THE WEATHER   The weather in the islands is unpredictable year-round. Thirty-mile-an-hour winds can blow for days, or sometimes a fog bank will settle in and smother the islands for weeks at a time. Winter rains can turn island trails into mud baths. In general, plan on wind, lots of sun (bring sunscreen), cool nights, and the possibility of hot days. Water temperatures are in the 50s and 60s year-round. If you're camping, bring a good tent—if you don't know the difference between a good and a bad tent, the island wind will gladly demonstrate it for you.

CAMPING   Camping is allowed on East Anacapa year-round, but don't bring more than you can carry the half mile from the landing cove. Bring earplugs and steer clear of the foghorn, which can leave permanent hearing damage. Most of the waters around the island, including the landing cove, are protected as a National Marine Sanctuary. Pack a good wet suit, mask, fins and snorkel; you can dive right off the landing cove dock. Fires and pets are prohibited. You must bring everything you'll need; there are no supplies. To reserve free camping permits for any of the islands, schedule your transportation, then call **805/658-5711** to reserve a permit no more than 90 days in advance (no more than 30 days in advance for San Miguel and Santa Rosa).

14 Los Angeles

by Stephanie Avnet

Los Angeles is not a humble city. Like a celebrity who chooses a front table at Spago, Los Angeles is a star that just loves to be noticed.

And noticed it is. The movies, TV, and music that it issues forth are seen, heard, and felt throughout the world. The city is America's, and often the world's, popular tastemaker, its cultural barometer. When it comes to what's hot and what's not, Angelenos can confidently say that they heard, or started, the buzz here first.

Los Angeles is a cosmopolitan city in the true sense of the word. It's a cornucopia of lifestyles and cultures and a sometimes uneasy mix of races that's at once both thrilling and uncomfortable. It's not an easy place to master. The sprawling city has no cultural center, and its layout is difficult to grasp. Despite all appearances, however, Los Angeles is a very welcoming place. Often criticized for having little historical or cultural attributes, Los Angeles is anxious to prove its critics wrong, and any resident will gladly tell of the hidden corners and secret treasures that make living here a nonstop adventure.

And the adventure isn't reserved for the gold-card set, either; personality oozes from every geographical and economic corner of the city. We'll show you how to enjoy all that Los Angeles has to offer without breaking the bank.

The best way to approach this colossal, Technicolor city is with a critical conscience and tongue firmly in cheek. Recognize its influence, and humor its self-importance. Keep in mind your media-made preconceptions, then discover Los Angeles for what it is: glitzy, grimy, glittery, powerful—the world capital of pop culture—and a city still basking in the sunny climate that has drawn admirers here for centuries. Put on your shades, take the top down, and get ready to roll—this is Hollywood.

1 Orientation

ARRIVING

BY PLANE

LOS ANGELES INTERNATIONAL AIRPORT (LAX) Most visitors to the area fly into Los Angeles International Airport, better known as LAX (☎ 310/646-5252). Situated oceanside just off I-405, between Santa Monica and Manhattan Beach, LAX is a convenient place to land; it's minutes away from all the city's beach

Area Code Change Notice

Please note that, effective June 14, 1997, the phone company plans to split the 818 area code. The eastern portion, including Burbank, Glendale, and Pasadena, will change to the new area code **626.** You will be able to dial 818 until January 17, 1998, after which you will have to use 626.

communities, and about a half-hour drive from the Westside, Hollywood, or downtown.

TRANSPORTATION FROM LAX   You'll probably be renting a car from LAX; you'll need one (see "Getting Around," below). All the major car-rental firms provide shuttles from the terminals to their off-site branches. To reach Santa Monica and other northern beach communities, exit the airport, take Sepulveda Boulevard north, then follow the signs to Calif. 1 (Pacific Coast Highway or PCH) north. To reach the southern beach communities, take Sepulveda Boulevard south, then follow the signs to Calif. 1 (PCH) south. To reach Beverly Hills or Hollywood, exit the airport via Century Boulevard, then take I-405 north to Santa Monica Boulevard east. To reach downtown, exit the airport via Century Boulevard, then take I-405 north to I-10 east. To reach Pasadena, exit the airport, turn right onto Sepulveda Boulevard south, then take I-105 east to I-110 north.

Many city hotels provide free shuttles for their guests; ask about transportation when you make reservations. You can also catch a **taxi** from your terminal. Taxis line up outside each terminal, and rides are metered. Expect to pay about $30 to Hollywood and downtown, $25 to Beverly Hills, $20 to Santa Monica, and $45 to Pasadena, including a $2.50 service charge for rides originating at LAX.

Super Shuttle (☎ 310/782-6600) offers regularly scheduled minivans from LAX to any location in the city. When traveling to the airport for your trip home, reserve your shuttle at least one day in advance. The city's MTA buses also go between LAX and many parts of the city; phone **MTA Airport Information** (☎ 800/252-7433 or 213/626-4455) for the schedules and fares.

OTHER AREA AIRPORTS   One of the area's smaller airports might be more convenient for you, landing you closer to your destination and enabling you to avoid the traffic and bustle of LAX. **Burbank-Glendale-Pasadena Airport** (☎ 818/840-8840) is the best place to land if you're locating in Hollywood or the valleys. The small airport has especially good links to Las Vegas and other southwestern cities. **Long Beach Municipal Airport** (☎ 310/421-8293), south of LAX, is the best place to land if you are visiting Long Beach or northern Orange County, and want to avoid Los Angeles entirely. **Orange County/John Wayne International Airport** in Anaheim (☎ 714/252-5200) is closest to Disneyland, Knott's Berry Farm, and other Anaheim area attractions (see Chapter 15).

BY CAR

If you're driving in from the north, you have two choices: the quick route, along I-5 through the middle of the state; or the scenic route along the coast.

Heading south along I-5, you'll pass a small town called Grapevine. This marks the start of a mountain pass known as the Grapevine. Once you've reached the southern end of the mountain pass, you'll be in the San Fernando Valley, and you've arrived in Los Angeles County. To reach the beach communities and L.A.'s Westside take I-405 south; to get to Hollywood, take Calif. 170 south to U.S. 101 south (this route is called the Hollywood Freeway the entire way); the I-5 will take you through downtown and into Orange County.

If you're taking the scenic coastal route in from the north, take U.S. 101 to I-405, I-5, or stay on U.S. 101, following the instructions as listed above to your final destination.

If you're approaching from the east, you'll be driving in on I-10. For Orange County, take Calif. 57 south. I-10 continues through downtown and terminates at the beach. If you're heading to Hollywood, take U.S. 101 north; if you're heading to the Westside, take I-405 north. To get to the beaches, take Calif. 1 (PCH) north or south, depending on your destination.

From the south, head north on I-5. At the southern end of Orange County, I-405 splits off to the west; take this road to the Westside and beach communities. Stay on I-5 to reach downtown.

BY TRAIN

Passengers arriving via **Amtrak** (☎ **800/USA-RAIL**) will disembark at Union Station, on downtown's northern edge. From the station, travelers can take one of the many taxis that line up outside the station.

BY BUS

The main Los Angeles bus station for arriving **Greyhound/Trailways** (☎ **800/ 231-2222**) buses is downtown at 1716 E. 7th St., east of Alameda (☎ 213/ 262-1514). For additional area terminal locations, call their toll-free number.

VISITOR INFORMATION

The **Los Angeles Convention and Visitors Bureau,** 633 W. 5th St., Suite 600, Los Angeles, CA 90071 (☎ **213/624-7300**), is the city's main source for information. Call or write for a free visitors kit, which contains a book of coupons for discounts on various attractions, accommodations, and restaurants. The bureau staffs a Visitors' Information Center at 685 S. Figueroa St., between Wilshire Boulevard and 7th Street; it's open Monday to Friday 8am to 5:30pm and Saturday 8:30am to 5pm.

Many Los Angeles-area communities also have their own tourist offices: **Visitor Information Center Hollywood** (☎ 213/236-2331); **Beverly Hills Visitors Bureau** (☎ 800/345-2210 or 310/271-8174; fax 310/858-8032); **Marina del Rey Chamber of Commerce** (☎ 213/821-0555); **Redondo Beach Chamber of Commerce** (☎ 310/376-6911); **Santa Monica Convention and Visitors Bureau** (☎ 310/393-7593; Internet Web site http://www.ci.santa-monica.ca.us); and **West Hollywood Convention and Visitors Bureau** (☎ 800/368-6020 or 310/ 289-2525). Call for information, hours, and locations.

OTHER INFORMATION SOURCES   Several city-oriented newspapers and magazines offer up-to-date information on current happenings. *L.A. Weekly,* a free weekly listings magazine, is packed with information on current events around town. It's available from sidewalk news racks and in many stores and restaurants around the city, and often offers discount or two-for-one coupons at area restaurants. The *Los Angeles Times* "**Calendar**" section of the Sunday paper is an excellent guide to the world of entertainment in and around Los Angeles, and includes listings of what's doing and where to do it. The *Times* also maintains an Internet "Guide to Tinseltown" at **http://www.latimes.com/HOME/ENT/TINSEL.** *Los Angeles Magazine* and the even trendier upstart *Buzz* are city-based monthlies full of news, information, and previews of L.A.'s art, music, and food scenes.

CITY LAYOUT

Los Angeles is not a single compact city, but a sprawling suburbia comprising dozens of disparate communities. Most of the city's communities are located between mountains and ocean, on the flatlands of a huge basin. Even if you've never visited Los Angeles before, you'll recognize the names of many of these areas: Hollywood, Beverly Hills, Santa Monica, and Malibu. Ocean breezes push the city's infamous smog inland, toward dozens of less well-known communities, and through mountain passes into the suburban sprawl of the San Fernando and San Gabriel valleys.

Downtown Los Angeles, which isn't where most visitors will stay, is in the center of the basin, about 12 miles east of the Pacific Ocean. You'll probably spend the bulk of your time either on the coast, or on the city's Westside (see "The Neighborhoods in Brief," below, for complete details on all of the city's sectors).

THE MAJOR FREEWAYS & BOULEVARDS

Los Angeles's extensive freeway system connects the city's patchwork of communities; they work well together to get you where you need to be, although rush-hour traffic can sometimes be bumper-to-bumper. You might only drive on a couple, but here is an overview of the entire system:

U.S. 101, called the Ventura Freeway in the San Fernando Valley and the Hollywood Freeway in the city, runs across Los Angeles in a roughly northwest-southeast direction, from the San Fernando Valley to the center of downtown.

Calif. 134 continues as the Ventura Freeway after U.S. 101 turns into the city and becomes the Hollywood Freeway. The Calif. 134 branch of the Ventura Freeway continues directly east, through the valley towns of Burbank and Glendale, to **I-210** (the Foothill Freeway), which will take you through Pasadena and out toward the eastern edge of Los Angeles County.

I-5, otherwise known as the Golden State Freeway north of I-10, and the Santa Ana Freeway south of I-10, bisects downtown on its way from San Francisco to San Diego.

I-10, labeled the Santa Monica Freeway west of I-5 and the San Bernardino Freeway east of I-5, is the city's major east-west freeway, connecting the San Gabriel Valley to downtown and Santa Monica.

I-405, also known as the San Diego Freeway, runs north-south through Los Angeles's Westside, connecting the San Fernando Valley with LAX and the southern beach areas.

I-105, Los Angeles's newest freeway, called the Century Freeway, extends from LAX east to I-605.

I-110, commonly known as the Harbor Freeway, starts in Pasadena as Calif. 110 (the Pasadena Freeway); it turns into the interstate in downtown Los Angeles and runs directly south, where it dead-ends in San Pedro. The section that is now the Pasadena Freeway is Los Angeles's historic first freeway, known as the Arroyo Seco when it opened in 1940.

I-710, also called the Long Beach Freeway, runs in a north-south direction through East Los Angeles and dead-ends at Long Beach.

I-605, the San Gabriel River Freeway, runs roughly parallel to the I-710 further east, through the cities of Hawthorne and Lynwood and into the San Gabriel Valley.

Calif. 1—called Highway 1, the Pacific Coast Highway, or simply PCH—is really a highway (more like a surface thruway) rather than a freeway. It skirts the ocean, linking all of Los Angeles's beach communities, from Malibu to the Orange Coast.

The Los Angeles Area at a Glance

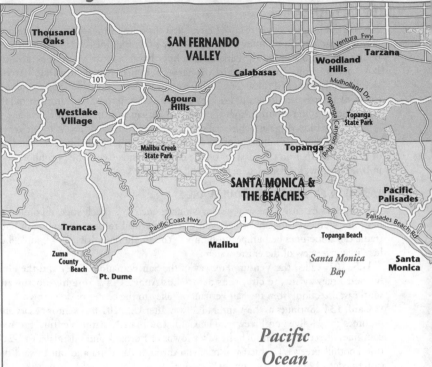

SAN FERNANDO VALLEY

Thousand Oaks

Tarzana

Woodland Hills

Calabasas

Agoura Hills

Westlake Village

Topanga State Park

Malibu Creek State Park

Topanga

SANTA MONICA & THE BEACHES

Pacific Palisades

Trancas

Pacific Coast Hwy

Palisades Beach Rd

Zuma County Beach

Pt. Dume

Malibu

Topanga Beach

Santa Monica

Santa Monica Bay

Pacific Ocean

Ventura Fwy

Mulholland Dr.

Topanga Canyon Blvd

(1) Lincoln Blvd.
Sepulveda Blvd.
Pacific Coast Hwy.

(2) Santa Monica Blvd.
Glendale Fwy.

(5) Golden State Fwy.
Santa Ana Fwy.

(10) Santa Monica Fwy.
San Bernardino Fwy.

(22) Garden Grove Fwy.

(27) Topanga Canyon Blvd.

(39) Beach Blvd.
San Gabriel Canyon Rd.

(47) Terminal Fwy.
Ocean Blvd.

(55) Newport Fwy. and Blvd.

(57) Orange Fwy.

(60) Pomona Fwy.

(90) Marina Fwy.

(91) Artesia Blvd. & Fwy.
Gardena Fwy.
Riverside Fwy.

(101) Ventura Fwy.
Hollywood Fwy.

(105) Glenn Anderson-
Century Fwy.

(110) Pasadena Fwy.

(110) Harbor Fwy.

(134) Ventura Fwy.

(170) Hollywood Fwy.

(210) Foothill Fwy.

(405) San Diego Fwy.

(605) San Gabriel
River Fwy.

(710) Long Beach Fwy.

LEGEND

(22) **State Highway**

(101) **U.S. Highway**

(210) **Interstate Highway**

The freeways are complemented by a complex web of surface streets. From north to south, the major east-west thoroughfares connecting downtown to the beaches are Sunset Boulevard, Santa Monica Boulevard, Wilshire Boulevard, and Olympic, Pico, and Venice boulevards. The section of Sunset Boulevard that runs between Crescent Heights Boulevard and Doheny Drive is the famed Sunset Strip.

STREET MAPS

Because Los Angeles is so spread out, a good map of the area is essential. Foldout maps are available at gas stations, hotels, bookshops, and tourist-oriented shops around the city. If you're going to be in Los Angeles for a week or more, or plan on doing some extensive touring, you might want to invest in the all-inclusive *Thomas Guide,* a comprehensive book of city maps that depicts every single road in the city. The ring-bound edition is sold in most area bookstores and costs about $16.

THE NEIGHBORHOODS IN BRIEF

Los Angeles is a very confusing city, with fluid neighborhood lines and equally elastic labels. I've found that the best way to grasp the city is to break it into five regions—**Santa Monica and the Beaches, L.A.'s Westside and Beverly Hills, Hollywood, Downtown,** and **the San Fernando Valley**—each of which encompasses a more or less distinctive patchwork of city neighborhoods and independently incorporated communities.

SANTA MONICA & THE BEACHES

These are my favorite L.A. communities. The 60-mile beachfront stretching southward from Malibu to the Palos Verdes Peninsula has milder weather and less smog than the inland communities, and traffic is nominally lighter, except on summer weekends, of course. The towns along the coast each have their own mood and charm. I've listed them below from north to south.

Malibu, at the northern border of Los Angeles County, is 25 miles from downtown. Its wide beaches, sparsely populated hills, and relative remoteness from the inner city make it extremely popular with rich recluses. With plenty of green space and dramatic rocky outcroppings, Malibu's rural beauty is unsurpassed in L.A.

Pretty **Santa Monica,** Los Angeles's premier beach community, is known for its long ocean pier, artsy atmosphere, and somewhat wacky residents. It's also noted for its particularly acute homeless problem. The 3rd Street Promenade, a pedestrian-only thoroughfare lined with great shops and restaurants, is one of the country's most successful revitalization projects.

Venice, a planned community in the spirit of its Italian forebear, was constructed with a series of narrow canals connected by quaint one-lane bridges. The area has been infested with grime and crime, but gentrification is in full swing. Some of Los Angeles's most innovative and interesting architecture lines funky Main Street. Without question, Venice is best known for its Ocean Front Walk, a nonstop circus of skaters, sellers, and posers of all ages, colors, and sizes.

Marina del Rey, just south of Venice, is a somewhat quieter, more upscale community best known for its small-craft harbor, one of the largest in the world.

Manhattan, Hermosa, and **Redondo Beaches** are relatively sleepy residential neighborhoods with modest homes, mild weather, and easy parking. There are excellent beaches for volleyballers, surfers, and sun-worshippers, but there's not much else about these South Bay suburbs for visitors to get very excited about—except some good bargains on places to stay at or near the beach.

L.A.'s WESTSIDE & BEVERLY HILLS

The Westside, an imprecise, misshapen "L" sandwiched between Hollywood and the city's coastal communities, includes some of L.A.'s most prestigious neighborhoods, all with names you're sure to recognize. It's also home to the primary center of gay life in Los Angeles.

Beverly Hills is roughly bounded by Olympic Boulevard on the south, Robertson Boulevard on the east, and Westwood and Century City on the west; it extends into the hills to the north. Politically distinct from the rest of Los Angeles, this famous enclave is best known for its palm tree–lined streets of palatial homes and high-priced shops (does Rodeo Drive ring a bell?), but it is the healthy mix of the filthy rich, tourists, and wanna-bes that creates a unique, and sometimes bizarre, atmosphere.

West Hollywood is a key-shaped community (go ahead, look at your map) whose epicenter is the intersection of Santa Monica and La Cienega boulevards. It's bounded on the west by Doheny Drive and on the south roughly by Melrose; the tip of the key extends east for several blocks north and south of Santa Monica Boulevard as far as La Brea Avenue, but it's primarily located to the west of Fairfax Avenue. Nestled between Beverly Hills and Hollywood, this politically independent town can feel either tony or tawdry, depending on which end of it you're in. In addition to being home to the city's best restaurants, shops, and art galleries, West Hollywood is the center of L.A.'s gay community.

Bel Air and **Holmby Hills,** located in the hills north of Westwood and west of the Beverly Hills city limits, comprise a wealthy residential area and feature prominently on most maps to the stars' homes.

Brentwood, the world-famous backdrop for the O. J. Simpson melodrama, is really just a tiny, quiet, relatively upscale neighborhood with the typical L.A. mixture of homes, restaurants, and strip malls. It's west of I-405 and north of Santa Monica and West Los Angeles.

Westwood, an urban village that the University of California, Los Angeles (UCLA), calls home, is bounded by I-405, Santa Monica Boulevard, Sunset Boulevard, and Beverly Hills. The village, which used to be a hot destination for a night on the town, lost much of its appeal due to overcrowding, rudeness, and even street violence. There is still a high concentration of movie theaters, but we're all waiting for Westwood to regain the charm it once had.

Century City is a compact, busy, rather bland high-rise area sandwiched between West Los Angeles and Beverly Hills. Once the back lot of 20th Century-Fox studios, Century City is home to the Shubert Theatre and the outdoor Century City Marketplace. Its three main thoroughfares are Century Park East, Avenue of the Stars, and Century Park West; it's bounded on the north by Santa Monica Boulevard and on the south by Pico Boulevard.

West Los Angeles is a label that basically applies to everything that isn't one of the other Westside neighborhoods. It's basically the area south of Santa Monica Boulevard, north of Venice Boulevard, east of Santa Monica and Venice, and west and south of Century City.

HOLLYWOOD

Yes, they still come. Young aspirants are attracted to this town like moths fluttering in the glare of neon lights. But Hollywood is now much more a state of mind than a glamour center. Many of the neighborhood's former movie studios have moved to less expensive, more spacious venues. Hollywood Boulevard is one of the city's seediest strips. The area is now just a less-than-admirable part of the whole of Los Angeles, but the legend of the neighborhood as the movie capital of the world endures, and it's still home to several important attractions, such as the Walk of Fame and Mann's Chinese Theatre.

For our purposes, the label *Hollywood* extends beyond seedy Hollywood itself—centered around Hollywood and Sunset boulevards—to surrounding neighborhoods. It generally encompasses everything between Western Avenue to the east and Fairfax Avenue to the west and from the Hollywood Hills (with its dazzling homes and million-dollar views) south.

Melrose Avenue, a scruffy but fun neighborhood, is the city's funkiest shopping district.

The stretch of Wilshire Boulevard that runs through the southern part of Hollywood is known as the **Mid-Wilshire district.** It's lined with contemporary apartment houses and office buildings; the stretch just east of Fairfax Avenue, now known as **Museum Row,** is home to almost a dozen museums, including the Los Angeles County Museum of Art, the La Brea Tar Pits, and that brand-new shrine to L.A. car culture, the Petersen Automotive Museum.

Griffith Park, up Western Avenue in the northernmost reaches of Hollywood, is one of the country's largest urban parks, and home to the Los Angeles Zoo and the famous Griffith Observatory.

DOWNTOWN

Roughly bounded by the U.S. 101, I-110, I-10, and I-5 freeways, L.A.'s downtown is home to a tight cluster of high-rise offices, the **El Pueblo de Los Angeles Historic District,** and the neighborhoods of **Koreatown, Chinatown,** and **Little Tokyo.** For our purposes, the residential neighborhoods of **Silverlake** and **Los Feliz, Exposition Park** (home to Los Angeles Memorial Coliseum, the L.A. Sports Area, and several downtown museums), and **East** and **South-Central** Los Angeles, the city's famous barrios, all fall under the downtown umbrella.

The construction of skyscrapers, facilitated by earthquake-proof technology, transformed downtown Los Angeles into the business center of the city. Despite the relatively recent construction of numerous cultural centers, including the Music Center and the Museum of Contemporary Art, and a few smart restaurants, downtown is not the hub it would be in most cities; the Westside, Hollywood, and the beach communities are all more popular.

THE SAN FERNANDO VALLEY

The San Fernando Valley, known locally as the *Valley,* was nationally popularized in the 1980s by the notorious mall-loving "Valley Girl" stereotype. Snuggled between the Santa Monica and the San Gabriel mountain ranges, most of the Valley is residential and commercial, and off the beaten tourist track. But there are some attractions bound to draw you over the hill: Universal City, located west of the Griffith Park between U.S. 101 and Calif. 134, is home to Universal Studios and Citywalk, the new shopping and entertainment complex. And you might make a trip to Burbank, just north of Universal City, to see one of your favorite TV shows being filmed at the NBC or Warner Bros. studios. There are also many good restaurants and shops along Ventura Boulevard in and around **Studio City.**

Glendale is a largely residential community sandwiched between the San Fernando Valley and downtown. You'll find the city's best sightseeing cemetery, Forest Lawn, there.

2 Getting Around

BY CAR

Despite its hassles, driving is the way to get around Los Angeles. The golden rule is this: Always allow more time to get to your destination than you reasonably think it will take, especially during morning and evening rush hours.

RENTALS   Los Angeles is one of the cheapest places in America to rent a car. Among the national firms operating in L.A. are: **Alamo** (☎ 800/327-9633), **Avis** (☎ 800/331-1212), **Budget** (☎ 800/527-0700), **Dollar** (☎ 800/800-4000), **Hertz** (☎ 800/654-3131), **National** (☎ 800/328-4567), and **Thrifty** (☎ 800/367-2277).

PARKING   Parking in Los Angeles is usually ample, but in some sections—most notably downtown and in Santa Monica, West Hollywood, and Hollywood—finding a space can be wrought with frustration. In most places, you'll be able to find metered street parking, but carry plenty of quarters. When you can't, expect to valet or garage your car for somewhere between $4 and $10. Many restaurants and nightclubs, and even some shopping centers, offer valet parking; they usually charge about $3 to $5. Most of the hotels listed in this book offer off-street parking; it's often complimentary, but can cost as much as $20 per day in high-density areas.

DRIVING TIPS   Many Southern California freeways have designated carpool lanes, also known as high-occupancy-vehicle (HOV) lanes. Some require two passengers, others three. The minimum fine for an HOV violation is $246. Most on-ramps are metered to control the traffic flow; carpools are exempt and pass in their own lane.

When it comes to radio traffic reporter jargon, the names of L.A.'s freeways (as opposed to their numbers) are usually used. A "SigAlert" is the term used for an unplanned freeway crisis (a serious accident) that will affect the movement of traffic for 30 minutes or more. When you hear "a big rig is blocking the number-one lane," you can determine the lane by counting out from the center divider.

On surface roads, you may turn right at a red light (unless otherwise indicated) after making a complete stop and yielding to traffic and pedestrians. Pedestrians have the right-of-way at intersections and crosswalks.

BY PUBLIC TRANSPORTATION

I've heard rumors about visitors to Los Angeles who have toured the city entirely by public transportation, but they can't be more than that: rumors. It's hard to believe that anyone can comprehensively tour this "Auto Land" without a car of their own. Still, if you're in the city for only a short time, are on a very tight budget, or don't expect to be moving around a lot, public transport might be for you. The city's trains and buses are operated by the **Los Angeles County Metropolitan Transit Authority (MTA),** 425 S. Main St., Los Angeles, CA 90013 (☎ **213/626-4455**).

FAST FACTS: Los Angeles

American Express   In addition to those at 327 N. Beverly Dr., Beverly Hills (☎ 310/274-8277), and downtown at 901 W. 7th St., downtown (☎ 213/627-4800), offices are located throughout the city. To report lost or stolen cards, call **800/528-4800.** To report lost or stolen traveler's checks, call **800/221-7282.**

Baby-Sitters   If you're staying at one of the larger hotels, the concierge can usually recommend a reliable baby-sitter. If not, contact the **Baby-Sitters Guild** in Glendale (☎ **818/552-2229**); or **Sitters Unlimited** (☎ **800/328-1191**).

Dentists To find an area dentist, call the national **Dental Referral Service** (☎ 800/422-8338).

Doctors Contact the **Uni-Health Information and Referral Hot Line** (☎ 800/922-0000) for a free, confidential physician referral.

Emergencies For police, fire, highway patrol, or in case of life-threatening medical emergencies, dial **911.**

Liquor Laws Liquor and grocery stores can sell packaged alcoholic beverages between 6am and 2am. Most restaurants, nightclubs, and bars are licensed to serve alcoholic beverages during the same hours. The legal age for purchase and consumption is 21; proof of age is required.

Newspapers/Magazines See "Other Information Sources" under "Orientation" above.

Police See "Emergencies," above. For nonemergency police matters, phone **213/485-2121** or, in Beverly Hills, **213/550-4951.**

Post Office Call **213/586-1467** to find the one closest to you.

Taxes The combined L.A. County and California state sales taxes amount to 8.25%; hotel taxes range from 12% to 17%, depending on the municipality you're in.

Taxis You can order a taxi in advance from **Checker Cab** (☎ 213/221-2355), **L.A. Taxi** (☎ 213/627-7000), or **United Independent Taxi** (☎ 213/483-7604).

Time Call for the correct time at 853-1212 (good for all area codes).

Weather Call **L.A. Weather Information** (☎ 213/554-1212) for the daily forecast. For beach conditions, call the **Zuma Beach Lifeguard** recorded information (☎ 310/457-9701).

3 Accommodations

by Jim Moore and Stephanie Avnet

In sprawling Los Angeles, location is everything. Choosing the right neighborhood as a base can make or break your vacation; if you plan to while away a few days at the beach but base yourself downtown, for example, you're going to lose a lot of valuable relaxation time on the freeway. Take into consideration where you'll be wanting to spend your time before you commit yourself to a base. But, wherever you stay, count on doing a good deal of driving—no hotel in Los Angeles is convenient to everything.

The hotels listed below are categorized first by area, then by price. While there are rates of $60 and below to be had in certain L.A. neighborhoods, the city ranks highly on a list of the nation's expensive destinations, and any room under $100 is considered a bargain. Rates given are the regular rack rates (published rates) for a standard room for two with private bath (unless otherwise noted). Be sure to read past the price heading for your budget; you'll be pleasantly surprised at how many hotels can be had for much less than the advertised rates. Throughout the listings, and in the box entitled "Suite Deals (& Other Bargains)," we've indicated what kinds of deals were available at press time. However, special rates are constantly in flux; be sure to ask for the best available rate or package before you book.

Consider also whether the inn or hotel offers breakfast or kitchen facilities; these bonuses can save two people as much as $30 a day over dining out. At the Mansion Inn in Venice, for example, that savings makes a $79 room an even sweeter deal.

Prices given do not include Los Angeles's hotel tax, which runs from 12% to a whopping 16%. Be aware that hotels in the more densely populated areas charge extra for parking (with in-and-out privileges, except where noted) and some levy heavy surcharges for telephone use.

Several hotel reservations services offer one-stop shopping; they'll tell you what's available at many of L.A.'s hotels and book you into the one of your choice, all at no additional charge. These services are particularly helpful for last-minute reservations, when rooms are often scarce or discounted. The following companies serve the L.A. area: **Central Reservation Service,** 505 Maitland Ave., Suite 100, Altamonte Springs, FL 32701 (☎ **800/548-3311** or 417/339-4116; fax 407/339-4736); and **Hotel Reservations Network,** 8140 Walnut Hill Lane, Suite 203, Dallas, TX 75231 (☎ **800/96-HOTEL** or 214/361-7311; fax 214/361-7299).

In a pinch, you can avail yourself of one of the profusion of chain hotels around town that are generally a reliable source of cheap, clean sleeps. Some of the more noteworthy are listed in full below. **Best Western** has dozens of properties in the greater L.A. area, most at bargain-basement prices. Call **800/528-1234** or browse their listings on the World Wide Web at http://www.bestwestern.com/best.html. Other options include **Travelodge** (☎ **800/367-2250**) and **Days Inn** (☎ **800/ DAYS-INN**).

SANTA MONICA & THE BEACHES

In addition to the listings below, other affordable options in Santa Monica include the new **Best Western Ocean View Hotel,** 1447 Ocean Ave. (☎ **800/528-1234** or 310/458-4888), just blocks from the Third Street Promenade; the **Best Western Gateway Hotel,** 1920 Santa Monica Blvd., at 20th Street (☎ **800/528-1234** or 310/829-9100); **Days Inn Santa Monica,** 3007 Santa Monica Blvd. (☎ **800/ 591-5995** or 310/829-6333), close to UCLA and Beverly Hills; and the **Comfort Inn Santa Monica,** 2815 Santa Monica Blvd. (☎ **800/228-5150** or 310/828-5517), which boasts the largest outdoor pool in the area.

DOUBLES FOR $80 OR LESS

Best Western Redondo Beach Inn. 1850 S. Pacific Coast Hwy., Redondo Beach, CA 90277. ☎ **800/528-1234** or 310/540-3700. Fax 310/540-3675. 108 rooms. A/C TEL TV. $89 double. Extra person $5; children under 18 stay free. Off-season rates and discounts available. AE, CB, DC, DISC, MC, V. Free parking.

Location is this hotel's claim to fame: The sands of beautiful Redondo Beach are only five blocks away, and the hotel offers guests a fleet of one-speed bicycles to get them there. Modern and ultraclean, this '80s-style white stucco building's nicer rooms are in the front wing, off quiet interior corridors. United Airlines flight personnel from nearby LAX have chosen this as their overnight crash pad. I suspect they feel strangely at home in the airport-style bar/lounge upstairs. There's also an outdoor heated pool, whirlpool, exercise room and coffee shop.

The Mansion Inn. 327 Washington Blvd., Marina del Rey, CA 90291. ☎ **800/828-0688** or 310/821-2557. Fax 310/827-0289. 38 rooms, 5 suites. A/C TV. $79–$89 double; $125 suite. Extra person $10; children under 12 stay free. Rates include breakfast. AE, CB, DC, DISC, EU, JCB, MC, V. No cash or checks accepted. Free parking.

It sounds too good to be true for L.A. lodging: a charming, friendly inn with affordable rates that include breakfast. But the Mansion Inn is all that and more. Three blocks from the ocean, straddling the communities of Venice and Marina del Rey, it features thoughtful touches like hair dryers, complimentary weekday newspapers, free movies, separate vanity areas, and a refrigerator in every room. Out front, there's an endless parade of people exploring the Marina, the beach, or the Venice canals on

Suite Deals (& Other Bargains)

There's no getting around it—Los Angeles is an expensive city. However, there are some terrific deals to be had out there—even on rooms that you thought were way out of your price range. The key to finding all these bargains is being flexible—and knowing where to look.

Low occupancy, the winter months (excluding holidays), and even just the on-set of the weekend regularly bring sky-high rates down to earth all around town. Just look at the scene in downtown L.A.: At such renowned hotels as the **New Otani Hotel and Gardens,** 120 S. Los Angeles St., at 1st Street (☎ **800/421-8795** or 213/629-1200), and the **Hyatt Regency Los Angeles,** 711 S. Hope St., at 7th Street (☎ **800/233-1234** or 213/683-1234), regular rates start at around $190 on most nights. On the weekends, however, when the business travelers who normally fill these towers have all gone home, rates plummet, often to bargain-basement levels of $95 or $100 a night.

The same holds true in the Valley. At the **Radisson Valley Center,** 15443 Ventura Blvd., Sherman Oaks (☎ **800/333-3333** or 818/981-5400), conveniently sitting at the crossroads of San Diego (I-405) and Ventura (U.S. 101) freeways, a spacious room with a private balcony can be had for as little as $99 a night—quite a discount from the regular room rates, which start at $160. Similar deals can be had at the **Universal City Hilton and Towers** (see p. 411), at the gate of Universal Studios, where rooms go for as little as $110 once all the out-of-town movie moguls go home for the weekend; and at the **Beverly Garland Holiday Inn** in North Hollywood (see p. 411), where off-season visitors can book a pleasant room for as litttle as $69—less than half of the regular rate.

You don't have to go downtown or to the Valley to get deals like these, either. At the 13-story **Hyatt on Sunset,** 8401 Sunset Blvd. (2 blocks east of La Cienega Blvd.; ☎ **800/233-1234** or 213/656-1234), a record-industry favorite situated right

---

foot, bike, or in-line skates (rentals are two blocks away; inquire at the front desk). All rooms have a small balcony, and breakfast is served in a cobblestone courtyard shielded from the noisy boulevard. About the only thing missing is a swimming pool (they'll cheerfully lend you beach towels, though, for an ocean dip). AAA members can take advantage of the $95 rate for suites, which are the best deal here.

Travelodge at LAX. 5547 W. Century Blvd., Los Angeles, CA 90045. ☎ **800/421-3939** or 310/649-4000. Fax 310/649-0311. 147 rms. A/C TEL TV. $69–$74 double. Extra person $8; children under 18 stay free. Lower rates off-season. AE, DISC, DC, MC, V. Free parking.

The lobby is nondescript and the rooms standard, but there's a surprisingly beautiful tropical garden surrounding the pool area. Some units have terraces, and no-smoking rooms are available. Services include free airport transportation, baby-sitting, 24-hour room service (a rarity for a hotel in this price range), and a car rental desk. A Denny's is attached to the hotel.

DOUBLES FOR $100 OR LESS

If you're going to be in town on the weekend, also consider **Barnaby's Hotel** (under "Worth a Splurge," below), where weekend rack rates run $109 to $129.

Best Western Sunrise–Redondo Beach Marina. 400 N. Harbor Drive, Redondo Beach, CA 90277. ☎ **800/334-7384** or 310/376-0746. Fax 310/376-7384. 111 rooms. A/C TEL TV. From $69 double. Extra person $10; children under 12 stay free. AE, CB, DC, DISC, MC, V. Free parking.

in the heart of the action on the world-famous Sunset Strip, rooms that go for $170 on weekdays go for $105 once the weekend rolls around. At the historic **Hollywood Roosevelt,** in the heart of Tinseltown (see p. 408), there's no need to pay the $109 to $129 rack rate; off-season and weekend specials start at $79!

Just across the street from the beach in Santa Monica is **Hotel Oceana,** 849 Ocean Ave. (☎ **800/777-0758** or 310/393-0486), a recently renovated, wonderfully hip all-suite hotel where you can book you and your family a $200 suite for as little as $90 in the winter months. Since the suites come with fully equipped kitchens, you can save even more by cooking for yourself. Another great all-suite option worth checking out is **Le Montrose Suite Hotel,** 900 Hammond St., West Hollywood (☎ **800/776-0666** or 310/855-1115). These upscale condo-like one-bedroom apartments, which come complete with gas fireplace, fax machine, and Nintendo games, normally start at a budget-crushing $220; however, they've often got a deal going on, so call and inquire.

If you need a comfortable place to stay at the airport, try the **Sheraton Gateway Hotel—Los Angeles Airport,** 6101 W. Century Blvd., near Sepulveda Blvd. (☎ **800/325-3535** or 310/642-1111), where rooms that officially start at $135 and go as high as $450 can be booked for as little as $89 on the weekends—with breakfast! Auto club members can get a rate of $101 anytime; if you're smart enough to ask for the corporate rate, you can get a room for $119 just about any day of the week. Not bad for a hotel with an outdoor pool, Jacuzzi, and 24-hour room service.

Wherever you book, always ask about package deals (some include breakfast or bargain tickets to local attractions), corporate rates, family plans, auto club member discounts—many L.A. hotels offer sizable discounts every day to AAA members—and military and senior discounts.

Across the street from charming King Harbor (the Redondo Beach marina), the Sunrise is clean and comfy, with pleasant and quiet interior hallways, a heated outdoor pool, and extralarge whirlpool. Casual, beachy watercolors adorn the hallways and rooms, which have refrigerators and cable TV. Guests can rent bicycles on the premises to explore the marina and adjacent beaches, plus there's a bike and skate rental hut directly across the street. The restaurant, formerly a grill, was recently transformed into a classier northern Italian seafood establishment; if that doesn't interest you, there are a half-dozen restaurants within two blocks.

❂ **The Venice Beach House Historic Inn.** 15 30th Ave. (off Pacific Ave.), Venice, CA 90291. ☎ **310/823-1966.** Fax 310/823-1842. 4 rms, 5 suites. TEL TV. $85–$95 double w/shared bath; $130–$165 suite. All rates include continental breakfast. AE, EU, MC, V. Free parking.

This former family home, built in 1911, is now a fine bed-and-breakfast on one of Venice's unique sidewalk streets (a service alley provides access to rear garages). The interiors of this Victorian, with its hardwood floors, bay windows, lattice porch, and large Oriental rugs, will make you forget the hustle and bustle of the beach that's just steps away. Each of the nine guest rooms is different, outfitted with white rattan or antique wood furnishings; some are punctuated with country prints, others with shelves of worn hardcover books. Breakfast is served in the comfortable downstairs sitting room, where you'll also find tea, cool lemonade, and fresh-baked cookies every afternoon. The inn can also prepare picnic baskets for day trips. *Beware:* The inn can get noisy, and despite its relative homeyness, it's not for everyone. Smoking is not permitted.

Doubles for $130 or Less

Courtyard by Marriott. 13480 Maxella Ave., Marina del Rey, CA 90292. ☎ **800/628-0908** or 310/822-8555. Fax 310/823-2996. 276 rms. A/C TEL TV. $119 double. Weekend and off-season rates. Children under 10 stay free. AE, DISC, DC, MC, V.

This resortlike hotel is conveniently located a few blocks from the marina and the Villa Marina Center, where you'll find good dining options and shopping. Rooms have been recently renovated and feature two phones and coffeemakers; many have patios or balconies. Take advantage of the spa, pool, sauna, steam room, and whirlpool; you'll also have free use of a nearby fitness center. Your AAA membership brings the weekend rate to $80, nonmembers pay $89; $95 buys a bonus breakfast for two on the weekends.

Hotel Shangri-La. 1301 Ocean Ave., Santa Monica, CA 90401. ☎ **800/345-STAY** or 310/394-2791. Fax 310/451-3351. 8 rms, 47 suites. A/C TEL TV. $115 studio; suites from $155. $99 AAA rate. AE, EU, DC, DISC, MC, V. Free parking.

Perched right on Ocean Avenue overlooking the Pacific and just two blocks from the Third Street Promenade, the Shangri-La has a great location. The small lobby opens to a large plant-filled courtyard (suprisingly lacking a pool) bordered on the north and west by the hotel. Rooms are accessed motel-style, from outside balconies overlooking the courtyard. The rooms themselves are spacious, and almost all offer ocean views. The overall art deco feel of the hotel permeates the rooms—the lamps and mirrors, even the faucets and doorknobs, evoke the early part of the century. The large Formica-topped furniture, however, evokes the Starship *Enterprise* more than the Golden Age of Hollywood. Complimentary continental breakfast is served daily, and there's a small ocean-view exercise room.

Marina International. 4200 Admiralty Way (west of Lincoln Blvd.), Marina del Rey, CA 90292. ☎ **800/529-2525** or 310/301-2000. Fax 310/301-6687. 110 rms, 25 bungalows. A/C TEL TV. $119–$139 double; bungalows from $119. Senior & auto club discounts. AE, CB, DC, EU, MC, V. Free parking.

This hotel's lovely rooms are bright, contemporary, and very private. Most are decorated in a casual California style, with soft pastels and textured fabrics; all have balconies or patios. The bungalows are plush and absolutely huge—some are even split-level duplexes—with sitting areas and sofa beds. The Crystal Fountain serves continental fare indoors or out, and the hotel offers concierge, room service, and complimentary airport shuttle. Other bonuses include an outdoor heated pool, whirlpool, sundeck, nearby golf and tennis, a business center, and a tour desk. AAA member rates, when available, bring the tariff down to $82.

Pacific Shore Hotel. 1819 Ocean Ave. (at Pico Blvd.), Santa Monica, CA 90401. ☎ **800/622-8711** or 310/451-8711. Fax 310/394-6657. 168 rms. A/C TEL TV. $125–$150 double. Lower rates off-season. AE, EU, MC, V. Free parking.

A rectangular, eight-story glass and concrete monolith located about a block from the beach, this is a good choice for those who want to be in the heart of Santa Monica. There's nothing to get too excited about, but the rooms are decent and well priced. Every room is chain-hotel identical. Great sunsets can be seen from the ocean-facing rooms on the high floors, but you'll have to look over busy Ocean Avenue, a vacant lot, and the ritzy roofs of oceanfront beach resort Shutters on the Beach. You'll find a busy cocktail lounge downstairs, and a heated swimming pool and Jacuzzi out back. Auto club membership earns a discount rate of $89 year-round, making this a surprising bargain if you simply must be by the sea.

WORTH A SPLURGE

Barnaby's Hotel. 3501 Sepulveda Blvd. (at Rosecrans Blvd.), Manhattan Beach, CA 90266. ☎ **800/552-5285** or 310/545-8466. 123 rms. A/C. Weekdays $149–$174 double, weekends $109–$129 double. AAA discount. All rates include breakfast. AE, DC, DISC, EU, MC, V. Valet parking $4.

The most unusual hotel on the coast, Barnaby's sounds like a guest house, operates like a bed-and-breakfast, and feels like a quaint old hotel. The stuccoed pink facade and trademark green awnings give way to European-styled guest rooms. Each is decorated with antique headboards, lace curtains, hardcover books, and 19th-century prints. Some rooms feature balconies, chandeliers, and attractive but nonfunctioning fireplaces. The best rooms are in back and overlook the courtyard, where weddings and other functions are held. Romantic Barnaby's is an excellent place for couples and celebrants. Full English breakfasts are served buffet style. The hotel offers complimentary airport service as well as a glass-enclosed heated pool and Jacuzzi, and a sundeck. Ask about reduced weekend rates and AAA member discounts, which can bring rooms down to less than $100 a night, with breakfast.

✪ **Casa Malibu.** 22752 Pacific Coast Hwy. (about ¼ mile south of Malibu Pier), Malibu, CA 90265. ☎ **800/831-0858** or 310/456-2219. Fax 310/456-5418. 19 rms, 2 suites. TEL TV. $99–$135 double with garden view, $150 double with ocean view, $169 beachfront double. Suites from $169. Room with kitchen $10 extra. AE, EU, MC, V. Free parking.

I'm hesitant to crow too loudly about Casa Malibu, one of my favorite L.A. hotels, for fear that it'll be even harder to get a room here. The modest two-story motel wraps around a palm-studded inner courtyard with well-tended flowerbeds and cuppa d'oro vines climbing the facade. Just past the garden is the blue Pacific and a large swath of private Malibu beach for the exclusive use of hotel guests. The king-bedded oceanfront rooms have balconies directly over the sand, making them some of the city's most coveted accommodations—they're a great place to watch the pelicans dive for fish in the late afternoon. If you've got a room without a view, you can only see the ocean from the communal balcony; but because the sound of the waves will put you soundly to sleep in any of the rooms, that criticism seems like complaining that the caviar is too cold.

L.A.'S WESTSIDE & BEVERLY HILLS
DOUBLES FOR $60 OR LESS

Beverly Laurel Motor Hotel. 8018 Beverly Blvd. (west of Fairfax), Los Angeles, CA 90048. ☎ **800/962-3824** or 213/651-2441. Fax 213/651-5225. 52 rooms, 10 with kitchen. A/C TEL TV. $60 double; $70 w/kitchen. Senior & Auto Club 10% discount. AE, CB, DC, MC, V. Free parking.

We admit it: This slightly dingy motel wouldn't rate a mention without the enormously popular Swingers Coffee Shop downstairs (see Section 4, "Dining"). After taking a look, though, we have to concede that its location is ideal for exploring most of Los Angeles. Beverly Hills, downtown, Universal Studios, and the beaches are all equidistant from this little dive near Farmer's Market and the orthodox Jewish Fairfax district. Catering mostly to an elderly European and Australian clientele, the Beverly Laurel does offer clean, safe rooms; if you can overlook some tacky, mismatched furniture, you'll appreciate the ample closet space and almost full-size kitchens. The postage stamp–sized outdoor swimming pool is a little public for carefree sunbathing, but does the job on hot summer days. This place is cheap, cheap, cheap—and did we mention the great coffee shop?

DOUBLES FOR $80 OR LESS

Los Angeles West Travelodge. 10740 Santa Monica Blvd. (at Overland Ave.), Los Angeles, CA 90025. ☎ **310/474-4576.** Fax 310/470-3117. 55 rms. A/C TEL TV. $75–$96 double. Rates include continental breakfast. AE, CB, DC, EU, MC, V. Free parking.

This clean and friendly motel offers good value in a high-priced area. The pleasant, modern rooms were renovated in 1990 and come with coffeemakers and refrigerators, though some rooms have only a shower stall (no tub). There's also an enclosed, heated swimming pool with a sundeck.

Park Sunset Hotel. 8462 Sunset Blvd., West Hollywood, CA 90069. ☎ **800/821-3660** or 213/654-6470. Fax 213/654-5918. 62 rms, 20 suites. A/C TEL TV. $79 double; $150 suite. AE, CB, DC, DISC, EU, MC, V. Parking $5.

You'd think that the Park Sunset's location right on the Strip would make this one of the noisiest places to sleep in Los Angeles. But all the guest rooms are in the back of the modest three-story hotel, away from the cars and cacophony. The rooms are well kept and surprisingly well decorated, though the carpets are a bit worn and the bathroom color schemes are a tad dated. Some rooms have balconies and/or kitchens, and corner rooms have panoramic city views. There's a small heated pool in a lush courtyard, and a continental restaurant on the lobby level.

✪ Ramada Limited Hotel. 1052 Tiverton Ave. (near Glendon Ave.), Los Angeles, CA 90024. ☎ **800/631-0100** or 310/208-6677. Fax 310/824-3732. 27 rms, 9 suites. A/C TEL TV. $66–$76 double; suites from $75. AE, CB, DC, DISC, EU, MC, V. Free parking.

This place isn't fancy by any stretch of the imagination, but the rooms are comfortable and have recently been updated—they're in better condition than those in many hotels that cost more. Some have stoves, refrigerators, and stainless-steel countertops; others have microwave ovens. Bathrooms have marble vanities. Facilities include an exercise room, a lounge, and an activities desk.

DOUBLES FOR $100 OR LESS

Century Wilshire Hotel. 10776 Wilshire Blvd. (between Malcolm and Selby aves.), Los Angeles, CA 90024. ☎ **800/421-7223** (outside CA), or 310/474-4506. Fax 310/474-2535. 42 rms, 58 suites. TEL TV. $85 double; $125 junior suite; $150–$175 1-bedroom suite. All rates include continental breakfast. AE, CB, DC, EU, MC, V. Free parking.

The units here are large, sparsely decorated, and well located, near UCLA and Beverly Hills. Most of the rooms in this three-story hotel have kitchenettes, and some have French doors that open onto balconies; furnishings, however, are worn and outdated. The hotel surrounds a quiet courtyard and has an Olympic-size swimming pool. Breakfast is served each morning either inside or out in the courtyard. For the money, it's hard to do better in Westwood.

✪ Hotel Del Capri. 10587 Wilshire Blvd. (at Westholme Ave.), Los Angeles, CA 90024. ☎ **800/444-6835** or 310/474-3511. Fax 310/470-9999. 36 rms, 45 suites. A/C TEL TV. $85–$105 double; suites from $110. Rates include continental breakfast. AE, CB, DC, EU, MC, V. Free parking.

The Del Capri is one of the best values in trendy Westwood. This well-located and fairly priced hotel is popular with tourists, business travelers, and parents visiting their UCLA offspring. There are two parts to the property: a four-story building on the boulevard, and a quieter two-story motel that surrounds a kidney-shaped swimming pool. Though the rooms are beginning to show wear and tear, all are of good quality and have electrically adjustable beds, a decidedly novel touch. The more expensive rooms are slightly larger, and have whirlpool baths and an extra phone in the bathroom. Most of the suites have kitchenettes. The hotel provides free shuttle service to nearby shopping and attractions in Westwood, Beverly Hills, and Century City.

San Vicente Inn. 837 N. San Vicente Blvd., West Hollywood, CA 90069. ☎ **310/854-6915.** 20 rms, suites, and cottages. TEL TV. $89–$109 double. All rates include continental breakfast. AE, CB, DC, EU, MC, V. Free parking.

West Hollywood's only gay owned and operated B&B is a thoroughly charming place, with rooms that are individually and cozily decorated. Some rooms have kitchens, but you won't really need one; lots of restaurants (and shops and bars) are just steps away. Guests have use of the garden patio, swimming pool, spa-bath, and clothing-optional redwood sundeck.

DOUBLES FOR $130 OR LESS

Ⓢ **Carlyle Inn.** 1119 S. Robertson Blvd. (south of Wilshire Blvd.), Los Angeles, CA 90035. ☎ **800/322-7595** or 310/275-4445. Fax 310/859-0496. 24 rms, 8 suites. A/C TEL TV. $110–$120 double; $190 suite. All rates include full breakfast. AE, DC, DISC, EU, MC, V. Parking $8.

Hidden on an uneventful stretch of Robertson Boulevard, just south of Beverly Hills, this four-story inn is one of the best-priced finds in Los Angeles. The hotel's exceedingly clever design has transformed an ordinary square lot in a high-density district into a delightfully airy hostelry. Despite its small size and unlikely location, architects have managed to create a multistory interior courtyard, which almost every room faces. Well-planned, contemporary interiors are fitted with recessed lighting, art deco wall lamps, pine furnishings, and well-framed classical architectural monoprints. Amenities include coffeemakers and VCRs. The hotel's primary drawback is that it lacks views; curtains must remain drawn at all times to maintain any sense of privacy. Suites are only slightly larger than standard rooms.

WORTH A SPLURGE

Beverly Hills Inn. 125 South Spalding Dr., Beverly Hills, CA 90212. ☎ **800/463-4466** or 310/278-0303. Fax 310/278-1728. 45 rms, 4 suites. A/C TEL TV. $135 double; suites from $180. All rates include full breakfast. AE, DC, EC, EU, MC, V. Free parking.

Once the nondescript Beverly Crest Hotel, this property underwent an enormous year-long renovation and reopened in 1995; it's now a terrific place to stay. The inn is well located, within walking distance of both Rodeo Drive and Century City. Rooms, thoughtfully designed in a slightly Asian style, tend to be on the small side, but you get what you pay for here. Larger rooms are more expensive, and the best overlook the pool and courtyard; guests on the other side can keep an eye on their cars in the parking lot. Every room has a refrigerator. There's a sauna and exercise room, and a small bar aptly named the Garden Hideaway. At press time, a new bar and restaurant were scheduled to open shortly. The full breakfast and free parking make this an extra-good deal in the most expensive part of town.

HOLLYWOOD
DOUBLES FOR $60 OR LESS

Ⓢ **Banana Bungalow.** 2775 Cahuenga Blvd. (north of U.S. 101), West Hollywood, CA 90068. ☎ **800/4-HOSTEL** or 213/851-1129. Fax 213/851-2022. 200 beds, 25 doubles. TV. $45 double; $12–$18 per person in multibed room. EU, MC, V. Free parking.

With a loose, carefree atmosphere reminiscent of a European backpackers' hostel, this is a great choice if you're under 35. It's probably the most fun place to stay in the city; it's often filled with international guests and there's almost always something going on. Nestled on 6.8 acres in the Hollywood Hills, a short drive from the Walk of Fame and Universal Studios, Banana Bungalow has double and multishare rooms, kitchen facilities, a restaurant, a lounge, a free movie theater, and an arcade/game room. The hostel offers free airport pickup and regular excursions to the beach, Disneyland, and other L.A. area destinations. And they've begun offering tours of the star's homes as well as tours to Tijuana, the Grand Canyon, or Las Vegas for an additional charge.

Hollywood Celebrity Hotel. 1775 Orchid Ave. (north of Hollywood Blvd.), Hollywood, CA 90028. ☎ **800/222-7017,** 800/222-7090 in California, or 213/850-6464. Fax 213/850-7667. 32 rms, 6 suites. A/C TEL TV. $65 double; suites from $75. All rates include continental breakfast. AE, CB, DC, DISC, EU, MC, V. Free parking.

This small but centrally located hotel is one of the best budget buys in Hollywood. Located just half a block behind Mann's Chinese Theatre, it offers spacious, comfortable, art deco–style units. Breakfast is delivered to your door along with the newspaper every morning. Small pets are allowed, but a $50 deposit is required.

DOUBLES FOR $80 OR LESS

Best Western Hollywood Motor Hotel. 6141 Franklin Ave. (between Vine & Gower sts.), Hollywood, CA 90028. ☎ **800/287-1700** (in CA only), or 213/464-5181. Fax 213/962-0536. 82 rooms. $69–$79 double. Senior & auto club discounts. DC, DISC, MC, V. Free parking.

Location is a big selling point for this chain representative just off U.S. 101 and within walking distance of the famed Hollywood and Vine intersection. They know it, too; the walls inside showcase images from the Golden Age of movies, and the front desk offers an endless variety of arranged tours, ranging from the Hollywood Walk of Fame to Six Flags Magic Mountain. Rooms are plain and clean, but lack warmth. Outer walls are painted cinder block, and closets are hidden behind institutional metal accordion doors. On the plus side, however, all come with a refrigerator and cable TV. Although the front wing overlooking the street has indoor hallways, the rooms in back have an attractive view of the neighboring hillside. Outside is a gleaming blue-tiled heated pool, off the lobby you'll find one of the city's most trendy retro-eateries, the Hollywood Hills Coffee Shop (see Section 4, "Dining").

DOUBLES FOR $130 OR LESS

Ⓢ **Hollywood Roosevelt.** 7000 Hollywood Blvd., Hollywood, CA 90028. ☎ **800/252-7466** or 213/466-7000. 311 rms, 19 suites. $109–$129 double, suites from $200. Off-season and weekend specials $79–$95. AE, CB, DC, DISC, EU, MC, V. Valet parking $9.50.

This 12-story movie-city landmark is located on a slightly seedy, very touristy part of Hollywood Boulevard, across from Mann's Chinese Theatre and just down the street from the Walk of Fame. The Roosevelt was one of the city's grandest hotels when it opened its doors in 1927, and home to the first Academy Awards ceremony. But, like the starlets who once filled the lobby, its beauty faded; until a relatively recent makeover, it seemed well on its way to Forest Lawn. The exquisitely restored two-story lobby features a Hollywood minimuseum. Rooms, however, are typical of chain hotels, far less appealing in size and decor than the public areas; but a few are charmed with their original 1920s-style bathrooms. High floors have unbeatable skyline views. David Hockney decorated the famous Olympic-size pool. The Cinegrill supper club draws locals with a zany cabaret show and guest chanteuses from Eartha Kitt to Cybill Shepherd.

WORTH A SPLURGE

Holiday Inn Hollywood. 1755 N. Highland Ave. (between Franklin and Hollywood blvds.), Hollywood, CA 90028. ☎ **800/465-4329** or 213/462-7181. Fax 213/466-9072. 448 rms, 22 suites. A/C TEL TV. $159 double; suites from $170. AE, DC, DISC, EU, MC, V. Parking $6.50.

This 23-story hotel in the heart of Hollywood offers perfectly acceptable rooms that are both pleasant and comfortable—as long as you don't mind being on a busy thoroughfare and sharing the pavement with bikers, wannabe rockers, and the other colorful characters that make up the neighborhood melange. The plus side is, in this neighborhood nobody expects you to pay rack rates. You can generally get a room for $100 or less, with off-season specials as low as $79. A major guest room renovation was completed in 1995, so the hotel's standard furnishings are now stain-free. Suites, which include small kitchenettes, are particularly good buys. There's a swimming pool, a sundeck, and a revolving rooftop restaurant.

DOWNTOWN
DOUBLES FOR $100 OR LESS

The Kawada Hotel. 200 S. Hill St. (at 2nd St.), Los Angeles, CA 90012. ☎ **800/752-9232** or 213/621-4455. Fax 213/687-4455. 115 rms, 1 suite. A/C TEL TV. $89–$95 double; $145 suite. AE, DC, DISC, EU, MC, V. Parking $6.60.

This pretty, well-kept, and efficiently managed hotel is a pleasant oasis in the otherwise gritty heart of downtown, conveniently located close to the Civic Center, the Museum of Contemporary Art, and Union Station. Behind the clean three-story, red-brick exterior are over a hundred pristine rooms, all with handy kitchenettes and simple furnishings. The rooms aren't large, but they're extremely functional, each outfitted with a VCR (movies are available free of charge) and two phones. No-smoking rooms are available. The hotel's lobby-level restaurant features an eclectic international menu all day.

THE SAN FERNANDO VALLEY

The Valley, a suburb-filled basin pressing Los Angeles from the north, sometimes gets a bad rap for not being as hip as Los Angeles proper. But many people make it their exclusive destination—those who are visiting family or doing business in the Valley, and the throngs who come to experience Universal Studios. It also makes sense to make the Valley your base if you're here to see the Burbank Studios, Warner Brothers Studios, or Six Flags Magic Mountain.

DOUBLES FOR $100 OR LESS

Best Western Mikado Hotel. 12600 Riverside Dr. (east of Coldwater Canyon), North Hollywood, CA 91607. ☎ **800/826-2759** or 818/763-9141. Fax 818/752-1045. 58 rooms, 2 with kitchenette. A/C TEL TV. $89 double; $100–$150 kitchenette units. Extra person $10; children under 12 stay free. Corporate, senior and auto club 10% discount. Rates include full breakfast. AE, CB, DC, DISC, JCB, MC, V. Free parking.

A Valley feature for 40 years, the Mikado is still fabulously kitschy, with a Japanese theme running from the pagoda-style exterior to the sushi bar (the Valley's oldest) across the driveway. Two-story motel buildings face onto well-maintained courtyards, one with a koi pond and wooden footbridge, the other with a shimmering blue-tiled pool and spa. Recent redecorating has stripped most of the Asian vibe from the room interiors, which are nevertheless comfortable and provide such extras as hair dryers and free cable TV and movies. American breakfasts are served at a cluster of tables off the lobby, and room service is available for lunch and dinner (Japanese dishes

⊕ Affordable Family-Friendly Hotels

In addition to these affordable family options, L.A. also has some terrific all-suite hotels that bring their rates down to manageable levels on occasion, particularly on weekends and during the winter months. See "Suite Deals (& Other Bargains)" on p. 402 for details.

The Mansion Inn *(see p. 401)*   Three blocks from Venice Beach and across the street from Marina del Rey, families can save a bundle at this charming inn. Breakfast is included in the already excellent rates, rooms are spacious and comfortable, and kids under 12 stay (and eat) free. Two parents and two children can easily share an $89 two-double-bed room or a $125 ($95 for AAA members) two-level suite. Plus, bicycles, in-line skates, and other recreational equipment can be rented nearby.

Sportsmen's Lodge *(see p. 410)*   Ideally located for families visiting Universal Studios and other San Fernando Valley attractions, the Lodge is situated near affordable restaurants and offers a number of discounts if you take the time to inquire. The fist thing kids gravitate to here is the Olympic-sized swimming pool (fenced in for safety), but there's also a nice lawn and garden area near the pool for rambunctious youngsters to let off a little steam. You can also take them down the street to the popular Sports Center bowling alley and arcade.

only). Lovers of the pagoda motif will dislike the planned 1997 exterior remodel; you should check ahead to see whether construction will affect the little serenity allowed so close to the freeway.

La Maida House. 11159 La Maida St. (west of Lankershim Blvd.), North Hollywood, CA 91601. ☎ **818/769-3857.** Fax 818/753-9363. 6 rooms, 5 suites. A/C TEL TV. $85–$125 double; $155–$210 suite. Discounts on stays over 7 days. Rates include breakfast and evening aperitif. MC, V. Free parking.

Comprised of four different converted homes on the same quiet, entirely residential street in North Hollywood, this bed-and-breakfast inn is elegant and discreet, with a carefully assembled decor of antiques and treasures from the owners' many travels. Without ever advertising, they've stayed full for 13 years with mostly entertainment industry folks working at the nearby NBC, Warner Bros., or Universal studios. You'll feel like an honored houseguest, particularly in one of the four rooms in the main house, a lovingly restored 1920s Italianate that contains the sunlit dining room. Behind one of the bungalows you'll find a swimming pool and exercise room for use by all guests, and each room has a private telephone, with answering machines available upon request. In addition to prohibiting smoking, the animal rights activist owners refuse to allow furs on the premises.

DOUBLES FOR $130 OR LESS

Sportsmen's Lodge. 12825 Ventura Blvd. (east of Coldwater Canyon), Studio City, CA 91604. ☎ **800/821-8511** or 818/769-4700. Fax 213/877-3898. 178 rms, 13 suites. A/C TEL TV. $109–$160 double; suites from $180. AAA member rates start at $89. AE, DC, DISC, EU, MC, V. Free parking.

It's been a long time since this part of Studio City was wilderness enough to justify the lodge's name; this sprawling motel has been enlarged and upgraded since those days, the most recent improvements, sprucing up the worn room furnishings, made within the last three years. Walking around the ponds and waterfalls out back, you come upon the surprise luxury of a heated, Olympic-size swimming pool surrounded by a fleet of chaise lounges. It's hard to imagine that busy Ventura Boulevard is just across the parking lot. Rooms are large and comfortable, but not luxurious; many have balconies, and refrigerators are available. The poolside executive studios are the largest and best located of the accommodations here. There's a well-equipped exercise room, a variety of shops and service desks, and both golf and bowling are nearby. Complimentary afternoon tea is served in the lobby at 4pm. Caribou, the latest incarnation of the hotel's stunning glass-enclosed dining room, serves meat and game dishes in a hunting-lodge setting (but we hope not any of the pretty swans frolicking out back!).

WORTH A SPLURGE

Beverly Garland Holiday Inn. 4222 Vineland Ave., North Hollywood, CA 91602. ☎ **800/ BEVERLY** or 818/980-8000. Fax 818/766-5230. 258 rms, 12 suites. A/C TEL TV. $149 double; suites from $199. AAA members and off-season visitors enjoy rates starting at $69. AE, DISC, DC, MC, V. Free parking.

Don't get confused by the name: This hotel is named for its owner, the actress Beverly Garland (of *My Three Sons* fame), not Beverly Hills. Grassy areas and greenery abound at this North Hollywood Holiday Inn, a virtual oasis in the concrete jungle that is most of Los Angeles. The Southern California Mission–style buildings that make up the hotel are a bit dated, but if you grew up with *Brady Bunch* reruns, this only adds to the charm—it looks like something Mike Brady would have designed. Southwestern fabrics complement the natural pine furnishings in the recently renovated guest rooms; unfortunately, the painted cinder-block walls give off something of a college dorm feel. And if you don't smoke, make sure to ask for a nonsmoking room; the smoking rooms smell musty. There are two tennis courts, a pool, a sauna, and all rooms feature balconies. The Paradise Restaurant serves Polynesian-influenced cuisine throughout the day. Complimentary shuttle to Universal is available. Even if you don't score the ultracheap rates, it's easy to stay here for around $100.

Universal City Hilton and Towers. 555 Universal Terrace Pkwy., Universal City, CA 91608. ☎ **800/HILTONS** or 818/506-2500. Fax 818/509-2031. 446 rms, 26 suites. A/C TEL TV. $130–$212 double; suites from $175. Weekend rates start at $110. AE, DC, DISC, EU, MC, V. Valet parking $13.

Although this 24-story hotel sits right outside of the Universal Studios theme park, there's more of a conservative business traveler feel than the raucous family with young children feel you might expect here. The large lobby is built almost entirely of glass, giving it an openness that doesn't feel hollow or empty. Rooms are tastefully decorated in light earth tones with English-style furniture. Cafe Sierra serves California cuisine and is open for breakfast, lunch, dinner, and Sunday brunch.

4 Dining

Any way you look at it—food, decor, service—Los Angeles is one of the world's great dining cities. When it comes to culinary innovation and architectural design, L.A.'s restaurants are tops. Even better, recent economic and social trends have led to a whole new crop of places serving bone china cuisine at blue-plate prices. Budget-minded coffee shops, cafes, and fast-food vendors (especially those serving Mexican fare) abound in this town, but I recommend splurging at least once at one of L.A.'s top-notch restaurants, as much for the people-watching as the food.

Here are some tips on approaching L.A.'s finer restaurants with a budget:

- See if the restaurant serves lunch. Many finer eateries have a moderately priced lunch menu offering smaller portions of their signature dishes. Some of my favorites are Campanile (also good for breakfast), Talesai, Valentino, and Joss.

- Consider keeping the meal tab down by skipping alcoholic beverages, which can add as much as $10 to $15 per person in the blink of an eye (or the bend of an elbow!). Alternately, you might want to visit the bar for *just* cocktails and hors d'oeuvres, which is another excellent way to experience the ambience and cuisine without breaking the bank. The tapas bar at Cava, for example, lends itself perfectly to this ploy.
- Check out L.A.'s newest downsize trend: the upscale coffee shops like Swingers and Hollywood Hills Coffee Shop, where you can get gourmet- and ethnic-tinged versions of comfort food at old-fashioned blue-plate prices.

The restaurants listed below are categorized first by geographic area, then by price. Our limited space forced us to make tough choices; for a greater selection of reviews, see *Frommer's Los Angeles.*

Reservations are recommended almost everywhere in Los Angeles, particularly on weekends and during peak lunch (from noon to 1:30pm) and dinner (7pm to 8:30pm) times.

SANTA MONICA & THE BEACHES
MEALS FOR $10 OR LESS

Benny's Bar-B-Q. 4077 Lincoln Blvd. (south of Washington Blvd.), Marina del Rey. ☎ **310/ 821-6939.** Sandwiches $4–$6, dinner specials $7–$10. AE, MC, V. Mon–Sat 11am–10pm, Sun 2–10pm. BARBECUE.

It's mostly take-out at this dive, but there are a few tables, where Angelenos gorge themselves on the best barbecued pork and beef ribs and hot-link sausages in town. Like almost everything on the menu, barbecued chicken is bathed in a tangy hot sauce and served with baked beans and a choice of coleslaw, potato salad, fries, or corn on the cob. Beef, ham, and pork sandwiches are also available.

☺ **Bread and Porridge.** 2315 Wilshire Blvd. (3 blocks west of 26th St.), Santa Monica. ☎ **310/453-4941.** Main courses $4.50–$9. No credit cards. Tues–Sun 8am–8pm. INTERNATIONAL.

A dozen tables are all that comprise this neighborhood cafe, but a steady stream of locals mills outside, reading their newspapers and waiting for a vacant seat. Once inside, surrounded by the vintage fruit crate labels adorning the walls and tabletops, you too can sample the delicious breakfasts, fresh salads and sandwiches, and super-affordable entrees. There's a vaguely international twist to the menu, which leaps from Mexican omelets to the Cajun crab cakes with corn on the cob and coleslaw to traditional pastas adorned with roma tomatoes and plenty of garlic. All menu items are amazingly cheap, but it's their inventive elegance that makes Bread and Porridge one of L.A.'s best-kept secrets. Get a short stack ($3 to $4) of one of five varieties of pancakes with any meal; they thoughtfully serve breakfast till 3pm.

Gallegos Mexican Deli. 1424 Broadway (corner of 15th St.), Santa Monica. ☎ **310/ 395-0162.** Most items under $4. No credit cards. Mon–Fri 7:30am–6pm, Sat 7:30am–4pm. MEXICAN.

The main order of business at Gallegos is catering, but they'll sell you a single homemade tamale as happily as a tray of 50! Choose from six varieties of the corn husk–wrapped delicacies (plus a "dessert" tamale made with vanilla, raisins, and sugar) and from eight different fresh salsas to top it off. Tacos, burritos, chile rellenos, and enchiladas are prepared with the freshest of ingredients, and the chips (can't eat just one) are made from Gallegos's homemade yellow- and blue-corn tortillas. Office workers, car mechanics, and art gallery curators from the surrounding light industrial/residential neighborhood all converge on the outdoor patio, where simple plastic furniture, vine-covered fences, and a communal copy of today's paper provide a simple setting for a cheap, quick, and enormously satisfying meal.

Jody Maroni's Sausage Kingdom. 2011 Ocean Front Walk (north of Venice Blvd.), Venice. ☎ **310/306-1995.** Sandwiches $4–$6. No credit cards. Daily 10am–5:30pm. SANDWICHES/ SAUSAGES.

Your cardiologist might not approve, but Jody Maroni's all-natural, preservative-free "haut dogs" are some of the best wieners served anywhere. The grungy walk-up (or Rollerblade-up) counter looks fairly foreboding—you wouldn't know there was gourmet fare behind the aging hot dog stand facade. At least 14 different grilled sausage sandwiches are served here. Bypass the traditional hot Italian and try the Toulouse garlic, Bombay curried lamb, all-chicken apple, or orange-garlic-cumin. Each is served on a freshly baked onion roll and smothered with onions and peppers. Burgers, hot dogs, BLTs, and rotisserie chicken are also served, but why bother?

Other locations include Santa Monica's Third Street Promenade, the Valley's Universal CityWalk (☎ 818/622-JODY), and inside LAX's Terminal 5, where you can pick up some last minute vacuum-packed sausages to go.

⑤ Kay 'n' Dave's Cantina. 262 26th St. (south of San Vicente), Santa Monica. ☎ **310/ 260-1355.** Main courses $5–$12. AE, MC, V. Mon–Thurs 7:30am–9:30pm, Fri 7:30am–10pm, Sat 8am–10pm, Sun 8am–9:30pm. HEALTHFUL MEXICAN.

A beach community favorite for "really big portions of really good food at really low prices," this dynamic duo cooks with no lard and has a vegetarian-friendly menu with plenty of meat items too. Come early (and be prepared to wait) for breakfast, as local devotees line up for five kinds of fluffy pancakes, zesty omelets, or one of the best breakfast burritos in town. Grilled tuna Veracruz, spinach-and-chicken enchiladas in tomatillo salsa, seafood fajitas tostada, vegetable-filled corn tamales, and other Mexican specialties are served in huge portions, making this minichain a great choice to fill up for (or re-energize after) an action-packed day of beach sightseeing. Bring the family—there's a kids' menu and crayons on every table. They also run cantinas in Malibu, 18763 Pacific Coast Hwy. (☎ 310/456-8800), and Pacific Palisades, 15246 Sunset Blvd. (☎ 310/459-8118). The Malibu location opens later in the mornings.

Sidewalk Cafe. 1401 Ocean Front Walk (between Horizon Ave. and Market St.), Venice. ☎ **310/399-5547.** Reservations not accepted. Main courses $6–$13. MC, V. Sun–Thurs 8am– 11pm, Fri–Sat 8am–midnight. AMERICAN.

Nowhere in Los Angeles is the people watching better than along Ocean Front Walk. The constantly bustling Sidewalk Cafe is ensconced in one of Venice's few remaining early 20th-century buildings. The best seats, of course, are out front, around overcrowded open-air tables, all with a perfect view of the crowd, which provides nonstop entertainment. The menu is extensive, and the food is a whole lot better than it has to be at a location like this. Choose from the overstuffed sandwiches or other oversize American favorites including omelets, salads, and burgers.

MEALS FOR $20 OR LESS

Alice's. 23000 Pacific Coast Hwy. (at the Malibu Pier), Malibu. ☎ **310/456-6646.** Reservations recommended. Main courses $9–$18; lunch $7–$15. MC, V. Mon–Fri 11:30am–10pm, Sat–Sun 11am–11pm. CALIFORNIA.

Alice's has a long history as a Malibu fixture, situated on Pacific Coast Highway on the pier above the beach. The dining room is glassed in on three sides and faces the ocean; rear tables sit on a raised platform so that everyone has a million-dollar view. It's a light and airy place, with a casual menu to match. Admittedly, most people are here for the one-of-a-kind atmosphere, but the food is a lot better than it needs to be. Seared yellowtail tuna is served simply, on a bed of spinach, with lemon and tarragon butter. The grilled chicken breast is marinated in garlic and soy and served with tomato-cilantro relish. Pastas and pizzas are also available, and there's a full bar.

Aunt Kizzy's Back Porch. 4325 Glencove Ave. (in the Villa Marina Shopping Center), Marina del Rey. ☎ **310/578-1005.** Reservations not accepted. Main courses $8–$13. AE. Mon–Sat 11am–4pm; Sun–Thurs 4–11pm, Fri–Sat 4pm–midnight; Sun 11am–3pm. SOUTHERN.

This is a real Southern restaurant, owned by genuine Southerners from Texas and Oklahoma. Kizzy's chicken creole, jambalaya, and smothered pork chops are just about as good as it gets in this city. Almost everything comes with vegetables, red beans and rice, and corn muffins. Fresh-squeezed lemonade is served by the mason jar. These are huge meals that, as corny as it sounds, are as filling as they are delicious. Sunday brunches are all-you-can-eat affairs, served buffet style. The biggest problem with Aunt Kizzy's is its location, hidden in a shopping center that has too few parking spaces to accommodate its customers. Look for the restaurant to the right of Vons supermarket.

Worth a Splurge

Camelions. 246 26th St. (south of San Vicente Blvd.), Santa Monica. ☎ **310/395-0746.** Reservations required. Main courses $14–$22; lunch $10–$13. AE, CB, DC, MC, V. Tues–Sun 11:30am–2:30pm, 6–9:30pm. CALIFORNIA/FRENCH.

Either indoors or out, dining here is one of Los Angeles's most romantic dining experiences. Camelions's three 1920s stucco cottages, each with beamed ceilings and a crackling fireplace, are built around an ivy-trellised brick patio. Contrary to its provincial setting, the tasty French-inspired cuisine is plenty trendy. Red lentil crepes arrive garnished with smoked salmon and arugula salad, and roasted duck breast is sliced thin and fanned out over a plate of walnut Merlot sauce, accompanied by a risotto and berry timbale. There are traditional French dishes like sautéed rabbit stewed in a clay pot with sweet garlic. A large selection of sandwiches and salads (like spinach with warm new potatoes, bacon, and mustard vinaigrette) are available at lunch.

Valentino. 3115 Pico Blvd. (west of Bundy Dr.), Santa Monica. ☎ **310/829-4313.** Reservations required. Pasta $12–$16, meat and fish $18–$25. AE, CB, DC, DISC, MC, V. Fri 11:30am–2:30pm; Mon–Thurs 5:30–10:30pm, Fri–Sat 5:30–11pm. ITALIAN.

All of Los Angeles ached for charming owner Piero Selvaggio when he lost 20,000 bottles of wine in the 1994 earthquake. But elegant Valentino never lost its position as *Wine Spectator* magazine's top wine cellar. *The New York Times* food critic Ruth Reichl calls this the best Italian restaurant in America. The creations of Selvaggio and his brilliant young chef, Angelo Auriana, make dinners here lengthy, multicourse affairs (often involving several bottles of wine). You might begin with a crisp Pinot Grigio paired with caviar-filled cannoli; or crespelle, thin little pancakes with fresh porcini mushrooms and a rich melt of fontina cheese. Handmade pastas tossed with tender baby squid or sweet tiny clams are typical of first courses, though it really depends on what came to market the morning you visit. A rich Barolo is the perfect accompaniment to rosemary-infused roasted rabbit; the fantastically fragrant risotto with white truffles is one of the most magnificent dishes I've ever had. Jackets are all but required in the elegant dining room. What more can I say: Go!

L.A.'s WESTSIDE & BEVERLY HILLS
Meals for $10 or Less

✪ **The Apple Pan.** 10801 Pico Blvd. (east of Westwood Blvd.). ☎ **310/475-3585.** Main courses $6–$7. No credit cards. Tues–Thurs, and Sun 11am–midnight; Fri–Sat 11am–1am. SANDWICHES/AMERICAN.

There are no tables, just a U-shaped counter, at this classic American burger shack and L.A. landmark. Open since 1947, it's a diner that looks and acts the part. Juicy burgers, bullet service, and the authentic frills-free atmosphere have made it famous. The hickory burger is best, though the tuna sandwich also has its huge share of fans. Definitely order fries and, if you're in the mood, the home-baked apple pie, too.

Dive! 10250 Santa Monica Blvd. (in the Century City Marketplace). ☎ **310/788-3483.** Reservations accepted only for parties of 10 or more. Main courses $6–$15. AE, DC, MC, V. Sun–Thurs 11:30am–10pm, Fri–Sat 11:30am–11pm. SANDWICHES/AMERICAN.

Owned by Steven Spielberg and Jeffrey Katzenberg, two-thirds of the new mega-company, Dreamworks SKG, Dive! is the first of what the investors hope to be a series of submarine-themed restaurants. The insulated underwater ambience is the ultimate in dining entertainment. Except for the fries and the thin-cut onion rings, however, the same cannot be said of the food, which is decent at best. The menu is mainly submarine sandwiches (get it?), along with salads and some wood-roasted dishes like salmon served with assorted dipping sauces like homemade ketchup and cheddar cheese sauce. My advice: Stick with the subs. The restaurant is perpetually packed; waiting patrons get a beeper that conveniently won't work outside, so they have to hang out at the expensive bar, where there's a voyeuristic periscope exposing the goings-on down on Santa Monica Boulevard.

La Salsa. 9631 Little Santa Monica Blvd. (between Camden and Bedford drives), Beverly Hills. ☎ **310/276-2373.** Main courses $5–$7. MC, V. Mon–Fri 10:30am–9:30pm, Sat 10:30am–9pm, Sun 10:30am–7pm. MEXICAN.

L.A.'s best Mexican fast food is served at this bright and spotless taqueria chain, well-known throughout the city for its excellent, healthful, lard-free burritos and tacos. The Gourmet Burrito is a hefty mix of grilled chicken or steak, cheese, and guacamole; the Grande adds rice and beans. True to its name, La Salsa excels in the preparation of fresh sauces, offering four types varying in spiciness, texture, and flavor. The restaurants serve soda and beer, and (sometimes) horchata, a traditional Mexican drink made with rice flour and cinnamon. Order at the counter.

Other locations include 22800 Pacific Coast Hwy., Malibu (☎ 310/456-6299); 44 N. Fair Oaks Ave., Pasadena (☎ 818/793-0723); downtown at 727 Flower St. (☎ 213/892-8227); and 245 Pine Ave., Long Beach (☎ 310/491-1104).

Mishima. 11301 Olympic Blvd. (at Sawtelle Blvd.). ☎ **310/473-5297.** Reservations not accepted. Main courses $4–$9. MC, V. Tues–Sun 11:30am–9pm. JAPANESE.

Hidden on the second floor of an unobtrusive strip mall, this small Japanese eatery has nevertheless become extraordinarily popular with neighborhood residents and workers. A dead ringer for any number of noodle shops in Tokyo, Mishima sports a contemporary Asian decor, complete with matte black tables and chairs, Japanese prints on white walls, and plastic reproductions of every menu item. A loyal clientele fills the small, bright dining room that resonates with noodle slurps and chopstick clacks. Udon (thick wheat noodles) or soba (narrow buckwheat linguine) are the main choices here; both are served either hot or cold in a variety of soups and sauces that true aficionados might find too bland and too thin. Sushi, chicken dishes, and a variety of tempuras are also available. It all seems so authentically Japanese, except, thankfully, for the prices.

⑤ Skewer. 8939 Santa Monica Blvd. (between Robertson and San Vicente blvds.), West Hollywood. ☎ **310/271-0555.** Main courses $7–$9; salads & pitas $4–$7. AE, MC, V. Daily 11am–midnight. MIDDLE EASTERN.

Santa Monica Boulevard is the heart of West Hollywood's commercial strip, and Skewer's sidewalk tables are a great place to see all kinds of neighborhood activity.

Inside is a New York–like narrow space with changing artwork adorning the bare brick walls. From the zesty marinated carrot sticks you get the moment you're seated, to sweet, sticky squares of baklava for dessert, this Mediterranean grill is sure to please. The cuisine is naturally healthful, including baskets of warm pita bread for dipping in traditional salads like *baba ghanoush* (grilled eggplant with tahini and lemon) and *tabbouleh* (cracked wheat, parsley, and tomatoes). Try marinated chicken and lamb off the grill, or *dolmades* (rice and meat–stuffed grape leaves) seared with a tangy tomato glaze.

Swingers. 8020 Beverly Blvd. (west of Fairfax). ☎ **213/653-5858.** Reservations not accepted. Most items under $8. AE, MC, V. Sun–Thurs 6am–2am; Fri–Sat 9am–4am. DINER/AMERICAN.

Resurrected from a motel coffee shop so dismal I can't even remember it, Swingers was transformed by a couple of L.A. nightclub owners into a '90s version of comfy Americana. The interior seems like a slice of the '50s until you notice the plaid upholstery and Warhol-esque graphics that contrast nicely with the red, white, and blue "Swingers" logo adorning *everything*. Guests at the attached Beverly Laurel Motor Hotel (see Section 3, "Accommodations") chow down alongside body-pierced entertainment industry hounds from nearby Maverick Records (Madonna's company), while outside orthodox Jews stroll to and from Fairfax Avenue. Listening to a soundtrack that runs the gamut from punk rock to "Schoolhouse Rock," you'll enjoy high-quality diner favorites spiked with trendy crowd-pleasers like steel-cut Irish oatmeal, challah French toast, grilled Jamaican jerk chicken, and a nice selection of tofu-enhanced vegetarian dishes. Sometimes I just "swing" by for a malt or milkshake to go—theirs are among the best in town.

Versailles. 1415 S. La Cienega Blvd. (south of Pico Blvd.). ☎ **310/289-0392.** Reservations not accepted. Main courses $5–$11. AE, MC, V. Daily 11am–10pm. CUBAN.

Outfitted with Formica tabletops and looking something like an ethnic International House of Pancakes, Versailles feels very much like any number of Miami restaurants that cater to the exiled Cuban community. Because meals are good, bountiful, and cheap, there's often a wait. The menu reads like a veritable survey of Havana-style cookery and includes specialties like "Moors and Christians" (flavorful black beans with white rice), *ropa vieja* (a stringy beef stew), *eastin lechón* (suckling pig with sliced onions), and fried whole fish (usually sea bass). Shredded roast pork is particularly recommendable, especially when tossed with the restaurant's trademark garlic-citrus sauce. But what everyone comes for is the chicken: succulent, slow roasted, smothered in onions, and either the garlic-citrus sauce or barbecue sauce. Most everything is served with black beans and rice; wine and beer are also available.

Additional Versailles restaurants are located in Culver City at 10319 Venice Blvd. (☎ 310/558-3168); and in Encino at 17410 Ventura Blvd. (☎ 818/906-0756).

MEALS FOR $20 OR LESS

Barney Greengrass. 9570 Wilshire Blvd. (in Barney's New York), Beverly Hills. ☎ **310/ 777-5877.** Reservations suggested. Main courses $12–$23; breakfast $5–$11; lunch $8–$15. AE, DC, MC, V. Mon–Wed & Fri 7:30am–7pm, Thurs 7:30am–8pm, Sat 9am–7pm, Sun 9am–6pm. DELI.

It was a big deal in Beverly Hills when the celebrated New York clothier Barney's opened a satellite store here. But it was a very big deal in Hollywood when New York's celebrated "sturgeon king," Barney Greengrass, opened on the department store's top floor. This upscale deli has quickly become an important power lunch spot for the entertainment industry crowd. Famous for sturgeon and smoked fish (at caviar prices), Barney Greengrass seems more than a bit like a fish out of water here. As soon as you get off the elevator you can tell that the restaurant is joyful, clean, and bright, without the attitude (and none of the atmosphere) of New York's nosheries. In addition to having a separate caviar, champagne, and vodka bar, the restaurant makes its own oven-baked matzos, claims to import its bagels from New York's famed H&H bagelry, and sets its paper-covered tables with designer utensils and stemware. The best meals are matzo brei with onions and wild mushrooms, orange-challah french toast, and smoked-salmon soufflé.

Bombay Cafe. 12113 Santa Monica Blvd. (at Bundy Dr.) ☎ **310/820-2070.** Reservations not accepted. Main courses $9–$15. MC, V. Tues–Sun 11:30am–4pm, Tues–Thurs 4–10pm, Fri–Sat 4–11pm. INDIAN.

Indian is the cuisine of the moment in Los Angeles, and nowhere is it done better than at Bombay Cafe. The unlikely McRestaurant interior and storefront location (on the second floor of a nondescript minimall) belie excellent curries and kormas that are typical of South Indian street food. Once seated, immediately order sev puri for the table; these crispy little chips topped with chopped potatoes, onions, cilantro, and chutneys are the perfect accompaniment to what is sure to be an extended menu-reading session. Also recommended are the burrito-like "frankies," juicy little bread rolls stuffed with lamb, chicken, or cauliflower. The best dishes come from the 800° tandoor, and include spicy yogurt-marinated swordfish, lamb, and chicken. The food is served authentically spicy, unless you specify otherwise. The restaurant is phenomenally popular, and gets its share of celebrities: Meg Ryan and Dennis Quaid hired Bombay Cafe to cater an affair at their Montana ranch. Only beer and wine are served.

Cava. 8384 W. 3rd St. (in the Beverly Plaza Hotel, at Orlando Ave.). ☎ **213/658-8898.** Reservations recommended on weekends. Main courses $8–$17; breakfast $3–$9; lunch $4–$14. AE, CB, DC, DISC, MC, V. Daily 6:30am–midnight. SPANISH.

Trendy types in the mood for some fun are attracted to Cava's great mambo atmosphere; their tapas bar is made festive with flamboyant colors and loud, lively flamenco really is live on weekends. The dining room is less raucous, with velvet drapes and tassels adorning the walls and comfortable booths. The cuisine is Spanish livened up with Caribbean touches (Cava is the invention of the team responsible for Cha Cha Cha in Silverlake), an influence reflected in dishes like black bean tamales with tomatillo salsa and golden caviar; thick, dark tortilla soup; jerk chicken with sweet jams; and pan-seared shrimp in spicy peppercorn sauce. Spanish paella is stewed up three ways—with seafood, chicken, and sausage, or all-vegetable—and is featured in Monday's all-you-can-eat "Paella Festival." If you have room for dessert, try the ruby-colored pears poached in port, the rice pudding, or the flan.

⑤ Il Pastaio. 400 N. Canon Dr. (at Brighton Way), Beverly Hills. ☎ **310/205-5444.** Reservations not accepted. Main courses $8–$13;. AE, MC, V. Mon–Sat 11:30am–11pm. ITALIAN.

Sicilian-born Celestino Drago is a terrific chef who has been running the kitchens of high-profile L.A. restaurants for years. Branching out on his own, Drago hit the jackpot with this hugely successful, value-priced eatery. The restaurant is a simple pasta place with white walls, a long bar, and a pasta-making area. It's as narrow as a bowling alley and almost as loud. Only starters, pastas, and desserts are served, but the selections are vast and great for grazing. Swordfish carpaccio with shaved fennel and blood oranges, and seafood "spaghetti" in a flaky envelope are Drago's signature dishes. Drago offered a sautéed foie gras appetizer with a buttery balsamic vinegar glaze when he worked at Chianti, and he continues to serve it here to those who know enough to ask for it. Pastas include lobster-stuffed ravioli in a silky lobster reduction, and garganelli: wheat pasta curls in amatriciana sauce (pureed tomato, pancetta, percorino, and onion). Two risottos are offered nightly, and both usually hit the proverbial bull's-eye. Unfortunately, Il Pastaio is too small. There's almost always a wait, and an uncomfortable one at that. But by meal's end, it always seems worth it.

A second Il Pastaio, on South Lake Street in Pasadena (☎ 818/795-4006), is identical in spirit but thankfully larger inside.

Joss. 9255 Sunset Blvd. (west of Doheny Dr.), West Hollywood. ☎ **310/276-1886.** Reservations suggested. Main courses $8–$18; dim sum $3.75 per order. AE, DC, DISC, MC, V. Mon–Fri noon–3pm; daily 6–11pm. HAUTE CHINESE.

Located on the fringe between Beverly Hills and the Sunset Strip, Joss has a minimalist yet welcoming decor. The entry's ever-present sherry decanter hints at the surprisingly well-chosen and affordable wine list compiled by owner Cecile Tang Shu Shuen. Her inventive menu takes Chinese essentials beyond your expectations, not by creating fussy "fusion" dishes, but by subtly manipulating ingredients and preparations according to her superb artist's palate. Fried rice is spiked with the tang of dried black beans and ginger; velvety curry sauce is creamed with coconut milk and tossed with chicken; and tender beef is marinated with spicy red chiles but mellowed with tangerine liqueur. You could make a meal of the dozen dim sum varieties that include delicately steamed dumplings (spinach and chicken, shrimp with bamboo shoot, or vegetable and black mushroom) served in stacked bamboo steaming trays, crisp-bottom potstickers filled with Peking duck or lamb and leeks, and crispy wonton or spring rolls. Desserts, never overly sweet, complement Joss's sublime meals perfectly. The restaurant's location draws many celebrities and entertainment industry honchos, but gawking is definitely uncool.

Kate Mantilini. 9101 Wilshire Blvd. (corner of Doheny Dr.), Beverly Hills. ☎ **310/278-3699.** Reservations suggested. Main courses $7–$16. AE, MC, V. Mon–Thurs 7:30am–1am, Fri 7:30am–3am, Sat noon–3am, Sun 10am–midnight. AMERICAN.

It's rare to find a restaurant that feels comfortably familiar yet trendy and cutting edge, and is one of L.A.'s few late-night eateries. Kate Mantilini fits the bill perfectly. One of the first to bring meatloaf back into fashion, Kate's offers a huge menu of upscale truck stop favorites like "white" chili (made with chicken, white beans, and Jack cheese), grilled steaks and fish, a few token pastas, and just about anything you could crave. At 2am nothing quite beats a steaming bowl of lentil vegetable soup and some garlic-cheese toast, unless your taste runs to fresh oysters and a dry martini. Kate has it all. The huge mural of the Hagler-Hearns boxing match that dominates the stark, open interior provides the only clue to the namesake's identity: Mantilini was an early female boxing promoter, circa 1947.

Nate and Al's. 414 N. Beverly Dr. (at Brighton Way), Beverly Hills. ☎ **310/274-0101.** Main courses $8–$13. AE, DISC, MC, V. Daily 7:30am–9pm. DELI.

Although located in the center of Beverly Hills' "Golden Triangle," this deli has remained unchanged since they opened in 1945, from the Naugahyde booths to the motherly waitresses, who treat you the same whether you're a house-account celebrity regular or just stopping in for an overstuffed pastrami on rye. Their too-salty chicken soup keeps Nate and Al from being the best L.A. deli, but staples like chopped liver, dense potato pancakes, blintzes, borscht, and well-dilled pickles more than make up for it. If you want to know where Jimmy Stewart, Debbie Reynolds, and other rich and famous types go for comfort food, look no further.

Replay Country Store Cafe. 8607 Melrose Ave. (between San Vicente and La Cienega blvds.), West Hollywood. ☎ **310/657-6404.** Reservations suggested on weekends. Main courses $6–$13. AE, DISC, MC, V. Daily 10am–10pm. ITALIAN/CONTINENTAL.

The two things to remember at Replay are don't buy the clothes and always order the soup. Most of the café's tables are on the wraparound wood porch of the overpriced boutique to which it is attached. This faux country general store on trendy Melrose near the Pacific Design Center won't fool anyone into plunking down $150 for denim overalls, but their restaurant is one of West Hollywood's hidden treasures. Everything on their casual, vaguely Italian menu is outstanding, from gourmet pizzas to pasta with delicately pureed tomato/basil sauce; from the Warm Chicken Salad's surprise combination of blue cheese, walnuts, and mandarin orange wedges, to exquisite pastries for dessert. Each day a different soup, always a simple puree allowing the fresh ingredients to shine through, is ladled into wide bowls at your table from heavy copper saucepans.

WORTH A SPLURGE

Four Oaks. 2181 N. Beverly Glen Blvd., Los Angeles. ☎ **310/470-2265.** Reservations required. Main courses $22–$29. AE, MC, V. Tues–Sat 11:30am–9:30pm, Sun 10:30am–2pm; daily 6–10pm. CALIFORNIA.

Just looking at the menu here makes me swoon. The country-cottage ambience and chef Peter Roelant's superlative blend of fresh ingredients with luxurious Continental flourishes make a meal at the Four Oaks one of my favorite luxuries. Dinner is served beneath trees festooned with twinkling lights. Appetizers like lavender-smoked salmon with crisp potatoes and horseradish crème fraîche complement mouthwatering dishes like roasted chicken with sage, Oregon forest mushrooms, artichoke hearts, and port-balsamic sauce. If you're looking for someplace special, head to this canyon hideaway—you won't be disappointed.

Spago. 1114 Horn Ave. (at Sunset Blvd.), West Hollywood. ☎ **310/652-4025.** Reservations required. Main courses $18–$28. DC, DISC, MC, V. Daily 6–11:30pm. CALIFORNIA.

Wolfgang Puck is more than a great chef: He's also a masterful businessman and publicist who has made Spago one of the best-known restaurants in America. Despite all the hoopla —and more than 15 years of service —Spago remains one of L.A.'s top-rated eateries. German-born Puck originally won fame serving imaginative "gourmet" pizzas. These individually sized thin-crust pies are baked in a wood-burning oven, topped with goodies like duck sausage, shiitake mushrooms, leeks, and artichokes, and other combinations once considered to be on the culinary edge. Of meat dishes, roast Sonoma lamb with braised shallots and grilled chicken with garlic and parsley are two perennial favorites. The celebrated (and far from secret) off-menu meal is Jewish Pizza, a crispy pie topped with smoked salmon, crème fraîche, dill, red onion, and dollops of caviar. The restaurant has plans to move from its quirky, hard-to-find location into Beverly Hills early in 1997, so be sure to call ahead.

HOLLYWOOD
MEALS FOR $10 OR LESS

Flora Kitchen. 460 S. La Brea Ave. (at 6th St.). ☎ **213/931-9900.** Reservations not accepted. Main courses $5–$10. AE, MC, V. Sun–Thurs 8am–10pm, Fri–Sat 8am–11pm. AMERICAN.

Picture an upscale, funky Carrow's or Denny's and you've imagined Flora Kitchen. Known for its tuna and chicken salads served on exalted La Brea Bakery breads, the restaurant is equally comfortable dishing out more eclectic fare like cayenne-spiced potato soup, poached salmon with dill sauce, and seared ahi with roast vegetables. Flora is popular with art-gallery strollers by day, and with music lovers, who take the restaurant's boxed dinners to the Hollywood Bowl, on warm summer nights. Unfortunately, service at Denny's is better.

Hollywood Hills Coffee Shop. 6145 Franklin Ave. (between Gower & Vine sts.). ☎ 213/467-7678. Reservations not accepted. Most items under $8. AE, DISC, MC, V. Tues–Sat 7am–10pm; Sun–Mon 7am–4pm. DINER.

Having served as the run-of-the-mill coffee shop for years for the attached freeway-side Best Western, this place took on a life of its own when chef Susan Fine commandeered the kitchen and spruced up the menu with quirky Mexican and Asian touches. Hotel guests still spill in from the lobby to rub noses with the actors, screenwriters, and other artistic types who converge from nearby canyons while awaiting that sitcom casting call or feature film deal. This community was immortalized in the 1996 film *Swingers*, with scenes actually taped in the restaurant. Prices have gone up (to pay for the industrial-strength cappuccino maker visible behind the counter?) and the dinner menu features surprisingly sophisticated entrees. But breakfast and lunch are still bargains, and the comfy Americana atmosphere is a nice break from the bright lights of nearby Hollywood Boulevard.

Pink's Hot Dogs. 709 N. La Brea Ave. (at Melrose Ave.). ☎ 213/931-4223. Hot dogs $2.10. Sun–Thurs 9:30am–2am, Fri–Sat 9:30am–3am. HOT DOGS.

Pink's isn't your usual guidebook recommendation, but then again, this crusty corner stand is not your usual doggery. The heartburn-inducing chili dogs are so decadent that otherwise upstanding, health-conscious Angelenos crave them; Bruce Willis reportedly proposed to Demi Moore at the 58-year-old shack that grew around the late Paul Pink's 10¢ wiener cart. Pray the bulldozers stay away from this little nugget of a place.

Roscoe's House of Chicken 'n' Waffles. 1514 N. Gower St. (at Sunset Blvd.). ☎ 213/466-7453. Main courses $4–$11. No credit cards. Sun–Thurs 9am–midnight, Fri–Sat 9am–4am. AMERICAN.

It sounds like a bad joke: Only chicken and waffle dishes are served here, a rubric that also encompasses eggs and chicken livers. Its close proximity to CBS Television City has turned this simple restaurant into a kind of de facto commissary for the network. A chicken-and-cheese omelet isn't everyone's ideal way to begin the day, but it's de rigueur at Roscoe's. At lunch, few calorie-unconscious diners can resist the chicken smothered in gravy and onions, a house specialty that's served with waffles or grits and biscuits. Large chicken-salad bowls and chicken sandwiches also provide plenty of cluck for the buck. Homemade cornbread, sweet-potato pie, homemade potato salad, and corn on the cob are available as side orders; wine and beer are sold.

Roscoe's can also be found at 4907 W. Washington Blvd., at La Brea Ave. (☎ 213/936-3730); and 5006 West Pico Blvd. (☎ 213/934-4405).

MEALS FOR $20 OR LESS

✪ **Authentic Cafe.** 7605 Beverly Blvd. (at Curson Ave.). ☎ 213/939-4626. Reservations not accepted. Main courses $8–$13; lunch $8–$13. AE, MC, V. Mon–Thurs 11:30am–10pm, Fri 11:30am–11pm, Sat 10am–11pm, Sun 10am–10pm. SOUTHWESTERN.

True to its name, this excellent restaurant serves authentic Southwestern food in a casual atmosphere; it's a winning combination that has made it an L.A. favorite. The trendy dining room is known for hip people watching, large portions, and good food; they recently expanded the dining room, easing what used to be an unbearable wait for tables. You'll sometimes find an Asian flair to Chef Roger Hayot's Southwestern-style meals. Look for brie, papaya, and chile quesadillas; other worthwhile dishes are the chicken casserole with a cornbread crust; fresh corn and red peppers in chile-cream sauce; and meat loaf with caramelized onions.

Boxer. 7615 Beverly Blvd., Los Angeles. ☎ **213/932-6178.** Reservations required. Main courses $10–$18. AE, MC, V. Tues–Fri 11:30am–2:30pm; Tues–Sun 6–11pm; Sat–Sun brunch 10:30am–2:30pm. CALIFORNIA.

L.A. foodies are watching Boxer carefully, agreeing that young, enthusiastic chef Neal Fraser has definitely stumbled onto something at this intimate eatery on the same block as the ever-expanding Authentic Cafe. The dark wood and weathered wrought iron decor is simple, classy and welcoming for the suited yuppies, Chanel-garbed socialites, and chunky-shoed 20-somethings who blend inside as well as the varied ingredients on the menu. At first glance, the menu appears fussy, an illusion created by the listing of every component in a dish; the perception is heightened by the almost architectural arrangement of food on the plate. True, Fraser invents some fanciful combos, like pancetta-wrapped Numidean hen with caramelized shallot sauce; grilled pork chop served with a tower of apple slices and sage polenta discs; and goat cheese and fennel crusted swordfish with gazpacho vinaigrette. Side dishes are carefully chosen—you get the overall feeling that your satisfaction is of primary importance to the chef. Desserts are equally inventive and tasty, everything from tangerine flan with a pomegranate glaze to bread pudding baked in a small pumpkin. Eschew the valet for the always-plentiful street parking, and bring your own wine (there's a nominal $3 corkage fee).

Ca' Brea. 346 S. La Brea Ave. (north of Wilshire Blvd.). ☎ **213/938-2863.** Reservations recommended. Main courses $9–$21; lunch $7–$20. AE, CB, DC, MC, V. Mon–Sat 11:30am–2:30pm; Mon–Thurs 5:30–10:30pm, Fri–Sat 5:30pm–midnight. NORTHERN ITALIAN.

With Ca' Brea opened in 1991, its talented chef/owner Antonio Tommasi was catapulted into a public spotlight that's shared by only a handful of L.A. chefs: Wolfgang Puck, Michel Richard, Joachim Splichal. Since then, Tommasi has opened two other celebrated restaurants, Locanda Veneta in Hollywood and Ca' Del Sole in the Valley, but, for many, Ca' Brea remains tops. The restaurant's refreshingly bright two-story dining room is a happy place, hung with colorful, oversize contemporary paintings and backed by an open prep kitchen where you can watch as your seafood cakes are sautéed and your napa cabbage braised. Booths are the most coveted seats, but with only 20 tables in all, be thankful you are sitting anywhere. Detractors might complain that Ca' Brea isn't what it used to be since Tommasi began splitting his time between three restaurants. But Tommasi stops in daily and keeps a very close watch over his hand-picked staff. Consistently excellent dishes include the roasted pork sausage, butternut squash–stuffed ravioli, and a different risotto each day, always rich, creamy and delightfully indulgent.

Chianti Cucina. 7383 Melrose Ave. (between Fairfax and La Brea aves.). ☎ **213/653-8333.** Reservations recommended. Pasta $9–$14; main courses $12–$19. AE, CB, DC, MC, V. Chianti Cucina: Mon–Thurs, Sun 11:30am–11:30pm, Fri–Sat 11:30am–midnight. Ristorante Chianti: Sun–Thurs 5:30–10:30pm, Fri–Sat 5:30–11pm. TUSCAN/ITALIAN.

Innocent passersby, and locals in search of a secret hideaway, go to the dimly lit, crimson-colored Ristorante Chianti, where waiters whip out flashlights so customers can read the menu. Cognoscenti, on the other hand, bypass this 60-year-old standby and head straight for Chianti Cucina, the bright, bustling eat-in "kitchen" of the more formal restaurant next door. Chianti Cucina features excellent meals at fair prices. The menu, which changes frequently, is always interesting and often exceptional. Hot and cold appetizers range from fresh handmade mozzarella and prosciutto to lamb carpaccio with asparagus and marinated grilled eggplant filled with goat cheese, arugula, and sun-dried tomatoes. As for main dishes, the homemade pasta is both superior and deliciously inventive. Try the black tortellini filled with fresh salmon, or the giant ravioli filled with spinach and ricotta.

○ **El Cholo.** 1121 S. Western Ave. (south of Olympic). ☎ **213/734-2773.** Reservations recommended. Main courses $7–$13. AE, DC, MC, V. Mon–Thurs 11am–10pm, Fri–Sat 11am–11pm; Sun 11am–9pm. MEXICAN.

There's authentic Mexican, and then there's traditional Mexican. El Cholo is comfort food of the latter variety, south-of-the-border cuisine traditionally craved by Angelenos. They've been serving it up in their pink adobe hacienda since 1927, even though the once outlying Mid-Wilshire neighborhood around them has turned into Koreatown. El Cholo's expertly blended margaritas, invitingly messy nachos, and classic combination dinners don't break new culinary ground, but their kitchen has perfected these standards over 70 years. El Cholo is the best of the bunch, and we wish they bottled their rich, dark red enchilada sauce! Other specialties include seasonally available green corn tamales, and creative sizzling vegetarian fajitas that go way beyond just eliminating the meat. The atmosphere is festive, as people from all parts of town dine happily in the restaurant's many rambling rooms. They have valet parking as well as a free self-park lot directly across the street.

○ **Sofi Estiatorion.** 8030³/₄ W. Third St. (between Fairfax and Crescent Heights) ☎ **213/651-0346.** Reservations suggested. Main courses $7–$14. AE, DC, MC, V. Mon–Sat noon–2:30pm; Sun–Thurs 5:30–10:30pm, Fri–Sat 5:30–11pm. GREEK.

Look for the Aegean-blue awning over the narrow passageway leading from the street to this hidden Athenian treasure. Be sure to ask for a table on the romantic patio amid twinkling lights, and immediately order a plate of their thick, satisfying *tzatziki* (yogurt-cucumber-garlic spread) and a basket of warm pitas for dipping. Other specialties (recipes courtesy of Sofi's old-world grandmother) include herbed rack of lamb with rice, fried calamari salad, *saganaki* (kasseri cheese flamed with ouzo), and other hearty taverna favorites. Located near Farmer's Market in a popular part of town, Sofi's odd, off-street setting has made it an insiders' secret (until now!).

WORTH A SPLURGE

Campanile. 624 S. La Brea Ave. (north of Wilshire Blvd.). ☎ **213/938-1447.** Reservations required. Main courses $18–$28. AE, MC, V. Mon–Fri 7:30am–2:30am, Sat–Sun 8am–1:30pm; Mon–Thurs 6–10pm, Fri–Sat 5:30–11pm. CALIFORNIA/MEDITERRANEAN.

Built as Charlie Chaplin's private offices in 1928, this lovely building is now home to crisply contemporary dining rooms that comprise one of the most attractive restaurant spaces in Los Angeles. The kitchen, headed by Spago alumnus chef/owner Mark Peel, gets a giant leg up from baker (and wife) Nancy Silverton, who runs the now-legendary La Brea Bakery next door. Meals here might begin with fried zucchini flowers drizzled with melted mozzarella, or lamb carpaccio surrounded by artichoke leaves, a dish that arrives looking like one of van Gogh's sunflowers. Chef Peel is particularly known for his grills and roasts. And don't skip dessert here; the restaurant's many enthusiastic sweets fans have turned Nancy Silverton's dessert book into a best-seller. *Tip:* Breakfast in their skylit front courtyard is a favorite among locals who want to skip the pretension (and expense) of dinner or lunch.

Musso and Frank Grill. 6667 Hollywood Blvd. (at Cahuenga Blvd.). ☎ **213/467-7788.** Reservations recommended. Main courses $13–$22. AE, CB, DC, MC, V. Tues–Sat 11am–11pm. AMERICAN/CONTINENTAL.

A survey of Hollywood eateries that leaves out Musso and Frank is like a study of Las Vegas showrooms that fails to mention Wayne Newton. It's not that this is the best restaurant in town, nor is it the most famous, but as L.A.'s oldest eatery (since 1919), Musso and Frank is the paragon of Old Hollywood grill rooms, an almost kitschy glimpse into a meat-and-potatoes world that's remained the same for generations. This is where Faulkner and Hemingway drank during their screenwriting days, where

Orson Welles used to hold court. The restaurant is still known for their bone-dry martinis and perfectly seasoned Bloody Marys. The setting is what you'd expect: oak-beamed ceilings, red-leather booths and banquettes, chandeliers with tiny shades. The extensive menu is a veritable survey of American/continental cookery. Hearty dinners include veal scaloppini marsala, roast spring lamb with mint jelly, and broiled lobster. Grilled meats are the restaurant's specialties, as is the Thursday-only chicken pot pie. Regulars also flock in for Musso's trademark "flannel cakes," crepe-thin pancakes flipped to order.

DOWNTOWN
MEALS FOR $10 OR LESS
The Original Pantry Cafe. 877 S. Figueroa St. (at 9th St.). ☎ **213/972-9279.** Main courses $6–$11. No credit cards. Daily 24 hours. AMERICAN.

An L.A. institution if there ever was one, this place has been serving huge portions of comfort food around the clock for more than 60 years; they don't even have a key to the front door. Owned by L.A. Mayor Richard Riordan, the Pantry is especially popular with politicos, who come here for weekday lunches, and conference-goers en route to the nearby L.A. Convention Center. The well-worn restaurant is also a welcoming beacon to late-night clubbers (downtown becomes a virtual ghost town). A bowl of celery stalks, carrot sticks, and whole radishes greets you at your Formica table, and creamy coleslaw and sourdough bread come free with every meal. Famous for quantity rather than quality, the Pantry serves huge T-bone steaks, densely packed meat loaf, macaroni and cheese, and other American favorites. A typical breakfast (served all day) might consist of a huge stack of hotcakes, a big slab of sweet cured ham, home fries, and coffee.

Philippe the Original. 1001 N. Alameda St. (at Ord St.). ☎ **213/628-3781.** Reservations not accepted. Main courses $3–$7. No credit cards. Daily 6am–10pm. SANDWICHES/AMERICAN.

Good old-fashioned value is what this legendary landmark cafeteria is all about. Popular with both South-Central projects dwellers and Beverly Hills elite, Philippe's decidedly unspectacular dining room is a microcosm of the entire city; it's one of the few places, it seems, where everyone can get along. Philippe's claims to have invented the French-dipped sandwich at this location in 1908; these remain the most popular menu items. Patrons push trays along the counter and watch while their choice of beef, pork, ham, turkey, or lamb is sliced and layered onto crusty French bread that's been dipped in meat juices. Other menu items include homemade beef stew, chili, and pickled pigs' feet. A hearty breakfast, served daily until 10:30am, is worth attending if only for Philippe's uncommonly good cinnamon-dipped French toast. Beer and wine are available.

MEALS FOR $20 OR LESS
Cha Cha Cha. 656 N. Virgil Ave. (at Melrose Ave.), Silver Lake. ☎ **213/664-7723.** Reservations recommended. Main courses $8–$15. AE, DC, DISC, MC, V. Sun–Thurs 8am–10:30pm; Fri–Sat 8am–11:30pm. CARIBBEAN.

Cha Cha Cha serves the West Coast's best Caribbean food in a fun and funky space on the seedy fringe of downtown. The restaurant is a festival of flavors and colors that are both upbeat and offbeat. It's impossible to feel down when you're part of this eclectic hodgepodge of pulsating Caribbean music, wild decor, and kaleidoscopic clutter; still, the intimate dining rooms cater to lively romantics, not obnoxious frat boys. Claustrophobes should choose seats in the airy covered courtyard. The very spicy black-pepper jumbo shrimp gets top marks, as does the paella, a generous mixture

🅐 Affordable Family-Friendly Restaurants

Dive! *(see p. 415)*   This place was created by Steven Spielberg and Jeffrey Katzenberg with kids specifically in mind. It's a fun place, with surroundings designed to take your mind off the food.

Grand Central Market *(see p. 426)*   No, this isn't a restaurant per se, but this Downtown venue is a great dining bargain for families. You'll have to keep smaller hands from grabbing at the displayed produce and other wares, but the sights, smells and flavors of this bustling food market are sure to thrill both grown-ups and kids. If the little ones want tacos while you'd prefer a salad or maybe some stir-fry, try assembling a mix-and-match lunch from the many prepared-food counters inside the market (tables are set up at either end for eating). You've never had such good eats at such cheap prices!

Jerry's Famous Deli *(see p. 425)*   This Studio City delicatessen is frequented mostly by industry types who populate this Valley community; their kids often sport baseball caps or production T-shirts from Mom or Dad's latest project. With the most extensive deli menu in town and a casual, coffee shop atmosphere, families flock to Jerry's for lunch, early dinner and (crowded) weekend breakfast.

Pink's Hot Dogs *(see p. 420*   Pink's is an institution in its own right; they've been serving franks here for what seems like forever. Everyone loves Pink's chili dogs, but you may never get the orange stains out of your kid's clothes.

---

of chicken, sausage and seafood blended with saffroned rice. Other Jamaican, Haitian, Cuban, and Puerto Rican inspired recommendations include jerk pork and mambo gumbo, a zesty soup of okra, shredded chicken, and spices. Hard-core Caribbeanites might visit for breakfast, when the fare ranges from plantain, yucca, onion, and herb omelets to scrambled eggs with fresh tomatillos served on hot grilled tortillas.

Clay Pit. 3465 W. 6th St. (in Chapman Market, between Normandie and Vermont aves.). ☎ **213/382-6300.** Reservations recommended on weekends. Main courses $12–$17; lunch $7–$11; weekday lunch buffet $7.75; Sunday brunch buffet $9.95. AE, CB, DC, DISC, MC, V. Mon–Sat 11:30am–2:30pm; daily 5:30–10pm; Sun 11:30am–2:30pm. INDIAN.

When you're in the mood for very good, inexpensive Indian cooking, you can do no better than this cozy and reliable Mid-Wilshire tandoori room. Physically, Clay Pit is just an unremarkable neighborhood place, with standard furnishings and decor. But, in nice weather, you can dine by the splashing fountain on an outdoor patio overlooking the action in the landmark Chapman Market arcade. Doting waiters serve flavorful traditional curries, some with California twists. If you're in the mood for authentic, order creamy saag paneer (spinach and homemade cheese), chunky aloo motor kabi (potato and peas in a coriander-based tomato sauce), or juicy lamb tikka (marinated in a yogurt sauce and cooked in the clay oven). If you're not, order rosemary-scented lamb, succulent pork chops, or moist ahi. Excellent nan breads and unbeatable all-you-can-eat buffets keep this value-packed place popular.

✪ **La Serenata de Garibaldi.** 1842 E. 1st St. (between Boyle and State sts.), Boyle Heights. ☎ **213/265-2887.** Reservations recommended. Main courses $9–$18; lunch $6–$11. AE, MC, V. Tues–Sun 11am–10pm. MEXICAN.

Once a humble neighborhood hang-out indistinguishable from the many tiny and thriving Latino businesses on this Boyle Heights street, La Serenata grew to prominence as word of their superior cuisine spread to business lunchers in nearby downtown. Soon affluent patrons came from far and wide—menu prices are decidedly more Westside than East L.A.—including O. J.'s legal "dream team" who lunched here often during his trial. Seafood is the focus of the hard-working kitchen. Trademark dishes include shrimp in cilantro sauce and Mexican sea bass fillets in a tangy chipotle sauce, plus a rich, simmered-all-day mole sauce served on giant shrimp or chicken. This brand of authentic Mexican cuisine, done so expertly, has made La Serenata a consistent draw despite its simple surroundings. The restaurant has a secure rear parking lot, and the food is worth the drive.

A smaller-scale sister restaurant called **La Serenata Gourmet** recently opened near the Westside Pavilion at 10924 W. Pico Blvd., Los Angeles (☎ 310/441-9667).

THE SAN FERNANDO VALLEY
MEALS FOR $10 OR LESS

Casa Vega. 13371 Ventura Blvd. (at Fulton), Sherman Oaks. ☎ **818/788-4868.** Reservations recommended. Main courses $5–$11. AE, MC, V. Daily 5pm–1am. MEXICAN.

I believe everyone loves a friendly dive, and Casa Vega is one of my local favorites. A faux-weathered adobe exterior with no windows conceals red Naugahyde booths lurking among fake potted plants and 1960s amateur oil paintings of dark-eyed Mexican children and red-cape-waving bullfighters. At Christmas the decor achieves critical mass: Tinsel garlands are dripping everywhere. Locals love it for good, cheap margaritas (order on the rocks), bottomless baskets of hot, salty chips, and traditional combination dinners (order by number), which all come with Casa Vega's patented tostada-style dinner salad. Street parking is so plentiful here you should use the valet only as a last resort.

Du-par's Coffee Shop. 12036 Ventura Blvd. (1 block east of Laurel Canyon), Studio City. ☎ **818/766-4437.** All items under $10. AE, MC, V. Sun–Thurs 6am–1am; Fri–Sat 6am–4am. AMERICAN/DINER.

It's been called a "culinary wax museum," the last of a dying breed, the kind of coffee shop Donna Reed took the family to for blue-plate specials. This isn't a trendy new theme place, it's the real deal, and that motherly waitress who calls everyone under 60 "Hon" might've had this job for 20 or 30 years! Du-par's is popular among old-timers who made it part of their daily routine decades ago, show-business denizens who eschew the standard watering holes, and a new generation who appreciates a tasty, cheap meal. It's common knowledge that they makes the best buttermilk pancakes in town, though some prefer the eggy French toast (extracrispy around the edges, please). Mouth-watering pies (blueberry cream cheese, coconut cream) line the front display case, and can be had for a song.

Du-par's is also in Los Angeles at Farmer's Market, 6333 W. Third St.; ☎ 213/933-8446 (but they don't stay open as late).

Jerry's Famous Deli. 12655 Ventura Blvd. (east of Coldwater Canyon), Studio City. ☎ **818/980-4245.** Reservations not accepted. Main courses $9–$14; breakfast $2–$11; sandwiches and salads $4–$12. AE, MC, V. Daily 24 hours. DELI.

Just east of Coldwater Canyon Avenue there's a simple yet sizable deli where all the Valley's hipsters go to relieve their late-night munchies. This place probably has one of the largest menus in America, a tome that spans cultures and continents, from Central America to China to New York. From salads to sandwiches to steak and seafood platters, everything, including breakfast, is served all day. Jerry's is consistently good at lox and eggs, pastrami sandwiches, potato pancakes, and all the deli staples; it's also an integral part of L.A.'s cultural landscape, and a favorite of the show-business types who populate the adjacent foothill neighborhoods. It also has a full bar.

Miceli's. 3655 Cahuenga Blvd. (east of Lankershim), Universal City. ☎ **818/508-1221.** Reservations not accepted. Main courses $7– pizza $9– AE, DC, MC, V. Mon–Thurs 5pm–midnight; Fri 5pm–1am; Sat 4pm–1am; Sun 4–11pm. ITALIAN.

Mostaccioli marinara, lasagna, thin-crust pizza, and eggplant parmigiana are indicative of the Sicilian-style fare at this cavernous, stained-glass-windowed Italian restaurant whose wait staff sings show tunes or opera favorites in between serving dinner (and sometimes instead of). Make sure you have enough Chianti to get into the spirit of it all—this is a great place for kids but way too rollicking for romance.

MEALS FOR $20 OR LESS

Iroha Sushi. 12953 Ventura Blvd. (west of Coldwater Canyon), Studio City. ☎ **818/990-9559.** Reservations recommended. Main courses $7–$15 sushi $3–$6. AE, DC, MC, V. Mon–Sat 5:30–10:15pm. JAPANESE.

You can't help feeling special at this tiny Japanese cottage hidden behind an ethnic art gallery—there are only about a dozen tables and a short sushi bar. Enter from a Zen gardenlike gravel courtyard to the demure welcome of kimono-clad waitresses and bowing waiters. Service is discreetly efficient; everything on the simple menu is excellent, from the airy tempura to tangy teriyaki, and especially the sushi. Dinner ends with an artistically carved orange to sweetly cleanse the palate, then it's back to the reality of busy Ventura Boulevard.

BAGELS & BAKERIES

For an inexpensive breakfast or lunch and a taste of Old New York, stop into **Noah's Bagels,** which operates several locations throughout the L.A. area. Large and chewy in the style of New York's legendary H&H bagel bakery, Noah's come in 14 varieties with your choice of 10 cream cheese "shmears;" since this Bay Area chain set up shop in the Southland they've quickly established themselves as the best bagelry around. You'll find them at 2710 Main St., Santa Monica (☎ **310/396-4339**); 8919 Santa Monica Blvd., West Hollywood (☎ **310/289-1795**); 200 S. Beverly Dr., Beverly Hills (☎ **310/550-7392**); and 12215 Ventura Blvd., Studio City (☎ **818/760-1446**).

Other quick (and cheap) fixes can be had at **Mani's Bakery,** 8801 Santa Monica Blvd. (at Palm, east of San Vicente), West Hollywood (☎ **310/659-5955**), serving cakes, muffins, cookies, and pastries that are all sweetened with fruit juice and other sugar-free alternatives; many are even approved for hard-core diabetics. But all this health consciousness hasn't kept Mani's from the enormous popularity it enjoys throughout Los Angeles as both a bakery and hip coffee joint. My favorite remains the carrot-pineapple muffin. Other Mani's locations include 519 S. Fairfax Blvd. (between Third Street and Wilshire Boulevard), Los Angeles (☎ **213/938-8800**); and 3960 Laurel Canyon Blvd. (south of Ventura Boulevard), Studio City (☎ **818/762-7200**).

Head downtown for the freshest, flakiest, sweetest almond cookies baked daily at **Phoenix Bakery,** 969 N. Broadway (Chinatown), Los Angeles (☎ **213/628-4642**); they come in three sizes and cost only pennies each. The bakery is also remarkable for their endless selection of special-occasion cake decorations; whatever theme you desire, from *Pocahontas* to *Star Trek,* they have the plastic figures and accessories to make it memorable.

FRUIT SHAKES & PRODUCE

Ⓢ **Grand Central Market.** 317 S. Broadway (between 3rd and 4th sts.), downtown. ☎ **213/624-2378.**

This bustling market, opened in 1917, has watched the face of downtown Los Angeles change, but has changed little itself. Today it serves Latino families, enterprising restaurateurs and home cooks in search of unusual ingredients and bargain fruits and vegetables. On weekends you'll be greeted by a lively mariachi band at the Hill Street entrance, near my favorite Market feature: the fruit juice counter that dispenses 20 fresh varieties from wall spigots and blends up the tastiest, healthiest "shakes" in town. Further into the market you'll find produce sellers and prepared food counters, plus spice vendors straight out of a Turkish alley and a grain and bean seller who'll scoop out dozens of exotic rices and dried legumes.

5 The Top Attractions

SANTA MONICA & THE BEACHES

✪ **J. Paul Getty Museum.** 17985 Pacific Coast Hwy. (Calif. 1), Malibu. ☎ **310/458-2003.** Free admission. Tues–Sun 10am–5pm (last entrance at 4:30pm).

When it opened in 1974, the Getty Museum was mocked as a filthy-rich upstart with a spotty art collection. It didn't help that the museum was pompously designed after a Roman villa buried at Pompeii. With about $60 million a year to spend, the Getty has repeatedly made headlines by paying record prices for some of the art world's trophies. But far from snatching up everything, the museum is buying intelligently and selectively, perhaps realizing its detractors worst fears, methodically transforming what was once a rich man's pastime into a connoisseur's delight.

The most notable piece in the rich antiquities collection is *The Victorious Athlete,* a 4th-century B.C. Greek sculpture known as the Getty Bronze; it's believed to have been crafted by Lysippus, court sculptor to Alexander the Great. But the most compelling antiquity is the *Kouros,* a Greek sculpture of a nude youth. It's now widely believed to be fake, but, after years of scientific testing and scholarly debate, the legitimacy of the statue has yet to be resolved. In a classic example of turning lemons into lemonade, rather than shirking from the controversial spotlight, the museum has turned the debate into the focal point of their exhibit, displaying all the evidence both for and against the statue's authenticity.

Construction of the new Getty Center in Brentwood will be completed by the end of 1997, and the Malibu villa will close for three years of renovation. Some pieces will be displayed at the new facility, which will have extensive research facilities in addition to public galleries. The Malibu Getty is a quintessential L.A. experience; try to visit while you still can.

Important: Parking is free, but you must phone for a parking reservation 7 to 10 days in advance. If you can't get a reservation, your best bet is to park in the lot of any restaurant on the Pacific Coast Highway (Calif. 1) and phone a cab (see "Getting Around," above). Walk-in visitors are not permitted.

Venice Ocean Front Walk. On the beach, between Venice Blvd. and Rose Ave.

Venice is one of the world's most engaging bohemias. It's not an exaggeration to say that no visit to L.A. would be complete without a stroll along the famous beach path, an almost surreal assemblage of every L.A. stereotype, and then some. Among stalls and stands selling cheap sunglasses, Mexican blankets, and "herbal ecstasy" pills swirls a carnival of humanity that includes bikini-clad roller-skaters, tattooed bikers, muscle-bound pretty boys, panhandling vets, beautiful wanna-bes, and plenty of tourists and gawkers. On any given day, you're bound to come across all kinds of performers: white-faced mimes, break dancers, buskers, chain saw jugglers, talking parrots, and an occasional apocalyptic evangelist. Last time I was there, a man stood behind a table and railed against the evils of circumcision. "It's too late for us, guys, but we can save

Hollywood Area Attractions

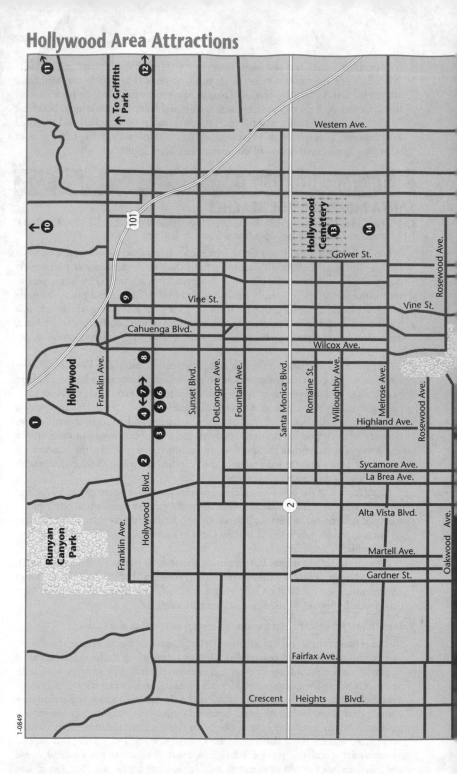

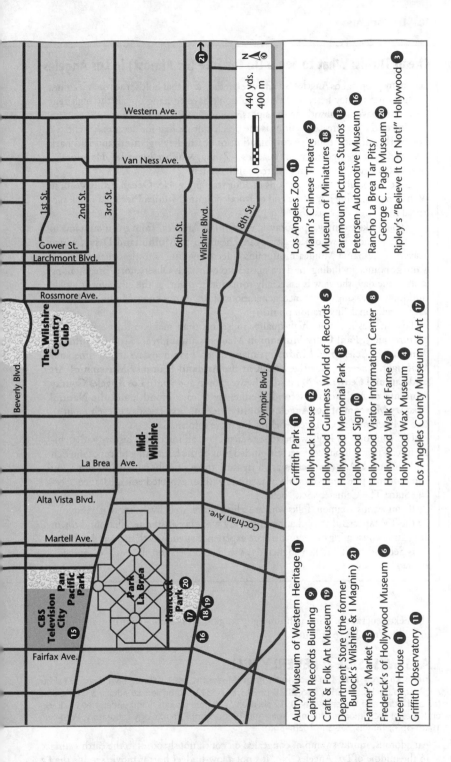

Western Ave.

Van Ness Ave.

1st St.
2nd St.
3rd St.

Gower St.
Larchmont Blvd.

Rossmore Ave.

The Wilshire
Country
Club

Beverly Blvd.

6th St.

Wilshire Blvd.

8th St.

Mid-
Wilshire

La Brea   Ave.

Olympic Blvd.

Alta Vista Blvd.

Martell Ave.

Cochran Ave.

CBS
Television
City 15

Pan
Pacific
Park

Park
La Brea

Fairfax Ave.

Hancock
Park 20

17
18 19
16

21

N

0   440 yds.
     400 m

Los Angeles Zoo 11
Mann's Chinese Theatre 2
Museum of Miniatures 18
Paramount Pictures Studios 13
Petersen Automotive Museum 16
Rancho La Brea Tar Pits/
George C. Page Museum 20
Ripley's "Believe It Or Not!" Hollywood 3

Griffith Park 11
Hollyhock House 12
Hollywood Guinness World of Records 5
Hollywood Memorial Park 13
Hollywood Sign 10
Hollywood Visitor Information Center 8
Hollywood Walk of Fame 7
Hollywood Wax Museum 4
Los Angeles County Museum of Art 17

Autry Museum of Western Heritage 11
Capitol Records Building 9
Craft & Folk Art Museum 19
Department Store (the former
Bullock's Wilshire & I Magnin) 21
Farmer's Market 15
Frederick's of Hollywood Museum 6
Freeman House 1
Griffith Observatory 11

Cheap Thrills: What to See & Do for Free (or Almost) in Los Angeles

To many people, Los Angeles is a city of extremes, and that holds true when it comes to spending money here, too. But, you don't have to hang out in the high-rent district to have fun absorbing the sights, sounds, and flavors of the city.

One of the best free attractions is the beach culture that for decades has enticed the world with its seductive combination of death-defying stunts and laid-back lifestyle. Visit the legendary surf beaches—**Zuma, Malibu Surfrider, Hermosa**—and watch a new generation of daredevils hang-ten.

Other colorful coastal diversions include strolling wacky **Ocean Front Walk** in Venice or clomping out to the end of wooden **Santa Monica Pier** for a quick pictorial history of the coastline.

If you'd like to enjoy a panoramic view of Los Angeles "from the mountains to the sea" (a local news broadcast slogan), head up to **Mulholland Drive,** which traverses the Santa Monica mountains ridge providing countless turn-outs and vantage points, including the deco masterpiece Griffith Observatory. Breathtaking during the day, the view is especially romantic at night, as the city lights twinkle alluringly. Speaking of romance, generations of Angelenos know Mulholland as the city's traditional "inspiration point."

Los Angeles has more high-quality museums than many visitors expect. The picturesque **J. Paul Getty Museum** in Malibu is always free, as is the **California Museum of Science and Industry;** many others have free days if you time your visit right. These include the **UCLA at the Armand Hammer Museum of Art and Cultural Center** (free Thursdays between 6pm and 9pm); **Los Angeles County Museum of Art** (free the second Wednesday of each month); and **the Natural History Museum of Los Angeles County** (free the first Tuesday of each month). See "Museums and Galleries," below, for more information.

Did you come to Hollywood to see stars? Have an interest in history and architecture? Try an absolutely free, self-guided tour of the last resting places of the rich and famous. **L.A.'s cemeteries** are a treasure trove of elaborate mausoleums and monuments, plus some humble headstones with unexpected epitaphs. (See "Seeing Stars: The Cemetery Set," below).

If you want see famous folks who are a little more, well, lively, try to get into one of the **TV tapings** that are happening every weekday at studios all around town. It's a time-consuming but very intimate experience as you watch sitcom friends like Jerry Seinfeld and Tim Allen do their day's work, bloopers and all (see "TV Tapings," below).

the next generation." But a chubby guy singing "Kokomo"—out of tune but with all his heart—cheered me up.

L.A.'S WESTSIDE & BEVERLY HILLS

Rancho La Brea Tar Pits/George C. Page Museum. 5801 Wilshire Blvd. (east of Fairfax Ave.), Los Angeles. ☎ **213/936-2230** or 213/857-6311. Admission $6 adults, $3.50 seniors (62 and older) and students with ID, $2 children 5–12, free for kids 4 and under; free to all second Tues of every month. Museum, Tues–Sun 10am–5pm; Paleontology Laboratory, Wed–Sun 10am–5pm; Tar Pits, Sat–Sun 10am–5pm.

An odorous, murky swamp of congealed oil continuously oozes to the earth's surface in the middle of Los Angeles. No, it's not a low-budget horror movie set, it's the La *stars shopping*

If you don't have the time—or the patience—to sit through a TV taping, not to worry: Stargazing is a good do-it-yourself activity, too. Often, the best places to see members of the A-list aren't as obvious as a back-alley stage door or the front room of Spago. Shops along Sunset Boulevard, like **Tower Records** and the **Virgin Megastore,** are often star-heavy. **Book Soup,** that browser's paradise across the street from Tower, is usually good for a star or two. You'll often find them casually browsing the international newsstand (if they're not there to sign their latest tell-all autobiography). You might even pop into **Sunset Strip Tattoo,** where Cher, Charlie Sheen, Lenny Kravitz, and members of Guns 'N' Roses all got inked. A midafternoon stroll along Melrose Avenue might also produce a familiar face; check out **Drake's Gift and Novelty Shop, Retail Slut,** and **Billy Martin's.**

And don't forget that celebrities keep their larders stocked just like the rest of us. You haven't lived until you've stumbled upon Ralph Bellamy or Rosanna Arquette sifting for unbruised tomatoes in the supermarket. Good bets are **Gelson's,** at Sunset Boulevard and Swarthmore Avenue in Pacific Palisades; **Hughes Market,** at Ventura Boulevard and Coldwater Canyon Avenue in Studio City; and **Mayfair Market,** at Franklin and Bronson avenues in Hollywood Hills.

Window shopping doesn't get much better than in **Beverly Hills' "Golden Triangle,"** a tony few blocks that includes legendary Rodeo Drive. If Prada handbags, Hermès scarves, or Cartier watches don't catch your fancy, turn your attention to the Beverly Hills denizens strolling alongside and *actually shopping;* they're a different kind of sight altogether.

Downtown Los Angeles, an area often bypassed by tourists who remember its all-too-recent gritty past, is an ongoing regentrification project with hours (or days) worth of cost-free activities for the entire family. Check out the spectacular architecture of the **Bradbury Building** and the **Central Library.** If the Library's courtyard art installations inspire you, venture on to **Pershing Square** and beyond to take advantage of the city's largest free gallery. **Grand Central Market** is another feast for the senses, where you might be tempted to part with a few dollars in exchange for an authentic food treat.

Even prime evening entertainment can be had for a song. While L.A.'s elite dine in $75-a-head box seats at the **Hollywood Bowl,** the venue's excellent acoustics guarantee an enjoyable time even if you're in "the trees" ($3 bench seats at the very top). Baseball fans visiting in season can take in a game at **Dodger Stadium** for as little as $3, but remember, Dodger dogs are extra!

Brea Tar Pits, an awesome, primal pool right on Museum Mile, where hot tar has been bubbling from the earth for more than 40,000 years. The glistening pools, which look like murky water, have enticed thirsty animals throughout history. Thousands of mammals, birds, amphibians, and insects, many of which are now extinct, mistakenly crawled into the sticky sludge and stayed forever. In 1906, scientists began a systematic removal and classification of entombed specimens, including ground sloths, giant vultures, mastodons, camels, bears, lizards, even prehistoric relatives of today's beloved superrats. The best finds are on display in the adjacent George C. Page Museum of La Brea Discoveries, where an excellent 15-minute film documenting the recoveries is also shown. Archaeology work is ongoing; you can watch as scientists clean, identify, and catalog new finds in the Paleontology Laboratory.

The Tar Pits themselves are only open on weekends; guided tours are given Saturdays and Sundays at 1pm. Swimming is prohibited.

HOLLYWOOD

Farmer's Market. 6333 W. 3rd St. (near Fairfax Ave.). ☎ **213/933-9211.** Mon–Sat 9am–6:30pm, Sun 10am–5pm.

The original Farmer's Market was little more than a field clustered with stands set up by farmers during the Depression so they could sell directly to city dwellers. It slowly grew into permanent buildings recognizable by the trademark shingled 10-story clock tower, and has evolved into a sprawling food marketplace with a carnival atmosphere, a kind of "turf" version of San Francisco's surfy Fisherman's Wharf. About 100 restaurants, shops, and grocers cater to a mix of workers from the adjacent CBS Television City complex, locals, and tourists, who are brought here by the busload. Retailers sell greeting cards, kitchen implements, candles, and souvenirs. But everyone comes here for the food stands, which offer oysters, Cajun gumbo, fresh-squeezed orange juice, roast beef sandwiches, fresh-pressed peanut butter, and all kinds of international fast foods. You can still buy produce here, no longer a farm-fresh bargain, but a better selection than the grocery stores offer. Don't miss Kokomo, a "gourmet" outdoor coffee shop that has become power breakfast spot for show-biz types. Red turkey hash and sweet potato fries are the dishes that keep them coming back.

Griffith Observatory. 2800 E. Observatory Rd. (in Griffith Park, at the end of Vermont Ave.). ☎ **213/664-1191,** or 213/663-8171 for the Sky Report, a recorded message on current planet positions and celestial events. Admission $4 adults, $2 children, $3 seniors. Sept–May, Tues–Fri 2–10pm, Sat–Sun 12:30–10pm; Jun–Aug, daily 12:30–10pm.

Made world famous in the film *Rebel Without a Cause*, Griffith Observatory's bronze domes have been Hollywood Hills landmarks since 1935. Most visitors never actually go inside; they come to this spot on the south slope of Mt. Hollywood for unparalleled city views. On warm nights, with the lights twinkling below, this is one of the most romantic places in Los Angeles.

The main dome houses a **planetarium,** where narrated projection shows reveal the stars and planets that are hidden from the naked eye by the city's lights and smog. Mock excursions into space search for extraterrestrial life, or examine the causes of earthquakes, moonquakes, and starquakes. Presentations last about an hour. Show times vary, so call for information. The adjacent **Hall of Science** holds exhibits on galaxies, meteorites, and other cosmic objects, including a telescope trained on the sun; a Foucault Pendulum; and six-foot-diameter earth and moon globes. On clear nights, you can gaze at the heavens through the powerful 12-inch telescope.

Hollywood Sign. At the top of Beachwood Dr., Hollywood.

These 50-foot-high white sheet-metal letters have come to symbolize both the movie industry and the city itself. Erected in 1923 as an advertisement for a fledgling real estate development, the full text originally read "HOLLYWOODLAND." The recent installation of motion detectors around the sign just made this graffiti tagger's coup a target even more worth boasting about. A thorny hiking trail leads to it from Durand Drive near Beachwood Drive, but the best view is from down below, at the corner of Sunset Boulevard and Bronson Avenue.

Hollywood Walk of Fame. Hollywood Blvd., between Gower St. and La Brea Ave; and Vine St., between Yucca St. and Sunset Blvd. ☎ **213/469-8311.**

More than 2,500 celebrities are honored along the world's most famous sidewalk. Each bronze medallion, set into the center of a granite star, pays homage to a famous television, film, radio, theater, or recording personality. Although about a third of them are just about as obscure as Andromeda—their fame simply hasn't withstood the test of time—millions of visitors are thrilled by the sight of famous names like James Dean (at 1719 Vine St.), John Lennon (at 1750 Vine St.), Marlon Brando (at 1765 Vine St.), Rudolph Valentino (at 6164 Hollywood Blvd.), Greta Garbo (6901 Hollywood Blvd.), Louis Armstrong (7000 Hollywood Blvd.), and Barbra Streisand (6925 Hollywood Blvd).

The sight of bikers, metalheads, druggies, hookers, and hordes of disoriented tourists all treading on memorials to Hollywood's greats, makes for quite a bizarre tribute indeed. But the Hollywood Chamber of Commerce has been doing a terrific job sprucing up the pedestrian experience with filmstrip crosswalks, swaying palms, and more. And at least one weekend a month, a privately organized group of fans calling themselves Star Polishers busy themselves scrubbing tarnished medallions.

Recent subway digging under the Boulevard has caused the street to sink several inches. When John Forsythe's star cracked, authorities removed many others to prevent further damage. In the next few years, up to 250 stars, including those of Marilyn Monroe (6744 Hollywood Blvd.) and Elvis Presley (6777 Hollywood Blvd.) will be temporarily removed as the subway project expands.

The legendary sidewalk is continually adding new names. The public is invited to attend dedication ceremonies; the honoree is usually in attendance. Contact the **Hollywood Chamber of Commerce,** 6255 Sunset Blvd., Suite 911, Hollywood, CA 90028 (☎ **213/469-8311**), for information on who's being honored this week.

Mann's Chinese Theatre. 6925 Hollywood Blvd. (3 blocks west of Highland). ☎ **213/461-3331.** Movie tickets $7.50. Call for show times.

This is one of the world's great movie palaces, and one of Hollywood's finest landmarks. The Chinese Theatre was opened in 1927 by entertainment impresario Sid Grauman, a brilliant promoter who's credited with originating the idea of the paparazzi-packed movie premiere. Outrageously conceived, with both authentic and simulated Chinese embellishments, gaudy Grauman's theater was designed to impress. Original Chinese heaven doves top the facade, and two of the theater's exterior columns once propped up a Ming Dynasty temple.

Visitors flock to the theater by the millions for its world-famous entry court, where stars like Elizabeth Taylor, Paul Newman, Ginger Rogers, Humphrey Bogart, Frank Sinatra, Marilyn Monroe, and about 160 others set their signatures and hand- and footprints in concrete. It's not always hands and feet, though: Betty Grable made an impression with her shapely leg, Gene Autry with the hoofprints of his horse Champion, and Jimmy Durante and Bob Hope used their trademark noses.

DOWNTOWN

El Pueblo de Los Angeles Historic District. ☎ **213/628-1274.** Enter on Alameda across the street from Union Station.

This Los Angeles Historic District was built in the 1930s, on the site where the city was founded, as an alternative to the wholesale razing of a particularly unsightly slum. The result is a contrived nostalgic fantasy of the city's beginnings, a kitschy theme park portraying Latino culture in a Disneyesque fashion. Nevertheless, El Pueblo has proven wildly successful, as L.A.'s Latinos have adopted it as an important cultural monument.

El Pueblo is not entirely without authenticity. Some of L.A.'s oldest extant buildings are located here, and the area really does exude the ambience of Old Mexico. At its core is a Mexican-style marketplace on old Olvera Street. The carnival of sights and sounds is heightened by mariachis, colorful piñatas, and more than occasional folkloric dancing. Olvera Street, the district's primary pedestrian thoroughfare, and adjacent Main Street, are home to about two dozen 19th-century buildings; one houses an authentic Mexican restaurant, **La Golondrina.** Stop in at the Visitor's Center, 622 N. Main St. (☎ 213/628-1274); it's open Monday to Saturday from 10am to 3pm). Don't miss Avila Adobe, at E-10 Olvera St.; built in 1818, it's the oldest building in the city (open Monday to Saturday from 10am to 5pm).

THE SAN FERNANDO VALLEY

Universal Studios. Hollywood Fwy. (Lankershim Blvd. exit), Universal City. ☎ **818/ 508-9600.** Admission $34 adults, $28 seniors (65 and older) and children 3–11, kids under 3 free. Parking $5. Summer daily 7am–11pm; rest of the year daily 9am–7pm.

Believing that filmmaking itself was a bona fide attraction, Universal Studios began offering tours to the public in 1964. The concept worked, and today, Universal is more than just one of the largest movie studios in the world—it's one of the biggest amusement parks.

The main attraction continues to be the Studio Tour, a one-hour guided tram ride around the company's 420 acres. En route, you pass stars' dressing rooms and production offices before visiting famous back-lot sets that include an eerily familiar Old West town, a clean New York City street, and the famous town square from the *Back to the Future* films. Along the way, the tram encounters several staged "disasters," which I won't divulge here lest I ruin the surprise for you.

Other attractions are more typical of high-tech theme park fare, but all have a film-oriented slant. On **Back to the Future: The Ride,** you're seated in mock time-traveling DeLorean and thrust into a fantastic multimedia rollercoasting extravaganza—it's far and away Universal's best ride. The **Backdraft** ride surrounds visitors with brilliant balls of very real fire spewing from imitation ruptured fuel lines. Kids love it. Like the movie that inspired it, the **E.T. Adventure** appeals to the heart; you ride simulated bicycles on an extraordinary special-effects adventure through principal parts of the film. A **Waterworld** live-action stunt show is thrilling to watch (and probably more successful than the film which inspired it), while the latest special effects showcase **Jurassic Park: The Ride** is short in duration but tall on dinosaur illusions and computer magic lifted from the Universal blockbuster.

Universal Studios is really a fun place. But, just like any theme park, lines can be long; the wait for a five-minute ride can sometimes last more than an hour. In summer, the stifling Valley heat can dog you all day. To avoid the crowds, skip weekends, school vacations, and Japanese holidays. Many local hotels offer discount coupons which can shave a few dollars off admission; also inquire about any auto club discounts that might be in effect.

6 TV Tapings

Being part of the audience for the taping of a television show might be the quintessential L.A. experience. This is a great, cost-free way to see Hollywood at work, to find out how your favorite sitcom or talk show is made, and to catch a glimpse of your favorite TV personalities. But you might end up with tickets to a show that may never make an appearance in your *TV Guide* rather than for one of your favorites, like *Mad About You* or *Friends.* Tickets to top shows are in greater demand than others, and getting your hands on them usually takes advance planning and possibly some time waiting in line.

Request tickets as far in advance as possible. Several episodes may be shot on a single day, so you may be required to remain in the theater for up to four hours (in addition to the recommended one-hour early check-in). If you phone at the last moment, you may luck into tickets for your top choice. More likely, however, you'll be given a list of shows that are currently filming, and you won't recognize many of the titles; studios are always taping pilots, few of which end up on the air. But you never know who may be starring in them—look at all the famous faces that have launched new sitcoms in the past couple of years. Tickets are always free, usually limited to two per person, and are distributed on a first-come, first-served basis. Many shows do not admit children under the age of 10; in some cases, no one under the age of 18 is admitted.

Audiences Unlimited (☎ **818/506-0043**; ticket information hot line 818/506-0067) distributes tickets for the top sitcoms, including *Murphy Brown, Seinfeld,* and *Frasier.* **Television Tickets** (☎ **213/467-4697**) distributes tickets for the most popular talk and game shows. Their services are free, and you can reserve by phone. Or you can get tickets directly from the networks:

ABC, 4151 Prospect Ave., Hollywood, CA 90027 (☎ **310/557-7777**). Taped messages on the hot line let you know what's currently going on. Order tickets for a taping either by writing three weeks in advance or by showing up the day of the taping.

CBS, 7800 Beverly Blvd., Los Angeles, CA 90036 (☎ **213/852-2345**; ticket information hot line 213/852-2458). Call to see what's being filmed while you're in town. Tickets for tapings are distributed on a first-come, first-served basis; you can write in advance to reserve them or pick them up directly at the studios up to an hour before taping.

NBC, 3000 West Alameda Ave., Burbank, CA 91523 (☎ **818/840-4444** or 818/840-3537). Call to see what's on while you're in Los Angeles. Tickets for NBC tapings, including the *Tonight Show with Jay Leno,* can be obtained in two ways: Pick them up on the day of the show you want to see at the NBC ticket counter—they're distributed on a first-come, first-served basis at the ticket counter off California Avenue; or, at least three weeks before your visit, send a self-addressed, stamped envelope with your ticket request to the address above.

Shows that appear on FOX, WBN, and UPN as well as many "Big Three" network shows are taped at a variety of studio complexes throughout the city. It's best to call one of the ticket services listed above if you don't have the individual production office numbers for each show. (There are far too many production offices, and production schedules change too frequently, to include a list of them here; you can always try calling information for the number of the company that appears at the end of your favorite show, or calling the network at the numbers listed above for the production office phone number).

7 Exploring the City

ARCHITECTURAL HIGHLIGHTS

Los Angeles is a veritable hodgepodge of architecture. The city is home to an amalgam of distinctive styles, from art deco to Spanish revival to coffee-shop kitsch to suburban ranch to postmodern, and much more.

SANTA MONICA & THE BEACHES

When you're strolling the historic canals and streets of Venice, be sure to check out **Chiat/Day/Mojo Headquarters** at 340 Main St. What would otherwise be an unspectacular contemporary office building is made fantastic by a three-story pair of binoculars that frames the entrance to this advertising agency. The sculpture is modeled after a design created by Claes Oldenburg and Coosje van Bruggen.

Seeing Stars: The Cemetery Set

Almost everybody who visits Los Angeles hopes to see a celebrity—they are, after all, our most common export item. Celebrities usually don't cooperate, failing to gather in readily viewable herds. They occasionally trod predictable paths, frequenting certain watering holes, but on the whole, celeb-spotting is a chancy proposition.

There's a much better alternative. An absolutely, guaranteed method of being within six feet of your favorite star: Cemeteries.

Cemeteries are *the* place for star (or at least headstone) gazing: The star is always available, and you're going to get a lot more up close and personal than you probably would to anyone who's actually alive. And L.A.'s a big place, with a lot of cemeteries, and there are a lot of stars in them thar hills. What follows is a guide to the most fruitful cemeteries, listed in order (more or less) of their friendliness to stargazers.

Weathered Victorian and art deco memorials add to the decaying charm of **Hollywood Memorial Park,** 6000 Santa Monica Blvd., Hollywood (☎ 213/469-1181). Fittingly, there's a terrific view of the Hollywood sign over the graves, as many of the founders of the community rest here. You'll see their names on the nearby street signs: the Gowers, the Wilcoxes, the Coles. The most notable tenant is Rudolph Valentino, who rests in an interior crypt. And there's silent film director William Desmond Taylor (under his real name, William Deane Tanner), whose 1922 murder was an enormous scandal, ruining the careers of silent stars Mary Miles Minter and Mabel Normand, who were considered guilty by association. (Sidney Kirkpatrick's excellent *A Cast of Killers* delves into this decades-old mystery in great detail, even solving the crime at last.) Outside are Tyrone Power Jr.; Douglas Fairbanks; *Shiek* co-star Agnes Ayres; Cecil B. DeMille (facing Paramount, his old studio); Alfalfa from the Little Rascals (contrary to what you might think, the dog on his grave is not Petey); Hearst mistress Marion Davies; Charlie Chaplin's mother, Hannah, and son Charlie; John Huston; and a headstone for Jayne Mansfield (she's really buried in Pennsylvania with family). In other mausoleums are the Talmadge Sisters and "Bugsy" Siegel.

Catholic **Holy Cross Cemetery,** 5835 W. Slauson Ave., Culver City (☎ 310/670-7697), hands out maps to the stars' graves. Religion makes for strange gravefellows: In one area, within feet of each other, lies Bing Crosby, Bela Lugosi (buried in his Dracula cape), and Sharon Tate (the name of her unborn son, Richard, is also on her marker—she was more than eight months pregnant when the Manson family murdered her); not far away are Rita Hayworth and Jimmy Durante. Also here are Tin Man Jack Haley and Scarecrow Ray Bolger, Mary Astor, John Ford, Spike Jones, gossip queen Louella Parsons, Mack Sennett, Elizabeth Taylor's first husband, Conrad "Nicky" Hilton, and Rosalind Russell, as well as Gloria Morgan Vanderbilt (whose daughter is quite well known for her jeans hawking).

The front office at **Hillside Memorial Park,** 6001 Centinela Ave., Baldwin Hills (☎ 310/641-0707), can provide a guide to this Jewish cemetery, which has an L.A. landmark: the behemoth tomb of Al Jolson, another humble star. His rotunda, complete with bronze reproduction of Jolson in his Mammy pose and cascading fountain, is visible from I-405. Also on hand are Georgie Jessel, Jack Benny, Eddie Cantor, Vic Morrow, comic Dick Shawn, and *Fugitive* star David Janssen.

You just know developers get stomach aches looking at **Westwood Memorial Park,** 1218 Glendon Ave., Westwood (☎ 310/474-1579; the staff can direct you around), smack-dab in the middle of some of L.A.'s priciest real estate. But it's not going anywhere. Especially when you consider its most famous resident: Marilyn Monroe. They've also got Truman Capote, John Cassavetes, Armand Hammer, Donna Reed, Edith Massey (John Waters's Egg Lady), Natalie Wood, *Playboy* playmate Dorothy Stratten (who was murdered by her husband; remember *Star 80?*), Darryl Zanuck, and Will and Ariel Durant, the husband and wife historian/writer team (most notably, the 11-volume *Story of Civilization*), who died within days of each other after a nearly 70-year romance. Peter Lawford was here, but he got evicted after nonpayment of rent, and his ashes were scattered.

Forest Lawn Glendale, 1712 South Glendale Ave. (☎ 213/254-3131), likes to pretend it has no celebrities. The most prominent of L.A. cemeteries, it's also the most humorless, which is pretty silly when you realize it's done its darndest to turn its graveyard into an amusement park. What else would you call its regular "dramatic" (read: cheesy) unveilings (complete with music and narration) of such works of "art" as a reproduction of DaVinci's *Last Supper* in stained glass? The place is full of Bad Art, all part of the continuing vision of founder Hubert Eaton, bane of cemetery buffs everywhere. Eaton thought cemeteries—excuse me, *memorial parks*—should be happy places, uninterrupted by nasty thoughts of, ick, death. So he banished all those gloomy upright tombstones and monuments in favor of flat, pleasant, character-free, flush-to-the-ground slabs. Voilà! A rolling, parklike vista, easy on the eyes and easy to mow.

Contrary to what you've heard, Walt Disney was *not* frozen and placed under Cinderella's castle at Disneyland. He was cremated, and resides in a little garden to the left of the Freedom Mausoleum. Turn around and just behind you are Errol Flynn (in the Garden of Everlasting Peace) and Spencer Tracy (to right of the George Washington statue). In the Freedom Mausoleum are Alan Ladd, Clara Bow, Nat King Cole, Chico Marx, Gummo Marx, Larry Fine (of the Three Stooges), and Gracie Allen, finally joined by George Burns. In a columbarium near the Mystery of Life is Humphrey Bogart. Keep moving to your left, and you should find Mary Pickford. Unfortunately, some of the best celebs, such as Clark Gable and Carole Lombard, W. C. Fields, and Jean Harlow, are in the Great Mausoleum, which you often can't get into unless you're visiting a relative.

You'd think a place that encourages people just to visit for fun would understand what the real attraction is. But no, Forest Lawn Glendale won't tell you where any of its illustrious guests are, so don't even bother asking. And this place is immense and, frankly, dull in comparison to the previous cemeteries, unless you appreciate the kitsch value of the Forest Lawn approach to art.

Forest Lawn Hollywood Hills, 6300 Forest Lawn Dr. (☎ 800/204-3131), is slightly less anal than the Glendale branch, but the same basic attitude prevails. On the right lawn, beside the wall near the statue of George Washington, is Buster Keaton. Marty Feldman is in front of the next garden, over on the left. From Buster's grave, go up several flights of stairs to the last wall on the right: There's Stan Laurel. In the Courts of Remembrance are Lucille Ball, Charles Laughton, Freddie Prinze, George Raft, Forrest Tucker, and the not-quite-gaudy-enough tomb of Liberace, with his mother and brother George. Outside, in a vault on the Ascension Road side, is Andy Gibb. Bette Davis's sarcophagus is in front of the wall, to the left of the entrance to the Courts. Also on the grounds are Ozzie Nelson, Ricky Nelson, Sammy Davis Jr., Ernie Kovacs, Jack Soo, Jack Webb, and John Travolta's mother Helen.

—*Mary Susan Herczog*

When you're flying in or out of LAX, be sure to stop for a moment to admire the **Control Tower and Theme Building.** The spacey Jetsons-style "Theme Building," which has always loomed over LAX, has been joined by a brand-new silhouette. The main control tower, designed by local architect Kate Diamond to evoke a stylized palm tree, is tailored to present Southern California in its best light. You can go inside to enjoy the view from the Theme Building's observation lounge.

L.A.'S WESTSIDE & BEVERLY HILLS

In addition to the Argyle and Beverly Hills Hotels (see "Accommodations," above), be sure to wind your way through the streets of Beverly Hills off Sunset Boulevard. Modern architecture lovers should check out the **Pacific Design Center** at 8687 Melrose Ave. (see "Shopping," below). Designed by Argentinean Cesar Pelli, the bold architecture and overwhelming scale of the Pacific Design Center aroused plenty of controversy when it was erected in 1975. Sheathed in cobalt-blue glass that's designed with a gentle curve, the seven-story building, housing over 750,000 square feet of wholesale interior design showrooms, is known to locals as "the Blue Whale." Nearby on San Vicente Boulevard, on a totally different scale, is the iconic **Tail o' the Pup.** This is roadside art, and the wiener, at its best.

HOLLYWOOD

In addition to the Griffith Observatory and Mann's Chinese Theatre (see "Top Attractions," above), and the Hollywood Roosevelt Hotel (see "Accommodations," above), don't miss the **Capitol Records Building.** This 12-story tower, just north of the legendary intersection of Hollywood and Vine, is one of the city's most recognizable buildings. Often, but incorrectly, rumored to have been made to resemble a stack of 45s under a turntable stylus (it kinda does, really), this circular tower is nevertheless unmistakable. Nat "King" Cole, songwriter Johnny Mercer, and other 1950s Capitol artists populate a giant exterior mural.

Built between 1917 and 1920, **Hollyhock House** was the first Frank Lloyd Wright residence to be constructed in Los Angeles. The centerpiece of art-filled Barnsdall Park (4800 Hollywood Blvd.; ☎ **213/485-4581**), the house is now owned by the city and operates as a small gallery and house museum, although it is undergoing extensive repairs for structural damage form the 1994 earthquake.

DOWNTOWN

Built in 1928, 27-story **City Hall** (200 N. Spring St.) remained the tallest building in the city for more than 30 years. The structure's distinctive ziggurat roof was featured in the film *War of the Worlds,* but is probably best known as the headquarters of the *Daily Planet* in the *Superman* TV series. On a clear day, the top floor observation deck (open Monday to Friday 10am to 4pm) offers views to Mount Wilson, 15 miles away.

On West 5th Street, between Flower Street and Grand Avenue, is one of L.A.'s early architectural achievements, the carefully restored **Central Library** (the majestic main entrance is actually on Flower Street). Working in the 1920s, architect Bertram G. Goodhue played on the Egyptian motifs and materials popularized by the discovery of King Tut's tomb, combining them with modern concrete block to great effect.

The 1893 **Bradbury Building,** at South Broadway and 3rd Street, is Los Angeles's oldest commercial building, and one of the city's most revered architectural landmarks. You've got to go inside to appreciate it. The glass-topped atrium is often used as a movie and TV set; you've seen it in *Chinatown* and *Blade Runner*.

Union Station (at Macy and Alameda Streets) is one of the finest examples of California Mission-style architecture, built with the opulence and attention to detail that characterize 1930s WPA projects. The cathedral-size, richly paneled ticket lobby and waiting area of this fantastic cream-colored structure stand sadly empty most of the time, but the MTA does use Union Station for Blue Line commuter trains.

The **Watts Towers,** at 1765 E. 107th St. (☎ **213/847-4646**), are more than a bit off the beaten track, but they warrant a visit. The fantastically colorful, 99-foot-tall cement-and-steel sculptures are ornamented with mosaics of bottles, sea shells, cups, plates, generic pottery, and ceramic tiles. They were completed in 1954 by folk artist Simon Rodia, an immigrant Italian tile setter who worked on them for 33 years. Call for tour schedule.

THE SAN FERNANDO VALLEY

At first glance, the **Walt Disney Corporate Office,** at 500 S. Buena Vista St. (at Alameda Avenue) in Burbank, is just another neoclassical building. But wait a minute: Those aren't Ionic columns holding up the building's pediment, they're the Seven Dwarfs (giant-size, of course).

MUSEUMS & GALLERIES
SANTA MONICA & THE BEACHES

Museum of Flying. Santa Monica Airport, 2772 Donald Douglas Loop North, Santa Monica. ☎ **310/392-8822.** Admission $7 adults, $5 seniors, $3 children. Wed–Sun 10am–5pm.

Once headquarters to the McDonald Douglas corporation, the Santa Monica Airport is the birthplace of the DC-3 and other pioneers of commercial aviation. The museum celebrates this bit of local history with 24 authentic aircraft displays and some interactive exhibits. In addition to antique Spitfires and Sopwith Camels, there's a new kid-oriented learning area, where "hands-on" exhibits detail airplane parts, pilot procedures, and the properties of air and aircraft design. The shop is full of scale models of World War II birds; the coffee-table book *The Best of the Past* beautifully illustrates 50 years of aviation history.

L.A.'S WESTSIDE & BEVERLY HILLS

The Museum of Television and Radio. 465 N. Beverly Dr. (at Santa Monica Blvd.), Beverly Hills. ☎ **310/786-1000.** Admission $6 adults, $4 students & seniors; $3 kids under 13. Wed–Sun noon–5pm (Thursdays till 9pm). Closed Thanksgiving, Christmas and New Year's Days, July 4. Internet Web site http://www.mtr.org.

Want to see the Beatles on the *Ed Sullivan Show* (1964), Edward R. Murrow's examination of Joseph McCarthy (1954), watch Arnold Palmer win the 1958 Masters Tournament, relive childhood's *Winky Dink and You,* or listen to radio excerpts like FDR's first Fireside Chat (1933) and Orson Welles's famous *War of the Worlds* UFO hoax (1938)? You can watch all these, plus a zillion episodes of *The Twilight Zone, I Love Lucy,* and other beloved series at this new West Coast branch of the 20-year-old New York facility. Like the ritzy Beverly Hills shopping district that surrounds it, the museum is more flash than substance. It becomes quickly apparent that "library" would be a more fitting name for this collection, since the main attractions are requested via sophisticated computer "catalogs" and viewed in private consoles. Although no one sets out to spend their vacation watching TV, it can be tempting once you start browsing the archives. Ultimately, the museum succeeds in treating our favorite pastime as a legitimate art form, with the respect history will prove it deserves.

Museum of Tolerance. 9786 W. Pico Blvd. (at Roxbury Dr.). ☎ **310/553-8403.** Admission $8 adults, $6 seniors, $5 students, $3 children 3–12, children under 3 free. Advance purchase recommended. Mon–Thurs 10am–5pm, Fri 10am–3pm (to 1pm Nov–Mar), Sun 11am–5pm. Closed many Jewish and secular holidays; call for schedule.

The Museum of Tolerance is designed to expose prejudices and teach racial and cultural tolerance; it's located in the Simon Wiesenthal Center, an institute founded by the legendary Nazi-hunter. While the Holocaust figures prominently here, this is not just a Jewish museum; it's an academy that broadly campaigns for a live-and-let-live world. Tolerance is an abstract idea that's hard to display, so most of this $50 million museum's exhibits are high-tech and conceptual in nature. Fast-paced interactive displays are designed to touch the heart as well as the mind, and engage both serious investigators and the MTV crowd. One of two major museums in America that deal with the Holocaust, the Museum of Tolerance is considered by some to be inferior to its Washington, D.C., counterpart, and visitors can be frustrated by their policy insisting that you follow a proscribed 2^1/$_2$-hour route through the exhibits.

UCLA at the Armand Hammer Museum of Art and Cultural Center. 10899 Wilshire Blvd. (corner of Westwood Blvd.) ☎ **310/443-7000.** Admission $4.50 adults, $3 students and seniors 55 and over, $1 kids 17 and under; free to everyone Thurs 6–9pm. Tues–Wed & Fri–Sat 11am–7pm; Thurs 11am–9pm; Sun 11am–5pm.

Created in 1990 by the former Chairman and CEO of Occidental Petroleum, the Armand Hammer Museum has had a hard time winning the respect of critics and the public alike. Barbs are usually aimed at both the museum's relatively flat collection and its patron's tremendous ego. Ensconced in a two-story Carrara marble building attached to the oil company's offices, the Hammer is better known for its high-profile and often provocative visiting exhibits, such as the opulent pre-Revolution treasures of Russian ruler Catherine the Great, or an exhibition entitled "Sexual Politics" assembled around avant-garde artist Judy Chicago's controversial 1970s feminist creation *The Dinner Party*. In conjunction with UCLA's Wight Gallery, a feisty gallery with a reputation for championing contemporary political and experimental art, the Hammer continues to present often daring and usually popular special exhibits, and it is most definitely worth calling ahead to find out what will be there during your visit to Los Angeles.

HOLLYWOOD

The Autry Museum of Western Heritage. 4700 Western Heritage Way, in Griffith Park. ☎ **213/667-2000.** Admission $7 adults, $5 seniors (60 and over) and students 13–18, $3 children 2–12, kids under 2 free. Tues–Sun 10am–5pm. Internet Web site http://www.questorsys.com/autry-museum.

If you're under the age of 45, you might not be familiar with Gene Autry, a Texas-born actor who starred in 82 Westerns and became known as the "Singing Cowboy." Opened in 1988, Autry's museum is one of L.A.'s best. The enormous collection of art and artifacts of the European conquest of the West is remarkably comprehensive and intelligently displayed. Evocative exhibits illustrate the everyday lives of early pioneers, not only with antique firearms, tools, saddles, and the like, but with many hands-on exhibits that successfully stir the imagination and the heart. There's footage from Buffalo Bill's Wild West Show, movie clips from the silent days, contemporary films, the works of wild West artists, and plenty of memorabilia from Autry's own film and television projects. The "Hall of Merchandising" displays Roy Rogers bedspreads, Hopalong Cassidy radios, and other items from the collective consciousness, and material collections, of baby boomers.

Craft and Folk Art Museum. 5800 Wilshire Blvd. (at Curson Ave.). ☎ **213/937-5544.** Admission $4 adults, $2.50 seniors students, children under 12 free. Tues–Sat 11am–5pm.

This gallery has grown into one of the city's largest, opening in a prominent Museum Row building in 1995. "Craft and folk art" is quite a large rubric that encompasses everything from clothing, tools, religious artifacts, and other everyday objects to wood carvings, papier-mâché, weaving, and metalwork. The museum displays folk objects from around the world, but its strongest collection is masks from India, America, Mexico, Japan, and China. Special exhibitions planned for 1997 include a retrospective of California woodworker Sam Maloof (whose custom-made chairs grace many a celebrity home) and a collection examining parallels between Italy's rich textile heritage and traditional bread shapes and textures. The museum is well known for its annual International Festival of Masks, a colorful and ethnic celebration held each October in Hancock Park, across the street.

Hollywood Entertainment Museum. 7021 Hollywood Blvd. (at Sycamore Ave.). ☎ **213/ 469-9151.** Admission $7.50 adults, discounts for students, seniors and children over 5. Tues–Sun 10am–6pm.

Opened in fall 1996, this facility in the heart of Hollywood's tourist district is devoted to the entertainment arts, and displays rotating selections from its sizable collection of original sets and props from film, TV, and radio. Initial exhibits include the complete *Cheers* bar and the Starship Enterprise bridge from the '60s *Star Trek* series. Fans of the former Max Factor Museum of Beauty will be happy to learn the collection from Hollywood's premier motion-picture cosmetic designer will be shown at the Entertainment Museum: antique make-up pots, glamour photos, and superstar toupees intact.

✪ Los Angeles County Museum of Art. 5905 Wilshire Blvd. ☎ **213/857-6111,** or 213/ 857-6000 for a recording. Admission $6 adults, $4 students and seniors (62 and over); $1 children 6–17, kids under 6 free; regular exhibitions free to all the second Wed of every month. Tues–Thurs 10am–5pm, Fri 10am–9pm, Sat–Sun 11am–6pm. Internet Web site http:// www.lacma.org.

This is one of the finest art museums in the United States. The huge complex was designed by three very different architects over a span of 30 years; the architectural fusion can be migraine inducing, but this city landmark is well worth delving into. If you fear getting lost forever, head straight for the Japanese Pavilion, which holds the museum's highest concentration of great art. Its exterior walls are made of Kalwall, a translucent material that, like shoji screens, permits the entry of soft natural light. Inside is a collection of Japanese Edo paintings that's rivaled only by the holdings of the emperor of Japan.

The Anderson Building, the museum's contemporary wing, is home to 20th-century painting and sculpture. Here you'll find works by Matisse, Magritte, and a good number of Dada artists.

The Ahmanson Building houses the rest of museum's permanent collections. Here you'll find everything from 2,000-year-old pre-Columbian Mexican ceramics to a unique glass collection spanning the centuries to 19th-century portraiture. The museum also has one of the nation's largest holdings of costumes and textiles, and an important Indian and Southeast Asian art collection.

The Hammer Building is primarily used for major special loan exhibitions. Free guided tours covering the museum's highlights depart on a regular basis from here.

✪ Petersen Automotive Museum. 6060 Wilshire Blvd. (at Fairfax Ave.). ☎ **213/930-2277.** Admission $7 adults, $5 seniors and students, $3 children 5–12, kids under 5 free. Tues–Sun 10am–6pm. Internet Web site http://www.lam.mus.ca.us/petersen.

When the Petersen opened in 1994, many locals were surprised that it had taken this long for the City of Freeways to salute its most important shaper. Indeed, this museum says more about the city than probably any other one in Los Angeles. Named for Robert Petersen, the publisher responsible for *Hot Rod* and *Motor Trend* magazines, the four-story museum displays more than 200 cars and motorcycles, from the historic to the futuristic. Cars on the first floor are depicted chronologically, in period settings. Other floors are devoted to frequently changing shows of race cars, early motorcycles, and famous movie vehicles. Recent exhibits have included the Flintstones' fiberglass and cotton movie car; a customized dune buggy, with seats made from surfboards, created for the Elvis Presley movie *Easy Come, Easy Go;* and a three-wheeled scooter that folds into a Samsonite briefcase, created in a competition by a Mazda engineer.

DOWNTOWN

California Museum of Science and Industry. 700 State Dr., Exposition Park. ☎ **213/744-7400;** IMAX theater ☎ 213/744-2014. Free admission to the museum; IMAX theater $6 adults, $4.75 ages 18–21, $4 seniors and children. Multishow discounts available. Daily 10am–5pm.

Celebrating Los Angeles's long-standing romance with the aerospace industry, this museum is best known for its collection of airplanes and other flying objects, including a Boeing DC-3 and a DC-8, and several rockets and satellites. Other industrial science exhibits include a working winery and a behind-the-scenes look at a functioning McDonald's restaurant. Exhibits on robotics and fiber optics thrill kids, as does the hatchery, where almost 200 chicks are born daily. Temporary exhibits are well planned and thoughtfully executed. The museum's IMAX theater shows up to three different films daily, from about 10am to 9pm. Most of the films are truly awesome exposes of events on earth and in space.

Los Angeles Children's Museum. 310 N. Main St. (at Los Angeles St.). ☎ **213/687-8800.** Admission $5; kids under 2 free. Summer, Tues–Fri 11:30am–5pm, Sat–Sun 10am–5pm; the rest of the year, Sat–Sun 10am–5pm.

This thoroughly enchanting museum is a place where children learn by doing. Everyday experiences are demystified with interesting interactive exhibits displayed in a playlike atmosphere. In the Art Studio, kids are encouraged to make finger puppets from a variety of media, and shiny rockets out of Mylar. Turn the corner, and you're in the unrealistically clean and safe City Street, where kids can sit on a policeman's motorcycle or pretend to drive a bus or a fire truck. Kids (and adults) can see their shadows freeze in the Shadow Box, and play with giant foam-filled, Velcro-edged building blocks in Sticky City. Because this is Hollywood, the museum wouldn't be complete without its own recording and TV studios, where kids can become "stars."

Museum of Contemporary Art. 250 S. Grand Ave. and 152 N. Central Ave. ☎ **213/621-2766.** Admission $6 adults, $4 seniors and students, children under 12 free. Tues–Wed and Fri–Sun 11am–5pm, Thurs 11am–8pm.

This is Los Angeles's only institution exclusively devoted to art from 1940 to the present. Displaying works in a variety of media, the museum is particularly strong in works by Cy Twombly, Jasper Johns, and Mark Rothko, and shows are often superb. For many experts, MOCA's collections are too spotty to be considered world-class, and the conservative museum board blushes when offered controversial shows (they passed on a Whitney exhibit that included photographs by Robert Maplethorpe); but I've seen some excellent exhibitions here.

MOCA is one museum with two buildings that are close to one another, but not within walking distance. The Grand Avenue main building is a contemporary red sandstone structure by renowned Japanese architect Arata Isozaki. The museum restaurant, **Patinette** (☎ 213/626-1178), located here, is the casual dining creation of celebrity chef Joachim Splichal. The museum's second space, on Central Avenue in Little Tokyo, was the "temporary" Contemporary while the Grand structure was being built, and now houses a superior permanent collection in a fittingly neutral warehouse-type space. An added feature here is a detailed timeline corresponding to the progression of works. Unless there is a visiting exhibit of great interest at the main museum, I recommend you start at the Temporary— it's also easier to park down here!

Natural History Museum of Los Angeles County. 900 Exposition Blvd., Exposition Park. ☎ 213/744-3466. Admission $6 adults; $3.50 children 12–17, seniors, and students with ID; $2 children 5–12; kids under 5 free; free to all the first Tues of every month. Tues–Sun 10am–5pm; closed Thanksgiving, Christmas and New Year's Day. Free docent-led tours are offered daily at 1pm. Internet Web site http://www.lam.mus.ca.us.

The "Fighting Dinosaurs" are not a high school football team but the trademark symbol of this massive museum, Tyrannosaurus rex and Triceratops skeletons poised in a stance so realistic every kid feels inspired to imitate their *Jurassic Park* bellows. Opened in 1913 in a beautiful columned and domed Spanish Renaissance building, the museum is a 35-hall warehouse of Earth's history, chronicling the planet and its inhabitants from 600 million years ago to the present day. There's a mind-numbing number of exhibits of prehistoric fossils, bird and marine life, rocks and minerals, and North American mammals. The best permanent displays include the world's rarest shark, a walk-through vault of priceless gems, and an Insect Zoo.

PIERS

Slightly raffish and somewhat shabby, **Santa Monica Pier,** on Ocean Avenue at the end of Colorado Boulevard, is everything an old wharf is supposed to be. Built in 1909 as a passenger and cargo ship pier, the wooden wharf, which just underwent a $45 million renovation, is now home to seafood restaurants and amusement arcades, as well as a gaily colored turn-of-the-century indoor wooden carousel (which Paul Newman operated in *The Sting*). Fishers head to the end to angle, and nostalgia buffs to view the photographic display of the pier's history. This is the last of the great pleasure piers, offering rides, romance, and perfect panoramic views of the bay and mountains. The pier is about 1 mile up Ocean Front Walk from Venice; it's a great round-trip stroll.

PARKS
SANTA MONICA & THE BEACHES

Will Rogers State Historic Park. 1501 Will Rogers State Park Rd., Pacific Palisades. ☎ 310/454-8212. Park entrance $5 per vehicle, including all passengers. From Santa Monica, take PCH (Calif. 1) north; turn right onto Sunset Blvd., and continue to the park entrance.

Will Rogers (1879–1935) was born in Oklahoma and became a cowboy in the Texas Panhandle before drifting into a Wild West show as a folksy philosophizing roper. The "cracker-barrel philosopher" performed lariat tricks while carrying on a humorous deadpan monologue on current events. The showman moved to Los Angeles in 1919, where he become a movie actor as well as the author of numerous books detailing his down-home cowboy philosophy.

Located between Santa Monica and Malibu, Will Rogers State Historic Park was once Will Rogers's private ranch and grounds. Willed to the state of California in 1944, the 168-acre estate is now both a park and historic site, supervised by the Department of Parks and Recreation. Visitors may explore the grounds, the former stables, and the 31-room house filled with the original furnishings, including a porch swing in the living room and many Native American rugs and baskets. Charles Lindbergh and his wife, Anne Morrow Lindbergh, hid out here in the 1930s during part of the craze that followed the kidnap and murder of their first son.

Downtown Area Attractions

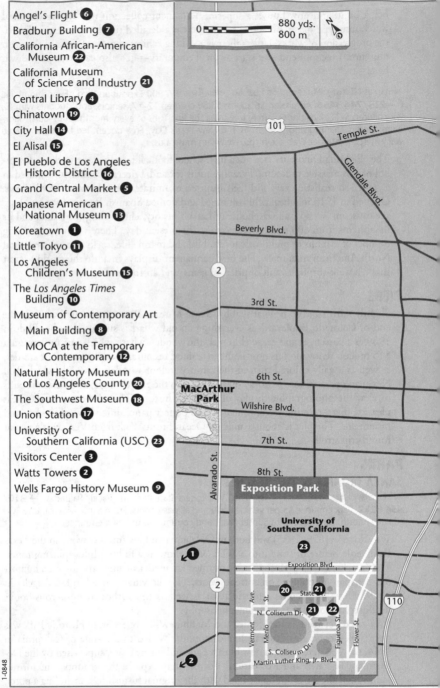

1-0848

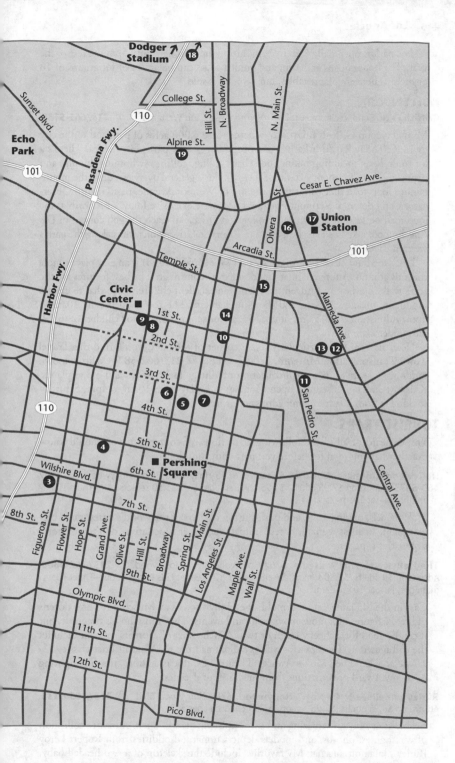

The park is open daily 8am to 7pm during the summer, until 5pm the rest of the year. The house opens at 10am, and guided tours can be arranged for groups of 10 or more. There are picnic tables, but no food is sold.

HOLLYWOOD

Griffith Park. Entrances from Feliz Blvd., Vermont Ave., and Western Ave. ☎ **213/665-5188.**

Mining tycoon Griffith J. Griffith donated these 4,000 acres of parkland to the city in 1896. Today, Griffith Park is one of the largest city parks in America. There's a lot to do here, including hiking, horseback riding, golfing, swimming, biking, and picnicking (see "Outdoor Activities," below). For a general overview, drive the mountainous loop road that winds from the top of Western Avenue, past Griffith Observatory, and down to Vermont Avenue. For a more extensive foray, turn north at the loop road's midsection, onto Mt. Hollywood Drive. To reach the golf courses or Los Angeles Zoo, take Los Feliz Boulevard to Riverside Drive, which runs along the park's western edge.

L.A.'s medium-sized **Los Angeles Zoo** (☎ **213/666-4090**) is an easy place to tote the kids around. Animal habitats are divided by continent. The best features are the zoo's walk-in aviary and Adventure Island, an excellent children's zoo that re-creates mountain, meadow, desert, and shoreline habitats. The zoo is open daily 10am to 5pm. Admission is $8.25 for adults, $5.25 for seniors, $3.25 for children 2 to 12; kids under 2 are free.

Near the zoo, in a particularly dusty corner of the park, you'll find the **Travel Town Transportation Museum,** 5200 Zoo Dr. (☎ **213/662-5874**), a little-known outdoor museum with a small collection of vintage locomotives and old airplanes. Kids love it. The museum is open Monday to Friday from 10am to 4pm, Saturday to Sunday from 10am to 5pm; admission is free.

TOURIST TRAPS

You've heard of all of the following attractions, of course, but you should know exactly what you're in for before you part with your dollars.

Hollywood Guinness World of Records. 6746 Hollywood Blvd., Hollywood. ☎ **213/463-6433.** Admission $7.95 adults, $4.95 children ages 6–1, $6.50 seniors. Sun–Thurs 10am–midnight, Fri–Sat 10am–2am.

Scale models, photographs, and push-button displays of the world's fattest man, biggest plant, smallest woman, fastest animal, and other superlatives don't make for a superlative experience.

The Hollywood Wax Museum. 6767 Hollywood Blvd., Hollywood. ☎ **213/462-8860.** Admission $9 adults, $7.50 seniors, $7 children 6–12, free for kids under 6. Sun–Thurs 10am–midnight, Fri–Sat 10am–2am.

Cast in the Madame Tussaud mold, the Hollywood Wax Museum features dozens of lifelike figures of famous movie stars and events. The "museum" is not great, but it can be good for a cheeky laugh or two. A "Chamber of Horrors" exhibit includes the coffin used in *The Raven,* as well as a diorama from the Vincent Price classic, *The House of Wax.* The "Movie Awards Theatre" exhibit is a short film highlighting Academy Award presentations from the last four decades.

Ripley's "Believe It Or Not!" Hollywood. 6780 Hollywood Blvd. ☎ **213/466-6335.** Admission $8.95 adults, $7.95 seniors, $5.95 children ages 5–11.

Believe it or not, this amazing and silly "museum" is still open. A bizarre collection of wax figures, photos, and models depicts unnatural oddities from Robert Leroy Ripley's infamous arsenal. My favorites include the skeleton of a two-headed baby, a statue of Marilyn Monroe sculpted with shredded money, and a portrait of John Wayne made from laundry lint.

8 Organized Tours

STUDIO TOURS

HOLLYWOOD

Paramount Pictures. 5555 Melrose Ave. ☎ **213/956-1777.** Tours $15 per person. Mon–Fri 9am–2pm.

Paramount's two-hour walking tour around their Hollywood headquarters is both a historical ode to filmmaking and a real-life look at a working studio. Tours depart hourly; the itinerary varies, depending on what productions are in progress. Visits might include a walk through the sound stages of TV shows like *Entertainment Tonight, Frasier,* and *Wings.* Cameras, recording equipment, and children under 10 are not allowed.

THE SAN FERNANDO VALLEY

NBC Studios. 3000 W. Alameda Ave., Burbank. ☎ **818/840-3537.** Tours $6 adults, $5.50 seniors, $3.75 children ages 6–12. Weekdays 9am–3pm.

According to a security guard, John Wayne and Redd Foxx once got into a fight here after Wayne refused to ride in the same limousine as Foxx, who called the movie star a "redneck." Well, your NBC tour will probably be a bit more docile than that. The guided one-hour tour includes a behind-the-scenes look at *The Tonight Show* set, wardrobe, make-up, and set-building departments, and several sound studios. The tour includes some cool video demonstrations of high-tech special effects.

✪ **Warner Brothers Studios.** Olive Ave. (at Hollywood Way), Burbank. ☎ **818/972-TOUR.** Admission $29 per person. Mon–Fri 9am–4:00pm, Sat (summer only) 10am–2pm.

This is the most comprehensive, and the least theme parklike, of the studio tours. The tour takes visitors on a two-hour informational drive-and-walk jaunt around the studio's movie set streets. After a brief introductory film, you'll pile into glorified golf carts and cruise past parking spaces marked "Clint Eastwood," "Michael Douglas," and "Sharon Stone," then walk through active film and television sets. Whether it's an orchestra scoring a film or a TV show being taped or edited, you'll get a glimpse of how it's done. Stops may include the wardrobe department or the mills where sets are made. Whenever possible, guests visit working sets to watch actors filming actual productions. Reservations are required; children under 10 are not admitted.

SIGHTSEEING TOURS

Oskar J's Tours (☎ **818/501-2217**), operates regularly scheduled panoramic motorcoach tours of the city. Buses (or plush minivans) pick up passengers from major hotels for morning or afternoon tours of Sunset Strip, the movie studios, Farmer's Market, Hollywood, homes of the stars, and other attractions. Tours vary in length from two to five hours and cost from $25 to $50. Call for details and to make reservations.

Next Stage Tour Company offers a unique **Insomniacs' Tour of L.A.** (☎ **213/939-2688**), a 3am tour of the predawn city that usually includes trips to the *Los Angeles Times;* flower, produce, and fish markets; and to the top of a skyscraper to watch the sun rise over the city. The fact-filled tour lasts about 6½ hours and includes breakfast. Tours depart twice monthly and cost $47 per person. Phone for information and reservations.

Grave Line Tours (☎ 213/469-4149), is a terrific journey through Hollywood's darker side. You're picked up in a renovated hearse and taken to the murder sites and final residences of the stars. You'll see the Hollywood Boulevard hotel where female impersonator-actor Divine died, the liquor store where John Belushi threw a temper tantrum shortly before his overdose, and the telephone pole that Montgomery Clift crashed his car into. Tours are $40 per person and last about 2¹/₂ hours. They depart at 9:30am daily from the corner of Orchid Street and Hollywood Boulevard, by Mann's Chinese Theatre. Reservations are required.

The **L.A. Conservancy** (☎ 213/623-2489) conducts a dozen fascinating, information-packed walking tours of historic downtown Los Angeles, seed of today's sprawling metropolis. The most popular is "Broadway Theaters," a loving look at movie palaces. Other intriguing ones include "Marble Masterpieces," "Art Deco," "Mecca for Merchants," "Terra-Cotta," and tours of the landmark Biltmore Hotel and City Hall. They're usually held on Saturday mornings, and cost $5. Call Monday to Friday between 9am and 5pm for exact schedule and information.

9 L.A.'s Best Beaches

Los Angeles County's 72-mile coastline sports more than 30 miles of beaches, most of which are operated by the **Department of Beaches and Harbors,** 13837 Fiji Way, Marina del Rey (☎ 310/305-9503). County-run beaches usually charge for parking ($4 to $8). Alcohol, bonfires, and pets are prohibited, so you'll have to leave Fido at home. For recorded Zuma Beach surf conditions (and coastal weather forecast), call 310/457-9701. The following are the county's best beaches, listed from north to south:

EL PESCADOR, LA PIEDRA & EL MATADOR BEACHES   These relatively rugged and isolated beaches front a 2-mile stretch of the Pacific Coast Highway (Calif. 1) between Broad Beach and Decker Canyon Roads, about 10 minutes driving from the Malibu Pier. Picturesque coves with unusual rock formations, they're perfect for sunbathing and picnicking, but swim with caution as there are no lifeguards or other facilities. These beaches can be difficult to find, marked only by small signs on the highway. Visitors are limited by a small number of parking spots atop the bluffs. Descend to the beach via stairs that cling to the cliffs.

ZUMA BEACH COUNTY PARK   Jam-packed on warm weekends, L.A. County's largest beach park is located off the Pacific Coast Highway (Calif. 1) a mile past Kanan Dume Road. While it can't claim to be the most lovely beach in the Southland, Zuma has the most comprehensive facilities: plenty of rest rooms, lifeguards, playgrounds, volleyball courts, and snack bars. The southern stretch, toward Point Dume, is Westward Beach, separated from the noisy highway by sandstone cliffs. A trail leads over the point's headlands to Pirate's Cove, once a popular nude beach.

✪ MALIBU LAGOON STATE BEACH   Not just a pretty white-sand beach, but an estuary and wetlands area as well, Malibu Lagoon is the historic home of Chumash Indians. The entrance is on the Pacific Coast Highway (Calif. 1) south of Cross Creek Road, and there is a small admission charge. Marine life and shorebirds teem where the creek empties into the sea, and waves are always mild. The historic Adamson House is here, a showplace of Malibu tile now operating as a museum.

SURFRIDER BEACH   Without a doubt, L.A.'s best waves roll ashore here. One of the city's most popular surfing spots, this beach is located between the Malibu Pier and the lagoon. In surf lingo, few "locals only" wave wars are ever fought here—

surfing is not as territorial here as it can be in other areas, where out-of-towners can be made to feel unwelcome. Surrounded by all of Malibu's hustle and bustle, don't come to Surfrider for peace and quiet.

WILL ROGERS STATE BEACH   Three miles along the Pacific Coast Highway (Calif. 1) between Sunset Boulevard and the Santa Monica border are named for the American humorist whose ranch-turned-state historic park (see "Parks," above) is nestled above the palisades that provide the striking backdrop for this popular beach. A pay parking lot extends the entire length of Will Rogers, and facilities include rest rooms, lifeguards, and a snack hut in season. While surfing is only so-so, the waves are friendly for swimmers of all ages.

SANTA MONICA STATE BEACH   The beaches on either side of the Santa Monica Pier are popular for their white sands and easy accessibility. There are big parking lots, eateries, and lots of well-maintained bathrooms. A paved beach path runs along here, allowing you to walk, bike, or skate to Venice and points south. Colorado Boulevard leads to the pier; turn north on the Pacific Coast Highway (Calif. 1) below the coastline's striking bluffs, or south along Ocean Avenue; you'll find parking lots in both directions.

VENICE BEACH   Moving south from the city of Santa Monica, the paved pedestrian Promenade becomes Ocean Front Walk, and gets progressively weirder until it reaches an apex at Washington Boulevard and the Venice fishing pier. Although there are people who swim and sunbathe, Venice Beach's character is defined by the sea of humanity that gathers here, plus the bevy of boardwalk vendors and old-fashioned "walk-streets" a block away (see "The Top Attractions," above). Park on the side streets or in plentiful lots west of Pacific Avenue.

MANHATTAN STATE BEACH   The Beach Boys used to hang out (and surf, of course) at this wide, friendly beach backed by beautiful ocean-view homes. Plenty of parking on 36 blocks of side streets (between Rosecrans Avenue and the Hermosa Beach border) draw weekend crowds from the L.A. area. Manhattan has some of the best surfing around, along with rest rooms, lifeguards, and volleyball courts. Manhattan Beach Boulevard leads west to the fishing pier and adjacent seafood restaurants.

HERMOSA CITY BEACH   A very wide white-sand beach with tons to recommend it, Hermosa extends to either side of the pier and includes "The Strand," a pedestrian lane that runs its entire length. Main access is at the foot of Pier Avenue, which itself is lined with interesting shops. There's plenty of street parking, rest rooms, lifeguards, volleyball courts, fishing pier, playgrounds, and good surfing.

REDONDO STATE BEACH   Popular with surfers, bicyclists, and joggers, Redondo's white sand and ice plant-carpeted dunes are just south of tiny King Harbor, along "The Esplanade" (South Esplanade Drive). Get there via Pacific Coast Highway (Calif. 1) or Torrance Boulevard. Facilities include rest rooms, lifeguards, and volleyball courts.

10 Outdoor Activities

BICYCLING   Los Angeles is great for biking. If you're into distance peddling, you can do no better than the flat 22-mile paved Ocean Front Walk that runs along the sand from Pacific Palisades in the north to Torrance in the south. The path attracts all levels of riders, so it gets pretty busy on weekends. For information on this and other city bike routes, phone the **Metropolitan Transportation Authority** (☎ **213/ 244-6539**).

Beaches & Coastal Attractions

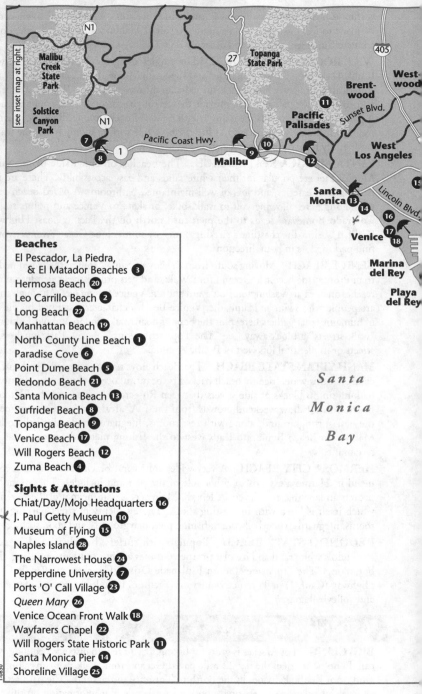

Beaches

El Pescador, La Piedra,
& El Matador Beaches **3**
Hermosa Beach **20**
Leo Carrillo Beach **2**
Long Beach **27**
Manhattan Beach **19**
North County Line Beach **1**
Paradise Cove **6**
Point Dume Beach **5**
Redondo Beach **21**
Santa Monica Beach **13**
Surfrider Beach **8**
Topanga Beach **9**
Venice Beach **17**
Will Rogers Beach **12**
Zuma Beach **4**

Sights & Attractions

Chiat/Day/Mojo Headquarters **16**
J. Paul Getty Museum **10**
Museum of Flying **15**
Naples Island **28**
The Narrowest House **24**
Pepperdine University **7**
Ports 'O' Call Village **23**
Queen Mary **26**
Venice Ocean Front Walk **18**
Wayfarers Chapel **22**
Will Rogers State Historic Park **11**
Santa Monica Pier **14**
Shoreline Village **25**

1-0850

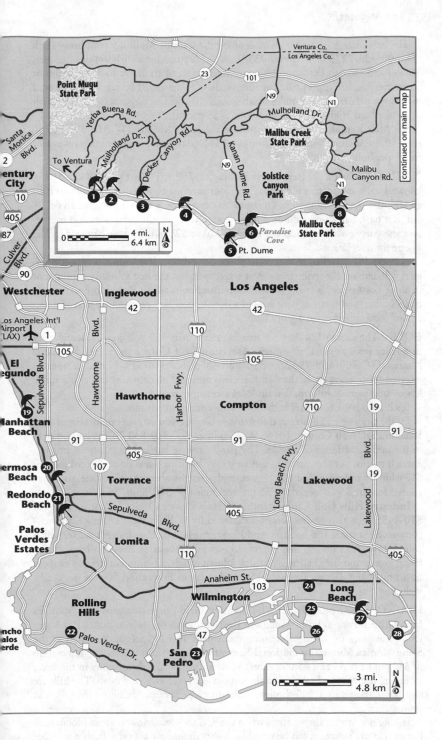

continued on main map

Ventura Co.
Los Angeles Co.

101

Point Mugu
State Park

Yerba Buena Rd.

N9

Mulholland Dr.

N1

23

Mulholland Dr.

Santa
Monica
Blvd.

2

To Ventura

century
City

10

Decker Canyon Rd.

Malibu Creek
State Park

Kanan Dume Rd.

N9

Solstice
Canyon
Park

405

87

1

2

3

Malibu
Canyon Rd.

N1

7

8

Culver
Blvd.

90

4

1

6 *Paradise
Cove*

Malibu Creek
State Park

0   4 mi.
       6.4 km

N

5 Pt. Dume

Westchester

Inglewood

Los Angeles

42

42

Los Angeles Int'l
Airport
(LAX)

1

Blvd.

110

105

105

El
Segundo

Sepulveda Blvd.

Hawthorne

Harbor Fwy.

Hawthorne

Compton

710

19

91

19

Manhattan
Beach

91

91

ermosa
Beach

20

107

405

Lakewood Blvd.

19

Redondo
Beach

21

Sepulveda
Blvd.

Torrance

405

Lakewood

Palos
Verdes
Estates

Lomita

110

405

ncho
alos
erde

22 Palos Verdes Dr.

Rolling
Hills

Anaheim St.

103

24

Long
Beach

25

Wilmington

47

26

27

San
Pedro

23

28

0   3 mi.
       4.8 km

N

461

The best place to mountain bike is along the trails of **Malibu Creek State Park** (☎ **800/533-7275** or 818/880-0350), in the Santa Monica Mountains between Malibu and the San Fernando Valley. Fifteen miles of trails rise to a maximum of 3,000 feet and are appropriate for intermediate to advanced bikers. Pick up a trail map at the park entrance, 4 miles south of U.S. 101 off Las Virgenes Road, just north of Mulholland Highway. Park admission is $5 per car.

Sea Mist Rental, 1619 Ocean Front Walk, Santa Monica (☎ **310/395-7076**), rents 10-speed cruisers for $5 per hour and $14 a day; 15-speed mountain bikes rent for $6 per hour and $20 a day.

FISHING   Marina del Rey Sports Fishing, 13759 Fiji Way (☎ **310/822-3625**), known locally as "Captain Frenchy's," has four deep-sea boats departing daily on half- and full-day ocean fishing trips. Of course, it depends on what's running when you're out, but bass, barracuda halibut, and yellowtail tuna are the most common catches on these party boats. Excursions cost from $20 to $25, and include bait and tackle. Phone for reservations.

No permit is required to cast from shore or to drop a line from a pier. Local anglers will hate me for giving away their secret spot, but the best saltwater fishing spot in all of Los Angeles is at the foot of Torrance Boulevard in Redondo Beach. Centuries of tides and currents have created a deep underwater canyon here that's known among local fisherman as a glory hole.

GOLF   The greater Los Angeles area has more than 100 golf courses, which vary in quality from abysmal to superb. **American Golf Corp.,** 1633 26th St., Santa Monica (☎ **800/468-7952** or 310/829-4653; fax 310/829-4990), guarantees reserved tee times at more than 16 top area courses. The company can also arrange lessons and provide information on local tournaments.

It's best to book tee times at the following courses in advance:

Of the city's seven 18-hole and five 9-hole courses, you can't get more central than **Rancho Park Golf Course,** 10460 W. Pico Blvd. (☎ **310/838-7373**), located right in the middle of L.A.'s Westside. The par-71 course has lots of tall trees, but not enough to blot out the towering Century City buildings next door. Greens fees are $17 Monday to Friday, and $22 on weekends. Rancho also has a nine-hole, par-three course; fees are $5 on weekdays, $6 on weekends (☎ **310/838/7561**).

Industry Hills Golf Club, 1 Industry Hills Pkwy., City of Industry (☎ **818/810-4455**), has two 18-hole courses designed by William Bell. Together, they encompass eight lakes, 160 bunkers, and long fairways. The Eisenhower Course, which consistently ranks among *Golf Digest's* top-25 public courses, has extra-large, undulating greens and the challenge of thick kikuyu rough. An adjacent driving range is lit for night use. Greens fees are $45 on Monday to Friday and $60 on weekends, including cart.

HIKING   The Santa Monica Mountains, a small range that runs only 50 miles from Griffith Park to Point Mugu, on the coast north of Malibu, makes Los Angeles a great place for hiking. The mountains peak at 3,111 feet and are part of the **Santa Monica Mountains National Recreation Area,** a contiguous conglomeration of 350 public parks and 65,000 acres. Many animals make their homes in this area, including deer, coyote, rabbit, skunk, rattlesnake, fox, hawk, and quail. The hills are also home to almost 1,000 drought-resistant plant species, including live oak and coastal sage.

Hiking is best after spring rains, when the hills are green, flowers are in bloom, and the air is clear. Summers can be very hot; hikers should always carry fresh water. Beware of poison oak, a hearty shrub that's common on the West Coast. Usually found among oak trees, poison oak has leaves in groups of three, with waxed surfaces and prominent veins. If you come into contact with this itch-producing plant, bathe yourself in calamine lotion, or the ocean.

Santa Ynez Canyon, in Pacific Palisades, is a long and difficult climb that rises steadily for about 3 miles. At the top, hikers are rewarded with fantastic views over the Pacific. Also at the top is Trippet Ranch, a public facility providing water, rest rooms, and picnic tables. From Santa Monica, take Pacific Coast Highway (Calif. 1) north. Turn right onto Sunset Boulevard, then left onto Palisades Drive. Continue for 2¹/₂ miles, turn left onto Verenda de la Montura, and park at the cul-de-sac at the end of the street, where you'll find the trailhead.

Temescal Canyon, in Pacific Palisades, is far easier than the Santa Ynez trail and, predictably, far more popular with locals. It's one of the quickest routes into the wilderness. Hikes here are anywhere from 1 to 5 miles. From Santa Monica, take Pacific Coast Highway (Calif. 1) north; turn right onto Temescal Canyon Road, and follow it to the end. Sign in with the gatekeeper, who can also answer your questions.

Will Rogers State Historic Park, Pacific Palisades, is also a terrific place for hiking. An intermediate-level hike from the park's entrance ends at Inspiration Point, a plateau from which you can see a good portion of L.A.'s Westside. See "Parks," above, for complete information.

SKATING The 22-mile-long Ocean Front Walk that runs from Pacific Palisades to Torrance is one of the premier skating spots in the country. In-line skating is especially popular, but conventionals are often seen here too. Roller-skating is allowed just about everywhere bicycling is, but be aware that cyclists have the right-of-way. **Spokes 'n' Stuff,** 4175 Admiralty Way, Marina del Rey (☎ **310/ 306-3332**), is just one of many places to rent wheels near the Venice portion of Ocean Front Walk. Skates cost $5 per hour; kneepads and wrist guards come with every rental.

SURFING Shops near all top surfing beaches in the L.A. area rent boards, including **Zuma Jay Surfboards,** 22775 Pacific Coast Highway, Malibu (☎ **310/ 456-8044**). You'll find the shop about ¹/₄ mile south of Malibu Pier. Rentals are $20 per day, plus $8 to $10 for wetsuits in winter.

TENNIS You'll find mostly hard-surface courts in California. If your hotel doesn't have a court, and can't suggest any courts nearby, try the well-maintained, well-lit **Griffith Park Tennis Courts,** on Commonwealth Road, just east of Vermont Avenue. Or, call the **City of Los Angeles Department of Recreation and Parks** (☎ **213/485-5555**) to make a reservation at a municipal court near you.

11 Shopping

Here's a rundown of the most interesting shopping areas of Los Angeles, from the fine and chic to the funky and cheap, along with some highlights of each neighborhood. For a more complete selection, see *Frommer's Los Angeles.*

MAJOR SHOPPING AREAS
SANTA MONICA & THE BEACHES
Third Street Promenade (3rd Street, from Broadway to Wilshire Boulevard, Santa Monica)

Packed with chain stores and boutiques as well as dozens of restaurants and a large movie theater, Santa Monica's pedestrian-only section of 3rd Street is one of the most popular shopping areas in the city. The promenade bustles on into the evening with a seemingly endless assortment of street performers, and an endless parade of souls. Stores stay open late (often till 1 or 2am on the weekends) for the movie-going crowds. There's plenty of metered parking in structures on the adjacent streets, so be sure to bring lots of quarters.

Midnight Special Bookstore. 1318 Third St. Promenade. ☎ **310/393-2923.**

This medium-size general bookshop is known for its good small-press selection and regular poetry readings.

Na Na. 1228 Third St. Promenade. ☎ **310/394-9690.**

This is what punk looks like in the nineties: clunky shoes, knit hats, narrow-striped shirts, and baggy streetwear.

Pyramid Music. 1340 Third St. Promenade. ☎ **310/393-5877.**

Seemingly endless bins of used CDs and cassette tapes line the walls of this long, narrow shop on the Promenade. LPs, posters, cards, buttons, and accessories are also available.

Main Street in Santa Monica and Venice (between Pacific Street and Rose Avenue)

South of Pico Boulevard, this stretch of Main Street is ideal for strolling and boasts a healthy combination of mall standards plus many left-of-center individual boutiques. A couple of these can appear pricey, but there's always something on sale, and the stores further toward Venice cater to a scruffier crowd with trendy taste but few dollars. You'll also find plenty of casually hip cafes, restaurants, and an espresso shop on every block. The primary strip connecting Santa Monica and Venice, Main Street has a relaxed, beach-community vibe that sets it apart from similar streets; the stores along it straddle the fashion fence between upscale trendy and beach-bum edgy.

The Bey's Garden. 2919 Main St. (between Ashland & Pier sts.) ☎ **310/399-5420.**

A fragrant, esoteric shop selling aromatic oils, candles, herbal body treatments, and exotic soaps, most of which come in affordable sample sizes. Check out their porous clay "diffuser" pots; when filled with the essential oil of your choice, they slowly disperse aromatherapy scent into the room.

CP Shades. 2925 Main St. ☎ **310/392-0949.**

CP Shades is a San Francisco ladies' clothier whose line is carried by many department stores and boutiques. Fans will love this store devoted solely to their loose, casual cotton and linen separates. Their trademark monochromatic neutrals are meticulously arranged within an airy, well-lit store. Take a tip from this frequent shopper and head straight for the sale rack.

Horizons West. 2011 Main St. (south of Pico Blvd.). ☎ **310/392-1122.**

Brand-name surfboards, wet suits, leashes, magazines, waxes, lotions, and everything else you need to catch the perfect wave are found here. Stop in and say hi to Randy, and pick up a free tide table.

Just In Case. 2718 Main St. ☎ **310/399-3096.**

Featuring "cruelty-free" handbags, backpacks, luggage, agendas, wallets, and other items made from fabric and innovative materials like recycled rubber instead of animal skins.

L.A. (The Bookstore). 208 Pier Ave. (¹/₂ block east of Main St.). ☎ **310/4-LA-BOOK.**

Fiction or nonfiction, pulp or classic, if it's about the Southland, written by a native author, or has anything to do with Los Angeles, this is the place to find it. Tucked away next to the Novel Cafe, this specialty shop also maintains a Web site for catalog information and other tidbits at http://www.labooks.com.

Venice Beach/Ocean Front Walk (along the beach, between Venice Boulevard & Rose Avenue)

For bargain-hunting along the waterfront, there's simply nothing like Venice Beach. Whether you seek traditional souvenirs like postcards, baseball caps, or T-shirts emblazoned with Southern California images or ethnic handcrafts like batik backpacks and fanny packs, Mexican huarache sandals, or leather goods, Venice is the place. Food vendors are interspersed with the dizzying array of sellers just waiting to barter with you on their wares. Insiders know the best deals are on cheap sunglasses and sterling silver jewelry.

Bergamot Station

Once a station for the Red Car trolley line, Bergamot Station's (2525 Michigan Ave., ☎ 310/829-5854) industrial space is now home to about two dozen art galleries, a cafe, a bookstore, and offices. Most of the galleries are closed Mondays; the train yard is located at the terminus of Michigan Avenue east of Cloverfield Boulevard. Exhibits change often and vary widely, ranging from a Julius Shulman B&W photo retrospective of L.A.'s Case Study Houses to a provocative exhibit of Vietnam War propaganda posters from the United States and Vietnam, to whimsical furniture constructed entirely of corrugated cardboard, this is a great place to browse away an afternoon without spending a dime. Here's just a sampling of offerings:

The **Gallery of Functional Art** (☎ 310/829-6990) sells tables, chairs, beds, sofas, lighting, screens, dressers, bathroom fixtures, and other functional art piece; all work is one of a kind or limited edition. The **Rosamund Felson Gallery** (☎ 310/828-8488) is well known for showcasing L.A.-based contemporary artists, and **Track 16 Gallery** (☎ 310/264-4678) has exhibitions ranging from pop art to avant-garde inventiveness. Be sure to see what's going on here.

Fisherman's Village

Marina Del Ray's waterfront village is touristy, yes; but it's still pleasant for strolling and souvenir shopping. International imports (an umbrella phrase that covers everything from rare $800 Niihau-shell necklaces to $2 plastic coin purses from Hong Kong) are available in shops lining the cobblestone walks. Restaurants and stores surround an authentic 60-foot-tall lighthouse.

L.A.'S WESTSIDE & BEVERLY HILLS

West Third Street (between Fairfax and Robertson boulevards)

You can shop till you drop on this newly trendy strip, which is anchored on the east end by **Farmer's Market.** Many of Melrose Avenue's shops have relocated here, alongside some terrific newcomers and several cafes. "Fun" is more the catchword here than "funky," and the shops (including the vintage clothing stores) tend to be more refined than those along Melrose, but not as outrageously priced.

✪ **Chado Tea Room.** 8422 W. Third St. ☎ 213/655-4681.

A temple for tea lovers, Chado is designed with a nod to Paris's renowned *Mariage Frères* tea purveyor. One wall is lined with nooks whose recognizable brown tins are filled with over 250 different varieties of tea from around the world. Among the choices are 15 kinds of Darjeeling, Indian teas blended with rose petals, and ceremonial Chinese and Japanese blends. They also serve tea meals here, featuring delightful sandwiches and individual pots brewed from any loose tea in the store; two can eat for about $23.

GOAT Cadeaux. 306 S. Edinburgh (at Third St. east of Crescent Heights). ☎ 213/651-3133.

Cadeaux means "gifts" in French, and this is the kind of shop where you can always find just the right last-minute present. From unusual candles to antique bookends to carved wooden boxes to art deco picture frames, GOAT carries a variety, all of it intriguing.

Polkadots and Moonbeams. 8367 & 8381 W. Third St. ☎ 213/651-1746.

This is actually two stores several doors apart, one carrying (slightly overpriced) hip young fashions for women, the other a vintage store with clothing, accessories and fabrics from the '20s to the '60s, all affordably priced and in remarkable condition.

Traveler's Bookcase. 8375 W. Third St. ☎ 213/655-0575.

This store, one of the best travel bookshops in the West, stocks a huge selection of guidebooks and travel literature, as well as maps and travel accessories. A quarterly newsletter chronicles the travel adventures of the genial owners, who know first-hand the most helpful items to carry. Look for regular readings by well-known travel writers.

The Beverly Center

When the Beverly Center, 8500 Beverly Blvd. (at La Cienega Blvd.), Los Angeles (☎ 310/854-0070), opened on L.A.'s Westside, there was more than a bit of concern about the impending "mallification" of Los Angeles. Loved for its convenience and disdained for its penitentiary-style architecture (and the "no validations" parking fee), Beverly Center contains about 170 standard mall shops (leaning a bit toward the high end) anchored on each side by **Macy's** and **Bloomingdales.** You can see it blocks away, looking like a gigantic angular boulder punctuated on one corner with the roof-mounted Cadillac of the **Hard Rock Cafe** (☎ 310/276-7605).

The Sunset Strip (between La Cienega Boulevard and Doheny Drive, 🏃 West Hollywood)

The monster-size billboards advertising the latest rock god make it clear that this is rock 'n' roll territory. The "Strip" is lined with trendy restaurants, industry-oriented hotels, and dozens of shops offering outrageous fashions and chunky stage accessories. One anomaly is Sunset Plaza, an upscale cluster of Georgian-style shops resembling Beverly Hills at its snootiest. Although the Strip isn't a great place for walking more than a block or two, you might cruise along and stop if something catches your eye.

✪ **Book Soup.** 8800 Sunset Blvd., West Hollywood. ☎ 310/657-1072.

This has long been one of L.A.'s most celebrated bookshops, selling both mainstream and small-press books and hosting regular book signings. Book Soup is a great browsing shop, with a large selection of show-biz books and an extensive news and magazine stand outside. The owners recently annexed an adjacent cafe space so they can better cater to hungry intellectuals.

Tower Records. 8811 W. Sunset Blvd., Hollywood. ☎ 310/657-7300.

Tower insists that it has L.A.'s largest selection of compact discs—more than 125,000 titles—despite the Virgin Megastore's (see below) contrary claim. Even if Virgin has more, Tower's collection tends to be more interesting and browser friendly. And the enormous shop's blues, jazz, and classical selections are definitely greater than the competition's. Open 365 days a year.

Virgin Megastore. 8000 Sunset Blvd., Hollywood. ☎ 213/650-866

Some 100 CD "listening posts" and an in-store "radio station' a music lover's paradise. Virgin claims to stock 150,000 title. sive collection of hard-to-find artists.

Beverly Boulevard (from Robertson Boulevard to La Brea Avenue)

These few blocks are a diverse pedestrian magnet—across the street from CBS Television City yet around the corner from Jewish Fairfax Avenue—that are slowly filling up with art galleries, small quirky shops, and casual eateries.

Every Picture Tells a Story. 7525 Beverly Blvd. (between Fairfax & LaBrea), Los Angeles. ☎ 213/932-6070.

This gallery, devoted to the art of children's literature, is frequented by young-at-heart art aficionados as well as parents introducing their kids to the concept of an art gallery. It features works by Maurice Sendak (*Where the Wild Things Are*), Tim Burton (*The Nightmare Before Christmas*), and original lithos of *Curious George* and *Charlotte's Web*. Call to see what's going on; they usually combine exhibitions of illustrators with story readings and interactive workshops. Another great place to look even if you have no intention of buying.

Re-Mix. 7605^1/$_2$ Beverly Blvd. (between Fairfax and La Brea aves.), Los Angeles. ☎ 213/936-6210.

If you complain that they just don't make 'em like they used to, head to Re-Mix, where they do. Selling only vintage (1940s to 1970s) but brand-new (unworn) shoes for men and women, it's more like a shoe store museum featuring wingtips, Hush Puppies, Joan Crawford pumps, and platform shoes. A rackful of unworn vintage socks all display their original tags and stickers, and the prices are downright reasonable. Celebrity hipsters and hep cats from Madonna to Roseanne are often spotted here.

La Brea Avenue (north of Wilshire Boulevard)

This is L.A.'s artsiest shopping strip, and the stores are less concentrated than elsewhere in town; luckily, metered street parking is pretty easy to find, except after 4pm, when the curb lane is put into rush-hour-traffic use. Anchored by the giant **American Rag, Cie.** alterna-complex, 150 S. La Brea Ave., (☎ 213/935-3154). La Brea is home to lots of great urban antique stores dealing in art deco, arts and crafts, 1950s modern, and the like (there's even a great antique hardware store). You'll also find vintage clothiers, furniture galleries, and other warehouse-size stores, as well as some of the city's hippest restaurants, such as Campanile.

⑤ Dishes a la Carte. 5650 W. Third St. (at LaBrea), Los Angeles. ☎ 213/938-6223.

Modeled after New York's *Fish's Eddie,* this little ceramics shop carries factory seconds and obsolete patterns of well- and little-known brands alike. You'll find Fiesta Ware next to locally hand-painted pieces and durable restaurant dishes.

Liz's Antique Hardware. 453 S. LaBrea Ave., Los Angeles. ☎ 213/939-4403.

Stuffed to the rafters with hardware and fixtures of the last 100 years, Liz's thoughtfully keeps a canister of wet-wipes at the register. Believe me, you'll need one after sifting through bags and crates of doorknobs, latches, finials, and any other home hardware you can imagine needing. Perfect sets of Bakelite drawer pulls and antique ceramic bathroom fixtures are some of the more intriguing items. Be prepared to browse for hours, whether you're redecorating or not!

Drive & Beverly Hills's Golden Triangle (between Santa Monica
vard, Wilshire Boulevard & Crescent Drive)

Everyone knows about Rodeo Drive, Beverly Hills's most famous shopping street, and everyone, rich or poor, wants to take a look. Names like **Cartier, Hermès, Louis Vuitton, Tiffany and Co.**, and **Gucci** need no introduction. Believe it or not, the several blocks surrounding Rodeo (known as the "Golden Triangle") do offer wares for the cost-conscious shopper; like the nicest **Gap** you're likely to ever see, and comfy Naugahyde **Nate and Al's** delicatessen. See two examples of the Beverly Hills version of minimalls, each a tiny, tony diorama: the **Rodeo Collection** (421 N. Rodeo Dr.), and **Two Rodeo** (at Wilshire Boulevard).

HOLLYWOOD

Melrose Avenue (Between Fairfax & La Brea avenues)

It's showing some wear—some stretches have become downright ugly—but this is still one of the most exciting shopping streets in the country for cutting-edge fashions and eye-popping people watching. Melrose is a playful stroll, dotted with plenty of hip restaurants and funky shops that are sure to shock. Where else could you find green patent-leather cowboy boots, a working 19th-century pocket watch, and an inflatable girlfriend in the same shopping spree?

Condomania. 7306 Melrose Ave., Los Angeles. ☎ **213/933-7865.**

A vast selection of condoms, lubricants, and kits creatively encourage safe sex. Glow-in-the-dark condoms, anyone?

Maya. 7452 Melrose Ave., Los Angeles. ☎ **213/655-2708.**

This rather plain-looking store houses a huge and fascinating variety of silver and turquoise rings and earrings from South America, Nepal, Bali, and central Asia, all at reasonable prices. The shop's walls are cluttered with Asian and South American ceremonial and ornamental masks.

Retail Slut. 7308 Melrose Ave., Los Angeles. ☎ **213/934-1339.**

You'll find new clothing and accessories for men and women at this famous rock 'n' roll shop. The unique designs are for a select crowd (the name says it all); don't expect to find anything for your next PTA meeting here.

Wasteland. 7428 Melrose Ave., Los Angeles. ☎ **213/653-3028.**

An enormous steel-sculpted facade fronts this L.A. branch of the Berkeley/Haight-Ashbury hipster hangout that sells vintage and contemporary clothes for men and women. There's a lot of leathers, denim, and some classic vintage, but mostly funky '70s garb. This ultratrendy store is a packed with the flamboyantly colorful polyester halters and bell-bottoms from the decade we'd rather forget.

Hollywood Boulevard (between Gower Street & La Brea Avenue)

One of Los Angeles's most famous streets is, for the most part, a sleazy strip. But along the Walk of Fame, between the T-shirt shops and greasy pizza parlors, you'll find some excellent poster shops, souvenir stores, and Hollywood memorabilia dealers. It's a silly, tourist-oriented strip that's worth getting out of your car for, especially if there's a chance of getting your hands on that long-sought-after Ethel Merman autograph or a 200 Motels poster.

Frederick's of Hollywood. 6606 Hollywood Blvd., Hollywood. ☎ **213/466-8506.**

Behind the garish pink and purple facade lies one of the most well-known panty shops in the world. Everything from spandex suits to "wonder" bras and sophisticated nighties is here. Even if you're not buying, stop in and pick up one of their famous catalogs.

Hollywood Book and Poster Company. 6349 Hollywood Blvd., Hollywood. ☎ **213/ 465-8764.**

Owner Eric Caidin's excellent collection of movie posters (from about $15 each) is particularly strong in horror and exploitation flicks. Photocopies of about 5,000 movie and television scripts are also sold for $10 to $15 each, and the store also carries music posters and photos.

DOWNTOWN

Since the late, lamented department store grande dame Bullock's closed in 1993 (her art deco masterpiece salons rescued to house Southwestern Law School's library), downtown has become less of a shopping destination. Savvy Angelenos still go for bargains in the **garment and fabric districts;** florists and bargain-hunters arrive at the vast **Flower Mart,** 742 Maple Ave. (between 7th and 8th streets; ☎ 213/627-2482), before dawn for the city's best selection of fresh blooms; and families of all ethnicities stroll the Grand Central Market (see "Dining," above). Many of the once-splendid streets are lined with cut-rate luggage and cheap electronics storefronts, however; shopping downtown can be a rewarding experience for the adventuresome.

Cooper Building. 860 S. Los Angeles St., downtown. ☎ **213/622-1139.**

The centerpiece of downtown's Garment District, the Cooper Building and surrounding blocks are full of shops selling name-brand clothes for men, women, and children at significantly discounted prices.

Ⓢ **La Plata Cigars.** 1026 S. Grand Ave. (between 11th St. and Olympic Blvd.). ☎ **213/ 747-8561.**

Los Angeles's only cigar factory, family run La Plata has been hand rolling them since 1947. The public is welcome to visit their compact downtown factory and watch how Cuban artisans create these premium prizes; afterward enter the shop's humidor to choose from thousands of fresh cigars in all sizes, for about half what the fancy places charge. Open Monday to Friday 7am to 4:30pm.

THE SAN FERNANDO VALLEY

Universal CityWalk (Universal Center Drive, Universal City)

Technically an outdoor mall rather than a shopping area, Universal CityWalk (☎ 818/622-4455) gets mention here because it's so utterly unique. A pedestrian promenade next door to Universal Studios, CityWalk is dominated by brightly colored, outrageously surreal oversize storefronts. The heavily touristed faux street is home to an inordinate number of restaurants, including B. B. King's Blues Club, the newest Hard Rock Cafe, and a branch of the Hollywood Athletic Club featuring a restaurant and pool hall. The bad news is, CityWalk is no bargain-hunter's paradise, catering primarily to tourists milling around Universal Studios.

STORES WORTH SEEKING OUT ELSEWHERE IN THE CITY

Ⓢ **Aardvark's Odd Ark.** 58 Market St. (corner of Pacific), Venice. ☎ **310/392-2996.**

This large storefront near the Venice Beach Walk is crammed with racks of antique and used clothes from the sixties, seventies, and eighties. They stock vintage everything, from suits and dresses to neckties, hats, handbags, and jewelry. And they manage to anticipate some of the hottest new street fashions. There's another Aardvark's at 7579 Melrose Ave. (☎ 213/655-6769).

Dressing the Part—for Less

Admit it: You've dreamed of being a glamorous movie or TV star—everyone has. Well, you shouldn't expect to be "discovered" during your L.A. vacation, but you can live out your fantasy by dressing the part. Costumes from famous movies, TV show wardrobes, castoffs from celebrity closets—they're easier to find (and more affordable to own) than you might think.

A good place to start is **Star Wares,** 2817 Main St., Santa Monica (☎ **310/ 399-0224;** open daily noon to 6pm). This deceptively small shop regularly has left-overs from Cher's closet, as well as celebrity-worn apparel from the likes of Joan Rivers, Tim Curry, and Kathleen Turner. They also stock movie production ward-robes and genuine collector's items. If the $5,000 *Star Trek: The Next Generation* uniform or *Planet of the Apes* military regalia you covet is out of your price range, don't worry: You can still pick up one of Johnny Depp's *Benny and Joon* outfits, dresses from the closets of Lucille Ball and Greer Garson, or ET's bathrobe, all of which are surprisingly affordable. Many pieces have accompanying photos or movie stills, so you'll know exactly who donned your piece before you.

For sheer volume, you can't beat **It's a Wrap,** 3315 W. Magnolia Blvd., Burbank (☎ **818/567-7366;** open Monday to Saturday from 11am to 6pm, Sunday 11am to 4pm). Every item here is marked with its place of origin, and the list is stagger-ing: *Beverly Hills, 90210; Melrose Place; Seinfeld; Baywatch; All My Children; Forrest Gump; The Brady Bunch Movie;* and so on. Many of these wardrobes (which in-clude shoes and accessories) aren't outstanding but for their Hollywood origins: Jerry Seinfeld's trademark polo shirts, for instance, are standard mall-issue. Some collectible pieces, like Sylvester Stallone's *Rocky* stars-and-stripes boxers, are framed and on display.

When you're done at It's a Wrap, stop in across the street at **Junk For Joy,** 3314 W. Magnolia Blvd., Burbank (☎ **818/569-4903;** open Tuesday to Friday from 10am to 6pm, Saturday 11am to 6pm). A Hollywood wardrobe coordinator or two will probably be hunting through this wacky little store right beside you. The emphasis here is on funky items more suitable as costumes than everyday wear (the store is mobbed each year around Halloween). At press time, they were loaded with 1970s polyester shirts and tacky slacks, but you never know what you'll find when you get there.

The grande dame of all wardrobe and costume outlets is **Western Costume,** 11041 Vanowen St., North Hollywood (☎ **818/760-0900;** open for rentals Mon-day to Friday from 8am to 5:30pm, for sales Tuesday to Friday 10am to 5pm). In business since 1912, Western Costume still designs and executes entire wardrobes for major motion pictures; when filming is finished, the garments are added to their staggering rental inventory. This place is perhaps best known for outfitting Vivien Leigh in *Gone with the Wind.* Several of Scarlett O'Hara's memorable gowns were even available for rent until they were recently auctioned off at a charity event. Western maintains an "outlet store" on the premises, where damaged garments are sold at rock-bottom (nothing over $15) prices. If you're willing to do some rescue work, there are definitely some hidden treasures here.

California Map and Travel Center. 3211 Pico Blvd., Santa Monica. ☎ **310/829-6277.**

Like the name says, this store carries a good selection of domestic and international maps and travel accessories, including guides for hiking, biking, and touring. Globes and atlases are also sold. Visit their Web site at http://www.mapper.com.

Dutton's Brentwood Books. 11975 San Vicente Blvd. (west of Montana Ave.), Los Angeles. ☎ **310/476-6263.**

This huge bookshop is well known not only for an extensive selection of new books, but for its good children's section and an eclectic collection of used and rare books. There are more than 120,000 in-stock titles at any one time. They host regular author readings and signings, and sell cards, stationery, prints, CDs, and selected software.

L.A. Wine Co. 4935 McConnell Ave. No. 8, Los Angeles. ☎ **310/306-9463.**

Known for low mark-ups on recent releases, this supplier near Marina Del Rey is one of the best places to buy young wines by the bottle or case (they ship throughout the United States), with an eye on aging them in your own cellar.

LAX Luggage. 2233 S. Sepulveda Blvd. (south of Olympic), West Los Angeles. ☎ **310/478-2661.**

Stop in for a vast assortment of all the popular luggage brands at substantial mark-downs. These aren't last season's styles or some manufacturer rejects, either, but current merchandise from Samsonite, Tumi, Travelpro, and the like.

✪ **Rhino Records.** 1720 Westwood Blvd., Westwood. ☎ **310/474-3786.**

This is L.A.'s premier alternative shop, specializing in new artists and independent-label releases. In addition to new releases, there's a terrific used selection; music industry types come here to trade in the records they don't want for the records they do, so you'll be able to find never-played promotional copies of brand-new releases at half the retail price. You'll also find the definitive collection of records on the Rhino label.

Samuel French Book Store. 7623 Sunset Blvd. (between Fairfax & LaBrea), Hollywood. ☎ **213/876-0570.** Also in Studio City at 11963 Ventura Blvd. (☎ 818/762-0535).

This is L.A.'s biggest theater and movie bookstore. Plays, screenplays, and film books are all sold here, as well as scripts for Broadway and Hollywood blockbusters.

Trashy Lingerie. 402 N. La Cienega Blvd., Hollywood. ☎ **310/652-4543.**

This shop will tailor-fit its house-designed clothes for you —everything from patent-leather bondage wear to elegant bridal underthings. There's a $2 "membership" fee to enter the store, but, even for browsers, it's worth it.

12　Los Angeles After Dark

The *L.A. Weekly,* a free weekly paper available at sidewalk stands, shops, and restaurants is the best place to find out what's going on about town, especially for club happenings. The "Calendar" section of the *Los Angeles Times* is also a good place to find out what's going on after dark.

For weekly updates on music, art, dance, theater, special events, and festivals, call the **Cultural Affairs Hot Line** (☎ 213/688-ARTS), a 24-hour directory listing a wide variety of events, most of which are free.

Ticketmaster (☎ 213/480-3232) and **Telecharge** (☎ 800/447-7400) are the major charge-by-phone ticket agency in the city, selling tickets to concerts, sporting events, plays, and special events.

THE PERFORMING ARTS

Enjoying live music and theater in L.A. doesn't have to cost a fortune; sometimes you can experience a world-class performance for as little as a few dollars. We've included all the details below.

THEATER
How to Save on Same-Day Theater Tickets

Theater L.A., an association of live theaters and theatrical producers in the greater Los Angeles area (and the organization that puts on the L.A. version of Broadway's Tony Awards each year), has plans to operate a half-price ticket booth beginning early in 1997. Modeled after New York City's highly successful TKTS, they expect to open a booth called "Theater Times" in the Beverly Center, 8500 Beverly Blvd. (at La Ciengega Blvd.), for same-day, walk-up sales only; it should be in place by the time you hold this book. For updated information, call them at **213/614-0556.**

Major Theaters & Companies

The **Ahmanson Theater** and **Mark Taper Forum,** the city's top two playhouses, are both part of the all-purpose **Music Center,** 135 N. Grand Ave., downtown. The **Ahmanson** (☎ 213/972-7401) is active year round, either with shows produced by the in-house Center Theater Group, or with traveling Broadway productions. In-house shows are usually revivals of major Broadway plays, starring famous film and TV actors.

The **Mark Taper Forum** (☎ 213/972-0700) is a more intimate, circular theater staging contemporary works by international and local playwrights. Kenneth Branagh's Renaissance Theatre Company staged their only American productions of *King Lear* and *A Midsummer Night's Dream* at the Mark Taper, to give you an idea of the quality of the shows here. Productions are usually excellent.

Ticket prices vary depending on the performance. Discounted tickets are usually available on the day of performance for students and seniors; call the box office the morning of the show to check availability.

Top-quality Broadway-caliber productions are also staged at the **Shubert Theater** (in the ABC Entertainment Center, 2020 Ave. of the Stars, Century City; ☎ **800/233-3123**) and the **UCLA James A. Doolittle Theater** (1615 N. Vine St., Hollywood; ☎ **213/462-6666** or 213/972-0700).

For the current theater schedule, check the listings in *Los Angeles* magazine or the "Calendar" section of the Sunday *Los Angeles Times,* or call the box offices directly.

Smaller Playhouses

Like New York's Off-Broadway or London's fringe, Los Angeles's small-scale theaters often outdo the slick, high-budget shows. Because this is Tinseltown, movie and TV stars sometimes headline, but more often than not, the talent is up and coming. Who knows? The unknown on stage today might be the next David Schwimmer tomorrow.

There are about 100 other stages of varying quality throughout the city. Good bets are the **Colony Studio Theater,** 1944 Riverside Dr., Silver Lake (☎ **213/665-3011**), which has an award-winning resident company; the **Actors Circle Theater,** 7313 Santa Monica Blvd., West Hollywood (☎ **213/882-8043**); and the grand **Los Angeles Theater,** 615 S. Broadway, downtown (☎ **213/629-2939**). Tickets for most plays usually cost from $10 to $30. Check newspaper listings for current offerings.

Classical Music & Opera

Beyond the pop realms, music in Los Angeles generally falls short of that found in other cities. For the most part, Angelenos rely on visiting orchestras and companies to fulfill their classical music appetites; scan the papers to find out who's playing and dancing while you're in the city.

The **Los Angeles Philharmonic** (☎ 213/850-2000) isn't just the city's top symphony; it's the only major classical music company in Los Angeles. Finnish-born music director Esa-Pekka Salonen concentrates on contemporary compositions; despite complaints from traditionalists, he does an excellent job attracting younger audiences. In addition to regular performances at the **Music Center's Dorothy Chandler Pavilion,** 135 N. Grand Ave., downtown, the Philharmonic also plays a popular summer season at the Hollywood Bowl (see "Concerts Under the Stars," below). Tickets, which regularly run $10 to $60 a seat, are discounted 50% at the box office on the day of the show when a large number go unsold. Call after 10am the day of performance to check on availability.

Slowly but surely, the **L.A. Opera** (☎ 213/972-8001), is gaining both respect and popularity with inventive stagings of classic operas, usually with guest divas. The Opera, which also calls the **Music Center** home, offers "rush" tickets at $15 (regularly $23 to $130) for students and seniors (65+) only. They can be purchased at the box office (cash only) beginning one hour before the performance.

CONCERTS UNDER THE STARS

✪ **Hollywood Bowl.** 2301 N. Highland Ave. (at Odin St.), Hollywood. ☎ **213/850-2000.**

Built in the early 1920s, the Hollywood Bowl is an elegant Greek-style natural outdoor amphitheater cradled in a small mountain canyon. This is the summer home of the Los Angeles Philharmonic Orchestra; internationally known conductors and soloists often sit in on Tuesday and Thursday nights. Friday and Saturday concerts are often feature orchestral swing or pops concerts. The summer season also includes a jazz series; past performers have included Natalie Cole, Mel Torme, Dionne Warwick, and Chick Corea. Other events, from Tom Petty concerts to an annual Mariachi Festival, are often on the season's schedule. A night at the bowl can be a real bargain; tickets can usually be had for as little as $3.

For many concert-goers, a visit to the Bowl is an excuse for an accompanied picnic under the stars; gourmet picnics at the Bowl, complete with a bottle of wine or two, are one of L.A.'s grandest traditions. You can prepare your own, or order a picnic basket with a choice of hot and cold dishes and a selection of wines and desserts from the theater's catering department. À la carte baskets run from $16.95 to $25.95 per person; appetizers and drinks are extra. Call **213/851-3588** the day before you go.

THE CLUB & MUSIC SCENE

by Steve Hochman and Heidi Siegmund Cuda

The L.A. club scene is truly something-for-everybody territory, from blues fanatics to leather freaks. *But be forewarned:* You're not in Kansas anymore. Or for that matter, San Francisco. Friendlier cities greet out-of-towners with arms extended and advice at hand. Travel to the City by the Bay, and a waiter might tip you off to the best restaurant or the hottest dance club for that moment in time. Sit in a Los Angeles cafe, however, and be grateful if you're acknowledged. It's nothing personal, it's more a matter of Social Darwinism. This is a town where the only the strongest, and the most resourceful, survive, and too many folks are angling to get out of the cattle line, past the velvet rope and into clubland's hot zones.

The competition is compounded by L.A.'s short attention span. What might have been the hip ticket last week, could be belly up by the time you find the door. That said, don't lose all hope. A smart visitor has ammo: This guide, along with a current *L.A. Weekly* (which can be found for free at numerous outlets on Thursdays), offers a plethora of dance and music club info for the adventurous at heart.

LIVE MUSIC

It's a good bet that someone of interest will be in town during any one stay. The best way to see what's on is by checking the *L.A. Weekly*, available just about everywhere.

Midsize Concerts

B. B. King's Blues Club. CityWalk, Universal City. ☎ **818/622-5464.**

B. B. King's is a bit more "real" than the House of Blues. It's three-floor seating area, resembling an old Southern club, is tastefully decorated, the music stays closer to authentic blues and the ribs are terrific. Also offers a fine, though overpriced, Sunday gospel brunch.

House of Blues. 8430 Sunset Blvd., West Hollywood. ☎ **213/650-0247.**

This club is co-owned by some really strange bedfellows, including, Hard Rock founder Issac Tigrett, Jim Belushi, Dan Ackroyd, Aerosmith, and Harvard University. Despite its Disneyland-ish decor, it earnestly honors its namesake music with informative displays and a wealth of colorful folk art. Still, it's permeated with industry types more interested in being seen than seeing the music. Even so, there's enough top-notch music here to keep many who routinely bad-mouth the place coming back, and the food in the upstairs restaurant can be superb (reservations are a must). The Sunday gospel brunch, though a bit overpriced, is a rousing diversion.

John Anson Ford Theatre. 2580 Cahuenga Blvd. West, Hollywood. ☎ **213/464-2826.**

Once, during a late '80s Ramones concert at this lovely al fresco facility, the punk sounds carried across U.S. 101 and into the ears of people who were trying to hear the L.A. Symphony play Beethoven at the Hollywood Bowl. They were not amused, and rock was virtually banned from the Ford for some time. But lately it's been back, and a night with a rising star under the stars (Alanis Morissette played there on her way to superstardom) can be wonderful. Parking, though, is nightmarish; prepare for a long walk up hill.

The Palace. 1735 N. Vine St., Hollywood. ☎ **213/461-3504.**

A classic vaudeville house, the 1,200-capacity theater, just across Vine from the famed Capitol Records tower, has been the site of numerous significant alternative rock shows in the '90s, including key appearances by Nirvana and Smashing Pumpkins. But its dominance has been challenged of late by several other venues of similar size.

✪ Wiltern Theatre. 3790 Wilshire Blvd., ☎ **213/380-5005.**

Saved from the wrecking ball in the mid-'80s, this WPA-era art deco showcase is perhaps the most beautiful theater in town. You could have an entertaining evening just sitting and staring at the ornate ceiling, but usually you don't have to. Countless national and international acts have played here, from Jerry Garcia to Joan Osborne, with such nonpop music events as Penn and Teller and top ballet troupes complementing the schedule.

Club Shows

Al's Bar. 305 S. Hewitt St., downtown. ☎ **213/625-9703.** 21 & over, cover varies.

Al's is the last of a dying breed of downtown hellholes that regularly attracts fun underground music. If you can brave the neighborhood, which is sketchy at best, a good time can almost always be had here.

Bar Deluxe. 1710 N. Las Palmas Ave., Hollywood. ☎ **213/469-1991.** 21 & over, generally no cover.

This is the club to go to when you're looking for a hassle-free, no lines affair. This dimly lit, black and red, voodoo-meets-hoodoo haven specializes in surf, blues, and rockabilly bands and is as comfortable as an old pair of Doc Martens.

✪ Billboard Live. 9039 Sunset Blvd., West Hollywood. ☎ **310/786-1712.** Cover varies.

This club hosted a gala opening in August 1996 that closed down the Sunset Strip for the first time in history so thousands of revelers could help Tony Bennett celebrate the birth of this three-tier, $5.5 million club. It promises to breathe some life into the legendary Strip. Located on the former site of the seminal rock 'n' roll club Gazzari's, Billboard Live's ambitions loom large. Two gigantic exterior "Jumbotrons" reveal the on-stage performances to passersby and, during the day, feature continuous music programming. Features also include a unique "industrial plush" interior design (think corrugated metal draped in velvet); a "Tequila Library," where card-carrying members can order any tequila concoction under the sun; and numerous monthly performances selected from *Billboard*'s "Heatseekers" charts. Ultimately, the 400-capacity club, the first of a dozen Billboard Live venues scheduled to be built over the next four years, is an excellent live-music showcase.

Coconut Teaszer. 8117 Sunset Blvd. ☎ **213/654-4773.**

In some ways a carryover of the '80s, prealternative rock ethos, with hard-rockin' dudes mostly trying to impress record company talent scouts. A good place for local acts that you've never heard of, and most likely will never hear of again. But who knows, the night you're there may be the night a future superstar is discovered.

Doug Weston's Troubadour. 9081 Santa Monica Blvd., West Hollywood. ☎ **310/ 276-6168.** All ages, cover varies.

The Troubadour has worked long and hard to shed its creepy '80s spandex 'n' big hair image, and it's emerged vibrant and vigorous once again. Turning 40 in 1997, the club counts the Byrds and the Eagles among the bands that virtually formed here, and even in the metal years saw Motley Crue and others rise to the big time. Today the Troub can be counted on for excellent sound, and a wide array of up-and-coming break-out bands and already made-its. A fine, fine venue.

Jack's Sugar Shack. 1707 Vine St., Hollywood. ☎ **213/466-7005.**

Jack doesn't mess around. The *Gilligan's Island* meets *Love Boat* decor combined with a select booking policy makes this night club a tasty treat. Less interested in trends than in quality music, Jack's books national and local blues, country and western, and alternative music and is the current host to Ronnie Mack's Barndance, an always free Tuesday-night affair of alternative country music.

Lava Lounge. 1533 La Brea Ave., Hollywood. ☎ **213/876-6612.** 21 & over, cover varies.

Described by its lovely owner, a former set decorator, as a "Vegas in hell" motif, the interior of this small bar and performance space located in a seriously ugly strip mall is very inventive. Think tiky-tacky coupled with big-city chic. Live music includes jazz and surfabilly, and live regulars include Quentin Tarantino.

LunaPark. 665 N. Robertson Blvd., West Hollywood. ☎ **310/652-0611.** Cover varies, none–$10.

Proprietor Jean-Pierre Boccarra has turned this bilevel restaurant/performance space into one of the most unpredictable yet reliable venues in the area. This holds true not just for music, which ranges from up-and-coming sensations (Ani DiFranco played her first L.A. show here) to global music stars (Cape Verde's "barefoot diva" Cesaria Evora), but for performance art, cabaret, and comedy, too.

McCabe's. 3101 Pico Blvd., Santa Monica. ☎ **213/828-4497.**

Since the early '70s, the back room of this earthy guitar shop has been the leading folk club in Los Angeles, and possibly west of the Mississippi. Bonnie Raitt, Jackson Browne, and Linda Ronstadt are among those who played here early in their careers, and top-flight folk, country, and even rock musicians still return regularly to perform in an unbeatable, low-key, almost living room-esque setting.

The Opium Den. 1605½ Ivar St., Hollywood. ☎ **213/466-7800.** 21 & over, cover varies.

Brent Bolthouse, a superpromoter on the Hollywood nightlife circuit, opened his first club on the site of the old Gaslight so his friends would have a comfortable, quality venue to perform in. With pals who appear in nearly every issue of *People,* this works in everyone's favor. Live alternative music is scheduled seven nights a week, with late-night dance parties occurring on Thursday, Friday, and Saturday. Stand-out performances include the Geraldine Fibbers, Rickie Lee Jones, Spain, and X.

The Roxy. 9009 Sunset Blvd. ☎ **213/276-2222.**

Veteran record producer/executive Lou Adler opened this Sunset Strip club in the mid-'70s with concerts by Neil Young and a lengthy run of the premovie *Rocky Horror Show.* Since, it has remained among the top showcase venues in Hollywood, though its lost its unchallenged preeminence among cozy clubs to increased competition from the revitalized Troubadour and such new entries as the House of Blues.

Spaceland at Dreams. 1717 Silver Lake Blvd., Silver Lake. ☎ **213/413-4442.** 21 & over, cover varies.

In less than a year, promoter Mitchell Frank took over a spacious, dowdy bar on the eastern edge of Hollywood and turned it into one of the most happening night spots in Los Angeles. With his eclectic booking (everyone from the Foo Fighters and the Beasties to hometown faves Extra Fancy), Frank built a scene from scratch; Spaceland now rivals such Hollywood fixtures as the Whisky and Roxy as a place to see and be seen.

Union. 8210 Sunset Blvd., West Hollywood. ☎ **213/654-1001.** 21 & over, no cover Thurs–Tues, $5 on Wed.

Otherwise known as the club that books avant-garde acid jazz artiste Toledo every Monday night, the Union is a comfortable bilevel venue with an outdoor patio and a piano bar. Averaging five nights of live music weekly, guests will hear acid jazz, straight jazz, and blues. On Wednesdays, promoter Brent Bolthouse takes over with "Soap," an inspired cocktail lounge atmosphere. But if you want something to remember L.A. by, see Toledo on Mondays. A true original.

✪ Viper Room. 8852 Sunset Blvd., West Hollywood. ☎ **310/358-1880.** 21 & over, cover varies.

This place is so delightfully hot you might get singed on the way out. Definitely a club to witness first-hand before exiting town, despite what you might have heard. Yes, Johnny Depp owns it (with partner Sal Jenco) and yes, River Phoenix overdosed here, and the combo either attracts or repulses clubgoers. But hands down, the Viper Room has the most varied and exciting live music bookings in town. From Johnny Cash to Iggy Pop, the small, bilevel venue doesn't disappoint. The expensive sound system is a delight to true music fans, and there's enough stars on hand nightly to keep gazers excited.

✪ **The Whisky.** 8901 Sunset Blvd., West Hollywood. ☎ **310/535-0579.** All ages, cover varies.

If you don't go to any other club in Los Angeles, you must a go-go to the Whisky. The bilevel venue personifies L.A. rock 'n' roll, from Jim Morrison to X to Guns 'N' Roses. Every trend has passed through this club, and it continues to be the most vital venue of its kind. Recently, an in-house booker was hired to bring more local music to the club, which already offers one of the best local showcases in town: Bianca's Hole on Monday nights, an always-free night of mostly L.A. bands.

DANCE CLUBS & BARS

To give outsiders an idea of the lightning speed with which dance clubs come and go in this town, the Roxbury doesn't even register on the map right now. It's still there, but folks aren't lining up like they used to, so we can't recommend it this time out. But no worries: There's plenty of sonic offerings to take its place, but best to move quickly and precisely. Take great pains to follow the recommended nights closely—you'll be glad you did. Of course, check out the *L.A. Weekly* for the most complete, up-to-the-minute listings.

7969. 7969 Santa Monica Blvd., West Hollywood. ☎ **213/654-0280.** 21 & over, cover varies.

Here's a fetish club that can't miss: Saturdays feature Sin-A-Matic, L.A.'s long-running, popular S&M industrial dance club, complete with whipping room. Mondays and Fridays offer a drag party. 7969's most popular night to date is Thursday's Grand Ville, a sexy dance club with a midnight striptease, emphasis on *tease*. Also quite popular, among the ladies, that is, is Michelle's XXX Revue, a Tuesday night lesbian hangout with an enormous number of topless women.

Cherry. Fri at the Love Lounge, 657 N. Robertson Blvd., West Hollywood. ☎ **310/659-0472.** 21 & over, $10 cover.

Deejay Mike Messex's Friday night gig finds him digging deep into the '80s for loads of glam rock, New Wave, and disco, keeping the dance floor packed all evening. Promoter Bryan Rabin knows how to keep the energy level high, with selective live performances, often with a homoerotic edge, as well as theme nights. A celebration of *Showgirls* was a must-see.

The Derby. 4500 Los Feliz Blvd., Los Feliz. ☎ **213/663-8979.** 21 & over, $5 cover.

This east Hollywood swing club is one class-A joint. The luscious club, located at a former Brown Derby site, was restored to its original luster and detailed with a heavy '40s edge. This would explain the inordinate number of guests who come decked out in garb from that era to swing the night away to such musical acts as Big Bad Voodoo Daddy and the Royal Crown Revue (whose popularity soared after weekly bookings by at the club).

El Floridita. 1253 N. Vine St., Hollywood. ☎ **213/871-8612.** 21 & over, cover varies.

This Cuban restaurant-cum-salsa joint is hot, hot, hot. Despite its modest strip lot locale, the tiny club attracts the likes of Jennifer Lopez, Sandra Bullock, Jimmy Smits, and Jack Nicholson, and the hippest nights continue to be Monday and Thursday, when Johnny Polanco and his swinging New York–flavored salsa band get the dance floor jumpin'.

The Garage. 4519 Santa Monica Blvd., Silver Lake. ☎ **213/683-3447.** 21 & over, cover varies.

This key Silver Lake club, sprang up from the underground and remains firmly planted therein. With a wide variety of weekly dance club promotions, this sparkling erstwhile garage attracts a comfortable gay/straight clientele with such events as Sucker, a Sunday beer bust hosted by drag diva Miss Vaginal Creme Davis; Hai Karate, a dazzling Friday night funky fest; and Ultra Saturdays, with hot Hollywood deejay Victor Rodriguez spinning deep house and soul.

Saturday Night Fever. Sat at the Diamond Club, 7070 Hollywood Blvd., Hollywood. ☎ **213/848-9300** for location. 21 & over, $10 cover.

For nearly five years now, this weekly disco party continues to be the biggest Saturday night dance bash in Hollywood. Although it's moved numerous times since its inception, it continues to outgrow each venue, and the last consistent spot was at the Roxbury. Fever's currently going off at the Diamond Club, but owner Brent Bolthouse indicated at press time he plans to move it yet again. Wherever it lands, it's sure to be the bomb: With popular L.A. DJ Mike Messex behind the main console, the temperature's always sizzling.

Soul Mama. Fri at Checca, 7323 Santa Monica Blvd., Hollywood. ☎ 213/850-7471. 21 & over, $15 cover.

Los Angeles used to be chock-full of decent hip-hop clubs, but in the past few years, they've dropped like flies. Until things straighten up, Soul Mama, with its ample supply of hip-hop, funk, and old school soul, will have to suffice.

HANGING OUT FOR THE PRICE OF A DRINK: GREAT L.A. COCKTAIL LOUNGES

Hanging out in one of these fabulous cocktail lounges is a great way to soak in lots of L.A. style for only the price of a Cosmopolitan, or even just a Coke:

Four Seasons Hotel Los Angeles. 300 S. Doheny Dr. (at Burton Way), Los Angeles. ☎ **310/273-2222.** No cover.

The sprawling lobby bar of this slightly pretentious but always eventful hotel serves as both celebrity magnet and unofficial parlor for monied regulars who virtually live in the high-rise. Decorated in the same comfortable but unremarkable neutral tones as the rest of the hotel, the bar is actually comprised of several sitting rooms and an outdoor patio, through which waft the sounds of the house pianist tinkling the ivories. The bartenders here have seen it all: No request is too outrageous, from a platter of oysters courtesy of the hotel's restaurant to a bowl of water for a canine companion (dogs served on patio only). The current cigar trend has found a home here: You may select from the bar's expansive humidor, but stay away if the smoke will offend you (or your dry cleaner).

Good Luck Bar. 1514 Hillhurst Ave. (between Hollywood and Sunset blvds.), Los Angeles. ☎ **213/666-3524.** No cover.

Until they installed a flashing sign that simply reads "Good Luck," only locals and hipsters knew about this Kung Fu–themed room in the Los Feliz/Silverlake area. The dark red windowless interior boasts Oriental ceiling tiles, fringed Chinese paper lanterns, sweet-but-deadly drinks like the "Yee Mee Loo" (translated as "blue drink"), and a jukebox with selections from Thelonius Monk to Cher's "Half Breed." The spacious sitting room, furnished with mismatched sofas, armchairs, and banquettes, provide a great atmosphere for conversation or romance. Arrive early to avoid the throngs of L.A. scenesters.

Lounge 217. 217 Broadway (between Second and Third streets), Santa Monica. ☎ **310/ 281-6692.** Cover varies.

A lounge in the true sense of the word, these plush art deco surroundings just scream "martini"—and the bartenders stand ready to shake or stir up your favorite. Comfortable seating lends itself well to intimate socializing, or enjoying Monday's classical guitarist; Thursday night brings a torch singer and cigar bar. Come early on the weekends, when Lounge 217 hosts a more raucous late-night crowd.

Windows on Hollywood. In the Holiday Inn, 1755 N. Highland Ave., Hollywood. ☎ **213/462-7181.** No cover.

There's nothing like a revolving bar/restaurant to enjoy a panoramic view of the city; this one is 23 floors above the heart of Hollywood. While it scores low on the hipness scale, we're glad trendy bar-hoppers have taken their scene elsewhere, freeing up the prime window tables for you and me. The slowly revolving outer circle will show you downtown's skyline, the lights of Hollywood, and the hills to the north; the noncirculating center offers entertainment and dancing. If you're lucky, there'll be some young Sinatra wanna-be providing a schmaltzy soundtrack for your cocktail hour.

COMEDY & CABARET

Except for the Cinegrill, which is in its own league, each of the following venues claims, and justly so, to have launched the careers of the comics that are now household names. The funniest up-and-comers are playing all the clubs (except for the Groundlings, which is an improvisation group), so you're probably best off choosing a club for its location. In addition to the venues listed below, see what's on at **LunaPark** (see "The Club and Music Scene," above).

Cover charges vary, but usually hover in the reasonable $10 to $15 range; however, be sure to ask about drink minimums (a two-drink minimum is common), so you don't get any surprises when the bill comes.

The Cinegrill. 7000 Hollywood Blvd., in the Hollywood Roosevelt Hotel, Hollywood. ☎ **213/ 466-7000.**

There's something going on every night of the week here, at one of L.A.'s most historic hotels. Some of the country's best cabaret singers pop up here regularly. The Cinegrill draws locals with a zany cabaret show and guest chanteuses from Eartha Kitt to Cybill Shepherd.

Comedy Store. 8433 Sunset Blvd., West Hollywood. ☎ **213/656-6225.**

You can't go wrong here: New comics develop their material, and established ones work out the kinks from theirs, at owner Mitzi Shore's (Pauly's mom) landmark venue. The talent here is almost always first rate, and includes comics who regularly appear on the *Tonight Show* and other shows.

Groundling Theater. 7307 Melrose Ave., Los Angeles. ☎ **213/934-9700.**

L.A.'s answer to Chicago's Second City has been around for more than 20 years, yet remains the most innovative and funny group in town. Their collection of skits changes every year or so, but they take new improvisational twists every night, and the satire is often savage. The Groundlings were the springboard to fame for Pee-Wee Herman, Elvira, and former *Saturday Night Live* stars Jon Lovitz, Phil Hartman, and Julia "It's Pat" Sweeney. Trust me, you haven't laughed this hard in ages. Phone for show times and reservations.

Igby's Comedy Cabaret. 11637 W. Pico Blvd., West Los Angeles. ☎ **310/477-3553.**

Igby's is the best spot for comedy on the Westside. There's not a bad seat in the place. The comics are well "stacked," so the night usually becomes racier the later it gets.

The Improvisation. 8162 Melrose Ave., West Hollywood. ☎ **213/651-2583.**

A showcase for top stand-ups since 1975, the Improv offers something different each night. Although there used to be a fairly active music schedule, the Improv is now mostly doing what it does best: showcasing comedy. Owner Bud Freedman's buddies, like Jay Leno, Billy Crystal, and Robin Williams, hone their skills here more often than you would expect. But even if the comedians on the bill the night you go are all unknowns, they won't be for long.

THE OTHER BAR SCENE: L.A.'S TOP COFFEEHOUSES

by Steve Hochman

Coffee is the fuel of the grunge culture. Actually, it's just the latest application of the sacred bean to boho lifestyle (imagine Maynard G. Krebs without access to a coffeehouse). Today, though, coffee has gone beyond cliché and into ubiquitousness, with funky little coffeehouses practically on every corner—in addition, of course, to the Starbucks that are overrunning the city.

L.A.'s romance with '90s coffee culture is hardly unique; every major urban city in America is similarly enthralled. But a few of L.A.'s coffeehouses are distinctly Angeleno in their funky characters, which basically range from seedy funky to arty funky. They're definitely worth checking out if you're craving a half-caf cap nonfat with a twist—and maybe some music or poetry to go with it.

The Abbey. 692 N. Robertson Blvd., West Hollywood. ☎ **310/289-8410.**

This coffeehouse in the heart of West Hollywood is really a cafe, offering full meals. But it's also perhaps the best casual hangout in the heavily gay neighborhood, with desserts galore. Lingering over an iced mocha on the patio with a few friends makes for a perfect evening time-waster.

Bourgeois Pig. 5931 Franklin Ave., Hollywood. ☎ **213/962-6366.**

With a bit more of a bar atmosphere than the usual coffeehouse, this veteran, on a hot business strip at the Hollywood/Los Feliz border, is a youth and show-biz drone favorite. An added draw is the terrific newsstand next door.

Highland Grounds. 742 N. Highland Ave., Hollywood. ☎ **213/466-1507.**

Predating the coffeehouse explosion, this comfortable, relatively unpretentious place set the L.A. standard with a vast assortment of food and drink, not just coffee, and often first-rate live music, ranging from nationally known locals, such Victoria Williams, to open-mike Wednesdays for all comers. The ample patio is often used for readings and record release parties.

Jabberjaw. 3711 W. Pico Blvd., Los Angeles. ☎ **213/732-3463.** All ages, cover varies.

This sweaty, arty coffeehouse is only fun if you like the national indie rock scene and a lot of java (no alcohol is served). When temperatures begin to soar, so does the discomfort factor, but guests are granted a reprieve on the club's outdoor patio. Nevertheless, this club is so tied in to the indie scene, a regular can cancel his subscription to *Flipside*.

Onyx/Sequel. 1804 N. Vermont Ave., Los Angeles. No phone.

These two cozy, adjacent rooms in the Los Feliz district offer generally friendly service, as well as a decent line-up of soup, sandwiches, and desserts to go with the beverages. Owner John has long supported local performers and visual artists, giving a home to spoken word and music nights that have drawn such luminaries as Ann

Magnuson and Beck. But if you're looking for something fancy, go elsewhere. Caveat: The art on the walls generally tends toward the scary tortured-soul variety, which doesn't always sit well after a double espresso.

LATE-NIGHT BITES

Los Angeles is no 24-hour town. Surprisingly, the city has only about a dozen bona fide restaurants that are open after hours; even fewer serve all night.

If you want a serious meal after 2am, head for one of these affordable places, both of which are open 24 hours: **The Original Pantry Cafe,** 877 S. Figueroa St. (at 9th Street; ☎ 213/972-9279), has been serving huge portions of comfort food around the clock for more than 60 years (in fact, they don't even have a key to the front door). **Jerry's Famous Deli,** 12655 Ventura Blvd. (at Coldwater Canyon Boulevard), Studio City (☎ 818/980-4245), is where Valley hipsters go to relieve their late-night munchies.

Kate Mantilini, 9101 Wilshire Blvd. (at Doheny Drive), Beverly Hills (☎ 310/ 278-3699), serves up stylish fare until 1am most weeknights, and to 3am on weekends; the menu is a little on the expensive side, but is so expansive that you can put together a decent late-night snack for as little as $15.

If you're looking for an after-hours hangout during the week, **Du-par's Coffee Shop,** 12036 Ventura Blvd. (one block east of Laurel Canyon), Studio City (☎ 818/ 766-4437), probably isn't the place to go; they're only serving blue-plate specials till 1am. However, come the weekend, they're slinging affordable hash until 4am.

Another late-night option is **Canter's Fairfax Restaurant, Delicatessen, and Bakery,** 419 N. Fairfax Ave. (☎ 213/651-2030), a Jewish deli that's been a hit with late-nighters since it opened more than 65 years ago. If you show up after the clubs close, you're sure to spot a bleary-eyed celebrity or two alongside the rest of the after-hours crowd, chowing down on a giant pastrami sandwich, matzoh-ball soup, potato pancakes, or another deli favorite. Try a potato knish with a side of brown gravy—trust me, you'll love it.

15 Side Trips from Los Angeles

by Stephanie Avnet

The area within a 100-mile radius of Los Angeles is one of the most diverse regions in the world. There are arid deserts, rugged mountains, industrial cities, historic towns, alpine lakes, rolling hillsides, and sophisticated seaside resorts. You'll also find an offshore island that's been transformed into the ultimate city-dweller's hideaway, not to mention the Happiest Place on Earth.

1 Pasadena & Environs

11 miles NE of Los Angeles

Pasadena is part of the greater Los Angeles area, but this community is so far removed from the rest of the city, both physically and in spirit, that we think of it as a side trip.

Founded by midwesterners fleeing the cold winter of 1873, Pasadena by the turn of the 20th century had grown into a warm resort destination nestled among the orange groves. The demolition craze that swept Los Angeles mercifully passed over Pasadena, allowing the city a refreshing old-time feel. Historic homes along tree-lined streets coexist with a revitalized downtown respectful of its old brick and stone commercial buildings.

Angelenos flock here to shop and dine, enjoying the opportunity to stroll a compact, manageable downtown area. Best known to the world as the site of the Tournament of Roses Parade each New Year's Day, Pasadena is also home to the California Institute of Technology. Caltech's scientists are the first to report earthquake activity worldwide. In addition, the school boasts 22 Nobel Prize winners among its alumni, and the Caltech-operated Jet Propulsion Laboratory is the birthplace of America's space program. Pasadena offers a richly diverse arts and entertainment scene, and is a favorite location for feature films and TV.

ESSENTIALS

GETTING THERE   If you are flying to Los Angeles, and are planning to make Pasadena or another San Fernando or San Gabriel Valley town your base, see if you can land at the quiet, convenient **Burbank-Glendale-Pasadena Airport,** 2627 N. Hollywood Way, Burbank (☎ 818/840-8840). See Section 1 in Chapter 14 for more airport and airline information.

Area Code Change Notice

Please note that, effective June 14, 1997, the area code for Pasadena and the San Gabriel Valley is scheduled to change to **626**. You will be able to dial 818 until January 17, 1998, after which you will have to use 626.

California's first freeway, the 6-mile Arroyo Seco Parkway, opened in 1940, linking downtown Los Angeles and Pasadena. It later connected to greater Los Angeles's planned 1,500-mile freeway system as the **Pasadena Freeway (Calif. 110).** Narrower and curvier than modern freeways, the Pasadena Freeway, with its lush, overgrown landscaping, now seems like a quaint relic of an earlier era. Though bumper-to-bumper during rush hours, it's refreshingly traffic-free in the late morning, and a lot of fun to drive. If you approach Pasadena from the San Fernando Valley, take the Calif. 134 Freeway east and exit directly onto Colorado Boulevard.

VISITOR INFORMATION   For a free destination guide and information, contact the **Pasadena Convention and Visitors Bureau,** 171 S. Los Robles Ave., Pasadena, CA 91101 (☎ **818/795-9311;** fax 818/795-9656). They are open Monday to Friday from 8am to 5pm and Saturdays from 10am to 4pm. There's also a city-run Web site (**http://www.ci.pasadena.ca.us**), which offers tourist information as well as business and government listings.

GETTING AROUND   Street parking can be scarce around the few blocks at the core of Old Town, but there are abundant public garages with friendly rates (often less than the change you'd feed your meter anyway). Look for the Old Pasadena Parking signs.

An alternative is to take advantage of the free **Arts Buses** that run along Colorado Boulevard and Green Street through Old Town and the Lake Avenue shopping district. Shuttles come every 20 minutes (12 minutes during lunchtime) between 11am and 8pm, Monday through Saturday.

SEEING THE SIGHTS IN & AROUND PASADENA

Various tours spotlighting architecture or neighborhoods are lots of fun, given this area's history of wealthy estates and ardent preservation. Call **Pasadena Heritage** (☎ **818/793-0617**) for a schedule of guided tours, or pick up "Ten Tours of Pasadena," self-guided walking or driving maps available at the Visitor's Bureau (see "Essentials," above). For a quick but profound architectural fix, stroll past Pasadena's grandiose and Baroque **City Hall,** 100 N. Garfield Ave., two blocks north of Colorado; closer inspection will reveal its classical colonnaded courtyard, formal gardens, and spectacular tiled dome.

Descanso Gardens. 1418 Descanso Dr., La Cañada. ☎ **818/952-4402** or 818/952-4401. Admission $5 adults, $3 students and seniors (over 62), $1 children 5–12, kids under 5 free. Daily 9am–4:30pm.

Camellias (evergreen flowering shrubs from China and Japan) were the passion of amateur gardener E. Manchester Boddy, who began planting them here in 1941. Today, his Descanso Gardens contains more than 100,000 camellias in over 600 varieties, blooming under a 30-acre canopy of California oak trees. The shrubs now share the limelight with a five-acre Rose Garden, home to hundreds of varieties.

This is really a magical place, with paths and streams that wind through the towering forest, bordering a lake and bird sanctuary. Each season features different plants: daffodils, azaleas, tulips, and lilacs in the spring; chrysanthemums in the fall; and so on. Monthly art exhibits are held in the garden's hospitality house.

There's also a beautifully landscaped Japanese-style teahouse that serves tea and cookies on Saturday and Sunday from 11am to 4pm. Free docent-guided walking tours are offered every Sunday at 1pm; guided tram tours, which cost $1.50, run Tuesday through Friday at 1, 2, and 3pm, and on Saturday and Sunday at 11am and 1, 2, and 3pm. Picnicking is allowed in specified areas.

✪ **Gamble House.** 4 Westmoreland Pl., Pasadena. ☎ **818/793-3334.** Admission $5 adults, $4 seniors, $3 students, children under 12 free. Thurs–Sun noon–3pm; closed holidays.

The huge two-story Gamble House, built in 1908 as a California vacation home for the wealthy family of Procter and Gamble fame, is a sublime example of Arts and Crafts architecture. Designed by the famous Pasadena-based Greene and Greene architectural team, the interior abounds with craftsmanship, including intricately carved teak cornices, custom-designed furnishings, elaborate carpets, and a fantastic Tiffany glass door. No detail was overlooked. Every oak wedge, downspout, air vent, and switch plate contributes to the unified design. Admission is by one-hour guided tour only, which departs every 15 minutes. No reservations are necessary.

✪ **The Huntington Library, Art Collections and Botanical Gardens.** 1151 Oxford Rd., San Marino. ☎ **818/405-2141.** Admission $7.50 adults, $6 seniors ages 65 and above, $4 students and children under 12, free for children under 12. Tues–Fri noon–4:30pm, Sat–Sun 10:30am–4:30pm. Closed major holidays.

The Huntington Library is the jewel in Pasadena's crown. The 207-acre hilltop estate was once home to industrialist and railroad magnate Henry E. Huntington (1850–1927), who bought books on the same massive scale that he acquired businesses. The continually expanding collection includes dozens of Shakespeare's original works; Benjamin Franklin's handwritten autobiography; a Gutenberg Bible from the 1450s; and the earliest known manuscript of Chaucer's *Canterbury Tales*. Although these rarer works are only available to visiting scholars, the library has a regularly changing (and always excellent) exhibit showcasing different items in the collection.

If you prefer canvas to parchment, Huntington also put together a terrific 18th-century British and French art collection. His most celebrated paintings are Gainsborough's *The Blue Boy,* and *Pinkie,* a companion piece by Sir Thomas Lawrence depicting the youthful aunt of Elizabeth Barrett Browning. These and other works are displayed in the stately Italianate mansion on the crest of this hillside estate, so you can get also get a glimpse of its splendid furnishings.

But it's the botanical gardens that draw most locals to the Huntington. The Japanese Garden is complete with traditional open-air Japanese house, koi-filled stream and serene Zen garden; the cactus garden is exotic, the jungle garden intriguing, the lily ponds soothing, and there are plentiful benches scattered about encouraging you to sit and enjoy.

Because the Huntington surprises many with its size and the wealth of activities from which to choose, first-timers might want to start by attending one of the regularly scheduled 12-minute introductory slide shows; or take the more in-depth one-hour garden tour, given each day at 1pm.

I also recommend you tailor your visit to include the popular English high tea served Tuesday to Sunday from 1:30 to 3:30pm. The charming tea room overlooks the Rose Garden (home to 1,000 varieties displayed in chronological order of their breeding), and since the finger sandwiches and desserts are served buffet-style, it's a

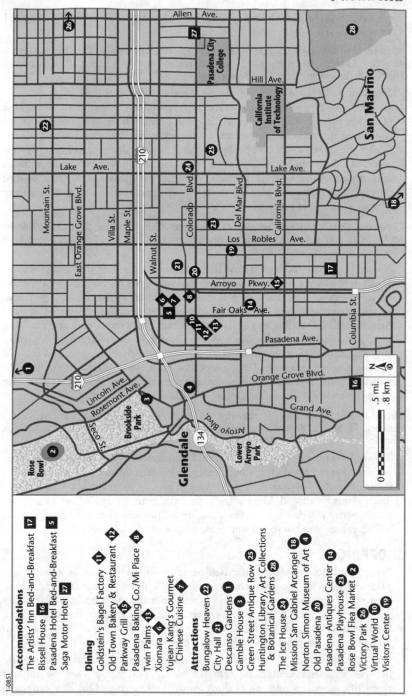

Pasadena

Accommodations
The Artists' Inn Bed-and-Breakfast **17**
Bissell House **16**
Pasadena Hotel Bed-and-Breakfast **5**
Saga Motor Hotel **27**

Dining
Goldstein's Bagel Factory **11**
Old Town Bakery & Restaurant **12**
Parkway Grill **15**
Pasadena Baking Co./Mi Piace **8**
Twin Palms **13**
Xiomara **6**
Yujean Kang's Gourmet
Chinese Cuisine **7**

Attractions
Bungalow Heaven **22**
City Hall **21**
Descanso Gardens **1**
Gamble House **3**
Green Street Antique Row **25**
Huntington Library, Art Collections
& Botanical Gardens **28**
The Ice House **24**
Mission San Gabriel Arcangel **18**
Norton Simon Museum of Art **4**
Old Pasadena **20**
Pasadena Antiques Center **14**
Pasadena Playhouse **23**
Rose Bowl Flea Market **2**
Victory Park **26**
Virtual World **10**
Visitors Center **19**

1-0851

genteel bargain (even for hearty appetites) at $11 per person. Phone 818/683-8131 for reservations.

Mission San Gabriel Arcangel. 537 W. Mission Dr., San Gabriel. ☎ **818/457-3035.** Admission $3 adults, $1 children 6–12 years, kids under 6 free. Daily 9am–4:30pm (Oct–May); 10am–5:30 (June–Sept). Closed holidays.

Founded in 1771, Mission San Gabriel Arcangel still retains its original facade, notable for its high oblong windows and large capped buttresses that are said to have been influenced by the cathedral in Cordova, Spain. The mission's self-contained compound encompasses an aqueduct, a cemetery, a tannery, and a working winery. Within the church stands a copper font with the dubious distinction of being the first one used to baptize a Native Californian. The most notable contents of the mission's museum are Native American paintings depicting the stations of the cross, painted on sailcloth, with colors made from crushed desert flower petals. The mission is about 15 minutes south of Pasadena.

✪ **Norton Simon Museum of Art.** 411 Colorado Blvd., Pasadena. ☎ **818/449-6840.** Admission $4 adults, $2 students and seniors, children under 12 free. Thurs–Sun noon–6pm; bookshop, Thurs–Sun noon–5:30pm.

Named for a food-packing king and financier who reorganized the failing Pasadena Museum of Modern Art, the Norton Simon Museum has become one of California's most important museums. Comprehensive collections of masterpieces by Degas, Picasso, Rembrandt, and Goya are augmented by sculptures by Henry Moore and Auguste Rodin, including *Burghers of Calais,* which greets you at the gates. The "Blue Four" collection of works by Kandinsky, Jawlensky, Klee, and Feininger is particularly impressive, as is a superb collection of Southeast Asian sculpture. *Still Life with Lemons, Oranges, and a Rose* (1633), an oil by Francisco de Zurbaràn, is one of the museum's most important holdings. One of the most popular pieces is Mexican artist Diego Rivera's *The Flower Vendor/Girl with Lilies.*

Virtual World. In the One Colorado Mall, 35 Hugus Alley (Colorado and Fair Oaks blvds.), Pasadena. ☎ **818/577-9896.** Admission $7 Mon–Fri before 5pm, $8 after 5pm; $9 Sat–Sun. Mon–Fri 10am–9pm, Sat–Sun 10am–8pm.

This is the ultimate "easy side trip" from Los Angeles. Several different adventures are offered at the world's first virtual reality play center, including a run through the mining tunnels of Mars in the year 2053 and a jousting tournament on the fictitious desert planet Solaris VII. Many of the virtual worlds are set up like intergalactic war games, where you don heavy helmets and try to "neutralize" your friends. After the VR adventure, you can review your game from various angles on videotape.

SHOPPING

Pretty, compact Pasadena lends itself perfectly to many travelers' number-one pastime: shopping. The city's recent renovation efforts have focused unabashedly on creating an alternative to Los Angeles's behemoth shopping malls, so Pasadena's streets are a true pleasure to stroll. As a general rule, stores are open seven days a week from about 10am, and, while some close at the standard 5 or 6pm, many stay open till 8 or 9pm to accommodate the pre- and post-dinner/movie crowd.

OLD PASADENA   The focus of consumerism is along Colorado Boulevard between Pasadena Avenue and Arroyo Parkway, where you'll see the ongoing regentrification of a once-dingy downtown. It's known as **Old Pasadena,** and some old-time residents hate it as much as the scores of visitors love it. In our opinion it's one of the best parts about the L.A. area, but we hope they retain more of the "mom-and-pop" businesses currently being pushed out by the likes of Banana Republic, Urban Outfitters, Crate and Barrel, and Victoria's Secret.

Penny Lane, 12 W. Colorado Blvd. (☎ **818/564-0161**), a new and used CD store, also has a great selection of music magazines and kitschy postcards. The selection is less picked over here than at many record stores in Hollywood. Around the corner at **Rebecca's Dream,** 16 S. Fair Oaks Ave. (☎ **818/796-1200**), both men and women can find vintage clothing treasures in this small and meticulously organized (by color scheme) store. Be sure to look up; vintage hats adorn the walls. Around the corner is the **Del Mano** gallery of contemporary crafts, 33 E. Colorado Blvd. (☎ **818/793-6648**), and it's a whole lot of fun to see the creations—some whimsical, some exquisite—of American artists working with glass, wood, ceramics or jewelry.

On the corner of Colorado and Raymond, even if you don't stop in, have a look at **Crown City Loan and Jewelry,** a pawn shop that survived regentrification as musty as ever! Their haphazard window display (wooden elephant carvings, assorted wristwatches, an old accordion) thumbs its nose at the order all around. Further down is **Tournament Souvenirs,** 88 E. Colorado Blvd. (☎ **808/395-7066**), which is exactly as it sounds: Rose Parade and Rose Bowl clothing, hats, pennants, glassware and sports sippers for anyone visiting during the 51 *other* weeks of the year. Around the corner is a duo of related stores, **Distant Lands Bookstore and Outfitters,** 54 and 62 S. Raymond Ave. (☎ **818/449-3220**). The bookstore has a terrific selection of maps, guides and travel-related literature, while the recently-opened outfitters two doors away offers everything from luggage and pith helmets to space-saving and convenient travel accessories.

TAKING A BREAK Serious shopping requires occasional periods of rest and refreshment, and there's no place better than one of Pasadena's many, many coffee cafes. In addition to the ubiquitous **Starbucks,** 117 W. Colorado Blvd. (☎ **818/577-4622**), there's sleek, spacious **Espresso Cabaret,** 17 E. Colorado Blvd. (☎ **818/584-6505**), and the outdoor patio at **Micah's,** 88 N. Fair Oaks at Holly (☎ **818/795-9733**). But our favorite is **Chatz of Pasadena,** 53 E. Union St. (☎ **818/584-9110**), tucked away one block north of busy Colorado Boulevard. It's cozy and friendly, the kind of place that runs out of the best muffins early but never takes down old flyers from the cluttered bulletin board on the wall by the door.

OTHER SHOPPING VENUES In addition to Old Town Pasadena, there are numerous good hunting grounds in the surrounding area. For example, antique hounds might want to head to the **Green Street Antique Row,** 985 to 1005 E. Green St., east of Lake Avenue, or **Pasadena Antique Center,** South Fair Oaks Boulevard south of Del Mar). Each has a rich concentration of collectibles dealers, and can captivate browsers for hours.

You never know what you'll find at the ✪ **Rose Bowl Flea Market,** at the Rose Bowl, 991 Rosemont Ave., Pasadena (☎ **818/577-3100**). Built in 1922, the horseshoe-shaped Rose Bowl is one of the world's most famous stadiums, home to UCLA's football Bruins, the annual Rose Bowl Game, and an occasional Super Bowl. California's largest monthly swap meet, on the second Sunday of every month from 9am to 3pm, is a favorite of Los Angeles antique hounds (who know to arrive as early as 6:30am for the best finds). Antique furnishings, clothing, jewelry, and other collectibles are assembled in the parking area to the left of the entrance, while the rest of the flea market surrounds the exterior of the Bowl. Here, look for everything from used surfboards and car stereos to one-of-a-kind lawn statuary and bargain athletic shoes. Admission is $5.

Book lovers will want to prowl through the rare and out-of-print treasures at **The Browser's Bookshop,** 659 E. Colorado Blvd. at El Molino (☎ **818/585-8308**), or its dusty neighbor **House of Fiction,** 663 E. Colorado Blvd. (☎ **818/449-9861**). For a world-class selection of big band, swing, pop vocalist, soundtracks, and other nonrock 'n' roll CDs, don't miss **Canterbury Records,** 805 E. Colorado, corner of Hudson (☎ **818/792-7184**).

Anglophiles will delight in **Rose Tree Cottage,** 824 E. California Blvd., just west of Lake Avenue (☎ **818/793-3337**), and their charming array of all things British. This cluster of historic Tudor cottages surrounded by traditional English gardens hold three gift shops and a tea room, where a superb $19.50 high tea is served thrice daily among the knickknacks (and supervised by the resident cat, Miss Moffett). In addition to imported teas, linens, and silver trinkets, Rose Tree Cottage sells homemade English delicacies like steak and kidney pies, hot cross buns, and shortbread. They are also the local representative of the British Tourist Authority and offer a comprehensive array of travel publications.

WHERE TO STAY
DOUBLES FOR $60 OR LESS

In this price range, you'll mainly find representatives of the national chains, for most Pasadena area accommodations cater to convention attendees on expense accounts or travelers in the higher price brackets. The good news is, they tend to be clean and politely managed, if not exceptional in other ways. Try the **Comfort Inn,** 2462 E. Colorado Blvd. (☎ **800/221-2222** or 818/405-0811; fax 818/796-0966). Their location, east of Sierra Madre Boulevard, about 10 minutes from the center of Old Town, might be inconvenient to some, but a room rate of $58 makes it a worthwhile consideration. The **Westway Inn,** 1599 E. Colorado Blvd. (☎ **818/304-9678;** fax 818/449-3493), is across the street from Pasadena City College and offers a friendly $50 rate year-round. Be sure to inquire about auto club and other discounts.

DOUBLES FOR $80 OR LESS

Pasadena Hotel Bed and Breakfast. 76 N. Fair Oaks Ave. (between Union and Holly sts.), Pasadena, CA 91103. ☎ **800/653-8886** or 818/568-8172. Fax 818/793-6409. 10 rooms, one with half bath. A/C TEL TV. Rooms $65–$165. Rates include continental breakfast. AE, MC, V.

This old-style hostelry is definitely not for everyone. In true turn-of-the-century rooming house style, the guest rooms have only washbasins; all but one must share hallway bathrooms (three full, two half). Part of the attraction here is the well-restored National Historic Register building, and part the hotel's flawless location: It's the only accommodation *literally* in the heart of Old Pasadena. Guest quarters are small but comfortable, and all are second-story exterior rooms. The central sitting room/lounge is elegant and welcoming, and there is a lively coffeehouse in the courtyard behind the hotel where you can enjoy your breakfast and complimentary afternoon teas. Shuttle buses to the Rose Bowl depart one block away during major events.

Saga Motor Hotel. 1633 E. Colorado Blvd. (between Allen and Sierra Bonita aves.), Pasadena, CA 91106. ☎ **818/795-0431.** 69 rms, 1 suite. A/C TEL TV. $62–$69 double, $75 suite. Rates include continental breakfast. AE, CB, DC, MC, V.

This motel is a 1950s relic of old Route 66, a little bland by modern standards but with far more character than most others in its price range. The rooms are small, clean, and simply furnished with just the basics. The best rooms are in the front building surrounding the gated swimming pool, which is shielded from the street and inviting in warm weather. The grounds are attractive and surprisingly well kept, if you don't count the AstroTurf "lawn" around the pool. The motel is about a mile from the Huntington Library and within 10 minutes of both the Rose Bowl and Old Pasadena.

DOUBLES FOR $100 OR LESS

The Artists' Inn Bed-and-Breakfast. 1038 Magnolia St., South Pasadena, CA 91030. ☎ and fax **818/799-5668.** 5 rms. A/C. Rooms $100–$120, additional person $20. Rates include full breakfast. AC, MC, V.

This Victorian-style inn, an unpretentious yellow-shingled home that's tastefully furnished throughout with wicker, was built in 1895 as a farmhouse. Each of the four rooms is thematically decorated to reflect the style of a particular artist or period, including Impressionist, Fauve, and Van Gogh. The English Room, fitted with good quality antique furnishings and cheerful rose-patterned wallpaper, is the best room in the house; it's also the only one with a king-size bed. The Italian Suite has a queen bed and adjoining sun room with twin beds, a perfect choice for families. The Inn is on a quiet residential street five minutes from the heart of downtown.

Bissell House. 201 Orange Grove Ave. (SW corner of Columbia St.), South Pasadena, CA 91030. ☎ **818/441-3535.** 4 rms. A/C. Rooms $100–$150. Rates include full breakfast on weekends, expanded continental breakfast weekdays; plus afternoon snack and all-day beverages. AE, MC, V.

Hidden behind tall hedges that carefully isolate it from busy Orange Grove Avenue, this 1887 gingerbread Victorian is furnished with antiques and offers a delightful taste of life on what was once Pasadena's "Millionaire's Row." All rooms have private bath with both shower and tub (one an antique claw foot, one a private whirlpool). There's a swimming pool and Jacuzzi on the beautifully landscaped grounds, and a downstairs library offers a telephone and fax machine for guests' use.

WHERE TO DINE

Within the past decade or so, Pasadena has grown into one of the premier dining destinations for Angelenos "in the know." Superstar chefs have fled the super competitive Westside restaurant scene to shine in this friendly suburb. Remember, this isn't really out-of-town, and no one thinks twice about hopping on the freeway for dinner and a movie. As with most of the greater Los Angeles area, you'll find the finer restaurants significantly more affordable for lunch.

MEALS FOR $10 OR LESS

Goldstein's Bagel Bakery. 86 W. Colorado Blvd. (corner of Delacey Ave.), Old Pasadena. ☎ **818/79-BAGEL.** Most items under $3. AE, MC, V. Mon–Thurs & Sun 6am–9pm, Fri–Sat 6am–10:30pm. BAKERY/DELI.

Join the locals who storm Goldstein's each morning for freshly baked (in the authentic New York style) bagels; reliable plain and onion are as good as exotic honey oat raisin or banana nut. In addition to six flavored cream cheeses, you can choose a bagel sandwich prepared with your choice of deli ingredients. Centrally located in the heart of Old Town, this is a good choice for snacks and light meals without interrupting the rhythm of your day or your budget.

Old Town Bakery and Restaurant. 166 W. Colorado Blvd. (at Pasadena Ave.), Pasadena. ☎ **818/792-7943.** Main courses $5–$11. DISC, MC, V. Sun–Thurs 7:30am–10pm, Fri–Sat 7:30am–midnight. CONTINENTAL.

Set back from the street in a quaint fountain courtyard, this cheery bakery is a popular place to read the morning paper over tasty breakfasts like pumpkin pancakes or zesty omelets. The display counters are packed with cakes, muffins, scones, and other confections, all baked expressly for this shop. The rest of the menu is a mishmash of pastas, salads and the like, borrowing heavily from Latin and Mediterranean cuisine. Old Town Bakery is a great place to spy on local Pasadenans in their natural habitat.

Pasadena Baking Company/Mi Piace. 25–29 E. Colorado Blvd. (east of Fair Oaks Ave.), Old Pasadena. ☎ **818/796-9966.** Bakery items under $3, main courses $6–$15. AE, MC, V. Mon–Thurs 7am–11pm, Fri 7am–midnight, Sat 8am–midnight, Sun 8am–11pm. BAKERY/ITALIAN CAFE.

This little cafe holds just a handful of small tables, which spill out onto the sidewalk during nice weather (90% of the time). Their particularly large and sweet-smelling selection of fresh pastries, tarts, truffles, cakes, and candies are all proudly displayed. There's also an assortment of fresh breads and a fresh fruit stand to accompany their breakfast and lunch menu.

Mi Piace is the adjoining, casual trattoria, offering usual pastas and Northern Italian dishes prepared unusually well. The Baking Company commandeers their sidewalk tables during breakfast, but starting around 11:30am it's not unusual to see locals enjoying an espresso with their dogs tethered to a table leg.

MEALS FOR $20 OR LESS

Parkway Grill. 510 S. Arroyo Parkway (at California Blvd.), Pasadena. ☎ **818/795-1001.** Reservations recommended. Main courses $8–$23. AE, CB, DC, MC, V. Mon–Fri 11:30am–2:30pm, Mon–Thurs 5:30–11pm, Fri–Sat 5pm–midnight, Sun 10am–2pm & 5–11pm. CALIFORNIA ECLECTIC.

This quintessentially Southern California restaurant has been one of the L.A. area's top-rated spots since it opened in 1985, quickly gaining a reputation for avant-garde flavor combinations and gourmet pizzas to rival Spago's. Although some critics find many of chef Hugo Molina's dishes too fussy, others thrill to appetizer innovations like lobster-stuffed cocoa crepes or Dungeness crab cakes with ginger cream and two salsas. The star entrees are meat and game from the iron mesquite grill, followed by richly sweet (and substantial) desserts. The interior is vibrantly colored and architecturally, well, eclectic, for the building once knew life as a transmission shop! Located where the old Arroyo Seco Parkway glides into an ordinary city street, the Parkway Grill is within a couple of minutes' drive from Old Pasadena and thoughtfully offers free valet parking.

☉ Twin Palms. 101 W. Green St. (at Delacey Ave.), Pasadena. ☎ **818/577-2567.** Reservations recommended on weekends. Main courses $9–$17. AE, DC, CB, MC, V. Mon–Thurs 11:30am–midnight, Fri–Sat 11:30am–1:30am, Sun 10:30am–midnight. MEDITERRANEAN/FRENCH.

Twin Palms is able to seat nearly 400 at spacious tables (no postage-stamp two-seaters here!) shaded by the fronds of 100-year-old palm trees. It's also busy, having become a hit with recession-weary Angelenos who come here for some of the best-value meals in the entire L.A. area. The quasi-outdoor and tented space creates a festival atmosphere augmented by two lively bars, and a bandstand with entertainment every night except Monday. Or come Sundays until 1:30pm for the "Gospel Brunch," during which Twin Palms also offers alternative entertainment for children. Co-owner/chef Michael Roberts is as well known for his celebrity backers (including Kevin Costner) as he is for the French "comfort food" he created as a backlash against pricey haute cuisine. Everyone talks about the salt cod mashed potato *brandade*, a delicious appetizer that's big enough to serve four, for only $5. The best main courses come off the crackling rotisserie and outdoor grill; they include juicy, roasted sage-infused pork and honey-glazed coriander-scented duck. Sautéed dishes and salads are not as successful. A number of exciting wines are priced well, under $20.

Yujean Kang's Gourmet Chinese Cuisine. 67 N. Raymond Ave. (between Walnut St. and Colorado Blvd.), Pasadena. ☎ **818/585-0855.** Reservations recommended. Main courses $14–$21. AE, MC, V. Daily 11:30am–2:30pm, 5–10pm. CHINESE CONTEMPORARY.

Many Chinese restaurants put the word *gourmet* in their name, but few really mean, or deserve, it. Not so at Yujean Kang, where Chinese cuisine is taken to an entirely new level. A master of "fusion" cuisine, the eponymous chef/owner snatches bits of techniques and flavors from both China and the West, commingling them in an entirely fresh way. Can you resist such provocative dishes as "Ants on Tree" (beef sautéed with glass noodles in chile and black sesame seeds), or lobster with caviar and fava beans, or Chilean sea bass in passion-fruit sauce? Kang is a wine aficionado and has assembled a magnificent cellar of California, French, and particularly German wines. Try pairing a German Spatlese with tea-smoked duck salad. The red-wrapped dining room is less subtle, but just as elegant, as the food.

WORTH A SPLURGE

✪ **Xiomara.** 69 N. Raymond Ave. (one block north of Colorado Blvd.), Pasadena. ☎ **818/796-2520.** Reservations recommended. Main courses $18–$23; fixed-price menu $25. AE, MC, V. Mon–Fri 11:30am–2:30pm; Mon–Sat 5:30–10:30pm, Sun 5–10:30pm. COUNTRY FRENCH.

By any other name, Xiomara (*see*-o-ma-ra) would still be one of the top restaurants in Los Angeles, despite the fact that it has never made Zagat's "top rated" list. Chef Patrick Healy's best dishes are rustic country concoctions like sausage-laden cassoulet, and veal shanks braised so long the meat practically falls off the bone. Chicken is simmered for an eternity in a sealed cast-iron pot with artichokes and carrots. The nightly fixed-price meal, a three-course menu determined by the chef's mood and the fresh ingredients at hand, is a remarkably good value. A long list of obscure country wines complements the menu. The dining room, a sleek black bistro setting, is as pleasing as the food, fitted with comfortable armchairs, and presided over by the enthusiastic Xiomara herself. An oyster and clam bar features oyster shooters, ceviche, and a large selection of raw oysters and clams on the half shell.

COFFEEHOUSES

Equator. 22 Mills Place, Pasadena. ☎ **818/564-8656.**

Airy and comfy, this brick room on a busy alleyway in the heart of resurgent Old Town Pasadena has withstood the challenge of a Starbucks that moved in a block away. The menu—with smoothies, soup, and desserts in addition to a wide variety of coffee drinks—and the friendly service keep people coming back. Even the post-Haring art on the walls gives a distinctive character, which has been used for scenes in such films and TV shows as *Beverly Hills, 90210* to *A Very Brady Sequel.*

Espresso Bar. 1039 E. Green St. (near Catalina) ☎ **818/577-9113.** Coffee drinks and baked goodies $1–$4. No credit cards. Mon–Thurs 9am–1am, Fri–Sat 9am–2am, Sun noon–midnight.

This simply named coffeehouse has been around so long that it almost seems as though Pasadena grew up around it. Formerly hidden down a hard-to-find alleyway, their new location is on Green Street's Antique Row, outside of Old Town but close to Pasadena City College. Open mike nights are popular with beat poets and singers, and bands play Friday and Saturday nights to an eclectic crowd lounging on the hodgepodge of dingy furniture typical of Espresso Bar's Greenwich Village ambience.

There's a spacious upstairs loft, and a beverage menu with some exotic entries like steamed milk with molasses.

2　Long Beach & the *Queen Mary*

21 miles S of Downtown L.A.

The fifth-largest incorporated city in California, Long Beach consists mostly of business and industrial areas interspersed with unremarkable neighborhoods. The city is best known as the permanent home of the former cruise liner *Queen Mary* (see "What to See and Do" and "Where to Stay," below) and for the annual Long Beach Grand Prix in mid-April, whose star-studded warm-up race sends the likes of young hipster Jason Priestly (*Beverly Hills, 90210*) and perennial racer Paul Newman burning rubber through the streets of the city. Although Long Beach is too far away to be considered part of Los Angeles as a tourist destination, and it's not as attractive as most of the smaller coastal communities to either the north or south, the *Queen Mary* makes a trip here worthwhile.

ESSENTIALS

GETTING THERE　See Section 1 in Chapter 14 for airport and airline information. When driving from Los Angeles on either I-5 or I-405, take I-710 south; it follows the Los Angeles River on its path to the ocean and leads directly to both downtown Long Beach and the *Queen Mary Seaport.*

ORIENTATION　Most of seaside Long Beach is in vast San Pedro Harbor, L.A.'s busy industrial port. Terminal Island sits right in the middle. To the west across pretty Vincent Thomas bridge is the city of San Pedro, home the nautical and touristy **Ports O' Call Village.** The *Queen Mary* is docked near the eastern end of Long Beach, looking out over the actual "long beach" extending along peaceful, affluent Belmont Shore to tiny Long Beach Marina, home to charming Naples Island.

VISITOR INFORMATION　Contact the **Long Beach Area Convention and Visitors Bureau,** One World Trade Center, No. 300 (☎ **800/4LB-STAY** or 562/436-3645). There's a city-run Web site at **http://www.ci.long-beach.ca.us,** which offers, in addition to business and government information, a section with tourism listings. For further information on the **Long Beach Grand Prix,** call **562/981-2600** or visit their Web site at **http://www.longbeachgp.com.**

THE *QUEEN MARY* & OTHER PORT ATTRACTIONS

The *Queen Mary.* Pier J (at the end of I-710), Long Beach. ☎ **562/435-3511.** Admission $10 adults, $8 seniors 55 & over and military, $6 children 4–11, under 4 free. Daily 10am–6pm (last entry at 5:30pm). Extended summer hours. Charge for parking.

It's easy to dismiss the *Queen Mary* as a barnacle-laden tourist trap, but it *is* the only surviving example of this particular kind of 20th-century elegance and excess. From staterooms paneled lavishly in now-extinct tropical hardwoods, to miles of hallway handrails made of once-pedestrian Bakelite and perfectly preserved crew quarters which are an art-deco homage, wonders never cease aboard this luxury liner. Stroll the teakwood decks with just a bit of imagination, and you're back in 1936 on the maiden voyage from Southampton, England. Kiosk displays of photographs and memorabilia are everywhere, and the ship has been virtually unaltered since her heyday. Especially evocative is the first-class observation lounge, a Streamline Moderne masterpiece you might recognize from *Barton Fink, Beverly Hills, 90210,* and others. Regular admission includes a self-guided tour. For an additional $6 adults or $3 for kids, you can take a behind-the-scenes guided tour of the ship, peppered with worthwhile anecdotes and details.

Shoreline Village. 407 Shoreline Drive (at Pine Ave. across the channel from the *Queen Mary*). ☎ 562/435-2668, or 562/432-3053 for information. Open daily 10am–9pm, or later in summer and holidays.

If you've seen the real thing in New England you won't be overly impressed, but Long Beach likes to promote this cluster of shops, restaurants, and waterside cafes as a replica 19th-century seaport village. But our favorite surprise was an ornate merry-go-round hand carved in 1906 by Charles Looff, master carousel maker who helped build The Pike, an old-fashioned seaside amusement park that stood on this spot in the 1930s. The 62 wooden carousel animals include not only horses but leaping camels, giraffes and rams, all illuminated by glittering Austrian crystal; rides are $1.

THE TALL SHIP CALIFORNIAN

Literally the flagship of the Nautical Heritage Society, the *Californian* sails from Long Beach between late August and mid-April (it's based in Northern California during summer). At 145 feet long, this two-masted wooden cutter-class vessel offers bare-footers the opportunity to help raise and lower eight sails, steer by compass, and generally experience the "romance of the high seas." Landlubbers will want to choose the four-hour day sail for $75 ($113 for two), including lunch, while old salts can take two-, three- or four-day cruises to Catalina or the Channel Islands at $140 per person per day. For reservations call **800/432-2201.**

WHERE TO STAY

✪ **Hotel *Queen Mary*.** 1126 Queen's Hwy. (off I-710 south), Long Beach, CA 90802-6390. ☎ **800/437-2934**, 562/435-3511, or 562/432-6964. Fax 562/437-4531. 365 rms, 17 suites. A/C TEL TV. Rooms $75–$160; suites from $350. AE, DC, EU, MC, V. Charge for parking.

Although the *Queen Mary* is considered the most luxurious ocean liner ever to sail the Atlantic, with the largest rooms ever built aboard a ship, the quarters aren't exceptional when compared to those on terra firma today, nor are its amenities. The idea is to enjoy the novelty and charm of the original bathtub handles ("cold salt," "cold fresh," "hot salt," "hot fresh"). The ship's beautifully carved interior is a festival for the eye and fun to explore, plus the weekday rates are hard to beat. Three on-board restaurants are overpriced but convenient, and the original shopping arcade has a decidedly British feel (one shop sells great *Queen Mary* souvenirs). An elegant Sunday champagne brunch, complete with ice sculpture and harpist, is served in the ship's Grand Salon, and it's always worth having a cocktail in the art deco Observation Bar. If you're too young or too poor to have traveled on the old luxury liners, this is the perfect opportunity to experience the romance of an Atlantic crossing, with no seasickness, cabin fever, or week of formal dinners.

WHERE TO DINE

Belmont Brewing Company. 25 Thirty-Ninth Place (at the Belmont Pier), Long Beach. ☎ **562/433-3891.** Main courses $5–$11. AE, CB, DC, MC, V. Mon–Fri 11:30am–9:30pm, Sat–Sun 10:30am–10pm (bar till midnight daily). BREWPUB/AMERICAN.

This brewed-on-premises beer restaurant's outdoor patio has a million-dollar harbor view of the *Queen Mary*, fiery sunsets, and the pier's unusual chameleon streetlamps. The five house brews include "Top Sail" (amber) and "Long Beach Crude" (porter). The menu consists of salads, sandwiches, pizzas, pasta, and happy hour appetizer favorites, including a deep-fried whole onion "flower" served with sweet-spicy dipping sauce.

Papadakis Taverna. 301 W. Sixth St. (at Centre St.), San Pedro. ☎ **562/548-1186.** Reservations recommended. Main courses $8–$16. CB, DC, MC, V. Sun–Thurs 5–9pm, Fri–Sat 5–10pm. GREEK.

The food here rates higher than the ambience—even genial host John Papadakis's hand-kissing greeting doesn't soften the blunt lines and bright lights of this banquet room–like space decorated with equal parts Aegean murals and football art (in deference to Papadakis's glory days as a USC football legend). The waiters dance and sing loudly when they're not bringing plates of spanikopita (spinach filled filo pastries) or thick, satisfying tsatziki (garlic-laced cucumber and yogurt spread) to your table. Servings are very generous, prices reasonable, and the wine list has something for everyone.

Parker's Lighthouse. 435 Shoreline Village Dr., Long Beach. ☎ **562/432-6500.** Reservations recommended on weekends. Lunches $6–$15, dinners $9–$27. AE, DC, DISC, MC, V. Mon–Thurs 11am–10pm, Fri 11am–11pm, Sat 3–11pm, Sun 3:30–9:30pm. SEAFOOD GRILL.

Built to look like a giant Cape Cod lighthouse, Parker's fits right into the Shoreline Village motif. It's actually kind of fun to wind upstairs to one of three dining levels, including the circular bar on the top floor which looks out over the harbor and the behemoth *Queen Mary.* The main dining room specializes in mesquite-fired fresh seafood, but also offers steaks and chicken.

3 Santa Catalina Island

22 miles W of mainland Los Angeles

Santa Catalina, which everyone calls simply Catalina, is a small, cove-fringed island famous for its laid-back inns, largely unspoiled landscape, and crystal-clear waters. Many devotees consider it Southern California's alternative to Capri or Malta. Because of its relative isolation, out-of-state tourists tend to ignore it; but those who do show up have plenty of elbow room to boat, fish, swim, scuba, and snorkel. There are miles of hiking and biking trails, plus golf, tennis, and horseback riding.

Catalina is so different from the mainland that it almost seems like a different country, remote and unspoiled. In 1915, the island was purchased by William Wrigley Jr., the chewing gum manufacturer, in order to develop a fashionable pleasure resort. To publicize the new vacation land, Wrigley brought big-name bands to the Avalon Ballroom and moved the Chicago Cubs, which he owned, to the island for spring training. His marketing efforts succeeded, and this charming and tranquil retreat became a favorite vacation resort for mainlanders, which it remains.

Today about 86% of the island remains undeveloped, owned and preserved by the Santa Catalina Island Conservancy. Some of the spectacular outlying areas can only be reached by arranged tour (see "Exploring the Island," below).

ESSENTIALS

GETTING THERE The most common way to get to and from the island is via the *Catalina Express* (☎ 562/519-1212), which operates up to 20 daily departures year-round to Catalina from San Pedro and Long Beach. The trip takes about an hour. One-way fares from San Pedro are $17.75 for adults, $16 for seniors, $13 for children 2 to 11, and $1 for infants. Long Beach fares are about $2 higher for all except infants, who are still charged $1. The trip is an additional $1.80 if you travel to Two Harbors. The *Catalina Express* departs from the Sea/Air Terminal at Berth 95, Port of Los Angeles in San Pedro; from the *Catalina Express* port at the *Queen Mary* in Long Beach; and from the *Catalina Express* port at 161 N. Harbor Dr. in Redondo Beach. Call for information and reservations.

Catalina Cruises (☎ 800/CATALINA) also ferries passengers from Long Beach to Avalon Harbor. They have the best rates going (about $5 cheaper than above) because they run monstrous 700-passenger boats that take longer to make the crossing (about one hour and 50 minutes). But they do offer twice-daily sailings during the high season, plus frequent runs to Twin Harbors. If you want to save money, particularly if you're staying overnight and don't have to maximize your island time, Catalina Cruises is the choice for you.

Note: Luggage on the *Catalina Express* is limited to 50 pounds per person; reservations are necessary for bicycles, surfboards, and dive tanks; and there are restrictions on transporting domestic pets. Call for information.

Island Express Helicopter Service, (☎ 310/510-2525; fax 310/510-9671), flies from Long Beach or San Pedro to Catalina in about 15 minutes. They fly on demand between 8am and sunset year-round, charging $66 each way. If you just want a airborne tour of Catalina, they'll spend 10 to 30 minutes showing you island sights. There's a four-passenger minimum and the cost is $50 to $90 per person.

ORIENTATION   The picturesque town of Avalon is the island's only city. Named for a passage in Tennyson's *Idylls of the King,* Avalon is also the port of entry for the island. From the ferry dock you can wander along Crescent Avenue, the main road along the beachfront, admire the Catalina tile on the Serpentine Wall opposite the beach, and easily explore adjacent side streets.

Visitors are not allowed to drive cars on the island. There are only a limited number of autos permitted; most residents motor around in golf carts (many of the homes only have golf cart–sized driveways). But don't worry, you'll be able to get everywhere you want to go by renting a cart yourself or just hoofing it, which is what most visitors do.

Northwest of Avalon is the village of Two Harbors (see below), accessible only by boat or the most intrepid of hikers. Its twin bays are favored by pleasure yachts from Los Angeles's various marinas, so there's more camaraderie and a less touristy ambience overall.

VISITOR INFORMATION   The **Catalina Island Chamber of Commerce and Visitor's Bureau,** P.O. Box 217, Avalon, CA 90704 (☎ **310/510-1520;** fax 310/510-7606), located on the Green Pleasure Pier, distributes brochures and information on island activities, including sightseeing tours, camping, hiking, fishing, and boating. It also offers information on hotels and boat and helicopter transport. Call for a free 100-page visitor's guide.

The Santa Catalina Island Company-run **Visitor's Information Center,** which is just across from the chamber of commerce, on Crescent Avenue (☎ 310/510-2000), handles hotel reservations, sightseeing tours, and other island activities.

There's also a colorful Internet site at **http://www.catalina.com,** which offers current news from the *Catalina Islander* newspaper in addition to updated activities, events and general information.

GETTING AROUND   If you want to explore the area around Avalon beyond where your feet can comfortably carry you, try renting a mountain bike or tandem from **Brown's Bikes,** 107 Pebbly Beach Rd., Avalon (☎ 310/510-0986) or even a gas-powered golf cart from **Cartopia,** 615 Crescent Ave., Avalon (☎ 310/510-2493), where rates are $30 per hour.

EXPLORING THE ISLAND

ORGANIZED TOURS   The Santa Catalina Island Company's **Discovery Tours,** Avalon Harbor Pier (☎ **800/626-7489** or 310/510-TOUR), operates several motorcoach excursions that depart from the tour plaza in the center of town on Sumner Avenue.

The **Skyline Drive tour** basically follows the perimeter of the island and takes about 1³/₄ hours. Trips leave several times a day from 11am to 3pm and cost $18 for adults, $16 for seniors, and $10 for children 3 to 11.

The **Inland Motor Tour** is more comprehensive; it includes some of the 66 square miles of preserve owned by the Santa Catalina Island Conservancy. You'll see El Rancho Escondido, and probably have a chance to view buffalo, deer, goats, and boars. Tours, which take about 3³/₄ hours, leave at 9am; from June to October, they leave at other times too. Tours are $29 for adults, $26 for seniors, and $16 for children 3 to 11; free for children under 3.

Other excursions offered by the company include the 40-minute **Casino Tour**, which explores Catalina's most famous landmark; the 50-minute **Avalon Scenic Tour**, a 9-mile introductory tour of the town; and the one-hour Flying Fish Boat Trip, during which an occasional flying fish lands right on the boat.

Check with the Catalina Island Company for other tour offerings, as well as for information on multiple excursion packages.

VISITING TWO HARBORS   If you want to get a better look at the rugged natural beauty of Catalina and escape the throngs of beachgoers, head over to Two Harbors, the ¹/₄-mile "neck" at the island's northwest end which gets its name from the "twin harbors" on each side, known as the Isthmus and "Cat" Harbor. An excellent starting point for campers and hikers, Two Harbors offers just enough civilization for the less intrepid traveler.

The **Banning House Lodge** (☎ 310/510-7265) is an 11-room bed-and-breakfast overlooking the Isthmus. The clapboard house was built in 1910 for Catalina's pre-Wrigley owners, and has seen duty as girls' camp, army barracks, and on-location lodging for movie stars like Errol Flynn and Dorothy Lamour. The innkeepers are gracious, the atmosphere peaceful and isolated. Call from the pier and they'll even drive you up to the lodge.

Everyone eats at **Doug's Harbor Reef** (☎ 310/510-7265) down on the beach. This nautical/South Seas themed saloon/restaurant serves breakfast, lunch and dinner, the latter being hearty steaks, ribs, swordfish, chicken teriyaki, and buffalo burgers in the summer. The house drink is sweet "buffalo milk," a potent concoction of vodka, creme de cacao, banana liqueur, milk, and whipped cream.

Avalon Casino and Catalina Island Museum. At the end of Crescent Ave. ☎ **310/510-2414.** Museum admission $1.50 adults, $1 seniors, 50¢ ages 6–11; children under 5 free. Daily 10:30am–4pm.

The Avalon Casino is the most famous structure on the island, and one of its oldest. Built in 1929 to house a ballroom and theater, its massive circular rotunda topped with a red-tile roof is its most notable feature. The Avalon Casino is widely known for its beautiful art deco ballroom, which once hosted the Tommy Dorsey and Glen Miller orchestras and other top bands. You can see the inside of the building by attending a ballroom event or watching a film (the Casino is Avalon's primary movie theater). Otherwise, admission is by guided tour only, operated daily by the Santa Catalina Island Company (see "Organized Tours," above).

The Catalina Island Museum, located on the ground floor of the Casino, features exhibits on island history, archaeology, and natural history; they also have a contour relief map of the island which can be helpful to anyone planning to venture into the interior.

SNORKELING, DIVING & KAYAKING

Snorkeling, scuba-diving, and sea kayaking are among the main reasons mainlanders head to Catalina. Purists will prefer the less-spoiled waters of Two Harbors, but Avalon's many coves have plenty to offer as well. **Banana Boat Riders,** 107 Pebbly Beach Rd., Avalon (☎ **800/708-2262** or 310/510-1774), offers snorkel gear and sea kayak rentals, as well as half- and full-day excursions to Two Harbors and other island coves. **Catalina Divers Supply** (☎ **800/353-0330** or 310/510-0330) offers guided snorkel and scuba tours with certified instructors, in addition to gear rental at three Avalon locations. **Descanso Beach Ocean Sports** (☎ **310/510-1226**) offers sea kayak and snorkel rentals with instruction, plus specialty expeditions and kids' programs.

At Two Harbors, sit-on-top beginner kayaks as well as advanced touring types can be rented at **Two Harbors Kayak Center** (☎ **310/510-7265**). They offer instruction and guided tours of the secluded coves on the northern end of the island.

WHERE TO STAY

Catalina's accommodations range from old-salt motels to yachting-set luxury. If you plan to stay overnight, be sure to reserve a room in advance because most places fill up pretty quickly during the summer and holiday seasons. **Catalina Island Accommodations** (☎ **310/510-3000**) might be able to help you out in a pinch; they're a reservations service with updated information on the whole island. Budget travelers who are interested in camping on the island should contact **Catalina Island Camping** (☎ **800/848-1632** or 310/510-7265), which coordinates the reservations (and equipment rentals) for all campgrounds, which range from seaside sites to secluded inland spots.

DOUBLES FOR $60 OR LESS

This is a rate category unheard of during Catalina's high season, and on most weekends. During those periods, the real bargain-hunters may want to consider camping out. If you visit midweek, however, or between October and February, nice rooms may be available for around $60 at the following smaller hotels: **El Terado Terrace,** 230 Marilla Ave. (☎ **310/510-083;** fax 310/510-1495); **Hotel Macrae,** 409 Crescent Ave. (☎ **800/698-2266** or 310/510-0246; fax 310/510-9632); and **Hotel Villa Portofino,** 111 Crescent Ave. (☎ **800/346-2326** or 310/510-0555; fax 310/510-0839). Be sure to inquire about auto club and other discounts when reserving a room at the above hotels.

DOUBLES FOR $80 OR LESS

Zane Grey Pueblo Hotel. Off Chimes Tower Rd. (north of Hill St.), (P.O. Box 216), Avalon, CA 90704. ☎ **800/378-3256** or 310/510-0966. 17 rms. Rooms $75–$125 Apr–Oct, $59 Nov–Mar. Rates include continental breakfast. AE, MC, V.

You'll have the most superb views on the island from this Shangri-la mountain retreat, the former home of novelist Zane Grey, who spent his last 20 years in Avalon. He wrote many books here, including *Tales of Swordfish and Tuna,* which tells of his fishing adventures off Catalina Island.

The hotel has teak beams that the novelist brought from Tahiti on one of his fishing trips. Most of the rooms also have large windows and ocean or mountain views. They have all been renovated with new furniture, carpeting, and ceiling fans. An outdoor patio has an excellent view. The original living room has a grand piano, a fireplace, and a TV. The hotel also has a pool and sundeck, with chairs overlooking Avalon and the ocean. Coffee is served all day, and there's a courtesy bus to town.

DOUBLES FOR $100 OR LESS

Catalina Island Inn. 125 Metropole (north of Crescent Ave.), P.O. Box 467, Avalon, CA 90704. ☎ **800/246-8134** or 310/510-1623. Fax 310/510-7218. 35 rms, 1 minisuite. TEL TV. May–Sept, holidays, and weekends year-round, $89–$179 double; $189 minisuite. Oct–Apr except holidays and weekends, $45–$99 double; $155 minisuite. All rates include continental breakfast. AE, DISC, MC, V.

Innkeepers Martin and Bernadine Curtin provide clean, comfortable rooms simply furnished with a vaguely tropical motif. Many rooms have balconies with views of the harbor, and you can't beat the location right in the center of bustling Avalon.

WHERE TO DINE

The Busy Bee. 306 Crescent Ave. (north of Pleasure Pier). ☎ **310/510-1983.** Reservations not accepted. Main courses $7–$15. AE, CB, DC, DISC, MC, V. Summer, daily 8am–10pm. Winter, daily 8am–8pm. AMERICAN.

The Busy Bee, an Avalon institution since 1923, is located right on the beach. The fare is light deli style, and the extensive menu offers breakfast, lunch, and dinner at all times. The restaurant grinds its own beef and cuts its own potatoes for french fries; salad dressings are also made on the premises. Even if you're not hungry, come here for a drink; it's Avalon's only waterfront bar.

El Galleon. 411 Crescent Ave. ☎ **310/510-1188.** Reservations recommended on weekends. Main courses $11–$37 at dinner. AE, DISC, MC, V. Daily 11am–2:30pm and 5–10pm. Bar daily 10am–1:30am. AMERICAN.

El Galleon is big, warm, and woody, complete with portholes, rigging, anchors, wrought-iron chandeliers, oversize leather booths, and tables with red-leather captain's chairs. There's additional balcony seating, plus outdoor cafe tables overlooking the ocean harbor. Lunch and dinner always feature seafood. Favorite dinner entrees include fresh swordfish steak and broiled Catalina lobster tails in drawn butter. The main "turf" dishes range from country-fried chicken to broiled rack of lamb with mint jelly.

Sand Trap. Avalon Canyon Rd. (north of Tremont St.). ☎ **310/510-1349.** Reservations not accepted. Main courses $4–$12. No credit cards. Daily 7:30am–3:30pm. CALIFORNIA/MEXICAN.

This local favorite is a great place to escape from the bayfront crowds. Enjoy breakfast, lunch, or snacks while overlooking the golf course. Specialties of the house include delectable omelets served until noon, and soft tacos served all day. Either can be made with any number of fillings. Burgers, sandwiches, salads, and chili are also on the menu, and beer and wine are available.

4 Big Bear Lake & Lake Arrowhead

100 miles NE of Los Angeles

These two deep blue lakes lie close to one another in the San Bernardino mountains, and have long been a favorite weekend getaway for city-weary Angelenos. Both were created in the early 20th century by damming what had been known as Little Bear and Big Bear Valleys. In addition to bringing power and water to the Inland Empire communities below, they provide Southern California with a year-round alpine playground.

Big Bear Lake has always been popular with skiers as well as avid boaters (it's much larger than Arrowhead and equipment rentals abound). In the past decade, the area has been given a much-needed face-lift. Big Bear Boulevard was substantially

Big Bear Lake & Lake Arrowhead

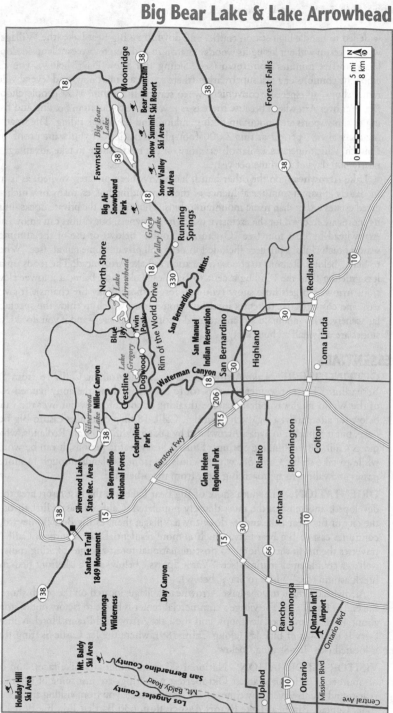

Moonridge

Forest Falls

Bear Mountain Ski Resort

Snow Summit Ski Area

Big Bear Lake

Fawnskin

Snow Valley Ski Area

Big Air Snowboard Park

Running Springs

Green Valley Lake

Redlands

North Shore

Lake Arrowhead

San Bernardino Mtns.

Blue Jay

Twin Peaks

Lake Gregory

Rim of the World Drive

San Manuel Indian Reservation

Loma Linda

Crestline

Dogwood

Waterman Canyon

San Bernardino

Highland

Silverwood Lake

Miller Canyon

Cedarpines Park

Barstow Fwy

Glen Helen Regional Park

Rialto

Bloomington

Colton

Silverwood Lake State Rec. Area

San Bernardino National Forest

Fontana

Santa Fe Trail 1849 Monument

Day Canyon

Cucamonga Wilderness

Rancho Cucamonga

Ontario Int'l Airport

Ontario Blvd

Holiday Hill Ski Area

Mt. Baldy Ski Area

Mt. Baldy Road

San Bernardino County

Los Angeles County

Upland

Ontario

Mission Blvd

Central Ave

N

5 mi
8 km
0

1-0852

widened to handle high-season traffic, and downtown Big Bear Lake (the "Village") was spiffed up without losing its woodsy charm. In addition to two excellent ski slopes less than five minutes from town (see "Skiing and Snow Play," below), you can enjoy the comforts of a real supermarket (there's even a Kmart now) and several video rental shops, all especially convenient when staying in a cabin! Most people choose Big Bear over Arrowhead because there is *so much* more to do, from boating and fishing to snow sports and mountain biking, hiking, and horseback riding. The weather is nearly always perfect at this 7,000-foot-plus elevation. If you want proof, ask Caltech, which operates a solar observatory on the north shore to take advantage of nearly 300 days of sunshine per year.

Lake Arrowhead, on the other hand, has always been privately owned, as is immediately apparent from the affluence of the surrounding homes, many of which are gated estates rather than rustic mountain cabins. The lake and the private docks lining its shores are reserved for the exclusive use of homeowners, but visitors can enjoy Lake Arrowhead by boat tour (see "Organized Tours," below) or use of the summer-season beach clubs, a privilege included in nearly all private home rentals (see "Where to Stay," below). Reasons to choose a vacation at Lake Arrowhead? The roads up are less grueling than the winding ascent to Big Bear Lake, and being at a lower elevation, Arrowhead gets little snow (you can forget those pesky tire chains). It's very easy and cost-effective to rent a luxurious house from which to enjoy the spectacular scenery, crisp mountain air, and relaxed resort atmosphere—and if you do ski, the slopes are only half an hour away.

ESSENTIALS

GETTING THERE   Lake Arrowhead is reached by taking Calif. 18 from San Bernardino. The last segment of this route takes you along the aptly named Rim of the World Highway, offering a breathtaking panoramic view out over the valley below (or alternately, a big ditch of smog). Calif. 18 then continues east to Big Bear Lake, but it's quicker to bypass Arrowhead by taking Calif. 330 from Redlands, which meets Calif. 18 in Running Springs. During heavy traffic periods, it can be worthwhile to take scenic Calif. 38, which winds up from Redlands through mountain passes and valleys to approach Big Bear from the other side.

ORIENTATION   The south shore of Big Bear Lake was the first resort area to be developed, and remains the most densely populated. Calif. 18 passes first through the city of Big Bear Lake and its downtown Village; then, as Big Bear Boulevard, it continues east to Big Bear City, which is more residential and suburban. Calif. 38 traverses the north shore, home to pristine national forest and great hiking trails, as well as a couple small marinas (see "Water Sports," below) and a lakefront bed-and-breakfast inn (see "Where to Stay," below).

Arrowhead's main town is Lake Arrowhead Village, located on the south shore at the end of Calif. 173. The village's commercial center is home to factory outlet stores, about 40 chain and specialty shops, and the Lake Arrowhead Resort Hotel. Minutes away is the town of Blue Jay (along Calif. 189), where the Ice Castle Skating Rink is located (see "Ice-Skating," below).

VISITOR INFORMATION   National ski tours, mountain bike races, and one of Southern California's largest Oktoberfest gatherings are just some of the many year-round events which may either entice or discourage you from visiting at the same time. Contact **Big Bear Lake Resort Association,** 630 Bartlett Rd., Big Bear Lake Village (☎ **909/866-7000**), for schedules and information. The Association also provides information on sightseeing and lodging, will send you a free visitors guide, and is open seven days a week. Visit their Web site at **http://www.bigbear.com**. In Lake Arrowhead, contact the **Lake Arrowhead Communities Chamber of Commerce** (☎ **800/337-3716** Lodging Info Line, or 909/337-3715; fax 909/ 336-1548). Their visitor center, located in the Lake Arrowhead Village lower shopping center, is open Monday to Friday from 10am to 5pm (till 3pm on Saturdays). Their Web site is **http://www.apsm.com/lakearrow**.

WATER SPORTS

BOATING   You can rent all kinds of boats, including speedboats, rowboats, paddleboats, pontoons, sailboats, and canoes at a number of Big Bear Lake marinas. Rates vary only slightly place to place: a 14-foot dinghy with outboard runs around $10 per hour or $30 for a half-day; pontoon (patio) boats which can hold large groups range in size and price from $25 to $45 per hour or $80 to $150 for half-day. **Pine Knot Landing** (☎ **909/866-BOAT**) is the most centrally located, behind the post office at the foot of Pine Knot Boulevard in Big Bear Lake. **Gray's Landing** (☎ **909/866-2443**) is just across the dam on the north shore and offers the best prices and the least attitude. **Big Bear Marina,** Paine Road at Lakeview (☎ **909/ 866-3218**), is also close to Big Bear Lake Village and provides take-along chicken dinners when you rent a pontoon boat for a sunset cruise ($75 for three hours).

FISHING   Big Bear Lake brims with rainbow trout, bass, and catfish in spring and summer, the best fishing seasons. Call 562/590-5020 to hear recorded stocking information. A fishing license is required and costs $8.95 per day, $24.95 per year. **Pine Knot Landing, Gray's Landing,** and **Big Bear Marina** (see "Boating," above) all rent fishing boats and have bait and tackle shops which sell licenses.

WATERSKIING   **Pine Knot Landing, North Shore Landing,** and **Big Bear Marina** (see "Boating," above) all offer water-ski lessons and speedboat rentals. Lake Arrowhead is home to **McKenzie Water Ski School,** dockside in Lake Arrowhead Village (☎ **909/337-3814**), famous for teaching Kirk Douglas, George Hamilton, and other Hollywood stars to ski. They're open from Memorial Day through the end of September, and offer group lessons for $115 per hour, short refresher lessons for $35, and boat rental (including driver) for $95 an hour.

OTHER WARM-WEATHER ACTIVITIES

In addition to the activities below, there's a great recreation spot for families near the heart of Big Bear Lake: **Magic Mountain,** on Calif. 18/Big Bear Boulevard (☎ **909/ 866-4626**), has a year round bobsled-style Alpine Slide, splashy double water slide open from mid-June to mid-September, and bunny slopes for snow tubing from November through Easter. The dry Alpine Slide is $3 a ride, the water slide $1 (or $10 for a day pass), and snowplay $10 per day including tube and rope-tow.

GOLF   **Bear Mountain Golf Course,** Goldmine Drive, Big Bear Lake (☎ **909/ 585-8002**), is a nine-hole, par 35, links-style course that winds through a gently sloping meadow at the base of Bear Mountain Ski Resort. The course is open daily from April to November. Greens fees are $17 and $23 for 9 and 18 holes, respectively. Both riding carts and pull carts are available. Phone for tee times.

HIKING   Hikers will love San Bernardino National Forest. The gray squirrel is a popular native; you may see him scurrying around gathering acorns or material for his nest. You can sometimes spot deer, coyotes, and American bald eagles, which come here with their young during winter months. The black-crowned Steller's jay and the talkative red, white, and black acorn woodpecker are the most common of the great variety of birds in this pine forest.

Stop in at the **Big Bear Ranger Station** (☎ 909/866-3437) on Calif. 38, 3 miles east of Fawnskin on Big Bear Lake's north shore. There you can pick up free trail maps, as well as other information on the area's plants, animals, and geology. The best trail for a short mountain hike is **Woodland Trail,** which begins near the ranger station. The best long hike is the **Pacific Crest Trail,** which travels 39 miles through the mountains above Big Bear and Arrowhead lakes. The most convenient trailhead is located at Cougar Crest, ¹/₂ mile west of the Big Bear Ranger Station.

The best place to begin a hike in Lake Arrowhead is at the **Arrowhead Ranger Station** (☎ 909/337-2444), located in the town of Skyforest on Calif. 18, ¹/₄ mile east of the Lake Arrowhead turn-off (Calif. 173). They will provide you with maps and information on the best area trails, which range from easy to difficult. The **Enchanted Loop Trail,** near the town of Blue Jay, is an easy half-hour hike. The **Heaps Peak Arboretum Trail** winds through a grove of redwoods; the trailhead is located on the north side of Calif. 18, ¹/₂ mile east of Santa's Village.

The area is home to a **National Children's Forest,** a 20-acre area developed so that children, the wheelchair-bound, and the visually impaired could enjoy nature. To get to the Children's Forest from Lake Arrowhead, take Calif. 330 to Calif. 18 east, past Deer Lick Station; when you reach a road marked IN96 (only open in the summer season), turn right and go 3 miles.

HORSEBACK RIDING   Horses are permitted on all the mountain trails through the national forest. **Magic Mountain Stables,** 40355 Big Bear Blvd., City of Big Bear Lake (☎ 909/878-HORSE), offers one- and two-hour guided rides for $20 per hour, 1¹/₂-hour sunset rides for $30. The stables are open daily from May through December. Phone for reservations. **Baldwin Lake Stables,** southeast of Big Bear City (☎ 909/585-6482), also conducts hourly, lunch and sunset specialty rides in addition to offering lessons.

MOUNTAIN BIKING   Big Bear Lake has become a mountain-bicycling center, with most of the action around **Snow Summit Ski Area** (see "Skiing & Snow Play," below), where a $7 lift ticket will take you and your bike to a scenic web of trails, fire roads, and meadows at about 8,000 feet. Call its **Summer Activities Hot Line** at **909/866-4621.** The lake's north shore is also a popular biking destination; the Forest Service Ranger Stations (see "Hiking," above) has maps to the historic gold rush–era Holcomb Valley or the 2-mile Alpine Pedal Path (an easy lakeside ride).

Big Bear Bikes, 41810 Big Bear Blvd. (☎ 909/866-4565), rents mountain bikes for $6 an hour or $21 for four hours. **Bear Valley Bikes,** 40298 Big Bear Blvd. (☎ 909/866-8000), rents bikes and offers free lessons on Sundays. **Team Big Bear** (☎ 909/866-4565) is located at the base of Snow Summit; they rent bicycles and provide detailed maps and guides for all Big Bear area trails.

At Lake Arrowhead, bicycles are permitted on all hiking trails and back roads except the Pacific Crest Trail (see the local Ranger Station for an area map), and gear can be rented from **Above and Beyond Sports,** 32877 Calif. 18, Running Springs (☎ 909/867-5517).

WINTER FUN

SKIING & SNOW PLAY   When the L.A. basin gets wintertime rain, skiers everywhere rejoice, for they know snow is falling up in the mountains. The last few seasons have seen abundant natural snowfall at Big Bear, augmented by sophisticated snowmaking equipment which also compensates during drier years. While the slopes can't compare with Utah or Colorado, they do offer diversity, difficulty and convenience.

Snow Summit at Big Bear Lake (☎ 909/866-5766) is the skier's choice, especially since they installed their second high-speed quad express from the 7,000-foot base to the 8,200-foot summit. Another nice feature is green (easy) runs *even* from the summit so beginners can also enjoy the Summit Haus lodge and breathtaking lake views from the top. Extreme skiers will appreciate the three *double* black diamond runs. Lift tickets range from $30 to $42. The resort offers midweek, beginner, half-day, night, and family specials as well as ski and snowboard rentals. Other helpful Snow Summit phone numbers include **Advance Lift Ticket Sales** (☎ 909/866-5841), **Ski School Info** (☎ 909/866-4546), and **Snow Report** (☎ 310/390-1498 in Los Angeles county). Or you can visit the facility's Web site at **http://www.bigbear.com/summit. instruction.** Hey, you can even ski free on your birthday here!

Bear Mountain Ski Resort at Big Bear Lake (☎ 909/585-2519; snow report from L.A. 213/683-8100) is smaller than the other two, but experts flock to the double black diamond "Geronimo" run from the 8,805-foot Bear Peak. Natural terrain skiers and snowboarders will enjoy legal access to off-trail canyons, but the limited beginner slopes and kids' areas get pretty crowded in-season. One high-speed quad express rises from the 7,140-foot base to 8,440-foot Goldmine Mountain; most runs from there are intermediate. Bear Mountain has a ski school, abundant dining facilities, and a well-stocked ski shop.

Snow Valley Ski Resort (☎ 800/680-SNOW or 909/867-2751) in Arrowbear, midway between Arrowhead and Big Bear, has improved its snowmaking and facilities to be competitive with the other two major ski areas, and is the primary choice of skiers staying at Arrowhead. From a base elevation of 6,800 feet, Snow Valley's 13 chair lifts (including five triples) can take you from the beginner runs all the way up to black diamond challenges at the 7,898-foot peak. Lift tickets cost $35 to $40 for adults; children's programs, night skiing, and lesson packages are available. Snow Valley's Internet address is **http://www.aminews.com/snowvalley.**

Big Air Snowboard Park (☎ 909/867-2338) in Green Valley is the answer to a snowboarder's dream. To get there take Green Valley Lake Road from Arrowbear. Absolutely no skiers are allowed on Big Air's 50 ridable acres full of hits, bonks, spines, and more. Use the rope tow or take the high-speed chair to untouched forest full of natural hits. They offer equipment rentals, lessons, and package deals. All-day passes are $24 for adults, $18 kids 12 and under, half-day passes are $20 and $14.

ICE-SKATING   The **Blue Jay Ice Castle,** North Bay Road and Calif. 189 (☎ 909/33-SKATE), near Lake Arrowhead Village, is a training site for world champion Michelle Kwan, and boasts Olympic gold medalist Robin Cousins on its staff. Several public sessions each day give amateurs a chance to enjoy this impeccably groomed "outdoor" rink (it's open on three sides to the scenery and fresh air). Hockey, broomball, group lessons, and book-in-advance private parties are also available.

ORGANIZED TOURS

LAKE TOURS   The *Big Bear Queen* (☎ 909/866-3218), a midget Mississippi-style paddle wheeler, cruises Big Bear Lake on 90-minute tours daily from late April through November. The boat departs from Big Bear Marina (at the end of Paine Avenue). Tours are $9.50 for adults, $5 for children ages 3 to 12, and $8 for seniors 65 or better. Call for reservations and information on special Sunday brunch, champagne sunset or dinner cruises. Fifty-minute tours of Lake Arrowhead are offered year-round by the *Arrowhead Queen* (☎ 909/336-6992), a sister ship that departs hourly each day between 10am and 6pm from Lake Arrowhead Village. Tours cost $9.50 for adults, $6.50 for children ages 2 to 12, $8.50 for seniors. This is about the only way for visitors to really see this alpine jewel, unless you know a resident with a boat.

FOREST TOURS　Big Bear Jeep Tours (☎ 909/878-JEEP) journeys into Big Bear Lake's back country, including historic Holcomb Valley, relic of the gold rush, plus the panoramic viewpoint "Butler Peak." Their off-road adventures range in length from 2 to 4¹/₂ hours, and from $38 to $80 per person. Bring your own snack though, because although the guide carries ample water, the longer excursions have short but appetite-building hikes scheduled into the itinerary. Phone for reservations, particularly on weekends and holidays.

WHERE TO STAY AT BIG BEAR LAKE

Vacation rentals are plentiful around the Big Bear area, from cabins to condos to private homes. Some can accommodate up to 20 people and be rented on a weekly or monthly basis. The oldest Realtor, with seven area offices and a wide range of rental properties, is **Spencer Real Estate** (☎ 800/237-3725 or 909/866-7591). **Village Reservation Service** (☎ 909/866-8583 or 909/585-5850) can arrange for everything from Jacuzzi condos to lakefront homes. For general information and referrals on all types of lodging call **Big Bear Lake Resort Association** (☎ 909/866-7000).

A word about seasons: The most popular times at Big Bear are the ski season, usually January through March, and the summer, between Memorial and Labor Day. Rates vary widely at all other times, so be sure to ask about off-season deals.

Grey Squirrel Resort. 39372 Big Bear Blvd., Big Bear Lake, CA 92315. ☎ **909/866-4335.** Fax 909/866-6271. 18 cabins, most with fireplace and kitchen. TEL TV. 1-bedroom cabin $75–$95, 2-bedroom $99–$125; 3-bedroom $125–$275. Value rates available, higher rates on holidays. AE, DISC, MC, V.

This is the most attractive of the many cabin-cluster type motels near the city of Big Bear Lake, offering rustic cottages that are adequately, though not attractively, furnished. The real appeal of the Grey Squirrel is the flexibility and privacy it gives long-term or large parties. A heated pool is enclosed in winter; there's an indoor spa, barbecue pits, volleyball and basketball courts, laundry facilities, and fully equipped kitchens. Pets are welcome for a $5 daily surcharge.

Janet Kay's Bed and Breakfast. 695 Paine Rd., Big Bear Lake, CA 92315. ☎ **800/243-7031** or 909/866-6800. 19 rms and suites. TEL TV. Rooms and suites $59–$175. Rates include full breakfast and afternoon tea with snacks. AE, DISC, MC, V.

This large, colonial-style inn within walking distance of Big Bear Lake Village is more comfortable than the standard hotel but less personal than most true B&Bs. Still, it offers a centrally located alternative and spacious, comfortable rooms each decorated to a theme (Victorian, Jungle, Garden). All have Jacuzzis; some have terraces and/ or fireplaces. The hotel offers winter ski and summer fun packages.

Windy Point Inn. 39015 North Shore Dr., Fawnskin, CA 92333. ☎ **909/866-2746.** 3 rms with fireplace. Rooms $105–$225. Rates include full breakfast and afternoon hors d'oeuvres. AE, DISC, MC, V.

A contemporary home on the scenic North Shore, Windy Point is the only shorefront B&B in Big Bear, and two rooms have a spectacular view of the sunrise over the lake. Hosts Val and Kent Jessler's attention to detail is impeccable. If you're tired of knotty pine and Victorian frills, this is a grown-up place for you. There's an outdoor Jacuzzi, romantic master suite, private whirlpools in two rooms, casual sunken living room with floor-to-ceiling windows on the lake, and custom gourmet breakfast served on the deck in summertime. The city of Big Bear Lake is only a 10-minute drive across the dam.

WHERE TO STAY AT LAKE ARROWHEAD

There are far more private homes than tourist accommodations in Arrowhead; many residents even live here full time and commute down to Redlands or San Bernardino. Rental properties abound, from cozy cottages to palatial mansions, and many can be surprisingly economical for families or other groups. Two of the largest agencies are **Arrowhead Cabin Rentals** (☎ 800/244-5138 or 909/337-2403) and **Arrowhead Mountain Resorts Rentals** (☎ 800/743-0865 or 909/337-4413). **The Forrester Homes of Lake Arrowhead** (☎ 800/587-5576 or 909/845-1004) is worth a call; they represent only six private homes, but have a warm, personal touch. Overnight guests enjoy some resident lake privileges—be sure to ask when you reserve.

A word about seasons: The most popular season at Arrowhead is summer, between Memorial and Labor Day, and, to a lesser extent than neighboring Big Bear, the ski season between January and March. Rates vary widely all other periods, so be sure to ask about off-season deals.

Lake Arrowhead Resort. 27984 Calif. 189, Lake Arrowhead, CA 92352. ☎ **800/800-6792** or 909/336-1511. Fax 909/336-1378. 261 rms & suites. A/C MINIBAR TEL TV. Rooms $125–$305, suites $255–$395; rates start at $99 off season. AE, CB, DC, MC, V.

This sprawling resort has been somewhat upgraded since it was part of the Hilton chain, but location is still its most outstanding feature, coupled with service and facilities unavailable anywhere else in the mountains. Situated on the lakeshore adjacent to Lake Arrowhead Village, the hotel has its own beach, plus docks ideal for fishing. Rooms are fitted with good-quality contemporary furnishings, and most have balconies, king-size beds, and fireplaces. Suites, some in private cottages, are equipped with full kitchens and whirlpool tubs.

The hotel offers a casual restaurant serving all meals (and room service), plus the elegant California/Continental "Seasons," which has only limited hours during off-peak seasons. Facilities include fully equipped health club, heated outdoor pool and whirlpool, racquetball courts, massage, and video arcade. A full program of supervised children's activities is offered on weekends year-round; it includes fishing, arts and crafts, nature hikes, and T-shirt painting. Be sure to inquire about auto-club membership discounts, which can shave up to 20% off your room bill.

Pine Rose Cabins. 25994 Calif. 189, Twin Peaks, CA 92391. ☎ **800/429-PINE** or 909/ 337-2341. 15 cabins. $69–$159 for up to 4 people; $700 for 5-bedroom lodge. AE, MC, V.

The only place of its kind in Lake Arrowhead, Pine Rose Cabins is a good choice for families. Sitting on five forested acres about 3 miles from the lake, the wonderful, free-standing cabins offer lots of privacy. Innkeepers Tricia and David Dufour have 15 cabins, ranging in size from romantic studios to a large five-bedroom lodge; each is decorated in a different theme. For example, the Indian cabin has a tepeelike bed, and the bed in Wild Bill's cabin is covered like a wagon. One- and two-bedroom units have a fully stocked kitchen and a separate living area. There's a large heated swimming pool on the premises, plus swing sets, croquet, tetherball, and Ping-Pong. Ski packages are offered in season.

WHERE TO DINE AT BIG BEAR LAKE
MEALS FOR $10 OR LESS

Old Country Inn. 41126 Big Bear Blvd., Big Bear Lake. ☎ **909/866-5600.** Main courses $5–$14. AE, DC, DISC, MC, V. Mon–Fri 7am–9pm, Sat–Sun 7am–10pm. DINER/GERMAN.

The Old Country Inn has long been a favorite for hearty preski breakfasts and stick-to-your-ribs dinners. The restaurant is casual and welcoming, but the adjacent cocktail lounge can get raucous on weekends. At breakfast enjoy German apple pancakes or colossal omelets, or for lunch, choose from the list of salads, sandwiches, and burgers. You can feast on Wiener schnitzel, sauerbraten, and other gravy-topped German standards for lunch or dinner, along with grilled steaks and chicken.

Paoli's Italian Country Kitchen. Corner of Pine Knot Blvd. and Village Dr., Big Bear Lake. ☎ **909/866-2020.** Pizza $11–$17, pasta & main courses $7–$15. MC, V. Mon–Thurs 10:30am–10pm, Fri 10:30am–midnight, Sat 8am–midnight, Sun 8am–10pm. ITALIAN.

You can't beat Paoli's for authentic thin-crust pizzas, tangy antipastos, and saucy lasagna. Although they've updated their traditional menu a bit, Paoli's will always be a checked tablecloth/woven Chianti bottle kind of place. As such, it's perfect in Big Bear.

MEALS FOR $20 OR LESS

Blue Whale Lakeside. 350 Alden Rd. (2 blocks east of Pine Knot Blvd.), Big Bear Lake. ☎ **909/866-5771.** Reservations recommended. Main courses $10–$22. AE, MC, V. Daily 4pm–9pm. SEAFOOD/STEAK.

This nautically themed restaurant has great views of Big Bear Lake from every table. Fresh fish and lobsters are delivered three times a week, and the broiled steaks and roasted poultry are imaginatively prepared. A guitar/piano duo entertains while you dine. *Tail of the Whale* is the adjoining lounge and oyster bar; they're open and serving lunch Thursday through Sunday from 11am and have their own dancing and entertainment, clambakes, and beach parties in the summer.

The Captain's Anchorage. Moonridge Way at Big Bear Blvd., Big Bear Lake. ☎ **909/866-3997.** Reservations recommended. Full dinners $10–$23. AE, MC, V. Sun–Thurs 4:30–9pm, Fri–Sat 4:30–10pm. STEAK/SEAFOOD.

Historic and rustic, this knotty-pine restaurant has been serving fine steaks, prime rib, seafood, and lobster since 1947. Inside, the dark, nautical decor and fire-warmed bar hit the spot on blustery winter nights; they've got one of those mile-long soup and salad bars, plus some great early bird and weeknight bargain specials.

Madlon's. 829 W. Big Bear Blvd., Big Bear City. ☎ **909/585-3762.** Reservations recommended. Main courses $8–$16. AE, MC, V. Wed–Mon 11am–3pm and 5–9pm, Sat–Sun from 8am. AMERICAN/CONTINENTAL.

One of the few nonretro-fare dining rooms at the mountain resorts, Madlon brings a bit of European flair to her fairy-tale cottage with the tulip-shaped white picket fence. A variety of creative croissant sandwiches at lunch are complemented by dinner selections like black pepper filet mignon with mushroom and brandy sauce, and lemon-pepper marinated chicken breast over pasta; everything is prepared with a sophisticated touch.

WHERE TO DINE AT LAKE ARROWHEAD

Surprisingly for an affluent residential community, there aren't many dining options around Lake Arrowhead. But not surprisingly, what there is tends to run to pricey elegance—elegant for a rustic mountain resort, that is. Although there are both a California/Continental restaurant and a casual family eatery in the Lake Arrowhead Resort (see "Where to Stay," above), you might want to venture out to some of the locals' choices. These include the **Chef's Inn and Tavern,** 29020 Oak Terrace, Cedar Glen (☎ **909/336-4488**), a moderate to expensive Continental restaurant in a turn-of-the-century former bordello; **Antler's Inn,** 26125 Calif. 189, Twin Peaks

(☎ 909/337-4020), serving prime rib, seafood, and buffalo in a historic log lodge; the **Royal Oak,** 27187 Calif. 189, Blue Jay Village (☎ 909/337-6018), an expensive American steakhouse with pub; or **Belgian Waffle Works,** dockside at Lake Arrowhead Village (☎ 909/337-5222), an inexpensive coffee shop with Victorian decor known for their generous, crispy waffles with tasty toppings.

5 Disneyland & Other Anaheim Area Attractions

27 miles SE of downtown Los Angeles

The sleepy Orange County town of Anaheim grew up around Disneyland, the West's most famous theme park. Now, even beyond this Happiest Place on Earth, the city and its neighboring communities are kid central. Otherwise unspectacular, sprawling suburbs have become a playground of family oriented hotels, restaurants, and unabashedly tourist-oriented attractions. Among the nearby draws are Knott's Berry Farm, another family oriented theme park, in nearby Buena Park. At the other end of the scale is the Richard Nixon Library and Birthplace, a surprisingly compelling presidential library and museum, just 7 miles northeast of Disneyland in Yorba Linda.

ESSENTIALS

GETTING THERE   **Los Angeles International Airport** (LAX) is located about 30 minutes from Anaheim via I-5 south (see Section 1 in Chapter 14). If you're heading directly to Anaheim and want to avoid Los Angeles altogether, try to land at **John Wayne International Airport** (☎ 714/252-5200) in Irvine, Orange County's largest airport. It's about 15 miles from Disneyland. The airport is served by Alaska, American, Continental, Delta, Northwest, TWA, and United airlines. Check to see if your hotel has a free shuttle to and from either airport, or call one of the following commercial shuttle services (fares are generally $10 one-way from John Wayne or $12 from LAX): **L.A. Xpress** (☎ 800/I-ARRIVE); **Prime Time** (☎ 800/262-7433); **SuperShuttle** (☎ 714/517-6600). Car-rental companies located at John Wayne Airport include **Budget** (☎ 800/221-1203) and **Hertz** (☎ 800/654-3131).

VISITOR INFORMATION   The **Anaheim/Orange County Visitor and Convention Bureau,** at 800 W. Katella Ave. (P.O. Box 4270), Anaheim, CA 92803 (☎ 714/999-8999), can fill you in on area activities and shopping shuttles. They are located just inside the convention center (across the street from Disneyland), next to the dramatic cantilevered arena, and welcome visitors Monday to Friday from 8:30am to 5:30pm. The **Buena Park Convention and Visitors Office,** 6280 Manchester Blvd., Suite 103 (☎ 800/541-3953 or 714/562-3560), will provide specialized information on their area, including Knott's Berry Farm.

DISNEYLAND

Walt Disney was the originator of the mega-theme park. Opened in 1955, Disneyland remains unsurpassed. Despite constant threats from pretenders to the crown, Disneyland and its sister park, Walt Disney World in Orlando, Florida, remain the kings of the theme parks. At no other park is fantasy elevated to an art form. Nowhere else is as fresh and fantastic every time you walk through the gates, whether you're 6 or 60, and no matter how many times you've done it before. There's nothing like Disney Magic.

The park stays on the cutting edge by continually updating and expanding, while still maintaining the hallmarks that make it the world's top amusement park (a term coined by Walt Disney himself). Look for the most recent Disney additions during your visit—**Toontown,** an interactive cartoon area added in 1993, and 1995's

Disneyland

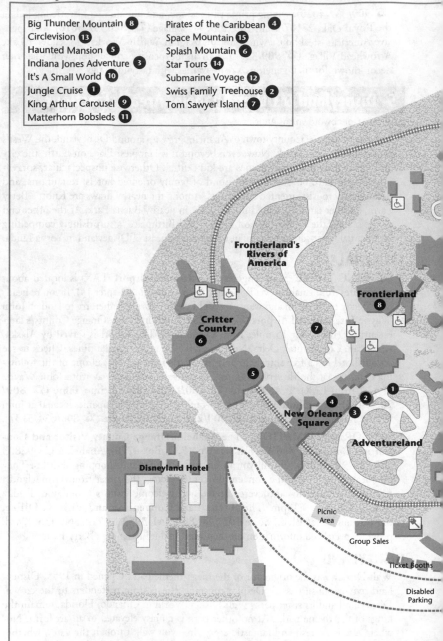

Big Thunder Mountain **8**
Circlevision **13**
Haunted Mansion **5**
Indiana Jones Adventure **3**
It's A Small World **10**
Jungle Cruise **1**
King Arthur Carousel **9**
Matterhorn Bobsleds **11**

Pirates of the Caribbean **4**
Space Mountain **15**
Splash Mountain **6**
Star Tours **14**
Submarine Voyage **12**
Swiss Family Treehouse **2**
Tom Sawyer Island **7**

Frontierland's
Rivers of
America

Frontierland
8

Critter
Country
6

7

5

New Orleans
Square
4 **2** **1**
3

Adventureland

Disneyland Hotel

Picnic
Area

Group Sales

Ticket Booths

Disabled
Parking

1-0853

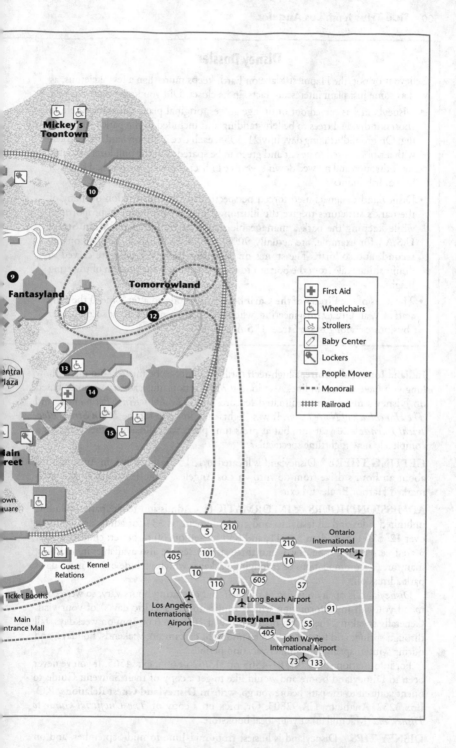

Mickey's
Toontown

10

9
Fantasyland

11

Tomorrowland

12

13

14

15

entral
Plaza

**Main
Street**

own
quare

Key:

	First Aid
	Wheelchairs
	Strollers
	Baby Center
	Lockers
—	People Mover
----	Monorail
++++	Railroad

Guest
Relations   Kennel

Ticket Booths

Main
Entrance Mall

Ontario
International
Airport

210

5   210

405   101

1   10

110   710   605   57

Los Angeles
International
Airport   Long Beach Airport

91

Disneyland   5   55

405

John Wayne
International
Airport

73   133

Disney Dossier

Believe it or not, the Happiest Place on Earth keeps more than a few skeletons, as well as some just plain interesting facts, in its closet. Did you know that:

- Disneyland was carved out of orange groves; original plans called for carefully chosen individual trees to be left standing and included in the park's landscaping. On groundbreaking day, July 21, 1954, each tree in the orchard was marked with a ribbon—red to be cut and green to be spared. But the bulldozer operator went through and mowed down *every* tree indiscriminately; no one had foreseen his color blindness.

- Disneyland designers used forced perspective in the construction of many of the park's structures to give the illusion of height and dramatic proportions while keeping the park a manageable size. The buildings on **Main Street U.S.A.**, for example, are actually 90% scale on the first floor, 80% on the second, and so forth. The stones on **Sleeping Beauty Castle** are carved in diminishing scale from the bottom to the top, giving it the illusion of towering height.

- The faces of the **Pirates of the Caribbean** were modeled after some of the early staff of Walt Disney Imagineering, who also lent their names to the second-floor "businesses" along **Main Street U.S.A.**

Indiana Jones Adventure, a high-tech thrill that's not to be missed—no matter how long you have to wait in line. Also look for live-action musical extravaganzas based on Disney's most recent animated features like *The Lion King, Pocahontas,* and *The Hunchback of Notre Dame.* It was "lights out" in 1996 for the *Main Street Electrical Parade's* 20-year run, but at press time plans were already in the works for a completely new nighttime spectacular.

GETTING THERE   Disneyland is located at 1313 Harbor Blvd. in Anaheim. It's about an hour's drive from downtown Los Angeles. Take I-5 south to the well-marked Harbor Boulevard exit.

ADMISSION, HOURS & INFORMATION   Admission to the park, including unlimited rides and all festivities and entertainment, is $34 for adults and children over 12, $26 for children 3 to 11, and $30 for seniors 60 or better; children under 3 are free. Parking is $6. Two- and three-day passes are also available; in addition, many area accommodations offer lodging packages which include one or more day's park admission.

Disneyland is open every day of the year, but operating hours vary, so we recommend you call for information which applies to the specific day(s) of your visit. Generally speaking, the park is open from 9 or 10am to 6 or 7pm on weekdays, fall through spring; and from 8 or 9am to midnight or 1am on weekends, holidays, and during winter, spring, or summer vacation periods.

For information, call **714/781-4565** or 213/626-8605, ext. 4565. If you've never been to Disneyland before and would like to get a copy of their Souvenir Guide to orient yourself to the park before you go, write to **Disneyland Guest Relations,** P.O. Box 3232, Anaheim, CA 92803. Or, pick up a copy of *The Unofficial Guide to Disneyland* (Macmillan) at your local bookstore.

DISNEY TIPS   Disneyland is busiest from mid-June to mid-September, and on weekends and holidays year-round. Peak hours are from noon to 5pm; visit the most

- Walt Disney maintained two apartments inside Disneyland. His private apartment above the **Town Square Fire Station** has been kept just as it was when he lived there.

- The elaborately carved horses on Fantasyland's **King Arthur Carousel** are between 100 and 120 years old; Walt Disney found them lying neglected in storage at Coney Island in New York, and brought them home to be restored.

- **It's a Small World** was touted at its opening as "mingling the waters of the oceans and seas around the world with Small World's Seven Seaways." This was more than a publicity stunt—records from that time show such charges as $21.86 for a shipment of sea water from the Caribbean.

- The peaceful demeanor of Disneyland was broken during the summer of 1970 by a group of radical Vietnam protesters who invaded the park. They seized **Tom Sawyer Island** and raised the Viet Cong flag over the fort before being expelled by riot specialists.

- **Indiana Jones: Temple of the Forbidden Eye,** Disneyland's newest attraction, won't be experienced the same way by any two groups of riders. Like a sophisticated computer game, the course is programmed with so many variables in the action that there are 160,000 possible combinations of events.

popular rides before and after these hours and you'll cut your waiting times substantially. If you plan on arriving during a busy time, purchase your tickets in advance and get a jump on the crowds at the ticket counters.

Disneyland's attendance falls dramatically during the wintertime, so the park offers discounted (about 25% off) admission to Southern California residents who may purchase up to six tickets per zip code verification. If you will be visiting the park with someone who lives here, be sure to take advantage of this money-saving opportunity.

A common gripe about Disneyland is the high cost of food while inside: Burgers and fries for a family of four can set you back $20 to $25, and meals at the sit-down restaurants are even pricier. Our advice: Remember how easy it is to exit the park and return again. You can take the monorail directly to the Disneyland Hotel, where dining options from casual to dressy are also somewhat overpriced, but not as badly as inside the park. Also, consider simply walking out the front gates, leaving your car safely in the lot, and eating at one of the coffee shop/diner-type places on Harbor Boulevard.

Many visitors tackle Disneyland systematically, beginning at the entrance and working their way clockwise around the park. But a better plan of attack is to arrive early and run to the most popular rides first: the Indiana Jones Adventure, Star Tours, Space Mountain, Big Thunder Mountain Railroad, Splash Mountain, the Haunted Mansion, and Pirates of the Caribbean. Lines for these rides can last an hour or more in the middle of the day.

TOURING THE PARK

The Disneyland complex is divided into several themed "lands," each of which has a number of rides and attractions that are, more or less, related to that land's theme.

Main Street U.S.A., at the park's entrance, is a cinematic version of turn-of-the-century small-town America. This whitewashed Rockwellian fantasy is lined with gift shops, candy stores, a soda fountain, and a silent theater that continuously runs early Mickey Mouse films. You'll find the practical things you might need here, too, such as stroller rentals and storage lockers. Because there are no rides here, it's best to tour Main Street during the middle of the afternoon, when lines for rides are longest, and in the evening, when you can rest your feet in the theater that features "Great Moments with Mr. Lincoln," a patriotic (and animatronic) look at America's 16th president. There's always something happening on Main Street; stop in at the information booth to the left of the main entrance for a schedule of the day's events.

You might start your day by circumnavigating the park by train. An authentic 19th-century steam engine pulls open-air cars around the park's perimeter. Board at the Main Street Depot and take a complete turn around the park, or disembark at any one of the lands.

Adventureland is inspired by most the exotic regions of Asia, Africa, India, and the South Pacific. There are several popular rides here. This is where you'll find the Swiss Family Treehouse. On the Jungle Cruise, passengers board a large authentic-looking Mississippi River paddleboat and float along an Amazon-like river. En route, the boat is threatened by "animatronic" wild animals and hostile natives, while a tour guide entertains with a running patter. A spear's throw away is The Enchanted Tiki Room, one of the most sedate attractions in Adventureland. Inside, you can sit down and watch a 20-minute musical comedy featuring electronically animated tropical birds, flowers, and "tiki gods."

The Indiana Jones Adventure is Adventureland's newest ride. Based on the Steven Spielberg series of films, this ride takes adventurers into the Temple of the Forbidden Eye, in joltingly realistic all-terrain vehicles. Riders follow Indy and experience the perils of bubbling lava pits, whizzing arrows, fire-breathing serpents, collapsing bridges, and the familiar cinematic tumbling boulder (this effect is *very* realistic in the front seats!). Disney "imagineers" reached new heights with the design of this ride's line which, take my word for it, has so much detail throughout its twisting path that 30 minutes or more simply flies by.

New Orleans Square, a large, grassy, gas lamp–dotted green, is home to the Haunted Mansion, the most high-tech ghost house I've ever seen. The spookiness has been toned down so kids won't get nightmares anymore, so the events inside are as funny as they are scary. Even more fanciful is Pirates of the Caribbean, one of Disneyland's most popular rides. Here, visitors float on boats through mock underground caves, entering an enchanting world of swashbuckling, rum-running, and buried treasure. Even in the middle of the afternoon you can dine by the cool moonlight and to the sound of crickets in the Blue Bayou Restaurant, the best eatery in the land.

Critter Country is supposed to be an ode to the backwoods—a sort of Frontierland without those pesky settlers. Little kids like to sing along with the animatronic critters in the musical Country Bear Jamboree show. Older kids and grown-ups head straight for Splash Mountain, one of the largest water flume rides in the world. Loosely based on the Disney movie *Song of the South,* the ride is lined with about 100 characters who won't stop singing "Zip-A-Dee-Doo-Dah." Be prepared to get wet, especially if someone sizable is in the front seat of your log-shaped boat.

Frontierland gets its inspiration from 19th-century America. It's full of dense "forests" and broad "rivers" inhabited by hearty looking (but, luckily, not smelling) "pioneers." You can take a raft to Tom Sawyer's Island, a do-it-yourself play island with balancing rocks, caves, and a rope bridge, and board the Big Thunder Mountain Railroad, a runaway roller coaster that races through a deserted 1870s gold mine.

You'll also find a petting zoo and an Abe Lincoln–style log cabin here; both are great for exploring with the little ones.

On Saturdays, Sundays, holidays, and vacation periods, head to Frontierland's Rivers of America after dark to see the FANTASMIC! show—a mix of magic, music, live performers, and sensational special effects. Just as he did in *Sorcerer's Apprentice,* Mickey Mouse appears and uses his magical powers to create giant water fountains, enormous flowers, and fantasy creatures. There's plenty of pyrotechnics, lasers, and fog, as well as a 45-foot-tall dragon that breathes fire and sets the water of the Rivers of America aflame. Cool.

Mickey's Toontown, opened in 1993, is a colorful, wacky, whimsical world inspired by the Roger Rabbit films. This is a gag-filled land populated by toons. There are several rides here, including Roger Rabbit's CarToonSpin, but these take a back seat to Toontown itself, a trippy smile-inducing world without a straight line or right angle in sight. This is a great place to talk with Mickey, Minnie, Goofy, Roger Rabbit, and the rest of your favorite toons. You can even visit their "houses" here. Mickey's red-shingled house and movie barn is filled with props from some of his greatest cartoons.

Fantasyland has a storybook theme and is the catchall "land" for all the stuff that doesn't quite seem to fit anywhere else. Most of the rides here are geared to the under-six set, including the King Arthur Carousel, Dumbo the Flying Elephant ride, and the Casey Jr. Circus Train. But grown-ups have an irrational attachment to some as well, like Mr. Toad's Wild Ride and Peter Pan's Flight. You'll also find Alice in Wonderland, Snow White's Scary Adventures, Pinocchio's Daring Journey, and more in Fantasyland. The most lauded attraction is It's a Small World, a slow-moving indoor river ride through a saccharine nightmare of all the world's children singing the song everybody loves to hate. For a different kind of thrill, try the Matterhorn Bobsleds, a zippy roller coaster through chilled caverns and drifting fog banks. It's one of the park's most popular rides.

Tomorrowland may now seem a bit dated, but it still offers some of the park's best attractions. Space Mountain, a pitch-black indoor roller coaster, is one of Disneyland's best rides. Star Tours, the original Disney/George Lucas joint venture, is a 40-passenger StarSpeeder that encounters a spaceload of misadventures on the way to the Moon of Endor, achieved with wired seats and video effects (not for the queasy); the line can last an hour or more, but it's worth the wait. In addition to all this, you can take a dive in a submarine and soar in a rocket jet in Tomorrowland; there's also a huge video arcade.

The "lands" themselves are only half the adventure. Other joys include roaming Disney characters, penny arcades, restaurants and snack bars galore, summer fireworks, mariachi and ragtime bands, parades, shops, marching bands, and much more. Oh yeah, there's also the storybook Sleeping Beauty Castle—can you spot the evil witch peering from one of the top windows?

KNOTT'S BERRY FARM

Cynics say that Knott's Berry Farm is for people who aren't smart enough to find Disneyland. Well, there's no doubt that visitors should tour Disney first, but it's worth staying in a hotel nearby so you can play at Knott's during your stay.

Like Disneyland, Knott's Berry Farm is not without its historical merit. Rudolph Boysen crossed a loganberry with a raspberry, calling the resulting hybrid the "boysenberry." In 1933, Buena Park farmer Walter Knott planted the boysenberry, thus launching Knott's Berry Farm on 10 acres of leased land. When things got tough during the Great Depression, Mrs. Knott set up a roadside stand, selling pies, preserves, and home-cooked chicken dinners. Within a year, she was selling 90 meals a day. Lines became so long that Walter decided to create an Old West Ghost Town as a diversion for waiting customers.

The Knott family now owns the farm that surrounds the world-famous Chicken Dinner Restaurant, an eatery serving more than a million fried meals a year. And Knott's Berry Farm is the nation's third most attended family entertainment complex (after the two Disney parks, of course).

During the last half of October, locals flock to Knott's Berry Farm. Why? Because the entire park is revamped as "Knott's *Scary* Farm"—the ordinary attractions are made spooky and haunted, every grassy area is transformed into a graveyard or gallows, and even the already scary rides get special surprise extras, like costumed ghouls who grab your arm in the middle of a roller-coaster ride!

GETTING THERE   Knott's Berry Farm is located at 8039 Beach Blvd. in Buena Park. It's about an hour's drive from downtown Los Angeles, and about a five-minute ride north on I-5 from Disneyland. From I-5 or Calif. 91, exit south onto Beach Boulevard. The park is located about half a mile south of Calif. 91.

ADMISSION, HOURS & INFORMATION   Admission to the park, including unlimited access to all rides, shows, and attractions, is $29 for adults and children over 12, $19 for seniors over 60 and children ages 3 to 11, free for children under 3. Admission is $14 for everyone after 4pm. Like Disneyland, Knott's offers discounted admission during off-peak seasons for Southern California residents, so if you're bringing local friends or family members along, be sure to take advantage of the bargain. Also like Disneyland, Knott's Berry Farm's hours vary from week to week, so you should call about the day you plan to visit. Generally speaking, the park is open during the summer every day from 9am to midnight. The rest of the year, they open at 10am and close at 6 or 8pm, except Saturdays when they stay open till 10pm. Knott's is closed Christmas Day. Special hours and prices are in effect during Knott's Scary Farm in late October.

For recorded information, call **714/220-5200.**

TOURING THE PARK

Knott's Berry Farm still maintains its original Old West motif. It's divided into five "Old Time Adventures" areas.

Old West Ghost Town, the original attraction, is a collection of refurbished 19th-century buildings that have been relocated from actual deserted Old West towns. Here, you can pan for gold, ride aboard an authentic stagecoach, ride rickety train cars through the Calico Mine, get held up aboard the Denver and Rio Grande Calico Railroad, and hiss at the villain during a melodrama in the Birdcage Theater.

Fiesta Village has a south-of-the-border theme that means festive markets, strolling mariachis, and wild rides like Montezooma's Revenge and Jaguar!, a huge new roller coaster that includes two heart-in-the-mouth drops and a loop that turns you upside down.

The Roaring '20s Amusement Area contains Sky Tower, a parachute jump drop with a 20-story free-fall. Other white-knuckle rides include XK-1, an excellent flight simulator "piloted" by the riders; and Boomerang, a state-of-the-art roller coaster that turns riders upside down six times in less than a minute. Kingdom of the Dinosaurs features extremely realistic *Jurassic Park*-like creatures. It's quite a thrill, but it may scare the little kids.

Wild Water Wilderness is a $10 million, $3\frac{1}{2}$-acre attraction styled like a turn-of-the-century California wilderness park. The top ride here is a white-water adventure called Bigfoot Rapids, featuring a long stretch of artificial rapids; it's the longest ride of its kind in the world.

Camp Snoopy will probably be the youngsters' favorite area. It's meant to re-create a wilderness camp in the picturesque High Sierra. Its six rustic acres are the play grounds of Charles Schulz's beloved beagle and his pals, Charlie Brown and Lucy, who greet guests and pose for pictures. The rides here, including Beary Tales Playhouse, are tailor made for the six-and-under set.

Thunder Falls, Knott's newest area, contains Mystery Lodge, a truly amazing high-tech, trick-of-the-eye attraction based on the legends of Northwestern Indians. Don't miss this wonderful theater piece.

Stage shows and special activities are scheduled throughout the day. Pick up a schedule at the ticket booth.

ATTRACTIONS BEYOND THE THEME PARKS

To locate these attractions, see map on p. 511 of this chapter.

Crystal Cathedral. 12141 Lewis St., Garden Grove. ☎ **714/971-4000.**

This angular, mirror-sheathed church (think movie Superman's Fortress of Solitude), otherwise known as the Garden Grove Community Church, is a shocking architectural oddity, with nine-story-high doors and a vast, open interior that's shaped like a four-pointed star. Opened in 1980, it's the pulpit for televangelist Robert Schuller, who broadcasts sermons and hymns of praise on radio and television to an international audience of millions. Each Sunday, an overflow crowd listens to the service blaring from loudspeakers into the parking lot. Annual Christmas and Easter pageants feature live animals, floating "angels," and other theatrics. A $5 million stainless steel carillon, which began ringing in 1991, has prompted some of the Cathedral's neighbors to complain that they want less joyful noise and more peace on earth.

Medieval Times Dinner and Tournament. 7662 Beach Blvd., Buena Park. ☎ **800/ 899-6600** or 714/521-4740. Admission $33–$36 adults, $23–$26 children 12 and under. Shows Mon–Thurs at 7pm, Fri at 6:30 and 8:45pm; Sat at 6 and 8:15pm, Sun at 5 and 7:15pm. Call for reservations (be sure to inquire about auto club discounts).

Guests crowd around long wooden tables and enjoy a four-course banquet of roast chicken, ribs, herbed potatoes, and pastries—all eaten with the hands in medieval fashion, of course. More than 1,100 people can fit into the castle, where sword fights, jousting tournaments, and various feats of skill are performed by colorfully costumed actors, including fake knights on real horseback. It's kind of ridiculous, but kids of all ages love it. *A word of warning:* The horses (and horseplay) kick up lots of dirt, so if you have any allergies to dust or animal dander, keep an eye on the nearest exit.

Movieland Wax Museum. 7711 Beach Blvd. (Calif. 39), Buena Park. ☎ **714/522-1155.** Admission $12.95 adults, $10.55 seniors, $6.95 children 4–11, free for children under 4. Daily 9am–7pm. Discount combination admission includes Ripley's Believe It Or Not (across the street).

At this goofy museum, located one block north of Knott's Berry Farm in Buena Park, you can see wax-molded figures of all your favorite film stars, from Bela Lugosi as Dracula and Marilyn Monroe in *Gentlemen Prefer Blondes,* to Leslie Nielsen in the *Naked Gun* movies. "America's Sweetheart," Mary Pickford, dedicated the museum on May 4, 1962; it has risen steadily in popularity ever since, with new stars added yearly, taking their place next to the time-tested favorites. The museum was created by film addict Allen Parkinson, who saw to it that some of the most memorable scenes in motion pictures were re-created in exacting detail in wax. In the seemingly unrelated Chamber of Horrors, you almost expect the torture victims to scream "tourist trap!" Discount combination admission tickets include the new **Ripley's Believe It Or Not Museum** across the street—grown-ups yawn but young kids marvel at the "astounding" facts presented in a sensational manner.

Richard Nixon Library and Birthplace. 18001 Yorba Linda Blvd., Yorba Linda. ☎ **714/ 993-5075.** Fax 714/528-0544. Admission $5.95 adults, $3.95 seniors, $2 children 8–11; children under 8 free. Mon–Sat 10am–5pm, Sun 11am–5pm.

Although he was the most vilified U.S. president in modern history, there's always been a warm place in the hearts of Orange County locals for Richard Nixon. This presidential library, located in Nixon's boyhood town, celebrates the roots, life, and legacy of America's 37th president. The nine-acre site contains the modest farmhouse where Nixon was born, manicured flower gardens, a modern museum containing presidential archives, and the final resting place of both Nixon and his wife, Pat.

Displays include videos of the famous Nixon-Kennedy TV debates, an impressive life-size statuary summit of world leaders, gifts of state (including a gun from Elvis Presley), and exhibits on China and Russia. There's also an exhibit of the late Pat Nixon's sparkling First Lady gowns. There's a 12-foot-high graffiti-covered chunk of the Berlin Wall, symbolizing the defeat of Communism, but hardly a mention of Nixon's leading role in the anti-Communist "witch hunts" of the 1950s. There are exhibits on Vietnam, yet no mention of Nixon's illegal expansion of that war into neighboring Cambodia. Only the Watergate Gallery is relatively forthright, where visitors can listen to actual White House tapes and view a montage of the president's last day in the White House.

WHERE TO STAY
DOUBLES FOR $60 OR LESS

Best Western Anaheim Stardust. 1057 W. Ball Rd., Anaheim, CA 92802. ☎ **800/ 222-3639** or 714/774-7600. Fax 714/535-6953. 103 rms, 18 suites. A/C TEL TV. Rooms $58–$70, suites $95. Rates include full breakfast. AE, DISC, DC, MC, V. Free parking.

Located on the back side of Disneyland, this modest hotel will appeal to the budget-conscious traveler who isn't willing to sacrifice absolutely everything. All rooms have refrigerator and microwave; breakfast is served in a refurbished train dining car; and you can relax by the large outdoor heated pool and spa while doing wash in the laundry room. Large family suites will accommodate virtually any brood, and shuttles run regularly to the park.

Colony Inn. 7800 Crescent Ave. (west of Beach Blvd.), Buena Park, CA 90620. ☎ **800/ 98-COLONY** or 714/527-2201. Fax 714/826-3826. 130 rms & suites. A/C TEL TV. Rooms (1–4 guests)/suites (up to 8 guests) $49–$98. AE, MC, V. Free parking.

Although it consists of two modest, U-shaped motels, the newly refurbished Colony Inn has a lot to offer. It's the closest lodging to Knott's Berry Farm's south entrance and is just 10 minutes away from Disneyland. They cheerfully offer discount coupons for Knott's and other nearby attractions, as well as complimentary coffee and donuts to jump-start your morning. Rooms are spacious and comfortably outfitted with conservative furnishings. There are two pools, two wading pools for kids, two saunas, and coin-operated laundry on the premises.

DOUBLES FOR $80 OR LESS

Anaheim Plaza Hotel. 1700 S. Harbor Blvd., Anaheim, CA 92802. ☎ **800/228-1357** or 714/772-5900. Fax 714/772-8386. 300 rms & suites. A/C TEL TV. Rooms $79–$119, suites from $175. AE, DISC, DC, MC, V. Free parking, shuttle to Disneyland.

You can easily cross the street to Disneyland's main gate, or you can take advantage of the Anaheim Plaza's free shuttle to the park. Once you return however, you'll appreciate the way this 30-year old hotel's clever design shuts out the noisy world. In fact, the seven two-story garden buildings remind me of 1960s Waikiki more than busy Anaheim. The olympic-size heated outdoor pool and whirlpool are unfortunately surrounded by AstroTurf, but new management was doing a total room renovation in 1996, so there's always hope. They won't change a thing about the light-filled modern lobby, nor the friendly rates. The hotel will still offer room service from the casual cafe in the lobby, plus laundry valet and coin-operated laundry.

Candy Cane Inn. 1747 S. Harbor Blvd., Anaheim, CA 92802. ☎ **800/345-7057** or 714/ 774-5284. Fax 714/772-5462. 173 rms. A/C TEL TV. Rooms $70–$84. Rates include breakfast. AE, DISC, DC, MC, V. Free parking, shuttle to Disneyland.

Take your standard U-shaped motel court with outdoor corridors, spruce it up with cobblestone walkways, old-time streetlamps, flowering vines engulfing the balconies of attractively painted rooms, and you have the Candy Cane. The face-lift worked, making this motel near Disneyland's main gate a real treat for the stylish bargain-hunter. Guest rooms are decorated in bright floral motifs with comfortable furnishings, including queen-size beds and a separate dressing and vanity area. Complimentary breakfast is served in the courtyard, where you can also splash around in a heated pool, spa, or kids' wading pool.

Howard Johnson Hotel. 1380 S. Harbor Blvd., Anaheim, CA 92802. ☎ **800/422-4228** or 714/776-6120. Fax 714/533-3578. 320 rms. A/C TEL TV. Rooms $64–$94. AE, CB, DC, DISC, MC, V. Free parking.

The hotel occupies an enviable location, directly opposite Disneyland, and a cute San Francisco trolley car runs to and from the park every 30 minutes. Rooms are divided among several low-profile buildings, all with balconies opening onto a central garden with two heated pools for adults and one for children. Garden paths lead under eucalyptus and olive trees to a splashing, circular fountain. During the summer, you can see the nightly fireworks display at Disneyland from the upper balconies of parkside rooms. Try to avoid rooms in the back buildings, for they get some freeway noise. Services and facilities include in-room movies and cable, room service from the attached Coco's Restaurant, gift shop, game room, laundry service plus coin laundry room, airport shuttle, and family lodging/Disney admission packages. We think it's pretty classy for a HoJo's.

The Jolly Roger Hotel. 640 W. Katella Ave. (west of Harbor Blvd.), Anaheim, CA 92802. ☎ **800/446-1555** or 714/772-7621. Fax 714/772-2308. 225 rms, 11 suites. A/C TEL TV. Rooms $65–$118; suites $78–$185. AE, DISC, DC, MC, V. Free parking, shuttles to Disneyland.

The only thing still sporting a buccaneer theme here is the adjoining Jolly Roger Restaurant, and that's just fine. The comfortable but blandly furnished rooms are in either an older, two-story L-shaped motel or two newer five-story annexes. We prefer the older units for their peace and quiet and also for the palm-shaded heated pool in the center of it all. Across the driveway is the swashbuckling restaurant; dinner will set you back a few doubloons, but the all-day coffee shop is more reasonable. There's also nightly entertainment and dancing in the lounge. Conveniently located across the street from Disneyland, the Jolly Roger also has meeting and banquet rooms, plus a second pool, spa, beauty salon, and gift shop.

DOUBLES FOR $100 OR LESS

Buena Park Hotel. 7675 Crescent Ave. (at Grand), Buena Park, CA 90620. ☎ **800/422-4444** or 714/995-1111. Fax 714/828-8590. 350 rms & suites. A/C TEL TV. Rooms $89–$99; suites $175–$250. AE, DC, DISC, MC, V. Free parking, shuttle to Disneyland.

Within easy walking distance of Knott's Berry Farm, the Buena Park Hotel also offers a free shuttle to Disneyland just 7 miles away. The pristine lobby has the look of a business-oriented hotel, and that it is. But vacationers can also benefit from the elevated level of service designed for the business traveler. Be sure to inquire about Executive Club rates as well as Knott's or Disneyland package deals. Rooms in the nine-story tower are tastefully decorated, and facilities and services include room service, charming heated outdoor pool and spa, two restaurants and a 1950s–60s dance club, and rental car desk.

WORTH A SPLURGE

✪ **Disneyland Hotel.** 1150 W. Cerritos Ave. (west of the Disneyland parking lot), Anaheim, CA 92802. ☎ **714/778-6600.** Fax 714/965-6597. 1,136 rms, 62 suites. A/C MINIBAR TEL TV. Rooms $155–$250; suites from $425. AE, MC, V. Parking $10.

The "Official Hotel of the Magic Kingdom," attached to Disneyland via a monorail system that runs right to the hotel, is the perfect place to stay if you're doing the park. You'll be able to return to your room anytime during the day, whether it's to take a much-needed nap or to change your soaked shorts after your Splash Mountain Adventure. Best of all, hotel guests get to enter the park early almost every day and enjoy the major rides before the lines form—usually you can enter $1^{1}/_{2}$ hours early. Call ahead to check the schedule for your specific day.

The theme hotel is a wild attraction unto itself. The rooms aren't fancy, but they're comfortably and attractively furnished like a good-quality business hotel. Many rooms feature framed reproductions of rare Disney conceptual art, and The Disney Channel is free on TV. The beautifully landscaped hotel is an all-inclusive resort, offering six restaurants, five cocktail lounges, every kind of service desk imaginable, a "wharfside" bazaar, a walk-under waterfall, and even an artificial white sand beach. Disneyland has also just taken over the adjoining Pacific Hotel, whose Asian tranquility (including a fine and pricey Japanese restaurant) bring a slightly higher tariff.

When you're planning your trip, ask the hotel about multiday packages that allow you to take on the park at your own pace.

Dining/Entertainment: The best restaurant is Stromboli's, an Italian/American eatery that serves all the pasta staples. Kids love Goofy's Kitchen, where the family can enjoy breakfast and dinner with the Disney characters.

Services: Concierge, room service, shoeshine, laundry, nightly turndown, baby-sitting, express check-out.

Facilities: Three large outdoor heated pools, complete health club, putting green, shuffleboard and croquet courts, sundeck, special children's programs, beauty salon, and 20 shops and boutiques.

WHERE TO DINE

Inland Orange County isn't known for its restaurants, most of which are branches of reliable upscale California or national chains you'll easily recognize. We've listed a few intriguing options, but if you're visiting the area just for the day, you'll probably eat inside the theme parks; there are plenty of restaurants to choose from at both

Disneyland and Knott's Berry Farm. At Disneyland, in the creole-themed **Blue Bayou,** you can sit under the stars inside the Pirates of the Caribbean ride, no matter what time of day it is. At Knott's, try the fried chicken dinners and boysenberry pies at Mrs. Knott's historic **Chicken Dinner Restaurant.** For the most unusual dinner you've ever had with the kids, see **Medieval Times** (see "Attractions Beyond the Theme Parks," above).

MEALS FOR $10 OR LESS

Belisle's Restaurant. 12001 Harbor Blvd. (at Chapman), Garden Grove. ☎ **714/750-6560.** Main courses $3–$23 (but most will feed more than one). MC, V. Sun–Thurs 7am–midnight, Fri–Sat 7am–2am. AMERICAN.

Harvey Belisle's modest pink cottage has been doling out "Texas-size" portions of diner-style food since before Disneyland opened in 1955. This is the place to bring a ravenous football team, or just your hollow-legged teenage boys. From the four-egg omelets accompanied by mountains of hash browns to the 12-ounce chicken fried steak to a chocolate eclair the size of a log, we think Paul Bunyan would feel right at home.

Felix Continental Cafe. 36 Plaza Square (intersection of Chapman & Glassell), Orange. ☎ **714/633-5842.** Reservations recommended for dinner. Main courses $6–$14. AE, DC, MC, V. Mon–Thurs 7am–9pm, Fri till 10pm; Sat 8am–10pm; Sun 8am–9pm. CUBAN/SPANISH.

If you like the re-created Main Street in the Magic Kingdom, then you'll love the historic 1886 town square in the city of Orange, and the cozy sidewalk tables outside Felix Continental Cafe. Dining on traditional Cuban specialties and watching traffic spin around the magnificent fountain and rosebushes of the plaza evokes old Havana or Madrid rather than the cookie-cutter Orange County communities just blocks away. The food receives glowing praise from restaurant reviewers and loyal locals alike.

MEALS FOR $20 OR LESS

Mr. Stox. 1105 E. Katella Ave. (east of Harbor Blvd.), Anaheim. ☎ **714/634-2994.** Reservations recommended on weekends. Main courses $12–$23. AE, DC, MC, V. Mon–Fri 11am–2:30pm; Mon–Sat 5:30–10pm, Sun 5–9pm. AMERICAN.

Hearty steaks and fresh seafood are served in an early California manor-house where specialties include roast prime rib and mesquite-broiled fish, veal, and lamb; chef Scott Raczek particularly excels at reduction sauces and innovative herbal preparations. Sandwiches and salads are also available, and homemade breads and desserts, such as chocolate mousse cake, are unexpectedly good. Mr. Stox has an enormous and renowned wine cellar, and there's live entertainment every night.

Peppers Restaurant and Nightclub. 12361 Chapman Ave. (west of Harbor Blvd.), Garden Grove. ☎ **714/740-1333.** Reservations recommended on weekends. Main courses $9–$14. AE, CB, DC, DISC, MC, V. Mon–Thurs 11am–10pm; Fri–Sat 11am–11pm; Sun 10am–10pm. CALIFORNIA/MEXICAN.

This colorful Californian/Mexican-themed restaurant just south of Disneyland looks like a partying kind of place, and it doesn't disappoint. The varied menu features mesquite-broiled dishes and fresh seafood daily. Mexican specialties include lots of variations of tacos and burritos, but the grilled meats and fish are best, especially Pepper's signature King Fajitas with crab legs or lobster tails. Dancing is available nightly to Top 40 hits starting at 9pm, and Monday nights a Mexican group plays live music. There's a free shuttle to and from six area hotels between 6pm and the nightclub closing time of 2am.

Renata's Caffe Italiano. 227 E. Chapman Ave. (corner of Grand), Orange. ☎ **714/ 771-4740.** Reservations recommended for dinner. Main courses $8–$15. AE, MC, V. Mon–Thurs 11am–9pm, Fri 11am–10pm; Sat–Sun 4–10pm. Closed Sun in summer. ITALIAN.

Near Felix Cafe in the historic plaza district, owner Renata Cerchiari draws a steady stream of regulars with good (but not great) contemporary Italian specialties. We found the charming patio dining in this small town atmosphere a welcome change from Orange County's frantic pace (particularly if you're staying by the amusement parks), and the wide selection of appetizers and pasta dishes more authentic and reasonably priced than anywhere else, although the creamy Caesar salad wins higher marks than the disappointing cannoli.

WORTH A SPLURGE

Chanteclair. 18912 MacArthur Blvd. (opposite John Wayne Airport), Irvine. ☎ **714/ 752-8001.** Reservations required. Main courses $15–$24. AE, CB, DC, MC, V. Mon–Fri 11am– 3pm; Mon–Sat 6–11pm. CONTINENTAL/FRENCH.

Chanteclair is expensive and a little difficult to reach, but it's worth seeking out. The restaurant is designed in the style of a provincial French inn. The rambling stucco structure, built around a central garden court, houses several dining and drinking areas, all with their own unique ambience. The antique-furnished restaurant has five fireplaces. At lunch, you might order grilled lamb chops with herb-and-garlic sauce, chicken-and-mushroom crepes, or Cajun charred ahi. Dinner is a worthwhile splurge that might begin with a lobster bisque with brandy or Beluga caviar with blinis. For a main dish, I recommend the rack of lamb with thyme sauce and roasted garlic.

6 The Orange Coast

Whatever you do, don't say "Orange County." The mere name evokes images of smoggy industrial parks, cookie-cutter housing developments, and the staunch Republicanism that prevail behind the so-called orange curtain.

We're talking instead about the Orange Coast, one of Southern California's best-kept secrets, a string of seaside jewels that have been compared with the French Riviera or the Costa del Sol. Forty-two miles of beaches offer pristine stretches of sand, tide pools teeming with marine life, ecological preserves, charming secluded coves, quaint pleasure-boat harbors, and legendary surfers atop breaking waves. Whether your bare feet want to stroll a funky wooden boardwalk or your gold card gravitates toward a yacht-club, you've come to the right place.

ESSENTIALS

GETTING THERE See Section 1 of Chapter 14 for airport and airline information. By car from Los Angeles, take I-5 or I-495 south. The scenic, shore-hugging Pacific Coast Highway (Calif. 1, or just P.C.H. to the locals) links the Orange Coast communities from Seal Beach in the north to Capistrano Beach just south of Dana Point, where it merges with I-5. To reach the beach communities directly, take the following freeway exits: **Seal Beach:** Seal Beach Blvd. from I-405. **Huntington Beach:** Beach Blvd./Calif. 39 from either I-405 or I-5. **Newport Beach:** Calif. 55 from either I-405 or I-5. Calif. **Laguna Beach:** Calif. 133 from I-5. **San Juan Capistrano:** Ortega Hwy./Calif. 74 from I-5. **Dana Point:** Pacific Coast Hwy./ Calif. 1 from I-5.

VISITOR INFORMATION The **Seal Beach Chamber of Commerce,** 201 8th St., corner of Central (☎ **310/799-0179**) is open Monday to Friday from 10am to 2pm.

Anaheim Area & Orange County Coast Attractions

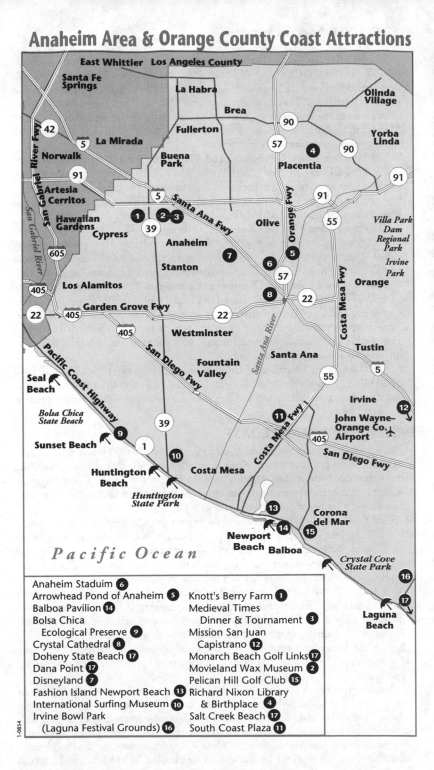

Anaheim Staduim 6
Arrowhead Pond of Anaheim 5
Balboa Pavilion 14
Bolsa Chica
　Ecological Preserve 9
Crystal Cathedral 8
Doheny State Beach 17
Dana Point 17
Disneyland 7
Fashion Island Newport Beach 13
International Surfing Museum 10
Irvine Bowl Park
　(Laguna Festival Grounds) 16

Knott's Berry Farm 1
Medieval Times
　Dinner & Tournament 3
Mission San Juan
　Capistrano 12
Monarch Beach Golf Links 17
Movieland Wax Museum 2
Pelican Hill Golf Club 15
Richard Nixon Library
　& Birthplace 4
Salt Creek Beach 17
South Coast Plaza 11

The **Huntington Beach Conference and Visitors Bureau,** 101 Main St., Suite A2 (☎ **800/SAY-OCEAN** or 714/969-3492; fax 714/969-5592) makes up for being *really* hard to find by genially offering tons of information, enthusiasm and personal anecdotes. They're at the corner of Pacific Coast Highway and Main Street—from the rear parking lot take the elevator to the second floor. Open Monday to Friday from 8:30am to noon and 1:30pm to 5pm. Their Internet Web site is at **http://www.imark.com/hbcvb.**

The **Newport Beach Conference and Visitors Bureau,** 3300 W. Coast Hwy. (☎ **800/94-COAST** or 714/722-1611; fax 714/722-1612), distributes brochures, sample menus, a calendar of events, and their free and very helpful Visitor's Guide. Call or stop in Monday to Friday from 8am to 5pm. Their Internet Web site is at **http://www.newport.lib.ca.us/default.htm.**

The **Laguna Beach Visitors Bureau,** 252 Broadway (☎ **800/877-1115** or 714/497-9229), is in the heart of town and distributes lodging, dining and art gallery guides. They're open Monday to Friday from 9am to 5pm and Saturday 10am to 4pm. Their Internet Web site is at **http://www.orangecounty.com/lagunabeach.**

The **San Juan Capistrano Chamber of Commerce,** 31931 Camino Capistrano, Suite D (☎ **714/493-4700**), is located in El Adobe Plaza at the corner of Camino Capistrano and Del Abispo, conveniently within walking distance of the mission. They're open Monday to Friday from 8:30am to 4pm, and publish a Walking Tour Guide to historic sites. Their Internet Web site with lots of helpful links is at **http://www.sanjuancapistrano.com.**

The **Dana Point Chamber of Commerce,** 24681 La Plaza, No. 120 (☎ **800/290-DANA** or 714/496-1555), is open Monday to Friday from 9am to 4:30pm and carries some restaurant and lodging info as well as a comprehensive recreation brochure.

DRIVING THE ORANGE COAST

You'll most likely be exploring the coast by car, so we cover the beach communities in order, from north to south. Keep in mind, however, that if you're traveling the interstates between Los Angeles and San Diego, the Pacific Coast Highway (Calif. 1) is a splendidly scenic detour that adds less than an hour to the commute. So pick out a couple of destinations, and go for it.

Seal Beach, on the border between Los Angeles and Orange Counties and neighbor to Long Beach's Naples harbor, is geographically isolated both by the adjacent U.S. Naval Weapons Station and the self-contained Leisure World retirement community. As a result, the charming beach town appears untouched by modern development—Orange County's answer to small-town America. Taking a stroll down Main Street is a walk back in time which culminates in the Seal Beach Pier. Although there are no longer clusters of the sunbathing, squawking seals which gave the town its name, old-timers fish hopefully, lovers stroll swooningly, and families cavort by the seaside, perhaps capping off the afternoon with an old-fashioned double dip from **Main Street Ice Cream and Yogurt** at the corner of Main Street and Ocean Avenue, where the walls are decorated with sepia-toned photographs of Seal Beach's yesteryear.

Huntington Beach is probably the largest Orange Coast city; it stretches quite a ways inland and has seen the most urbanization. To some extent, this has changed the old boardwalk and pier to a modern outdoor mall where cliques of gang kids co-exist with families and the surfers who continue to flock here, for Huntington is legendary in surf lore. Hawaiian surfer Duke Kahanamoka brought the sport here in the 1920s, and some say the breaks around the pier and Bolsa Chica are the best in

California. The world's top wave-riders flock to Huntington each August for the rowdy but professional **U.S. Open of Surfing** (☎ **310/286-3700**). If you'll be around during Christmastime, try to see the gaily decorated marina homes and boats in Huntington Harbour by taking the **Cruise of Lights,** a 45-minute narrated sail through and around the harbor islands. The festivities generally last from mid-December until Christmas; call **714/840-7542** for schedules and ticket information.

The name **Newport Beach** conjures comparisons with Rhode Island's Newport, where the well-to-do enjoy seaside living with all the creature comforts. That's the way it is here too, on a less grandiose scale. From the million-dollar Cape Cod–style cottages on sunny Balboa Island in the bay, to elegant shopping complexes like Fashion Island (surrounded by ultra-manicured country club lawns) and South Coast Plaza (a supermall with valet parking, car detailing, limo service, and concierge), this is where fashionable socialites, right-wing celebrities and business mavens can all be found. Alternately, you could explore **Balboa** peninsula's historic Pavilion and old-fashioned pier; or board a passenger ferry to Catalina Island.

Laguna Beach, whose breathtaking geography is marked by bold elevated headlands, coastal bluffs, and pocket coves, is known as an artist enclave, but the truth is Laguna has became so *in* (read: expensive) that it drove most of the true Bohemians *out*. Their legacy remains with the annual **Festival of the Arts and Pageant of the Masters** (see "Seeing the Sights," below), as well as a proliferation of art galleries intermingling with high-priced boutiques along the town's cozy streets. In warm weather Laguna Beach has an overwhelming Mediterranean-island ambience that makes *everyone* feel beautifully, idly rich.

San Juan Capistrano, nestled in the verdant headlands just inland of Dana Point, is defined by Spanish missions and its loyal flock of swallows. The "mission" architecture is authentic, and history abounds here. Consider San Juan Capistrano a compact, life-size diorama illustrating the evolution of a Western small town from Spanish mission era to secular rancho period, into statehood and the 20th century. Ironically, Mission San Juan Capistrano (see "Seeing the Sights," below) is once again the center of the community, just as the founding friars intended 200 years ago.

Dana Point, the last town south, has been called a "marina development in search of a soul." Overlooking the harbor stands a monument to 19th-century author Richard Henry Dana, who gave his name to the area and described it in *Two Years Before the Mast.* Activities generally center around yachting and Dana Point's jewel of a harbor. Nautical themes are everywhere; particularly charming are the series of streets named for old-fashioned shipboard lights, a rainbow that includes Street of the Amber Lantern, Violet Lantern, Golden Lantern, and so on. Bordering the harbor is **Doheny State Beach** (see "Beaches and Nature Preserves," below), which sets the standard on seaside park and camping facilities.

BEACHES & NATURE PRESERVES

Bolsa Chica Ecological Reserve (☎ **714/897-7003**), in Huntington Beach, is a 300-acre restored urban salt marsh that's haven to more than 200 bird species, as well as a wide variety of protected plants and animals. Naturalists come to spot herons and egrets as well as California horn snails, jackknife clams, sea sponges, common jellyfish, and shore crabs. An easy $1^1/2$-mile loop trail begins from a parking lot on Pacific Coast Highway (Calif. 1) 1 mile south of Warner Boulevard; docents lead a narrated walk every first Saturday. The trail heads inland, over Inner Bolsa Bay and up Bolsa Chica bluffs. It then loops back toward the ocean over a dike that separates the Inner and Outer Bolsa Bays and traverses a coastal sand dune system. This beautiful hike is a terrific afternoon adventure. The Bolsa Chica Conservancy has been working since 1978 on reclaiming the wetlands from oil companies that began drilling here 70 years ago. It is an ongoing process, and you can still see those "see-saw" drills dotting the outer areas of the Reserve. Although Bolsa Chica State Beach across the road has superb facilities, fantastic surfing and well-equipped campsites, you might find that the hulking offshore oil rigs spoil the view.

Huntington City Beach, adjacent to Huntington Pier, is a haven for volleyball players and surfers; dense crowds abound, but at least so do amenities like outdoor showers, beach rentals and rest rooms. Just south of the city beach is 3-mile-long **Huntington State Beach.** Both popular beaches have lifeguards and concession stands seasonally. The state beach also has rest rooms, showers, barbecue pits, and a waterfront bike path. Main entrance is at Beach Boulevard, plus access points all along Pacific Coast Highway (Calif. 1).

Newport Beach runs for about 5 miles and includes both Newport and Balboa piers. There are outdoor showers, rest rooms, volleyball nets, and a vintage board-walk that just may make you feel like you've stepped 50 years back in time. **Balboa Bike and Beach Stuff** (☎ 714/723-1516), at the corner of Balboa and Palm near the pier, can rent you a variety of items, from pier fishing poles to bikes, beach umbrellas, and bodyboards. **Southwind Kayak Center,** 2801 W. Pacific Coast Hwy. (☎ 800/768-8494 or 714/261-0200), rents sea kayaks for use in the bay or open ocean at rates of $8 to $10 per hour; instructional classes are available on weekends only. They also conduct bird-watching kayak expeditions into Upper Newport Bay Ecological Reserve at rates of $40 to $65.

Crystal Cove State Park, which covers 3 miles of coastline between Corona Del Mar and Laguna Beach plus extends up into the hills around El Moro Canyon, is a good alternative to the more popular beaches for you seekers of solitude. There are, however, lifeguards and rest rooms. The beach is a winding sandy strip, backed with grassy terraces; high tide sometimes sections it into coves. The entire area offshore is an underwater nature preserve. There are four entrances including Pelican Point and El Moro Canyon. Call **714/494-3539** or 714/848-1566.

Salt Creek Beach Park lies below the palatial Ritz-Carlton Laguna Niguel; guests who tire of the pristine swimming pool just venture down the staircase to wiggle their toes in the sand. The setting is marvelous, wide white sand beaches looking out toward Catalina Island (why do you think Ritz-Carlton built here?). There are lifeguards, rest rooms, a snack bar, and convenient parking near the hotel.

Doheny State Beach in Dana Point has long been known as a premier surfing spot and camping site. Just south of lovely Dana Point Marina (enter off Del Abispo Street), Doheny has the friendly vibe of beach parties in days gone by: tree-shaded lawns give way to wide beaches, and picnicking and beach camping are encouraged. There are 121 sites for both tents and RVs, and a state-run visitor's center featuring several small aquariums of sea and tide pool life. For more information and camping availability call **714/492-0802.**

BIKING & GOLFING

BICYCLE RENTALS   Bicycling is the most popular beach activity up and down the coast. A slower-paced alternative to driving, it allows you to enjoy the clean fresh air and notice smaller details of these laid-back beach towns and harbors. Bikes and safety equipment are available for rent at **Zack's Too,** Pacific Coast Highway at Beach Boulevard, Huntington Beach (☎ 714/536-2696); **Balboa Bike and Beach Stuff,** 601 Balboa Blvd., Newport Beach (☎ 714/723-1516); **Laguna Beach Cyclery,** 240 Thalia St. (☎ 714/494-1522); and **Dana Point Bicycle,** 34155 Pacific Coast Hwy. (☎ 714/661-8356).

GOLF Many golf course architects use the geography of the Orange Coast to its full advantage, molding challenging and scenic courses from the rolling bluffs. Unfortunately, most of the courses in this region are private and the few that are open to the public are pricey. But, if you're willing to splurge, we recommend **Monarch Beach Golf Links,** 23841 Stonehill Dr., Dana Point (☎ 714/240-8247) and **Pelican Hill Golf Club,** 22651 Pelican Hill Rd. South, Newport Beach (☎ 714/760-0707).

SEEING THE SIGHTS

Balboa Pavilion. 400 Main St., Balboa, Newport Beach. ☎ 714/673-5245. From Calif. 1, turn south onto Newport Blvd. (which becomes Balboa Blvd. on the peninsula); turn left at Main St.

This historic cupola-topped structure, a California Historical Landmark, was built in 1905 as a bathhouse for swimmers in ankle-length bathing costumes. Later during the Big Band era, dancers rocked the Pavilion doing the "Balboa Hop." Now it serves as the terminal for Catalina Island passenger service, harbor and whale-watching cruises, and fishing charters. The surrounding boardwalk is the Balboa Fun Zone, a collection of carnival rides, game arcade and vendors of hot dogs and cotton candy. For Newport Harbor or Catalina cruise information, call 714/673-5245; for sportfishing and whale-watching information, call 714/673-1434.

International Surfing Museum. 411 Olive Ave., Huntington Beach. ☎ 714/960-3483. Admission $2 adults, $1 students, kids under 6 free. Mid-June to late Sept, daily 12 noon–5pm; rest of year, Wed–Sun noon–5pm.

Nostalgic Gidgets and Moondoggies shouldn't miss this monument to the laid-back sport that has become synonymous with California beaches. There are gargantuan longboards from the sport's early days, memorabilia of Duke Kahanamoka and the other surfing greats represented on the "Walk of Fame" near Huntington Pier, and a gift shop where a copy of the "Surfin'ary" can help you bone up on your surfer slang even if you can't hang ten.

Balboa Island.

The charm of this pretty little neighborhood isn't diminished by knowing that the island is artificial—and it certainly hasn't affected the price of real estate. Tiny clapboard cottages in the island's center and modern houses with two-story windows and private docks along the perimeter make a colorful and romantic picture. You can drive onto the island on Jamboree Road to the north, or take the three-car ferry from Balboa Peninsula (about $1 per vehicle). It's generally more fun to park and take the ferry as a pedestrian, since the tiny alleys they call streets are more suitable for strolling, there usually are crowds, and parking spaces are scarce. Marine Avenue, the main commercial street, is lined with small shops and cafes which evoke a New England fishing village. Refreshing shaved ices sold by sidewalk vendors will relieve the heat of summer.

Mission San Juan Capistrano. Ortega Hwy. (Calif. 74), San Juan Capistrano. ☎ 714/248-2049. Admission $4 adults, $3 children and seniors. Daily 8:30am–5pm. Closed Thanksgiving, Christmas, and Good Friday.

The seventh of the 21 California coastal missions, Mission San Juan Capistrano is continually being restored, a mix of old ruins and working buildings that are home to small museum collections and various adobe rooms that are as quaint as they are interesting. The intimate mission chapel with its ornate Baroque altar is still regularly used for religious services, and the mission complex is the center of the community, hosting performing arts, children's programs, and other cultural events year-round.

This mission is best known for its swallows, who are said to return to nest each year at their favorite sanctuary. According to legend, the birds wing their way back to the mission annually on March 19, St. Joseph's Day, arriving here at dawn; they are said to take flight again on October 23, after bidding the mission farewell. In reality, however, you can probably see the well-fed birds here any day of the week, winter or summer.

A SPECIAL ARTS FESTIVAL

A 60-year tradition in arts-friendly Laguna, the ✪ **Festival of Arts and Pageant of the Masters** is held each summer throughout July and August. It's pretty large now, including the formerly "alternative" Sawdust Festival across the street and the unique Pageant of the Masters. Amidst the artists exhibiting (and selling) original works in every medium, local volunteers perform a series of *tableaux vivants,* re-creating well-known paintings by posing perfectly still in accurate costumes and elaborate make-up against carefully re-created backdrops. The Pageant is one-of-a-kind, creating an extraordinary sense of two-dimentionality. Musical groups ranging from jazz ensembles to ethnic groups perform throughout the day, and there are workshops for adults and children, plus demonstrations of printmaking, *raku* (Japanese pottery), and other arts. The festival grounds are at 650 Laguna Canyon Rd., Laguna Beach (☎ 800/487-3378 for advance tickets, or 714/494-1145). Grounds admission is $3 adults, $2 seniors and students. Pageant tickets cost $15 to $40, depending on performance night and seat location. Check it out on the Web at **http:// www.coolsville.com/festival.**

SHOPPING

Just as the communities along the coast range from casually barefoot summer playgrounds to meticulously groomed yacht-clubby enclaves, so does the shopping scene stretch to both ends of the spectrum.

Seal Beach, indifferent to tourists, has charming low-tech shops designed to service the year-round residents, while Huntington Beach offers a plethora of surf and water-sport shops, reflecting its sporty nature. Both Huntington and Balboa have more than their share of T-shirt and souvenir stands, while tony Newport Beach has been called "Beverly Hills south" because of the many European designer boutiques and high-priced shops there. Corona Del Mar, immediately south of Newport Beach on Calif. 1, is more like "Pasadena south," with branches of stylish but affordable L.A. boutiques sharing several fun blocks with local boutiques and services. Laguna Beach is art gallery intensive; there are too many to list, but most are along Pacific Coast Highway or Ocean, Forest, and Park avenues. There's little shopping in Dana Point and mostly Mission-themed souvenirs in San Juan Capistrano. Shoppers from all over the Southland flock to the two excellent malls listed below. If that isn't to your taste, a drive along Pacific Coast Highway will yield many other opportunities for browsing and souvenir purchases.

Fashion Island Newport Beach. 401 Newport Center Dr., Newport Beach. ☎ **714/ 721-2000.** Mon–Fri 10am–9pm, Sat 10am–7pm, Sun 11am–6pm.

Not an island at all, this shopping center is located next to the harbor and designed to resemble an open-air Mediterranean village. A pretty upscale village, that is, with tiled streets and plazas dotted with strolling pull-cart vendors and lined with upscale stores and boutiques, including Neiman-Marcus and Macy's department stores as well as Baywatch (they sell timepieces) and other specialty shops.

South Coast Plaza. 3333 Bristol St. (at I-405), Costa Mesa. ☎ 800/782-8̶&̶
435-2000. Mon–Fri 10am–9pm, Sat 10am–7pm, Sun 11am–6:30pm.

South Coast Plaza is one of the most upscale shopping complexes in the world, and it's so big that it's a day's adventure unto itself—even if you can only afford to browse. This beautifully designed center is home to some of fashion's most prominent boutiques, including Emporio Armani, Chanel, Alfred Dunhill, and Coach, beautiful branches of the nation's top department stores such as Saks Fifth Avenue and Nordstrom, and outposts of the best high-end specialty shops like Williams Sonoma, L.A. Eyeworks, and Rizzoli Booksellers.

The mall is home to many impressive works of art, including a 1.6-acre environmental sculpture by Isamu Noguchi. In between shoe-store browsing or sale-rack pillaging, you can stroll along the sculpture garden path, climb its hill, listen to its rushing water, cross its bubbling stream, and wonder at the sculpture's striking geometric forms from the garden benches. Not the usual rest in the food court, is it?

Speaking of food, here you won't find Hot-Dog-On-A-Stick among the forty or so restaurants scattered throughout. Wolfgang Puck Cafe, Morton's of Chicago, Ghirardelli Soda Fountain, Planet Hollywood, and Scott's Seafood Grill lure the hungry away from Del Taco and McDonald's.

WHERE TO STAY
DOUBLES FOR $80 OR LESS

Budget options along the mostly glitzy Orange Coast do exist, they're just few and far between. Some of the national chains have motels near (not on) the beach, but it's not impossible to find a comfortable, but small-scale, beachfront motel. Here are some options along the coast: **Harbour Inn,** 16912 Pacific Coast Hwy., Huntington/Sunset Beach (☎ 800/546-4770 or 310/592-4770; fax 310/592-3547); **Best Western Bay Shores Inn,** 1800 W. Balboa Blvd., Newport Beach (☎ 800/ 222-6675 or 714/675-3463; fax 714/675-4977); **Best Western Laguna Brisas,** 1600 So. Coast Hwy., Laguna Beach (☎ 800/624-4442 or 714/497-7272; fax 714/497-8306); **Best Western Marina Inn,** 24800 Dana Point Harbor Dr., Dana Point (☎ 800/255-6843 or 714/496-1203; fax 714/248-0360).

DOUBLES FOR $100 OR LESS

Blue Lantern Inn. 34343 Street of the Blue Lantern, Dana Point, CA 92629. ☎ 800/ 950-1236 or 714/661-1304. Fax 714/496-1483. 29 rms, all with fireplace & Jacuzzi tub. A/C TEL TV. Rooms $125–$275, including breakfast for two. AE, MC, V.

A newly constructed New England–style gray clapboard inn, the Blue Lantern is a pleasant cross between romantic B&B and sophisticated small hotel. Almost all of the rooms, which are decorated with reproduction traditional furniture and plush bedding, have a balcony or deck overlooking the harbor. Have your breakfast here in private (clad perhaps in the fluffy robe provided), or choose to go downstairs to the sunny dining room, which also serves complimentary afternoon tea. There's an exercise room, a cozy lounge with menus for many area restaurants, and a staff so genuine and friendly they welcome you with home-baked cookies at the front desk.

Vacation Village. 647 S. Coast Hwy., Laguna Beach, CA 92651. ☎ 800/843-6895 or 714/ 494-8566. Fax 714/494-1386. 100 rms, 38 suites. TV. $80–$155 double; from $175 suite. AE, CB, DC, DISC, MC, V.

Vacation Village has something for everyone. This cluster of seven oceanfront and near-the-ocean motels offers rooms, studios, suites, and apartments. Most of the accommodations are standard motel fare: bed, TV, table, basic bath. The best rooms are in a four-story, oceanfront structure overlooking the Village's private beach.

Umbrellas and backrests for beachgoers are available in summer. Facilities include a private beach, two pools, and a whirlpool. There's also a separately owned restaurant, The Beach House, on the premises that serves up affordable American cuisine.

WHERE TO DINE
MEALS FOR $10 OR LESS

El Adobe de Capistrano. 31891 Camino Capistrano (near the Mission), San Juan Capistrano. ☎ **714/493-1163** or 714/830-8620. Dinners $8–$15; lunch $5–$10. AE, DISC, MC, V. Mon–Thurs 11:30am–10pm, Fri–Sat 11:30am–11pm, Sun 10:30am–2:30pm and 4–10pm. CLASSIC MEXICAN.

This restaurant is housed in a historic landmark 1778 Spanish adobe near San Juan Capistrano's main attraction, the Mission. Understandably touristy, there's some interesting history inside, like the enclosed lobby that was originally a dirt pathway between two buildings. A former jail cell makes a fine wine cellar, and El Adobe proudly offers a menu combination named "the President's Choice" after Richard Nixon, who visited often from his summer house at the shore nearby. Hot plates overflow with cheesy combinations featuring chile rellenos, tamales and enchiladas topped with rich, red sauce; dinner selections also include steak and seafood.

Ruby's. 1 Balboa Pier, Balboa. ☎ **714/675-7829.** Most items under $5. AE, MC, V. Sun–Thurs 7am–10pm, Fri–Sat 7am–11pm. AMERICAN DINER.

With their trademark red and white hamburger stand decor sprouting up all over the Southland, Ruby's is fast becoming a local institution. The Balboa Pier Ruby's (a former baithouse) is the original, and several others can be found on or near the end of Orange Coast piers, including Seal Beach, Huntington, and Laguna. Ruby's sells nostalgia and food in equal measure; their hamburgers, fries, milkshakes, and flavored sodas are reasonably priced, and the fun, kid-friendly atmosphere really suits the surroundings.

MEALS FOR $20 OR LESS

Five Feet. 328 Glenneyre, Laguna Beach. ☎ **714/497-4955.** Reservations recommended on weekends. Main courses $14–$24. AE, MC, V. Fri 11:30am–2:30pm; Sun–Thurs 5–10pm, Fri–Sat 5–11pm. CALIFORNIA/ASIAN.

Chef/proprietor Michael Kang has created one of the area's most innovative and interesting restaurants, combining the best in California cuisine with Asian technique and ingredients. If the atmosphere were as good as the food, Five Feet would be one of the best restaurants in California. Main courses run the gamut from tea-smoked filet mignon topped with Roquefort cheese and candied walnuts to a hot Thai-style mixed grill of veal, beef, lamb, and chicken stir-fried with sweet peppers, onions, and mushrooms in curry-mint sauce. Unfortunately, the dining room's gray-concrete walls are not much to look at, and the exposed vents on an airplane hangar-scale wooden ceiling just look unfinished, not trendy industrial. Fortunately this unspectacular decor is brightened by an exceedingly friendly staff and unparalleled food.

Harbor Grille. 34499 Street of the Golden Lantern, Dana Point. ☎ **714/240-1416.** Reservations suggested on weekends. Main courses $8–$18. AE, DC, MC, V. Mon–Sat 11:30am–10pm, Sun 9am–10pm. SEAFOOD.

In a business/commercial mall right in the center of pretty Dana Point Marina, Harbor Grille is enthusiastically recommended by local inns for mesquite-broiled, ocean-fresh seafood. Hawaiian mahimahi with a mango chutney baste is on the menu, along with Pacific swordfish, grilled shark steaks, and teriyaki chicken.

Las Brisas. 361 Cliff Drive (off Pacific Coast Hwy. north of Laguna Canyon), Laguna Beach. ☎ 714/497-5434. Reservations recommended. Main courses $8–$17. AE, MC, V. Mon–Sat 8am–10:30pm, Sun 9am–10:30pm. MEXICAN.

Boasting a breathtaking view of the Pacific, Las Brisas is popular for sunset drinks and alfresco appetizers—so much so that it can get pretty crowded during the summer months. Affordable during lunch but pricey at dinner, the menu consists mostly of seafood recipes from the Mexican Riviera. Even the standard enchiladas and tacos get a zesty update with crab or lobster meat and fresh herbs. Calamari steak is sautéed with bell peppers, capers, and herbs in a garlic butter sauce, and king salmon is mesquite broiled and served with a creamy lime sauce. Although a bit on the touristy side, Las Brisas can be a fun part of the Laguna Beach experience.

Twin Palms. 630 Newport Center Drive, Newport Beach. ☎ **714/721-8288.** Reservations suggested. Main courses $9–$17. AE, DC, CB, MC, V. Sun–Wed 11:30am–10pm, Thurs–Sat 11:30am–1am. MEDITERRANEAN/FRENCH.

Opened in late 1995, this sister restaurant to one of Pasadena's most popular eateries seems to be leading the Newport Beach pack as well. From the famous original, which was started by, among others, movie star Kevin Costner, comes the high-tented, palm-accented, huge circuslike space that is Twin Palms's trademark. Amid this festival atmosphere you can enjoy the French "comfort food" original chef Michael Roberts created as a backlash against pricey haute cuisine. Favorites include juicy, roasted sage-infused pork, and honey-glazed coriander-scented duck from the rotisserie grill, as well as the popular salt cod mashed potato *brandade* appetizer. Sautéed dishes and salads are not as successful, but Twin Palms has brought its traditional Sunday "Gospel Brunch" to the new location.

WORTH A SPLURGE

Splashes Restaurant and Bar. In the Surf and Sand Hotel, 1555 S. Coast Hwy., Laguna Beach. ☎ **714/497-4477.** Reservations recommended. Main courses $16–$22. DC, DISC, MC, V. Daily 7am–10pm. MEDITERRANEAN.

Splashes is truly stunning. Almost directly on the surf, this light and bright restaurant basks in sunlight and the calming crash of the waves. At dinner, a basket of fresh-baked crusty bread prefaces a long list of appetizers that might include wild mushroom ravioli with lobster sauce, or sautéed Louisiana shrimp with red chiles and lemon. Gourmet pizzas also make great starters; they come topped with interesting combinations like grilled lamb, roasted fennel, artichokes, mushrooms, and feta cheese. Main courses change daily and might offer baked striped bass and braised duck in a cabernet sauce.

16 The Southern California Desert

by Stephanie Avnet

To the casual observer, Southern California's desert seems like a desolate place—nothing but vast landscapes baking under a relentless sun. Its splendor is subtle, letting each traveler discover its beauty in his or her own time. For some it will be the surprising lushness of unique varieties of trees, flowering cacti, fragrant shrubs, and other plants—many of them found only here—that have adapted ingeniously to the harsh climate. The unique Joshua tree, majestic to some and ugly to others, thrives in the upper Mojave Desert. Each spring, the ground throughout the Lancaster area is carpeted with brilliant golds and oranges of the poppy, California's state flower. Like the autumn leaves in New England, the poppies along Calif. 14 draw seasonal tourists in droves.

If it looks like nothing except insects could survive here, look again: You're bound to see the speedy roadrunner or a tiny gecko dart across your path. Close your eyes and listen for the cry of a hawk or an owl. Check the ground for coyote or bobcat tracks. Notice the sparkle of fish in the streams running through flourishing palm oases. Road signs near Barstow warn of desert tortoise crossing. The tortoise is just one of the many endangered species found only here. Fortunately, most of the Southern California desert's flora and fauna is protected by the federal government as a wildlife sanctuary.

Or perhaps the beauty you seek is that of personal renewal surrounded by spectacular desert landscape. In the shadow of purple-tinged mountains, amid ancient, otherworldly rock formations, or beside a sparkling swimming pool, you'll find as much or as little to occupy your time as you desire. Destinations range from gloriously untouched national parks to ultraluxurious resorts. And let's not forget that it's a rare day when the sun doesn't shine out here.

1 En Route to Palm Springs

If you're making the drive from Los Angeles via I-10, the first hour or more will be spent just, well, getting out of the L.A. metropolitan sprawl. Soon you'll leave the Inland Empire auto plazas behind, sail past the last of the bedroom community shopping malls, and edge ever closer to the (if you're lucky) snow-capped San Bernardino and San Jacinto mountain ranges. Coming from San Diego via I-15, the areas discussed below are east of the junction with I-10.

Antiquing is a very popular pastime in Southern California (we're not talking Louis XIV here, though, mostly late 19th- and early

20th-century stuff), and there will be some great opportunities to stop and poke around. What used to be a ramshackle string of junk shops along the I-10 service road in **Yucaipa** is now a respectable "antique row" worth exiting the freeway. Farther along I-10 lies **Beaumont,** touting itself as "City of Antiques," for it holds almost a dozen (at last count) mall-style antique and collectible emporiums.

If all this sifting through tchotchkes has made you hungry, how about some kitschy roadside dining? Although their fare is coffee-shop standard, don't tell the enthusiastic gingham and overall-clad waitstaff at **The Farm House** in **Banning** (signs will direct you off the freeway). From the giant rooster and rusty agricultural implements out front to the proudly framed photos of Banning's heyday as "Stagecoach Town U.S.A," this is just the kind of place you'd expect the rural Kiwanis club to meet in each week, and a far sight more interesting than the Denny's next door.

Or, as the horse- and silo-dotted fields give way to pale, dry desert, keep your eyes peeled for the dinosaurs which stand guard over the **Wheel Inn Restaurant** in **Cabazon.** That's right, a four-story-tall brontosaurus and his Tyrannosaurus rex pal. They were built in the 1960s by Claude K. Bell, a sketch artist and sculptor at Knott's Berry Farm with a way-before-his-time dream of an entire dinosaur amusement park. These two behemoths were all he completed. You can stop and climb up into the belly of the larger one, where you'll find a remarkably spacious gift shop selling dinosaur toys, books and souvenirs.

Cabazon is also the home of **Hadley's Orchards,** a fixture on this stretch of road since 1931. They're always packed with folks shopping for dates, dried fruits, nuts, honey, preserves, and other regional products. A snack bar serves the date shake so beloved in this region and sells gift packs of tasty treats to carry home (for more about the date mystique, see "More to See and Do," in section 2, below). Nearby, you'll either love or hate the **Desert Hills Factory Stores** (☎ 909/849-6641). Southern California's largest outlet mall contains more than 100 stores, the most intriguing of which is **Barney's New York** (☎ 909/849-1600), presenting a nice opportunity to pick up designer threads at a fraction of the cost.

Soon after leaving Cabazon you'll enter the **San Gorgonio Pass.** Be prepared for an awesome and otherworldly sight: never-ending windmill fields that harness the powerful force of the wind gusting through this passage, converting it to electricity for air-conditioners throughout the Coachella Valley. The Calif. 111 turn-off leads you past the Albert Frey–designed "hyperbolic paraboloid" gas station at Tramway Road, which for 30 years has served as the unofficial gateway to Palm Springs and the symbol that you have arrived!

2 The Palm Springs Desert Resorts

Palm Springs had been known for years as a golf course–studded retirement mecca annually invaded by raucous herds of libidinous college kids at spring break. Well, the city of Palm Springs has been quietly changing its image and attracting a whole new crowd. Former mayor (now U.S. congressman) Sonny Bono's revolutionary "antithong" ordinance in 1991 put a lightning-quick halt to the spring break migration by eliminating public display of the bare derriere, and the upscale fairway-condo crowd has been sticking to the tiny outlying resort cities of Rancho Mirage, Palm Desert, Indian Wells, and La Quinta. From the billboards on the highway it seems *all* the newly developed communities are endorsed by Arnold Palmer!

These days, there are no billboards allowed in Palm Springs itself, all the palm trees in the center of town are appealingly backlit at night, and you won't see the word "motel" on any establishment. Senior citizens are everywhere, dressed to the nines in brightly colored leisure suits and keeping alive the retro-kitsch establishments from

---

Area Code Change Notice

Please note that, effective March 22, 1997, the area code for the Southern California desert areas is scheduled to change to **760**. You will be able to dial 619 until September 27, 1997, after which you will have to use 760.

---

the days when Elvis, Liberace, and Sinatra made the balmy desert a swingin' place. But they're not alone: Baby boomers and yuppies nostalgic for the kidney-shaped swimming pools and backyard luaus of their Eisenhower/Kennedy glory years upbringing are buying ranch-style vacation homes and restoring them to their 1950s splendor. Hollywood's young glitterati are returning, too. Today the city fancies itself a cross between a European Riviera-style destination and a good old American small town combining Jetson-like architecture and the crushed-velvet vibe of piano bars with the colors and attitude of a laid-back Aegean island village. One thing hasn't changed: Swimming, sunbathing, golfing, and playing tennis are still the primary pastimes in this convenient little oasis.

An important presence in Palm Springs has little to do with socialites and Americana, for the Agua Caliente band of Cahuilla Indians settled in this area 1,000 years before the first golf ball was ever teed up. Recognizing the beauty and spirituality of this wide-open space, they lived a simple life around the natural mineral springs on the desert floor and would migrate into the cool canyons during the hot summer months. Under a treaty with the railroad companies and the U.S. government, the tribe owns half the land on which Palm Springs is built and actively works to preserve Native American heritage. It's easy to learn about the American Indians during your visit, and it will definitely add to your appreciation of this part of California.

ESSENTIALS

GETTING THERE   Several airlines service the **Palm Springs Regional Airport,** 3400 E. Tahquitz Canyon Way (☎ 619/323-8161), including **Alaska Airlines** (☎ 800/426-0333), **America West** (☎ 800/235-9292), **American** (☎ 800/433-7300), **Delta/Skywest** (☎ 800/453-9417), **United** (☎ 800/241-6522), and **USAir** (☎ 800/428-4322). Flights from Los Angeles International Airport (see Section 1 in Chapter 14) take about 40 minutes.

If you're driving from Los Angeles, take I-10 to the Calif. 111 turnoff to Palm Springs. You'll breeze into town on North Palm Canyon Drive, the main thoroughfare. The trip from downtown Los Angeles takes about two hours. If you're driving from San Diego, take I-15 north to I-10 east; it's 135 miles.

ORIENTATION   The commercial downtown area of Palm Springs stretches about a half mile along North Palm Canyon Drive between Alejo and Ramon streets. The street is one way through the heart of town, but its other-way counterpart is Indian Canyon Drive, one block east. The mountains lie directly west and south, while the rest of Palm Springs is laid out in a grid to the southeast. Palm Canyon forks into South Palm Canyon (leading to the Indian Canyons) and East Palm Canyon (the continuation of Calif. 111) traversing the resort towns of Cathedral City, Rancho Mirage, Palm Desert, Indian Wells, and La Quinta before looping up to rejoin I-10 at Indio. Desert Hot Springs is north of Palm Springs, straight up Gene Autry Trail. Tahquitz Canyon Way creates North Palm Canyon's primary intersection, tracking a straight line between the airport and the heart of town.

VISITOR INFORMATION   Be sure to pick up *Palm Springs Life* magazine's free monthly "Desert Guide." It contains tons of visitor information including a comprehensive calendar of events. Copies are distributed in hotels and newsstands and by the **Palm Springs Desert Resorts Convention and Visitors Bureau,** in the Atrium Design Centre, 69-930 Calif. 111, Suite 201, Rancho Mirage, CA 92270 (☎ **800/41-RELAX** or 619/770-9000). The bureau's office staff can help with maps, brochures, and advice Monday to Friday from 8:30am to 5pm. They also operate a 24-hour information and activities hot line (☎ **619/770-1992**), and an Internet site at **http://www.desert-resorts.com.**

   Palm Springs Visitors Information Center, 2781 N. Palm Canyon Dr. (☎ **800/34-SPRINGS;** fax 619/323-3021), offers maps, brochures, advice, souvenirs, and a free hotel reservation service. The office is open Monday to Sunday from 9am to 5pm, Sunday from 8am to 4pm.

ENJOYING THE OUTDOORS

The Coachella Valley desert is truly a playground, and what follows is but a sampling of opportunities to enjoy the abundant sunshine during your vacation here. Please keep in mind, however, that the strong sun and dry air that are so appealing can also sneak up in the form of sunburn and heat exhaustion. Especially during the summer, but even in milder times, always drink and carry plenty of water. And remember to bring sunscreen and wear a wide-brimmed hat. A little common sense will ensure hours of outdoor enjoyment!

TENNIS   Virtually all the larger hotels and resorts have tennis courts, but if you choose the intimate B&B option you might want to play at **The Tennis Center,** 1300 Baristo Rd., Palm Springs (☎ **619/320-0020**), which has nine courts and offers day and evening clinics for adults, juniors, and seniors, as well as ball machines for solo practice. USPTA pros are on hand.

   If you'd like to play for free, the night-lighted courts at **Palm Springs High School,** 2248 E. Ramon Rd., are open to the public on weekends, holidays, and during the summer. There are also eight free night-lighted courts in beautiful Ruth Hardy Park at Tamarisk and Caballero streets.

HORSEBACK RIDING   Equestrians from novice to advanced can experience the natural solitude and quiet of the desert on horseback at **Smoke Tree Stables** (☎ **619/327-1372**). Located south of downtown and ideal for exploring the nearby Indian Canyon trails, Smoke Tree offers guided rides for $25 per hour. But don't expect your posse leader to be primed with facts on the nature you'll encounter; this is strictly a do-it-yourself experience.

BICYCLING   The clean, dry air here just cries out to be enjoyed. What could be better than to pedal your way around town or into the desert? **Adventure Bike Tours** (☎ **619/328-2089**) will outfit you with bike, helmet, souvenir water bottle, and certified guide. If you're just looking to rent some wheels and a helmet, **Mac's Bicycle Rental** (☎ **619/321-9444**) offers hourly, daily, and weekly rentals on bikes, including children's and mountain models. **The Bike Man** (☎ **619/771-3619**) sweetens his deals by including water bottles, locks, maps, and free delivery. **Bighorn Bicycle Rental and Tour Company** (☎ **619/325-3367**) has hourly and daily rental rates in addition to guided bike treks.

HIKING   The most popular spot for hiking is the nearby **Indian Canyons** (for information call **619/325-5673**). The Agua Caliente tribe made their home here centuries ago, and remnants of their simple lifestyle can be seen among the streams, waterfalls, and astounding palm groves in Andreas, Murray, and Palm Canyons.

Hitting the Low-Cost Links

The Palm Springs desert resorts are world-famous meccas for golfers. There are 85 public, semiprivate, and private courses in the area; if you're the kind who starts polishing your irons the moment you begin planning your vacation, you're best off staying at one of the valley's many golf resorts, where you can enjoy the proximity of your hotel facilities as well as economically smart package deals that can give you a taste of country club membership (see "The Art of the Package Deal," below). If, on the other hand, you'd like to fit a round of golf into an otherwise varied trip and aren't staying at a hotel with its own links, there are courses at all levels and prices open to the general public, most of them in Palm Springs. Call ahead to see which will rent clubs or other equipment to the spontaneous player.

Greens fees vary throughout the year in the desert resorts. Contrary to popular belief, not all courses will cost you $100 or more per round. Also, prices drop drastically during the off-season, usually June or July through September, when the volume of play decreases due to the unbearably high temperatures (if you do choose to play in the summer, we suggest you tee it up early). A valuable service for the budget traveler is **Stand-By Golf** (☎ 619/321-2665), which helps more than 20 area courses fill their bookings by offering players a healthy discount. Call after 5pm and you'll be told which courses, some of them private, have slots open the following day.

Here are our favorite affordable courses for all types of players.

Beginners will enjoy **Tommy Jacobs' Bel-Air Greens,** 1001 El Cielo, Palm Springs (☎ 619/322-6062), a scenic nine-hole, 32-par executive course that has some water and sand trap challenges but also allows for a few confidence-boosting successes. Generally flat fairways and mature trees characterize the relatively short (3,350 yards) course. The complex also offers an 18-hole miniature golf course. Green fees range from $23 to $27; off-season, $9.50 for nine holes or $14 for all day.

Slightly more intermediate amateurs will want to check out the **Tahquitz Creek Golf Resort,** 1885 Golf Club Dr., Palm Springs (☎ 619/328-1005), whose two diverse courses appeal to midhandicappers. The "Legend's" wide, water-free holes will appeal to anyone frustrated by the "target" courses popular with many architects, while the new Ted Robinson–designed "Resort" course offers all those accuracy-testing bells and whistles more common to lavish private clubs. Green fees range from $35 to $85 depending on day and cart rental; off-season, $17 to $25.

Striking rock formations and herds of Bighorn sheep and wild ponies will probably be more appealing than the Trading Post in Palm Canyon, but it does sell detailed trail maps. This is Indian land, and the Tribal Council charges admission of $6 per adult with discounts for seniors, children, students, and military. The canyons are closed to visitors from late June to early September.

Ten miles east of Palm Springs is the 13,000-acre **Coachella Valley Preserve** (☎ 619/343-1234), which is open from sunrise to sunset. There are springs, mesas, both hiking and riding trails, the Thousand Palms Oasis, a visitors center, and picnic areas. If you're heading up to Joshua Tree National Park (see below), consider stopping at **Big Morongo Canyon Preserve** (☎ 619/363-7190), which was once an Indian village and later a cattle ranch. Open for visitors Wednesday to Sunday from 7:30am until sunset, the park's high water table makes it a magnet for birds and other wildlife; the lush springs and streams are an unexpected desert treat.

✪ **Palm Springs Country Club,** 2500 Whitewater Club Dr. (☎ 619/323-8625), is the oldest public-access golf course within the city of Palm Springs, and is especially popular with budget-conscious golfers, with green fees of only $40 to $50 (off-season, $20 to $25) including the required cart. The challenge of bunkers and rough can be amplified by the oft-blowing wind along the 5,885 yards of this unusually laid-out course.

If you're a golf fanatic whose looking to splurge, the **Westin Mission Hills Resort Course,** Dinah Shore and Bob Hope drives, Rancho Mirage (☎ 619/328-3198), is worth the extra bucks. It's somewhat more forgiving than most of legendary architect Pete Dye's courses, but don't play the back tees unless you've got a consistent 220-yard drive and won't be fazed by the Dye-trademark giant sand bunkers and elevated greens. Water only comes into play on four holes, and the scenery is an exquisite reward for low-handicappers. Nonguest green fees are $120 to $130 including cart; off-season, $65 to $25 and $25 after 2pm.

Be aware that many courses close completely for anywhere from one week to one month during the summer and early fall for reseeding. Since most desert facilities have more than one 18-hole course, the process is usually staggered enough so that there's always a playable course. But, if you have your heart set on one particular course, call before you go to make sure it will be open.

For the nonplaying spectator (or anyone longing to see the pros make it look *so* easy) there are dozens of golf tournaments year-round, including many celebrity and pro-am events in addition to regular PGA, LPGA, and Senior Tour stops. February brings the PGA Tour **Bob Hope Chrysler Classic** at the Bermuda Dunes Country Club and the **Frank Sinatra Celebrity Invitational** at Marriott's Desert Springs Resort and Spa. In March, catch the LPGA Tour **Nabisco Dinah Shore** at Mission Hills Country Club, then in April the Senior PGA **Liberty Mutual Legends of Golf** comes to PGA West. November brings two of the desert's longest running charity events, the **22nd Annual Frostig Center/Chris Korman Celebrity Tournament** at Westin Mission Hills and the 24-year **Billy Barty/7Up Celebrity Golf Classic** at Mesquite Country Club in Palm Springs. Also in November, check out the wacky **Palm Desert Golf Cart Parade** along El Paseo.

For more information you can call the **Palm Springs Desert Resorts Convention and Visitors Bureau** at **800/41-RELAX** or 619/770-9000. The Bureau also maintains an Activities Hot Line at **619/770-1992.**

A FAMILY WATERPARK   Palm Springs Oasis Waterpark, off I-10 south on Gene Autry Trail between Ramon Road and East Palm Canyon Drive (☎ 619/325-7873), is a water playground with 13 water slides, body- and board-surfing, an inner tube ride, beach volleyball, and more. Dressing rooms, lockers, and private beach cabanas (with food service) are available. Admission is $16.95 for visitors over 60 inches tall, $11.50 for 40 to 60 inches, free for kids under 40 inches, $9.95 for seniors. The park is open daily from 11am to 6pm mid-March through Labor Day, plus weekends through all of October.

MORE TO SEE & DO

Haven't seen any celebrities wandering the streets? You may want to hook up with **Celebrity Tours** (☎ 619/770-2700) located on E. Palm Canyon at Gene Autry Trail. Advance reservations are required for their one- and 2¹/₂-hour tours of Palm

Springs, which include some history and lore but mostly the opportunity to gawk at the homes of movie stars and celebrities. The longer tours take in the estates of surrounding Rancho Mirage and Palm Desert, "playground of the internationally elite."

The Living Desert Wildlife and Botanical Park. 47-900 Portola Ave., Palm Desert. ☎ 619/346-5694. Admission $7 adults, $6 seniors over 62, $3.50 children 3–12, under 2 free. Mon–Sun 9am–5pm (last admission 4:30). Call for summer schedule. Closed Aug, Christmas Day. No pets allowed.

This 1,200-acre desert reserve, museum, zoo, and educational center is designed to acquaint visitors with the unique habitats that make up the Southern California deserts. You can walk or take a tram tour through sectors that re-create life in several distinctive desert zones. See and learn about a dizzying variety of plants, insects, and wildlife, including bighorn sheep, mountain lions, rattlesnakes, lizards, owls, golden eagles, and the ubiquitous roadrunner.

Palm Springs Aerial Tramway. Tramway Rd. off Calif. 111, Palm Springs. ☎ 619/325-1391. Tickets $17 adults, $14 seniors, $11 children ages 5–12, under 5 ride free. Ride 'n' Dine combination (available after 2:30pm, dinner served after 4pm) $21 adults, $14 children. Mon–Fri 10am–8pm, Sat–Sun 8am–8pm; 1 hour later during daylight saving time.

To gain a birds-eye perspective of the Coachella Valley, take this 14-minute ascent up 2$^1/_2$ miles to the top of Mt. San Jacinto. The whole experience has a fabulous 1960s feel, from the original Swiss funicular equipment to the scratchy recording broadcast during the trip up (often drowned out by the periodic squeals of white-knuckled passengers). There's a whole other world once you arrive: alpine scenery, a ski lodge–flavored restaurant and gift shop, and temperatures typically 40° cooler than the desert floor. The most dramatic contrast is during the winter when the mountaintop is a snowy wonderland, irresistible to hikers and bundled-up kids with saucers. The excursion might not be worth the expense during the rest of the year. Guided mule rides and cross-country ski equipment are available at the top.

The Palm Springs Desert Museum. 101 Museum Dr. (just west of Palm Canyon/Tahquitz intersection), Palm Springs. ☎ 619/325-7186. Admission $5 adults, $4 military and seniors over 62, $2 children 6–17, free children under 6. Free to all first Fri of every month. Tues–Thurs and Sat–Sun 10am–4pm, Fri 10am–8pm.

This well-endowed museum combines a world-class Western and Native American art collection, the natural history of the desert, and an outstanding anthropology department, primarily representing the local Cahuilla tribe. Traditional Indian life as it was conducted for centuries before the white presence is illustrated by tools, baskets, and other relics. Check local schedules to find out about (usually excellent) visiting exhibits; plays, lectures and other events are presented in the Museum's Annenberg Theater.

Shields Date Gardens. 80225 Calif. 111, Indio. ☎ 619/347-0996. Daily 8am–6pm.

In a splendid display of wishful thinking and clever engineering, the Coachella Valley has grown into a rich agricultural region, known internationally for grapefruit, figs, and grapes, but mostly dates. The fascination of 1920s entrepreneurs with Arabian lore fueled by the Sahara-like conditions of the desert around Indio led to the planting of date palm groves. Started with just a few parent trees imported from the Middle East, the groves now produce 95% of the world's date crop. The trees are hand-pollinated by farmers, a process detailed in *The Romance and Sex Life of the Date*, a film running continuously (its racy title is the best part). Also housed in the splendid 1930s Moderne building is a lunch counter (date shake anyone?) and store selling an endless variety of dates and related goodies.

The Palm Springs Desert Resorts

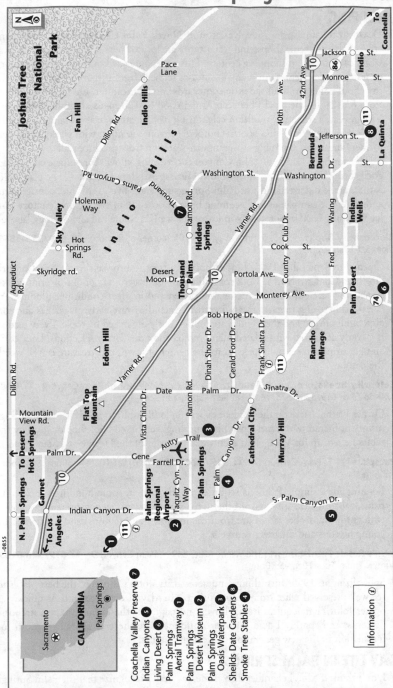

SHOPPING

Downtown Palm Springs revolves around **North Palm Canyon Drive,** and many art galleries, souvenir shops, and restaurants are located here, along with a couple of large scale hotels and shopping centers. This wide, one-way boulevard is designed for pedestrian enjoyment, with many businesses set back from the street itself—don't be shy about poking around the little courtyards you'll encounter. On Thursday nights from 6 to 10pm the blocks between Amado and Baristo roads are transformed into **VillageFest,** a street fair tradition celebrating its fifth anniversary. Handmade crafts vendors and aromatic food booths compete for your attention with wacky street performers and locals shopping at the mouth-watering fresh produce stalls.

The northern section of Palm Canyon is becoming known for vintage collectibles and is being touted as the **"Antique and Heritage Gallery District."** The plain truth is that, as the older residents of Palm Springs say good-bye to this life, consignment and estate sale companies are becoming better stocked than ever before. **Factory outlet shopping** is 20 minutes away in Cabazon (see "En Route to Palm Springs,"above).

Bloomsbury Books. 555 S. Sunrise Way No. 105 (corner of Ramon). ☎ **619/325-3862.** Mon–Sat 11am–9pm.

Opened in September 1995, Bloomsbury is a treat to browse through, and proprietor Brad Confer is hard at work compiling an impressive array of out-of-print books, signed and rare editions, all reasonably priced and in great condition. Bloomsbury is especially strong in gay-lesbian literature (including rare early magazines and foreign publications) and their books are meticulously organized by topic. Every section is cleverly decorated with related memorabilia and noteworthy selections. Located in an ugly strip mall several blocks from the center of town, this treasure is well worth the detour.

Celebrity Bookstore. 170 E. Tahquitz Canyon (¹/₂ block east of Palm Canyon). ☎ **800/ 320-6575** or 619/320-6575. Mon–Sat 9am–8pm, Sun 9am–4pm.

Owner Darrell Meeks is the resident expert on local publications: If it's Palm Springs history or literature you seek, visit his appealingly cluttered bookshop or stroll by the tables he sets up for VillageFest each week (in front of the Hollywood Stars Diner).

Patsy's. 4121 E. Palm Canyon Dr. ☎ **619/324-8825.** Wed–Sat 10am–4:30pm, Sun noon–4:30pm.

Looking for a simply fabulous sequined evening frock, some blindingly tacky golf pants, gabardine leisure suits, or other retro-garb? Patsy's is a consignment shop filled with entire wardrobes (some are from the local rich and famous) and frequented by young hipsters and cabaret costumers.

John's Resale Furnishings. In The Village Attic, 849 N. Palm Canyon Dr. ☎ **619/320-6165.** Winter, Thurs–Tues 10am–5:30pm.

Specializing in 1950s furnishings and accessories, John's is one of the best places to see well-preserved relics from Palm Springs's heyday of development. As quickly as owner John Hall acquires items, buyers nostalgic for the kidney shapes, starburst patterns, and sparkly Lucite of their childhood are there to snatch them up for installation in the new generation of weekend homes.

GAY LIFE IN PALM SPRINGS

Don't think the local chamber of commerce doesn't recognize that the Palm Springs area is one of the current top three American destinations for gay travelers. After just a short while in town, it's easy to tell how the gay tourism dollar is courted as aggressively as straight spending. Real estate agents cater to gay shoppers for vacation properties, and entire condo communities are marketed toward the gay resident. Advertisements for these and scores of other proudly gay-owned businesses can be found in *The Bottom Line,* the desert's free biweekly magazine of articles, events, and community guides for the gay reader, available at hotels, newsstands, and select merchants.

Throughout the year events are held that transcend the gay community to include everyone. In March, the Desert AIDS Walk benefits the Desert AIDS Project, while the world's largest organized gathering of lesbians coincides with the Nabisco Dinah Shore Golf Tournament.

Be sure to visit **Between The Pages Bookstore,** on Arenas Road east of Indian Canyon (☎ **619/320-7158**). Besides offering an extensive selection of gay- and lesbian-oriented books and videos, you'll find a wealth of free brochures and guides in the adjacent espresso bar, which also serves as a lobby for the **Between the Pages Playhouse.** This short block of Arenas is home to a score of gay establishments, including **Streetbar** (☎ **619/320-1266**), a neighborhood gathering spot for tourists and locals alike.

Just a few blocks away is a cozy neighborhood of modest homes and small hotels, concentrated on Warm Sands Drive south of Ramon. Known simply as **"Warm Sands,"** this area holds the very nicest "private resorts"—mostly discreet and gated B&B-style inns. Locals recommend the coed **El Mirasol Villas** (☎ **800/327-2985** or 619/326-5913) and the all-male **Warm Sands Villas** (☎ **619/323-3006**). Near the center of town lies the historic **Harlow Club Hotel,** 175 E. El Alameda (☎ **800/ 223-4073** or 619/320-4333), where men enjoy luxury haciendas amid lush gardens. The **Bee Charmer Inn,** 1600 E. Palm Canyon (☎ **619/778-5883**), caters to a female clientele, as does the party-atmosphere **Delilah's Enclave**, 641 San Lorenzo Rd. (☎ **800/621-6973** or 619/325-5269).

Gay nightlife is everywhere in the Valley, and especially raucous on holiday weekends. Pick up *The Bottom Line* for the latest restaurant, nightclub, theater, and special events listings.

WHERE TO STAY

The city of Palm Springs offers a wide range of accommodations. We particularly like the B&B-type inns becoming more prevalent as new owners renovate the many fabulous 40- to 60-year-old cottage complexes in the wind-shielded "Tennis Club" area west of Palm Canyon Drive. The other desert resort cities (Rancho Mirage, La Quinta, Palm Desert) have little diversity in lodgings, consisting mostly of luxurious resort complexes, many boasting world-class golf, tennis, or spa facilities and multiple on-site restaurants. If you're looking for a good base from which to shop or sightsee, Palm Springs, which has the most affordable lodgings in the area, is your best bet. Regardless of your choice, remember that rates given below are high-season (winter, generally October through May). Peak-season, off-season, midweek, or golf packages are common, so always ask about them when making your reservation.

If you're planning on staying for a week or more, you may consider renting a privately owned condo or villa. The **Rental Connection** (☎ **800/GO-2-PALM** or 619/ 320-7336) has a variety of units, all of which require a three-night minimum stay (one week for houses).

Remember: If you're calling to make a reservation directly (not via a toll-free number) after September 27, 1997, you must replace the local 619 area code with the region's new area code, **760,** when dialing.

DOUBLES FOR $80 OR LESS

In addition to the accommodations listed below, most of the recognized national chains have branches in the Palm Springs area, including the **Quality Inn,** 1269 E. Palm Canyon Dr., Palm Springs (☎ **800/472-4339** or 619/323-2775; $59 to $99); **Travelodge Palm Springs,** 333 E. Palm Canyon Dr. (☎ **800/578-7878** or 619/327-1211; $49 to $75); and **Best Western Las Brisas,** 222 S. Indian Canyon Dr., Palm Springs (☎ **800/346-5714** or 619/325-4372; $56 to $119).

Casa Cody. 175 S. Cahuilla Road (between Tahquitz Way & Arenas Rd.) Palm Springs, CA 92262. ☎ **619/320-9346.** 17 rms, suites, and villas, many with fireplace & full-size kitchen. A/C TEL TV. Rooms $55–$69, studio suites $69–$115, 1-bedroom villa $115–$135, 2-bedroom villa $165–$185. Rates include continental breakfast. AE, DISC, MC, V. Free parking.

Once owned by "Wild" Bill Cody's niece, this 1920s double courtyard (each with swimming pool) has been restored to fine condition, sporting a vaguely Southwestern decor and peaceful grounds marked by large lawns and mature, blossoming fruit trees. You'll feel more like a houseguest than a hotel client at the Casa Cody; it's located in the primarily residential "Tennis Club" area of town, a couple of easy blocks from Palm Canyon. Breakfast is served poolside, as is complimentary wine and cheese on Saturday afternoons.

Desert Patch Inn. 73758 Shadow Mountain Dr., Palm Desert, CA 92260. ☎ **800/350-9758** or 619/346-9161; Fax 619/776-9661. 14 rms & suites, most with kitchen. A/C TEL TV. Rooms and suites $52–$94. AE, DISC, MC, V. Small pets allowed. Closed Aug. Free parking.

Located in a quiet residential area near Palm Desert's fancy El Paseo, the Desert Patch Inn offers terrific prices and a friendly setting in a city not known for bargain accommodations. The grounds are well maintained and diverse, with shuffleboard courts and a putting green, plus a swimming pool and whirlpool. The rooms are nicely furnished, and many have living rooms and kitchens; all have refrigerators, microwaves, and coffeemakers. Rates fall even lower in July and September, making the Desert Patch a nice alternative to impersonal chain hotels.

DOUBLES FOR $100 OR LESS

Holiday Inn Palm Mountain Resort. 155 S. Belardo Rd., Palm Springs, CA 92262. ☎ **800/622-9451** or 619/325-1301; Fax 619/323-8937. 122 rms. A/C TEL TV. $79–$169 double, high season. AE, CB, DC, DISC, JCB, MC, V. Free parking.

Located within easy walking distance of Palm Springs's main drag, this Holiday Inn (like most in the chain) welcomes kids under 18 free in their parents' room, making it a terrific choice for families. Rooms are located in either the two- or the three-story wing, and many have a patio or balcony, with a view of either the mountains or the heated swimming pool in the hotel's large AstroTurf courtyard; all offer the convenience of refrigerators, microwaves, and coffeemakers. Midweek, summer rates can be as low as $49 a night; there's also a restaurant, lounge, and poolside cabana bar.

✪ **Korakia Pensione.** 257 S. Patencio Rd., Palm Springs, CA 92262. ☎ **619/864-6411.** 12 rms and suites, 8 with kitchen, 5 with fireplace. $79–$169 double, high season. Rates include breakfast. No credit cards. Free parking.

If you can work within the Korakia's rigid deposit/cancellation policy and tolerate the lackadaisical staff, you're in for a special stay at this Greek/Moroccan oasis just a few blocks from Palm Canyon Drive. The simply furnished rooms and unbelievably spacious suites are peaceful and private, surrounded by flagstone courtyards and flowering gardens. Eight have kitchens, while five sport fireplaces. This former artist's villa from the 1920s draws a fashionable international crowd of artists, writers, and musicians. All beds are blessed with thick feather duvets, and windows are shaded with flowing white canvas draperies in the Mediterranean style. Add a sumptuous breakfast served in-room or poolside (*korakia* is Greek for "crow," and a tile mosaic example graces the pool bottom), and this unusual B&B shapes up as a pleasant and cost-efficient treat.

Orchid Tree Inn. 261 S. Belardo Rd. (at Baristo Rd.), Palm Springs, CA 92262. ☎ **800/ 733-3435** or 619/325-2791. Fax 619/325-3855. 40 rms and suites (30 with kitchen), one 2-bedroom bungalow. A/C TEL TV. Rooms $95–$110, suites $100–$155, bungalow $290. AE, MC, V. Free parking.

Although it bills itself as a "1930s desert garden retreat," both the interior and exterior of the Orchid Tree bear many marks (like contemporary sliding glass doors) of a 1970s remodel. If you're not too picky about authenticity, however, the inn's beautifully landscaped grounds and three swimming pools (complemented by two outdoor whirlpools) make this a good choice in the genuinely historic "Tennis Club" area near the heart of town. Red-tile roofed buildings surrounded by flowering shrubs, mature citrus trees, and other foliage make for pleasant and private accommodations; an added treat are the multitudes of twittering hummingbirds, sparrows, and quail drawn by the many bird feeders and baths.

Villa Royale. 1620 Indian Trail (off East Palm Canyon), Palm Springs, CA 92264. ☎ **800/ 245-2314** or 619/327-2314. Fax 619/322-3794. 31 rms and suites. A/C TEL TV. Rooms $75–$165, suites/villas $150–$225. Extra person $25. Rates include breakfast. AE, MC, V. Free parking.

Located five minutes from the hustle and bustle of downtown Palm Springs, this bed-and-breakfast evokes the image of a European cluster of villas, complete with climbing bougainvillea and rooms filled with international antiques and artwork. The main building was once home to Olympic and silver screen ice-skater Sonya Henie. Present owner Bob Lee later commandeered two adjacent apartment buildings. Rooms vary widely in quality, so you might find the trade-off for quiet seclusion is a small, dark room in back. Some rooms and suites, on the other hand, are spacious and have fireplaces and/or private patios with spa. Continental breakfast is served in an intimate garden setting surrounding the main pool. At lunch and dinner this patio becomes Europa Restaurant, serving slightly pricey but inventive continental fare. Europa is heavily advertised as a "romantic" dining spot, but you'd better bring your own romantic distraction, since the service can sometimes be frustratingly leisurely. Not advisable for children.

WORTH A SPLURGE

Ingleside Inn. 200 W. Ramon Rd. (corner of Belardo), Palm Springs, CA 92264. ☎ **800/ 772-6655** or 619/325-0046. Fax 619/325-0710. 29 rms, 16 suites. A/C MINIBAR TEL TV. Rooms $110–$235, minisuites $205–$285, villas $135–$265, suites from $295. Rates include continental breakfast. AE, DISC, MC, V. Complimentary valet parking.

Once the 1920s estate of the Humphrey Birge family, manufacturers of the Pierce Arrow automobile, this hideaway estate offers some of the most charming rooms in town. Each guest room and suite is uniquely decorated with antiques, perhaps a canopied bed or a 15th-century vestment chest. Many rooms have wood-burning fireplaces; all have in-room whirlpools and steam baths.

There's an old-world charm here matched with fine service. The Ingleside is hardly low key, however, for they are quick to mention on brochures and wall plaques celebrities such as Elizabeth Taylor, Howard Hughes, John Wayne, Bette Davis, Salvador Dalí, John Travolta, and Goldie Hawn who have stayed here (the celebrity watching is still first rate). They also like to boast of the Inn's *two* appearances on *Lifestyles of the Rich and Famous.*

The Art of the Package Deal

The desert is one of California's best-kept secrets for the budget traveler. No need to book that cheap motel; you can live like royalty here at bargain-basement rates. The caveat, of course, is that you must be willing to be flexible—which usually means heading to the desert when everyone else is fleeing the 100°-plus temperatures. Once their rich-and-famous regulars have gone, many of the area's ritziest resorts offer more-than-generous packages to entice regular folks like you and me to fill their empty rooms. During the summer months, tariffs literally plummet; it's common to find $300 rooms going for $89 or less as part of off-season packages. If you're willing to brave the heat, you're likely to get quite a deal.

At the ultra-luxurious **La Quinta Resort & Club** in La Quinta (☎ **800/ 854-1271** or 619/564-4111), *the* place to be if you're serious about your golf or tennis game, mid-summer deals can often get you into a *casita* for as little as $90, including a weekend of mariachi music or a round of golf. Many other fine resorts also offer generous golf packages, among them **Marriott's Desert Springs Spa and Resort** in Palm Desert (☎ **800/228-9290** or 619/341-2211), an artificial desert oasis—complete with an indoor "rain forest" and moat, as well as a gaggle of pink flamingos—that's a tourist attraction in its own right; at the other end of the scale, **Marriott's Rancho Las Palmas** in Rancho Mirage (☎ **800/I-LUV-SUN** or 619/ 568-2727), a relaxing Spanish hacienda that's one of the desert's least pretentious luxury resorts; **Hyatt Grand Champions** in Indian Wells (☎ **800/228-9000** or 619/341-1000); and the **Estrella Inn** in downtown Palm Springs (☎ **800/ 237-3687** or 619/320-4417), a 1930s property that was recently restored to its early Hollywood charm. Since the Estrella Inn is the most reasonably priced of the desert resorts—rack rates start at $150—this may be your best bet for a good deal; they often offer attractive golf packages that include play at one of several nearby courses.

If the idea of spending summer in the desert is too much for you, don't despair; there are deals to be had in the more palatable months, too. Midweek, family, and golf packages are common year-round, and AAA members can almost always do better than the rack rates. If your timing is right, you may land a great deal even in peak season. Who knows? You may be sunning yourself by the pool before you know it.

Melvyn's is the expensive continental dining room, and the adjacent piano bar and lounge attract a fancy, old-money crowd. Frank and Barbara Sinatra hosted a dinner here on the eve of their wedding. Services and facilities include concierge, room service, in-room massage, complimentary limousine service, large outdoor heated pool, Jacuzzi, sundeck, croquet, shuffleboard, business center, car-rental desk, tour desk, and boutiques.

WHERE TO DINE
MEALS FOR $10 OR LESS

Big Weenys. 238 N. Palm Canyon Dr., Palm Springs. ☎ **619/416-0766.** $2.45–$6.25. MC, V. Mon–Fri 9:30am–9pm, Sat–Sun 9:30am–10pm. HOT DOGS/SAUSAGE SANDWICHES.

Feed your inner adolescent with the double entendres abundant at this surprisingly varied hot dog shop. The "big weeny" is fine quality meat, though, and equivalent in mass to three or four state-fair standards. Or choose the "normal," "long," or "teeny weeny." For the culinary adventurer, they offer designer sausages such as

Chicken and Jalapeño, Italian Antelope, or Smoked Pheasant. Which of the eleven available toppings would *you* choose for an Alligator or Kangaroo wiener?

Hollywood Stars Diner. 103 S. Palm Canyon Dr. (at Tahquitz Canyon), Palm Springs. ☎ **619/416-1555.** Reservations not accepted. Most items under $10. MC, V. Daily 8am–9pm. AMERICAN.

Centrally located and flashy, this restaurant offers great people-watching from its expansive patio, while serving up reliably tasty blue-plate specials and soda fountain treats. If you can't get into the superior, but often-packed Louise's, you'll do fine to cross the street to the Hollywood Diner.

Lincoln View Café. 278 N. Palm Canyon Dr. (back of courtyard), Palm Springs. ☎ **619/327-6365.** Breakfast $2–$7, salads & sandwiches $4–$6, coffee drinks $1.25–$3.75. AE, DISC, DC, MC, V. Daily 7:30am–5pm.

Tucked in the same quiet courtyard as Palmie restaurant (see below), this tasteful purveyor of coffee specialties, baked treats, and light meals is named for the unlikely "historic" view of Abraham Lincoln. Okay, it's not quite Mt. Rushmore, but the city makes the most of it. Use the purple scope outside the cafe's entrance to help fix your gaze on the former president's profile, formed in the scraggy hillside beyond the skyline. Enjoy live jazz here on the weekends.

Louise's Pantry. 124 S. Palm Canyon Dr., Palm Springs. ☎ **619/325-5124.** Most items under $10. MC, V. Daily 7am–8:30pm. AMERICAN.

A real old-fashioned diner, Louise's has been a fixture in Palm Springs since it opened as a drugstore lunch counter in 1945. Locals line up for the very few booths (expect a wait during popular mealtimes) to enjoy premium quality comfort foods such as Cobb salad, Reuben and French dip sandwiches, chicken and dumplings, hearty breakfasts with biscuits and gravy, and tasty fresh-baked pies. (A second location is in Palm Desert in the Town Center Plaza, Fred Waring Drive and Town Center Way, ☎ **619/346-1315.**)

Mykonos. 139 Andreas (just off Palm Canyon), Palm Springs. ☎ **619/322-0223.** Reservations not accepted. Most items under $10. MC, V. Wed–Mon 11am–10pm. GREEK.

Sit at the simple, candle-lit tables in this off-street brick courtyard with locals who've been enjoying authentic Greek specialties at this family run spot for nine years. Mykonos is supercasual (vinyl tablecloths) and decorated white and blue like its Aegean namesake. Nevertheless, it's a pleasant treat in a town of mostly mediocre retro-diner fare. Traditional lamb shanks over rice, *dolmades* (stuffed grape leaves), tangy salad with crumbled feta cheese, and sweet, sticky *baklava* are among their best items.

MEALS FOR $20 OR LESS

In addition to what's listed below, there's also an ever-reliable **Chart House,** 69934 Calif. 111 (between Country Club and Frank Sinatra drives; ☎ **619/324-5613**) to satisfy the carnivore in you.

La Provence. 254 N. Palm Canyon Dr. (upstairs from arcade), Palm Springs. ☎ **619/416-4418.** Reservations recommended. Main courses $10–$21. AE, DC, DISC, MC, V. Thurs–Tues 5:30–10:30pm. COUNTRY FRENCH.

A favorite among erudite locals and recommended by knowledgeable innkeepers, the casually elegant La Provence eschews heavy traditional French cream sauces in favor of carefully married herbs and spices. The second-story terrace is filled with tables and sets a lovely mood on balmy desert evenings, whether or not it "subtly infuses the diner with an elevated sense of tranquility," as the restaurant pretentiously promises.

The menu offers some expected items—escargots in mushroom caps, seafood bouillabaisse, steak au poivre, as well as inventive pastas like wild mushroom raviolis in a sun-dried tomato and sweet onion sauce. Like Palmie (see "Worth a Splurge," below), La Provence is run by French expatriates who've brought their culinary expertise to the desert.

Las Casuelas Terraza. 222 S. Palm Canyon Dr., Palm Springs. ☎ **619/325-2794.** Reservations recommended on weekends. Main courses $7–$13. AE, DC, DISC, MC, V. Mon–Thurs 11am–10pm, Fri–Sat 11am–11pm, Sun 10am–10pm. CLASSIC MEXICAN.

The original Las Casuelas is still open, a tiny storefront several blocks from this popular *terraza* (terrace) offspring, but the bougainvillea-draped front patio here is a much better place to people-watch over Mexican standards like quesadillas, enchiladas, and mountainous nachos washed down with equally supersize margaritas. Inside the action heats up with live music and raucous happy-hour crowds. During hot weather the patio and even sidewalk passersby are cooled by the restaurant's well-placed misters, making this a perfect late-afternoon, early evening choice.

Livreri's. 350 Indian Canyon Dr. (between Tahquitz & Ramon), Palm Springs. ☎ **619/327-1419.** Reservations recommended. Pizza, pasta, and main courses $8–$24. AE, MC, V. Wed–Mon 4:30–10pm. OLD-WORLD ITALIAN.

The Livreri family came to the desert from Long Island, New York, in the mid-1970s and began preparing traditional Italian cuisine served in generous portions: steaming pastas, cheesy pizzas, and garlicky seafood specialties. It's not the glamorous, old-money Sinatra spot (for that try Dominick's or Alberto's in Rancho Mirage), but it's conveniently located and satisfying. Separate rooms hold a long, leather-upholstered bar and the "Celebrity Room," where a retirement-age crowd gathers to enjoy dinner-theater performances of Broadway show tunes.

Max's Opera Cafe. 73-030 El Paseo (Monterey at Calif. 111), Palm Desert. ☎ **619/776-6635.** Reservations not accepted. Salads and sandwiches $9–$11, dinner main courses $12–$19. AE, MC, V, DISC, DC. Mon–Thurs 11:30am–10pm, Fri 11:30am–11pm, Sat 11am–11pm, Sun 11am–10pm. DELI.

There's plenty of schmaltz at this upscale deli in the Beverly Hills of the desert, from the "secret recipe" of the "Matzoh Ball Queen" to cute menu Sinatra-isms like "Luck Be a Latke Tonight." Their robust, overstuffed pastrami sandwich falls just shy of New York deli authenticity, but after 7pm nightly the place swings to opera and show tunes performed by the wait staff!

WORTH A SPLURGE

✪ **Palmie.** 276 N. Palm Canyon Dr. (across from the Hyatt), Palm Springs. ☎ **619/320-3375.** Reservations recommended. Main courses $15–$22 at dinner. AE, MC, V. Mon–Fri 11am–2pm, Mon–Sat 5:30–9:30pm. CLASSIC FRENCH.

You can't see Palmie from the street, and once you are seated inside their softly lit, lattice-enclosed dining patio, you won't see the bustle outside anymore either. Art deco posters of French seaside resorts abound, transporting you to the cozy bistro of owners Martine and Alain Clerc. Chef Alain sends out dishes of traditional French masterpieces such as bubbling cheese soufflé, green lentil salad dotted with pancetta, steak au poivre rich with cognac sauce, and lobster raviolis garnished with caviar; every carefully garnished plate is a work of art. To the charming background strains of French chanteuses, hostess/manager Martine circulates between tables, determined that all should enjoy their meals as much as the loyal regulars she greets by name. Forget your cardiologist for one night, and don't leave without sampling dessert: Our favorite is the trio of petite crème brûlées, flavored with ginger, vanilla, and Kahlua.

DRINKS & SNACKS

Lalajava. 300 N. Palm Canyon Dr. (corner of Amado), Palm Springs. ☎ 619/325-3494. Coffee drinks $1.25–$3.75. MC, V ($10 minimum). Sun–Thurs 7:30am–7pm, Fri 7:30am–10pm, Sat 7:30am–11pm.

Do you know the difference between an espresso, latte, and macchiato? The cheerful staff at Lalajava will help you navigate their extensive menu of coffee items that run the gamut from steaming hot cappuccinos to blended ice mochas, including flavored lattes, mochas, and cocoas. Nibble on a fresh muffin or bagel with plain or honey-walnut cream cheese, and you'll be well prepared for your day.

ICE CREAM

Swenson's Ice Cream Parlor. 204 S. Palm Canyon Dr., Palm Springs. ☎ 619/325-7073. Cones and sundaes $1.50–$5. No credit cards. Daily 11am–9pm.

Still reliable for creamy sundaes and shakes featuring their signature ice cream flavors Swiss Orange Chip and Sticky Chewy Chocolate, Swenson's is conveniently located in the center of town. There's also a second location in the **Palm Desert Town Center,** Calif. 111 at Monterey (☎ 619/340-6229).

PALM SPRINGS AFTER DARK

Every month a different club or disco is the hot spot in the Springs, and the best way to tap into the trend is by consulting *The Desert Guide, The Bottom Line* (see "Gay Life in Palm Springs," above), or one of the many other free newsletters available from area hotels and merchants. **VillageFest** (see "Shopping," above) turns Palm Canyon Drive into an outdoor party each Thursday night; here are a few more of the enduring arts and entertainment attractions around the desert resorts.

Cactus Corral. 67–501 Calif. 111, Cathedral City. ☎ 619/321-8558. Limited summer days 6pm–2am; call ahead for exact days.

Billing itself as "the Coachella Valley's Country Music Nightclub," the Cactus Corral has stood the test of time with billiards, sports bar, and live country bands, plus firewater and good, greasy grub. Early in the evening they offer Western-style dance lessons.

The Fabulous Palm Springs Follies. At the Plaza Theatre, 128 S. Palm Canyon Dr., Palm Springs. ☎ 619/327-0225.

This vaudeville-style show filled with lively production numbers is celebrating its fifth year of running in the historic Plaza Theatre in the heart of Palm Springs. With a cast of energetic retired showgirls, singers, dancers, and comedians, this revue has been enormously popular around town. Call for show schedule. Tickets range from $25 to $37.

McCallum Theatre for the Performing Arts. 73–000 Fred Waring Dr., Palm Desert. ☎ 619/340-ARTS.

For urban sophisticates who move to the Palm Springs desert, the McCallum Theatre offers the only cultural high road around. Frequent symphony performances with visiting virtuosos such as conductor Seiji Ozawa or violinist Itzhak Perlman, musicals like Tommy Tune's *Grease,* and pop performers like The Captain and Tennille or The Ink Spots are among the theater's recent offerings. Call for upcoming event information.

Touché Restaurant and Nightclub. 42–250 Bob Hope Dr., Rancho Mirage. ☎ 619/773-1111. Wed–Sun from 6:30pm.

Run by the same team who keep Melvyn's piano lounge (at the Ingleside Inn) one of the desert's "in" spots for the old money/celebrity set, Touché offers dining and dancing in the old style, and hip devotees of the "cocktail nation" movement can be seen swinging alongside perfectly coifed retirees.

3 Joshua Tree National Park

by John McKinney

For many visitors to Joshua Tree National Park, the trees themselves are not only the essence but the whole of their park experience. The park is much more than a tableau of twisted yucca, however, for it beckons the explorer with a diversity of desert environments, including sand dunes, native palm oases, cactus gardens, and jumbles of jumbo granite.

The Joshua trees' distribution defines the very boundaries of the Mojave Desert. Here in their namesake national park, they reach the southernmost limit of their range.

Sometimes known as the "in between" desert because of its location between the Mojave and the Colorado deserts, the parkland shares characteristics of each. The mountainous, Joshua tree–studded Mojave Desert is relatively cooler, wetter, and higher; it forms the northern and western parts of the park. Hotter, drier, lower, and characterized by a wide variety of desert flora including ironwood, smoketree, and native California fan palms, the Colorado Desert comprises the southern and eastern sections of the park. Cacti, especially cholla and ocotillo, thrive in the more southerly Colorado Desert (a part of the larger Sonoran Desert).

During the 1920s, a worldwide fascination with the desert emerged, and cactus gardens were very much in vogue. Entrepreneurs hauled truckloads of desert plants into Los Angeles for quick sale or export. The Mojave was in danger of being picked clean of its cacti, yucca, and ocotillo. Wealthy socialite Minerva Hoyt organized the International Desert Conservation League to halt this destructive practice. Almost single-handedly, she successfully lobbied for the establishment of Joshua Tree National Monument in 1936.

In 1994, under provisions of the federal California Desert Protection Act, Joshua Tree was "upgraded" to national park status and expanded by a quarter-million acres.

The Joshua tree is said to have been given its name by early Mormon settlers traveling West. The tree's upraised limbs and bearded appearance reminded them of the prophet Joshua leading them to the promised land.

Other observers were not so kind. Explorer John C. Fremont called it "the most repulsive tree in the vegetable kingdom." Nature writer Charles Francis Saunders opined: "The trees themselves were as grotesque as the creations of a bad dream; the shaggy trunks and limbs were twisted and seemed writhing as though in pain, and dagger-pointed leaves were clenched in bristling fists of inhospitality."

Despite its harsh appearance, the Joshua tree belongs to the lily family. Like lilies and other flowers, it must be pollinated in order to reproduce. The Tegeticula moth does the job for the Joshua tree, which in turn provides seeds for the newly hatched larvae of the moth. Long ago, during the evolutionary history of the Mojave Desert, the Joshua tree and the moth joined together to produce a partnership that continues to this day.

The trees grow at the foot of mountain slopes and capture the surface and groundwater draining from higher elevations. Once in a while you'll see a Joshua tree clumsily embrace one of its fellows but, generally, its water requirements keep it distant from other trees. Pale yellow, lilylike flowers festoon the limbs of the Joshuas when they bloom (depending on rainfall) in March, April, or May.

Area Code Change Notice

Please note that, effective March 22, 1997, the area code for the Southern California desert areas is scheduled to change to **760.** You will be able to dial 619 until September 27, 1997, after which you will have to use 760.

SEEING THE HIGHLIGHTS

An excellent first stop is the main **Oasis Visitor Center,** located alongside the Oasis of Mara, also known as the Twentynine Palms Oasis. For many generations, the native Serrano lived at this "place of little springs and much grass." Get maps, books and the latest in road, trail, and weather conditions before beginning your tour.

Two paved roads explore the heart of the park. The first loops through the high northwest section, visiting Queen and Lost Horse Valleys, as well as the awesome boulder piles at Jumbo Rocks and Wonderland of Rocks. The second angles northwest-southeast across the park and crosses both the Mojave Desert Joshua tree woodland and cactus gardens of the Colorado Desert.

From Oasis Visitor Center, drive south to **Jumbo Rocks,** which captures the complete essence of the park: a vast array of rock formations, a Joshua tree forest, the yucca-dotted desert open and wide. Check out Skull Rock (one of the many rocks in the area that appear to resemble humans, dinosaurs, monsters, cathedrals, and castles) via a 1½-mile-long nature trail that provides an introduction to the park's flora, wildlife, and geology.

In Queen Valley, just west of Jumbo Rocks, is the signed beginning of **Geology Tour Road,** a rough dirt road (four-wheel drive recommended) extending 18 miles into the heart of the park. Motorists get close-up looks at the considerable erosive forces that shaped this land, forming the flattest of desert playas, or dry lake beds, as well as massive heaps of boulders that tower over the valley floor. Geology Tour Road also delivers a Joshua tree woodland, a historic spring, abandoned mines, and some fascinating native petroglyphs.

Farther west of Jumbo Rocks is **Indian Cave,** typical of the kind of shelter sought by the nomadic Cahuilla and Serrano Indian clans that traveled this desert land. A number of bedrock mortars found in the cave suggest its use as a work site by its aboriginal inhabitants. A 4-mile round-trip trail climbs through a lunar landscape of rocks and Joshua trees to the top of 5,470-foot Ryan Mountain. Your reward for making this climb is one of the park's best panoramic views.

At Cap Rock Junction, the paved park road swings north toward the **Wonderland of Rocks,** 12 square miles of massive jumbled granite. This curious maze of stone hides groves of Joshua trees, trackless washes, and several small pools of water.

The easiest and certainly the safest way to explore the Wonderland is to follow the 1¼-mile Barker Dam Loop Trail. The first part of the journey is on a nature trail that interprets botanical highlights; the second part visits some native petroglyphs and a little lake created a century ago by cattle ranchers.

From Cap Rock Junction, dirt Keys View Road dead-ends at mile-high **Keys View.** From the crest of the Little San Bernardino Mountains, enjoy grand desert views that encompass both the highest (Mt. San Gorgonio) and lowest (Salton Sea) points in Southern California.

Pinto Basin Road tours the Colorado Desert side of the park. **Cholla Cactus Garden** preserves an unusually thick concentration of cholla, often called teddy-bear

This Is Our Life: The Roy Rogers & Dale Evans Museum

Passing through Victorville, it's tough to miss a log fort visible from I-15, with the words "Roy Rogers and Dale Evans Museum" emblazoned on the side, Las Vegas–style: larger than life, brightly lit, embellished with stars.

Fans of cowboy lore, Western movies, or country music can all tell you the museum is legendary for being the final resting place of Roy's faithful horse Trigger, whom he had stuffed and mounted. For company, Trigger has Buttermilk (Dale's golden horse), Bullet (their canine companion), and a veritable Noah's Ark of taxidermy—Roy's trophies from safaris in every corner of the globe.

These are among the many surprises awaiting visitors to the museum, a glorified attic containing the relics and souvenirs of two lifetimes. The displays are folksy, accented by tags saying "my first cowboy boots" (bronzed, of course), "the 1923 Dodge I came to California in, in 1930," and other personal remarks. But because of Roy and Dale's wealth, years of travel, varied interests, and an apparent inability to throw anything away, this museum truly has something for everyone. Some of the highlights are:

- Beautifully arranged cases commemorating three of Roy and Dale's children who died in childhood. On display are photos, toys, letters, and report cards, as well as the inspirational books written in tribute by Dale Evans Rogers after each of their deaths. The Rogers's many living children and grandchildren are also well represented; in fact, by the end of your visit you might feel as if you know the whole family personally!

- Gifts from the couple's fans all over the world, including a pair of stitched samplers framed near the entrance, containing poetic tributes both epic and homespun.

- Every piece of Roy Rogers and/or Dale Evans merchandise from over the years: comic books, breakfast cereal boxes, fan club items, war effort promotions, and more. See the 1950s era "den/playroom" filled with vintage furniture and littered with dozens of Roy and Dale toys, storybooks, dolls, model horses, and board games.

- Roy's personal collection of Western memorabilia from his role models—real-life and movie cowboys—includes Tom Mix's director's chair, Buck Jones's saddle, Hoot Gibson's piano, and last but not least, an autographed picture of Lee Majors (remember him in *The Big Valley?*).

The museum is open daily from 9am to 5pm except Thanksgiving and Christmas. For more information call **619/243-4547.**

—Stephanie Avnet

cactus because of the soft, fluffy appearance of its spines. Don't be deceived; the spines stick in the skin with only the lightest touch.

Pinto Basin is, to say the least, forbidding: a barren lowland surrounded by austere mountains and punctuated by trackless sand dunes. Nevertheless, some 2,000 to 4,000 years ago, a hardy group of natives managed to live here by forging some specialized tools; so unique were these ancients that anthropologists describe them as "Pinto Man." Try to imagine how even the most primitive people could have survived in the harsh environs of Pinto Basin as you enjoy a mellow stroll to a group of low sand dunes.

HIKING, ROCK CLIMBING & MOUNTAIN BIKING

HIKING The national park holds a couple of California's loveliest palm oases. **Fortynine Palms Oasis Trail** (3 miles round-trip) winds up and over a hot rocky crest to the dripping springs, pools, and the blessed shade of palms and cottonwoods.

Cottonwood Spring, near the south end of the park is a little palm and cottonwood-shaded oasis that attracts desert birds and bird-watchers. From Cottonwood Campground, a 3-mile round-trip trail leads to the old Mastodon Gold Mine, then climbs behemoth-looking Mastodon Peak for a view from Mt. San Jacinto above Palm Springs to the Salton Sea.

Lost Palms Oasis Trail (8 miles round-trip) visits the park's premier palm grove.

Black Rock Canyon Trail (6 miles round-trip) follows a classic desert wash, then ascends to the crest of the Little San Bernardino Mountains at Warren Peak. Desert and mountain views from the peak are stunning.

Lost Horse Mine Trail (3¹/₂ miles round-trip) visits one of the area's most successful gold mines and offers a close-up look back into a colorful era and some fine views into the heart of the park.

ROCK CLIMBING From Hidden Valley to the Wonderland of Rocks, the park has emerged as one of the world's premier rock-climbing destinations. The park offers some 3,000 climbing routes, ranging from the easiest of bouldering to some of the sport's most difficult technical climbs. During the November through May climbing season, the superstars of the sport from Europe, Japan, and America can be seen surmounting flared chimneys and difficult jam cracks.

MOUNTAIN BIKING Although they are not encouraged by park officials, mountain bikes are a good tool for touring Joshua Tree. Much of the park is designated wilderness, meaning mountain bikes are limited to roads; they will damage the fragile ecosystem if you venture off the beaten track. Try the 18-mile **Geology Tour Road.** Hammer out the miles on the rarely traveled, rough washboard roads in **Hidden Valley** and **Queen Valley.**

CAMPING & ACCOMMODATIONS

Nine campgrounds scattered throughout the park offer pleasant though often spartan accommodations, just picnic tables and pit toilets for the most part. Only two have water: **Black Rock Canyon** and **Cottonwood.**

If you're staying in the Palm Springs area, it's entirely possible to make a day trip to the national park. But if you'd like to stay close by and spend more time here, Twentynine Palms and Yucca Valley, just outside the north boundary of the national park on Calif. 62, offer budget to moderate lodging. In Twentynine Palms is the 71-room **Best Western Gardens Motel** (☎ 619/367-9141). In Yucca Valley is the **Yucca Inn** (☎ 619/365-3311). For a complete listing of Yucca Valley lodging, contact the **Yucca Valley Chamber of Commerce,** 56300 Twentynine Palms Highway, Yucca Valley, CA 92284 (☎ 619/365-6323).

JUST THE FACTS

No restaurants, lodging, gas stations, or stores are found within Joshua Tree National Park. In fact, water is only available from four park locations: Cottonwood Springs, Blackrock Canyon Campground, Indian Cove Ranger Station, and Oasis Visitors Center.

Yucca Valley has lots of restaurants and every fast-food franchise imaginable.

ACCESS POINTS From metropolitan Los Angeles, the usual route to the Oasis Visitor Center in Joshua Tree National Park is via I-10 to its intersection with

Calif. 62 (some 45 miles east of San Bernardino). Calif. 62 leads north and east for about 43 miles to the town of Twentynine Palms. From town, follow the park signs a short distance to the visitor center.

VISITOR CENTERS In addition to the main Oasis Visitor Center at the Twentynine Palms entrance, there is Cottonwood at the south entrance, and Black Rock Canyon, located at the campground southeast of Yucca Valley.

Oasis Visitor Center is open daily from 8am to 4:30pm except Christmas. Check here for a schedule of ranger-guided walks and evening interpretive programs. Ask about the weekend tours of the Desert Queen Ranch, once a working ranch and now part of the park.

INFORMATION For information, contact Superintendent, Joshua Tree National Park, 74485 National Park Dr., Twentynine Palms, CA 92277 (☎ **619/367-7511**).

4 Mojave National Preserve

by John McKinney

Two decades of park politicking finally ended in 1994 when President Clinton signed into law the California Desert Protection Act that transferred the East Mojave National Scenic Area, previously administered by the U.S. Bureau of Land Management, to the national park service and established the new Mojave National Preserve. Thus far, the Mojave's elevated status has not attracted hordes of sightseers.

To most Americans, the East Mojave is that vast, bleak, interminable stretch of desert to be crossed as quickly as possible while driving I-15 from Los Angeles to Las Vegas. Few realize that I-15 is the northern boundary of what desert rats have long considered the crown jewel of the California desert.

With few campgrounds, even fewer motels, and no visitors center, this land is a hard one to get to know. But it's an easy one to get to like. Its 1.4 million acres include the world's largest Joshua tree forest, wild burros and grazing cattle, spec-tacular canyons and volcanic formations, nationally honored scenic back roads and footpaths to historic mining sites, tabletop mesas, and a dozen mountain ranges.

One of the preserve's spectacular sights is the **Kelso Dunes,** the most extensive dune field in the West. The 45-square-mile formation of magnificently sculpted sand is famous for its "booming": Visitors' footsteps cause miniavalanches and the dunes to go "sha-boom-sha-boom-sha-boom." Geologists speculate that the extreme dryness of the East Mojave Desert, combined with the wind-polished, rounded nature of the individual sand grains, has something to do with their musical ability. Sometimes the low rumbling sound resembles a Tibetan gong; other times it sounds like a 1950s doo-wop musical group.

From atop the **Kelso Dunes** is a stunning view: the Kelso Mountains to the north, the Bristol Mountains to the southwest, the Granite Mountains to the south, the Providence Mountains to the east. Everywhere you look there are mountain ranges, small and large, from the jagged, red-colored spirelike Castle Peaks to the flat-topped Table Mountain. In fact, despite evidence to the contrary, most notably the stunning Kelso Dunes, the East Mojave is really a desert of mountains, not sand.

A 10-mile drive from the Kelso Dunes is **Kelso Depot,** built by Union Pacific in 1924. The Spanish Revival–style structure was designed with a red-tiled roof, graceful arches, and a brick platform. Train passengers and visitors ate meals in a restaurant nicknamed "The Beanery." The depot continued to be open for freight train crew use through the mid-1980s, although it ceased to be a railroad stop for passengers after World War II. The national park service is considering refurbishing the building for use as the preserve's visitors center.

Another preserve highlight is **Cima Dome,** a 75-square-mile chunk of uplifted volcanic rock. A geological rarity, Cima has been called the most symmetrical natural dome in the United States. Another distinctive feature of the dome is its handsome rock outcroppings, the same type found in Joshua Tree National Park to the south, and a lure for rock climbers and hikers.

On and around Cima Dome grows the world's largest and densest **Joshua tree forest.** Botanists say Cima's Joshuas are more symmetrical than their cousins elsewhere in the Mojave. The dramatic colors of the sky at sunset provide a breathtaking backdrop for Cima's Joshua trees, some more than 25 feet high and several hundred years old.

A half-hour drive from the Joshuas brings the tiny, blink-and-you'll-miss-it **Nipton,** located in the northeast corner of the preserve a few miles from the California-Nevada state line. The town consists of a few houses, a general store, and the Hotel Nipton, a Southwestern-style bed-and-breakfast.

Jerry Freeman, a former hard-rock miner who purchased the entire town in 1984, says hotel occupancy is up 80% since the East Mojave became a national preserve. He and his wife, Roxanne, moved from the famous sands of Malibu to the abandoned ghost town and have gradually brought it back to life.

While you can see the lights of Vegas (50 miles away) from Nipton, this is testimonial to the clarity of the desert sky, not Nipton's proximity to civilization. The opalescent light and the spectacular sunrises and sunsets in the East Mojave are grand. And for city dwellers all too accustomed to viewing murky night skies, gazing at the Milky Way on display is a revelation. This is a place where shooting stars and constellations appear with startling clarity and the nearby New York Mountains seem sprinkled with stardust.

Hole-in-the-Wall and Mid Hills are the centerpieces of Mojave National Preserve. Both locales offer diverse desert scenery, fine campgrounds, and the feeling of being in the middle of nowhere, though in fact, they're located right in the middle of the preserve.

Linking the two sites is the preserve's best drive. In 1989, **Wildhorse Canyon Road,** which loops from Mid Hills Campground to Hole-in-the-Wall Campground, was declared the nation's first official "Back Country Byway," an honor federal agencies bestow upon America's most scenic back roads. The 11-mile, horseshoe-shaped road crosses wide-open country dotted with cholla, and in season, delicate purple, yellow, and red wildflowers. Dramatic volcanic slopes and flattop mesas tower over the low desert. I stopped to scramble among large piñon pine trees and lichen-covered granite rocks and to visit a "Devil's Garden," a grouping of several types of cactus interspersed with boulders.

Mile-high **Mid Hills,** so named because of its location halfway between the Providence and New York Mountains, recalls the Great Basin Desert topography of Nevada and Utah. Mid Hills Campground offers a grand observation point from which to gaze out at the coffee-with-cream-colored Pinto Mountains to the north and the rolling Kelso Dunes shining on the western horizon.

Hole-in-the-Wall is the kind of place Butch Cassidy and the Sundance Kid would have chosen as a hideout. This twisted maze of rocks called rhyolite is a form of crystallized red lava rock. A series of iron rings aids descent into Hole-in-the-Wall; they're not particularly difficult for those who are reasonably agile and take their time.

The heart of the new preserve—Kelso Dunes, the Joshua trees, a night at Nipton, Hole-in-the-Wall, and Mid Hills—can be viewed in a weekend. But you'll need a week just to see all the major sights and maybe a lifetime to really get to know the East Mojave. And right now, without much in the way of services, the traveler to this desert must be well prepared and self reliant. For many, it's this that makes a trip to the East Mojave an adventure.

If Mojave National Preserve attracts you, you'll want to return again and again to see the wonders of this desert, including **Caruthers Canyon,** a "botanical island" of piñon pine and juniper woodland, and **Ivanpah Valley,** which supports the largest desert tortoise population in the California Desert. You'll want to climb atop enormous volcanic cinder cones, then with flashlights crawl through narrow lava tubes; explore the ruins of Fort Piute and wonder about the lonely life of the soldiers stationed there and marvel at the ruts carved into rock by the wheels of pioneer wagon trains; and guess at the meaning of the petroglyphs left behind by the Native Americans who roamed this land long ago.

Just west of the preserve is **Afton Canyon,** often called the Grand Canyon of the Mojave. Afton Canyon, a geological wonderland sculpted by the Mojave River, is a dramatic 8-mile-long, narrow gorge with some sheer walls that rise 600 feet above the canyon floor.

Afton Canyon is one of the few places where the Mojave River runs year-round. The dependable source of water supports a variety of plants, including cottonwoods, willows, rabbit bush, smoketrees, and grasses.

HIKING & MOUNTAIN BIKING

HIKING   The climb to the top of the Kelso Dunes is 3 miles round-trip. A cool, inviting, piñon pine and juniper woodland is explored by **Caruthers Canyon Trail** (3 miles round-trip).

The longest pathway is the 8-mile (one-way) **Mid Hills to Hole-in-the-Wall Trail,** a grand tour of basin and range tabletop mesas, large piñon trees and colorful cactus. If you're not up for a long day hike, the ³/₄-mile trip from Hole-in-the-Wall Campground to Banshee Canyon and the 5-mile jaunt to Wildhorse Canyon offer some easier alternatives.

MOUNTAIN BIKING   Opportunities are as extensive as the preserve's hundreds of miles of lonesome dirt roads. The 140-mile-long historic **Mojave Road,** a rough four-wheel drive route, visits many of the most scenic areas in the East Mojave; sections of this road are excellent bike tours. Prepare well: The Mojave Road and other dirt roads are rugged routes through desert wilderness.

CAMPING

Mid Hills Campground is located in a piñon pine and juniper woodland and offers outstanding views. This mile-high camp is the coolest in the East Mojave. Nearby **Hole-in-the-Wall Campground** is perched above two dramatic canyons.

Afton Canyon Campground, 33 miles east of Barstow, can be easily reached via the Afton exit off I-15 and a well-graded 3-mile dirt road.

One of the highlights of the East Mojave Desert is camping in the open desert all by your lonesome, but certain rules apply. Call the California Desert Information Center for suggestions.

JUST THE FACTS

GETTING THERE   I-15, the major route taken between the Southern California metropolis and the state line by Las Vegas–bound travelers, extends along the northern boundary of Mojave National Preserve. I-40 is the southern access route to the East Mojave.

WHEN TO GO   Spring is a splendid time (autumn is another) to visit this desert. From March through May, temperatures are mild, the Joshua trees are in bloom, and the lower Kelso Dunes are bedecked with yellow and white desert primrose and pink sand verbena.

REGULATIONS   Most national park service regulations apply, but certain land uses permitted in Mojave National Preserve that would not be found in the more pristine national parks include cattle grazing, mining, and hunting.

INFORMATION   For further information, call **619/928-2573** or 619/733-4040, or stop into one of the information centers in Barstow and Baker (see below).

NEARBY TOWNS WITH TOURIST SERVICES

BARSTOW   The Bureau of Land Management's **California Desert Information Center,** 831 Barstow Rd., Barstow (☎ **619/255-8760**), is a logical first stop for any desert tour. Maps, brochures, information about area camping, lodging, and desert attractions, and a selection of guidebooks are available. Nature exhibits, as well as personable National Park Service and U.S. Bureau of Land Management staff are on hand to help the visitor get oriented. Open 9am to 5pm daily.

Barstow has a great many restaurants and motels. Call the **Barstow Chamber of Commerce** (☎ **619/256-8617**) for suggestions.

BAKER   Accommodations and food are available in this small desert town, a good point to fill up your gas tank and purchase supplies before entering Mojave National Preserve. Check out the world's tallest thermometer in front of the National Park Service's **Desert Visitor Center,** 72157 Baker Blvd. (☎ **619/733-4040**), which provides information about Mojave National Preserve, Death Valley National Park, and surrounding U.S. Bureau of Land Management lands; open daily from 9am to 5pm.

The **Bun Boy Coffee Shop** is open 24 hours. For a tasty surprise, stop at the **Mad Greek Restaurant.** Order a Greek salad, a souvlaki, or zucchini sticks and marvel at your good fortune; imagine finding such tasty food and pleasant surroundings in the middle of nowhere.

Inexpensive lodging can be secured at a couple of motels, including the **Bun Boy Motel** (☎ **619/733-4363**).

NIPTON   This tiny town boasts a general store and the **Hotel Nipton** (☎ **619/856-2335**), a B&B with a sitting room, two bathrooms down the hall, and four guest rooms, each going for $45 a night. Nipton is located on Nipton Road, a few miles from I-15 near the Nevada state line.

STATELINE   The aptly named town on the California-Nevada border features **Whiskey Pete's** (☎ **702/382-4388**), a casino-hotel-restaurant-truck stop in ersatz Wild West decor; it boasts of "Nevada's loosest slots." Pete's sister, **The Prima Donna Casino and Hotel** (☎ **702/386-7867**), also vies for your attention.

5 Death Valley National Park

by John McKinney

Entering Death Valley at Towne Pass, Calif. 190 crests the rolling Panamint Range and descends into Emigrant Wash. Along the road is a new sign: Death Valley National Park.

Park? Death Valley National Park? The Forty-niners, whose suffering gave the valley its name, would have howled at the notion. "Death Valley National Park" seems a contradiction in terms, an oxymoron of the great outdoors. To them, other four-letter words would have been more appropriate: gold, mine, heat, lost, dead. And the four-letter words shouted by teamsters who drove the 20-mule team borax wagons need not be repeated.

Visitors to Death Valley have long linked the Creator with the place, not as a heavenly spot, but as the closest place to Hell on earth. It's been called the land that God forgot, a land God made in anger.

Mountains stand naked, unadorned. The bitter waters of saline lakes evaporate into bizarre, razor-sharp crystal formations. Jagged canyons jab deep into the earth. Ovenlike heat, frigid cold, and the driest air imaginable combine to make this one of the most inhospitable locations in the world.

In Death Valley, the forces of the earth are exposed to view with dramatic clarity: A sudden fault and a sink became a lake. The water evaporated, leaving behind borax and above all, fantastic scenery. Although Death Valley is called a valley, in actuality it is not. Valleys are carved by rivers, but Death Valley is what geologists call a graben. Here a block of the earth's crust has dropped down along fault lines in relation to its mountain walls.

At **Racetrack Playa,** a dry lake bed, visitors puzzle over rocks that weigh as much as one-quarter ton and move mysteriously across the mud floor, leaving trails as a record of their movement. Research suggests that a combination of powerful winds and rain may skid the rocks over slick clay.

Badwater, the lowest point in the western hemisphere at 282 feet below sea level, is also one of the hottest places in the world, with regularly recorded summer temperatures of 120°F.

Death Valley is raw, bare earth, the way it must have looked before life began. Just looking out on the landscape, it's impossible to know what year, or even what century, it is.

Today's visitor to Death Valley drives in air-conditioned comfort, stays in comfortable hotel rooms or well-maintained campgrounds, orders meals and provisions at park concessions, even quaffs a cold beer at the local saloon. He or she may take a swim in the Olympic-size pool, tour a Moorish castle, shop for souvenirs, and enjoy the desert landscape while hiking along a nature trail with a park ranger.

It hasn't always been so.

Americans looking for gold in California's mountains in 1849 were forced to cross the burning sands to avoid severe snowstorms in the nearby Sierra Nevada. Some perished along the way, and the land became known as Death Valley.

Many of Death Valley's topographical features are associated with hellish images— Funeral Mountains, Furnace Creek, Dante's View, Coffin Peak, and Devil's Golf Course. But it can be a place of serenity.

In one of his last official acts, President Herbert Hoover signed a proclamation on February 11, 1933, designating Death Valley as a National Monument. With the stroke of a pen he not only legislated the protection of a vast and wondrous land, but also helped to transform one of the earth's least hospitable spots into a popular tourist destination.

The naming of Death Valley National Monument came at a time when Americans began to discover the romance of the desert. Land that had previously been considered hideously devoid of life was now celebrated for its spare beauty; places that had once been feared for their harshness were now admired for their uniqueness.

Death Valley National Park became the largest national park outside Alaska, with more than 3.3 million acres, when President Clinton signed the California Desert Protection Act of 1994. Numerous parts of the mountain ranges surrounding Death Valley, as well as two other large valleys, Eureka and Saline, were added to the park.

This land may as well be a national park because it cannot be settled and will never be tamed. The urbanization of other parts of the Mojave notwithstanding, this is a land that will never see suburbs or shopping centers. It's too naked, too harsh. It's a land that meets you face to face on its own terms—and it always wins. Formerly rich mining sites stand empty. Once-bustling towns silently crumble into dust. Broken slabs of asphalt mark where roads have been demolished by powerful flash floods.

Death Valley is an alien land, so apart from the rest of America that it may just as well be located on Mars. But this harsh land attracts visitors, more than a million a year, from all over the world. During the winter months, much of the visitation is by retired snowbirds camping in their motor homes or trailers. But during the summer months, you're more likely to hear visitors speaking German, French, or Japanese.

SEEING THE HIGHLIGHTS

A good first stop after checking in at the main park visitor center in Furnace Creek is the **Harmony Borax Works,** a rock salt landscape as tortured as you'll ever find. Death Valley prospectors called borax "white gold," and though it was not exactly a glamorous substance, it was a profitable one. From 1883 to 1888, more than 20 million pounds of borax were transported from the Harmony Borax Works. A short trail with interpretive signs leads past the ruins of the old borax refinery and some outlying buildings.

Transport of the borax was the stuff of legends, too. The famous 20-mule teams hauled the huge loaded wagons 165 miles to the rail station at Mojave. (To learn more about this colorful era, visit the Borax Museum at Furnace Creek Ranch and the park visitor center, also located in Furnace Creek.)

Salt Creek is the home of the **Salt Creek pupfish,** found nowhere else on earth. The little fish, which has made some amazing adaptations to survive in this arid land, can be glimpsed from a wooden boardwalk nature trail. In spring, a million pupfish might be wriggling in the creek; by summer's end, only a few thousand remain.

Before sunrise, photographers set up their tripods at **Zabriskie Point** and point their cameras down at the pale mudstone hills of Golden Canyon and the great valley beyond. The panoramic view of Golden Canyon is magnificent, but don't miss getting right into the canyon itself, possible only by hitting the trail.

Another grand park vista is seen at **Dante's View.** From this 5,475-foot viewpoint in the Black Mountains, one can see the Funeral Mountains, Greenwater Valley, and the shimmering Death Valley floor backed by the high Panamint Mountains.

A 14-square-mile field of dunes and some bizarre geology are some of the attractions of a visit to the **Stove Pipe Wells** area. Death Valley's dunes lie between Towne Pass on the west and Daylight Pass to the east; there's quite a sand-laden draft between the two passes. The sand in the dunes is actually tiny pieces of rock, most of them quartz fragments.

Those surreal corn stalks you see across Calif. 190 from the dunes are actually clumps of arrowweed. The **Devil's Cornstalks** are perched on wind- and water-eroded pedestals.

Mosaic Canyon, located near Stovepipe Wells, displays mosaics of water-polished white, gray, and black rock. Nature has cemented the canyon's stream gravels into mosaics large and small. It's easy to imagine you've entered an art gallery when you view the mosaics on the canyon walls; not only are nature's works of art on display, but the long, narrow, white marble walls of the canyon seem quite "gallery"-like.

Scotty's Castle, the Mediterranean-to-the-max mega-hacienda in the northern part of the park, is unabashedly Death Valley's premier tourist attraction. Visitors are wowed by the elaborate Spanish tiles, well-crafted furnishings, and innovative construction that included solar water heating. Even more compelling is the colorful history of this villa in remote Grapevine Canyon, brought to life by park rangers dressed in 1930s period clothing. Don't be surprised if the castle cook or a friend of Scotty's gives you a special insight into castle life.

Construction of the "castle"—more officially Death Valley Ranch—began in 1924. It was to be a winter retreat for eccentric Chicago millionaire Albert Johnson. The insurance tycoon's unlikely friendship with prospector/cowboy/spinner-of-tall-tales Walter Scott put the $2.3 million structure on the map and captured the public's imagination. Scotty greeted visitors and told them fanciful stories from the early hard-rock mining days of Death Valley.

The one-hour walking tour of Scotty's Castle is excellent, both for its inside look at the mansion and for what it reveals about the eccentricities of Johnson and Scotty. Tours fill up quickly; arrive early for the first available spots (there's a small fee). A snack bar and gift shop make the wait more comfortable. To learn more about the castle grounds, pick up the pamphlet "A Walking Tour of Scotty's Castle," which leads you on an exploration from stable to swimming pool, from bunkhouse to powerhouse.

Near Scotty's Castle is **Ubehebe Crater.** It is known as an explosion crater; one look and you know why. Hot magma rose from the depths of the earth to meet the ground water; the resultant steam blasted out a crater and scattered cinders.

To the native Shoshone of Death Valley, the crater was known as *Temp-pin-tta Wo' sah,* "Basket in the Rock"—an apt description indeed. A half-mile in diameter Ubehebe is not the only basket around; to the south is Little Hebe Crater and a cluster of smaller craters.

HIKING & MOUNTAIN BIKING

HIKING   The **Keane Wonder Mine Trail** (2 miles round-trip) climbs very steeply to a historic mine and terrific valley view.

Golden Canyon (5 miles round-trip) explores a colorful canyon and climbs to one of the park's grandest vistas at Zabriskie Point. The first mile of Golden Canyon Trail is a self-guided interpretive trail. At the end of the nature trail, the path branches. One fork heads for Red Cathedral, also called Red Cliffs. The red color is essentially iron oxide (rust) produced by the weathering of rocks with high iron content. Enjoy the grand view of the valley, framed by the badlands just below and the Panamint Mountains to the west.

Telescope Peak Trail (14 miles round-trip) is an all-day trek to the 11,049-foot summit, where as one pioneer declared: "You can see so far, it's just like looking through a telescope." Snow-covered during the winter, the peak is best climbed from May to November. Nearby **Wildrose Peak** (8^1/$_2$ miles round-trip) also offers an awesome panorama with somewhat less effort.

Eureka Valley Dunes, newly added to the national park, offer free-form hiking. California's highest at nearly 700-feet tall, they are a delight to roam.

MOUNTAIN BIKING   Because most (94%) of the park is federally designated wilderness, cycling is allowed only on roads used by automobiles. Cycling is not allowed on hiking trails.

Good routes for bikers include Racetrack (28 miles, mainly level), Greenwater Valley (30 miles, mostly level), Cottonwood Canyon (20 miles), and West Side Road (40 miles, fairly level with some washboard sections). Artists Drive is 8 miles long, paved, with some steep uphills. A favorite is Titus Canyon (28 miles on a hilly road—it's highly recommended that you make this a one-way descent).

CAMPING & ACCOMMODATIONS

The park's nine campgrounds are located at elevations ranging from below sea level to 8,000 feet. In Furnace Creek, Sunset offers 1,000 spaces with water and flush toilets. Furnace Creek Campground has 200 similarly appointed spaces. Stovepipe Wells has 200 spaces with water and flush toilets.

Furnace Creek Ranch (☎ 619/786-2345) has 225 no-frills cottage units with air-conditioning and showers. The swimming pool is a popular hangout for tired lodgers. Nearby are a coffee shop, cafeteria, steak house, Mexican restaurant, and general store. The **Furnace Creek Inn** (☎ 619/786-2345), an elegant resort, boasts 67 deluxe rooms with a formal dining room, heated pool, golf, and tennis courts. **Stove Pipe Wells Village** (☎ 619/786-2387) has 74 modest rooms with air-conditioning and showers.

Because accommodations in Death Valley are both limited and expensive, consider spending a night at one of the two gateway towns: **Lone Pine** on the west side of the park, and **Baker** on the south. **Beatty, Nevada,** which has inexpensive lodging, is only a 20-mile drive from the park's eastern boundary. The restored **Amargosa Hotel** (☎ 619/852-4441) in Death Valley Junction offers 14 rooms in a historic, out-of-the-way place.

JUST THE FACTS

The **Death Valley Visitor Center** at Furnace Creek, 15 miles inside the eastern park boundary on Calif. 190 (☎ 619/786-3244), offers well-done interpretive exhibits and an hourly slide program. Ask at the information desk for ranger-led nature walks and evening naturalist programs. Visitor Center hours are 8am to 7pm in the winter, 8am to 5pm in the summer.

Perhaps the most scenic entry to the park is via Calif. 190, east from Calif. 395 through Towne Pass. Another scenic drive to the park is by way of Calif. 127 and Calif. 190 from Baker.

INFORMATION For more information, contact Superintendent, **Death Valley National Park,** Death Valley, CA 92328 (☎ 619/786-2331).

17

San Diego & Environs

by Elizabeth Hansen

San Diego is best known for its benign climate and bodacious beaches, but my hometown has much more to offer than sunny skies, offshore breezes, and miles of clean sand. The sixth-largest city in the United States, San Diego is home to top-notch tourist attractions, a wide variety of dining and lodging options, and the country's best regional theater. And the best news is that this nearly perfect destination is also quite reasonably priced. In the pages that follow, I'll tell you how to cut the cost of admission at the major attractions, where to sleep and eat at moderate prices, and how to stretch your travel budget by enjoying the area's many *free* activities. Welcome to San Diego! I think you're going to have a great time.

1 Orientation

ARRIVING

BY PLANE   **San Diego International Airport,** 3707 N. Harbor Dr. (☎ 619/231-7361), locally known as Lindbergh Field, is just 3 miles from downtown. Most of the major domestic carriers fly here, including **Alaska Airlines** (☎ 800/426-0333), **American** (☎ 800/433-7300), **America West** (☎ 800/235-9292), **Continental** (☎ 800/525-0280), **Delta** (☎ 800/221-1212), **Northwest** (☎ 800/447-4747), **Southwest** (☎ 800/435-9792), **TWA** (☎ 619/295-7009), **United** (☎ 800/241-6522), and **USAir** (☎ 800/428-4322 or 619/574-6233).

Two adjacent airport terminals, "East" and "West," are both supported by a number of transportation options. San Diego Transit's Bus no. 2 stops at the center traffic aisle of the East Terminal and at the far west end of the West Terminal. The no. 2 bus runs weekdays every 20 minutes from 5:30am to midnight (every 30 minutes on weekends); the fare is $1.50. The bus connects the airport with downtown, stopping at Broadway and Fourth Avenue. Just a couple of blocks away, at Broadway and First Avenue, is the **Transit Store** (☎ **619/233-3004**), where the staff can answer your transit questions and provide free route maps to help you get where you're going.

Several shuttles run regularly from the airport to downtown hotels. They charge about $5, and you'll see designated shuttle stops outside each terminal. Taxis line up outside both terminals and charge about $8 to take you to a downtown location.

Several major car-rental companies operate at the airport, including Avis, Budget, Dollar, Hertz, and National. However, off-site agencies are less expensive (see "Getting Around," below, for details). If you're driving into the city from the airport, take Harbor Drive south to Broadway, the main east-west thoroughfare, and turn left.

BY CAR   From Los Angeles, you'll enter San Diego via coastal route I-5. From points northeast of the city, you'll come down on I-15 (link up with I-8 West and Calif. 163 South to drive into downtown). From the east, you'll come in on I-8, connecting with Calif. 163 south. (Calif. 163 turns into Tenth Avenue). The freeways are well marked, pointing the way to downtown streets.

BY TRAIN   Amtrak (☎ 800/USA-RAIL) trains connect San Diego to Los Angeles and the rest of the country. Trains pull into San Diego's pretty mission-style Santa Fe Station, (1850 Kettner Blvd. at Broadway), within walking distance of many downtown hotels and 1½ blocks from the Embarcadero.

VISITOR INFORMATION

San Diego's excellent **International Visitors Information Center,** 11 Horton Plaza (at First Avenue and F Street; ☎ 619/236-1212) offers a free San Diego visitor's guide and the **Visitor Value Pack,** which is full of money-saving coupons. The center employs a multilingual staff and sells street maps, phone cards, and the Annual Major Events Calendar. The office is open Monday through Saturday from 8:30am to 5pm; June through August it's also open Sunday from 11am to 5pm. Cybernauts can access the Visitors Guide on the San Diego Convention and Visitors Bureau's home page at **http://www.sandiego.org.** *Tip:* The Visitor Value Pack is produced annually in March and is available as long as supplies last, so request a copy by phone in March or April regardless of when you plan to visit.

    Traveler's Aid (☎ 619/231-7361) has booths at both the East and the West Terminal of the airport and at the San Diego Cruise Terminal, B Street Pier.

    Specialized visitor information outlets include the **Balboa Park Visitors Center,** 1549 El Prado (☎ 619/239-0512); **Coronado Visitor Information Center,** 1111 Orange Ave., Suite A, Coronado (☎ 800/622-8300 or 619/437-8788); **Old Town Visitor Information Center,** 4002 Wallace St. (☎ 619/220-5422); and the **Mission Bay Visitors Information Center,** 2688 E. Mission Bay Dr., San Diego, CA 92109 (☎ 619/276-8200).

    The **North County Convention and Visitors Bureau,** 720 N. Broadway, Escondido (☎ 800/848-3336 24 hours, or 619/745-4741) can provide information on La Jolla and excursion areas in San Diego County, including Escondido, Julian, and Anza Borrego State Park.

    To find out what's on at the theater and who's playing in the clubs during your visit, pick up a copy of *The Reader,* a free weekly newspaper available all over the city. There's also a Thursday entertainment supplement called *Night and Day* in the *San Diego Union-Tribune.*

CITY LAYOUT

San Diego is more a chain of separate neighborhoods than a single cohesive city, but each is well defined and relatively compact. The street system is straightforward, so getting around is fairly easy.

MAIN ARTERIES & STREETS

Interstate 5 is the most important thoroughfare in San Diego, connecting the city's divergent parts with one another and the entire region with the rest of the state. Access to the Coronado Bay Bridge is via I-5.

The San Diego Area at a Glance

N

To Oceanside & Carlsbad

To Temecula

15

Del Mar

S21

5

Torrey Pines State Beach

Torrey Pines State Reserve

Black's Beach

La Jolla Shores Beach

La Jolla Cove

La Jolla

Mt. Soledad

5

52

Windansea Beach

Pacific Beach

Clairemont

274

Mission Beach

Mission Bay Park

Sea World

8

Ocean Beach

Harbor Island

8

Old Town

209

San Diego Int'l Airport

Shelter Island

North Island

282

Point Loma

Coronado

75

Silver Strand State Beach

Chula Vista Wildlife Reserve

Imperial Beach

Mira Mesa

Miramar

Miramar Naval Air Station

River

52

San Diego

Mission Trails Regional Park

Lake Murray

Fletcher Pkwy

15

La Mesa

125

163

Balboa Park

805

15

94

Sweetwater Reservoir

National City

South Bay Fwy

S17

5

Chula Vista

805

117

San Ysidro

Pacific Ocean

San Diego Bay

Tijuana

Tijuana Int'l Airport

Agua Caliente

I D

1-0856

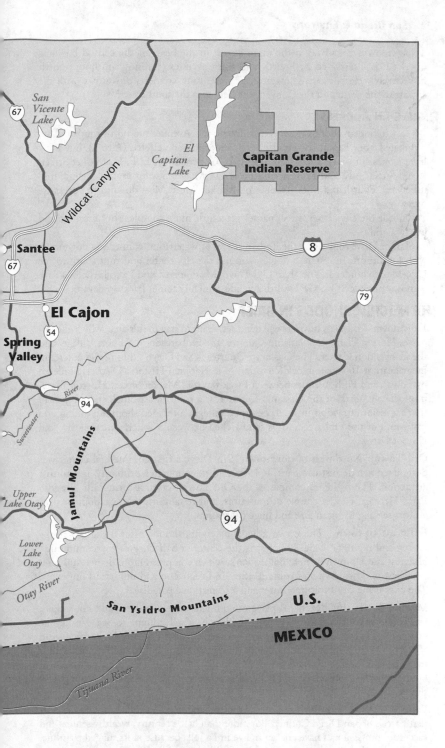

San Vicente Lake

67

Wildcat Canyon

El Capitan Lake

Capitan Grande Indian Reserve

8

79

Santee

67

El Cajon

54

Spring Valley

Sweetwater

River

94

Jamul Mountains

Upper Lake Otay

Lower Lake Otay

Otay River

94

San Ysidro Mountains

U.S.

MEXICO

Tijuana River

Downtown, Broadway is the main street; in the heart of the central business district it is intersected by Fourth and Fifth avenues (running south and north respectively). Harbor Drive, hugging the waterfront, connects downtown with the airport to the north and the Convention Center to the south.

FINDING AN ADDRESS

It's easy to find an address when you're downtown. Avenues run north-south and are numbered from 1 to 12. Streets run east-west; most are lettered (A to L), but a few have names. In order, the streets are: A, B, C, Broadway, E, F, G, Market Street, Island Street, J, K, and L. If the address is 411 Market St., for example, you'll find it between Fourth and Fifth Avenues on Market Street. Most downtown streets are one way.

Outside the city center, street names get a little more complex, but most are laid out in a grid.

Harbor Drive runs along the Embarcadero, or waterfront, connecting downtown with the airport. Interstate 5 doglegs around the city center and runs south to the U.S.-Mexico border and north to Old Town, Mission Bay, and La Jolla. Balboa Park is most easily accessible via Twelfth Avenue, which becomes Park Boulevard.

THE NEIGHBORHOODS IN BRIEF

Downtown   Business travelers will definitely want to stay in this area, which encompasses Horton Plaza, the Gaslamp Quarter, the Embarcadero, Seaport Village, and the Convention Center. The **Gaslamp Quarter** is San Diego's dining and entertainment heart, a 16-square-block Victorian-style National Historic District, bordered by Fourth and Fifth Avenues between Broadway and Market Street. **Horton Plaza,** immediately north of the Gaslamp Quarter, is a colorful six-block shopping mall that's a major attraction in itself. **Seaport Village,** a themed shopping/dining area just south of the Embarcadero, is sandwiched between a waterfront walkway and Harbor Drive.

Old Town   Northwest of downtown, San Diego's first commercial center was designated a state historic park in 1968 and now operates primarily as a tourist attraction. The region encompasses the Old Town State Historic Park, Presidio Park, Heritage Park, a couple of museums, and restaurants that are popular with visitors seeking Mexican fare and huge Margaritas.

Hillcrest/Uptown   These two adjacent neighborhoods offer a slightly funky dining and nightlife scene. Hillcrest is the center of San Diego's gay community. Hillcrest and Uptown lie near Balboa Park, which comprises more than 1,400 acres northeast of downtown and contains the San Diego Zoo and numerous museums. The park is the city's cultural center and a recreational paradise.

Mission Bay/Pacific Beach   A playground for swimmers, boaters, and sun-seekers, this is one of your options for hitting the beach. It's also home to Sea World, one of San Diego's top attractions. The area between Mission Bay and the Pacific Ocean is one of the city's most colorful regions, known for its nightlife and hip, casual dining. The boardwalk runs from South Mission Beach through Pacific Beach (known by the common abbreviation "PB") and is popular for in-line skating, biking, and sunset watching.

La Jolla   About 12 miles north of downtown San Diego, La Jolla is one of the prettiest parcels of San Diego County. For more than half a century, wealthy seniors and successful professionals have chosen to live in La Jolla because of its rugged coastline, lush landscaping, good restaurants, beautiful homes, great beaches, and proximity to the city. La Jolla still retains its "old-money" image despite its openness to adventurous yuppies, immigrants from various foreign countries, and retirees from the Midwest. The University of California San Diego and the Museum of Contemporary Art are here.

Coronado   Coronado is actually an incorporated city in its own right, but we have included it as a neighborhood because it's so easily reached from downtown San Diego. It's a lovely, upscale community, full of retired naval officers; here you'll find a terrific beach, several good restaurants, and the famed Hotel del Coronado.

2 Getting Around

BY CAR

Traffic is heavy on the freeways during rush hours, but in general, the city is pretty easy to negotiate.

Many streets run one way, which may hamper you until you learn the lay of the land. The map from the International Visitor Information Center or the AAA ones are extremely helpful, since arrows indicate which way each street runs.

You can turn right on a red light unless a sign at the intersection indicates otherwise.

RENTALS   All the large national car-rental firms have counters at the airport, in the major hotels, and at other locations around the city. However, frugal travelers will want to check out some of the local companies that don't allow one-way rentals, but are usually cheaper for use around the area. For instance, **Dirt Cheap Car Rental,** 2559 Kettner Blvd., San Diego (☎ **619/234-9300**), rents used compact cars for about $119 a week (including 100 free miles a day). Their vehicles must stay in San Diego County, and renters must be 21 or over. Another good-value company is **7 Days Rent-A-Car** (☎ **619/455-1644;** fax 619/455-1757), which delivers their compact cars to customers age 21 or over. Their rate changes seasonally, but is usually around $19.95 a day (including 100 miles) or $119 a week (including 500 miles), and their cars can be driven anywhere in California or to Las Vegas or Mexico with permission. Before deciding where to rent you should also check with **Bargain Auto Rentals,** 3860 Rosecrans St. (☎ **619/299-0009;** fax 619/299-9057). Their daily rate for used compacts is $16.95 a day with 150 free miles or $95 a week with 500 miles, and the minimum age for renters is 18. Bargain's cars can go to Mexico, but no farther north than Santa Barbara and not east of the state border.

If you plan to drive to Mexico, it's essential that you rent from a company that allows their cars south of the border. In addition to the ones mentioned above, **Avis** (☎ **619/231-7155**) and **Courtesy Auto Rentals** (☎ **800/252-9756** or 619/ 497-4800) allow their cars into Mexico. Most companies that allow their cars to be driven in Mexico limit travel to as far as Ensenada, several hours beyond the border. However, you must stop before crossing the border and buy Mexican auto insurance. You would also be *very* wise to buy insurance if you drive your own car into Mexico.

PARKING   For the most part you'll find plenty of metered parking on San Diego streets. Things tighten up downtown, where you'll probably have to put your car in an enclosed garage. The one at Horton Plaza, G Street and Fourth Avenue, is free to shoppers for the first three hours, then costs $1 for each additional hour; it's free daily after 5pm. The parking lot at G Street and Sixth Avenue charges $3.25 for the day and $3 at night and on weekends and holidays.

BY PUBLIC TRANSPORTATION

BY BUS   San Diego has an adequate, but not remarkable, bus system that will get you where you're going, eventually. Most drivers are friendly and helpful and have a good rapport with their passengers. The system, which includes 101 routes in the greater San Diego area, provides a special plus for travelers: the **Transit Store** (102 Broadway, at First Avenue). This information center supplies passes, tokens, timetables, maps, brochures, lost-and-found information, and ID cards for disabled travelers and seniors 60 and older (who pay only 75¢ per ride). Request a copy of the useful brochure *Your Open Door to San Diego*, which details the city's most popular tourist attractions and the buses that take you to them. You can also call the helpful **Regional Transit Information** (☎ 619/233-3004 or, for the hearing impaired, TTY/TDD 619/234-5005) and tell them where you are and where you want to go—they'll tell you the nearest appropriate bus stop and what time the next couple of buses will pass by. If you know your route and just need schedule information, call **619/685-4900** from any touch-tone phone. You can call between 5:30am and 8:30pm daily except Thanksgiving and Christmas. The line is often busy, and the best times to call are noon to 3pm and on weekends. The Transit Store office is open Monday through Friday from 8:30am to 5:30pm, and Saturday and Sunday from noon to 4pm.

Dedicated budgeteers may want to plot their way around the city before arrival. If that's the case, send $1 to **MTDB**, 1255 Imperial Ave., Suite 100, San Diego, CA 92101-7490, and request a copy of the Regional Transit Map.

Bus stops are marked by rectangular blue signs every other block or so on local routes. More than 20 bus routes pass through the downtown area, among them nos. 2, 4, 7, 9, 29, 34, and 901. Local fare is $1.50 one way and you must have the exact change ($1 bills are accepted); express buses, whose numbers end in "0," cost $1.75. Route timetables let you know exactly when the buses will pass by; often it's every 15 to 20 minutes. Board buses through the front door and exit through the rear.

You can get a **transfer** at no extra charge as long as you continue on a bus or trolley with an equal or lower fare (if it's higher, you simply pay the difference). Transfers must be used within an hour, and you can actually loop back to where you started as long as you use a different route on a different timetable.

A particular saving is the **Day Tripper** pass, which allows unlimited rides on any Metropolitan Transit System bus or trolley route for one day for only $5 (four days for $15). These passes also provide free passage on the San Diego–Coronado ferry. Buses that go to popular tourist attractions include nos. 7, 7A, 7B, 1, 3, and 25 to Balboa Park; nos. 7, 7A, and 7B to the San Diego Zoo and Seaport Village; nos. 9 and 34 to Kemper and Midway, then no. 6 to the Cabrillo National Monument; no. 9 to Sea World and Pacific Beach; no. 2 to the Maritime Museum at the Embarcadero; and nos. 5, 6, 8, 9, 26, 28, 34, 35, 81, and 5/105 to Old Town. No. 2 goes to the airport, and nos. 30 and 34 go to Mission Beach and La Jolla. Most buses serving the downtown area pass by or close to Horton Plaza; double-check with the driver just to be sure.

BY TRAIN   The **Coaster** (☎ 800/COASTER) travels between downtown and Oceanside, with stops en route at Old Town, Sorrento Valley, Solana Beach, Encinitas, and Carlsbad. Fares range from $4.75 to $6.20 round-trip, depending how far you go (senior fares are lower); it takes an hour to get to Oceanside from downtown. Trains run Monday to Saturday; call for current schedule. **Amtrak** service (☎ 800/USA-RAIL) from San Diego to Los Angeles stops at Solana Beach, Oceanside, San Juan Capistrano, and Anaheim (Disneyland), on its way up the coast. Round-trip tickets to Oceanside, San Juan Capistrano, and Anaheim are $18, $22, and $28, respectively.

BY TROLLEY   The bright-red **San Diego Trolley** is both fun to ride and an efficient form of transportation. There are two trolley lines: the East Line, which runs between Centre City and El Cajon/Santee, and the North-South Line, which runs between Old Town and the U.S. Border at San Ysidro. In December 1997, a third line will open from Old Town through Mission and Fashion Valleys to the Stadium (just in time for the '97 Holiday Bowl).

Downtown trolley stops include C Street at 5th Avenue, the Civic Center on C Street at Third Avenue, America Plaza, Santa Fe Station, County Center/Little Italy, Seaport Village, the Convention Center West, and Gaslamp Quarter/Convention Center. Trolleys operate on a self-service fare collection system: Before boarding, passengers purchase tickets from machines at the trolley stops. The machines list fares for each destination and should give you your ticket and any change you require, after you push the button to specify how much you are paying. (Some machines require exact change.) Tickets are good for two hours from the time of purchase in one direction only except in the "Center Zone" where the ticket is good in any direction. Fare inspectors randomly board trains and check proof of payment.

Trolleys generally run every 15 minutes (the North-South Line operates every 10 minutes during weekday morning and evening rush hours) and stop for less than half a minute at each stop; to board, push the lighted green button beside the doors. Stations are announced as the trolley approaches them. To exit the car, push the lighted white button beside the doors if they do not open automatically. Trolley travel within the downtown area costs $1; the fare to the border is $1.75. Senior citizens 60 and over and disabled riders pay a flat fee of 75¢, and children five and under ride free. For recorded trolley information, call **619/231-8549;** to get a real person on the line, call **619/233-3004** or TTY/TDD 619/234-5005 from 5:30am to 8:30pm daily. The trolley generally operates daily from 5am to about 12:30am, although the San Ysidro line runs 24 hours on Saturday.

BY FERRY & WATER TAXI   There's regularly scheduled ferry service between San Diego and Coronado (☎ **619/234-4111** for information). It's a 15-minute ride. Ferries leave from the Broadway Pier on the hour from 9am to 9pm Sunday through Thursday and from 9am to 10pm Friday and Saturday. They return from the Old Ferry Landing in Coronado to San Diego every hour on the half hour 9:30am to 9:30pm Sunday through Thursday and from 9:30am to 10:30pm Friday and Saturday. The fare is $2 one way (50¢ extra if you bring your bike). MTS Day Tripper Pass-holders ride the ferry for free. Purchase tickets in advance at the Harbor Excursion kiosk on the pier in San Diego or at the Old Ferry Landing in Coronado. Water taxis (☎ **619/235-TAXI**) will take you anywhere you want to go on San Diego Bay for $5.

BY TAXI

Cab companies don't have standardized rates, except from the airport into town, which costs $1.80 per mile. Taxis may be hailed in the street, but you'll be lucky if you can find one; phone for a guaranteed pick-up. Companies include **Orange Cab** (☎ 619/291-3333), **San Diego Cab** (☎ 619/226-TAXI), and **Yellow Cab** (☎ 619/ 234-6161). The **Coronado Cab Company** (☎ 619/435-6211) serves Coronado. In La Jolla use **La Jolla Cab** (☎ 619/453-4222).

BY TOUR TROLLEY

The **Old Town Trolley,** 4040 Twiggs St. (☎ **619/298-8687**), is not a trolley at all; it's a privately operated open-air tour bus that travels in a continuous loop around the city, providing access to sightseeing highlights.

It stops at more than a dozen places and you can hop on and off as many times as you please during one entire loop (but once you've completed the circuit, you can't go around again). A nonstop tour takes 90 minutes and is accompanied by a fast-moving live commentary on city history and sights. Major stops include Old Town, Presidio Park, Bazaar del Mundo, Balboa Park, the San Diego Zoo, the Embarcadero, Seaport Village, and the Gaslamp Quarter. Old Town Trolley is the only company allowed on military bases in San Diego. Their passengers view the ships at Naval Station San Diego, ride alongside an aircraft carrier at North Island Naval Air Station, or see recruits undergoing training at the Marine Corps Recruit Depot (MCRD). City tours operate daily from 9am to 5pm in summer, to 4pm the rest of the year; they cost $17 for adults and $8 for children 6 to 12; kids under five ride free. For information on base tours call **800/NAVY-TOUR.** There's usually a discount coupon in the Visitor Value Pack (see "Visitor Information," above).

BY BICYCLE

San Diego is great for bikers; it's pretty flat and many roads have designated bike lanes. If you didn't bring your own wheels, you can rent from **Pennyfarthing's,** 314 G St. in the Gaslamp Quarter (☎ 619/233-7696), or **Hamel's Action Sports Center,** 704 Ventura Place, off Mission Boulevard at the roller coaster in North Mission Beach (☎ 619/488-5050). In Coronado, there's **Bikes and Beyond** at the Old Ferry Landing (☎ 619/435-7180).

If a bus stop has a bike-route sign attached (not all of them do), you can place your bike on the bus's bike rack for free while you ride. The San Diego Trolley also allows bikes on board for free during certain hours. You just need a bike permit, which is available for $4 from the **Transit Store,** 102 Broadway (☎ 619/234-1060). Bikes can be brought aboard the San Diego–Coronado ferry as well.

FAST FACTS: San Diego

American Express   A convenient downtown office is at 258 Broadway (☎ 619/ 234-4455), open Monday through Friday from 9am to 5pm.

Dentists/Doctors   For dental referrals, contact the **San Diego County Dental Society** at 800/201-0244 or call 800/DENTIST. **Hotel Docs** (☎ 619/275-2663) is a 24-hour network of physicians, dentists, optometrists, chiropractors, and podiatrists who'll come to your hotel room within 45 minutes of your call. They accept credit cards and their services are covered by most insurance policies.

Emergencies   For police, fire, highway patrol, or life-threatening medical emergencies, dial **911** from any phone. No coins are required.

Hospitals   **UCSD Medical Center,** 200 W. Arbor Dr. in Hillcrest (☎ 619/ 543-6400), has the best-located, almost-downtown emergency room. **Coronado Hospital,** 250 Prospect Place (☎ 619/435-6251), is a good pick in Coronado. In La Jolla, bring your bruises to **Scripps Memorial,** 9888 Genesee Ave. (☎ 619/ 457-4123).

Information   See "Visitor Information," earlier in this chapter.

Liquor Laws   Liquor shops, grocery stores, and most supermarkets sell packaged alcoholic beverages between 6am and 2am. Most restaurants, nightclubs, and bars are licensed to serve alcoholic beverages during the same hours. The legal age for purchase and consumption is 21, and it is strictly enforced.

Newspapers/Magazines   The *San Diego Union-Tribune* is published daily, and its informative entertainment section, *Night and Day,* is in the Thursday edition. *The Reader,* published weekly (on Thursday), is more alternative and offers dining and entertainment information, too. *San Diego* magazine is also filled with extensive entertainment and dining listings. The free *San Diego This Week* has restaurant listings and information about shopping, attractions, nightlife, and the latest goings-on about town.

Police   In an emergency, dial **911** from any phone. No coins are needed. For other matters, contact the downtown precinct, 1401 Broadway (☎ **619/531-2000**).

Post Office   The main post office, 2535 Midway Dr., San Diego, CA 92110 (☎ **800/333-8777**), is between Barnett Avenue and Rosecrans Street. It's open to 1am Monday through Friday. A convenient downtown branch is at 815 E St. (open Monday through Friday from 8:30am to 5pm and Saturday from 8:30am to noon).

Safety   As cities go, San Diego is pretty safe. But use particular caution on beaches after dark (romantic as they may seem), and stay on designated walkways and away from secluded areas in Balboa Park, night or day. In the Gaslamp Quarter, don't wander east of 5th Avenue.

Taxes   A 7.75% sales tax is applied at the register to all goods and services purchased in San Diego. The city hotel tax is 10.5%.

Transit Information   Public transportation is operated by the **Metropolitan Transit System** (☎ **619/233-3004**). See "Getting Around" in this chapter for complete information.

Useful Telephone Numbers   Time (☎ **619/853-1212**); local highway conditions (☎ **800/427-7623**).

Weather   For local weather information and surf reports, call **619/289-1212**.

3 Accommodations

San Diego offers the cost-conscious traveler a good selection of lodgings. Remember to factor in the city's 10.5% hotel tax and to keep in mind that rates are often higher in summer (especially true of beach hotels). Also keep in mind that hotel rates are usually negotiable. When you call to make a reservation, ask for the off-season discount, the AAA discount, the AARP discount, the midweek rate, the long-stay rate, and the senior or military discount—whatever is applicable. If you can't wheedle a better price, see if any packages are available. Some motels, for instance, offer a deal that includes passes to the zoo. The Dine-A-Mate coupon book (see ordering instructions in "Dining," below) also offers hotel discounts, as does the Visitor Value Pack (mentioned in "Visitor Information," above).

You might want to compare the price you're quoted with those available through **San Diego Hotel Reservations** (☎ **800/SAVE-CASH** or 619/627-9300; or if you're on-line: http://www.savecash.com). For information on 30 bed-and-breakfasts in the San Diego area, send $3.95 for a 20-page directory to **B&B Resources,** P.O. Box 3292, San Diego, CA 92163 (☎ **800/619-ROOM** or 619/297-3130). You can also get information from the **Bed and Breakfast Guild** of San Diego (☎ **619/ 523-1300**).

If you like B&Bs, you might want to contact **Eye Openers Bed and Breakfast Reservations,** P.O. Box 694, Altadena, CA 91003-0694 (☎ **213/684-4428** or 818/797-2055; fax 818/798-3640 or E-mail eobb@loop.com). They can find you a bed (and breakfast) in a cozy inn or private home in the San Diego area from $40 a night for two.

Travelers over 40 years of age can join the **Affordable Travel Club,** 6556 Snug Harbor Lane, Gig Harbor, WA 98335 (☎ **206/858-2172;** voice and fax). Founded by John and Suzanne Miller in 1992, members stay in each others' homes for $20 to $40 a night for two. According to the Millers, "host members are genuinely friendly people who enjoy offering their extra bedroom and breakfast to fellow travelers." It costs $50 to $90 to join the club depending on whether or not you also want to be a host. There are about 15 members in the San Diego area.

If you really want to get away from it all, try one of the properties described in *Guide to Retreat Center Guest Houses* by John and Mary Jensen (CTS Publications, P.O. Box 8355, Newport Beach, CA 92660; $15.95). This 160-page paperback lists restful lodgings in the United States and worldwide that cost $35 to $45 a day including three meals. The retreat centers are abbeys, priories, missions, and sanctuaries that furnish a quiet setting and serene surroundings. The San Diego–area offerings include rooms at the beautiful Mission San Luis Rey near Oceanside.

Since I can't give you complete accommodations coverage here, you might want to check out my *Frommer's San Diego*, which offers many more options. *Note:* You'll also find additional information on the Internet at **http://www.infopost.com/sandiego/hotels.**

DOWNTOWN
DOUBLES FOR $60 OR LESS

Grand Pacific Hostel (AAIH). 437 J St., San Diego, CA 92101. ☎ **800/GET-TO-CA** (800/438-8622) or 619/232-3100. Fax 619/232-3106. 60 beds. Dorm $14 per person, $35 double. Rates include breakfast and bedding. Lower weekly rates. MC, V. No off-street parking. Bus: 1, 3, 5, 105, 16, or 25. Trolley: Gaslamp/Convention Center.

This handy hostel is located in a historic (1887) building in the Gaslamp District, with myriad bars and bistros nearby. It probably isn't the best area for fraidy cats, but the hardy backpackers who stay here think it's great. Host Ashley Walton caters to international travelers, and only accepts passport-carrying adults (no kids). He provides inexpensive evening meals (about $3), operates tours to Tijuana, and provides lots of information on local attractions. He also offers transportation to and from the airport, shuttle service to L.A. hostels, laundry facilities, and activities such as keg parties and beach barbecues. Five private rooms are available in addition to single-sex and coed dorms. Occupants share four toilets, four showers, and four sinks—each housed separately. My favorite area is the communal kitchen where "Clean up your own mess. Your mother doesn't live here" is written on the wall in 14 languages. No handicapped access.

Hostelling International—San Diego. 500 W. Broadway (between Columbia and India sts.), San Diego, CA 92101. ☎ **619/525-1531.** Fax 619/338-0129. E-mail HISDDWNTWN@aol.com. 84 beds. In dorm, $12 members, $15 nonmembers; semiprivate room, $13 members, $16 nonmembers; couple's room, $14 per person members, $17 per person nonmembers. MC, V. Limited metered parking available on street. Bus: 2, 4, 7, or 29. Trolley: America Plaza.

San Diego's downtown Youth Hostel Association (YHA) hostel is conveniently located one block from a trolley stop, two blocks from the train station, and three blocks from the bus station. The men's dorm has 16 beds; three women's dorms have four beds each. There are 24 semiprivate rooms with two single beds, and four private rooms with double beds. These rooms can be coed or single sex. Guests may use the TV room and the large common room with a full kitchen and plenty of books for swapping, but no alcohol or smoking are permitted. Both the women's and the men's bathrooms are large. Vending machines are on the premises. Guests have 24-hour access to the hostel and are given a key to operate the elevator. There are two-hour metered street parking and pay-to-park lots nearby. You can reserve a bed or room with a credit card. *Note:* As we went to press, the YHA announced it will be moving in April 1997 to 521 Market St. (corner of 5th Avenue) and will be known in the future as Hostelling International–Metropolitan Hostel. The phone and fax numbers and E-mail address will remain the same.

DOUBLES FOR $80 OR LESS

Comfort Inn—Downtown. 719 Ash St. (at 7th Ave.), San Diego, CA 92101. ☎ **800/228-5150** or 619/232-2525. Fax 619/687-3024. 67 rms. A/C TEL TV. $61–$71 double, extra person $5. Children 17 and under stay free with parents. Dine-A-Mate discount available. Lower weekly rates. Rates include continental breakfast. AE, DISC, MC, V. Free parking. Free shuttle to train, bus, and airport. Bus: 1, 3, 5, 25, or 105.

Located across the street from the landmark El Cortez Hotel (sadly closed for several years now), this three-story Comfort Inn has an eye-catching butterscotch and teal exterior. The rooms are modern, bright, spacious, and surprisingly quiet given the central location just four blocks north of Broadway. Guests have the choice of one queen bed or two doubles, and no-smoking rooms are available. Room doors open onto exterior walkways, which I found kind of scary on the top floor in spite of the sturdy railings decorated with window boxes. This dollarwise property also offers free coffee in the lobby and a heated spa.

✪ **La Pensione.** 1700 India St. (at Date St.), San Diego, CA 92101. ☎ **619/236-8000.** Fax 619/236-8088. 80 rms. TEL TV. $44–$70 double. Packages available. AE, CB, DC, MC, V. Free daily parking, or $10 per week. Bus: 5 or 105. Trolley: County Center/Little Italy.

This place has a lot going for it: modernity, cleanliness, remarkable value, a quiet location within walking distance of the central business district, a friendly staff, and parking, which is a premium for small hotels in San Diego. The lobby is small but inviting, and the rooms, while not overly large, make the most of their space and leave you with area to move around. Each room offers a tub/shower combination, ceiling fan, wet bar, microwave, and small refrigerator. Quarters are cleaned once a week for weekly guests, daily for those who stay a shorter period. La Pensione is built around a courtyard and feels like a small European hotel. It has two restaurants: Caffè Italia, which offers sandwiches and salads, as well as Sunday brunch and jazz on Friday and Saturday; and Indigo Grill, which serves Southwestern fare. There is also a self-service Laundromat on the premises. The fourth floor is for nonsmokers. One reader complained about noise filtering up to his room from the restaurants on the ground level; others rave about this property. La Pensione has a similarly priced sibling hotel of the same name at 1654 Columbia St. between Cedar and Date streets (☎ 619/232-3400), which is rented by the week or month only, and offers similar accommodations but no parking. Both properties are centrally located and within walking distance of eateries (mostly Italian) and nightspots.

DOUBLES FOR $100 OR LESS

Best Western Bayside Inn. 555 W. Ash St. (at Columbia St.), San Diego, CA 92101. ☎ **800/341-1818** or 619/233-7500. Fax 619/239-8060. 122 rms. A/C TEL TV. $85–$105 double. Harbor view $10 extra. Children under 12 stay free in parents' room. All rates include continental breakfast. Weekend rates (except in summer) and packages available. AE, AM (Amoco), CB, DC, DISC, ER, MC, V. Free covered parking. Free shuttle to train, bus, and airport. Bus: 5 or 105. Trolley: America Plaza.

The accommodating staff, city and harbor views, and good location of this quiet, unassuming hotel may very well please you. It's an easy walk to the Embarcadero (it should be called Bay*view* rather than Bayside), farther to Horton Plaza, four blocks to the trolley stop, and five blocks to the train station. The hotel has comfortable rooms decorated with traditional furnishings in restful colors, with king- or beds as well as balconies overlooking the bay or downtown. No-smoking available. The lobby, glass-enclosed on the street side, is sunny and inviting.

The hotel's restaurant, the Bayside Bar and Grill, serves breakfast, lunch, and dinner; the bar has a 50-inch TV. Good restaurants and bars are nearby and meals are available from room service. Facilities include cable TV, in-room movies, an outdoor pool, and Jacuzzi.

WORTH A SPLURGE

Clarion Hotel Bay View San Diego. 660 K St. (at Sixth), San Diego, CA 92101. ☎ **800/ 766-0234** or 619/696-0234. Fax 619/231-8199. 312 rms and suites. A/C TEL TV. $109–$139 double, $149–$169 suites. Dine-A-Mate discounts available. Visitor Value Pack discount offered. Children under 18 stay free in parents' room. Additional person $10. AE, CB, DC, DISC, MC, V. Parking $8 per day. Bus: 1. Trolley: Gaslamp/Convention Center.

This newish entry on the San Diego hotel scene provides an economical alternative for those attending meetings at the Convention Center—it's very nearly as close as the Marriott and the Hyatt, but considerably less expensive. The Clarion is also close to the Gaslamp Quarter and an excellent choice for those who plan to enjoy the nightlife here and want to avoid walking far late at night. All quarters are spacious, bright and modern, and more than half offer views of San Diego Bay and the Coronado Bridge. All rooms have sliding-glass doors that provide ample fresh air, and many have minibars. In-room safes are standard, as are tub/shower combinations; and 80% of the rooms are reserved for nonsmokers. The carpeted rooftop sundeck offers a great view as well as a Jacuzzi, sauna, workout room, and video games arcade.

Dining/Entertainment: The 6th and K Cafe is just off the marble-floored lobby. Breakfast, lunch, and dinner are served seven days a week. There's a big-screen TV in the bar, and karaoke is popular on Friday and Saturday nights.

Services: Concierge, room service 6am to 10pm, dry cleaning/laundry, express checkout.

Facilities: In-room pay-per-view movies; workout room with Nautilus equipment; Jacuzzi; sauna; sundeck; video games room; conference rooms; coin-operated washer and dryer; in-room touch-screen TVs can be used for express checkout, ordering breakfast, and retrieving voice-mail messages.

Holiday Inn on the Bay. 1355 N. Harbor Dr. (at Ash St.), San Diego, CA 92101-3385. ☎ **800/HOLIDAY** or 619/232-3861. Fax 619/232-4924. 563 rms, 17 suites. A/C TEL TV. $140–$160 single or double; from $400 suite. Children under 18 stay free in parents' room. Visitor Value Pack discount offered. Bed-and-breakfast packages available. AE, DC, MC, V. Parking $10. Bus: 2, 9, 29, 34, 34A, or 35.

Renovated in 1992, this hotel is ideally located on the harbor, overlooking the Maritime Museum, the cruise-ship terminal, and Harbor Island. It's only 1 1/2 miles from the airport (you can watch the planes landing and taking off, as well as flight attendants and pilots checking in and out) and two blocks from the train station and trolley. The rooms are California contemporary, offering harbor views. King rooms, which are a little larger, are a good choice for families. Rooms with a king bed or two double beds also have voice-mail message service. In general, the hotel's baths are small, but they have a separate sink with a lot of counter space.

Dining/Entertainment: The Elephant and Castle Restaurant and Ruth's Chris Steak House serves lunch and dinner. Shells Bar is small and intimate, while the lobby lounge is larger and has live entertainment.

Services: Room service (6am to 2pm and 5:30pm to midnight); baby-sitting; laundry; valet.

Facilities: Cable TV and in-room movies; no-smoking rooms; outdoor pool; self-service laundry; meeting rooms; minibars in some rooms.

HILLCREST/UPTOWN
DOUBLES FOR $60 OR LESS

The Cottage. 3829 Albatross St. (off Robinson), San Diego, CA 92103. ☎ **619/299-1564.**
Fax 619/299-6213. 1 rm, 1 cottage (both with bath). TEL TV. $55–$65 Garden Room for
1 or 2; $75–$85 cottage for 1 or 2. Third person in cottage $10. Rates include continental break-
fast. AE, MC, V. Limited on-street parking. Bus: 11, 1, 3, or 25.

The two-room cottage, which dates from the 1940s, is a private hideaway tucked
behind a Homestead-style house (1913) at the end of a cul-de-sac in a quiet residential neighborhood. There's an herb garden out front, birdbaths, and a flower-lined
walkway to the back. Owner Carol Emerick used to have an antiques shop, and her
house has inherited its treasures. The cottage has a living room with a working wood-
burning stove, a pump organ, a queen-size sofa bed, and a tiny kitchen. The bedroom
features a king-size bed and a hidden TV, as does the Garden Room in the main
house. Both accommodations are filled with fresh flowers and mid–19th-century
antiques put to clever uses, and both feature a private entrance and bath. Besides serving guests a scrumptious breakfast, Carol also supplies a copy of the morning paper.
Guests are welcome to use the dining room and parlor in the main house, where they
sometimes light a fire and rev up the 19th-century player piano. In this haven,
expect to wake up to the gentle chirping of birds. The cottage is a block from Front
Street, 1¹/₂ miles from the zoo, and only 4 miles from the airport.

DOUBLES FOR $100 OR LESS

Park Manor Suites. 525 Spruce St. (at Fifth Ave.), San Diego, CA 92103. ☎ **800/874-2649**
or 619/291-0999. Fax 619/291-8844. 80 rms. TEL TV. $69 studio for 1 or 2; $99 one-bedroom
unit for 1 or 2; $149 2-bedroom unit for up to 4. All rates include continental breakfast. Chil-
dren under 12 stay free in parents' room. Weekly and monthly rates available. AE, MC, V. Free
parking. Bus: 1, 3, 3A, or 25.

The stately Park Manor Suites with the red-brick facade, built across the street from
Balboa Park in 1926, includes an elegant lobby with a hand-painted ceiling, a baby
grand piano, and a glittering chandelier; a young, enthusiastic staff; old-world–style
rooms; cable TVs; computer data ports; voice mail; and separate kitchen and dining
areas. And what's more, a market is just a block away. Rooms facing the park are
quietest, and baths include tubs and showers. There's a restaurant on the ground
floor, open for lunch and dinner, and many others are within walking distance. The
bus stops a block away. The hotel, which has undergone extensive, tasteful renovation, attracts visiting actors in local productions, especially those at the nearby Old
Globe Theatre. The main entrance to Balboa Park is six blocks away. The Park
Manor Suites is a good, convenient choice for a longer stay in the area. Laundry and
dry-cleaning services are offered. There's no air conditioning, but you would rarely
need it; there's steam heat for chilly days.

✪ **Sommerset Suites Hotel.** 606 Washington St. (at Fifth Ave.), San Diego, CA 92103.
☎ **800/356-1787** in California, 800/962-9665 elsewhere, or 619/692-5200. Fax 619/
299-6065. 80 suites. A/C TEL TV. $90 studio suite; $160 1-bedroom suite; $180 executive suite.
Dine-A-Mate discounts available. Children under 12 stay free in parents' room. Rates include
large continental breakfast. AE, CB, DC, DISC, MC, V. Free covered parking. Bus: 16 or 25. Take
Washington St. exit off I-5.

This terrific bargain is a good choice for those who find traditional hotels too
impersonal. The staff is friendly and helpful, and in the late afternoon they serve
complimentary snacks, soda, beer, and wine in the cozy guest lounge. The poolside
patio, set up for barbecues, encourages impromptu gatherings and picnics among
guests. Your options here include studio, one-bedroom, and executive suites. All are
tastefully furnished and have in-room safes and fully equipped modern kitchens

(including dishwashers in the executive suites), large closets, and balconies. Even the studios are spacious.

Services include a concierge; laundry and dry cleaning; baby-sitting; courtesy van service (7am to 9pm) to the airport, Sea World, the zoo, and other attractions within a 5-mile radius; video rentals; and two-line phones and voice mail. Rollaway beds and cribs are available. Facilities include a small heated outdoor pool, a Jacuzzi, a roof-top sundeck, gas barbecue grills, a snack room, and a coin-operated laundry. No-smoking rooms are available.

OLD TOWN, HOTEL CIRCLE & BEYOND

In addition to the places described below, you might also want to check out the **EZ-8 Motel** (2484 Hotel Circle, San Diego, CA 92108; ☎ 800/326-6835 or 619/291-8252) and **Motel 6** (2424 Hotel Circle N., San Diego, CA 92108; ☎ 800/466-8356 or 619/296-1612, fax 619/543-9305). It's also worth noting that **San Diego State University** (SDSU), 5500 Campanile Dr., San Diego, CA 92182-1802 (☎ 619/594-4610) offers rooms ($25 double) on a cash-only basis between academic terms.

DOUBLES FOR $60 OR LESS

Old Town Travelodge. 2380 Moore St., San Diego, CA 92110. ☎ 800/292-9928 or 619/291-9100. Fax 619/291-4717. 79 rms. A/C TEL TV. $44–$59 double winter, extra person $5. Higher summer rates. Children 17 and under stay free. Visitor Value Pack discount offered. AE, DC, DISC, MC, V. Free parking. Bus: 5, 6, or 81. Trolley: Old Town Transit Center. Take I-5 to the Old Town Ave. exit.

Perched alongside Interstate 5, this good-value Travelodge offers comfortable rooms that come equipped with coffeemakers. Suites also offer skylights, therapy jets in the bathtub, sitting areas, microwaves, refrigerators, and wet bars. The majority of rooms are reserved for nonsmokers, and guests enjoy a nice pool and Jacuzzi. The staff is very friendly, and they help to make this property much more inviting than others in this nationwide chain. It's only a five-minute walk to Old Town attractions and eateries.

DOUBLES FOR $80 OR LESS

✪ **The Blom House.** 1372 Minden Dr., San Diego, CA 92104. ☎ 800/797-BLOM or 619/467-0890. Fax 619/467-0890. 4 rms (all with bath). A/C TEL TV. $69 double midweek; $80 double weekend. Lower weekly, monthly, senior, and cash rates. Rates include full breakfast. Packages also available. DISC, MC, V. Take Calif. 163 to Friars Rd.; head west to Ulrich St.; turn right. Take next 3 rights, on Linbrook, Babette, and Minden.

Bette Blom is the consummate B&B hostess, offering her guests extensive breakfasts served on Bavarian china, homemade cookies, a video library, and rooms that offer robes, small refrigerators, coffee- and tea-making facilities, VCRs, and hair dryers. Guests feel at home here and enjoy sitting in the hot tub on the deck that overlooks Mission Valley and in the living room—some even use the kitchen to prepare evening meals. Breakfast fare ranges from huevos rancheros to blueberry pancakes. The house is a little cluttered, but if you stay here, this former schoolteacher's kind heart will be your lasting impression. No smoking is permitted inside.

WORTH A SPLURGE

Hacienda Hotel. 4041 Harney St. (just east of San Diego Ave.), San Diego, CA 92110. ☎ 800/888-1991 or 619/298-4707. Fax 619/298-4771. 150 suites. A/C TEL TV. $109–$119 double. Children under 16 stay free in parents' room. AE, CB, DC, DISC, ER, MC, V. Free underground parking. Bus: 5, 6, or 81. Trolley: Old Town Transit Center. From I-5 take Old Town Ave. exit, turn left onto San Diego Ave. and right onto Harney St.

Perched above Old Town, this Best Western all-suite hotel is brightly lit and creates an impressive sight at night. It affords excellent views of Old Town from its outdoor pool and patio. The comfortable suites have 20-foot-high ceilings, ceiling fans, refrigerators, microwave ovens, coffeemakers, VCRs, and furnishings right out of the American Southwest. The one-room units have either one or two queen-size beds, and they feature desert tones. Walkways thread through courtyards with bubbling fountains, palm trees, lampposts, and bougainvillea-trimmed balconies.

Dining/Entertainment: The Acapulco restaurant (yes, it's Mexican) serves breakfast, lunch, and dinner daily from its perch atop the hotel.

Services: Concierge Monday through Friday, room service (6:30am to 2pm and 4 to 10pm), hosted manager's social Monday through Thursday, complimentary airport/train transportation.

Facilities: Movie rentals with complimentary bag of microwave popcorn, pool, Jacuzzi, spa, fitness center, conference suites, meeting rooms, coin-operated laundry.

MISSION BAY, PACIFIC BEACH & POINT LOMA

In addition to the places described below, you might also be interested in the budget beds at **Point Loma Nazarene College,** 3900 Lomaland Dr., San Diego, CA 92106 (☎ **619/221-2220**). Rooms run $18 for a single and $36 for a double and are available from June 10 to August 10. All beds are singles, two to a room, and they don't accept credit cards.

DOUBLES FOR $40 OR LESS

Campland on the Bay. 2211 Pacific Beach Dr., San Diego (Mission Bay), CA 92109-5699. ☎ **800/4BAYFUN,** 619/581-4200, or 619/581-4212 (24 hours). 600 hookup sites. Summer $26–$52 for up to 4 people; off-season $19–$37 for up to 4 people. Lowest-priced sites do not have hookups. Senior rates available. MC, V. Take I-5 to Grand/Garnet exit, and follow Grand to Olney and turn left; turn left again onto Pacific Beach Dr.

This family oriented bayside campground draws RVs, campers (with or without vans), and boaters. Conveniently located nearby are parks, a beach, a bird sanctuary, and a dog walk. Other facilities include pools, a Jacuzzi, catamaran and Windsurfer rentals and lessons, bike and boat rentals, a game room, a cafe, a market, and a laundry. Sea World is five minutes away.

De Anza Bay Resort RV Park. 2727 De Anza Rd., San Diego (Mission Bay), CA 92109. ☎ **800/924-PLAY** in California, or 619/273-3211. 250 hookup sites. Summer, $40. Off-season, $28. Weekly and monthly rates available off-season. MC, V. Bus: 34 or 34A. Take I-5 to the Clairemont Dr. exit, go west and turn right onto E. Mission Bay Dr. at the Visitor Information Center; follow E. Mission Bay Dr. for about a mile to the north end of the bay.

Directly across an inlet from Campland on the Bay and under the same management, this serenely situated park caters only to RV vacationers, and it offers them a market, a laundry, a private beach, a floating dock and diving platform, fishing, boating, water sports, bike rental, auto rental, free movies, potluck dinners, dancing, beach parties, and bingo. Small pets are welcome. A plus for golfers: It's adjacent to an executive 18-hole course that's open day and night.

Hostelling International—Elliott Hostel. 3790 Udall St., San Diego (Point Loma), CA 92107. ☎ **619/223-4778.** 61 beds. $12 dorm; $14 semiprivate (2-person room); $14 double bed; rates are per person, per night for members; nonmembers add $3. MC, V. Free parking. Bus: 35 (to Ocean Beach); catch it on Broadway (downtown) and get off at Voltaire (in front of Subway); it's about a 20-minute ride. Cross the street to Worden. The hostel is on the corner of Worden and Udall sts. From Los Angeles, take I-5 south to Sea World Drive exit and go west. Follow signs to Sunset Cliffs Blvd. Turn left on Voltaire; after 1 mile make a right on Worden. Hostel is on the corner of Worden and Udall. From downtown San Diego or airport, follow N. Harbor Dr.; turn right on Nimitz and follow it to Chatsworth and turn right; left on Poinsettia, which merges with Udall; the hostel will be on the right.

The Elliott (Point Loma) YHA Hostel offers budget digs in a residential neighborhood 6 miles from downtown San Diego and 3 miles from the airport. It's a short drive, or figure 30 minutes to get there by city bus from downtown San Diego. Dorm rooms sleep two to twelve people, and there are six couples rooms with double beds, and four family rooms. Facilities include showers, an impressive kitchen, a large common room, a TV room, a coin-operated laundry, and a patio with picnic tables. The hostel is a short distance to the beaches and Sea World; inexpensive Tijuana tours are offered; and bike rentals cost $10 a day. Biweekly events include taco tasting, bonfires, and movie nights. It's no wonder that this spot is popular with Europeans and others looking for clean, inexpensive lodging. Cash, traveler's checks, and a couple of credit cards (see above) are accepted; reception is open from 8am to 10pm every day. Quiet hours are 10pm to 8am. No alcohol is allowed on the premises.

DOUBLES FOR $80 OR LESS

Bears at the Beach. 1047 Grand Ave., San Diego (Pacific Beach), CA 92109. ☎ **619/ 272-2578.** 2 rms (shared or private bath; see below). TV. $78 double with shared bath. $88 double with private bath. Rates include breakfast. No credit cards. Parking only on street. Bus: 30 or 34.

Doña Denson just loves bears—cute little stuffed ones, others flying on kites, even the one on the California state flag—and they are everywhere in her pretty little two-bedroom unit at the rear of a neat and tidy fourplex located just 2 1/2 blocks from the beach. This dainty decor may not appeal to everyone, but I think it's great. Guests get as much mollycoddling or privacy as they want—Doña lives around the corner and comes in every morning to cook breakfast, which she serves on the patio, and is available to answer questions throughout the day. Both rooms have TVs, ceiling fans, and robes. One has an oversize double bed, the other a queen. Guests who don't want to share the bathroom can pay an extra $10 and have the whole place to themselves (only using one bedroom, of course). Bears is immaculate—it's no wonder that smoking is not permitted.

Pacific Shores Inn. 4802 Mission Blvd., San Diego (Pacific Beach), CA 92109. ☎ **800/ 826-0715** or 619/483-6300. Fax 619/483-9276. 55 rms. A/C TEL TV. $58–$78 double winter. Extra person $5. Higher rates June 15–Sept 15. Visitor Value Pack discount offered. Children under 16 stay free. Rates include continental breakfast. AE, DC, DISC, MC, V. Free parking. Bus: 30 or 34.

If the beach is going to be a major feature of your San Diego vacation, you couldn't stay in a better location than the one enjoyed by this two-story motel located at the north (quiet) end of Pacific Beach. The sand starts about 100 yards to the west, and there's also a nice heated pool. They don't advertise "beach views," but I happen to know that rooms 29, 31, 33, 35, and 23 have them. Half the units have kitchens; the others offer small refrigerators. There's a little deferred maintenance, but the modern furnishings are in good condition. Nonsmoking rooms are available, and there's free HBO and a coin-op laundry. Pets (not huge ones) are accepted for a small extra charge. Ask for a room away from the street.

DOUBLES FOR $100 OR LESS

✪ **The Beach Cottages.** 4255 Ocean Blvd. (a block south of Grand Ave.), San Diego (Pacific Beach), CA 92109. ☎ **619/483-7440.** Fax 619/273-9365. 78 units including 28 motel rms, 12 studios, 18 apts, 17 cottages, and 3 suites. TEL TV. Winter (Oct through mid-May), $60–$70 double motel room; $80 studio for up to 4; $95–$120 apt for up to 6; $90–$130 cottage for up to 6; $180–$200 2-bedroom, 2-bath suite for up to 6. Extra person $7. Higher fall and summer rates. Weekly rates available except in summer. AE, CB, DC, DISC, MC, V. Free parking. Take I-5 to Grand/Garnet exit, then go west on Grand Ave., and left on Mission Blvd. Free parking. Bus: 30 or 34.

I just love this place. Even though I live nearby, I've often been tempted to check in. If I did, I'd request cottage number 506, which is 12 steps from the sand (look both ways for speeding cyclists before crossing the boardwalk). There's a wide variety of accommodation, and it all comes with country decor. All accommodations except the motel rooms have fully equipped kitchens. The balcony/walkway on the third floor offers a great ocean view. The Beach Cottages are particularly suited for young couples (especially honeymooners) and families who want to stay directly on the beach. It's also within walking distance of shops and restaurants and has barbecue grills, shuffleboard courts, table tennis, and a laundry. The rustic cottages contain either one or two bedrooms and sleep up to six; each has a patio with tables and chairs.

To make a reservation, call between 9am and 9pm, when the office is open. It's advisable to reserve the most popular cottages well in advance.

Beach Haven Inn. 4740 Mission Blvd. (at Missouri St.), San Diego (Pacific Beach), CA 92109. ☎ **800/831-6323** or 619/272-3812. Fax 619/272-3532. 23 rms, including 18 with eat-in kitchens. A/C TEL TV. $55–$90 double winter. Extra person $5. Higher rates June 15–Sept 15. Children under 12 stay free. Rates include continental breakfast. AE, DC, DISC, MC, V. Free parking. Bus: 30 or 34.

Another great spot for beach lovers, this motel is about half a block from the sand. Rooms face an inner courtyard, where there is a nice pool and Jacuzzi. On the street side it looks kind of marginal, but once on the property I found all quarters well maintained and sporting modern furnishings. The friendly staff provides free coffee in the lobby and rents VCRs and movies; HBO is free.

WORTH A SPLURGE

✪ **Crystal Pier Hotel.** 4500 Ocean Blvd., San Diego (Pacific Beach), CA 92109. ☎ **800/ 748-5894** or 619/483-6983. Fax 619/483-6811. 26 cottages. TV. Cottages for up to 4 people, $145–$225 mid-June to mid-Sept; $95–$190 rest of the year. Three-day minimum in summer; weekly and monthly rates available. DISC, MC, V. Free parking. Take I-5 to Grand/Garnet exit; follow Garnet to the pier. Bus: 30 or 34.

This historic property, which dates from 1927, offers a unique opportunity to sleep *over* the water. Built on a private pier jutting into the ocean in the center of Pacific Beach, 20 older cottages date from 1936; six more were added in 1992 (and 12 units were recently renovated). The management did a great job on the remodeling; try not to get one of the older, untouched units. All quarters have a living room, bedroom, kitchenette, and private deck. The quietest units are furthest out on the pier, away from the noise of the boardwalk. Boogie boards, fishing poles, beach chairs, and umbrellas are available.

To make a reservation, call between 8am and 8pm, when the office is open.

Ocean Park Inn. 710 Grand Ave., San Diego (Pacific Beach), CA 92109. ☎ **800/231-7735** or 619/483-5858. Fax 619/274-0823. 73 rms, 4 suites. A/C TEL TV. Summer $99–$149 double; from $159 suite. Lower rates rest of the year. Rates include continental breakfast. AE, DC, DISC, MC, V. Free indoor parking. Take Grand/Garnet exit off I-5, and follow Grand Ave. to the ocean. Bus: 30 or 34.

On Pacific Beach's lively beach boardwalk, this three-story standout is visually appealing both inside and out. Behind the hotel's modern Spanish-Mediterranean facade is a sharply designed marble lobby that gives way to the less splendid but completely comfortable guest rooms. The accommodations are contemporary; all units have terraces and refrigerators. The most expensive rooms have oceanfront

---

🏨 Affordable Family-Friendly Hotels

The Beach Cottages *(see p. 564)* Kids enjoy the informality and the terrific location near the beach.

Crystal Pier Hotel *(see p. 565)* Where else can you sleep *over* the surf? Your offspring will love this exciting location.

El Cordova Hotel *(see p. 567)* El Cordova will welcome the kids and even the family dog to comfortable surroundings that your family will enjoy.

---

balconies but can be a bit noisy. King suites are extra large and have Roman tubs; some also have kitchenettes. Hotel facilities include a sun deck, a heated pool, an outdoor Jacuzzi, vending machines, and a coin laundry.

LA JOLLA
DOUBLES FOR $80 OR LESS

La Jolla Cove Travelodge. 1141 Silverado St. (corner Herschel St.), La Jolla, CA 92037. ☎ **800/578-7878** or 619/454-0791. Fax 619/459-8534. 30 rms. A/C TEL TV. $49–$89 double winter, extra person $5. Children 17 and under stay free. Higher summer rates. AE, DC, DISC, MC, V. Free parking. Bus: 30 or 34.

It's unusual to find a motel in this price range without an objectionable amount of deferred maintenance, but I really can't detect any here. All rooms were refurbished in 1996 and offer a choice of queen, king, or two double beds. All quarters come with coffeemakers and free HBO. Rooms for nonsmokers are available. The motel, with its cheery blue and white exterior, is very handy to La Jolla shopping, dining, and nightlife. There's a modest sundeck on the third floor.

DOUBLES FOR $100 OR LESS

Andrea Villa Inn. 2402 Torrey Pines Rd., La Jolla, CA 92037. ☎ **619/459-3311.** Fax 619/459-1320. 49 rms, including 30 with kitchenettes and 2 suites. A/C TEL TV. $60–$95 double winter, extra person $5–$10. Higher rates June 15–Sept 15. Lower rates for Scripps Clinic patients and their families. Rates include continental breakfast. AE, DC, DISC, MC, V. Free parking. Bus: 30.

Don't be put off by the dated exterior here. Once inside, you'll find an attractive lobby filled with caged birds and green plants and a pleasant breakfast room overlooking the pool. Spacious rooms have modern decor, and guests have a choice of king or queen beds; kitchenette units have a microwave or oven, a two-burner stove, a fridge, a sink, and cooking utensils. The pool's excellent, and there's also a Jacuzzi, several quiet sitting areas, and a coin-op laundry on the grounds. There are rooms for nonsmokers, but not for people with handicaps. La Jolla Shores beach is less than a mile away.

WORTH A SPLURGE

Empress Hotel of La Jolla. 7766 Fay Ave. (at Silverado), La Jolla, CA 92037. ☎ **800/525-6552** or 619/454-3001. Fax 619/454-6387. 73 rms and suites. A/C TEL TV. $109–$135 double; $250 Jacuzzi suite. Extra person $10. Children under 18 stay free in parents' room. Lower off-season and long-stay rates. Rates include continental breakfast. AE, BC, DC, DISC, MC, V. Valet parking $5. Take Ardath Rd. exit off I-5 north; or the La Jolla Village Dr. west exit off I-5 south. Take Torrey Pines Rd. to Girard, turn right; then left on Silverado to Fay. Bus: 30 or 34.

The Empress Hotel offers spacious quarters with traditional furnishings a block or two away from La Jolla's main drag. It's definitely quieter here than at the Prospect Park Inn (described below).

All rooms come equipped with hair dryers, coffeemakers, and terry robes. The four Empress Rooms have a sitting area with a full-size sofa sleeper. While these rooms have only a microwave, four suites have complete cooking facilities. Two suites come equipped with a grand piano. The top two floors in this five-story building have partial ocean views. I like the European ambiance, marble bathrooms with large mirrors, and tasteful decor. Room service comes from the award-winning Manhattan Restaurant located on the ground floor.

○ **Prospect Park Inn.** 1110 Prospect St. (at Coast Blvd.), La Jolla, CA 92037. ☎ **800/ 433-1609** or 619/454-0133. Fax 619/454-2056. 23 rms and suites. A/C TEL TV. $95–$140 double. Lower off-season rates. Rates include continental breakfast. AE, DC, DISC, MC, V. Take the Ardath Rd. exit off I-5 north; or the La Jolla Village Dr. west exit off I-5 south. Take Torrey Pines Rd. to Prospect Pl. and turn right. Prospect Pl. becomes Prospect St. Indoor parking off-site free of charge. Bus: 30 or 34.

This place is a real gem. It's a small property that offers charming rooms, some with ocean views. Built in 1947 as a boarding house for women, this spotless boutique hotel feels more European than Californian. There is no elevator in the three-story building, but fruit, cookies, and beverages are offered in the library area every afternoon and breakfast is served on a sundeck that affords a great ocean view. Prospect Park Inn enjoys essentially the same location as La Valencia (which is right next door) and the Colonial Inn—the beach, park, shops, and myriad restaurants are within steps—at much lower prices. The Cove Suite is extra large and has an outstanding ocean view; other units have balconies or terraces. Beach towels and chairs are provided for guest use free of charge. This is a nonsmoking establishment.

CORONADO

DOUBLES FOR $80 OR LESS

El Rancho Motel. 370 Orange Ave. (at 4th St.), Coronado, CA 92118. ☎ **619/435-2251.** 6 rms. A/C TEL TV. Summer, $45–$85 single or double. Winter, $65–$70 single or double. AE, DC, DISC, JCB, MC, V. Free parking. Bus: 901, 902, or 904. Ferry or water taxi: From Broadway Pier. Driving: Take I-5 to the Coronado Bridge, turn left onto Orange Ave.

This pretty, Spanish-style hotel is owned and lovingly tended by Cecilia Leith, one of the most helpful hosts I've ever met. The smallish rooms are pleasant and clean, and they feature walk-in closets, cable TV with HBO, small refrigerators, facilities and supplies for making coffee, tea, and cocoa, and microwaves. Some units have VCRs, and two have Jacuzzi jets in the bath tub. The motel's reception area is tiny, but Ms. Leith supplies brochures that you can take to your room. A tiny garden blooms in the courtyard, and guests enjoy using the table and chairs on the brick patio. The front units are a little noisy.

DOUBLES FOR $100 OR LESS

Also consider the **Glorietta Bay Inn** (under "Worth a Splurge," below), which offers economy doubles for $79 to $89.

○ **El Cordova Hotel.** 1351 Orange Ave. (at Adella St.), Coronado, CA 92118. ☎ **800/ 229-2032** or 619/435-4131. Fax 619/435-0632. 14 rms, 26 suites. TEL TV. $75–$95 double; $85–$105 studio with kitchen; $110–$140 1-bedroom suite; $135–$170 2-bedroom suite. Weekly and monthly rates available off-season. Visitor Value Pack discount offered. Children under 12 stay free in parents' room. AE, DC, DISC, MC, V. Take I-5 to the Coronado Bridge, and turn left onto Orange Ave. No off-street parking. Bus: 901, 902, or 904. Ferry: from Broadway Pier to Ferry Landing Marketplace. Water taxi: to Glorietta Bay.

Entering the El Cordova is like stepping into a village south of the border. Colorful little shops and an atmospheric Mexican restaurant are woven into this property, which was built as a mansion in 1902 and converted into a hotel in 1930. The

Spanish-style low-rise is located across a busy street from the beachfront Hotel del Coronado. The lobby has a quarry-tile floor and hacienda-style furnishings, a decor that extends to the comfortable rooms and suites. Each room is slightly different from the next: The best accommodations are the suites, with oak floors and bay windows. Several come with kitchenettes, which, like baths and stairways, are decorated with hand-crafted Mexican designs. About half the rooms offer air-conditioning. El Cordova is a good family choice; you're welcome to bring the kids and even the family dog. All the family activity does increase the noise level at times, however, so if you're looking for a really quiet retreat, the El Cordova probably isn't for you. If you do decide to give it a try, reserve well in advance. In addition to Miguel's Cocina, an on-site Mexican restaurant, there's a heated pool, a barbecue area with a picnic table, and a coin-op laundry.

WORTH A SPLURGE

Glorietta Bay Inn. 1630 Glorietta Blvd. (near Orange Ave.), Coronado, CA 92118. ☎ **800/ 283-9383** or 619/435-3101. Fax 619/435-6182. 81 rms, 17 suites. A/C TEL TV. In the mansion, $145–$155 double; $165–$179 suite; $279–$299 penthouse. Annex, $79–$89 economy double; $109–$139 contemporary double; $139–$179 family suite with kitchen. AE, DC, DISC, MC, V. Free parking. Bus: 901, 902, or 904. Ferry: from Broadway Pier to Ferry Landing Marketplace. Water taxi: to Glorietta Bay. Take I-5 to the Coronado Bridge and turn left on Orange Ave. After 2 miles, turn left onto Glorietta Blvd.; it's across the street from the Hotel del Coronado.

Once the summer mansion of 19th-century multimillionaire sugar baron John Spreckels, former owner of the Hotel del Coronado, the Glorietta Bay Inn is a beautifully restored 1908 house surrounded by lush gardens, with intricate moldings and a fine brass-and-marble staircase leading to well-appointed rooms. The rooms in the original mansion have a nice Victorian style; those in the less charming annex are contemporary, with bright furnishings and large windows overlooking Glorietta Bay. The hotel is within walking distance (one block) of the beach. There's a heated pool, a spa pool, bike rentals, and a guest laundry. Free morning coffee is offered, and continental breakfast is available for a charge.

4 Dining

San Diego offers a good selection of cheap eats. What follows is only a sampling—for a greater selection, see *Frommer's San Diego.*

Keep in mind that you can stretch your budget with the two-for-one coupons found in the *Night & Day* section of *The Union-Tribune* and in *The Reader* on Thursdays. If you're going to be in town for more than a few days, you might also profit from **Dine-A-Mate,** a book of two-for-one and discount coupons to *many* area eateries. Dine-A-Mate costs $25; to order call **800/248-DINE** or 619/578-4800, or write to Dine-A-Mate, 7960 Silverton Ave., Ste. 123, San Diego, CA 92126. Be sure to specify that you want the San Diego book.

DOWNTOWN

MEALS FOR $10 OR LESS

Galaxy Grill. Horton Plaza (top level). ☎ **619/234-7211.** Main courses $3.50–$6.50. AE, DISC, MC, V. Sun 11am–8pm, Mon–Thurs 11am–9pm, Fri–Sat 11am–10pm. Trolley: America Plaza. 3 hours' free parking with validation. AMERICAN/DINER.

At the Galaxy, waitresses in 1950s garb serve up good old-fashioned burgers, shakes, tuna melts, cherry Cokes, and the like. Pop a quarter in the jukebox and you'll get two songs.

⭐ **Mandarin House.** 2604 Fifth Ave. (at Maple). ☎ **619/232-1101.** Most main courses $6.50–$9.95. AE, DC, MC, V. Mon–Thurs 11am–10pm; Fri 11am–11pm; Sat noon–11pm; Sun 2–10pm. CHINESE.

This is the most popular Chinese restaurant in San Diego and the winner of many awards. My favorite dish is the kung pao chicken, which is hot and spicy in the traditional Szechuan style and laced with lots of peanuts. Not spicy, but just as delicious, is the moo-shu pork—tender shredded beef mixed with eggs, mushrooms, bamboo shoots, and vegetables. This dish is served with crepe-type pancakes onto which the server spreads plum sauce. (I think of it as a Chinese burrito.) The Peking duck (the most expensive item on the menu) also comes with pancakes. If you expect the usual Chinese-red decor, you'll be surprised by the pleasant sea-foam-and-peach color scheme. Mandarin House also has locations in La Jolla and Pacific Beach.

Old Spaghetti Factory. Fifth Ave. and K St. ☎ **619/233-4323.** Main courses $4.25–$8.10. DISC, MC, V. Mon–Thurs 11:30am–10pm; Fri 11:30am–10pm; Sat–Sun noon–10pm. Trolley: Gaslamp Quarter. ITALIAN.

A family restaurant with a Victorian atmosphere, this place allows you and your kids to dine in a trolley car that's been converted into a dining room. Main courses, mostly old standbys such as lasagna and spaghetti, come with lots of extras, such as salad, sourdough bread, ice cream, and coffee or tea with refills. The word is out about what a great deal this place offers, so there's always a wait. There's a small play area for kids.

MEALS FOR $20 OR LESS

⭐ **Croce's Restaurant and Jazz Bar.** 802 Fifth Ave. (at F St.). ☎ **619/233-4355.** Fax 619/232-9836. Reservations recommended. Main courses $13.50–$17.95. AE, DC, DISC, MC, V. Daily 7:30am–3pm and 4pm–midnight. Valet parking $5 with validation. AMERICAN.

This very popular jazz restaurant/bar is named after the late musician Jim Croce and is owned by his wife, Ingrid. You might think the food would be an afterthought to the scene here, but that's not the case. The menu runs the gamut from casual breakfast and lunch fare to salmon baked in puff pastry, served with wild spinach hollandaise, and grilled breast of chicken with figs and goat cheese, served with a peach and caramelized onion chutney. The above-mentioned salmon is one of my favorite dishes in San Diego. In addition to the main restaurant, there's Ingrid's Cantina and Sidewalk Cafe next door for Southwestern cuisine, and Upstairs at Croce's for cocktails, coffee, and desserts. Two adjacent nightspots, The Jazz Bar and The Top Hat, serve up jazz and R&B; if you have dinner in one of the restaurants, you won't have to pay the cover charge.

Filippi's Pizza Grotto. 1747 India St. (between Date and Fir sts. in Little Italy). ☎ **619/232-5095.** Fax 619/695-8591. Main courses $4.75–$12.50. AE, DC, DISC, MC, V. Mon–Sat 11am–11pm, Sun 11am–10pm. Free parking. Trolley: America Plaza. ITALIAN.

This is one of those down-home Italian places, right down to the Chianti bottles lining the dining areas. It's been around since the 1950s, and has given birth to a dozen spin-off locations throughout the city. You enter through an Italian deli that will stir your hunger pangs with a selection of cheeses, pastas, wines, and salamis. Choose from 15 pizzas and the requisite pasta dishes. Kids will feel right at home here.

Planet Hollywood. 197 Horton Plaza. ☎ **619/702-STAR.** Reservations not accepted. Main courses $6.50–$13.95. AE, DC, MC, V. Daily 11am–2am. Bus: 1, 2, 3, 25, 34, or 34A. Trolley: America Plaza. Parking: Horton Plaza Garage, 3 hours free with validation. CALIFORNIA/AMERICAN.

Twenty thousand gawkers gathered here in March 1995, when this Planet Hollywood—number 19 in the chain—opened. They came to see celebrity shareholders Arnold Schwarzenegger, Bruce Willis, Sylvester Stallone, and Demi Moore frolic with their celebrity friends. Today folks stand in line for a turn to eat here and ogle the movie memorabilia. Glass cases contain more than 300 objects, including an animatronic owl from *Indiana Jones and the Temple of Doom*, Roddy McDowell's costume from *Planet of the Apes*, and a submachine gun from *Die Hard*. This is a noisy, friendly, enjoyable place, which is understandably popular with families. Menu items include pizza, pasta, burgers, sandwiches, salads, and a handful of light California cuisine choices. (On a recent visit I enjoyed grilled salmon served on a bed of trendy salad greens, atop a crisp pizza crust.) Kids can drink a "Home Alone" (an ice-cold combination of strawberry, banana, and grenadine), an "E.T." (grapefruit and orange juice topped with soda), or a "Predator" (pineapple, ginger ale, and grenadine). If you don't relish standing in line, be there at 11am when they open, between 2 and 5pm, or after 9pm. There's a retail outlet adjacent, of course.

WORTH A SPLURGE

✪ **Osteria Panevino.** 722 Fifth Ave. (between F and G sts.). ☎ **619/595-7959.** Reservations recommended. Main courses $8.95–$19.95. AE, CB, DC, DISC, MC, V. Sun–Thurs 11:30am–10pm; Fri–Sat 11:30am–11:30pm. ITALIAN.

One of the most popular Italian restaurants in a town filled with them, Osterino Panevino deserves its loyal clientele because it offers top-notch food and wine and a decidedly unself-conscious atmosphere often lacking elsewhere. The interior is reminiscent of a Tuscan farmhouse, with ceramics and large terra-cotta tiles from Italy; old wine barrels are stacked in a rear alcove. Other nice touches include a mural of Florence opposite the bar, a brick wall, inviting picture windows looking onto the street, high ceilings, good lighting (you can actually see your food), and a brick oven for making pizzas. For antipasto, consider the assorted marinated vegetables with prosciutto, fresh mozzarella, and tomatoes; fried squid and parsley; or bite-size mozzarella in prosciutto, baked over sautéed spinach. More than a dozen dishes feature homemade pasta, among them egg-and-spinach noodles with radicchio and grilled chicken in a light cream sauce; spinach-and-meat ravioli tossed with butter, sage, and diced tomatoes; and angel-hair pasta with wild mushrooms and shrimp in garlic, white wine, and a touch of tomatoes. Fish and meat dishes include veal medaillons topped with French string beans, smoked mozzarella, and tomato bruschetta; grilled boneless chicken with diced vegetables, crushed red pepper, and drizzled with olive oil and rosemary; and poached salmon filet with wild mushrooms, carrots, and pine nuts in white-wine sauce. Or you could opt for the risotto, lasagna, gnocchi of the day, or a simple pizza or focaccia. From the time you enter Panevino, you'll feel welcome, and you're bound to leave satisfied.

HILLCREST/UPTOWN
MEALS FOR $10 OR LESS

Corvette Diner. 3946 Fifth Ave. (between Washington and University). ☎ **619/542-1001.** Reservations not accepted. Main courses $4.50–$9.95. AE, DC, DISC, MC, V. Sun–Thurs 11am–11pm, Fri–Sat 11am–midnight. Bus: 1 or 3. AMERICAN.

The slightly faded facade lets you know you're in for something a little unusual: a trompe l'oeil painting of a cafe with a giant female strolling across the roof. Inside, the decor is art deco; the centerpiece is a sleek Corvette. The walls are filled with portraits of popular singers by local artist Gina Falk—from the Beatles to Connie Francis. Do pay your respects to Norma Jean. There's a DJ at night to play your requests. The menu features burgers, sandwiches, and other diner fare. Besides the old-fashioned soda fountain, there's a full bar, and on Tuesday and Wednesday evenings, a magician performs at the diner, a tradition for the past eight years. This is a fun place with a young crowd, and it's great for kids; expect a line on weekends.

✪ **Kung Food.** 2949 Fifth Ave. (between Palm and Quince). ☎ **619/298-7302** or 619/298-9232 for deli/take-out. Reservations not accepted. Main courses $6.50–$9.55. DISC, MC, V. Mon–Thurs 11:30am–9pm, Fri 11:30am–10pm, Sat 8:30–10pm, Sun 8:30–9pm. VEGETARIAN.

San Diego's best-known vegetarian eatery offers an extensive menu created from natural ingredients—no meat products, no bleached flours, no sugar, and lots of low-fat choices. But that doesn't mean the food is boring or bland. The menu includes Greek spinach pie, tofu vegetable enchiladas, lentil-walnut loaf, and garden burgers. There is indoor and outdoor seating, and soothing music sets the scene. Beer and wine are served. Smoking is not allowed.

MEALS FOR $20 OR LESS

Hob Nob Hill. 2271 First Ave. (at Juniper). ☎ **619/239-8176.** Breakfast and lunch $3.25–$8.25; dinner $8–$14. AE, DISC, MC, V. Daily 7am–9pm. Bus: 1 or 3. AMERICAN.

Consider this your kitchen away from home, as do many professional and retired San Diegans. It's been serving up home-style cooking since 1946, and some of the waitresses have been greeting patrons here for 30 years. Everything is made from scratch, and the rolls are tops. The large breakfast menu includes eggs (from fried to Florentine), pancakes, waffles, and heartier fare like beef hash; there's even champagne by the glass (pretty fancy for a mom-and-pop place), and you can order a side of Canadian bacon or fresh pork sausage. Lunch features sandwiches, salads, and meat or fish meals; dinner, old-fashioned chicken and dumplings, roast turkey, prime rib, turkey croquettes, and a vegetarian plate. A children's menu is available.

OLD TOWN, HOTEL CIRCLE & BEYOND
MEALS FOR $10 OR LESS

✪ **Old Town Mexican Cafe.** 2489 San Diego Ave. ☎ **619/297-4330.** Reservations accepted for parties of 10 or more. Most main courses under $10. AE, DISC, MC, V. Daily 7am–11pm. MEXICAN.

A fun margarita bar and homemade tortillas are the primary draws of this boisterous Mexican restaurant that's popular with both families and couples. (Expect a wait.) It's nothing fancy; the food speaks for itself. All the south-of-the-border standards are available—tacos, burritos, fajitas, and the like—served with excellent salsa. You'll see the staff in the window facing the street making each day's fresh tortillas by hand. Check out the Mexican-style rotisserie pork ribs.

MEALS FOR $20 OR LESS

Casa de Bandini. Opposite Old Town Plaza, Old Town. ☎ **619/297-8211.** Reservations not accepted. Main courses $6.50–$14. AE, CB, DC, MC, V. Sun 10am–9:30pm, Mon–Thurs 11am–9:30pm, Fri–Sat 11am–10pm. Bus: 4 or 5/105. MEXICAN.

As much an Old Town tradition as the mariachi music that's played here on weekends, this lively restaurant, with its appealing balcony and courtyard, fills the nooks and crannies of an adobe hacienda. The house was built in 1823 for Juan Bandini, once a merchant and politician in these parts; later, with a second floor added, it became a hotel. Today it's the scene of many a happy repast over dishes like crab enchiladas, chicken-and-avocado salad, crab brochette with mild green chiles, and jumbo cod filet with sautéed vegetables. Some of the dishes are gourmet Mexican, others simple south-of-the-border fare; you'll never run short of refried beans, guacamole, or jumbo margaritas. It's the house itself that makes the restaurant extra special.

WORTH A SPLURGE

Cafe Pacifica. 2414 San Diego Ave. ☎ **619/291-6666.** Reservations recommended. Main courses $11–$18. AE, CB, DC, DISC, MC, V. Tues–Fri 11:30am–2pm; daily 5:30–10pm. Valet parking at lunch free, at dinner $4. CALIFORNIA.

Excellent fresh fish, grilled over mesquite, keeps visitors happy and locals returning. The setting is charming, with tiny twinkling lights overhead and candles adorning the tables, and slightly formal. On my last visit, I started with the Dungeness crab salad, an intriguing combination of flavors that included papaya, avocado, and endive. Then I moved onto the Hawaiian ahi with shiitake mushrooms and ginger butter. The menu changes daily but always offers excellent dishes like panfried catfish, shrimp tacos, and perfect crab cakes (crunchy outside, moist inside).

MISSION BAY, PACIFIC BEACH & POINT LOMA

In addition to the dining options described below, there is also a **D'Lish** in Pacific Beach (4150 Mission Blvd., in the Promenade Shopping Center.; ☎ **619/483-4949**). The menu here is the same as for the D'Lish described in the La Jolla section of this chapter. There are also a **Mandarin House** (1820 Garnet St., in Pacific Plaza; ☎ **619/273-2288**) and a **Filippi's Pizza Grotto** (962 Garnet St.; ☎ 619/483-6222) similar to the ones described under "Downtown."

You can get a tasty, all-you-can-eat, vegetarian meal at the **Hare Krishna Center,** 1030 Grand Ave., Pacific Beach (☎ **619/483-2500**). The schedule varies, but as we went to press, dinner was served Monday, Wednesday, and Friday from 6:30 to 8:30pm and cost $3.50 for adults and $2.50 for children. There's no proselytizing, but you do have to sit on the floor.

MEALS FOR $10 OR LESS

Mitsuru. 1130 Garnet Ave., Pacific Beach. ☎ **619/272-2389** or 619/272-0831. Reservations accepted. All-you-can-eat lunch buffet $5.49, dinner buffet $8.99. AE, MC, V. Mon–Thurs 11:30am–9:30pm, Fri–Sat 11:30am–10pm. CHINESE/JAPANESE.

This is a great spot for those with a hearty appetite and a passion for Asian food. Popular with the hip, but income-deficient PB crowd, Mitsuru's buffet offers about 45 dishes, including a variety of sushi, a salad bar, and a selection of desserts. I particularly like that the vegetables aren't overcooked and that none of the dishes I sampled were too salty. If you dine here, you can enjoy a cold Tsingtao, Sapporo, or Kirin beer with your meal. Look for this budget-stretcher across the street from McDonald's. They also do take-out.

✪ **Notis Cafe.** 4864 Cass St., Pacific Beach. ☎ **619/272-2077.** Reservations not accepted. Main courses $3.80–$8. No credit cards. 9am–9pm daily. AMERICAN/GREEK/MEXICAN.

My favorite little PB "dive"—and I say that with affection, not disdain—serves up great moussaka, really good gyros, and tasty dolmades. Dining in is also a good option as long as you aren't disturbed by the sound from the constantly blaring TV. A few Greek travel posters constitute the total "decor," but the lack of fancy decorations doesn't deter folks from the surrounding neighborhood who appreciate the friendly service, good food, bargain prices, and low-key ambience.

Souplantation. 3960 W. Point Loma Blvd., Point Loma. ☎ **619/222-7404.** Reservations not accepted. All-you-can-eat buffet $7.19. DC, DISC, MC, V. Sun–Thurs 11am–9pm, Fri–Sat 11am–10pm. SOUP/SALAD BAR.

Understandably popular with families, the Souplantation really does have something for everyone. You can make your own salad from a huge assortment of ingredients, and there's a selection of serve-yourself soups. In addition to assorted rolls and breads, you can also help yourself to slices of pizza, baked potatoes with various toppings,

🐧 Affordable Family-Friendly Restaurants

Corvette Diner *(see p. 570)*   Resembling a '50s diner, this place appeals to teens and preteens who like the sock-hop surroundings, as well as the short-order fare.

Galaxy Grill *(see p. 568)*   How could burgers, shakes, and an old-time jukebox let you down?

Hard Rock Cafe *(see p. 576)*   This is a great place for kids—the music is so loud that no one will notice if they get a little rambunctious.

Old Spaghetti Factory *(see p. 569)*   The wait staff here makes kids feel especially welcome, and the ambience is definitely family friendly. Kids get their own toys, and there's a special play area for them.

Planet Hollywood *(see p. 569)*   This noisy, friendly place is popular with families because of the more than 300 pieces of movie memorabilia which hang from the walls and ceiling and the great casual fare.

and nachos. If you still have room, waddle up to the dessert bar where the self-serve frozen yogurt is a popular item. The atmosphere is light, bright, modern, and abuzz with the chatter of boisterous families.

There is a similar restaurant, **The Soup Exchange,** at 1840 Garnet Ave., in Pacific Beach (☎ **619/272-7766**).

MEALS FOR $20 OR LESS

Firehouse Beach Cafe. 722 Grand Ave. ☎ **619/272-1999.** Reservations recommended on weekends. Main courses $8–$12. AE, CB, DC, DISC, MC, V. Sun–Thurs 7am–9pm, Fri–Sat 7am–10pm. Free parking. AMERICAN.

This casual place is always packed (though not oppressively so), and if you're lucky, you can get an umbrella table on the upstairs deck with an ocean view. The locals love eating breakfast here; the omelets are especially popular. The kitchen turns out one of the best burgers in San Diego, in addition to perennial favorites like taco salad, fish and chips, and lasagna. A patio bar overlooking the ocean was added in 1996.

WORTH A SPLURGE

✪ **The Atoll.** In the Catamaran Resort Hotel, 3999 Mission Blvd. ☎ **619/539-8635.** Reservations recommended for Sunday brunch. Main courses $8–$20. AE, CB, DC, DISC, MC, V. Sun–Thurs 6:30am–10pm, Fri–Sat 6:30am–11pm. Valet parking $7, free self-parking with validation. CALIFORNIA.

You can dine at a wrought-iron table on the waterfront patio here and take in the view of Mission Bay, or inside, where the interior is made elegant by rattan chairs, crisp tablecloths, and Villeroy and Boch china. I'd start with the spicy crab cakes with lime and ginger-butter sauce, then move on to the broiled lamb chops. If you're looking for something light and simple, though, there are selections like club sandwiches to keep you happy. The service is friendly and polished.

The Green Flash. 701 Thomas Ave. (at Mission Blvd.). ☎ **619/270-7715.** Main courses $10–$25. AE, DC, DISC, MC, V. Mon–Thurs 8am–9:30pm, Fri 8am–10pm, Sat 7:30am–10pm, Sun 7:30am–9:30pm. Bus: 34 or 34A. SEAFOOD/INTERNATIONAL.

You can spend as much or as little as you choose in this oceanfront place, which has a menu to match a variety of budgets and hankerings. It's known for its fresh fish, but you may also order steaks and prime rib, steak-and-seafood combos, chicken dishes, or burgers. Or simply make a meal of appetizers: fresh oysters, steamed clams, shrimp cocktail, and ceviche. Salads and sandwiches are available at lunch, and there are sunset dinner specials Sunday through Thursday from 5 to 7pm for $9.95. The outdoor tables here are prime real estate, especially when the sky begins to blush. The ambience couldn't be livelier. Ask your wait person to explain how the restaurant got its name.

LA JOLLA

This community is known for its mansions and Mercedes, but it also offers a surprising number of reasonably priced places to eat. Most restaurants are clustered along Prospect Street and Pearl Street in the village.

MEALS FOR $10 OR LESS

✪ **The Cottage.** 7702 Fay Ave. (at Kline). ☎ **619/454-8409.** Reservations accepted for dinner only. Breakfast and lunch $4.95–$6.95; dinner main courses $6.95–$11.95. MC, V. Daily 7:30am–3pm; daily June–Sept 4–9pm. LIGHT FARE.

The turn-of-the-century Cottage, on a sunny corner in downtown La Jolla, is light and airy inside, with booths and tables under a skylight; outside there's a welcoming white fence, trellis, and large brick patio, which also offers seating. You can start the day with farm-fresh eggs most any style, granola and fresh fruit, oatmeal pancakes, Belgian waffles, or a vegetable frittata. The dinner menu (summer only) features California bistro cuisine. The Cottage bakery makes their own *wonderful* desserts, pastries, and bread (with the exception of foccacia). There's no smoking inside or out.

✪ **D'Lish.** 7514 Girard Ave. (at Pearl St.). ☎ **619/459-8118.** Main courses $5.95–$8.99. AE, DC, DISC, MC, V. Sun–Thurs 11:30am–10pm, Fri–Sat 11:30am–11pm. Free off-street parking. CONTEMPORARY ITALIAN.

This is the place for one of those trendy wood-fired pizzas with designer toppings you wouldn't have imagined a decade ago. My favorite is the Greek grilled chicken, but I also like the pizza with shrimp, mozzarella, roma tomatoes, kalamata olives, sun-dried tomatoes, pesto sauce, and pine nuts. Their salads make it painless to feel virtuous when ordering. There are also good pasta dishes, especially the shrimp-scallop angel hair, one of many heart-healthy choices. Here's a hot tip: Don't sit upstairs when the weather's warm.

Harry's Coffee Shop. 7545 Girard Ave. (across from Vons). ☎ **619/454-7381.** Reservations not accepted. Breakfast $3.15–$7.75, lunch $3.25–$7.50. AE, DISC, MC, V. 6am–2:30pm daily. COFFEE SHOP.

Harry Rudolph has been running this La Jolla institution since 1960, and I can't even imagine how many deals have been made, problems solved, and victories celebrated over one of his popular breakfasts or "fountain favorites." The decor hasn't changed since the day he opened: The walls are covered with posters and the friendly wait staff seems to have stepped out of one of the ones by Norman Rockwell. Breakfast is served all day, and you can get bacon and eggs here for the cost of a cup of coffee at one of the trendy cafes just down the street. Be prepared to wait if you come Saturday or Sunday morning, although you can call ahead and get your name on the list. There's free parking at the rear of the restaurant.

MEALS FOR $20 OR LESS

Also consider the 5-course feast at **Marrakesh** (under "Worth a Splurge," below), which can be had for as little as $16.50 per person.

Brockton Villa. 1235 Coast Blvd. (across from the La Jolla Cove). ☎ **619/454-7393.** Reservations: call by Thurs for Sun brunch. Breakfast $3.95–$7.25. Dinner main courses $7.95–$13.95. AE, DISC, MC, V. Mon–Wed 8am–5pm; Thurs–Sun 8am–9pm (later in summer). Validated parking in Coast Walk Shopping Center. CALIFORNIA.

Cheap Eats to Go

Southern Californians have a reputation for living in their cars. While this is more true of Los Angelenos, I have to admit that the automotive culture is alive and well in the San Diego area, too. Enter fast food, also known as "car cuisine." How can we live in our vehicles if we can't eat there?

One of the local favorites is **Rubios,** home of the fish taco, mahimahi burrito, and other Cali-Mex specialties. You'll find these emporia scattered around the city. Some of the most convenient locations are 901 Fourth Ave. (at E Street; ☎ **619/231-7731**); in Pacific Beach at 910 Grand Ave. (☎ **619/270-4800**); and at 3555 Rosecrans St. (near Midway Drive; ☎ **619/223-2631**).

You might also like to try **In-N-Out Burgers.** Even some of my most highbrow friends admit to having a private passion for these thin meat patties, doused in secret sauce and served with fresh lettuce and tomato on toasted buns. There's an In-N-Out just off I-5 in Pacific Beach (2910 Damon Ave., near E. Mission Bay Drive; no phone).

Because our benign climate lends itself to alfresco dining, portable meals can, and often do, take the form of picnics. My favorite spot to pick up sandwiches is **The Cheese Shop,** 401 G St., downtown (☎ **619/232-2303**); or in La Jolla Shores at 2165 Avenida de la Playa (☎ **619/459-3921**). Another spot that's very popular with San Diegans is **Point Loma Seafoods,** located on the water's edge in front of the Municipal Sportfishing Pier (2805 Emerson, near Scott Street, south of Rosecrans and west of Harbor Drive; ☎ **619/223-1109**); it's a fish market where they sell seafood sandwiches and salads to go.

Located in a beach cottage that dates from 1894, Brockton Villa offers good food, a great view of the La Jolla Cove, and charming historic surroundings. The blue-and-white bungalow has a wooden floor that's appropriately worn and perhaps not entirely level. Diners can sit inside, outside on the patio, or on a semienclosed porch. My favorite dinner is the basil ravioli with saffron shrimp sauce, and my lunch choice is Shari's turkey meat loaf sandwich on toasted sourdough bread with spicy tomato mint chutney. For breakfast I have a hard time choosing between homemade granola, "coast toast" (French toast that resembles a soufflé), and Greek steamers (three eggs steam scrambled using the espresso machine and mixed with feta, tomato, and basil). There's no smoking allowed, and no access for people with disabilities.

⭕ **George's Ocean Terrace and Café/Bar.** 1250 Prospect St. ☎ **619/454-4244.** Reservations not accepted. Lunch main courses $7.50–$10.75; dinner main courses $9.50–$14.95. AE, DC, DISC, MC, V. Sun–Thurs 11am–10pm, Fri–Sat 11am–11pm. CALIFORNIA.

The main dining room on level one at George's is legendary and has won numerous awards for its haute cuisine. It isn't, however, in the price range of budget travelers. However, the level three Ocean Terrace and the level two cafe/bar serve some of the same dishes and others prepared in the same kitchen as the high-price fare. These two areas offer indoor and outdoor seating overlooking La Jolla Cove and the same great service as the main dining room. For dinner you could choose from one of several seafood or pasta dishes, or have something out of the ordinary like George's meat loaf served with mushroom and corn mashed potatoes. The smoked chicken soup is to die for. Valet parking is available for $3 during the day, $4 at night, but if you drive around long enough, you'll find a place on the street.

Hard Rock Cafe. 909 Prospect St. (at Fay Ave.). ☎ **619/454-5101.** Reservations not accepted. Main courses $6.95–$13.95. AE, DC, MC, V. Sun–Thurs 11:30am–11pm, Fri–Sat 11:30am–midnight. Bus: 34 or 34A. AMERICAN.

San Diego's branch of "the Smithsonian of rock 'n' roll," as Andy Warhol described the Hard Rock Cafe, is a great spot for families. In fact, pre-teens, teens, and tourists seem to comprise the majority of their customers. It isn't *just* the huge inventory of music memorabilia on display: The Hard Rock also serves generous portions of really good food, with most main courses costing about $6.95. Burgers are the specialty of the house, but they also offer salads and sandwiches. The service isn't swift, but there's plenty to look at and listen to in the interim. This includes items such as Madonna's bustier from the "Who's That Girl" tour, a vintage Cher doll, and one of John Lennon's band leader coats from the Sgt. Pepper era. If the line is long and you're really starving, see if there's a place at the counter. You can also eat at the bar, the only place where smoking is allowed.

WORTH A SPLURGE

Marrakesh. 634 Pearl St. (at Draper). ☎ **619/454-2500.** Main courses $15–$16.95; 5-course "feasts" $16.50–$23. AE, DC, DISC, MC, V. Sun–Thurs 5–10pm; Fri–Sat 5–11pm. MOROCCAN.

What diners get here isn't just a meal, it's a total experience that starts when you're seated on cushions around a low table, and continues when your server washes your hands in the traditional Moroccan style. The decor consists of colorful North African fabrics and objets d'art. I recommend ordering one of the feasts, a multicourse experience that starts with soup, salad, and bastilla (a wonderful pastry) and includes a choice of lemon chicken, lamb in honey sauce, or lamb couscous, my favorite. The latter is the national Moroccan dish and consists of steamed semolina topped with lamb and vegetables. These meals conclude with fruit, pastry, and mint tea poured from a lofty three feet above your cup. If you aren't up for a feast, you can order a dinner, solely accompanied by soup or salad and bastilla. Did I mention that Moroccan meals are eaten with fingers, not knives and forks?

Marrakesh also has a location downtown at 756 Fifth Ave. (☎ 619/231-8353), but it isn't as traditional and therefore, in my opinion, not as much fun.

CORONADO
MEALS FOR $10 OR LESS

Mandarin Cafe. 1330 Orange Ave. (in Coronado Plaza, second floor). ☎ **619/435-2771.** Most main courses under $10. AE, MC, V. Mon–Thurs 11:30am–10pm, Fri 11:30am–11pm, Sat 3–11pm, Sun 1–10pm. Free parking with validation. MANDARIN/SZECHUAN.

Located within steps of the beach, this is a local favorite, a reliable standby for those times when nothing but Chinese food will satisfy the munchies. House favorites are the honey shrimp and the sizzling seafood noodles. The kitchen will hold the MSG, sugar, and salt on request.

MEALS FOR $20 OR LESS

Bay Beach Cafe. 1201 1st St. (in the Ferry Landing Marketplace). ☎ **619/435-4900.** Main courses $8.95–$16.95. AE, DISC, MC, V. Daily 7am–10:30pm. Free parking. AMERICAN/SEAFOOD.

You can't beat the views at the Bay Beach Cafe: the San Diego skyline across the water. Dine indoors or alfresco, and choose from items such as daily fresh fish specials, vegetarian pasta, and roasted free-range chicken with wild mushroom sauce. There's also a bar menu featuring sandwiches and burgers.

Rhinoceros Cafe and Grill. 1166 Orange Ave. (between 10th and 11th). ☎ **619/435-2121.**
Main courses $8.95–$17.95. AE, MC, V. Sat–Sun 8am–12:30pm; Mon–Sat 11am–3pm; Fri–Sat
5–10pm; Sun–Thurs 5–9pm. AMERICAN CONTINENTAL.

Owner Scott Hanlon won't explain to the wait staff why he named this place as
he did, so they made up a story. If they tell you it refers to the large portions served
here, they're pulling your leg. This light, bright bistro is a good place for people-
watching, as large windows face the sidewalk outside. Inside, white walls, hung with
large, colorful abstract paintings, reach up to the very high ceiling, which is also white.
Lunch possibilities include salads, burgers, sandwiches, and pasta. Favorite dinner
specials are charbroiled swordfish with citrus glaze, halibut with cucumber dill sauce,
and fresh Maine lobster. There's a good wine list, or you might decide to try Rhino
Chaser's American Ale. This spot would be a good choice for dinner before attending a production at Lamb's Players Theatre, which is next door.

WORTH A SPLURGE

✪ **Primavera.** 932 Orange Ave. ☎ **619/435-0454.** Reservations recommended. Main
courses $10.95–$19.95. AE, DC, DISC, MC, V. Mon–Fri 11am–2:30pm; daily 5–10:30pm. Free
parking. NORTHERN ITALIAN.

The lovely dining room at Primavera is the setting for delicious, creatively prepared
Italian dishes. One of the most popular appetizers is bagna caoda primavera—grilled
eggplant, roasted red peppers, sun-dried tomatoes, Montrachet, and Parmesan cheese
with bagna caoda sauce. Main courses include angel-hair pasta with mushrooms,
garlic, prosciutto, capers, anchovies, and herbs; osso buco; and chicken breast with
eggplant, mozzarella cheese, mushrooms, and wine sauce. For dessert, I can't resist
the homemade tiramisu. This is the best restaurant in Coronado, but the last time I
dined there the service felt slightly robotic.

5 Beaches

San Diego County is blessed with 70 miles of sandy coastline and more than 30
beaches that attract surfers, snorkelers, swimmers, and sunbathers. In summer, the
beaches teem with locals and visitors alike. The rest of the year they're popular places
to walk and jog, and surfers don wet suits to pursue their passion.

The following are some of San Diego's most accessible beaches, each with its own
personality and devotees. If you're interested in others, *The California Coastal Access
Handbook*, published by the California Coastal Commission, is helpful. All California beaches are public to the mean high-tide line. If you plan to poke around in tide
pools, get a tide chart, available free or for a nominal charge from many surf and
diving shops, including **Emerald City Surf and Sport,** at 118 Orange Ave.,
Coronado (☎ 619/435-6677), and **San Diego Divers Supply,** at 5701 La Jolla
Blvd., La Jolla (☎ 619/459-2691).

OCEAN BEACH   Near the pier off I-8 and Sunset Cliffs Boulevard, this is surfers' and sunset-lovers' heaven and the stuff Beach Boys songs are made of. Not far
away are Dog Beach, where four-legged beach lovers roam unleashed, and Garbage
Beach, another surfing spot (happily, it doesn't live up to its name).

MISSION BAY PARK   In this 4,600-acre aquatic playground you'll discover
27 miles of bay front, 17 miles of oceanfront beaches, picnic areas, children's
playgrounds, and paths for biking, roller-skating, and jogging. The bay lends itself
to windsurfing, sailing, jet-skiing, waterskiing, and fishing. There are dozens of

access points; one of the most popular is off I-5 at Clairemont Drive, where there's a visitor information center.

PACIFIC BEACH   Here you'll find a popular beach and boardwalk for meeting friends, grabbing a bite to eat, jogging, biking, or in-line skating. It runs along Ocean Boulevard (just west of Mission Boulevard), north of Pacific Beach Drive.

MISSION BEACH   Surfing is popular year-round here. The long beach and board-walk extend from Pacific Beach Drive south to Belmont Park and beyond to the jetty.

BONITA COVE/MARINER'S POINT AND MISSION POINT   Facing Mission Bay in South Mission Beach, these spots are perfect for families, with calm waters, grassy areas for picnicking, and playground equipment.

WINDANSEA   One of California's finest surfing beaches, this area along Neptune Street in La Jolla achieved cult status in 1968, when the serious surfers who rode its waves were the subject of Tom Wolfe's book *The Pumphouse Gang*. Hang around for the usually memorable sunset.

✪ LA JOLLA COVE   The protected, calm waters here, praised as the clearest along the California coast, attract swimmers, snorkelers, scuba divers, and families on outings. There's a small sandy beach and on the cliffs above, the Ellen Browning Scripps Park. The Cove's "look but don't touch" policy protects the colorful Garibaldi, California's state fish, plus other marine life, including abalone, octopus, and lobster. The unique Underwater Park stretches from here to the northern end of Torrey Pines State Reserve and incorporates kelp forests, artificial reefs, two deep submarine canyons, and tidal pools.

LA JOLLA SHORES BEACH   A mile-long flat stretch of beach, it's popular for jogging, swimming, and body and board surfing for beginners. Families often come here, where lifeguards are on duty year-round.

BLACK'S BEACH   The area's unofficial nude beach, it lies between La Jolla Shores Beach and Torrey Pines State Beach. Below some steep cliffs, it's out of the way and not easy to reach. To get here, take North Torrey Pines Road, park at the Glider Port, and walk from there. *Note:* Though the water is shallow and pleasant for wading, this area is known for its rip currents.

DEL MAR   After a visit to the famous fairgrounds that host the Del Mar Thor-oughbred Club, you may want to make tracks for the beach, a long stretch of sand backed by grassy cliffs and a playground area. Del Mar is about 15 miles from down-town San Diego.

NORTHERN SAN DIEGO COUNTY   Those inclined to venture even farther north in San Diego County won't be disappointed. Pacific Coast Highway leads to some inviting beaches, such as these in Encinitas: peaceful Boneyards Beach, Swami's Beach for surfing, and Moonlight Beach, popular with families and volleyball buffs. Farthest north in this beach-blessed county is Oceanside, which has one of the West Coast's longest wooden piers and several popular surfing areas. For further discussion of the beaches here, see "North County Beach Towns," below.

CORONADO BEACH   Lovely, wide, and sparkling white, this romantic beach is conducive to strolling and lingering, especially in late afternoon. It fronts Ocean Boulevard and is especially pretty in front of the Hotel del Coronado. The islands visible from here, 18 miles off the coast, are named Los Coronados, and they belong to Mexico.

IMPERIAL BEACH   Half an hour south of San Diego by car or trolley and only a few minutes from the Mexican border lies Imperial Beach. Besides being popular

San Diego & North County Beaches

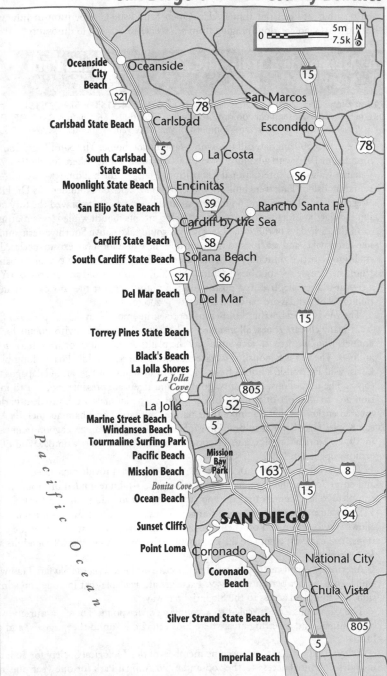

Oceanside City Beach
Oceanside
S21
Carlsbad State Beach
Carlsbad
South Carlsbad State Beach
Moonlight State Beach
San Elijo State Beach
Cardiff State Beach
South Cardiff State Beach
Del Mar Beach
Torrey Pines State Beach
Black's Beach
La Jolla Shores
La Jolla Cove
Marine Street Beach
Windansea Beach
Tourmaline Surfing Park
Pacific Beach
Mission Beach
Bonita Cove
Ocean Beach
Sunset Cliffs
Point Loma
Coronado Beach
Silver Strand State Beach
Imperial Beach

San Marcos
Escondido
La Costa
78
S6
Encinitas
S9
Rancho Santa Fe
Cardiff by the Sea
S8
Solana Beach
S21
S6
Del Mar
15
805
52
5
Mission Bay Park
163
15
8
SAN DIEGO
94
La Jolla
Coronado
National City
Chula Vista
805
5

15
78

Pacific Ocean

0   5m   N
    7.5k

with surfers, it hosts the annual U.S. Open Sandcastle Competition in July, with world-class sand creations ranging from sea scenes to dragons to dinosaurs.

6 Ménagerie à Trois: The Zoo, Wild Animal Park & Sea World

✪ **San Diego Zoo.** 2920 Zoo Dr., Balboa Park. ☎ **619/234-3153** or 619/231-1515. On the Internet: http//www.sandiegozoo.org. Admission $15 adults, $6 children 3–11. AE, DISC, MC, V. July to Labor Day daily 9am–9pm; rest of year daily 9am–4pm. Bus: 7, 7A, or 7B.

More than 3,500 animals call this world-famous zoo home. The San Diego Zoo was founded in 1916 with a handful of animals originally brought here for the 1915–16 Panama-California International Exposition. Many of the buildings you see in surrounding Balboa Park were built for the Exposition. The zoo's founder was Dr. Harry Wegeforth, local physician and lifelong animal lover, who once braved the fury of an injured tiger in order to toss needed medicine into its mouth while it was roaring.

In the early days of the zoo, "Dr. Harry" would take native Southwestern animals like rattlesnakes and sea lions to trade around the world for more exotic species. This tradition is carried on today: In September 1996, the zoo received two giant pandas from the People's Republic of China. Shi Shi, a 16-year-old male, and Bai Yun, a 5-year-old female, live in a posh panda-minium that cost the zoo more than $1 million. The pandas are expected to be at the zoo for 12 years.

The zoo is also a botanical museum, representing more than 6,500 species of flora from many climate zones, all installed to help simulate native environments for the animals who live here. In fact, some say the plants are actually worth more than the animals. The zoo is famous for its rare and exotic species: cuddly koalas, long-billed kiwis, wild Przewalski's horses from Mongolia, lowland gorillas, and Galapagos tortoises. The usual lions, elephants, giraffes, and tigers are present, too, not to mention a great number of tropical birds. Most of the animals are housed in barless, moated enclosures that resemble their natural habitats. These habitats include African Kopje, Tiger River, Sun Bear Forest, Scripps Aviary, Flamingo Lagoon (renovated in 1996), Gorilla Tropics, and Hippo Beach. New polar bear, wombat, and okapi exhibits opened in 1996.

The zoo offers two types of bus tours, both of which provide a narrated overview and cover 75% of the park. You can choose the 35-minute guided bus tour, which completes one circuit around the zoo (the cost is $4 for adults and $3 for kids 3 to 11). Or you might opt to take the Kangaroo Bus, which provides unlimited use and allows you to get on and off the bus as many times as you desire at any of the eight stops. You can even complete the circuit more than once; this costs $8 for adults and $5 for children.

Alternatively, you can get an aerial perspective of the zoo via the Skyfari Tramway, which costs $1 per person each way. Packages are available that include zoo admission, bus tour, and access to the Skyfari Tramway.

The Children's Zoo is scaled to a youngster's viewpoint. There's a nursery with baby animals and a petting area where kids can cuddle up to sheep, goats, and the like.

Budget tip: Two adults can become members of the Zoological Society for $68; this includes unlimited access to the zoo and Wild Animal Park for one year plus two guest passes to either the zoo or Wild Animal Park, six discount passes, four twofer bus passes, and free parking at the Wild Animal Park. This is a great deal when you consider that the regular admission price for two adults to these two attractions is $67.90. If you don't buy the annual pass, the best discount is the one for AAA members. The next best deal is using the coupons in the Visitor Value Pack available from the International Visitor Center. Also, keep in mind that the San Diego Zoo is free to everyone on the first Monday in October and free to children ages 11 and under all through October.

Sea World. 1720 S. Shores Rd., Mission Bay. ☎ **619/226-3901.** Admission $30.95 adults, $25.45 seniors 55 and older, $21.95 children 3–11; children under 3 free. DISC, MC, V. Parking $5 per car, $2 per motorcycle, and $7 per RV. Mid-June to Aug daily 9am–11pm; rest of the year daily 10am–5pm. Bus: 9. Exit I-5 west onto Sea World Dr.

Sea World is one of the best-promoted attractions in California. The 150-acre multimillion-dollar aquatic playground is a zoo and showplace for marine mammals in a nominally "educational" atmosphere. Several successive four-ton black-and-white killer whales have functioned as the park's mascot, all named Shamu. At its heart, Sea World is a family entertainment center where the performers are dolphins, otters, sea lions, walruses, and seals. Shows are presented continuously throughout the day, while visitors rotate to various theaters to watch the performances.

The park expanded dramatically in 1995, adding a two-acre hands-on park called Shamu's Happy Harbor. These attractions encourage kids to handle everything, including a pretend pirate ship, with plenty of netted towers, tubes to crawl through, slides, and chances to get wet. The newest attractions are Baywatch at Sea World, a water-ski show named for the popular TV show; Bermuda Triangle, an adventure ride; and Shamu Backstage, which makes it possible for visitors to get up close and personal with killer whales.

The Dolphin Interaction Program introduced at Sea World in late 1995 has created an opportunity for people to interact with bottlenose dolphins. Although this program does not allow you to swim with the dolphins, it gives you the opportunity to wade waist-deep into the water and plenty of time to stroke the mammals and give commands like the trainers. This two-hour program (one hour of education and instruction, 15 minutes of wet-suit fitting, and 45 minutes of interaction in the water with the dolphins) costs $125 per person ($95 per person for Sea World members). Space is limited to eight people per day, so advance reservations are required and participants must be at least 13 years old.

Although Sea World is best known as Shamu's home, the facility also plays an important role in rescuing and rehabilitating animals found beached along the San Diego coast—more than 300 seals, sea lions, marine birds, and dolphins in a recent year. Sea World also helps out with injured marine species in other parts of the world, such as the oil-soaked victims of the *Exxon Valdez* disaster. You might like to take a guided tour of the park and get an insider's view for $6 per adult and $5 per child.

Budget tip: The best deal is the discount for AAA members. The next best is the coupon in the Visitor Value Pack available from the International Visitor Center.

✪ **Wild Animal Park.** 15500 San Pasqual Valley Rd., Escondido (30 miles north of San Diego). ☎ **619/747-8702.** Admission $18.95 adults, $11.95 children 3–11, free for children 2 and under. AE, DISC, MC, V. Daily 9am–4pm; extended summer hours. Parking costs $3 per vehicle. Take I-15 to Via Rancho Pkwy.; follow signs from here for about 3 miles.

Many zoos could learn a lesson from the Wild Animal Park: More than 3,000 animals, many of them endangered species, roam freely over 2,200 acres, while the humans are enclosed. The animals don't usually eat each other because the predatory ones are kept separate from the ones that they might like to make a meal out of. This living arrangement encourages breeding colonies, so it's not surprising that more than 75 white rhinoceroses have been born here. Several species of rare animals that had vanished from the wilds and have been reintroduced to their natural habitats from stock bred here.

Cheap Thrills: What to See & Do for Free (or Almost) in San Diego

It's easy to get charged up on a vacation—$10 here, $5 there, and pretty soon your credit card statement looks like the national debt. To keep that from happening, I've compiled a list of San Diego–area activities that won't break your budget.

Downtown and Beyond   It doesn't cost a penny to stroll around the **Gaslamp Quarter,** along the Embarcadero, and around **Seaport Village** or **Horton Plaza.** And **Walkabout International** (☎ 619/231-7463) sponsors 150 free walking tours every month, led by volunteers. If you'd rather drive around, ask for the map of the 52-mile **San Diego Scenic Drive** when you're at the International Visitor Information Center. The downtown branch of the **Museum of Contemporary Art,** San Diego, is free the first Tuesday of each month. Another fun activity is the Sunset Cinema discussed under "Movies," below. And you can fish free of charge off any municipal pier (see "Fishing," below).

For Military Buffs   At the Broadway Pier, near the intersection of Broadway and Harbor Drive, a navy ship is in port and open for free tours most Saturdays and Sundays from 1 to 4pm (☎ 619/532-1430, ext. 9). There is usually a marine corps recruit parade at the **Marine Corps Recruit Depot** (MCRD) off Pacific Coast Highway on Friday mornings (☎ 619/225-3141); and a navy recruit review at the **Naval Training Center** off Rosecrans in Point Loma most Friday afternoons at 1:15, featuring a marching band, drum-and-bugle corps, flag teams, and color guards (☎ 619/225-5311).

Balboa Park   The **San Diego Zoo** is free to all on the first Monday of October, Founders Day. Children 11 and under are free every day during October.

All of the **museums in Balboa Park** are open to the public free of charge one day a month. The following is a list of free days (if you can't get there on a free day, buy a Passport to Balboa Park (10 museums for $18) at the **Balboa Park Visitors Information Center** (☎ 619/239-0512).

- **First Tuesday of the month**   Natural History Museum, Reuben H. Fleet Science Center, and Model Railroad Museum.
- **Second Tuesday of the month**   Museum of Photographic Arts, Hall of Champions, and Museum of San Diego History.
- **Third Tuesday of the month**   Museum of Art, Museum of Man, and Japanese Friendship Garden.
- **Fourth Tuesday of the month**   Aerospace Museum and San Diego Automotive Museum.

The following attractions in Balboa Park are always free: The Botanical Building and Lily Pond, House of Pacific Relations International Cottages, and Timken Museum of Art. Free one-hour Sunday concerts and free Summer Festival concerts are given at the Spreckels Organ Pavilion.

The best way to see the animals is by riding the 5-mile monorail (included in the price of admission); for the best views sit on the right side. During the 50-minute ride, as you pass through areas resembling Africa and Asia you'll learn interesting tidbits—did you know that rhinos are susceptible to sunburn and mosquito bites? Trains leave every 20 minutes; you can watch informative videos while you wait in the stations.

Old Town and Beyond   You can walk around **Heritage Park, Presidio Park, or Old Town State Historic Park** without paying a dime, and there's no charge to enjoy the entertainment (mariachis and folk dancers) at the **Bazaar del Mundo** on Saturday and Sunday. If you're interested in art, you might want to watch the glass blowers at Lowery's, 3985 Harney St. There's also no admission charge to **Mission Trails Regional Park,** where there are hiking trails and an interpretive center. Admission to **Mission Basilica San Diego de Alcala** is a suggested $2 donation.

Mission Bay and Pacific Beach   Walk along the beach or around the bay—not only is it free and fun, it's good for you.

La Jolla   Enjoy the ✪ **free outdoor concerts at Scripps Park** on Sundays from 2 to 4pm, mid-June through mid-September (☎ 619/525-3160). Anytime is a good time to take a walk around the **La Jolla Cove, Ellen Browning Scripps Park,** and **Torrey Pines State Reserve.** As you walk along the ocean in La Jolla you're bound to notice the harbor seal colony at the **Children's Pool** (near the intersection of Coast Boulevard and Jenner). If you're a diver check out the 6,000-acre **San Diego–La Jolla Underwater Park,** which stretches from La Jolla Cove to the northern end of Torrey Pines State Reserve. It's also fun to meander around the campus of **University of California at San Diego (UCSD)** and view the Stuart Collection of Outdoor Sculpture. The La Jolla branch of the **Museum of Contemporary Art,** San Diego, is free the first Tuesday of each month. For the best vista, follow the "Scenic Drive" signs to Mount Soledad and a 360° view of the area.

Coronado   Drive across the **Coronado Bay Bridge** (free for two or more people in a car) and take a self-guided tour of the ✪ **Hotel Del Coronado's** grounds and photo gallery. Take a walk on the beach and continue on to the **Coronado Beach Historical Museum.**

North County   My favorite thing to do in and around Leucadia and Encinitas is to **visit the garden nurseries.** Because I'm a plant junkie, this isn't a free activity for *me,* since I'm usually looking to add to my collection, but it might be for you if you're just visiting and prefer only to look. My favorites nurseries are **Weidners's Gardens,** 695 Normandy Rd. (☎ 619/436-2194), and **Encinitas Gardens,** 1452 Santa Fe Dr., Encinitas (☎ 619/753-2852). You can request a copy of the *Nursery Hopper's Guide* from North County Nursery Hoppers Association, P.O. Box 231208, Encinitas, CA 92023-1208.

I also enjoy watching the hot-air balloons as they take off and float over the polo field and golf courses around **Del Mar** and **Rancho Santa Fe.** If you'd like to watch them launch, head to the intersection of El Camino Real and San Dieguito Road.

Parts of the park can be visited on foot. On the 1³/₄-mile Kilimanjaro hiking trail, you'll see tigers, elephants, and cheetahs close up (the animals are separated from the hikers by chain-link fences that are well disguised with landscaping), as well as the Australian rain forest and views of East Africa.

Approximately 650 baby animals are born every year in the park, which also is a botanical preserve with more than two million plants, including 300 endangered species.

San Diego Attractions

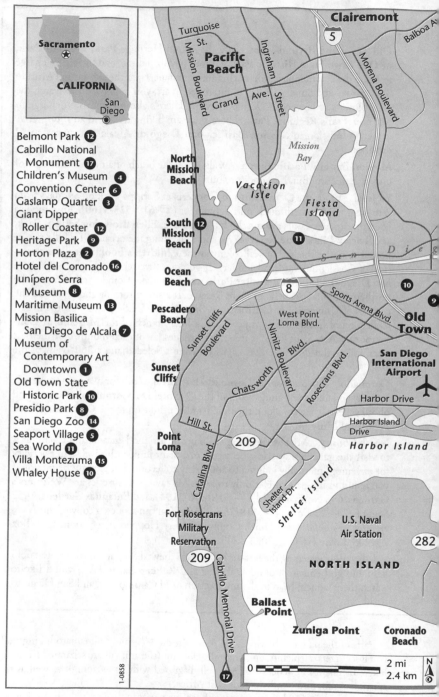

Belmont Park ⑫
Cabrillo National
  Monument ⑰
Children's Museum ④
Convention Center ⑥
Gaslamp Quarter ③
Giant Dipper
  Roller Coaster ⑫
Heritage Park ⑨
Horton Plaza ②
Hotel del Coronado ⑯
Junípero Serra
  Museum ⑧
Maritime Museum ⑬
Mission Basilica
  San Diego de Alcala ⑦
Museum of
  Contemporary Art
  Downtown ①
Old Town State
  Historic Park ⑩
Presidio Park ⑧
San Diego Zoo ⑭
Seaport Village ⑤
Sea World ⑪
Villa Montezuma ⑮
Whaley House ⑩

Downtown

Date Street
Cedar Street
Beech Street
Ash Street
A Street
B Street
C Street
Broadway

4th Ave.
5th Ave.
6th Ave.
7th Ave.
8th Ave.
9th Ave.
10th Ave.
11th Ave.

Drive
Highway
Harbor
Pacific
Kettner Blvd.
State Street
Union Street
Front Street
Market Street
1st Ave.
2nd Ave.
3rd Ave.
Harbor Dr.

E Street
F Street
G Street
Island Avenue
J Street
K Street

Gaslamp Quarter

Vista Rd.
Linda
Friars Rd.
River

8

Hillcrest/ Uptown

Pacific Hwy.
1st Ave.
5th Ave.
163
Park Blvd.

Balboa Park

805
15
94

Ash Street
Broadway

SAN DIEGO

Euclid Ave.

National Ave.
Logan Ave.

3rd St.
4th St.
Orange Ave.

San Diego–Coronado Bay Bridge (Toll)

Division St.

National City
8th St.

Silver
75
805

Photo tours take place May through September on Wednesday, Thursday, Saturday, and Sunday, costing $60 or $85 depending on the tour. Stroller and wheelchair rentals are available. Take a jacket along; it can get cold in the open-air monorail. Local public transportation will get you here, but it takes three buses and 3¹/₂ hours; Gray Line, a local tour company, offers a seven-hour tour for $40 for adults and $24 for kids, including admission and transportation (for more information, call 619/491-0011).

7 Exploring the Area

BALBOA PARK

Balboa Park is one of the nation's largest, loveliest, and most important municipal greenbelts. This is no simple city park: It boasts walkways, gardens, historical buildings, a couple of restaurants, an ornate pavilion with one of the world's largest outdoor organs, and a world-famous zoo that's been covered earlier in this chapter. Stroll along El Prado, the park's main street, and admire the distinctive Spanish-Mediterranean buildings, which house an amazing array of museums.

Entry to the park is free, of course, but most of its museums have admission charges and varying open hours. A free tram will transport you around the park. It might be worth your while to buy the Balboa Park Pass (10 museums for $18) from the Visitors Center. Below is a list of highlights. (See "Cheap Thrills," above, for a list of free days at these museums.)

✪ **Aerospace Museum & International Aerospace Hall of Fame** (☎ 619/234-8291): Great achievers and achievements in the history of aviation and aerospace are celebrated by this superb collection of historical aircraft and related artifacts, including art, models, dioramas, and films.

Museum of Art (☎ 619/232-7931): The impressive painting and sculpture collections here include outstanding Italian Renaissance and Dutch and Spanish baroque art. Exhibits in the ground-floor Grant-Munger Gallery include works by Monet, Toulouse-Lautrec, Renoir, Pissarro, and Van Gogh. Upstairs in the Fitch Gallery is El Greco's *Penitent St. Peter,* and in the Gluck Gallery hangs Modigliani's *Boy with Blue Eyes* and Braque's *Coquelicots.*

✪ **Museum of Photographic Arts** (☎ 619/239-5262): One of the finest museums in the city, the Museum of Photographic Arts occupies an imitation Spanish baroque building that served as part of Charles Foster Kane's Xanadu in the film *Citizen Kane.* The museum displays a wide range of historic and contemporary work and has made a commitment to issue-oriented photography.

Natural History Museum (☎ 619/232-3821): The best exhibits display the plants, animals, and minerals of the San Diego and Baja California region. There's also a Foucault pendulum, a seismograph, and a life-size Allosaurus skeleton. The Hall of Desert Ecology features a discovery lab, with living desert denizens.

Reuben H. Fleet Space Theater and Science Center (☎ 619/238-1233, or 619/232-6866 for advance ticket sales): Easily the park's busiest museum, this large complex contains a Science Center with 65 hands-on exhibits, a laser light show, and an OMNIMAX movie theater with a 76-foot screen. In the theater, sophisticated effects give simulated journeys an incredible feeling of reality. The giant dome is also the setting for thrilling travelogues and voyages under the sea and inside a volcano. Call to charge tickets in advance; you may save yourself a long wait in line.

Museum of Man (☎ 619/239-2001): This museum is devoted to the sociology and anthropology of the peoples of North and South America, and includes life-size replicas of a dozen varieties of Homo sapiens.

Balboa Park

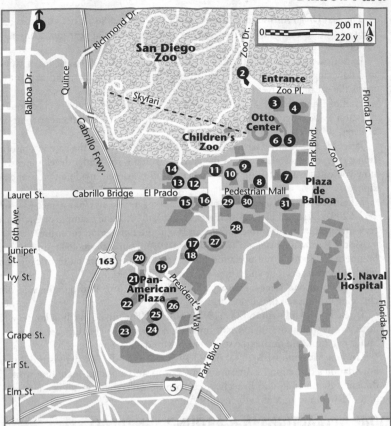

Aerospace Museum 23
Alcazar Gardens 15
Balboa Park Club 20
Balboa Park Visitors Center 29
Botanical Building 9
Carousel 4
Casa de Balboa 30
  Hall of Champions Sports Museum
  Museum of Photographic Arts
  Museum of San Diego History
  Model Railroad Museum
Casa del Prado 8
Federal Building 26
Hall of Nations 17
House of Charm
  Mingei International
    Museum of World Folk Art
  San Diego Art Institure 16
House of Pacific Relations
  International Cottages 19
Japanese Friendship Garden 28
Marston House 1
Municipal Museum 25

Museum of Art 11
Museum of Man 13
Photographic Arts Building 5
Natural History Museum 7
Palisades Building
  Marie Hitchcock Puppet Theater
  Recital Hall 21
Reuben H. Fleet Space Theater
  & Science Center 31
San Diego Automotive Museum 22
San Diego Miniature Railroad 3
San Diego Zoo 2
Sculpture Garden 12
Simon Edison Centre for the Performing Arts 14
  Old Globe Theatre
  Cassius Carter Centre Stage
  Lowell Davies Festival Theatre
Spanish Village Art Center 6
Spreckels Organ Pavilion 27
Starlight Bowl 24
Timken Museum of Art 10
United Nations Building 18

1-0859

The **San Diego Automotive Museum** (☎ 619/231-2886): Check out that classic Bentley and the rare 1948 Tucker, among other gems that appear in a changing array of shows featuring classic, antique, and exotic cars.

Botanical Museum (☎ 619/235-1100): More than 1,000 varieties of tropical and flowering plants are sheltered within this structure. The lily pond out front attracts the occasional street performer.

Hall of Champions (☎ 619/234-2544): Sports fans will want to check out this museum, which highlights dozens of different professional and amateur sports and athletes.

Japanese Friendship Garden (☎ 619/232-2780): Stop in the garden's information center to see a scale model of the garden, which is still under development. For now you can see a sekitei, the most ancient kind of garden, made only of sand and stone.

Marston House Museum, located on Balboa Drive at Upas Street (☎ 619/232-6203): Designed by local architect Irving Gill, this fine example of Craftsman-style architecture exhibits fine antique and reproduction period furniture.

Model Railroad Museum (☎ 619/696-0199): Four scale-model railroads depict Southern California's transportation history and terrain. There's a terrific gift shop, plus multimedia exhibits and hands-on Lionel trains for kids.

Museum of San Diego History (☎ 619/232-6203): Photographs and other changing exhibits tell the city's story.

Sprekels Organ Pavilion (☎ 619/226-0819): The ornate pavilion houses a fantastic organ with more than 4,000 individual pipes. Free concerts are given every Sunday at 2pm, and during the summer on Mondays at 8pm.

Timken Museum of Art (☎ 619/239-5548): On display here is the Putnam Foundation's collection of American and European paintings, including works by Boucher, Rembrandt, and Brueghel. The private gallery also exhibits a rare collection of Russian icons and 19th-century American paintings.

MORE ATTRACTIONS IN & AROUND SAN DIEGO

✪ **Cabrillo National Monument.** 1800 Cabrillo Memorial Dr., Point Loma. ☎ 619/557-5450. Admission $4 per vehicle, $2 for walk-ins; ages 62 and over (with a National Parks Service Golden Age Passport) and 16 and younger free. Daily 9am–5:15pm. Follow I-5 or I-8 to Rosecrans St. (Calif. 209), which leads to Point Loma and the monument via Catalina Blvd.

Enjoy stunning views while you're learning about California history at this monument commemorating Juan Rodríguez Cabrillo, the European discoverer of America's west coast. At the restored Old Point Loma Lighthouse, visitors are treated to a sweeping vista of the ocean, bays, islands, mountains, valleys, and plains that make up San Diego. From mid-December to February the lighthouse is a good vantage point for watching the migration of the Pacific gray whales. National Park rangers offer free 30-minute films about the monument daily from 10am to 4pm, and there are tide pools that beg for exploration. A free film about the whale migration is shown during winter.

Children's Museum of San Diego. 200 W. Island Ave. ☎ 619/233-8792. Admission $5 for adults and children over 2, $2.50 for seniors; children under 2 free. Tues–Sat 10am–4:30pm, Sun 11am–4:30pm. Trolley: Convention Center stop; the museum is a block away.

This is an interactive museum that encourages hands-on participation. It provides ongoing supervised activities, as well as a monthly special celebration, with changing exhibits every month. A big draw for kids ages 2 to 10 is the indoor and outdoor art studio. There is also a theater with costumes for budding actors to don.

Maritime Museum. 1306 N. Harbor Dr. ☎ **619/234-9153.** Admission (to all 3 ships) $5 adults, $4 seniors and children 13–17, $2 children 6–12. DISC, MC, V. Daily 9am–8pm. Bus: 4, 9, 29, 34, 34A, or 35.

This nautical museum consists of three restored historic vessels docked downtown at the Embarcadero. *The Berkeley,* a propeller-driven ferry launched in 1898, participated in the evacuation of San Francisco after the great earthquake and fire of 1906. *The Medea,* a steam yacht built in Scotland in 1904, was used in both world wars. *The Star of India,* launched in 1863, is the oldest square-rigged merchant vessel still afloat. Each vessel can be boarded and explored. April through October you can even watch movies on the deck.

Museum of Contemporary Art, Downtown (MCA). 1001 Kettner Blvd. (at Broadway). ☎ **619/234-1001.** Admission $4 adults; $2 students, military with ID, and seniors; 50¢ children 5–12; free on first Tues of the month. AE, MC, V. Tues–Sun 10:30am–5:30pm; Fri 10:30am–8pm. Parking $2 with validation at America Plaza Complex. Trolley: America Plaza.

Two large galleries and two smaller ones present changing exhibitions of distinguished contemporary artists. Lectures and tours for adults and children are offered.

Villa Montezuma. 1925 K St. (at 20th Ave.). ☎ **619/239-2211.** Admission $3 adults, $5 in combination with Marston House, free for children 12 and under. MC, V. Sat–Sun noon–4:30pm; during Dec Thurs–Sun noon–4:30pm. Bus: 3, 3A, 4, 5, 16, or 105 to Market and Imperial sts.

Just east of downtown, this stunning mansion was built in 1887 for then internationally acclaimed musician and author Jesse Shepard. Lush with Victoriana, it features stained-glass windows depicting Mozart, Beethoven, Sappho, Rubens, St. Cecilia (patron saint of musicians), and other notables. The San Diego Historical Society painstakingly restored the house, on the National Register of Historic Places, and furnished it with period pieces. Unfortunately, the neighborhood is not as fashionable as the house, but it's safe to park your car here in the daytime. If you love Victorian houses, don't miss this one for its quirkiness.

OLD TOWN & BEYOND: A LOOK AT CALIFORNIA'S BEGINNINGS

The birthplace of San Diego—indeed, of California—Old Town brings back to life Mexican California, which existed here until the mid-1800s. You can get to Old Town on the trolley. Free walking tours leave daily at 2pm from the Old Town State Historic Park's visitors center (☎ 619/220-5422), located at the head of the pedestrian walkway that is the continuation of San Diego Avenue. Admission to the center, open daily from 10am to 5pm, is free. Among the highlights are the following:

Heritage Park. 2455 Heritage Park Row (corner of Juan and Harney sts.), Old Town. ☎ **619/694-3049.** Free admission. Daily 9:30am–3pm. Bus: 4 or 5/105.

This small 7.8-acre park is filled with seven original 19th-century houses moved here from other places and given new uses, among them a bed-and-breakfast inn, a doll shop, and a gift shop. Take a tour and have tea for $10 Tuesday to Sunday from 2:30 to 5pm.

Junípero Serra Museum. 2727 Presidio Dr., Presidio Park, Old Town. ☎ **619/297-3258.** Admission $3 adults, free for children 12 and under. MC, V. Tues–Sat 10am–4:30pm, Sun noon–4:30pm. Take I-8 to Taylor St. exit; turn right on Taylor, then left on Presidio Dr. or take a bus to the intersection of Taylor and Juan sts. and walk uphill.

Perched on a hill above Old Town, the stately mission-style building overlooks the spot where California began. Here in 1769, the first mission and first nonnative settlement on the west coast of the United States and Canada were founded. Inside, the museum's exhibits introduce visitors to California's origins, and to the Native American, Spanish, and Mexican people who first called this place home. On display are their belongings, from cannons to cookware. The mission remained San Diego's only settlement until the 1820s, when families began to move down the hill into what is now known as Old Town. Watch an ongoing archaeological dig uncover more of the items used by early settlers.

The museum is located in Presidio Park, called the "Plymouth Rock of the Pacific." The large cross in the park was made from floor tile from the Presidio ruins. Sculptor Arthur Puntnam made the statues of Father Serra, founder of the missions in California, and the Native American. Climb up to Inspiration Point for a sweeping view of the area.

Mission Basilica San Diego de Alcala. 10818 San Diego Mission Rd., Mission Valley. ☎ **619/281-8449.** Admission $2 adults, $1 seniors and students, 50¢ children 12 and under. Daily 9am–5pm; mass daily 7am and 5:30pm. Bus: 6, 16, 25, 43, or 81. Take I-8 to Mission Gorge Rd. to Twain Ave.

Established in 1769, this was the first link in a chain of 21 missions founded by Spanish missionary Junípero Serra. In 1774, the mission was moved to its present site for agricultural reasons and to separate Native American converts from a fortress that included the original building. A few bricks belonging to the original mission can be seen in Presidio Park in Old Town. Mass is held regularly in this still-active Catholic parish.

Whaley House. 2482 San Diego Ave. ☎ **619/298-2482.** Admission $4 adults, $3 seniors 65 and over, $2 juniors 5–16. Daily 10am–5pm.

In 1856, this striking two-story house (the first one in these parts) just outside Old Town State Historic Park was built for Thomas Whaley and his family. Whaley was a New Yorker who arrived here via San Francisco, where he had been lured by the gold rush. The house is one of only two authenticated haunted houses in California, and 10,000 schoolchildren come here each year hoping to see the unexplained paranormal activity for themselves. Exhibits include a life mask of Abraham Lincoln, one of only six made; the spinet piano used in the movie *Gone with the Wind;* and the concert piano that accompanied Swedish soprano Jenny Lind on her final U.S. tour in 1852. Director June Reading will make you feel at home, in spite of the ghost.

LA JOLLA

Some folks just enjoy driving around La Jolla, taking in the sea views and the 360° vista from the top of Mount Soledad. However, La Jolla also offers other attractions.

Torrey Pines State Reserve (☎ **619/755-2063**) has hiking trails with wonderful ocean views and a chance to see the rare torrey pine. Access is via N. Torrey Pines Road. The trails are free of charge; parking costs $4 per car, $3 for seniors.

Museum of Contemporary Art, San Diego. 700 Prospect St., La Jolla, CA 92037. ☎ **619/ 454-3541.** Admission $4 adults; $2 students, military with ID, and seniors; children under 12 free; free to all first Tues of each month. Take Ardath Rd. and exit off I-5 north, or La Jolla Village Dr. West and exit off I-5 south. Take Torrey Pines Rd. to Prospect Pl. and turn right; Prospect Pl. becomes Prospect St.

Focusing primarily on work produced since 1950, the museum is known internationally for its permanent collection and thought-provoking exhibitions. After being closed for two years while it underwent a major renovation and expansion, MCA, San Diego reopened in March of 1996. The ocean views from the galleries are gorgeous.

La Jolla

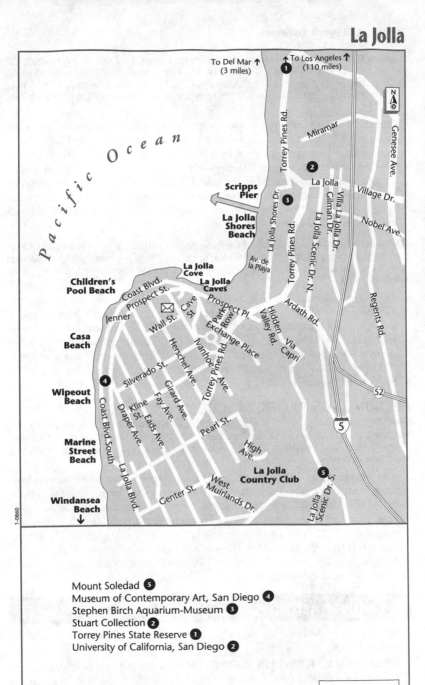

Mount Soledad ❺
Museum of Contemporary Art, San Diego ❹
Stephen Birch Aquarium-Museum ❸
Stuart Collection ❷
Torrey Pines State Reserve ❶
University of California, San Diego ❷

Post Office ✉

Stephen Birch Aquarium-Museum. At the Scripps Institution of Oceanography, 2300 Expedition Way, La Jolla, CA 92037. ☎ **619/534-3474** for a recording. Admission $6.50 adults, $5.50 seniors, $4.50 students, $3.50 children 3–12. AE, MC, V. Daily 9am–5pm. Take I-5 to La Jolla Village Dr. West, which turns into North Torrey Pines Rd., then turn left at Expedition Way. Parking $3.

Part of the Scripps Institution of Oceanography, a branch of the University of California San Diego, the aquarium-museum offers close-up views of the Pacific Ocean in 33 marine life tanks. The giant kelp forest is particularly impressive. World renowned for its oceanic research, Scripps offers visitors a chance to view its marine aquarium and artificial outdoor tide pools. The museum has interpretive exhibits on the current and historical research done at the institution, which has been in existence since 1903. In 1997, the aquarium will highlight The Year of the Reef with special exhibits and programs.

Stuart Collection. At the University of California San Diego (UCSD). ☎ **619/534-2117.** Free admission. From La Jolla, take Torrey Pines Rd. to La Jolla Village Dr., turn right, go 2 blocks to Gilman Dr., and turn left into the campus; in about a block the information booth will be visible on the right.

The Stuart Collection is a work in progress on a large scale. The still-growing collection consists of site-related sculptures by leading contemporary artists placed throughout the 1,200-acre UCSD campus. Among the 12 diverse sculptures on view are Niki de Saint-Phalle's *Sun God,* a jubilant 14-foot fiberglass bird on a 15-foot concrete base, nicknamed "Big Bird" and made an unofficial mascot by the students. Pick up a brochure and map with marked sculpture locations from the information booth at the Northview Drive or Gilman Drive entrance to the campus.

MISSION BAY & PACIFIC BEACH

Giant Dipper Roller Coaster. 3146 Mission Blvd. ☎ **619/488-1549.** Admission to park is free; ride on Giant Dipper is $2.50. Summer hours: Sun, Mon, and Thurs 11am–8pm, Tues–Wed 11am–9pm, Fri–Sat 11am–10pm. Closes earlier rest of the year. Take I-5 to the Sea World exit, and follow W. Mission Bay Dr. to Belmont Park.

A local landmark for 70 years, the Giant Dipper is one of two surviving fixtures from the original Belmont Amusement Park (the other is the Plunge indoor swimming pool). After sitting dormant for 15 years, this vintage wooden roller coaster, with more than 2,600 feet of track and 13 hills, underwent an extensive restoration and reopened in 1991. You can also ride on the Giant Dipper's neighbor, the Liberty Carousel ($1), or the newer rides: Tilt-a-Whirl, Crazy Sub, Thunder Boats, and Baja Buggies. You can also watch the Dive-In Movies shown at the Plunge (☎ 619/488-3110), an indoor swimming pool (see "Movies," below, for details).

8 Outdoor Activities

For coverage of the San Diego area's best beaches, see the "Beaches" section earlier in this chapter.

BICYCLING & MOUNTAIN BIKING   Mission Bay and Coronado are especially good for leisurely bike rides. The boardwalk in Pacific Beach and Mission Beach can get very crowded, especially on weekends. Most major thoroughfares offer a bike lane. Just remember to wear a helmet; it's the law. For information on bike rentals, see Section 2, "Getting Around," earlier in this chapter.

For a downhill thrill of a lifetime, take the **Palomar Plunge.** From the top of Palomar Mountain to its base, you'll experience, courtesy of gravity, a 5,000-foot vertical drop stretched out over 16 miles. Or try the **Desert Descent,** a 12-mile,

3,700-foot descent down the Montezuma Valley Grade to the desert floor, followed by a tour of the Visitor Center and a delicious lunch. **Gravity Activated Sports** (☎ **800/985-4427** or 619/742-2294) supplies the mountain bike, helmet, gloves, souvenir photo, and T-shirt.

Adventure Bike Tours, based at the Hyatt (☎ **619/234-1500,** ext. 6514) offers a "Bay to Breakers" bike ride that starts in downtown San Diego and includes Coronado. The cost of $39 covers bikes, helmets, the ferry, and a guide.

Backroads Bicycle Touring, (☎ **800/BIKE-TRIP** or 415/527-1555) offers cycling packages to San Diego.

BOATING   Club Nautico, a concession at the San Diego Marriott Marina, 333 W. Harbor Dr. (☎ **619/233-9311;** fax 619/689-2363), provides guests and non-guests an exhilarating way to see the bay by the hour, half day, or full day in 20- to 27-foot offshore power boats. Rentals start at $89 per hour. They also rent wave runners and allow their boats to be taken into the ocean, and also provide diving, waterskiing, and fishing packages.

Seaforth Boat Rental, 1641 Quivira Rd., Mission Bay (☎ **619/223-1681**), has a wide variety of fishing boats for bay and ocean, powerboats for $50 to $90 per hour, and 14- to 27-foot sailboats for $20 to $45 per hour; with half-day and full-day rates. Canoes, pedal boats, kayaks, and rowboats are available for those who prefer a slower pace. If you don't want to go out on the water they also rent bicycles and equipment with which you can fish off the Municipal Pier (see below). **Downtown Boat Rental** (at the Marriott), 33 W. Harbor Dr. (☎ **619/239-2628**), has similar rentals.

Coronado Boat Rental, 1715 Strand Way, in Coronado (☎ **619/437-1514**), has powerboats renting from $65 to $90 per hour, with half- and full-day rates; 14- to 30-foot sailboats from $25 to $40 per hour; and jet skis, skiboats, canoes, pedal boats, kayaks, fishing skiffs, and charter boats.

Sail USA (☎ **619/298-6822**) offers custom-tailored skippered cruises on a 34-foot Catalina sloop. A half-day bay cruise costs $275 for up to six passengers. Full-day and overnight trips are also available, as are trips up the coast and to Catalina.

FISHING   Public fishing piers are at Shelter Island (where there's a statue dedicated to anglers), Ocean Beach, and Imperial Beach. Anglers of any age can fish free of charge without a license off any municipal pier in California. Fishing charters depart from Harbor and Shelter islands, Point Loma, the Imperial Beach pier, and Quivira Basin in Mission Bay (near the Hyatt Islandia Hotel). Participants in these trips over the age of 16 need a California fishing license.

For **sportfishing,** you can go out on a large boat for about $25 for a half-day, or $40 to $100 for three-quarters to a full day. Call around and compare prices. Summer and fall are excellent times for excursions; it's worth the splurge if you're into sportfishing. Locally, the waters around Point Loma are filled with bass, bonita, and barracuda; the Coronado Islands, which belong to Mexico but are only about 18 miles from San Diego, are popular for abalone, yellowtail, yellow fin, and big-eyed tuna. Some outfitters will take you farther into Baja California waters.

The following outfitters offer short or extended outings with daily departures: **H&M Landing** (☎ 619/222-1144), **Islandia Sportfishing** (☎ 619/222-1164), **Lee Palm Sportfishers** (☎ 619/224-3857), **Point Loma Sportfishing** (☎ 619/223-1627), and **Seaforth Boat Rentals** (☎ 619/223-1681).

GOLF   With nearly 80 courses, 50 of them open to the public, San Diego County has much to offer the golf enthusiast. Courses are diverse, some with vistas of the Pacific, others with views of country hillsides or of desert. **Par-Tee Golf** (☎ **800/PAR-TEE-1**) and **M&M Tee Times** (☎ **619/456-8366**) can arrange tee times for you at most golf courses. **Greenlink** (☎ 619/I-LOVE-GOLF—that's 619/456-8346) is also a valuable source of information about golf courses, schools, and equipment.

And where else but San Diego can you practice your golf swing in the middle of the central business district? The **Harborside Golf Center,** on Broadway at Pacific Highway (☎ 619/239-GOLF), is open from 8am to 11pm daily. Here you will find 80 tees, 40 with automatic pop-up; a USGA putting and chipping area; night lighting; a pro shop; golf school; and golf simulators. Club rental is available at $1 each; a large bucket of balls costs $6; a small bucket, $3.

Space constraints prevent us from listing all of the San Diego area's fine golf courses (for a more extensive listing, see *Frommer's San Diego)*, but a partial listing follows.

Coronado Municipal Golf Course. 2000 Visalia Row, Coronado. ☎ **619/435-3121.**

This is the first sight that welcomes you as you cross the Coronado Bay Bridge (the course is off to the left). It is an 18-hole, par-72 course overlooking Glorietta Bay, and there's a coffee shop, pro shop, and driving range. Two-day prior reservations are strongly recommended; call anytime after 7am. Greens fees are $20 for 18 holes; $10 after 4pm.

☉ Torrey Pines Golf Course. 11480 Torrey Pines Rd., La Jolla ☎ **619/552-1784** for information; 619/570-1234 to book a tee time; 619/452-3226 for the pro shop.

Two gorgeous 18-hole championship courses are located on the coast between La Jolla and Del Mar, only 15 minutes from downtown San Diego. Home of the Buick Invitational Tournament, these municipal courses are very popular. Both overlook the ocean; the north course is more picturesque, the south course more challenging. Tee times are taken by computer starting at 5am up to 7 days in advance by telephone only. Confirmation numbers are issued, and you must have the number and photo identification with you when you check in with the starter 15 minutes ahead of time. If you're late, your time may be forfeited. Golf professionals are available for lessons, and the pro shop rents clubs, if you left yours at home. Greens fees for out-of-towners are $42 during the week and $49.50 Saturday and Sunday for 18 holes; $21 for nine holes.

HIKING The **Sierra Club** sponsors regular hikes in the San Diego area, and nonmembers are welcome to participate. There's always a Wednesday mountain hike, usually in the Cuyamaca Mountains, though sometimes in the Lagunas; there are evening and day hikes as well. Most are free. For a recorded message of upcoming hikes, call **619/299-1744,** box no. 4000, or call the office Monday through Friday from noon to 5pm and on Saturday from 10am to 4pm (☎ **619/299-1743**).

The Bayside Trail near **Cabrillo National Monument** is popular because hikers can stop and look in the tide pools. Drive to the Monument and follow signs to the trail. **Mission Trails Regional Park,** 8 miles northeast of downtown, offers a glimpse of what San Diego looked like before development. Located between Calif. 52 and I-8 and east of I-15, rugged hills, valleys, and open areas provide a quick escape from urban hustle-bustle. A visitor and interpretive center (☎ **619/668-3275**) is open daily from 9am to 5pm. Access is via Mission Gorge Road. Torrey Pines State Park in La Jolla is another great spot for hiking.

HORSEBACK RIDING Hosts Earl and Liz Hammond at **Holidays on Horseback** (☎ **619/445-3997**), located 40 miles east of San Diego in Descanso, offer half- and full-day outings, as well as overnight camping trips, through Cuyamaca Rancho State Park. Riders pass through beautiful scenery that includes native chaparral, live oak, and manzanita. A four-hour ride with a picnic lunch on the trail costs $60 and a 1¹/₂ hour ride is $25.

IN-LINE SKATING Gliding around San Diego, especially the Mission Bay area, on in-line skates is as much a Southern California experience as sailing or surfing. In Mission Beach, rent a pair of regular or in-line skates from **Skates Plus,** 3830 Mission Blvd. (☎ **619/488-PLUS**), or **Hamel's Action Sports Center,** 704 Ventura Place, off Mission Boulevard at the roller coaster (☎ **619/488-5050**); and in Pacific Beach, at **Pacific Beach Sun and Sea,** 4539 Ocean Blvd. (☎ **619/483-6613**). In Coronado, go to **Mike's Bikes,** at 1343 Orange Ave. (☎ **619/435-7744**); or **Bikes and Beyond,** 1201 First St. and at the Ferry Landing (☎ **619/435-7180**).

SCUBA DIVING & SNORKELING The **San Diego–La Jolla Underwater Park,** especially the La Jolla Cove, is the best spot for scuba diving and snorkeling. For more information see "Beaches," earlier in this chapter. The **Underwater Pumpkin Carving Contest,** held at Halloween, is a fun local event. For information phone **619/565-6054.**

TENNIS There are 1,200 public and private tennis courts in San Diego. Public courts are located throughout the city, including the **La Jolla Recreation Center** (☎ **619/295-9278**) and **Morley Field** (☎ **619/459-9950**) in Balboa Park.

9 Great Shopping Areas

Shops in San Diego tend to stay open late. Expect to find the welcome mat out until 9pm on weeknights, 8pm on Saturdays, and 6pm and sometimes 8pm on Sundays. In addition to the specific shopping clusters listed below you might like to checkout the following malls: **Fashion Valley,** 352 Fashion Valley Rd., (☎ 619/ 297-3381); **Mission Valley,** 1640 Camino del Rio North, (☎ 619/296-6375); **University Towne Center,** 4545 La Jolla Village Dr., San Diego, (☎ 619/ 546-8858). The favorite department store of many a San Diegan is **Nordstrom,** located in Fashion Valley, University Towne Center, and Horton Plaza. Its upscale stock may be beyond your budget, but go if there's a sale on; the savings can be great.

In addition to the areas described below, remember that it's fun to shop in **Tijuana,** Mexico, just across the border from San Diego. You can also shop on the north side of the international border at the **San Diego Factory Outlet Center.** In addition, bargain hunters will want to attend **Kobey's Swap Meet,** which takes place at the San Diego Sports Arena Thursday through Sunday.

Bazaar del Mundo. 2754 Calhoun St., Old Town State Historic Park. ☎ **619/296-3161.** Bus: 4 or 5/105. Trolley: Old Town.

Always festive, the central courtyard here vibrates with folk music, mariachis, and a splashing fountain. Shops are pricey, but feature one-of-a-kind folk art, home furnishings, clothing, and textiles from Mexico and South America. You'll find a top-notch bookstore called Libros, with a large kids' selection. If you're pooped, collapse at Casa de Pico and enjoy one of their bathtub-sized margaritas.

The Ferry Landing Market Place. 1201 1st St. (at B Ave.), Coronado. ☎ **619/435-8895.** Bus: 901. Ferry: From Broadway Pier. Take I-5 to Coronado Bay Bridge, to B Ave., and turn right.

The entrance of this shopping center is impressive—turreted red rooftops with jaunty blue flags that draw closer as the ferry to Coronado pulls into the slip. A stroll up the pier puts you in the midst of shops filled with gifts, imported and designer fashions, jewelry, and crafts. You can get a quick bite to eat or have a leisurely dinner with a view, wander along landscaped walkways, or laze on a friendly beach or grassy bank.

Homegrown San Diego: Farmers' Markets

Farmers' markets throughout San Diego County sell fresh local fruits, vegetables, and flowers, as well as specialty items such as raw apple cider (in the fall), macadamia nuts, and rhubarb pies.

Sunday: In uptown **San Diego** at "The Boulevard," El Cajon at Marlborough (three blocks east of 40th Street), 10am to 2pm.

Tuesday: In **Coronado** (Old Ferry Landing) at the corner of First and B streets, 2:30 to 6pm; and in **Escondido,** Grand Avenue and Broadway, 3 to 7pm.

Wednesday: In **Escondido** at North County Market, 3660 Sunset Dr. (across from North County Fair), 9am to noon; in **Ocean Beach,** along 4900 block Newport Avenue (west of Sunset Cliffs Boulevard), 4 to 8pm; and in **Carlsbad,** along Roosevelt Street between Grand Avenue and Carlsbad Village Dr., 3 to 6pm.

Thursday: In downtown **Oceanside** at the corner of North Hill and 3rd Street, 9am to 12:30pm; in **Mission Valley,** at the Hazard Center, Friars Road at Calif. 163, 3 to 6:30pm; and in **Chula Vista,** at Third Avenue and E Street, 3 to 6pm.

Friday: In **Rancho Bernardo** at Bernardo Winery, 13330 Paseo del Verano Norte, 9am to noon; and in **La Mesa,** 8500 Allison St. (east of Spring Street), 3 to 6pm.

Saturday: In **Pacific Beach** at Promenade Mall, Mission Boulevard between Reed and Pacific Beach Drive, 8am to noon; in **Vista,** at the corner of Eucalyptus and Escondido Avenue (city hall parking lot), 8 to 11am; in **Poway** (at Old Poway Park); at the corner of Midland and Temple, 8 to 11am; in **Del Mar** (city hall parking lot), at the corner of El Camino Del Mar and 10th Street, 1 to 4pm; and in **Carlsbad,** at the parking lot north of Andersen's Pea Soup, 2 to 5pm.

Horton Plaza. 324 Horton Plaza. ☎ **619/238-1596.** Bus: 2, 7, 9, 29, 34, or 35. Trolley: City Center.

The Disneyland of shopping malls, Horton Plaza is right in the heart of San Diego; in fact, it *is* the heart of the revitalized city center, bounded by Broadway, First and Fourth Avenues, and G Street. Covering 6½ city blocks, this multilevel shopping center has 140 specialty shops, including art galleries, clothing and shoe stores, several fun shops for kids, bookstores, a seven-screen cinema, three major department stores, and a variety of restaurants and short-order eateries. It's almost as much a San Diego attraction as Sea World or the San Diego Zoo, partly for its unusual, eclectic designs and colors. The plaza is purposefully designed for meandering, so expect to take some wrong turns and make some delightful discoveries (or stay close to the escalator, which you can pick up at the front of the plaza beside Long's Pharmacy, or take the elevator beside Nordstrom). Horton Plaza usually has free entertainment daily from noon to 2pm. Parking is free the first three hours with validation, $1 per half hour thereafter; parking levels are confusing, and temporarily losing your car is part of the Horton Plaza experience.

La Jolla. Prospect St. and Girard Ave. Bus: 34 or 34A.

"The village," as it is still referred to by long-time locals, has become sort of a cross between Rodeo Drive and a shopping mall. A few of the old-time stores remain—Warwick's (books and stationery), Burns Drugs, John Cole's Book Shop, Meanley Hardware—but these are outnumbered by the glossy newcomers, such as The Gap, Talbots (a personal favorite), and Tina's Boutique. Bargain hunters might also like to browse the resale shops; **Encore,** at 7850 Herschel St., is just one of many. You can park on the street, but watch your time. The local parking enforcement officers are slightly overzealous.

Seaport Village. 849 W. Harbor Dr. (at Kettner Blvd.). ☎ **619/235-4014,** or 619/235-4013 for events information. Two hours free parking with validation; $1 per half hour thereafter. Bus: 7. Trolley: Seaport Village.

This 14-acre ersatz village snuggled alongside San Diego Bay was built to resemble a small Cape Cod community, but the 75 shops are very much of the Southern California cutesy variety. Favorites include the Tile Shop; the Seasick Giraffe for resort wear; and the Upstart Crow bookshop/coffeehouse with the Crow's Nest children's bookstore inside. Be sure to see the 1890 carousel imported from Coney Island, New York.

10 San Diego After Dark

San Diego is hardly the wild and crazy nightlife capital of America, but pockets of lively after-dark entertainment *do* exist around the city. On the more sedate side of things, the city offers wonderful and varied live theater experiences. This isn't just civic pride speaking: Both the Old Globe and La Jolla Playhouse have won Tonys for best regional theater.

For a rundown of the latest performances, gallery openings, and other events in the city, check the listings in *Night and Day,* the Thursday entertainment section of the *San Diego Union-Tribune,* or *The Reader,* San Diego's free alternative newspaper, published weekly on Thursday. For what's happening at the gay clubs, get the weekly *San Diego Gay and Lesbian Times.* The *San Diego Performing Arts Guide,* produced every two months by the San Diego Theatre Foundation is also very helpful. You can pick one up at the Times Art Tix booth.

THE PERFORMING ARTS
HOW TO SAVE ON TICKETS

Half-price tickets to theater, music, and dance events are available at the **Times Arts Tix** booth, in Horton Plaza Park, at Broadway and Third Avenue. Park in the Horton Plaza parking garage and have your parking validated or pause at the curb nearby. The kiosk is open Tuesday through Saturday from 10am to 7pm. Half-price tickets for Sunday performances are sold on Saturday. Only cash payments are accepted. For a daily listing of half-price offerings, call **619/497-5000.** Full-price advance tickets are also sold; the kiosk doubles as a Ticketmaster outlet, selling tickets to concerts throughout California.

You might also find a way to take advantage of **Bargain Arts Day,** held at the Arts Tix booth once a year in May. On this occasion, tickets for shows and concerts at almost every performing arts venue in the San Diego area are sold on a pay-what-you-can basis. A list of the events and the days for which tickets are available is distributed from the booth a week or more ahead of time. If you plan ahead, maybe you could get a friend or relative in San Diego to stand in line for you and snag some tickets that you can use during your vacation here. It isn't unusual to pay 25 cents for $30 tickets.

THEATER

The **San Diego Repertory Theatre** offers professional, culturally diverse productions of contemporary and classic dramas, comedies, and musicals at the Lyceum Theatre,

79 Horton Plaza (☎ **619/235-8025** or 619/231-3586; fax 619/235-0939). It's annual "A Christmas Carol" is a perennial favorite.

In Coronado, **Lamb's Players Theatre,** at 1142 Orange Ave. (☎ **619/437-0600;** fax 619/437-6053), is a professional repertory company whose season runs from February through December. Shows take place in their 340-seat theater in Coronado's historic Spreckels building, where no seat is more than seven rows from the stage.

La Jolla Playhouse. La Jolla Village Dr. and Torrey Pines Rd., La Jolla. ☎ **619/550-1010.**

Winner of the 1993 Tony Award for outstanding American regional theater, the La Jolla Playhouse stages six productions each year in its 500-seat Mandell Weiss Theater and 400-seat Mandell Weiss Forum on the campus of UCSD. Performances are held May through November. Playhouse audiences cheered *The Who's Tommy,* and Matthew Broderick in *How to Succeed in Business Without Really Trying* before they went on to Broadway fame and fortune. The original La Jolla Playhouse was founded by Gregory Peck, Dorothy McGuire, and Mel Ferrer in 1947 and closed in 1964; this stellar reincarnation emerged on the theatrical scene in 1983. The box office is open Monday from noon to 6pm, and Tuesday through Sunday from noon to 8pm. Each show designates one Saturday matinee as a "pay-what-you-can performance." Reduced-price "Public Rush" tickets are available 10 minutes before curtain, subject to availability. Tickets run $19 to $39. Self parking is $3.

✪ **Old Globe Theatre.** Balboa Park. ☎ **619/239-2255,** or 619/23-GLOBE for 24-hour hot line. Tickets $28.50–$39 (previews $22); seniors and students $25 matinees, $29 weeknights. Bus: 7 or 25.

Near the entrance to Balboa Park and just behind the Museum of Man, this Tony Award–winning theater, fashioned after Shakespeare's, has produced the revival of *Damn Yankees,* and has billed such notable performers as John Goodman, Marsha Mason, Cliff Robertson, Jon Voight, and Christopher Walken.

The 581-seat Old Globe is part of the Simon Edison Centre for the Performing Arts, which also includes the 245-seat Cassius Carter Centre Stage and the 620-seat open-air Lowell Davies Festival Theatre, and mounts a dozen plays a year on the three stages between January and October. Tours are offered Saturday and Sunday at 11am and cost $3 ($1 students, seniors, and military). The box office is open Tuesday through Sunday from noon to 8:30pm.

OPERA & CLASSICAL MUSIC

The **San Diego Opera** performs at the Civic Theater, 202 C St. (☎ **619/232-7636**), and often showcases international stars. The 1997 season, January through May, will include *Carmen, The Italian Girl in Algiers, The Conquistadore* (world premiere)*, La Traviata,* and *Turandot.* Placido Domingo will be featured in concert on April 10. The box office is located across the plaza from the theater and is open Monday through Friday from 9am to 5pm. Tickets run from $25 to $100. Student and senior discounts and $17 standing room tickets are available an hour before the performance. Find the opera in cyberspace at http://www.sdopera.com.

The future of **San Diego's Symphony,** whose home is Copley Symphony Hall, 750 B St. (☎ **619/699-4205**), is up in the air. In early 1996 it was announced that the symphony would play no more due to financial problems, and in mid-1996 they filed for bankruptcy. Will a wealthy, civic-minded angel rescue them? Should the symphony play again, it will probably be led by Israeli-born conductor Yoav Talmi.

In the past, the regular season has lasted from October to May, and from June through September the symphony has offered outdoor pops concerts at Embarcadero

Marina Park. These latter events have been a part of San Diego's summer for as long as I can remember and will be sorely missed if they are discontinued. During its winter concert season the Symphony accompanies **silent movies,** October through May.

MOVIES, SAN DIEGO STYLE

In addition to the usual multiplex theaters, movie venues in San Diego include ✪ **Movies Before the Mast** aboard the *Star of India.* Here movies of the nautical genre (such as *Black Beard the Pirate* and *Hook*) are shown on a special "screensail" April through October (☎ **619/234-9153**).

At the **Sunset Cinema Film Festival** in August you can view a mix of classic and current films free of charge from a blanket or chair on the beach. Films are projected on screens mounted on floating barges from San Diego to Imperial Beach (☎ **619/454-7373**).

Dive-In Movies are shown at the Plunge (☎ **619/488-3110**), an indoor swimming pool in Mission Beach. Viewers float on rafts in 91° water and watch water-related movies projected onto the wall. *Jaws* is a perennial favorite.

THE CLUB & MUSIC SCENE

Clubs do come and go, so your best bet for finding the latest, hottest spot is to stroll through the Gaslamp Quarter. The current favorites are **Johnny Loves,** 664 Fifth Ave. (☎ **619/595-0123**), which endears itself to an over-30 crowd; **Club 66,** at 901 Fifth Ave. (☎ **619/234-4166**), which has a Route 66 motif and caters to those aged 25 to 45; **E Street Alley,** on the north side of E Street between Fourth and Fifth avenues (☎ **619/231-9200**), which is a dressier club; **Ole Madrid,** 751 Fifth Ave. (☎ **619/557-0146**), the destination of choice for Europhiles; and **Dick's Last Resort,** 345 Fourth Ave., with entrances on both Fourth and Fifth avenues (☎ **619/231-9100**), popular with the college crowd; **Buffalo Joe's Saloon,** 600 Fifth Ave. (☎ **619/236-1616**), a country western nightclub. Cover charges vary from nil to $10, depending on who's playing and the night of the week.

Fans of alternative music might enjoy the **Casbah,** 2501 Kettner Blvd. (☎ **619/232-4355**), where breakthrough bands are the norm, or **Bodies,** 528 F St. (☎ **619/236-8988**), where live original music is played nightly.

If you're under 21, **SOMA Live,** 5305 Metro St., Mission Bay (☎ **619/239-SOMA**), is the place for you. This concert venue in a warehouse-like building has hosted Courtney Love, Social Distortion, and Faith No More.

From May through October a series of contemporary concerts takes place outdoors at **Humphrey's,** 2241 Shelter Island Dr., San Diego (☎ **619/523-1010**). During the 1996 season Ray Charles, Willie Nelson, and Wayne Newton were just three of the popular performers who appeared here. For the 1997 schedule, call or check their Web site: http://user.aol.com/humconcert.

Videos and live bands (sometimes local, sometimes nationally known) take center stage in the **Cannibal Bar,** 3999 Mission Blvd. (in the Catamaran Hotel; ☎ **619/539-8650**). Open Wednesday through Sunday till about 2am; weekend cover charges range from $3 to $15.

The nautical theme and waterfront location, with a curving window wall looking onto the marina, make **The Yacht Club,** 333 W. Harbor Dr. (in the San Diego Marriott Marina; ☎ **619/234-1500**), a comfortable spot. There's live dance music nightly, with appetizers and light fare available until 11pm, along with a dinner menu served from 5 to 11pm. A band plays five nights a week, a DJ two nights at 9pm. No cover, no drink minimum.

COMEDY

Top L.A. comics regularly visit the **Comedy Store,** 916 Pearl St., La Jolla (☎ 619/454-9176). Monday and Tuesday are amateur nights; the acts improve as the week progresses. Showtime is 8pm Sunday through Thursday, 8 and 10:30pm Friday and Saturday. The cover is $8 to $10, with a two-drink minimum.

JAZZ & BLUES

Croce's. 802 Fifth Ave. (at F St.). ☎ **619/233-4355.** No cover to either Croce's Jazz Bar or Croce's Top Hat if you have dinner at Croce's Restaurant or Ingrid's Cantina. Cover for regional bands $3–$7, for national acts $10–$18. Minimum at both bars $5.

There's traditional jazz every night in Croce's Jazz Bar and rhythm and blues at Croce's Top Hat, both named after the late musician Jim Croce and owned by his wife, Ingrid. Jim Croce's son, A. J., an accomplished musician in his own right, sometimes performs. Jazz holds sway in the Jazz Bar and drifts easily into the adjoining restaurant; it opens nightly at 5pm and music starts at 8:30pm. Next door, in Croce's Top Hat, balcony seating overlooks the stage; it's open daily, with music starting at 9pm.

BIG BAND

Hotel del Coronado. 1500 Orange Ave., Coronado. ☎ **619/435-6611.** Cover $15 without dinner.

The West Coast's most glorious Victorian hotel kicks up its heels on Sunday nights, when it's swing time in the Crown Room. Besides the music and dancing, the architecturally memorable room makes the trip here worthwhile. Prices are $24.95 with buffet dinner.

BARS & BEYOND
FOR A QUIET COCKTAIL

The **Top o' The Cove,** 1216 Prospect St., La Jolla (☎ 619/454-7779), is an intimate setting, where the pianist plays old favorites, and leans heavily toward Gershwin. Nab the corner table next to the piano. On nice evenings, the music is piped to the patio, another idyllic spot to sit and sip. Valet parking is $5.

BREWPUBS

Karl Strauss' Old Columbia Brewery, at 1157 Columbia St. (☎ 619/234-BREW), serving great beer and hearty American fare, opened several years ago and started something of a microbrewery trend in San Diego. Strauss named his brews after local attractions—Gaslamp Gold Ale, Red Trolley Ale, Black's Beach Extra Dark, Star of India Pale Ale—but he brought the recipes from the Old World. Want to try them all and still be able to walk? You can order a Taster Series, four ounces of eight different brews for only $5.95. Hours are 11:30am to 10pm Sunday through Thursday and 11:30am to midnight Friday and Saturday.

While an upscale crowd of "suits" gathers at Karl's place, **R. J.'s Riptide Brewery,** at 5th and K in the Gaslamp Quarter (☎ 619/231-7700), attracts a sportshappy bunch who appreciate the pub's big-screen TV. The copper-clad brewing tanks take center stage here, with the large U-shaped bar curving around them. R. J.'s produces top-fermented English-, German-, Irish-, and Belgian-style ales, stouts, and porters (no lagers). This is an upbeat, lighthearted place, where the slogan is *Save the Ales.*

In contrast, the **La Jolla Brewing Company,** at 7536 Fay Ave., La Jolla (☎ 619/456-BREW), feels more like a neighborhood pub. The wood floor is appropriately worn, and pool and darts are played in the back room. Brewmaster John Atwater makes his handcrafted beers from his own recipes and names them after local spots. John offers TVs for sports fans and serves meals such as Baja fish tacos, brewhouse pasta, and a "cheeseburger in paradise."

COFFEEHOUSES

Pannikin Hillcrest, 523 University Ave., Hillcrest (☎ **619/295-1600**), is a laid-back place to enjoy your latte or espresso. The desserts are rich, and the art on the wall is the work of local artists. Open Sunday to Thursday 6am to 11pm, Friday and Saturday 6am to midnight.

Upstart Crow, on the central plaza at Seaport Village (☎ **619/232-4855**), is a coffeehouse/bookstore where tables and chairs fill cozy spaces surrounded by books. The selection of books, coffees, and desserts is scrumptious. And coffee refills are only 25¢. Open Sunday through Thursday from 9am to 10pm (until 11pm in summer), Friday and Saturday from 9am to 11pm.

Centrally located in the Gaslamp Quarter and particularly popular with students, **Cafe Lulu,** 419 F St. (near Fourth Avenue; ☎ **619/238-0114**), is open daily till 2am (till 4am on Fridays and Saturdays). Light fare at this sparsely decorated coffeehouse runs the gamut from Brie or pizza baguettes to bagels to croissants to quiche to lasagna. The emphasis is on coffees, but you can also get teas, natural sodas, Aqua Libra, sarsaparilla, and beer or wine by the glass or bottle. No credit cards.

In La Jolla try the **Wall Street Cafe,** at 1044 Wall St., between Girard and Herschel Avenues (☎ **619/551-1044**), which was once a bank (today the old vault contains the rest rooms.) Live entertainment, such as light jazz or a mellow guitar, makes this a particularly popular place on Friday and Saturday nights.

GAY & LESBIAN HANGOUTS

The Flame. 3780 Park Blvd. ☎ **619/295-4163.** Cover Sun–Fri $2, Sat $3.

The Flame has a large dance floor and two bars, including a video bar open Tuesday through Saturday. The club features a different style of music every night of the week: Tuesday is "Boys Night Out"; Wednesday is "trash disco"; on Saturday Top 40 dance music is played; Sunday night there's Latin music. The Flame is open daily till 2am.

Kickers/Hamburger Mary's. 308 University Ave. (between 3rd and 4th aves.). ☎ **619/491-0400.** No cover.

This is a foot-stomping gay owned and operated bar with an adjacent outdoor restaurant, Hamburger Mary's. The atmosphere is relaxed and informal, and though country music is the standard musical fare, no Western garb is expected (the waiters are likely to be in shorts). If you're unschooled in the art of country-western dancing, just show up on Monday and Friday for lessons from 7 to 8:30pm, then put what you've learned to the test for the rest of the evening. Beginner classes are taught Monday and Tuesday, tougher moves the rest of the week. There's line dancing, too. Before, during, or after an evening at Kickers, head outside to the patio and Hamburger Mary's for a burger or sandwich and a chance to catch your breath. This place, which is equally popular among men and women, is a definite kick. Open daily till 2am.

Rich's. 1051 University Ave. (between 10th and 11th aves.). ☎ **619/295-2195,** or 619/497-4588 for upcoming events. Thurs–Sat $4–$5; Sun, no cover before 9pm, $3 afterward.

This popular club/dance space welcomes primarily gay men 21 and older. Sunday is popular for Tea and Me, when there is no cover between 7 and 9pm, and Thursday for Club Hedonism, with techno tunes and more. On Friday and Saturday nights, go-go dancers and high-energy music set the tone for the night. Always check the events hot line, since the schedules can change. Open Thursday through Sunday till 2am.

11 North County Beach Towns

Picturesque beach towns, each poised over a stretch of sand, dot the coast of San Diego County from Del Mar to Oceanside. These make great day-trip destinations for sun worshippers and surfers.

Getting there is easy: Del Mar is only 18 miles north of downtown San Diego; Carlsbad about 33; and Oceanside approximately 36. If you're driving, follow I-5 north: You'll find freeway exits for Del Mar, Solana Beach, Cardiff by the Sea, Encinitas, Leucadia, Carlsbad, and Oceanside. The farthest point, Oceanside, will take you about 45 minutes. The other choice by car is to wander up the coast road—known variously along the way as Camino del Mar, Pacific Coast Highway, Old Highway 101, and County Highway S21.

Amtrak and **The Coaster** provide service to Solana Beach and Oceanside; The Coaster also stops in Carlsbad and Encinitas. Check with Amtrak (☎ **800/ USA-RAIL**), The Coaster (☎ **800/COASTER**), or the local tourist information offices for schedules.

The **San Diego North County Convention AND Visitors Bureau** (☎ **800/ 848-3336**) is also a good information source.

DEL MAR

Less than 20 miles up the coast from San Diego lies Del Mar, a community with just over 5,000 inhabitants in a 2-square-mile municipality. The town has adamantly maintained its independence, eschewing incorporation into the city of San Diego. Sometimes known as "the people's republic of Del Mar," this community was one of the nation's first to ban smoking. The upscale folks who live here grin and bear it during the summer racing season when the Del Mar Thoroughbred Club attracts droves of out-of-towners.

Del Mar Beach connects with **Torrey Pines Beach,** providing miles of sand for walking; swimmers congregate north of Jake's seaside restaurant, surfers go south. On the **Del Mar Beach,** Powerhouse Park has picnic tables and a children's playground. On the cliff above it overlooking the ocean is **Seagrove Park,** the scene of free concerts in July and August (☎ **619/755-9313**).

Del Mar is best known for its **racetrack,** founded in 1937 by Bing Crosby and Pat O'Brien. Thoroughbred racing still takes place here from late July to mid-September. The new grandstand seats 14,300 and, like the 1937 original, is in Spanish Mission style. In addition to the Del Mar Thoroughbred Club, the Fairgrounds also host the **Del Mar Fair,** one of the country's largest, during the last two weeks in June, culminating on the Fourth of July.

On Camino del Mar in the town center, the stylish **Del Mar Plaza** has well-selected shops and a variety of restaurants, as well as jazz concerts in summer. ✪ **Esmeralda Books and Coffee** on the upper level provides food and food for thought. Parking is under the plaza.

For more information about Del Mar, contact or visit the **Del Mar Chamber of Commerce Visitor Information Center,** 1104 Camino del Mar, Del Mar, CA 92014 (☎ **619/793-5292**).

WHERE TO STAY

In addition to the places listed below, both campers and RVers are welcome at the oceanfront **San Elijo State Beach,** located on the west side of S21 near Birmingham

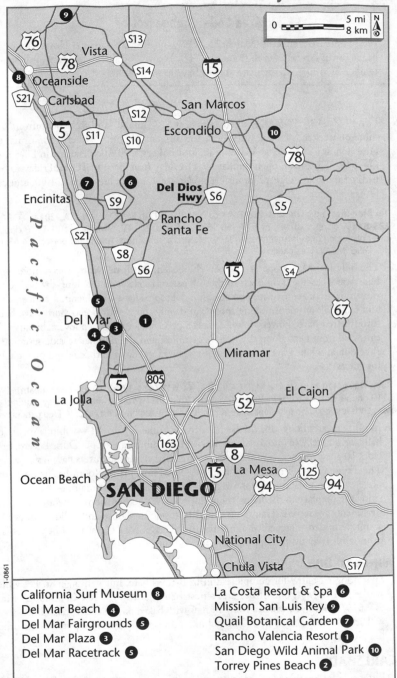

North County Beach Towns

Pacific Ocean

Oceanside
Carlsbad
Vista
San Marcos
Escondido
Encinitas
Del Dios Hwy
Rancho Santa Fe
Del Mar
La Jolla
Miramar
El Cajon
Ocean Beach
SAN DIEGO
La Mesa
National City
Chula Vista

76
78
S13
S14
15
S21
5
S11
S10
S12
78
7
6
S9
S6
S5
S21
S8
S6
15
S4
67
5
805
52
163
8
15
94
125
94
S17

California Surf Museum **8**
Del Mar Beach **4**
Del Mar Fairgrounds **5**
Del Mar Plaza **3**
Del Mar Racetrack **5**

La Costa Resort & Spa **6**
Mission San Luis Rey **9**
Quail Botanical Garden **7**
Rancho Valencia Resort **1**
San Diego Wild Animal Park **10**
Torrey Pines Beach **2**

1-0861

Area Code Change Notice

Please note that, effective March 22, 1997, the area code for the North County beach towns is scheduled to change to **760.** You will be able to dial 619 until September 27, 1997, after which you will have to use 760.

Drive (☎ **619/753-5091**), where sites cost $17 "inland" and $22 "oceanfront" ($1 more on weekends). Book well ahead for summer. (If you stay here, don't miss the great donuts and scones at **VG Donuts and Bakery,** 109 Aberdeen at San Elijo Road (☎ **619/753-2400**), open Sunday to Thursday from 5am to 10pm, Friday to Saturday 5am to midnight. Donuts are 45¢ to 50¢, scones are six for $1.40, and coffee is 65¢ a cup.

Del Mar Motel on the Beach. 1702 Coast Blvd. (at 17th St.), Del Mar, CA 92014. ☎ **800/ 223-8449** for reservations, or 619/755-1534. 45 rms. TEL TV. Summer $100–$130 double; lower off-season rates; sometimes higher weekends and holidays. Additional person $5. AE, CB, DC, DISC, MC, V. Free parking.

The only Del Mar property right on the beach, this little white-stucco motel with blue trim is clean and simply furnished. Upstairs rooms have one king-size bed, while those downstairs come with two doubles. All rooms have a refrigerator, coffeemaker, and fan. Half are nonsmoking rooms, and only those with ocean views have bathtubs (the rest have showers only). This is a good choice for beach lovers, because you can walk from here along the beach for miles, and the popular seaside restaurants Poseidon and Jake's are right next door. The motel has a barbecue and picnic table for guests' use.

Rock Haus. 410 15th St., Del Mar, CA 92014. ☎ **619/481-3764.** 10 rms (4 with bath). $90– $110 double without bath, $120–150 double with bath. Two-night minimum stay required on weekends and holidays July–Sept. Rates include continental breakfast. MC, V. Free parking.

In other incarnations, this has been a private home, a place of worship, a gambling hall, and a hotel. Now restored, the Rock Haus, run by innkeeper Doris Lucero, provides 10 guest rooms (six of them share three baths); most quarters have ocean views. The Triple Crown Room is my favorite. The Huntsman's Room has its own fireplace, which is great, but the shower stall here is really tiny. It might be better to just enjoy the fireplace in the living room and choose another room. Late-afternoon refreshments are served. There's no smoking inside the house and children under 13 aren't permitted. Perched on a hill behind the Del Mar Plaza, the Rock Haus is a short stroll away from shopping, dining, and the beach.

WHERE TO DINE

Space doesn't allow for complete dining listings here, but if hunger strikes while you're in Del Mar, one of the area's best bets is **Bully's,** 1404 Camino del Mar, (☎ **619/755-1660**), where a Bully Burger with baked potato and a great dinner salad will set you back only $5.75. The publike atmosphere and large portions are other big pluses.

CARLSBAD

Fifteen miles north of Del Mar and 33 miles from downtown San Diego (a 45-minute drive), the pretty beach community of Carlsbad provides many reasons to linger: good swimming and surfing beaches (with a mile-long two-tiered beach walk that's accessible for travelers with disabilities); three lagoons perfect for walks or bird watching; landscaped streets; memorable restaurants; and an abundance of antique and gift shops.

There's a small-town atmosphere—the population is 63,000, but it actually feels smaller than Del Mar. You won't see any high-rise buildings (and none are on the drawing board). The town extends a warm welcome to travelers in the recycled train depot (1887) that's now home to the **Visitors Information Center** (☎ 619/ 434-6093).

Carlsbad was named for Karlsbad, Bohemia, because of the similar mineral (some say curative) waters they both produced, but the town's once-famous artesian well has long been plugged up. You can picnic in small **Florence Magee Park;** while there, peek into tiny **St. Michael's by the Sea** Episcopal Church (1894); the original organ is to the right.

In spring, visit the 200 acres of cultivated flower fields that transform the hills south of town into a startling rainbow from March through May; in winter witness a profusion of poinsettias here. The latest flower fields information is available at 619/ 431-0352 or on the Internet at FlowerFlds@aol.com. You can also see 3,000 varieties of flowers, plants, and trees year-round at the serene, 30-acre **Quail Botanical Garden** in nearby Encinitas (☎ 619/436-3036), open daily from 8am to 5pm.

Legoland, a Danish theme park made of the world-famous LEGO blocks, is scheduled to open here in 1999, making many children ecstatic.

WHERE TO STAY

Beach Terrace Inn. 2775 Ocean St., Carlsbad, CA 92003. ☎ **800/622-3224** in California, 800/433-5415 elsewhere, or 619/729-5951. Fax 619/729-1078. 41 rms, 5 suites. A/C TEL TV. Summer $108–$219 double, from $139 suite; winter $97–$177 double, from $117 suite. Extra person $10. Rates include continental breakfast. AE, CB, DC, DISC, ER, MC, V. Free parking.

Carlsbad's only beachside hostelry (others are across the road or a little farther away), this Best Western property has a helpful staff, a living roomlike lobby, and rooms and an outdoor pool with ocean views. The rooms, though not elegant, are extra large, and some have balconies, fireplaces, and kitchenettes; suites have separate living rooms and bedrooms. VCRs and films are available at the front desk. This place is good for families. You can walk everywhere from here, and there's street parking as well as carports.

✪ Pelican Cove Inn. 320 Walnut Ave., Carlsbad, CA 92008. ☎ **619/434-5995.** 8 rms. $85–$175 double. Extra person $15. Rates include full breakfast. AE, MC, V. Free parking. Complimentary transfer from Oceanside train station or Palomar Airport.

This Cape Cod–style hideaway near the beach combines romance with luxury, down to the bed covers, which resemble clouds more than comforters. All rooms have fireplaces and private entrances; two have spa tubs. You can lounge or have breakfast in the garden with a gazebo and a sundeck. Hosts Kris and Nancy Nayudu can provide beach towels and chairs or prepare a wonderful picnic basket (with 24-hour notice) you can enjoy on the lovely local beaches or parks. All guest rooms are nonsmoking.

WHERE TO DINE

If you find yourself in Leucadia looking for something to eat, head for **Leucadia Pizzeria,** Corner of U.S. 101 and Encinitas Boulevard (☎ 619/942-2222). The food is great, and the prices are very reasonable.

In Carlsbad the best value for the money is **Tip Top Meats,** 6118 Paseo del Norte (☎ **619/438-2620**), where you can get a full meal for only $4.95. Other local favorites include **Branci's Caldo Pomodoro,** 2907 State St. (☎ **619/720-9998**); and **Neiman's,** 2978 Carlsbad Blvd. (☎ **619/729-4131**).

OCEANSIDE

The most northerly town in San Diego County (actually it's a city of 100,000) and 36 miles from San Diego, Oceanside claims almost 4 miles of beaches and one of the West Coast's longest wooden piers, where a tram does nothing but transport people from the street to the end of the 1,600-foot-long pier and back for 25¢ one way. The restaurant at the end of the pier is a great place for lunch over the ocean. The beach, the pier, and a well-tended recreational area with playground equipment and an outdoor amphitheater are within easy walking distance of the train station. The small **California Surf Museum,** across from the pier, at 308 Pacific St. (☎ **619/ 721-6876**), is open Monday, Thursday, and Friday from 10am to 4pm, Saturday and Sunday from 10am to 4pm.

Try not to miss **Mission San Luis Rey** (☎ **619/757-3651**), a few miles inland. Founded in 1798, it's the largest of California's 21 missions. There's a small charge to tour the mission's impressive church, exhibits, grounds, and cemetery. You might recognize it as the backdrop for several Zorro movies.

For an information packet about Oceanside and its attractions, send a check for $3 to the **Oceanside Chamber of Commerce,** P.O. Box 1578, Oceanside, CA 92051 (☎ **619/722-1534**).

A SIDE TRIP INLAND

The coastal and inland sections of North County are as different as night and day. Beaches and laid-back villages where work seems to be the curse of the surfing class characterize the coast, while inland you'll find beautiful barren hills, citrus groves, and conservative communities where agriculture plays an important role.

Rancho Santa Fe is located about 27 miles north of downtown San Diego. Certainly one of the county's loveliest communities, exclusive Rancho Santa Fe was once the property of the Santa Fe Railroad, and the eucalyptus trees they grew there create a stately atmosphere. From there, the Del Dios Highway (S6) leads to **Escondido,** almost 32 miles from the city and home to Wild Animal Park (see p. 581). This road affords views of Lake Hodges, as well as glimpses of expansive estates, some of the most expensive in the country. **San Marcos, Vista,** and **Fallbrook** are even farther north. Nearly 70 miles away is **Palomar Mountain** in the Cleveland National Forest, which spills over the border into Riverside County.

The **San Diego North County Convention and Visitors Bureau** (☎ **800/ 848-3336**) can answer all your questions about these areas.

12 Julian: Apples, Pies & a Slice of Small-Town California

A trip 60 miles northeast of San Diego to Julian (pop. 1,500) is a trip back in time. The old gold-mining town, now best known for its apples, has some good eateries and a handful of cute B&Bs, but its popularity is based on the fact that it provides a chance for city-weary folks to get away from it all. However, when it's sunny in San Diego it may be snowing in Julian, perched 4,235 feet above sea level.

Before you leave, try Julian's apple pies; whether the best pies come from Mom's Pies, Mrs. Glad's Bakery, or the Julian Pie Company is a toss-up. It's fun to sample all of them and decide for yourself.

Area Code Change Notice

Please note that, effective March 22, 1997, the area code for Julian is scheduled to change to **760.** You will be able to dial 619 until September 27, 1997, after which you will have to use 760.

ESSENTIALS

GETTING THERE The 90-minute drive from San Diego can be made via Calif. 78 or I-8 to Calif. 79. I suggest taking one route going and the other coming back. Calif. 79 winds through scenic Rancho Cuyamaca State Park, while Calif. 78 traverses open country and farmland.

If you come by Calif. 78, you'll pass the mission church of **Santa Ysabel** (1812), where there's a tiny museum and a large Native American cemetery, on your right, as well as **Dudley's Bakery,** off to the left at the junction with Calif. 79 and just 7 miles from Julian. The bakery, here since 1963, is known for its breads, from raisin date nut to jalapeño, and on weekends 5,000 to 6,000 loaves come out of the ovens. Dudley's is open 8am to 5pm Wednesday through Sunday.

SPECIAL EVENTS Julian's popular fall apple harvest starts mid-September and continues for an entire month (it used to be only one weekend, but the traffic in town got way out of hand); the annual wildflower show lasts for a week in early May; there is also a Spring Fine Arts Show in May; and the annual weed show, a tradition since 1961, is usually held the last few weeks in August or the beginning of September.

VISITOR INFORMATION Town maps and flyers for accommodations are available from the Town Hall on Main Street at Washington Street. The town has a **24-hour hot line** (☎ 619/765-0707) to provide information on lodging, dining, shopping, activities, upcoming events, weather, and road conditions. For a brochure on what to see and do, contact the **Julian Chamber of Commerce** (☎ 619/765-1857). **The Julian Arts Guild** (☎ 619/765-0560) can answer questions about the Fine Arts Show.

WHAT TO SEE & DO

It's fun to learn about the town and surrounding area by visiting the **Julian Cider Mill,** which moved in about 20 years ago when a service station moved out. The father-and-son team of Turk and Fred Slaughter run the place, an actual mill where you can see cider being made; homemade peanut butter is ground on the premises too, and in the spring a glass-enclosed beehive bustles with activity. It's hard not to feel like a kid in this store filled with jawbreakers, preserves, nuts, trail mix, and easy conversation around a potbellied stove.

On the right as you come into town is the **Julian Pioneer Museum** (☎ 619/765-0227), at 4th and Washington streets, housed in an old brewery and open Tuesday through Sunday from 10am to 4pm April through November, weekends and holidays December through March. Here you can learn about some of the old-timers buried up the hill in the Haven of Rest Cemetery.

The **Eagle and High Peak Mines** (☎ 619/765-0036), six blocks from Main Street via C Street, operate daily from 9am to 4pm but only for educational reasons, since the gold is long gone.

It's fun to dart in and out of the little shops in Julian. My favorites are the **Julian Farms Antiques Shop,** 2818 Washington St. (☎ 619/765-0250), for gifts and patio accessories, and **Warm Hearth,** 2125 Main St. (☎ **619/765-1022**), for gifts, cassettes, and wood-burning stoves, if you're in the market for one. **Applewood,** next door to Julian Farms Antiques, is also very good.

You can mix culture with barbecue at the **Pine Hills Dinner Theater** on Friday and Saturday nights at Pine Hills Lodge, a few miles from Julian off Pine Hills Road (☎ **619/765-1100**). The rustic lodge opened its doors on July 4, 1912; in 1980, Dave and Donna Goodman bought it and opened the 96-seat dinner theater, which has staged almost 70 productions, among them *I'm Not Rappaport* and *Last of the Red-Hot Lovers.* The dinner buffet of delicious baby back pork ribs or barbecue chicken starts promptly at 7pm; give them 24-hour notice and you can get a vegetarian plate. Showtime is at 8pm, and the price for the dinner and the theater is $28.50; for the show alone it's $14.50. The playhouse is boxing champ Jack Dempsey's former gym, built for Dempsey in 1926 when he was in training for his fight against Gene Tunney.

To hear some music—folk music or piano or maybe the strains of a hammered dulcimer—head out to the **Wynola Coffee Company** (☎ **619/765-2023**), in a big red barn just over 3 miles south of town on Calif. 78; it'll be on the left. The musicians are on hand only on Saturday from 7pm, and people of all ages come to this local hangout with its mismatched tables and chairs to hear them and indulge in dessert and coffee. The cover is about $3.

EXPLORING THE COUNTRYSIDE

If there's something about being in the country that makes you want to hop in the car and drive down one rural road after another, Julian is an ideal starting point. You'll pass rolling hills, country stores, rambling houses, and fruit stands and come upon towns with names like Ramona, Ballena, and Wynola.

One of my favorite short drives is along the road leading to the **Menghini Winery,** owned and run by Toni and Michael Menghini; it's 2 miles out on Farmer's Road (follow it west out of town until you see the winery sign, then bear to the left down the hill). The winery is usually open Monday, Friday, Saturday, and Sunday from 10am to 4pm, daily in October and December, or call for an appointment (☎ **619/765-2072**). The grapes come from Ramona and Temecula, and the local favorite wine is Julian Blossom. The tanks are right in the tasting room, and the wines are sold only locally, for $7 to $10 per bottle. You may enjoy your purchase right away in the picnic area in the apple orchard.

If you don't make it to the desert this trip, at least take a moment to gaze out at it and the Salton Sea from **Inspiration Point,** just 1¹/₂ miles south of Julian on Calif. 79, opposite Pinecroft Park. **Lake Cuyamaca** (pronounced *kwee-yah-mack*-ah), 10 miles south on Calif. 79, offers boating, fishing (bass, trout, and crappie), and recreational vehicle camping on a first-come, first-served basis. Its facilities are open from sunrise to sunset daily (☎ **619/765-0515** or 619/447-8123). There are motorboat and rowboat rentals, a 3¹/₂-mile hiking trail around the lake, and a charge for fishing ($4.50 for adults, $2.50 for children 8 to 15). A restaurant with a deck and adjoining store overlook the lake.

Back in Julian, **Country Carriages** (☎ **619/765-1471**) will show you the sights and give you a spin down a country lane in a horse-drawn wagon for $20 per couple or around the town for $5 per adult, $2 per child. Hop on in front of or catercorner to the drugstore; the ride lasts half an hour.

For a different way to tour, try **Llama Trek** (☎ **800/LAMAPAK** or 619/765-1890; fax 619/765-1512), in which luggage is packed onto llamas while the tour group hikes alongside them on foot. Trips include rural neighborhoods, a historic gold mine, mountain and lake views, and apple orchards. They even conduct a trek to the local winery. Rates vary from $55 to $75 per person and include lunch (the winery trek also includes wine tasting).

WHERE TO STAY

Julian Farms Lodging. 2818 Washington St., Julian, CA 92036. ☎ **619/765-0250.** 4 attached cottages, 1 cabin. TV. $69 double; $99 cabin. Extra person $5. AE, DISC, MC, V.

Driving into town, you'll find it easy to pass right by this little place on the left. That would be a shame because the yellow cottages with blue shutters and a grape arbor in front make the perfect secret hideaway. Three of the cottages have a double bed and a daybed in a single room; one has two double beds in two rooms and is perfect for families. All have small private baths with showers, hot pots, country antiques, goose-down comforters, and a split of Julian Blossom wine. A nearby cabin has a queen-size bed and a sitting area. You can pick all the grapes you want and eat them in the vine-covered gazebo. It's just down the hill from Main Street. Reserve three to four months ahead for weekends. Smoking is permitted outside only.

Julian Hotel. Main St. and B St. (P.O. Box 1856), Julian, CA 92036. ☎ **619/765-0201.** 15 rms (3 with bath), 2 cottages. $72–$90 double second floor (without bath), $82–$110 double first floor (with bath); $125–$160 cottage. Rates include full breakfast. AE, MC, V.

The Julian Hotel has been putting a roof over travelers' heads since the days when the Butterfield stagecoach stopped across the street. A potbellied stove still sits in the parlor, along with an upright piano that arrived from Philadelphia via Cape Horn. The hotel's original owners, Albert and Margaret Robinson, were former slaves; their photograph hangs on the parlor wall. There are a dozen rooms in the original part of the house—with "necessary rooms" at the end of the hall—and each room is decorated in a variation of a Victorian theme. Another three rooms (with bath) were added off the front porch in 1920. First floor rooms are slightly larger and offer queen-size beds; rooms on the second floor have queen-length double beds. One of the cottages, the Honeymoon House, features a Franklin (freestanding) fireplace and an old-fashioned tub. The cottages book up two months in advance. The hotel's generous breakfast menu includes omelets and apple-filled pancakes. Coffee, tea, cakes, and cookies are served in the parlor at 5pm.

BED-AND-BREAKFASTS

For a list and a description of a dozen interesting B&Bs, contact the **Julian Bed and Breakfast Guild,** P.O. Box 1711, Julian, CA 92036 (☎ 619/765-1555 daily from 9am to 9pm). All members are within a few miles of the town center, and accommodations range from a tree house to cottages tucked away in the woods.

My favorites are the ✪ **Julian White House** (☎ **800/WHT-HOUS** or 619/765-1764) and the **Artists' Loft** (☎ 619/765-0765).

CAMPING

Cuyamaca Rancho State Park is 11 miles from Julian, and a new camp store and interpretive center are located a mile from the entrance. It's another 2 miles to a little museum and park headquarters where you can stock up on maps, information, and even books to help you identify local flora and fauna. The park has more than 100 miles of trails, and you can see Mexico from Cuyamaca Peak (6,512 feet).

Campsites are set in the midst of trees and scrubs; each one has a table and fire ring. Reserve a spot in Paso Picacho or Green Valley Campground, both with about

80 sites (☎ **800/444-PARK** for reservations; 619/765-0755 for park information only). The camping fee is $14 in summer, $12 off-season, or $5 for day use only. They book up fast on weekends from Easter to Thanksgiving, so plan ahead. Park headquarters is open Monday through Friday from 8am to 5pm.

WHERE TO DINE

Julian Cafe. Main St. ☎ **619/765-2712.** Menu items $2.50–$9. MC, V. Mon–Fri 8am–7:30pm; Sat–Sun 7am–8pm. AMERICAN.

A tasty, filling chicken pie is the specialty here; buy it at lunch for $6.95 or pay $8.95 for the full dinner. Mashed potatoes come the old-fashioned way, smothered in country gravy. Other home-cooked offerings include fried chicken, liver and onions, meat loaf dinner, and a hot vegetable plate. This is a good place to bring kids; the waitresses are friendly and service is quick, even when it's packed.

13 Anza-Borrego Desert State Park

The vast, striking landscapes of Anza-Borrego comprise the largest state park in the Lower 48. Most visitors come during the spring **wildflower season,** when a colorful carpet of flowers blankets the desert floor and climbs into the surrounding hills and mountains. Call the Wildflower Hot Line at **619/767-4684** to find out what's blooming during your trip.

JUST THE FACTS

Anza-Borrego Desert State Park (☎ **619/767-4205** or 619/767-5311) is open from October through May daily from 9am to 5pm; June through September, it's only open Saturdays, Sundays, and holidays from 9am to 5pm.

The park lies about 90 miles northeast of San Diego or 150 miles southwest of Los Angeles between I-10 and I-8. It's reached by Calif. 78 and Calif. 79 from the east and by I-8 from the south.

Information on the park is available from the Borrego Springs Chamber of Commerce (☎ **619/767-5555**); the California Desert Tourism Association (☎ **619/328-9256**); and the Julian Chamber of Commerce (☎ **619/765-1857**).

The telephone area code here will change from 619 to 760 in March of 1997.

SEEING THE HIGHLIGHTS

At the **Visitors Center,** you're introduced to the park and desert with a 15-minute slide show and exhibits that cover the local ecosystem and the history of the Native Americans who once lived here. Hiking maps are on sale here as well.

Hikers can choose from more than 100 miles of designated trails. About 35 miles are part of the **Pacific Crest Trail** that goes from Mexico to Canada. Register at the Visitors Center before setting out. If you don't want to attempt a serious hike, there are a number of shorter **nature trails.** The **Borrego Palm Canyon Trail** starts at the main campground and will take you to a grove of California fan palms, the largest palm species in North America, and a year-round stream, one of the 25 oases in the park. Brochures are available at the Visitors Center for a number of these nature trails.

A few hundred rare bighorn sheep live in the park's rough, rocky terrain, and other animal residents include rabbits, desert mice, the chuckwalla (the largest lizard in the park), coyotes, mule deer, and bobcats.

Horseback trails surround the park's Vernon Whitaker horse camp. One trail ascends 12 miles to the top of the mountains for a spectacular vista. Riders may use all the dirt roads in the park, but not the nature or hiking trails.

CAMPING

There are two developed campgrounds in the park. **Borrego Palm Canyon Campground** has 52 full hookup sites (fees are $16 to $22) and 65 multiuse sites without hookups ($10 to $16). Another 27 multiuse nonhookup sites are situated at **Tamarisk Grove** ($10 to $16). All of the park's nonhookup sites have shade ramadas.

You and your horse can stay at the park's **Vernon Whitaker horse camp.** All of the 10 campsites can hold up to eight people and have corrals for four horses. Reservations for the campgrounds and horse camp are made through **DESTINET** (☎ **800/444-PARK** (7275)). Payment can be made with MC, VISA, or personal check. The horse camp is the hub of many miles of riding trails.

Bow Willow is a primitive camping site off S2. It has picnic tables and portable toilet facilities. Once you are out of the developed areas of the park, you can camp just about anywhere along its 500 miles of primitive roads. Only two restrictions apply. First, you must keep your vehicle within one car length of the road so as not to damage the fragile plant life. Second, you can't camp near a watering hole or spring, as it scares away the wildlife.

WHERE TO STAY NEARBY IN BORREGO SPRINGS

The nearby town of Borrego Springs, just down the road from the Visitors Center, offers tourist services, including restaurants, shops, and motels, plus one very special accommodation.

✪ **La Casa del Zorro.** 3845 Yaqui Pass Rd., Borrego Springs, CA 92004. ☎ **800/824-1884** or 619/767-5323. Fax 619/767-5963. 79 rms and suites, 19 cottages/villas. A/C TEL TV. $85–$100 double; from $125 suite; from $150 cottage/villa. Lower summer and midweek rates. Children under 12 stay free in parent's room. Special packages available. AE, DC, DISC, MC, V.

This is a beautiful oasis in the desert, surrounded by more than 500,000 acres of the unforgettable scenery of Anza-Borrego State Park. Each room is accented with pieces that reflect the early California heritage of Borrego Springs, and comes with thoughtful touches such as bathrobes, hair dryers, and coffeemakers. Some units have terraces, fireplaces, or Jacuzzis. The resort's facilities include three swimming pools, bicycles, six tennis courts, a fitness center, a whirlpool, and a beauty salon. There's a restaurant on the premises, as well as a bar that offers live entertainment.

14 Temecula: Southern California's Wine Country

Located over the line in Riverside County, 60 miles north of San Diego, Temecula is known for its wineries and the excellent vintages they produce. To get there, travel north from San Diego on I-15 for 50 miles; when the Temecula Valley comes into view, it'll take your breath away. To reach the vineyards, head east on Rancho California Road.

For information on accommodations and maps and brochures on Old Town Temecula and the vineyards, contact the **Temecula Valley Chamber of Commerce,** 27450 Ynez Rd., Suite 104, Temecula, CA 92591 (☎ **909/676-5090**), or visit their home page at http://www.temecula.org; and the **Temecula Valley Vintners Association,** Box 1601, Temecula, CA 92593–1601 (☎ **909/699-3626**). The telephone area code for Temecula is 909.

Temecula (pronounced te-*mec*-u-la) is a Native American word meaning "where the sun shines through the mist." If you gaze out over the vineyards early in the morning or in the middle of the afternoon, the name still holds true. It's the only town on California's west coast that still goes by its original name. The region was used as the setting for Helen Hunt Jackson's novel *Ramona*, first published in 1884.

Temecula has a couple of unique claims to fame. Granite from its quarries (most of which closed down in 1915, when reinforced concrete became popular) constitutes most of the street curbs in San Francisco. The last person sentenced to death by hanging in California was Temecula's blacksmith, John McNeil, who killed his wife in 1936.

When you turn onto Rancho California Road, all you'll see at first is new construction, but soon the vineyards come into view and the countryside turns natural again. Temecula's microclimate, allowing grapes to flourish, is due to a notch in the coastal mountains called Rainbow Gap, which lets breezes blow through from the ocean, 22 miles away. They result both in temperatures that are 8° to 10° cooler than on the coast and in a longer growing season; this lets grapes ripen more slowly. Most vineyards here are more than 1,400 feet above sea level.

Temecula is not as well known for its wines as Napa or Sonoma because those wine-producing regions have been at it 100 years longer. Franciscan missionaries planted the first grapevines here in the early 1800s, but the land ended up being used primarily for cattle raising on the 87,000-acre Vail Ranch from 1904 until 1964, when it was sold. Grapevines began to take root in the receptive soil again in 1968, and the first Temecula wines were produced in 1971.

WHAT TO SEE & DO

Today there are 11 wineries in the region, most of them strung side by side for a couple of miles along Rancho California Road, producing white, red, and rosé wines. Most of them are not sold outside of California or the West, although some have made it as far as the White House. Since the wineries in Temecula are smaller than their counterparts in Northern California, and are mostly family owned and operated, you're more likely to meet and talk with the owners when you come to their property than you would be at a larger northern vineyard. You're not likely to be there alone, however; 300 to 400 people can show up on the weekends.

Harvest time is usually mid-August through September, and visitors are welcome then and throughout the year to tour, taste, and stock up. In addition, a half-dozen local companies offer balloon rides over the vineyards, an unforgettable sight. Two that have been around for about 20 years are **DAE Flights** (☎ **909/676-3902**) and **Sunrise Balloons** (☎ **800/548-9912**).

On a spring or fall afternoon, head over to the **Thornton Winery** (see below) to hear jazz (there's an admission charge).

TOURING THE WINERIES

All the Temecula wineries welcome visitors and are well marked along the road. The following ones are listed in the order you'll come to them as you drive along Rancho California Road.

✪ **Thornton Winery.** 32575 Rancho California Rd., Temecula. ☎ **909/699-0099.** Daily 10am–5pm (tours Sat–Sun).

The first wine-making establishment you come to along Rancho California Road is housed in a striking stone building with a waterfall and sloping lawn in front and an herb garden in back. Today Thornton produces Culbertson sparkling wine, *à la méthode champenoise*, as well as Brindiamo premium varietal wines. The wines, sold nationwide, have been poured at the White House for after-dinner toasts. The gift shop sells a nice range of wine-related items. There is a champagne bar with a jukebox where drinks are about $5 a glass, or you can pay $6 to taste two champagnes and two still wines. The bar opens daily at noon. Café Champagne, the vineyard's award-winning restaurant, is open for lunch and dinner and serves California cuisine (see "Where to Dine," below). The winery hosts jazz concerts from April through October.

Callaway. 32720 Rancho California Rd. ☎ **909/676-4001.** Daily 10:30am–5pm; free tours at 11am, 1pm, and 3pm (11am–4pm on the hour weekends). Closed New Year's Day, Easter, Thanksgiving, Christmas.

Across the road from Thornton, in a long, low white building with brown trim, set in grounds lush with 2,500 rose bushes and orange trees, the winery is the area's oldest and now, at 720 acres, its largest. Producing wine here since 1974—nine labels in all, mostly whites—it offers the most in-depth tour. Each year some 75,000 visitors look down on the operations from a raised, enclosed walkway. There's a $3 charge to sample four different wines; you get to keep the glass. The large gift shop features not only the Callaway Vintages, but also gift baskets, books on wine, aprons, cups, and T-shirts. A vine-covered picnic area overlooks the vineyards. In 1981 the Callaway winery was bought by Hiram Walker of Canada, which was in turn bought by Allied Lyons of England in 1987, but its operation remains pure California.

Mount Palomar Winery. 33820 Rancho California Rd. ☎ **909/676-5047.** Tastings of four wines of your choice cost $2, including the souvenir glass. Daily 10am–5pm Oct–March; daily 10am–6pm Apr–Sept. Free tours 1:30 and 3:30pm weekdays; 11:30am, 1:30, and 3:30pm weekends. Turn off the main road and follow the blacktop up and over the hill to the winery.

This 105-acre vineyard also has a visitor center and shop, where deli snacks are always available, and a full-service deli operates Friday through Sunday. Mount Palomar's Reisling and chardonnay are particularly popular, along with their port and cream sherry. The sherry is aged by the Spanish method, in old brandy barrels set out in the sun for 24 to 30 months. One of the first vineyards in the region, Mount Palomar has continued its innovative style by introducing two new labels. The Castelletto label featuring classic Italian varieties Sangiovese and Cortese and its newest Mediterranean varietals like Syrah and Rhône style blends under the Rey Sol label.

Ribbons won in wine competitions over the years are proudly displayed on the walls. Outside, 60 tables are available for picnicking, some on a spot overlooking the property belonging to the vineyard. From the winery, you can gaze out at Mount San Jacinto and, behind it, Mount San Gorgonio, the highest mountain in Southern California.

The establishment opened in 1975, founded by John Poole, and it is run by his eldest son, Peter. Try to come before 1pm on weekends, when people may stand five deep for tastings, and be sure to heed the quotation on the wall of the tasting room: *Donde el vino entra, la verdad sale* ("Where wine enters, truth departs").

Cilurzo Vineyard and Winery. 41220 Calle Contento (just off Rancho California Rd.). ☎ **909/676-5250.** Daily 9:30am–4:45pm.

Vince Cilurzo may be better known in some circles in Los Angeles as the man who has lighted the TV game show *Jeopardy!* for many years (he still does so a couple of days a week; he also lit the Lawrence Welk Show for many years), but out in Temecula he's known as a vintner who established his 52-acre vineyard in 1968 and started producing wines in 1978. One of the most popular Cilurzo labels is the petite syrah, which, Vince claims, can be served with anything from tomato sauce to curry. The winery also produces a nouveau and a late harvest version of the petite syrah, along with a number of other wines. Unlike many other Temecula wineries, this one has no bar for tastings; instead, visitors sit in chairs and Vince Cilurzo or his wife, Audrey, serves them. A tasting of five or six wines costs $1, refundable with a purchase. Photos on the wall at the back of the tasting room capture moments from Vince's star-studded career. A picnic area overlooks the pond.

Maurice Carrie. 34225 Rancho California Rd. ☎ **909/676-1711.** Daily 10am–5pm.

This is the last of the wineries on Rancho California Road, off to your right. You can't miss the large two-story pseudo-Southern building with veranda and gazebo—a "Victorian farmhouse," Maurice Van Roekel likes to call it. She and her husband, Budd, came here to retire, but soon were producing red and white wines instead. Four of their wines are named after their grandchildren. The property has a wine boutique, a resident cat named Butterscotch, and a lovely oak bar trimmed with black and white tiles that draws a good afternoon crowd. The boutique sells wine and champagne glasses and insulated wine coolers, among other items. A deli section carries juice, crackers, and cold wine. Tastings are available.

EXPLORING OLD TOWN TEMECULA

A wonderful, eccentric counterpoint to the vineyards is the old part of the city of Temecula, preserved as it was in the 1890s, Western storefronts and all. It lies 4 miles west of the vineyards off Rancho California Road, stretches along six short blocks, and has a reputation as an antique-hunter's haven.

Park at the south end of town near the Swing Inn Café or Butterfield Plaza and walk north along Main Street to Sixth Street and back, going up one side of the street and back on the other; take time to read the plaques on the old buildings along the way. Be forewarned that Temecula has become a traffic-clogged town, and you will hear the drone of cars most everywhere, even on the golf course.

One of my favorite spots in town, partly for the name, is the **Swing Inn Café,** which you'll find at 28676 Front St., where a sign on the door announces No Checks or Credit Cards. Another sign claims that the cafe's been in existence since 1927. I asked my waitress if that was true. "Look around," she said. "Some of our customers have been here that long."

Continue along the same side of Front Street as the Swing Inn Café one block to Main Street to visit the **Temecula Valley Museum,** at 41950 Main St. On the right (unless it has moved by the time you pass through), the museum houses Native American artifacts from the area that are more than 1,000 years old, along with memorabilia from 1846 to the 1940s, and a model of the town from 1914. The museum, which is open Wednesday through Sunday from 11am to 4pm and by appointment, will eventually move into a new space three times larger a few blocks from here, at Sam Hicks Park, across from the post office on Moreno Drive (☎ **909/676-0021**).

At 28532 Front St. (at Fifth Street), check out **Ronnie's House** for antiques. While a number of the "antique" stores in the town sell more of what I'd call "collectibles," Ronnie has the real thing—all more than 100 years old. She's originally from Brooklyn, New York, and has had her store here since 1980. A lot of the items come from back East and beyond (☎ **909/676-4229**).

At Front and Sixth streets, turn right and walk a short block to **Sam Hicks Park,** home to the "They Passed This Way" Monument and the Old St. Catherine's Church, which dates from the early 1920s and is now part of the Temecula Valley Museum, which will relocate to the park.

Cross Front Street and walk back down the west side of the street. At Front and Sixth Streets is the **Chaparral Antique Mall,** with more than 70 dealers under one roof (☎ **909/676-0070**). Down at Front and Main Streets stands the **First National Bank,** which was built in 1912 and managed to stay open during the Great Depression, gaining it the nickname the "Pawn Shop." The bank finally closed in 1941 and is now a Mexican restaurant. For many years, its second floor was the town's community center and dance hall.

Nearby are two plunderable antiques malls: **Morgan's Antiques** (☎ **909/ 676-2722**), in a brick building dating from 1891 that, for 60 years, was Burnham's Store, the mainstay of local ranchers, and beside it, the **Temecula Trading Post** (☎ **909/676-5759**). Across the street stands the Old Welty/Temecula Hotel, built in 1882, the year the railroad came to Temecula; it burned and was rebuilt in 1891 and now is a private residence. Check out the store beside it, **Country Seller and Friends** (☎ **909/676-2322**), which sells furniture and antiques.

At the southwest corner of Main and Front streets, the **Welty Building,** which dates from the 1880s, now houses a deli, but it used to be a gym where Jack Dempsey worked out.

A NEARBY NATURE PRESERVE

For an outing in more than 3,000 acres of unspoiled terrain, take I-15 north to Clinton Keith Road and drive west on it for about 5 miles to get to the **Santa Rosa Plateau Ecological Reserve,** owned and maintained by the Nature Conservancy (☎ **909/677-6951**). Here walking trails, coyotes, hawks, migrating birds, and maybe even an eagle or two await you.

WHERE TO STAY

Butterfield Inn Motel. 28718 Front St., Temecula, CA 92390. ☎ **909/676-4833.** Fax 909/ 676-2019. 39 rms. A/C TEL TV. Weekdays, $35 single; $45–$89 double. Weekends $55 single; $55–$94 double. Extra person $5. AE, DISC, MC, V. Take I-15 north to Rancho California Rd. West to Front St.

Within walking distance of Old Town Temecula shops, the motel (not really an inn) has an Old West facade—it's easy to imagine the Butterfield stagecoach pulling up any moment. The rooms have double or king-size beds, and the motel has a small, unheated outdoor pool, and a Jacuzzi. There's complimentary coffee in the lobby in the morning.

Loma Vista. 33350 La Serena Way, Temecula, CA 92591. ☎ **909/676-7047.** 6 rms. A/C. $95–$135 single or double, $75–$115 midweek. Rates include full champagne breakfast. DISC, MC, V. Take I-15 to Rancho California Rd. East; inn is on left just beyond Callaway vineyard.

Betty and Dick Ryan came here from Los Angeles in 1988 and designed and built this tiled-roof mission-style house for their bed-and-breakfast inn. Perfectly named, it sits on a hill (*loma* in Spanish) overlooking the best vista around. From the living room, you can look out at the Callaway vineyard and the Santa Ana Mountains. All of the guest rooms have full private bath and a queen- or king-size bed; four have private wisteria-covered balconies. Favorite balconied rooms are sauvignon blanc, with Southwestern furnishings made of white pine and a four-poster queen-size bed; and fumé blanc, in California garden style with white wicker. Besides complimentary fruit and a decanter of sherry in each room, free wine and cheese are served by the fire at 6pm. A spa bubbles away on the back patio, while the front patio, a great place just to while away the hours, has a fire pit. The property is a real oasis, with 85 rosebushes, ranunculus, daisies, Australian tea bushes, and 325 grapefruit trees. The Ryans are both from Montana; she actually runs the operation and does all the cooking. Old Town Temecula is 5 miles away.

WHERE TO DINE

Baily Wine Country Cafe. 27644 Ynez Rd. (in Miller's Outpost shopping center at Rancho California Rd.). ☎ **909/676-9567.** Reservations recommended, especially on weekends. Main courses $8.75–$19. AE, CB, DC, MC, V. Mon–Thurs and Sun 11:30am–9pm, Fri–Sat 11:30am–9:30pm. CALIFORNIA/CONTINENTAL.

If you aren't interested in winery tours and tastings, just come here. Baily's has the largest selection of Temecula Valley wines anywhere, including those from the Baily family's own winery on Rancho California Road. To show them off to the best advantage, the cafe's chef has concocted some mouth-watering dishes, which change every few months. Consider such appetizers as crab cakes with roasted red bell pepper sauce and mixed greens, Caesar salad with shaved Parmesan cheese, and fresh mixed greens with balsamic shallot vinaigrette. At lunch, try the penne with roasted garlic, fresh vegetables, and tomato sauce made chunky with Italian sausage; Southwestern-style grilled cheese sandwich with cilantro (a regional prize winner); and grilled chicken picata salad with mixed greens and lemon-caper vinaigrette. Dinner favorites include Southwestern pork tenderloin with garlic mashed potatoes, salmon Wellington with cucumber and papaya relish and fresh vegetables, and chicken ravioli in a basil pesto. Finish off the meal with Carol Baily's white chocolate cheesecake, a top choice with local diners. If you're in luck, the Baily family, who are always in evidence at the cafe, will be hosting one of their celebrated Dinners in the Wine Cellar. Smoking is allowed on the patio but not inside the restaurant. They can provide picnics to go with 24 hours' notice. The restaurant is to your right and up the hill after you enter the shopping center.

✪ **Cafe Champagne.** Thornton Winery, 32575 Rancho California Rd. ☎ **909/699-0088.** Reservations recommended. Main courses $13–$21. AE, MC, V. Daily 11am–9pm. CALIFORNIA.

The toast of the Temecula wine country, this bistro and cafe features tasty dishes specially created to be served with nine Thornton champagnes. The wine list also features other Temecula and California labels. The lunch and dinner menus, California cuisine at its best, feature appetizers like soup du jour, warm brie en crôute with honey-walnut sauce, crab and shrimp strudel, and smoked salmon carpaccio. Among the entrees are angel-hair pasta primavera or angel-hair seafood pasta, mesquite-grilled tuna, and baked pecan chicken. The list of mesquite-grilled entrees expands at dinner, and at lunch tempting lighter fare includes hearty salads and sandwiches filled with mesquite-grilled hamburger, steak, or chicken. The setting, overlooking the vineyard, is sublime. It's a small place, so do reserve ahead. If you have a high regard for really good food, you're going to like it here.

Temet Grill. in the Temecula Creek Inn, 44501 Rainbow Canyon Rd. ☎ **909/676-5631.** Reservations recommended. Main courses $15.50–$19.50. AE, DC, DISC, MC, V. Mon–Sat 6:30am–10pm, Sun 6am–10pm. CALIFORNIA/SOUTHWESTERN.

The very attractive dining room has five striking chandeliers, Native American artifacts in glass cases, and floor-to-ceiling picture windows overlooking the golf course. The menu changes frequently, but you might find such specialties of the house as grilled tortilla pizza or grilled chiles rellenos with chipotle salsa. Main courses might include roasted sea bass in a five-spice crust, sautéed or grilled chicken breast with beer mustard and chipotle hollandaise, or grilled swordfish or steak. All the dishes are creatively presented. The wine list emphasizes California vintages, along with some from Oregon and Washington and a few French champagnes.

TEMECULA AFTER DARK

Any time of year for a fun evening out in Old Town Temecula, indulge in a little bit of country-western dancing at **The Temecula Stampede,** 28721 Front St., opposite the Butterfield Inn (☎ **909/695-1760**). This may be California's biggest saloon/dance hall, with 4,000 square feet incorporating dance areas for two-steppers, swing dancers, and line dancers. There's room left for eight pool tables, tables and chairs, and two impressive bars, one 110 feet long and the other 60 feet long. It's open Tuesday through Sunday from 6pm, with dance lessons given on Tuesday and Thursday nights; live bands are on hand from 8:30pm until 2am Thursday through Saturday nights, when there is a $5 cover; otherwise, there's a DJ. Devotees range in age from the minimum of 21 to 80-plus, most decked out in Western garb; weekends are crowded. The entrance is at the back of the building.

Appendix: Useful Toll-Free Numbers & Web Sites

A Major Airlines

Alaska Airlines
☎ 800/426-0333

America West Airlines
☎ 800/235-9292

American Airlines
☎ 800/433-7300
http://www.americanair.com/aa_home/aa_home.html

Continental Airlines
☎ 800/525-0280
http://www.flycontinental.com:80/index.html

Delta Air Lines
☎ 800/221-1212
http://www.delta-air.com/index.html

Northwest Airlines
☎ 800/225-2525
http://www.nwa.com

Southwest Airlines
☎ 800/435-9792
http://iflyswa.com

TWA
☎ 800/221-2000
http://www2.twa.com/TWA/Airlines/home/home.htm

United Airlines
☎ 800/241-6522
http://www.ual.com

USAir
☎ 800/428-4322
http://www.usair.com

B Car-Rental Agencies

Advantage
☎ 800/777-5500

Airways
☎ 800/952-9200

Alamo
☎ 800/327-9633
http://www.goalamo.com

Avis
☎ 800/331-1212 Continental USA
☎ 800/TRY-AVIS Canada
http://www.avis/com

Budget
☎ 800/527-0700

Dollar
☎ 800/800-4000

Enterprise
☎ 800/325-8007

Hertz
☎ 800/654-3131

National
☎ 800/CAR-RENT
http://www.nationalcar.com/index.html

Payless
☎ 800/PAYLESS

Rent-A-Wreck
☎ 800/535-1391

Sears
☎ 800/527-0770

Thrifty
☎ 800/367-2277

Value
☎ 800/327-2501
http://www.go-value.com

C Major Hotel & Motel Chains

Best Western
☎ 800/528-1234

Clarion Hotels
☎ 800/CLARION
http://www.hotelchoice.com/cgi-bin/res/webres?clarion.html

Comfort Inns
☎ 800/228-5150
http://www.hotelchoice.com/cgi-bin/res/webres?comfort.html

Courtyard by Marriott
☎ 800/321-2211
http://www.marriott.com/lodging/courtyar.htm

Days Inn
☎ 800/325-2525
http://www.daysinn.com/daysinn.html

Doubletree Hotels
☎ 800/222-TREE

Econo Lodges
☎ 800/55-ECONO
http://www.hotelchoice.com/cgi-bin/res/webres?econo.html

Embassy Suites
☎ 800/362-2779
http://www.embassy-suites.com

Fairfield Inns by Marriott
☎ 800/228-2800
http://www.marriott.com/lodging/fairf.htm

Hampton Inns
☎ 800/HAMPTON
http://www.hampton-inn.com

Holiday Inn
☎ 800/HOLIDAY
http://www.holiday-inn.com

Howard Johnson
☎ 800/654-2000
http://www.hojo.com/hojo.html

La Quinta Motor Inns
☎ 800/531-5900

Motel 6
☎ 800/466-8536

Quality Inns
☎ 800/228-5151
http://www.hotelchoice.com/cgi-bin/res/webres?quality.html

Ramada
☎ 800/2-RAMADA
http://www.ramada.com/ramada.html

Red Carpet Inns
☎ 800/251-1962

Red Lion Hotels and Inns
☎ 800/547-8010

Red Roof Inns
☎ 800/843-7663
http://www.redroof.com

Residence Inn by Marriott
☎ 800/331-3131
http://www.marriott.com/lodging/resinn.htm

Rodeway Inns
☎ 800/228-2000
http://www.hotelchoice.com/cgi-bin/res/webres?rodeway.html

Super 8 Motels
☎ 800/800-8000
http://www.super8motels.com/super8.html

Travelodge
☎ 800/255-3050

Vagabond Hotels
☎ 800/522-1555

Index

WHEREVER YOU TRAVEL, *H*ELP IS NEVER FAR AWAY.

From planning your trip to

providing travel assistance along

the way, American Express®

Travel Service Offices are

always there to help.

For the office nearest you in California, call
1-800-AXP-3429.

THE RICHARD NIXON
LIBRARY & BIRTHPLACE

Valid for up to TWO complimentary ADULT ADMISSIONS
when up to TWO ADULT ADMISSIONS
of equal or greater value are purchased.

valid anytime

18001 Yorba Linda Boulevard, Yorba Linda, California
(714) 993-5075

Valid for all shows except Saturday. Limit six people per coupon.
Not valid for gift certificate purchase. Not valid for groups of 15
or more. Not valid Ticketmaster outlets. Cannot be combined with
any other discount. Valid only at the Buena Park Castle. Not valid
12/30/97 & 12/31/97. Expires 12/29/98. Reservations required.
(714) 521-4740 or (800) 899-6600.

Sea World.

Present this coupon at any Sea World of California ticket window for your discount.
One coupon is good for your entire group (limit 6). Not valid with any other discount,
special event, special pricing, senior discount, or 12-Month Pass purchase.
Not for sale. Expires 12/31/98. **A-3900 C-3899**.

©1997 Sea World, Inc. An Anheuser-Busch Theme Park®

For Your Information:

Offer available at participating Hertz U.S. Corporate locations through
12/31/98. Leisure Weekly rentals require a 5 day minimum keep,
including Saturday night. Minimum age is 25. Advanced reservations are
required . Black out periods apply. This coupon has no cash value, must
be surrendered at time of rental and may not be combined with any other
discount, offer, coupon or promotion. Standard rental qualifications and
return restrictions must be met Car must be returned to renting location.
Taxes and optional services, such as refueling, are extra and are not
subject to discount.

Hertz®

Hertz rents Fords and other fine cars.

SAVE UP TO $12

at the

SAN DIEGO ZOO

Present this coupon at any ticket booth to SAVE $2 off the Deluxe Package, which includes a 35 minute double-deck bus tour, round trip Skyfari aerial tram ride, all animal shows & exhibits.

Gates open 9:00 A.M. daily. For more information and directions to the San Diego Zoo, call (619) 234-3153. Not valid with any other offer or membership. Prices subject to change. Good for up to six (6) persons per coupon.

Valid through January 31, 1998.

8376Z

SAVE UP TO $12
SAN DIEGO WILD ANIMAL PARK

Present this coupon at any ticket booth to SAVE $2 off the
Nairobi Ticket Package, including the Wgasa Bush Line monorail
tour, The Hidden Jungle and all animal shows & exhibits.

10% OFF

Follow the Sun to **Days Inn**
Now you can save even more at any of more than 1,700 Days Inns
throughout the United States and internationally.
Just present this coupon upon check-in and Days Inn will take 10%
off your regular room rate for your entire length of stay!
Advance reservations required, so call now!
1-800-DAYS INN
See details on back

Not valid with any other offer or on membership. Prices subject to change. Good for up to six (6) persons per coupon.

P3767

UP TO **$100.00 OFF**

Save up to $100.00 off when you buy your airline ticket from Travel Discounters.

Call 1-800-355-1065 and give code FRO in order to receive the discount. See reverse side for discount prices.

$5.00 Off Per Night

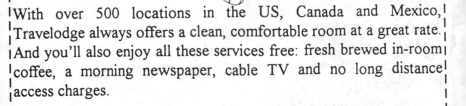

Travelodge

With over 500 locations in the US, Canada and Mexico, Travelodge always offers a clean, comfortable room at a great rate. And you'll also enjoy all these services free: fresh brewed in-room coffee, a morning newspaper, cable TV and no long distance access charges.

And if you present this certificate upon check-in we'll take $5.00 off the regular room rate for each night of your stay at a Travelodge location. It just makes sense to stay with us and save.

For reservations, call **1-800-578-7878** or your travel agent and ask for the 5CPN discount.

Savings are subject to certain restrictions and availability. Good for domestic and international travel that originates in the U.S. Valid for flights on most airlines worldwide.

Minimum Ticket Price	Save
$200.00	$25.00
$250.00	$50.00
$350.00	$75.00
$450.00	$100.00

Terms and Conditions

1. Advance reservations require.
2. Coupon must be presented at check-in.
3. Coupon cannot be combined with any other special offers, discounted rates.
4. Subject to availability.
5. No photo copies allowed

For reservations, call **1-800-578-7878** or your travel agent and ask for the 5CPN discount.

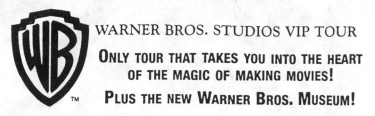

MARINE WORLD
AFRICA USA™

Marine World Africa USA, Marine World Parkway, Vallejo. Located 30 miles northeast of San Francisco and 12 miles south of Napa, at the intersection of I-80 and Hwy. 37. 707-643-ORCA (6722) (tape).

Present this coupon at Marine World's main gate and save **$4.00** per person off each full price adult and child general admission. One coupon good for up to six people. Coupon valid through **October 31, 1998** during regular park hours. Cannot be used or combined with any other discount program or special offer. Not for resale. For operating schedule and information, call (707) 643-ORCA (6722).

1067 A
1068 C

Knott's
BERRY FARM®

Present this coupon at any Knott's ticket booth and receive $3 off full-priced adult admission, or $3 off full-priced child admission (ages 3-11). Limit six discounts per coupon. Not valid for special-ticket events. Cannot be combined with any other offer or discount. Offer expires 12/31/98.

#1112

California Academy of Sciences--Home of Steinhart Aquarium, Morrison Planetarium and the Natural History Museum in San Francisco's beautiful Golden Gate Park.

Present this coupon for one free child age 6-11 ($1.50 value) with paid adult. Planetarium sky shows are an additional fee.

Open daily 10 a.m. to 5 p.m. (with extended summer hours). Located on the Music Concourse, near 9th Ave. and Lincoln Way.

Information (415) 750-7145
www.calacademy.org